W9-CRY-252

Contents

Chapter 3   **Decision Structures   111**

Chapter 4   **Loops and Files** 189

Chapter 6   **A First Look at Classes   319**

Chapter 7   **Arrays and the `ArrayList` Class   405**

Chapter 10 **Inheritance   613**

Chapter 11 **Exceptions and Advanced File I/O** **703**

Chapter 12 **A First Look at GUI Applications** **761**

Chapter 16 **Recursion   1041**

Chapter 17 **Sorting, Searching, and Algorithm Analysis   1069**

Chapter 18 **Generics**   **1121**

Chapter 19 **Collections and the Stream API   1167**

Chapter 20 **Linked Lists**   **1237**

Chapter 21 **Stacks and Queues**   **1289**

Chapter 22   **Binary Trees, AVL Trees, and Priority Queues   1335**

Companion Website:

LOCATION OF VIDEONOTES IN THE TEXT ▶

(continued on the next page)

LOCATION OF VIDEONOTES IN THE TEXT *(continued)* ▶

Preface

Welcome to *Starting Out with Java: From Control Structures through Data Structures, Third Edition.* This book is intended for a traditional two-semester CS1/CS2 sequence of courses. The first half of the book, intended for a CS1 class, teaches fundamental programming and problem-solving concepts using Java. The second half of the book, intended for a CS2 class, teaches advanced concepts and provides an introduction to algorithms and data structures. The book is written for students with no prior programming background, but experienced students will also benefit from its depth of detail.

Control Structures First, Then Objects, Then Data Structures

The text introduces students to the fundamentals of data types, input/output, control structures, methods, and objects created from standard library classes. Next, students learn to use arrays. Then, a series of more advanced topics are presented, including inheritance, polymorphism, GUI development, recursion, searching, sorting, algorithm analysis, and generics. Finally, students are introduced to the world of data structures, beginning with an overview of the Java Collections Framework (JCF), and continuing through a series of chapters in which students learn to develop their own data structures, including linked lists, stacks, queues, priority queues, binary trees, and AVL trees. Students are shown how to implement data structures either with or without generics, which gives instructors a great deal of flexibility in presenting the material.

As with all the books in the *Starting Out With* series, the hallmark of the text is its clear, friendly, and easy-to-understand writing. In addition, it is rich in concise, practical example programs.

Changes in This Edition

This book's pedagogy, organization, and clear writing style remain the same as in the previous edition. Many improvements have been made, which are summarized here:

- **New GUI Organization:** In previous editions, GUI programming with Swing was introduced in Chapter 7, and then revisited in Chapter 13. Many of the reviewers requested that GUI programming be postponed until inheritance had been covered. In this edition, the *First Look at GUI Applications* chapter has been moved to Chapter 12. However, the chapter has been written in a manner that it can still be covered after Chapter 6, as in the previous editions. Instructors who prefer to follow the previous sequence of topics can still do so. (See the chapter dependency chart in Figure P-1 for possible sequencing of the chapters.)

- **A New Chapter on JavaFX:** New to this edition is *Chapter 15 Creating GUI Applications with JavaFX.* JavaFX is the next generation toolkit for creating GUIs and graphical applications in Java, and is bundled with Java 8. The chapter is written in such a way that it is independent from the existing chapters on Swing and AWT. The instructor can choose to skip the Swing and AWT chapters and go straight to JavaFX, or cover all of the GUI chapters.
- **`System.out.printf` Is Primarily Used For Formatting Console Output:** In this edition, `System.out.printf` is used as the primary method for formatting output in console programs.
- **`String.format` Is Used Instead of `DecimalFormat`:** In previous editions, the `DecimalFormat` class was used to format strings for GUI output. In this edition, the `String.format` method is used instead. With `String.format`, the student can use the same format specifiers and flags that were learned with the `System.out.printf` method.
- **Expanded Coverage of the `switch` Statement:** In Chapter 3, the introduction to the `switch` statement has been rewritten, and enhanced with a flowchart. A section covering the ability to `switch` on a string has also been added.
- **Discussion of Nested Loops Has Been Expanded:** In Chapter 4, the section on nested loops has been expanded to include an *In the Spotlight* section highlighting the use of nested loops to print patterns.
- **Usage of Random Numbers Has Been Expanded:** In Chapter 4, the section on random numbers has been expanded, and now includes *In the Spotlight* sections demonstrating how random numbers can be used to simulate the rolling of dice, and how random numbers can be used to determine the results of a coin toss.
- **A New Introduction to Objects Has Been Added to Chapter 6:** In Chapter 6, a new introduction to objects has been added to the beginning of the chapter. The new introduction is much more practical and concrete than the previous introduction, discussing Java objects that the student has already used. The goal of this new introduction is to show, in a familiar way, how programs consist of objects. This reinforces an object-oriented mindset, and prepares the student to write his or her own classes.
- **New Motivational Examples of Classes Have Been Added to Chapter 6:** In Chapter 6, new motivational examples of classes have been added. One of the new examples introduces a `Die` class that simulates a die that can be rolled in a game. Another example shows how a variation of the game of Cho-Han can be simulated with classes that represent the players, a dealer, and the dice.
- **The Diamond Operator (`<>`):** Type inference with the diamond operator is discussed in Chapter 7.
- **`StringTokenizer` Is No Longer Used:** In previous editions, the `StringTokenizer` class was introduced as a way to tokenize strings. In this edition, all string tokenizing is done with the `String.split` method.
- **Introduction of `@Override` annotation:** Chapter 10 now introduces the use of `@Override` annotation, and explains how it can prevent subtle errors.
- **A New Section on Anonymous Inner Classes:** Chapter 10 now has a new section that introduces anonymous inner classes.
- **The Introduction to Interfaces Has Been Improved:** The introductory material on interfaces in Chapter 10 has been revised for greater clarity.
- **Default Methods:** In this edition, Chapter 10 provides new material on default methods in interfaces, a new feature in Java 8.

- **Functional Interfaces and Lambda Expressions:** Java 8 introduces functional interfaces and lambda expressions, and in this edition, Chapter 10 has a new section on these topics. The new material gives a detailed, stepped-out explanation of lambda expressions, and discusses how they can be used to instantiate objects of anonymous classes that implement functional interfaces.
- **Multi-catch Exception Handling:** Multi-catch exception handling is discussed in Chapter 11.
- **New Exercises and Programming Problems:** New shorter algorithm workbench exercises, and new, motivational programming problems have been added to many of the chapters.
- **The `java.util.stream` Package Is Introduced:** A new section covering the `java.util.stream` package has been added to the *Collections* chapter, which is now Chapter 20.
- **The Array-Based List Chapter Has Been Removed:** In the previous edition, Chapter 19 covered array-based lists. Because Java (and most other programming languages) provide built-in lists, it is less important for students to learn how to implement them. The chapter has been removed, to make room for other new material.
- **Discussion of the `Vector` Class Has Been Removed:** `Vector` is now considered as a legacy class, and is not recommended for use in new code. The discussion of the `Vector` class (section 18.2 in the previous edition) has been removed.
- **A New Online Database Chapter:** The book's companion Web site provides a new online chapter that introduces the students to databases and SQL using JavaDB.

Organization of the Text

The text teaches Java step by step. Each chapter covers a major set of topics and builds knowledge as students progress through the book. Although the chapters can be easily taught in their existing sequence, there is some flexibility. Figure P-1 shows chapter dependencies. Each box represents a chapter or a group of chapters. An arrow points from a chapter to the chapter that must be previously covered.

Brief Overview of Each Chapter

Chapter 1: Introduction to Computers and Java. This chapter provides an introduction to the field of computer science, and covers the fundamentals of hardware, software, and programming languages. The elements of a program, such as key words, variables, operators, and punctuation are discussed by examining a simple program. An overview of entering source code, compiling, and executing a program is presented. A brief history of Java is also given.

Chapter 2: Java Fundamentals. This chapter gets students started in Java by introducing data types, identifiers, variable declarations, constants, comments, program output, and simple arithmetic operations. The conventions of programming style are also introduced. Students learn to read console input with the `Scanner` class and with dialog boxes using `JOptionPane`.

Figure P-1 Chapter Dependencies

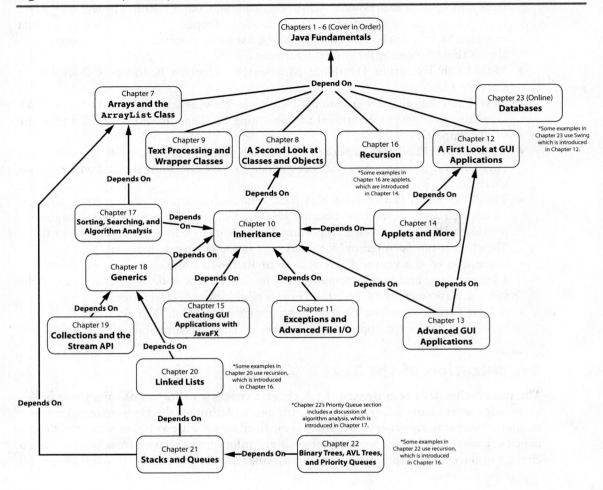

Chapter 3: Decision Structures. In this chapter students explore relational operators and relational expressions, and are shown how to control the flow of a program with the `if`, `if-else`, and `if-else-if` statements. Nested `if` statements, logical operators, the conditional operator, and the `switch` statement are also covered. The chapter discusses how to compare `String` objects with the `equals`, `compareTo`, `equalsIgnoreCase`, and `compareToIgnoreCase` methods. Formatting numeric output with the `System.out.printf` method and the `String.format` method is discussed.

Chapter 4: Loops and Files. This chapter covers Java's repetition control structures. The `while` loop, `do-while` loop, and `for` loop are taught, along with common uses for these devices. Counters, accumulators, running totals, sentinels, and other application-related topics are discussed. Simple file operations for reading and writing text files are included.

Chapter 5: Methods. In this chapter students learn how to write void methods, value-returning methods, and methods that do and do not accept arguments. The concept of functional decomposition is discussed.

Chapter 6: A First Look at Classes. This chapter introduces students to designing classes for the purpose of instantiating objects. Students learn about class fields and methods, and UML diagrams are introduced as a design tool. Then constructors and overloading are discussed. A BankAccount class is presented as a case study, and a section on object-oriented design is included. This section leads the students through the process of identifying classes and their responsibilities within a problem domain. There is also a section that briefly explains packages and the import statement.

Chapter 7: Arrays and the ArrayList Class. In this chapter students learn to create and work with single and multi-dimensional arrays. Numerous array-processing techniques are demonstrated, such as summing the elements in an array, finding the highest and lowest values, and sequentially searching an array are also discussed. Other topics, including ragged arrays and variable-length arguments (varargs) are also discussed. The ArrayList class is introduced and Java's generic types are briefly discussed and demonstrated.

Chapter 8: A Second Look at Classes and Objects. This chapter shows students how to write classes with added capabilities. Static methods and fields, interaction between objects, passing objects as arguments, and returning objects from methods are discussed. Aggregation and the "has a" relationship is covered, as well as enumerated types. A section on object-oriented design shows how to use CRC cards to determine the collaborations among classes.

Chapter 9: Text Processing and More about Wrapper Classes. This chapter discusses the numeric and Character wrapper classes. Methods for converting numbers to strings, testing the case of characters, and converting the case of characters are covered. Autoboxing and unboxing are also discussed. More String class methods are covered, including using the split method to tokenize strings. The chapter also covers the StringBuilder class.

Chapter 10: Inheritance. The study of classes continues in this chapter with the subjects of inheritance and polymorphism. The topics covered include superclasses, subclasses, how constructors work in inheritance, method overriding, polymorphism and dynamic binding, protected and package access, class hierarchies, abstract classes, abstract methods, anonymous inner classes, interfaces, and lambda expressions.

Chapter 11: Exceptions and Advanced File I/O. In this chapter students learn to develop enhanced error trapping techniques using exceptions. Handling exceptions is covered, as well as developing and throwing custom exceptions. The chapter discusses advanced techniques for working with sequential access, random access, text, and binary files.

Chapter 12: A First Look at GUI Applications. This chapter presents the basics of developing GUI applications with Swing. Fundamental Swing components and the basic concepts of event-driven programming are covered.

Chapter 13: Advanced GUI Applications. This chapter continues the study of GUI application development with Swing. More advanced components, menu systems, and look-and-feel are covered.

Chapter 14: Applets and More. In this chapter students apply their knowledge of GUI development to the creation of applets. In addition to using Swing applet classes, AWT classes are discussed for portability. Drawing simple graphical shapes is discussed.

Chapter 15: Creating GUI Applications with JavaFX. This chapter introduces JavaFX, which is the next generation library for creating graphical applications in Java. This chapter is written in such a way that it is independent from the existing chapters on Swing and AWT. You can choose to skip chapters 12, 13, and 14, and go straight to Chapter 15, or cover all of the GUI chapters.

Chapter 16: Recursion. This chapter presents recursion as a problem-solving technique. Numerous examples of recursive methods are demonstrated.

Chapter 17: Sorting, Searching, and Algorithm Analysis. In this chapter students learn the basics of sorting arrays and searching for data stored in them. The chapter covers the bubble sort, selection sort, insertion sort, Quicksort, sequential search, and binary search algorithms. A section on algorithm analysis is also provided, which covers basic steps, complexity, and Big O notation.

Chapter 18: Generics. This chapter shows students how to write generic classes and methods. Topics include erasure, passing instances of a generic class as arguments to a method, constraining type parameters, generics and inheritance, and generics and interfaces. Restrictions on the use of generic types are also discussed.

Chapter 19: Collections and the Stream API. This chapter introduces students to the Java Collections Framework (JCF). Lists, sets, maps, and the `Collections` class are discussed. The chapter concludes with a discussion of the classes and interfaces in the `java.util.stream` package.

Chapter 20: Linked Lists. This chapter introduces concepts and techniques for writing a linked list class. Basic linked list operations, such as adding, inserting, removing, and traversing, are covered. Doubly-linked lists, circularly-linked lists, and using recursion with linked lists are discussed.

Chapter 21: Stacks and Queues. In this chapter students learn about the operations of stacks and queues, and how to write array-based and linked list-based stack and queue classes.

Chapter 22: Binary Trees, AVL Trees, and Priority Queues. This chapter covers various aspects of binary trees and binary tree operations. The specific binary tree implementations covered are binary search trees, AVL trees, and priority queues.

Chapter 23 (Online): Databases. This chapter is available on the book's companion Web site (at www.pearsonhighered.com/gaddis). It introduces the students to database programming. The basic concepts of database management systems and SQL are first introduced. Then the students learn to use JDBC to write database applications in Java. Relational data is covered, and numerous example programs are presented throughout the chapter.

Features of the Text

Concept Statements. Each major section of the text starts with a concept statement that concisely summarizes the focus of the section.

Example Programs. The text has an abundant number of complete and partial example programs, each designed to highlight the current topic. In most cases the programs are practical, real-world examples.

Program Output. Each example program is followed by a sample of its output, which shows students how the program functions.

 Checkpoints. Checkpoints, highlighted by the checkmark icon, appear at intervals throughout each chapter. They are designed to check students' knowledge soon after learning a new topic. Answers for all Checkpoint questions can be downloaded from the book's companion Web site at www.pearsonhighered.com/gaddis.

 NOTE: Notes appear at several places throughout the text. They are short explanations of interesting or often misunderstood points relevant to the topic at hand.

 TIP: Tips advise the student on the best techniques for approaching different programming problems and appear regularly throughout the text.

 WARNING! Warnings caution students about certain Java features, programming techniques, or practices that can lead to malfunctioning programs or lost data.

 In the Spotlight. Many of the chapters provide an *In the Spotlight* section that presents a programming problem, along with detailed, step-by-step analysis showing the student how to solve it.

 VideoNotes. A series of online videos, developed specifically for this book, are available for viewing at www.pearsonhighered.com/cs-resources/. Icons appear throughout the text, alerting the student to videos about specific topics.

Case Studies. Case studies that simulate real-world business applications are introduced throughout the text and are available for download from the Gaddis resource page at www.pearsonhighered.com/gaddis.

Common Errors to Avoid. Most chapters provide a list of common errors and explanations of how to avoid them.

Review Questions and Exercises. Each chapter presents a thorough and diverse set of review questions and exercises. They include Multiple Choice and True/False, Find the Error, Algorithm Workbench, and Short Answer.

Programming Challenges. Each chapter offers a pool of programming challenges designed to solidify students' knowledge of topics at hand. In most cases the assignments present real-world problems to be solved.

Supplements

Student Online Resources

Many student resources are available for this book from the publisher. The following items are available on the Gaddis Series resource page at www.pearsonhighered.com/cs-resources:

- The source code for each example program in the book
- Access to the book's companion VideoNotes
- Appendixes A–K (listed in the Contents)
- A collection of seven valuable Case Studies (listed in the Contents)
- Links to download the Java™ Edition Development Kit
- Links to download numerous programming environments, including jGRASP™, Eclipse™, TextPad™, NetBeans™, JCreator, and DrJava

Instructor Resources

The following supplements are available to qualified instructors:

- Answers to all of the Review Questions
- Solutions for the Programming Challenges
- PowerPoint presentation slides for each chapter

Acknowledgments

There have been many helping hands in the development and publication of this book. We would like to thank the following faculty reviewers for their helpful suggestions and expertise:

Carl Stephen Guynes
University of North Texas

Alan G. Jackson
Oakland Community College

Zhen Jiang
West Chester University

Neven Jurkovic
Palo Alto College

Dennis Lang
Kansas State University

Jiang Li
Austin Peay State University

Cheng Luo
Coppin State University

Felix Rodriguez
Naugatuck Valley Community College

Diane Rudolph
John A Logan College

Timothy Urness
Drake University

Zijiang Yang
Western Michigan University

Reviewers for Previous Editions

Ahmad Abuhejleh
University of Wisconsin, River Falls

Colin Archibald
Valencia Community College

Ijaz Awani
Savannah State University

Bill Bane
Tarleton State University

N. Dwight Barnette
Virginia Tech

Asoke Bhattacharyya
Saint Xavier University, Chicago

Marvin Bishop
Manhattan College

Heather Booth
University of Tennessee, Knoxville

David Boyd
Valdosta State University

Julius Brandstatter
Golden Gate University

Kim Cannon
Greenville Tech

Jesse Cecil
College of the Siskiyous

James Chegwidden
Tarrant County College

Kay Chen
Bucks County Community College

Brad Chilton
Tarleton State University

Diane Christie
University of Wisconsin, Stout

Cara Cocking
Marquette University

Jose Cordova
University of Louisiana, Monroe

Walter C. Daugherity
Texas A&M University

Michael Doherty
University of the Pacific

Jeanne M. Douglas
University of Vermont

Sander Eller
*California Polytechnic University,
Pomona*

Brooke Estabrook-Fishinghawk
Mesa Community College

Mike Fry
Lebanon Valley College

David Goldschmidt
College of St. Rose

Georgia R. Grant
College of San Mateo

Nancy Harris
James Madison University

Chris Haynes
Indiana University

Ric Heishman
Northern Virginia Community College

Deedee Herrera
Dodge City Community College

Mary Hovik
Lehigh Carbon Community College

Brian Howard
DePauw University

Alan Jackson
Oakland Community College (MI)

Norm Jacobson
University of California, Irvine

Stephen Judd
University of Pennsylvania

Harry Lichtbach
Evergreen Valley College

Michael A. Long
California State University, Chico

Tim Margush
University of Akron

Blayne E. Mayfield
Oklahoma State University

Scott McLeod
Riverside Community College

Dean Mellas
Cerritos College

Georges Merx
San Diego Mesa College

Martin Meyers
California State University, Sacramento

Pati Milligan
Baylor University

Laurie Murphy
Pacific Lutheran University

Steve Newberry
Tarleton State University

Lynne O'Hanlon
Los Angeles Pierce College

Merrill Parker
Chattanooga State Technical Community College

Bryson R. Payne
North Georgia College and State University

Rodney Pearson
Mississippi State University

Peter John Polito
Springfield College

Charles Robert Putnam
California State University, Northridge

Y. B. Reddy
Grambling State University

Elizabeth Riley
Macon State College

Carolyn Schauble
Colorado State University

Bonnie Smith
Fresno City College

Daniel Spiegel
Kutztown University

Caroline St. Clair
North Central College

Karen Stanton
Los Medanos College

Peter van der Goes
Rose State College

Tuan A Vo
Mt. San Antonio College

Xiaoying Wang
University of Mississippi

Yu Wu
University of North Texas

The authors would like to thank their families for their tremendous support during the development of this book. We also want to thank everyone at Pearson for making the *Starting Out With* series so successful. We are extremely fortunate to have Matt Goldstein as our editor and Kelsey Loanes as editorial assistant. Their support and encouragement makes it a pleasure to write chapters and meet deadlines. We are also fortunate to have Demetrius Hall and Bram Van Kempen as marketing managers. They have done a great job getting this book out to the academic community. We had a great production team, led by Camille Trentacoste. She worked tirelessly to make this edition a reality. Thanks to you all!

About the Authors

Tony Gaddis is the principal author of the *Starting Out With* series of textbooks. Tony has nearly 20 years experience teaching computer science courses at Haywood Community College in North Carolina. He is a highly acclaimed instructor who was previously selected as the North Carolina Community College Teacher of the Year and has received the Teaching Excellence award from the National Institute for Staff and Organizational Development. The *Starting Out With* series includes introductory books using the C++ programming language, the Java™ programming language, Microsoft® Visual Basic®, Microsoft® C#®, Python, Programming Logic and Design, MIT App Inventor, and Alice, all published by Pearson.

Godfrey Muganda is Professor of Computer Science at North Central College. He teaches a wide variety of courses at the undergraduate and graduate levels including courses in Linux and Unix programming, Windows and .NET programming, web application development, web services, data structures, and algorithms. He is a past winner of the North Central College faculty award for outstanding scholarship. His primary research interests are in the area of fuzzy sets and systems.

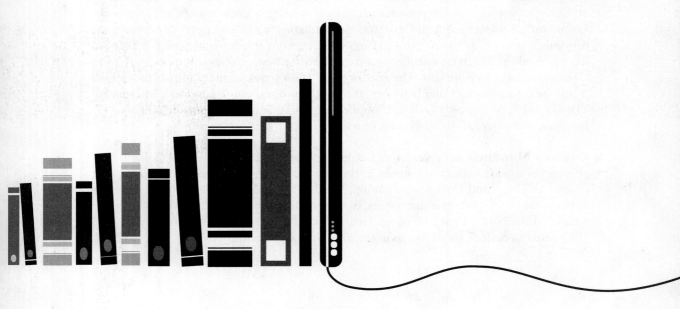

1

Introduction to Computers and Java

1.1 Introduction

This book teaches programming using Java. Java is a powerful language that runs on practically every type of computer. It can be used to create large applications or small programs that are part of a Web site. Before plunging right into learning Java, however, this chapter will review the fundamentals of computer hardware and software, and then take a broad look at computer programming in general.

1.2 Why Program?

CONCEPT: Computers can do many different jobs because they are programmable.

Every profession has tools that make the job easier to do. Carpenters use hammers, saws, and measuring tapes. Mechanics use wrenches, screwdrivers, and ratchets. Electronics technicians use probes, scopes, and meters. Some tools are unique and can be categorized as belonging to a single profession. For example, surgeons have certain tools that are designed specifically for surgical operations. Those tools probably aren't used by anyone other than surgeons. There are some tools, however, that are used in several professions. Screwdrivers, for instance, are used by mechanics, carpenters, and many others.

The computer is a tool used by so many professions that it cannot be easily categorized. It can perform so many different jobs that it is perhaps the most versatile tool ever made. To the accountant, computers balance books, analyze profits and losses, and prepare tax reports. To the factory worker, computers control manufacturing machines and track production. To the mechanic, computers analyze the various systems in an automobile and pinpoint hard-to-find problems. The computer can do such a wide variety of tasks because it can be *programmed*. It is a machine specifically designed to follow instructions. Because of the computer's programmability, it doesn't belong to any single profession. Computers are designed to do whatever job their programs, or *software*, tell them to do.

Computer programmers do a very important job. They create software that transforms computers into the specialized tools of many trades. Without programmers, the users of computers would have no software, and without software, computers would not be able to do anything.

Computer programming is both an art and a science. It is an art because every aspect of a program should be carefully designed. Here are a few of the things that must be designed for any real-world computer program:

- The logical flow of the instructions
- The mathematical procedures
- The layout of the programming statements
- The appearance of the screens
- The way information is presented to the user
- The program's "user friendliness"
- Manuals, help systems, and/or other forms of written documentation

There is also a science to programming. Because programs rarely work right the first time they are written, a lot of analyzing, experimenting, correcting, and redesigning is required. This demands patience and persistence of the programmer. Writing software demands discipline as well. Programmers must learn special languages such as Java because computers do not understand English or other human languages. Programming languages have strict rules that must be carefully followed.

Both the artistic and scientific nature of programming makes writing computer software like designing a car: Both cars and programs should be functional, efficient, powerful, easy to use, and pleasing to look at.

1.3   Computer Systems: Hardware and Software

CONCEPT: All computer systems consist of similar hardware devices and software components.

Hardware

Hardware refers to the physical components that a computer is made of. A computer, as we generally think of it, is not an individual device, but a system of devices. Like the instruments in a symphony orchestra, each device plays its own part. A typical computer system consists of the following major components:

- The central processing unit (CPU)
- Main memory
- Secondary storage devices
- Input devices
- Output devices

The organization of a computer system is shown in Figure 1-1.

Figure 1-1   The organization of a computer system

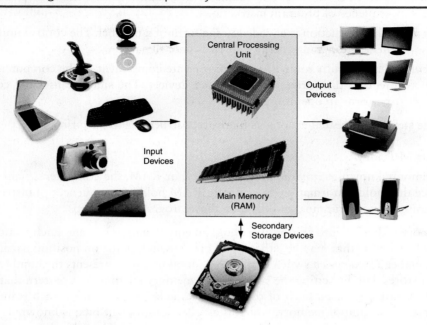

Let's take a closer look at each of these devices.

The CPU

At the heart of a computer is its *central processing unit*, or *CPU*. The CPU's job is to fetch instructions, follow the instructions, and produce some resulting data. Internally, the central processing unit consists of two parts: the *control unit* and the *arithmetic and logic unit (ALU)*. The control unit coordinates all of the computer's operations. It is responsible for determining where to get the next instruction and regulating the other major components of the computer with control signals. The arithmetic and logic unit, as its name suggests, is designed to perform mathematical operations. The organization of the CPU is shown in Figure 1-2.

Figure 1-2   The organization of the CPU

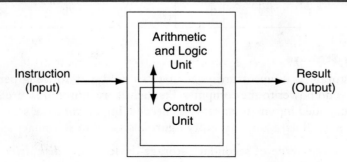

A program is a sequence of instructions stored in the computer's memory. When a computer is running a program, the CPU is engaged in a process known formally as the *fetch/decode/execute cycle*. The steps in the fetch/decode/execute cycle are as follows:

Fetch   The CPU's control unit fetches, from main memory, the next instruction in the sequence of program instructions.

Decode   The instruction is encoded in the form of a number. The control unit decodes the instruction and generates an electronic signal.

Execute   The signal is routed to the appropriate component of the computer (such as the ALU, a disk drive, or some other device). The signal causes the component to perform an operation.

These steps are repeated as long as there are instructions to perform.

Main Memory

Commonly known as *random access memory*, or *RAM*, the computer's main memory is a device that holds information. Specifically, RAM holds the sequences of instructions in the programs that are running and the data those programs are using.

Memory is divided into sections that hold an equal amount of data. Each section is made of eight "switches" that may be either on or off. A switch in the on position usually represents the number 1, whereas a switch in the off position usually represents the number 0. The computer stores data by setting the switches in a memory location to a pattern that represents a character or a number. Each of these switches is known as a *bit*, which stands for *binary digit*. Each section of memory, which is a collection of eight bits, is known as a *byte*. Each byte is assigned a unique number known as an *address*. The addresses are ordered from lowest to highest. A byte is identified by its address in much the same way a post office box is identified by an address. Figure 1-3 shows a series of bytes with their addresses. In the illustration, sample data is stored in memory. The number 149 is stored in the byte at address 16, and the number 72 is stored in the byte at address 23.

RAM is usually a volatile type of memory, used only for temporary storage. When the computer is turned off, the contents of RAM are erased.

Figure 1-3   Memory bytes and their addresses

0	1	2	3	4	5	6	7	8	9
10	11	12	13	14	15	16 149	17	18	19
20	21	22	23 72	24	25	26	27	28	29

Secondary Storage

Secondary storage is a type of memory that can hold data for long periods of time—even when there is no power to the computer. Frequently used programs are stored in secondary memory and loaded into main memory as needed. Important data, such as word processing documents, payroll data, and inventory figures, is saved to secondary storage as well.

The most common type of secondary storage device is the *disk drive*. A traditional disk drive stores data by magnetically encoding it onto a spinning circular disk. *Solid state drives*, which store data in solid-state memory, are increasingly becoming popular. A solid-state drive has no moving parts, and operates faster than a traditional disk drive.

Most computers have some sort of secondary storage device, either a traditional disk drive or a solid-state drive, mounted inside their case. External drives are also available, which connect to one of the computer's communication ports. External drives can be used to create backup copies of important data or to move data to another computer.

In addition to external drives, many types of devices have been created for copying data, and for moving it to other computers. *Universal Serial Bus drives,* or *USB drives* are small devices that plug into the computer's USB (Universal Serial Bus) port, and appear to the system as a disk drive. These drives do not actually contain a disk, however. They store data in a special type of memory known as *flash memory.* USB drives are inexpensive, reliable, and small enough to be carried in your pocket.

Optical devices such as the *CD* (compact disc) and the *DVD* (digital versatile disc) are also popular for data storage. Data is not recorded magnetically on an optical disc, but is encoded as a series of pits on the disc surface. CD and DVD drives use a laser to detect the pits and thus read the encoded data. Optical discs hold large amounts of data, and because recordable CD and DVD drives are now commonplace, they make a good medium for creating backup copies of data.

Input Devices

Input is any data the computer collects from the outside world. The device that collects the data and sends it to the computer is called an *input device.* Common input devices are the keyboard, mouse, scanner, and digital camera. Disk drives, optical drives, and USB drives can also be considered input devices because programs and data are retrieved from them and loaded into the computer's memory.

Output Devices

Output is any data the computer sends to the outside world. It might be a sales report, a list of names, or a graphic image. The data is sent to an output device, which formats and presents it. Common output devices are monitors and printers. Disk drives, USB drives, and CD recorders can also be considered output devices because the CPU sends data to them to be saved.

Software

As previously mentioned, software refers to the programs that run on a computer. There are two general categories of software: operating systems and application software. An operating system is a set of programs that manages the computer's hardware devices and controls their processes. Most all modern operating systems are multitasking, which means they are capable of running multiple programs at once. Through a technique called time sharing, a multitasking system divides the allocation of hardware resources and the attention of the CPU among all the executing programs. UNIX, Linux, Mac OS, and Windows are multitasking operating systems.

Application software refers to programs that make the computer useful to the user. These programs solve specific problems or perform general operations that satisfy the needs of the user. Word processing, spreadsheet, and database packages are all examples of application software.

Checkpoint

1.1   Why is the computer used by so many different people, in so many different professions?

1.2   List the five major hardware components of a computer system.

1.3   Internally, the CPU consists of what two units?

1.4   Describe the steps in the fetch/decode/execute cycle.

1.5   What is a memory address? What is its purpose?

1.6   Explain why computers have both main memory and secondary storage.

1.7   What does the term *multitasking* mean?

1.4   Programming Languages

CONCEPT: A program is a set of instructions a computer follows in order to perform a task. A programming language is a special language used to write computer programs.

What Is a Program?

Computers are designed to follow instructions. A computer program is a set of instructions that enable the computer to solve a problem or perform a task. For example, suppose we want the computer to calculate someone's gross pay. The following is a list of things the computer should do to perform this task.

1. Display a message on the screen: "How many hours did you work?"
2. Allow the user to enter the number of hours worked.
3. Once the user enters a number, store it in memory.
4. Display a message on the screen: "How much do you get paid per hour?"
5. Allow the user to enter an hourly pay rate.
6. Once the user enters a number, store it in memory.
7. Once both the number of hours worked and the hourly pay rate are entered, multiply the two numbers and store the result in memory.
8. Display a message on the screen that shows the amount of money earned. The message must include the result of the calculation performed in Step 7.

Collectively, these instructions are called an *algorithm*. An algorithm is a set of well-defined steps for performing a task or solving a problem. Notice that these steps are sequentially ordered. Step 1 should be performed before Step 2, and so forth. It is important that these instructions be performed in their proper sequence.

Although you and I might easily understand the instructions in the pay-calculating algorithm, it is not ready to be executed on a computer. A computer's CPU can only process instructions that are written in *machine language*. If you were to look at a machine language program, you would see a stream of binary numbers (numbers consisting of only 1s and 0s). The binary numbers form machine language instructions, which the CPU interprets as commands. Here is an example of what a machine language instruction might look like:

1011010000000101

As you can imagine, the process of encoding an algorithm in machine language is very tedious and difficult. In addition, each different type of CPU has its own machine language. If you wrote a machine language program for computer A and then wanted to run it on computer B, which has a different type of CPU, you would have to rewrite the program in computer B's machine language.

Programming languages, which use words instead of numbers, were invented to ease the task of programming. A program can be written in a programming language, which is much easier to understand than machine language, and then translated into machine language. Programmers use software to perform this translation. Many programming languages have been created. Table 1-1 lists a few of the well-known ones.

Table 1-1 Programming languages

Language	Description
BASIC	Beginners All-purpose Symbolic Instruction Code is a general-purpose, procedural programming language. It was originally designed to be simple enough for beginners to learn.
FORTRAN	FORmula TRANslator is a procedural language designed for programming complex mathematical algorithms.
COBOL	Common Business-Oriented Language is a procedural language designed for business applications.
Pascal	Pascal is a structured, general-purpose, procedural language designed primarily for teaching programming.
C	C is a structured, general-purpose, procedural language developed at Bell Laboratories.
C++	Based on the C language, C++ offers object-oriented features not found in C. C++ was also invented at Bell Laboratories.
C#	Pronounced "C sharp." It is a language invented by Microsoft for developing applications based on the Microsoft .NET platform.
Java	Java is an object-oriented language invented at Sun Microsystems, and is now owned by Oracle. It may be used to develop stand-alone applications that operate on a single computer, applications that run over the Internet from a Web server, and applets that run in a Web browser.
JavaScript	JavaScript is a programming language that can be used in a Web site to perform simple operations. Despite its name, JavaScript is not related to Java.
Perl	A general-purpose programming language used widely on Internet servers.
PHP	A programming language used primarily for developing Web server applications and dynamic Web pages.
Python	Python is an object-oriented programming language used in both business and academia. Many popular Web sites contain features developed in Python.
Ruby	Ruby is a simple but powerful object-oriented programming language. It can be used for a variety of purposes, from small utility programs to large Web applications.
Visual Basic	Visual Basic is a Microsoft programming language and software development environment that allows programmers to create Windows-based applications quickly.

A History of Java

In 1991 a team was formed at Sun Microsystems (a company that is now owned by Oracle) to speculate about the important technological trends that might emerge in the near future. The team, which was named the Green Team, concluded that computers would merge with consumer appliances. Their first project was to develop a handheld device named *7 (pronounced star seven) that could be used to control a variety of home entertainment devices. For the unit to work, it had to use a programming language that could be processed by all the devices it controlled. This presented a problem because different brands of consumer devices use different processors, each with its own machine language.

Because no such universal language existed, James Gosling, the team's lead engineer, created one. Programs written in this language, which was originally named Oak, were not translated into the machine language of a specific processor, but were translated into an intermediate language known as *byte code*. Another program would then translate the byte code into machine language that could be executed by the processor in a specific consumer device.

Unfortunately, the technology developed by the Green Team was ahead of its time. No customers could be found, mostly because the computer-controlled consumer appliance industry was just beginning. But rather than abandoning their hard work and moving on to other projects, the team saw another opportunity: the Internet. The Internet is a perfect environment for a universal programming language such as Oak. It consists of numerous different computer platforms connected together in a single network.

To demonstrate the effectiveness of its language, which was renamed Java, the team used it to develop a Web browser. The browser, named HotJava, was able to download and run small Java programs known as applets. This gave the browser the capability to display animation and interact with the user. HotJava was demonstrated at the 1995 SunWorld conference before a wowed audience. Later the announcement was made that Netscape would incorporate Java technology into its Navigator browser. Other Internet companies rapidly followed, increasing the acceptance and the influence of the Java language. Today, Java is very popular for developing not only applets for the Internet but also stand-alone applications.

Java Applications and Applets

There are two types of programs that may be created with Java: applications and applets. An application is a stand-alone program that runs on your computer. You have probably used several applications already, such as word processors, spreadsheets, database managers, and graphics programs. Although Java may be used to write these types of applications, other languages such as C, C++, and Visual Basic are also used.

In the previous section you learned that Java may also be used to create applets. The term *applet* refers to a small application, in the same way that the term *piglet* refers to a small pig. Unlike applications, an applet is designed to be transmitted over the Internet from a Web server, and then executed in a Web browser. Applets are important because they can be used to extend the capabilities of a Web page significantly.

Web pages are normally written in Hypertext Markup Language (HTML). HTML is limited, however, because it merely describes the content and layout of a Web page. HTML does not have sophisticated abilities such as performing math calculations and interacting with the user. A Web designer can write a Java applet to perform operations that are normally performed by an application and embed it in a Web site. When someone visits the Web site, the applet is downloaded to the visitor's browser and executed.

Security

Any time content is downloaded from a Web server to a visitor's computer, security is an important concern. Because Java is a full-featured programming language, at first you might be suspicious of any Web site that transmits an applet to your computer. After all, couldn't a Java applet do harmful things, such as deleting the contents of the disk drive or transmitting private information to another computer? Fortunately, the answer is no. Web browsers run Java applets in a secure environment within your computer's memory and do not allow them to access resources, such as a disk drive, that are outside that environment.

1.5 What Is a Program Made Of?

CONCEPT: There are certain elements that are common to all programming languages.

Language Elements

All programming languages have some things in common. Table 1-2 lists the common elements you will find in almost every language.

Table 1-2 The common elements of a programming language

Language Element	Description
Key Words	These are words that have a special meaning in the programming language. They may be used for their intended purpose only. Key words are also known as *reserved words*.
Operators	Operators are symbols or words that perform operations on one or more operands. An operand is usually an item of data, such as a number.
Punctuation	Most programming languages require the use of punctuation characters. These characters serve specific purposes, such as marking the beginning or ending of a statement, or separating items in a list.
Programmer-Defined Names	Unlike key words, which are part of the programming language, these are words or names that are defined by the programmer. They are used to identify storage locations in memory and parts of the program that are created by the programmer. Programmer-defined names are often called *identifiers*.
Syntax	These are rules that must be followed when writing a program. Syntax dictates how key words and operators may be used, and where punctuation symbols must appear.

Let's look at an example Java program and identify an instance of each of these elements. Code Listing 1-1 shows the code listing with each line numbered.

 NOTE: The line numbers are not part of the program. They are included to help point out specific parts of the program.

Code Listing 1-1   `Payroll.java`

```
 1   public class Payroll
 2   {
 3      public static void main(String[] args)
 4      {
 5         int hours = 40;
 6         double grossPay, payRate = 25.0;
 7
 8         grossPay = hours * payRate;
 9         System.out.println("Your gross pay is $" + grossPay);
10      }
11   }
```

Key Words (Reserved Words)

Two of Java's key words appear in line 1: `public` and `class`. In line 3, the words `public`, `static`, and `void` are all key words. The words `int` in line 5 and `double` in line 6 are also key words. These words, which are always written in lowercase, each have a special meaning in Java and can only be used for their intended purpose. As you will see, the programmer is allowed to make up his or her own names for certain things in a program. Key words, however, are reserved and cannot be used for anything other than their designated purpose. Part of learning a programming language is learning the commonly used key words, what they mean, and how to use them.

Table 1-3 shows a list of the Java key words.

Table 1-3   The Java key words

abstract	const	final	int	public	throw
assert	continue	finally	interface	return	throws
boolean	default	float	long	short	transient
break	do	for	native	static	true
byte	double	goto	new	strictfp	try
case	else	if	null	super	void
catch	enum	implements	package	switch	volatile
char	extends	import	private	synchronized	while
class	false	instanceof	protected	this	

Programmer-Defined Names

The words `hours`, `payRate`, and `grossPay` that appear in the program in lines 5, 6, 8, and 9 are programmer-defined names. They are not part of the Java language but are names made up by the programmer. In this particular program, these are the names of variables. As you will learn later in this chapter, variables are the names of memory locations that may hold data.

Operators

In line 8 the following line appears:

8 `grossPay = hours * payRate;` *Equation*

The = and * symbols are both operators. They perform operations on items of data, known as operands. The * operator multiplies its two operands, which in this example are the variables `hours` and `payRate`. The = symbol is called the assignment operator. It takes the value of the expression that appears at its right and stores it in the variable whose name appears at its left. In this example, the = operator stores in the `grossPay` variable the result of the `hours` variable multiplied by the `payRate` variable. In other words, the statement says, "the `grossPay` variable is assigned the value of `hours` times `payRate`."

Punctuation

Notice that lines 5, 6, 8, and 9 end with a semicolon. A semicolon in Java is similar to a period in English: It marks the end of a complete sentence (or statement, as it is called in programming jargon). Semicolons do not appear at the end of every line in a Java program, however. There are rules that govern where semicolons are required and where they are not. Part of learning Java is learning where to place semicolons and other punctuation symbols.

Lines and Statements

Often, the contents of a program are thought of in terms of lines and statements. A *line* is just that—a single line as it appears in the body of a program. Code Listing 1-1 is shown with each of its lines numbered. Most of the lines contain something meaningful; however, line 7 is empty. Blank lines are only used to make a program more readable.

A statement is a complete instruction that causes the computer to perform some action. Here is the statement that appears in line 9 of Code Listing 1-1:

```
System.out.println("Your gross pay is $" + grossPay);
```

This statement causes the computer to display a message on the screen. Statements can be a combination of key words, operators, and programmer-defined names. Statements often occupy only one line in a program, but sometimes they are spread out over more than one line.

Variables

The most fundamental way that a Java program stores an item of data in memory is with a variable. A *variable* is a named storage location in the computer's memory. The data stored in a variable may change while the program is running (hence the name "variable"). Notice that in Code Listing 1-1 the programmer-defined names `hours`, `payRate`, and `grossPay` appear in several places. All three of these are the names of variables. The hours variable is used to store the number of hours the user has worked. The payRate variable stores the user's hourly pay rate. The grossPay variable holds the result of hours multiplied by payRate, which is the user's gross pay.

Variables are symbolic names made up by the programmer that represent locations in the computer's RAM. When data is stored in a variable, it is actually stored in RAM. Assume that a program has a variable named length. Figure 1-4 illustrates the way the variable name represents a memory location.

In Figure 1-4, the variable length is holding the value 72. The number 72 is actually stored in RAM at address 23, but the name length symbolically represents this storage location. If it helps, you can think of a variable as a box that holds data. In Figure 1-4, the number 72 is stored in the box named length. Only one item may be stored in the box at any given time. If the program stores another value in the box, it will take the place of the number 72.

Figure 1-4 A variable name represents a location in memory

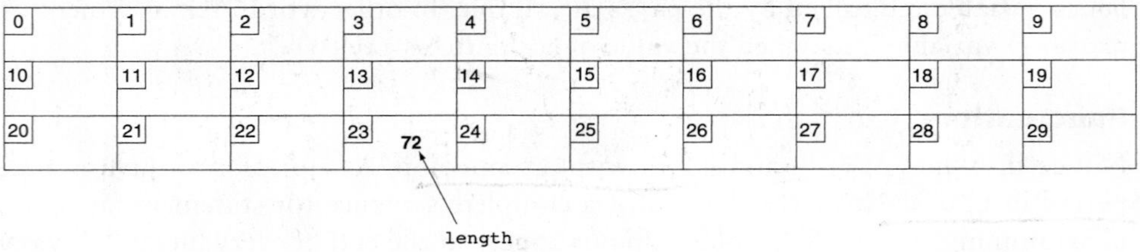

The Compiler and the Java Virtual Machine

When a Java program is written, it must be typed into the computer and saved to a file. A *text editor*, which is similar to a word processing program, is used for this task. The Java programming statements written by the programmer are called *source code*, and the file they are saved in is called a *source file*. Java source files end with the *.java* extension.

After the programmer saves the source code to a file, he or she runs the Java compiler. A *compiler* is a program that translates source code into an executable form. During the translation process, the compiler uncovers any syntax errors that may be in the program. *Syntax errors* are mistakes that the programmer has made that violate the rules of the programming language. These errors must be corrected before the compiler can translate the source code. Once the program is free of syntax errors, the compiler creates another file that holds the translated instructions.

Most programming language compilers translate source code directly into files that contain machine language instructions. These are called *executable files* because they may be executed directly by the computer's CPU. The Java compiler, however, translates a Java source file into a file that contains byte code instructions. Byte code instructions are not machine language, and therefore cannot be directly executed by the CPU. Instead, they are executed by the *Java Virtual Machine* (JVM). The JVM is a program that reads Java byte code instructions and executes them as they are read. For this reason, the JVM is often called an interpreter, and Java is often referred to as an interpreted language. Figure 1-5 illustrates the process of writing a Java program, compiling it to byte code, and running it.

Although Java byte code is not machine language for a CPU, it can be considered as machine language for the JVM. You can think of the JVM as a program that simulates a computer whose machine language is Java byte code.

Portability

The term *portable* means that a program may be written on one type of computer and then run on a wide variety of computers, with little or no modification necessary. Because Java byte code is the same on all computers, compiled Java programs are highly portable. In fact, a compiled Java program may be run on any computer that has a JVM. Figure 1-6 illustrates the concept of a compiled Java program running on Windows, Linux, Mac, and UNIX computers.

With most other programming languages, portability is achieved by the creation of a compiler for each type of computer that the language is to run on. For example, in order for the C++ language to be supported by Windows, Linux, and Mac computers, a separate C++ compiler must be created for each of those environments. Compilers are very complex programs, and more difficult to develop than interpreters. For this reason, a JVM has been developed for many types of computers.

Figure 1-5
Program development process

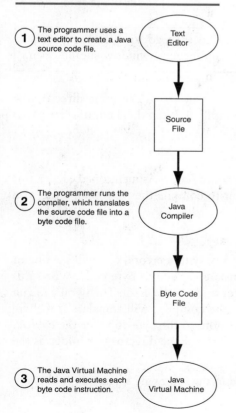

1. The programmer uses a text editor to create a Java source code file.
2. The programmer runs the compiler, which translates the source code file into a byte code file.
3. The Java Virtual Machine reads and executes each byte code instruction.

Figure 1-6 Java byte code may be run on any computer with a Java Virtual Machine

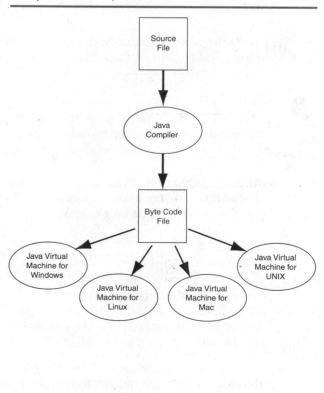

Java Software Editions

The software that you use to create Java programs is referred to as the *JDK* (Java Development Kit) or the *SDK* (Software Development Kit). There are the following different editions of the JDK available from Oracle:

- *Java SE*—The Java Standard Edition provides all the essential software tools necessary for writing Java applications and applets.
- *Java EE*—The Java Enterprise Edition provides tools for creating large business applications that employ servers and provide services over the Web.
- *Java ME*—The Java Micro Edition provides a small, highly optimized runtime environment for consumer products such as cell phones, pagers, and appliances.

These editions of Java may be downloaded from Oracle by going to:

> http://java.oracle.com

NOTE: You can follow the instructions in Appendix E, which can be downloaded from the book's companion Web site, to install the JDK on your system. You can access the book's companion Web site by going to www.pearsonhighered.com/gaddis.

Compiling and Running a Java Program

Compiling a Java program is a simple process. Once you have installed the JDK, go to your operating system's command prompt.

TIP: In Windows click Start, go to All Programs, and then go to Accessories. Click Command Prompt on the Accessories menu. A command prompt window should open.

VideoNote

Compiling and
Running a Java
Program

At the operating system command prompt, make sure you are in the same directory or folder where the Java program that you want to compile is located. Then, use the javac command, in the following form:

```
javac Filename
```

Filename is the name of a file that contains the Java source code. As mentioned earlier, this file has the *.java* extension. For example, if you want to compile the *Payroll.java* file, you would execute the following command:

```
javac Payroll.java
```

This command runs the compiler. If the file contains any syntax errors, you will see one or more error messages and the compiler will not translate the file to byte code. When this happens you must open the source file in a text editor and fix the error. Then you can run the compiler again. If the file has no syntax errors, the compiler will translate it to byte code. Byte code is stored in a file with the *.class* extension, so the byte code for the *Payroll.java* file will be stored in *Payroll.class*, which will be in the same directory or folder as the source file.

To run the Java program, you use the java command in the following form:

```
java ClassFilename
```

ClassFilename is the name of the *.class* file that you wish to execute; however, you do not type the *.class* extension. For example, to run the program that is stored in the *Payroll.class* file, you would enter the following command:

```
java Payroll
```

This command runs the Java interpreter (the JVM) and executes the program.

Integrated Development Environments

VideoNote
Using an IDE

In addition to the command prompt programs, there are also several Java integrated development environments (IDEs). These environments consist of a text editor, compiler, debugger, and other utilities integrated into a package with a single set of menus. A program is compiled and executed with a single click of a button, or by selecting a single item from a menu. Figure 1-7 shows a screen from the NetBeans IDE.

Figure 1-7   An integrated development environment (IDE)   (Oracle Corporate Counsel)

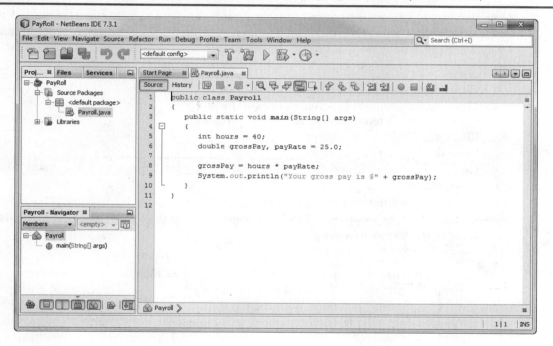

Checkpoint

MyProgrammingLab™   *www.myprogramminglab.com*

1.8   Describe the difference between a key word and a programmer-defined symbol.

1.9   Describe the difference between operators and punctuation symbols.

1.10   Describe the difference between a program line and a statement.

1.11   Why are variables called "variable"?

1.12   What happens to a variable's current contents when a new value is stored there?

1.13   What is a compiler?

1.14   What is a syntax error?

1.15   What is byte code?

1.16   What is the JVM?

1.6   The Programming Process

CONCEPT: The programming process consists of several steps, which include design, creation, testing, and debugging activities.

Now that you have been introduced to what a program is, it's time to consider the process of creating a program. Quite often when inexperienced students are given programming assignments, they have trouble getting started because they don't know what to do first. If you find yourself in this dilemma, the following steps may help.

1. Clearly define what the program is to do.
2. Visualize the program running on the computer.
3. Use design tools to create a model of the program.
4. Check the model for logical errors.
5. Enter the code and compile it.
6. Correct any errors found during compilation. Repeat Steps 5 and 6 as many times as necessary.
7. Run the program with test data for input.
8. Correct any runtime errors found while running the program. Repeat Steps 5 through 8 as many times as necessary.
9. Validate the results of the program.

These steps emphasize the importance of planning. Just as there are good ways and bad ways to paint a house, there are good ways and bad ways to create a program. A good program always begins with planning. With the pay-calculating algorithm that was presented earlier in this chapter serving as our example, let's look at each of the steps in more detail.

1. Clearly define what the program is to do

This step commonly requires you to identify the purpose of the program, the data that is to be input, the processing that is to take place, and the desired output. Let's examine each of these requirements for the pay-calculating algorithm.

Purpose   To calculate the user's gross pay.

Input   Number of hours worked, hourly pay rate.

Process   Multiply number of hours worked by hourly pay rate. The result is the user's gross pay.

Output   Display a message indicating the user's gross pay.

2. Visualize the program running on the computer

Before you create a program on the computer, you should first create it in your mind. Try to imagine what the computer screen will look like while the program is running. If it helps, draw pictures of the screen, with sample input and output, at various points in the program. For instance, Figure 1-8 shows the screen we might want produced by a program that implements the pay-calculating algorithm.

Figure 1-8   Screen produced by the pay-calculating algorithm

```
How many hours did you work? 10
How much do you get paid per hour? 15
Your gross pay is $150.0
```

In this step, you must put yourself in the shoes of the user. What messages should the program display? What questions should it ask? By addressing these concerns, you can determine most of the program's output.

3. Use design tools to create a model of the program

While planning a program, the programmer uses one or more design tools to create a model of the program. For example, *pseudocode* is a cross between human language and a programming language and is especially helpful when designing an algorithm. Although the computer can't understand pseudocode, programmers often find it helpful to write an algorithm in a language that's "almost" a programming language, but still very similar to natural language. For example, here is pseudocode that describes the pay-calculating algorithm:

> *Get payroll data.*
> *Calculate gross pay.*
> *Display gross pay.*

Although this pseudocode gives a broad view of the program, it doesn't reveal all the program's details. A more detailed version of the pseudocode follows:

> *Display "How many hours did you work?"*
> *Input hours.*
> *Display "How much do you get paid per hour?"*
> *Input rate.*
> *Store the value of hours times rate in the pay variable.*
> *Display the value in the pay variable.*

Notice that the pseudocode uses statements that look more like commands than the English statements that describe the algorithm in Section 1.4. The pseudocode even names variables and describes mathematical operations.

4. Check the model for logical errors

Logical errors are mistakes that cause the program to produce erroneous results. Once a model of the program is assembled, it should be checked for these errors. For example, if pseudocode is used, the programmer should trace through it, checking the logic of each step. If an error is found, the model can be corrected before the next step is attempted.

5. Enter the code and compile it

Once a model of the program has been created, checked, and corrected, the programmer is ready to write source code on the computer. The programmer saves the source code to a file and begins the process of compiling it. During this step the compiler will find any syntax errors that may exist in the program.

6. Correct any errors found during compilation. Repeat Steps 5 and 6 as many times as necessary

If the compiler reports any errors, they must be corrected. Steps 5 and 6 must be repeated until the program is free of compile-time errors.

7. Run the program with test data for input

Once an executable file is generated, the program is ready to be tested for runtime errors. A runtime error is an error that occurs while the program is running. These are usually logical errors, such as mathematical mistakes.

Testing for runtime errors requires that the program be executed with sample data or sample input. The sample data should be such that the correct output can be predicted. If the program does not produce the correct output, a logical error is present in the program.

8. Correct any runtime errors found while running the program. Repeat Steps 5 through 8 as many times as necessary

When runtime errors are found in a program, they must be corrected. You must identify the step where the error occurred and determine the cause. If an error is a result of incorrect logic (such as an improperly stated math formula), you must correct the statement or statements involved in the logic. If an error is due to an incomplete understanding of the program requirements, then you must restate the program purpose and modify the program model and source code. The program must then be saved, recompiled, and retested. This means Steps 5 though 8 must be repeated until the program reliably produces satisfactory results.

9. Validate the results of the program

When you believe you have corrected all the runtime errors, enter test data and determine whether the program solves the original problem.

Software Engineering

The field of software engineering encompasses the whole process of crafting computer software. It includes designing, writing, testing, debugging, documenting, modifying, and maintaining complex software development projects. Like traditional engineers, software engineers use a number of tools in their craft. Here are a few examples:

- Program specifications
- Diagrams of screen output
- Diagrams representing the program components and the flow of data
- Pseudocode
- Examples of expected input and desired output
- Special software designed for testing programs

Most commercial software applications are large and complex. Usually a team of programmers, not a single individual, develops them. It is important that the program requirements be thoroughly analyzed and divided into subtasks that are handled by individual teams, or individuals within a team.

Checkpoint

MyProgrammingLab™ *www.myprogramminglab.com*

1.17　What four items should you identify when defining what a program is to do?

1.18　What does it mean to "visualize a program running"? What is the value of such an activity?

1.19　What is pseudocode?

1.20　Describe what a compiler does with a program's source code.

1.21　What is a runtime error?

1.22　Is a syntax error (such as misspelling a key word) found by the compiler or when the program is running?

1.23　What is the purpose of testing a program with sample data or input?

1.7 Object-Oriented Programming

> **CONCEPT:** Java is an object-oriented programming (OOP) language. OOP is a method of software development that has its own practices, concepts, and vocabulary.

There are primarily two methods of programming in use today: procedural and object-oriented. The earliest programming languages were procedural, meaning a program was made of one or more procedures. A *procedure* is a set of programming statements that, together, perform a specific task. The statements might gather input from the user, manipulate data stored in the computer's memory, and perform calculations or any other operation necessary to complete the procedure's task.

Procedures typically operate on data items that are separate from the procedures. In a procedural program, the data items are commonly passed from one procedure to another, as shown in Figure 1-9.

Figure 1-9　Data is passed among procedures

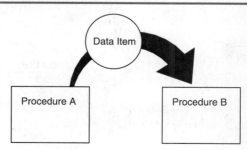

As you might imagine, the focus of procedural programming is on the creation of procedures that operate on the program's data. The separation of data and the code that operates on the data often leads to problems, however. For example, the data is stored in a particular format, which consists of variables and more complex structures that are created from variables. The procedures that operate on the data must be designed with that format in mind. But, what happens if the format of the data is altered? Quite often, a program's specifications change, resulting in a redesigned data format. When the structure of the data changes, the code that operates on the data must also be changed to accept the new format. This results in added work for programmers and a greater opportunity for bugs to appear in the code.

This has helped influence the shift from procedural programming to object-oriented programming (OOP). Whereas procedural programming is centered on creating procedures, object-oriented programming is centered on creating objects. An object is a software entity that contains data and procedures. The data contained in an object is known as the object's *attributes*. The procedures, or behaviors, that an object performs are known as the object's *methods*. The object is, conceptually, a self-contained unit consisting of data (attributes) and procedures (methods). This is illustrated in Figure 1-10.

OOP addresses the problem of code/data separation through encapsulation and data hiding. *Encapsulation* refers to the combining of data and code into a single object. *Data hiding* refers to an object's ability to hide its data from code that is outside the object. Only the object's methods may then directly access and make changes to the object's data. An object typically hides its data, but allows outside code to access the methods that operate on the data. As shown in Figure 1-11, the object's methods provide programming statements outside the object with indirect access to the object's data.

When an object's internal data is hidden from outside code and access to that data is restricted to the object's methods, the data is protected from accidental corruption. In addition, the programming code outside the object does not need to know about the format or

Figure 1-10 An object contains data and procedures

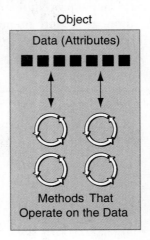

Figure 1-11 Code outside the object interacts with the object's methods

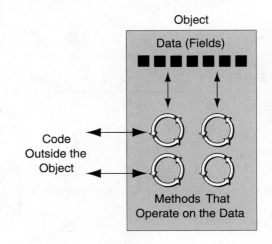

internal structure of the object's data. The code only needs to interact with the object's methods. When a programmer changes the structure of an object's internal data, he or she also modifies the object's methods so they may properly operate on the data. The way in which outside code interacts with the methods, however, does not change.

These are just a few of the benefits of object-oriented programming. Because Java is fully object-oriented, you will learn much more about OOP practices, concepts, and terms as you progress through this book.

 Checkpoint

MyProgrammingLab™ *www.myprogramminglab.com*

1.24   In procedural programming, what two parts of a program are typically separated?

1.25   What are an object's attributes?

1.26   What are an object's methods?

1.27   What is encapsulation?

1.28   What is data hiding?

Review Questions and Exercises

Multiple Choice

1. This part of the computer fetches instructions, carries out the operations commanded by the instructions, and produces some outcome or resultant information.
    a. memory
    b. CPU
    c. secondary storage
    d. input device

2. A byte is made up of eight
    a. CPUs
    b. addresses
    c. variables
    d. bits

3. Each byte is assigned a unique
    a. address
    b. CPU
    c. bit
    d. variable

4. This type of memory can hold data for long periods of time—even when there is no power to the computer.
    a. RAM
    b. primary storage
    c. secondary storage
    d. CPU storage

5. If you were to look at a machine language program, you would see _____.
   a. Java source code
   b. a stream of binary numbers
   c. English words
   d. circuits

6. This type of program is designed to be transmitted over the Internet and run in a Web browser.
   a. application
   b. applet
   c. machine language
   d. source code

7. These are words that have a special meaning in the programming language.
   a. punctuation
   b. programmer-defined names
   c. key words
   d. operators

8. These are symbols or words that perform operations on one or more operands.
   a. punctuation
   b. programmer-defined names
   c. key words
   d. operators

9. These characters serve specific purposes, such as marking the beginning or ending of a statement, or separating items in a list.
   a. punctuation
   b. programmer-defined names
   c. key words
   d. operators

10. These are words or names that are used to identify storage locations in memory and parts of the program that are created by the programmer.
   a. punctuation
   b. programmer-defined names
   c. key words
   d. operators

11. These are the rules that must be followed when writing a program.
   a. syntax
   b. punctuation
   c. key words
   d. operators

12. This is a named storage location in the computer's memory.
   a. class
   b. key word
   c. variable
   d. operator

13. The Java compiler generates _____.
    a. machine code
    b. byte code
    c. source code
    d. HTML

14. JVM stands for _____.
    a. Java Variable Machine
    b. Java Variable Method
    c. Java Virtual Method
    d. Java Virtual Machine

Find the Error

1. The following pseudocode algorithm has an error. The program is supposed to ask the user for the length and width of a rectangular room, and then display the room's area. The program must multiply the width by the length to determine the area. Find the error.

   area = width × length
   Display "What is the room's width?"
   Input width.
   Display "What is the room's length?"
   Input length.
   Display area.

Algorithm Workbench

Write pseudocode algorithms for the programs described as follows:

1. **Available Credit**

   A program that calculates a customer's available credit should ask the user for the following:

   - The customer's maximum amount of credit
   - The amount of credit used by the customer

   Once these items have been entered, the program should calculate and display the customer's available credit. You can calculate available credit by subtracting the amount of credit used from the maximum amount of credit.

2. **Sales Tax**

   A program that calculates the total of a retail sale should ask the user for the following:

   - The retail price of the item being purchased
   - The sales tax rate

   Once these items have been entered, the program should calculate and display the following:

   - The sales tax for the purchase
   - The total of the sale

3. **Account Balance**

   A program that calculates the current balance in a savings account must ask the user for the following:

   - The starting balance
   - The total dollar amount of deposits made
   - The total dollar amount of withdrawals made
   - The monthly interest rate

   Once the program calculates the current balance, it should be displayed on the screen.

Predict the Result

The following are programs expressed as English statements. What would each display on the screen if they were actual programs?

1. The variable x starts with the value 0.

   The variable y starts with the value 5.
   Add 1 to x.
   Add 1 to y.
   Add x and y, and store the result in y.
   Display the value in y on the screen.

2. The variable a starts with the value 10.

   The variable b starts with the value 2.

   The variable c starts with the value 4.
   Store the value of a times b in a.
   Store the value of b times c in c.
   Add a and c, and store the result in b.
   Display the value in b on the screen.

Short Answer

1. Both main memory and secondary storage are types of memory. Describe the difference between the two.

2. What type of memory is usually volatile?

3. What is the difference between operating system software and application software?

4. Why must programs written in a high-level language be translated into machine language before they can be run?

5. Why is it easier to write a program in a high-level language than in machine language?

6. What is a source file?

7. What is the difference between a syntax error and a logical error?

8. What is an algorithm?

9. What is a compiler?

10. What is the difference between an application and an applet?

11. Why are Java applets safe to download and execute?

12. What must a computer have in order for it to execute Java programs?

13. What is the difference between machine language code and byte code?

14. Why does byte code make Java a portable language?

15. Is encapsulation a characteristic of procedural or object-oriented programming?

16. Why should an object hide its data?

17. What part of an object forms an interface through which outside code may access the object's data?

18. What type of program do you use to write Java source code?

19. Will the Java compiler translate a source file that contains syntax errors?

20. What does the Java compiler translate Java source code to?

21. Assuming you are using the JDK, what command would you type at the operating system command prompt to compile the program `LabAssignment.java`?

22. Assuming there are no syntax errors in the *LabAssignment.java* program when it is compiled, answer the following questions.

    a. What file will be produced?
    b. What will the file contain?
    c. What command would you type at the operating system command prompt to run the program?

Programming Challenge

MyProgrammingLab™ *Visit www.myprogramminglab.com to complete many of these Programming Challenges online and get instant feedback.*

1. Your First Java Program

This assignment will help you get acquainted with your Java development software. Here is the Java program you will enter:

VideoNote
Your First Java
Program

```java
// This is my first Java program.
public class MyFirstProgram
{
    public static void main(String[] args)
    {
        System.out.println("Hello World!");
    }
}
```

If You Are Using the JDK at the Command Prompt:

1. Use a text editor to type the source code exactly as it is shown. Be sure to place all the punctuation characters and be careful to match the case of the letters as they are shown. Save it to a file named *MyFirstProgram.java*.

2. After saving the program, go to your operating system's command prompt and change your current directory or folder to the one that contains the Java program you just created. Then use the following command to compile the program:

```
javac MyFirstProgram.java
```

If you typed the contents of the file exactly as shown, you shouldn't have any syntax errors. If you see error messages, open the file in the editor and compare your code to that shown. Correct any mistakes you have made, save the file, and run the compiler again. If you see no error messages, the file was successfully compiled.

3. Next, enter the following command to run the program:

```
java MyFirstProgram
```

Be sure to use the capitalization of `MyFirstProgram` exactly as it is shown here. You should see the message "Hello World!" displayed on the screen.

If You Are Using an IDE:

Because there are many Java IDEs, we cannot include specific instructions for all of these. The following are general steps that should apply to most of them. You will need to consult your IDE's documentation for specific instructions.

1. Start your Java IDE and perform any necessary setup operations, such as starting a new project and creating a new Java source file.

2. Use the IDE's text editor to type the source code exactly as it is shown. Be sure to place all the punctuation characters and be careful to match the case of the letters as they are shown. Save it to a file named *MyFirstProgram.java*.

3. After saving the program, use your IDE's command to compile the program. If you typed the contents of the file exactly as shown, you shouldn't have any syntax errors. If you see error messages, compare your code to that shown. Correct any mistakes you have made, save the file, and run the compiler again. If you see no error messages, the file was successfully compiled.

Use your IDE's command to run the program. You should see the message "Hello World!" displayed.

2 Java Fundamentals

TOPICS

2.1 The Parts of a Java Program

CONCEPT: A Java program has parts that serve specific purposes.

Java programs are made up of different parts. Your first step in learning Java is to learn what the parts are. We will begin by looking at a simple example, shown in Code Listing 2-1.

Code Listing 2-1 (Simple.java)

```
1  // This is a simple Java program.
2
3  public class Simple
4  {
5     public static void main(String[] args)
6     {
7        System.out.println("Programming is great fun!");
8     }
9  }
```

TIP: Remember, the line numbers shown in the program listings are not part of the program. The numbers are shown so we can refer to specific lines in the programs.

As mentioned in Chapter 1, the names of Java source code files end with *.java*. The program shown in Code Listing 2-1 is named *Simple.java*. Using the Java compiler, this program may be compiled with the following command:

```
javac Simple.java
```

The compiler will create another file named *Simple.class*, which contains the translated Java byte code. This file can be executed with the following command:

```
java Simple
```

 TIP: Remember, you do not type the *.class* extension when using the java command.

The output of the program is as follows. This is what appears on the screen when the program runs.

Program Output

```
Programming is great fun!
```

Let's examine the program line by line. Here's the statement in line 1:

```
// This is a simple Java program.
```

Other than the two slash marks that begin this line, it looks pretty much like an ordinary sentence. The // marks the beginning of a comment. The compiler ignores everything from the double-slash to the end of the line. That means you can type anything you want on that line and the compiler never complains. Although comments are not required, they are very important to programmers. Most programs are much more complicated than this example, and comments help explain what's going on.

Line 2 is blank. Programmers often insert blank lines in programs to make them easier to read. Line 3 reads:

```
public class Simple
```

This line is known as a *class header*, and it marks the beginning of a *class definition*. One of the uses of a class is to serve as a container for an application. As you progress through this book, you will learn more and more about classes. For now, just remember that a Java program must have at least one class definition. This line of code consists of three words: public, class, and Simple. Let's take a closer look at each word.

- public is a Java key word, and it must be written in all lowercase letters. It is known as an *access specifier*, and it controls where the class may be accessed from. The public specifier means access to the class is unrestricted. (In other words, the class is "open to the public.")
- class, which must also be written in lowercase letters, is a Java key word that indicates the beginning of a class definition.

- `Simple` is the class name. This name was made up by the programmer. The class could have been called `Pizza`, or `Dog`, or anything else the programmer wanted. Programmer-defined names may be written in lowercase letters, uppercase letters, or a mixture of both.

In a nutshell, this line of code tells the compiler that a publicly accessible class named `Simple` is being defined. Here are two more points to know about classes:

- You may create more than one class in a file, but you may have only one `public class` per Java file.
- When a Java file has a `public class`, the name of the public class must be the same as the name of the file (without the *.java* extension). For instance, the program in Code Listing 2-1 has a `public class` named `Simple`, so it is stored in a file named *Simple.java*.

> **NOTE:** Java is a case-sensitive language. That means it regards uppercase letters as being entirely different characters than their lowercase counterparts. The word `Public` is not the same as `public`, and `Class` is not the same as `class`. Some words in a Java program must be entirely in lowercase, while other words may use a combination of lower and uppercase characters. Later in this chapter, you will see a list of all the Java key words, which must appear in lowercase.

Line 4 contains only a single character:

[handwritten: Left Brace / Opening brace]   *[handwritten: Closi... / Brace...]*

```
{
```

This is called a left brace, or an opening brace, and is associated with the beginning of the class definition. All of the programming statements that are part of the class are enclosed in a set of braces. If you glance at the last line in the program, line 9, you'll see the closing brace. Everything between the two braces is the *body* of the class named `Simple`. Here is the program code again, this time the body of the class definition is shaded.

```
// This is a simple Java program.
public class Simple
{
    public static void main(String[] args)
    {
        System.out.println("Programming is great fun!");
    }
}
```

> **WARNING!** Make sure you have a closing brace for every opening brace in your program!

Line 5 reads:

```
public static void main(String[] args)
```

This line is known as a *method header*. It marks the beginning of a *method*. A method can be thought of as a group of one or more programming statements that collectively has a name. When creating a method, you must tell the compiler several things about it. That is why this line contains so many words. At this point, the only thing you should be concerned about is that the name of the method is main, and the rest of the words are required for the method to be properly defined. This is shown in Figure 2-1.

Recall from Chapter 1 that a stand-alone Java program that runs on your computer is known as an application. Every Java application must have a method named main. The main method is the starting point of an application.

Figure 2-1   The main method header

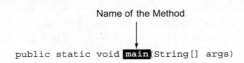

Name of the Method

```
public static void main(String[] args)
```

The other parts of this line are necessary
for the method to be properly defined.

> **NOTE:** For the time being, all the programs you will write will consist of a class with a main method whose header looks exactly like the one shown in Code Listing 2-1. As you progress through this book you will learn what public static void and (String[] args) mean. For now, just assume that you are learning a "recipe" for assembling a Java program.

Line 6 has another opening brace:

```
{
```

This opening brace belongs to the main method. Remember that braces enclose statements, and every opening brace must have an accompanying closing brace. If you look at line 8 you will see the closing brace that corresponds with this opening brace. Everything between these braces is the *body* of the main method.

Line 7 appears as follows:

```
System.out.println("Programming is great fun!");
```

To put it simply, this line displays a message on the screen. The message, "Programming is great fun!" is printed without the quotation marks. In programming terms, the group of characters inside the quotation marks is called a *string literal*.

> **NOTE:** This is the only line in the program that causes anything to be printed on the screen. The other lines, like public class Simple and public static void main(String[] args), are necessary for the framework of your program, but they do not cause any screen output. Remember, a program is a set of instructions for the computer. If something is to be displayed on the screen, you must use a programming statement for that purpose.

At the end of the line is a *semicolon*. Just as a period marks the end of a sentence, a semicolon marks the end of a statement in Java. Not every line of code ends with a semicolon, however. Here is a summary of where you do not place a semicolon:

- Comments do not have to end with a semicolon because they are ignored by the compiler.
- Class headers and method headers do not end with a semicolon because they are terminated with a body of code inside braces.
- The brace characters, { and }, are not statements, so you do not place a semicolon after them.

It might seem that the rules for where to put a semicolon are not clear at all. For now, just concentrate on learning the parts of a program. You'll soon get a feel for where you should and should not use semicolons.

As has already been pointed out, lines 8 and 9 contain the closing braces for the main method and the class definition:

```
        }
    }
```

Before continuing, let's review the points we just covered, including some of the more elusive rules.

- Java is a case-sensitive language. It does not regard uppercase letters as being the same character as their lowercase equivalents.
- All Java programs must be stored in a file with a name that ends with .*java*.
- Comments are ignored by the compiler.
- A .*java* file may contain many classes, but may have only one public class. If a .*java* file has a public class, the class must have the same name as the file. For instance, if the file *Pizza.java* contains a public class, the class's name would be Pizza.
- Every Java application program must have a method named main.
- For every left brace, or opening brace, there must be a corresponding right brace, or closing brace.
- Statements are terminated with semicolons. This does not include comments, class headers, method headers, or braces.

In the sample program, you encountered several special characters. Table 2-1 summarizes how they were used.

Table 2-1   Special characters

Characters	Name	Meaning
//	Double slash	Marks the beginning of a comment
( )	Opening and closing parentheses	Used in a method header
{ }	Opening and closing braces	Encloses a group of statements, such as the contents of a class or a method
" "	Quotation marks	Encloses a string of characters, such as a message that is to be printed on the screen
;	Semicolon	Marks the end of a complete programming statement

 **Checkpoint**

MyProgrammingLab™ *www.myprogramminglab.com*

2.1 The following program will not compile because the lines have been mixed up.

```
public static void main(String[] args)
}
// A crazy mixed up program
public class Columbus
{
System.out.println("In 1492 Columbus sailed the ocean blue.");
{
}
```

When the lines are properly arranged, the program should display the following on the screen:

```
In 1492 Columbus sailed the ocean blue.
```

Rearrange the lines in the correct order. Test the program by entering it on the computer, compiling it, and running it.

2.2 When the program in Question 2.1 is saved to a file, what should the file be named?

2.3 Complete the following program skeleton so it displays the message "Hello World" on the screen.

```
public class Hello
{
    public static void main(String[] args)
    {
        // Insert code here to complete the program
    }
}
```

2.4 On paper, write a program that will display your name on the screen. Place a comment with today's date at the top of the program. Test your program by entering, compiling, and running it.

2.5 All Java source code filenames must end with _____.
a) a semicolon
b) *.class*
c) *.java*
d) none of the above

2.6 Every Java application program must have _____.
a) a method named main
b) more than one class definition
c) one or more comments

2.2 The `print` and `println` Methods, and the Java API

CONCEPT: The **print** and **println** methods are used to display text output. They are part of the Java API, which is a collection of prewritten classes and methods for performing specific operations.

In this section, you will learn how to write programs that produce output on the screen. The simplest type of output that a program can display on the screen is console output. *Console output* is merely plain text. When you display console output in a system that uses a graphical user interface, such as Windows or Mac OS, the output usually appears in a window similar to the one shown in Figure 2-2.

Figure 2-2 A console window (Microsoft Corporation)

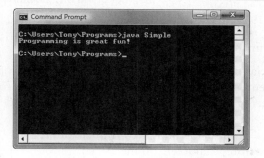

VideoNote
Displaying
Console Output

The word *console* is an old computer term. It comes from the days when the operator of a large computer system interacted with the system by typing on a terminal that consisted of a simple screen and keyboard. This terminal was known as the *console*. The console screen, which displayed only text, was known as the standard output device. Today, the term *standard output device* typically refers to the device that displays console output.

Performing output in Java, as well as many other tasks, is accomplished by using the Java API. The term *API* stands for *Application Programmer Interface*. The API is a standard library of prewritten classes for performing specific operations. These classes and their methods are available to all Java programs. The print and println methods are part of the API and provide ways for output to be displayed on the standard output device.

The program in Code Listing 2-1 (`Simple.java`) uses the following statement to print a message on the screen:

```
System.out.println("Programming is great fun!");
```

System is a class that is part of the Java API. The System class contains objects and methods that perform system-level operations. One of the objects contained in the System class is named out. The out object has methods, such as print and println, for performing output on the system console, or standard output device. The hierarchical relationship among System, out, print, and println is shown in Figure 2-3.

Figure 2-3 Relationship among the `System` class, the `out` object, and the
`print` and `println` methods

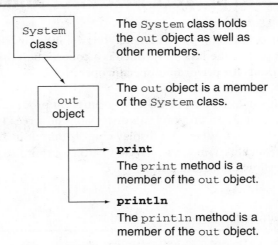

Here is a brief summary of how it all works together:

- The `System` class is part of the Java API. It has member objects and methods for performing system-level operations, such as sending output to the console.
- The `out` object is a member of the `System` class. It provides methods for sending output to the screen.
- The `print` and `println` methods are members of the `out` object. They actually perform the work of writing characters on the screen.

This hierarchy explains why the statement that executes `println` is so long. The sequence `System.out.println` specifies that `println` is a member of `out`, which is a member of `System`.

NOTE: The period that separates the names of the objects is pronounced "dot." `System.out.println` is pronounced "system dot out dot print line."

The value that is to be displayed on the screen is placed inside the parentheses. This value is known as an *argument*. For example, the following statement executes the `println` method using the string `"King Arthur"` as its argument. This will print "King Arthur" on the screen. (The quotation marks are not displayed.)

```
System.out.println("King Arthur");
```

An important thing to know about the `println` method is that after it displays its message, it advances the cursor to the beginning of the next line. The next item printed on the screen will begin in this position. For example, look at the program in Code Listing 2-2.

Because each string is printed with separate `println` statements in Code Listing 2-2, they appear on separate lines in the Program Output.

Code Listing 2-2   (TwoLines.java)

```java
 1   // This is another simple Java program.
 2
 3   public class TwoLines
 4   {
 5      public static void main(String[] args)
 6      {
 7         System.out.println("Programming is great fun!");
 8         System.out.println("I can't get enough of it!");
 9      }
10   }
```

Program Output

```
Programming is great fun!
I can't get enough of it!
```

The print Method

The print method, which is also part of the System.out object, serves a purpose similar to that of println—to display output on the screen. The print method, however, does not advance the cursor to the next line after its message is displayed. Look at Code Listing 2-3.

Code Listing 2-3   (GreatFun.java)

```java
 1   // This is another simple Java program.
 2
 3   public class GreatFun
 4   {
 5      public static void main(String[] args)
 6      {
 7         System.out.print("Programming is ");
 8         System.out.println("great fun!");
 9      }
10   }
```

Program Output

```
Programming is great fun!
```

An important concept to understand about Code Listing 2-3 is that, although the output is broken up into two programming statements, this program will still display the message on one line. The data that you send to the print method is displayed in a continuous stream. Sometimes this can produce less-than-desirable results. The program in Code Listing 2-4 is an example.

Code Listing 2-4   (`Unruly.java`)

```
 1   // An unruly printing program
 2
 3   public class Unruly
 4   {
 5      public static void main(String[] args)
 6      {
 7         System.out.print("These are our top sellers:");
 8         System.out.print("Computer games");
 9         System.out.print("Coffee");
10         System.out.println("Aspirin");
11      }
12   }
```

Program Output

```
These are our top sellers:Computer gamesCoffeeAspirin
```

The layout of the actual output looks nothing like the arrangement of the strings in the source code. First, even though the output is broken up into four lines in the source code (lines 7 through 10), it comes out on the screen as one line. Second, notice that some of the words that are displayed are not separated by spaces. The strings are displayed exactly as they are sent to the print method. If spaces are to be displayed, they must appear in the strings.

There are two ways to fix this program. The most obvious way is to use `println` methods instead of print methods. Another way is to use escape sequences to separate the output into different lines. An *escape sequence* starts with the backslash character (\), and is followed by one or more *control characters*. It allows you to control the way output is displayed by embedding commands within the string itself. The escape sequence that causes the output cursor to go to the next line is \n. Code Listing 2-5 illustrates its use.

Code Listing 2-5   (`Adjusted.java`)

```
 1   // A well adjusted printing program
 2
 3   public class Adjusted
 4   {
 5      public static void main(String[] args)
 6      {
 7         System.out.print("These are our top sellers:\n");
 8         System.out.print("Computer games\nCoffee\n");
 9         System.out.println("Aspirin");
10      }
11   }
```

Program Output

```
These are our top sellers:
Computer games
Coffee
Aspirin
```

The \n characters are called the newline escape sequence. When the print or println method encounters \n in a string, it does not print the \n characters on the screen, but interprets them as a special command to advance the output cursor to the next line. There are several other escape sequences as well. For instance, \t is the tab escape sequence. When print or println encounters it in a string, it causes the output cursor to advance to the next tab position. Code Listing 2-6 shows it in use.

Code Listing 2-6   (Tabs.java)

```
 1   // Another well-adjusted printing program
 2
 3   public class Tabs
 4   {
 5      public static void main(String[] args)
 6      {
 7         System.out.print("These are our top sellers:\n");
 8         System.out.print("\tComputer games\n\tCoffee\n");
 9         System.out.println("\tAspirin");
10      }
11   }
```

Program Output

```
These are our top sellers:
        Computer games
        Coffee
        Aspirin
```

 NOTE: Although you have to type two characters to write an escape sequence, they are stored in memory as a single character.

Table 2-2 lists the common escape sequences and describes them.

Table 2-2 Common escape sequences

Escape Sequence	Name	Description
\n	Newline	Advances the cursor to the next line for subsequent printing
\t	Horizontal tab	Causes the cursor to skip over to the next tab stop
\b	Backspace	Causes the cursor to back up, or move left, one position
\r	Return	Causes the cursor to go to the beginning of the current line, not the next line
\\	Backslash	Causes a backslash to be printed
\'	Single quote	Causes a single quotation mark to be printed
\"	Double quote	Causes a double quotation mark to be printed

WARNING! Do not confuse the backslash (\) with the forward slash (/). An escape sequence will not work if you accidentally start it with a forward slash. Also, do not put a space between the backslash and the control character.

 Checkpoint

MyProgrammingLab™ *www.myprogramminglab.com*

2.7 The following program will not compile because the lines have been mixed up.

```
System.out.print("Success\n");
}
public class Success
{
System.out.print("Success\n");
public static void main(String[] args)
System.out.print("Success ");
}
// It's a mad, mad program.
System.out.println("\nSuccess");
{
```

When the lines are arranged properly, the program should display the following output on the screen:

Program Output

```
Success
Success Success

Success
```

Rearrange the lines in the correct order. Test the program by entering it on the computer, compiling it, and running it.

2.8 Study the following program and show what it will print on the screen.

```
// The Works of Wolfgang
public class Wolfgang
{
    public static void main(String[] args)
    {
        System.out.print("The works of Wolfgang\ninclude ");
        System.out.print("the following");
        System.out.print("\nThe Turkish March ");
        System.out.print("and Symphony No. 40 ");
        System.out.println("in G minor.");
    }
}
```

2.9 On paper, write a program that will display your name on the first line; your street address on the second line; your city, state, and ZIP code on the third line; and your telephone number on the fourth line. Place a comment with today's date at the top of the program. Test your program by entering, compiling, and running it.

2.3 Variables and Literals

CONCEPT: A variable is a named storage location in the computer's memory. A literal is a value that is written into the code of a program.

As you discovered in Chapter 1, variables allow you to store and work with data in the computer's memory. Part of the job of programming is to determine how many variables a program will need and what types of data they will hold. The program in Code Listing 2-7 is an example of a Java program with a variable.

Code Listing 2-7   (Variable.java)

```
1   // This program has a variable.
2
3   public class Variable
4   {
5       public static void main(String[] args)
6       {
7           int value;
8
9           value = 5;
10          System.out.print("The value is ");
11          System.out.println(value);
12      }
13  }
```

Program Output

```
The value is 5
```

Let's look more closely at this program. Here is line 7:

```
    int value;
```

VideoNote
Declaring
Variables

This is called a *variable declaration*. Variables must be declared before they can be used. A variable declaration tells the compiler the variable's name and the type of data it will hold. This line indicates the variable's name is value. The word int stands for integer, so value will only be used to hold integer numbers. Notice that variable declarations end with a semicolon. The next statement in this program appears in line 9:

```
    value = 5;
```

This is called an *assignment statement*. The equal sign is an operator that stores the value on its right (in this case 5) into the variable named on its left. After this line executes, the value variable will contain the value 5.

NOTE: This line does not print anything on the computer screen. It runs silently behind the scenes.

Now look at lines 10 and 11:

```
System.out.print("The value is ");
System.out.println(value);
```

The statement in line 10 sends the string literal "The value is " to the print method. The statement in line 11 sends the name of the value variable to the println method. When you send a variable name to print or println, the variable's contents are displayed. Notice there are no quotation marks around value. Look at what happens in Code Listing 2-8.

Code Listing 2-8   **(Variable2.java)**

```
1   // This program has a variable.
2
3   public class Variable2
4   {
5      public static void main(String[] args)
6      {
7         int value;
8
9         value = 5;
10        System.out.print("The value is ");
11        System.out.println("value");
12     }
13 }
```

Program Output

```
The value is value
```

When double quotation marks are placed around the word value it becomes a string literal, not a variable name. When string literals are sent to print or println, they are displayed exactly as they appear inside the quotation marks.

Displaying Multiple Items with the + Operator

When the + operator is used with strings, it is known as the *string concatenation operator*. To concatenate means to append, so the string concatenation operator appends one string to another. For example, look at the following statement:

```
System.out.println("This is " + "one string.");
```

This statement will print:

```
This is one string.
```

The + operator produces a string that is the combination of the two strings used as its operands. You can also use the + operator to concatenate the contents of a variable to a string. The following code shows an example:

```
number = 5;
System.out.println("The value is " + number);
```

The second line uses the + operator to concatenate the contents of the number variable with the string "The value is ". Although number is not a string, the + operator converts its value to a string and then concatenates that value with the first string. The output that will be displayed is:

```
The value is 5
```

Sometimes the argument you use with print or println is too long to fit on one line in your program code. However, a string literal cannot begin on one line and end on another. For example, the following will cause an error:

```
// This is an error!
System.out.println("Enter a value that is greater than zero
                    and less than 10." );
```

You can remedy this problem by breaking the argument up into smaller string literals, and then using the string concatenation operator to spread them out over more than one line. Here is an example:

```
System.out.println("Enter a value that is " +
                    "greater than zero and less " +
                    "than 10." );
```

In this statement, the argument is broken up into three strings and joined using the + operator. The following example shows the same technique used when the contents of a variable are part of the concatenation:

```
sum = 249;
System.out.println("The sum of the three " +
                    "numbers is " + sum);
```

Be Careful with Quotation Marks

As shown in Code Listing 2-8, placing quotation marks around a variable name changes the program's results. In fact, placing double quotation marks around anything that is not intended to be a string literal will create an error of some type. For example, in Code Listings 2-7 and 2-8, the number 5 was assigned to the variable value. It would have been an error to perform the assignment this way:

```
value = "5";    // Error!
```

In this statement, 5 is no longer an integer, but a string literal. Because value was declared as an integer variable, you can only store integers in it. In other words, 5 and "5" are not the same thing.

The fact that numbers can be represented as strings frequently confuses students who are new to programming. Just remember that strings are intended for humans to read. They are to be printed on computer screens or paper. Numbers, however, are intended primarily for mathematical operations. You cannot perform math on strings, and before numbers can be displayed on the screen, first they must be converted to strings. (Fortunately, print and println handle the conversion automatically when you send numbers to them.) Don't fret if this still bothers you. Later in this chapter, we will shed more light on the differences among numbers, characters, and strings by discussing their internal storage.

More about Literals

A literal is a value that is written in the code of a program. Literals are commonly assigned to variables or displayed. Code Listing 2-9 contains both literals and a variable.

Code Listing 2-9   (Literals.java)

```
 1   // This program has literals and a variable.
 2
 3   public class Literals
 4   {
 5      public static void main(String[] args)
 6      {
 7         int apples;
 8
 9         apples = 20;
10         System.out.println("Today we sold " + apples +
11                            " bushels of apples.");
12      }
13   }
```

Program Output

```
Today we sold 20 bushels of apples.
```

Of course, the variable in this program is apples. It is declared as an integer. Table 2-3 shows a list of the literals found in the program.

Table 2-3   Literals

Literal	Type of Literal
20	Integer literal
"Today we sold "	String literal
" bushels of apples."	String literal

Identifiers

An *identifier* is a programmer-defined name that represents some element of a program. Variable names and class names are examples of identifiers. You may choose your own variable names and class names in Java, as long as you do not use any of the Java key words. The *key words* make up the core of the language and each has a specific purpose. Table 1-3 in Chapter 1 and Appendix D (available on the book's companion Web site) show a complete list of Java key words.

You should always choose names for your variables that give an indication of what they are used for. You may be tempted to declare variables with names like this:

```
    int x;
```

The rather nondescript name, x, gives no clue as to what the variable's purpose is. Here is a better example.

```
int itemsOrdered;
```

The name `itemsOrdered` gives anyone reading the program an idea of what the variable is used for. This method of coding helps produce *self-documenting programs*, which means you get an understanding of what the program is doing just by reading its code. Because real-world programs usually have thousands of lines of code, it is important that they be as self-documenting as possible.

You have probably noticed the mixture of uppercase and lowercase letters in the name `itemsOrdered`. Although all of Java's key words must be written in lowercase, you may use uppercase letters in variable names. The reason the O in `itemsOrdered` is capitalized is to improve readability. Normally "items ordered" is used as two words. Variable names cannot contain spaces, however, so the two words must be combined. When "items" and "ordered" are stuck together, you get a variable declaration like this:

```
int itemsordered;
```

Capitalization of the letter O makes `itemsOrdered` easier to read. Typically, variable names begin with a lowercase letter, and after that, the first letter of each individual word that makes up the variable name is capitalized.

The following are some specific rules that must be followed with all identifiers:

- The first character must be one of the letters a–z or A–Z, an underscore (_), or a dollar sign ($).
- After the first character, you may use the letters a–z or A–Z, the digits 0–9, underscores (_), or dollar signs ($).
- Uppercase and lowercase characters are distinct. This means `itemsOrdered` is not the same as `itemsordered`.
- Identifiers cannot include spaces.

 NOTE: Although the $ is a legal identifier character, it is normally used for special purposes. So, don't use it in your variable names.

Table 2-4 shows a list of variable names and tells whether each is legal or illegal in Java.

Table 2-4   Some variable names

Variable Name	Legal or Illegal?
dayOfWeek	Legal
3dGraph	Illegal because identifiers cannot begin with a digit
june1997	Legal
mixture#3	Illegal because identifiers may use only alphabetic letters, digits, underscores, or dollar signs
week day	Illegal because identifiers cannot contain spaces

Class Names

As mentioned before, it is standard practice to begin variable names with a lowercase letter, and then capitalize the first letter of each subsequent word that makes up the name. It is also a standard practice to capitalize the first letter of a class name, as well as the first letter of each subsequent word it contains. This helps differentiate the names of variables from the names of classes. For example, payRate would be a variable name, and Employee would be a class name.

Checkpoint

MyProgrammingLab™ *www.myprogramminglab.com*

2.10 Examine the following program.

```
// This program uses variables and literals.
public class BigLittle
{
    public static void main(String[] args)
    {
        int little;
        int big;

        little = 2;
        big = 2000;
        System.out.println("The little number is " + little);
        System.out.println("The big number is " + big);
    }
}
```

List the variables and literals found in the program.

2.11 What will the following program display on the screen?

```
public class CheckPoint
{
    public static void main(String[] args)
    {
        int number;
        number = 712;
        System.out.println("The value is " + "number");
    }
}
```

2.4 Primitive Data Types

CONCEPT: There are many different types of data. Variables are classified according to their data type, which determines the kind of data that may be stored in them.

Computer programs collect pieces of data from the real world and manipulate them in various ways. There are many different types of data. In the realm of numeric data, for example, there are whole and fractional numbers, negative and positive numbers, and numbers so large and others so small that they don't even have a name. Then there is textual information. Names and addresses, for instance, are stored as strings of characters. When you write a program you must determine what types of data it is likely to encounter.

Each variable has a *data type*, which is the type of data that the variable can hold. Selecting the proper data type is important because a variable's data type determines the amount of memory the variable uses, and the way the variable formats and stores data. It is important to select a data type that is appropriate for the type of data that your program will work with. If you are writing a program to calculate the number of miles to a distant star, you need variables that can hold very large numbers. If you are designing software to record microscopic dimensions, you need variables that store very small and precise numbers. If you are writing a program that must perform thousands of intensive calculations, you want variables that can be processed quickly. The data type of a variable determines all of these factors.

Table 2-5 shows all of the Java *primitive data types* for holding numeric data.

The words listed in the left column of Table 2-5 are the key words that you use in variable declarations. A variable declaration takes the following general format:

```
DataType VariableName;
```

Table 2-5 Primitive data types for numeric data

Data Type	Size	Range
byte	1 byte	Integers in the range of −128 to +127
short	2 bytes	Integers in the range of −32,768 to +32,767
int	4 bytes	Integers in the range of −2,147,483,648 to +2,147,483,647
long	8 bytes	Integers in the range of −9,223,372,036,854,775,808 to +9,223,372,036,854,775,807
float	4 bytes	Floating-point numbers in the range of $\pm 3.4 \times 10^{-38}$ to $\pm 3.4 \times 10^{38}$, with 7 digits of accuracy
double	8 bytes	Floating-point numbers in the range of $\pm 1.7 \times 10^{-308}$ to $\pm 1.7 \times 10^{308}$, with 15 digits of accuracy

DataType is the name of the data type and *VariableName* is the name of the variable. Here are some examples of variable declarations:

```
byte inches;
int speed;
short month;
float salesCommission;
double distance;
```

The size column in Table 2-5 shows the number of bytes that a variable of each of the data types uses. For example, an int variable uses 4 bytes, and a double variable uses 8 bytes.

The range column shows the ranges of numbers that may be stored in variables of each data type. For example, an int variable can hold numbers from –2,147,483,648 up to +2,147,483,647. One of the appealing characteristics of the Java language is that the sizes and ranges of all the primitive data types are the same on all computers.

> **NOTE:** These data types are called "primitive" because you cannot use them to create objects. Recall from Chapter 1's discussion on object-oriented programming that an object has attributes and methods. With the primitive data types, you can only create variables, and a variable can only be used to hold a single value. Such variables do not have attributes or methods.

The Integer Data Types

The first four data types listed in Table 2-5, byte, int, short, and long, are all integer data types. An integer variable can hold whole numbers such as 7, 125, –14, and 6928. The program in Code Listing 2-10 shows several variables of different integer data types being used.

Code Listing 2-10   (IntegerVariables.java)

```
 1  // This program has variables of several of the integer types.
 2
 3  public class IntegerVariables
 4  {
 5     public static void main(String[] args)
 6     {
 7        int checking; // Declare an int variable named checking.
 8        byte miles; // Declare a byte variable named miles.
 9        short minutes; // Declare a short variable named minutes.
10        long days; // Declare a long variable named days.
11
12        checking = -20;
13        miles = 105;
14        minutes = 120;
15        days = 189000;
16        System.out.println("We have made a journey of " + miles +
17                           " miles.");
18        System.out.println("It took us " + minutes + " minutes.");
19        System.out.println("Our account balance is $" + checking);
20        System.out.println("About " + days + " days ago Columbus " +
21                           "stood on this spot.");
22     }
23  }
```

Program Output

```
We have made a journey of 105 miles.
It took us 120 minutes.
Our account balance is $-20
About 189000 days ago Columbus stood on this spot.
```

In most programs you will need more than one variable of any given data type. If a program uses three integers, length, width, and area, they could be declared separately, as follows:

```
int length;
int width;
int area;
```

It is easier, however, to combine the three variable declarations:

```
int length, width, area;
```

You can declare several variables of the same type, simply by separating their names with commas.

Integer Literals

When you write an integer literal in your program code, Java assumes it to be of the int data type. For example, in Code Listing 2-10, the literals –20, 105, 120, and 189000 are all treated as int values. You can force an integer literal to be treated as a long, however, by suffixing it with the letter L. For example, the value 57L would be treated as a long. Although you can use either an uppercase or a lowercase L, it is advisable to use the uppercase L because the lowercase l looks too much like the number 1.

> **WARNING!** You cannot embed commas in numeric literals. For example, the following statement will cause an error:
>
> ```
> number = 1,257,649;        // ERROR!
> ```
>
> This statement must be written as:
>
> ```
> number = 1257649;          // Correct.
> ```

Floating-Point Data Types

Whole numbers are not adequate for many jobs. If you are writing a program that works with dollar amounts or precise measurements, you need a data type that allows fractional values. In programming terms, these are called *floating-point* numbers. Values such as 1.7 and –45.316 are floating-point numbers.

In Java there are two data types that can represent floating-point numbers. They are float and double. The float data type is considered a single precision data type. It can store a floating-point number with 7 digits of accuracy. The double data type is considered a double precision data type. It can store a floating-point number with 15 digits of accuracy. The double data type uses twice as much memory as the float data type, however. A float variable occupies 4 bytes of memory, whereas a double variable uses 8 bytes.

Code Listing 2-11 shows a program that uses three double variables.

Code Listing 2-11   (Sale.java)

```
1   // This program demonstrates the double data type.
2
3   public class Sale
4   {
```

```
 5      public static void main(String[] args)
 6      {
 7         double price, tax, total;
 8
 9         price = 29.75;
10         tax = 1.76;
11         total = 31.51;
12         System.out.println("The price of the item " +
13                            "is " + price);
14         System.out.println("The tax is " + tax);
15         System.out.println("The total is " + total);
16      }
17 }
```

Program Output

```
The price of the item is 29.75
The tax is 1.76
The total is 31.51
```

Floating-Point Literals

When you write a floating-point literal in your program code, Java assumes it to be of the double data type. For example, in Code Listing 2-11, the literals 29.75, 1.76, and 31.51 are all treated as double values. Because of this, a problem can arise when assigning a floating-point literal to a float variable. Java is a *strongly typed language*, which means that it only allows you to store values of compatible data types in variables. A double value is not compatible with a float variable because a double can be much larger or much smaller than the allowable range for a float. As a result, code such as the following will cause an error:

```
float number;
number = 23.5;            // Error!
```

You can force a double literal to be treated as a float, however, by suffixing it with the letter F or f. The preceding code can be rewritten in the following manner to prevent an error:

```
float number;
number = 23.5F;           // This will work.
```

 WARNING! If you are working with literals that represent dollar amounts, remember that you cannot embed currency symbols (such as $) or commas in the literal. For example, the following statement will cause an error:

```
grossPay = $1,257.00;     // ERROR!
```

This statement must be written as:

```
grossPay = 1257.00;       // Correct.
```

Scientific and E Notation

Floating-point literals can be represented in scientific notation. Take the number 47,281.97. In scientific notation this number is 4.728197×10^4. (10^4 is equal to 10,000, and 4.728197 × 10,000 is 47,281.97.)

Java uses E notation to represent values in scientific notation. In E notation, the number 4.728197×10^4 would be 4.728197E4. Table 2-6 shows other numbers represented in scientific and E notation.

Table 2-6 Floating-point representations

Decimal Notation	Scientific Notation	E Notation
247.91	2.4791×10^2	2.4791E2
0.00072	7.2×10^{-4}	7.2E–4
2,900,000	2.9×10^6	2.9E6

NOTE: The E can be uppercase or lowercase.

Code Listing 2-12 demonstrates the use of floating-point literals expressed in E notation.

Code Listing 2-12   (SunFacts.java)

```
1   // This program uses E notation.
2
3   public class SunFacts
4   {
5      public static void main(String[] args)
6      {
7         double distance, mass;
8
9         distance = 1.495979E11;
10        mass = 1.989E30;
11        System.out.println("The sun is " + distance +
12                           " meters away.");
13        System.out.println("The sun's mass is " + mass +
14                           " kilograms.");
15     }
16  }
```

Program Output

```
The sun is 1.495979E11 meters away.
The sun's mass is 1.989E30 kilograms.
```

The boolean Data Type

The boolean data type allows you to create variables that may hold one of two possible values: true or false. Code Listing 2-13 demonstrates the declaration and assignment of a boolean variable.

Code Listing 2-13   (TrueFalse.java)

```
 1   // A program for demonstrating boolean variables
 2
 3   public class TrueFalse
 4   {
 5      public static void main(String[] args)
 6      {
 7         boolean bool;
 8
 9         bool = true;
10         System.out.println(bool);
11         bool = false;
12         System.out.println(bool);
13      }
14   }
```

Program Output

```
true
false
```

Variables of the boolean data type are useful for evaluating conditions that are either true or false. You will not be using them until Chapter 3, however, so for now just remember the following things:

- boolean variables may hold only the value true or false.
- The contents of a boolean variable may not be copied to a variable of any type other than boolean.

The char Data Type

The char data type is used to store characters. A variable of the char data type can hold one character at a time. Character literals are enclosed in *single quotation marks*. The program in Code Listing 2-14 uses a char variable. The character literals 'A' and 'B' are assigned to the variable.

Code Listing 2-14   (Letters.java)

```
 1   // This program demonstrates the char data type.
 2
 3   public class Letters
 4   {
 5      public static void main(String[] args)
```

```
 6     {
 7         char letter;
 8
 9         letter = 'A';
10         System.out.println(letter);
11         letter = 'B';
12         System.out.println(letter);
13     }
14 }
```

Program Output

```
A
B
```

It is important that you do not confuse character literals with string literals, which are enclosed in double quotation marks. String literals cannot be assigned to char variables.

Unicode

Characters are internally represented by numbers. Each printable character, as well as many non-printable characters, is assigned a unique number. Java uses Unicode, which is a set of numbers that are used as codes for representing characters. Each Unicode number requires two bytes of memory, so char variables occupy two bytes. When a character is stored in memory, it is actually the numeric code that is stored. When the computer is instructed to print the value on the screen, it displays the character that corresponds with the numeric code.

You may want to refer to Appendix B, available on the book's companion Web site (at www.pearsonhighered.com/gaddis), which shows a portion of the Unicode character set. Notice that the number 65 is the code for A, 66 is the code for B, and so on. Code Listing 2-15 demonstrates that when you work with characters, you are actually working with numbers.

Code Listing 2-15   **(Letters2.java)**

```
 1 // This program demonstrates the close relationship between
 2 // characters and integers.
 3
 4 public class Letters2
 5 {
 6     public static void main(String[] args)
 7     {
 8         char letter;
 9
10         letter = 65;
11         System.out.println(letter);
12         letter = 66;
13         System.out.println(letter);
14     }
15 }
```

Program Output

```
A
B
```

Figure 2-4 illustrates that when you think of the characters A, B, and C being stored in memory, it is really the numbers 65, 66, and 67 that are stored.

Figure 2-4 Characters and how they are stored in memory

These characters are stored in memory as...

Variable Assignment and Initialization

As you have already seen in several examples, a value is put into a variable with an *assignment statement*. For example, the following statement assigns the value 12 to the variable unitsSold:

```
unitsSold = 12;
```

The = symbol is called the assignment operator. Operators perform operations on data. The data that operators work with are called operands. The assignment operator has two operands. In the statement above, the operands are unitsSold and 12.

In an assignment statement, the name of the variable receiving the assignment must appear on the left side of the operator, and the value being assigned must appear on the right side. The following statement is incorrect:

```
12 = unitsSold;        // ERROR!
```

The operand on the left side of the = operator must be a variable name. The operand on the right side of the = symbol must be an expression that has a value. The assignment operator takes the value of the right operand and puts it in the variable identified by the left operand. Assuming that length and width are both int variables, the following code illustrates that the assignment operator's right operand may be a literal or a variable:

```
length = 20;
width = length;
```

It is important to note that the assignment operator only changes the contents of its left operand. The second statement assigns the value of the length variable to the width variable. After the statement has executed, length still has the same value, 20.

You may also assign values to variables as part of the declaration statement. This is known as *initialization*. Code Listing 2-16 shows how it is done.

The variable declaration statement in this program is in line 7:

```
int month = 2, days = 28;
```

Code Listing 2-16   (Initialize.java)

```
 1   // This program shows variable initialization.
 2
 3   public class Initialize
 4   {
 5      public static void main(String[] args)
 6      {
 7         int month = 2, days = 28;
 8
 9         System.out.println("Month " + month + " has " +
10                            days + " days.");
11      }
12   }
```

Program Output

Month 2 has 28 days.

This statement declares the month variable and initializes it with the value 2, and declares the days variable and initializes it with the value 28. As you can see, this simplifies the program and reduces the number of statements that must be typed by the programmer. Here are examples of other declaration statements that perform initialization:

```
double payRate = 25.52;
float interestRate = 12.9F;
char stockCode = 'D';
int customerNum = 459;
```

Of course, there are always variations on a theme. Java allows you to declare several variables and initialize only some of them. Here is an example of such a declaration:

```
int flightNum = 89, travelTime, departure = 10, distance;
```

The variable flightNum is initialized to 89 and departure is initialized to 10. The travelTime and distance variables remain uninitialized.

> **WARNING!** When a variable is declared inside a method, it must have a value stored in it before it can be used. If the compiler determines that the program might be using such a variable before a value has been stored in it, an error will occur. You can avoid this type of error by initializing the variable with a value.

Variables Hold Only One Value at a Time

Remember, a variable can hold only one value at a time. When you assign a new value to a variable, the new value takes the place of the variable's previous contents. For example, look at the following code.

```
int x = 5;
System.out.println(x);
x = 99;
System.out.println(x);
```

In this code, the variable x is initialized with the value 5 and its contents are displayed. Then the variable is assigned the value 99. This value overwrites the value 5 that was previously stored there. The code will produce the following output:

```
5
99
```

 Checkpoint

 MyProgrammingLab™ *www.myprogramminglab.com*

2.12   Which of the following are illegal variable names and why?

```
x
99bottles
july97
theSalesFigureForFiscalYear98
r&d
grade_report
```

2.13   Is the variable name Sales the same as sales? Why or why not?

2.14   Refer to the Java primitive data types listed in Table 2-5 for this question.
    a)   If a variable needs to hold whole numbers in the range 32 to 6,000, what primitive data type would be best?
    b)   If a variable needs to hold whole numbers in the range –40,000 to +40,000, what primitive data type would be best?
    c)   Which of the following literals use more memory? 22.1 or 22.1F?

2.15   How would the number 6.31×10^{17} be represented in E notation?

2.16   A program declares a float variable named number, and the following statement causes an error. What can be done to fix the error?

```
number = 7.4;
```

2.17   What values can boolean variables hold?

2.18   Write statements that do the following:
    a)   Declare a char variable named letter.
    b)   Assign the letter A to the letter variable.
    c)   Display the contents of the letter variable.

2.19   What are the Unicode codes for the characters 'C', 'F', and 'W'? (You may need to refer to Appendix B on the book's companion Web site, at www.pearsonhighered. com/gaddis.)

2.20   Which is a character literal, 'B' or "B"?

2.21   What is wrong with the following statement?

```
char letter = "Z";
```

2.5   Arithmetic Operators

CONCEPT: There are many operators for manipulating numeric values and performing arithmetic operations.

Java offers a multitude of operators for manipulating data. Generally, there are three types of operators: *unary*, *binary*, and *ternary*. These terms reflect the number of operands an operator requires.

VideoNote

Simple Math
Expressions

Unary operators require only a single operand. For example, consider the following expression:

```
-5
```

Of course, we understand this represents the value negative five. We can also apply the operator to a variable, as follows:

```
-number
```

This expression gives the negative of the value stored in number. The minus sign, when used this way, is called the *negation operator*. Because it requires only one operand, it is a unary operator.

Binary operators work with two operands. The assignment operator is in this category. Ternary operators, as you may have guessed, require three operands. Java has only one ternary operator, which is discussed in Chapter 3.

Arithmetic operations are very common in programming. Table 2-7 shows the arithmetic operators in Java.

Table 2-7 Arithmetic operators

Operator	Meaning	Type	Example
+	Addition	Binary	total = cost + tax;
-	Subtraction	Binary	cost = total - tax;
*	Multiplication	Binary	tax = cost * rate;
/	Division	Binary	salePrice = original / 2;
%	Modulus	Binary	remainder = value % 3;

Each of these operators works as you probably expect. The addition operator returns the sum of its two operands. Here are some example statements that use the addition operator:

```
amount = 4 + 8;            // Assigns 12 to amount
total = price + tax;       // Assigns price + tax to total
number = number + 1;       // Assigns number + 1 to number
```

The subtraction operator returns the value of its right operand subtracted from its left operand. Here are some examples:

```
temperature = 112 - 14;    // Assigns 98 to temperature
sale = price - discount;   // Assigns price - discount to sale
number = number - 1;       // Assigns number - 1 to number
```

The multiplication operator returns the product of its two operands. Here are some examples:

```
markUp = 12 * 0.25;              // Assigns 3 to markUp
commission = sales * percent;    // Assigns sales * percent to commission
population = population * 2;      // Assigns population * 2 to population
```

The division operator returns the quotient of its left operand divided by its right operand. Here are some examples:

```
points = 100 / 20;              // Assigns 5 to points
teams = players / maxEach;      // Assigns players / maxEach to teams
half = number / 2;              // Assigns number / 2 to half
```

The modulus operator returns the remainder of a division operation involving two integers. The following statement assigns 2 to leftOver:

```
leftOver = 17 % 3;
```

Situations arise where you need to get the remainder of a division. Computations that detect odd numbers or are required to determine how many items are left over after division use the modulus operator.

The program in Code Listing 2-17 demonstrates some of these operators used in a simple payroll calculation.

Code Listing 2-17   (Wages.java)

```
 1  // This program calculates hourly wages plus overtime.
 2
 3  public class Wages
 4  {
 5     public static void main(String[] args)
 6     {
 7        double regularWages;        // The calculated regular wages.
 8        double basePay = 25;        // The base pay rate.
 9        double regularHours = 40;   // The hours worked less overtime.
10        double overtimeWages;       // Overtime wages
11        double overtimePay = 37.5;  // Overtime pay rate
12        double overtimeHours = 10;  // Overtime hours worked
13        double totalWages;          // Total wages
14
15        regularWages = basePay * regularHours;
16        overtimeWages = overtimePay * overtimeHours;
17        totalWages = regularWages + overtimeWages;
18        System.out.println("Wages for this week are $" +
19                            totalWages);
20     }
21  }
```

Program Output

```
Wages for this week are $1375.0
```

Code Listing 2-17 calculates the total wages an hourly paid worker earned in one week. As mentioned in the comments, there are variables for regular wages, base pay rate, regular hours worked, overtime wages, overtime pay rate, overtime hours worked, and total wages.

Line 15 in the program multiplies `basePay` times `regularHours` and stores the result, which is 1000, in `regularWages`:

```
regularWages = basePay * regularHours;
```

Line 16 multiplies `overtimePay` times `overtimeHours` and stores the result, which is 375, in `overtimeWages`:

```
overtimeWages = overtimePay * overtimeHours;
```

Line 17 adds the regular wages and the overtime wages and stores the result, 1375, in `totalWages`:

```
totalWages = regularWages + overtimeWages;
```

The `println` statement in lines 18 and 19 displays the message on the screen reporting the week's wages.

Integer Division

When both operands of the division operator are integers, the operator will perform *integer division*. This means the result of the division will be an integer as well. If there is a remainder, it will be discarded. For example, look at the following code:

```
double number;
number = 5 / 2;
```

This code divides 5 by 2 and assigns the result to the `number` variable. What value will be stored in `number`? You would probably assume that 2.5 would be stored in `number` because that is the result your calculator shows when you divide 5 by 2; however, that is not what happens when the previous Java code is executed. Because the numbers 5 and 2 are both integers, the fractional part of the result will be thrown away, or *truncated*. As a result, the value 2 will be assigned to the `number` variable.

In the previous code, it doesn't matter that `number` is declared as a `double` because the fractional part of the result is discarded before the assignment takes place. In order for a division operation to return a floating-point value, one of the operands must be of a floating-point data type. For example, the previous code could be written as follows:

```
double number;
number = 5.0 / 2;
```

In this code, 5.0 is treated as a floating-point number, so the division operation will return a floating-point number. The result of the division is 2.5.

Operator Precedence

It is possible to build mathematical expressions with several operators. The following statement assigns the sum of 17, x, 21, and y to the variable `answer`:

```
answer = 17 + x + 21 + y;
```

Some expressions are not that straightforward, however. Consider the following statement:

```
outcome = 12 + 6 / 3;
```

What value will be stored in outcome? The 6 is used as an operand for both the addition and division operators. The outcome variable could be assigned either 6 or 14, depending on when the division takes place. The answer is 14 because the division operator has higher *precedence* than the addition operator.

Mathematical expressions are evaluated from left to right. When two operators share an operand, the operator with the highest precedence works first. Multiplication and division have higher precedence than addition and subtraction, so the statement above works like this:

1. 6 is divided by 3, yielding a result of 2
2. 12 is added to 2, yielding a result of 14

It could be diagrammed as shown in Figure 2-5.

Figure 2-5   Precedence illustrated

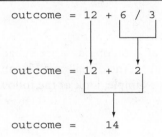

Table 2-8 shows the precedence of the arithmetic operators. The operators at the top of the table have higher precedence than the ones below them.

Table 2-8   Precedence of arithmetic operators (highest to lowest)

Highest Precedence →	– (unary negation)
	* / %
Lowest Precedence →	+ –

The multiplication, division, and modulus operators have the same precedence. The addition and subtraction operators have the same precedence. If two operators sharing an operand have the same precedence, they work according to their *associativity*. Associativity is either *left to right* or *right to left*. Table 2-9 shows the arithmetic operators and their associativity.

Table 2-9   Associativity of arithmetic operators

Operator	Associativity
– (unary negation)	Right to left
* / %	Left to right
+ –	Left to right

Table 2-10 shows some expressions and their values.

Table 2-10 Some expressions and their values

Expression	Value
5 + 2 * 4	13
10 / 2 - 3	2
8 + 12 * 2 - 4	28
4 + 17 % 2 - 1	4
6 - 3 * 2 + 7 - 1	6

Grouping with Parentheses

Parts of a mathematical expression may be grouped with parentheses to force some operations to be performed before others. In the statement below, the sum of a, b, c, and d is divided by 4.0.

```
average = (a + b + c + d) / 4.0;
```

Without the parentheses, however, d would be divided by 4 and the result added to a, b, and c. Table 2-11 shows more expressions and their values.

Table 2-11 More expressions and their values

Expression	Value
(5 + 2) * 4	28
10 / (5 - 3)	5
8 + 12 * (6 - 2)	56
(4 + 17) % 2 - 1	0
(6 - 3) * (2 + 7) / 3	9

In the Spotlight:
Calculating Percentages and Discounts

Determining percentages is a common calculation in computer programming. Although the % symbol is used in general mathematics to indicate a percentage, most programming languages (including Java) do not use the % symbol for this purpose. In a program, you have to convert a percentage to a floating-point number, just as you would if you were using a calculator. For example, 50 percent would be written as 0.5 and 2 percent would be written as 0.02.

Let's look at an example. Suppose you earn $6,000 per month and you are allowed to contribute a portion of your gross monthly pay to a retirement plan. You want to determine the amount of your pay that will go into the plan if you contribute 5 percent, 8 percent, or 10 percent of your gross wages. To make this determination you write a program like the one shown in Code Listing 2-18.

Code Listing 2-18   (Contribution.java)

```java
 1 // This program calculates the amount of pay that
 2 // will be contributed to a retirement plan if 5%,
 3 // 8%, or 10% of monthly pay is withheld.
 4
 5 public class Contribution
 6 {
 7    public static void main(String[] args)
 8    {
 9       // Variables to hold the monthly pay and
10       // the amount of contribution.
11       double monthlyPay = 6000.0;
12       double contribution;
13
14       // Calculate and display a 5% contribution.
15       contribution = monthlyPay * 0.05;
16       System.out.println("5 percent is $" +
17                          contribution +
18                          " per month.");
19
20       // Calculate and display an 8% contribution.
21       contribution = monthlyPay * 0.08;
22       System.out.println("8 percent is $" +
23                          contribution +
24                          " per month.");
25
26       // Calculate and display a 10% contribution.
27       contribution = monthlyPay * 0.1;
28       System.out.println("10 percent is $" +
29                          contribution +
30                          " per month.");
31    }
32 }
```

Program Output

```
5 percent is $300.0 per month.
8 percent is $480.0 per month.
10 percent is $600.0 per month.
```

Lines 11 and 12 declare two variables: monthlyPay and contribution. The monthlyPay variable, which is initialized with the value 6000.0, holds the amount of your monthly pay. The contribution variable will hold the amount of a contribution to the retirement plan.

The statements in lines 15 through 18 calculate and display 5 percent of the monthly pay. The calculation is done in line 15, where the monthlyPay variable is multiplied by 0.05. The result is assigned to the contribution variable, which is then displayed by the statement in lines 16 through 18.

Similar steps are taken in lines 21 through 24, which calculate and display 8 percent of the monthly pay, and lines 27 through 30, which calculate and display 10 percent of the monthly pay.

Calculating a Percentage Discount

Another common calculation is determining a percentage discount. For example, suppose a retail business sells an item that is regularly priced at $59, and is planning to have a sale where the item's price will be reduced by 20 percent. You have been asked to write a program to calculate the sale price of the item.

To determine the sale price you perform two calculations:

- First, you get the amount of the discount, which is 20 percent of the item's regular price.
- Second, you subtract the discount amount from the item's regular price. This gives you the sale price.

Code Listing 2-19 shows how this is done in Java.

Code Listing 2-19   (Discount.java)

```java
1 // This program calculates the sale price of an
2 // item that is regularly priced at $59, with
3 // a 20 percent discount subtracted.
4
5 public class Discount
6 {
7    public static void main(String[] args)
8    {
9       // Variables to hold the regular price, the
10      // amount of a discount, and the sale price.
11      double regularPrice = 59.0;
12      double discount;
13      double salePrice;
14
15      // Calculate the amount of a 20% discount.
16      discount = regularPrice * 0.2;
17
18      // Calculate the sale price by subtracting
19      // the discount from the regular price.
20      salePrice = regularPrice - discount;
21
22      // Display the results.
23      System.out.println("Regular price: $" + regularPrice);
24      System.out.println("Discount amount $" + discount);
25      System.out.println("Sale price: $" + salePrice);
26   }
27 }
```

Program Output

```
Regular price: $59.0
Discount amount $11.8
Sale price: $47.2
```

Lines 11 through 13 declare three variables. The regularPrice variable holds the item's regular price, and is initialized with the value 59.0. The discount variable will hold the amount of the discount once it is calculated. The salePrice variable will hold the item's sale price.

Line 16 calculates the amount of the 20 percent discount by multiplying regularPrice by 0.2. The result is stored in the discount variable. Line 20 calculates the sale price by subtracting discount from regularPrice. The result is stored in the salePrice variable. The statements in lines 23 through 25 display the item's regular price, the amount of the discount, and the sale price.

The Math Class

The Java API provides a class named Math, which contains numerous methods that are useful for performing complex mathematical operations. In this section we will briefly look at the Math.pow and Math.sqrt methods.

The Math.pow Method

In Java, raising a number to a power requires the Math.pow method. Here is an example of how the Math.pow method is used:

```
result = Math.pow(4.0, 2.0);
```

The method takes two double arguments. It raises the first argument to the power of the second argument, and returns the result as a double. In this example, 4.0 is raised to the power of 2.0. This statement is equivalent to the following algebraic statement:

$$result = 4^2$$

Here is another example of a statement using the Math.pow method. It assigns 3 times 6^3 to x:

```
x = 3 * Math.pow(6.0, 3.0);
```

And the following statement displays the value of 5 raised to the power of 4:

```
System.out.println(Math.pow(5.0, 4.0));
```

The Math.sqrt Method

The Math.sqrt method accepts a double value as its argument and returns the square root of the value. Here is an example of how the method is used:

```
result = Math.sqrt(9.0);
```

In this example the value 9.0 is passed as an argument to the Math.sqrt method. The method will return the square root of 9.0, which is assigned to the result variable. The following statement shows another example. In this statement the square root of 25.0 (which is 5.0) is displayed on the screen:

```
System.out.println(Math.sqrt(25.0));
```

For more information about the Math class, see Appendix G, available on the book's companion Web site at www.pearsonhighered.com/gaddis.

 Checkpoint

MyProgrammingLab™ *www.myprogramminglab.com*

2.22 Complete the following table by writing the value of each expression in the Value column.

Expression	Value
6 + 3 * 5	_____
12 / 2 - 4	_____
9 + 14 * 2 - 6	_____
5 + 19 % 3 - 1	_____
(6 + 2) * 3	_____
14 / (11 - 4)	_____
9 + 12 * (8 - 3)	_____

2.23 Is the division statement in the following code an example of integer division or floating-point division? What value will be stored in portion?

```
double portion;
portion = 70 / 3;
```

2.6 Combined Assignment Operators

CONCEPT: The combined assignment operators combine the assignment operator with the arithmetic operators.

Quite often, programs have assignment statements of the following form:

```
x = x + 1;
```

On the right side of the assignment operator, 1 is added to x. The result is then assigned to x, replacing the value that was previously there. Effectively, this statement adds 1 to x. Here is another example:

```
balance = balance + deposit;
```

Assuming that balance and deposit are variables, this statement assigns the value of balance + deposit to balance. The effect of this statement is that deposit is added to the value stored in balance. Here is another example:

```
balance = balance - withdrawal;
```

Assuming that balance and withdrawal are variables, this statement assigns the value of balance - withdrawal to balance. The effect of this statement is that withdrawal is subtracted from the value stored in balance.

If you have not seen these types of statements before, they might cause some initial confusion because the same variable name appears on both sides of the assignment operator. Table 2-12 shows other examples of statements written this way.

Table 2-12 Various assignment statements (assume x = 6 in each statement)

Statement	What It Does	Value of **x** after the Statement
x = x + 4;	Adds 4 to x	10
x = x - 3;	Subtracts 3 from x	3
x = x * 10;	Multiplies x by 10	60
x = x / 2;	Divides x by 2	3
x = x % 4	Assigns the remainder of x / 4 to x.	2

These types of operations are common in programming. For convenience, Java offers a special set of operators designed specifically for these jobs. Table 2-13 shows the *combined assignment operators*, also known as *compound operators*.

Table 2-13 Combined assignment operators

Operator	Example Usage	Equivalent To
+=	x += 5;	x = x + 5;
-=	y -= 2;	y = y - 2;
*=	z *= 10;	z = z * 10;
/=	a /= b;	a = a / b;
%=	c %= 3;	c = c % 3;

As you can see, the combined assignment operators do not require the programmer to type the variable name twice. The following statement:

```
balance = balance + deposit;
```

could be rewritten as

```
balance += deposit;
```

Similarly, the statement

```
balance = balance - withdrawal;
```

could be rewritten as

```
balance -= withdrawal;
```

 Checkpoint

MyProgrammingLab™ *www.myprogramminglab.com*

2.24   Write statements using combined assignment operators to perform the following:
   a)   Add 6 to x
   b)   Subtract 4 from amount

c) Multiply y by 4
d) Divide total by 27
e) Store in x the remainder of x divided by 7

2.7 Conversion between Primitive Data Types

CONCEPT: Before a value can be stored in a variable, the value's data type must be compatible with the variable's data type. Java performs some conversions between data types automatically, but does not automatically perform any conversion that can result in the loss of data. Java also follows a set of rules when evaluating arithmetic expressions containing mixed data types.

Java is a *strongly typed* language. This means that before a value is assigned to a variable, Java checks the data types of the variable and the value being assigned to it to determine whether they are compatible. For example, look at the following statements:

```
int x;
double y = 2.5;
x = y;
```

The assignment statement is attempting to store a `double` value (2.5) in an `int` variable. When the Java compiler encounters this line of code, it will respond with an error message. (The JDK displays the message "possible loss of precision.")

Not all assignment statements that mix data types are rejected by the compiler, however. For instance, look at the following program segment:

```
int x;
short y = 2;
x = y;
```

This assignment statement, which stores a `short` in an `int`, will work with no problems. So why does Java permit a `short` to be stored in an `int`, but does not permit a `double` to be stored in an `int`? The obvious reason is that a `double` can store fractional numbers and can hold values much larger than an `int` can hold. If Java were to permit a `double` to be assigned to an `int`, a loss of data would be likely.

Just like officers in the military, the primitive data types are ranked. One data type outranks another if it can hold a larger number. For example, a `float` outranks an `int`, and an `int` outranks a `short`. Figure 2-6 shows the numeric data types in order of their rank. The higher a data type appears in the list, the higher is its rank.

Figure 2-6 Primitive data type ranking

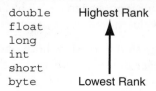

In assignment statements where values of lower-ranked data types are stored in variables of higher-ranked data types, Java automatically converts the lower-ranked value to the higher-ranked type. This is called a *widening conversion*. For example, the following code demonstrates a widening conversion, which takes place when an int value is stored in a double variable:

```
double x;
int y = 10;
x = y;          // Performs a widening conversion
```

A *narrowing conversion* is the conversion of a value to a lower-ranked type. For example, converting a double to an int would be a narrowing conversion. Because narrowing conversions can potentially cause a loss of data, Java does not automatically perform them.

Cast Operators

The *cast operator* lets you manually convert a value, even if it means that a narrowing conversion will take place. Cast operators are unary operators that appear as a data type name enclosed in a set of parentheses. The operator precedes the value being converted. Here is an example:

```
x = (int)number;
```

The cast operator in this statement is the word int inside the parentheses. It returns the value in number, converted to an int. This converted value is then stored in x. If number were a floating-point variable, such as a float or a double, the value that is returned would be *truncated*, which means the fractional part of the number is lost. The original value in the number variable is not changed, however.

Table 2-14 shows several statements using cast operators.

Table 2-14   Example uses of cast operators

Statement	Description
littleNum = (short)bigNum;	The cast operator returns the value in bigNum, converted to a short. The converted value is assigned to the variable littleNum.
x = (long)3.7;	The cast operator is applied to the expression 3.7. The operator returns the value 3, which is assigned to the variable x.
number = (int)72.567;	The cast operator is applied to the expression 72.567. The operator returns 72, which is used to initialize the variable number.
value = (float)x;	The cast operator returns the value in x, converted to a float. The converted value is assigned to the variable value.
value = (byte)number;	The cast operator returns the value in number, converted to a byte. The converted value is assigned to the variable value.

Note that when a cast operator is applied to a variable, it does not change the contents of the variable. It only returns the value stored in the variable, converted to the specified data type.

Recall from our earlier discussion that when both operands of a division are integers, the operation will result in integer division. This means that the result of the division will be an integer, with any fractional part of the result thrown away. For example, look at the following code:

```
int pies = 10, people = 4;
double piesPerPerson;
piesPerPerson = pies / people;
```

Although 10 divided by 4 is 2.5, this code will store 2 in the `piesPerPerson` variable. Because both `pies` and `people` are `int` variables, the result will be an `int`, and the fractional part will be thrown away. We can modify the code with a cast operator, however, so it gives the correct result as a floating-point value:

```
piesPerPerson = (double)pies / people;
```

The variable `pies` is an `int` and holds the value 10. The expression `(double)pies` returns the value in `pies` converted to a `double`. This means that one of the division operator's operands is a `double`, so the result of the division will be a `double`. The statement could also have been written as follows:

```
piesPerPerson = pies / (double)people;
```

In this statement, the cast operator returns the value of the `people` variable converted to a `double`. In either statement, the result of the division is a `double`.

> **WARNING!** The cast operator can be applied to an entire expression enclosed in parentheses. For example, look at the following statement:
>
> ```
> piesPerPerson = (double)(pies / people);
> ```
>
> This statement does not convert the value in `pies` or `people` to a `double`, but converts the result of the expression `pies / people`. If this statement were used, an integer division operation would still have been performed. Here's why: The result of the expression `pies / people` is 2 (because integer division takes place). The value 2 converted to a `double` is 2.0. To prevent the integer division from taking place, one of the operands must be converted to a `double`.

Mixed Integer Operations

One of the nuances of the Java language is the way it internally handles arithmetic operations on `int`, `byte`, and `short` variables. When values of the `byte` or `short` data types are used in arithmetic expressions, they are temporarily converted to `int` values. The result of an arithmetic operation using only a mixture of `byte`, `short`, or `int` values will always be an `int`.

For example, assume that `b` and `c` in the following expression are `short` variables:

```
b + c
```

Although both `b` and `c` are `short` variables, the result of the expression `b + c` is an `int`. This means that when the result of such an expression is stored in a variable, the variable must be an `int` or higher data type. For example, look at the following code:

```
short firstNumber = 10,
      secondNumber = 20,
      thirdNumber;
```

```
    // The following statement causes an error!
    thirdNumber = firstNumber + secondNumber;
```

When this code is compiled, the following statement causes an error:

```
    thirdNumber = firstNumber + secondNumber;
```

The error results from the fact that `thirdNumber` is a `short`. Although `firstNumber` and `secondNumber` are also `short` variables, the expression `firstNumber + secondNumber` results in an `int` value. The program can be corrected if `thirdNumber` is declared as an `int`, or if a cast operator is used in the assignment statement, as shown here:

```
    thirdNumber = (short)(firstNumber + secondNumber);
```

Other Mixed Mathematical Expressions

In situations where a mathematical expression has one or more values of the `double`, `float`, or `long` data types, Java strives to convert all of the operands in the expression to the same data type. Let's look at the specific rules that govern evaluation of these types of expressions.

1. If one of an operator's operands is a `double`, the value of the other operand will be converted to a `double`. The result of the expression will be a `double`. For example, in the following statement assume that b is a `double` and c is an `int`:

   ```
   a = b + c;
   ```

   The value in c will be converted to a `double` prior to the addition. The result of the addition will be a `double`, so the variable a must also be a `double`.

2. If one of an operator's operands is a `float`, the value of the other operand will be converted to a `float`. The result of the expression will be a `float`. For example, in the following statement assume that x is a `short` and y is a `float`:

   ```
   z = x * y;
   ```

   The value in x will be converted to a `float` prior to the multiplication. The result of the multiplication will be a `float`, so the variable z must also be either a `double` or a `float`.

3. If one of an operator's operands is a `long`, the value of the other operand will be converted to a `long`. The result of the expression will be a `long`. For example, in the following statement assume that a is a `long` and b is a `short`:

   ```
   c = a - b;
   ```

   The variable b will be converted to a `long` prior to the subtraction. The result of the subtraction will be a `long`, so the variable c must also be a `long`, `float`, or `double`.

 **Checkpoint**

MyProgrammingLab™ *www.myprogramminglab.com*

2.25 The following declaration appears in a program:

```
    short totalPay, basePay = 500, bonus = 1000;
```

The following statement appears in the same program:

```
    totalPay = basePay + bonus;
```

a) Will the statement compile properly or cause an error?
b) If the statement causes an error, why? How can you fix it?

2.26 The variable a is a `float` and the variable b is a `double`. Write a statement that will assign the value of b to a without causing an error when the program is compiled.

2.8 Creating Named Constants with `final`

> **CONCEPT:** The **`final`** key word can be used in a variable declaration to make the variable a named constant. Named constants are initialized with a value, and that value cannot change during the execution of the program.

Assume that the following statement appears in a banking program that calculates data pertaining to loans:

```
amount = balance * 0.069;
```

In such a program, two potential problems arise. First, it is not clear to anyone other than the original programmer what 0.069 is. It appears to be an interest rate, but in some situations there are fees associated with loan payments. How can the purpose of this statement be determined without painstakingly checking the rest of the program?

The second problem occurs if this number is used in other calculations throughout the program and must be changed periodically. Assuming the number is an interest rate, what if the rate changes from 6.9 percent to 8.2 percent? The programmer would have to search through the source code for every occurrence of the number.

Both of these problems can be addressed by using named constants. A *named constant* is a variable whose value is read only and cannot be changed during the program's execution. You can create such a variable in Java by using the `final` key word in the variable declaration. The word `final` is written just before the data type. Here is an example:

```
final double INTEREST_RATE = 0.069;
```

This statement looks just like a regular variable declaration except that the word `final` appears before the data type, and the variable name is written in all uppercase letters. It is not required that the variable name appear in all uppercase letters, but many programmers prefer to write them this way so they are easily distinguishable from regular variable names.

An initialization value must be given when declaring a variable with the `final` modifier, or an error will result when the program is compiled. A compiler error will also result if there are any statements in the program that attempt to change the value of a `final` variable.

An advantage of using named constants is that they make programs more self-documenting. The following statement:

```
amount = balance * 0.069;
```

can be changed to read

```
amount = balance * INTEREST_RATE;
```

A new programmer can read the second statement and know what is happening. It is evident that balance is being multiplied by the interest rate. Another advantage to this approach is that widespread changes can easily be made to the program. Let's say the interest rate appears in a dozen different statements throughout the program. When the rate changes, the initialization value in the definition of the named constant is the only value that needs to be modified. If the rate increases to 8.2 percent, the declaration can be changed to the following:

```
final double INTEREST_RATE = 0.082;
```

The program is then ready to be recompiled. Every statement that uses INTEREST_RATE will use the new value.

The Math.PI Named Constant

The Math class, which is part of the Java API, provides a predefined named constant, Math.PI. This constant is assigned the value 3.14159265358979323846, which is an approximation of the mathematical value pi. For example, look at the following statement:

```
area = Math.PI * radius * radius;
```

Assuming the radius variable holds the radius of a circle, this statement uses the Math.PI constant to calculate the area of the circle.

> For more information about the Math class, see Appendix F, available on the book's companion Web site at www.pearsonhighered.com/gaddis.

2.9   The String Class

> **CONCEPT:** The String class allows you to create objects for holding strings. It also has various methods that allow you to work with strings.

You have already encountered strings and examined programs that display them on the screen, but let's take a moment to make sure you understand what a string is. A string is a sequence of characters. It can be used to represent any type of data that contains text, such as names, addresses, warning messages, and so forth. String literals are enclosed in double-quotation marks, such as the following:

```
"Hello World"
"Joe Mahoney"
```

Although programs commonly encounter strings and must perform a variety of tasks with them, Java does not have a primitive data type for storing them in memory. Instead, the Java API provides a class for handling strings. You use this class to create objects that are capable of storing strings and performing operations on them. Before discussing this class, let's briefly discuss how classes and objects are related.

Objects Are Created from Classes

Chapter 1 introduced you to objects as software entities that can contain attributes and methods. An object's attributes are data values that are stored in the object. An object's methods are procedures that perform operations on the object's attributes. Before an object can be created, however, it must be designed by a programmer. The programmer determines the attributes and methods that are necessary, and then creates a class that describes the object.

You have already seen classes used as containers for applications. A class can also be used to specify the attributes and methods that a particular type of object may have. Think of a class as a "blueprint" that objects may be created from. So a class is not an object, but a description of an object. When the program is running, it can use the class to create, in memory, as many objects as needed. Each object that is created from a class is called an *instance* of the class.

> **TIP:** Don't worry if these concepts seem a little fuzzy to you. As you progress through this book, the concepts of classes and objects will be reinforced again and again.

The String Class

The class that is provided by the Java API for handling strings is named String. The first step in using the String class is to declare a variable of the String class data type. Here is an example of a String variable declaration:

```
String name;
```

> **TIP:** The S in String is written in an uppercase letter. By convention, the first character of a class name is always written in an uppercase letter.

This statement declares name as a String variable. Remember that String is a class, not a primitive data type. Let's briefly look at the difference between primitive type variables and class type variables.

Primitive Type Variables and Class Type Variables

A variable of any type can be associated with an item of data. *Primitive type variables* hold the actual data items with which they are associated. For example, assume that number is an int variable. The following statement stores the value 25 in the variable:

```
number = 25;
```

This is illustrated in Figure 2-7.

Figure 2-7 A primitive type variable holds the data with which it is associated

The **number** variable holds the actual data with which it is associated.   `25`

A *class type variable* does not hold the actual data item that it is associated with, but holds the memory address of the data item it is associated with. If name is a String class variable, then name can hold the memory address of a String object. This is illustrated in Figure 2-8.

Figure 2-8 A String class variable can hold the address of a String object

The name variable can hold the address of a String object.   `address` → A String object `[ ]`

When a class type variable holds the address of an object, it is said that the variable references the object. For this reason, class type variables are commonly known as *reference variables*.

Creating a `String` Object

Any time you write a string literal in your program, Java will create a `String` object in memory to hold it. You can create a `String` object in memory and store its address in a `String` variable with a simple assignment statement. Here is an example:

```
name = "Joe Mahoney";
```

Here, the string literal causes a `String` object to be created in memory with the value "Joe Mahoney" stored in it. Then the assignment operator stores the address of that object in the name variable. After this statement executes, it is said that the name variable references a `String` object. This is illustrated in Figure 2-9.

Figure 2-9   The name variable holds the address of a `String` object

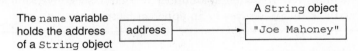

You can also use the = operator to initialize a `String` variable, as shown here:

```
String name = "Joe Mahoney";
```

This statement declares name as a `String` variable, creates a `String` object with the value "Joe Mahoney" stored in it, and assigns the object's memory address to the name variable. Code Listing 2-20 shows `String` variables being declared, initialized, and then used in a println statement.

Code Listing 2-20   (StringDemo.java)

```java
 1  // A simple program demonstrating String objects.
 2
 3  public class StringDemo
 4  {
 5     public static void main(String[] args)
 6     {
 7        String greeting = "Good morning, ";
 8        String name = "Herman";
 9
10        System.out.println(greeting + name);
11     }
12  }
```

Program Output

```
Good morning, Herman
```

Because the String type is a class instead of a primitive data type, it provides numerous methods for working with strings. For example, the String class has a method named length that returns the length of the string stored in an object. Assuming the name variable references a String object, the following statement stores the length of its string in the variable stringSize (assume that stringSize is an int variable):

```
stringSize = name.length();
```

This statement calls the length method of the object that name refers to. To *call* a method means to execute it. The general form of a method call is as follows:

```
referenceVariable.method(arguments. . .)
```

referenceVariable is the name of a variable that references an object, *method* is the name of a method, and *arguments. . .* is zero or more arguments that are passed to the method. If no arguments are passed to the method, as is the case with the length method, a set of empty parentheses must follow the name of the method.

The String class's length method *returns* an int value. This means that the method sends an int value back to the statement that called it. This value can be stored in a variable, displayed on the screen, or used in calculations. Code Listing 2-21 demonstrates the length method.

Code Listing 2-21   (StringLength.java)

```
 1  // This program demonstrates the String class's length method.
 2
 3  public class StringLength
 4  {
 5     public static void main(String[] args)
 6     {
 7        String name = "Herman";
 8        int stringSize;
 9
10        stringSize = name.length();
11        System.out.println(name + " has " + stringSize +
12                           " characters.");
13     }
14  }
```

Program Output

```
Herman has 6 characters.
```

 NOTE: The String class's length method returns the number of characters in the string, including spaces.

You will study the String class methods in detail in Chapter 9, but let's look at a few more examples now. In addition to length, Table 2-15 describes the charAt, toLowerCase, and toUpperCase methods.

Table 2-15 A few `String` class methods

Method	Description and Example
`charAt(index)`	The argument *index* is an int value and specifies a character position in the string. The first character is at position 0, the second character is at position 1, and so forth. The method returns the character at the specified position. The return value is of the type char. **Example:** <code>char letter;</code> <code>String name = "Herman";</code> <code>letter = name.charAt(3);</code> After this code executes, the variable letter will hold the character 'm'.
`length()`	This method returns the number of characters in the string. The return value is of the type int. **Example:** <code>int stringSize;</code> <code>String name = "Herman";</code> <code>stringSize = name.length();</code> After this code executes, the stringSize variable will hold the value 6.
`toLowerCase()`	This method returns a new string that is the lowercase equivalent of the string contained in the calling object. **Example:** <code>String bigName = "HERMAN";</code> <code>String littleName = bigName.toLowerCase();</code> After this code executes, the object referenced by littleName will hold the string "herman".
`toUpperCase()`	This method returns a new string that is the uppercase equivalent of the string contained in the calling object. **Example:** <code>String littleName = "herman";</code> <code>String bigName = littleName.toUpperCase();</code> After this code executes, the object referenced by bigName will hold the string "HERMAN".

The program in Code Listing 2-22 demonstrates these methods.

Code Listing 2-22   (**StringMethods.java**)

```
1   // This program demonstrates a few of the String methods.
2
3   public class StringMethods
4   {
5      public static void main(String[] args)
6      {
7         String message = "Java is Great Fun!";
8         String upper = message.toUpperCase();
```

```
 9          String lower = message.toLowerCase();
10          char letter = message.charAt(2);
11          int stringSize = message.length();
12
13          System.out.println(message);
14          System.out.println(upper);
15          System.out.println(lower);
16          System.out.println(letter);
17          System.out.println(stringSize);
18      }
19  }
```

Program Output

```
Java is Great Fun!
JAVA IS GREAT FUN!
java is great fun!
v
18
```

 Checkpoint

MyProgrammingLab™ *www.myprogramminglab.com*

2.27 Write a statement that declares a String variable named city. The variable should be initialized so it references an object with the string "San Francisco".

2.28 Assume that stringLength is an int variable. Write a statement that stores the length of the string referenced by the city variable (declared in Checkpoint 2.27) in stringLength.

2.29 Assume that oneChar is a char variable. Write a statement that stores the first character in the string referenced by the city variable (declared in Checkpoint 2.27) in oneChar.

2.30 Assume that upperCity is a String reference variable. Write a statement that stores the uppercase equivalent of the string referenced by the city variable (declared in Checkpoint 2.27) in upperCity.

2.31 Assume that lowerCity is a String reference variable. Write a statement that stores the lowercase equivalent of the string referenced by the city variable (declared in Checkpoint 2.27) in lowerCity.

 2.10 Scope

CONCEPT: A variable's scope is the part of the program that has access to the variable.

Every variable has a *scope*. The scope of a variable is the part of the program where the variable may be accessed by its name. A variable is visible only to statements inside the variable's scope. The rules that define a variable's scope are complex, and you are only introduced to the concept here. In other chapters of the book we revisit this topic and expand on it.

So far, you have only seen variables declared inside the main method. Variables that are declared inside a method are called *local variables*. Later you will learn about variables that are declared outside a method, but for now, let's focus on the use of local variables.

A local variable's scope begins at the variable's declaration and ends at the end of the method in which the variable is declared. The variable cannot be accessed by statements that are outside this region. This means that a local variable cannot be accessed by code that is outside the method, or inside the method but before the variable's declaration. The program in Code Listing 2-23 shows an example.

Code Listing 2-23   (Scope.java)

```
1   // This program can't find its variable.
2
3   public class Scope
4   {
5      public static void main(String[] args)
6      {
7         System.out.println(value); // ERROR!
8         int value = 100;
9      }
10  }
```

The program does not compile because it attempts to send the contents of the variable value to println before the variable is declared. It is important to remember that the compiler reads your program from top to bottom. If it encounters a statement that uses a variable before the variable is declared, an error will result. To correct the program, the variable declaration must be written before any statement that uses it.

 NOTE: If you compile this program, the compiler will display an error message such as "cannot resolve symbol." This means that the compiler has encountered a name for which it cannot determine a meaning.

Another rule that you must remember about local variables is that you cannot have two local variables with the same name in the same scope. For example, look at the following method.

```
public static void main(String[] args)
{
   // Declare a variable named number and
   // display its value.
   int number = 7;
   System.out.println(number);
```

```
    // Declare another variable named number and
    // display its value.
    int number = 100;              // ERROR!!!
    System.out.println(number);    // ERROR!!!
}
```

This method declares a variable named number and initializes it with the value 7. The variable's scope begins at the declaration statement and extends to the end of the method. Inside the variable's scope a statement appears that declares another variable named number. This statement will cause an error because you cannot have two local variables with the same name in the same scope.

2.11 Comments

> **CONCEPT:** Comments are notes of explanation that document lines or sections of a program. Comments are part of the program, but the compiler ignores them. They are intended for people who may be reading the source code.

Comments are short notes that are placed in different parts of a program, explaining how those parts of the program work. Comments are not intended for the compiler. They are intended for programmers to read, to help them understand the code. The compiler skips all of the comments that appear in a program.

As a beginning programmer, you might resist the idea of writing a lot of comments in your programs. After all, it's a lot more fun to write code that actually does something! However, it's crucial that you take the extra time to write comments. They will almost certainly save you time in the future when you have to modify or debug the program. Even large and complex programs can be made easy to read and understand if they are properly commented.

In Java there are three types of comments: single-line comments, multiline comments, and documentation comments. Let's briefly discuss each type.

Single-Line Comments

You have already seen the first way to write comments in a Java program. You simply place two forward slashes (//) where you want the comment to begin. The compiler ignores everything from that point to the end of the line. Code Listing 2-24 shows that comments may be placed liberally throughout a program.

Code Listing 2-24 (Comment1.java)

```
1  // PROGRAM: Comment1.java
2  // Written by Herbert Dorfmann
3  // This program calculates company payroll
4
5  public class Comment1
```

```
 6  {
 7      public static void main(String[] args)
 8      {
 9         double payRate;       // Holds the hourly pay rate
10         double hours;         // Holds the hours worked
11         int employeeNumber;   // Holds the employee number
12
13         // The Remainder of This Program is Omitted.
14      }
15  }
```

In addition to telling who wrote the program and describing the purpose of variables, comments can also be used to explain complex procedures in your code.

Multi-Line Comments

The second type of comment in Java is the multi-line comment. *Multi-line comments* start with /* (a forward slash followed by an asterisk) and end with */ (an asterisk followed by a forward slash). Everything between these markers is ignored. Code Listing 2-25 illustrates how multi-line comments may be used.

Code Listing 2-25   (Comment2.java)

```
 1  /*
 2      PROGRAM: Comment2.java
 3      Written by Herbert Dorfmann
 4      This program calculates company payroll
 5  */
 6
 7  public class Comment2
 8  {
 9      public static void main(String[] args)
10      {
11         double payRate;       // Holds the hourly pay rate
12         double hours;         // Holds the hours worked
13         int employeeNumber;   // Holds the employee number
14
15         // The Remainder of This Program is Omitted.
16      }
17  }
```

Unlike a comment started with //, a multi-line comment can span several lines. This makes it more convenient to write large blocks of comments because you do not have to mark every line. Consequently, the multi-line comment is inconvenient for writing single-line comments because you must type both a beginning and an ending comment symbol.

Remember the following advice when using multi-line comments:

- Be careful not to reverse the beginning symbol with the ending symbol.
- Be sure not to forget the ending symbol.

Many programmers use asterisks or other characters to draw borders or boxes around their comments. This helps to visually separate the comments from surrounding code. These are called block comments. Table 2-16 shows four examples of block comments.

Table 2-16   Block comments

```
/*                                     //**********************************
 *    This program demonstrates the    //    This program demonstrates the *
 *    way to write comments.           //    way to write comments.        *
 */                                    //**********************************


//////////////////////////////////    //----------------------------------
//    This program demonstrates the    //    This program demonstrates the
//    way to write comments.           //    way to write comments.
//////////////////////////////////    //----------------------------------
```

Documentation Comments

The third type of comment is known as a documentation comment. *Documentation comments* can be read and processed by a program named `javadoc`, which comes with the JDK. The purpose of the `javadoc` program is to read Java source code files and generate attractively formatted HTML files that document the source code. If the source code files contain any documentation comments, the information in the comments becomes part of the HTML documentation. The HTML documentation files may be viewed in a Web browser.

Any comment that starts with `/**` and ends with `*/` is considered a documentation comment. Normally you write a documentation comment just before a class header, giving a brief description of the class. You also write a documentation comment just before each method header, giving a brief description of the method. For example, Code Listing 2-26 shows a program with documentation comments. This program has a documentation comment just before the class header, and just before the `main` method header.

Code Listing 2-26 (`Comment3.java`)

```
 1  /**
 2     This class creates a program that calculates company payroll.
 3  */
 4
 5  public class Comment3
 6  {
 7     /**
 8         The main method is the program's starting point.
 9     */
10
11     public static void main(String[] args)
12     {
13        double payRate;       // Holds the hourly pay rate
14        double hours;         // Holds the hours worked
15        int employeeNumber;   // Holds the employee number
16
17        // The Remainder of This Program is Omitted.
18     }
19  }
```

You run the `javadoc` program from the operating system command prompt. Here is the general format of the `javadoc` command:

```
javadoc SourceFile.java
```

`SourceFile`.java is the name of a Java source code file, including the .java extension. The file will be read by `javadoc` and documentation will be produced for it. For example, the following command will produce documentation for the *Comment3.java* source code file, which is shown in Code Listing 2-26:

```
javadoc Comment3.java
```

After this command executes, several documentation files will be created in the same directory as the source code file. One of these files will be named *index.html*. Figure 2-10 shows the *index.html* file being viewed in a Web browser. Notice that the text that was written in the documentation comments appears in the file.

TIP: When you write a documentation comment for a method, the HTML documentation file that is produced by `javadoc` will have two sections for the method: a summary section and a detail section. The first sentence in the method's documentation comment is used as the summary of the method. Note that `javadoc` considers the end of the sentence as a period followed by a whitespace character. For this reason, when a method description contains more than one sentence, you should always end the first sentence with a period followed by a whitespace character. The method's detail section will contain all of the description that appears in the documentation comment.

Figure 2-10   Documentation generated by `javadoc`   (Google Inc.)

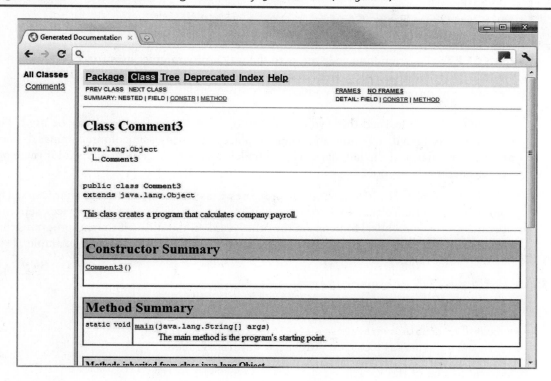

If you look at the JDK documentation, which are HTML files that you view in a Web browser, you will see that they are formatted in the same way as the files generated by javadoc. A benefit of using javadoc to document your source code is that your documentation will have the same professional look and feel as the standard Java documentation.

From this point forward in the book, we will use documentation comments in the example source code. As we progress through various topics, you will see additional uses of documentation comments and the javadoc program.

 **Checkpoint**

MyProgrammingLab™ *www.myprogramminglab.com*

2.32   How do you write a single line comment? How do you write a multi-line comment? How do you write a documentation comment?

2.33   How are documentation comments different from other types of comments?

2.12 Programming Style

CONCEPT: Programming style refers to the way a programmer uses spaces, indentations, blank lines, and punctuation characters to visually arrange a program's source code.

In Chapter 1, you learned that syntax rules govern the way a language may be used. The syntax rules of Java dictate how and where to place key words, semicolons, commas, braces, and other elements of the language. The compiler checks for syntax errors, and if there are none, generates byte code.

When the compiler reads a program it processes it as one long stream of characters. The compiler doesn't care that each statement is on a separate line, or that spaces separate operators from operands. Humans, on the other hand, find it difficult to read programs that aren't written in a visually pleasing manner. Consider Code Listing 2-27 for example.

Code Listing 2-27   (Compact.java)

```
1  public class Compact {public static void main(String [] args){int
2  shares=220; double averagePrice=14.67; System.out.println(
3  "There were "+shares+" shares sold at $"+averagePrice+
4  " per share.");}}
```

Program Output

```
There were 220 shares sold at $14.67 per share.
```

Although the program is syntactically correct (it doesn't violate any rules of Java), it is very difficult to read. The same program is shown in Code Listing 2-28, written in a more understandable style.

Code Listing 2-28   (Readable.java)

```
1   /**
2      This example is much more readable than Compact.java.
3   */
4
5   public class Readable
6   {
7      public static void main(String[] args)
8      {
9         int shares = 220;
10        double averagePrice = 14.67;
11
12        System.out.println("There were " + shares +
13                           " shares sold at $" +
14                           averagePrice + " per share.");
```

```
15      }
16  }
```

Program Output

There were 220 shares sold at $14.67 per share.

The term *programming style* usually refers to the way source code is visually arranged. It includes techniques for consistently putting spaces and indentations in a program so visual cues are created. These cues quickly tell a programmer important information about a program.

For example, notice in Code Listing 2-28 that inside the class's braces each line is indented, and inside the main method's braces each line is indented again. It is a common programming style to indent all the lines inside a set of braces, as shown in Figure 2-11.

Figure 2-11   Indentation

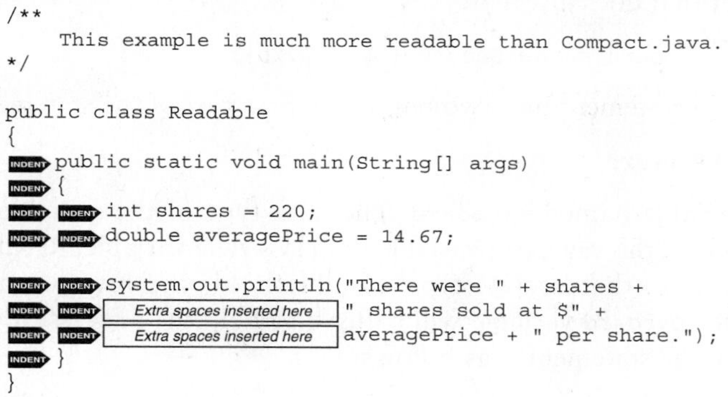

```
/**
      This example is much more readable than Compact.java.
*/

public class Readable
{
INDENT public static void main(String[] args)
INDENT {
INDENT INDENT int shares = 220;
INDENT INDENT double averagePrice = 14.67;

INDENT INDENT System.out.println("There were " + shares +
INDENT INDENT [Extra spaces inserted here] " shares sold at $" +
INDENT INDENT [Extra spaces inserted here] averagePrice + " per share.");
INDENT }
}
```

Another aspect of programming style is how to handle statements that are too long to fit on one line. Notice that the println statement is spread out over three lines. Extra spaces are inserted at the beginning of the statement's second and third lines, which indicate that they are continuations.

When declaring multiple variables of the same type with a single statement, it is a common practice to write each variable name on a separate line with a comment explaining the variable's purpose. Here is an example:

```
int fahrenheit,    // To hold the Fahrenheit temperature
    celsius,       // To hold the Celsius temperature
    kelvin;        // To hold the Kelvin temperature
```

You may have noticed in the example programs that a blank line is inserted between the variable declarations and the statements that follow them. This is intended to separate the declarations visually from the executable statements.

There are many other issues related to programming style. They will be presented throughout the book.

2.13   Reading Keyboard Input

CONCEPT: Objects of the **Scanner** class can be used to read input from the keyboard.

Previously we discussed the System.out object, and how it refers to the standard output device. The Java API has another object, System.in, which refers to the standard input device. The *standard input device* is normally the keyboard. You can use the System.in object to read keystrokes that have been typed at the keyboard. However, using System.in is not as simple and straightforward as using System.out because the System.in object reads input only as byte values. This isn't very useful because programs normally require values of other data types as input. To work around this, you can use the System.in object in conjunction with an object of the Scanner class. The Scanner class is designed to read input from a source (such as System.in), and it, provides methods that you can use to retrieve the input formatted as primitive values or strings.

First, you create a Scanner object and connect it to the System.in object. Here is an example of a statement that does just that:

```
Scanner keyboard = new Scanner(System.in);
```

Let's dissect the statement into two parts. The first part of the statement,

```
Scanner keyboard
```

declares a variable named keyboard. The data type of the variable is Scanner. Because Scanner is a class, the keyboard variable is a class type variable. Recall from our discussion on String objects that a class type variable holds the memory address of an object. Therefore, the keyboard variable will be used to hold the address of a Scanner object. The second part of the statement is as follows:

```
= new Scanner(System.in);
```

The first thing we see in this part of the statement is the assignment operator (=). The assignment operator will assign something to the keyboard variable. After the assignment operator we see the word new, which is a Java key word. The purpose of the new key word is to create an object in memory. The type of object that will be created is listed next. In this case, we see Scanner(System.in) listed after the new key word. This specifies that a Scanner object should be created, and it should be connected to the System.in object. The memory address of the object is assigned (by the = operator) to the variable keyboard. After the statement executes, the keyboard variable will reference the Scanner object that was created in memory.

Figure 2-12 points out the purpose of each part of this statement. Figure 2-13 illustrates how the keyboard variable references an object of the Scanner class.

Figure 2-12 The parts of the statement

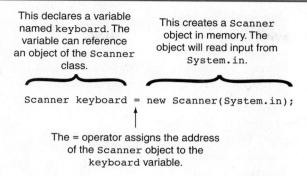

This declares a variable named keyboard. The variable can reference an object of the Scanner class.

This creates a Scanner object in memory. The object will read input from System.in.

```
Scanner keyboard = new Scanner(System.in);
```

The = operator assigns the address of the Scanner object to the keyboard variable.

Figure 2-13 The keyboard variable references a Scanner object

The keyboard variable can hold the address of a Scanner object.

address →

A Scanner object

This Scanner object is configured to read input from System.in.

NOTE: In the preceding code, we chose keyboard as the variable name. There is nothing special about the name keyboard. We simply chose that name because we will use the variable to read input from the keyboard.

The Scanner class has methods for reading strings, bytes, integers, long integers, short integers, floats, and doubles. For example, the following code uses an object of the Scanner class to read an int value from the keyboard and assign the value to the number variable.

```
int number;
Scanner keyboard = new Scanner(System.in);
System.out.print("Enter an integer value: ");
number = keyboard.nextInt();
```

The last statement shown here calls the Scanner class's nextInt method. The nextInt method formats an input value as an int, and then returns that value. Therefore, this statement formats the input that was entered at the keyboard as an int, and then returns it. The value is assigned to the number variable.

Table 2-17 lists several of the Scanner class's methods and describes their use.

Table 2-17 Some of the Scanner class methods

Method	Example and Description

nextByte	**Example Usage:**
	<pre>byte x;
	Scanner keyboard = new Scanner(System.in);
	System.out.print("Enter a byte value: ");
	x = keyboard.nextByte();</pre>**Description:** Returns input as a byte.

nextDouble	**Example Usage:**
	<pre>double number;
	Scanner keyboard = new Scanner(System.in);
	System.out.print("Enter a double value: ");
	number = keyboard.nextDouble();</pre>**Description:** Returns input as a double.

nextFloat	**Example Usage:**
	<pre>float number;
	Scanner keyboard = new Scanner(System.in);
	System.out.print("Enter a float value: ");
	number = keyboard.nextFloat();</pre>**Description:** Returns input as a float.

nextInt	**Example Usage:**
	<pre>int number;
	Scanner keyboard = new Scanner(System.in);
	System.out.print("Enter an integer value: ");
	number = keyboard.nextInt();</pre>**Description:** Returns input as an int.

nextLine	**Example Usage:**
	<pre>String name;
	Scanner keyboard = new Scanner(System.in);
	System.out.print("Enter your name: ");
	name = keyboard.nextLine();</pre>**Description:** Returns input as a String.

nextLong	**Example Usage:**
	<pre>long number;
	Scanner keyboard = new Scanner(System.in);
	System.out.print("Enter a long value: ");
	number = keyboard.nextLong();</pre>**Description:** Returns input as a long.

nextShort	**Example Usage:**
	<pre>short number;
	Scanner keyboard = new Scanner(System.in);
	System.out.print("Enter a short value: ");
	number = keyboard.nextShort();</pre>**Description:** Returns input as a short.

Using the `import` Statement

There is one last detail about the Scanner class that you must know before you will be ready to use it. The Scanner class is not automatically available to your Java programs. Any program that uses the Scanner class should have the following statement near the beginning of the file, before any class definition:

```java
import java.util.Scanner;
```

This statement tells the Java compiler where in the Java library to find the Scanner class, and makes it available to your program.

Code Listing 2-29 shows the Scanner class being used to read a String, an int, and a double.

Code Listing 2-29   (Payroll.java)

```java
 1  import java.util.Scanner;  // Needed for the Scanner class
 2
 3  /**
 4    This program demonstrates the Scanner class.
 5  */
 6
 7  public class Payroll
 8  {
 9     public static void main(String[] args)
10     {
11        String name;         // To hold a name
12        int hours;           // Hours worked
13        double payRate;      // Hourly pay rate
14        double grossPay;     // Gross pay
15
16        // Create a Scanner object to read input.
17        Scanner keyboard = new Scanner(System.in);
18
19        // Get the user's name.
20        System.out.print("What is your name? ");
21        name = keyboard.nextLine();
22
23        // Get the number of hours worked this week.
24        System.out.print("How many hours did you work this week? ");
25        hours = keyboard.nextInt();
26
27        // Get the user's hourly pay rate.
28        System.out.print("What is your hourly pay rate? ");
29        payRate = keyboard.nextDouble();
30
31        // Calculate the gross pay.
32        grossPay = hours * payRate;
33
```

```
34            // Display the resulting information.
35            System.out.println("Hello, " + name);
36            System.out.println("Your gross pay is $" + grossPay);
37        }
38  }
```

Program Output with Example Input Shown in Bold

What is your name? **Joe Mahoney [Enter]**
How many hours did you work this week? **40 [Enter]**
What is your hourly pay rate? **20 [Enter]**
Hello, Joe Mahoney
Your gross pay is $800.0

 NOTE: Notice that each `Scanner` class method that we used waits for the user to press the ⌈Enter⌋ key before it returns a value. When the ⌈Enter⌋ key is pressed, the cursor automatically moves to the next line for subsequent output operations.

Reading a Character

Sometimes you will want to read a single character from the keyboard. For example, your program might ask the user a yes/no question, and specify that he or she type Y for yes or N for no. The `Scanner` class does not have a method for reading a single character, however. The approach that we will use in this book for reading a character is to use the `Scanner` class's `nextLine` method to read a string from the keyboard, and then use the `String` class's `charAt` method to extract the first character of the string. This will be the character that the user entered at the keyboard. Here is an example:

```
String input;  // To hold a line of input
char answer;   // To hold a single character

// Create a Scanner object for keyboard input.
Scanner keyboard = new Scanner(System.in);

// Ask the user a question.
System.out.print("Are you having fun? (Y=yes, N=no) ");
input = keyboard.nextLine();  // Get a line of input.
answer = input.charAt(0);     // Get the first character.
```

The `input` variable references a `String` object. The last statement in this code calls the `String` class's `charAt` method to retrieve the character at position 0, which is the first character in the string. After this statement executes, the `answer` variable will hold the character that the user typed at the keyboard.

Mixing Calls to `nextLine` with Calls to Other `Scanner` Methods

When you call one of the `Scanner` class's methods to read a primitive value, such as `nextInt` or `nextDouble`, and then call the `nextLine` method to read a string, an annoying and hard-to-find problem can occur. For example, look at the program in Code Listing 2-30.

Code Listing 2-30   (`InputProblem.java`)

```java
1   import java.util.Scanner;  // Needed for the Scanner class
2
3   /*
4      This program has a problem reading input.
5   */
6
7   public class InputProblem
8   {
9      public static void main(String[] args)
10     {
11        String name;     // To hold the user's name
12        int age;         // To hold the user's age
13        double income;   // To hold the user's income
14
15        // Create a Scanner object to read input.
16        Scanner keyboard = new Scanner(System.in);
17
18        // Get the user's age.
19        System.out.print("What is your age? ");
20        age = keyboard.nextInt();
21
22        // Get the user's income
23        System.out.print("What is your annual income? ");
24        income = keyboard.nextDouble();
25
26        // Get the user's name.
27        System.out.print("What is your name? ");
28        name = keyboard.nextLine();
29
30        // Display the information back to the user.
31        System.out.println("Hello, " + name + ". Your age is " +
32                           age + " and your income is $" +
33                           income);
34     }
35  }
```

Program Output with Example Input Shown in Bold

```
What is your age? 24 [Enter]
What is your annual income? 50000.00 [Enter]
What is your name? Hello, . Your age is 24 and your income is $50000.0
```

Notice in the example output that the program first allows the user to enter his or her age. The statement in line 20 reads an int from the keyboard and stores the value in the age variable. Next, the user enters his or her income. The statement in line 24 reads a double from the keyboard and stores the value in the income variable. Then the user is asked to enter his or her name, but it appears that the statement in line 28 is skipped. The name is never read from the keyboard. This happens because of a slight difference in behavior between the nextLine method and the other Scanner class methods.

When the user types keystrokes at the keyboard, those keystrokes are stored in an area of memory that is sometimes called the *keyboard buffer*. Pressing the Enter key causes a new-line character to be stored in the keyboard buffer. In the example running of the program in Code Listing 2-30, the user was asked to enter his or her age, and the statement in line 20 called the nextInt method to read an integer from the keyboard buffer. Notice that the user typed 24 and then pressed the Enter key. The nextInt method read the value 24 from the keyboard buffer, and then stopped when it encountered the newline character. So the value 24 was read from the keyboard buffer, but the newline character was not read. The newline character remained in the keyboard buffer.

Next, the user was asked to enter his or her annual income. The user typed 50000.00 and then pressed the Enter key. When the nextDouble method in line 24 executed, it first encoun-tered the newline character that was left behind by the nextInt method. This does not cause a problem because the nextDouble method is designed to skip any leading newline charac-ters it encounters. It skips over the initial newline, reads the value 50000.00 from the key-board buffer, and stops reading when it encounters the next newline character. This newline character is then left in the keyboard buffer.

Next, the user is asked to enter his or her name. In line 28 the nextLine method is called. The nextLine method, however, is not designed to skip over an initial newline character. If a newline character is the first character that the nextLine method encounters, then nothing will be read. Because the nextDouble method, back in line 24, left a newline char-acter in the keyboard buffer, the nextLine method will not read any input. Instead, it will immediately terminate and the user will not be given a chance to enter his or her name.

Although the details of this problem might seem confusing, the solution is easy. The program in Code Listing 2-31 is a modification of Code Listing 2-30, with the input problem fixed.

Code Listing 2-31   (CorrectedInputProblem.java)

```
 1   import java.util.Scanner;   // Needed for the Scanner class
 2
 3   /*
 4      This program correctly reads numeric and string input.
 5   */
 6
 7   public class CorrectedInputProblem
 8   {
 9      public static void main(String[] args)
10      {
11         String name;   // To hold the user's name
```

```
12          int age;        // To hold the user's age
13          double income;  // To hold the user's income
14
15          // Create a Scanner object to read input.
16          Scanner keyboard = new Scanner(System.in);
17
18          // Get the user's age.
19          System.out.print("What is your age? ");
20          age = keyboard.nextInt();
21
22          // Get the user's income
23          System.out.print("What is your annual income? ");
24          income = keyboard.nextDouble();
25
26          // Consume the remaining newline.
27          keyboard.nextLine();
28
29          // Get the user's name.
30          System.out.print("What is your name? ");
31          name = keyboard.nextLine();
32
33          // Display the information back to the user.
34          System.out.println("Hello, " + name + ". Your age is " +
35                             age + " and your income is $" +
36                             income);
37    }
38 }
```

Program Output with Example Input Shown in Bold

What is your age? **24 [Enter]**
What is your annual income? **50000.00 [Enter]**
What is your name? **Mary Simpson [Enter]**
Hello, Mary Simpson. Your age is 24 and your income is $50000.0

Notice that after the user's income is read by the nextDouble method in line 24, the nextLine method is called in line 27. The purpose of this call is to consume, or remove, the newline character that remains in the keyboard buffer. Then, in line 31, the nextLine method is called again. This time it correctly reads the user's name.

 NOTE: Notice that in line 27, where we consume the remaining newline character, we do not assign the method's return value to any variable. This is because we are simply calling the method to remove the newline character, and we do not need to keep the method's return value.

2.14   Dialog Boxes

CONCEPT: The **JOptionPane** class allows you to quickly display a dialog box, which is a small graphical window displaying a message or requesting input.

A *dialog box* is a small graphical window that displays a message to the user or requests input. You can quickly display dialog boxes with the JOptionPane class. In this section we will discuss the following types of dialog boxes and how you can display them using JOptionPane:

- Message Dialog   A dialog box that displays a message; an OK button is also displayed
- Input Dialog   A dialog box that prompts the user for input and provides a text field where input is typed; an OK button and a Cancel button are also displayed

Figure 2-14 shows an example of each type of dialog box.

Figure 2-14   A message dialog and an input dialog

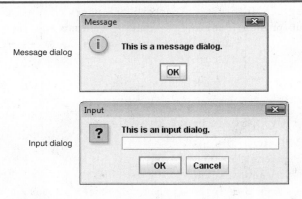

The JOptionPane class is not automatically available to your Java programs. Any program that uses the JOptionPane class must have the following statement near the beginning of the file:

```
import javax.swing.JOptionPane;
```

This statement tells the compiler where to find the JOptionPane class and makes it available to your program.

Displaying Message Dialogs

The showMessageDialog method is used to display a message dialog. Here is a statement that calls the method:

```
JOptionPane.showMessageDialog(null, "Hello World");
```

The first argument is only important in programs that display other graphical windows. You will learn more about this in Chapter 12. Until then, we will always pass the key word null as the first argument. This causes the dialog box to be displayed in the center of the screen. The second argument is the message that we wish to display in the dialog box. This code will cause the dialog box in Figure 2-15 to appear. When the user clicks the OK button, the dialog box will close.

Figure 2-15   Message dialog

Displaying Input Dialogs

An input dialog is a quick and simple way to ask the user to enter data. You use the JOptionPane class's showInputDialog method to display an input dialog. The following code calls the method:

```
String name;
name = JOptionPane.showInputDialog("Enter your name.");
```

The argument passed to the method is a message to display in the dialog box. This statement will cause the dialog box shown in Figure 2-16 to be displayed in the center of the screen. If the user clicks the OK button, name will reference the string value entered by the user into the text field. If the user clicks the Cancel button, name will reference the special value null.

Figure 2-16   Input dialog

An Example Program

The program in Code Listing 2-32 demonstrates how to use both types of dialog boxes. This program uses input dialogs to ask the user to enter his or her first, middle, and last names, and then displays a greeting with a message dialog. When this program executes, the dialog boxes shown in Figure 2-17 will be displayed, one at a time.

Code Listing 2-32   (`NamesDialog.java`)

```
1   import javax.swing.JOptionPane;
2
3   /**
4      This program demonstrates using dialogs with
5      JOptionPane.
6   */
7
8   public class NamesDialog
9   {
10     public static void main(String[] args)
11     {
12        String firstName;  // The user's first name
13        String middleName; // The user's middle name
14        String lastName;   // The user's last name
15
16        // Get the user's first name.
17        firstName =
18             JOptionPane.showInputDialog("What is " +
19                                  "your first name? ");
20
21        // Get the user's middle name.
22        middleName =
23             JOptionPane.showInputDialog("What is " +
24                                  "your middle name? ");
25
26        // Get the user's last name.
27        lastName =
28             JOptionPane.showInputDialog("What is " +
29                                  "your last name? ");
30
31        // Display a greeting
32        JOptionPane.showMessageDialog(null, "Hello " +
33                         firstName + " " + middleName +
34                         " " + lastName);
35        System.exit(0);
36     }
37  }
```

Notice the last statement in the main method:

```
System.exit(0);
```

This statement causes the program to end, and is required if you use the `JOptionPane` class to display dialog boxes. Unlike a console program, a program that uses `JOptionPane` does not automatically stop executing when the end of the main method is reached, because the `JOptionPane` class causes an additional task to run in the JVM. If the `System.exit` method

Figure 2-17 Dialog boxes displayed by the `NamesDialog` program

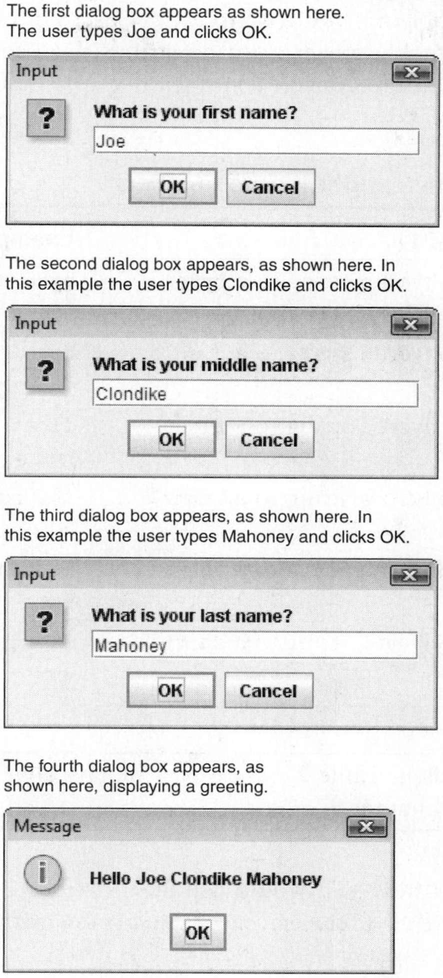
The first dialog box appears as shown here.
The user types Joe and clicks OK.
Input
What is your first name?
Joe
OK
Cancel
The second dialog box appears, as shown here. In
this example the user types Clondike and clicks OK.
Input
What is your middle name?
Clondike
OK
Cancel
The third dialog box appears, as shown here. In
this example the user types Mahoney and clicks OK.
Input
What is your last name?
Mahoney
OK
Cancel
The fourth dialog box appears, as
shown here, displaying a greeting.
Message
Hello Joe Clondike Mahoney
OK

is not called, this task, also known as a *thread*, will continue to execute, even after the end of the `main` method has been reached.

The `System.exit` method requires an integer argument. This argument is an exit code that is passed back to the operating system. Although this code is usually ignored, it can be used outside the program to indicate whether the program ended successfully or as the result of a failure. The value 0 traditionally indicates that the program ended successfully.

Converting String Input to Numbers

Unlike the `Scanner` class, the `JOptionPane` class does not have different methods for reading values of different data types as input. The `showInputDialog` method always returns the user's input as a `String`, even if the user enters numeric data. For example, if the user enters the number 72 into an input dialog, the `showInputDialog` method will return the string `"72"`. This can be a problem if you wish to use the user's input in a math operation because, as you know, you cannot perform math on strings. In such a case, you must convert the input to a numeric value. To convert a string value to a numeric value, you use one of the methods listed in Table 2-18.

Table 2-18 Methods for converting strings to numbers

Method	Use This Method To . . .	Example Code
`Byte.parseByte`	Convert a string to a byte.	`byte num;` `num = Byte.parseByte(str);`
`Double.parseDouble`	Convert a string to a double.	`double num;` `num = Double.parseDouble(str);`
`Float.parseFloat`	Convert a string to a float.	`float num;` `num = Float.parseFloat(str);`
`Integer.parseInt`	Convert a string to an int.	`int num;` `num = Integer.parseInt(str);`
`Long.parseLong`	Convert a string to a long.	`long num;` `num = Long.parseLong(str);`
`Short.parseShort`	Convert a string to a short.	`short num;` `num = Short.parseShort(str);`

 NOTE: The methods in Table 2-18 are part of Java's wrapper classes, which you will learn more about in Chapter 9.

Here is an example of how you would use the `Integer.parseInt` method to convert the value returned from the `JOptionPane.showInputDialog` method to an int:

```
int number;
String str;
str = JOptionPane.showInputDialog("Enter a number.");
number = Integer.parseInt(str);
```

After this code executes, the `number` variable will hold the value entered by the user, converted to an int. Here is an example of how you would use the `Double.parseDouble` method to convert the user's input to a double:

```
double price;
String str;
str = JOptionPane.showInputDialog("Enter the retail price.");
price = Double.parseDouble(str);
```

After this code executes, the `price` variable will hold the value entered by the user, converted to a double. Code Listing 2-33 shows a complete program. This is a modification of the `Payroll.java` program in Code Listing 2-29. When this program executes, the dialog boxes shown in Figure 2-18 will be displayed, one at a time.

Code Listing 2-33   (`PayrollDialog.java`)

```java
 1   import javax.swing.JOptionPane;
 2
 3   /**
 4      This program demonstrates using dialogs with
 5      JOptionPane.
 6   */
 7
 8   public class PayrollDialog
 9   {
10      public static void main(String[] args)
11      {
12         String inputString;      // For reading input
13         String name;             // The user's name
14         int hours;               // The number of hours worked
15         double payRate;          // The user's hourly pay rate
16         double grossPay;         // The user's gross pay
17
18         // Get the user's name.
19         name = JOptionPane.showInputDialog("What is " +
20                                        "your name? ");
21
22         // Get the hours worked.
23         inputString =
24            JOptionPane.showInputDialog("How many hours " +
25                                   "did you work this week? ");
26
27         // Convert the input to an int.
28         hours = Integer.parseInt(inputString);
29
30         // Get the hourly pay rate.
31         inputString =
32            JOptionPane.showInputDialog("What is your " +
33                                   "hourly pay rate? ");
34
35         // Convert the input to a double.
36         payRate = Double.parseDouble(inputString);
37
38         // Calculate the gross pay.
39         grossPay = hours * payRate;
40
41         // Display the results.
42         JOptionPane.showMessageDialog(null, "Hello " +
43                       name + ". Your gross pay is $" +
44                       grossPay);
45
46         // End the program.
47         System.exit(0);
48      }
49   }
```

Figure 2-18 Dialog boxes displayed by `PayrollDialog.java`

The first dialog box appears as shown here. The user enters his or her name and then clicks OK.

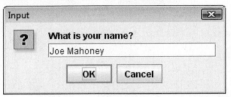

The second dialog box appears, as shown here. The user enters the number of hours workded and then clicks OK.

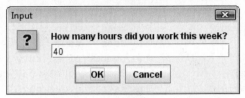

The third dialog box appears, as shown here. The user enters his or her hourly pay rate and then clicks OK.

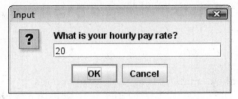

The fourth dialog box appears, as shown here.

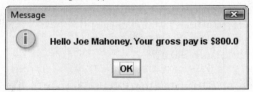

 **Checkpoint**

MyProgrammingLab™ *www.myprogramminglab.com*

2.34 What is the purpose of the following types of dialog boxes?

Message dialog

Input dialog

2.35 Write code that will display each of the dialog boxes shown in Figure 2-19.

Figure 2-19 Dialog boxes

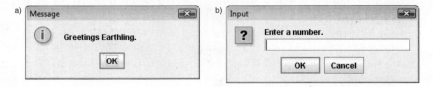

2.36   Write code that displays an input dialog asking the user to enter his or her age. Convert the input value to an `int` and store it in an `int` variable named `age`.

2.37   What `import` statement do you write in a program that uses the `JOptionPane` class?

2.15   Common Errors to Avoid

- **Mismatched braces, quotation marks, or parentheses.** In this chapter you saw that the statements making up a class definition are enclosed in a set of braces. Also, you saw that the statements in a method are also enclosed in a set of braces. For every opening brace, there must be a closing brace in the proper location. The same is true of double-quotation marks that enclose string literals and single-quotation marks that enclose character literals. Also, in a statement that uses parentheses, such as a mathematical expression, you must have a closing parenthesis for every opening parenthesis.
- **Misspelling key words.** Java will not recognize a key word that has been misspelled.
- **Using capital letters in key words.** Remember that Java is a case-sensitive language, and all key words are written in lowercase. Using an uppercase letter in a key word is the same as misspelling the key word.
- **Using a key word as a variable name.** The key words are reserved for special uses; they cannot be used for any other purpose.
- **Using inconsistent spelling of variable names.** Each time you use a variable name, it must be spelled exactly as it appears in its declaration statement.
- **Using inconsistent case of letters in variable names.** Because Java is a case-sensitive language, it distinguishes between uppercase and lowercase letters. Java will not recognize a variable name that is not written exactly as it appears in its declaration statement.
- **Inserting a space in a variable name.** Spaces are not allowed in variable names. Instead of using a two-word name such as `gross pay`, use one word, such as `grossPay`.
- **Forgetting the semicolon at the end of a statement.** A semicolon appears at the end of each complete statement in Java.
- **Assigning a `double` literal to a `float` variable.** Java is a strongly typed language, which means that it only allows you to store values of compatible data types in variables. All floating-point literals are treated as `doubles`, and a `double` value is not compatible with a `float` variable. A floating-point literal must end with the letter `f` or `F` in order to be stored in a `float` variable.
- **Using commas or other currency symbols in numeric literals.** Numeric literals cannot contain commas or currency symbols, such as the dollar sign.
- **Unintentionally performing integer division.** When both operands of a division statement are integers, the statement will result in an integer. If there is a remainder, it will be discarded.
- **Forgetting to group parts of a mathematical expression.** If you use more than one operator in a mathematical expression, the expression will be evaluated according to the order of operations. If you wish to change the order in which the operators are used, you must use parentheses to group part of the expression.
- **Inserting a space in a combined assignment operator.** A space cannot appear between the two operators that make a combined assignment operator.
- **Using a variable to receive the result of a calculation when the variable's data type is incompatible with the data type of the result.** A variable that receives the result of a calculation must be of a data type that is compatible with the data type of the result.

- **Incorrectly terminating a multi-line comment or a documentation comment.** Multi-line comments and documentation comments are terminated by the */ characters. Forgetting to place these characters at a comment's desired ending point, or accidentally switching the * and the /, will cause the comment not to have an ending point.
- **Forgetting to use the correct import statement in a program that uses the Scanner class or the JOptionPane class.** In order for the Scanner class to be available to your program, you must have the import java.util.Scanner; statement near the top of your program file. In order for the JOptionPane class to be available to your program, you must have the import javax.swing.JOptionPane; statement near the top of the program file.
- **When using an input dialog to read numeric input, not converting the showInput-Dialog method's return value to a number.** The showInputDialog method always returns the user's input as a string. If the user enters a numeric value, it must be converted to a number before it can be used in a math statement.

Review Questions and Exercises

Multiple Choice and True/False

1. Every complete statement ends with a _____.
   a. period
   b. parenthesis
   c. semicolon
   d. ending brace

2. The following data

   ```
   72
   'A'
   "Hello World"
   2.8712
   ```

   are all examples of _____.
   a. variables
   b. literals
   c. strings
   d. none of these

3. A group of statements, such as the contents of a class or a method, are enclosed in _____.
   a. braces {}
   b. parentheses ()
   c. brackets []
   d. any of these will do

4. Which of the following are *not* valid assignment statements? (Indicate all that apply.)
   a. total = 9;
   b. 72 = amount;
   c. profit = 129
   d. letter = 'W';

5. Which of the following are not valid `println` statements? (Indicate all that apply.)
   a. `System.out.println + "Hello World";`
   b. `System.out.println("Have a nice day");`
   c. `out.System.println(value);`
   d. `println.out(Programming is great fun);`

6. The negation operator is _____.
   a. unary
   b. binary
   c. ternary
   d. none of these

7. This key word is used to declare a named constant.
   a. `constant`
   b. `namedConstant`
   c. `final`
   d. `concrete`

8. These characters mark the beginning of a multi-line comment.
   a. `//`
   b. `/*`
   c. `*/`
   d. `/**`

9. These characters mark the beginning of a single-line comment.
   a. `//`
   b. `/*`
   c. `*/`
   d. `/**`

10. These characters mark the beginning of a documentation comment.
    a. `//`
    b. `/*`
    c. `*/`
    d. `/**`

11. Which `Scanner` class method would you use to read a string as input?
    a. `nextString`
    b. `nextLine`
    c. `readString`
    d. `getLine`

12. Which `Scanner` class method would you use to read a `double` as input?
    a. `nextDouble`
    b. `getDouble`
    c. `readDouble`
    d. None of these; you cannot read a `double` with the `Scanner` class

13. You can use this class to display dialog boxes.
    a. `JOptionPane`
    b. `BufferedReader`
    c. `InputStreamReader`
    d. `DialogBox`

14. When Java converts a lower-ranked value to a higher-ranked type, it is called a(n)
_____.
   a. 4-bit conversion
   b. escalating conversion
   c. widening conversion
   d. narrowing conversion

15. This type of operator lets you manually convert a value, even if it means that a narrowing conversion will take place.
   a. cast
   b. binary
   c. uploading
   d. dot

16. **True or False:** A left brace in a Java program is always followed by a right brace later in the program.

17. **True or False:** A variable must be declared before it can be used.

18. **True or False:** Variable names may begin with a number.

19. **True or False:** You cannot change the value of a variable whose declaration uses the `final` key word.

20. **True or False:** Comments that begin with `//` can be processed by `javadoc`.

21. **True or False:** If one of an operator's operands is a `double`, and the other operand is an `int`, Java will automatically convert the value of the `double` to an `int`.

Predict the Output

What will the following code segments print on the screen?

1.
```java
int freeze = 32, boil = 212;
freeze = 0;
boil = 100;
System.out.println(freeze + "\n"+ boil + "\n");
```

2.
```java
int x = 0, y = 2;
x = y * 4;
System.out.println(x + "\n" + y + "\n");
```

3.
```java
System.out.print("I am the incredible");
System.out.print("computing\nmachine");
System.out.print("\nand I will\namaze\n)";
System.out.println("you.");
```

4.
```java
System.out.print("Be careful\n)";
System.out.print("This might/n be a trick ");
System.out.println("question.");
```

5.
```java
int a, x = 23;
a = x % 2;
System.out.println(x + "\n" + a);
```

Find the Error

There are a number of syntax errors in the following program. Locate as many as you can.

```
*/  What's wrong with this program?  /*
public MyProgram
{
   public static void main(String[] args);
   }
      int a, b, c    \\ Three integers
      a = 3
      b = 4
      c = a + b
      System.out.println('The value of c is' + C);
   {
```

Algorithm Workbench

1. Show how the `double` variables `temp`, `weight`, and `age` can be declared in one statement.

2. Show how the `int` variables `months`, `days`, and `years` may be declared in one statement, with `months` initialized to 2 and `years` initialized to 3.

3. Write assignment statements that perform the following operations with the variables a, b, and c.
   a. Adds 2 to a and stores the result in b
   b. Multiplies b times 4 and stores the result in a
   c. Divides a by 3.14 and stores the result in b
   d. Subtracts 8 from b and stores the result in a
   e. Stores the character 'K' in c
   f. Stores the Unicode code for 'B' in c

4. Assume the variables `result`, w, x, y, and z are all integers, and that w = 5, x = 4, y = 8, and z = 2. What value will be stored in `result` in each of the following statements?
   a. `result = x + y;`
   b. `result = z * 2;`
   c. `result = y / x;`
   d. `result = y - z;`
   e. `result = w % 2;`

5. How would each of the following numbers be represented in E notation?
   a. 3.287×10^6
   b. -9.7865×10^{12}
   c. 7.65491×10^{-3}

6. Modify the following program so it prints two blank lines between each line of text.

```
public class
{
   public static void main(String[] args)
   {
      System.out.print("Hearing in the distance");
      System.out.print("Two mandolins like creatures in the");
      System.out.print("dark");
      System.out.print("Creating the agony of ecstasy.");
      System.out.println("                - George Barker");
   }
}
```

7.   What will the following code output?

```
int apples = 0, bananas = 2, pears = 10;
apples += 10;
bananas *= 10;
pears /= 10;
System.out.println(apples + " " +
                   bananas + " " +
                   pears);
```

8.   What will the following code output?

```
double d = 12.9;
int i = (int)d;
System.out.println(i);
```

9.   What will the following code output?

```
String message = "Have a great day!";
System.out.println(message.charAt(5));
```

10.   What will the following code output?

```
String message = "Have a great day!";
System.out.println(message.toUpperCase());
System.out.println(message);
```

11.   Convert the following pseudocode to Java code. Be sure to declare the appropriate variables.

Store 20 in the speed variable.
Store 10 in the time variable.
Multiply speed by time and store the result in the distance variable.
Display the contents of the distance variable.

12.   Convert the following pseudocode to Java code. Be sure to declare the appropriate variables.

Store 172.5 in the force variable.
Store 27.5 in the area variable.
Divide area by force and store the result in the pressure variable.
Display the contents of the pressure variable.

13.   Write the code to set up all the necessary objects for reading keyboard input. Then write code that asks the user to enter his or her desired annual income. Store the input in a `double` variable.

14.   Write the code to display a dialog box that asks the user to enter his or her desired annual income. Store the input in a `double` variable.

15.   A program has a `float` variable named `total` and a `double` variable named `number`. Write a statement that assigns `number` to `total` without causing an error when compiled.

Short Answer

1.   Is the following comment a single-line style comment or a multi-line style comment?

```
/* This program was written by M. A. Codewriter */
```

2.   Is the following comment a single-line style comment or a multi-line style comment?

```
// This program was written by M. A. Codewriter
```

3.   Describe what the phrase "self-documenting program" means.

4. What is meant by "case-sensitive"? Why is it important for a programmer to know that Java is a case-sensitive language?

5. Briefly explain how the print and println methods are related to the System class and the out object.

6. What does a variable declaration tell the Java compiler about a variable?

7. Why are variable names like x not recommended?

8. What things must be considered when deciding on a data type to use for a variable?

9. Briefly describe the difference between variable assignment and variable initialization.

10. What is the difference between comments that start with the // characters and comments that start with the /* characters?

11. Briefly describe what programming style means. Why should your programming style be consistent?

12. Assume that a program uses the named constant PI to represent the value 3.14. The program uses the named constant in several statements. What is the advantage of using the named constant instead of the actual value 3.14 in each statement?

13. Assume the file *SalesAverage.java* is a Java source file that contains documentation comments. Assuming you are in the same folder or directory as the source code file, what command would you enter at the operating system command prompt to generate the HTML documentation files?

14. An expression adds a byte variable and a short variable. Of what data type will the result be?

Programming Challenges

MyProgrammingLab™ *Visit www.myprogramminglab.com to complete many of these Programming Challenges online and get instant feedback.*

1. Name, Age, and Annual Income

Write a program that declares the following:

- a String variable named name
- an int variable named age
- a double variable named annualPay

Store your age, name, and desired annual income as literals in these variables. The program should display these values on the screen in a manner similar to the following:

```
My name is Joe Mahoney, my age is 26 and
I hope to earn $100000.0 per year.
```

2. Name and Initials

Write a program that has the following String variables: firstName, middleName, and lastName. Initialize these with your first, middle, and last names. The program should also have the following char variables: firstInitial, middleInitial, and lastInitial. Store your first, middle, and last initials in these variables. The program should display the contents of these variables on the screen.

3. Personal Information

Write a program that displays the following information, each on a separate line:

- Your name
- Your address, with city, state, and ZIP
- Your telephone number
- Your college major

Although these items should be displayed on separate output lines, use only a single `println` statement in your program.

4. Star Pattern

Write a program that displays the following pattern:

```
   *
  ***
 *****
*******
 *****
  ***
   *
```

5. Sales Prediction

The East Coast sales division of a company generates 62 percent of total sales. Based on that percentage, write a program that will predict how much the East Coast division will generate if the company has $4.6 million in sales this year. *Hint: Use the value 0.62 to represent 62 percent.*

6. Land Calculation

One acre of land is equivalent to 43,560 square feet. Write a program that calculates the number of acres in a tract of land with 389,767 square feet. *Hint: Divide the size of the tract of land by the size of an acre to get the number of acres.*

7. Sales Tax

Write a program that will ask the user to enter the amount of a purchase. The program should then compute the state and county sales tax. Assume the state sales tax is 4 percent and the county sales tax is 2 percent. The program should display the amount of the purchase, the state sales tax, the county sales tax, the total sales tax, and the total of the sale (which is the sum of the amount of purchase plus the total sales tax). *Hint: Use the value 0.02 to represent 2 percent, and 0.04 to represent 4 percent.*

8. Cookie Calories

A bag of cookies holds 40 cookies. The calorie information on the bag claims that there are 10 servings in the bag and that a serving equals 300 calories. Write a program that lets the user enter the number of cookies he or she actually ate and then reports the number of total calories consumed.

VideoNote
The Miles-per-
Gallon Problem

9. Miles-per-Gallon

A car's miles-per-gallon (MPG) can be calculated with the following formula:

$$MPG = Miles\ driven\ /\ Gallons\ of\ gas\ used$$

Write a program that asks the user for the number of miles driven and the gallons of gas used. It should calculate the car's miles-per-gallon and display the result on the screen.

10. Test Average

Write a program that asks the user to enter three test scores. The program should display each test score, as well as the average of the scores.

11. Circuit Board Profit

An electronics company sells circuit boards at a 40 percent profit. If you know the retail price of a circuit board, you can calculate its profit with the following formula:

$$Profit = Retail\ price \times 0.4$$

Write a program that asks the user for the retail price of a circuit board, calculates the amount of profit earned for that product, and displays the results on the screen.

12. String Manipulator

Write a program that asks the user to enter the name of his or her favorite city. Use a `String` variable to store the input. The program should display the following:

- The number of characters in the city name
- The name of the city in all uppercase letters
- The name of the city in all lowercase letters
- The first character in the name of the city

13. Restaurant Bill

Write a program that computes the tax and tip on a restaurant bill. The program should ask the user to enter the charge for the meal. The tax should be 6.75 percent of the meal charge. The tip should be 20 percent of the total after adding the tax. Display the meal charge, tax amount, tip amount, and total bill on the screen.

14. Male and Female Percentages

Write a program that asks the user for the number of males and the number of females registered in a class. The program should display the percentage of males and females in the class.

Hint: Suppose there are 8 males and 12 females in a class. There are 20 students in the class. The percentage of males can be calculated as 8 ÷ 20 = 0.4, or 40%. The percentage of females can be calculated as 12 ÷ 20 = 0.6, or 60%.

15. Stock Commission

Kathryn bought 600 shares of stock at a price of $21.77 per share. She must pay her stockbroker a 2 percent commission for the transaction. Write a program that calculates and displays the following:

- The amount paid for the stock alone (without the commission)
- The amount of the commission
- The total amount paid (for the stock plus the commission)

16. Energy Drink Consumption

A soft drink company recently surveyed 12,467 of its customers and found that approximately 14 percent of those surveyed purchase one or more energy drinks per week. Of those customers who purchase energy drinks, approximately 64 percent of them prefer citrus-flavored energy drinks. Write a program that displays the following:

- The approximate number of customers in the survey who purchase one or more energy drinks per week
- The approximate number of customers in the survey who prefer citrus-flavored energy drinks

17. Ingredient Adjuster

A cookie recipe calls for the following ingredients:

- 1.5 cups of sugar
- 1 cup of butter
- 2.75 cups of flour

The recipe produces 48 cookies with these amounts of the ingredients. Write a program that asks the user how many cookies he or she wants to make, and then displays the number of cups of each ingredient needed for the specified number of cookies.

18. Word Game

Write a program that plays a word game with the user. The program should ask the user to enter the following:

- His or her name
- His or her age
- The name of a city
- The name of a college
- A profession
- A type of animal
- A pet's name

After the user has entered these items, the program should display the following story, inserting the user's input into the appropriate locations:

> There once was a person named **NAME** who lived in **CITY**. At the age of **AGE**, **NAME** went to college at **COLLEGE**. **NAME** graduated and went to work as a **PROFESSION**. Then, **NAME** adopted a(n) **ANIMAL** named **PETNAME**. They both lived happily ever after!

19. Stock Transaction Program

Last month Joe purchased some stock in Acme Software, Inc. Here are the details of the purchase:

- The number of shares that Joe purchased was 1,000.
- When Joe purchased the stock, he paid $32.87 per share.
- Joe paid his stockbroker a commission that amounted to 2% of the amount he paid for the stock.

Two weeks later Joe sold the stock. Here are the details of the sale:

- The number of shares that Joe sold was 1,000.
- He sold the stock for $33.92 per share.

- He paid his stockbroker another commission that amounted to 2% of the amount he received for the stock.

Write a program that displays the following information:

- The amount of money Joe paid for the stock.
- The amount of commission Joe paid his broker when he bought the stock.
- The amount that Joe sold the stock for.
- The amount of commission Joe paid his broker when he sold the stock.
- Display the amount of profit that Joe made after selling his stock and paying the two commissions to his broker. (If the amount of profit that your program displays is a negative number, then Joe lost money on the transaction.)

TOPICS

3.1 The if Statement

CONCEPT: The if statement is used to create a decision structure, which allows a program to have more than one path of execution. The if statement causes one or more statements to execute only when a boolean expression is true.

VideoNote
The if
Statement

In all the programs you have written so far, the statements are executed one after the other, in the order they appear. You might think of sequentially executed statements as the steps you take as you walk down a road. To complete the journey, you must start at the beginning and take each step, one after the other, until you reach your destination. This is illustrated in Figure 3-1.

Figure 3-1 Sequence structure

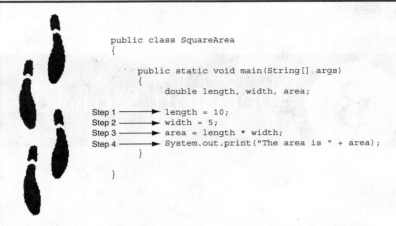

```
public class SquareArea
{
        public static void main(String[] args)
        {
                double length, width, area;
Step 1 ─────▶  length = 10;
Step 2 ─────▶  width = 5;
Step 3 ─────▶  area = length * width;
Step 4 ─────▶  System.out.print("The area is " + area);
        }

}
```

The type of code shown in Figure 3-1 is called a *sequence structure*, because the statements are executed in sequence, without branching off in another direction. Programs often need more than one path of execution, however. Many algorithms require a program to execute some statements only under certain circumstances. This can be accomplished with a *decision structure*.

In a decision structure's simplest form, a specific action is taken only when a condition exists. If the condition does not exist, the action is not performed. The flowchart in Figure 3-2 shows the logic of a decision structure. The diamond symbol represents a yes/no question or a true/false condition. If the answer to the question is yes (or if the condition is true), the program flow follows one path, which leads to an action being performed. If the answer to the question is no (or the condition is false), the program flow follows another path, which skips the action.

Figure 3-2 Simple decision structure logic

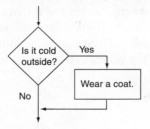

In the flowchart, the action "Wear a coat" is performed only when it is cold outside. If it is not cold outside, the action is skipped. The action is *conditionally executed* because it is performed only when a certain condition (cold outside) exists. Figure 3-3 shows a more elaborate flowchart, where three actions are taken only when it is cold outside.

Figure 3-3   Three-action decision structure logic

One way to code a decision structure in Java is with the if statement. Here is the general format of the if statement:

```
if (BooleanExpression)
    statement;
```

The if statement is simple in the way it works: The BooleanExpression that appears inside the parentheses must be a boolean expression. A boolean *expression* is one that is either true or false. If the boolean expression is true, the very next statement is executed. Otherwise, it is skipped. The statement is conditionally executed because it executes only under the condition that the expression in the parentheses is true.

Using Relational Operators to Form Conditions

Typically, the boolean expression that is tested by an if statement is formed with a relational operator. A *relational operator* determines whether a specific relationship exists between two values. For example, the greater than operator (>) determines whether one value is greater than another. The equal to operator (==) determines whether two values are equal. Table 3-1 lists all of the Java relational operators.

Table 3-1   Relational operators

Relational Operators (in Order of Precedence)	Meaning
>	Greater than
<	Less than
>=	Greater than or equal to
<=	Less than or equal to
==	Equal to
!=	Not equal to

All of the relational operators are binary, which means they use two operands. Here is an example of an expression using the greater than operator:

```
length > width
```

This expression determines whether `length` is greater than `width`. If `length` is greater than `width`, the value of the expression is `true`. Otherwise, the value of the expression is `false`. Because the expression can be only `true` or `false`, it is a `boolean` expression. The following expression uses the less than operator to determine whether `length` is less than `width`:

```
length < width
```

Table 3-2 shows examples of several `boolean` expressions that compare the variables x and y.

Table 3-2 `boolean` expressions using relational operators

Expression	Meaning
x > y	Is x greater than y?
x < y	Is x less than y?
x >= y	Is x greater than or equal to y?
x <= y	Is x less than or equal to y?
x == y	Is x equal to y?
x != y	Is x not equal to y?

Two of the operators, >= and <=, test for more than one relationship. The >= operator determines whether the operand on its left is greater than or equal to the operand on its right. Assuming that a is 4, b is 6, and c is 4, both of the expressions b >= a and a >= c are true, but a >= 5 is false. When using this operator, the > symbol must precede the = symbol, and there is no space between them. The <= operator determines whether the operand on its left is less than or equal to the operand on its right. Once again, assuming that a is 4, b is 6, and c is 4, both a <= c and b <= 10 are true, but b <= a is false. When using this operator, the < symbol must precede the = symbol, and there is no space between them.

The == operator determines whether the operand on its left is equal to the operand on its right. If both operands have the same value, the expression is true. Assuming that a is 4, the expression a == 4 is true and the expression a == 2 is false. Notice the equality operator is two = symbols together. Don't confuse this operator with the assignment operator, which is one = symbol.

The != operator is the not equal operator. It determines whether the operand on its left is not equal to the operand on its right, which is the opposite of the == operator. As before, assuming a is 4, b is 6, and c is 4, both a != b and b != c are true because a is not equal to b and b is not equal to c. However, a != c is false because a is equal to c.

Putting It All Together

Let's look at an example of the `if` statement:

```
if (sales > 50000)
    bonus = 500.0;
```

This statement uses the > operator to determine whether sales is greater than 50,000. If the expression sales > 50000 is true, the variable bonus is assigned 500.0. If the expression is false, however, the assignment statement is skipped. The program in Code Listing 3-1 shows another example. The user enters three test scores and the program calculates their average. If the average is greater than 95, the program congratulates the user on obtaining a high score.

Code Listing 3-1   **(AverageScore.java)**

```java
 1  import javax.swing.JOptionPane; // Needed for JOptionPane
 2
 3  /**
 4     This program demonstrates the if statement.
 5  */
 6
 7  public class AverageScore
 8  {
 9     public static void main(String[] args)
10     {
11        double score1;    // To hold score #1
12        double score2;    // To hold score #2
13        double score3;    // To hold score #3
14        double average;   // To hold the average score
15        String input;     // To hold the user's input
16
17        // Get the first test score.
18        input = JOptionPane.showInputDialog("Enter score #1:");
19        score1 = Double.parseDouble(input);
20
21        // Get the second score.
22        input = JOptionPane.showInputDialog("Enter score #2:");
23        score2 = Double.parseDouble(input);
24
25        // Get the third test score.
26        input = JOptionPane.showInputDialog("Enter score #3:");
27        score3 = Double.parseDouble(input);
28
29        // Calculate the average score.
30        average = (score1 + score2 + score3) / 3.0;
31
32        // Display the average score.
33        JOptionPane.showMessageDialog(null,
34                            "The average is " + average);
35
36        // If the score was greater than 95, let the user know
37        // that's a great score.
38        if (average > 95)
```

```
39                JOptionPane.showMessageDialog(null,
40                                 "That's a great score!");
41
42           System.exit(0);
43       }
44  }
```

Figures 3-4 and 3-5 show examples of interaction with this program. In Figure 3-4 the average of the test scores is not greater than 95. In Figure 3-5 the average is greater than 95.

Figure 3-4   Interaction with the AverageScore program

This input dialog box appears first. The user enters 82 and then clicks on the OK button.

This input dialog box appears next. The user enters 76 and then clicks on the OK button.

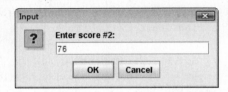

This input dialog box appears next. The user enters 91 and then clicks on the OK button.

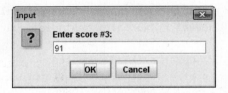

This message dialog box appears next. The average of the three test scores is displayed.

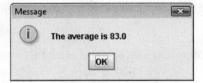

Figure 3-5   Interaction with the AverageScore program

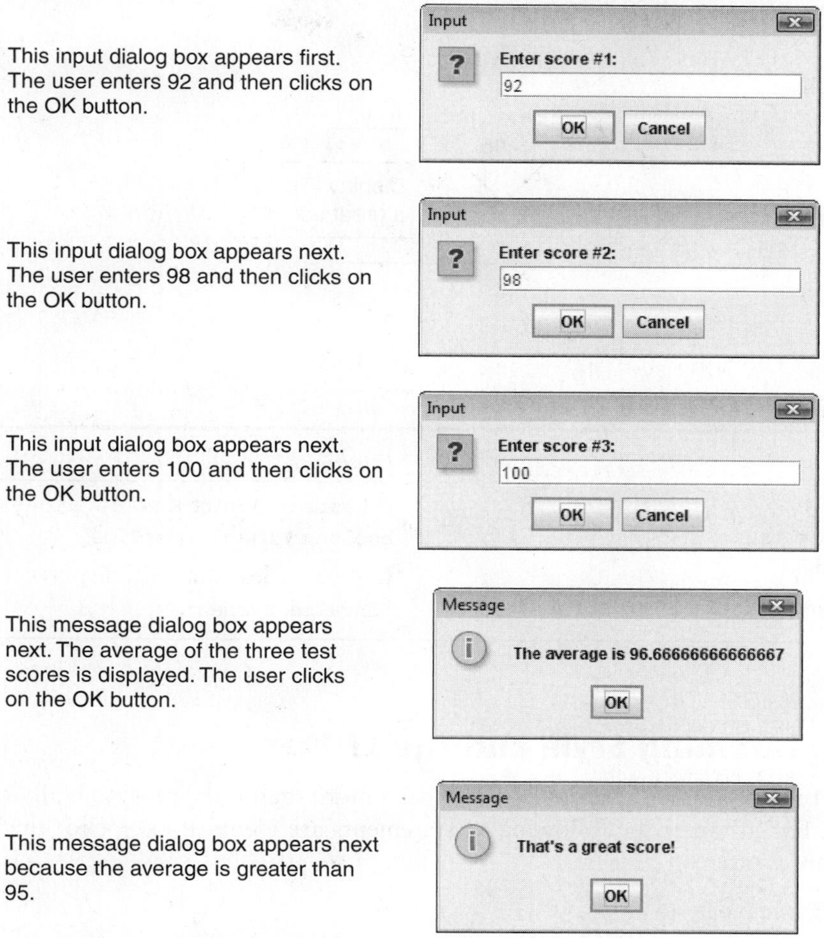

This input dialog box appears first. The user enters 92 and then clicks on the OK button.

> **Input**
> ? Enter score #1:
> 92
> [OK] [Cancel]

This input dialog box appears next. The user enters 98 and then clicks on the OK button.

> **Input**
> ? Enter score #2:
> 98
> [OK] [Cancel]

This input dialog box appears next. The user enters 100 and then clicks on the OK button.

> **Input**
> ? Enter score #3:
> 100
> [OK] [Cancel]

This message dialog box appears next. The average of the three test scores is displayed. The user clicks on the OK button.

> **Message**
> (i) The average is 96.66666666666667
> [OK]

This message dialog box appears next because the average is greater than 95.

> **Message**
> (i) That's a great score!
> [OK]

The code in lines 38 through 40 causes the congratulatory message to be printed:

```
if (average > 95)
    JOptionPane.showMessageDialog(null,
                        "That's a great score!");
```

Figure 3-6 shows the logic of this if statement.

Table 3-3 shows other examples of if statements and their outcomes.

Figure 3-6 Logic of the `if` statement

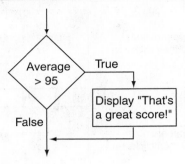

Table 3-3 Other examples of `if` statements

Statement	Outcome
`if (hours > 40)` `overTime = true;`	If `hours` is greater than 40, assigns `true` to the boolean variable `overTime`.
`if (value < 32)` `System.out.println("Invalid number");`	If `value` is less than 32, displays the message `"Invalid number"`.

Programming Style and the `if` Statement

Even though an `if` statement usually spans more than one line, it is really one long statement. For instance, the following `if` statements are identical except for the style in which they are written:

```
if (value > 32)
    System.out.println("Invalid number.");
if (value > 32) System.out.println("Invalid number.");
```

In both of these examples, the compiler considers the `if` statement and the conditionally executed statement as one unit, with a semicolon properly placed at the end. Indentions and spacing are for the human readers of a program, not the compiler. Here are two important style rules you should adopt for writing `if` statements:

- The conditionally executed statement should appear on the line after the `if` statement.
- The conditionally executed statement should be indented one level from the `if` statement.

In most editors, each time you press the tab key, you are indenting one level. By indenting the conditionally executed statement, you are causing it to stand out visually. This is so you can tell at a glance what part of the program the `if` statement executes. This is a standard way of writing `if` statements and is the method you should use.

Be Careful with Semicolons

You do not put a semicolon after the if (*expression*) portion of an if statement, as illustrated in Figure 3-7. This is because the if statement isn't complete without its conditionally executed statement.

Figure 3-7   Do not prematurely terminate an if statement with a semicolon

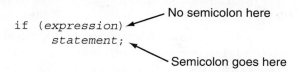

If you prematurely terminate an if statement with a semicolon, the compiler will not display an error message, but will assume that you are placing a *null statement* there. The null statement, which is an empty statement that does nothing, will become the conditionally executed statement. The statement that you intended to be conditionally executed will be disconnected from the if statement and will always execute.

For example, look at the following code:

```
int x = 0, y = 10;

// The following if statement is prematurely
// terminated with a semicolon.
if (x > y);
    System.out.println(x + " is greater than " + y);
```

The if statement in this code is prematurely terminated with a semicolon. Because the println statement is not connected to the if statement, it will always execute.

Having Multiple Conditionally Executed Statements

The previous examples of the if statement conditionally execute a single statement. The if statement can also conditionally execute a group of statements, as long as they are enclosed in a set of braces. Enclosing a group of statements inside braces creates a *block* of statements. Here is an example:

```
if (sales > 50000)
{
    bonus = 500.0;
    commissionRate = 0.12;
    daysOff += 1;
}
```

If sales is greater than 50,000, this code will execute all three of the statements inside the braces, in the order they appear. If the braces are accidentally left out, however, the if statement conditionally executes only the very next statement. Figure 3-8 illustrates this.

Figure 3-8   An if statement missing its braces

```
                    if (sales > 50000)
                        bonus = 500.0;  ◄──────────── Only this statement is
                        commissionRate = 0.12;        conditionally executed.
                        daysOff += 1;
```

These statements are
always executed.

Flags

A flag is a boolean variable that signals when some condition exists in the program. When the flag variable is set to false, it indicates the condition does not yet exist. When the flag variable is set to true, it means the condition does exist.

For example, suppose a program similar to the previous test averaging program has a boolean variable named highScore. The variable might be used to signal that a high score has been achieved by the following code:

```
if (average > 95)
    highScore = true;
```

Later, the same program might use code similar to the following to test the highScore variable, in order to determine whether a high score has been achieved:

```
if (highScore)
    System.out.println("That's a high score!");
```

You will find flag variables useful in many circumstances, and we will come back to them in future chapters.

Comparing Characters

You can use the relational operators to test character data as well as numbers. For example, assuming that ch is a char variable, the following code segment uses the == operator to compare it to the character 'A':

```
if (ch == 'A')
    System.out.println("The letter is A.");
```

The != operator can also be used with characters to test for inequality. For example, the following statement determines whether the char variable ch is not equal to the letter 'A':

```
if (ch != 'A')
    System.out.println("Not the letter A.");
```

You can also use the >, <, >=, and <= operators to compare characters. Computers do not actually store characters, such as A, B, C, and so forth, in memory. Instead, they store numeric codes that represent the characters. Recall from Chapter 2 that Java uses Unicode, which is a set of numbers that represents all the letters of the alphabet (both lowercase and uppercase), the printable digits 0 through 9, punctuation symbols, and special characters. When a character is stored in memory, it is actually the Unicode number that is stored. When the computer is instructed to print the value on the screen, it displays the character that corresponds with the numeric code.

> **NOTE:** Unicode is an international encoding system that is extensive enough to represent all the characters of all the world's alphabets.

In Unicode, letters are arranged in alphabetic order. Because 'A' comes before 'B', the numeric code for the character 'A' is less than the code for the character 'B'. (The code for 'A' is 65 and the code for 'B' is 66. Appendix B, available for download from this book's companion Web site, lists the codes for all of the printable English characters.) In the following if statement, the boolean expression 'A' < 'B' is true:

```
if ('A' < 'B')
    System.out.println("A is less than B.");
```

In Unicode, the uppercase letters come before the lowercase letters, so the numeric code for 'A' (65) is less than the numeric code for 'a' (97). In addition, the space character (code 32) comes before all the alphabetic characters.

Checkpoint

MyProgrammingLab™ *www.myprogramminglab.com*

3.1   Write an if statement that assigns 0 to x when y is equal to 20.

3.2   Write an if statement that multiplies payRate by 1.5 if hours is greater than 40.

3.3   Write an if statement that assigns 0.2 to commission if sales is greater than or equal to 10000.

3.4   Write an if statement that sets the variable fees to 50 if the boolean variable max is true.

3.5   Write an if statement that assigns 20 to the variable y and assigns 40 to the variable z if the variable x is greater than 100.

3.6   Write an if statement that assigns 0 to the variable b and assigns 1 to the variable c if the variable a is less than 10.

3.7   Write an if statement that displays "Goodbye" if the variable myCharacter contains the character 'D'.

3.2   The if-else **Statement**

CONCEPT: The if-else statement will execute one group of statements if its boolean expression is true, or another group if its boolean expression is false.

VideoNote

The if-else Statement

The if-else statement is an expansion of the if statement. Here is its format:

```
if (BooleanExpression)
    statement or block
else
    statement or block
```

Like the if statement, a boolean expression is evaluated. If the expression is true, a statement or block of statements is executed. If the expression is false, however, a separate group of statements is executed. The program in Code Listing 3-2 uses the if-else statement to handle a classic programming problem: division by zero. In Java, a program crashes when it divides an integer by 0. When a floating-point value is divided by 0, the program doesn't crash. Instead, the special value Infinity is produced as the result of the division.

Code Listing 3-2   (Division.java)

```
 1   import java.util.Scanner; // Needed for the Scanner class
 2
 3   /**
 4      This program demonstrates the if-else statement.
 5   */
 6
 7   public class Division
 8   {
 9      public static void main(String[] args)
10      {
11         double number1, number2; // Division operands
12         double quotient;          // Result of division
13
14         // Create a Scanner object for keyboard input.
15         Scanner keyboard = new Scanner(System.in);
16
17         // Get the first number.
18         System.out.print("Enter a number: ");
19         number1 = keyboard.nextDouble();
20
21         // Get the second number.
22         System.out.print("Enter another number: ");
23         number2 = keyboard.nextDouble();
24
25         if (number2 == 0)
26         {
27            System.out.println("Division by zero is not possible.");
28            System.out.println("Please run the program again and ");
29            System.out.println("enter a number other than zero.");
30         }
31         else
32         {
33            quotient = number1 / number2;
34            System.out.print("The quotient of " + number1);
35            System.out.print(" divided by " + number2);
36            System.out.println(" is " + quotient);
37         }
38      }
39   }
```

Program Output with Example Input Shown in Bold

```
Enter a number: 10 [Enter]
Enter another number: 0 [Enter]
Division by zero is not possible.
Please run the program again and
enter a number other than zero.
```

Program Output with Example Input Shown in Bold

```
Enter a number: 10 [Enter]
Enter another number: 5 [Enter]
The quotient of 10 divided by 5 is 2.0
```

The value of `number2` is tested before the division is performed. If the user enters 0, the block of statements controlled by the `if` clause executes, displaying a message that indicates the program cannot perform division by zero. Otherwise, the `else` clause takes control, which divides `number1` by `number2` and displays the result. Figure 3-9 shows the logic of the `if-else` statement.

Figure 3-9   Logic of the `if-else` statement

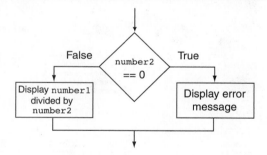

 **Checkpoint**

MyProgrammingLab™ *www.myprogramminglab.com*

3.8   Write an `if-else` statement that assigns 20 to the variable `y` if the variable `x` is greater than 100. Otherwise, it should assign 0 to the variable `y`.

3.9   Write an `if-else` statement that assigns 1 to `x` when `y` is equal to 100. Otherwise, it should assign 0 to `x`.

3.10   Write an `if-else` statement that assigns 0.10 to `commission` unless `sales` is greater than or equal to 50000.0, in which case it assigns 0.2 to `commission`.

3.11   Write an `if-else` statement that assigns 0 to the variable `b` and assigns 1 to the variable `c` if the variable `a` is less than 10. Otherwise, it should assign –99 to the variable `b` and assign 0 to the variable `c`.

3.3   Nested `if` Statements

CONCEPT: To test more than one condition, an `if` statement can be nested inside another `if` statement.

Sometimes an `if` statement must be nested inside another `if` statement. For example, consider a banking program that determines whether a bank customer qualifies for a special, low interest rate on a loan. To qualify, two conditions must exist: (1) the customer's salary must be at least $30,000, and (2) the customer must have held his or her current job for at least two years. Figure 3-10 shows a flowchart for an algorithm that could be used in such a program.

Figure 3-10   Logic of nested `if` statements

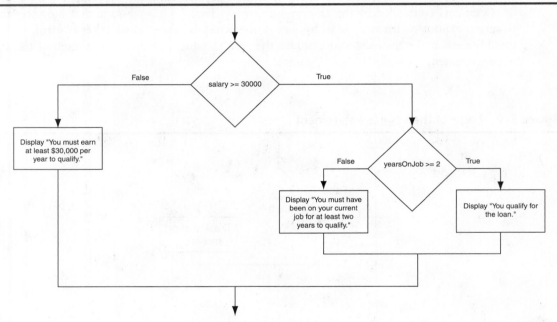

If we follow the flow of execution in the flowchart, we see that the expression `salary >= 30000` is tested. If this expression is false, there is no need to perform further tests; we know that the customer does not qualify for the special interest rate. If the expression is true, however, we need to test the second condition. This is done with a nested decision structure that tests the expression `yearsOnJob >= 2`. If this expression is true, then the customer qualifies for the special interest rate. If this expression is false, then the customer does not qualify. Code Listing 3-3 shows the complete program. Figures 3-11, 3-12, and 3-13 show what happens during three different sessions with the program.

Code Listing 3-3   (`LoanQualifier.java`)

```
1 import javax.swing.JOptionPane; // Needed for JOptionPane class
2
3 /**
```

```
 4      This program demonstrates a nested if statement.
 5  */
 6
 7  public class LoanQualifier
 8  {
 9     public static void main(String[] args)
10     {
11        double salary;         // Annual salary
12        double yearsOnJob;     // Years at current job
13        String input;          // To hold string input
14
15        // Get the user's annual salary.
16        input = JOptionPane.showInputDialog("Enter your " +
17                                       "annual salary.");
18        salary = Double.parseDouble(input);
19
20        // Get the number of years at the current job.
21        input = JOptionPane.showInputDialog("Enter the number of " +
22                                       "years at your current job.");
23        yearsOnJob = Double.parseDouble(input);
24
25        // Determine whether the user qualifies for the loan.
26        if (salary >= 30000)
27        {
28          if (yearsOnJob >= 2)
29          {
30             JOptionPane.showMessageDialog(null, "You qualify " +
31                                            "for the loan.");
32          }
33          else
34          {
35             JOptionPane.showMessageDialog(null, "You must have " +
36                         "been on your current job for at least " +
37                         "two years to qualify.");
38          }
39        }
40        else
41        {
42           JOptionPane.showMessageDialog(null, "You must earn " +
43                       "at least $30,000 per year to qualify.");
44        }
45
46      System.exit(0);
47     }
48  }
```

Figure 3-11 Interaction with the LoanQualifier program

This input dialog box appears first. The user enters 35000 and clicks on the OK button.

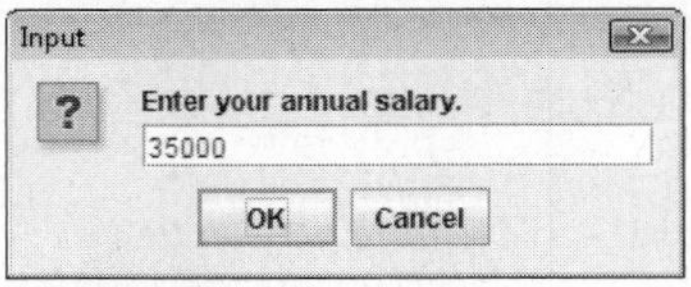

This input dialog box appears next. The user enters 1 and clicks on the OK button.

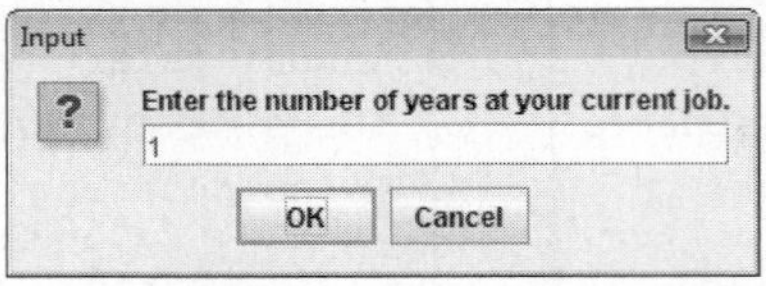

This message dialog box appears next.

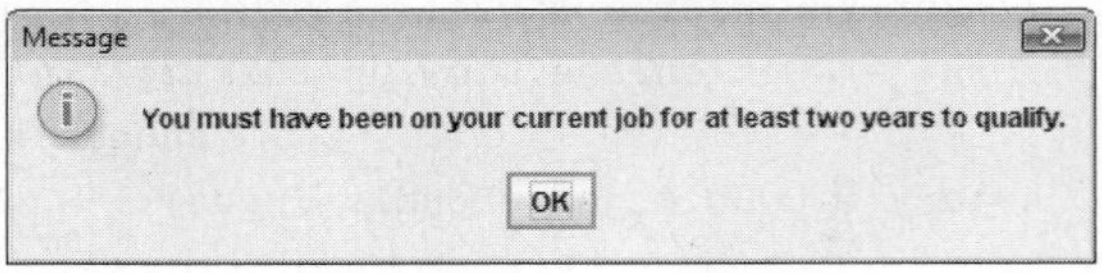

Figure 3-12 Interaction with the LoanQualifier program

This input dialog box appears first. The user enters 25000 and clicks on the OK button.

This input dialog box appears next. The user enters 5 and clicks on the OK button.

This message dialog box appears next.

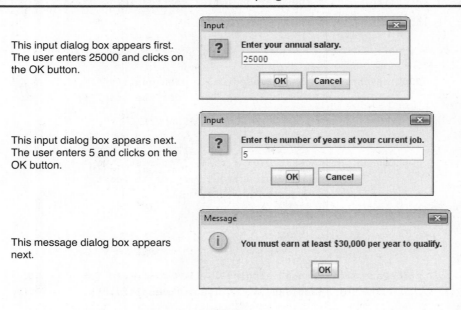

Figure 3-13   Interaction with the LoanQualifier program

This input dialog box appears first. The user enters 35000 and clicks on the OK button.

> Input
>
> ? Enter your annual salary.
>   35000
>
>   OK   Cancel

This input dialog box appears next. The user enters 5 and clicks on the OK button.

> Input
>
> ? Enter the number of years at your current job.
>   5
>
>   OK   Cancel

This message dialog box appears next.

> Message
>
> (i) You qualify for the loan.
>
>   OK

The first if statement (which begins in line 26) conditionally executes the second one (which begins in line 28). The only way the program will execute the second if statement is for the salary variable to contain a value that is greater than or equal to 30,000. When this is the case, the second if statement will test the yearsOnJob variable. If it contains a value that is greater than or equal to 2, a dialog box will be displayed informing the user that he or she qualifies for the loan.

It should be noted that the braces used in the if statements in this program are not required. They could have been written as follows:

```
if (salary >= 30000)
  if (yearsOnJob >= 2)
    JOptionPane.showMessageDialog(null, "You qualify " +
                                     "for the loan.");
  else
    JOptionPane.showMessageDialog(null, "You must have " +
            "been on your current job for at least " +
            "two years to qualify.");
else
  JOptionPane.showMessageDialog(null, "You must earn " +
            "at least $30,000 per year to qualify.");
```

Not only do the braces make the statements easier to read, but they also help in debugging code. When debugging a program with nested if-else statements, it's important to know which if clause each else clause belongs to. The rule for matching else clauses with if clauses is this: An else clause goes with the closest previous if clause that doesn't already have its own else clause. This is easy to see when the conditionally executed statements are enclosed in braces and are properly indented, as shown in Figure 3-14. Each else clause lines up with the if clause it belongs to. These visual cues are important because nested if statements can be very long and complex.

Figure 3-14   Alignment of `if` and `else` clauses

```
                                        if (salary >= 30000)
                                        {
                                            if (yearsOnJob >= 2)
                    This if and else          {
                    go together.                  JOptionPane.showMessageDialog(null, "You qualify " +
                                                                         "for the loan.");
    This if and else                            }
    go together.                            else
                                            {
                                                JOptionPane.showMessageDialog(null, "You must have " +
                                                                 "been on your current job for at least " +
                                                                 "two years to qualify.");
                                            }
                                        }
                                        else
                                        {
                                            JOptionPane.showMessageDialog(null, "You must earn " +
                                                             "at least $30,000 per year to qualify.");
                                        }
```

Testing a Series of Conditions

In the previous example, you saw how a program can use nested decision structures to test more than one condition. It is not uncommon for a program to have a series of conditions to test, and then perform an action depending on which condition is true. One way to accomplish this it to have a decision structure with numerous other decision structures nested inside it. For example, consider the program presented in the following *In the Spotlight* section.

In the Spotlight:
Multiple Nested Decision Structures

Suppose one of your professors uses the following 10-point grading scale for exams:

Test Score	Grade
90 and above	A
80–89	B
70–79	C
60–69	D
Below 60	F

Your professor has asked you to write a program that will allow a student to enter a test score and then display the grade for that score. Here is the algorithm that you will use:

Ask the user to enter a test score.
Determine the grade in the following manner:
If the score is less than 60, then the grade is F.
   Otherwise, if the score is less than 70, then the grade is D.
    Otherwise, if the score is less than 80, then the grade is C.
     Otherwise, if the score is less than 90, then the grade is B.
      Otherwise, the grade is A.

You decide that the process of determining the grade will require several nested decision structures, as shown in Figure 3-15. Code Listing 3-4 shows the complete program. The code for the nested decision structures is in lines 23 through 51. Figures 3-16 and 3-17 show what happens in two different sessions with the program.

Figure 3-15   Nested decision structure to determine a grade

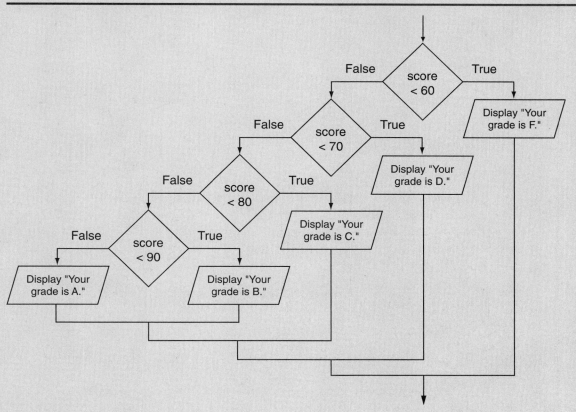

Code Listing 3-4   (NestedDecision.java)

```
1 import javax.swing.JOptionPane; // Needed for JOptionPane
2
3 /**
4     This program asks the user to enter a numeric test
5     score and displays a letter grade for the score. The
6     program uses nested decision structures
7     to determine the grade.
8 */
9
10 public class NestedDecision
11 {
```

```
12      public static void main(String[] args)
13      {
14          int testScore;     // Numeric test score
15          String input;      // To hold the user's input
16
17          // Get the numeric test score.
18          input = JOptionPane.showInputDialog("Enter your numeric " +
19                      "test score and I will tell you the grade: ");
20          testScore = Integer.parseInt(input);
21
22          // Display the grade.
23          if (testScore < 60)
24          {
25              JOptionPane.showMessageDialog(null, "Your grade is F.");
26          }
27          else
28          {
29             if (testScore < 70)
30             {
31                JOptionPane.showMessageDialog(null, "Your grade is D.");
32             }
33             else
34                {
35                if (testScore < 80)
36                {
37                   JOptionPane.showMessageDialog(null, "Your grade is C.");
38                }
39                else
40                {
41                   if (testScore < 90)
42                   {
43                      JOptionPane.showMessageDialog(null, "Your grade is B.");
44                   }
45                   else
46                   {
47                      JOptionPane.showMessageDialog(null, "Your grade is A.");
48                   }
49                }
50             }
51      }
52
53  System.exit(0);
54  }
55 }
```

Figure 3-16   Interaction with the NestedDecision program

This input dialog box appears first. The user enters 80 and then clicks the OK button.

Input

? Enter your numeric test score and I will tell you the grade:

80

OK   Cancel

This message dialog box appears next.

Message

(i) Your grade is B.

OK

Figure 3-17   Interaction with the NestedDecision program

This input dialog box appears first. The user enters 72 and then clicks the OK button.

Input

? Enter your numeric test score and I will tell you the grade:

72

OK   Cancel

This message dialog box appears next.

Message

(i) Your grade is C.

OK

Checkpoint

MyProgrammingLab™ *www.myprogramminglab.com*

3.12   Write nested if statements that perform the following test: If amount1 is greater than 10 and amount2 is less than 100, display the greater of the two.

3.13   Write code that tests the variable x to determine whether it is greater than 0. If x is greater than 0, the code should test the variable y to determine whether it is less than 20. If y is less than 20, the code should assign 1 to the variable z. If y is not less than 20, the code should assign 0 to the variable z.

3.4   The if-else-if Statement

CONCEPT: The if-else-if statement tests a series of conditions. It is often simpler to test a series of conditions with the if-else-if statement than with a set of nested if-else statements.

Even though Code Listing 3-4 is a simple example, the logic of the nested decision structure is fairly complex. You can alternatively test a series of conditions using the if-else-if

VideoNote

The if-else-if Statement

statement. The `if-else-if` statement makes certain types of nested decision logic simpler to write. Here is the general format of the `if-else-if` statement:

```
if (expression_1)
{
    statement
    statement
    etc.
}
else if (expression_2)
{
    statement
    statement
    etc.
}
Insert as many else if clauses as necessary
else
{
    statement
    statement
    etc.
}
```

If `expression_1` is true these statements are executed, and the rest of the structure is ignored.

Otherwise, if `expression_2` is true these statements are executed, and the rest of the structure is ignored.

These statements are executed if none of the expressions above are true.

When the statement executes, *expression_1* is tested. If *expression_1* is true, the block of statements that immediately follows is executed, and the rest of the structure is ignored. If *expression_1* is false, however, the program jumps to the next `else if` clause and tests *expression_2*. If it is true, the block of statements that immediately follows is executed, and then the rest of the structure is ignored. This process continues, from the top of the structure to the bottom, until one of the expressions is found to be true. If none of the expressions are true, the last `else` clause takes over and the block of statements immediately following it is executed.

The last `else` clause, which does not have an `if` statement following it, is referred to as the *trailing* `else`. The trailing `else` is optional, but in most cases you will use it.

> **NOTE:** The general format shows braces surrounding each block of conditionally executed statements. As with other forms of the `if` statement, the braces are required only when more than one statement is conditionally executed.

Code Listing 3-5 shows an example of the `if-else-if` statement. This program is a modification of Code Listing 3-4, which appears in the previous *In the Spotlight* section. The output of this program is the same as Code Listing 3-4.

Code Listing 3-5   (TestResults.Java)

```java
 1 import javax.swing.JOptionPane;    // Needed for JOptionPane
 2
 3 /**
 4    This program asks the user to enter a numeric test
 5    score and displays a letter grade for the score. The
 6    program uses an if-else-if statement to determine
 7    the letter grade.
 8 */
 9
10 public class TestResults
11 {
12  public static void main(String[] args)
13  {
14    int testScore;    // Numeric test score
15    String input;     // To hold the user's input
16
17    // Get the numeric test score.
18    input = JOptionPane.showInputDialog("Enter your numeric " +
19                    "test score and I will tell you the grade: ");
20    testScore = Integer.parseInt(input);
21
22    // Display the grade.
23    if (testScore < 60)
24       JOptionPane.showMessageDialog(null, "Your grade is F.");
25    else if (testScore < 70)
26       JOptionPane.showMessageDialog(null, "Your grade is D.");
27    else if (testScore < 80)
28       JOptionPane.showMessageDialog(null, "Your grade is C.");
29    else if (testScore < 90)
30       JOptionPane.showMessageDialog(null, "Your grade is B.");
31    else
32       JOptionPane.showMessageDialog(null, "Your grade is A.");
33
34    System.exit(0);
35  }
36 }
```

Let's analyze how the if-else-if statement in lines 23 through 32 works. First, the expression testScore < 60 is tested in line 23:

```java
→ if (testScore < 60)
      JOptionPane.showMessageDialog(null, "Your grade is F.");
   else if (testScore < 70)
      JOptionPane.showMessageDialog(null, "Your grade is D.");
   else if (testScore < 80)
```

```
        JOptionPane.showMessageDialog(null, "Your grade is C.");
    else if (testScore < 90)
        JOptionPane.showMessageDialog(null, "Your grade is B.");
    else
        JOptionPane.showMessageDialog(null, "Your grade is A.");
```

If testScore is less than 60, the message "Your grade is F." is displayed and the rest of the if-else-if statement is skipped. If testScore is not less than 60, the else clause in line 25 takes over and causes the next if statement to be executed:

```
    if (testScore < 60)
        JOptionPane.showMessageDialog(null, "Your grade is F.");
  → else if (testScore < 70)
        JOptionPane.showMessageDialog(null, "Your grade is D.");
    else if (testScore < 80)
        JOptionPane.showMessageDialog(null, "Your grade is C.");
    else if (testScore < 90)
        JOptionPane.showMessageDialog(null, "Your grade is B.");
    else
        JOptionPane.showMessageDialog(null, "Your grade is A.");
```

The first if statement handled all of the grades less than 60, so when this if statement executes, testScore will have a value of 60 or greater. If testScore is less than 70, the message "Your grade is D." is displayed and the rest of the if-else-if statement is skipped. This chain of events continues until one of the expressions is found to be true, or the last else clause at the end of the statement is encountered.

Notice the alignment and indentation that are used with the if-else-if statement: The starting if clause, the else if clauses, and the trailing else clause are all aligned, and the conditionally executed statements are indented.

Using the Trailing else to Catch Errors

The trailing else clause, which appears at the end of the if-else-if statement, is optional, but in many situations you will use it to catch errors. For example, Code Listing 3-5 will assign the grade 'A' to any test score that is 90 or greater. What if the highest possible test score is 100? We can modify the code as shown in Code Listing 3-6 so the trailing else clause catches any value greater than 100 and displays an error message. Figure 3-18 shows what happens when the user enters a test score that is greater than 100.

Code Listing 3-6   (TrailingElse.java)

```
1 import javax.swing.JOptionPane; // Needed for JOptionPane
2
3 /**
4    This program asks the user to enter a numeric test
5    score and displays a letter grade for the score. The
6    program displays an error message if an invalid
7    numeric score is entered.
8 */
9
```

```
10  public class TrailingElse
11  {
12      public static void main(String[] args)
13      {
14          int testScore;        // Numeric test score
15          String input;         // To hold the user's input
16
17          // Get the numeric test score.
18          input = JOptionPane.showInputDialog("Enter your numeric " +
19                          "test score and I will tell you the grade: ");
20          testScore = Integer.parseInt(input);
21
22          // Display the grade.
23          if (testScore < 60)
24              JOptionPane.showMessageDialog(null, "Your grade is F.");
25          else if (testScore < 70)
26              JOptionPane.showMessageDialog(null, "Your grade is D.");
27          else if (testScore < 80)
28              JOptionPane.showMessageDialog(null, "Your grade is C.");
29          else if (testScore < 90)
30              JOptionPane.showMessageDialog(null, "Your grade is B.");
31          else if (testScore <= 100)
32              JOptionPane.showMessageDialog(null, "Your grade is A.");
33          else
34              JOptionPane.showMessageDialog(null, "Invalid score.");
35
36          System.exit(0);
37      }
38  }
```

Figure 3-18 Interaction with the NestedDecision program

This input dialog box appears first. The user enters 105 and then clicks the OK button.

> **Input**
> ? Enter your numeric test score and I will tell you the grade:
> 105
> OK   Cancel

This message dialog box appears next.

> **Message**
> (i) Invalid score.
> OK

The if-else-if Statement Compared to a Nested Decision Structure

You never have to use the if-else-if statement because its logic can be coded with nested if-else statements. However, a long series of nested if-else statements has two particular disadvantages when you are debugging code:

- The code can grow complex and become difficult to understand.

- Because indenting is important in nested statements, a long series of nested `if-else` statements can become too long to be displayed on the computer screen without horizontal scrolling. Also, long statements tend to "wrap around" when printed on paper, making the code even more difficult to read.

The logic of an `if-else-if` statement is usually easier to follow than that of a long series of nested `if-else` statements. And, because all of the clauses are aligned in an `if-else-if` statement, the lengths of the lines in the statement tend to be shorter.

 Checkpoint

MyProgrammingLab™ *www.myprogramminglab.com*

3.14 What will the following program display?

```java
public class CheckPoint
{
    public static void main(String[] args)
    {
        int funny = 7, serious = 15;
        funny = serious % 2;
        if (funny != 1)
        {
            funny = 0;
            serious = 0;
        }
        else if (funny == 2)
        {
            funny = 10;
            serious = 10;
        }
        else
        {
            funny = 1;
            serious = 1;
        }
        System.out.println(funny + " " + serious);
    }
}
```

3.15 The following program is used in a bookstore to determine how many discount coupons a customer gets. Complete the table that appears after the program.

```java
import javax.swing.JOptionPane;
public class CheckPoint
{
    public static void main(String[] args)
    {
        int books, coupons;
        String input;
        input = JOptionPane.showInputDialog("How many books " +
                                "are being purchased? ");
        books = Integer.parseInt(input);
```

```
      if (books < 1)
         coupons = 0;
      else if (books < 3)
         coupons = 1;
      else if (books < 5)
         coupons = 2;
      else
         coupons = 3;
      JOptionPane.showMessageDialog(null,
               "The number of coupons to give is " +
               coupons);
      System.exit(0);
   }
}
```

If the customer purchases this many books . . .	this many coupons are given.
1	_____
2	_____
3	_____
4	_____
5	_____
10	_____

3.5 Logical Operators

CONCEPT: Logical operators connect two or more relational expressions into one or reverse the logic of an expression.

Java provides two binary logical operators, && and ||, which are used to combine two boolean expressions into a single expression. It also provides the unary ! operator, which reverses the truth of a boolean expression. Table 3-4 describes these logical operators.

Table 3-4   Logical operators

Operator	Meaning	Effect
&&	AND	Connects two boolean expressions into one. Both expressions must be true for the overall expression to be true.
||	OR	Connects two boolean expressions into one. One or both expressions must be true for the overall expression to be true. It is only necessary for one to be true, and it does not matter which one.
!	NOT	The ! operator reverses the truth of a boolean expression. If it is applied to an expression that is true, the operator returns false. If it is applied to an expression that is false, the operator returns true.

Table 3-5 shows examples of several `boolean` expressions that use logical operators.

Table 3-5 `boolean` expressions using logical operators

Expression	Meaning
x > y && a < b	Is x greater than y AND is a less than b?
x == y || x == z	Is x equal to y OR is x equal to z?
!(x > y)	Is the expression x > y NOT true?

Let's take a close look at each of these operators.

The `&&` Operator

The `&&` operator is known as the logical AND operator. It takes two `boolean` expressions as operands and creates a `boolean` expression that is `true` only when both subexpressions are true. Here is an example of an `if` statement that uses the `&&` operator:

```
if (temperature < 20 && minutes > 12)
{
        System.out.println("The temperature is in the " +
                            "danger zone.");
}
```

In this statement the two `boolean` expressions temperature < 20 and minutes > 12 are combined into a single expression. The message will be displayed only if `temperature` is less than 20 AND `minutes` is greater than 12. If either `boolean` expression is `false`, the entire expression is `false` and the message is not displayed.

Table 3-6 shows a truth table for the `&&` operator. The truth table lists expressions showing all the possible combinations of `true` and `false` connected with the `&&` operator. The resulting values of the expressions are also shown.

Table 3-6 Truth table for the `&&` operator

Expression	Value of the Expression
true && false	false
false && true	false
false && false	false
true && true	true

As the table shows, both sides of the `&&` operator must be `true` for the operator to return a `true` value.

The `&&` operator performs *short-circuit evaluation*. Here's how it works: If the expression on the left side of the `&&` operator is `false`, the expression on the right side will not be checked. Because the entire expression is `false` if only one of the subexpressions is `false`, it would waste CPU time to check the remaining expression. So, when the `&&` operator finds that the expression on its left is `false`, it short-circuits and does not evaluate the expression on its right.

The `&&` operator can be used to simplify programs that otherwise would use nested `if` statements. The program in Code Listing 3-7 is a different version of the `LoanQualifier` program in Code Listing 3-3, written to use the `&&` operator. Figures 3-19 and 3-20 show the interaction during two different sessions with the program.

Code Listing 3-7   (`LogicalAnd.java`)

```java
 1  import javax.swing.JOptionPane; // Needed for JOptionPane class
 2
 3  /**
 4     This program demonstrates the logical && operator.
 5  */
 6
 7  public class LogicalAnd
 8  {
 9     public static void main(String[] args)
10     {
11        double salary;         // Annual salary
12        double yearsOnJob;     // Years at current job
13        String input;          // To hold string input
14
15        // Get the user's annual salary.
16        input = JOptionPane.showInputDialog("Enter your " +
17                                        "annual salary.");
18        salary = Double.parseDouble(input);
19
20        // Get the number of years at the current job.
21        input = JOptionPane.showInputDialog("Enter the number of " +
22                                        "years at your current job.");
23        yearsOnJob = Double.parseDouble(input);
24
25        // Determine whether the user qualifies for the loan.
26        if (salary >= 30000 && yearsOnJob >= 2)
27        {
28                JOptionPane.showMessageDialog(null, "You qualify " +
29                                        "for the loan.");
30        }
31        else
32        {
33                JOptionPane.showMessageDialog(null, "You do not " +
34                                        "qualify for the loan.");
35        }
36
37        System.exit(0);
38     }
39  }
```

Figure 3-19 Interaction with the `LogicalAnd` program

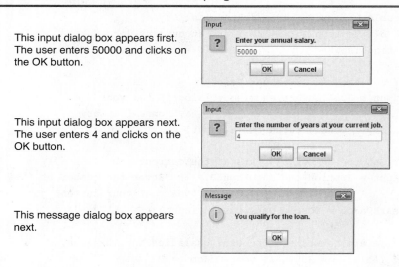

This input dialog box appears first. The user enters 50000 and clicks on the OK button.

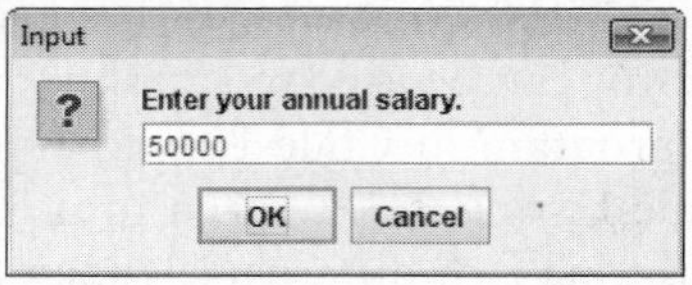

This input dialog box appears next. The user enters 1 and clicks on the OK button.

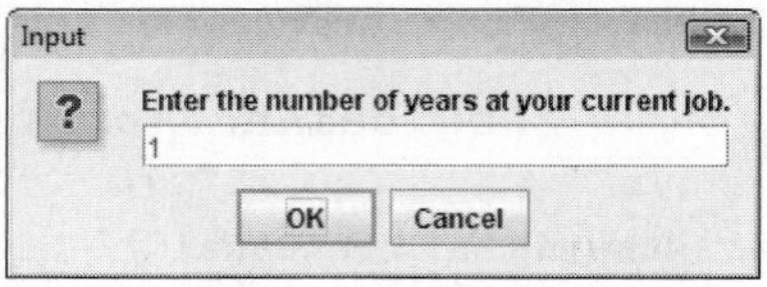

This message dialog box appears next.

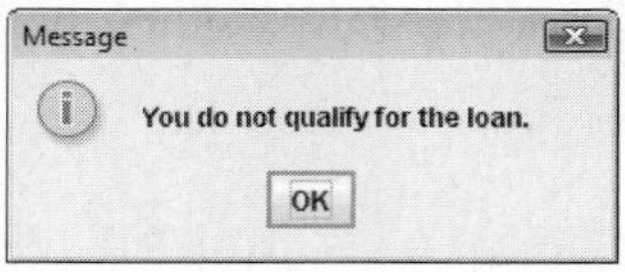

Figure 3-20 Interaction with the `LogicalAnd` program

This input dialog box appears first. The user enters 50000 and clicks on the OK button.

This input dialog box appears next. The user enters 4 and clicks on the OK button.

This message dialog box appears next.

The message `"You qualify for the loan."` is displayed only when both the expressions `salary >= 30000` and `yearsOnJob >= 2` are true. If either of these expressions is `false`, the message `"You do not qualify for the loan."` is displayed.

You can also use logical operators with `boolean` variables. For example, assuming that `isValid` is a `boolean` variable, the following `if` statement determines whether `isValid` is true and `x` is greater than 90.

```
if (isValid && x > 90)
```

The || Operator

The || operator is known as the logical OR operator. It takes two boolean expressions as operands and creates a boolean expression that is true when either of the subexpressions is true. Here is an example of an if statement that uses the || operator:

```
if (temperature < 20 || temperature > 100)
{
        System.out.println("The temperature is in the " +
                        "danger zone.");
}
```

The message will be displayed if temperature is less than 20 OR temperature is greater than 100. If either relational test is true, the entire expression is true.

Table 3-7 shows a truth table for the || operator.

All it takes for an OR expression to be true is for one side of the || operator to be true. It doesn't matter if the other side is false or true. Like the && operator, the || operator performs short-circuit evaluation. If the expression on the left side of the || operator is true, the expression on the right side will not be checked. Because it is necessary for only one of the expressions to be true, it would waste CPU time to check the remaining expression.

Table 3-7 Truth table for the || operator

Expression	Value
true || false	true
false || true	true
false || false	false
true || true	true

The program in Code Listing 3-8 is a different version of the previous program, shown in Code Listing 3-7. This version uses the || operator to determine whether salary >= 30000 is true OR yearsOnJob >= 2 is true. If either expression is true, then the person qualifies for the loan. Figure 3-21 shows example interaction with the program.

Code Listing 3-8   **(LogicalOr.java)**

```
 1  import javax.swing.JOptionPane; // Needed for JOptionPane class
 2
 3  /**
 4      This program demonstrates the logical || operator.
 5  */
 6
 7  public class LogicalOr
 8  {
 9     public static void main(String[] args)
10     {
```

```
11          double salary;        // Annual salary
12          double yearsOnJob;    // Years at current job
13          String input;         // To hold string input
14
15          // Get the user's annual salary.
16          input = JOptionPane.showInputDialog("Enter your " +
17                                        "annual salary.");
18          salary = Double.parseDouble(input);
19
20          // Get the number of years at the current job.
21          input = JOptionPane.showInputDialog("Enter the number of " +
22                                        "years at your current job.");
23          yearsOnJob = Double.parseDouble(input);
24
25          // Determine whether the user qualifies for loan.
26          if (salary >= 30000 || yearsOnJob >= 2)
27          {
28                  JOptionPane.showMessageDialog(null, "You qualify " +
29                                        "for the loan.");
30          }
31          else
32          {
33                  JOptionPane.showMessageDialog(null, "You do not " +
34                                        "qualify for the loan.");
35          }
36
37          System.exit(0);
38      }
39  }
```

Figure 3-21 Interaction with the `LogicalOr` program

This input dialog box appears first. The user enters 20000 and clicks on the OK button.

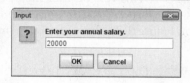

This input dialog box appears next. The user enters 7 and clicks on the OK button.

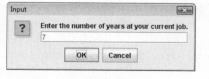

This message dialog box appears next.

The ! Operator

The ! operator performs a logical NOT operation. It is a unary operator that takes a boolean expression as its operand and reverses its logical value. In other words, if the expression is true, the ! operator returns false, and if the expression is false, it returns true. Here is an if statement using the ! operator:

```
if (!(temperature > 100))
    System.out.println("This is below the maximum temperature.");
```

First, the expression (temperature > 100) is tested and a value of either true or false is the result. Then the ! operator is applied to that value. If the expression (temperature > 100) is true, the ! operator returns false. If the expression (temperature > 100) is false, the ! operator returns true. The previous code is equivalent to asking: "Is the temperature not greater than 100?"

Table 3-8 shows a truth table for the ! operator.

Table 3-8   Truth table for the ! operator

Expression	Value
!true	false
!false	true

The Precedence of Logical Operators

Like other operators, the logical operators have orders of precedence and associativity. Table 3-9 shows the precedence of the logical operators, from highest to lowest.

Table 3-9   Logical operators in order of precedence

!
&&
||

The ! operator has a higher precedence than many of Java's other operators. You should always enclose its operand in parentheses unless you intend to apply it to a variable or a simple expression with no other operators. For example, consider the following expressions (assume x is an int variable with a value stored in it):

```
!(x > 2)
!x > 2
```

The first expression applies the ! operator to the expression x > 2. It is asking "is x not greater than 2?" The second expression, however, attempts to apply the ! operator to x only. It is asking "is the logical complement of x greater than 2?" Because the ! operator can only be applied to boolean expressions, this statement would cause a compiler error.

The `&&` and `||` operators rank lower in precedence than the relational operators, so precedence problems are less likely to occur. If you are unsure, however, it doesn't hurt to use parentheses anyway.

```
(a > b) && (x < y)  is the same as  a > b && x < y
(x == y) || (b > a)  is the same as  x == y || b > a
```

The logical operators evaluate their expressions from left to right. In the following expression, a < b is evaluated before y == z.

```
a < b || y == z
```

In the following expression, y == z is evaluated first, however, because the `&&` operator has higher precedence than `||`.

```
a < b || y == z && m > j
```

This expression is equivalent to the following:

```
(a < b) || ((y == z) && (m > j))
```

Table 3-10 shows the precedence of all the operators we have discussed so far. This table includes the assignment, arithmetic, relational, and logical operators.

Table 3-10 Precedence of all operators discussed so far

Order of Precedence	Operators	Description
1	- (unary negation) !	Unary negation, logical NOT
2	* / %	Multiplication, division, modulus
3	+ -	Addition, subtraction
4	< > <= >=	Less than, greater than, less than or equal to, greater than or equal to
5	== !=	Equal to, not equal to
6	&&	Logical AND
7	||	Logical OR
8	= += -= *= /= %=	Assignment and combined assignment

Checking Numeric Ranges with Logical Operators

Sometimes you will need to write code that determines whether a numeric value is within a specific range of values or outside a specific range of values. When determining whether a number is inside a range, it's best to use the `&&` operator. For example, the following `if` statement checks the value in x to determine whether it is in the range of 20 through 40:

```
if (x >= 20 && x <= 40)
    System.out.println(x + " is in the acceptable range.");
```

The `boolean` expression in the `if` statement will be `true` only when x is greater than or equal to 20 AND less than or equal to 40. The value in x must be within the range of 20 through 40 for this expression to be `true`.

When determining whether a number is outside a range, it's best to use the || operator. The following statement determines whether x is outside the range of 20 through 40:

```
if (x < 20 || x > 40)
    System.out.println(x + " is outside the acceptable range.");
```

It's important not to get the logic of these logical operators confused. For example, the boolean expression in the following if statement would never test true:

```
if (x < 20 && x > 40)
    System.out.println(x + " is outside the acceptable range.");
```

Obviously, x cannot be less than 20 and at the same time be greater than 40.

 Checkpoint

MyProgrammingLab™ *www.myprogramminglab.com*

3.16   The following truth table shows various combinations of the values true and false connected by a logical operator. Complete the table by circling T or F to indicate whether the result of such a combination is true or false.

Logical Expression	Result (true or false)
true && false	T F
true && true	T F
false && true	T F
false && false	T F
true || false	T F
true || true	T F
false || true	T F
false || false	T F
!true	T F
!false	T F

3.17   Assume the variables a = 2, b = 4, and c = 6. Circle the T or F for each of the following conditions to indicate whether it is true or false.

a == 4 || b > 2	T F
6 <= c && a > 3	T F
1 != b && c != 3	T F
a >= -1 || a <= b	T F
!(a > 2)	T F

3.18   Write an if statement that displays the message "The number is valid" if the variable speed is within the range 0 through 200.

3.19   Write an if statement that displays the message "The number is not valid" if the variable speed is outside the range 0 through 200.

3.6   Comparing String Objects

CONCEPT: You cannot use relational operators to compare String objects. Instead you must use a String method.

You saw in the preceding sections how numeric values can be compared using the relational operators. You should not use the relational operators to compare String objects, however.

Remember that a String object is referenced by a variable that contains the object's memory address. When you use a relational operator with the reference variable, the operator works on the memory address that the variable contains, not the contents of the String object. For example, suppose a program has the following declarations:

```
String name1 = "Mark";
String name2 = "Mary";
```

And later, the same program has the following if statement:

```
if (name1 == name2)
```

The expression name1 == name2 will be false, but not because the strings "Mark" and "Mary" are different. The expression will be false because the variables name1 and name2 reference different objects. Figure 3-22 illustrates how the variables reference the String objects.

Figure 3-22 The name1 and name2 variables reference different String objects

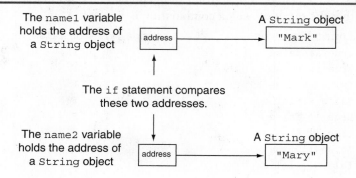

To compare the contents of two String objects correctly, you should use the String class's equals method. The general form of the method is as follows:

```
StringReference1.equals(StringReference2)
```

StringReference1 is a variable that references a String object, and *StringReference2* is another variable that references a String object. The method returns true if the two strings are equal, or false if they are not equal. Here is an example:

```
if (name1.equals(name2))
```

Assuming that name1 and name2 reference String objects, the expression in the if statement will return true if they are the same, or false if they are not the same. The program in Code Listing 3-9 demonstrates.

Code Listing 3-9   (StringCompare.java)

```
1  /**
2     This program correctly compares two String objects using
3     the equals method.
```

```
 4   */
 5
 6   public class StringCompare
 7   {
 8      public static void main(String[] args)
 9      {
10         String name1 = "Mark",
11                name2 = "Mark",
12                name3 = "Mary";
13
14         // Compare "Mark" and "Mark"
15
16         if (name1.equals(name2))
17         {
18             System.out.println(name1 + " and " + name2 +
19                                       " are the same.");
20         }
21         else
22         {
23             System.out.println(name1 + " and " + name2 +
24                                     " are NOT the same.");
25         }
26
27         // Compare "Mark" and "Mary"
28
29         if (name1.equals(name3))
30         {
31             System.out.println(name1 + " and " + name3 +
32         " are the same.");
33         }
34         else
35         {
36             System.out.println(name1 + " and " + name3 +
37                                     " are NOT the same.");
38         }
39      }
40   }
```

Program Output

```
Mark and Mark are the same.
Mark and Mary are NOT the same.
```

You can also compare String objects to string literals. Simply pass the string literal as the argument to the equals method, as follows:

```
if (name1.equals("Mark"))
```

To determine whether two strings are not equal, simply apply the ! operator to the `equals` method's return value. Here is an example:

```
if (!name1.equals("Mark"))
```

The `boolean` expression in this `if` statement performs a not-equal-to operation. It determines whether the object referenced by `name1` is not equal to "Mark".

The `String` class also provides the `compareTo` method, which can be used to determine whether one string is greater than, equal to, or less than another string. The general form of the method is as follows:

```
StringReference.compareTo(OtherString)
```

StringReference is a variable that references a `String` object, and *OtherString* is either another variable that references a `String` object or a string literal. The method returns an integer value that can be used in the following manner:

- If the method's return value is negative, the string referenced by *StringReference* (the calling object) is less than the *OtherString* argument.
- If the method's return value is 0, the two strings are equal.
- If the method's return value is positive, the string referenced by *StringReference* (the calling object) is greater than the *OtherString* argument.

For example, assume that `name1` and `name2` are variables that reference `String` objects. The following `if` statement uses the `compareTo` method to compare the strings:

```
if (name1.compareTo(name2) == 0)
    System.out.println("The names are the same.");
```

Also, the following expression compares the string referenced by `name1` to the string literal "Joe":

```
if (name1.compareTo("Joe") == 0)
    System.out.println("The names are the same.");
```

The program in Code Listing 3-10 more fully demonstrates the `compareTo` method.

Code Listing 3-10   (`StringCompareTo.java`)

```java
1  /**
2     This program compares two String objects using
3     the compareTo method.
4  */
5
6  public class StringCompareTo
7  {
8     public static void main(String[] args)
9     {
10        String name1 = "Mary",
11               name2 = "Mark";
12
13        // Compare "Mary" and "Mark"
```

```
14
15          if (name1.compareTo(name2) < 0)
16          {
17              System.out.println(name1 + " is less than " + name2);
18          }
19              else if (name1.compareTo(name2) == 0)
20          {
21              System.out.println(name1 + " is equal to " + name2);
22          }
23              else if (name1.compareTo(name2) > 0)
24          {
25              System.out.println(name1 + " is greater than " + name2);
26          }
27      }
28  }
```

Program Output

```
Mary is greater than Mark
```

Let's take a closer look at this program. When you use the compareTo method to compare two strings, the strings are compared character by character. This is often called a *lexicographical comparison*. The program uses the compareTo method to compare the strings "Mary" and "Mark", beginning with the first, or leftmost, characters. This is illustrated in Figure 3-23.

Figure 3-23   String comparison of "Mary" and "Mark"

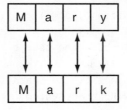

Here is how the comparison takes place:

1. The "M" in "Mary" is compared with the "M" in "Mark." Because these are the same, the next characters are compared.
2. The "a" in "Mary" is compared with the "a" in "Mark." Because these are the same, the next characters are compared.
3. The "r" in "Mary" is compared with the "r" in "Mark." Because these are the same, the next characters are compared.
4. The "y" in "Mary" is compared with the "k" in "Mark." Because these are not the same, the two strings are not equal. The character "y" is greater than "k", so it is determined that "Mary" is greater than "Mark."

If one of the strings in a comparison is shorter than the other, Java can only compare the corresponding characters. If the corresponding characters are identical, then the shorter string is considered less than the longer string. For example, suppose the strings "High" and "Hi" were being compared. The string "Hi" would be considered less than "High" because it is shorter.

Ignoring Case in String Comparisons

The `equals` and `compareTo` methods perform case-sensitive comparisons, which means that uppercase letters are not considered the same as their lowercase counterparts. In other words, "A" is not the same as "a". This can obviously lead to problems when you want to perform case-insensitive comparisons.

The `String` class provides the `equalsIgnoreCase` and `compareToIgnoreCase` methods. These methods work like the `equals` and `compareTo` methods, except the case of the characters in the strings is ignored. For example, the program in Code Listing 3-11 asks the user to enter the secret word, which is similar to a password. The secret word is `"PROSPERO"`, and the program performs a case-insensitive string comparison to determine whether the user has entered it.

Code Listing 3-11   **(SecretWord.java)**

```java
 1  import java.util.Scanner; // Needed for the Scanner class
 2
 3  /**
 4     This program demonstrates a case insensitive string comparison.
 5  */
 6
 7  public class SecretWord
 8  {
 9     public static void main(String[] args)
10     {
11        String input;     // To hold the user's input
12
13        // Create a Scanner object for keyboard input.
14        Scanner keyboard = new Scanner(System.in);
15
16        // Prompt the user to enter the secret word.
17        System.out.print("Enter the secret word: ");
18        input = keyboard.nextLine();
19
20        // Determine whether the user entered the secret word.
21        if (input.equalsIgnoreCase("PROSPERO"))
22        {
23           System.out.println("Congratulations! You know the " +
24                              "secret word!");
25        }
26        else
27        {
```

```
28            System.out.println("Sorry, that is NOT the " +
29                           "secret word!");
30        }
31    }
32 }
```

Program Output with Example Input Shown in Bold

Enter the secret word: **Ferdinand [Enter]**
Sorry, that is NOT the secret word!

Program Output with Example Input Shown in Bold

Enter the secret word: **Prospero [Enter]**
Congratulations! You know the secret word!

The `compareToIgnoreCase` method works exactly like the `compareTo` method, except the case of the characters in the strings being compared is ignored.

 Checkpoint

MyProgrammingLab™ *www.myprogramminglab.com*

3.20 Assume the variable `name` references a `String` object. Write an `if` statement that displays "Do I know you?" if the `String` object contains "Timothy".

3.21 Assume the variables `name1` and `name2` reference two different `String` objects, containing different strings. Write code that displays the strings referenced by these variables in alphabetical order.

3.22 Modify the statement you wrote in response to Checkpoint 3.20 so it performs a case-insensitive comparison.

3.7 More about Variable Declaration and Scope

CONCEPT: The scope of a variable is limited to the block in which it is declared.

Recall from Chapter 2 that a local variable is a variable that is declared inside a method. Java allows you to create local variables just about anywhere in a method. For example, look at the program in Code Listing 3-12. The `main` method declares two `String` reference variables: `firstName` and `lastName`. Notice that the declarations of these variables appear near the code that first uses the variables.

Code Listing 3-12   (`VariableScope.java`)

```
1 import javax.swing.JOptionPane; // Needed for JOptionPane
2
3 /**
4    This program demonstrates how variables may be declared
5    in various locations throughout a program.
```

```
 6   */
 7
 8   public class VariableScope
 9   {
10      public static void main(String[] args)
11      {
12         // Get the user's first name.
13         String firstName;
14         firstName = JOptionPane.showInputDialog("Enter your " +
15                                                 "first name.");
16
17         // Get the user's last name.
18         String lastName;
19         lastName = JOptionPane.showInputDialog("Enter your " +
20                                                "last name.");
21
22         JOptionPane.showMessageDialog(null, "Hello, " + firstName +
23                                       " " + lastName);
24         System.exit(0);
25      }
26   }
```

Although it is a common practice to declare all of a method's local variables at the beginning of the method, it is possible to declare them at later points. Sometimes programmers declare certain variables near the part of the program where they are used in order to make their purpose more evident.

Recall from Chapter 2 that a variable's scope is the part of the program where the variable's name may be used. A local variable's scope always starts at the variable's declaration, and ends at the closing brace of the block of code in which it is declared. In Code Listing 3-12, the `firstName` variable is visible only to the code in lines 13 through 24. The `lastName` variable is visible only to the code in lines 18 through 24.

NOTE: When a program is running and it enters the section of code that constitutes a variable's scope, it is said that the variable "comes into scope." This simply means the variable is now visible and the program may reference it. Likewise, when a variable "leaves scope" it may not be used.

3.8 The Conditional Operator (Optional)

CONCEPT: You can use the conditional operator to create short expressions that work like `if-else` statements.

The *conditional operator* is powerful and unique. Because it takes three operands, it is considered a ternary operator. The conditional operator provides a shorthand method of expressing a simple if-else statement. The operator consists of the question mark (?) and the colon (:). You use the operator to write a conditional expression, in the following format:

```
BooleanExpression ? Value1: Value2;
```

The `BooleanExpression` is like the boolean expression in the parentheses of an if statement. If the `BooleanExpression` is true, then the value of the conditional expression is `Value1`. Otherwise, the value of the conditional expression is `Value2`. Here is an example of a statement using the conditional operator:

```
y = x < 0 ? 10: 20;
```

This preceding statement performs the same operation as the following if-else statement:

```
if (x < 0)
    y = 10;
else
    y = 20;
```

The conditional operator gives you the ability to pack decision-making power into a concise line of code. With a little imagination it can be applied to many other programming problems. For instance, consider the following statement:

```
System.out.println("Your grade is: " +
          (score < 60 ? "Fail." : "Pass."));
```

Converted to an if-else statement, it would be written as follows:

```
if (score < 60)
    System.out.println("Your grade is: Fail.");
else
    System.out.println("Your grade is: Pass.");
```

 NOTE: The parentheses are placed around the conditional expression because the + operator has higher precedence than the ?: operator. Without the parentheses, the + operator would concatenate the value in score with the string "Your grade is: ".

For a complete example using the conditional operator, see the program named *ConsultantCharges.java* in this chapter's source code folder, available for download from the book's companion Web site (www.pearsonhighered.com/gaddis).

 Checkpoint

MyProgrammingLab™ *www.myprogramminglab.com*

3.23   Rewrite the following if-else statements as statements that use the conditional operator.

   a)   ```
if (x > y)
        z = 1;
else
        z = 20;
```
```

b) ```java
if (temp > 45)
    population = base * 10;
else
    population = base * 2;
```

c) ```java
if (hours > 40)
    wages *= 1.5;
else
    wages *= 1;
```

d) ```java
if (result >= 0)
    System.out.println("The result is positive.");
else
    System.out.println("The result is negative.");
```

## 3.9 The switch Statement

**CONCEPT:** The switch statement lets the value of a variable or expression determine where the program will branch to.

The *switch statement* is a *multiple alternative decision structure*. It allows you to test the value of a variable or an expression and then use that value to determine which statement or set of statements to execute. Figure 3-24 shows an example of how a multiple alternative decision structure looks in a flowchart.

**Figure 3-24** A multiple alternative decision structure

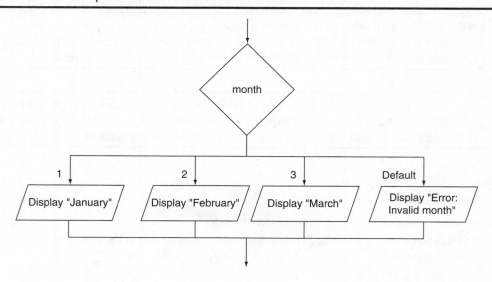

In the flowchart, the diamond symbol shows month, which is the name of a variable. If the month variable contains the value 1, the program displays *January*. If the month variable contains the value 2, the program displays *February*. If the month variable contains the
```

value 3, the program displays *March*. If the month variable contains none of these values, the action that is labeled *Default* is executed. In this case, the program displays *Error: Invalid month*.

Here is the general format of a switch statement in Java:

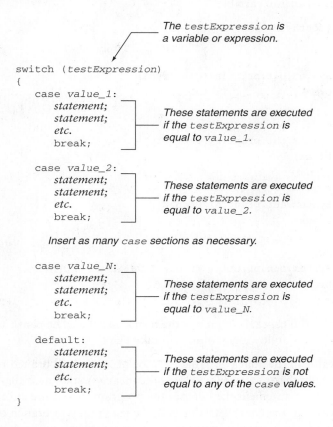

The first line of the statement starts with the word switch, followed by a *testExpression*, which is enclosed in parentheses. The *testExpression* is a variable or an expression that gives a char, byte, short, int, or string value. (If you are using a version of Java prior to Java 7, the *testExpression* cannot be a string.)

Beginning at the next line is a block of code enclosed in curly braces. Inside this block of code is one or more case sections. A case section begins with the word case, followed by a value, followed by a colon. Each case section contains one or more statements, followed by a break statement. After all of the case sections, an optional default section appears.

When the switch statement executes, it compares the value of the *testExpression* with the values that follow each of the case statements (from top to bottom). When it finds a case value that matches the *testExpression*'s value, the program branches to the case statement. The statements that follow the case statement are executed until a break statement is encountered. At that point, the program jumps out of the switch statement. If the *testExpression* does not match any of the case values, the program branches to the default statement and executes the statements that immediately follow it.

| **NOTE:** Each of the `case` values must be unique.

For example, the following code performs the same operation as the flowchart in Figure 3-24. Assume `month` is an `int` variable.

```
switch (month)
{
    case 1:
        System.out.println("January");
        break;

    case 2:
        System.out.println("February");
        break;

    case 3:
        System.out.println("March");
        break;

    default:
        System.out.println("Error: Invalid month");
        break;
}
```

In this example the *testExpression* is the `month` variable. The `month` variable will be evaluated and one of the following actions will take place:

- If the value in the `month` variable is 1, the program will branch to the `case 1:` section and execute the `System.out.println("January")` statement that immediately follows it. The `break` statement then causes the program to exit the `switch` statement.
- If the value in the `month` variable is 2, the program will branch to the `case 2:` section and execute the `System.out.println("February")` statement that immediately follows it. The `break` statement then causes the program to exit the `switch` statement.
- If the value in the `month` variable is 3, the program will branch to the `case 3:` section and execute the `System.out.println("March")` statement that immediately follows it. The `break` statement then causes the program to exit the `switch` statement.
- If the value in the `month` variable is not 1, 2, or 3, the program will branch to the `default:` section and execute the `System.out.println("Error: Invalid month")` statement that immediately follows it.

The `switch` statement can be used as an alternative to an `if-else-if` statement that compares the same variable or expression to several different values. For example, the previously shown `switch` statement works like this `if-else-if` statement:

```
if (month == 1)
{
    System.out.println("January");
}
```

```
        else if (month == 2)
        {
            System.out.println("February");
        }
        else if (month == 3)
        {
            System.out.println("March");
        }
        else
        {
            System.out.println("Error: Invalid month");
        }
```

NOTE: The default section is optional. If you leave it out, however, the program will have nowhere to branch to if the *testExpression* doesn't match any of the case values.

The program in Code Listing 3-13 shows how a simple switch statement works.

Code Listing 3-13   **(SwitchDemo.java)**

```
1   import java.util.Scanner; // Needed for Scanner class
2
3   /**
4      This program demonstrates the switch statement.
5   */
6
7   public class SwitchDemo
8   {
9      public static void main(String[] args)
10  {
11         int number;       // A number entered by the user
12
13         // Create a Scanner object for keyboard input.
14         Scanner keyboard = new Scanner(System.in);
15
16         // Get one of the numbers 1, 2, or 3 from the user.
17         System.out.print("Enter 1, 2, or 3: ");
18         number = keyboard.nextInt();
19
20         // Determine the number entered.
21         switch (number)
22         {
23             case 1:
24                 System.out.println("You entered 1.");
```

```
25                  break;
26              case 2:
27                  System.out.println("You entered 2.");
28                  break;
29              case 3:
30                  System.out.println("You entered 3.");
31                  break;
32              default:
33                  System.out.println("That's not 1, 2, or 3!");
34          }
35      }
36  }
```

Program Output with Example Input Shown in Bold

Enter 1, 2, or 3: **2 [Enter]**
You entered 2.

Program Output with Example Input Shown in Bold

Enter 1, 2, or 3: **5 [Enter]**
That's not 1, 2, or 3!

Notice the break statements that are in the case 1, case 2, and case 3 sections.

```
switch (number)
{
    case 1:
            System.out.println("You entered 1.");
            break;←
    case 2:
            System.out.println("You entered 2.");
            break;←
    case 3:
            System.out.println("You entered 3.");
            break;←
    default:
            System.out.println("That's not 1, 2, or 3!");
}
```

The case statements show the program where to start executing in the block and the break statements show the program where to stop. Without the break statements, the program would execute all of the lines from the matching case statement to the end of the block.

NOTE: The default section (or the last case section if there is no default) does not need a break statement. Some programmers prefer to put one there anyway for consistency.

The program in Code Listing 3-14 is a modification of Code Listing 3-13, without the break statements.

Code Listing 3-14   (NoBreaks.java)

```java
 1   import java.util.Scanner;    // Needed for Scanner class
 2
 3   /**
 4      This program demonstrates the switch statement.
 5   */
 6
 7   public class NoBreaks
 8   {
 9      public static void main(String[] args)
10      {
11         int number;       // A number entered by the user
12
13         // Create a Scanner object for keyboard input.
14         Scanner keyboard = new Scanner(System.in);
15
16         // Get one of the numbers 1, 2, or 3 from the user.
17         System.out.print("Enter 1, 2, or 3: ");
18         number = keyboard.nextInt();
19
20         // Determine the number entered.
21         switch (number)
22         {
23            case 1:
24               System.out.println("You entered 1.");
25            case 2:
26               System.out.println("You entered 2.");
27            case 3:
28               System.out.println("You entered 3.");
29            default:
30               System.out.println("That's not 1, 2, or 3!");
31         }
32      }
33   }
```

Program Output with Example Input Shown in Bold
Enter 1, 2, or 3: **1 [Enter]**
You entered 1.
You entered 2.
You entered 3.
That's not 1, 2, or 3!

Program Output with Example Input Shown in Bold

```
Enter 1, 2, or 3: 3 [Enter]
You entered 3.
That's not 1, 2, or 3!
```

Without the break statement, the program "falls through" all of the statements below the one with the matching case expression. Sometimes this is what you want. For instance, the program in Code Listing 3-15 asks the user to select a grade of pet food. The available choices are A, B, and C. The switch statement will recognize either uppercase or lowercase letters.

Code Listing 3-15   (PetFood.java)

```java
 1   import java.util.Scanner; // Needed for the Scanner class
 2
 3   /**
 4      This program demonstrates a switch statement.
 5   */
 6
 7   public class PetFood
 8   {
 9      public static void main(String[] args)
10      {
11         String input;      // To hold the user's input
12         char foodGrade;    // Grade of pet food
13
14         // Create a Scanner object for keyboard input.
15         Scanner keyboard = new Scanner(System.in);
16
17         // Prompt the user for a grade of pet food.
18         System.out.println("Our pet food is available in " +
19                            "three grades:");
20         System.out.print("A, B, and C. Which do you want " +
21                          "pricing for? ");
22         input = keyboard.nextLine();
23         foodGrade = input.charAt(0);
24
25         // Display pricing for the selected grade.
26         switch(foodGrade)
27         {
28            case 'a':
29            case 'A':
30               System.out.println("30 cents per lb.");
31               break;
32            case 'b':
33            case 'B':
34               System.out.println("20 cents per lb.");
35               break;
```

```
36                case 'c':
37                case 'C':
38                    System.out.println("15 cents per lb.");
39                    break;
40                default:
41                    System.out.println("Invalid choice.");
42            }
43        }
44  }
```

Program Output with Example Input Shown in Bold

Our pet food is available in three grades:
A, B, and C. Which do you want pricing for? **b [Enter]**
20 cents per lb.

Program Output with Example Input Shown in Bold

Our pet food is available in three grades:
A, B, and C. Which do you want pricing for? **B [Enter]**
20 cents per lb.

When the user enters 'a' the corresponding case has no statements associated with it, so the program falls through to the next case, which corresponds with 'A'.

```
case 'a':
case 'A':
        System.out.println("30 cents per lb.");
        break;
```

The same technique is used for 'b' and 'c'.

If you are using a version of Java prior to Java 7, a switch statement's *testExpression* can be a char, byte, short, or int value. Beginning with Java 7, however, the *testExpression* can also be a string. The program in Code Listing 3-16 demonstrates.

Code Listing 3-16   (Seasons.java)

```
1   import java.util.Scanner;
2
3   /**
4       This program translates the English names of
5       the seasons into Spanish.
6   */
7
8   public class Seasons
9   {
10      public static void main(String[] args)
11      {
12          String input;
13
```

```
14        // Create a Scanner object for keyboard input.
15        Scanner keyboard = new Scanner(System.in);
16
17        // Get a day from the user.
18        System.out.print("Enter the name of a season: ");
19        input = keyboard.nextLine();
20
21        // Translate the season to Spanish.
22        switch (input)
23        {
24           case "spring":
25              System.out.println("la primavera");
26              break;
27           case "summer":
28              System.out.println("el verano");
29              break;
30           case "autumn":
31           case "fall":
32              System.out.println("el otono");
33              break;
34           case "winter":
35              System.out.println("el invierno");
36              break;
37           default:
38              System.out.println("Please enter one of these words:\n"
39                        + "spring, summer, autumn, fall, or winter.");
40        }
41     }
42  }
```

Program Output with Example Input Shown in Bold

Enter the name of a season: **summer [Enter]**
el verano

Program Output with Example Input Shown in Bold

Enter the name of a season: **fall [Enter]**
el otono

 Checkpoint

MyProgrammingLab™ *www.myprogramminglab.com*

3.24 Complete the following program skeleton by writing a switch statement that displays "one" if the user has entered 1, "two" if the user has entered 2, and "three" if the user has entered 3. If a number other than 1, 2, or 3 is entered, the program should display an error message.

```
import java.util.Scanner;
public class CheckPoint
{
```

```
        public static void main(String[] args)
        {
            int userNum;
            Scanner keyboard = new Scanner(System.in);
            System.out.print("Enter one of the numbers " +
                            "1, 2, or 3: ");
            userNum = keyboard.nextInt();
            //
            // Write the switch statement here.
            //
        }
    }
```

3.25   Rewrite the following if-else-if statement as a switch statement.

```
    if (selection == 'A')
        System.out.println("You selected A.");
    else if (selection == 'B')
        System.out.println("You selected B.");
    else if (selection == 'C')
        System.out.println("You selected C.");
    else if (selection == 'D')
        System.out.println("You selected D.");
    else
        System.out.println("Not good with letters, eh?");
```

3.26   Explain why you cannot convert the following if-else-if statement into a switch statement.

```
    if (temp == 100)
        x = 0;
    else if (population > 1000)
        x = 1;
    else if (rate < .1)
        x = -1;
```

3.27   What is wrong with the following switch statement?

```
    // This code has errors!!!
    switch (temp)
    {
        case temp < 0 :
            System.out.println("Temp is negative.");
            break;
        case temp = 0:
            System.out.println("Temp is zero.");
            break;
        case temp > 0 :
            System.out.println("Temp is positive.");
            break;
    }
```

3.28   What will the following code display?

```java
int funny = 7, serious = 15;
funny = serious * 2;
switch (funny)
{   case 0 :
        System.out.println("That is funny.");
        break;
    case 30:
        System.out.println("That is serious.");
        break;
    case 32:
        System.out.println("That is seriously funny.");
        break;
    default:
        System.out.println(funny);
}
```

3.10 Displaying Formatted Output with `System.out.printf` and `String.format`

CONCEPT: The `System.out.printf` method allows you to format output in a variety of ways. The `String.format` method allows you to format a string, without displaying it. The string can be displayed at a later time.

When you display numbers with the `System.out.println` or `System.out.print` method, you have little control over the way the numbers appear. For example, a value of the `double` data type can be displayed with as many as 15 decimal places, as demonstrated by the following code:

```java
double number = 10.0 / 6.0;
System.out.println(number);
```

This code will display:

```
1.666666666666667
```

Quite often, you want to format numbers so they are displayed in a particular way. For example, you might want to round a floating-point number to a specific number of decimal places, or insert comma separators to make a number easier to read. Fortunately, Java gives us a way to do just that, and more, with the `System.out.printf` method. The method's general format is as follows:

```java
System.out.printf(FormatString, ArgumentList)
```

In the general format, *FormatString* is a string that contains text, special formatting specifiers, or both. *ArgumentList* is a list of zero or more additional arguments, which will be formatted according to the format specifiers listed in the format string.

The simplest way you can use the `System.out.printf` method is with only a format string, and no additional arguments. Here is an example:

```java
System.out.printf("I love Java programming.\n");
```

The format string in this example is `"I love Java programming.\n"`. This method call does not perform any special formatting, however. It simply prints the string `"I love Java programming.\n"`. Using the method in this fashion is exactly like using the `System.out.print` method.

In most cases you will call the `System.out.printf` method in the following manner:

- The format string will contain one or more format specifiers. A *format specifier* is a placeholder for a value that will be inserted into the string when it is displayed.
- After the format string, one or more additional arguments will appear. Each of the additional arguments will correspond to a format specifier that appears inside the format string.

The following code shows an example:

```
double sales = 12345.67;
System.out.printf("Our sales are %f for the day.\n", sales);
```

Notice the following characteristics of the `System.out.printf` method call:

- Inside the format string, the `%f` is a format specifier. The letter `f` indicates that a floating-point value will be inserted into the string when it is displayed.
- Following the format string, the `sales` variable is passed as an argument. This argument corresponds to the `%f` format specifier that appears inside the format string.

When the `System.out.printf` method executes, the `%f` will not be displayed on the screen. In its place, the value of the `sales` argument will be displayed. Here is the output of the code:

```
Our sales are 12345.670000 for the day.
```

The diagram in Figure 3-25 shows how the `sales` variable corresponds to the `%f` format specifier.

Figure 3-25   The value of the `sales` variable is displayed in the place of the `%f` format specifier

```
System.out.printf("Our sales is %f for the day.\n", sales);
```

Here is another example:

```
double temp1 = 72.5, temp2 = 83.7;
System.out.printf("The temperatures are %f and %f degrees.\n", temp1, temp2);
```

First, notice that this example uses two `%f` format specifiers in the format string. Also notice that two additional arguments appear after the format string. The value of the first argument, `temp1`, will be printed in place of the first `%f`, and the value of the second argument, `temp2`, will be printed in place of the second `%f`. The code will produce the following output:

```
The temperatures are 72.500000 and 83.700000 degrees.
```

There is a one-to-one correspondence between the format specifiers and the arguments that appear after the format string. The diagram in Figure 3-26 shows how the first format specifier corresponds to the first argument after the format string (the `temp1` variable), and

Figure 3-26 The format specifiers and their corresponding arguments

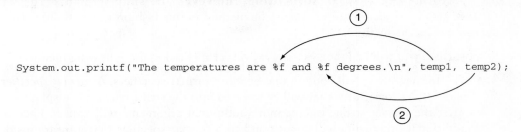

```
System.out.printf("The temperatures are %f and %f degrees.\n", temp1, temp2);
```

the second format specifier corresponds to the second argument after the format string (the `temp2` variable).

The following code shows another example:

```
double value1 = 3.0;
double value2 = 6.0;
double value3 = 9.0;
System.out.printf("%f %f %f\n", value1, value2, value3);
```

In the `System.out.printf` method call, there are three format specifiers and three additional arguments after the format string. This code will produce the following output:

```
3.000000 6.000000 9.000000
```

The diagram in Figure 3-27 shows how the format specifiers correspond to the arguments that appear after the format string.

Figure 3-27 The format specifiers and their corresponding arguments

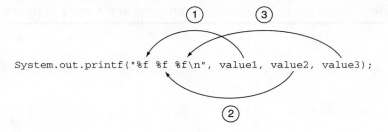

```
System.out.printf("%f %f %f\n", value1, value2, value3);
```

The previous examples demonstrated how to format floating-point numbers with the `%f` format specifier. The letter `f` in the format specifier is a *conversion character* that indicates the data type of the argument that is being formatted. You use the `f` conversion character with any argument that is a `float` or a `double`.

If you want to format an integer value, you must use the `%d` format specifier. The `d` conversion character stands for *decimal integer*, and it can be used with arguments of the `int`, `short`, and `long` data types. Here is an example that displays an `int`:

```
int hours = 40;
System.out.printf("I worked %d hours this week.\n", hours);
```

In this example, the `%d` format specifier corresponds with the `hours` argument. This code will display the following:

```
I worked 40 hours this week.
```

Here is an example that displays two `int` values:

```
int dogs = 2;
int cats = 4;
System.out.printf("We have %d dogs and %d cats.\n", dogs, cats);
```

This code will display the following:

```
We have 2 dogs and 4 cats.
```

Keep in mind that `%f` must be used with floating-point values, and `%d` must be used with integer values. Otherwise, an error will occur at runtime.

Format Specifier Syntax

In the previous examples you saw how format specifiers correspond to the arguments that appear after the format string. Now you can learn how to use format specifiers to actually format the values that they correspond to. When displaying numbers, the general syntax for writing a format specifier is:

```
%[flags][width][.precision]conversion
```

The items that appear inside brackets are optional. Here is a summary of each item:

- `%`—All format specifiers begin with a `%` character.
- `flags`—After the `%` character, one or more optional flags may appear. Flags cause the value to be formatted in a variety of ways.
- `width`—After any flags, you can optionally specify the minimum field width for the value.
- `.precision`—If the value is a floating-point number, after the minimum field width, you can optionally specify the precision. This is the number of decimal places that the number should be rounded to.
- `conversion`—All format specifiers must end with a conversion character, such as `f` for floating-point, or `d` for decimal integer.

Let's take a closer look at each of the optional items, beginning with precision.

Precision

You probably noticed in the previous examples that the `%f` format specifier causes floating-point values to be displayed with six decimal places. You can change the number of decimal points that are displayed, as shown in the following example:

```
double temp = 78.42819;
System.out.printf("The temperature is %.2f degrees.\n", temp);
```

Notice that this example doesn't use the regular `%f` format specifier, but uses `%.2f` instead. The `.2` that appears between the `%` and the `f` specifies the *precision* of the displayed value. It will cause the value of the `temp` variable to be rounded to two decimal places. This code will produce the following output:

```
The temperature is 78.43 degrees.
```

The following example displays the same value, rounded to one decimal place:

```
double temp = 78.42819;
System.out.printf("The temperature is %.1f degrees.\n", temp);
```

This code will produce the following output:

```
The temperature is 78.4 degrees.
```

The following code shows another example:

```
double value1 = 123.45678;
double value2 = 123.45678;
double value3 = 123.45678;
System.out.printf("%.1f %.2f %.3f\n", value1, value2, value3);
```

In this example, `value1` is rounded to one decimal place, `value2` is rounded to two decimal places, and `value3` is rounded to three decimal places. This code will produce the following output:

```
123.5 123.46 123.457
```

Keep in mind that you can specify precision only with floating-point point values. If you specify a precision with the `%d` format specifier, an error will occur at runtime.

Specifying a Minimum Field Width

A format specifier can also include a *minimum field width*, which is the minimum number of spaces that should be used to display the value. The following example prints a floating-point number in a field that is 20 spaces wide:

```
double number = 12345.6789;
System.out.printf("The number is:%20f\n", number);
```

Notice that the number 20 appears in the format specifier, between the `%` and the `f`. This code will produce the following output:

```
The number is:        12345.678900
```

In this example, the 20 that appears inside the `%f` format specifier indicates that the number should be displayed in a field that is a minimum of 20 spaces wide. This is illustrated in Figure 3-28.

Figure 3-28 The number is displayed in a field that is 20 spaces wide

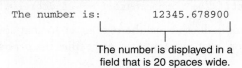

```
The number is:        12345.678900
```
The number is displayed in a
field that is 20 spaces wide.

In this case, the number that is displayed is shorter than the field in which it is displayed. The number 12345.678900 uses only 12 spaces on the screen, but it is displayed in a field that is 20 spaces wide. When this is the case, the number will be right-justified in the field. If a value is too large to fit in the specified field width, the field is automatically enlarged to accommodate it. The following example prints a floating-point number in a field that is only one space wide:

```java
double number = 12345.6789;
System.out.printf("The number is:%1f\n", number);
```

The value of the number variable requires more than one space, however, so the field width is expanded to accommodate the entire number. This code will produce the following output:

```
The number is:12345.678900
```

You can specify a minimum field width for integers, as well as for floating-point values. The following example displays an integer with a minimum field width of six characters:

```java
int number = 200;
System.out.printf("The number is:%6d", number);
```

This code will display the following:

```
The number is:   200
```

Combining Minimum Field Width and Precision in the Same Format Specifier

When specifying the minimum field width and the precision of a floating-point number in the same format specifier, remember that the field width must appear first, followed by the precision. For example, the following code displays a number in a field of 12 spaces, rounded to two decimal places:

```java
double number = 12345.6789;
System.out.printf("The number is:%12.2f\n", number);
```

This code will produce the following output:

```
The number is:    12345.68
```

Field widths can help when you need to print numbers aligned in columns. For example, look at Code Listing 3-17. Each of the variables is displayed in a field that is eight spaces wide, and rounded to two decimal places. The numbers appear aligned in a column.

Code Listing 3-17 (Columns.java)

```java
1  /**
2     This program displays a variety of
3     floating-point numbers in a column
4     with their decimal points aligned.
5  */
6
7  public class Columns
```

```
 8  {
 9      public static void main(String[] args)
10      {
11          // Declare a variety of double variables.
12          double num1 = 127.899;
13          double num2 = 3465.148;
14          double num3 = 3.776;
15          double num4 = 264.821;
16          double num5 = 88.081;
17          double num6 = 1799.999;
18
19          // Display each variable in a field of
20          // 8 spaces with 2 decimal places.
21          System.out.printf("%8.2f\n", num1);
22          System.out.printf("%8.2f\n", num2);
23          System.out.printf("%8.2f\n", num3);
24          System.out.printf("%8.2f\n", num4);
25          System.out.printf("%8.2f\n", num5);
26          System.out.printf("%8.2f\n", num6);
27      }
28  }
```

Program Output

```
  127.90
 3465.15
    3.78
  264.82
   88.08
 1800.00
```

Flags

There are several optional flags that you can insert into a format specifier to cause a value to be formatted in a particular way. In this book, we will use flags for the following purposes:

- To display numbers with comma separators
- To pad numbers with leading zeros
- To left-justify numbers

If you use a flag in a format specifier, you must write the flag before the field width and the precision.

Comma Separators

Large numbers are easier to read if they are displayed with comma separators. You can format a number with comma separators by inserting a comma (,) flag into the format specifier. Here is an example:

```
double amount = 1234567.89;
System.out.printf("%,f\n", amount);
```

This code will produce the following output:

```
1,234,567.890000
```

Quite often, you will want to format a number with comma separators, and round the number to a specific number of decimal places. You can accomplish this by inserting a comma, followed by the precision value, into the %f format specifier, as shown in the following example:

```
double sales = 28756.89;
System.out.printf("Sales for the month are %,.2f\n", sales);
```

This code will produce the following output:

```
Sales for the month are 28,756.89
```

Code Listing 3-18 demonstrates how the comma separator and a precision of two decimal places can be used to format a number as a currency amount.

Code Listing 3-18   **(CurrencyFormat.java)**

```
1   /**
2      This program demonstrates how to use the System.out.printf
3      method to format a number as currency.
4   */
5
6   public class CurrencyFormat
7   {
8      public static void main(String[] args)
9      {
10         double monthlyPay = 5000.0;
11         double annualPay = monthlyPay * 12;
12         System.out.printf("Your annual pay is $%,.2f\n", annualPay);
13      }
14   }
```

Program Output

```
Your annual pay is $60,000.00
```

The following example displays a floating-point number with comma separators, in a field of 15 spaces, rounded to two decimal places:

```
double amount = 1234567.8901;
System.out.printf("%,15.2f\n", amount);
```

This code will produce the following output:

```
   1,234,567.89
```

The following example displays an int with a minimum field width of six characters:

```
int number = 200;
System.out.printf("The number is:%6d", number);
```

This code will display the following:

```
The number is:    200
```

The following example displays an `int` with comma separators, with a minimum field width of 10 characters:

```
int number = 20000;
System.out.printf("The number is:%,10d", number);
```

This code will display the following:

```
The number is:    20,000
```

Padding Numbers with Leading Zeros

Sometimes, when a number is shorter than the field in which it is displayed, you want to pad the number with leading zeros. If you insert a 0 flag into a format specifier, the resulting number will be padded with leading zeros, if it is shorter than the field width. The following code shows an example:

```
double number = 123.4;
System.out.printf("The number is:%08.1f\n", number);
```

This code will produce the following output:

```
The number is:000123.4
```

The diagram in Figure 3-29 shows the purpose of each part of the format specifier in the previous example.

Figure 3-29   Format specifier that pads with leading zeros

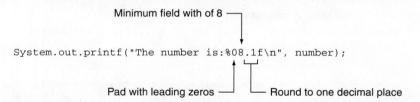

The following example displays an `int` padded with leading zeros, with a minimum field width of seven characters:

```
int number = 1234;
System.out.printf("The number is:%07d", number);
```

This code will display the following:

```
The number is:0001234
```

The program in Code Listing 3-19 shows another example. This program displays a variety of floating-point numbers with leading zeros, in a field of nine spaces, rounded to two decimal places.

Code Listing 3-19 (`LeadingZeros.java`)

```
 1   /**
 2       This program displays numbers padded with leading zeros.
 3   */
 4
 5   public class LeadingZeros
 6   {
 7       public static void main(String[] args)
 8       {
 9           // Declare a variety of double variables.
10           double number1 = 1.234;
11           double number2 = 12.345;
12           double number3 = 123.456;
13
14           // Display each variable with leading
15           // zeros, in a field of 9 spaces, rounded
16           // to 2 decimal places.
17           System.out.printf("%09.2f\n", number1);
18           System.out.printf("%09.2f\n", number2);
19           System.out.printf("%09.2f\n", number3);
20       }
21   }
```

Program Output

```
000001.23
000012.35
000123.46
```

Left-Justifying Numbers

By default, when a number is shorter than the field in which it is displayed, the number is right-justified within that field. If you want a number to be left-justified within its field, you insert a minus sign (-) flag into the format specifier. Code Listing 3-20 shows an example.

Code Listing 3-20 (`LeftJustified.java`)

```
 1   /**
 2       This program displays a variety of
 3       numbers left-justified in columns.
 4   */
 5
 6   public class LeftJustified
 7   {
 8       public static void main(String[] args)
 9       {
10           // Declare a variety of int variables.
```

```
11          int num1 = 123;
12          int num2 = 12;
13          int num3 = 45678;
14          int num4 = 456;
15          int num5 = 1234567;
16          int num6 = 1234;
17
18          // Display each variable left-justified
19          // in a field of 8 spaces.
20          System.out.printf("%-8d%-8d\n", num1, num2);
21          System.out.printf("%-8d%-8d\n", num3, num4);
22          System.out.printf("%-8d%-8d\n", num5, num6);
23      }
24  }
```

Program Output

```
123     12
45678   456
1234567 1234
```

Formatting String Arguments

If you wish to print a string argument, use the %s format specifier. Here is an example:

```
String name = "Ringo";
System.out.printf("Your name is %s\n", name);
```

This code produces the following output:

```
Your name is Ringo
```

You can also use a field width when printing strings. For example, look at the following code:

```
String name1 = "George";
String name2 = "Franklin";
String name3 = "Jay";
String name4 = "Ozzy";
String name5 = "Carmine";
String name6 = "Dee";
System.out.printf("%10s%10s\n", name1, name2);
System.out.printf("%10s%10s\n", name3, name4);
System.out.printf("%10s%10s\n", name5, name6);
```

The %10s format specifier prints a string in a field that is ten spaces wide. This code displays the values of the variables in a table with three rows and two columns. Each column has a width of ten spaces. Here is the output of the code:

```
  George  Franklin
     Jay      Ozzy
 Carmine       Dee
```

Notice that the strings are right-justified. You can use the minus flag (–) to left-justify a string within its field. The following code demonstrates:

```
String name1 = "George";
String name2 = "Franklin";
String name3 = "Jay";
String name4 = "Ozzy";
String name5 = "Carmine";
String name6 = "Dee";
System.out.printf("%-10s%-10s\n", name1, name2);
System.out.printf("%-10s%-10s\n", name3, name4);
System.out.printf("%-10s%-10s\n", name5, name6);
```

Here is the output of the code:

```
George    Franklin
Jay       Ozzy
Carmine   Dee
```

The following example shows how you can print arguments of different data types:

```
int hours = 40;
double pay = hours * 25;
String name = "Jay";
System.out.printf("Name: %s, Hours: %d, Pay: $%,.2f\n",
                  name, hours, pay);
```

In this example, we are displaying a `String`, an `int`, and a `double`. The code will produce the following output:

```
Name: Jay, Hours: 40, Pay: $1,000.00
```

 NOTE: The format specifiers we have shown in this section are the basic ones. Java provides much more powerful format specifiers for more complex formatting needs. The API documentation gives an overview of them all.

The `String.format` Method

The `System.out.printf` method formats a string and displays it in the console window. Sometimes you need to format a string without displaying it in the console. For example, you might need to display formatted output in a graphical interface, such as a message dialog. When this is the case, you can use the `String.format` method.

The `String.format` method works exactly like the `System.out.printf` method, except that it does not display the formatted string on the screen. Instead, it returns a reference to the formatted string. You can assign the reference to a variable, and then use it later. Here is the method's general format:

```
String.format(FormatString, ArgumentList)
```

In the general format, *FormatString* is a string that contains text, special formatting specifiers, or both. *ArgumentList* is a list of zero or more additional arguments, which will be formatted according to the format specifiers listed in the format string. The syntax for writing the format specifiers is the same as with the `System.out.printf` method. The method creates a string in memory that is formatted as specified, and returns a reference to that string. For example, look at the program in Code Listing 3-21. The program's output is shown in Figure 3-30.

Code Listing 3-21   (`CurrencyFormat2.java`)

```java
 1  import javax.swing.JOptionPane;
 2
 3  /**
 4     This program demonstrates how to use the String.format
 5     method to format a number as currency.
 6  */
 7
 8  public class CurrencyFormat2
 9  {
10     public static void main(String[] args)
11     {
12        double monthlyPay = 5000.0;
13        double annualPay = monthlyPay * 12;
14        String output = String.format("Your annual pay is $%,.2f", annualPay);
15
16        JOptionPane.showMessageDialog(null, output);
17     }
18  }
```

Figure 3-30   Output of Code Listing 3-21

Let's take a closer look at the program. Line 12 declares a `double` variable named `monthlyPay`, initialized with the value 5000.0, and line 13 declares a `double` variable named `annualPay`, initialized with the result of the calculation `monthlyPay * 12`. Line 14 declares a `String` variable named `output`, and initializes it with the string that is returned from the `String.format` method. In line 16, the `output` variable is passed as an argument to the `JOptionPane.showMessageDialog` method.

The program in Code Listing 3-21 can be simplified. We can combine the steps of calling the `String.format` method, and passing the value that it returns to the `JOptionPane.showMessageDialog` method. This allows us to eliminate the declaration of the output variable. Code Listing 3-22 shows how this is done. The program's output is the same as shown in Figure 3-30.

Code Listing 3-22   (`CurrencyFormat3.java`)

```
 1  import javax.swing.JOptionPane;
 2
 3  /**
 4     This program demonstrates how to use the String.format
 5     method to format a number as currency.
 6  */
 7
 8  public class CurrencyFormat3
 9  {
10     public static void main(String[] args)
11     {
12        double monthlyPay = 5000.0;
13        double annualPay = monthlyPay * 12;
14
15        JOptionPane.showMessageDialog(null,
16           String.format("Your annual pay is $%,.2f", annualPay));
17     }
18  }
```

Checkpoint

MyProgrammingLab™ *www.myprogramminglab.com*

3.29   Assume the following variable declaration exists in a program:

```
double number = 1234567.456;
```

Write a statement that uses `System.out.printf` to display the value of the `number` variable formatted as:

```
1,234,567.46
```

3.30   Assume the following variable declaration exists in a program:

```
double number = 123.456;
```

Write a statement that uses `System.out.printf` to display the value of the `number` variable rounded to one decimal place, in a field that is 10 spaces wide. (Do not use comma separators.)

3.31   Assume the following variable declaration exists in a program:

```
double number = 123.456;
```

Write a statement that uses `System.out.printf` to display the value of the `number` variable padded with leading zeros, in a field that is eight spaces wide, rounded to one decimal place. (Do not use comma separators.)

3.32 Assume the following variable declaration exists in a program:

```
int number = 123456;
```

Write a statement that uses System.out.printf to display the value of the number variable in a field that is 10 spaces wide, with comma separators.

3.33 Assume the following variable declaration exists in a program:

```
double number = 123456.789;
```

Write a statement that uses System.out.printf to display the value of the number variable left-justified, with comma separators, in a field that is 20 spaces wide, rounded to two decimal places.

3.34 Assume the following declaration exists in a program:

```
String name = "James";
```

Write a statement that uses System.out.printf to display the value of name in a field that is 20 spaces wide.

3.11 Common Errors to Avoid

The following list describes several errors that are commonly committed when learning this chapter's topics.

- **Using = instead of == to compare primitive values.** Remember, = is the assignment operator and == tests for equality.
- **Using == instead of the equals method to compare String objects.** You cannot use the == operator to compare the contents of a String object with another string. Instead you must use the equals or compareTo method.
- **Forgetting to enclose an if statement's boolean expression in parentheses.** Java requires that the boolean expression being tested by an if statement is enclosed in a set of parentheses. An error will result if you omit the parentheses or use any other grouping characters.
- **Writing a semicolon at the end of an if clause.** When you write a semicolon at the end of an if clause, Java assumes that the conditionally executed statement is a null or empty statement.
- **Forgetting to enclose multiple conditionally executed statements in braces.** Normally the if statement conditionally executes only one statement. To conditionally execute more than one statement, you must enclose them in braces.
- **Omitting the trailing else in an if-else-if statement.** This is not a syntax error, but can lead to logical errors. If you omit the trailing else from an if-else-if statement, no code will be executed if none of the statement's boolean expressions are true.
- **Not writing complete boolean expressions on both sides of a logical && or || operator.** You must write a complete boolean expression on both sides of a logical && or || operator. For example, the expression x > 0 && < 10 is not valid because < 10 is not a complete expression. The expression should be written as x > 0 && x < 10.
- **Trying to perform case-insensitive string comparisons with the String class's equals and compareTo methods.** To perform case-insensitive string comparisons, use the String class's equalsIgnoreCase and compareToIgnoreCase methods.

- Using a `SwitchExpression` that is not an `int`, `short`, `byte`, `char`, or `String`. The switch statement can only evaluate expressions that are of the `int`, `short`, `byte`, `char`, or `String` data types.
- Using a `CaseExpression` that is not a literal or a `final` variable. Because the compiler must determine the value of a `CaseExpression` at compile time, `CaseExpressions` must be either literal values or `final` variables.
- Forgetting to write a colon at the end of a `case` statement. A colon must appear after the `CaseExpression` in each case statement.
- Forgetting to write a `break` statement in a `case` section. This is not a syntax error, but it can lead to logical errors. The program does not branch out of a `switch` statement until it reaches a `break` statement or the end of the `switch` statement.
- Forgetting to write a `default` section in a `switch` statement. This is not a syntax error, but can lead to a logical error. If you omit the `default` section, no code will be executed if none of the `CaseExpressions` match the `SwitchExpression`.
- Reversing the `?` and the `:` when using the conditional operator. When using the conditional operator, the `?` character appears first in the conditional expression, then the `:` character.
- When formatting a number with `System.out.printf` or `String.format`, writing the flags, field width, and precision in an incorrect order.
- When writing a format specifier for the `System.out.printf` or `String.format` methods, using the wrong type indicator (`%f` = floating-point, `%d` = integer, `%s` = string).

Review Questions and Exercises

Multiple Choice and True/False

1. The `if` statement is an example of a _____.
   a. sequence structure
   b. decision structure
   c. pathway structure
   d. class structure

2. This type of expression has a value of either `true` or `false`.
   a. binary expression
   b. decision expression
   c. unconditional expression
   d. boolean expression

3. `>`, `<`, and `==` are _____.
   a. relational operators
   b. logical operators
   c. conditional operators
   d. ternary operators

4. `&&`, `||`, and `!` are _____.
   a. relational operators
   b. logical operators
   c. conditional operators
   d. ternary operators

5. This is an empty statement that does nothing.
   a. missing statement
   b. virtual statement
   c. `null` statement
   d. conditional statement

6. To create a block of statements, you enclose the statements in these.
   a. parentheses `( )`
   b. square brackets `[ ]`
   c. angled brackets `<>`
   d. braces `{ }`

7. This is a `boolean` variable that signals when some condition exists in the program.
   a. flag
   b. signal
   c. sentinel
   d. siren

8. How does the character 'A' compare to the character 'B'?
   a. 'A' is greater than 'B'
   b. 'A' is less than 'B'
   c. 'A' is equal to 'B'
   d. You cannot compare characters

9. This is an `if` statement that appears inside another `if` statement.
   a. nested `if` statement
   b. tiered `if` statement
   c. dislodged `if` statement
   d. structured `if` statement

10. An `else` clause always goes with _____.
    a. the closest previous `if` clause that doesn't already have its own `else` clause
    b. the closest `if` clause
    c. the `if` clause that is randomly selected by the compiler
    d. none of these

11. When determining whether a number is inside a range, it's best to use this operator.
    a. `&&`
    b. `!`
    c. `||`
    d. `? :`

12. This determines whether two different `String` objects contain the same string.
    a. the `==` operator
    b. the `=` operator
    c. the `equals` method
    d. the `stringCompare` method

13. The conditional operator takes this many operands.
    a. one
    b. two
    c. three
    d. four

14. This section of a switch statement is branched to if none of the case expressions match the switch expression.
    a. else
    b. default
    c. case
    d. otherwise

15. You can use this method to display formatted output in a console window.
    a. Format.out.println
    b. Console.format
    c. System.out.printf
    d. System.out.formatted

16. True or False: The = operator and the == operator perform the same operation.

17. True or False: A conditionally executed statement should be indented one level from the if clause.

18. True or False: All lines in a conditionally executed block should be indented one level.

19. True or False: When an if statement is nested in the if clause of another statement, the only time the inner if statement is executed is when the boolean expression of the outer if statement is true.

20. True or False: When an if statement is nested in the else clause of another statement, the only time the inner if statement is executed is when the boolean expression of the outer if statement is true.

21. True or False: The scope of a variable is limited to the block in which it is defined.

Find the Error

Find the errors in the following code:

1.
```
// Warning! This code contains ERRORS!
if (x == 1);
    y = 2;
else if (x == 2);
    y = 3;
else if (x == 3);
    y = 4;
```

2.
```
// Warning! This code contains an ERROR!
if (average = 100)
    System.out.println("Perfect Average!");
```

3.
```
// Warning! This code contains ERRORS!
if (num2 == 0)
    System.out.println("Division by zero is not possible.");
    System.out.println("Please run the program again ");
    System.out.println("and enter a number besides zero.");
else
    Quotient = num1 / num2;
    System.out.print("The quotient of " + Num1);
    System.out.print(" divided by " + Num2 + " is ");
    System.out.println(Quotient);
```

4.  ```
    // Warning! This code contains ERRORS!
    switch (score)
    {
       case (score > 90):
          grade = 'A';
          break;
       case(score > 80):
          grade = 'b';
          break;
       case(score > 70):
          grade = 'C';
          break;
       case (score > 60):
          grade = 'D';
          break;
       default:
          grade = 'F';
    }
    ```

5. The following statement should determine whether x is not greater than 20. What is wrong with it?

    ```
    if (!x > 20)
    ```

6. The following statement should determine whether count is within the range of 0 through 100. What is wrong with it?

    ```
    if (count >= 0 || count <= 100)
    ```

7. The following statement should determine whether count is outside the range of 0 through 100. What is wrong with it?

    ```
    if (count < 0 && count > 100)
    ```

8. The following statement should assign 0 to z if a is less than 10; otherwise, it should assign 7 to z. What is wrong with it?

    ```
    z = (a < 10) : 0 ? 7;
    ```

9. Assume that partNumber references a String object. The following if statement should perform a case-insensitive comparison. What is wrong with it?

    ```
    if (partNumber.equals("BQ789W4"))
       available = true;
    ```

10. What is wrong with the following code?

    ```
    double value = 12345.678;
    System.out.printf("%.2d", value);
    ```

Algorithm Workbench

1. Write an if statement that assigns 100 to x when y is equal to 0.

2. Write an if-else statement that assigns 0 to x when y is equal to 10. Otherwise, it should assign 1 to x.
    ```

3. Using the following chart, write an `if-else-if` statement that assigns .10, .15, or .20 to `commission`, depending on the value in `sales`.

Sales	Commission Rate
Up to $10,000	10%
$10,000 to $15,000	15%
Over $15,000	20%

4. Write an `if` statement that sets the variable `hours` to 10 when the `boolean` flag variable `minimum` is equal to `true`.

5. Write nested `if` statements that perform the following tests: If `amount1` is greater than 10 and `amount2` is less than 100, display the greater of the two.

6. Write an `if` statement that prints the message "The number is valid" if the variable `grade` is within the range 0 through 100.

7. Write an `if` statement that prints the message "The number is valid" if the variable `temperature` is within the range −50 through 150.

8. Write an `if` statement that prints the message "The number is not valid" if the variable `hours` is outside the range 0 through 80.

9. Write an `if-else` statement that displays the `String` objects `title1` and `title2` in alphabetical order.

10. Convert the following `if-else-if` statement into a `switch` statement:

```
if (choice == 1)
{
   System.out.println("You selected 1.");
}
else if (choice == 2 || choice == 3)
{
   System.out.println("You selected 2 or 3.");
}
else if (choice == 4)
{
    System.out.println("You selected 4.");
}
else
{
    System.out.println("Select again please.");
}
```

11. Match the conditional expression with the `if-else` statement that performs the same operation.

```
a. q = x < y ? a + b : x * 2;
b. q = x < y ? x * 2 : a + b;
c. q = x < y ? 0 : 1;
_____      if (x < y)
               q = 0;
           else
               q = 1;
```

```
____        if (x < y)
                q = a + b;
            else
                q = x * 2;
____        if (x < y)
                q = x * 2;
            else
                q = a + b;
```

12. Assume the `double` variable `number` contains the value 12345.6789. Write a statement that uses `System.out.printf` to display the number as 12345.7.

13. Assume the `double` variable `number` contains the value 12345.6789. Write a statement that uses `System.out.printf` to display the number as 12,345.68.

14. Assume the `int` variable `number` contains the value 1234567. Write a statement that uses `System.out.printf` to display the number as 1,234,567.

Short Answer

1. Explain what is meant by the phrase "conditionally executed."

2. Explain why a misplaced semicolon can cause an `if` statement to operate incorrectly.

3. Why is it good advice to indent all the statements inside a set of braces?

4. What happens when you compare two `String` objects with the `==` operator?

5. Explain the purpose of a flag variable. Of what data type should a flag variable be?

6. What risk does a programmer take when not placing a trailing `else` at the end of an `if-else-if` statement?

7. Briefly describe how the `&&` operator works.

8. Briefly describe how the `||` operator works.

9. Why are the relational operators called "relational"?

10. When does a constructor execute? What is its purpose?

Programming Challenges

MyProgrammingLab™ *Visit www.myprogramminglab.com to complete many of these Programming Challenges online and get instant feedback.*

1. Roman Numerals

Write a program that prompts the user to enter a number within the range of 1 through 10. The program should display the Roman numeral version of that number. If the number is outside the range of 1 through 10, the program should display an error message.

2. Magic Dates

The date June 10, 1960, is special because when we write it in the following format, the month times the day equals the year:

6/10/60

Write a program that asks the user to enter a month (in numeric form), a day, and a two-digit year. The program should then determine whether the month times the day is equal to the year. If so, it should display a message saying the date is magic. Otherwise, it should display a message saying the date is not magic.

3. Body Mass Index

Write a program that calculates and displays a person's body mass index (BMI). The BMI is often used to determine whether a person with a sedentary lifestyle is overweight or underweight for his or her height. A person's BMI is calculated with the following formula:

$$BMI = Weight \times 703 / Height^2$$

where *weight* is measured in pounds and *height* is measured in inches. The program should display a message indicating whether the person has optimal weight, is underweight, or is overweight. A sedentary person's weight is considered optimal if his or her BMI is between 18.5 and 25. If the BMI is less than 18.5, the person is considered underweight. If the BMI value is greater than 25, the person is considered overweight.

4. Test Scores and Grade

Write a program that has variables to hold three test scores. The program should ask the user to enter three test scores and then assign the values entered to the variables. The program should display the average of the test scores and the letter grade that is assigned for the test score average. Use the grading scheme in the following table:

Test Score Average	Letter Grade
90–100	A
80–89	B
70–79	C
60–69	D
Below 60	F

5. Mass and Weight

Scientists measure an object's mass in kilograms and its weight in Newtons. If you know the amount of mass that an object has, you can calculate its weight, in Newtons, with the following formula:

$$Weight = Mass \times 9.8$$

Write a program that asks the user to enter an object's mass, and then calculate its weight. If the object weighs more than 1,000 Newtons, display a message indicating that it is too heavy. If the object weighs less than 10 Newtons, display a message indicating that the object is too light.

6. Time Calculator

VideoNote
The Time
Calculator
Problem

Write a program that asks the user to enter a number of seconds.

- There are 60 seconds in a minute. If the number of seconds entered by the user is greater than or equal to 60, the program should display the number of minutes in that many seconds.

- There are 3,600 seconds in an hour. If the number of seconds entered by the user is greater than or equal to 3,600, the program should display the number of hours in that many seconds.
- There are 86,400 seconds in a day. If the number of seconds entered by the user is greater than or equal to 86,400, the program should display the number of days in that many seconds.

7. Sorted Names

Write a program that asks the user to enter three names, and then displays the names sorted in ascending order. For example, if the user entered "Charlie", "Leslie", and "Andy", the program would display:

Andy
Charlie
Leslie

8. Software Sales

A software company sells a package that retails for $99. Quantity discounts are given according to the following table:

Quantity	Discount
10–19	20%
20–49	30%
50–99	40%
100 or more	50%

Write a program that asks the user to enter the number of packages purchased. The program should then display the amount of the discount (if any) and the total amount of the purchase after the discount.

9. Shipping Charges

The Fast Freight Shipping Company charges the following rates:

Weight of Package	Rate per 500 Miles Shipped
2 pounds or less	$1.10
Over 2 pounds but not more than 6 pounds	$2.20
Over 6 pounds but not more than 10 pounds	$3.70
Over 10 pounds	$3.80

The shipping charges per 500 miles are not prorated. For example, if a 2-pound package is shipped 550 miles, the charges would be $2.20. Write a program that asks the user to enter the weight of a package and then displays the shipping charges.

10. Fat Gram Calculator

Write a program that asks the user to enter the number of calories and fat grams in a food item. The program should display the percentage of the calories that come from fat. One gram of fat has 9 calories; therefore:

*Calories from fat = Fat grams * 9*

The percentage of calories from fat can be calculated as follows:

Calories from fat ÷ Total calories

If the calories from fat are less than 30 percent of the total calories of the food, it should also display a message indicating the food is low in fat.

 NOTE: The number of calories from fat cannot be greater than the total number of calories in the food item. If the program determines that the number of calories from fat is greater than the number of calories in the food item, it should display an error message indicating that the input is invalid.

11. Running the Race

Write a program that asks for the names of three runners and the time, in minutes, it took each of them to finish a race. The program should display the names of the runners in the order that they finished.

12. The Speed of Sound

The following table shows the approximate speed of sound in air, water, and steel:

Medium	Speed
Air	1,100 feet per second
Water	4,900 feet per second
Steel	16,400 feet per second

Write a program that asks the user to enter "air", "water", or "steel", and the distance that a sound wave will travel in the medium. The program should then display the amount of time it will take. You can calculate the amount of time it takes sound to travel in air with the following formula:

Time = Distance / 1,100

You can calculate the amount of time it takes sound to travel in water with the following formula:

Time = Distance / 4,900

You can calculate the amount of time it takes sound to travel in steel with the following formula:

Time = Distance / 16,400

13. Internet Service Provider

An Internet service provider has three different subscription packages for its customers:

Package A: For $9.95 per month 10 hours of access are provided. Additional hours are $2.00 per hour.

Package B: For $13.95 per month 20 hours of access are provided. Additional hours are $1.00 per hour.

Package C: For $19.95 per month unlimited access is provided.

Write a program that calculates a customer's monthly bill. It should ask the user to enter the letter of the package the customer has purchased (A, B, or C) and the number of hours that were used. It should then display the total charges.

14. Internet Service Provider, Part 2

Modify the program you wrote for Programming Challenge 13 so it also calculates and displays the amount of money Package A customers would save if they purchased Package B or C, and the amount of money Package B customers would save if they purchased Package C. If there would be no savings, no message should be printed.

15. Bank Charges

A bank charges a base fee of $10 per month, plus the following check fees for a commercial checking account:

> $.10 each for less than 20 checks
> $.08 each for 20–39 checks
> $.06 each for 40–59 checks
> $.04 each for 60 or more checks

Write a program that asks for the number of checks written for the month. The program should then calculate and display the bank's service fees for the month.

16. Book Club Points

Serendipity Booksellers has a book club that awards points to its customers based on the number of books purchased each month. The points are awarded as follows:

- If a customer purchases 0 books, he or she earns 0 points.
- If a customer purchases 1 book, he or she earns 5 points.
- If a customer purchases 2 books, he or she earns 15 points.
- If a customer purchases 3 books, he or she earns 30 points.
- If a customer purchases 4 or more books, he or she earns 60 points.

Write a program that asks the user to enter the number of books that he or she has purchased this month and then displays the number of points awarded.

CHAPTER

4

Loops and Files

TOPICS

4.1 The Increment and Decrement Operators

CONCEPT: ++ and -- are operators that add and subtract one from their operands.

To *increment* a value means to increase it by one, and to *decrement* a value means to decrease it by one. Both of the following statements increment the variable number:

```
number = number + 1;
number += 1;
```

And number is decremented in both of the following statements:

```
number = number - 1;
number -= 1;
```

Java provides a set of simple unary operators designed just for incrementing and decrementing variables. The increment operator is ++ and the decrement operator is --. The following statement uses the ++ operator to increment number:

```
number++;
```

And the following statement decrements number:

```
number--;
```

> **NOTE:** The expression number++ is pronounced "number plus plus," and number--
> is pronounced "number minus minus."

The program in Code Listing 4-1 demonstrates the ++ and -- operators.

Code Listing 4-1   (IncrementDecrement.java)

```
 1  /**
 2      This program demonstrates the ++ and -- operators.
 3  */
 4
 5  public class IncrementDecrement
 6  {
 7     public static void main(String[] args)
 8     {
 9         int number = 4; // number starts out with 4
10
11         // Display the value in number.
12         System.out.println("number is " + number);
13         System.out.println("I will increment number.");
14
15         // Increment number.
16         number++;
17
18         // Display the value in number again.
19         System.out.println("Now, number is " + number);
20         System.out.println("I will decrement number.");
21
22         // Decrement number.
23         number--;
24
25         // Display the value in number once more.
26         System.out.println("Now, number is " + number);
27     }
28  }
```

Program Output

```
number is 4
I will increment number.
Now, number is 5
I will decrement number.
Now, number is 4
```

The statements in Code Listing 4-1 show the increment and decrement operators used in *postfix mode*, which means the operator is placed after the variable. The operators also work in *prefix mode*, where the operator is placed before the variable name as follows:

```
++number;

--number;
```

In both postfix and prefix mode, these operators add one to or subtract one from their operand. Code Listing 4-2 demonstrates this.

Code Listing 4-2 **(Prefix.java)**

```
 1  /**
 2      This program demonstrates the ++ and -- operators
 3      in prefix mode.
 4  */
 5
 6  public class Prefix
 7  {
 8      public static void main(String[] args)
 9      {
10          int number = 4; // number starts out with 4
11
12          // Display the value in number.
13          System.out.println("number is " + number);
14          System.out.println("I will increment number.");
15
16          // Increment number.
17          ++number;
18
19          // Display the value in number again.
20          System.out.println("Now, number is " + number);
21          System.out.println("I will decrement number.");
22
23          // Decrement number.
24          --number;
25
26          // Display the value in number once again.
27          System.out.println("Now, number is " + number);
28      }
29  }
```

Program Output

```
number is 4
I will increment number.
Now, number is 5
I will decrement number.
Now, number is 4
```

The Difference between Postfix and Prefix Modes

In Code Listings 4-1 and 4-2, the statements number++ and ++number increment the variable number, while the statements number-- and --number decrement the variable number. In these simple statements, it doesn't matter whether the operator is used in postfix or prefix mode. The difference is important, however, when these operators are used in statements that do more than just increment or decrement. For example, look at the following code:

```
number = 4;
System.out.println(number++);
```

The statement that calls the println method does two things: (1) calls println to display the value of number, and (2) increments number. But which happens first? The println method will display a different value if number is incremented first than if number is incremented last. The answer depends upon the mode of the increment operator.

Postfix mode causes the increment to happen after the value of the variable is used in the expression. In the previously shown statement, the println method will display 4 and then number will be incremented to 5. Prefix mode, however, causes the increment to happen first. Here is an example:

```
number = 4;
System.out.println(++number);
```

In these statements, number is incremented to 5, then println will display the value in number (which is 5). For another example, look at the following code:

```
int x = 1, y;
y = x++;                 // Postfix increment
```

The first statement declares the variable x (initialized with the value 1) and the variable y. The second statement does the following:

- It assigns the value of x to the variable y.
- The variable x is incremented.

The value that will be stored in y depends on when the increment takes place. Because the ++ operator is used in postfix mode, it acts after the assignment takes place. So, this code will store 1 in y. After the code has executed, x will contain 2. Let's look at the same code, but with the ++ operator used in prefix mode as follows:

```
int x = 1, y;
y = ++x;                 // Prefix increment
```

The first statement declares the variable x (initialized with the value 1) and the variable y. In the second statement, the ++ operator is used in prefix mode, so it acts on the variable before the assignment takes place. So, this code will store 2 in y. After the code has executed, x will also contain 2.

 **Checkpoint**

MyProgrammingLab™ *www.myprogramminglab.com*

4.1   What will the following program segments display?

a)
```java
x = 2;
y = x++;
System.out.println(y);
```

b)
```java
x = 2;
System.out.println(x++);
```

c)
```java
x = 2;
System.out.println(--x);
```

d)
```java
x = 8;
y = x--;
System.out.println(y);
```

4.2   The while Loop

CONCEPT: A loop is part of a program that repeats.

In Chapter 3, you were introduced to the concept of control structures, which direct the flow of a program. A *loop* is a control structure that causes a statement or group of statements to repeat. Java has three looping control structures: the while loop, the do-while loop, and the for loop. The difference among each of these is how they control the repetition. In this section we will focus on the while loop.

VideoNote

The while
Loop

The while loop has two important parts: (1) a boolean expression that is tested for a true or false value, and (2) a statement or block of statements that is repeated as long as the expression is true. Figure 4-1 shows the logic of a while loop.

Figure 4-1   Logic of a while loop

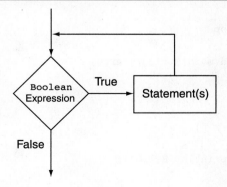

Here is the general format of the while loop:

```java
while (BooleanExpression)
    Statement;
```

In the general format, *BooleanExpression* is any valid boolean expression, and *Statement* is any valid Java statement. The first line shown in the format is sometimes called the *loop header*. It consists of the key word while followed by the *BooleanExpression* enclosed in parentheses.

Here's how the loop works: The *BooleanExpression* is tested, and if it is true, the *Statement* is executed. Then, the *BooleanExpression* is tested again. If it is true, the *Statement* is executed. This cycle repeats until the *BooleanExpression* is false.

The statement that is repeated is known as the *body* of the loop. It is also considered a conditionally executed statement, because it is only executed under the condition that the *BooleanExpression* is true.

Notice there is no semicolon at the end of the loop header. Like the if statement, the while loop is not complete without the conditionally executed statement that follows it.

If you wish the while loop to repeat a block of statements, the format is as follows:

```
while (BooleanExpression)
{
    Statement;
    Statement;
    // Place as many statements here
    // as necessary.
}
```

The while loop works like an if statement that executes over and over. As long as the expression in the parentheses is true, the conditionally executed statement or block will repeat. The program in Code Listing 4-3 uses the while loop to print "Hello" five times.

Code Listing 4-3 **(WhileLoop.java)**

```
1   /**
2       This program demonstrates the while loop.
3   */
4
5   public class WhileLoop
6   {
7       public static void main(String[] args)
8       {
9           int number = 1;
10
11          while (number <= 5)
12          {
13              System.out.println("Hello");
14              number++;
15          }
```

```
16
17            System.out.println("That's all!");
18      }
19   }
```

Program Output

```
Hello
Hello
Hello
Hello
Hello
That's all!
```

Let's take a closer look at this program. An integer variable, number, is declared and initialized with the value 1. The while loop begins with the following statement:

```
while (number <= 5)
```

This statement tests the variable number to determine whether it is less than or equal to 5. If it is, then the statements in the body of the loop are executed as follows:

```
System.out.println("Hello");
number++;
```

The first statement in the body of the loop prints the word "Hello". The second statement uses the increment operator to add one to number. This is the last statement in the body of the loop, so after it executes, the loop starts over. It tests the boolean expression again, and if it is true, the statements in the body of the loop are executed. This cycle repeats until the boolean expression number <= 5 is false, as illustrated in Figure 4-2.

Figure 4-2   The while loop

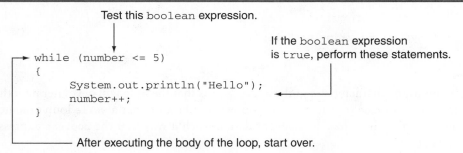

Each repetition of a loop is known as an *iteration*. This loop will perform five iterations because the variable number is initialized with the value 1, and it is incremented each time the body of the loop is executed. When the expression number <= 5 is tested and found to be false, the loop will terminate and the program will resume execution at the statement that immediately follows the loop. Figure 4-3 shows the logic of this loop.

In this example, the number variable is referred to as the *loop control variable* because it controls the number of times that the loop iterates.

Figure 4-3 Logic of the example while loop

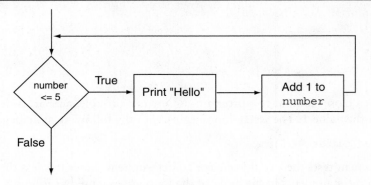

The while Loop Is a Pretest Loop

The while loop is known as a *pretest* loop, which means it tests its expression before each iteration. Notice the variable declaration of number in Code Listing 4-3:

```
int number = 1;
```

The number variable is initialized with the value 1. If number had been initialized with a value that is greater than 5, as shown in the following program segment, the loop would never execute:

```
int number = 6;
while (number <= 5)
{
    System.out.println("Hello");
    number++;
}
```

An important characteristic of the while loop is that the loop will never iterate if the boolean expression is false to start with. If you want to be sure that a while loop executes the first time, you must initialize the relevant data in such a way that the boolean expression starts out as true.

Infinite Loops

In all but rare cases, loops must contain a way to terminate within themselves. This means that something inside the loop must eventually make the boolean expression false. The loop in Code Listing 4-3 stops when the expression number <= 5 is false.

If a loop does not have a way of stopping, it is called an *infinite loop* as it continues to repeat until the program is interrupted. Here is an example of an infinite loop:

```
int number = 1;
while (number <= 5)
{
    System.out.println("Hello");
}
```

This is an infinite loop because it does not contain a statement that changes the value of the number variable. Each time the boolean expression is tested, number will contain the value 1.

It's also possible to create an infinite loop by accidentally placing a semicolon after the first line of the while loop. Here is an example:

```
int number = 1;
while (number <= 5); // This semicolon is an ERROR!
{
    System.out.println("Hello");
    number++;
}
```

The semicolon at the end of the first line is assumed to be a null statement and disconnects the while statement from the block that comes after it. To the compiler, this loop looks like the following:

```
while (number <= 5);
```

This while loop will forever execute the null statement, which does nothing. The program will appear to have "gone into space" because there is nothing to display screen output or show activity.

Don't Forget the Braces with a Block of Statements

If you are using a block of statements, don't forget to enclose all of the statements in a set of braces. If the braces are accidentally left out, the while statement conditionally executes only the very next statement. For example, look at the following code:

```
int number = 1;
// This loop is missing its braces!
while (number <= 5)
    System.out.println("Hello");
    number++;
```

In this code the number++ statement is not in the body of the loop. Because the braces are missing, the while statement executes only the statement that immediately follows it. This loop will execute infinitely because there is no code in its body that changes the number variable.

Programming Style and the `while` Loop

It's possible to create loops that look like the following:

```java
while (number <= 5) { System.out.println("Hello"); number++; }
```

Avoid this style of programming. The programming style you should use with the `while` loop is similar to that of the `if` statement as follows:

- If there is only one statement repeated by the loop, it should appear on the line after the `while` statement and be indented one additional level. The statement can optionally appear inside a set of braces.
- If the loop repeats a block, each line inside the braces should be indented.

This programming style should visually set the body of the loop apart from the surrounding code. In general, you'll find a similar style being used with the other types of loops presented in this chapter.

In the Spotlight:

Designing a Program with a `while` Loop

A project currently underway at Chemical Labs, Inc., requires that a substance be continually heated in a vat. A technician must check the substance's temperature every 15 minutes. If the substance's temperature does not exceed 102.5 degrees Celsius, then the technician does nothing. However, if the temperature is greater than 102.5 degrees Celsius, the technician must turn down the vat's thermostat, wait 5 minutes, and check the temperature again. The technician repeats these steps until the temperature does not exceed 102.5 degrees Celsius. The director of engineering has asked you to write a program that guides the technician through this process.

Here is the algorithm:

1. *Prompt the user to enter the substance's temperature.*
2. *Repeat the following steps as long as the temperature is greater than 102.5 degrees Celsius:*
   (a) *Tell the technician to turn down the thermostat, wait 5 minutes, and check the temperature again.*
   (b) *Prompt the user to enter the substance's temperature.*
3. *After the loop finishes, tell the technician that the temperature is acceptable and to check it again in 15 minutes.*

After reviewing this algorithm, you realize that Steps 2(a) and 2(b) should not be performed if the test condition (temperature is greater than 102.5) is `false` to begin with. The `while` loop will work well in this situation, because it will not execute even once if its condition is `false`. Code Listing 4-4 shows the program.

Code Listing 4-4   (`CheckTemperature.java`)

```java
1  import java.util.Scanner;
2
```

```java
 3   /**
 4       This program assists a technician in the process
 5       of checking a substance's temperature.
 6   */
 7   public class CheckTemperature
 8   {
 9       public static void main(String[] args)
10       {
11           final double MAX_TEMP = 102.5;      // Maximum temperature
12           double temperature;                 // To hold the temperature
13
14           // Create a Scanner object for keyboard input.
15           Scanner keyboard = new Scanner(System.in);
16
17           // Get the current temperature.
18           System.out.print("Enter the substance's Celsius temperature: ");
19           temperature = keyboard.nextDouble();
20
21           // As long as necessary, instruct the technician
22           // to adjust the temperature.
23           while (temperature > MAX_TEMP)
24           {
25               System.out.println("The temperature is too high. Turn the");
26               System.out.println("thermostat down and wait 5 minutes.");
27               System.out.println("Then, take the Celsius temperature again");
28               System.out.print("and enter it here: ");
29               temperature = keyboard.nextDouble();
30           }
31
32           // Remind the technician to check the temperature
33           // again in 15 minutes.
34           System.out.println("The temperature is acceptable.");
35           System.out.println("Check it again in 15 minutes.");
36       }
37   }
```

Program Output with Example Input Shown in Bold

Enter the substance's Celsius temperature: **104.7 [Enter]**
The temperature is too high. Turn the
thermostat down and wait 5 minutes.
Then, take the Celsius temperature again
and enter it here: **103.2 [Enter]**
The temperature is too high. Turn the
thermostat down and wait 5 minutes.
Then, take the Celsius temperature again
and enter it here: **102.1 [Enter]**
The temperature is acceptable.
Check it again in 15 minutes.

Checkpoint

MyProgrammingLab™ *www.myprogramminglab.com*

4.2 How many times will "Hello World" be printed in the following program segment?

```
int count = 10;
while (count < 1)
{
    System.out.println("Hello World");
    count++;
}
```

4.3 How many times will "I love Java programming!" be printed in the following program segment?

```
int count = 0;
while (count < 10)
    System.out.println("I love Java programming!);
```

4.3 Using the while Loop for Input Validation

CONCEPT: The while loop can be used to create input routines that repeat until acceptable data is entered.

Perhaps the most famous saying of the computer industry is "garbage in, garbage out." The integrity of a program's output is only as good as its input, so you should try to make sure garbage does not go into your programs. *Input validation* is the process of inspecting data given to a program by the user and determining whether it is valid. A good program should give clear instructions about the kind of input that is acceptable, and not assume the user has followed those instructions.

The while loop is especially useful for validating input. If an invalid value is entered, a loop can require that the user reenter it as many times as necessary. For example, the following loop asks for a number in the range of 1 through 100:

```
input = JOptionPane.showInputDialog("Enter a number " +
                    "in the range of 1 through 100.");
number = Integer.parseInt(input);
// Validate the input.
while (number < 1 || number > 100)
{
    input = JOptionPane.showInputDialog("Invalid input. " +
                    "Enter a number in the range of " +
                    "1 through 100.");
    number = Integer.parseInt(input);
}
```

This code first allows the user to enter a number. This takes place just before the loop. If the input is valid, the loop will not execute. If the input is invalid, however, the loop will display an error message and require the user to enter another number. The loop will continue to execute until the user enters a valid number. The general logic of performing input validation is shown in Figure 4-4.

Figure 4-4   Input validation logic

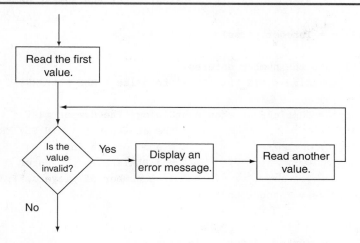

The read operation that takes place just before the loop is called a *priming read*. It provides the first value for the loop to test. Subsequent values are obtained by the loop.

The program in Code Listing 4-5 calculates the number of soccer teams a youth league may create, based on a given number of players and a maximum number of players per team. The program uses while loops (in lines 28 through 36 and lines 44 through 49) to validate the user's input. Figure 4-5 shows an example of interaction with the program.

Code Listing 4-5   **(SoccerTeams.java)**

```java
 1  import javax.swing.JOptionPane;
 2
 3  /**
 4     This program calculates the number of soccer teams
 5     that a youth league may create from the number of
 6     available players. Input validation is demonstrated
 7     with while loops.
 8  */
 9
10  public class SoccerTeams
11  {
12     public static void main(String[] args)
13     {
14        final int MIN_PLAYERS = 9;    // Minimum players per team
15        final int MAX_PLAYERS = 15;   // Maximum players per team
16        int players;                  // Number of available players
17        int teamSize;                 // Number of players per team
18        int teams;                    // Number of teams
```

```
19        int leftOver;                    // Number of leftover players
20        String input;                    // To hold the user input
21
22        // Get the number of players per team.
23        input = JOptionPane.showInputDialog("Enter the number of " +
24                                            "players per team.");
25        teamSize = Integer.parseInt(input);
26
27        // Validate the number entered.
28        while (teamSize < MIN_PLAYERS || teamSize > MAX_PLAYERS)
29        {
30           input = JOptionPane.showInputDialog("The number must " +
31                                    "be at least " + MIN_PLAYERS +
32                                    " and no more than " +
33                                    MAX_PLAYERS + ".\n Enter " +
34                                    "the number of players.");
35           teamSize = Integer.parseInt(input);
36        }
37
38        // Get the number of available players.
39        input = JOptionPane.showInputDialog("Enter the available " +
40                                            "number of players.");
41        players = Integer.parseInt(input);
42
43        // Validate the number entered.
44        while (players < 0)
45        {
46           input = JOptionPane.showInputDialog("Enter 0 or " +
47                                            "greater.");
48           players = Integer.parseInt(input);
49        }
50
51        // Calculate the number of teams.
52        teams = players / teamSize;
53
54        // Calculate the number of leftover players.
55        leftOver = players % teamSize;
56
57        // Display the results.
58        JOptionPane.showMessageDialog(null, "There will be " +
59                                    teams + " teams with " +
60                                    leftOver +
61                                    " players left over.");
62        System.exit(0);
63     }
64  }
```

Figure 4-5   Interaction with the SoccerTeams program

This input dialog box appears first. The user enters 4 (an invalid value) and clicks the OK button.

> **Input**
>
> **?**   Enter the number of players per team.
>
> `4`
>
> [OK]   [Cancel]

This input dialog box appears next. The user enters 12 and clicks the OK button.

> **Input**
>
> **?**   The number must be at least 9 and no more than 15.
>   Enter the number of players.
>
> `12`
>
> [OK]   [Cancel]

This input dialog box appears next. The user enters −142 (an invalid value) and clicks the OK button.

> **Input**
>
> **?**   Enter the available number of players.
>
> `-142`
>
> [OK]   [Cancel]

This input dialog box appears next. The user enters 142 and clicks the OK button.

> **Input**
>
> **?**   Enter 0 or greater.
>
> `142`
>
> [OK]   [Cancel]

This message dialog box appears next.

> **Message**
>
> **(i)**   There will be 11 teams with 10 players left over.
>
> [OK]

Checkpoint

MyProgrammingLab™ *www.myprogramminglab.com*

4.4   Write an input validation loop that asks the user to enter a number in the range of 10 through 24.

4.5   Write an input validation loop that asks the user to enter 'Y', 'y', 'N', or 'n'.

4.6   Write an input validation loop that asks the user to enter "Yes" or "No".

4.4 The do-while Loop

CONCEPT: The do-while loop is a posttest loop, which means its boolean expression is tested after each iteration.

The do-while loop looks something like an inverted while loop. Here is the do-while loop's format when the body of the loop contains only a single statement:

```
do
    Statement;
while (BooleanExpression);
```

Here is the format of the do-while loop when the body of the loop contains multiple statements:

```
do
{
    Statement;
    Statement;
    // Place as many statements here as necessary.
} while (BooleanExpression);
```

NOTE: The do-while loop must be terminated with a semicolon.

The do-while loop is a *posttest* loop. This means it does not test its boolean expression until it has completed an iteration. As a result, the do-while loop always performs at least one iteration, even if the boolean expression is false to begin with. This differs from the behavior of a while loop, which you will recall is a pretest loop. For example, in the following while loop the println statement will not execute at all:

```
int x = 1;
while (x < 0)
    System.out.println(x);
```

But the println statement in the following do-while loop will execute once because the do-while loop does not evaluate the expression x < 0 until the end of the iteration:

```
int x = 1;
do
    System.out.println(x);
while (x < 0);
```

Figure 4-6 illustrates the logic of the do-while loop.

You should use the do-while loop when you want to make sure the loop executes at least once. For example, the program in Code Listing 4-6 averages a series of three test scores for a student. After the average is displayed, it asks the user whether he or she wants to average another set of test scores. The program repeats as long as the user enters Y for yes.

Figure 4-6   Logic of the do-while loop

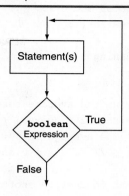

Code Listing 4-6   (`TestAverage1.java`)

```java
 1  import java.util.Scanner; // Needed for the Scanner class
 2
 3  /**
 4     This program demonstrates a user controlled loop.
 5  */
 6
 7  public class TestAverage1
 8  {
 9     public static void main(String[] args)
10     {
11        int score1, score2, score3;      // Three test scores
12        double average;                  // Average test score
13        char repeat;                     // To hold 'y' or 'n'
14        String input;                    // To hold input
15
16        System.out.println("This program calculates the " +
17                           "average of three test scores.");
18
19        // Create a Scanner object for keyboard input.
20        Scanner keyboard = new Scanner(System.in);
21
22        // Get as many sets of test scores as the user wants.
23        do
24        {
25           // Get the first test score in this set.
26           System.out.print("Enter score #1: ");
27           score1 = keyboard.nextInt();
28
29           // Get the second test score in this set.
30           System.out.print("Enter score #2: ");
31           score2 = keyboard.nextInt();
32
```

```
33              // Get the third test score in this set.
34              System.out.print("Enter score #3: ");
35              score3 = keyboard.nextInt();
36
37              // Consume the remaining newline.
38              keyboard.nextLine();
39
40              // Calculate and print the average test score.
41              average = (score1 + score2 + score3) / 3.0;
42              System.out.println("The average is " + average);
43              System.out.println(); // Prints a blank line
44
45              // Does the user want to average another set?
46              System.out.println("Would you like to average " +
47                                 "another set of test scores?");
48              System.out.print("Enter Y for yes or N for no: ");
49              input = keyboard.nextLine();     // Read a line.
50              repeat = input.charAt(0);        // Get the first char.
51
52        } while (repeat == 'Y' || repeat == 'y');
53    }
54 }
```

Program Output with Example Input Shown in Bold

```
This program calculates the average of three test scores.
Enter score #1: 89 [Enter]
Enter score #2: 90 [Enter]
Enter score #3: 97 [Enter]
The average is 92.0

Would you like to average another set of test scores?
Enter Y for yes or N for no: y [Enter]
Enter score #1: 78 [Enter]
Enter score #2: 65 [Enter]
Enter score #3: 88 [Enter]
The average is 77.0

Would you like to average another set of test scores?
Enter Y for yes or N for no: n [Enter]
```

When this program was written, the programmer had no way of knowing the number of times the loop would iterate. This is because the loop asks the user whether he or she wants to repeat the process. This type of loop is known as a *user controlled loop,* because it allows the user to decide the number of iterations.

4.5 The for Loop

CONCEPT: The for loop is ideal for performing a known number of iterations.

In general, there are two categories of loops: conditional loops and count-controlled loops. A *conditional loop* executes as long as a particular condition exists. For example, an input validation loop executes as long as the input value is invalid. When you write a conditional loop, you have no way of knowing the number of times it will iterate.

Sometimes you do know the exact number of iterations that a loop must perform. A loop that repeats a specific number of times is known as a *count-controlled loop*. For example, if a loop asks the user to enter the sales amounts for each month in the year, it will iterate 12 times. In essence, the loop counts to 12 and asks the user to enter a sales amount each time it makes a count.

A count-controlled loop must possess three elements:

1. It must initialize a control variable to a starting value.
2. It must test the control variable by comparing it to a maximum value. When the control variable reaches its maximum value, the loop terminates.
3. It must update the control variable during each iteration. This is usually done by incrementing the variable.

In Java, the for loop is ideal for writing count-controlled loops. It is specifically designed to initialize, test, and update a loop control variable. Here is the format of the for loop when used to repeat a single statement:

```
for (Initialization; Test; Update)
    Statement;
```

The format of the for loop when used to repeat a block is as follows:

```
for (Initialization; Test; Update)
{
    Statement;
    Statement;
    // Place as many statements here as necessary.
}
```

The first line of the for loop is known as the *loop header*. After the key word for, there are three expressions inside the parentheses, separated by semicolons. (Notice there is not a semicolon after the third expression.) The first expression is the *initialization expression*. It is normally used to initialize a control variable to its starting value. This is the first action performed by the loop, and it is done only once. The second expression is the *test expression*. This is a boolean expression that controls the execution of the loop. As long as this expression is true, the body of the for loop will repeat. The for loop is a pretest loop, so it evaluates the test expression before each iteration. The third expression is the *update expression*. It executes at the end of each iteration. Typically, this is a statement that increments the loop's control variable.

Here is an example of a simple for loop that prints "Hello" five times:

```
for (count = 1; count <= 5; count++)
    System.out.println("Hello");
```

In this loop, the initialization expression is count = 1, the test expression is count <= 5, and the update expression is count++. The body of the loop has one statement, which is the println statement. Figure 4-7 illustrates the sequence of events that takes place during the loop's execution. Notice that Steps 2 through 4 are repeated as long as the test expression is true.

Figure 4-7   Sequence of events in the for loop

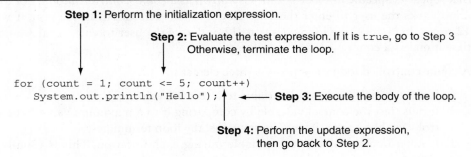

Figure 4-8 shows the loop's logic in the form of a flowchart.

Figure 4-8   Logic of the for loop

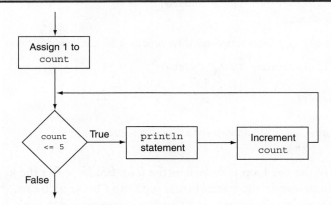

Notice how the control variable, count, is used to control the number of times that the loop iterates. During the execution of the loop, this variable takes on the values 1 through 5, and when the test expression count <= 5 is false, the loop terminates. Because this variable keeps a count of the number of iterations, it is often called a *counter variable*.

Also notice that in this example the count variable is used only in the loop header, to control the number of loop iterations. It is not used for any other purpose. It is also possible to use the control variable within the body of the loop. For example, look at the following code:

```
for (number = 1; number <= 10; number++)
    System.out.print(number + " ");
```

The control variable in this loop is `number`. In addition to controlling the number of iterations, it is also used in the body of the loop. This loop will produce the following output:

```
1 2 3 4 5 6 7 8 9 10
```

As you can see, the loop displays the contents of the `number` variable during each iteration. The program in Code Listing 4-7 shows another example of a `for` loop that uses its control variable within the body of the loop. This program displays a table showing the numbers 1 through 10 and their squares.

Code Listing 4-7   (`Squares.java`)

```
 1  /**
 2      This program demonstrates the for loop.
 3  */
 4
 5  public class Squares
 6  {
 7     public static void main(String[] args)
 8     {
 9        int number; // Loop control variable
10
11        System.out.println("Number Number Squared");
12        System.out.println("-----------------------");
13
14        for (number = 1; number <= 10; number++)
15        {
16           System.out.println(number + "\t\t" +
17                              number * number);
18        }
19     }
20  }
```

Program Output

```
Number      Number Squared
--------------------------------
1                 1
2                 4
3                 9
4                 16
5                 25
6                 36
7                 49
8                 64
9                 81
10                100
```

Figure 4-9 illustrates the sequence of events performed by this for loop.

Figure 4-9 Sequence of events with the for loop in Code Listing 4-7

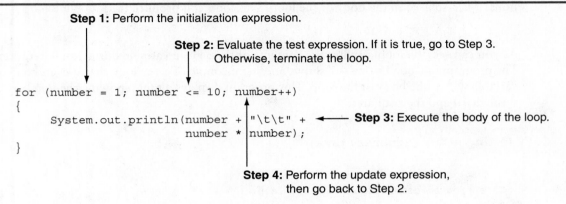

Figure 4-10 shows the logic of the loop.

Figure 4-10 Logic of the for loop in Code Listing 4-7

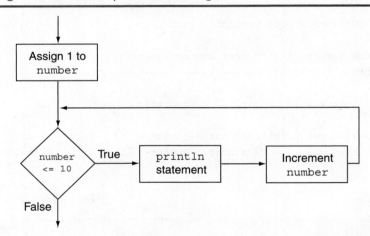

The for Loop Is a Pretest Loop

Because the for loop tests its boolean expression before it performs an iteration, it is a pretest loop. It is possible to write a for loop in such a way that it will never iterate. Here is an example:

```
for (count = 11; count <= 10; count++)
    System.out.println("Hello");
```

Because the variable count is initialized to a value that makes the boolean expression false from the beginning, this loop terminates as soon as it begins.

Avoid Modifying the Control Variable in the Body of the `for` Loop

Be careful not to place a statement that modifies the control variable in the body of the `for` loop. All modifications of the control variable should take place in the update expression, which is automatically executed at the end of each iteration. If a statement in the body of the loop also modifies the control variable, the loop probably will not terminate when you expect it to. The following loop, for example, increments x twice for each iteration:

```
for (x = 1; x <= 10; x++)
{
   System.out.println(x);
   x++; // Wrong!
}
```

Other Forms of the Update Expression

You are not limited to using increment statements in the update expression. Here is a loop that displays all the even numbers from 2 through 100 by adding 2 to its counter:

```
for (number = 2; number <= 100; number += 2)
   System.out.println(number);
```

And here is a loop that counts backward from 10 to 0:

```
for (number = 10; number >= 0; number--)
   System.out.println(number);
```

Declaring a Variable in the `for` Loop's Initialization Expression

Not only may the control variable be initialized in the initialization expression, but also it may be declared there. The following code shows an example. The following is a modified version of the loop in Code Listing 4-7:

```
for (int number = 1; number <= 10; number++)
{
   System.out.println(number + "\t\t" +
                       number * number);
}
```

In this loop, the number variable is both declared and initialized in the initialization expression. If the control variable is used only in the loop, it makes sense to declare it in the loop header. This makes the variable's purpose clearer.

When a variable is declared in the initialization expression of a `for` loop, the scope of the variable is limited to the loop. This means you cannot access the variable in statements outside the loop. For example, the following program segment will not compile because the last `println` statement cannot access the variable count:

```
        for (int count = 1; count <= 10; count++)
            System.out.println(count);
        System.out.println("count is now " + count); // ERROR!
```

Creating a User Controlled for Loop

Sometimes you want the user to determine the maximum value of the control variable in a for loop, and therefore determine the number of times the loop iterates. For example, look at the program in Code Listing 4-8. It is a modification of Code Listing 4-7. Instead of displaying the numbers 1 through 10 and their squares, this program allows the user to enter the maximum value to display.

Code Listing 4-8   (UserSquares.java)

```java
1   import java.util.Scanner;        // Needed for the Scanner class
2
3   /**
4       This program demonstrates a user controlled for loop.
5   */
6
7   public class UserSquares
8   {
9       public static void main(String[] args)
10      {
11          int number;       // Loop control variable
12          int maxValue;     // Maximum value to display
13
14          System.out.println("I will display a table of " +
15                              "numbers and their squares.");
16
17          // Create a Scanner object for keyboard input.
18          Scanner keyboard = new Scanner(System.in);
19
20          // Get the maximum value to display.
21          System.out.print("How high should I go? ");
22          maxValue = keyboard.nextInt();
23
24          // Display the table.
25          System.out.println("Number Number Squared");
26          System.out.println("-----------------------");
27          for (number = 1; number <= maxValue; number++)
28          {
29              System.out.println(number + "\t\t" +
30                                  number * number);
31          }
32      }
33  }
```

Program Output with Example Input Shown in Bold

```
I will display a table of numbers and their squares.
How high should I go? 7 [Enter]
Number        Number Squared
----------------------------------
1                1
2                4
3                9
4                16
5                25
6                36
7                49
```

In lines 21 and 22, which are before the loop, this program asks the user to enter the highest value to display. This value is stored in the maxValue variable as follows:

```
System.out.print("How high should I go? ");
maxValue = keyboard.nextInt();
```

In line 27, the for loop's test expression uses the value in the maxValue variable as the upper limit for the control variable as follows:

```
for (number = 1; number <= maxValue; number++)
```

In this loop, the number variable takes on the values 1 through maxValue, and then the loop terminates.

Using Multiple Statements in the Initialization and Update Expressions

It is possible to execute more than one statement in the initialization expression and the update expression. When using multiple statements in either of these expressions, simply separate the statements with commas. For example, look at the loop in the following code, which has two statements in the initialization expression:

```
int x, y;
for (x = 1, y = 1; x <= 5; x++)
{
    System.out.println(x + " plus " + y +
                    " equals " + (x + y));
}
```

This loop's initialization expression is as follows:

```
x = 1, y = 1
```

This initializes two variables, x and y. The output produced by this loop is as follows:

```
1 plus 1 equals 2
2 plus 1 equals 3
3 plus 1 equals 4
```

```
4 plus 1 equals 5
5 plus 1 equals 6
```

We can further modify the loop to execute two statements in the update expression. Here is an example:

```
int x, y;
for (x = 1, y = 1; x <= 5; x++, y++)
{
    System.out.println(x + " plus " + y +
                       " equals " + (x + y));
}
```

The loop's update expression is as follows:

```
x++, y++
```

This update expression increments both the x and y variables. The output produced by this loop is as follows:

```
1 plus 1 equals 2
2 plus 2 equals 4
3 plus 3 equals 6
4 plus 4 equals 8
5 plus 5 equals 10
```

Connecting multiple statements with commas works well in the initialization and update expressions, but don't try to connect multiple boolean expressions this way in the test expression. If you wish to combine multiple boolean expressions in the test expression, you must use the && or || operators.

In the Spotlight:

Designing a Count-Controlled for Loop

Your friend Amanda just inherited a European sports car from her uncle. Amanda lives in the United States, and she is afraid she will get a speeding ticket because the car's speedometer indicates kilometers per hour (KPH). She has asked you to write a program that displays a table of speeds in kilometers per hour with their values converted to miles per hour (MPH). The formula for converting KPH to MPH is

$$MPH = KPH * 0.6214$$

In the formula, *MPH* is the speed in miles per hour and *KPH* is the speed in kilometers per hour.

The table that your program displays should show speeds from 60 kilometers per hour through 130 kilometers per hour, in increments of 10, along with their values converted to miles per hour. The table should look something like this:

KPH	MPH
60	37.3
70	43.5
80	49.7
etc.	
130	80.8

After thinking about this table of values, you decide that you will write a for loop that uses a counter variable to hold the KPH speeds. The counter's starting value will be 60, its ending value will be 130, and you will add 10 to the counter variable after each iteration. Inside the loop you will use the counter variable to calculate a speed in MPH. Code Listing 4-9 shows the code.

Code Listing 4-9   (SpeedConverter.java)

```
 1  /**
 2      This program displays a table of speeds in
 3      kph converted to mph.
 4  */
 5
 6  public class SpeedConverter
 7  {
 8     public static void main(String[] args)
 9     {
10        // Constants
11        final int STARTING_KPH = 60;        // Starting speed
12        final int MAX_KPH = 130;            // Maximum speed
13        final int INCREMENT = 10;           // Speed increment
14
15        // Variables
16        int kph;        // To hold the speed in kph
17        double mph;     // To hold the speed in mph
18
19        // Display the table headings.
20        System.out.println("KPH\t\tMPH");
21        System.out.println("-------------------");
22
23        // Display the speeds.
24        for (kph = STARTING_KPH; kph <= MAX_KPH; kph += INCREMENT)
25        {
26           // Calculate the mph.
27           mph = kph * 0.6214;
28
29           // Display the speeds in kph and mph.
30           System.out.printf("%d\t\t%.1f\n", kph, mph);
31        }
32     }
33  }
```

Program Output

```
KPH     MPH
--------------------
60      37.3
70      43.5
80      49.7
90      55.9
100     62.1
110     68.4
120     74.6
130     80.8
```

Checkpoint

MyProgrammingLab™   *www.myprogramminglab.com*

4.7   Name the three expressions that appear inside the parentheses in the for loop's header.

4.8   You want to write a for loop that displays "I love to program" 50 times. Assume that you will use a control variable named count.
   a)   What initialization expression will you use?
   b)   What test expression will you use?
   c)   What update expression will you use?
   d)   Write the loop.

4.9   What will the following program segments display?
   a)   ```
for (int count = 0; count < 6; count++)
    System.out.println(count + count);
```
   b)   ```
for (int value = -5; value < 5; value++)
    System.out.println(value);
```
   c)   ```
int x;
for (x = 5; x <= 14; x += 3)
    System.out.println(x);
System.out.println(x);
```

4.10   Write a for loop that displays your name 10 times.

4.11   Write a for loop that displays all of the odd numbers, 1 through 49.

4.12   Write a for loop that displays every fifth number, zero through 100.

## 4.6    Running Totals and Sentinel Values

**CONCEPT:** A running total is a sum of numbers that accumulates with each iteration of a loop. The variable used to keep the running total is called an accumulator. A sentinel is a value that signals when the end of a list of values has been reached.

Many programming tasks require you to calculate the total of a series of numbers. For example, suppose you are writing a program that calculates a business's total sales for a week. The program would read the sales for each day as input and calculate the total of those numbers.
```

Programs that calculate the total of a series of numbers typically use two elements:

- A loop that reads each number in the series.
- A variable that accumulates the total of the numbers as they are read.

The variable used to accumulate the total of the numbers is called an *accumulator*. It is often said that the loop keeps a *running total* because it accumulates the total as it reads each number in the series. Figure 4-11 shows the general logic of a loop that calculates a running total.

Figure 4-11   Logic for calculating a running total

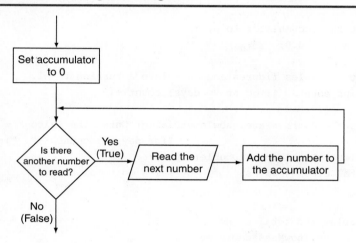

When the loop finishes, the accumulator will contain the total of the numbers that were read by the loop. Notice that the first step in the flowchart is to set the accumulator variable to 0. This is a critical step. Each time the loop reads a number, it adds it to the accumulator. If the accumulator starts with any value other than 0, it will not contain the correct total when the loop finishes.

Let's look at a program that calculates a running total. Code Listing 4-10 calculates a company's total sales over a period of time by taking daily sales figures as input and calculating a running total of them as they are gathered. Figure 4-12 shows an example of interaction with the program.

Code Listing 4-10   (**TotalSales.java**)

```
1 import javax.swing.JOptionPane;
2
3 /**
4    This program calculates a running total.
5 */
6
7 public class TotalSales
8 {
9    public static void main(String[] args)
```

```
10      {
11          int days;            // The number of days
12          double sales;        // A day's sales figure
13          double totalSales;   // Accumulator
14          String input;        // To hold the user's input
15
16          // Get the number of days.
17          input = JOptionPane.showInputDialog("For how many days " +
18                                  "do you have sales figures?");
19          days = Integer.parseInt(input);
20
21          // Set the accumulator to 0.
22          totalSales = 0.0;
23
24          // Get the sales figures and calculate a running total.
25          for (int count = 1; count <= days; count++)
26          {
27              input = JOptionPane.showInputDialog("Enter the sales " +
28                                  "for day " + count + ": ");
29              sales = Double.parseDouble(input);
30              totalSales += sales;    // Add sales to totalSales.
31          }
32
33          // Display the total sales.
34          JOptionPane.showMessageDialog(null,
35              String.format("The total sales are $%,.2f", totalSales));
36
37          System.exit(0);
38      }
39 }
```

Figure 4-12 Interaction with the TotalSales program

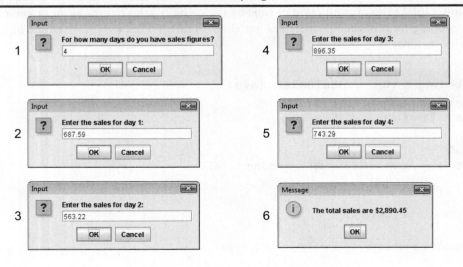

Let's take a closer look at this program. In lines 17 and 18 the user is asked to enter the number of days for which he or she has sales figures. The number is read from an input dialog box and assigned to the days variable. Then, in line 22 the totalSales variable is assigned 0.0. In general programming terms, the totalSales variable is referred to as an accumulator. An *accumulator* is a variable that is initialized with a starting value, which is usually zero, and then accumulates a sum of numbers by having the numbers added to it. As you will see, it is critical that the accumulator is set to zero before values are added to it.

Next, the for loop in lines 25 through 31 executes. During each iteration of the loop, the user enters the amount of sales for a specific day, which are assigned to the sales variable. This is done in lines 27 through 29. Then, in line 30 the contents of sales is added to the existing value in the totalSales variable. (Note that line 30 does not assign sales to totalSales, but adds sales to totalSales. Put another way, this line increases totalSales by the amount in sales.)

Because totalSales was initially assigned 0.0, after the first iteration of the loop, totalSales will be set to the same value as sales. After each subsequent iteration, totalSales will be increased by the amount in sales. After the loop has finished, totalSales will contain the total of all the daily sales figures entered. Now it should be clear why we assigned 0.0 to totalSales before the loop executed. If totalSales started at any other value, the total would be incorrect.

Using a Sentinel Value

The program in Code Listing 4-10 requires the user to know in advance the number of days for which he or she has sales figures. Sometimes the user has a very long list of input values, and doesn't know the exact number of items. In other cases, the user might be entering values from several lists and it is impractical to require that every item in every list is counted.

A technique that can be used in these situations is to ask the user to enter a sentinel value at the end of the list. A *sentinel value* is a special value that cannot be mistaken as a member of the list, and signals that there are no more values to be entered. When the user enters the sentinel value, the loop terminates.

The program in Code Listing 4-11 shows an example. It calculates the total points earned by a soccer team over a series of games. It allows the user to enter the series of game points, and then −1 to signal the end of the list.

Code Listing 4-11   (SoccerPoints.java)

```
1   import java.util.Scanner;      // Needed for the Scanner class
2
3   /**
4      This program calculates the total number of points a
5      soccer team has earned over a series of games. The user
6      enters a series of point values, then -1 when finished.
7   */
8
9   public class SoccerPoints
```

```
10  {
11      public static void main(String[] args)
12      {
13          int points;                 // Game points
14          int totalPoints = 0;        // Accumulator initialized to 0
15
16          // Create a Scanner object for keyboard input.
17          Scanner keyboard = new Scanner(System.in);
18
19          // Display general instructions.
20          System.out.println("Enter the number of points your team");
21          System.out.println("has earned for each game this season.");
22          System.out.println("Enter -1 when finished.");
23          System.out.println();
24
25          // Get the first number of points.
26          System.out.print("Enter game points or -1 to end: ");
27          points = keyboard.nextInt();
28
29          // Accumulate the points until -1 is entered.
30          while (points != -1)
31          {
32              // Add points to totalPoints.
33              totalPoints += points;
34
35              // Get the next number of points.
36              System.out.print("Enter game points or -1 to end: ");
37              points = keyboard.nextInt();
38          }
39
40          // Display the total number of points.
41          System.out.println("The total points are " +
42                             totalPoints);
43      }
44  }
```

Program Output with Example Input Shown in Bold

Enter the number of points your team
has earned for each game this season.
Enter -1 when finished.

Enter game points or -1 to end: **7 [Enter]**
Enter game points or -1 to end: **9 [Enter]**
Enter game points or -1 to end: **4 [Enter]**
Enter game points or -1 to end: **6 [Enter]**
Enter game points or -1 to end: **8 [Enter]**
Enter game points or -1 to end: **-1 [Enter]**
The total points are 34

The value –1 was chosen for the sentinel because it is not possible for a team to score negative points. Notice that this program performs a priming read to get the first value. This makes it possible for the loop to terminate immediately if the user enters –1 as the first value. Also note that the sentinel value is not included in the running total.

Checkpoint

MyProgrammingLab™ *www.myprogramminglab.com*

4.13   Write a for loop that repeats seven times, asking the user to enter a number. The loop should also calculate the sum of the numbers entered.

4.14   In the following program segment, which variable is the loop control variable (also known as the counter variable) and which is the accumulator?

```
int a, x = 0, y = 0;
while (x < 10)
{
    a = x * 2;
    y += a;
    x++;
}
System.out.println("The sum is " + y);
```

4.15   Why should you be careful when choosing a sentinel value?

4.7   Nested Loops

CONCEPT: A loop that is inside another loop is called a nested loop.

Nested loops are necessary when a task performs a repetitive operation and that task itself must be repeated. A clock is a good example of something that works like a nested loop. The program in Code Listing 4-12 uses nested loops to simulate a clock.

Code Listing 4-12   (**Clock.java**)

```
 1  /**
 2      This program uses nested loops to simulate a clock.
 3  */
 4
 5  public class Clock
 6  {
 7      public static void main(String[] args)
 8      {
 9          // Simulate the clock.
10          for (int hours = 1; hours <= 12; hours++)
11          {
12              for (int minutes = 0; minutes <= 59; minutes++)
13              {
14                  for (int seconds = 0; seconds <= 59; seconds++)
```

```
15                  {
16                      System.out.printf("%02d:%02d:%02d\n", hours, minutes, seconds);
17                  }
18              }
19          }
20      }
21 }
```

Program Output

```
01:00:00
01:00:01
01:00:02
01:00:03
```

(The loop continues to count . . .)

```
12:59:57
12:59:58
12:59:59
```

The innermost loop (which begins at line 14) will iterate 60 times for each single iteration of the middle loop. The middle loop (which begins at line 12) will iterate 60 times for each single iteration of the outermost loop. When the outermost loop (which begins at line 10) has iterated 12 times, the middle loop will have iterated 720 times and the innermost loop will have iterated 43,200 times.

The simulated clock example brings up a few points about nested loops:

- An inner loop goes through all of its iterations for each iteration of an outer loop.
- Inner loops complete their iterations before outer loops do.
- To get the total number of iterations of a nested loop, multiply the number of iterations of all the loops.

The program in Code Listing 4-13 shows another example. It is a program that a teacher might use to get the average of each student's test scores. In line 22 the user enters the number of students, and in line 26 the user enters the number of test scores per student. The `for` loop that begins in line 29 iterates once for each student. The nested inner `for` loop, in lines 36 through 41, iterates once for each test score.

Code Listing 4-13   **(TestAverage2.java)**

```
1 import java.util.Scanner;
2
3 /**
4    This program demonstrates a nested loop.
5 */
6
7 public class TestAverage2
```

```
 8 {
 9     public static void main(String [] args)
10     {
11         int numStudents,      // Number of students
12             numTests,         // Number of tests per student
13             score,            // Test score
14             total;            // Accumulator for test scores
15         double average;       // Average test score
16
17         // Create a Scanner object for keyboard input.
18         Scanner keyboard = new Scanner(System.in);
19
20         // Get the number of students.
21         System.out.print("How many students do you have? ");
22         numStudents = keyboard.nextInt();
23
24         // Get the number of test scores per student.
25         System.out.print("How many test scores per student? ");
26         numTests = keyboard.nextInt();
27
28         // Process all the students.
29         for (int student = 1; student <= numStudents; student++)
30         {
31             total = 0; // Set the accumulator to zero.
32
33             // Get the test scores for a student.
34             System.out.println("Student number " + student);
35             System.out.println("--------------------");
36             for (int test = 1; test <= numTests; test++)
37             {
38                 System.out.print("Enter score " + test + ": ");
39                 score = keyboard.nextInt();
40                 total += score; // Add score to total.
41             }
42
43             // Calculate and display the average.
44             average = total / numTests;
45             System.out.printf("The average for student %d is %.1f.\n\n",
46                               student, average);
47         }
48     }
49 }
```

Program Output with Example Input Shown in Bold

How many students do you have? **3 [Enter]**
How many test scores per student? **3 [Enter]**

```
Student number 1
----------------------
Enter score 1: 100 [Enter]
Enter score 2: 95 [Enter]
Enter score 3: 90 [Enter]
The average for student number 1 is 95.0.

Student number 2
---------------------
Enter score 1: 80 [Enter]
Enter score 2: 81 [Enter]
Enter score 3: 82 [Enter]
The average for student number 2 is 81.0.

Student number 3
----------------------
Enter score 1: 75 [Enter]
Enter score 2: 85 [Enter]
Enter score 3: 80 [Enter]
The average for student number 3 is 80.0.
```

In the Spotlight:

Using Nested Loops to Print Patterns

One interesting way to learn about nested loops is to use them to display patterns on the screen. Let's look at a simple example. Suppose we want to print asterisks on the screen in the following rectangular pattern:

```
******
******
******
******
******
******
******
******
```

If you think of this pattern as having rows and columns, you can see that it has eight rows, and each row has six columns. The following code can be used to display one row of asterisks:

```java
final int COLS = 6;
for (int col = 0; col < COLS; col++)
{
    System.out.print("*");
}
```

If we run this code in a program, it will produce the following output:

```
******
```

To complete the entire pattern, we need to execute this loop eight times. We can place the loop inside another loop that iterates eight times, as shown here:

```
1       final int COLS = 6;
2       final int ROWS = 8;
3       for (int row = 0; row < ROWS; row++)
4       {
5           for (int col = 0; col < COLS; col++)
6           {
7               System.out.print("*");
8           }
9           System.out.println();
10      }
```

The outer loop iterates eight times. Each time it iterates, the inner loop iterates six times. (Notice that in line 9, after each row has been printed, we call the `System.out.println()` method. We have to do that to advance the screen cursor to the next line at the end of each row. Without that statement, all the asterisks will be printed in one long row on the screen.)

We could easily write a program that prompts the user for the number of rows and columns, as shown in Code Listing 4-14.

Code Listing 4-14   **(RectangularPattern.java)**

```
1 import java.util.Scanner;
2
3 /**
4    This program displays a rectangular pattern
5    of asterisks.
6 */
7
8 public class RectangularPattern
9 {
10    public static void main(String[] args)
11    {
12       int rows, cols;
13
14       // Create a Scanner object for keyboard input.
15       Scanner keyboard = new Scanner(System.in);
16
17       // Get the number of rows and columns.
18       System.out.print("How many rows? ");
19       rows = keyboard.nextInt();
20       System.out.print("How many columns? ");
21       cols = keyboard.nextInt();
22
23       for (int r = 0; r < rows; r++)
24       {
25          for (int c = 0; c < cols; c++)
```

```
26              {
27                  System.out.print("*");
28              }
29              System.out.println();
30          }
31      }
32 }
```

Program Output with Example Input Shown in Bold

```
How many rows? 5 [Enter]
How many columns? 10 [Enter]
**********
**********
**********
**********
**********
```

Let's look at another example. Suppose you want to print asterisks in a pattern that looks like the following triangle:

```
*
**
***
****
*****
******
*******
********
```

Once again, think of the pattern as being arranged in rows and columns. The pattern has a total of eight rows. In the first row, there is one column. In the second row, there are two columns. In the third row, there are three columns. This continues to the eighth row, which has eight columns. Code Listing 4-15 shows the program that produces this pattern.

Code Listing 4-15   (TrianglePattern.java)

```
1 import java.util.Scanner;
2
3 /**
4    This program displays a triangle pattern.
5 */
6
7 public class TrianglePattern
8 {
9    public static void main(String[] args)
10   {
11       final int BASE_SIZE = 8;
12
13       for (int r = 0; r < BASE_SIZE; r++)
```

```
14        {
15            for (int c = 0; c < (r + 1); c++)
16            {
17                System.out.print("*");
18            }
19            System.out.println();
20        }
21    }
22 }
```

Program Output

```
*
**
***
****
*****
******
*******
********
```

The outer loop (which begins in line 13) will iterate eight times. As the loop iterates, the variable r will be assigned the values 0 through 7.

For each iteration of the outer loop, the inner loop will iterate r + 1 times. So,

- During the outer loop's first iteration, the variable r is assigned 0. The inner loop iterates one time, printing one asterisk.
- During the outer loop's second iteration, the variable r is assigned 1. The inner loop iterates two times, printing two asterisks.
- During the outer loop's third iteration, the variable r is assigned 2. The inner loop iterates three times, printing three asterisks.
- And so forth.

Let's look at another example. Suppose you want to display the following stair-step pattern:

```
#
 #
  #
   #
    #
     #
```

The pattern has six rows. In general, we can describe each row as having some number of spaces followed by a # character. Here's a row-by-row description:

First row: 0 spaces followed by a # character.
Second row: 1 space followed by a # character.
Third row: 2 spaces followed by a # character.
Fourth row: 3 spaces followed by a # character.
Fifth row: 4 spaces followed by a # character.
Sixth row: 5 spaces followed by a # character.

To display this pattern, we can write code containing a pair of nested loops that work in the following manner:

- The outer loop will iterate six times. Each iteration will perform the following:
  - The inner loop will display the correct number of spaces, side by side.
  - Then, a # character will be displayed.

Code Listing 4-16 shows the Java code.

Code Listing 4-16   **(StairStepPattern.java)**

```
 1 import java.util.Scanner;
 2
 3 /**
 4    This program displays a stairstep pattern.
 5 */
 6
 7 public class StairStepPattern
 8 {
 9    public static void main(String[] args)
10    {
11       final int NUM_STEPS = 6;
12
13       for (int r = 0; r < NUM_STEPS; r++)
14       {
15          for (int c = 0; c < r; c++)
16          {
17             System.out.print(" ");
18          }
19          System.out.println("#");
20       }
21    }
22 }
```

Program Output

```
#
 #
  #
   #
    #
     #
```

The outer loop (which begins in line 13) will iterate six times. As the loop iterates, the variable r will be assigned the values 0 through 5.

For each iteration of the outer loop, the inner loop will iterate r times. So,

- During the outer loop's first iteration, the variable r is assigned 0. The inner loop will not execute at this time.

- During the outer loop's second iteration, the variable r is assigned 1. The inner loop iterates one time, printing one space.
- During the outer loop's third iteration, the variable r is assigned 2. The inner loop iterates two times, printing two spaces.
- And so forth.

4.8 The break and continue Statements (Optional)

CONCEPT: The break statement causes a loop to terminate early. The continue statement causes a loop to stop its current iteration and begin the next one.

The break statement, which was used with the switch statement in Chapter 3, can also be placed inside a loop. When it is encountered, the loop stops and the program jumps to the statement immediately following the loop. Although it is perfectly acceptable to use the break statement in a switch statement, it is considered taboo to use it in a loop. This is because it bypasses the normal condition that is required to terminate the loop, and it makes code difficult to understand and debug. For this reason, you should avoid using the break statement in a loop when possible.

The continue statement causes the current iteration of a loop to end immediately. When continue is encountered, all the statements in the body of the loop that appear after it are ignored, and the loop prepares for the next iteration. In a while loop, this means the program jumps to the boolean expression at the top of the loop. As usual, if the expression is still true, the next iteration begins. In a do-while loop, the program jumps to the boolean expression at the bottom of the loop, which determines whether the next iteration will begin. In a for loop, continue causes the update expression to be executed, and then the test expression is evaluated.

The continue statement should also be avoided. Like the break statement, it bypasses the loop's logic and makes the code difficult to understand and debug.

4.9 Deciding Which Loop to Use

CONCEPT: Although most repetitive algorithms can be written with any of the three types of loops, each works best in different situations.

Each of Java's three loops is ideal to use in different situations. The following is a short summary of when each loop should be used:

- **The while loop.** The while loop is a pretest loop. It is ideal in situations where you do not want the loop to iterate if the condition is false from the beginning. It is also ideal if you want to use a sentinel value to terminate the loop.
- **The do-while loop.** The do-while loop is a posttest loop. It is ideal in situations where you always want the loop to iterate at least once.
- **The for loop.** The for loop is a pretest loop that has built-in expressions for initializing, testing, and updating. These expressions make it very convenient to use a loop control variable as a counter. The for loop is ideal in situations where the exact number of iterations is known.

4.10 Introduction to File Input and Output

CONCEPT: The Java API provides several classes that you can use for writing data to a file and reading data from a file. To write data to a file, you can use the **PrintWriter** class and, optionally, the **FileWriter** class. To read data from a file, you can use the **Scanner** class and the **File** class.

The programs you have written so far require you to reenter data each time the program runs. This is because the data stored in variables and objects in RAM disappears once the program stops running. To retain data between the times it runs, a program must have a way of saving the data.

Data may be saved in a *file*, which is usually stored on a computer's disk. Once the data is saved in a file, it will remain there after the program stops running. The data can then be retrieved and used at a later time. In general, there are three steps that are taken when a file is used by a program:

1. The file must be *opened*. When the file is opened, a connection is created between the file and the program.
2. Data is then written to the file or read from the file.
3. When the program is finished using the file, the file must be *closed*.

In this section we will discuss how to write Java programs that write data to files and read data from files. The terms *input file* and *output file* are commonly used. An *input file* is a file that a program reads data from. It is called an input file because the data stored in it serves as input to the program. An *output file* is a file that a program writes data to. It is called an output file because the program stores output in the file.

In general, there are two types of files: text and binary. A *text file* contains data that has been encoded as text, using a scheme such as Unicode. Even if the file contains numbers, those numbers are stored in the file as a series of characters. As a result, the file may be opened and viewed in a text editor such as Notepad. A *binary file* contains data that has not been converted to text. As a consequence, you cannot view the contents of a binary file with a text editor. In this chapter, we will discuss how to work with text files. Binary files are discussed in Chapter 11.

The Java API provides a number of classes that you will use to work with files. To use these classes, you will place the following import statement near the top of your program:

```
import java.io.*;
```

Using the PrintWriter Class to Write Data to a File

To write data to a file you will create an instance of the PrintWriter class. The PrintWriter class allows you to open a file for writing. It also allows you to write data to the file using the same print and println methods that you have been using to display data on the screen. You pass the name of the file that you wish to open, as a string, to the PrintWriter class's constructor. For example, the following statement creates a PrintWriter object and passes the file name *StudentData.txt* to the constructor.

```
PrintWriter outputFile = new PrintWriter("StudentData.txt");
```

This statement will create an empty file named *StudentData.txt* and establish a connection between it and the PrintWriter object that is referenced by outputFile. The file will be created in the current directory or folder.

You may also pass a reference to a `String` object as an argument to the `PrintWriter` constructor. For example, in the following code the user specifies the name of the file.

```
String filename;
filename = JOptionPane.showInputDialog("Enter the filename.");
PrintWriter outputFile = new PrintWriter(filename);
```

WARNING! If the file that you are opening with the `PrintWriter` object already exists, it will be erased and an empty file by the same name will be created.

Once you have created an instance of the `PrintWriter` class and opened a file, you can write data to the file using the `print` and `println` methods. You already know how to use `print` and `println` with `System.out` to display data on the screen. They are used the same way with a `PrintWriter` object to write data to a file. For example, assuming that `outputFile` references a `PrintWriter` object, the following statement writes the string `"Jim"` to the file:

```
outputFile.println("Jim");
```

When the program is finished writing data to the file, it must close the file. To close the file use the `PrintWriter` class's `close` method. Here is an example of the method's use:

```
outputFile.close();
```

Your application should always close files when finished with them. This is because the system creates one or more buffers when a file is opened. A *buffer* is a small "holding section" of memory. When a program writes data to a file, that data is first written to the buffer. When the buffer is filled, all the information stored there is written to the file. This technique increases the system's performance because writing data to memory is faster than writing it to a disk. The `close` method writes any unsaved data remaining in the file buffer.

Once a file is closed, the connection between it and the `PrintWriter` object is removed. In order to perform further operations on the file, it must be opened again.

More about the `PrintWriter` Class's `println` Method

The `PrintWriter` class's `println` method writes a line of data to a file. For example, assume an application creates a file and writes three students' first names and their test scores to the file with the following code:

```
PrintWriter outputFile = new PrintWriter("StudentData.txt");
outputFile.println("Jim");
outputFile.println(95);
outputFile.println("Karen");
outputFile.println(98);
outputFile.println("Bob");
outputFile.println(82);
outputFile.close();
```

The `println` method writes data to the file and then writes a newline character immediately after the data. You can visualize the data written to the file in the following manner:

Jim*<newline>*95*<newline>*Karen*<newline>*98*<newline>*Bob*<newline>*82*<newline>*

The newline characters are represented here as *<newline>*. You do not actually see the newline characters, but when the file is opened in a text editor such as Notepad, its contents will appear as shown in Figure 4-13. As you can see from the figure, each newline character causes the data that follows it to be displayed on a new line.

Figure 4-13   File contents displayed in Notepad

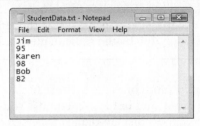

In addition to separating the contents of a file into lines, the newline character also serves as a delimiter. A *delimiter* is an item that separates other items. When you write data to a file using the `println` method, newline characters will separate the individual items of data. Later you will see that the individual items of data in a file must be separated in order for them to be read from the file.

The `PrintWriter` Class's `print` Method

The `print` method is used to write an item of data to a file without writing the newline character. For example, look at the following code:

```
String name = "Jeffrey Smith";
String phone = "555-7864";
int idNumber = 47895;
PrintWriter outputFile = new PrintWriter("PersonalData.txt");
outputFile.print(name + " ");
outputFile.print(phone + " ");
outputFile.println(idNumber);
outputFile.close();
```

This code uses the `print` method to write the contents of the `name` object to the file, followed by a space (`" "`). Then it uses the `print` method to write the contents of the `phone` object to the file, followed by a space. Then it uses the `println` method to write the contents of the `idNumber` variable, followed by a newline character. Figure 4-14 shows the contents of the file displayed in Notepad.

Figure 4-14   Contents of file displayed in Notepad

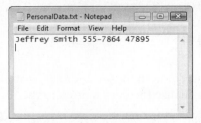

Adding a `throws` Clause to the Method Header

When an unexpected event occurs in a Java program, it is said that the program throws an exception. For now, you can think of an *exception* as a signal indicating that the program cannot continue until the unexpected event has been dealt with. For example, suppose you create a `PrintWriter` object and pass the name of a file to its constructor. The `PrintWriter` object attempts to create the file, but unexpectedly, the disk is full and the file cannot be created. Obviously the program cannot continue until this situation has been dealt with, so an exception is thrown, which causes the program to suspend normal execution.

When an exception is thrown, the method that is executing must either deal with the exception or throw it again. If the `main` method throws an exception, the program halts and an error message is displayed. Because `PrintWriter` objects are capable of throwing exceptions, we must either write code that deals with the possible exceptions, or allow our methods to rethrow the exceptions when they occur. In Chapter 12 you will learn all about exceptions and how to respond to them, but for now, we will simply allow our methods to rethrow any exceptions that might occur.

To allow a method to rethrow an exception that has not been dealt with, you simply write a `throws` clause in the method header. The `throws` clause must indicate the type of exception that might be thrown. The following is an example:

```
public static void main(String[] args) throws IOException
```

This header indicates that the `main` method is capable of throwing an exception of the `IOException` type. This is the type of exception that `PrintWriter` objects are capable of throwing. So, any method that uses `PrintWriter` objects and does not respond to their exceptions must have this `throws` clause listed in its header.

In addition, any method that calls a method that uses a `PrintWriter` object should have a `throws IOException` clause in its header. For example, suppose the `main` method does not perform any file operations, but calls a method named `buildFile` that opens a file and writes data to it. Both the `buildFile` and `main` methods should have a `throws IOException` clause in their headers. Otherwise a compiler error will occur.

An Example Program

Let's look at an example program that writes data to a file. The program in Code Listing 4-17 writes the names of your friends to a file.

Code Listing 4-17   (FileWriteDemo.java)

```java
 1  import java.util.Scanner;      // Needed for Scanner class
 2  import java.io.*;              // Needed for File I/O classes
 3
 4  /**
 5     This program writes data to a file.
 6  */
 7
 8  public class FileWriteDemo
 9  {
```

```
10      public static void main(String[] args) throws IOException
11      {
12          String filename;      // File name
13          String friendName;    // Friend's name
14          int numFriends;       // Number of friends
15
16          // Create a Scanner object for keyboard input.
17          Scanner keyboard = new Scanner(System.in);
18
19          // Get the number of friends.
20          System.out.print("How many friends do you have? ");
21          numFriends = keyboard.nextInt();
22
23          // Consume the remaining newline character.
24          keyboard.nextLine();
25
26          // Get the filename.
27          System.out.print("Enter the filename: ");
28          filename = keyboard.nextLine();
29
30          // Open the file.
31          PrintWriter outputFile = new PrintWriter(filename);
32
33          // Get data and write it to the file.
34          for (int i = 1; i <= numFriends; i++)
35          {
36              // Get the name of a friend.
37              System.out.print("Enter the name of friend " +
38                               "number " + i + ": ");
39              friendName = keyboard.nextLine();
40
41              // Write the name to the file.
42              outputFile.println(friendName);
43          }
44
45          // Close the file.
46          outputFile.close();
47          System.out.println("Data written to the file.");
48      }
49  }
```

Program Output with Example Input Shown in Bold

```
How many friends do you have? 5 [Enter]
Enter the filename: MyFriends.txt [Enter]
Enter the name of friend number 1: Joe [Enter]
Enter the name of friend number 2: Rose [Enter]
Enter the name of friend number 3: Greg [Enter]
```

```
Enter the name of friend number 4: Kirk [Enter]
Enter the name of friend number 5: Renee [Enter]
Data written to the file.
```

The import statement in line 2 is necessary because this program uses the PrintWriter class. In addition, the main method header, in line 10, has a throws IOException clause because objects of the PrintWriter class can potentially throw an IOException.

This program asks the user to enter the number of friends he or she has (in lines 20 and 21), then a name for the file that will be created (in lines 27 and 28). The filename variable references the name of the file, and is used in the following statement, in line 31:

```
PrintWriter outputFile = new PrintWriter(filename);
```

This statement opens the file and creates a PrintWriter object that can be used to write data to the file. The for loop in lines 34 through 43 performs an iteration for each friend that the user has, each time asking for the name of a friend. The user's input is referenced by the friendName variable. Once the name is entered, it is written to the file with the following statement, which appears in line 42:

```
outputFile.println(friendName);
```

After the loop finishes, the file is closed in line 46. After the program is executed with the input shown in the example run, the file *MyFriends.txt* will be created. If we open the file in Notepad, we will see its contents as shown in Figure 4-15.

Figure 4-15 Contents of the file displayed in Notepad

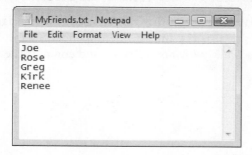

Review

Before moving on, let's review the basic steps necessary when writing a program that writes data to a file:

1. You need the import java.io.*; statement in the top section of your program.
2. Because we have not yet learned how to respond to exceptions, any method that uses a PrintWriter object must have a throws IOException clause in its header.
3. You create a PrintWriter object and pass the name of the file as a string to the constructor.

4. You use the `PrintWriter` class's `print` and `println` methods to write data to the file.

5. When finished writing to the file, you use the `PrintWriter` class's `close` method to close the file.

Appending Data to a File

When you pass the name of a file to the `PrintWriter` constructor, and the file already exists, it will be erased and a new empty file with the same name will be created. Sometimes, however, you want to preserve an existing file and append new data to its current contents. Appending to a file means writing new data to the end of the data that already exists in the file.

To append data to an existing file, you first create an instance of the `FileWriter` class. You pass two arguments to the `FileWriter` constructor: a string containing the name of the file, and the `boolean` value `true`. Here is an example:

```
FileWriter fwriter = new FileWriter("MyFriends.txt", true);
```

This statement creates a `FileWriter` object and opens the file *MyFriends.txt* for writing. Any data written to the file will be appended to the file's existing contents. (If the file does not exist, it will be created.)

You still need to create a `PrintWriter` object so you can use the `print` and `println` methods to write data to the file. When you create the `PrintWriter` object, you pass a reference to the `FileWriter` object as an argument to the `PrintWriter` constructor. For example, look at the following code:

```
FileWriter fwriter = new FileWriter("MyFriends.txt", true);
PrintWriter outputFile = new PrintWriter(fwriter);
```

This creates a `PrintWriter` object that can be used to write data to the file *MyFriends.txt*. Any data that is written to the file will be appended to the file's existing contents. For example, assume the file *MyFriends.txt* exists and contains the following data:

```
Joe
Rose
Greg
Kirk
Renee
```

The following code opens the file and appends additional data to its existing contents:

```
FileWriter fwriter = new FileWriter("MyFriends.txt", true);
PrintWriter outputFile = new PrintWriter(fwriter);
outputFile.println("Bill");
outputFile.println("Steven");
outputFile.println("Sharon");
outputFile.close();
```

After this code executes, the *MyFriends.txt* file will contain the following data:

```
Joe
Rose
Greg
Kirk
Renee
Bill
Steven
Sharon
```

> **NOTE:** The `FileWriter` class also throws an `IOException` if the file cannot be opened for any reason.

Specifying the File Location

When you open a file you may specify its path along with its filename. On a Windows computer, paths contain backslash characters. Remember that when a single backslash character appears in a string literal, it marks the beginning of an escape sequence such as `"\n"`. Two backslash characters in a string literal represent a single backslash. So, when you provide a path in a string literal, and the path contains backslash characters, you must use two backslash characters in the place of each single backslash character.

For example, the path `"E:\\Names.txt"` specifies that *Names.txt* is in the root folder of drive E:, and the path `"C:\\MyData\\Data.txt"` specifies that *Data.txt* is in the *MyData* folder on drive C:. In the following statement, the file *Pricelist.txt* is created in the root folder of drive A:.

```
PrintWriter outputFile = new PrintWriter("A:\\PriceList.txt");
```

You only need to use double backslashes if the file's path is in a string literal. If your program asks the user to enter a path into a `String` object, which is then passed to the `PrintWriter` or `FileWriter` constructor, the user does not have to enter double backslashes.

> **TIP:** Java allows you to substitute forward slashes for backslashes in a Windows path. For example, the path `"C:\\MyData\\Data.txt"` could be written as `"C:/MyData/Data.txt"`. This eliminates the need to use double backslashes.

On a UNIX or Linux computer, you can provide a path without any modifications. Here is an example:

```
PrintWriter outputFile = new PrintWriter("/home/rharrison/names.txt");
```

Reading Data from a File

In Chapter 2 you learned how to use the `Scanner` class to read input from the keyboard. To read keyboard input, recall that we create a `Scanner` object, passing `System.in` to the `Scanner` class constructor. Here is an example:

```
Scanner keyboard = new Scanner(System.in);
```

Recall that the `System.in` object represents the keyboard. Passing `System.in` as an argument to the `Scanner` constructor specifies that the keyboard is the `Scanner` object's source of input.

You can also use the `Scanner` class to read input from a file. Instead of passing `System.in` to the `Scanner` class constructor, you pass a reference to a `File` object. Here is an example:

```
File myFile = new File("Customers.txt");
Scanner inputFile = new Scanner(myFile);
```

The first statement creates an instance of the `File` class. The `File` class is in the Java API, and is used to represent a file. Notice that we have passed the string `"Customers.txt"` to the constructor. This creates a `File` object that represents the file *Customers.txt*.

In the second statement we pass a reference to this `File` object as an argument to the `Scanner` class constructor. This creates a `Scanner` object that uses the file *Customers.txt* as its source of input. You can then use the same `Scanner` class methods that you learned about in Chapter 2 to read items from the file. (See Table 2-17 for a list of commonly used methods.)

When you are finished reading from the file, you use the `Scanner` class's `close` method to close the file. For example, assuming the variable `inputFile` references a `Scanner` object, the following statement closes the file that is the object's source of input:

```
inputFile.close();
```

Reading Lines from a File with the `nextLine` Method

The `Scanner` class's `nextLine` method reads a line of input, and returns the line as a `String`. The program in Code Listing 4-18 demonstrates how the `nextLine` method can be used to read a line from a file. This program asks the user to enter a filename. It then displays the first line in the file on the screen.

Code Listing 4-18   (ReadFirstLine.java)

```
 1   import java.util.Scanner;   // Needed for Scanner class
 2   import java.io.*;           // Needed for File and IOException
 3
 4   /**
 5      This program reads the first line from a file.
 6   */
 7
 8   public class ReadFirstLine
 9   {
10      public static void main(String[] args) throws IOException
11      {
12         // Create a Scanner object for keyboard input.
13         Scanner keyboard = new Scanner(System.in);
14
```

```
15          // Get the file name.
16          System.out.print("Enter the name of a file: ");
17          String filename = keyboard.nextLine();
18
19          // Open the file.
20          File file = new File(filename);
21          Scanner inputFile = new Scanner(file);
22
23          // Read the first line from the file.
24          String line = inputFile.nextLine();
25
26          // Display the line.
27          System.out.println("The first line in the file is:");
28          System.out.println(line);
29
30          // Close the file.
31          inputFile.close();
32      }
33  }
```

Program Output with Example Input Shown in Bold

```
Enter the name of a file: MyFriends.txt [Enter]
The first line in the file is:
Joe
```

This program gets the name of a file from the user in line 17. A `File` object is created in line 20 to represent the file, and a `Scanner` object is created in line 21 to read data from the file. Line 24 reads a line from the file. After this statement executes, the `line` variable references a `String` object holding the line that was read from the file. The line is displayed on the screen in line 28, and the file is closed in line 31.

It's worth pointing out that this program creates two separate `Scanner` objects. The `Scanner` object that is created in line 13 reads data from the keyboard, and the `Scanner` object that is created in line 21 reads data from a file.

When a file is opened for reading, a special value known as a *read position* is internally maintained for that file. A file's read position marks the location of the next item that will be read from the file. When a file is opened, its read position is set to the first item in the file. When the item is read, the read position is advanced to the next item in the file. As subsequent items are read, the internal read position advances through the file. For example, consider the file *Quotation.txt*, shown in Figure 4-16. As you can see from the figure, the file has three lines.

You can visualize that the data is stored in the file in the following manner:

```
Imagination is more<newline>important than knowledge.<newline>
Albert Einstein<newline>
```

Suppose a program opens the file with the following code:

```
File file = new File("Quotation.txt");
Scanner inputFile = new Scanner(file);
```

Figure 4-16 File with three lines

Quotation.txt - Notepad
File Edit Format View Help
Imagination is more
important than knowledge.
Albert Einstein

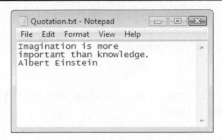

When this code opens the file, its read position is at the beginning of the first line, as illustrated in Figure 4-17.

Figure 4-17 Initial read position

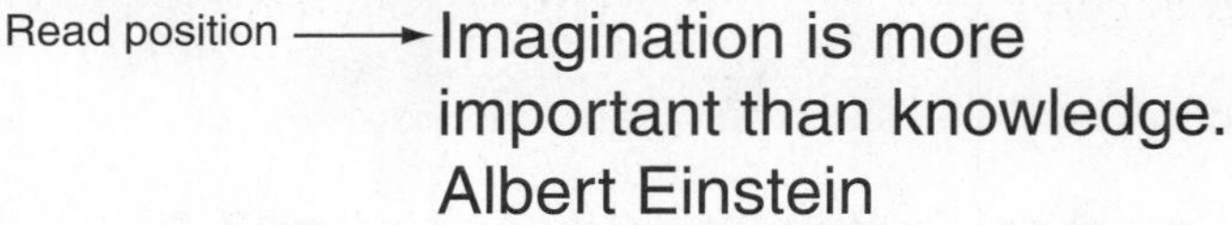

Read position
Imagination is more
important than knowledge.
Albert Einstein

Now, suppose the program uses the following statement to read a line from the file:

```
String str = inputFile.nextLine();
```

This statement will read a line from the file, beginning at the current read position. After the statement executes, the object referenced by `str` will contain the string "Imagination is more". The file's read position will be advanced to the next line, as illustrated in Figure 4-18.

Figure 4-18 Read position after first line is read

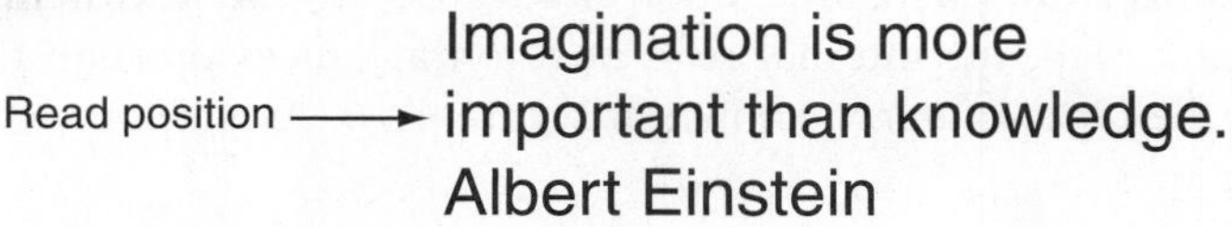

Imagination is more
Read position
important than knowledge.
Albert Einstein

If the `nextLine` method is called again, the second line will be read from the file and the file's read position will be advanced to the third line. After all the lines have been read, the read position will be at the end of the file.

NOTE: The string that is returned from the `nextLine` method will not contain the newline character.

Adding a `throws` Clause to the Method Header

When you pass a `File` object reference to the `Scanner` class constructor, the constructor will throw an exception of the `IOException` type if the specified file is not found. So, you will need to write a throws `IOException` clause in the header of any method that passes a `File` object reference to the `Scanner` class constructor.

Detecting the End of a File

Quite often a program must read the contents of a file without knowing the number of items that are stored in the file. For example, the *MyFriends.txt* file that was created by the program in Code Listing 4-17 can have any number of names stored in it. This is because the program asks the user for the number of friends that he or she has. If the user enters 5 for the number of friends, the program creates a file with five names in it. If the user enters 100, the program creates a file with 100 names in it.

The `Scanner` class has a method named `hasNext` that can be used to determine whether the file has more data that can be read. You call the `hasNext` method before you call any other methods to read from the file. If there is more data that can be read from the file, the `hasNext` method returns `true`. If the end of the file has been reached and there is no more data to read, the `hasNext` method returns `false`.

Code Listing 4-19 shows an example. The program reads the file containing the names of your friends, which was created by the program in Code Listing 4-17.

Code Listing 4-19   **(FileReadDemo.java)**

```
 1  import java.util.Scanner;   // Needed for the Scanner class
 2  import java.io.*;           // Needed for the File and IOException
 3
 4  /**
 5     This program reads data from a file.
 6  */
 7
 8  public class FileReadDemo
 9  {
10     public static void main(String[] args) throws IOException
11     {
12        // Create a Scanner object for keyboard input.
13        Scanner keyboard = new Scanner(System.in);
14
15        // Get the filename.
16        System.out.print("Enter the filename: ");
17        String filename = keyboard.nextLine();
```

```
18
19          // Open the file.
20          File file = new File(filename);
21          Scanner inputFile = new Scanner(file);
22
23          // Read lines from the file until no more are left.
24          while (inputFile.hasNext())
25          {
26             // Read the next name.
27             String friendName = inputFile.nextLine();
28
29             // Display the last name read.
30             System.out.println(friendName);
31          }
32
33          // Close the file.
34          inputFile.close();
35       }
36 }
```

Program Output with Example Input Shown in Bold

Enter the filename: **MyFriends.txt [Enter]**
Joe
Rose
Greg
Kirk
Renee

The file is opened and a Scanner object to read it is created in line 21. The loop in lines 24 through 31 reads all of the lines from the file and displays them. In line 24 the loop calls the Scanner object's hasNext method. If the method returns true, then the file has more data to read. In that case, the next line is read from the file in line 27, and is displayed in line 30. The loop repeats until the hasNext method returns false in line 24. Figure 4-19 shows the logic of reading a file until the end is reached.

Reading Primitive Values from a File

Recall from Chapter 2 that the Scanner class provides methods for reading primitive values. These methods are named nextByte, nextDouble, nextFloat, nextInt, nextLine, nextLong, and nextShort. Table 2-17 gives more information on each of these methods, which can be used to read primitive values from a file.

The program in Code Listing 4-20 demonstrates how the nextDouble method can be used to read floating-point values from a file. The program reads the contents of a file named *Numbers.txt*. The contents of the *Numbers.txt* file are shown in Figure 4-20. As you can see, the file contains a series of floating-point numbers. The program reads all of the numbers from the file and calculates their total.

Figure 4-19   Logic of reading a file until the end is reached

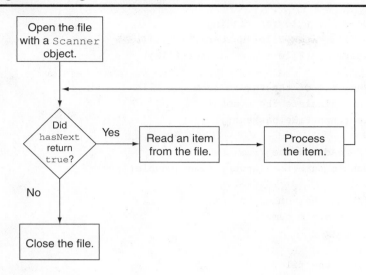

Figure 4-20   Contents of *Numbers.txt*

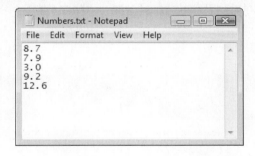

Code Listing 4-20   (`FileSum.java`)

```
1   import java.util.Scanner;
2   import java.io.*;
3
4   /**
5      This program reads a series of numbers from a file and
6      accumulates their sum.
7   */
8
9   public class FileSum
10  {
11     public static void main(String[] args) throws IOException
12     {
```

```
13          double sum = 0.0; // Accumulator, initialized to 0
14
15          // Open the file for reading.
16          File file = new File("Numbers.txt");
17          Scanner inputFile = new Scanner(file);
18
19          // Read all of the values from the file
20          // and calculate their total.
21          while (inputFile.hasNext())
22          {
23             // Read a value from the file.
24             double number = inputFile.nextDouble();
25
26             // Add the number to sum.
27             sum = sum + number;
28          }
29
30          // Close the file.
31          inputFile.close();
32
33          // Display the sum of the numbers.
34          System.out.println("The sum of the numbers in " +
35                             "Numbers.txt is " + sum);
36      }
37 }
```

Program Output

```
The sum of the numbers in Numbers.txt is 41.4
```

Review

Let's quickly review the steps necessary when writing a program that reads data from a file:

1. You will need the import java.util.Scanner; statement in the top section of your program, so you can use the Scanner class. You will also need the import java.io.*; statement in the top section of your program. This is required by the File class.
2. Because we have not yet learned how to respond to exceptions, any method that uses a Scanner object to open a file must have a throws IOException clause in its header.
3. You create a File object and pass the name of the file as a string to the constructor.
4. You create a Scanner object and pass a reference to the File object as an argument to the constructor.
5. You use the Scanner class's nextLine method to read a line from the file. The method returns the line of data as a string. To read primitive values, use methods such as nextInt, nextDouble, and so forth.

6. Call the Scanner class's hasNext method to determine whether there is more data to read from the file. If the method returns true, then there is more data to read. If the method returns false, you have reached the end of the file.
7. When finished writing to the file, you use the Scanner class's close method to close the file.

Checking for a File's Existence

It's usually a good idea to make sure that a file exists before you try to open it for input. If you attempt to open a file for input, and the file does not exist, the program will throw an exception and halt. For example, the program you saw in Code Listing 4-20 will throw an exception at line 17 if the file *Numbers.txt* does not exist. Here is an example of the error message that will be displayed when this happens:

```
Exception in thread "main" java.io.FileNotFoundException: Numbers.txt (The
system cannot find the file specified)
    at java.io.FileInputStream.open(Native Method)
    at java.io.FileInputStream.<init>(FileInputStream.java:106)
    at java.util.Scanner.<init>(Scanner.java:636)
    at FileSum.main(FileSum.java:17)
```

Rather than allowing the exception to be thrown and permitting this cryptic error message to be displayed, your program can check for the file's existence before it attempts to open the file. If the file does not exist, the program can display a more user-friendly error message and gracefully shut down.

After you create a File object representing the file that you want to open, you can use the File class's exists method to determine whether the file exists. The method returns true if the file exists, or false if the file does not exist. Code Listing 4-21 shows how to use the method. This is a modification of the *FileSum* program in Code Listing 4-20. This version of the program checks for the existence of the file *Numbers.txt* before it attempts to open it.

Code Listing 4-21   (FileSum2.java)

```
 1   import java.util.Scanner;
 2   import java.io.*;
 3
 4   /**
 5      This version of the program confirms that the
 6      Numbers.txt file exists before opening it.
 7   */
 8
 9   public class FileSum2
10   {
11      public static void main(String[] args) throws IOException
12      {
13         double sum = 0.0;    // Accumulator, initialized to 0
```

```
14
15          // Make sure the file exists.
16          File file = new File("Numbers.txt");
17          if (!file.exists())
18          {
19             System.out.println("The file Numbers.txt is not found.");
20             System.exit(0);
21          }
22
23          // Open the file for reading.
24          Scanner inputFile = new Scanner(file);
25
26          // Read all of the values from the file
27          // and calculate their total.
28          while (inputFile.hasNext())
29          {
30             // Read a value from the file.
31             double number = inputFile.nextDouble();
32
33             // Add the number to sum.
34             sum = sum + number;
35          }
36
37          // Close the file.
38          inputFile.close();
39
40          // Display the sum of the numbers.
41          System.out.println("The sum of the numbers in " +
42                          "Numbers.txt is " + sum);
43       }
44    }
```

Program Output (Assuming Numbers.txt Does Not Exist)

The file Numbers.txt is not found.

In line 16 the program creates a File object to represent the *Numbers.txt* file. In line 17, the if statement calls the file.exists() method. Notice the use of the ! operator. If the method returns false, indicating that the file does not exist, the code in lines 19 and 20 executes. Line 19 displays an error message, and line 20 calls the System.exit(0) method to shut the program down.

The previous example shows you how to make sure that a file exists before trying to open it for input. But, when you are opening a file for output, sometimes you want to make sure the file does *not* exist. When you use a PrintWriter object to open a file, the file will be erased if it already exists. If you do not want to erase the existing file, you have to check for its existence before creating the PrintWriter object. Code Listing 4-22 shows you how to use the File class's exists method in this type of situation. This is a modification of the program you saw in Code Listing 4-17.

Code Listing 4-22   `(FileWriteDemo2.java)`

```java
 1  import java.util.Scanner;        // Needed for Scanner class
 2  import java.io.*;                // Needed for File and IOException
 3
 4  /**
 5     This program writes data to a file. It makes sure the
 6     specified file does not exist before opening it.
 7  */
 8
 9  public class FileWriteDemo2
10  {
11     public static void main(String[] args) throws IOException
12     {
13        String filename;          // Filename
14        String friendName;        // Friend's name
15        int numFriends;           // Number of friends
16
17        // Create a Scanner object for keyboard input.
18        Scanner keyboard = new Scanner(System.in);
19
20        // Get the number of friends.
21        System.out.print("How many friends do you have? ");
22        numFriends = keyboard.nextInt();
23
24        // Consume the remaining newline character.
25        keyboard.nextLine();
26
27        // Get the filename.
28        System.out.print("Enter the filename: ");
29        filename = keyboard.nextLine();
30
31        // Make sure the file does not exist.
32        File file = new File(filename);
33        if (file.exists())
34        {
35           System.out.println("The file " + filename +
36                              " already exists.");
37           System.exit(0);
38        }
39
40        // Open the file.
41        PrintWriter outputFile = new PrintWriter(file);
42
43        // Get data and write it to the file.
44        for (int i = 1; i <= numFriends; i++)
45        {
46           // Get the name of a friend.
```

```
47            System.out.print("Enter the name of friend " +
48                          "number " + i + ": ");
49            friendName = keyboard.nextLine();
50
51            // Write the name to the file.
52            outputFile.println(friendName);
53        }
54
55        // Close the file.
56        outputFile.close();
57        System.out.println("Data written to the file.");
58    }
59 }
```

Program Output with Example Input Shown in Bold

```
How many friends do you have? 2 [Enter]
Enter the filename: MyFriends.txt [Enter]
The file MyFriends.txt already exists.
```

Line 32 creates a `File` object representing the file. The `if` statement in line 33 calls the `file.exists()` method. If the method returns `true`, then the file exists. In this case the code in lines 35 through 37 executes. This code displays an error message and shuts the program down. If the file does not exist, the rest of the program executes.

Notice that in line 41 we pass a reference to the `File` object to the `PrintWriter` constructor. In previous programs that created an instance `PrintWriter`, we passed a filename to the constructor. If you have a reference to a `File` object that represents the file you wish to open, as we do in this program, you have the option of passing it to the `PrintWriter` constructor.

 Checkpoint

MyProgrammingLab™ *www.myprogramminglab.com*

4.16   What is the difference between an input file and an output file?

4.17   What `import` statement will you need in a program that performs file operations?

4.18   What class do you use to write data to a file?

4.19   Write code that does the following: opens a file named *MyName.txt*, writes your first name to the file, and then closes the file.

4.20   What classes do you use to read data from a file?

4.21   Write code that does the following: opens a file named *MyName.txt*, reads the first line from the file and displays it, and then closes the file.

4.22   You are opening an existing file for output. How do you open the file without erasing it, and at the same time make sure that new data that is written to the file is appended to the end of the file's existing data?

4.23   What clause must you write in the header of a method that performs a file operation?

4.11 Generating Random Numbers with the Random Class

CONCEPT: Random numbers are used in a variety of applications. Java provides the Random class that you can use to generate random numbers.

Random numbers are useful for lots of different programming tasks. The following are just a few examples.

- Random numbers are commonly used in games. For example, computer games that let the player roll dice use random numbers to represent the values of the dice. Programs that show cards being drawn from a shuffled deck use random numbers to represent the face values of the cards.
- Random numbers are useful in simulation programs. In some simulations, the computer must randomly decide how a person, animal, insect, or other living being will behave. Formulas can be constructed in which a random number is used to determine various actions and events that take place in the program.
- Random numbers are useful in statistical programs that must randomly select data for analysis.
- Random numbers are commonly used in computer security to encrypt sensitive data.

The Java API provides a class named Random that you can use to generate random numbers. The class is part of the java.util package, so any program that uses it will need an import statement such as:

```
import java.util.Random;
```

You create an object from the Random class with a statement such as this:

```
Random randomNumbers = new Random();
```

This statement does the following:

- It declares a variable named randomNumbers. The data type is the Random class.
- The expression new Random() creates an instance of the Random class.
- The equal sign assigns the address of the Random class to the randomNumbers variable.

After this statement executes, the randomNumbers variable will reference a Random object. Once you have created a Random object, you can call its nextInt method to get a random integer number. The following code shows an example:

```
// Declare an int variable.
int number;

// Create a Random object.
Random randomNumbers = new Random();

// Get a random integer and assign it to number.
number = randomNumbers.nextInt();
```

After this code executes, the number variable will contain a random integer. If you call the nextInt method with no arguments, as shown in this example, the returned integer is somewhere between –2,147,483,648 and +2,147,483,647. Alternatively, you can pass an argument that specifies an upper limit to the generated number's range. In the following statement, the value assigned to number is somewhere between 0 and 99:

```java
number = randomNumbers.nextInt(100);
```

You can add or subtract a value to shift the numeric range upward or downward. In the following statement, we call the nextInt method to get a random number in the range of 0 through 9, and then we add 1 to it. So, the number assigned to number will be somewhere in the range of 1 through 10:

```java
number = randomNumbers.nextInt(10) + 1;
```

The following statement shows another example. It assigns a random integer to number between –50 and +49:

```java
number = randomNumbers.nextInt(100) - 50
```

The Random class has other methods for generating random numbers, and Table 4-1 summarizes several of them.

Table 4-1 Some of the Random class's methods

Method	Description
nextDouble()	Returns the next random number as a double. The number will be within the range of 0.0 through 1.0.
nextFloat()	Returns the next random number as a float. The number will be within the range of 0.0 through 1.0.
nextInt()	Returns the next random number as an int. The number will be within the range of an int, which is –2,147,483,648 to +2,147,483,648.
nextInt(int n)	This method accepts an integer argument, n. It returns a random number as an int. The number will be within the range of 0 through n.
nextLong()	Returns the next random number as a long. The number will be within the range of a long, which is –9,223,372,036,854,775,808 to +9,223,372,036,854,775,808.

The program in Code Listing 4-23 demonstrates using the Random class.

Code Listing 4-23   (MathTutor.java)

```java
 1  import java.util.Scanner;    // Needed for the Scanner class
 2  import java.util.Random;     // Needed for the Random class
 3
 4  /**
 5     This program demonstrates the Random class.
 6  */
 7
 8  public class MathTutor
```

```
 9  {
10     public static void main(String[] args)
11     {
12        int number1;        // A number
13        int number2;        // Another number
14        int sum;            // The sum of the numbers
15        int userAnswer;     // The user's answer
16
17        // Create a Scanner object for keyboard input.
18        Scanner keyboard = new Scanner(System.in);
19
20        // Create a Random class object.
21        Random randomNumbers = new Random();
22
23        // Get two random numbers.
24        number1 = randomNumbers.nextInt(100);
25        number2 = randomNumbers.nextInt(100);
26
27        // Display an addition problem.
28        System.out.println("What is the answer to the " +
29                           "following problem?");
30        System.out.print(number1 + " + " +
31                         number2 + " = ? ");
32
33        // Calculate the answer.
34        sum = number1 + number2;
35
36        // Get the user's answer.
37        userAnswer = keyboard.nextInt();
38
39        // Display the user's results.
40        if (userAnswer == sum)
41           System.out.println("Correct!");
42        else
43        {
44           System.out.println("Sorry, wrong answer. " +
45                              "The correct answer is " +
46                              sum);
47        }
48     }
49  }
```

Program Output with Example Input Shown in Bold

```
What is the answer to the following problem?
52 + 19 = ? 71 [Enter]
Correct!
```

Program Output with Example Input Shown in Bold
```
What is the answer to the following problem?
27 + 73 = ? 101 [Enter]
Sorry, wrong answer. The correct answer is 100
```

In the Spotlight:
Using Random Numbers

Dr. Kimura teaches an introductory statistics class, and has asked you to write a program that he can use in class to simulate the rolling of dice. The program should randomly generate two numbers in the range of 1 through 6 and display them. In your interview with Dr. Kimura, you learn that he would like to use the program to simulate several rolls of the dice, one after the other. Here is the pseudocode for the program:

While the user wants to roll the dice:
  Display a random number in the range of 1 through 6
  Display another random number in the range of 1 through 6
  Ask the user if he or she wants to roll the dice again

You will write a `while` loop that simulates one roll of the dice, and then asks the user whether another roll should be performed. As long as the user answers "y" for yes, the loop will repeat. Code Listing 4-24 shows the program.

Code Listing 4-24 **(RollDice.java)**

```java
 1 import java.util.Scanner;
 2 import java.util.Random;
 3
 4 /**
 5    This program simulates the rolling of dice.
 6 */
 7
 8 public class RollDice
 9 {
10    public static void main(String[] args)
11    {
12       String again = "y";    // To control the loop
13       int die1;              // To hold the value of die #1
14       int die2;              // to hold the value of die #2
15
16       // Create a Scanner object to read keyboard input.
17       Scanner keyboard = new Scanner(System.in);
18
19       // Create a Random object to generate random numbers.
20       Random rand = new Random();
21
22       // Simulate rolling the dice.
```

```
23        while (again.equalsIgnoreCase("y"))
24        {
25            System.out.println("Rolling the dice ...");
26            die1 = rand.nextInt(6) + 1;
27            die2 = rand.nextInt(6) + 1;
28            System.out.println("Their values are:");
29            System.out.println(die1 + " " + die2);
30
31            System.out.print("Roll them again (y = yes)? ");
32            again = keyboard.nextLine();
33        }
34    }
35 }
```

Program Output with Example Input Shown in Bold

```
Rolling the dice ...
Their values are:
4 3
Roll them again (y = yes)? y [Enter]
Rolling the dice ...
Their values are:
2 6
Roll them again (y = yes)? y [Enter]
Rolling the dice ...
Their values are:
1 5
Roll them again (y = yes)? n [Enter]
```

In the Spotlight:

Using Random Numbers to Represent Other Values

Dr. Kimura was so happy with the dice rolling simulator that you wrote for him, he has asked you to write one more program. He would like a program that he can use to simulate ten coin tosses, one after the other. Each time the program simulates a coin toss, it should randomly display either "Heads" or "Tails".

You decide that you can simulate the tossing of a coin by randomly generating a number in the range of 0 through 1. You will write an if statement that displays "Tails" if the random number is 0, or "Heads" otherwise. Here is the pseudocode:

Repeat 10 times:
    If a random number in the range of 0 through 1 equals 0, then:
        Display "Tails"
    Else:
        Display "Heads"

Because the program should simulate 10 tosses of a coin, you decide to use a for loop. The program is shown in Code Listing 4-25.

Code Listing 4-25   (CoinToss.java)

```java
 1 import java.util.Random;
 2
 3 /**
 4    This program simulates 10 tosses of a coin.
 5 */
 6
 7 public class CoinToss
 8 {
 9    public static void main(String[] args)
10    {
11       // Create a Random object to generate random numbers.
12       Random rand = new Random();
13
14       // Simulate the coin tosses.
15       for (int count = 0; count < 10; count++)
16       {
17          if (rand.nextInt(2) == 0)
18             System.out.println("Tails");
19          else
20             System.out.println("Heads");
21       }
22    }
23 }
```

Program Output

```
Tails
Tails
Heads
Tails
Heads
Heads
Heads
Tails
Heads
Tails
```

Checkpoint

MyProgrammingLab™ *www.myprogramminglab.com*

4.24   Assume x is an int variable, and rand references a Random object. What does the following statement do?

```java
x = rand.nextInt();
```

4.25 Assume x is an int variable, and rand references a Random object. What does the following statement do?

```
x = rand.nextInt(100);
```

4.26 Assume x is an int variable, and rand references a Random object. What does the following statement do?

```
x = rand.nextInt(9) + 1;
```

4.27 Assume x is a double variable, and rand references a Random object. What does the following statement do?

```
x = rand.nextDouble();
```

4.12 Common Errors to Avoid

The following list describes several errors that are commonly committed when learning this chapter's topics.

- **Using the increment or decrement operator in the wrong mode.** When the increment or decrement operator is placed in front of (to the left of) its operand, it is used in prefix mode. When either of these operators is placed behind (to the right of) its operand, it is used in postfix mode.
- **Forgetting to enclose the boolean expression in a while loop or a do-while loop inside parentheses.**
- **Placing a semicolon at the end of a while or for loop's header.** When you write a semicolon at the end of a while or for loop's header, Java assumes that the conditionally executed statement is a null or empty statement. This usually results in an infinite loop.
- **Forgetting to write the semicolon at the end of the do-while loop.** The do-while loop must be terminated with a semicolon.
- **Forgetting to enclose multiple statements in the body of a loop in braces.** Normally a loop conditionally executes only one statement. To conditionally execute more than one statement, you must place the statements in braces.
- **Using commas instead of semicolons to separate the initialization, test, and update expressions in a for loop.**
- **Forgetting to write code in the body of a while or do-while loop that modifies the loop control variable.** If a while or do-while loop's boolean expression never becomes false, the loop will repeat indefinitely. You must have code in the body of the loop that modifies the loop control variable so that the boolean expression will at some point become false.
- **Using a sentinel value that can also be a valid data value.** Remember, a sentinel is a special value that cannot be mistaken as a member of a list of data items and signals that there are no more data items from the list to be processed. If you choose as a sentinel a value that might also appear in the list, the loop will prematurely terminate if it encounters the value in the list.
- **Forgetting to initialize an accumulator to zero.** In order for an accumulator to keep a correct running total, it must be initialized to zero before any values are added to it.

Review Questions and Exercises

Multiple Choice and True/False

1. What will the `println` statement in the following program segment display?

   ```
   int x = 5;
   System.out.println(x++);
   ```

   a. 5
   b. 6
   c. 0
   d. None of these

2. What will the `println` statement in the following program segment display?

   ```
   int x = 5;
   System.out.println(++x);
   ```

   a. 5
   b. 6
   c. 0
   d. None of these

3. In the expression `number++`, the ++ operator is in what mode?
   a. prefix
   b. pretest
   c. postfix
   d. posttest

4. What is each repetition of a loop known as?
   a. cycle
   b. revolution
   c. orbit
   d. iteration

5. This is a variable that controls the number of iterations performed by a loop.
   a. loop control variable
   b. accumulator
   c. iteration register variable
   d. repetition meter

6. The `while` loop is this type of loop.
   a. pretest
   b. posttest
   c. prefix
   d. postfix

7. The `do-while` loop is this type of loop.
   a. pretest
   b. posttest
   c. prefix
   d. postfix

8. The `for` loop is this type of loop.
   a. pretest
   b. posttest
   c. prefix
   d. postfix

9. This type of loop has no way of ending and repeats until the program is interrupted.
   a. indeterminate
   b. interminable
   c. infinite
   d. timeless

10. This type of loop always executes at least once.
    a. `while`
    b. `do-while`
    c. `for`
    d. any of these

11. This expression is executed by the `for` loop only once, regardless of the number of iterations.
    a. initialization expression
    b. test expression
    c. update expression
    d. pre-increment expression

12. This is a variable that keeps a running total.
    a. sentinel
    b. sum
    c. total
    d. accumulator

13. This is a special value that signals when there are no more items from a list of items to be processed. This value cannot be mistaken as an item from the list.
    a. sentinel
    b. flag
    c. signal
    d. accumulator

14. To open a file for writing, you use the following class.
    a. `PrintWriter`
    b. `FileOpen`
    c. `OutputFile`
    d. `FileReader`

15. To open a file for reading, you use the following classes.
    a. `File` and `Writer`
    b. `File` and `Output`
    c. `File` and `Input`
    d. `File` and `Scanner`

16. When a program is finished using a file, it should do this.
    a. erase the file
    b. close the file
    c. throw an exception
    d. reset the read position

17. This class allows you to use the print and println methods to write data to a file.
    a. File
    b. FileReader
    c. OutputFile
    d. PrintWriter

18. This class allows you to read a line from a file.
    a. FileWriter
    b. Scanner
    c. InputFile
    d. FileReader

19. **True or False:** The while loop is a pretest loop.

20. **True or False:** The do-while loop is a pretest loop.

21. **True or False:** The for loop is a posttest loop.

22. **True or False:** It is not necessary to initialize accumulator variables.

23. **True or False:** One limitation of the for loop is that only one variable may be initialized in the initialization expression.

24. **True or False:** A variable may be defined in the initialization expression of the for loop.

25. **True or False:** In a nested loop, the inner loop goes through all of its iterations for every iteration of the outer loop.

26. **True or False:** To calculate the total number of iterations of a nested loop, add the number of iterations of all the loops.

Find the Error

Find the errors in the following code:

1.
```java
// This code contains ERRORS!
// It adds two numbers entered by the user.
int num1, num2;
String input;
char again;

Scanner keyboard = new Scanner(System.in);
while (again == 'y' || again == 'Y')
   System.out.print("Enter a number: ");
   num1 = keyboard.nextInt();
   System.out.print("Enter another number: ";
```

```
        num2 = keyboard.nextInt();
        System.out.println("Their sum is "+ (num1 + num2));
        System.out.println("Do you want to do this again? ");
        keyboard.nextLine();  // Consume remaining newline
        input = keyboard.nextLine();
        again = input.charAt(0);
```

2. ```
   // This code contains ERRORS!
   int count = 1, total;
   while (count <= 100)
       total += count;
   System.out.print("The sum of the numbers 1 - 100 is ");
   System.out.println(total);
   ```

3. ```
   // This code contains ERRORS!
   int choice, num1, num2;
   Scanner keyboard = new Scanner(System.in);
   do
   {
       System.out.print("Enter a number: ");
       num1 = keyboard.nextInt();
       System.out.print("Enter another number: ");
       num2 = keyboard.nextInt();
       System.out.println("Their sum is " + (num1 + num2));
       System.out.println("Do you want to do this again? ");
       System.out.print("1 = yes, 0 = no ");
       choice = keyboard.nextInt();
   } while (choice = 1)
   ```

4. ```
   // This code contains ERRORS!
   // Print the numbers 1 through 10.
   for (int count = 1, count <= 10, count++;)
   {
           System.out.println(count);
           count++;
   }
   ```

Algorithm Workbench

1. Write a while loop that lets the user enter a number. The number should be multiplied by 10, and the result stored in the variable product. The loop should iterate as long as product contains a value less than 100.

2. Write a do-while loop that asks the user to enter two numbers. The numbers should be added and the sum displayed. The loop should ask the user whether he or she wishes to perform the operation again. If so, the loop should repeat; otherwise it should terminate.

3. Write a for loop that displays the following set of numbers:

   0, 10, 20, 30, 40, 50 ... 1000
   ```

4. Write a loop that asks the user to enter a number. The loop should iterate 10 times and keep a running total of the numbers entered.

5. Write a `for` loop that calculates the total of the following series of numbers:

$$\frac{1}{30} + \frac{2}{29} + \frac{3}{28} + \cdots \frac{30}{1}$$

6. Write a nested loop that displays 10 rows of '#' characters. There should be 15 '#' characters in each row.

7. Convert the `while` loop in the following code to a `do-while` loop:

```
Scanner keyboard = new Scanner(System.in);
int x = 1;
while (x > 0)
{
   System.out.print("Enter a number: ");
   x = keyboard.nextInt();
}
```

8. Convert the `do-while` loop in the following code to a `while` loop:

```
Scanner keyboard = new Scanner(System.in);
String input;
char sure;
do
{
   System.out.print("Are you sure you want to quit? ");
   input = keyboard.next();
   sure = input.charAt(0);
} while (sure != 'Y' && sure != 'N');
```

9. Convert the following `while` loop to a `for` loop:

```
int count = 0;
while (count < 50)
{
   System.out.println("count is " + count);
   count++;
}
```

10. Convert the following `for` loop to a `while` loop:

```
for (int x = 50; x > 0; x--)
{
   System.out.println(x + " seconds to go.");
}
```

11. Write an input validation loop that asks the user to enter a number in the range of 1 through 4.

12. Write an input validation loop that asks the user to enter the word "yes" or "no".

13. Write nested loops to draw this pattern:

```
*******
******
*****
****
***
**
*
```

14. Write nested loops to draw this pattern:

```
##
# #
#  #
#   #
#    #
#     #
```

15. Complete the following program so it displays a random integer in the range of 1 through 10.

```java
// Write the necessary import statement(s) here.
public class ReviewQuestion15
{
    public static void main(String[] args)
    {
        // Write the necessary code here.
    }
}
```

16. Complete the following program so it performs the following actions 10 times:

   • Generates a random number that is either 0 or 1.

   • Displays either the word "Yes" or the word "No" depending on the random number that was generated.

```java
// Write the necessary import statement(s) here.
public class ReviewQuestion16
{
    public static void main(String[] args)
    {
        // Write the necessary code here.
    }
}
```

17. Write code that does the following: opens a file named *NumberList.txt*, uses a loop to write the numbers 1 through 100 to the file, and then closes the file.

18. Write code that does the following: opens the *NumberList.txt* file that was created by the code in Question 17, reads all of the numbers from the file and displays them, and then closes the file.

19. Modify the code you wrote in Question 18 so it adds all of the numbers read from the file and displays their total.

20. Write code that opens a file named *NumberList.txt* for writing, but does not erase the file's contents if it already exists.

Short Answer

1. Briefly describe the difference between the prefix and postfix modes used by the increment and decrement operators.

2. Why should you indent the statements in the body of a loop?

3. Describe the difference between pretest loops and posttest loops.

4. Why are the statements in the body of a loop called conditionally executed statements?

5. Describe the difference between the `while` loop and the `do-while` loop.

6. Which loop should you use in situations where you want the loop to repeat until the `boolean` expression is `false`, and the loop should not execute if the test expression is `false` to begin with?

7. Which loop should you use in situations where you want the loop to repeat until the `boolean` expression is `false`, but the loop should execute at least once?

8. Which loop should you use when you know the number of required iterations?

9. Why is it critical that accumulator variables are properly initialized?

10. What is an infinite loop? Write the code for an infinite loop.

11. Describe a programming problem that would require the use of an accumulator.

12. What does it mean to let the user control a loop?

13. What is the advantage of using a sentinel?

14. Why must the value chosen for use as a sentinel be carefully selected?

15. Describe a programming problem requiring the use of nested loops.

16. How does a file buffer increase a program's performance?

17. Why should a program close a file when it's finished using it?

18. What is a file's read position? Where is the read position when a file is first opened for reading?

19. When writing data to a file, what is the difference between the `print` and the `println` methods?

20. What does the `Scanner` class's `hasNext` method return when the end of the file has been reached?

21. What is a potential error that can occur when a file is opened for reading?

22. What does it mean to append data to a file?

23. How do you open a file so that new data will be written to the end of the file's existing data?

Programming Challenges

MyProgrammingLab™   *Visit www.myprogramminglab.com to complete many of these Programming Challenges online and get instant feedback.*

1. Sum of Numbers

Write a program that asks the user for a positive nonzero integer value. The program should use a loop to get the sum of all the integers from 1 up to the number entered. For example, if the user enters 50, the loop will find the sum of 1, 2, 3, 4, . . . 50.

2. Distance Traveled

The distance a vehicle travels can be calculated as follows:

$$Distance = Speed * Time$$

For example, if a train travels 40 miles-per-hour for three hours, the distance traveled is 120 miles. Write a program that asks for the speed of a vehicle (in miles-per-hour) and the number of hours it has traveled. It should use a loop to display the distance a vehicle has traveled for each hour of a time period specified by the user. For example, if a vehicle is traveling at 40 mph for a three-hour time period, it should display a report similar to the one that follows:

```
Hour      Distance Traveled
--------------------------
1                  40
2                  80
3                 120
```

Input Validation: Do not accept a negative number for speed and do not accept any value less than 1 for time traveled.

3. Distance File

Modify the program you wrote for Programming Challenge 2 (Distance Traveled) so it writes the report to a file instead of the screen. Open the file in Notepad or another text editor to confirm the output.

4. Pennies for Pay

VideoNote
The Pennies
for Pay
Problem

Write a program that calculates the amount a person would earn over a period of time if his or her salary is one penny the first day, two pennies the second day, and continues to double each day. The program should display a table showing the salary for each day, and then show the total pay at the end of the period. The output should be displayed in a dollar amount, not the number of pennies.

Input Validation: Do not accept a number less than 1 for the number of days worked.

5. Letter Counter

Write a program that asks the user to enter a string, and then asks the user to enter a character. The program should count and display the number of times that the specified character appears in the string.

6. File Letter Counter

Write a program that asks the user to enter the name of a file, and then asks the user to enter a character. The program should count and display the number of times that the specified character appears in the file. Use Notepad or another text editor to create a simple file that can be used to test the program.

7. Hotel Occupancy

A hotel's occupancy rate is calculated as follows:

$$Occupancy\ rate = Number\ of\ rooms\ occupied \div Total\ number\ of\ rooms$$

Write a program that calculates the occupancy rate for each floor of a hotel. The program should start by asking for the number of floors in the hotel. A loop should then iterate once for each floor. During each iteration, the loop should ask the user for the number of rooms on the floor and the number of them that are occupied. After all the iterations, the program should display the number of rooms the hotel has, the number of them that are occupied, the number that are vacant, and the occupancy rate for the hotel.

Input Validation: Do not accept a value less than 1 for the number of floors. Do not accept a number less than 10 for the number of rooms on a floor.

8. Average Rainfall

Write a program that uses nested loops to collect data and calculate the average rainfall over a period of years. First the program should ask for the number of years. The outer loop will iterate once for each year. The inner loop will iterate 12 times, once for each month. Each iteration of the inner loop will ask the user for the inches of rainfall for that month. After all iterations, the program should display the number of months, the total inches of rainfall, and the average rainfall per month for the entire period.

Input Validation: Do not accept a number less than 1 for the number of years. Do not accept negative numbers for the monthly rainfall.

9. Population

Write a program that will predict the size of a population of organisms. The program should ask for the starting number of organisms, their average daily population increase (as a percentage), and the number of days they will multiply. For example, a population might begin with two organisms, have an average daily increase of 50 percent, and will be allowed to multiply for seven days. The program should use a loop to display the size of the population for each day.

Input Validation: Do not accept a number less than 2 for the starting size of the population. Do not accept a negative number for average daily population increase. Do not accept a number less than 1 for the number of days they will multiply.

10. Largest and Smallest

Write a program with a loop that lets the user enter a series of integers. The user should enter –99 to signal the end of the series. After all the numbers have been entered, the program should display the largest and smallest numbers entered.

11. Celsius to Fahrenheit Table

Write a program that displays a table of the Celsius temperatures 0 through 20 and their Fahrenheit equivalents. The formula for converting a temperature from Celsius to Fahrenheit is

$$F = \frac{9}{5}C + 32$$

where F is the Fahrenheit temperature and C is the Celsius temperature. Your program must use a loop to display the table.

12. Bar Chart

Write a program that asks the user to enter today's sales for five stores. The program should display a bar chart comparing each store's sales. Create each bar in the bar chart by displaying a row of asterisks. Each asterisk should represent $100 of sales. Here is an example of the program's output:

```
Enter today's sales for store 1: 1000 [Enter]
Enter today's sales for store 2: 1200 [Enter]
Enter today's sales for store 3: 1800 [Enter]
Enter today's sales for store 4: 800 [Enter]
Enter today's sales for store 5: 1900 [Enter]

SALES BAR CHART
Store 1: **********
Store 2: ************
Store 3: ******************
Store 4: ********
Store 5: *******************
```

13. File Head Display

Write a program that asks the user for the name of a file. The program should display only the first five lines of the file's contents. If the file contains fewer than five lines, it should display the file's entire contents.

14. Line Numbers

Write a program that asks the user for the name of a file. The program should display the contents of the file with each line preceded with a line number followed by a colon. The line numbering should start at 1.

15. Uppercase File Converter

Write a program that asks the user for the names of two files. The first file should be opened for reading and the second file should be opened for writing. The program should read the contents of the first file, change all characters to uppercase, and store the results in the second file. The second file will be a copy of the first file, except that all the characters will be uppercase. Use Notepad or another text editor to create a simple file that can be used to test the program.

16. Budget Analysis

Write a program that asks the user to enter the amount that he or she has budgeted for a month. A loop should then prompt the user to enter each of his or her expenses for the month, and keep a running total. When the loop finishes, the program should display the amount that the user is over or under budget.

17. Random Number Guessing Game

Write a program that generates a random number and asks the user to guess what the number is. If the user's guess is higher than the random number, the program should display "Too high, try again." If the user's guess is lower than the random number, the program should display "Too low, try again." The program should use a loop that repeats until the user correctly guesses the random number.

18. Random Number Guessing Game Enhancement

Enhance the program that you wrote for Programming Challenge 17 so it keeps a count of the number of guesses that the user makes. When the user correctly guesses the random number, the program should display the number of guesses.

19. ESP Game

Write a program that tests your ESP (extrasensory perception). The program should randomly select the name of a color from the following list of words:

Red, Green, Blue, Orange, Yellow

To select a word, the program can generate a random number. For example, if the number is 0, the selected word is *Red*, if the number is 1, the selected word is *Green*, and so forth.

Next, the program should ask the user to enter the color that the computer has selected. After the user has entered his or her guess, the program should display the name of the randomly selected color. The program should repeat this 10 times and then display the number of times the user correctly guessed the selected color.

20. Square Display

Write a program that asks the user for a positive integer no greater than 15. The program should then display a square on the screen using the character 'X'. The number entered by the user will be the length of each side of the square. For example, if the user enters 5, the program should display the following:

```
XXXXX
XXXXX
XXXXX
XXXXX
XXXXX
```

If the user enters 8, the program should display the following:

```
XXXXXXXX
XXXXXXXX
XXXXXXXX
XXXXXXXX
XXXXXXXX
XXXXXXXX
XXXXXXXX
XXXXXXXX
```

21. Dice Game

Write a program that plays a simple dice game between the computer and the user. When the program runs, a loop should repeat 10 times. Each iteration of the loop should do the following:

- Generate a random integer in the range of 1 through 6. This is the value of the computer's die.
- Generate another random integer in the range of 1 through 6. This is the value of the user's die.
- The die with the highest value wins. (In case of a tie, there is no winner for that particular roll of the dice.)

As the loop iterates, the program should keep count of the number of times the computer wins, and the number of times that the user wins. After the loop performs all of its iterations, the program should display who was the grand winner, the computer or the user.

22. Slot Machine Simulation

A slot machine is a gambling device that the user inserts money into and then pulls a lever (or presses a button). The slot machine then displays a set of random images. If two or more of the images match, the user wins an amount of money that the slot machine dispenses back to the user.

Create a program that simulates a slot machine. When the program runs, it should do the following:

- Asks the user to enter the amount of money he or she wants to enter into the slot machine.
- Instead of displaying images, the program will randomly select a word from the following list:

  Cherries, Oranges, Plums, Bells, Melons, Bars

  To select a word, the program can generate a random number in the range of 0 through 5. If the number is 0, the selected word is *Cherries*; if the number is 1, the selected word is *Oranges*; and so forth. The program should randomly select a word from this list three times and display all three of the words.

- If none of the randomly selected words match, the program will inform the user that he or she has won $0. If two of the words match, the program will inform the user that he or she has won two times the amount entered. If three of the words match, the program will inform the user that he or she has won three times the amount entered.

- The program will ask whether the user wants to play again. If so, these steps are repeated. If not, the program displays the total amount of money entered into the slot machine and the total amount won.Decision Structures

5 Methods

5.1 Introduction to Methods

CONCEPT: Methods can be used to break a complex program into small, manageable pieces. A **void** method simply executes a group of statements and then terminates. A value-returning method returns a value to the statement that called it.

In a general sense, a method is a collection of statements that performs a specific task. So far you have experienced methods in two ways: (1) You have created a method named main in every program you've written, and (2) you have executed predefined methods from the Java API, such as System.out.println, Integer.parseInt, and Math.pow. In this chapter, you will learn how to create your own methods, other than main, that can be executed just as you execute the API methods.

Methods are commonly used to break a problem into small, manageable pieces. Instead of writing one long method that contains all of the statements necessary to solve a problem, several small methods that each solve a specific part of the problem can be written. These small methods can then be executed in the desired order to solve the problem. This approach is sometimes called *divide and conquer* because a large problem is divided into several smaller problems that are easily solved. Figure 5-1 illustrates this idea by comparing two programs: one that uses a long, complex method containing all of the statements necessary to solve a problem, and another that divides a problem into smaller problems, each of which is handled by a separate method.

Figure 5-1 Using methods to divide and conquer a problem

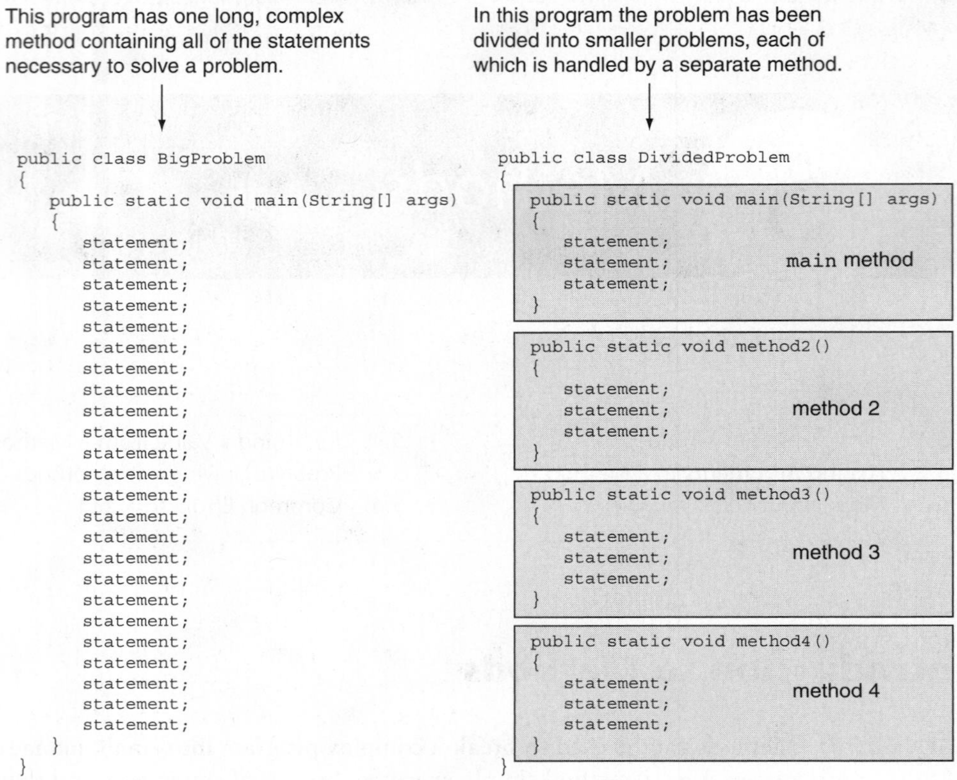

This program has one long, complex method containing all of the statements necessary to solve a problem.

In this program the problem has been divided into smaller problems, each of which is handled by a separate method.

```
public class BigProblem
{
    public static void main(String[] args)
    {
        statement;
        statement;
        statement;
        statement;
        statement;
        statement;
        statement;
        statement;
        statement;
        statement;
        statement;
        statement;
        statement;
        statement;
        statement;
        statement;
        statement;
        statement;
        statement;
        statement;
        statement;
        statement;
    }
}
```

```
public class DividedProblem
{
    public static void main(String[] args)
    {
        statement;
        statement;          main method
        statement;
    }

    public static void method2()
    {
        statement;
        statement;          method 2
        statement;
    }

    public static void method3()
    {
        statement;
        statement;          method 3
        statement;
    }

    public static void method4()
    {
        statement;
        statement;          method 4
        statement;
    }
}
```

Another reason to write methods is that they simplify programs. If a specific task is performed in several places in a program, a method can be written once to perform that task, and then be executed any time it is needed. This benefit of using methods is known as *code reuse* because you are writing the code to perform a task once and then reusing it each time you need to perform the task.

First, we will look at the general ways in which methods operate. At the end of the chapter we will discuss in greater detail how methods can be used in problem solving.

void **Methods and Value-Returning Methods**

In this chapter, you will learn about two general categories of methods: void methods and value-returning methods. A *void method* is one that simply performs a task and then terminates. System.out.println is an example of a void method. For example, look at the following code:

```
1    int number = 7;
2    System.out.println(number);
3    number = 0;
```

The statement in line 1 declares the number variable and initializes it with the value 7. The statement in line 2 calls the System.out.println method, passing number as an argument. The method does its job, which is to display a value on the screen, and then terminates. The code then resumes at line 3.

A *value-returning method* not only performs a task but also sends a value back to the code that called it. The Random class's nextInt method is an example of a value-returning method. For example, look at the following code:

```
1    int number;
2    Random rand = new Random();
3    number = rand.nextInt();
```

The statement in line 1 declares the number variable. Line 2 creates a Random object and assigns its address to a variable named rand. Line 3 is an assignment statement, which assigns a value to the number variable. Notice that on the right side of the = operator is a call to the rand.nextInt method. The method executes, and then returns a value. The value that is returned from the method is assigned to the number variable.

Defining a void Method

To create a method you must write its *definition*, which consists of two general parts: a header and a body. You learned about both of these in Chapter 2, but let's briefly review. The *method header*, which appears at the beginning of a method definition, lists several important things about the method, including the method's name. The *method body* is a collection of statements that are performed when the method is executed. These statements are enclosed inside a set of curly braces. Figure 5-2 points out the header and body of a main method.

Figure 5-2 The header and body of a main method

```
Header ──▶  public static void main(String[] args)

                {
Body ──▶            System.out.println("Hello World!");
                }
```

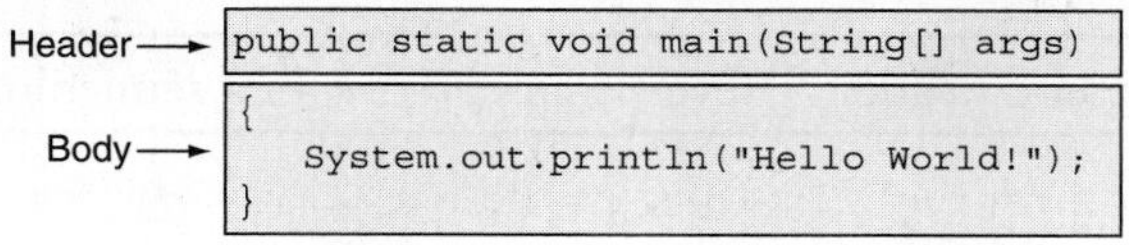

As you already know, every complete Java program must have a main method. Java programs can have other methods as well. Here is an example of a simple method that displays a message on the screen:

```
public static void displayMessage()
{
    System.out.println("Hello from the displayMessage method.");
}
```

This method has a header and a body. Figure 5-3 shows the different parts of the method header.

Figure 5-3   Parts of the method header

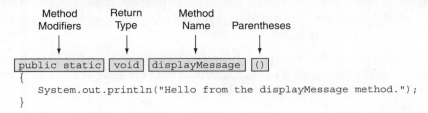

Let's take a closer look at the parts identified in the figure as follows:

- **Method modifiers**—The key words `public` and `static` are modifiers. You don't need to be too concerned with these modifiers now, but if your curiosity is getting the best of you, here's a brief explanation: The word `public` means that the method is publicly available to code outside the class. The word `static` means that the method belongs to the class, not a specific object. You will learn more about these modifiers in later chapters. For this chapter, every method that we write will begin with `public static`.
- **Return type**—Recall our previous discussion of `void` and value-returning methods. When the key word `void` appears here, it means that the method is a `void` method, and does not return a value. As you will see later, a value-returning method lists a data type here.
- **Method name**—You should give each method a descriptive name. In general, the same rules that apply to variable names also apply to method names. This method is named `displayMessage`, so we can easily guess what the method does: It displays a message.
- **Parentheses**—In the header, the method name is always followed by a set of parentheses. As you will learn later in this chapter, methods can be capable of receiving arguments. When this is the case, a list of one or more variable declarations will appear inside the parentheses. The method in this example does not receive any arguments, so the parentheses are empty.

 NOTE: The method header is never terminated with a semicolon.

Calling a Method

A method executes when it is called. The `main` method is automatically called when a program starts, but other methods are executed by method call statements. When a method is called, the JVM branches to that method and executes the statements in its body. Here is an example of a method call statement that calls the `displayMessage` method we previously examined:

```
displayMessage();
```

The statement is simply the name of the method followed by a set of parentheses. Because it is a complete statement, it is terminated with a semicolon.

TIP: Notice that the method modifiers and the void return type are not written in the method call statement. They are written only in the method header.

The program in Code Listing 5-1 demonstrates.

Code Listing 5-1 (`SimpleMethod.java`)

```
1  /**
2     This program defines and calls a simple method.
3  */
4
5  public class SimpleMethod
6  {
7     public static void main(String[] args)
8     {
9        System.out.println("Hello from the main method.");
10       displayMessage();
11       System.out.println("Back in the main method.");
12    }
13
14    /**
15       The displayMessage method displays a greeting.
16    */
17
18    public static void displayMessage()
19    {
20       System.out.println("Hello from the displayMessage method.");
21    }
22 }
```

Program Output

```
Hello from the main method.
Hello from the displayMessage method.
Back in the main method.
```

Notice how the program flows. It starts, of course, in the main method. When the call to the displayMessage method in line 10 is encountered, the JVM branches to that method and performs the statement in its body (at line 20). Once the displayMessage method has finished executing, the JVM branches back to the main method and resumes at line 11 with the statement that follows the method call. This is illustrated in Figure 5-4.

Figure 5-4 Branching in the `SimpleMethod.java` program

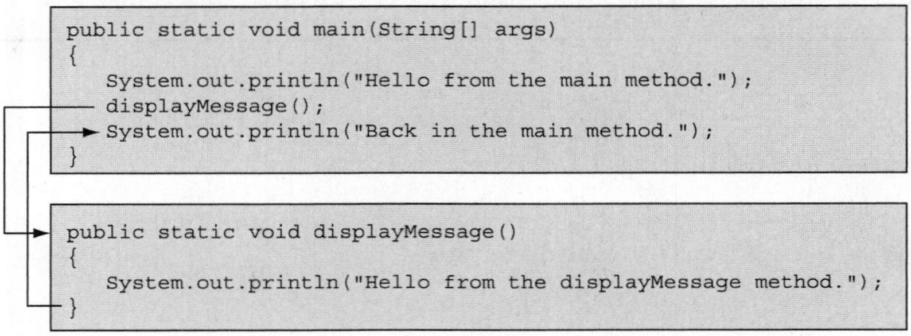

```
public static void main(String[] args)
{
    System.out.println("Hello from the main method.");
    displayMessage();
    System.out.println("Back in the main method.");
}

public static void displayMessage()
{
    System.out.println("Hello from the displayMessage method.");
}
```

Method call statements may be used in control structures like loops, `if` statements, and `switch` statements. The program in Code Listing 5-2 places the `displayMessage` method call inside a loop.

Code Listing 5-2   (LoopCall.java)

```
 1  /**
 2      This program defines and calls a simple method.
 3  */
 4
 5  public class LoopCall
 6  {
 7     public static void main(String[] args)
 8     {
 9        System.out.println("Hello from the main method.");
10        for (int i = 0; i < 5; i++)
11           displayMessage();
12        System.out.println("Back in the main method.");
13     }
14
15     /**
16         The displayMessage method displays a greeting.
17     */
18
19     public static void displayMessage()
20     {
21        System.out.println("Hello from the displayMessage method.");
22     }
23  }
```

Program Output

```
Hello from the main method.
Hello from the displayMessage method.
Hello from the displayMessage method.
Hello from the displayMessage method.
```

```
Hello from the displayMessage method.
Hello from the displayMessage method.
Back in the main method.
```

The program in Code Listing 5-3 shows another example. It asks the user to enter his or her annual salary and credit rating. The program then determines whether the user qualifies for a credit card. One of two void methods, `qualify` or `noQualify`, is called to display a message. Figures 5-5 and 5-6 show example interactions with the program.

Code Listing 5-3   (CreditCard.java)

```java
1   import javax.swing.JOptionPane; 2
2
3   /**
4      This program uses two void methods.
5   */
6
7   public class CreditCard
8   {
9      public static void main(String[] args)
10     {
11        double salary;        // Annual salary
12        int creditRating;     // Credit rating
13        String input;         // To hold the user's input
14
15        // Get the user's annual salary.
16        input = JOptionPane.showInputDialog("What is " +
17                                "your annual salary?");
18        salary = Double.parseDouble(input);
19
20        // Get the user's credit rating (1 through 10).
21        input = JOptionPane.showInputDialog("On a scale of " +
22             "1 through 10, what is your credit rating?\n" +
23             "(10 = excellent, 1 = very bad)");
24        creditRating = Integer.parseInt(input);
25
26        // Determine whether the user qualifies.
27        if (salary >= 20000 && creditRating >= 7)
28           qualify();
29        else
30           noQualify();
31
32        System.exit(0);
33     }
34
35     /**
36        The qualify method informs the user that he
37        or she qualifies for the credit card.
38     */
```

```
39
40     public static void qualify()
41     {
42        JOptionPane.showMessageDialog(null, "Congratulations! " +
43                                 "You qualify for the credit card!");
44     }
45
46     /**
47        The noQualify method informs the user that he
48        or she does not qualify for the credit card.
49     */
50
51     public static void noQualify()
52     {
53        JOptionPane.showMessageDialog(null, "I'm sorry. You " +
54                                 "do not qualify for the credit card.");
55     }
56  }
```

Figure 5-5   Interaction with the `CreditCard.java` program

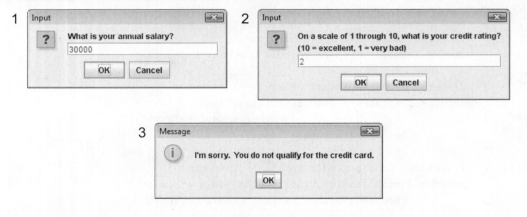

Figure 5-6   Interaction with the `CreditCard.java` program

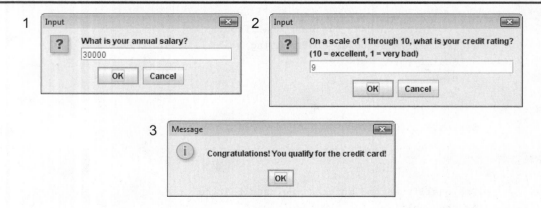

Hierarchical Method Calls

Methods can also be called in a hierarchical, or layered fashion. In other words, method A can call method B, which can then call method C. When method C finishes, the JVM returns to method B. When method B finishes, the JVM returns to method A. The program in Code Listing 5-4 demonstrates this with three methods: main, deep, and deeper. The main method calls the deep method, which then calls the deeper method.

Code Listing 5-4   (DeepAndDeeper.java)

```
 1  /**
 2      This program demonstrates hierarchical method calls.
 3  */
 4
 5  public class DeepAndDeeper
 6  {
 7     public static void main(String[] args)
 8     {
 9        System.out.println("I am starting in main.");
10        deep();
11        System.out.println("Now I am back in main.");
12     }
13
14     /**
15         The deep method displays a message and then calls
16         the deeper method.
17     */
18
19     public static void deep()
20     {
21        System.out.println("I am now in deep.");
22        deeper();
23        System.out.println("Now I am back in deep.");
24     }
25
26     /**
27         The deeper method simply displays a message.
28     */
29
30     public static void deeper()
31     {
32        System.out.println("I am now in deeper.");
33     }
34  }
```

Program Output

```
I am starting in main.
I am now in deep.
```

```
I am now in deeper.
Now I am back in deep.
Now I am back in main.
```

Using Documentation Comments with Methods

You should always document a method by writing comments that appear just before the method's definition. The comments should provide a brief explanation of the method's purpose. Notice that the programs we've looked at in this chapter use documentation comments. Recall from Chapter 2 that documentation comments begin with /** and end with */. These types of comments can be read and processed by a program named javadoc, which produces attractive HTML documentation. As we progress through this chapter, you will learn more about documentation comments and how they can be used with methods.

 Checkpoint

MyProgrammingLab™ *www.myprogramminglab.com*

5.1   What is the difference between a void method and a value-returning method?

5.2   Is the following line of code a method header or a method call?

```
calcTotal();
```

5.3   Is the following line of code a method header or a method call?

```
public static void calcTotal()
```

5.4   What message will the following program display if the user enters 5? What if the user enters 10? What if the user enters 100?

```java
import javax.swing.JOptionPane;
public class Checkpoint
{
    public static void main(String[] args)
    {
        String input;
        int number;

        input = JOptionPane.showInputDialog("Enter a number.");
        number = Integer.parseInt(input);

        if (number < 10)
            method1();
        else
            method2();

        System.exit(0);
    }

    public static void method1()
    {
        JOptionPane.showMessageDialog(null, "Able was I.");
    }
```

```
            public static void method2()
            {
                JOptionPane.showMessageDialog(null, "I saw Elba.");
            }
        }
```

5.5   Write a `void` method that displays your full name. The method should be named
       `myName`.

5.2   Passing Arguments to a Method

CONCEPT: A method may be written so it accepts arguments. Data can then be
passed into the method when it is called.

VideoNote

Passing
Arguments
to a Method

Values that are sent into a method are called *arguments*. You're already familiar with how
to use arguments in a method call. For example, look at the following statement:

```
System.out.println("Hello");
```

This statement calls the `System.out.println` method and passes `"Hello"` as an argument.
Here is another example:

```
number = Integer.parseInt(str);
```

This statement calls the `Integer.parseInt` method and passes the contents of the `str` variable as an argument. By using parameter variables, you can design your own methods that
accept data this way. A *parameter variable*, sometimes simply referred to as a *parameter*, is
a special variable that holds a value being passed into a method. Here is the definition of a
method that uses a parameter:

```
    public static void displayValue(int num)
    {
        System.out.println("The value is " + num);
    }
```

Notice the integer variable declaration that appears inside the parentheses (`int num`). This is
the declaration of a parameter variable, which enables the `displayValue` method to accept
an integer value as an argument. Here is an example of a call to the `displayValue` method,
passing 5 as an argument:

```
    displayValue(5);
```

This statement executes the `displayValue` method. The argument that is listed inside the
parentheses is copied into the method's parameter variable, `num`. This is illustrated in
Figure 5-7.

Figure 5-7 Passing 5 to the `displayValue` method

```
displayValue(5);          The argument 5 is copied into
                          the parameter variable num.


public static void displayValue(int num)
{
    System.out.println("The value is " + num);
}
```

Inside the `displayValue` method, the variable `num` will contain the value of whatever argument was passed into it. If we pass 5 as the argument, the method will display as follows:

    The value is 5

You may also pass the contents of variables and the values of expressions as arguments. For example, the following statements call the `displayValue` method with various arguments passed:

```
displayValue(x);
displayValue(x * 4);
displayValue(Integer.parseInt("700"));
```

The first statement is simple. It passes the value in the variable x as the argument to the `displayValue` method. The second statement is also simple, but it does a little more work: It passes the result of the expression x * 4 as the argument to the `displayValue` method. The third statement does even more work. It passes the value returned from the `Integer.parseInt` method as the argument to the `displayValue` method. (The `Integer.parseInt` method is called first, and its return value is passed to the `displayValue` method.) The program in Code Listing 5-5 demonstrates these method calls.

Code Listing 5-5   (`PassArg.java`)

```
 1  /**
 2      This program demonstrates a method with a parameter.
 3  */
 4
 5  public class PassArg
 6  {
 7     public static void main(String[] args)
 8     {
 9        int x = 10;
10
11        System.out.println("I am passing values to displayValue.");
12        displayValue(5);                                  // Pass 5
13        displayValue(x);                                  // Pass 10
14        displayValue(x * 4);                              // Pass 40
15        displayValue(Integer.parseInt("700"));            // Pass 700
```

```
16            System.out.println("Now I am back in main.");
17      }
18
19      /**
20          The displayValue method displays the value
21          of its integer parameter.
22      */
23
24      public static void displayValue(int num)
25      {
26            System.out.println("The value is " + num);
27      }
28 }
```

Program Output

```
I am passing values to displayValue.
The value is 5
The value is 10
The value is 40
The value is 700
Now I am back in main.
```

 WARNING! When passing a variable as an argument, simply write the variable name inside the parentheses of the method call. Do not write the data type of the argument variable in the method call. For example, the following statement will cause an error:

```
    displayValue(int x);     // Error!
```

The method call should appear as follows:

```
    displayValue(x);         // Correct
```

 NOTE: In this text, the values that are passed into a method are called arguments, and the variables that receive those values are called parameters. There are several variations of these terms in use. In some circles these terms are switched in meaning. Also, some call the arguments *actual parameters* and call the parameters *formal parameters*. Others use the terms *actual argument* and *formal argument*. Regardless of which set of terms you use, it is important to be consistent.

Argument and Parameter Data Type Compatibility

When you pass an argument to a method, be sure that the argument's data type is compatible with the parameter variable's data type. Java will automatically perform a widening conversion if the argument's data type is ranked lower than the parameter variable's data type. For example, the `displayValue` method has an `int` parameter variable. Both of the following code segments will work because the `short` and `byte` arguments are automatically converted to an `int`:

```
short s = 1;
displayValue(s);      // Converts short to int

byte b = 2;
displayValue(b);      // Converts byte to int
```

However, Java will not automatically convert an argument to a lower-ranking data type. This means that a `long`, `float`, or `double` value cannot be passed to a method that has an `int` parameter variable. For example, the following code will cause a compiler error:

```
double d = 1.0;
displayValue(d);   // Error! Can't convert double to int.
```

TIP: You can use a cast operator to convert a value manually to a lower-ranking data type. For example, the following code will compile:

```
double d = 1.0;
displayValue((int)d);   // This will work.
```

Parameter Variable Scope

Recall from Chapter 2 that a variable's scope is the part of the program where the variable may be accessed by its name. A variable is visible only to statements inside the variable's scope. A parameter variable's scope is the method in which the parameter is declared. No statement outside the method can access the parameter variable by its name.

Passing Multiple Arguments

Often it is useful to pass more than one argument to a method. Here is a method that accepts two arguments:

```
public static void showSum(double num1, double num2)
{
    double sum;     // To hold the sum

    sum = num1 + num2;
    System.out.println("The sum is " + sum);
}
```

Notice that two parameter variables, `num1` and `num2`, are declared inside the parentheses in the method header. This is often referred to as a *parameter list*. Also notice that a comma separates the declarations. Here is an example of a statement that calls the method:

```
showSum(5, 10);
```

This statement passes the arguments 5 and 10 into the method. The arguments are passed into the parameter variables in the order that they appear in the method call. In other words, the first argument is passed into the first parameter variable, the second argument is passed into the second parameter variable, and so forth. So, this statement causes 5 to be passed into the num1 parameter and 10 to be passed into the num2 parameter. This is illustrated in Figure 5-8.

Figure 5-8   Multiple arguments passed into multiple parameters

```
                          The argument 5 is copied into the num1 parameter.
                          The argument 10 is copied into the num2 parameter.
    showSum(5, 10);


    public static void showSum(double num1, double num2)
    {
        double sum;     // To hold the sum

        sum = num1 + num2;
        System.out.println("The sum is " + sum);
    }
```

Suppose we were to reverse the order in which the arguments are listed in the method call, as shown here:

```
    showSum(10, 5);
```

This would cause 10 to be passed into the num1 parameter and 5 to be passed into the num2 parameter. The following code segment shows one more example. This time we are passing variables as arguments.

```
    double value1 = 2.5;
    double value2 = 3.5;
    showSum(value1, value2);
```

When the showSum methods executes as a result of this code, the num1 parameter will contain 2.5 and the num2 parameter will contain 3.5.

WARNING! Each parameter variable in a parameter list must have a data type listed before its name. For example, a compiler error would occur if the parameter list for the showSum method were defined as shown in the following header:

```
    public static void showSum(double num1, num2) // Error!
```

A data type for both the num1 and num2 parameter variables must be listed, as shown here:

```
    public static void showSum(double num1, double num2)
```

> See the program TwoArgs.java in this chapter's source code folder for a complete program that demonstrates the showSum method. You can download the book's source code from www.pearsonhighered.com/gaddis.

Arguments Are Passed by Value

In Java, all arguments of the primitive data types are *passed by value*, which means that only a copy of an argument's value is passed into a parameter variable. A method's parameter variables are separate and distinct from the arguments that are listed inside the parentheses of a method call. If a parameter variable is changed inside a method, it has no effect on the original argument. For example, look at the program in Code Listing 5-6.

Code Listing 5-6 (PassByValue.java)

```java
 1  /**
 2      This program demonstrates that only a copy of an argument
 3      is passed into a method.
 4  */
 5
 6  public class PassByValue
 7  {
 8      public static void main(String[] args)
 9      {
10          int number = 99; // number starts with 99
11
12          // Display the value in number.
13          System.out.println("number is " + number);
14
15          // Call changeMe, passing the value in number
16          // as an argument.
17          changeMe(number);
18
19          // Display the value in number again.
20          System.out.println("number is " + number);
21      }
22
23      /**
24          The changeMe method accepts an argument and then
25          changes the value of the parameter.
26      */
27
28      public static void changeMe(int myValue)
29      {
30          System.out.println("I am changing the value.");
31
32          // Change the myValue parameter variable to 0.
33          myValue = 0;
```

```
34
35            // Display the value in myValue.
36            System.out.println("Now the value is " + myValue);
37       }
38  }
```

Program Output

```
number is 99
I am changing the value.
Now the value is 0
number is 99
```

Even though the parameter variable myValue is changed in the changeMe method, the argument number is not modified. The myValue variable contains only a copy of the number variable.

Passing Object References to a Method

So far you've seen examples of methods that accept primitive values as arguments. You can also write methods that accept references to objects as arguments. For example, look at the following method:

```
public static void showLength(String str)
{
   System.out.println(str + " is " + str.length() +
                      " characters long.");
}
```

This method accepts a String object reference as its argument, and displays a message showing the number of characters in the object. The following code shows an example of how to call the method:

```
String name = "Warren";
showLength(name);
```

When this code executes, the showLength method will display the following:

```
Warren is 6 characters long.
```

When an object, such as a String, is passed as an argument, it is actually a reference to the object that is passed. In this example code, the name variable is a String reference variable. It is passed as an argument to the showLength method. The showLength method has a parameter variable, str, which is also a String reference variable, that receives the argument.

Recall that a reference variable holds the memory address of an object. When the showLength method is called, the address that is stored in name is passed into the str parameter variable. This is illustrated in Figure 5-9. This means that when the showLength method is executing, both name and str reference the same object. This is illustrated in Figure 5-10.

Figure 5-9 Passing a reference as an argument

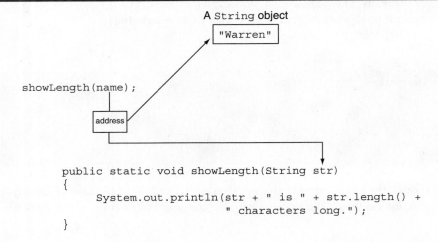

Figure 5-10 Both name and str reference the same object

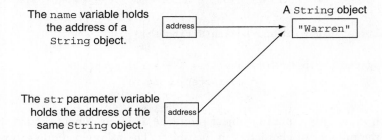

This might lead you to the conclusion that a method can change the contents of any String object that has been passed to it as an argument. After all, the parameter variable references the same object as the argument. However, String objects in Java are *immutable*, which means that they cannot be changed. For example, look at the program in Code Listing 5-7. It passes a String object to a method, which appears to change the object. In reality, the object is not changed.

Code Listing 5-7   (**PassString.java**)

```
1   /**
2       This program demonstrates that String arguments
3       cannot be changed.
4   */
5
6   public class PassString
7   {
8       public static void main(String[] args)
```

```
 9     {
10         // Create a String object containing "Shakespeare".
11         // The name variable references the object.
12         String name = "Shakespeare";
13
14         // Display the String referenced by the name variable.
15         System.out.println("In main, the name is " +
16                         name);
17
18         // Call the changeName method, passing the
19         // contents of the name variable as an argument.
20         changeName(name);
21
22         // Display the String referenced by the name variable.
23         System.out.println("Back in main, the name is " +
24                         name);
25     }
26
27     /**
28         The changeName method accepts a String as its argument
29         and assigns the str parameter to a new String.
30     */
31
32     public static void changeName(String str)
33     {
34         // Create a String object containing "Dickens".
35         // Assign its address to the str parameter variable.
36         str = "Dickens";
37
38         // Display the String referenced by str.
39         System.out.println("In changeName, the name " +
40                         "is now " + str);
41     }
42 }
```

Program Output

```
In main, the name is Shakespeare
In changeName, the name is now Dickens
Back in main, the name is Shakespeare
```

Let's take a closer look at this program. After line 12 executes, the name variable references a String object containing "Shakespeare". In line 20 the changeName method is called and the name variable is passed as an argument. This passes the address of the String object into the str parameter variable. At this point, both name and str reference the same object, as shown in Figure 5-11.

Figure 5-11   Before line 36 executes, both `name` and `str` reference the same object

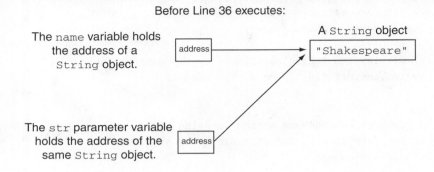

Before Line 36 executes:

The `name` variable holds
the address of a
`String` object.

A `String` object

"Shakespeare"

The `str` parameter variable
holds the address of the
same `String` object.

In the `changeName` method, line 36 executes as follows:

    str = "Dickens";

At first, you might think that this statement changes the `String` object's contents to "Dickens". What actually happens is that a new `String` object containing "Dickens" is created and its address is stored in the `str` variable. After this statement executes, the `name` variable and the `str` parameter variable reference different objects. This is shown in Figure 5-12.

Figure 5-12   After line 36 executes, `name` and `str` reference different objects

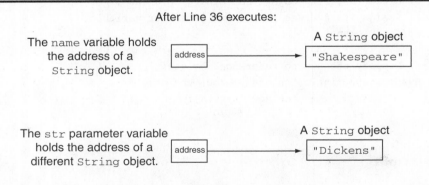

After Line 36 executes:

The `name` variable holds
the address of a
`String` object.

A `String` object

"Shakespeare"

The `str` parameter variable
holds the address of a
different `String` object.

A `String` object

"Dickens"

In Chapter 9 we will discuss the immutability of `String` objects in greater detail. Until then, just remember the following point: `String` objects cannot be changed. Any time you use the = operator to assign a string literal to a `String` reference variable, a new `String` object is created in memory.

Using the `@param` Tag in Documentation Comments

When writing the documentation comments for a method, you can provide a description of each parameter by using a `@param` tag. When the `javadoc` utility sees a `@param` tag inside a method's documentation comments, it knows that the documentation for a parameter variable appears next. The file *TwoArgs2.java*, in this chapter's source code (available at www.pearsonhighered.com/gaddis), has the following method, which uses @param tags in its documentation comments:

```
/**
    The showSum method displays the sum of two numbers.
    @param num1 The first number.
    @param num2 The second number.
*/

    public static void showSum(double num1, double num2)
    {
        double sum;    // To hold the sum

        sum = num1 + num2;
        System.out.println("The sum is " + sum);
    }
```

The general format of a @param tag comment is as follows:

```
@param parameterName Description
```

In the general format, parameterName is the name of the parameter and Description is a description of the parameter. Remember the following points about @param tag comments:

- All @param tags in a method's documentation comment must appear after the general description of the method.
- The description can span several lines. It ends at the end of the documentation comment (the */ symbol), or at the beginning of another tag.

When a method's documentation comments contain one or more @param tags, the javadoc utility will create a Parameters section in the method's documentation. This is where the descriptions of the method's parameters will be listed. Figure 5-13 shows the documentation generated by javadoc for the showSum method in the *TwoArgs2.java* file.

Figure 5-13   Documentation for the showSum method in *TwoArgs2.java*

showSum

```
public static void showSum(double num1,
                           double num2)
```

The showSum method displays the sum of two numbers.

Parameters:
 num1 - The first number.
 num2 - The second number.

Checkpoint

MyProgrammingLab™ *www.myprogramminglab.com*

5.6   What is the difference between an argument and a parameter?

5.7   Look at the following method header:

```
public static void myMethod(int num)
```

Which of the following calls to the method will cause a compiler error?

a) `myMethod(7);`
b) `myMethod(6.2);`
c) `long x = 99;`
    `myMethod(x);`
d) `short s = 2;`
    `myMethod(s);`

5.8   Suppose a method named showValues accepts two int arguments. Which of the
following method headers is written correctly?

a) `public static void showValues()`
b) `public static void showValues(int num1, num2)`
c) `public static void showValues(num1, num2)`
d) `public static void showValues(int num1, int num2)`

5.9   In Java, method arguments are passed by value. What does this mean?

5.10   What will the following program display?

```
public class Checkpoint
{
    public static void main(String[] args)
    {
        int num1 = 99;
        double num2 = 1.5;

        System.out.println(num1 + " " + num2);
        myMethod(num1, num2);
        System.out.println(num1 + " " + num2);
    }

    public static void myMethod(int i, double d)
    {
        System.out.println(i + " " + d);
        i = 0;
        d = 0.0;
        System.out.println(i + " " + d);
    }
}
```

5.3 More about Local Variables

CONCEPT: A local variable is declared inside a method and is not accessible to statements outside the method. Different methods can have local variables with the same names because the methods cannot see each other's local variables.

In Chapter 2 we introduced the concept of local variables, which are variables that are declared inside a method. They are called *local* because they are local to the method in which they are declared. Statements outside a method cannot access that method's local variables.

Because a method's local variables are hidden from other methods, the other methods may have their own local variables with the same name. For example, look at the program in Code Listing 5-8. In addition to the main method, this program has two other methods: texas and california. These two methods each have a local variable named birds.

Code Listing 5-8   (LocalVars.java)

```java
 1  /**
 2      This program demonstrates that two methods may have
 3      local variables with the same name.
 4  */
 5
 6  public class LocalVars
 7  {
 8     public static void main(String[] args)
 9     {
10        texas();
11        california();
12     }
13
14     /**
15         The texas method has a local variable named birds.
16     */
17
18     public static void texas()
19     {
20        int birds = 5000;
21
22        System.out.println("In texas there are " +
23                           birds + " birds.");
24     }
25
26     /**
27         The california method also has a local variable named birds.
28     */
```

```
29      public static void california()
30      {
31         int birds = 3500;
32
33         System.out.println("In california there are " +
34                           birds + " birds.");
35      }
36   }
```

Program Output

```
In texas there are 5000 birds.
In california there are 3500 birds.
```

Although there are two variables named birds, the program can see only one of them at a time because they are in different methods. When the texas method is executing, the birds variable declared inside texas is visible. When the california method is executing, the birds variable declared inside california is visible.

Local Variable Lifetime

A method's local variables exist only while the method is executing. This is known as the *lifetime* of a local variable. When the method begins, its local variables and its parameter variables are created in memory, and when the method ends, the local variables and parameter variables are destroyed. This means that any value stored in a local variable is lost between calls to the method in which the variable is declared.

Initializing Local Variables with Parameter Values

It is possible to use a parameter variable to initialize a local variable. Sometimes this simplifies the code in a method. For example, recall the following showSum method we discussed earlier:

```
public static void showSum(double num1, double num2)
{
   double sum;    // To hold the sum

   sum = num1 + num2;
   System.out.println("The sum is " + sum);
}
```

In the body of the method, the sum variable is declared and then a separate assignment statement assigns num1 + num2 to sum. We can combine these statements into one, as shown in the following modified version of the method.

```
public static void showSum(double num1, double num2)
{
   double sum = num1 + num2;
   System.out.println("The sum is " + sum);
}
```

Because the scope of a parameter variable is the entire method in which it is declared, we can use parameter variables to initialize local variables.

> **WARNING!** Local variables are not automatically initialized with a default value. They must be given a value before they can be used. If you attempt to use a local variable before it has been given a value, a compiler error will result. For example, look at the following method:
>
> ```
> public static void myMethod()
> {
>     int x;
>     System.out.println(x);   //Error! x has no value.
> }
> ```
>
> This code will cause a compiler error because the variable x has not been given a value, and it is being used as an argument to the System.out.println method.

5.4 Returning a Value from a Method

CONCEPT: A method may send a value back to the statement that called the method.

You've seen that data may be passed into a method by way of parameter variables. Data may also be returned from a method, back to the statement that called it. Methods that return a value are appropriately known as *value-returning methods*.

VideoNote

Returning a Value from a Method

You are already experienced at using value-returning methods. For instance, you have used the wrapper class parse methods, such as Integer.parseInt. Here is an example:

```
int num;
num = Integer.parseInt("700");
```

The second line in this code calls the Integer.parseInt method, passing "700" as the argument. The method returns the integer value 700, which is assigned to the num variable by the = operator. You have also seen the Math.pow method, which returns a value. Here is an example:

```
double x;
x = Math.pow(4.0, 2.0);
```

The second line in this code calls the Math.pow method, passing 4.0 and 2.0 as arguments. The method calculates the value of 4.0 raised to the power of 2.0 and returns that value. The value, which is 16.0, is assigned to the x variable by the = operator.

In this section, we will discuss how you can write your own value-returning methods.

Defining a Value-Returning Method

When you are writing a value-returning method, you must decide what type of value the method will return. This is because you must specify the data type of the return value in the method header. Recall that a void method, which does not return a value, uses the key word void as its return type in the method header. A value-returning method will use int, double, boolean, or any other valid data type in its header. Here is an example of a method that returns an int value:

```java
public static int sum(int num1, int num2)
{
    int result;

    result = num1 + num2;
    return result;
}
```

The name of this method is sum. Notice in the method header that the return type is int, as shown in Figure 5-14.

Figure 5-14 Return type in the method header

Return Type

↓

`public static int sum(int num1, int num2)`

This code defines a method named sum that accepts two int arguments. The arguments are passed into the parameter variables num1 and num2. Inside the method, a local variable, result, is declared. The parameter variables num1 and num2 are added, and their sum is assigned to the result variable. The last statement in the method is as follows:

```java
return result;
```

This is a return statement. You must have a return statement in a value-returning method. It causes the method to end execution and it returns a value to the statement that called the method. In a value-returning method, the general format of the return statement is as follows:

```java
return Expression;
```

Expression is the value to be returned. It can be any expression that has a value, such as a variable, literal, or mathematical expression. In this case, the sum method returns the value in the result variable. However, we could have eliminated the result variable and returned the expression num1 + num2, as shown in the following code:

```java
public static int sum(int num1, int num2)
{
    return num1 + num2;
}
```

 NOTE: The return statement's expression must be of the same data type as the return type specified in the method header, or compatible with it. Otherwise, a compiler error will occur. Java will automatically widen the value of the return expression, if necessary, but it will not automatically narrow it.

Calling a Value-Returning Method

The program in Code Listing 5-9 shows an example of how to call the sum method. Notice that the documentation comments for the sum method have a new tag, @return. This tag will be explained later.

Code Listing 5-9   **(ValueReturn.java)**

```java
 1  /**
 2      This program demonstrates a value-returning method.
 3  */
 4
 5  public class ValueReturn
 6  {
 7      public static void main(String[] args)
 8      {
 9          int total, value1 = 20, value2 = 40;
10
11          // Call the sum method, passing the contents of
12          // value1 and value2 as arguments. Assign the
13          // return value to the total variable.
14          total = sum(value1, value2);
15
16          // Display the contents of all these variables.
17          System.out.println("The sum of " + value1 +
18                          " and " + value2 + " is " +
19                          total);
20      }
21
22      /**
23          The sum method returns the sum of its two parameters.
24          @param num1 The first number to be added.
25          @param num2 The second number to be added.
26          @return The sum of num1 and num2.
27      */
28
29      public static int sum(int num1, int num2)
30      {
31          int result; // result is a local variable
32
33          // Assign the value of num1 + num2 to result.
34          result = num1 + num2;
35
36          // Return the value in the result variable.
37          return result;
38      }
39  }
```

Program Output

```
The sum of 20 and 40 is 60
```

The statement in line 14 calls the sum method, passing value1 and value2 as arguments. It assigns the value returned by the sum method to the total variable. In this case, the method will return 60. Figure 5-15 shows how the arguments are passed into the method and how a value is passed back from the method.

Figure 5-15 Arguments passed to sum and a value returned

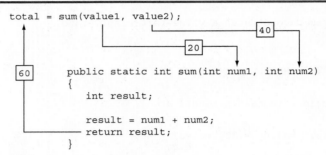

When you call a value-returning method, you usually want to do something meaningful with the value it returns. The ValueReturn.java program shows a method's return value being assigned to a variable. This is commonly how return values are used, but you can do many other things with them. For example, the following code shows a math expression that uses a call to the sum method:

```
int x = 10, y = 15;
double average;
average = sum(x, y) / 2.0;
```

In the last statement, the sum method is called with x and y as its arguments. The method's return value, which is 25, is divided by 2.0. The result, 12.5, is assigned to average. Here is another example:

```
int x = 10, y = 15;
System.out.println("The sum is " + sum(x, y));
```

This code sends the sum method's return value to System.out.println, so it can be displayed on the screen. The message "The sum is 25" will be displayed.

Remember, a value-returning method returns a value of a specific data type. You can use the method's return value anywhere that you can use a regular value of the same data type. This means that anywhere an int value can be used, a call to an int value-returning method can be used. Likewise, anywhere a double value can be used, a call to a double value-returning method can be used. The same is true for all other data types.

Using the @return Tag in Documentation Comments

When writing the documentation comments for a value-returning method, you can provide a description of the return value by using a @return tag. When the javadoc utility sees a @return tag inside a method's documentation comments, it knows that a description of the method's return value appears next.

The general format of a @return tag comment is as follows:

    @return *Description*

Description is a description of the return value. Remember the following points about @return tag comments:

- The @return tag in a method's documentation comment must appear after the general description of the method.
- The description can span several lines. It ends at the end of the documentation comment (the */ symbol), or at the beginning of another tag.

When a method's documentation comments contain a @return tag, the javadoc utility will create a Returns section in the method's documentation. This is where the description of the method's return value will be listed. Figure 5-16 shows the documentation generated by javadoc for the sum method in the *ValueReturn.java* file.

Figure 5-16 Documentation for the sum method in ValueReturn.java

sum

```
public static int sum(int num1,
                      int num2)
```

The sum method returns the sum of its two parameters.

Parameters:
    num1 - The first number to be added.
    num2 - The second number to be added.
Returns:
    The sum of num1 and num2.

In the Spotlight:
Using Methods

Your friend Michael runs a catering company. Some of the ingredients that his recipes require are measured in cups. When he goes to the grocery store to buy those ingredients, however, they are sold only by the fluid ounce. He has asked you to write a simple program that converts cups to fluid ounces.

You design the following algorithm:

1. *Get the number of cups from the user.*
2. *Convert the number of cups to fluid ounces.*
3. *Display the result.*

This algorithm lists the top level of tasks that the program needs to perform, and becomes the basis of the class's main method. The class will also have the following methods:

- getCups—This method will prompt the user to enter the number of cups, and then return that value as a double.

- cupsToOunces—This method will accept the number of cups as an argument and then return the equivalent number of fluid ounces as a double.
- displayResults—This method displays a message indicating the results of the conversion.

Code Listing 5-10 shows the program. Figure 5-17 shows interaction with the program during execution.

Code Listing 5-10   (CupConverter.java)

```java
 1  import javax.swing.JOptionPane;
 2
 3  /**
 4     This program converts cups to fluid ounces.
 5  */
 6
 7  public class CupConverter
 8  {
 9     public static void main(String[] args)
10     {
11        double cups;   // To hold the number of cups
12        double ounces; // To hold the number of ounces
13
14        // Get the number of cups.
15        cups = getCups();
16
17        // Convert the cups to fluid ounces.
18        ounces = cupsToOunces(cups);
19
20        // Display the results.
21        displayResults(cups, ounces);
22        System.exit(0);
23     }
24
25     /**
26        The getCups method prompts the user to enter a number
27        of cups.
28        @return The number of cups entered by the user.
29     */
30
31     public static double getCups()
32     {
33        String input;      // To hold input.
34        double numCups;    // To hold cups.
35
```

```
36        // Get the number of cups from the user.
37        input = JOptionPane.showInputDialog(
38                "This program converts measurements\n" +
39                "in cups to fluid ounces. For your\n" +
40                "reference the formula is:\n" +
41                "    1 cup = 8 fluid ounces\n\n" +
42                "Enter the number of cups.");
43
44        // Convert the input to a double.
45        numCups = Double.parseDouble(input);
46
47        // Return the number of cups.
48        return numCups;
49     }
50
51     /**
52        The cupsToOunces method converts a number of
53        cups to fluid ounces, using the formula
54        1 cup = 8 fluid ounces.
55        @param numCups The number of cups to convert.
56        @return The number of ounces.
57     */
58
59     public static double cupsToOunces(double numCups)
60     {
61        return numCups * 8.0;
62     }
63
64     /**
65        The displayResults method displays a message showing
66        the results of the conversion.
67        @param cups A number of cups.
68        @param ounces A number of ounces.
69     */
70
71     public static void displayResults(double cups, double ounces)
72     {
73        // Display the number of ounces.
74        JOptionPane.showMessageDialog(null,
75                cups + " cups equals " +
76                ounces + " fluid ounces.");
77     }
78  }
```

Figure 5-17 Interaction with the CupConverter program

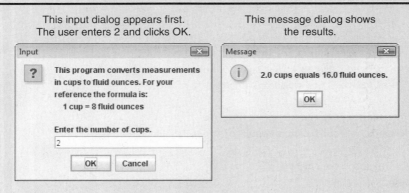

This input dialog appears first.
The user enters 2 and clicks OK.

This message dialog shows
the results.

Returning a boolean Value

Frequently there is a need for a method that tests an argument and returns a true or false value indicating whether or not a condition exists. Such a method would return a boolean value. For example, the following method accepts an argument and returns true if the argument is within the range of 1 through 100, or false otherwise:

```
public static boolean isValid(int number)
{
   boolean status;

   if (number >= 1 && number <= 100)
      status = true;
   else
      status = false;
   return status;
}
```

The following code shows an if-else statement that uses a call to the method:

```
int value = 20;
if (isValid(value))
   System.out.println("The value is within range.");
else
   System.out.println("The value is out of range.");
```

When this code executes, the message "The value is within range." will be displayed.

Returning a Reference to an Object

A value-returning method can also return a reference to a non-primitive type, such as a String object. The program in Code Listing 5-11 shows such an example.

Code Listing 5-11   `(ReturnString.java)`

```
 1  /**
 2      This program demonstrates a method that
 3      returns a reference to a String object.
 4  */
 5
 6  public class ReturnString
 7  {
 8      public static void main(String[] args)
 9      {
10          String customerName;
11
12          customerName = fullName("John", "Martin");
13          System.out.println(customerName);
14      }
15
16      /**
17          The fullName method accepts two String arguments
18          containing a first and last name. It concatenates
19          them into a single String object.
20          @param first The first name.
21          @param last The last name.
22          @return A reference to a String object containing
23                   the first and last names.
24      */
25
26      public static String fullName(String first, String last)
27      {
28          String name;
29
30          name = first + " " + last;
31          return name;
32      }
33  }
```

Program Output

```
John Martin
```

Line 12 calls the `fullName` method, passing `"John"` and `"Martin"` as arguments. The method returns a reference to a `String` object containing `"John Martin"`. The reference is assigned to the `customerName` variable. This is illustrated in Figure 5-18.

Figure 5-18 The `fullName` method returning a reference to a `String` object

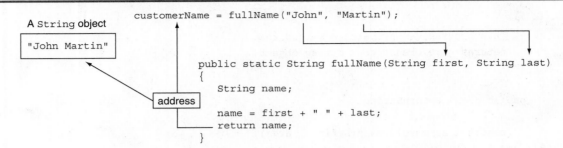

 Checkpoint

www.myprogramminglab.com

5.11 Look at the following method header. What type of value does the method return?

```
public static double getValue(int a, float b, String c)
```

5.12 Write the header for a method named days. The method should return an `int` and have three `int` parameter variables: years, months, and weeks.

5.13 Write the header for a method named `distance`. The method should return a `double` and have two `double` parameter variables: rate and time.

5.14 Write the header for a method named `lightYears`. The method should return a `long` and have one `long` parameter variable: miles.

 5.5 Problem Solving with Methods

CONCEPT: A large, complex problem can be solved a piece at a time by methods.

At the beginning of this chapter we introduced the idea of using methods to "divide and conquer" a problem. Often the best way to solve a complex problem is to break it down into smaller problems, and then solve the smaller problems. The process of breaking down a problem into smaller pieces is called *functional decomposition*.

In functional decomposition, instead of writing one long method that contains all of the statements necessary to solve a problem, small methods are written, which each solve a specific part of the problem. These small methods can then be executed in the desired order to solve the problem.

Let's look at an example. The program in Code Listing 5-12 reads 30 days of sales amounts from a file, and then displays the total sales and average daily sales. Here's a brief pseudo-code model of the algorithm:

Ask the user to enter the name of the file.
Get the total of the sales amounts in the file.
Calculate the average daily sales.
Display the total and average daily sales.

> The file `MonthlySales.txt`, in this chapter's source code (available at www.pearsonhighered.com/gaddis), is used to test the program. Figure 5-19 shows interaction with the program during execution.

Code Listing 5-12   (SalesReport.java)

```java
 1 import java.util.Scanner;         // For the Scanner class
 2 import java.io.*;                  // For file I/O classes
 3 import javax.swing.JOptionPane;    // For the JOptionPane class
 4
 5 /**
 6    This program opens a file containing the sales
 7    amounts for 30 days. It calculates and displays
 8    the total sales and average daily sales.
 9 */
10
11 public class SalesReport
12 {
13    public static void main(String[] args) throws IOException
14    {
15       final int NUM_DAYS = 30; // Number of days of sales
16       String filename;         // The name of the file to open
17       double totalSales;       // Total sales for period
18       double averageSales;     // Average daily sales
19
20       // Get the name of the file.
21       filename = getFileName();
22
23       // Get the total sales from the file.
24       totalSales = getTotalSales(filename);
25
26       // Calculate the average.
27       averageSales = totalSales / NUM_DAYS;
28
29       // Display the total and average.
30       displayResults(totalSales, averageSales);
31
32       System.exit(0);
33    }
34
35    /**
36       The getFileName method prompts the user to enter
37       the name of the file to open.
38       @return A reference to a String object containing
39               the name of the file.
40    */
```

```
41
42      public static String getFileName()
43      {
44         String file;   // To hold the file name
45
46         // Prompt the user to enter a file name.
47         file = JOptionPane.showInputDialog(
48                   "Enter the name of the file\n" +
49                   "containing 30 days of sales amounts.");
50
51         // Return the name.
52         return file;
53      }
54
55      /**
56         The getTotalSales method opens a file and
57         reads the daily sales amounts, accumulating
58         the total. The total is returned.
59         @param filename The name of the file to open.
60         @return The total of the sales amounts.
61      */
62
63      public static double getTotalSales(String filename) throws IOException
64      {
65         double total = 0.0;   // Accumulator
66         double sales;         // A daily sales amount
67
68         // Open the file.
69         File file = new File(filename);
70         Scanner inputFile = new Scanner(file);
71
72         // This loop processes the lines read from the file,
73         // until the end of the file is encountered.
74         while (inputFile.hasNext())
75         {
76            // Read a double from the file.
77            sales = inputFile.nextDouble();
78
79            // Add sales to the value already in total.
80            total += sales;
81         }
82
83         // Close the file.
84         inputFile.close();
85
86         // Return the total sales.
87         return total;
```

```
 88    }
 89
 90    /**
 91       The displayResults method displays the total and
 92       average daily sales.
 93       @param total The total sales.
 94       @param avg The average daily sales.
 95    */
 96
 97    public static void displayResults(double total, double avg)
 98    {
 99       // Display the formatted total and average sales.
100       JOptionPane.showMessageDialog(null,
101          String.format("The total sales for the period is $%,.2f\n" +
102                        "The average daily sales were $%,.2f",
103                        total, avg));
104    }
105 }
```

Instead of writing the entire program in the `main` method, the algorithm was broken down into the following methods:

- `getFileName`—This method displays an input dialog box asking the user to enter the name of the file containing 30 days of sales amounts. The method returns a reference to a `String` object containing the name entered by the user.
- `getTotalSales`—This method accepts the name of a file as an argument. The file is opened, the sales amounts are read from it, and the total of the sales amounts is accumulated. The method returns the total as a `double`.
- `displayResults`—This method accepts as arguments the total sales and the average daily sales. It displays a message dialog box indicating these values.

Figure 5-19 Interaction with the `SalesReport.java` program

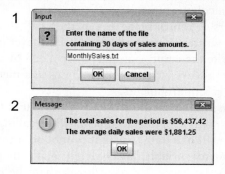

Calling Methods That Throw Exceptions

One last thing about the *SalesReport.java* program should be discussed. Notice that the main method header (in line 13) and the getTotalSales method header (in line 63) both have a throws IOException clause. The getTotalSales method has the clause because it uses a Scanner object to open a file. As you know from Chapter 4, any method that uses a Scanner object to open a file should have a throws IOException clause in its header. Let's quickly review why this is so.

When a Scanner object has a problem opening a file, it throws an exception known as IOException. Java requires that either (a) the exception is handled in the method that caused it to occur, or (b) the method terminates and throws the exception again. For now you must write your methods to throw the exception again because you will not learn how to handle exceptions until Chapter 11. By writing a throws IOException clause in a method's header, you are telling the compiler that the method does not handle the exception. Instead, it throws the exception again.

That explains why the getTotalSales method has the throws IOException clause, but it doesn't explain why the main method has one. After all, main doesn't use a Scanner object to perform any file operations. The reason main has to have the clause is because main calls the getTotalSales method. If the Scanner object in getTotalSales throws an IOException, the getTotalSales method terminates and throws the IOException again. That means that main must either handle the exception, or terminate and throw it once again. When the main method throws the exception, the JVM displays an error message on the screen.

 TIP: Until you learn how to handle exceptions in Chapter 11, just remember this when writing programs that throw exceptions: If a method calls another method that has a throws clause in its header, then the calling method should have the same throws clause.

5.6   Common Errors to Avoid

- **Putting a semicolon at the end of a method header.** Method headers are never terminated with a semicolon.
- **Writing modifiers or return types in a method call statement.** Method modifiers and return types are written in method headers, but never in method calls.
- **Forgetting to write the empty parentheses in a call to a method that accepts no arguments.** You must always write the parentheses in a method call statement, even if the method doesn't accept arguments.
- **Forgetting to pass arguments to methods that require them.** If a method has parameter variables, you must provide arguments when calling the method.
- **Passing an argument of a data type that cannot be automatically converted to the data type of the parameter variable.** Java will automatically perform a widening conversion if the argument's data type is ranked lower than the parameter variable's data type. But Java will not automatically convert an argument to a lower-ranking data type.
- **Attempting to access a parameter variable with code outside the method where the variable is declared.** A parameter variable is visible only within the method it is declared in.

- **Not writing the data type of each parameter variable in a method header.** Each parameter variable declaration inside the parentheses of a method header must include the variable's data type.
- **Changing the contents of a method's parameter variable and expecting the argument that was passed into the parameter to change as well.** Method arguments are passed by value, which means that a copy of the argument is passed into a parameter variable. Changes to the parameter variable have no effect on the argument.
- **Using a variable to receive a method's return value when the variable's data type is incompatible with the data type of the return value.** A variable that receives a method's return value must be of a data type that is compatible with the data type of the return value.
- **Not writing a `return` statement in a value-returning method.** If a method's return type is anything other than `void`, it should return a value.
- **Not writing a required `throws` clause in a method that calls another method.** Any method that calls a method with a `throws` clause in its header must either handle the potential exception or have the same `throws` clause. You will learn how to handle exceptions in Chapter 11.

Review Questions and Exercises

Multiple Choice and True/False

1. This type of method does not return a value.
   a. null
   b. void
   c. empty
   d. anonymous

2. This appears at the beginning of a method definition.
   a. semicolon
   b. parentheses
   c. body
   d. header

3. The body of a method is enclosed in _____.
   a. curly braces `{ }`
   b. square brackets `[ ]`
   c. parentheses `( )`
   d. quotation marks `" "`

4. A method header can contain _____.
   a. method modifiers
   b. the method return type
   c. the method name
   d. a list of parameter declarations
   e. all of these
   f. none of these

5. A value that is passed into a method when it is called is known as a(n) _____.
    a. parameter
    b. argument
    c. signal
    d. return value

6. A variable that receives a value that is passed into a method is known as a(n) _____.
    a. parameter
    b. argument
    c. signal
    d. return value

7. This `javadoc` tag is used to document a parameter variable.
    a. `@parameter`
    b. `@param`
    c. `@paramvar`
    d. `@arg`

8. This statement causes a method to end and sends a value back to the statement that called the method.
    a. `end`
    b. `send`
    c. `exit`
    d. `return`

9. This `javadoc` tag is used to document a method's return value.
    a. `@methodreturn`
    b. `@ret`
    c. `@return`
    d. `@returnval`

10. **True or False:** You terminate a method header with a semicolon.

11. **True or False:** When passing an argument to a method, Java will automatically perform a widening conversion (convert the argument to a higher-ranking data type), if necessary.

12. **True or False:** When passing an argument to a method, Java will automatically perform a narrowing conversion (convert the argument to a lower-ranking data type), if necessary.

13. **True or False:** A parameter variable's scope is the entire program that contains the method in which the parameter is declared.

14. **True or False:** When code in a method changes the value of a parameter, it also changes the value of the argument that was passed into the parameter.

15. **True or False:** When an object, such as a `String`, is passed as an argument, it is actually a reference to the object that is passed.

16. **True or False:** The contents of a `String` object cannot be changed.

17. **True or False:** When passing multiple arguments to a method, the order in which the arguments are passed is not important.

18. **True or False:** No two methods in the same program can have a local variable with the same name.

19. **True or False:** It is possible for one method to access a local variable that is declared in another method.

20. **True or False:** You must have a `return` statement in a value-returning method.

Find the Error

1. Find the error in the following method definition:

```
// This method has an error!
public static void sayHello();
{
    System.out.println("Hello");
}
```

2. Look at the following method header:

```
public static void showValue(int x)
```

The following code has a call to the `showValue` method. Find the error.

```
int x = 8;
showValue(int x);     // Error!
```

3. Find the error in the following method definition:

```
// This method has an error!
public static double timesTwo(double num)
{
    double result = num * 2;
}
```

4. Find the error in the following method definition:

```
// This method has an error!
public static int half(double num)
{
    double result = num / 2.0;
    return result;
}
```

Algorithm Workbench

1. Examine the following method header, and then write an example call to the method:

```
public static void doSomething(int x)
```

2. Here is the code for the `displayValue` method, shown earlier in this chapter:

```
public static void displayValue(int num)
{
    System.out.println("The value is " + num);
}
```

For each of the following code segments, indicate whether it will successfully compile or cause an error:

a. `displayValue(100);`
b. `displayValue(6.0);`
c. `short s = 5;`
   `displayValue(s);`
d. `long num = 1;`
   `displayValue(num);`
e. `displayValue(6.2f);`
f. `displayValue((int) 7.5);`

3. Look at the following method header:

```
public static void myMethod(int a, int b, int c)
```

Now look at the following call to `myMethod`:

```
myMethod(3, 2, 1);
```

When this call executes, what value will be stored in a? What value will be stored in b? What value will be stored in c?

4. What will the following program display?

```
public class ChangeParam
{
    public static void main(String[] args)
    {
        int x = 1;
        double y = 3.4;
        System.out.println(x + " " + y);
        changeUs(x, y);
        System.out.println(x + " " + y);
    }

    public static void changeUs(int a, double b)
    {
        a = 0;
        b = 0.0;
        System.out.println(a + " " + b);
    }
}
```

5. A program contains the following method definition:

```
public static int cube(int num)
{
    return num * num * num;
}
```

Write a statement that passes the value 4 to this method and assigns its return value to a variable named `result`.

6. A program contains the following method:

```
public static void display(int arg1, double arg2, char arg3)
{
    System.out.println("The values are " + arg1 + ", " +
                    arg2 + ", and " + arg3);
}
```

Write a statement that calls this method and passes the following variables as arguments:

```
char initial = 'T';
int age = 25;
double income = 50000.00;
```

7. Write a method named `timesTen`. The method should accept a `double` argument, and return a `double` value that is ten times the value of the argument.

8. Write a method named `square` that accepts an integer argument and returns the square of that argument.

9. Write a method named `getName` that prompts the user to enter his or her first name, and then returns the user's input.

10. Write a method named `quartersToDollars`. The method should accept an `int` argument that is a number of quarters, and return the equivalent number of dollars as a `double`. For example, if you pass 4 as an argument, the method should return 1.0; and if you pass 7 as an argument, the method should return 1.75.

Short Answer

1. What is the "divide and conquer" approach to problem solving?

2. What is the difference between a void method and a value-returning method?

3. What is the difference between an argument and a parameter variable?

4. Where do you declare a parameter variable?

5. Explain what is meant by the phrase "pass by value."

6. Why do local variables lose their values between calls to the method in which they are declared?

Programming Challenges

MyProgrammingLab™ *Visit www.myprogramminglab.com to complete many of these Programming Challenges online and get instant feedback.*

1. showChar Method

Write a method named showChar. The method should accept two arguments: a reference to a String object and an integer. The integer argument is a character position within the String, with the first character being at position 0. When the method executes, it should display the character at that character position. Here is an example of a call to the method:

```
showChar("New York", 2);
```

In this call, the method will display the character w because it is in position 2. Demonstrate the method in a complete program.

2. Retail Price Calculator

VideoNote
The Retail
Price
Calculator
Problem

Write a program that asks the user to enter an item's wholesale cost and its markup percentage. It should then display the item's retail price. For example:

- If an item's wholesale cost is 5.00 and its markup percentage is 100 percent, then the item's retail price is 10.00.
- If an item's wholesale cost is 5.00 and its markup percentage is 50 percent, then the item's retail price is 7.50.

The program should have a method named calculateRetail that receives the wholesale cost and the markup percentage as arguments, and returns the retail price of the item.

3. Rectangle Area—Complete the Program

If you have downloaded the book's source code from www.pearsonhighered.com/gaddis, you will find a partially written program named AreaRectangle.java in this chapter's source code folder. Your job is to complete the program. When it is complete, the program will ask the user to enter the width and length of a rectangle, and then display the rectangle's area. The program calls the following methods, which have not been written:

- getLength—This method should ask the user to enter the rectangle's length, and then return that value as a double.
- getWidth—This method should ask the user to enter the rectangle's width, and then return that value as a double.
- getArea—This method should accept the rectangle's length and width as arguments, and return the rectangle's area. The area is calculated by multiplying the length by the width.
- displayData—This method should accept the rectangle's length, width, and area as arguments, and display them in an appropriate message on the screen.

4. Paint Job Estimator

A painting company has determined that for every 115 square feet of wall space, one gallon of paint and eight hours of labor will be required. The company charges $18.00 per hour for labor. Write a program that allows the user to enter the number of rooms to be painted and the price of the paint per gallon. It should also ask for the square feet of wall space in each room. The program should have methods that return the following data:

- The number of gallons of paint required
- The hours of labor required

- The cost of the paint
- The labor charges
- The total cost of the paint job

Then it should display the data on the screen.

5. Falling Distance

When an object is falling because of gravity, the following formula can be used to determine the distance the object falls in a specific time period:

$$d = \frac{1}{2} gt^2$$

The variables in the formula are as follows: d is the distance in meters, g is 9.8, and t is the amount of time, in seconds, that the object has been falling.

Write a method named `fallingDistance` that accepts an object's falling time (in seconds) as an argument. The method should return the distance, in meters, that the object has fallen during that time interval. Demonstrate the method by calling it in a loop that passes the values 1 through 10 as arguments, and displays the return value.

6. Celsius Temperature Table

The formula for converting a temperature from Fahrenheit to Celsius is

$$C = \frac{5}{9} (F - 32)$$

where F is the Fahrenheit temperature and C is the Celsius temperature. Write a method named `celsius` that accepts a Fahrenheit temperature as an argument. The method should return the temperature, converted to Celsius. Demonstrate the method by calling it in a loop that displays a table of the Fahrenheit temperatures 0 through 20 and their Celsius equivalents.

7. Test Average and Grade

Write a program that asks the user to enter five test scores. The program should display a letter grade for each score and the average test score. Write the following methods in the program:

- `calcAverage`—This method should accept five test scores as arguments and return the average of the scores.
- `determineGrade`—This method should accept a test score as an argument and return a letter grade for the score, based on the following grading scale:

Score	Letter Grade
90–100	A
80–89	B
70–79	C
60–69	D
Below 60	F

8. Conversion Program

Write a program that asks the user to enter a distance in meters. The program will then present the following menu of selections:

1. Convert to kilometers
2. Convert to inches
3. Convert to feet
4. Quit the program

The program will convert the distance to kilometers, inches, or feet, depending on the user's selection. Here are the specific requirements:

- Write a void method named showKilometers, which accepts the number of meters as an argument. The method should display the argument converted to kilometers. Convert the meters to kilometers using the following formula:

  ```
  kilometers = meters * 0.001
  ```

- Write a void method named showInches, which accepts the number of meters as an argument. The method should display the argument converted to inches. Convert the meters to inches using the following formula:

  ```
  inches = meters * 39.37
  ```

- Write a void method named showFeet, which accepts the number of meters as an argument. The method should display the argument converted to feet. Convert the meters to feet using the following formula:

  ```
  feet = meters * 3.281
  ```

- Write a void method named menu that displays the menu of selections. This method should not accept any arguments.
- The program should continue to display the menu until the user enters 4 to quit the program.
- The program should not accept negative numbers for the distance in meters.
- If the user selects an invalid choice from the menu, the program should display an error message.

Here is an example session with the program, using console input. The user's input is shown in bold.

```
Enter a distance in meters: 500 [Enter]
1. Convert to kilometers
2. Convert to inches
3. Convert to feet
4. Quit the program

Enter your choice: 1 [Enter]
500 meters is 0.5 kilometers.

1. Convert to kilometers
2. Convert to inches
3. Convert to feet
4. Quit the program
```

```
Enter your choice: 3 [Enter]
500 meters is 1640.5 feet.

1. Convert to kilometers
2. Convert to inches
3. Convert to feet
4. Quit the program

Enter your choice: 4 [Enter]
Bye!
```

9. Distance Traveled Modification

The distance a vehicle travels can be calculated as follows:

$Distance = Speed * Time$

Write a method named distance that accepts a vehicle's speed and time as arguments, and returns the distance the vehicle has traveled. Modify the "Distance Traveled" program you wrote in Chapter 4 (Programming Challenge 2) to use the method.

10. Stock Profit

The profit from the sale of a stock can be calculated as follows:

$Profit = ((NS \times SP) - SC) - ((NS \times PP) + PC)$

where NS is the number of shares, PP is the purchase price per share, PC is the purchase commission paid, SP is the sale price per share, and SC is the sale commission paid. If the calculation yields a positive value, then the sale of the stock resulted in a profit. If the calculation yields a negative number, then the sale resulted in a loss.

Write a method that accepts as arguments the number of shares, the purchase price per share, the purchase commission paid, the sale price per share, and the sale commission paid. The method should return the profit (or loss) from the sale of stock. Demonstrate the method in a program that asks the user to enter the necessary data and displays the amount of the profit or loss.

11. Multiple Stock Sales

Use the method that you wrote for Programming Challenge 10 (Stock Profit) in a program that calculates the total profit or loss from the sale of multiple stocks. The program should ask the user for the number of stock sales, and the necessary data for each stock sale. It should accumulate the profit or loss for each stock sale and then display the total.

12. Kinetic Energy

In physics, an object that is in motion is said to have kinetic energy. The following formula can be used to determine a moving object's kinetic energy:

$KE = \frac{1}{2} mv^2$

The variables in the formula are as follows: KE is the kinetic energy, m is the object's mass in kilograms, and v is the object's velocity, in meters per second.

Write a method named `kineticEnergy` that accepts an object's mass (in kilograms) and velocity (in meters per second) as arguments. The method should return the amount of kinetic energy that the object has. Demonstrate the method by calling it in a program that asks the user to enter values for mass and velocity.

13. `isPrime` Method

A prime number is a number that is evenly divisible only by itself and 1. For example, the number 5 is prime because it can be evenly divided only by 1 and 5. The number 6, however, is not prime because it can be divided evenly by 1, 2, 3, and 6.

Write a method named `isPrime`, which takes an integer as an argument and returns `true` if the argument is a prime number, or `false` otherwise. Demonstrate the method in a complete program.

TIP: Recall that the `%` operator divides one number by another, and returns the remainder of the division. In an expression such as `num1 % num2`, the `%` operator will return 0 if `num1` is evenly divisible by `num2`.

14. Prime Number List

Use the `isPrime` method that you wrote in Programming Challenge 13 in a program that stores a list of all the prime numbers from 1 through 100 in a file.

15. Even/Odd Counter

You can use the following logic to determine whether a number is even or odd:

```
if ((number % 2) == 0)
{
    // The number is even.
}
else
{
    // The number is odd.
}
```

Write a program with a method named `isEven` that accepts an `int` argument. The method should return `true` if the argument is even, or `false` otherwise. The program's `main` method should use a loop to generate 100 random integers. It should use the `isEven` method to determine whether each random number is even, or odd. When the loop is finished, the program should display the number of even numbers that were generated, and the number of odd numbers.

16. Present Value

Suppose you want to deposit a certain amount of money into a savings account, and then leave it alone to draw interest for the next 10 years. At the end of 10 years, you would like to have $10,000 in the account. How much do you need to deposit today to make that happen? You can use the following formula, which is known as the present value formula, to find out:

$$P = \frac{F}{(1 + r)^n}$$

The terms in the formula are as follows:

- P is the **present value,** or the amount that you need to deposit today.
- F is the **future value** that you want in the account. (In this case, F is $10,000.)
- r is the **annual interest rate.**
- n is the **number of years** that you plan to let the money sit in the account.

Write a method named `presentValue` that performs this calculation. The method should accept the future value, annual interest rate, and number of years as arguments. It should return the present value, which is the amount that you need to deposit today. Demonstrate the method in a program that lets the user experiment with different values for the formula's terms.

17. Rock, Paper, Scissors Game

Write a program that lets the user play the game of Rock, Paper, Scissors against the computer. The program should work as follows.

1. When the program begins, a random number in the range of 1 through 3 is generated. If the number is 1, then the computer has chosen rock. If the number is 2, then the computer has chosen paper. If the number is 3, then the computer has chosen scissors. (Don't display the computer's choice yet.)
2. The user enters his or her choice of "rock", "paper", or "scissors" at the keyboard. (You can use a menu if you prefer.)
3. The computer's choice is displayed.
4. A winner is selected according to the following rules:

- If one player chooses rock and the other player chooses scissors, then rock wins. (The rock smashes the scissors.)
- If one player chooses scissors and the other player chooses paper, then scissors wins. (Scissors cuts paper.)
- If one player chooses paper and the other player chooses rock, then paper wins. (Paper wraps rock.)
- If both players make the same choice, the game must be played again to determine the winner.

Be sure to divide the program into methods that perform each major task.

18. ESP Game

Write a program that tests your ESP (extrasensory perception). The program should randomly select the name of a color from the following list of words:

> *Red, Green, Blue, Orange, Yellow*

To select a word, the program can generate a random number. For example, if the number is 0, the selected word is *Red*; if the number is 1, the selected word is *Green*; and so forth.

Next, the program should ask the user to enter the color that the computer has selected. After the user has entered his or her guess, the program should display the name of the randomly selected color. The program should repeat this 10 times and then display the number of times the user correctly guessed the selected color. Be sure to modularize the program into methods that perform each major task.

CHAPTER

6 A First Look at Classes

TOPICS

6.1 Objects and Classes

CONCEPT: An object is a software component that exists in memory and serves a specific purpose in a program. An object is created from a class that contains code describing the object.

If you have ever driven a car, you know that a car consists of a lot of components. It has a steering wheel, an accelerator pedal, a brake pedal, a gear shifter, a speedometer, and numerous other devices that the driver interacts with. There are also a lot of components under the hood, such as the engine, the battery, the radiator, and so forth. So, a car is not just one single object, but rather a collection of objects that work together.

This same notion applies to computer programming as well. Most programming languages in use today are object-oriented. With an object-oriented language, such as Java, you create programs that are made of objects. In programming, however, an object isn't a physical device, like a steering wheel or a brake pedal; it's a software component that exists in the computer's memory and performs a specific task. In software, an object has two general capabilities:

- An object can store data. The data stored in an object are commonly called *fields*.
- An object can perform operations. The operations that an object can perform are called *methods*.

319

Objects are very important in Java. Here are some examples of objects that you have previously learned about:

- If you need to read input from the keyboard, or from a file, you can use a Scanner object.
- If you need to generate random numbers, you can use a Random object.
- If you need to write output to a file, you can use a PrintWriter object.

When a program needs the services of a particular type of object, it creates that object in memory, and then calls that object's methods as necessary.

Classes: Where Objects Come From

Objects are very useful, but they don't just magically appear in your program. Before a specific type of object can be used by a program, that object has to be created in memory. And, before an object can be created in memory, you must have a class for the object.

A *class* is code that describes a particular type of object. It specifies the data that an object can hold (the object's fields), and the actions that an object can perform (the object's methods). You can think of a class as a code "blueprint" that can be used to create a particular type of object. It serves a purpose similar to that of the blueprint for a house. The blueprint itself is not a house, but rather a detailed description of a house. When we use the blueprint to build an actual house, we could say we are building an instance of the house described by the blueprint. If we so desire, we can build several identical houses from the same blueprint. Each house is a separate instance of the house described by the blueprint. This idea is illustrated in Figure 6-1.

Figure 6-1 A blueprint and houses built from the blueprint

Blueprint that describes a house

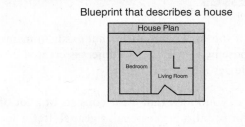

Instances of the house described by the blueprint

So, a class is not an object, but a description of an object. When a program is running, it can use the class to create, in memory, as many objects of a specific type as needed. Each object that is created from a class is called an *instance* of the class.

NOTE: Up to this chapter, you have used classes for a different purpose: as containers for a program's methods. All of the Java programs that you have written so far have had a class containing a main method, and possibly other methods. In this chapter, you will learn how to write classes from which objects can be created.

Classes in the Java API

So far, the objects that you have used in your programs are created from classes in the Java API. For example, each time you create a Scanner object, you are creating an instance of a class named Scanner, which is in the Java API. Likewise, when you create a Random object, you are creating an instance of a class named Random, which is in the Java API. The same is true for PrintWriter objects. When you need to write data to a file, you create an instance of the PrintWriter class, which is in the Java API. Look at Code Listing 6-1, a program that uses all of these types of objects.

Code Listing 6-1   (ObjectDemo.java)

```java
1   import java.util.Scanner; // Needed for the Scanner class
2   import java.util.Random;  // Needed for the Random class
3   import java.io.*;         // Needed for file I/O classes
4
5   /**
6      This program writes random numbers to a file.
7   */
8
9   public class ObjectDemo
10  {
11     public static void main(String[] args) throws IOException
12     {
13        int maxNumbers;    // Max number of random numbers
14        int number;        // To hold a random number
15
16        // Create a Scanner object for keyboard input.
17        Scanner keyboard = new Scanner(System.in);
18
19        // Create a Random object to generate random numbers.
20        Random rand = new Random();
21
22        // Create a PrintWriter object to open the file.
23        PrintWriter outputFile = new PrintWriter("numbers.txt");
24
25        // Get the number of random numbers to write.
26        System.out.print("How many random numbers should I write? ");
27        maxNumbers = keyboard.nextInt();
28
```

```
29          // Write the random numbers to the file.
30          for (int count = 0; count < maxNumbers; count++)
31          {
32             // Generate a random integer.
33             number = rand.nextInt();
34
35             // Write the random integer to the file.
36             outputFile.println(number);
37          }
38
39          // Close the file.
40          outputFile.close();
41          System.out.println("Done");
42       }
43    }
```

Program Output with Example Input Shown in Bold

How many random numbers should I write? **10 [Enter]**
Done

In a nutshell, this program writes a specified number of random numbers to a file named numbers.txt. When the program runs, it asks the user for the number of random numbers to write. It then writes that many numbers to the file. To do its job, it creates three objects:

- In line 17 it creates an instance of the Scanner class, and assigns the object's address to a variable named keyboard. The object will be used to read keyboard input.
- In line 20 it creates an instance of the Random class, and assigns the object's address to a variable named rand. The object will be used to generate random numbers.
- In line 23 it creates an instance of the PrintWriter class, and assigns the object's address to a variable named outputFile. The object will be used to write output to the numbers.txt file.

Figure 6-2 illustrates the three objects that the program creates. As the program runs, it uses these objects to accomplish certain tasks. For example:

- In line 27 the Scanner object's nextInt method is called to read the user's input (which is the number of random numbers to generate). The value that is returned from the method is assigned to the maxNumbers variable.
- In line 33 the Random object's nextInt method is called to get a random integer. The value that is returned from the method is assigned to the number variable.
- In line 36 the PrintWriter object's println method is called to write the value of the number variable to the file.
- In line 40 the PrintWriter object's close method is called to close the file.

This simple example demonstrates how most programs work. A program creates the various objects that it needs to complete its job. Each object has a set of methods that can be called, causing the object to perform an operation. When the program needs an object to do something, it calls the appropriate method.

Figure 6-2   Objects created by the `ObjectDemo` program

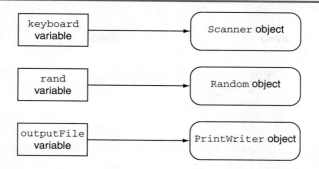

 NOTE: The `import` statements that appear in lines 1 through 3 of Code Listing 6-1 make the `Scanner`, `Random`, and `PrintWriter` classes available to the program. You will learn more about how the Java API is organized, and why you need these `import` statements later in this chapter.

Primitive Variables vs. Objects

Chapter 2 introduced you to the Java primitive data types: `byte`, `short`, `int`, `long`, `char`, `float`, `double`, and `boolean`. By now you have seen many programs that use both primitive data types and objects. In fact, the program in Code Listing 6-1 uses two primitive variables (`maxNumbers` and `number`, both `int` variables), as well as a `Scanner` object, a `Random` object, and a `PrintWriter` object.

You've probably noticed that the steps required to create an object differ from the steps required to create a primitive variable. For example, to create an `int` variable, you simply need a declaration such as the following:

```
int wholeNumber;
```

But, to create an object, you have to write some extra code. For example, the following statement creates a `Random` object:

```
Random rand = new Rand();
```

Primitive variables, such as `int`s, `double`s, and so forth, are simply storage locations in the computer's memory. A primitive data type is called "primitive" because a variable created with a primitive data type has no built-in capabilities other than storing a value. When you declare a primitive variable, the compiler sets aside, or allocates, a chunk of memory that is big enough for that variable. For example, look at the following variable declarations:

```
int wholeNumber;
double realNumber;
```

Recall from Chapter 2 that an `int` uses 4 bytes of memory and a `double` uses 8 bytes of memory. These declaration statements will cause memory to be allocated as shown in Figure 6-3.

Figure 6-3   Memory allocation

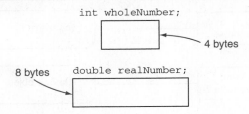

The memory that is allocated for a primitive variable is the actual location that will hold any value that is assigned to that variable. For example, suppose we use the following statements to assign values to the variables shown in Figure 6-3:

```
wholeNumber = 99;
realNumber = 123.45;
```

Figure 6-4 shows how the assigned values are stored in each variable's memory location.

Figure 6-4   Values assigned to the variables

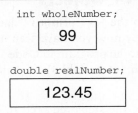

As you can see from these illustrations, primitive variables are very straightforward. When you are working with a primitive variable, you are using a storage location that holds a piece of data.

This is different from the way that objects work. When you are working with an object, you are typically using two things:

- The object itself, which must be created in memory
- A reference variable that refers to the object

The object that is created in memory holds data of some sort and performs operations of some sort. (Exactly what the data and operations are depends on what kind of object it is.) In order to work with the object in code, you need some way to refer to the object. That's where the reference variable comes in. The reference variable doesn't hold an actual piece of data that your program will work with. Instead, it holds the object's memory address. We say that the variable references the object. When you want to work with the object, you use the variable that references it.

Reference variables, also known as class type variables, can be used only to reference objects. Figure 6-5 illustrates two objects that have been created in memory, each referenced by a variable.

Figure 6-5 Two objects referenced by variables

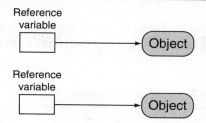

To understand how reference variables and objects work together, think about flying a kite. In order to fly a kite, you need a spool of string attached to it. When the kite is airborne, you use the spool of string to hold on to the kite and control it. This is similar to the relationship between an object and the variable that references the object. As shown in Figure 6-6, the object is like the kite, and the variable that references the object is like the spool of string.

Figure 6-6 The kite and string metaphor

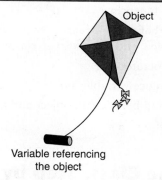

Creating an object typically requires the following two steps:

1. You declare a reference variable.
2. You create the object in memory, and assign its memory address to the reference variable.

After you have performed these steps, you can use the reference variable to work with the object. Once again, here is the familiar example of how you create an object from the Random class:

```
Random rand = new Random();
```

Let's look at the different parts of this statement:

- The first part of the statement, appearing on the left side of the = operator, reads Random rand. This declares a variable named rand, which can be used to reference an object of the Random type.
- The second part of the statement, appearing on the right side of the = operator, reads new Random(). The new operator creates an object in memory, and returns that object's memory address. So, the expression new Random() creates an object from the Random class, and returns that object's memory address.

- The = operator assigns the memory address that was returned from the new operator to the rand variable.

After this statement executes, the rand variable will reference a Random object, as shown in Figure 6-7. The rand variable can then be used to perform operations with the object, such as generating random numbers.

Figure 6-7 The rand variable references a Random object

 Checkpoint

MyProgrammingLab™ *www.myprogramminglab.com*

6.1 What does an object use its fields for?

6.2 What are an object's methods?

6.3 How is a class like a blueprint?

6.4 You have programs that create Scanner, Random, and PrintWriter objects. Where are the Scanner, Random, and PrintWriter classes?

6.5 What does the new operator do?

6.6 What values do reference variables hold?

6.7 How is the relationship between an object and a reference variable similar to a kite and a spool of string?

6.2 Writing a Simple Class, Step by Step

CONCEPT: You can write your own classes to create the objects that you need in a program. We will go through the process of writing a class in a step-by-step fashion.

The Java API provides many prewritten classes, ready for use in your programs. Sometimes, however, you will wish you had an object to perform a specific task, and no such class will exist in the Java API. This is not a problem, because you can write your own classes with the specific fields and methods that you need for any situation.

In this section we will write a class named Rectangle. Each object that is created from the Rectangle class will be able to hold data about a rectangle. Specifically, a Rectangle object will have the following fields:

- length. The length field will hold the rectangle's length.
- width. The width field will hold the rectangle's width.

The Rectangle class will also have the following methods:

- setLength. The setLength method will store a value in an object's length field.
- setWidth. The setWidth method will store a value in an object's width field.

- getLength. The getLength method will return the value in an object's length field.
- getWidth. The getWidth method will return the value in an object's width field.
- getArea. The getArea method will return the area of the rectangle, which is the result of an object's length multiplied by its width.

When designing a class it is often helpful to draw a UML diagram. UML stands for Unified Modeling Language. It provides a set of standard diagrams for graphically depicting object-oriented systems. Figure 6-8 shows the general layout of a UML diagram for a class. Notice that the diagram is a box that is divided into three sections. The top section is where you write the name of the class. The middle section holds a list of the class's fields. The bottom section holds a list of the class's methods.

Figure 6-8   General layout of a UML diagram for a class

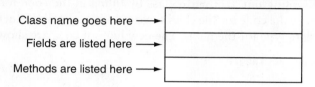

Following this layout, Figure 6-9 shows a UML diagram for our Rectangle class. Throughout this book we frequently use UML diagrams to illustrate classes.

Figure 6-9   UML diagram for the Rectangle class

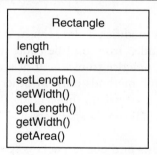

Writing the Code for a Class

Now that we have identified the fields and methods that we want the Rectangle class to have, let's write the Java code. First, we use an editor to create a new file named *Rectangle.java*. In the *Rectangle.java* file we will start by writing a general class "skeleton" as follows:

```
public class Rectangle
{
}
```

VideoNote

riting Classes and Creating Objects

The key word public, which appears in the first line, is an access specifier. An access specifier indicates how the class may be accessed. The public access specifier indicates that the class will be publicly available to code that is written outside the *Rectangle.java* file. Almost all of the classes that we write in this book are public.

Following the access specifier is the key word class, followed by Rectangle, which is the name of the class. On the next line an opening brace appears, which is followed by a closing brace. The contents of the class, which are the fields and methods, will be written inside these braces. The general format of a class definition is as follows:

```
AccessSpecifier class Name
{
    Members
}
```

In general terms, the fields and methods that belong to a class are referred to as the class's *members*.

Writing the Code for the Class Fields

Let's continue writing our Rectangle class by filling in the code for some of its members. First we will write the code for the class's two fields, length and width. We will use variables of the double data type for the fields. The new lines of code are shown in bold, as follows:

```
public class Rectangle
{
    private double length;
    private double width;
}
```

These two lines of code that we have added declare the variables length and width. Notice that both declarations begin with the key word private, preceding the data type. The key word private is an access specifier. It indicates that these variables may not be accessed by statements outside the class.

By using the private access modifier, a class can hide its data from code outside the class. When a class's fields are hidden from outside code, the data is protected from accidental corruption. It is a common practice to make all of a class's fields private and to provide access to those fields through methods only. In other words, a class usually has private fields, and public methods that access those fields. Table 6-1 summarizes the difference between the private and public access specifiers.

Table 6-1   Summary of the private and public access specifiers for class members

Access Specifier	Description
private	When the private access specifier is applied to a class member, the member cannot be accessed by code outside the class. The member can be accessed only by methods that are members of the same class.
public	When the public access specifier is applied to a class member, the member can be accessed by code inside the class or outside.

Writing the setLength Method

Now we will begin writing the class methods. We will start with the setLength method. This method will allow code outside the class to store a value in the length field.

Code Listing 6-2 shows the `Rectangle` class at this stage of its development. The `setLength` method is in lines 17 through 20. (This file is in the source code folder *Chapter 06\ Rectangle Class Phase 1.*)

Code Listing 6-2   (`Rectangle.java`)

```
 1  /**
 2      Rectangle class, phase 1
 3      Under construction!
 4  */
 5
 6  public class Rectangle
 7  {
 8      private double length;
 9      private double width;
10
11      /**
12          The setLength method stores a value in the
13          length field.
14          @param len The value to store in length.
15      */
16
17      public void setLength(double len)
18      {
19          length = len;
20      }
21  }
```

In lines 11 through 15, we write a block comment that gives a brief description of the method. It's important always to write comments that describe a class's methods so that in the future, anyone reading the code will understand it. The definition of the method appears in lines 17 through 20. Here is the method header:

```
    public void setLength(double len)
```

The method header looks very much like any other method header that you learned to write in Chapter 5. Let's look at the parts as follows:

- `public`. The key word `public` is an access specifier. It indicates that the method may be called by statements outside the class.
- `void`. This is the method's return type. The key word `void` indicates that the method returns no data to the statement that called it.
- `setLength`. This is the name of the method.
- `(double len)`. This is the declaration of a parameter variable of the `double` data type, named `len`.

Figure 6-10 labels each part of the header for the `setLength` method.

Figure 6-10   Header for the `setLength` method

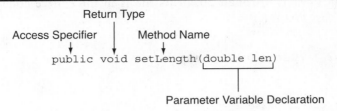

Notice that the word `static` does not appear in the method header. When a method is designed to work on an instance of a class, it is referred to as an *instance method*, and you do not write the word `static` in the header. Because this method will store a value in the `length` field of an instance of the `Rectangle` class, it is an instance method. We will discuss this in greater detail later.

After the header, the body of the method appears inside a set of braces:

```
{
    length = len;
}
```

The body of this method has only one statement, which assigns the value of `len` to the `length` field. When the method executes, the `len` parameter variable will hold the value of an argument that is passed to the method. That value is assigned to the `length` field.

Before adding the other methods to the class, it might help if we demonstrate how the `setLength` method works. First, notice that the `Rectangle` class does not have a `main` method. This class is not a complete program, but is a blueprint that `Rectangle` objects may be created from. Other programs will use the `Rectangle` class to create objects. The programs that create and use these objects will have their own `main` methods. We can demonstrate the class's `setLength` method by saving the current contents of the *Rectangle.java* file and then creating the program shown in Code Listing 6-3.

Code Listing 6-3   (`LengthDemo.java`)

```
 1  /**
 2      This program demonstrates the Rectangle class's
 3      setLength method.
 4  */
 5
 6  public class LengthDemo
 7  {
 8      public static void main(String[] args)
 9      {
10          // Create a Rectangle object and assign its
11          // address to the box variable.
```

```
12          Rectangle box = new Rectangle();
13
14          // Indicate what we are doing.
15          System.out.println("Sending the value 10.0 " +
16                             "to the setLength method.");
17
18          // Call the box object's setLength method.
19          box.setLength(10.0);
20
21          // Indicate we are done.
22          System.out.println("Done.");
23      }
24  }
```

Program Output

```
Sending the value 10.0 to the setLength method.
Done.
```

The program in Code Listing 6-3 must be saved as *LengthDemo.java* in the same folder or directory as the file *Rectangle.java*. The following command can then be used with the Sun JDK to compile the program:

```
javac LengthDemo.java
```

When the compiler reads the source code for LengthDemo.java and sees that a class named Rectangle is being used, it looks in the current folder or directory for the file *Rectangle. class*. That file does not exist, however, because we have not yet compiled *Rectangle.java*. So, the compiler searches for the file Rectangle.java and compiles it. This creates the file *Rectangle.class*, which makes the Rectangle class available. The compiler then finishes compiling LengthDemo.java. The resulting *LengthDemo.class* file may be executed with the following command:

```
java LengthDemo
```

The output of the program is shown at the bottom of Code Listing 6-3.

Let's look at each statement in this program's main method. First, the program uses the following statement, in line 12, to create a Rectangle object and associate it with a variable:

```
Rectangle box = new Rectangle();
```

Let's dissect the statement into two parts. The first part of the statement,

```
Rectangle box
```

declares a variable named box. The data type of the variable is Rectangle. (Because the word Rectangle is not the name of a primitive data type, Java assumes it to be the name of a class.) Recall that a variable of a class type is a reference variable, and it holds the memory address of an object. When a reference variable holds an object's memory address, it is said that the variable references the object. So, the variable box will be used to reference a Rectangle object. The second part of the statement is as follows:

```
= new Rectangle();
```

This part of the statement uses the key word new, which creates an object in memory. After the word new, the name of a class followed by a set of parentheses appears. This specifies the class that the object should be created from. In this case, an object of the Rectangle class is created. The memory address of the object is then assigned (by the = operator) to the variable box. After the statement executes, the variable box will reference the object that was created in memory. This is illustrated in Figure 6-11.

Figure 6-11 The box variable references a Rectangle class object

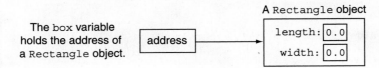

Notice that Figure 6-11 shows the Rectangle object's length and width fields set to 0. All of a class's numeric fields are initialized to 0 by default.

TIP: The parentheses in this statement are required. It would be an error to write the statement as follows:

```
Rectangle box = new Rectangle; // ERROR!!
```

The statement in lines 15 and 16 uses the System.out.println method to display a message on the screen. The next statement, in line 19, calls the box object's setLength method as follows:

```
box.setLength(10.0);
```

This statement passes the argument 10.0 to the setLength method. When the method executes, the value 10.0 is copied into the len parameter variable. The method assigns the value of len to the length field and then terminates. Figure 6-12 shows the state of the box object after the method executes.

Figure 6-12 The state of the box object after the setLength method executes

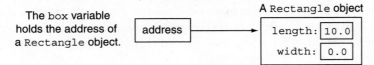

Writing the setWidth Method

Now that we've seen how the setLength method works, let's add the setWidth method to the Rectangle class. The setWidth method is similar to setLength. It accepts an argument, which is assigned to the width field. Code Listing 6-4 shows the updated Rectangle class. The setWidth method is in lines 28 through 31. (This file is stored in the source code folder *Chapter 06\Rectangle Class Phase 2.*)

Code Listing 6-4   (`Rectangle.java`)

```
 1  /**
 2      Rectangle class, phase 2
 3      Under construction!
 4  */
 5
 6  public class Rectangle
 7  {
 8      private double length;
 9      private double width;
10
11      /**
12          The setLength method stores a value in the
13          length field.
14          @param len The value to store in length.
15      */
16
17      public void setLength(double len)
18      {
19          length = len;
20      }
21
22      /**
23          The setWidth method stores a value in the
24          width field.
25          @param w The value to store in width.
26      */
27
28      public void setWidth(double w)
29      {
30          width = w;
31      }
32  }
```

The setWidth method has a parameter variable named w, which is assigned to the width field. For example, assume that box references a Rectangle object and the following statement is executed:

```
box.setWidth(20.0);
```

After this statement executes, the box object's width field will be set to 20.0.

Writing the getLength and getWidth Methods

Because the length and width fields are private, we wrote the setLength and setWidth methods to allow code outside the Rectangle class to store values in the fields. We must also write methods that allow code outside the class to get the values that are stored in these fields. That's what the getLength and getWidth methods will do. The getLength method will return the value stored in the length field, and the getWidth method will return the value stored in the width field.

Here is the code for the getLength method:

```
public double getLength()
{
    return length;
}
```

Assume that size is a double variable and that box references a Rectangle object, and the following statement is executed:

```
size = box.getLength();
```

This statement assigns the value that is returned from the getLength method to the size variable. After this statement executes, the size variable will contain the same value as the box object's length field.

The getWidth method is similar to getLength. The code for the method follows:

```
public double getWidth()
{
    return width;
}
```

This method returns the value that is stored in the width field. For example, assume that size is a double variable and that box references a Rectangle object, and the following statement is executed:

```
size = box.getWidth();
```

This statement assigns the value that is returned from the getWidth method to the size variable. After this statement executes, the size variable will contain the same value as the box object's width field.

Code Listing 6-5 shows the Rectangle class with all of the members we have discussed so far. The code for the getLength and getWidth methods is shown in lines 33 through 53. (This file is stored in the source code folder *Chapter 06\Rectangle Class Phase 3.*)

Code Listing 6-5   (Rectangle.java)

```
1 /**
2     Rectangle class, phase 3
3     Under construction!
4 */
5
6 public class Rectangle
7 {
8     private double length;
9     private double width;
10
11    /**
12        The setLength method stores a value in the
13        length field.
14        @param len The value to store in length.
15    */
16
17    public void setLength(double len)
18    {
19        length = len;
20    }
21
22    /**
23        The setWidth method stores a value in the
24        width field.
25        @param w The value to store in width.
26    */
27
28    public void setWidth(double w)
29    {
30        width = w;
31    }
32
33    /**
34        The getLength method returns a Rectangle
35        object's length.
36        @return The value in the length field.
37    */
38
39    public double getLength()
40    {
41        return length;
42    }
43
44    /**
45        The getWidth method returns a Rectangle
46        object's width.
```

```
47          @return The value in the width field.
48      */
49
50      public double getWidth()
51      {
52          return width;
53      }
54 }
```

Before continuing we should demonstrate how these methods work. Look at the program in Code Listing 6-6. (This file is also stored in the source code folder *Chapter 06\Rectangle Class Phase 3.*)

Code Listing 6-6   (`LengthWidthDemo.java`)

```
1   /**
2       This program demonstrates the Rectangle class's
3       setLength, setWidth, getLength, and getWidth methods.
4   */
5
6   public class LengthWidthDemo
7   {
8       public static void main(String[] args)
9       {
10          // Create a Rectangle object.
11          Rectangle box = new Rectangle();
12
13          // Call the object's setLength method, passing 10.0
14          // as an argument.
15          box.setLength(10.0);
16
17          // Call the object's setWidth method, passing 20.0
18          // as an argument.
19          box.setWidth(20.0);
20
21          // Display the object's length and width.
22          System.out.println("The box's length is " +
23                              box.getLength());
24          System.out.println("The box's width is " +
25                              box.getWidth());
26      }
27 }
```

Program Output

```
The box's length is 10.0
The box's width is 20.0
```

Let's take a closer look at the program. In line 11, this program creates a `Rectangle` object, which is referenced by the `box` variable. Then the following statements execute in lines 15 and 19:

```
box.setLength(10.0);
box.setWidth(20.0);
```

After these statements execute, the `box` object's `length` field is set to 10.0 and its `width` field is set to 20.0. The state of the object is shown in Figure 6-13.

Figure 6-13   State of the box object

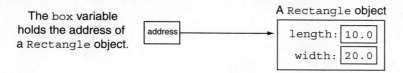

Next, the following statement in lines 22 and 23 executes as follows:

```
System.out.println("The box's length is " +
                   box.getLength());
```

This statement calls the `box.getLength()` method, which returns the value 10.0. The following message is displayed on the screen:

```
The box's length is 10.0
```

Then the following statement executes in lines 24 and 25:

```
System.out.println("The box's width is " +
                   box.getWidth());
```

This statement calls the `box.getWidth()` method, which returns the value 20.0. The following message is displayed on the screen:

```
The box's width is 20.0
```

Writing the `getArea` Method

The last method we will write for the `Rectangle` class is `getArea`. This method returns the area of a rectangle, which is its length multiplied by its width. Here is the code for the `getArea` method:

```
public double getArea()
{
    return length * width;
}
```

This method returns the result of the mathematical expression `length * width`. For example, assume that `area` is a `double` variable and that `box` references a `Rectangle` object, and the following code is executed:

```
box.setLength(10.0);
box.setWidth(20.0);
area = box.getArea();
```

The last statement assigns the value that is returned from the getArea method to the area variable. After this statement executes, the area variable will contain the value 200.0.

Code Listing 6-7 shows the Rectangle class with all of the members we have discussed so far. The getArea method appears in lines 61 through 64. (This file is stored in the source code folder *Chapter 06\Rectangle Class Phase 4*.)

Code Listing 6-7   (Rectangle.java)

```java
1  /**
2     Rectangle class, phase 4
3     Under construction!
4  */
5
6  public class Rectangle
7  {
8     private double length;
9     private double width;
10
11    /**
12       The setLength method stores a value in the
13       length field.
14       @param len The value to store in length.
15    */
16
17    public void setLength(double len)
18    {
19       length = len;
20    }
21
22    /**
23       The setWidth method stores a value in the
24       width field.
25       @param w The value to store in width.
26    */
27
28    public void setWidth(double w)
29    {
30       width = w;
31    }
32
33    /**
34       The getLength method returns a Rectangle
35       object's length.
36       @return The value in the length field.
37    */
38
```

```
39      public double getLength()
40      {
41          return length;
42      }
43
44      /**
45         The getWidth method returns a Rectangle
46         object's width.
47         @return The value in the width field.
48      */
49
50      public double getWidth()
51      {
52          return width;
53      }
54
55      /**
56         The getArea method returns a Rectangle
57         object's area.
58         @return The product of length times width.
59      */
60
61      public double getArea()
62      {
63          return length * width;
64      }
65  }
```

The program in Code Listing 6-8 demonstrates all the methods of the Rectangle class, including getArea. (This file is also stored in the source code folder *Chapter 06\Rectangle Class Phase 4.*)

Code Listing 6-8   (`RectangleDemo.java`)

```
1  /**
2     This program demonstrates the Rectangle class's
3     setLength, setWidth, getLength, getWidth, and
4     getArea methods.
5  */
6
7  public class RectangleDemo
8  {
9      public static void main(String[] args)
10     {
11         // Create a Rectangle object.
12         Rectangle box = new Rectangle();
13
```

```
14            // Set length to 10.0 and width to 20.0.
15            box.setLength(10.0);
16            box.setWidth(20.0);
17
18            // Display the length.
19            System.out.println("The box's length is " +
20                                box.getLength());
21
22            // Display the width.
23            System.out.println("The box's width is " +
24                                box.getWidth());
25
26            // Display the area.
27            System.out.println("The box's area is " +
28                                box.getArea());
29       }
30    }
```

Program Output

```
The box's length is 10.0
The box's width is 20.0
The box's area is 200.0
```

Accessor and Mutator Methods

As mentioned earlier, it is common practice to make all of a class's fields private and to provide public methods for accessing and changing those fields. This ensures that the object owning those fields is in control of all changes being made to them. A method that gets a value from a class's field but does not change it is known as an *accessor method*. A method that stores a value in a field or changes the value of a field in some other way is known as a *mutator method*. In the Rectangle class, the methods getLength and getWidth are accessors, and the methods setLength and setWidth are mutators.

 NOTE: Mutator methods are sometimes called "setters" and accessor methods are sometimes called "getters."

The Importance of Data Hiding

Data hiding is an important concept in object-oriented programming. An object hides its internal data from code that is outside the class that the object is an instance of. Only the class's methods may directly access and make changes to the object's internal data. You hide an object's internal data by making the class's fields private, and making the methods that access those fields public.

As a beginning student, you might be wondering why you would want to hide the data that is inside the classes you create. As you learn to program, you will be the user of your own classes, so it might seem that you are putting forth a great effort to hide data from yourself. If you write software in industry, however, the classes that you create will be used as components in large software systems, and programmers other than yourself will be using your classes. By hiding a class's data, and allowing it to be accessed only through the class's methods, you can better ensure that the class will operate as you intended it to.

Avoiding Stale Data

In the `Rectangle` class, the `getLength` and `getWidth` methods return the values stored in fields, but the `getArea` method returns the result of a calculation. You might be wondering why the area of the rectangle is not stored in a field, like the length and the width. The area is not stored in a field because it could potentially become stale. When the value of an item is dependent on other data and that item is not updated when the other data is changed, it is said that the item has become *stale*. If the area of the rectangle were stored in a field, the value of the field would become incorrect as soon as either the `length` or `width` field changed.

When designing a class, you should take care not to store in a field calculated data that can potentially become stale. Instead, provide a method that returns the result of the calculation.

Showing Access Specification in UML Diagrams

In Figure 6-9 we presented a UML diagram for the `Rectangle` class. The diagram listed all of the members of the class but did not indicate which members were private and which were public. In a UML diagram, you have the option to place a - character before a member name to indicate that it is private, or a + character to indicate that it is public. Figure 6-14 shows the UML diagram modified to include this notation.

Figure 6-14   UML diagram for the `Rectangle` class

Rectangle
− length − width
+ setLength() + setWidth() + getLength() + getWidth() + getArea()

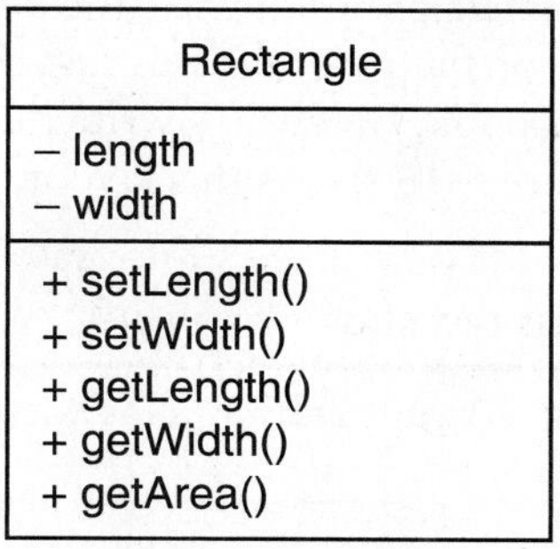

Data Type and Parameter Notation in UML Diagrams

The Unified Modeling Language also provides notation that you may use to indicate the data types of fields, methods, and parameter variables. To indicate the data type of a field, place a colon followed by the name of the data type after the name of the field. For example, the `length` field in the `Rectangle` class is a `double`. It could be listed in the UML diagram as follows:

```
- length : double
```

The return type of a method can be listed in the same manner: After the method's name, place a colon followed by the return type. The `Rectangle` class's `getLength` method returns a `double`, so it could be listed in the UML diagram as follows:

```
+ getLength() : double
```

Parameter variables and their data types may be listed inside a method's parentheses. For example, the `Rectangle` class's `setLength` method has a `double` parameter named `len`, so it could be listed in the UML diagram as follows:

```
+ setLength(len : double) : void
```

Figure 6-15 shows a UML diagram for the `Rectangle` class with parameter and data type notation.

Figure 6-15 UML diagram for the `Rectangle` class with parameter and data type notation

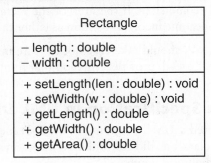

Rectangle
− length : double − width : double
+ setLength(len : double) : void + setWidth(w : double) : void + getLength() : double + getWidth() : double + getArea() : double

Layout of Class Members

Notice that in the `Rectangle` class, the field variables are declared first and then the methods are defined. You are not required to write field declarations before the method definitions. In fact, some programmers prefer to write the definitions for the public methods first and write the declarations for the private fields last. Regardless of the style you use, you should be consistent. In this book, we always write the field declarations first, followed by the method definitions. Figure 6-16 shows this layout.

Figure 6-16 Typical layout of class members

```
public class ClassName
{
```
> Field declarations

> Method definitions
```
}
```

 **Checkpoint**

MyProgrammingLab™ *www.myprogramminglab.com*

6.8 You hear someone make the following comment: "A blueprint is a design for a house. A carpenter can use the blueprint to build the house. If the carpenter wishes, he or she can build several identical houses from the same blueprint." Think of this as a metaphor for classes and objects. Does the blueprint represent a class, or does it represent an object?

6.9 In this chapter we used the metaphor of a kite attached to a spool of string to describe the relationship between an object and a reference variable. In this metaphor, does the kite represent an object, or a reference variable?

6.10 When a variable is said to reference an object, what is actually stored in the variable?

6.11 A string literal, such as `"Joe"`, causes what type of object to be created?

6.12 Look at the UML diagram in Figure 6-17 and answer the following questions:
a) What is the name of the class?
b) What are the fields?
c) What are the methods?
d) What are the private members?
e) What are the public members?

6.13 Assume that limo is a variable that references an instance of the class shown in Figure 6-17. Write a statement that calls `setMake` and passes the argument `"Cadillac"`.

Figure 6-17 UML diagram

```
             Car
 ─────────────────────────
  – make
  – yearModel
 ─────────────────────────
  + setMake()
  + setYearModel()
  + getMake()
  + getYearModel()
```

6.14 What does the key word `new` do?

6.15 What is an accessor? What is a mutator?

6.16 What is a stale data item?

6.3 Instance Fields and Methods

CONCEPT: Each instance of a class has its own set of fields, which are known as instance fields. You can create several instances of a class and store different values in each instance's fields. The methods that operate on an instance of a class are known as instance methods.

The program in Code Listing 6-8 creates one instance of the `Rectangle` class. It is possible to create many instances of the same class, each with its own data. For example, the `RoomAreas.java` program in Code Listing 6-9 creates three instances of the `Rectangle` class, referenced by the variables `kitchen`, `bedroom`, and `den`. Figure 6-18 shows example interaction with the program. (The file in Code Listing 6-9 is stored in the source code folder *Chapter 06\Rectangle Class Phase 4*.)

Code Listing 6-9 (`RoomAreas.java`)

```java
 1   import javax.swing.JOptionPane;
 2
 3   /**
 4      This program creates three instances of the
 5      Rectangle class.
 6   */
 7
 8   public class RoomAreas
 9   {
10      public static void main(String[] args)
11      {
12         double number;        // To hold a number
13         double totalArea;     // The total area
14         String input;         // To hold user input
15
16         // Create three Rectangle objects.
17         Rectangle kitchen = new Rectangle();
18         Rectangle bedroom = new Rectangle();
19         Rectangle den = new Rectangle();
20
21         // Get and store the dimensions of the kitchen.
22         input = JOptionPane.showInputDialog("What is the " +
23                                     "kitchen's length?");
24         number = Double.parseDouble(input);
25         kitchen.setLength(number);
26         input = JOptionPane.showInputDialog("What is the " +
27                                     "kitchen's width?");
28         number = Double.parseDouble(input);
29         kitchen.setWidth(number);
30
31         // Get and store the dimensions of the bedroom.
32         input = JOptionPane.showInputDialog("What is the " +
33                                     "bedroom's length?");
34         number = Double.parseDouble(input);
35         bedroom.setLength(number);
36         input = JOptionPane.showInputDialog("What is the " +
37                                     "bedroom's width?");
38         number = Double.parseDouble(input);
39         bedroom.setWidth(number);
40
41         // Get and store the dimensions of the den.
42         input = JOptionPane.showInputDialog("What is the " +
43                                     "den's length?");
44         number = Double.parseDouble(input);
45         den.setLength(number);
```

```
46            input = JOptionPane.showInputDialog("What is the " +
47                                                "den's width?");
48            number = Double.parseDouble(input);
49            den.setWidth(number);
50
51            // Calculate the total area of the rooms.
52            totalArea = kitchen.getArea() + bedroom.getArea()
53                        + den.getArea();
54
55            // Display the total area of the rooms.
56            JOptionPane.showMessageDialog(null, "The total area " +
57                                          "of the rooms is " + totalArea);
58
59            System.exit(0);
60        }
61  }
```

Figure 6-18   Interaction with the `RoomAreas.java` program

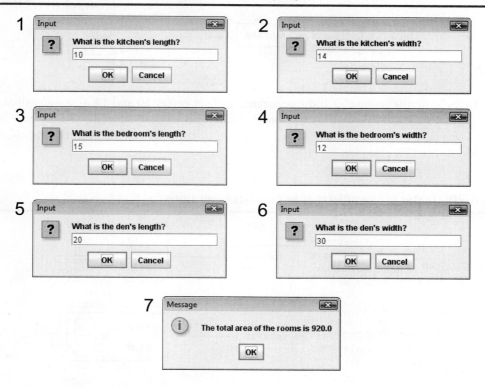

In lines 17, 18, and 19, the following code creates three objects, each an instance of the Rectangle class:

```
Rectangle kitchen = new Rectangle();
Rectangle bedroom = new Rectangle();
Rectangle den = new Rectangle();
```

Figure 6-19 illustrates how the kitchen, bedroom, and den variables reference the objects.

Figure 6-19   The kitchen, bedroom, and den variables reference Rectangle objects

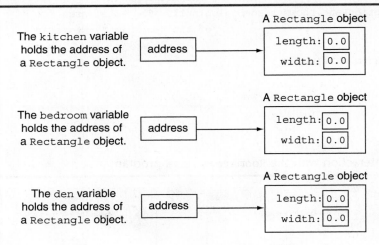

In the example session with the program, the user enters 10 and 14 as the length and width of the kitchen, 15 and 12 as the length and width of the bedroom, and 20 and 30 as the length and width of the den. Figure 6-20 shows the states of the objects after these values are stored in them.

Figure 6-20   States of the objects after data has been stored in them

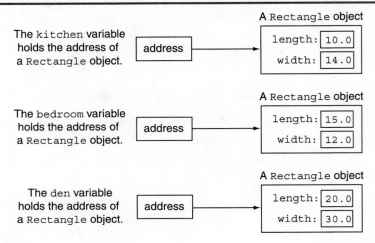

Notice from Figure 6-20 that each instance of the `Rectangle` class has its own `length` and `width` variables. For this reason, the variables are known as *instance variables*, or *instance fields*. Every instance of a class has its own set of instance fields and can store its own values in those fields.

The methods that operate on an instance of a class are known as *instance methods*. All of the methods in the `Rectangle` class are instance methods because they perform operations on specific instances of the class. For example, look at the following statement in line 25 of the `RoomAreas.java` program:

```
kitchen.setLength(number);
```

This statement calls the `setLength` method, which stores a value in the `kitchen` object's `length` field. Now look at the following statement in line 35:

```
bedroom.setLength(number);
```

This statement also calls the `setLength` method, but this time it stores a value in the `bedroom` object's `length` field. Likewise, the following statement in line 45 calls the `setLength` method to store a value in the `den` object's `length` field:

```
den.setLength(number);
```

The `setLength` method stores a value in a specific instance of the `Rectangle` class. This is true of all of the methods that are members of the `Rectangle` class.

> **NOTE:** As previously mentioned, instance methods do not have the key word `static` in their headers.

Checkpoint

MyProgrammingLab™ *www.myprogramminglab.com*

6.17 Assume that `r1` and `r2` are variables that reference `Rectangle` objects, and the following statements are executed:

```
r1.setLength(5.0);
r2.setLength(10.0);
r1.setWidth(20.0);
r2.setWidth(15.0);
```

Fill in the boxes in Figure 6-21 that represent each object's length and width fields.

Figure 6-21 Fill in the boxes for each field

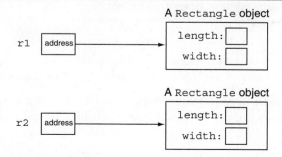

6.4   Constructors

CONCEPT: A constructor is a method that is automatically called when an object is created.

VideoNote
Initializing an
Object with a
Constructor

A constructor is a method that is automatically called when an instance of a class is created. Constructors normally perform initialization or setup operations, such as storing initial values in instance fields. They are called "constructors" because they help construct an object.

A constructor method has the same name as the class. For example, Code Listing 6-10 shows the first few lines of a new version of the Rectangle class. In this version of the class, a constructor has been added. (This file is stored in the source code folder *Chapter 06\ Rectangle Class Phase 5.*)

Code Listing 6-10   **(Rectangle.java)**

```
 1  /**
 2      Rectangle class, phase 5
 3  */
 4
 5  public class Rectangle
 6  {
 7      private double length;
 8      private double width;
 9
10      /**
11          Constructor
12          @param len The length of the rectangle.
13          @param w The width of the rectangle.
14      */
15
16      public Rectangle(double len, double w)
17      {
18          length = len;
19          width = w;
20      }
```

. . . The remainder of the class has not changed, and is not shown.

This constructor accepts two arguments, which are passed into the len and w parameter variables. The parameter variables are then assigned to the length and width fields.

Notice that the constructor's header doesn't specify a return type—not even void. This is because constructors are not executed by explicit method calls and cannot return a value.

The method header for a constructor takes the following general format:

> *AccessSpecifier ClassName(Parameters...)*

Here is an example statement that declares the variable box, creates a Rectangle object, and passes the values 7.0 and 14.0 to the constructor.

```
Rectangle box = new Rectangle(7.0, 14.0);
```

After this statement executes, box will reference a Rectangle object whose length field is set to 7 and whose width field is set to 14. The program in Code Listing 6-11 demonstrates the Rectangle class constructor. (This file is also stored in the source code folder *Chapter 06\ Rectangle Class Phase 5.*)

Code Listing 6-11   **(ConstructorDemo.java)**

```java
 1  /**
 2     This program demonstrates the Rectangle class's
 3     constructor.
 4  */
 5
 6  public class ConstructorDemo
 7  {
 8     public static void main(String[] args)
 9     {
10        // Create a Rectangle object, passing 5.0 and
11        // 15.0 as arguments to the constructor.
12        Rectangle box = new Rectangle(5.0, 15.0);
13
14        // Display the length.
15        System.out.println("The box's length is " +
16                           box.getLength());
17
18        // Display the width.
19        System.out.println("The box's width is " +
20                           box.getWidth());
21
22        // Display the area.
23        System.out.println("The box's area is " +
24                           box.getArea());
25     }
26  }
```

Program Output

```
The box's length is 5.0
The box's width is 15.0
The box's area is 75.0
```

Showing Constructors in a UML Diagram

There is more than one accepted way of showing a class's constructor in a UML diagram. In this book, we simply show a constructor just as any other method, except we list no return type. Figure 6-22 shows a UML diagram for the Rectangle class with the constructor listed.

Figure 6-22 UML diagram for the Rectangle class showing the constructor

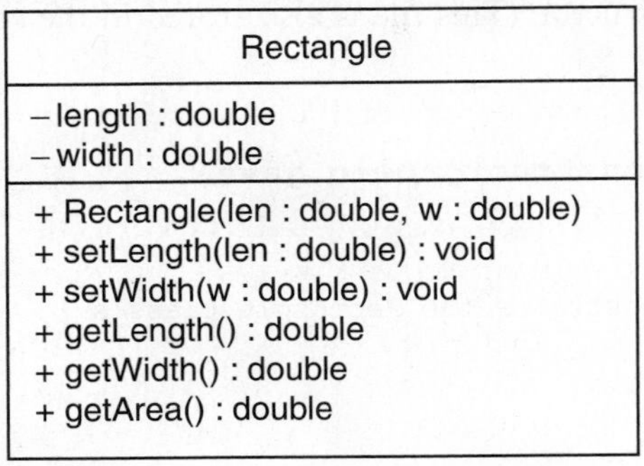

```
┌─────────────────────────────────────────┐
│                Rectangle                 │
├─────────────────────────────────────────┤
│ − length : double                        │
│ − width : double                         │
├─────────────────────────────────────────┤
│ + Rectangle(len : double, w : double)    │
│ + setLength(len : double) : void         │
│ + setWidth(w : double) : void            │
│ + getLength() : double                   │
│ + getWidth() : double                    │
│ + getArea() : double                     │
└─────────────────────────────────────────┘
```

Uninitialized Local Reference Variables

The program in Code Listing 6-11 initializes the box variable with the address of a Rectangle object. Reference variables can also be declared without being initialized, as in the following statement:

```
Rectangle box;
```

Note that this statement does not create a Rectangle object. It only declares a variable named box that can be used to reference a Rectangle object. Because the box variable does not yet hold an object's address, it is an *uninitialized reference variable*.

After declaring the reference variable, the following statement can be used to assign it the address of an object. This statement creates a Rectangle object, passes the values 7.0 and 14.0 to its constructor, and assigns the object's address to the box variable:

```
box = new Rectangle(7.0, 14.0);
```

Once this statement executes, the box variable will reference a Rectangle object.

You need to be careful when using uninitialized reference variables. Recall from Chapter 5 that local variables *must* be initialized or assigned a value before they can be used. This is also true for local reference variables. A local reference variable must reference an object before it can be used. Otherwise a compiler error will occur.

The Default Constructor

When an object is created, its constructor is *always* called. But what if we do not write a constructor in the object's class? If you do not write a constructor in a class, Java automatically provides one when the class is compiled. The constructor that Java provides is known as the *default constructor*. The default constructor doesn't accept arguments. It sets all of the object's numeric fields to 0 and boolean fields to false. If the object has any fields that are reference variables, the default constructor sets them to the special value null, which means that they do not reference anything.

The *only* time that Java provides a default constructor is when you do not write your own constructor for a class. For example, at the beginning of this chapter we developed the Rectangle class without writing a constructor for it. When we compiled the class, the compiler generated a default constructor that set both the length and width fields to 0.0. Assume that the following code uses that version of the class to create a Rectangle object:

```java
// We wrote no constructor for the Rectangle class.
Rectangle r = new Rectangle();  // Calls the default constructor
```

When we created Rectangle objects using that version of the class, we did not pass any arguments to the default constructor because the default constructor doesn't accept arguments.

Later we added our own constructor to the class. The constructor that we added accepts arguments for the length and width fields. When we compiled the class at that point, Java did not provide a default constructor. The constructor that we added became the only constructor that the class has. When we create Rectangle objects with that version of the class, we *must* pass the length and width arguments to the constructor. Using that version of the class, the following statement would cause an error because we have not provided arguments for the constructor:

```java
// Now we wrote our own constructor for the Rectangle class.
Rectangle box = new Rectangle(); // Error! Must now pass arguments.
```

Because we have added our own constructor, which requires two arguments, the class no longer has a default constructor.

Writing Your Own No-Arg Constructor

A constructor that does not accept arguments is known as a *no-arg constructor*. The default constructor doesn't accept arguments, so it is considered a no-arg constructor. In addition, you can write your own no-arg constructor. For example, suppose we wrote the following constructor for the Rectangle class:

```java
public Rectangle()
{
    length = 1.0;
    width = 1.0;
}
```

If we were using this constructor in our Rectangle class, we would not pass any arguments when creating a Rectangle object. The following code shows an example. After this code executes, the Rectangle object's length and width fields would both be set to 1.0.

```java
// Now we have written our own no-arg constructor.
Rectangle r = new Rectangle();  // Calls the no-arg constructor
```

The String Class Constructor

Earlier in this chapter (in Section 6.1) we discussed the difference between creating a primitive variable and creating an object. You create primitive variables with simple declaration statements, and you create objects with the new operator. There is one class, however, that can be instantiated without the new operator: the String class.

Because string operations are so common, Java allows you to create String objects in the same way that you create primitive variables. Here is an example:

```
String name = "Joe Mahoney";
```

This statement creates a String object in memory, initialized with the string literal "Joe Mahoney". The object is referenced by the name variable. If you wish, you can use the new operator to create a String object, and initialize the object by passing a string literal to the constructor, as shown here:

```
String name = new String("Joe Mahoney");
```

NOTE: String objects are a special case in Java. Because they are so commonly used, Java provides numerous shortcut operations with String objects that are not possible with objects of other types. In addition to creating a String object without using the new operator, you can use the = operator to assign values to String objects, the + operator to concatenate strings, and so forth. Chapter 9 discusses several of the String class methods.

In the Spotlight:

Creating the CellPhone Class

Wireless Solutions, Inc., is a business that sells cell phones and wireless service. You are a programmer in the company's information technology (IT) department, and your team is designing a program to manage all of the cell phones that are in inventory. You have been asked to design a class that represents a cell phone. The data that should be kept as fields in the class are as follows:

- The name of the phone's manufacturer will be assigned to the manufact field.
- The phone's model number will be assigned to the model field.
- The phone's retail price will be assigned to the retailPrice field.

The class will also have the following methods:

- A constructor that accepts arguments for the manufacturer, model number, and retail price.
- A setManufact method that accepts an argument for the manufacturer. This method will allow us to change the value of the manufact field after the object has been created, if necessary.
- A setModel method that accepts an argument for the model. This method will allow us to change the value of the model field after the object has been created, if necessary.
- A setRetailPrice method that accepts an argument for the retail price. This method will allow us to change the value of the retailPrice field after the object has been created, if necessary.

- A getManufact method that returns the phone's manufacturer.
- A getModel method that returns the phone's model number.
- A getRetailPrice method that returns the phone's retail price.

Figure 6-23 shows a UML diagram for the class. Code Listing 6-12 shows the class definition.

Figure 6-23 UML diagram for the CellPhone class

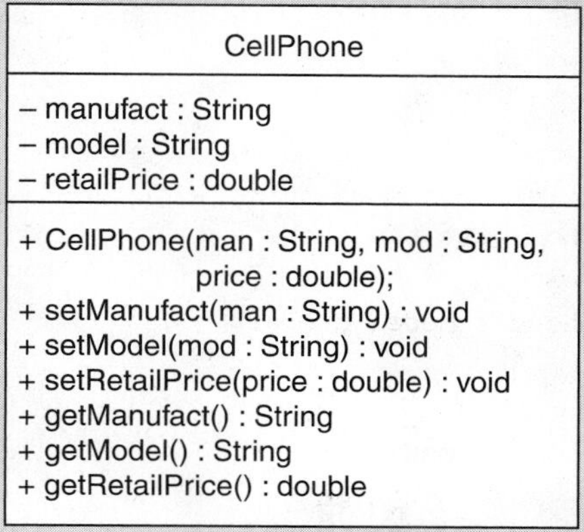

CellPhone
− manufact : String − model : String − retailPrice : double
+ CellPhone(man : String, mod : String,   price : double); + setManufact(man : String) : void + setModel(mod : String) : void + setRetailPrice(price : double) : void + getManufact() : String + getModel() : String + getRetailPrice() : double

Code Listing 6-12 (CellPhone.java)

```
1   /**
2      The CellPhone class holds data about a cell phone.
3   */
4
5   public class CellPhone
6   {
7      // Fields
8      private String manufact;      // Manufacturer
9      private String model;         // Model
10     private double retailPrice;   // Retail price
11
12     /**
13        Constructor
14        @param man The phone's manufacturer.
15        @param mod The phone's model number.
16        @param price The phone's retail price.
17     */
18
19     public CellPhone(String man, String mod, double price)
20     {
21        manufact = man;
22        model = mod;
23        retailPrice = price;
24     }
```

```
25
26      /**
27         The setManufact method sets the phone's
28         manufacturer name.
29         @param man The phone's manufacturer.
30      */
31
32      public void setManufact(String man)
33      {
34         manufact = man;
35      }
36
37      /**
38         The setModel method sets the phone's
39         model number.
40         @param mod The phone's model number.
41      */
42
43      public void setMod(String mod)
44      {
45         model = mod;
46      }
47
48      /**
49         The setRetailPrice method sets the phone's
50         retail price.
51         @param price The phone's retail price.
52      */
53
54      public void setRetailPrice(double price)
55      {
56         retailPrice = price;
57      }
58
59      /**
60         getManufact method
61         @return The name of the phone's manufacturer.
62      */
63
64      public String getManufact()
65      {
66         return manufact;
67      }
68
69      /**
70         getModel method
71         @return The phone's model number.
72      */
73
```

```
74    public String getModel()
75    {
76       return model;
77    }
78
79    /**
80       getretailPrice method
81       @return The phone's retail price.
82    */
83
84    public double getRetailPrice()
85    {
86       return retailPrice;
87    }
88 }
```

The CellPhone class will be used by several programs that your team is developing. To perform a simple test of the class, you write the program shown in Code Listing 6-13. This is a simple program that prompts the user for the phone's manufacturer, model number, and retail price. An instance of the CellPhone class is created and the data is assigned to its attributes.

Code Listing 6-13   (CellPhoneTest.java)

```
1  import java.util.Scanner;
2
3  /**
4     This program runs a simple test
5     of the CellPhone class.
6  */
7
8  public class CellPhoneTest
9  {
10    public static void main(String[] args)
11    {
12       String testMan;    // To hold a manufacturer
13       String testMod;    // To hold a model number
14       double testPrice;  // To hold a price
15
16       // Create a Scanner object for keyboard input.
17       Scanner keyboard = new Scanner(System.in);
18
19       // Get the manufacturer name.
20       System.out.print("Enter the manufacturer: ");
21       testMan = keyboard.nextLine();
22
23       // Get the model number.
24       System.out.print("Enter the model number: ");
25       testMod = keyboard.nextLine();
```

```
26
27         // Get the retail price.
28         System.out.print("Enter the retail price: ");
29         testPrice = keyboard.nextDouble();
30
31         // Create an instance of the CellPhone class,
32         // passing the data that was entered as arguments
33         // to the constructor.
34         CellPhone phone = new CellPhone(testMan, testMod, testPrice);
35
36         // Get the data from the phone and display it.
37         System.out.println();
38         System.out.println("Here is the data that you provided:");
39         System.out.println("Manufacturer: " + phone.getManufact());
40         System.out.println("Model number: " + phone.getModel());
41         System.out.println("Retail price: " + phone.getRetailPrice());
42     }
43 }
```

Program Output with Example Input Shown in Bold

```
Enter the manufacturer: Acme Electronics [Enter]
Enter the model number: M1000 [Enter]
Enter the retail price: 199.99 [Enter]

Here is the data that you provided:
Manufacturer: Acme Electronics
Model number: M1000
Retail price: $199.99
```

In the Spotlight:
Simulating Dice with Objects

Dice traditionally have six sides, representing the values 1 through 6. Some games, however, use specialized dice that have a different number of sides. For example, the fantasy role-playing game *Dungeons and Dragons®* uses dice with four, six, eight, ten, twelve, and twenty sides.

Suppose you are writing a program that needs to roll simulated dice with various numbers of sides. A simple approach would be to write a Die class with a constructor that accepts the number of sides as an argument. The class would also have appropriate methods for rolling the die, and getting the die's value. Figure 6-24 shows the UML diagram for such a class, and Code Listing 6-14 shows the code.

Figure 6-24 UML diagram for the Die class

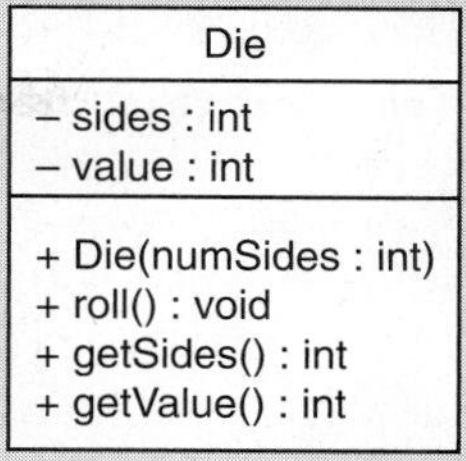

Die
– sides : int – value : int
+ Die(numSides : int) + roll() : void + getSides() : int + getValue() : int

Code Listing 6-14   (Die.java)

```java
1   import java.util.Random;
2
3   /**
4      The Die class simulates a six-sided die.
5   */
6
7   public class Die
8   {
9      private int sides;   // Number of sides
10     private int value;   // The die's value
11
12     /**
13        The constructor performs an initial
14        roll of the die.
15        @param numSides The number of sides for this die.
16     */
17
18     public Die(int numSides)
19     {
20        sides = numSides;
21        roll();
22     }
23
24     /**
25        The roll method simulates the rolling of
26        the die.
27     */
28
29     public void roll()
30     {
31        // Create a Random object.
32        Random rand = new Random();
33
34        // Get a random value for the die.
35        value = rand.nextInt(sides) + 1;
36     }
```

```
37
38      /**
39         getSides method
40         @return The number of sides for this die.
41      */
42
43      public int getSides()
44      {
45         return sides;
46      }
47
48      /**
49         getValue method
50         @return The value of the die.
51      */
52
53      public int getValue()
54      {
55         return value;
56      }
57   }
```

Let's take a closer look at the code for the class:

Lines 9 and 10: These statements declare two int fields. The sides field will hold the number of sides that the die has, and the value field will hold the value of the die once it has been rolled.

Lines 18–22: This is the constructor. Notice that the constructor has a parameter for the number of sides. The parameter is assigned to the sides field in line 20. Line 21 calls the roll method, which simulates the rolling of the die.

Lines 29–36: This is the roll method, which simulates the rolling of the die. In line 32 a Random object is created, and it is referenced by the rand variable. Line 35 uses the Random object to get a random number that is in the appropriate range for this particular die. For example, if the sides field is set to 6, the expression rand.nextInt(sides) + 1 will return a random integer in the range of 1 through 6. The random number is assigned to the value field.

Lines 43–46: This is the getSides method, an accessor that returns the sides field.

Lines 53–56: This is the getValue method, an accessor that returns the value field.

The program in Code Listing 6-15 demonstrates the class. It creates two instances of the Die class: one with six sides, and the other with twelve sides. It then simulates five rolls of the dice.

Code Listing 6-15   (DiceDemo.java)

```
1   /**
2      This program simulates the rolling of dice.
3   */
```

```
4
5   public class DiceDemo
6   {
7      public static void main(String[] args)
8      {
9         final int DIE1_SIDES = 6;     // Number of sides for die #1
10        final int DIE2_SIDES = 12;    // Number of sides for die #2
11        final int MAX_ROLLS = 5;      // Number of times to roll
12
13        // Create two instances of the Die class.
14        Die die1 = new Die(DIE1_SIDES);
15        Die die2 = new Die(DIE2_SIDES);
16
17        // Display the initial state of the dice.
18        System.out.println("This simulates the rolling of a " +
19                           DIE1_SIDES + " sided die and a " +
20                           DIE2_SIDES + " sided die.");
21
22        System.out.println("Initial value of the dice:");
23        System.out.println(die1.getValue() + " " + die2.getValue());
24
25        // Roll the dice five times.
26        System.out.println("Rolling the dice " + MAX_ROLLS + " times.");
27
28        for (int i = 0; i < MAX_ROLLS; i++)
29        {
30           // Roll the dice.
31           die1.roll();
32           die2.roll();
33
34           // Display the values of the dice.
35           System.out.println(die1.getValue() + " " + die2.getValue());
36        }
37     }
38  }
```

Program Output

```
This simulates the rolling of a 6 sided die and a 12 sided die.
Initial value of the dice:
2 7
Rolling the dice 5 times.
3 5
5 2
2 1
4 1
5 9
```

Let's take a closer look at the program:

Lines 9–11:   These statements declare three constants. DIE1_SIDES is the number of sides for the first die (6), DIE2_SIDES is the number of sides for the second die (12), and MAX_ROLLS is the number of times to roll the die (5).

Lines 14–15:   These statements create two instances of the Die class. Notice that DIE1_SIDES, which is 6, is passed to the constructor in line 14, and DIE2_SIDES, which is 12, is passed to the constructor in line 15. As a result, die1 will reference a Die object with six sides, and die2 will reference a Die object with twelve sides.

Lines 23:   This statement displays the initial value of both Die objects. (Recall that the Die class constructor performs an initial roll of the die.)

Lines 28–36:   This for loop iterates five times. Each time the loop iterates, line 31 calls the die1 object's roll method, and line 32 calls the die2 object's roll method. Line 35 displays the value of both dice.

Checkpoint

MyProgrammingLab™ *www.myprogramminglab.com*

6.18   How is a constructor named?

6.19   What is a constructor's return type?

6.20   Assume that the following is a constructor, which appears in a class:

```
ClassAct(int number)
{
    item = number;
}
```

a)   What is the name of the class that this constructor appears in?

b)   Write a statement that creates an object from the class and passes the value 25 as an argument to the constructor.

6.5 Passing Objects as Arguments

CONCEPT: When an object is passed as an argument to a method, the object's address is passed into the method's parameter variable. As a result, the parameter references the object.

When you are developing applications that work with objects, you will often need to write methods that accept objects as arguments. For example, suppose that a program is using the Die class that was previously shown in Code Listing 6-14. The following code shows a method named showDieSides that accepts a Die object as an argument:

```
void showDieSides(Die d)
{
    System.out.println("This die has " + d.getSides() +
                    " sides.");
}
```

The following code sample shows how we might create a `Die` object, and then pass it as an argument to the `showDieSides` method:

```
Die myDie = new Die(6);
showDieSides(myDie)
```

When you pass an object as an argument, the thing that is passed into the parameter variable is the object's memory address. As a result, the parameter variable references the object, and the method has access to the object.

The program shown in Code Listing 6-16 gives a complete demonstration. It creates two `Die` objects: one with six sides, and the other with twenty sides. It passes each object to a method named `rollDie` that displays the die's sides, rolls the die, and displays the die's value.

Code Listing 6-16   (`DieArgument.java`)

```
1  /**
2     This program rolls a 6-sided die and
3     a 20-sided die.
4  */
5
6  public class DieArgument
7  {
8     public static void main(String[] args)
9     {
10       final int SIX_SIDES = 6;
11       final int TWENTY_SIDES = 20;
12
13       // Create a 6-sided die.
14       Die sixDie = new Die(SIX_SIDES);
15
16       // Create a 20-sided die.
17       Die twentyDie = new Die(TWENTY_SIDES);
18
19       // Roll the dice.
20       rollDie(sixDie);
21       rollDie(twentyDie);
22    }
23
24    /**
25       This method simulates a die roll, displaying
26       the die's number of sides and value.
27       @param d The Die object to roll.
28    */
29
30    public static void rollDie(Die d)
31    {
32       // Display the number of sides.
```

```
33          System.out.println("Rolling a " + d.getSides() +
34                              " sided die.");
35
36          // Roll the die.
37          d.roll();
38
39          // Display the die's value.
40          System.out.println("The die's value: " + d.getValue());
41     }
42 }
```

Program Output

```
Rolling a 6 sided die.
The die's value: 3
Rolling a 20 sided die.
The die's value: 19
```

In the Spotlight:
Simulating the Game of Cho-Han

Cho-Han is a traditional Japanese gambling game in which a dealer uses a cup to roll two six-sided dice. The cup is placed upside down on a table so that the value of the dice is concealed. Players then wager on whether the sum of the dice values is even (Cho) or odd (Han). The winner or winners take all of the wagers, or the house takes them if there are no winners.

We will develop a program that simulates a simplified variation of the game. The simulated game will have a dealer and two players. The players will not wager money, but will simply guess whether the sum of the dice values is even (Cho) or odd (Han). One point will be awarded to the player, or players, correctly guessing the outcome. The game will play for five rounds, and the player with the most points is the grand winner.

In the program, we will use the Die class that was introduced in Code Listing 6-14. We will create two instances of the class to represent two six-sided dice. In addition to the Die class, we will write the following classes:

- Dealer class: We will create an instance of this class to represent the dealer. It will have the ability to roll the dice, report the value of the dice, and report whether the total dice value is Cho or Han.
- Player class: We will create two instances of this class to represent the players. Instances of the Player class can store the player's name, make a guess between Cho and Han, and be awarded points.

First, let's look at the Dealer class. Figure 6-25 shows a UML diagram for the class, and Code Listing 6-17 shows the code.

Figure 6-25 UML diagram for the `Dealer` class

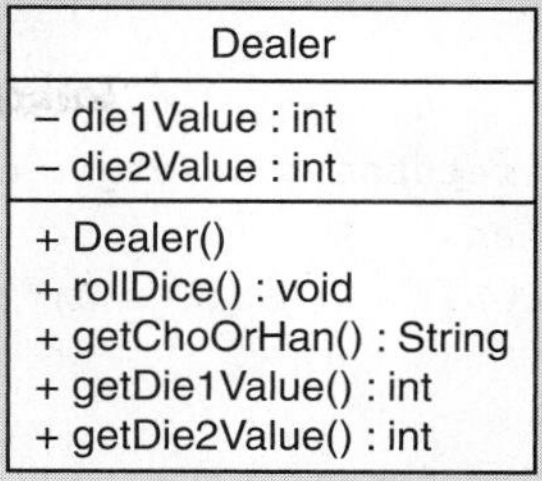

```
              Dealer
  – die1Value : int
  – die2Value : int
  + Dealer()
  + rollDice() : void
  + getChoOrHan() : String
  + getDie1Value() : int
  + getDie2Value() : int
```

Code Listing 6-17   (`Dealer.java`)

```java
 1 /**
 2     Dealer class for the game of Cho-Han
 3 */
 4
 5 public class Dealer
 6 {
 7    private int die1Value;  // The value of die #1
 8    private int die2Value;  // The value of die #2
 9
10    /**
11       Constructor
12    */
13
14    public Dealer()
15    {
16       die1Value = 0;
17       die2Value = 0;
18    }
19
20    /**
21       The rollDice method rolls the dice and saves
22       their values.
23    */
24
25    public void rollDice()
26    {
27       final int SIDES = 6; // Number of sides for the dice
28
29       // Create the two dice. (This also rolls them.)
30       Die die1 = new Die(SIDES);
31       Die die2 = new Die(SIDES);
32
33       // Record their values.
34       die1Value = die1.getValue();
```

```java
35          die2Value = die2.getValue();
36    }
37
38    /**
39       The getChoOrHan method returns the result of
40       the dice roll, Cho or Han.
41       @return Either "Cho (even)" or "Han (odd)"
42    */
43
44    public String getChoOrHan()
45    {
46       String result; // To hold the result
47
48       // Get the sum of the dice.
49       int sum = die1Value + die2Value;
50
51       // Determine even or odd.
52       if (sum % 2 == 0)
53          result = "Cho (even)";
54       else
55          result = "Han (odd)";
56
57       // Return the result.
58       return result;
59    }
60
61    /**
62       The getDie1Value method returns the value of
63       die #1.
64       @return The die1Value field
65    */
66
67    public int getDie1Value()
68    {
69       return die1Value;
70    }
71
72    /**
73       The getDie2Value method returns the value of
74       die #2.
75       @return The die2Value field
76    */
77
78    public int getDie2Value()
79    {
80       return die2Value;
81    }
82 }
```

Let's take a closer look at the code for the `Dealer` class:

- Lines 7 and 8 declare the fields `die1Value` and `die2Value`. These fields will hold the value of the two dice after they have been rolled.
- The constructor, in lines 14 through 18, initializes the `die1Value` and `die2Value` fields to 0.
- The `rollDice` method, in lines 25 through 36, simulates the rolling of the dice. Lines 30 and 31 create two `Die` objects. Recall that the `Die` class constructor performs an initial roll of the die, so there is no need to call the `Die` objects' `roll` method. Lines 34 and 35 save the value of the dice in the `die1Value` and `die2Value` fields.
- The `getChoOrHan` method, in lines 44 through 59, returns a string indicating whether the sum of the dice is Cho (even) or Han (odd).
- The `getDie1Value` method, in lines 67 through 70, returns the value of the first die (stored in the `die1Value` field).
- The `getDie2Value` method, in lines 78 through 81, returns the value of the second die (stored in the `die2Value` field).

Now let's look at the `Player` class. Figure 6-26 shows a UML diagram for the class, and Code Listing 6-18 shows the code.

Figure 6-26 UML diagram for the `Player` class

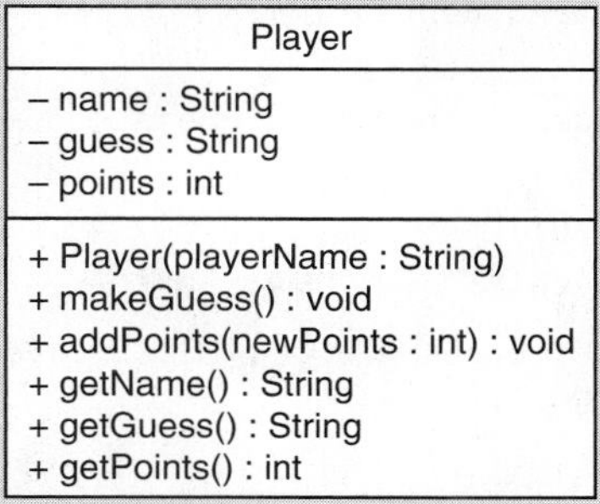

```
                    Player
          ──────────────────────────
          – name : String
          – guess : String
          – points : int
          ──────────────────────────
          + Player(playerName : String)
          + makeGuess() : void
          + addPoints(newPoints : int) : void
          + getName() : String
          + getGuess() : String
          + getPoints() : int
```

Code Listing 6-18   (`Player.java`)

```java
 1   import java.util.Random;
 2
 3   /**
 4       Player class for the game of Cho-Han
 5   */
 6
 7   public class Player
 8   {
 9      private String name;      // The player's name
10      private String guess;     // The player's guess
11      private int points;       // The player's points
12
13      /**
14          Constructor
```

```
15          @param playerName The player's name.
16       */
17
18       public Player(String playerName)
19       {
20          name = playerName;
21          guess = "";
22          points = 0;
23       }
24
25       /**
26          The makeGuess method causes the player to guess
27          either "Cho (even)" or "Han (odd)".
28       */
29
30       public void makeGuess()
31       {
32          // Create a Random object.
33          Random rand = new Random();
34
35          // Get a random number, either 0 or 1.
36          int guessNumber = rand.nextInt(2);
37
38          // Convert the random number to a guess of
39          // either "Cho (even)" or "Han (odd)".
40          if (guessNumber == 0)
41             guess = "Cho (even)";
42          else
43             guess = "Han (odd)";
44       }
45
46       /**
47          The addPoints method adds a specified number of
48          points to the player's current balance.
49          @newPoints The points to add.
50       */
51
52       public void addPoints(int newPoints)
53       {
54          points += newPoints;
55       }
56
57       /**
58          The getName method returns the player's name.
59          @return The value of the name field.
60       */
61
```

```
62      public String getName()
63      {
64         return name;
65      }
66
67      /**
68         The getGuess method returns the player's guess.
69         @return The value of the guess field.
70      */
71
72      public String getGuess()
73      {
74         return guess;
75      }
76
77      /**
78         The getPoints method returns the player's points
79         @return The value of the points field.
80      */
81
82      public int getPoints()
83      {
84         return points;
85      }
86   }
```

Here's a summary of the code for the `Player` class:

- Lines 9 through 11 declare the fields `name`, `guess`, and `points`. These fields will hold the player's name, the player's guess, and the number of points the player has earned.
- The constructor, in lines 18 through 23, accepts an argument for the player's name, which is assigned to the `name` field. The `guess` field is assigned an empty string, and the `points` field is set to 0.
- The `makeGuess` method, in lines 30 through 44, causes the player to make a guess. The method generates a random number that is either a 0 or a 1. The `if` statement that begins at line 40 assigns the string "Cho (even)" to the `guess` field if the random number is 0, or it assigns the string "Han (odd)" to the `guess` field if the random number is 1.
- The `addPoints` method, in lines 52 through 55, adds the number of points specified by the argument to the player's `point` field.
- The `getName` method, in lines 62 through 65, returns the player's name.
- The `getGuess` method, in lines 72 through 75, returns the player's guess.
- The `getPoints` method, in lines 82 through 85, returns the player's points.

Code Listing 6-19 shows the program that uses these classes to simulate the game. The `main` method simulates five rounds of the game, displaying the results of each round, and then displays the overall game results.

Code Listing 6-19   (`ChoHan.java`)

```java
 1  import java.util.Scanner;
 2
 3  public class ChoHan
 4  {
 5     public static void main(String[] args)
 6     {
 7        final int MAX_ROUNDS = 5;   // Number of rounds
 8        String player1Name;         // First player's name
 9        String player2Name;         // Second player's name
10
11        // Create a Scanner object for keyboard input.
12        Scanner keyboard = new Scanner(System.in);
13
14        // Get the players' names.
15        System.out.print("Enter the first player's name: ");
16        player1Name = keyboard.nextLine();
17        System.out.print("Enter the second player's name: ");
18        player2Name = keyboard.nextLine();
19
20        // Create the dealer.
21        Dealer dealer = new Dealer();
22
23        // Create the two players.
24        Player player1 = new Player(player1Name);
25        Player player2 = new Player(player2Name);
26
27        // Play the rounds.
28        for (int round = 0; round < MAX_ROUNDS; round++)
29        {
30           System.out.println("-----------------------------");
31           System.out.printf("Now playing round %d.\n", round + 1);
32
33           // Roll the dice.
34           dealer.rollDice();
35
36           // The players make their guesses.
37           player1.makeGuess();
38           player2.makeGuess();
39
40           // Determine the winner of this round.
41           roundResults(dealer, player1, player2);
42        }
43
44        // Display the grand winner.
45        displayGrandWinner(player1, player2);
46     }
```

```
47
48     /**
49        The roundResults method determines the results of
50        the current round.
51        @param dealer The Dealer object
52        @param player1 Player #1 object
53        @param player2 Player #2 object
54     */
55
56     public static void roundResults(Dealer dealer, Player player1,
57                                     Player player2)
58     {
59        // Show the dice values.
60        System.out.printf("The dealer rolled %d and %d.\n",
61                          dealer.getDie1Value(), dealer.getDie2Value());
62        System.out.printf("Result: %s\n", dealer.getChoOrHan());
63
64        // Check each player's guess and award points.
65        checkGuess(player1, dealer);
66        checkGuess(player2, dealer);
67     }
68
69     /**
70        The checkGuess method checks a player's guess against
71        the dealer's result.
72        @param player The Player object to check.
73        @param dealer The Dealer object.
74     */
75
76     public static void checkGuess(Player player, Dealer dealer)
77     {
78        final int POINTS_TO_ADD = 1; // Points to award winner
79        String guess = player.getGuess();            // Player's guess
80        String choHanResult = dealer.getChoOrHan(); // Cho or Han
81
82        // Display the player's guess.
83        System.out.printf("The player %s guessed %s.\n",
84                          player.getName(), player.getGuess());
85
86        // Award points if the player guessed correctly.
87        if (guess.equalsIgnoreCase(choHanResult))
88        {
89           player.addPoints(POINTS_TO_ADD);
90           System.out.printf("Awarding %d point(s) to %s.\n",
91                             POINTS_TO_ADD, player.getName());
92        }
93     }
94
```

```
 95      /**
 96          The displayGrandWinner method displays the game's grand winner.
 97          @param player1 Player #1
 98          @param player2 Player #2
 99      */
100
101      public static void displayGrandWinner(Player player1, Player player2)
102      {
103          System.out.println("----------------------------");
104          System.out.println("Game over. Here are the results:");
105          System.out.printf("%s: %d points.\n", player1.getName(),
106                              player1.getPoints());
107          System.out.printf("%s: %d points.\n", player2.getName(),
108                              player2.getPoints());
109
110          if (player1.getPoints() > player2.getPoints())
111              System.out.println(player1.getName() + " is the grand winner!");
112          else if (player2.getPoints() > player1.getPoints())
113              System.out.println(player2.getName() + " is the grand winner!");
114          else
115              System.out.println("Both players are tied!");
116      }
117  }
```

Program Output with Example Input Shown in Bold

```
Enter the first player's name: Chelsea [Enter]
Enter the second player's name: Chris [Enter]
----------------------------
Now playing round 1.
The dealer rolled 3 and 6.
Result: Han (odd)
The player Chelsea guessed Han (odd).
Awarding 1 point(s) to Chelsea.
The player Chris guessed Han (odd).
Awarding 1 point(s) to Chris.
----------------------------
Now playing round 2.
The dealer rolled 4 and 5.
Result: Han (odd)
The player Chelsea guessed Cho (even).
The player Chris guessed Cho (even).
----------------------------
Now playing round 3.
The dealer rolled 5 and 6.
Result: Han (odd)
The player Chelsea guessed Cho (even).
The player Chris guessed Han (odd).
Awarding 1 point(s) to Chris.
```

```
-----------------------------
Now playing round 4.
The dealer rolled 1 and 6.
Result: Han (odd)
The player Chelsea guessed Cho (even).
The player Chris guessed Cho (even).
-----------------------------
Now playing round 5.
The dealer rolled 6 and 6.
Result: Cho (even)
The player Chelsea guessed Han (odd).
The player Chris guessed Cho (even).
Awarding 1 point(s) to Chris.
-----------------------------
Game over. Here are the results:
Chelsea: 1 points.
Chris: 3 points.
Chris is the grand winner!
```

Let's look at the code. Here is a summary of the main method:

- Lines 7 through 9 make the following declarations: MAX_ROUNDS—the number of rounds to play, player1Name—to hold the name of player #1, and player2Name—to hold the name of player #2.
- Lines 15 through 18 prompt the user to enter the players' names.
- Line 21 creates an instance of the Dealer class. The object represents the dealer, and is referenced by the dealer variable.
- Line 24 creates an instance of the Player class. The object represents player #1, and is referenced by the player1 variable. Notice that player1Name is passed as an argument to the constructor.
- Line 25 creates another instance of the Player class. The object represents player #2, and is referenced by the player2 variable. Notice that player2Name is passed as an argument to the constructor.
- The for loop that begins in line 28 iterates five times, causing the simulation of five rounds of the game. The loop performs the following actions:
  - Line 34 causes the dealer to roll the dice.
  - Line 37 causes player #1 to make a guess (Cho or Han).
  - Line 38 causes player #2 to make a guess (Cho or Han).
  - Line 41 passes the dealer, player1, and player2 objects to the roundResults method. The method displays the results of this round.
- Line 45 passes the player1 and player2 objects to the displayGrandWinner method, which displays the grand winner of the game.

The roundResults method, which displays the results of a round, appears in lines 56 through 67. Here is a summary of the method:

- The method accepts references to the dealer, player1, and player2 objects as arguments.
- The statement in lines 60 and 61 displays the value of the two dice.

- Line 62 calls the `dealer` object's `getChoOrHan` method to display the results, Cho or Han.
- Line 65 calls the `checkGuess` method, passing the `player1` and `dealer` objects as arguments. The `checkGuess` method compares a player's guess to the dealer's result (Cho or Han), and awards points to the player, if the guess is correct.
- Line 66 calls the `checkGuess` method, passing the `player2` and `dealer` objects as arguments.

The `checkGuess` method, which compares a player's guess to the dealer's result, awarding points to the player for a correct guess, appears in lines 76 through 93. Here is a summary of the method:

- The method accepts references to a `Player` object and the `Dealer` object as arguments.
- Line 78 declares the constant `POINTS_TO_ADD`, set to the value 1, which is the number of points to add to the player's balance if the player's guess is correct.
- Line 79 assigns the player's guess to the `String` object `guess`.
- Line 80 assigns the dealer's results (Cho or Han) to the `String` object `choHanResult`.
- The statement in lines 83 and 84 displays the player's name and guess.
- The `if` statement in line 87 compares the player's guess to the dealer's result. If they match, then the player guessed correctly, and line 89 awards points to the player.

The `displayGrandWinner` method, which displays the grand winner of the game, appears in lines 101 through 116. Here is a summary of the method:

- The method accepts references to the `player1` and `player2` objects.
- The statements in lines 105 through 108 display both players' names and points.
- The `if-else-if` statement that begins in line 110 determines which of the two players has the highest score, and displays that player's name as the grand winner. If both players have the same score, a tie is declared.

6.6 Overloading Methods and Constructors

CONCEPT: Two or more methods in a class may have the same name as long as their parameter lists are different. This also applies to constructors.

Method overloading is an important part of object-oriented programming. When a method is *overloaded*, it means that multiple methods in the same class have the same name, but use different types of parameters. Method overloading is important because sometimes you need several different ways to perform the same operation. For example, suppose a class has the following two methods:

```
public int add(int num1, int num2)
{
    int sum = num1 + num2;
    return sum;
}
```

```java
public String add(String str1, String str2)
{
    String combined = str1 + str2;
    return combined;
}
```

Both of these methods are named `add`. They both take two arguments, which are added together. The first one accepts two `int` arguments and returns their sum. The second accepts two `String` references and returns a reference to a `String` that is a concatenation of the two arguments. When we write a call to the `add` method, the compiler must determine which one of the overloaded methods we intended to call.

The process of matching a method call with the correct method is known as *binding*. When an overloaded method is being called, Java uses the method's name and parameter list to determine which method to bind the call to. If two `int` arguments are passed to the `add` method, the version of the method with two `int` parameters is called. Likewise, when two `String` arguments are passed to `add`, the version with two `String` parameters is called.

Java uses a method's signature to distinguish it from other methods of the same name. A method's *signature* consists of the method's name and the data types of the method's parameters, in the order that they appear. For example, here are the signatures of the `add` methods that were previously shown:

```java
add(int, int)
add(String, String)
```

Note that the method's return type is *not* part of the signature. For this reason, the following `add` method cannot be added to the same class with the previous ones:

```java
public int add(String str1, String str2)
{
    int sum = Integer.parstInt(str1) + Integer.parseInt(str2);
    return sum;
}
```

Because the return type is not part of the signature, this method's signature is the same as that of the other `add` method that takes two `String` arguments. For this reason, an error message will be issued when a class containing all of these methods is compiled.

Constructors can also be overloaded, which means that a class can have more than one constructor. The rules for overloading constructors are the same for overloading other methods: Each version of the constructor must have a different parameter list. As long as each constructor has a unique signature, the compiler can tell them apart. For example, the `Rectangle` class that we discussed earlier could have the following two constructors:

```java
public Rectangle()
{
    length = 0.0;
    width = 0.0;
}
```

```
    public Rectangle(double len, double w)
    {
        length = len;
        width = w;
    }
```

The first constructor shown here accepts no arguments, and assigns 0.0 to the `length` and `width` fields. The second constructor accepts two arguments, which are assigned to the `length` and `width` fields. The following code shows an example of how each constructor is called:

```
    Rectangle box1 = new Rectangle();
    Rectangle box2 = new Rectangle(5.0, 10.0);
```

The first statement creates a `Rectangle` object, referenced by the `box1` variable, and executes the no-arg constructor. Its `length` and `width` fields will be set to 0.0. The second statement creates another `Rectangle` object, referenced by the `box2` variable, and executes the second constructor. Its `length` and `width` fields will be set to 5.0 and 10.0, respectively.

Recall that Java provides a default constructor only when you do not write any constructors for a class. If a class has a constructor that accepts arguments, but it does not have a no-arg constructor, you cannot create an instance of the class without passing arguments to the constructor. Therefore, any time you write a constructor for a class, and that constructor accepts arguments, you should also write a no-arg constructor if you want to be able to create instances of the class without passing arguments to the constructor.

The BankAccount Class

Now we will look at the `BankAccount` class. Objects that are created from this class will simulate bank accounts, allowing us to have a starting balance, make deposits, make withdrawals, and get the current balance. A UML diagram for the `BankAccount` class is shown in Figure 6-27. In the figure, the overloaded constructors and overloaded methods are pointed out. Note that the extra annotation is not part of the UML diagram. It is there to draw attention to the items that are overloaded.

Figure 6-27   UML diagram for the `BankAccount` class

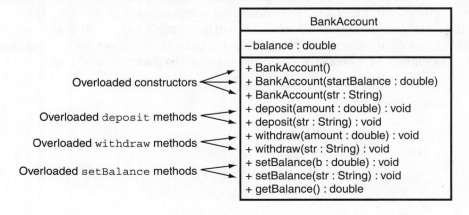

As you can see from the diagram, the class has three overloaded constructors. Also, the class has two overloaded methods named deposit, two overloaded methods named withdraw, and two overloaded methods named setBalance. The last method, getBalance, is not over-loaded. Code Listing 6-20 shows the code for the class.

Code Listing 6-20   **(BankAccount.java)**

```java
 1  /**
 2      The BankAccount class simulates a bank account.
 3  */
 4
 5  public class BankAccount
 6  {
 7     private double balance;        // Account balance
 8
 9     /**
10        This constructor sets the starting balance
11        at 0.0.
12     */
13
14     public BankAccount()
15     {
16        balance = 0.0;
17     }
18
19     /**
20        This constructor sets the starting balance
21        to the value passed as an argument.
22        @param startBalance The starting balance.
23     */
24
25     public BankAccount(double startBalance)
26     {
27        balance = startBalance;
28     }
29
30     /**
31        This constructor sets the starting balance
32        to the value in the String argument.
33        @param str The starting balance, as a String.
34     */
35
36     public BankAccount(String str)
37     {
38        balance = Double.parseDouble(str);
39     }
40
```

```
41      /**
42         The deposit method makes a deposit into
43         the account.
44         @param amount The amount to add to the
45                     balance field.
46      */
47
48      public void deposit(double amount)
49      {
50         balance += amount;
51      }
52
53      /**
54         The deposit method makes a deposit into
55         the account.
56         @param str The amount to add to the
57                     balance field, as a String.
58      */
59
60      public void deposit(String str)
61      {
62         balance += Double.parseDouble(str);
63      }
64
65      /**
66         The withdraw method withdraws an amount
67         from the account.
68         @param amount The amount to subtract from
69                     the balance field.
70      */
71
72      public void withdraw(double amount)
73      {
74         balance -= amount;
75      }
76
77      /**
78         The withdraw method withdraws an amount
79         from the account.
80         @param str The amount to subtract from
81                     the balance field, as a String.
82      */
83
84      public void withdraw(String str)
85      {
86         balance -= Double.parseDouble(str);
87      }
88
```

```
 89       /**
 90          The setBalance method sets the account balance.
 91          @param b The value to store in the balance field.
 92       */
 93
 94       public void setBalance(double b)
 95       {
 96          balance = b;
 97       }
 98
 99       /**
100          The setBalance method sets the account balance.
101          @param str The value, as a String, to store in
102                     the balance field.
103       */
104
105       public void setBalance(String str)
106       {
107          balance = Double.parseDouble(str);
108        }
109
110       /**
111          The getBalance method returns the
112          account balance.
113          @return The value in the balance field.
114       */
115
116       public double getBalance()
117       {
118          return balance;
119       }
120   }
```

The class has one field, `balance`, which is a `double`. This field holds an account's current balance. Here is a summary of the class's overloaded constructors:

- The first constructor is a no-arg constructor. It sets the `balance` field to 0.0. If we wish to execute this constructor when we create an instance of the class, we simply pass no constructor arguments. Here is an example:

    ```
    BankAccount account = new BankAccount();
    ```

- The second constructor has a `double` parameter variable, `startBalance`, which is assigned to the `balance` field. If we wish to execute this constructor when we create an instance of the class, we pass a `double` value as a constructor argument. Here is an example:

    ```
    BankAccount account = new BankAccount(1000.0);
    ```

- The third constructor has a String parameter variable, str. It is assumed that the String contains a string representation of the account's balance. The method uses the Double.parseDouble method to convert the string to a double, and then assigns it to the balance field. If we wish to execute this constructor when we create an instance of the class, we pass a reference to a String as a constructor argument. Here is an example:

  ```
  BankAccount account = new BankAccount("1000.0");
  ```

  This constructor is provided as a convenience. If the class is used in a program that reads the account balance from a dialog box, or from a text file, the amount does not have to be converted from a string before it is passed to the constructor.

Here is a summary of the overloaded deposit methods:

- The first deposit method has a parameter, amount, which is a double. When the method is called, an amount that is to be deposited into the account is passed into this parameter. The value of the parameter is then added to value in the balance field.
- The second deposit method has a parameter, str, which is a reference to a String. It is assumed that the String contains a string representation of the amount to be deposited. The method uses the Double.parseDouble method to convert the string to a double, and then adds it to the balance field. For example, if we call the method and pass "500.0" as the argument, it will add 500.0 to the balance field. As with the overloaded constructors, this method is provided as a convenience for programs that read the amount to be deposited from a dialog box or a text file.

Here is a summary of the overloaded withdraw methods:

- The first withdraw method has a parameter, amount, which is a double. When the method is called, an amount that is to be withdrawn from the account is passed into this parameter. The value of the parameter is then subtracted from the value in the balance field.
- The second withdraw method has a parameter, str, which is a reference to a String. It is assumed that the String contains a string representation of the amount to be withdrawn. This amount is converted to a double, and then subtracted from the balance field. As with the overloaded constructors and deposit methods, this method is provided as a convenience.

Here is a summary of the overloaded setBalance methods:

- The first setBalance method accepts a double argument, which is assigned to the balance field.
- The second setBalance method accepts a String reference as an argument. It is assumed that the String contains a string representation of the account's balance. The String is converted to a double and then assigned to the balance field. As with many of the other overloaded methods, this method is provided as a convenience.

The remaining method is getBalance. It returns the value in the balance field, which is the current account balance. The AccountTest.java program, shown in Code Listing 6-21, demonstrates the BankAccount class. Its output is shown in Figure 6-28.

Code Listing 6-21   (`AccountTest.java`)

```java
 1 import javax.swing.JOptionPane; // For the JOptionPane class
 2
 3 /**
 4     This program demonstrates the BankAccount class.
 5 */
 6
 7 public class AccountTest
 8 {
 9     public static void main(String[] args)
10     {
11         String input;    // To hold user input
12
13         // Get the starting balance.
14         input = JOptionPane.showInputDialog(
15                 "What is your account's starting balance?");
16
17         // Create a BankAccount object.
18         BankAccount account = new BankAccount(input);
19
20         // Get the amount of pay.
21         input = JOptionPane.showInputDialog(
22                 "How much were you paid this month?");
23
24         // Deposit the user's pay into the account.
25         account.deposit(input);
26
27         // Display the new balance.
28         JOptionPane.showMessageDialog(null,
29             String.format("Your pay has been deposited.\n" +
30                         "Your current balance is $%,.2f",
31                         account.getBalance()));
32
33         // Withdraw some cash from the account.
34         input = JOptionPane.showInputDialog(
35                 "How much would you like to withdraw?");
36         account.withdraw(input);
37
38         // Display the new balance
39         JOptionPane.showMessageDialog(null,
40             String.format("Now your balance is $%,.2f",
41                         account.getBalance()));
42
43         System.exit(0);
44     }
45 }
```

Figure 6-28   Interaction with the AccountTest program

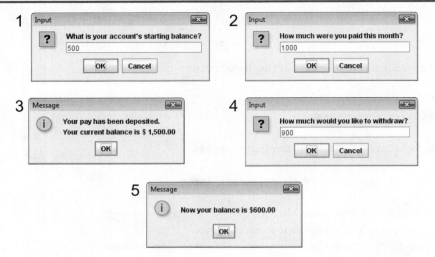

Overloaded Methods Make Classes More Useful

You might be wondering why all those overloaded methods appear in the BankAccount class, especially because many of them weren't used by the demonstration program in Code Listing 6-21. After all, wouldn't it be simpler if the class had only the methods we were going to use?

An object's purpose is to provide a specific service. The service provided by the BankAccount class is that it simulates a bank account. Any program that needs a simulated bank account can simply create a BankAccount object and then use its methods to put the simulation into action. Because the BankAccount class has numerous overloaded methods, it is much more flexible than it would be if it provided only one way to perform every operation. By providing overloaded constructors, deposit methods, withdraw methods, and setBalance methods, we made the BankAccount class useful to programs other than our simple demonstration program. This is an important consideration to keep in mind when you design classes of your own.

6.7 Scope of Instance Fields

CONCEPT: Instance fields are visible to all of the class's instance methods.

Recall from Chapter 2 that a variable's scope is the part of a program where the variable may be accessed by its name. A variable's name is visible only to statements inside the variable's scope. The location of a variable's declaration determines the variable's scope.

In this chapter you have seen variables declared as instance fields in a class. An instance field can be accessed by any instance method in the same class as the field. If an instance field is declared with the `public` access specifier, it can also be accessed by code outside the class.

Shadowing

In Chapter 2 you saw that you cannot have two local variables with the same name in the same scope. This applies to parameter variables as well. A parameter variable is, in essence, a local variable. So, you cannot give a parameter variable and a local variable in the same method the same name.

However, you can have a local variable or a parameter variable with the same name as a field. When you do, the name of the local or parameter variable *shadows* the name of the field. This means that the field name is hidden by the name of the local or parameter variable.

For example, assume that the `Rectangle` class's `setLength` method had been written in the following manner:

```
public void setLength(double len)
{
    int length;          // Local variable
    length = len;
}
```

In this code a local variable is given the same name as a field. Therefore, the local variable's name shadows the field's name. When the statement `length = len;` is executed, the value of `len` is assigned to the local variable `length`, not to the field. The unintentional shadowing of field names can cause elusive bugs, so you need to be careful not to give local variables the same names as fields.

Checkpoint

MyProgrammingLab™ *www.myprogramminglab.com*

6.21 Is it required that overloaded methods have different return values, different parameter lists, or both?

6.22 What is a method's signature?

6.23 Look at the following class:

```
public class CheckPoint
{
    public void message(int x)
    {
        System.out.print("This is the first version ");
        System.out.println("of the method.");
    }
    public void message(String x)
    {
        System.out.print("This is the second version ");
        System.out.println("of the method.");
    }
}
```

What will the following code display?

```
CheckPoint cp = new CheckPoint();
cp.message("1");
cp.message(1);
```

6.24 How many default constructors may a class have?

6.8 Packages and `import` Statements

> **CONCEPT:** The classes in the Java API are organized into packages. An `import` statement tells the compiler which package a class is located in.

In Chapter 2 you were introduced to the Java API, which is a standard library of prewritten classes. Each class in the Java API is designed for a specific purpose, and you can use the classes in your own programs. You've already used a few classes from the API, such as the `String` class, the `Scanner` class, the `JOptionPane` class, and the `Random` class.

All of the classes in the Java API are organized into packages. A *package* is simply a group of related classes. Each package also has a name. For example, the `Scanner` class is in the `java.util` package.

Many of the classes in the Java API are not automatically available to your program. Quite often, you have to *import* an API class in order to use it. You use the `import` key word to import a class. For example, the following statement is required to import the `Scanner` class:

```
import java.util.Scanner;
```

This statement tells the compiler that the `Scanner` class is located in the `java.util` package. Without this statement, the compiler will not be able to locate the `Scanner` class, and the program will not compile.

Explicit and Wildcard `import` Statements

There are two types of `import` statements: explicit and wildcard. An *explicit* `import` statement identifies the package location of a single class. For example, the following statement explicitly identifies the location of the `Scanner` class:

```
import java.util.Scanner;
```

The `java.util` package contains several other classes as well as the `Scanner` class. For example, the `Random` class is also part of the `java.util` package. If a program needs to use the `Scanner` class and the `Random` class, it will have to import both of these classes. One way to do this is to write explicit `import` statements for each class, as follows:

```
import java.util.Scanner;
import java.util.Random;
```

Another way to import both of these classes is to use a wildcard import statement. A *wildcard import* statement tells the compiler to import all of the classes in a package. Here is an example:

```
import java.util.*;
```

The .* that follows the package name tells the compiler to import all the classes that are part of the java.util package. Using a wildcard import statement does not affect the performance or the size of your program. It merely tells the compiler that you want to make every class in a particular package available to your program.

The `java.lang` Package

The Java API does have one package, java.lang, which is automatically imported into every Java program. This package contains general classes, such as String and System, that are fundamental to the Java programming language. You do not have to write an import statement for any class that is part of the java.lang package.

Other API Packages

There are numerous packages in the Java API. Table 6-2 lists a few of them.

Table 6-2 A few of the standard Java packages

Package	Description
java.applet	Provides the classes necessary to create an applet.
java.awt	Provides classes for the Abstract Windowing Toolkit. These classes are used in drawing images and creating graphical user interfaces.
java.io	Provides classes that perform various types of input and output.
java.lang	Provides general classes for the Java language. This package is automatically imported.
java.net	Provides classes for network communications.
java.security	Provides classes that implement security features.
java.sql	Provides classes for accessing databases using structured query language.
java.text	Provides various classes for formatting text.
java.util	Provides various utility classes.
javax.swing	Provides classes for creating graphical user interfaces.

See Appendix H, available on the book's companion Web site at www.pearsonhighered. com/gaddis, for a more detailed look at packages.

6.9 Focus on Object-Oriented Design: Finding the Classes and Their Responsibilities

So far you have learned the basics of writing a class, creating an object from the class, and using the object to perform operations. Although this knowledge is necessary to create an object-oriented application, it is not the first step. The first step is to analyze the problem that you are trying to solve and determine the classes that you will need. In this section, we will discuss a simple technique for finding the classes in a problem and determining their responsibilities.

Finding the Classes

When developing an object-oriented application, one of your first tasks is to identify the classes that you will need to create. Typically, your goal is to identify the different types of real-world objects that are present in the problem, and then create classes for those types of objects within your application.

Over the years, software professionals have developed numerous techniques for finding the classes in a given problem. One simple and popular technique involves the following steps:

1. Get a written description of the problem domain.
2. Identify all the nouns (including pronouns and noun phrases) in the description. Each of these is a potential class.
3. Refine the list to include only the classes that are relevant to the problem.

Let's take a closer look at each of these steps.

Writing a Description of the Problem Domain

The *problem domain* is the set of real-world objects, parties, and major events related to the problem. If you adequately understand the nature of the problem you are trying to solve, you can write a description of the problem domain yourself. If you do not thoroughly understand the nature of the problem, you should have an expert write the description for you.

For example, suppose we are programming an application that the manager of Joe's Automotive Shop will use to print service quotes for customers. Here is a description that an expert, perhaps Joe himself, might have written:

> Joe's Automotive Shop services foreign cars, and specializes in servicing cars made by Mercedes, Porsche, and BMW. When a customer brings a car to the shop, the manager gets the customer's name, address, and telephone number. Then the manager determines the make, model, and year of the car, and gives the customer a service quote. The service quote shows the estimated parts charges, estimated labor charges, sales tax, and total estimated charges.

The problem domain description should include any of the following:

- Physical objects such vehicles, machines, or products
- Any role played by a person, such as manager, employee, customer, teacher, student, and so forth
- The results of a business event, such as a customer order, or in this case a service quote
- Recordkeeping items, such as customer histories and payroll records

Identifying All of the Nouns

The next step is to identify all of the nouns and noun phrases. (If the description contains pronouns, include them too.) Here's another look at the previous problem domain description. This time the nouns and noun phrases appear in bold.

> **Joe's Automotive Shop** services **foreign cars,** and specializes in servicing **cars** made by **Mercedes, Porsche,** and **BMW.** When a **customer** brings a **car** to the **shop,** the **manager** gets the **customer's name, address,** and **telephone number.** Then the **manager** determines the **make, model,** and **year** of the **car,** and gives the **customer** a **service quote.** The **service quote** shows the **estimated parts charges, estimated labor charges, sales tax,** and **total estimated charges.**

Notice that some of the nouns are repeated. The following list shows all of the nouns without duplication.

address	foreign cars	Porsche
BMW	Joe's Automotive Shop	sales tax
car	make	service quote
cars	manager	shop
customer	Mercedes	telephone number
estimated labor charges	model	total estimated charges
estimated parts charges	name	year

Refining the List of Nouns

The nouns that appear in the problem description are merely candidates to become classes. It might not be necessary to make classes for them all. The next step is to refine the list to include only the classes that are necessary to solve the particular problem at hand. We will look at the common reasons that a noun can be eliminated from the list of potential classes.

1. Some of the nouns really mean the same thing.

In this example, the following sets of nouns refer to the same thing:

- **car, cars,** and **foreign cars**
  These all refer to the general concept of a car.

- **Joe's Automotive Shop** and **shop**
  Both of these refer to the company "Joe's Automotive Shop."

We can settle on a single class for each of these. In this example we will arbitrarily eliminate **cars** and **foreign cars** from the list, and use the word **car.** Likewise, we will eliminate **Joe's Automotive Shop** from the list and use the word **shop.** The updated list of potential classes is as follows:

address	~~foreign cars~~	Porsche
BMW	~~Joe's Automotive Shop~~	sales tax
car	make	service quote
~~cars~~	manager	shop
customer	Mercedes	telephone number
estimated labor charges	model	total estimated charges
estimated parts charges	name	year

Because **car, cars,** and **foreign cars** mean the same thing in this problem, we have eliminated **cars** and **foreign cars**. Also, because **Joe's Automotive Shop** and **shop** mean the same thing, we have eliminated **Joe's Automotive Shop.**

2. Some nouns might represent items that we do not need to be concerned with in order to solve the problem.

A quick review of the problem description reminds us of what our application should do: print a service quote. In this example we can eliminate two unnecessary classes from the list:

- We can cross **shop** off the list because our application only needs to be concerned with individual service quotes. It doesn't need to work with or determine any company-wide information. If the problem description asked us to keep a total of all the service quotes, then it would make sense to have a class for the shop.
- We will not need a class for the **manager** because the problem statement does not direct us to process any information about the manager. If there were multiple shop managers, and the problem description had asked us to record which manager generated each service quote, then it would make sense to have a class for the manager.

At this point the updated list of potential classes is as follows:

address	~~foreign cars~~	Porsche
BMW	~~Joe's Automotive Shop~~	sales tax
car	make	service quote
~~cars~~	~~manager~~	~~shop~~
customer	Mercedes	telephone number
estimated labor charges	model	total estimated charges
estimated parts charges	name	year

Our problem description does not direct us to process any information about the **shop,** or any information about the **manager,** so we have eliminated those from the list.

3. Some of the nouns might represent objects, not classes.

We can eliminate **Mercedes, Porsche,** and **BMW** as classes because, in this example, they all represent specific cars, and can be considered instances of a **car** class. In the description it refers to a specific car brought to the shop by a customer. Therefore, it would also represent an instance of a **cars** class. At this point the updated list of potential classes is as follows:

address	~~foreign cars~~	~~Porsche~~
~~BMW~~	~~Joe's Automotive Shop~~	sales tax
car	make	service quote
~~cars~~	~~manager~~	~~shop~~
customer	~~Mercedes~~	telephone number
estimated labor charges	model	total estimated charges
estimated parts charges	name	year

We have eliminated **Mercedes, Porsche,** and **BMW** because they are all instances of a car class. That means that these nouns identify objects, not classes.

> **TIP:** Some object-oriented designers take note of whether a noun is plural or singular. Sometimes a plural noun will indicate a class and a singular noun will indicate an object.

4. Some of the nouns might represent simple values that can be stored in a primitive variable and do not require a class.

Remember, a class contains fields and methods. Fields are related items that are stored within an object of the class, and define the object's state. Methods are actions or behaviors that may be performed by an object of the class. If a noun represents a type of item that would not have any identifiable fields or methods, then it can probably be eliminated from the list. To help determine whether a noun represents an item that would have fields and methods, ask the following questions about it:

- Would you use a group of related values to represent the item's state?
- Are there any obvious actions to be performed by the item?

If the answers to both of these questions are no, then the noun probably represents a value that can be stored in a primitive variable. If we apply this test to each of the nouns that remain in our list, we can conclude that the following are probably not classes: **address, estimated labor charges, estimated parts charges, make, model, name, sales tax, telephone number, total estimated charges,** and **year**. These are all simple string or numeric values that can be stored in primitive variables. Here is the updated list of potential classes:

~~address~~	~~foreign cars~~	~~Porsche~~
~~BMW~~	~~Joe's Automotive Shop~~	~~sales tax~~
car	~~make~~	service quote
~~cars~~	~~manager~~	~~shop~~
customer	~~Mercedes~~	~~telephone number~~
~~estimated labor charges~~	~~model~~	~~total estimated charges~~
~~estimated parts charges~~	~~name~~	~~year~~

We have eliminated **address, estimated labor charges, estimated parts charges, make, model, name, sales tax, telephone number, total estimated charges,** and **year** as classes because they represent simple values that can be stored in primitive variables.

As you can see from the list, we have eliminated everything except **cars, customer,** and **service quote**. This means that in our application, we will need classes to represent cars, customers, and service quotes. Ultimately, we will write a `Car` class, a `Customer` class, and a `ServiceQuote` class.

Identifying a Class's Responsibilities

Once the classes have been identified, the next task is to identify each class's responsibilities. A class's *responsibilities* are as follows:

- The things that the class is responsible for knowing
- The actions that the class is responsible for doing

When you have identified the things that a class is responsible for knowing, you have identified the class's attributes. These values will be stored in fields. Likewise, when you have identified the actions that a class is responsible for doing, you have identified its methods.

It is often helpful to ask the questions "In the context of this problem, what must the class know? What must the class do?" The first place to look for the answers is in the description of the problem domain. Many of the things that a class must know and do will be mentioned. Some class responsibilities, however, might not be directly mentioned in the problem domain, so brainstorming is often required. Let's apply this methodology to the classes we previously identified from our problem domain.

The Customer class

In the context of our problem domain, what must the Customer class know? The description directly mentions the following items, which are all attributes of a customer:

- The customer's name
- The customer's address
- The customer's telephone number

These are all values that can be represented as strings and stored in the class's fields. The Customer class can potentially know many other things. One mistake that can be made at this point is to identify too many things that an object is responsible for knowing. In some applications, a Customer class might know the customer's email address. This particular problem domain does not mention that the customer's email address is used for any purpose, so we should not include it as a responsibility.

Now let's identify the class's methods. In the context of our problem domain, what must the Customer class do? The only obvious actions are as follows:

- Create an object of the Customer class
- Set and get the customer's name
- Set and get the customer's address
- Set and get the customer's telephone number

From this list we can see that the Customer class will have a constructor, as well as accessor and mutator methods for each of its fields. Figure 6-29 shows a UML diagram for the Customer class.

Figure 6-29   UML diagram for the Customer class

```
┌─────────────────────────────┐
│          Customer           │
├─────────────────────────────┤
│ – name : String             │
│ – address : String          │
│ – phone : String            │
├─────────────────────────────┤
│ + Customer()                │
│ + setName(n : String) : void│
│ + setAddress(a : String) : void │
│ + setPhone(p : String) : void │
│ + getName() : String        │
│ + getAddress() : String     │
│ + getPhone() : String       │
└─────────────────────────────┘
```

The Car Class

In the context of our problem domain, what must an object of the Car class know? The following items are all attributes of a car, and are mentioned in the problem domain:

- The car's make
- The car's model
- The car's year

Now let's identify the class's methods. In the context of our problem domain, what must the Car class do? Once again, the only obvious actions are the standard set of methods that we will find in most classes (constructors, accessors, and mutators). Specifically, the actions are:

- Create an object of the Car class
- Set and get the car's make
- Set and get the car's model
- Set and get the car's year

Figure 6-30 shows a UML diagram for the Car class at this point.

Figure 6-30   UML diagram for the Car class

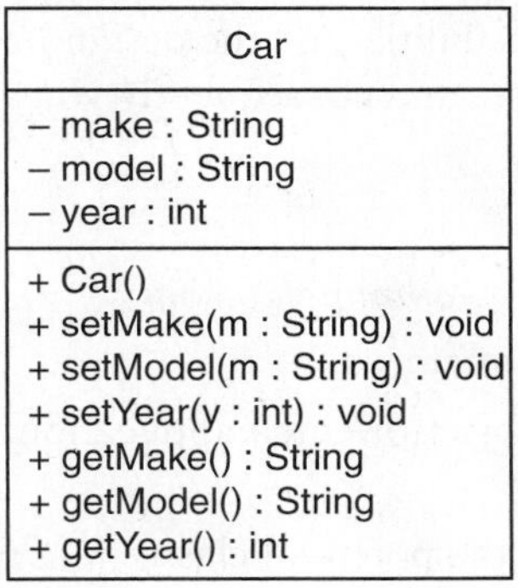

```
            Car
-------------------------------
– make : String
– model : String
– year : int
-------------------------------
+ Car()
+ setMake(m : String) : void
+ setModel(m : String) : void
+ setYear(y : int) : void
+ getMake() : String
+ getModel() : String
+ getYear() : int
```

The ServiceQuote Class

In the context of our problem domain, what must an object of the ServiceQuote class know? The problem domain mentions the following items:

- The estimated parts charges
- The estimated labor charges
- The sales tax
- The total estimated charges

Careful thought and a little brainstorming will reveal that two of these items are the results of calculations: sales tax and total estimated charges. These items are dependent on the values of the estimated parts and labor charges. In order to avoid the risk of holding stale data, we will not store these values in fields. Rather, we will provide methods that calculate these values and return them. The other methods that we will need for this class are a constructor and the accessors and mutators for the estimated parts charges and estimated labor charges fields. Figure 6-31 shows a UML diagram for the ServiceQuote class.

Figure 6-31 UML diagram for the ServiceQuote class

ServiceQuote
− partsCharges : double − laborCharges : double

+ ServiceQuote()
+ setPartsCharges(c : double):
    void
+ setLaborCharges(c : double):
    void
+ getPartsCharges() : double
+ getLaborCharges() : double
+ getSalesTax() : double
+ getTotalCharges() : double

This Is Only the Beginning

You should consider the process that we have discussed in this section merely as a starting point. It's important to realize that designing an object-oriented application is an iterative process. It may take you several attempts to identify all of the classes that you will need, and determine all of their responsibilities. As the design process unfolds, you will gain a deeper understanding of the problem, and consequently you will see ways to improve the design.

Checkpoint

MyProgrammingLab™ *www.myprogramminglab.com*

6.25 What is a problem domain?

6.26 When designing an object-oriented application, who should write a description of the problem domain?

6.27 How do you identify the potential classes in a problem domain description?

6.28 What are a class's responsibilities?

6.29 What two questions should you ask to determine a class's responsibilities?

6.30 Will all of a class's actions always be directly mentioned in the problem domain description?

See the Amortization Class Case Study, available on the book's companion Web site at www.pearsonhighered.com/gaddis, for an in-depth example using this chapter's topics.

6.10 ## Common Errors to Avoid

- **Putting a semicolon at the end of a method header.** A semicolon never appears at the end of a method header.
- **Declaring a variable to reference an object, but forgetting to use the new key word to create the object.** Declaring a variable to reference an object does not create an object. You must use the new key word to create the object.

- Forgetting the parentheses that must appear after the class name, which appears after the new **key word.** The name of a class appears after the new key word, and a set of parentheses appears after the class name. You must write the parentheses even if no arguments are passed to the constructor.
- Forgetting to provide arguments when a constructor requires them. When using a constructor that has parameter variables, you must provide arguments for them.
- Trying to overload methods by giving them different return types. Overloaded methods must have unique parameter lists.
- Forgetting to write a no-arg constructor for a class that you want to be able to create instances of without passing arguments to the constructor. If you write a constructor that accepts arguments, you must also write a no-arg constructor for the same class if you want to be able to create instances of the class without passing arguments to the constructor.
- Unintentionally declaring a local variable with the same name as a field of the same class in a method. When a method's local variable has the same name as a field in the same class, the local variable's name shadows the field's name.

Review Questions and Exercises

Multiple Choice and True/False

1. This is a collection of programming statements that specify the fields and methods that a particular type of object may have.
   a. class
   b. method
   c. parameter
   d. instance

2. A class is analogous to a(n) _____.
   a. house
   b. blueprint
   c. drafting table
   d. architect

3. An object is a(n) _____.
   a. blueprint
   b. primitive data type
   c. variable
   d. instance of a class

4. This is a class member that holds data.
   a. method
   b. instance
   c. field
   d. constructor

5. This key word causes an object to be created in memory.
   a. create
   b. new
   c. object
   d. construct

6. This is a method that gets a value from a class's field, but does not change it.
   a. accessor
   b. constructor
   c. void
   d. mutator

7. This is a method that stores a value in a field or in some other way changes the value of a field.
   a. accessor
   b. constructor
   c. void
   d. mutator

8. When the value of an item is dependent on other data, and that item is not updated when the other data is changed, what has the value become?
   a. bitter
   b. stale
   c. asynchronous
   d. moldy

9. This is a method that is automatically called when an instance of a class is created.
   a. accessor
   b. constructor
   c. void
   d. mutator

10. When a local variable has the same name as a field, the local variable's name does this to the field's name.
    a. shadows
    b. complements
    c. deletes
    d. merges with

11. This is automatically provided for a class if you do not write one yourself.
    a. accessor method
    b. default instance
    c. default constructor
    d. variable declaration

12. Two or more methods in a class may have the same name, as long as this is different.
    a. their return values
    b. their access specifier
    c. their parameter lists
    d. their memory address

13. The process of matching a method call with the correct method is known as _____.
    a. matching
    b. binding
    c. linking
    d. connecting

14. A class's responsibilities are _____.
    a. the objects created from the class
    b. things the class knows
    c. actions the class performs
    d. both b and c

15. **True or False:** The new operator creates an instance of a class.

16. **True or False:** Each instance of a class has its own set of instance fields.

17. **True or False:** When you write a constructor for a class, it still has the default constructor that Java automatically provides.

18. **True or False:** A class may not have more than one constructor.

19. **True or False:** To find the classes needed for an object-oriented application, you identify all of the verbs in a description of the problem domain.

Find the Error

1. Find the error in the following class:
```
public class MyClass
{
    private int x;
    private double y;
    public void MyClass(int a, double b)
    {
        x = a;
        y = b;
    }
}
```

2. Assume that the following method is a member of a class. Find the error.
```
public void total(int value1, value2, value3)
{
    return value1 + value2 + value3;
}
```

3. The following statement attempts to create a Rectangle object. Find the error.
```
Rectangle box = new Rectangle;
```

4. Find the error in the following class:
```
public class TwoValues
{
    private int x, y;
    public TwoValues()
    {
        x = 0;
    }
    public TwoValues()
    {
        x = 0;
        y = 0;
    }
}
```

5. Find the error in the following class:

```java
public class FindTheError
{
    public int square(int number)
    {
        return number * number;
    }
    public double square(int number)
    {
        return number * number;
    }
}
```

Algorithm Workbench

1. Design a class named Pet, which should have the following fields:

   - name. The name field holds the name of a pet.
   - animal. The animal field holds the type of animal that a pet is. Example values are "Dog", "Cat", and "Bird".
   - age. The age field holds the pet's age.

   The Pet class should also have the following methods:

   - setName. The setName method stores a value in the name field.
   - setAnimal. The setAnimal method stores a value in the animal field.
   - setAge. The setAge method stores a value in the age field.
   - getName. The getName method returns the value of the name field.
   - getAnimal. The getAnimal method returns the value of the animal field.
   - getAge. The getAge method returns the value of the age field.

   a. Draw a UML diagram of the class. Be sure to include notation showing each field and method's access specification and data type. Also include notation showing any method parameters and their data types.
   b. Write the Java code for the Pet class.

2. Look at the following partial class definition, and then respond to the questions that follow it:

```java
public class Book
{
    private String title;
    private String author;
    private String publisher;
    private int copiesSold;
}
```

   a. Write a constructor for this class. The constructor should accept an argument for each of the fields.
   b. Write accessor and mutator methods for each field.
   c. Draw a UML diagram for the class, including the methods you have written.

3. Consider the following class declaration:

```java
public class Square
{
   private double sideLength;
   public double getArea()
   {
      return sideLength * sideLength;
   }
   public double getSideLength()
   {
      return sideLength;
   }
}
```

a. Write a no-arg constructor for this class. It should assign the sideLength field the value 0.0.

b. Write an overloaded constructor for this class. It should accept an argument that is copied into the sideLength field.

4. Look at the following description of a problem domain:

The bank offers the following types of accounts to its customers: savings accounts, checking accounts, and money market accounts. Customers are allowed to deposit money into an account (thereby increasing its balance), withdraw money from an account (thereby decreasing its balance), and earn interest on the account. Each account has an interest rate.

Assume that you are writing an application that will calculate the amount of interest earned for a bank account.

a. Identify the potential classes in this problem domain.

b. Refine the list to include only the necessary class or classes for this problem.

c. Identify the responsibilities of the class or classes.

Short Answer

1. What is the difference between a class and an instance of a class?

2. A contractor uses a blueprint to build a set of identical houses. Are classes analogous to the blueprint or the houses?

3. What is an accessor method? What is a mutator method?

4. Is it a good idea to make fields private? Why or why not?

5. If a class has a private field, what has access to the field?

6. What is the purpose of the new key word?

7. Assume a program named MailList.java is stored in the DataBase folder on your hard drive. The program creates objects of the Customer and Account classes. Describe the steps that the compiler goes through in locating and compiling the Customer and Account classes.

8. Why are constructors useful for performing "start-up" operations?

9. Under what circumstances does Java automatically provide a default constructor for a class?

10. What do you call a constructor that accepts no arguments?

11. When the same name is used for two or more methods in the same class, how does Java tell them apart?

12. How does method overloading improve the usefulness of a class?

Programming Challenges

MyProgrammingLab™ *Visit www.myprogramminglab.com to complete many of these Programming Challenges online and get instant feedback.*

1. Employee Class

Write a class named Employee that has the following fields:

- name. The name field references a String object that holds the employee's name.
- idNumber. The idNumber is an int variable that holds the employee's ID number.
- department. The department field references a String object that holds the name of the department where the employee works.
- position. The position field references a String object that holds the employee's job title.

The class should have the following constructors:

- A constructor that accepts the following values as arguments and assigns them to the appropriate fields: employee's name, employee's ID number, department, and position.
- A constructor that accepts the following values as arguments and assigns them to the appropriate fields: employee's name and ID number. The department and position fields should be assigned an empty string ("").
- A no-arg constructor that assigns empty strings ("") to the name, department, and position fields, and 0 to the idNumber field.

Write appropriate mutator methods that store values in these fields and accessor methods that return the values in these fields. Once you have written the class, write a separate program that creates three Employee objects to hold the following data:

Name	ID Number	Department	Position
Susan Meyers	47899	Accounting	Vice President
Mark Jones	39119	IT	Programmer
Joy Rogers	81774	Manufacturing	Engineer

The program should store this data in the three objects and then display the data for each employee on the screen.

2. Car Class

Write a class named Car that has the following fields:

- yearModel. The yearModel field is an int that holds the car's year model.
- make. The make field references a String object that holds the make of the car.
- speed. The speed field is an int that holds the car's current speed.

In addition, the class should have the following constructor and other methods.

- Constructor. The constructor should accept the car's year model and make as arguments. These values should be assigned to the object's yearModel and make fields. The constructor should also assign 0 to the speed field.
- Accessors. Appropriate accessor methods should get the values stored in an object's yearModel, make, and speed fields.
- accelerate. The accelerate method should add 5 to the speed field each time it is called.
- brake. The brake method should subtract 5 from the speed field each time it is called.

Demonstrate the class in a program that creates a Car object, and then calls the accelerate method five times. After each call to the accelerate method, get the current speed of the car and display it. Then call the brake method five times. After each call to the brake method, get the current speed of the car and display it.

VideoNote
The Personal
Information
Class Problem

3. Personal Information Class

Design a class that holds the following personal data: name, address, age, and phone number. Write appropriate accessor and mutator methods. Demonstrate the class by writing a program that creates three instances of it. One instance should hold your information, and the other two should hold your friends' or family members' information.

4. RetailItem Class

Write a class named RetailItem that holds data about an item in a retail store. The class should have the following fields:

- description. The description field references a String object that holds a brief description of the item.
- unitsOnHand. The unitsOnHand field is an int variable that holds the number of units currently in inventory.
- price. The price field is a double that holds the item's retail price.

Write a constructor that accepts arguments for each field, appropriate mutator methods that store values in these fields, and accessor methods that return the values in these fields. Once you have written the class, write a separate program that creates three RetailItem objects and stores the following data in them:

	Description	Units on Hand	Price
Item #1	Jacket	12	59.95
Item #2	Designer Jeans	40	34.95
Item #3	Shirt	20	24.95

5. Payroll Class

Design a Payroll class that has fields for an employee's name, ID number, hourly pay rate, and number of hours worked. Write the appropriate accessor and mutator methods and a constructor that accepts the employee's name and ID number as arguments. The class should also have a method that returns the employee's gross pay, which is calculated as the number of hours worked multiplied by the hourly pay rate. Write a program that demonstrates the class by creating a `Payroll` object, then asking the user to enter the data for an employee. The program should display the amount of gross pay earned.

6. `TestScores` Class

Design a `TestScores` class that has fields to hold three test scores. The class should have a constructor, accessor and mutator methods for the test score fields, and a method that returns the average of the test scores. Demonstrate the class by writing a separate program that creates an instance of the class. The program should ask the user to enter three test scores, which are stored in the `TestScores` object. Then the program should display the average of the scores, as reported by the `TestScores` object.

7. `Circle` Class

Write a `Circle` class that has the following fields:

- `radius`: a double
- `PI`: a final double initialized with the value 3.14159

The class should have the following methods:

- **Constructor.** Accepts the radius of the circle as an argument.
- **Constructor.** A no-arg constructor that sets the `radius` field to 0.0.
- `setRadius`. A mutator method for the radius field.
- `getRadius`. An accessor method for the radius field.
- `getArea`. Returns the area of the circle, which is calculated as
  `area = PI * radius * radius`
- `getDiameter`. Returns the diameter of the circle, which is calculated as
  `diameter = radius * 2`
- `getCircumference`. Returns the circumference of the circle, which is calculated as
  `circumference = 2 * PI * radius`

Write a program that demonstrates the `Circle` class by asking the user for the circle's radius, creating a `Circle` object, and then reporting the circle's area, diameter, and circumference.

8. `Temperature` Class

Write a `Temperature` class that will hold a temperature in Fahrenheit, and provide methods to get the temperature in Fahrenheit, Celsius, and Kelvin. The class should have the following field:

- `ftemp` – A double that holds a Fahrenheit temperature.

The class should have the following methods:

- Constructor – The constructor accepts a Fahrenheit temperature (as a `double`) and stores it in the `ftemp` field.
- `setFahrenheit` – The `setFahrenheit` method accepts a Fahrenheit temperature (as a `double`) and stores it in the `ftemp` field.
- `getFahrenheit` – Returns the value of the `ftemp` field, as a Fahrenheit temperature (no conversion required).
- `getCelsius` – Returns the value of the `ftemp` field converted to Celsius.
- `getKelvin` – Returns the value of the `ftemp` field converted to Kelvin.

Use the following formula to convert the Fahrenheit temperature to Celsius:

$$Celsius = (5/9) \times (Fahrenheit - 32)$$

Use the following formula to convert the Fahrenheit temperature to Kelvin:

$$Kelvin = ((5/9) \times (Fahrenheit - 32)) + 273$$

Demonstrate the `Temperature` class by writing a separate program that asks the user for a Fahrenheit temperature. The program should create an instance of the `Temperature` class, with the value entered by the user passed to the constructor. The program should then call the object's methods to display the temperature in Celsius and Kelvin.

9. Days in a Month

Write a class named `MonthDays`. The class's constructor should accept two arguments:

- An integer for the month (1 = January, 2 February, etc.).
- An integer for the year

The class should have a method named `getNumberOfDays` that returns the number of days in the specified month. The method should use the following criteria to identify leap years:

1. Determine whether the year is divisible by 100. If it is, then it is a leap year if and if only it is divisible by 400. For example, 2000 is a leap year but 2100 is not.

2. If the year is not divisible by 100, then it is a leap year if and if only it is divisible by 4. For example, 2008 is a leap year but 2009 is not.

Demonstrate the class in a program that asks the user to enter the month (letting the user enter an integer in the range of 1 through 12) and the year. The program should then display the number of days in that month. Here is a sample run of the program:

```
Enter a month (1-12): 2 [Enter]
Enter a year: 2008 [Enter]
29 days
```

10. A Game of Twenty-One

For this assignment, you will write a program that lets the user play against the computer in a variation of the popular blackjack card game. In this variation of the game, two six-sided dice are used instead of cards. The dice are rolled, and the player tries to beat the computer's hidden total without going over 21.

Here are some suggestions for the game's design:

- Each round of the game is performed as an iteration of a loop that repeats as long as the player agrees to roll the dice, and the player's total does not exceed 21.
- At the beginning of each round, the program will ask the user whether or not he or she wants to roll the dice to accumulate points.
- During each round, the program simulates the rolling of two six-sided dice. It rolls the dice first for the computer, and then it asks the user whether he or she wants to roll. (Use the `Die` class that was shown in Code Listing 6-14 to simulate the dice.)
- The loop keeps a running total of both the computer's and the user's points.
- The computer's total should remain hidden until the loop has finished.
- After the loop has finished, the computer's total is revealed, and the player with the most points, without going over 21, wins.

11. Freezing and Boiling Points

The following table lists the freezing and boiling points of several substances.

Substance	Freezing Point	Boiling Point
Ethyl Alcohol	−173	172
Oxygen	−362	−306
Water	32	212

Design a class that stores a temperature in a `temperature` field and has the appropriate accessor and mutator methods for the field. In addition to appropriate constructors, the class should have the following methods:

- **isEthylFreezing.** This method should return the `boolean` value `true` if the temperature stored in the `temperature` field is at or below the freezing point of ethyl alcohol. Otherwise, the method should return `false`.
- **isEthylBoiling.** This method should return the `boolean` value `true` if the temperature stored in the `temperature` field is at or above the boiling point of ethyl alcohol. Otherwise, the method should return `false`.
- **isOxygenFreezing.** This method should return the `boolean` value `true` if the temperature stored in the `temperature` field is at or below the freezing point of oxygen. Otherwise, the method should return `false`.
- **isOxygenBoiling.** This method should return the `boolean` value `true` if the temperature stored in the `temperature` field is at or above the boiling point of oxygen. Otherwise, the method should return `false`.
- **isWaterFreezing.** This method should return the `boolean` value `true` if the temperature stored in the `temperature` field is at or below the freezing point of water. Otherwise, the method should return `false`.
- **isWaterBoiling.** This method should return the `boolean` value `true` if the temperature stored in the `temperature` field is at or above the boiling point of water. Otherwise, the method should return `false`.

Write a program that demonstrates the class. The program should ask the user to enter a temperature, and then display a list of the substances that will freeze at that temperature and those that will boil at that temperature. For example, if the temperature is −20 the class should report that water will freeze and oxygen will boil at that temperature.

12. SavingsAccount Class

Design a `SavingsAccount` class that stores a savings account's annual interest rate and balance. The class constructor should accept the amount of the savings account's starting balance. The class should also have methods for subtracting the amount of a withdrawal, adding the amount of a deposit, and adding the amount of monthly interest to the balance. The monthly interest rate is the annual interest rate divided by twelve. To add the monthly interest to the balance, multiply the monthly interest rate by the balance, and add the result to the balance.

Test the class in a program that calculates the balance of a savings account at the end of a period of time. It should ask the user for the annual interest rate, the starting balance, and the number of months that have passed since the account was established. A loop should then iterate once for every month, performing the following:

    a. Ask the user for the amount deposited into the account during the month. Use the class method to add this amount to the account balance.

    b. Ask the user for the amount withdrawn from the account during the month. Use the class method to subtract this amount from the account balance.

    c. Use the class method to calculate the monthly interest.

After the last iteration, the program should display the ending balance, the total amount of deposits, the total amount of withdrawals, and the total interest earned.

13. Deposit and Withdrawal Files

Use Notepad or another text editor to create a text file named `Deposits.txt`. The file should contain the following numbers, one per line:

```
100.00
124.00
78.92
37.55
```

Next, create a text file named `Withdrawals.txt`. The file should contain the following numbers, one per line:

```
29.88
110.00
27.52
50.00
12.90
```

The numbers in the `Deposits.txt` file are the amounts of deposits that were made to a savings account during the month, and the numbers in the `Withdrawals.txt` file are the amounts of withdrawals that were made during the month. Write a program that creates an instance of the `SavingsAccount` class that you wrote in Programming Challenge 12. The starting balance for the object is 500.00. The program should read the values from the `Deposits.txt` file and use the object's method to add them to the account balance. The program should read the values from the `Withdrawals.txt` file and use the object's method to subtract them from the account balance. The program should call the class method to calculate the monthly interest, and then display the ending balance and the total interest earned.

14. Dice Game

Write a program that uses the `Die` class that was presented in this chapter to play a simple dice game between the computer and the user. The program should create two instances of the `Die` class (each a 6-sided die). One `Die` object is the computer's die, and the other `Die` object is the user's die.

The program should have a loop that iterates 10 times. Each time the loop iterates, it should roll both dice. The die with the highest value wins. (In case of a tie, there is no winner for that particular roll of the dice.)

As the loop iterates, the program should keep count of the number of times the computer wins, and the number of times that the user wins. After the loop performs all of its iterations, the program should display who was the grand winner, the computer or the user.

15. Roulette Wheel Colors

On a roulette wheel, the pockets are numbered from 0 to 36. The colors of the pockets are as follows:

- Pocket 0 is green.
- For pockets 1 through 10, the odd numbered pockets are red and the even numbered pockets are black.
- For pockets 11 through 18, the odd numbered pockets are black and the even numbered pockets are red.
- For pockets 19 through 28, the odd numbered pockets are red and the even numbered pockets are black.
- For pockets 29 through 36, the odd numbered pockets are black and the even numbered pockets are red.

Write a class named `RoulettePocket`. The class's constructor should accept a pocket number. The class should have a method named `getPocketColor` that returns the pocket's color, as a string.

Demonstrate the class in a program that asks the user to enter a pocket number, and displays whether the pocket is green, red, or black. The program should display an error message if the user enters a number that is outside the range of 0 through 36.

16. Coin Toss Simulator

Write a class named `Coin`. The `Coin` class should have the following field:

- A `String` named `sideUp`. The `sideUp` field will hold either "heads" or "tails" indicating the side of the coin that is facing up.

The `Coin` class should have the following methods:

- A no-arg constructor that randomly determines the side of the coin that is facing up ("heads" or "tails") and initializes the `sideUp` field accordingly.
- A `void` method named `toss` that simulates the tossing of the coin. When the toss method is called, it randomly determines the side of the coin that is facing up ("heads" or "tails") and sets the `sideUp` field accordingly.
- A method named `getSideUp` that returns the value of the `sideUp` field.

Write a program that demonstrates the `Coin` class. The program should create an instance of the class and display the side that is initially facing up. Then, use a loop to toss the coin 20 times. Each time the coin is tossed, display the side that is facing up. The program should keep count of the number of times heads is facing up and the number of times tails is facing up, and display those values after the loop finishes.

17. Tossing Coins for a Dollar

For this assignment you will create a game program using the `Coin` class from Programming Challenge 16. The program should have three instances of the `Coin` class: one representing a quarter, one representing a dime, and one representing a nickel.

When the game begins, your starting balance is $0. During each round of the game, the program will toss the simulated coins. When a coin is tossed, the value of the coin is added to your balance if it lands heads-up. For example, if the quarter lands heads-up, 25 cents is added to your balance. Nothing is added to your balance for coins that land tails-up. The game is over when your balance reaches one dollar or more. If your balance is exactly one dollar, you win the game. You lose if your balance exceeds one dollar.

18. Fishing Game Simulation

For this assignment, you will write a program that simulates a fishing game. In this game, a six-sided die is rolled to determine what the user has caught. Each possible item is worth a certain number of fishing points. The points will remain hidden until the user is finished fishing, and then a message is displayed congratulating the user, depending on the number of fishing points gained.

Here are some suggestions for the game's design:

- Each round of the game is performed as an iteration of a loop that repeats as long as the player wants to fish for more items.
- At the beginning of each round, the program will ask the user whether or not he or she wants to continue fishing.
- The program simulates the rolling of a six-sided die (use the Die class that was shown in Code Listing 6-14).
- Each item that can be caught is represented by a number generated from the die; for example, 1 for "a huge fish", 2 for "an old shoe", 3 for "a little fish", and so on.
- Each item the user catches is worth a different amount of points.
- The loop keeps a running total of the user's fishing points.
- After the loop has finished, the total number of fishing points is displayed, along with a message that varies depending on the number of points earned.

Arrays and the ArrayList Class

TOPICS

7.1 Introduction to Arrays

CONCEPT: An array can hold multiple values of the same data type simultaneously.

The primitive variables you have worked with so far are designed to hold one value at a time. Each of the variable declarations in Figure 7-1 causes only enough memory to be reserved to hold one value of the specified data type.

An array, however, is an object that can store a group of values, all of the same type. Creating and using an array in Java is similar to creating and using any other type of object: You declare a reference variable and use the new key word to create an instance of the array in memory. Here is an example of a statement that declares an array reference variable:

```
int[] numbers;
```

This statement declares numbers as an array reference variable. The numbers variable can reference an array of int values. Notice that this statement looks like a regular int variable declaration except for the set of brackets that appears after the key word int. The brackets indicate that this variable is a reference to an int array. Declaring an array reference variable does not create an array. The next step in the process is to use the new key word to create an array and assign its address to the numbers variable. The following statement shows an example:

```
numbers = new int[6];
```

Figure 7-1 Variable declarations and their memory allocations

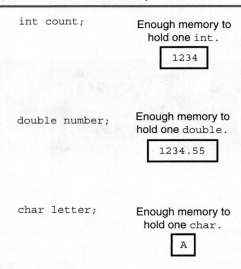

```
int count;
```
Enough memory to hold one `int`.

1234

```
double number;
```
Enough memory to hold one `double`.

1234.55

```
char letter;
```
Enough memory to hold one `char`.

A

The number inside the brackets is the array's *size declarator*. It indicates the number of elements, or values, the array can hold. When this statement is executed, `numbers` will reference an array that can hold six elements, each one an `int`. This is shown in Figure 7-2.

Figure 7-2 The numbers array

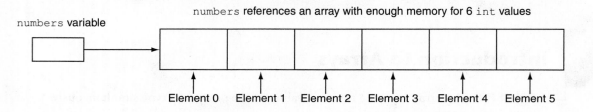

`numbers` **variable**

`numbers` references an array with enough memory for 6 `int` values

Element 0 Element 1 Element 2 Element 3 Element 4 Element 5

As with any other type of object, it is possible to declare a reference variable and create an instance of an array with one statement. Here is an example:

```
int[] numbers = new int[6];
```

Arrays of any data type can be declared. The following are all valid array declarations:

```
float[] temperatures = new float[100];
char[] letters = new char[41];
long[] units = new long[50];
double[] sizes = new double[1200];
```

An array's size declarator must be a non-negative integer expression. It can be a literal value, as shown in the previous examples, or a variable. It is a common practice to use a `final` variable as a size declarator. Here is an example:

```
final int NUM_ELEMENTS = 6;
int[] numbers = new int[NUM_ELEMENTS];
```

This practice can make programs easier to maintain. When we store the size of an array in a variable, we can use the variable instead of a literal number when we refer to the size of the array. If we ever need to change the array's size, we need only to change the value of the variable. The variable should be `final` so its contents cannot be changed during the program's execution.

> **NOTE:** Once an array is created, its size cannot be changed.

Accessing Array Elements

Although an array has only one name, the elements in the array may be accessed and used as individual variables. This is possible because each element is assigned a number known as a *subscript*. A subscript is used as an index to pinpoint a specific element within an array. The first element is assigned the subscript 0, the second element is assigned 1, and so forth. The six elements in the `numbers` array (described earlier) would have the subscripts 0 through 5. This is shown in Figure 7-3.

Figure 7-3   Subscripts for the numbers array

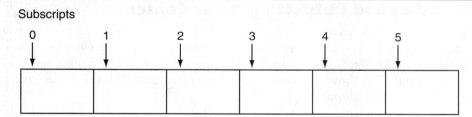

The `numbers` array has six elements, numbered 0 through 5.

Subscript numbering always starts at zero. The subscript of the last element in an array is one less than the total number of elements in the array. This means that for the `numbers` array, which has six elements, 5 is the subscript for the last element.

Each element in the `numbers` array, when accessed by its subscript, can be used as an `int` variable. For example, look at the following code. The first statement stores 20 in the first element of the array (element 0), and the second statement stores 30 in the fourth element (element 3).

```
numbers[0] = 20;
numbers[3] = 30;
```

> **NOTE:** The expression `numbers[0]` is pronounced "numbers sub zero." You read these assignment statements as "numbers sub zero is assigned twenty" and "numbers sub three is assigned thirty."

Figure 7-4 illustrates the contents of the array after these statements execute.

Figure 7-4 Contents of the array after 20 is assigned to numbers[0] and 30 is assigned to numbers[3]

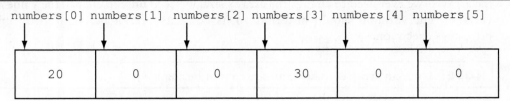

numbers[0] numbers[1] numbers[2] numbers[3] numbers[4] numbers[5]

| 20 | 0 | 0 | 30 | 0 | 0 |

NOTE: By default, Java initializes array elements with 0. In Figure 7-4, values have not been stored in elements 1, 2, 4, and 5, so they are shown as 0s.

By this point you should understand the difference between the array size declarator and a subscript. When you use the `new` key word to create an array object, the number inside the brackets is the size declarator. It indicates the number of elements in the array. The number inside the brackets in an assignment statement or any statement that works with the contents of an array is a subscript. It is used to access a specific element in the array.

Inputting and Outputting Array Contents

You can read values from the keyboard and store them in an array element just as you can a regular variable. You can also output the contents of an array element with `print` and `println`. Code Listing 7-1 shows an array being used to store and display values entered by the user. Figure 7-5 shows the contents of the `hours` array with the values entered by the user in the example output.

Code Listing 7-1   (`ArrayDemo1.java`)

```
 1  import java.util.Scanner;   // Needed for Scanner class
 2
 3  /**
 4     This program shows values being stored in an array's
 5     elements and displayed.
 6  */
 7
 8  public class ArrayDemo1
 9  {
10     public static void main(String[] args)
11     {
12        final int EMPLOYEES = 3;         // Number of employees
13        int[] hours = new int[EMPLOYEES]; // Array of hours
14
15        // Create a Scanner object for keyboard input.
16        Scanner keyboard = new Scanner(System.in);
17
18        System.out.println("Enter the hours worked by " +
```

```
19                            EMPLOYEES + " employees.");
20
21          // Get the hours worked by employee 1.
22          System.out.print("Employee 1: ");
23          hours[0] = keyboard.nextInt();
24
25          // Get the hours worked by employee 2.
26          System.out.print("Employee 2: ");
27          hours[1] = keyboard.nextInt();
28
29          // Get the hours worked by employee 3.
30          System.out.print("Employee 3: ");
31          hours[2] = keyboard.nextInt();
32
33          // Display the values entered.
34          System.out.println("The hours you entered are:");
35          System.out.println(hours[0]);
36          System.out.println(hours[1]);
37          System.out.println(hours[2]);
38      }
39  }
```

Program Output with Example Input Shown in Bold

```
Enter the hours worked by 3 employees.
Employee 1: 40 [Enter]
Employee 2: 20 [Enter]
Employee 3: 15 [Enter]
The hours you entered are:
40
20
15
```

Figure 7-5   Contents of the hours array

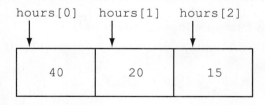

Subscript numbers can be stored in variables. This makes it possible to use a loop to "cycle through" an entire array, performing the same operation on each element. For example, Code Listing 7-1 could be simplified by using two `for` loops: one for inputting the values into the array and the other for displaying the contents of the array. This is shown in Code Listing 7-2.

VideoNote

Accessing Array
Elements in
a Loop

Code Listing 7-2   (`ArrayDemo2.java`)

```java
 1  import java.util.Scanner;    // Needed for Scanner class
 2
 3  /**
 4     This program shows an array being processed with loops.
 5  */
 6
 7  public class ArrayDemo2
 8  {
 9     public static void main(String[] args)
10     {
11        final int EMPLOYEES = 3;                // Number of employees
12        int[] hours = new int[EMPLOYEES];       // Array of hours
13
14        // Create a Scanner object for keyboard input.
15        Scanner keyboard = new Scanner(System.in);
16
17        System.out.println("Enter the hours worked by " +
18                           EMPLOYEES + " employees.");
19
20        // Get the hours for each employee.
21        for (int index = 0; index < EMPLOYEES; index++)
22        {
23           System.out.print("Employee " + (index + 1) + ": ");
24           hours[index] = keyboard.nextInt();
25        }
26
27        System.out.println("The hours you entered are:");
28
29        // Display the values entered.
30        for (int index = 0; index < EMPLOYEES; index++)
31           System.out.println(hours[index]);
32     }
33  }
```

Program Output with Example Input Shown in Bold

```
Enter the hours worked by 3 employees.
Employee 1: 40 [Enter]
Employee 2: 20 [Enter]
Employee 3: 15 [Enter]
The hours you entered are:
40
20
15
```

Let's take a closer look at the first loop in this program, which appears in lines 21 through 25. Notice that the loop's control variable, index, is used as a subscript in line 24:

```
hours[index] = keyboard.nextInt();
```

The variable index starts at 0. During the loop's first iteration, the user's input is stored in hours[0]. Then, index is incremented, so its value becomes 1. During the next iteration, the user's input is stored in hours[1]. This continues until values have been stored in all of the elements of the array. Notice that the loop correctly starts and ends the control variable with valid subscript values (0 through 2), as illustrated in Figure 7-6. This ensures that only valid subscripts are used.

Figure 7-6 Annotated loop

The variable index starts at 0, which is the first valid subscript value.

The loop ends before the variable index reaches 3, which is the first invalid subscript value.

```
for (int index = 0; index < EMPLOYEES; index++)
{
    System.out.print("Employee " + (index + 1) + ": ");
    hours[index] = keyboard.nextInt();
}
```

Java Performs Bounds Checking

Java performs array bounds checking, which means that it does not allow a statement to use a subscript that is outside the range of valid subscripts for an array. For example, the following statement creates an array with 10 elements. The valid subscripts for the array are 0 through 9.

```
int[] values = new int[10];
```

Java will not allow a statement to use a subscript that is less than 0 or greater than 9 with this array. Bounds checking occurs at runtime. The Java compiler does not display an error message when it processes a statement that uses an invalid subscript. Instead, when the statement executes, the program throws an exception and immediately terminates. For instance, the program in Code Listing 7-3 declares a three-element array, but attempts to store four values in the array. In line 17, when the program attempts to store a value in values[3], it halts and an error message is displayed.

Code Listing 7-3   (**InvalidSubscript.java**)

```
1  /**
2     This program uses an invalid subscript with an array.
3  */
4
```

```
 5  public class InvalidSubscript
 6  {
 7     public static void main(String[] args)
 8     {
 9        int[] values = new int[3];
10
11        System.out.println("I will attempt to store four " +
12                           "numbers in a three-element array.");
13
14        for (int index = 0; index < 4; index++)
15        {
16           System.out.println("Now processing element " + index);
17           values[index] = 10;
18        }
19     }
20  }
```

Program Output

```
I will attempt to store four numbers in a three-element array.
Now processing element 0
Now processing element 1
Now processing element 2
Now processing element 3
Exception in thread "main"
java.lang.ArrayIndexOutOfBoundsException: 3
        at InvalidSubscript.main(InvalidSubscript.java:17)
```

 NOTE: The error message you see may be different, depending on your system.

Watch Out for Off-by-One Errors

Because array subscripts start at 0 rather than 1, you have to be careful not to perform an off-by-one error. For example, look at the following code:

```
// This code has an off-by-one error.
final int SIZE = 100;
int[] numbers = new int[SIZE];
for (int index = 1; index <= SIZE; index++)
   numbers[index] = 0;
```

The intent of this code is to create an array of integers with 100 elements, and store the value 0 in each element. However, this code has an off-by-one error. The loop uses its control variable, index, as a subscript with the numbers array. During the loop's execution, the variable index takes on the values 1 through 100, when it should take on the values 0 through 99. As a result, the first element, which is at subscript 0, is skipped. In addition, the loop attempts to use 100 as a subscript during the last iteration. Because 100 is an invalid subscript, the program will throw an exception and halt.

Array Initialization

Like regular variables, Java allows you to initialize an array's elements when you create the array. Here is an example:

```
int[] days = {31, 28, 31, 30, 31, 30, 31, 31, 30, 31, 30, 31};
```

This statement declares the reference variable days, creates an array in memory, and stores initial values in the array. The series of values inside the braces and separated with commas is called an initialization list. These values are stored in the array elements in the order they appear in the list. (The first value, 31, is stored in days[0], the second value, 28, is stored in days[1], and so forth.) Note that you do not use the new key word when you use an initialization list. Java automatically creates the array and stores the values in the initialization list in it.

The Java compiler determines the size of the array by the number of items in the initialization list. Because there are 12 items in the example statement's initialization list, the array will have 12 elements. The program in Code Listing 7-4 demonstrates an array being initialized.

Code Listing 7-4   (**ArrayInitialization.java**)

```
 1  /**
 2      This program shows an array being initialized.
 3  */
 4
 5  public class ArrayInitialization
 6  {
 7     public static void main(String[] args)
 8     {
 9        int[] days = { 31, 28, 31, 30, 31, 30,
10                       31, 31, 30, 31, 30, 31 };
11
12        for (int index = 0; index < 12; index++)
13        {
14           System.out.println("Month " + (index + 1) +
15                              " has " + days[index] +
16                              " days.");
17        }
18     }
19  }
```

Program Output

```
Month 1 has 31 days.
Month 2 has 28 days.
Month 3 has 31 days.
Month 4 has 30 days.
Month 5 has 31 days.
Month 6 has 30 days.
```

```
Month 7 has 31 days.
Month 8 has 31 days.
Month 9 has 30 days.
Month 10 has 31 days.
Month 11 has 30 days.
Month 12 has 31 days.
```

Java allows you to spread the initialization list across multiple lines. Both of the following array declarations are equivalent:

```
double[] coins = { 0.05, 0.1, 0.25 };
double[] coins = { 0.05,
                   0.1,
                   0.25 };
```

Alternate Array Declaration Notation

Java allows you to use two different styles when declaring array reference variables. The first style is the one used in this book, with the brackets immediately following the data type, as shown here:

```
int[] numbers;
```

In the second style the brackets are placed after the variable name, as shown here:

```
int numbers[];
```

Both of these statements accomplish the same thing: They declare that numbers is a reference to an int array. The difference between the two styles is noticed when more than one variable is declared in the same statement. For example, look at the following statement:

```
int[] numbers, codes, scores;
```

This statement declares three variables: numbers, codes, and scores. All three are references to int arrays. This makes perfect sense because int[] is the data type for all the variables declared in the statement. Now look at the following statement, which uses the alternate notation:

```
int numbers[], codes, scores;
```

This statement declares the same three variables, but only numbers is a reference to an int array. The codes and scores variables are regular int variables. This is because int is the data type for all the variables declared in the statement, and only numbers is followed by the brackets. To declare all three of these variables as references to int arrays using the alternate notation, you need to write a set of brackets after each variable name. Here is an example:

```
int numbers[], codes[], scores[];
```

The first style is the standard notation for most Java programmers, so that is the style used in this book.

Checkpoint

MyProgrammingLab™ *www.myprogramminglab.com*

7.1 Write statements that create the following arrays:
   a) A 100-element `int` array referenced by the variable `employeeNumbers`.
   b) A 25-element `double` array referenced by the variable `payRates`.
   c) A 14-element `float` array referenced by the variable `miles`.
   d) A 1000-element `char` array referenced by the variable `letters`.

7.2 What's wrong with the following array declarations?

```
int[] readings = new int[-1];
double[] measurements = new double[4.5];
```

7.3 What would the valid subscript values be in a four-element array of `doubles`?

7.4 What is the difference between an array's size declarator and a subscript?

7.5 What does it mean for a subscript to be out-of-bounds?

7.6 What happens in Java when a program tries to use a subscript that is out-of-bounds?

7.7 What is the output of the following code?

```
int[] values = new int[5];
for (int count = 0; count < 5; count++)
    values[count] = count + 1;
for (int count = 0; count < 5; count++)
    System.out.println(values[count]);
```

7.8 Write a statement that creates and initializes a `double` array with the following values: 1.7, 6.4, 8.9, 3.1, and 9.2. How many elements are in the array?

7.2 Processing Array Elements

CONCEPT: Individual array elements are processed like any other type of variable.

Processing array elements is no different from processing other variables. For example, the following statement multiplies `hours[3]` by the variable `payRate`:

```
grossPay = hours[3] * payRate;
```

The following are examples of pre-increment and post-increment operations on array elements:

```
int[] score = {7, 8, 9, 10, 11};
++score[2];    // Pre-increment operation
score[4]++;    // Post-increment operation
```

When using increment and decrement operators, be careful not to use the operator on the subscript when you intend to use it on the array element. For example, the following statement decrements the variable count, but does nothing to the value stored in the array element `amount[count]`:

```
amount[count--];
```

Code Listing 7-5 demonstrates the use of array elements in a simple mathematical statement. A loop steps through each element of the array, using the elements to calculate the gross pay of five employees.

Code Listing 7-5 (PayArray.java)

```java
 1  import java.util.Scanner; // Needed for Scanner class
 2
 3  /**
 4     This program stores in an array the hours worked by
 5     five employees who all make the same hourly wage.
 6  */
 7
 8  public class PayArray
 9  {
10     public static void main(String[] args)
11     {
12        final int EMPLOYEES = 5;   // Number of employees
13        double payRate;            // Hourly pay rate
14        double grossPay;           // Gross pay
15
16        // Create an array to hold employee hours.
17        int[] hours = new int[EMPLOYEES];
18
19        // Create a Scanner object for keyboard input.
20        Scanner keyboard = new Scanner(System.in);
21
22        // Get the hours worked by each employee.
23        System.out.println("Enter the hours worked by " +
24                           EMPLOYEES + " employees who all earn " +
25                           "the same hourly rate.");
26
27        for (int index = 0; index < EMPLOYEES; index++)
28        {
29           System.out.print( "Employee #" + (index + 1) + ": ");
30           hours[index] = keyboard.nextInt();
31        }
32
33        // Get the hourly pay rate.
34        System.out.print("Enter the hourly rate for each employee: ");
35        payRate = keyboard.nextDouble();
36
37        // Display each employee's gross pay.
38        System.out.println( "Here is each employee's gross pay:");
39        for (int index = 0; index < EMPLOYEES; index++)
40        {
41           grossPay = hours[index] * payRate;
```

```
42                  System.out.println("Employee #" + (index + 1) +
43                              ": $" + grossPay);
44          }
45      }
46  }
```

Program Output with Example Input Shown in Bold

Enter the hours worked by 5 employees who all earn the same hourly rate.
Employee #1: **10 [Enter]**
Employee #2: **20 [Enter]**
Employee #3: **30 [Enter]**
Employee #4: **40 [Enter]**
Employee #5: **50 [Enter]**
Enter the hourly rate for each employee: **10 [Enter]**
Here is each employee's gross pay:
Employee #1: $100.0
Employee #2: $200.0
Employee #3: $300.0
Employee #4: $400.0
Employee #5: $500.0

In line 41, the following statement assigns the value of hours[index] times payRate to the grossPay variable:

```
grossPay = hours[index] * payRate;
```

Array elements may also be used in relational expressions. For example, the following if statement determines whether cost[20] is less than cost[0]:

```
if (cost[20] < cost[0])
```

And the following while loop iterates as long as value[count] does not equal 0:

```
while (value[count] != 0)
{
    Statements
}
```

In this chapter's source code (available at www.pearsonhighered.com/gaddis), you will find the file *Overtime.java*, which is a modification of the *PayArray.java* program in Code Listing 7-5. The *Overtime.java* program includes overtime wages in the gross pay. If an employee works more than 40 hours, an overtime pay rate of 1.5 times the regular pay rate is used for the excess hours.

Array Length

Each array in Java has a public field named length. This field contains the number of elements in the array. For example, consider an array created by the following statement:

```
double[] temperatures = new double[25];
```

Because the `temperatures` array has 25 elements, the following statement would assign 25 to the variable `size`:

```
size = temperatures.length;
```

The `length` field can be useful when processing the entire contents of an array. For example, the following loop steps through an array and displays the contents of each element. The array's `length` field is used in the test expression as the upper limit for the loop control variable:

```
for (int i = 0; i < temperatures.length; i++)
    System.out.println(temperatures[i]);
```

 WARNING! Be careful not to cause an off-by-one error when using the `length` field as the upper limit of a subscript. The `length` field contains the number of elements in an array. The largest subscript in an array is `length − 1`.

 NOTE: You cannot change the value of an array's `length` field.

The Enhanced `for` Loop

Java provides a specialized version of the `for` loop that, in many circumstances, simplifies array processing. It is known as the *enhanced `for` loop*. Here is the general format of the enhanced `for` loop:

```
for (dataType elementVariable : array)
    statement;
```

The enhanced `for` loop is designed to iterate once for every element in an array. Each time the loop iterates, it copies an array element to a variable. Let's look at the syntax more closely as follows:

- *dataType elementVariable* is a variable declaration. This variable will receive the value of a different array element during each loop iteration. During the first loop iteration, it receives the value of the first element; during the second iteration, it receives the value of the second element, and so on. This variable must be of the same data type as the array elements, or a type that the elements can automatically be converted to.
- *array* is the name of an array on which you wish the loop to operate. The loop will iterate once for every element in the array.
- *statement* is a statement that executes during a loop iteration.

For example, assume that we have the following array declaration:

```
int[] numbers = { 3, 6, 9 };
```

We can use the following enhanced `for` loop to display the contents of the `numbers` array:

```
for (int val : numbers)
    System.out.println(val);
```

Because the numbers array has three elements, this loop will iterate three times. The first time it iterates, the val variable will receive the value in numbers[0]. During the second iteration, val will receive the value in numbers[1]. During the third iteration, val will receive the value in numbers[2]. The code's output will be as follows:

```
3
6
9
```

If you need to execute more than one statement in the enhanced for loop, simply enclose the block of statements in a set of braces. Here is an example:

```
int[] numbers = { 3, 6, 9 };
for (int val : numbers)
{
    System.out.print("The next value is ");
    System.out.println(val);
}
```

This code will produce the following output:

```
The next value is 3
The next value is 6
The next value is 9
```

The Enhanced for Loop versus the Traditional for Loop

When you need to access the values that are stored in an array, from the first element to the last element, the enhanced for loop is simpler to use than the traditional for loop. With the enhanced for loop you do not have to be concerned about the size of the array, and you do not have to create an "index" variable to hold subscripts. However, there are circumstances in which the enhanced for loop is not adequate. You cannot use the enhanced for loop as follows:

- if you need to change the contents of an array element
- if you need to work through the array elements in reverse order
- if you need to access some of the array elements, but not all of them
- if you need to simultaneously work with two or more arrays within the loop
- if you need to refer to the subscript number of a particular element

In any of these circumstances, you should use the traditional for loop to process the array.

Letting the User Specify an Array's Size

Java allows you to use an integer variable to specify an array's size declarator. This makes it possible to allow the user to specify an array's size. Code Listing 7-6 demonstrates this, as well as the use of the length field. It stores a number of test scores in an array and then displays them.

Code Listing 7-6 (`DisplayTestScores.java`)

```java
 1 import java.util.Scanner; // Needed for Scanner class
 2
 3 /**
 4    This program demonstrates how the user may specify an
 5    array's size.
 6 */
 7
 8 public class DisplayTestScores
 9 {
10    public static void main(String[] args)
11    {
12       int numTests;     // The number of tests
13       int[] tests;      // Array of test scores
14
15       // Create a Scanner object for keyboard input.
16       Scanner keyboard = new Scanner(System.in);
17
18       // Get the number of test scores.
19       System.out.print("How many tests do you have? ");
20       numTests = keyboard.nextInt();
21
22       // Create an array to hold that number of scores.
23       tests = new int[numTests];
24
25       // Get the individual test scores.
26       for (int index = 0; index < tests.length; index++)
27       {
28          System.out.print("Enter test score " +
29                           (index + 1) + ": ");
30          tests[index] = keyboard.nextInt();
31       }
32
33       // Display the test scores.
34       System.out.println();
35       System.out.println("Here are the scores you entered:");
36       for (int index = 0; index < tests.length; index++)
37          System.out.print(tests[index] + " ");
38    }
39 }
```

Program Output with Example Input Shown in Bold

```
How many tests do you have? 5 [Enter]
Enter test score 1: 72 [Enter]
```

```
Enter test score 2: 85 [Enter]
Enter test score 3: 81 [Enter]
Enter test score 4: 94 [Enter]
Enter test score 5: 99 [Enter]

Here are the scores you entered:
72 85 81 94 99
```

This program allows the user to determine the size of the array. In line 23 the following statement creates the array, using the numTests variable to determine its size:

```
tests = new int[numTests];
```

The program then uses two for loops. The first, in lines 26 through 31, allows the user to input each test score. The second, in lines 36 and 37, displays all of the test scores. Both loops use the length member to control their number of iterations as follows:

```
for (int index = 0; index < tests.length; index++)
```

Reassigning Array Reference Variables

It is possible to reassign an array reference variable to a different array, as demonstrated by the following code:

```
// Create an array referenced by the numbers variable.
int[] numbers = new int[10];
// Reassign numbers to a new array.
numbers = new int[5];
```

The first statement creates a ten-element integer array and assigns its address to the numbers variable. This is illustrated in Figure 7-7.

Figure 7-7 The numbers variable references a ten-element array

The second statement allocates a five-element integer array and assigns its address to the numbers variable. The address of the five-element array takes the place of the address of the ten-element array. After this statement executes, the numbers variable references the five-element array instead of the ten-element array. This is illustrated in Figure 7-8. Because the ten-element array is no longer referenced, it cannot be accessed.

Figure 7-8 The `numbers` variable references a five-element array

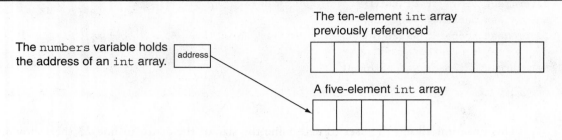

Copying Arrays

Because an array is an object, there is a distinction between an array and the variable that references it. The array and the reference variable are two separate entities. This is important to remember when you wish to copy the contents of one array to another. You might be tempted to write something like the following code, thinking that you are copying an array:

```
int[] array1 = { 2, 4, 6, 8, 10 };
int[] array2 = array1;    // This does not copy array1.
```

The first statement creates an array and assigns its address to the `array1` variable. The second statement assigns `array1` to `array2`. This does not make a copy of the array referenced by `array1`. Rather, it makes a copy of the address that is stored in `array1` and stores it in `array2`. After this statement executes, both the `array1` and `array2` variables will reference the same array. This type of assignment operation is called a *reference copy*. Only the address of the array object is copied, not the contents of the array object. This is illustrated in Figure 7-9.

Figure 7-9 Both `array1` and `array2` reference the same array

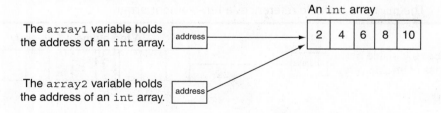

Code Listing 7-7 demonstrates the assigning of an array's address to two reference variables. Regardless of which variable the program uses, it is working with the same array.

Code Listing 7-7   (`SameArray.java`)

```
 1  /**
 2      This program demonstrates that two variables can
 3      reference the same array.
 4  */
 5
 6  public class SameArray
 7  {
 8      public static void main(String[] args)
 9      {
10          int[] array1 = { 2, 4, 6, 8, 10 };
11          int[] array2 = array1;
12
13          // Change one of the elements using array1.
14          array1[0] = 200;
15
16          // Change one of the elements using array2.
17          array2[4] = 1000;
18
19          // Display all the elements using array1
20          System.out.println("The contents of array1:");
21          for (int value : array1)
22              System.out.print(value + " ");
23          System.out.println();
24
25          // Display all the elements using array2
26          System.out.println("The contents of array2:");
27          for (int value : array2)
28              System.out.print(value + " ");
29          System.out.println();
30      }
31  }
```

Program Output

```
The contents of array1:
200 4 6 8 1000
The contents of array2:
200 4 6 8 1000
```

The program in Code Listing 7-7 illustrates that you cannot copy an array by merely assigning one array reference variable to another. Instead, to copy an array you need to copy the individual elements of one array to another. Usually, this is best done with a loop, such as the following:

```
int[] firstArray = { 5, 10, 15, 20, 25 };
int[] secondArray = new int[5];

for (int index = 0; index < firstArray.length; index++)
    secondArray[index] = firstArray[index];
```

The loop in this code copies each element of `firstArray` to the corresponding element of `secondArray`.

Checkpoint

MyProgrammingLab™ *www.myprogramminglab.com*

7.9 Look at the following statements:

```
int[] numbers1 = { 1, 3, 6, 9 };
int[] numbers2 = { 2, 4, 6, 8 };
int result;
```

Write a statement that multiplies element 0 of the `numbers1` array by element 3 of the `numbers2` array and assigns the result to the `result` variable.

7.10 A program uses a variable named `array` that references an array of integers. You do not know the number of elements in the array. Write a `for` loop that stores –1 in each element of the array.

7.11 A program has the following declaration:

```
double[] values;
```

Write code that asks the user for the size of the array and then creates an array of the specified size, referenced by the `values` variable.

7.12 Look at the following statements:

```
int[] a = { 1, 2, 3, 4, 5, 6, 7 };
int[] b = new int[7];
```

Write code that copies the a array to the b array.

7.3 Passing Arrays as Arguments to Methods

CONCEPT: An array can be passed as an argument to a method. To pass an array, you pass the value in the variable that references the array.

VideoNote

Passing an
Array to a
Method

Quite often you'll want to write methods that process the data in arrays. As you will see, methods can be written to store values in an array, display an array's contents, total all of an array's elements, calculate their average, and so forth. Usually, such methods accept an array as an argument.

When a single element of an array is passed to a method, it is handled like any other variable. For example, Code Listing 7-8 shows a loop that passes each element of the array `numbers` to the method `showValue`.

Code Listing 7-8   **(PassElements.java)**

```java
 1  /**
 2      This program demonstrates passing individual array
 3      elements as arguments to a method.
 4  */
 5
 6  public class PassElements
 7  {
 8      public static void main(String[] args)
 9      {
10          int[] numbers = {5, 10, 15, 20, 25, 30, 35, 40};
11
12          for (int index = 0; index < numbers.length; index++)
13              showValue(numbers[index]);
14      }
15
16      /**
17          The showValue method displays its argument.
18          @param n The value to display.
19      */
20
21      public static void showValue(int n)
22      {
23          System.out.print(n + " ");
24      }
25  }
```

Program Output

```
5 10 15 20 25 30 35 40
```

Each time showValue is called in this program, an array element is passed to the method. The showValue method has an int parameter variable named n, which receives the argument. The method simply displays the contents of n. If the method were written to accept the entire array as an argument, however, the parameter would have to be set up differently. For example, consider the following method definition. The parameter array is declared as an array reference variable. This indicates that the argument will be an array, not a single value.

```java
public static void showArray(int[] array)
{
    for (int i = 0; i < array.length; i++)
        System.out.print(array[i] + " ");
}
```

When you pass an array as an argument, you simply pass the value in the variable that references the array, as shown here:

```
showArray(numbers);
```

When an entire array is passed into a method, it is passed just as an object is passed: The actual array itself is not passed, but a reference to the array is passed into the parameter. Consequently, this means the method has direct access to the original array. This is illustrated in Figure 7-10.

Figure 7-10 An array passed as an argument

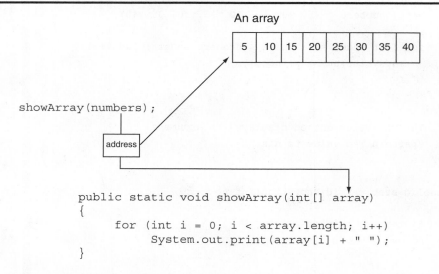

Code Listing 7-9 shows the `showArray` method in use, as well as another method, `getValues`. The `getValues` method accepts an array as an argument. It asks the user to enter a value for each element.

Code Listing 7-9 (`PassArray.java`)

```
1 import java.util.Scanner;  // Needed for Scanner class
2
3 /**
4    This program demonstrates passing an array
5    as an argument to a method.
6 */
7
8 public class PassArray
9 {
10    public static void main(String[] args)
11    {
12       final int ARRAY_SIZE = 4;  // Size of the array
13
```

```
14          // Create an array.
15          int[] numbers = new int[ARRAY_SIZE];
16
17          // Pass the array to the getValues method.
18          getValues(numbers);
19
20          System.out.println("Here are the " +
21                             "numbers that you entered:");
22
23          // Pass the array to the showArray method.
24          showArray(numbers);
25      }
26
27      /**
28         The getValues method accepts a reference
29         to an array as its argument. The user is
30         asked to enter a value for each element.
31         @param array A reference to the array.
32      */
33
34      private static void getValues(int[] array)
35      {
36          // Create a Scanner objects for keyboard input.
37          Scanner keyboard = new Scanner(System.in);
38
39          System.out.println("Enter a series of " +
40                             array.length + " numbers.");
41
42          // Read values into the array
43          for (int index = 0; index < array.length; index++)
44          {
45              System.out.print("Enter number " +
46                               (index + 1) + ": ");
47              array[index] = keyboard.nextInt();
48          }
49      }
50
51      /**
52         The showArray method accepts an array as
53         an argument and displays its contents.
54         @param array A reference to the array.
55      */
56
57      public static void showArray(int[] array)
58      {
59          // Display the array elements.
60          for (int index = 0; index < array.length; index++)
61              System.out.print(array[index] + " ");
```

```
62    }
63 }
```

Program Output with Example Input Shown in Bold

```
Enter a series of 4 numbers.
Enter number 1: 2 [Enter]
Enter number 2: 4 [Enter]
Enter number 3: 6 [Enter]
Enter number 4: 8 [Enter]
Here are the numbers that you entered:
2 4 6 8
```

 Checkpoint

 *www.myprogramminglab.com*

7.13 Look at the following method header:

```
public static void myMethod(double[] array)
```

Here is an array declaration:

```
double[] numbers = new double[100];
```

Write a statement that passes the `numbers` array to the `myMethod` method.

7.14 Write a method named `zero`, which accepts an `int` array as an argument and stores the value 0 in each element.

7.4 Some Useful Array Algorithms and Operations

Comparing Arrays

In the previous section you saw that you cannot copy an array by simply assigning its reference variable to another array's reference variable. In addition, you cannot use the `==` operator to compare two array reference variables and determine whether the arrays are equal. For example, the following code appears to compare two arrays, but in reality does not:

```
int[] firstArray = { 5, 10, 15, 20, 25 };
int[] secondArray = { 5, 10, 15, 20, 25 };
if (firstArray == secondArray)        // This is a mistake.
   System.out.println("The arrays are the same.");
else
   System.out.println("The arrays are not the same.");
```

When you use the `==` operator with reference variables, including those that reference arrays, the operator compares the memory addresses that the variables contain, not the contents of the objects referenced by the variables. Because the two array variables in this code reference different objects in memory, they will contain different addresses. Therefore, the result of the `boolean` expression `firstArray == secondArray` is `false` and the code reports that the arrays are not the same.

To compare the contents of two arrays, you must compare the elements of the two arrays.

For example, look at the following code:

```java
int[] firstArray = { 2, 4, 6, 8, 10 };
int[] secondArray = { 2, 4, 6, 8, 10 };
boolean arraysEqual = true;    // Flag variable
int index = 0;                 // Loop control variable

// First determine whether the arrays are the same size.
if (firstArray.length != secondArray.length)
   arraysEqual = false;

// Next determine whether the elements contain the same data.
while (arraysEqual && index < firstArray.length)
{
   if (firstArray[index] != secondArray[index])
      arraysEqual = false;
   index++;
}

if (arraysEqual)
   System.out.println("The arrays are equal.");
else
   System.out.println("The arrays are not equal.");
```

This code determines whether firstArray and secondArray contain the same values. A boolean flag variable, arraysEqual, which is initialized to true, is used to signal whether the arrays are equal. Another variable, index, which is initialized to 0, is used as a loop control variable.

First, this code determines whether the two arrays are the same length. If they are not the same length, then the arrays cannot be equal, so the flag variable arraysEqual is set to false. Then a while loop begins. The loop executes as long as arraysEqual is true and the control variable index is less than firstArray.length. During each iteration, it compares a different set of corresponding elements in the arrays. When it finds two corresponding elements that have different values, the flag variable arraysEqual is set to false. After the loop finishes, an if statement examines the arraysEqual variable. If the variable is true, then the arrays are equal and a message indicating so is displayed. Otherwise, they are not equal, so a different message is displayed.

Summing the Values in a Numeric Array

To sum the values in an array you must use a loop with an accumulator variable. The loop adds the value in each array element to the accumulator. For example, assume that the following statement appears in a program and that values have been stored in the units array:

```java
int[] units = new int[25];
```

The following loop adds the values of each element of the units array to the total variable. When the code is finished, total will contain the sum of all of the units array's elements.

```
int total = 0;      // Initialize accumulator
for (int index = 0; index < units.length; index++)
   total += units[index];
```

Getting the Average of the Values in a Numeric Array

The first step in calculating the average of all the values in an array is to sum the values. The second step is to divide the sum by the number of elements in the array. Assume that the following statement appears in a program and that values have been stored in the scores array:

```
double[] scores = new double[10];
```

The following code calculates the average of the values in the scores array. When the code completes, the average will be stored in the average variable.

```
double total = 0;     // Initialize accumulator
double average;       // Will hold the average
for (int index = 0; index < scores.length; index++)
   total += scores[index];
average = total / scores.length;
```

Notice that the last statement, which divides total by scores.length, is not inside the loop. This statement should execute only once, after the loop has finished its iterations.

Finding the Highest and Lowest Values in a Numeric Array

The algorithms for finding the highest and lowest values in an array are very similar. First, let's look at code for finding the highest value in an array. Assume that the following statement exists in a program and that values have been stored in the numbers array:

```
int[] numbers = new int[50];
```

The code to find the highest value in the array is as follows:

```
int highest = numbers[0];
for (int index = 1; index < numbers.length; index++)
{
   if (numbers[index] > highest)
      highest = numbers[index];
}
```

First we copy the value in the first array element to the variable highest. Then the loop compares all of the remaining array elements, beginning at subscript 1, to the value in highest. Each time it finds a value in the array that is greater than highest, it copies that value to highest. When the loop has finished, highest will contain the highest value in the array.

The following code finds the lowest value in the array. As you can see, it is nearly identical to the code for finding the highest value.

```
int lowest = numbers[0];
for (int index = 1; index < numbers.length; index++)
{
   if (numbers[index] < lowest)
      lowest = numbers[index];
}
```

When the loop has finished, `lowest` will contain the lowest value in the array.

The SalesData Class

To demonstrate these algorithms, look at the `SalesData` class shown in Code Listing 7-10. An instance of the class keeps sales amounts for any number of days in an array, which is a private field. Public methods are provided that return the total, average, highest, and lowest amounts of sales. The program in Code Listing 7-11 demonstrates the class, and Figure 7-11 shows an example of interaction with the program.

Code Listing 7-10   (`SalesData.java`)

```java
 1  /**
 2     This class keeps the sales figures for a number of
 3     days in an array and provides methods for getting
 4     the total and average sales, and the highest and
 5     lowest amounts of sales.
 6  */
 7
 8  public class SalesData
 9  {
10     private double[] sales; // The sales data
11
12     /**
13        The constructor copies the elements in
14        an array to the sales array.
15        @param s The array to copy.
16     */
17
18     public SalesData(double[] s)
19     {
20        // Create an array as large as s.
21        sales = new double[s.length];
22
23        // Copy the elements from s to sales.
24        for (int index = 0; index < s.length; index++)
25           sales[index] = s[index];
26     }
```

```
27
28      /**
29         getTotal method
30         @return The total of the elements in
31         the sales array.
32      */
33
34      public double getTotal()
35      {
36         double total = 0.0;        // Accumulator
37
38         // Accumulate the sum of the elements
39         // in the sales array.
40         for (int index = 0; index < sales.length; index++)
41            total += sales[index];
42
43         // Return the total.
44         return total;
45      }
46
47      /**
48         getAverage method
49         @return The average of the elements
50         in the sales array.
51      */
52
53      public double getAverage()
54      {
55         return getTotal() / sales.length;
56      }
57
58      /**
59         getHighest method
60         @return The highest value stored
61         in the sales array.
62      */
63
64      public double getHighest()
65      {
66         double highest = sales[0];
67
68         for (int index = 1; index < sales.length; index++)
69         {
70            if (sales[index] > highest)
71               highest = sales[index];
72         }
```

```
73
74        return highest;
75    }
76
77    /**
78       getLowest method
79       @return The lowest value stored
80       in the sales array.
81    */
82
83    public double getLowest()
84    {
85       double lowest = sales[0];
86
87       for (int index = 1; index < sales.length; index++)
88       {
89          if (sales[index] < lowest)
90             lowest = sales[index];
91       }
92
93       return lowest;
94    }
95 }
```

Code Listing 7-11   (Sales.java)

```
1 import javax.swing.JOptionPane;
2
3 /**
4    This program gathers sales amounts for the week.
5    It uses the SalesData class to display the total,
6    average, highest, and lowest sales amounts.
7 */
8
9 public class Sales
10 {
11    public static void main(String[] args)
12    {
13       final int ONE_WEEK = 7; // Number of elements
14
15       // Create an array to hold sales amounts for a week.
16       double[] sales = new double[ONE_WEEK];
```

```
17
18        // Get the week's sales figures.
19        getValues(sales);
20
21        // Create a SalesData object, initialized
22        // with the week's sales figures.
23        SalesData week = new SalesData(sales);
24
25        // Display the total, average, highest, and lowest
26        // sales amounts for the week.
27        JOptionPane.showMessageDialog(null,
28           String.format("The total sales were $%,.2f\n" +
29                         "The average sales were $%,.2f\n" +
30                         "The highest sales were $%,.2f\n" +
31                         "The lowest sales were $%,.2f",
32                         week.getTotal(),
33                         week.getAverage(),
34                         week.getHighest(),
35                         week.getLowest()));
36
37        System.exit(0);
38     }
39
40     /**
41        The getValues method asks the user to enter sales
42        amounts for each element of an array.
43        @param array The array to store the values in.
44     */
45
46     private static void getValues(double[] array)
47     {
48        String input;   // To hold user input.
49
50        // Get sales for each day of the week.
51        for (int i = 0; i < array.length; i++)
52        {
53           input = JOptionPane.showInputDialog(
54                   "Enter the sales for day " + (i + 1) + ".");
55           array[i] = Double.parseDouble(input);
56        }
57     }
58 }
```

Figure 7-11 Interaction with the `Sales.java` program

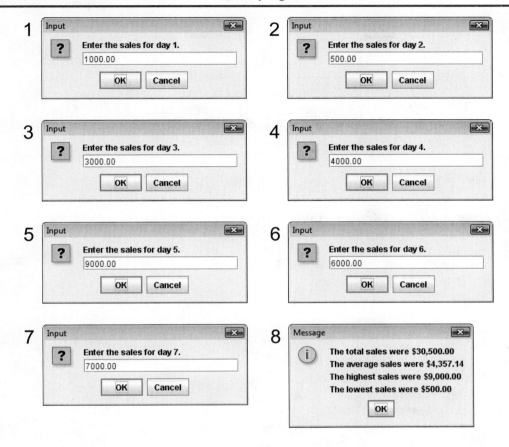

In the Spotlight:
Creating an Object That Processes an Array

Dr. LaClaire gives a set of exams during the semester in her chemistry class. At the end of the semester, she drops each student's lowest test score before averaging the scores. She has asked you to write a program that will read a student's test scores as input and calculate the average with the lowest score dropped.

The following pseudocode shows the steps for calculating the average of a set of test scores, with the lowest score dropped:

> *Calculate the total of the scores.*
> *Find the lowest score.*
> *Subtract the lowest score from the total. This gives the adjusted total.*
> *Divide the adjusted total by (number of scores − 1). This is the average.*

You decide to create a class named `Grader`, with a constructor that accepts a double array of test scores. The `Grader` class will have a method named `getLowestScore` that returns the lowest score in the array, and a method named `getAverage` that returns the average of the test scores with the lowest score dropped. Figure 7-12 shows a UML diagram for the class.

Figure 7-12 UML diagram for the `Grader` class

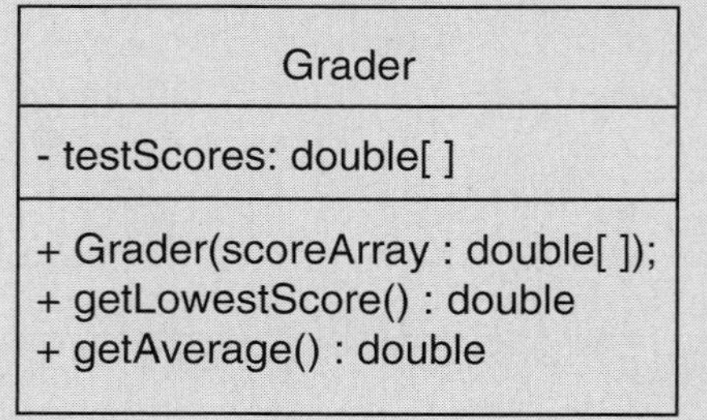

Grader
- testScores: double[ ]
+ Grader(scoreArray : double[ ]); + getLowestScore() : double + getAverage() : double

Code Listing 7-12 shows the code for the class.

Code Listing 7-12 (`Grader.java`)

```
1 /**
2     The Grader class calculates the average
3     of an array of test scores, with the
4     lowest score dropped.
5 */
6
7 public class Grader
8 {
9     // The testScores field is a variable
10    // that will reference an array
11    // of test scores.
12    private double[] testScores;
13
14    /**
15       Constructor
16       @param scoreArray An array of test scores.
17    */
18
19    public Grader(double[] scoreArray)
20    {
21       // Assign the array argument to
22       // the testScores field.
23       testScores = scoreArray;
24    }
25
26    /**
27       getLowestScore method
28       @return The lowest test score.
29    */
30
31    public double getLowestScore()
32    {
33       double lowest;     // To hold the lowest score
```

```
34
35        // Get the first test score in the array.
36        lowest = testScores[0];
37
38        // Step through the rest of the array. When
39        // a value less than lowest is found, assign
40        // it to lowest.
41        for (int index = 1; index < testScores.length; index++)
42        {
43           if (testScores[index] < lowest)
44              lowest = testScores[index];
45        }
46
47        // Return the lowest test score.
48        return lowest;
49     }
50
51     /**
52        getAverage method
53        @return The average of the test scores
54               with the lowest score dropped.
55     */
56
57     public double getAverage()
58     {
59        double total = 0;   // To hold the score total
60        double lowest;      // To hold the lowest score
61        double average;     // To hold the average
62
63        // If the array contains less than two test
64        // scores, display an error message and set
65        // average to 0.
66        if (testScores.length < 2)
67        {
68           System.out.println("ERROR: You must have at " +
69                              "least two test scores!");
70           average = 0;
71        }
72        else
73        {
74           // First, calculate the total of the scores.
75           for (double score : testScores)
76              total += score;
77
78           // Next, get the lowest score.
79           lowest = getLowestScore();
80
81           // Subtract the lowest score from the total.
82           total -= lowest;
```

```
83
84            // Get the adjusted average.
85            average = total / (testScores.length - 1);
86        }
87
88        // Return the adjusted average.
89        return average;
90    }
91 }
```

- Line 12 declares a field named `testScores`, which will be used to reference a `double` array of test scores.
- The constructor appears in lines 19 through 24. It accepts a `double` array as an argument, which is assigned to the `testScores` field.
- The `getLowestScore` method appears in lines 31 through 49. It finds the lowest value in the `testScores` array and returns that value.
- The `getAverage` method appears in lines 57 through 90. This method first determines whether there are less than 2 elements in the `testScores` array (in line 66). If that is the case, we cannot drop the lowest score, so an error message is displayed and the average variable is set to 0. Otherwise, the code in lines 74 through 85 calculates the average of the test scores with the lowest score dropped, and assigns that value to the average variable. Line 89 returns the value of the average variable.

Code Listing 7-13 shows the program that Dr. LaClaire will use to calculate a student's adjusted average. The program gets a series of test scores, stores those scores in an array, and uses an instance of the `Grader` class to calculate the average.

Code Listing 7-13   (`CalcAverage.java`)

```
1 import java.util.Scanner;
2
3 /**
4    This program gets a set of test scores and
5    uses the Grader class to calculate the average
6    with the lowest score dropped.
7 */
8
9 public class CalcAverage
10 {
11    public static void main(String[] args)
12    {
13       int numScores;    // To hold the number of scores
14
15       // Create a Scanner object for keyboard input.
16       Scanner keyboard = new Scanner(System.in);
17
18       // Get the number of test scores.
19       System.out.print("How many test scores do you have? ");
```

```
20          numScores = keyboard.nextInt();
21
22          // Create an array to hold the test scores.
23          double[] scores = new double[numScores];
24
25          // Get the test scores and store them
26          // in the scores array.
27          for (int index = 0; index < numScores; index++)
28          {
29              System.out.print("Enter score #" +
30                               (index + 1) + ": ");
31              scores[index] = keyboard.nextDouble();
32          }
33
34          // Create a Grader object, passing the
35          // scores array as an argument to the
36          // constructor.
37          Grader myGrader = new Grader(scores);
38
39          // Display the adjusted average.
40          System.out.println("Your adjusted average is " +
41                              myGrader.getAverage());
42
43          // Display the lowest score.
44          System.out.println("Your lowest test score was " +
45                              myGrader.getLowestScore());
46
47      }
48 }
```

Program Output with Example Input Shown in Bold

```
How many test scores do you have? 4 [Enter]
Enter score #1: 100 [Enter]
Enter score #2: 100 [Enter]
Enter score #3: 40 [Enter]
Enter score #4: 100 [Enter]
Your adjusted average is 100.0
Your lowest test score was 40.0
```

Partially Filled Arrays

Sometimes you need to store a series of items in an array, but you do not know the number of items that there are. As a result, you do not know the exact number of elements needed for the array. One solution is to make the array large enough to hold the largest possible number of items. This can lead to another problem, however. If the actual number of items stored in the array is less than the number of elements, the array will be only partially filled. When you process a partially filled array, you must process only the elements that contain valid data items.

A partially filled array is normally used with an accompanying integer variable that holds the number of items stored in the array. For example, suppose a program uses the following code to create an array with 100 elements, and an `int` variable named `count`, which will hold the number of items stored in the array:

```
final int ARRAY_SIZE = 100;
int[] array = new int[ARRAY_SIZE];
int count = 0;
```

Each time we add an item to the array, we must increment `count`. The following code demonstrates:

```
Scanner keyboard = new Scanner(System.in);
System.out.print("Enter a number or -1 to quit: ");
number = keyboard.nextInt();
while (number != -1 && count < array.length)
{
    array[count] = number;
    count++;
    System.out.print("Enter a number or -1 to quit: ");
    number = keyboard.nextInt();
}
```

Each iteration of this sentinel-controlled loop allows the user to enter a number to be stored in the array, or -1 to quit. The `count` variable is used as the subscript of the next available element in the array, and then incremented. When the user enters -1, or `count` reaches the size of the array, the loop stops. The following code displays all of the valid items in the array:

```
for (int index = 0; index < count; index++)
{
    System.out.println(array[index]);
}
```

Notice that this code uses `count` to determine the maximum array subscript to use.

> **NOTE:** If a partially filled array is passed as an argument to a method, the variable that holds the count of items in the array must also be passed as an argument. Otherwise, the method will not be able to determine the number of items that are stored in the array.

Working with Arrays and Files

Saving the contents of an array to a file is a straightforward procedure: Use a loop to step through each element of the array, writing its contents to the file. For example, assume a program declares an array as follows:

```
int[] numbers = { 10, 20, 30, 40, 50 };
```

The following code opens a file named *Values.txt* and writes the contents of each element of the `numbers` array to the file:

```
int[] numbers = { 10, 20, 30, 40, 50 };
```

```
// Open the file.
PrintWriter outputFile = new PrintWriter("Values.txt");

// Write the array elements to the file.
for (int index = 0; index < numbers.length; index++)
    outputFile.println(numbers[index]);
// Close the file.
outputFile.close();
```

The following code demonstrates how to open the *Values.txt* file and read its contents back into the numbers array.

```
final int SIZE = 5;
int[] numbers = new int[SIZE];
int index = 0;     // Loop control variable

// Open the file.
File file = new File("Values.txt");
Scanner inputFile = new Scanner(file);

// Read the file contents into the array.
while (inputFile.hasNext() && index < numbers.length)
{
    numbers[index] = inputFile.nextInt();
    index++;
}

// Close the file.
inputFile.close();
```

The file is opened, then a while loop reads all of the values from the file into the numbers array. The loop repeats as long as inputFile.hasNext() returns true, and index is less than numbers.length. The inputFile.hasNext() method is called to make sure there is a value remaining in the file. This prevents an error in case the file does not contain enough values to fill the array. The second condition (index < numbers.length) prevents the loop from writing outside the array boundaries.

7.5 Returning Arrays from Methods

CONCEPT: In addition to accepting arrays as arguments, methods may also return arrays.

A method can return a reference to an array. To do so, the return type of the method must be declared properly. For example, look at the following method definition:

```
public static double[] getArray()
{
    double[] array = { 1.2, 2.3, 4.5, 6.7, 8.9 };
    return array;
}
```

The `getArray` method returns an array of `doubles`. Notice that the return type listed in the method header is `double[]`. The method header is illustrated in Figure 7-13. It indicates that the method returns a reference to a `double` array.

Figure 7-13 Array reference return type

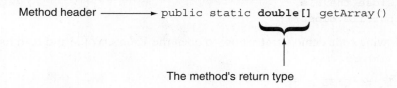

Inside the method an array of `doubles` is created, initialized with some values, and referenced by the `array` variable. Then the `return` statement returns the `array` variable. By returning the `array` variable, the method is returning a reference to the array. The method's return value can be stored in any compatible reference variable, as demonstrated in Code Listing 7-14.

Code Listing 7-14   (ReturnArray.java)

```
1   /**
2       This program demonstrates how a reference to an
3       array can be returned from a method.
4   */
5
6   public class ReturnArray
7   {
8       public static void main(String[] args)
9       {
10          double[] values;
11
12          values = getArray();
13          for (double num : values)
14              System.out.print(num + " ");
15      }
16
17      /**
18          getArray method
19          @return A reference to an array of doubles.
20      */
21
22      public static double[] getArray()
23      {
24          double[] array = { 1.2, 2.3, 4.5, 6.7, 8.9 };
25
26          return array;
```

```
27      }
28  }
```

Program Output

```
1.2    2.3    4.5    6.7    8.9
```

The following statement, which appears in line 12, assigns the array returned by the getArray method to the array variable values:

```
values = getArray();
```

Then the for loop in lines 13 and 14 displays the value of each element of the values array.

7.6 String **Arrays**

CONCEPT: An array of **String** objects may be created, but if the array is uninitialized, each **String** in the array must be created individually.

Java also allows you to create arrays of String objects. Here is a statement that creates an array of String objects initialized with values:

```
String[] names = { "Bill", "Susan", "Steven", "Jean" };
```

In memory, an array of String objects is arranged differently than an array of a primitive data type. In order to use a String object, you must have a reference to the String object. So, an array of String objects is really an array of references to String objects. Figure 7-14 illustrates how the names variable will reference an array of references to String objects.

Figure 7-14 The names variable references a String array

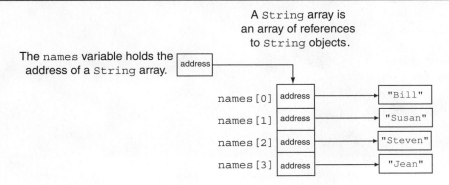

Each element in the names array is a reference to a String object. The names[0] element references a String object containing "Bill", the names[1] element references a String object containing "Susan", and so forth. The program in Code Listing 7-15 demonstrates an array of String objects.

Code Listing 7-15   (`MonthDays.java`)

```java
 1  /**
 2      This program demonstrates an array of String objects.
 3  */
 4
 5  public class MonthDays
 6  {
 7      public static void main(String[] args)
 8      {
 9          String[] months = { "January", "February", "March",
10                              "April", "May", "June", "July",
11                              "August", "September", "October",
12                              "November", "December" };
13
14          int[] days = { 31, 28, 31, 30, 31, 30, 31,
15                         31, 30, 31, 30, 31 };
16
17          for (int index = 0; index < months.length; index++)
18          {
19              System.out.println(months[index] + " has " +
20                                 days[index] + " days.");
21          }
22      }
23  }
```

Program Output

```
January has 31 days.
February has 28 days.
March has 31 days.
April has 30 days.
May has 31 days.
June has 30 days.
July has 31 days.
August has 31 days.
September has 30 days.
October has 31 days.
November has 30 days.
December has 31 days.
```

As with the primitive data types, an initialization list automatically causes an array of String objects to be created in memory. If you do not provide an initialization list, you must use the new key word to create the array. Here is an example:

```java
final int SIZE = 4;
String[] names = new String[SIZE];
```

This statement creates an array of four references to String objects, as shown in Figure 7-15. Notice that the array is an array of four uninitialized String references. Because they do not reference any objects, they are set to null.

Figure 7-15 An uninitialized String array

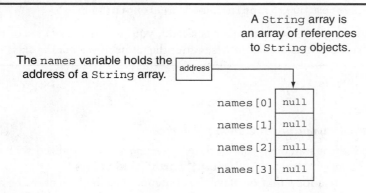

When you create an uninitialized array of String objects, you must assign a value to each element in the array that you intend to use. Here is an example:

```
final int SIZE = 4;
String[] names = new String[SIZE];
names[0] = "Bill";
names[1] = "Susan";
names[2] = "Steven";
names[3] = "Jean";
```

After these statements execute, each element of the names array will reference a String object.

Calling String Methods from an Array Element

Recall from Chapter 2 that String objects have several methods. For example, the toUpperCase method returns the uppercase equivalent of a String object. Because each element of a String array is a String object, you can use an element to call a String method. For example, the following statement uses element 0 of the names array to call the toUpperCase method:

```
System.out.println(names[0].toUpperCase());
```

The following code shows another example. It uses element 3 of the names array to call the charAt method. When this code executes, the first character of the string stored in names[3] will be assigned to the letter variable.

```
// Declare a char variable named letter.
char letter;
// Assign the first character in names[3] to letter.
letter = names[3].charAt(0);
```

TIP: Arrays have a field named `length` and `String` objects have a method named `length`. When working with `String` arrays, do not confuse the two. The following loop displays the length of each string held in names, which is assumed to be a `String` array. Note that the loop uses both the array's `length` field and each element's `length` method.

```
for (int i = 0; i < names.length; i++)
    System.out.println(names[i].length());
```

Because the array's `length` member is a field, you do not write a set of parentheses after its name. You do write the parentheses after the name of the `String` class's `length` method.

Checkpoint

MyProgrammingLab™ *www.myprogramminglab.com*

7.15 a) Write a statement that declares a `String` array initialized with the following strings: "Mercury", "Venus", "Earth", and "Mars".

  b) Write a loop that displays the contents of each element in the array you declared in A.

  c) Write a loop that displays the first character of the strings stored in each element of the array you declared in A. (*Hint*: Use the `String` class's `charAt` method discussed in Chapter 2.)

7.7 Arrays of Objects

CONCEPT: You may create arrays of objects that are instances of classes that you have written.

Like any other data type, you can create arrays of class objects. For example, recall the `BankAccount` class that we developed in Chapter 6. An array of `BankAccount` objects could be created to represent all of the bank accounts owned by a single person. The following code declares an array of five `BankAccount` objects:

```
final int NUM_ACCOUNTS = 5;
BankAccount[] accounts = new BankAccount[NUM_ACCOUNTS];
```

The variable that references the array is named `accounts`. As with `String` arrays, each element in this array is a reference variable, as illustrated in Figure 7-16.

Notice from the figure that each element of the array is initialized with the value `null`. This is a special value in Java that indicates the array elements do not yet reference objects. You must individually create the objects that each element will reference. The following code uses a loop to create objects for each element:

```
for (int index = 0; index < accounts.length; index++)
    accounts[index] = new BankAccount();
```

Figure 7-16 The accounts variable references an array of references

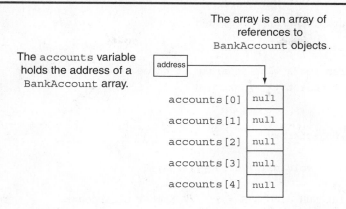

In this code, the no-arg constructor is called for each object. Recall that the BankAccount class has a no-arg constructor that assigns 0.0 to the balance field. After the loop executes, each element of the accounts array will reference a BankAccount object, as shown in Figure 7-17.

Figure 7-17 Each element of the array references an object

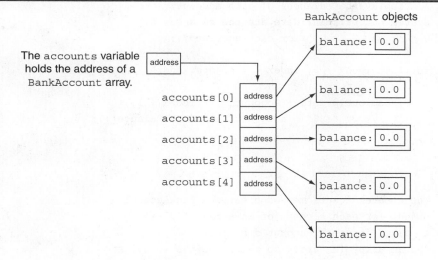

Objects in an array are accessed with subscripts, just like any other data type in an array. For example, the following code uses the accounts[2] element to call the setBalance and withdraw methods:

```
accounts[2].setBalance(2500.0);
accounts[2].withdraw(500.0);
```

Code Listing 7-16 shows a complete program that uses an array of objects.

Code Listing 7-16 (`ObjectArray.java`)

```java
 1 import java.util.Scanner; // Needed for the Scanner class
 2
 3 /**
 4    This program works with an array of three
 5    BankAccount objects.
 6 */
 7
 8 public class ObjectArray
 9 {
10    public static void main(String[] args)
11    {
12       final int NUM_ACCOUNTS = 3;  // Number of accounts
13
14       // Create an array that can reference
15       // BankAccount objects.
16       BankAccount[] accounts = new BankAccount[NUM_ACCOUNTS];
17
18       // Create objects for the array.
19       createAccounts(accounts);
20
21       // Display the balances of each account.
22       System.out.println("Here are the balances " +
23                          "for each account:");
24
25       for (int index = 0; index < accounts.length; index++)
26       {
27          System.out.println("Account " + (index + 1) +
28                     ": $" + accounts[index].getBalance());
29       }
30    }
31
32    /**
33       The createAccounts method creates a BankAccount
34       object for each element of an array. The user
35       is asked for each account's balance.
36       @param array The array to reference the accounts
37    */
38
39    private static void createAccounts(BankAccount[] array)
40    {
41       double balance;    // To hold an account balance
42
43       // Create a Scanner object.
44       Scanner keyboard = new Scanner(System.in);
45
```

```
46          // Create the accounts.
47          for (int index = 0; index < array.length; index++)
48          {
49              // Get the account's balance.
50              System.out.print("Enter the balance for " +
51                              "account " + (index + 1) + ": ");
52              balance = keyboard.nextDouble();
53
54              // Create the account.
55              array[index] = new BankAccount(balance);
56          }
57      }
58  }
```

Program Output with Example Input Shown in Bold

```
Enter the balance for account 1: 2500.0 [Enter]
Enter the balance for account 2: 5000.0 [Enter]
Enter the balance for account 3: 1500.0 [Enter]
Here are the balances for each account:
Account 1: $2500.0
Account 2: $5000.0
Account 3: $1500.0
```

 Checkpoint

MyProgrammingLab™ *www.myprogramminglab.com*

7.16   Recall that we discussed a `Rectangle` class in Chapter 6. Write code that declares a `Rectangle` array with five elements. Instantiate each element with a `Rectangle` object. Use the `Rectangle` constructor to initialize each object with values for the `length` and `width` fields.

7.8   The Sequential Search Algorithm

CONCEPT: A search algorithm is a method of locating a specific item in a larger collection of data. This section discusses the sequential search algorithm, which is a simple technique for searching the contents of an array.

It is very common for programs not only to store and process information stored in arrays, but also to search arrays for specific items. This section shows you how to use the simplest of all search algorithms—the sequential search.

The sequential search algorithm uses a loop to sequentially step through an array, starting with the first element. It compares each element with the value being searched for and stops when the value is found or the end of the array is encountered. If the value being searched for is not in the array, the algorithm unsuccessfully searches to the end of the array.

The `SearchArray` program shown in Code Listing 7-17 searches the five-element array `tests` to find a score of 100. It uses a method, `sequentialSearch`, to find the value in the array. The array that is passed as an argument into the `array` parameter is searched for an occurrence of the number passed into `value`. If the number is found, its array subscript is returned. Otherwise, −1 is returned, indicating the value did not appear in the array.

Code Listing 7-17   (`SearchArray.java`)

```
 1   /**
 2       This program sequentially searches an
 3       int array for a specified value.
 4   */
 5
 6   public class SearchArray
 7   {
 8      public static void main(String[] args)
 9      {
10         int[] tests = { 87, 75, 98, 100, 82 };
11         int results;
12
13         // Search the array for the value 100.
14         results = sequentialSearch(tests, 100);
15
16         // Determine whether 100 was found and
17         // display an appropriate message.
18         if (results == -1)
19         {
20            System.out.println("You did not " +
21                     "earn 100 on any test.");
22         }
23         else
24         {
25            System.out.println("You earned 100 " +
26                     "on test " + (results + 1));
27         }
28      }
29
30      /**
31          The sequentialSearch method searches an array for
32          a value.
33          @param array The array to search.
34          @param value The value to search for.
35          @return The subscript of the value if found in the
36                  array, otherwise -1.
37      */
```

```
38
39      public static int sequentialSearch(int[] array,
40                                         int value)
41      {
42         int index;          // Loop control variable
43         int element;        // Element the value is found at
44         boolean found;      // Flag indicating search results
45
46         // Element 0 is the starting point of the search.
47         index = 0;
48
49         // Store the default values element and found.
50         element = -1;
51         found = false;
52
53         // Search the array.
54         while (!found && index < array.length)
55         {
56            if (array[index] == value)
57            {
58               found = true;
59               element = index;
60            }
61            index++;
62         }
63
64         return element;
65      }
66   }
```

Program Output

You earned 100 on test 4

 NOTE: The reason −1 is returned when the search value is not found in the array is because −1 is not a valid subscript.

See the PinTester Class Case Study on this book's companion Web site (available at www. pearsonhighered.com/gaddis) for another example using arrays. Also, see the companion Web site for the Bonus Section on Parallel Arrays to learn about another programming technique using arrays.

7.9 Two-Dimensional Arrays

CONCEPT: A two-dimensional array is an array of arrays. It can be thought of as having rows and columns.

An array is useful for storing and working with a set of data. Sometimes, though, it's necessary to work with multiple sets of data. For example, in a grade-averaging program a teacher might record all of one student's test scores in an array of doubles. If the teacher has 30 students, that means she'll need 30 arrays to record the scores for the entire class. Instead of defining 30 individual arrays, however, it would be better to define a two-dimensional array.

The arrays that you have studied so far are one-dimensional arrays. They are called *one-dimensional* because they can hold only one set of data. Two-dimensional arrays, which are sometimes called *2D arrays*, can hold multiple sets of data. Although a two-dimensional array is actually an array of arrays, it's best to think of it as having rows and columns of elements, as shown in Figure 7-18. This figure shows an array of test scores, having three rows and four columns.

Figure 7-18 Rows and columns

	Column 0	Column 1	Column 2	Column 3
Row 0				
Row 1				
Row 2				

The array shown in the figure has three rows (numbered 0 through 2) and four columns (numbered 0 through 3). There are a total of 12 elements in the array.

To declare a two-dimensional array, two sets of brackets and two size declarators are required: The first one is for the number of rows and the second one is for the number of columns. Here is an example declaration of a two-dimensional array with three rows and four columns:

```
double[][] scores = new double[3][4];
```

The two sets of brackets in the data type indicate that the scores variable will reference a two-dimensional array. The numbers 3 and 4 are size declarators. The first size declarator specifies the number of rows, and the second size declarator specifies the number of columns. Notice that each size declarator is enclosed in its own set of brackets. This is illustrated in Figure 7-19.

Figure 7-19   Declaration of a two-dimensional array

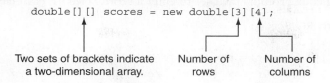

```
double[][] scores = new double[3][4];
```

Two sets of brackets indicate   Number of   Number of
a two-dimensional array.   rows   columns

When processing the data in a two-dimensional array, each element has two subscripts: one for its row and another for its column. In the scores array, the elements in row 0 are referenced as follows:

```
scores[0][0]
scores[0][1]
scores[0][2]
scores[0][3]
```

The elements in row 1 are as follows:

```
scores[1][0]
scores[1][1]
scores[1][2]
scores[1][3]
```

And the elements in row 2 are as follows:

```
scores[2][0]
scores[2][1]
scores[2][2]
scores[2][3]
```

Figure 7-20 illustrates the array with the subscripts shown for each element.

Figure 7-20   Subscripts for each element of the scores array

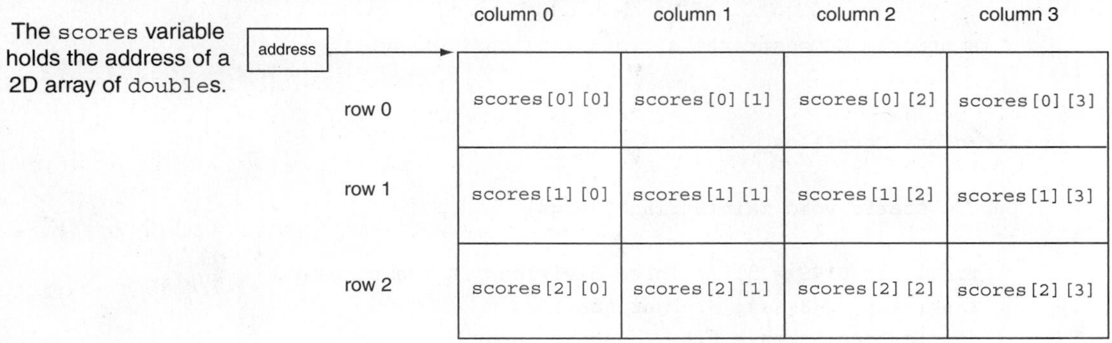

The scores variable holds the address of a 2D array of doubles.	address →	column 0	column 1	column 2	column 3
	row 0	scores[0][0]	scores[0][1]	scores[0][2]	scores[0][3]
	row 1	scores[1][0]	scores[1][1]	scores[1][2]	scores[1][3]
	row 2	scores[2][0]	scores[2][1]	scores[2][2]	scores[2][3]

To access one of the elements in a two-dimensional array, you must use both subscripts. For example, the following statement stores the number 95 in scores[2][1]:

```
scores[2][1] = 95;
```

Programs that process two-dimensional arrays can do so with nested loops. For example, the following code prompts the user to enter a score, once for each element in the array:

```
final int ROWS = 3;
final int COLS = 4;
double[][] scores = new double[ROWS][COLS];
for (int row = 0; row < ROWS; row++)
{
   for (int col = 0; col < COLS; col++)
   {
      System.out.print("Enter a score: ");
      scores[row][col] = keyboard.nextDouble();
   }
}
```

And the following code displays all the elements in the scores array:

```
for (int row = 0; row < ROWS; row++)
{
   for (int col = 0; col < COLS; col++)
   {
      System.out.println(scores[row][col]);
   }
}
```

The program in Code Listing 7-18 uses a two-dimensional array to store corporate sales data. The array has three rows (one for each division of the company) and four columns (one for each quarter).

Code Listing 7-18   (`CorpSales.java`)

```
 1 import java.util.Scanner;
 2
 3 /**
 4    This program demonstrates a two-dimensional array.
 5 */
 6
 7 public class CorpSales
 8 {
 9    public static void main(String[] args)
10    {
11       final int DIVS = 3; // Three divisions in the company
12       final int QTRS = 4; // Four quarters
13       double totalSales = 0.0; // Accumulator
14
15       // Create an array to hold the sales for each
16       // division, for each quarter.
```

```
17        double[][] sales = new double[DIVS][QTRS];
18
19        // Create a Scanner object for keyboard input.
20        Scanner keyboard = new Scanner(System.in);
21
22        // Display an introduction.
23        System.out.println("This program will calculate the " +
24                           "total sales of");
25        System.out.println("all the company's divisions. " +
26                           "Enter the following sales data:");
27
28        // Nested loops to fill the array with quarterly
29        // sales figures for each division.
30        for (int div = 0; div < DIVS; div++)
31        {
32           for (int qtr = 0; qtr < QTRS; qtr++)
33           {
34              System.out.printf("Division %d, Quarter %d: $",
35                                (div + 1), (qtr + 1));
36              sales[div][qtr] = keyboard.nextDouble();
37           }
38           System.out.println();   // Print blank line.
39        }
40
41        // Nested loops to add all the elements of the array.
42        for (int div = 0; div < DIVS; div++)
43        {
44           for (int qtr = 0; qtr < QTRS; qtr++)
45           {
46              totalSales += sales[div][qtr];
47           }
48        }
49
50        // Display the total sales.
51        System.out.printf("Total company sales: $%,.2f\n",
52                          totalSales);
53     }
54 }
```

Program Output with Example Input Shown in Bold

```
This program will calculate the total sales of
all the company's divisions. Enter the following sales data:
Division 1, Quarter 1: $35698.77 [Enter]
Division 1, Quarter 2: $36148.63 [Enter]
Division 1, Quarter 3: $31258.95 [Enter]
Division 1, Quarter 4: $30864.12 [Enter]
```

```
Division 2, Quarter 1: $41289.64 [Enter]
Division 2, Quarter 2: $43278.52 [Enter]
Division 2, Quarter 3: $40928.18 [Enter]
Division 2, Quarter 4: $42818.98 [Enter]

Division 3, Quarter 1: $28914.56 [Enter]
Division 3, Quarter 2: $27631.52 [Enter]
Division 3, Quarter 3: $30596.64 [Enter]
Division 3, Quarter 4: $29834.21 [Enter]

Total company sales: $419,262.72
```

Look at the following array declaration in line 17:

```
double[][] sales = new double[DIVS][QTRS];
```

As mentioned earlier, the array has three rows (one for each division) and four columns (one for each quarter) to store the company's sales data. The row subscripts are 0, 1, and 2, and the column subscripts are 0, 1, 2, and 3. Figure 7-21 illustrates how the quarterly sales data is stored in the array.

Figure 7-21   Division and quarter data stored in the `sales` array

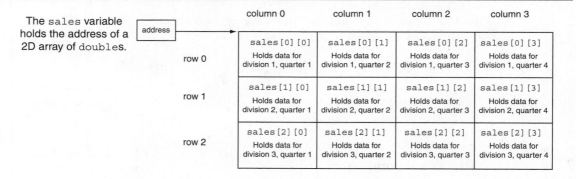

Initializing a Two-Dimensional Array

When initializing a two-dimensional array, you enclose each row's initialization list in its own set of braces. Here is an example:

```
int[][] numbers = { {1, 2, 3}, {4, 5, 6}, {7, 8, 9} };
```

As with one-dimensional arrays, you do not use the new key word when you provide an initialization list. Java automatically creates the array and fills its elements with the initialization values. In this example, the initialization values for row 0 are {1, 2, 3}, the initialization values for row 1 are {4, 5, 6}, and the initialization values for row 2 are {7, 8, 9}. So, this statement declares an array with three rows and three columns. For more clarity, the same statement could also be written as follows:

```
int[][] numbers = { {1, 2, 3},
                    {4, 5, 6},
                    {7, 8, 9} };
```

In either case, the values are assigned to the numbers array as illustrated in Figure 7-22.

Figure 7-22 The numbers array

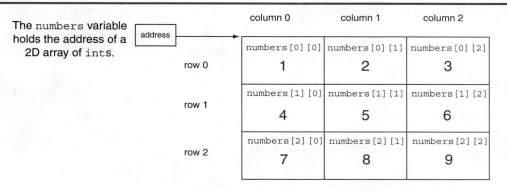

The length **Field in a Two-Dimensional Array**

A one-dimensional array has a length field that holds the number of elements in the array. A two-dimensional array, however, has multiple length fields. It has a length field that holds the number of rows, and then each row has a length field that holds the number of columns. This makes sense when you think of a two-dimensional array as an array of one-dimensional arrays. Figure 7-22 shows the numbers array depicted in rows and columns. Figure 7-23 shows another way of thinking of the numbers array: as an array of arrays.

Figure 7-23 The numbers array is an array of arrays

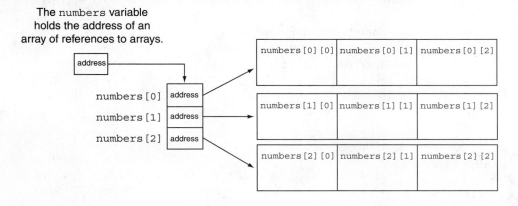

As you can see from the figure, the `numbers` variable references a one-dimensional array with three elements. Each of the three elements is a reference to another one-dimensional array. The elements in the array referenced by `numbers[0]` are `numbers[0][0]`, `numbers[0][1]`, and `numbers[0][2]`. This pattern continues with `numbers[1]` and `numbers[2]`. The figure shows a total of four arrays. Each of the arrays in the figure has its own `length` field. The program in Code Listing 7-19 uses these `length` fields to display the number of rows and columns in a two-dimensional array.

Code Listing 7-19   (`Lengths.java`)

```
 1 /**
 2    This program uses the length fields of a 2D array
 3    to display the number of rows, and the number of
 4    columns in each row.
 5 */
 6
 7 public class Lengths
 8 {
 9    public static void main(String[] args)
10    {
11       // Declare a 2D array with 3 rows
12       // and 4 columns.
13
14       int[][] numbers = { { 1,  2, 3,   4 },
15                           { 5,  6, 7,   8 },
16                           { 9, 10, 11, 12 } };
17
18       // Display the number of rows.
19       System.out.println("The number of " +
20                "rows is " + numbers.length);
21
22       // Display the number of columns in each row.
23       for (int index = 0; index < numbers.length; index++)
24       {
25          System.out.println("The number of " +
26                "columns in row " + index + " is " +
27                numbers[index].length);
28       }
29    }
30 }
```

Program Output

```
The number of rows is 3
The number of columns in row 0 is 4
The number of columns in row 1 is 4
The number of columns in row 2 is 4
```

Displaying All the Elements of a Two-Dimensional Array

As you have seen in previous example programs, a pair of nested loops can be used to display all the elements of a two-dimensional array. For example, the following code creates the numbers array with three rows and four columns, and then displays all the elements in the array:

```
int[][] numbers = { { 1,   2,   3,   4 },
                    { 5,   6,   7,   8 },
                    { 9, 10, 11, 12 } };

for (int row = 0; row < 3; row++)
{
   for (int col = 0; col < 4; col++)
      System.out.println(numbers[row][col]);
}
```

Although this code will display all of the elements, it is limited in the following way: The loops are specifically written to display an array with three rows and four columns. A better approach is to use the array's length fields for the upper limit of the subscripts in the loop test expressions. Here are the modified loops:

```
for (int row = 0; row < numbers.length; row++)
{
   for (int col = 0; col < numbers[row].length; col++)
      System.out.println(numbers[row][col]);
}
```

Let's take a closer look at the header for the outer loop:

```
for (int row = 0; row < numbers.length; row++)
```

This loop controls the subscript for the number array's rows. Because numbers.length holds the number of rows in the array, we have used it as the upper limit for the row subscripts. Here is the header for the inner loop:

```
for (int col = 0; col < numbers[row].length; col++)
```

This loop controls the subscript for the number array's columns. Because each row's length field holds the number of columns in the row, we have used it as the upper limit for the column subscripts. By using the length fields in algorithms that process two-dimensional arrays, you can write code that works with arrays of any number of rows and columns.

Summing All the Elements of a Two-Dimensional Array

To sum all the elements of a two-dimensional array, you can use a pair of nested loops to add the contents of each element to an accumulator. The following code shows an example:

```
int[][] numbers = { { 1,   2,   3,   4 },
                    { 5,   6,   7,   8 },
                    { 9, 10, 11, 12 } };
```

```
int total = 0;        // Accumulator, set to 0
// Sum the array elements.
for (int row = 0; row < numbers.length; row++)
{
   for (int col = 0; col < numbers[row].length; col++)
      total += numbers[row][col];
}

// Display the sum.
System.out.println("The total is " + total);
```

Summing the Rows of a Two-Dimensional Array

Sometimes you may need to calculate the sum of each row in a two-dimensional array. For example, suppose a two-dimensional array is used to hold a set of test scores for a set of students. Each row in the array is a set of test scores for one student. To get the sum of a student's test scores (perhaps so an average may be calculated), you use a loop to add all the elements in one row. The following code shows an example:

```
int[][] numbers = { { 1,  2,  3,  4 },
                    { 5,  6,  7,  8 },
                    { 9, 10, 11, 12 } };
int total;          // Accumulator
for (int row = 0; row < numbers.length; row++)
{
   // Set the accumulator to 0.
   total = 0;

   // Sum a row.
   for (int col = 0; col < numbers[row].length; col++)
      total += numbers[row][col];

   // Display the row's total.
   System.out.println("Total of row " + row +
                " is " + total);
}
```

Notice that the `total` variable, which is used as an accumulator, is set to zero just before the inner loop executes, because the inner loop sums the elements of a row and stores the sum in `total`. Therefore, the `total` variable must be set to zero before each iteration of the inner loop.

Summing the Columns of a Two-Dimensional Array

Sometimes you may need to calculate the sum of each column in a two-dimensional array. For example, suppose a two-dimensional array is used to hold a set of test scores for a set of students, and you wish to calculate the class average for each of the test scores. To do this, you calculate the average of each column in the array. This is accomplished with a set of nested loops. The outer loop controls the column subscript and the inner loop controls the row subscript. The inner loop calculates the sum of a column, which is stored in an accumulator. The following code demonstrates:

```
int[][] numbers = { { 1,  2,  3,  4 },
                    { 5,  6,  7,  8 },
                    { 9, 10, 11, 12 } };
int total;          // Accumulator

for (int col = 0; col < numbers[0].length; col++)
{
    // Set the accumulator to 0.
    total = 0;

    // Sum a column.
    for (int row = 0; row < numbers.length; row++)
        total += numbers[row][col];

    // Display the columns's total.
    System.out.println("Total of column " + col +
                    " is " + total);
}
```

Passing Two-Dimensional Arrays to Methods

When a two-dimensional array is passed to a method, the parameter must be declared as a reference to a two-dimensional array. The following method header shows an example:

```
private static void showArray(int[][] array)
```

This method's parameter, array, is declared as a reference to a two-dimensional int array. Any two-dimensional int array can be passed as an argument to the method. Code Listing 7-20 demonstrates two such methods.

Code Listing 7-20   (Pass2Darray.java)

```
1  /**
2     This program demonstrates methods that accept
3     a two-dimensional array as an argument.
4  */
5
6  public class Pass2Darray
7  {
8     public static void main(String[] args)
9     {
10        int[][] numbers = { { 1,  2,  3,  4 },
11                            { 5,  6,  7,  8 },
12                            { 9, 10, 11, 12 } };
```

```
13
14          // Display the contents of the array.
15          System.out.println("Here are the values " +
16                              " in the array.");
17          showArray(numbers);
18
19          // Display the sum of the array's values.
20          System.out.println("The sum of the values " +
21                              "is " + arraySum(numbers));
22      }
23
24      /**
25         The showArray method displays the contents
26         of a two-dimensional int array.
27         @param array The array to display.
28      */
29
30      private static void showArray(int[][] array)
31      {
32          for (int row = 0; row < array.length; row++)
33          {
34             for (int col = 0; col < array[row].length; col++)
35                 System.out.print(array[row][col] + " ");
36             System.out.println();
37          }
38      }
39
40      /**
41         The arraySum method returns the sum of the
42         values in a two-dimensional int array.
43         @param array The array to sum.
44         @return The sum of the array elements.
45      */
46
47      private static int arraySum(int[][] array)
48      {
49          int total = 0;      // Accumulator
50
51          for (int row = 0; row < array.length; row++)
52          {
53             for (int col = 0; col < array[row].length; col++)
54                 total += array[row][col];
55          }
56
```

```
57        return total;
58    }
59 }
```

Program Output

```
Here are the values in the array.
1 2 3 4
5 6 7 8
9 10 11 12
The sum of the values is 78
```

Ragged Arrays

Because the rows in a two-dimensional array are also arrays, each row can have its own length. When the rows of a two-dimensional array are of different lengths, the array is known as a ragged array. You create a ragged array by first creating a two-dimensional array with a specific number of rows, but no columns. Here is an example:

```
int[][] ragged = new int[4][];
```

This statement partially creates a two-dimensional array. The array can have four rows, but the rows have not yet been created. Next, you create the individual rows as shown in the following code:

```
ragged[0] = new int[3];    // Row 0 has 3 columns.
ragged[1] = new int[4];    // Row 1 has 4 columns.
ragged[2] = new int[5];    // Row 2 has 5 columns.
ragged[3] = new int[6];    // Row 3 has 6 columns.
```

This code creates the four rows. Row 0 has three columns, row 1 has four columns, row 2 has five columns, and row 3 has six columns. The following code displays the number of columns in each row:

```
for (int index = 0; index < ragged.length; index++)
{
    System.out.println("The number of columns " +
                    "in row " + index + " is " +
                    ragged[index].length);
}
```

This code will display the following output:

```
The number of columns in row 0 is 3
The number of columns in row 1 is 4
The number of columns in row 2 is 5
The number of columns in row 3 is 6
```

7.10 Arrays with Three or More Dimensions

CONCEPT: Java does not limit the number of dimensions that an array may have. It is possible to create arrays with multiple dimensions, to model data that occurs in multiple sets.

Java allows you to create arrays with virtually any number of dimensions. Here is an example of a three-dimensional array declaration:

```
double[][][] seats = new double[3][5][8];
```

This array can be thought of as three sets of five rows, with each row containing eight elements. The array might be used to store the prices of seats in an auditorium, where there are eight seats in a row, five rows in a section, and a total of three sections.

Figure 7-24 illustrates the concept of a three-dimensional array as "pages" of two-dimensional arrays.

Figure 7-24 A three-dimensional array

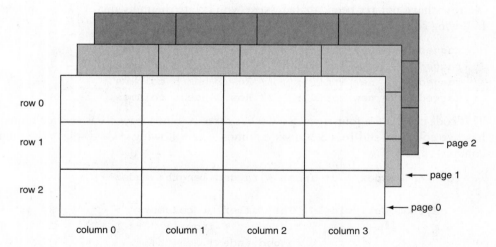

Arrays with more than three dimensions are difficult to visualize, but can be useful in some programming problems. For example, in a factory warehouse where cases of widgets are stacked on pallets, an array with four dimensions could be used to store a part number for each widget. The four subscripts of each element could represent the pallet number, case number, row number, and column number of each widget. Similarly, an array with five dimensions could be used if there were multiple warehouses.

 Checkpoint

MyProgrammingLab™ *www.myprogramminglab.com*

7.17 A video rental store keeps videos on 50 racks with 10 shelves each. Each shelf holds 25 videos. Declare a three-dimensional array large enough to represent the store's storage system.

7.11 The Selection Sort and the Binary Search Algorithms

CONCEPT: A sorting algorithm is used to arrange data into some order. A search algorithm is a method of locating a specific item in a larger collection of data. The selection sort and the binary search are popular sorting and searching algorithms.

The Selection Sort Algorithm

Often the data in an array must be sorted in some order. Customer lists, for instance, are commonly sorted in alphabetical order. Student grades might be sorted from highest to lowest. Product codes could be sorted so all the products of the same color are stored together. In this section we explore how to write your own sorting algorithm. A sorting algorithm is a technique for scanning through an array and rearranging its contents in some specific order. The algorithm that we will explore is called the selection sort.

The *selection sort* works like this: The smallest value in the array is located and moved to element 0. Then the next smallest value is located and moved to element 1. This process continues until all of the elements have been placed in their proper order. Let's see how the selection sort works when arranging the elements of the following array in Figure 7-25.

Figure 7-25 Values in an array

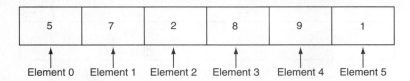

The selection sort scans the array, starting at element 0, and locates the element with the smallest value. The contents of this element are then swapped with the contents of element 0. In this example, the 1 stored in element 5 is swapped with the 5 stored in element 0. After the exchange, the array would appear as shown in Figure 7-26.

Figure 7-26 Values in array after first swap

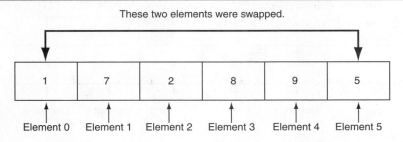

The algorithm then repeats the process, but because element 0 already contains the smallest value in the array, it can be left out of the procedure. This time, the algorithm begins the scan at element 1. In this example, the contents of element 2 are exchanged with that of element 1. The array would then appear as shown in Figure 7-27.

Figure 7-27   Values in array after second swap

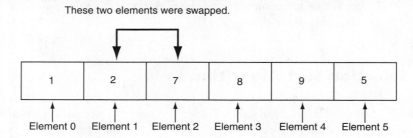

Once again the process is repeated, but this time the scan begins at element 2. The algorithm will find that element 5 contains the next smallest value. This element's value is swapped with that of element 2, causing the array to appear as shown in Figure 7-28.

Figure 7-28   Values in array after third swap

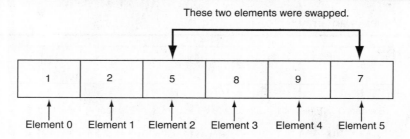

Next, the scanning begins at element 3. Its value is swapped with that of element 5, causing the array to appear as shown in Figure 7-29.

Figure 7-29   Values in array after fourth swap

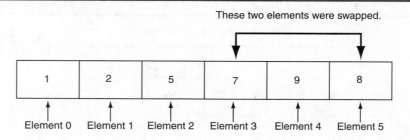

At this point there are only two elements left to sort. The algorithm finds that the value in element 5 is smaller than that of element 4, so the two are swapped. This puts the array in its final arrangement as shown in Figure 7-30.

Figure 7-30   Values in array after fifth swap

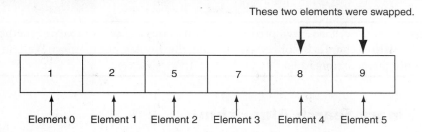

Here is the selection sort algorithm in pseudocode:

For `startScan` *is each subscript in array from 0 through the next-to-last subscript*
   Set `minIndex` *variable to* `startScan`.
   Set `minValue` *variable to* `array[startScan]`.
   For `index` *is each subscript in array from* (`startScan` + 1) *through the last subscript*
     If `array[index]` *is less than* `minValue`
       Set `minValue` *to* `array[index]`.
       Set `minIndex` *to* `index`.
     End If.
    Increment `index`.
   End For.
   Set `array[minIndex]` *to* `array[startScan]`.
   Set `array[startScan]` *to* `minValue`.
End For.

The following method performs a selection sort on an integer array. The array that is passed as an argument is sorted in ascending order.

```java
public static void selectionSort(int[] array)
{
    int startScan, index, minIndex, minValue;

    for (startScan = 0; startScan < (array.length-1); startScan++)
    {
        minIndex = startScan;
        minValue = array[startScan];
        for(index = startScan + 1; index < array.length; index++)
        {
            if (array[index] < minValue)
            {
                minValue = array[index];
```

```
                minIndex = index;
            }
        }
        array[minIndex] = array[startScan];
        array[startScan] = minValue;
    }
}
```

The `SelectionSortDemo.java` program demonstrates the `selectionSort` method. You can download this chapter's source code from the book's companion Web site at www.pearsonhighered.com/gaddis.

The Binary Search Algorithm

This chapter previously presented the sequential search algorithm for searching an array. The advantage of the sequential search is its simplicity. It is easy to understand and implement. Furthermore, it doesn't require the data in the array to be stored in any particular order. Its disadvantage, however, is its inefficiency. If the array being searched contains 20,000 elements, the algorithm will have to look at all 20,000 elements in order to find a value stored in the last element. In an average case, an item is just as likely to be found near the end of the array as near the beginning. Typically, for an array of N items, the sequential search will locate an item in N/2 attempts. If an array has 50,000 elements, the sequential search will make a comparison with 25,000 of them in a typical case.

This is assuming, of course, that the search item is consistently found in the array. (N/2 is the average number of comparisons. The maximum number of comparisons is always N.) When the sequential search fails to locate an item, it must make a comparison with every element in the array. As the number of failed search attempts increases, so does the average number of comparisons. Obviously, the sequential search should not be used on large arrays if speed is important.

The binary search is a clever algorithm that is much more efficient than the sequential search. Its only requirement is that the values in the array must be sorted in ascending order. Instead of testing the array's first element, this algorithm starts with the element in the middle. If that element happens to contain the desired value, then the search is over. Otherwise, the value in the middle element is either greater than or less than the value being searched for. If it is greater, then the desired value (if it is in the list) will be found somewhere in the first half of the array. If it is less, then the desired value (again, if it is in the list) will be found somewhere in the last half of the array. In either case, half of the array's elements have been eliminated from further searching.

If the desired value wasn't found in the middle element, the procedure is repeated for the half of the array that potentially contains the value. For instance, if the last half of the array is to be searched, the algorithm tests its middle element. If the desired value isn't found there, the search is narrowed to the quarter of the array that resides before or after that element. This process continues until the value being searched for is either found, or there are no more elements to test. Here is the pseudocode for a method that performs a binary search on an array:

Set first *to 0.*
Set last *to the last subscript in the array.*
Set position *to* − *1.*
Set found *to false.*
While found *is not true and* first *is less than or equal to* last
   Set middle *to the subscript half way between*
                    array[first] *and* array[last].
   If array[middle] *equals the desired value*
      Set found *to true.*
      Set position *to* middle.
   Else If array[middle] *is greater than the desired value*
      Set last *to* middle − 1.
   Else
      Set first *to* middle + 1.
   End If.
End While.
Return position.

This algorithm uses three variables to mark positions within the array: first, last, and middle. The first and last variables mark the boundaries of the portion of the array currently being searched. They are initialized with the subscripts of the array's first and last elements. The subscript of the element halfway between first and last is calculated and stored in the middle variable. If the element in the middle of the array does not contain the search value, the first or last variables are adjusted so that only the top or bottom half of the array is searched during the next iteration. This cuts the portion of the array being searched in half each time the loop fails to locate the search value.

The following method performs a binary search on an integer array. The first parameter, array, is searched for an occurrence of the number stored in value. If the number is found, its array subscript is returned. Otherwise, −1 is returned, indicating the value did not appear in the array.

```
public static int binarySearch(int[] array, int value)
{
    int first;        // First array element
    int last;         // Last array element
    int middle;       // Midpoint of search
    int position;     // Position of search value
    boolean found;    // Flag
    // Set the inital values.
    first = 0;
    last = array.length - 1;
    position = -1;
    found = false;
    // Search for the value.
    while (!found && first <= last)
    {
```

```
                // Calculate midpoint
                middle = (first + last) / 2;
                // If value is found at midpoint...
                if (array[middle] == value)
                {
                   found = true;
                   position = middle;
                }
                // else if value is in lower half...
                else if (array[middle] > value)
                   last = middle - 1;
                // else if value is in upper half....
                else
                   first = middle + 1;
         }
         // Return the position of the item, or -1
         // if it was not found.
         return position;
      }
```

The `BinarySearchDemo` program demonstrates this method. You can download this chapter's source code from the book's companion Web site at www.pearsonhighered.com/gaddis.

Checkpoint

MyProgrammingLab™ *www.myprogramminglab.com*

7.18 What value in an array does the selection sort algorithm look for first? When the selection sort finds this value, what does it do with it?

7.19 How many times will the selection sort swap the smallest value in an array with another value?

7.20 Describe the difference between the sequential search and the binary search.

7.21 On average, with an array of 20,000 elements, how many comparisons will the sequential search perform? (Assume the items being searched for are consistently found in the array.)

7.22 If a sequential search is performed on an array, and it is known that some items are searched for more frequently than others, how can the contents of the array be reordered to improve the average performance of the search?

7.12 Command-Line Arguments and Variable-Length Argument Lists

CONCEPT: When you invoke a Java program from the operating system command line, you can specify arguments that are passed into the `main` method of the program. In addition, you can write a method that takes a variable number of arguments. When the method runs, it can determine the number of arguments that were passed to it and act accordingly.

Command-Line Arguments

Every program you have seen in this book and every program you have written uses a static main method with a header that looks like this:

```
public static void main(String[] args)
```

Inside the parentheses of the method header is the declaration of a parameter named args. This parameter is an array name. As its declaration indicates, it is used to reference an array of Strings. The array that is passed into the args parameter comes from the operating system command line. For example, look at Code Listing 7-21.

Code Listing 7-21   (CommandLine.java)

```
 1  /**
 2      This program displays the arguments passed to
 3      it from the operating system command line.
 4  */
 5
 6  public class CommandLine
 7  {
 8      public static void main(String[] args)
 9      {
10          for (int index = 0; index < args.length; index++)
11              System.out.println(args[index]);
12      }
13  }
```

If this program is compiled and then executed with the following command:

```
java CommandLine How does this work?
```

its output will be as follows:

```
How
does
this
work?
```

Any items typed on the command line, separated by spaces, and after the name of the class are considered to be one or more arguments that are to be passed into the main method. In the previous example, four arguments are passed into args. The word "How" is passed into args[0], "does" is passed into args[1], "this" is passed into args[2], and "work?" is passed into args[3]. The for loop in main simply displays each argument.

NOTE: It is not required that the name of main's parameter array be args. You can name it anything you wish. It is a standard convention, however, for the name args to be used.

Variable-Length Argument Lists

Java provides a mechanism known as *variable-length argument lists,* which makes it possible to write a method that takes a variable number of arguments. In other words, you can write a method that accepts any number of arguments when it is called. When the method runs, it can determine the number of arguments that were passed to it and act accordingly.

For example, suppose we need to write a method named `sum` that can accept any number of `int` values and then return the sum of those values. We might call the method as shown here:

```
result = sum(10, 20);
```

Here we pass two arguments to the method: 10 and 20. After this code executes, the value 30 would be stored in the `result` variable. But, the method does not have to accept two arguments each time it is called. We could call the method again with a different number of arguments, as shown here:

```
int firstVal = 1, secondVal = 2, thirdVal = 3, fourthVal = 4;
result = sum(firstVal, secondVal, thirdVal, fourthVal);
```

Here we pass four arguments to the method: `firstVal` (which is set to 1), `secondVal` (which is set to 2), `thirdVal` (which is set to 3), and `fourthVal` (which is set to 4). After this code executes, the value 10 would be stored in the `result` variable. Here's the code for the `sum` method:

```
public static int sum(int... numbers)
{
   int total = 0;   // Accumulator

   // Add all the values in the numbers array.
   for (int val : numbers)
      total += val;

   // Return the total.
   return total;
}
```

Notice the declaration of the `numbers` parameter in the method header. The ellipsis (three periods) that follows the data type indicates that `numbers` is a special type of parameter known as a *vararg parameter.* A vararg parameter can take a variable number of arguments.

In fact, vararg parameters are actually arrays. In the `sum` method, the `numbers` parameter is an array of `int`s. All of the arguments that are passed to the `sum` method are stored in the elements of the `numbers` array. As you can see from the code, the method uses the enhanced `for` loop to step through the elements of the `numbers` array, adding up the values stored in its elements. (The *VarargsDemo1.java* program in this chapter's source code demonstrates the `sum` method.)

You can also write a method to accept a variable number of object references as arguments. For example, the program in Code Listing 7-22 shows a method that accepts a variable number of references to `BankAccount` objects. The method returns the total of the objects' `balance` fields.

Code Listing 7-22   (`VarargsDemo2.java`)

```java
 1 /**
 2     This program demonstrates a method that accepts
 3     a variable number of arguments (varargs).
 4 */
 5
 6 public class VarargsDemo2
 7 {
 8    public static void main(String[] args)
 9    {
10       double total;  // To hold the total balances
11
12       // Create BankAccount object with $100.
13       BankAccount account1 = new BankAccount(100.0);
14
15       // Create BankAccount object with $500.
16       BankAccount account2 = new BankAccount(500.0);
17
18       // Create BankAccount object with $1500.
19       BankAccount account3 = new BankAccount(1500.0);
20
21       // Call the method with one argument.
22       total = totalBalance(account1);
23       System.out.println("Total: $" + total);
24
25       // Call the method with two arguments.
26       total = totalBalance(account1, account2);
27       System.out.println("Total: $" + total);
28
29       // Call the method with three arguments.
30       total = totalBalance(account1, account2, account3);
31       System.out.println("Total: $" + total);
32    }
33
34    /**
35       The totalBalance method takes a variable number
36       of BankAccount objects and returns the total
37       of their balances.
38       @param accounts The target account or accounts.
39       @return The sum of the account balances
40    */
41
42    public static double totalBalance(BankAccount... accounts)
43    {
44       double total = 0.0;  // Accumulator
45
46       // Add all the values in the accounts array.
```

```
47         for (BankAccount acctObject : accounts)
48            total += acctObject.getBalance();
49
50         // Return the total.
51         return total;
52   }
53 }
```

Program Output

```
Total: $100.0
Total: $600.0
Total: $2100.0
```

You can write a method to accept a mixture of fixed arguments and a variable-length argument list. For example, suppose we want to write a method named `courseAverage`, which accepts the name of a course as a `String`, and a variable-length list of test scores as `doubles`. We could write the method header as follows:

```
public static void courseAverage(String course, double... scores)
```

This method has a regular `String` parameter named `course`, and a vararg parameter named `scores`. When we call this method, we always pass a `String` argument, then a list of `double` values. (This method is demonstrated in the program *VarargsDemo3.java*, which is in this chapter's source code folder.) Note that when a method accepts a mixture of fixed arguments and a variable-length argument list, the vararg parameter must be the last one declared.

> You can also pass an array to a vararg parameter. This is demonstrated in the program *VarargsDemo4.java*. You can download this chapter's source code from the book's companion Web site at www.pearsonhighered.com/gaddis.

7.13 The `ArrayList` Class

CONCEPT: `ArrayList` is a class in the Java API that is similar to an array and allows you to store objects. Unlike an array, an `ArrayList` object's size is automatically adjusted to accommodate the number of items being stored in it.

The Java API provides a class named `ArrayList`, which can be used for storing and retrieving objects. Once you create an `ArrayList` object, you can think of it as a container for holding other objects. An `ArrayList` object is similar to an array of objects, but offers many advantages over an array. Here are a few:

- An `ArrayList` object automatically expands as items are added to it.
- In addition to adding items to an `ArrayList`, you can remove items as well.
- An `ArrayList` object automatically shrinks as items are removed from it.

The ArrayList class is in the java.util package, so the following import statement is required:

```
import java.util.ArrayList;
```

Creating and Using an ArrayList Object

Here is an example of how you create an ArrayList object:

```
ArrayList<String> nameList = new ArrayList<String>();
```

This statement creates a new ArrayList object and stores its address in the nameList variable. Notice that in this example the word String is written inside angled brackets <> immediately after the word ArrayList. This specifies that the ArrayList can hold String objects. If we try to store any other type of object in this ArrayList, an error will occur. (Later in this section, you will see an example that creates an ArrayList for holding other types of objects.)

To add items to the ArrayList object, you use the add method. For example, the following statements add a series of String objects to nameList:

```
nameList.add("James");
nameList.add("Catherine");
nameList.add("Bill");
```

After these statements execute, nameList will hold three references to String objects. The first will reference "James", the second will reference "Catherine", and the third will reference "Bill".

The items that are stored in an ArrayList have a corresponding index. The index specifies the item's location in the ArrayList, so it is much like an array subscript. The first item that is added to an ArrayList is stored at index 0. The next item that is added to the ArrayList is stored at index 1, and so forth. After the previously shown statements execute, "James" will be stored at index 0, "Catherine" will be stored at index 1, and "Bill" will be stored at index 2.

The ArrayList class has a size method that reports the number of items stored in an ArrayList. It returns the number of items as an int. For example, the following statement uses the method to display the number of items stored in nameList:

```
System.out.println("The ArrayList has " +
                   nameList.size() +
                   " objects stored in it.");
```

Assuming that nameList holds the Strings "James", "Catherine", and "Bill", the following statement will display:

```
The ArrayList has 3 objects stored in it.
```

The ArrayList class's get method returns the item stored at a specific index. You pass the index as an argument to the method. For example, the following statement will display the item stored at index 1 of nameList:

```
System.out.println(nameList.get(1));
```

The program in Code Listing 7-23 demonstrates the topics discussed so far.

Code Listing 7-23 (ArrayListDemo1.java)

```
1   import java.util.ArrayList; // Needed for ArrayList class
2
3   /**
4      This program demonstrates an ArrayList.
5   */
6
7   public class ArrayListDemo1
8   {
9      public static void main(String[] args)
10     {
11        // Create an ArrayList to hold some names.
12        ArrayList<String> nameList = new ArrayList<String>();
13
14        // Add some names to the ArrayList.
15        nameList.add("James");
16        nameList.add("Catherine");
17        nameList.add("Bill");
18
19        // Display the size of the ArrayList.
20        System.out.println("The ArrayList has " +
21                            nameList.size() +
22                            " objects stored in it.");
23
24        // Now display the items in nameList.
25        for (int index = 0; index < nameList.size(); index++)
26           System.out.println(nameList.get(index));
27     }
28  }
```

Program Output

```
The ArrayList has 3 objects stored in it.
James
Catherine
Bill
```

Notice in line 25 that the for loop uses the value returned from nameList's size method to control the number of times the loop iterates. This is to prevent a bounds checking error from occurring. The last item stored in an `ArrayList` will have an index that is 1 less than the size of the `ArrayList`. If you pass a value larger than this to the get method, an error will occur.

Using the Enhanced for Loop with an ArrayList

Earlier in this chapter, you saw how the enhanced for loop can be used to iterate over each element in an array. You can also use the enhanced for loop to iterate over each item in an

ArrayList. Code Listing 7-24 demonstrates. The enhanced for loop is used in lines 26 and 27 to display all of the items stored in the ArrayList.

Code Listing 7-24   (ArrayListDemo2.java)

```java
 1 import java.util.ArrayList; // Needed for ArrayList class
 2
 3 /**
 4    This program demonstrates how the enhanced for loop
 5    can be used with an ArrayList.
 6 */
 7
 8 public class ArrayListDemo2
 9 {
10    public static void main(String[] args)
11    {
12       // Create an ArrayList to hold some names.
13       ArrayList<String> nameList = new ArrayList<String>();
14
15       // Add some names to the ArrayList.
16       nameList.add("James");
17       nameList.add("Catherine");
18       nameList.add("Bill");
19
20       // Display the size of the ArrayList.
21       System.out.println("The ArrayList has " +
22                          nameList.size() +
23                          " objects stored in it.");
24
25       // Now display the items in nameList.
26       for (String name : nameList)
27          System.out.println(name);
28    }
29 }
```

Program Output

```
The ArrayList has 3 objects stored in it.
James
Catherine
Bill
```

The ArrayList Class's toString method

The ArrayList class has a toString method that returns a string representing all of the items stored in an ArrayList object. For example, suppose we have set up the nameList object as previously shown, with the `String`s "James", "Catherine", and "Bill". We could use the following statement to display all of the names:

```
System.out.println(nameList);
```

The contents of the `ArrayList` will be displayed in the following manner:

```
[James, Catherine, Bill]
```

This is demonstrated in the program *ArrayListToString.java*, which is in this chapter's source code folder, available at www.pearsonhighered.com/gaddis.

Removing an Item from an `ArrayList`

The `ArrayList` class has a remove method that removes an item at a specific index. You pass the index as an argument to the method. The program in Code Listing 7-25 demonstrates.

Code Listing 7-25   (`ArrayListDemo3.java`)

```java
 1  import java.util.ArrayList; // Needed for ArrayList class
 2
 3  /**
 4     This program demonstrates an ArrayList.
 5  */
 6
 7  public class ArrayListDemo3
 8  {
 9     public static void main(String[] args)
10     {
11        // Create an ArrayList to hold some names.
12        ArrayList<String> nameList = new ArrayList<String>();
13
14        // Add some names to the ArrayList.
15        nameList.add("James");
16        nameList.add("Catherine");
17        nameList.add("Bill");
18
19        // Display the items in nameList and their indices.
20        for (int index = 0; index < nameList.size(); index++)
21        {
22           System.out.println("Index: " + index + " Name: " +
23                             nameList.get(index));
24        }
25
26        // Now remove the item at index 1.
27        nameList.remove(1);
28
29        System.out.println("The item at index 1 is removed. " +
30                         "Here are the items now.");
31
32        // Display the items in nameList and their indices.
```

```
33          for (int index = 0; index < nameList.size(); index++)
34          {
35              System.out.println("Index: " + index + " Name: " +
36                              nameList.get(index));
37          }
38      }
39 }
```

Program Output

```
Index: 0 Name: James
Index: 1 Name: Catherine
Index: 2 Name: Bill
The item at index 1 is removed. Here are the items now.
Index: 0 Name: James
Index: 1 Name: Bill
```

Note that when the item at index 1 was removed (in line 27), the item that was previously stored at index 2 was shifted in position to index 1. When an item is removed from an ArrayList, the items that come after it are shifted downward in position to fill the empty space. This means that the index of each item after the removed item will be decreased by one.

Note that an error will occur if you call the remove method with an invalid index.

Inserting an Item

The add method, as previously shown, adds an item at the last position in an ArrayList object. The ArrayList class has an overloaded version of the add method that allows you to add an item at a specific index. This causes the item to be inserted into the ArrayList object at a specific position. The program in Code Listing 7-26 demonstrates.

Code Listing 7-26   (ArrayListDemo4.java)

```java
1  import java.util.ArrayList; // Needed for ArrayList class
2
3  /**
4     This program demonstrates inserting an item.
5  */
6
7  public class ArrayListDemo4
8  {
9      public static void main(String[] args)
10     {
11         // Create an ArrayList to hold some names.
12         ArrayList<String> nameList = new ArrayList<String>();
13
14         // Add some names to the ArrayList.
15         nameList.add("James");
16         nameList.add("Catherine");
```

```
17            nameList.add("Bill");
18
19        // Display the items in nameList and their indices.
20        for (int index = 0; index < nameList.size(); index++)
21        {
22            System.out.println("Index: " + index + " Name: " +
23                               nameList.get(index));
24        }
25
26        // Now insert an item at index 1.
27        nameList.add(1, "Mary");
28
29        System.out.println("Mary was added at index 1. " +
30                           "Here are the items now.");
31
32        // Display the items in nameList and their indices.
33        for (int index = 0; index < nameList.size(); index++)
34        {
35            System.out.println("Index: " + index + " Name: " +
36                               nameList.get(index));
37        }
38    }
39 }
```

Program Output

```
Index: 0 Name: James
Index: 1 Name: Catherine
Index: 2 Name: Bill
Mary was added at index 1. Here are the items now.
Index: 0 Name: James
Index: 1 Name: Mary
Index: 2 Name: Catherine
Index: 3 Name: Bill
```

Note that when a new item was added at index 1 (in line 27), the item that was previously stored at index 1 was shifted in position to index 2. When an item is added at a specific index, the items that come after it are shifted upward in position to accommodate the new item. This means that the index of each item after the new item will be increased by one.

Note that an error will occur if you call the add method with an invalid index.

Replacing an Item

The `ArrayList` class's set method can be used to replace an item at a specific index with another item. For example, the following statement will replace the item currently at index 1 with the String "Becky":

```
nameList.set(1, "Becky");
```

This is demonstrated in the program *ArrayListDemo5.java*, which is in this chapter's source code folder, available at www.pearsonhighered.com/gaddis. Note that an error will occur if you specify an invalid index.

Capacity

Previously you learned that an `ArrayList` object's size is the number of items stored in the `ArrayList` object. When you add an item to the `ArrayList` object, its size increases by one, and when you remove an item from the `ArrayList` object, its size decreases by one.

An `ArrayList` object also has a *capacity*, which is the number of items it can store without having to increase its size. When an `ArrayList` object is first created, using the no-arg constructor, it has an initial capacity of 10 items. This means that it can hold up to 10 items without having to increase its size. When the eleventh item is added, the `ArrayList` object must increase its size to accommodate the new item. You can specify a different starting capacity, if you desire, by passing an `int` argument to the `ArrayList` constructor. For example, the following statement creates an `ArrayList` object with an initial capacity of 100 items:

```
ArrayList<String> list = new ArrayList<String>(100);
```

All of the examples we have looked at so far use `ArrayList` objects to hold `Strings`. You can create an `ArrayList` to hold any type of object. For example, the following statement creates an `ArrayList` that can hold `BankAccount` objects:

```
ArrayList<BankAccount> accountList = new ArrayList<BankAccount>();
```

By specifying `BankAccount` inside the angled brackets, we are declaring that the `ArrayList` can hold only `BankAccount` objects. Code Listing 7-27 demonstrates such an `ArrayList`.

Code Listing 7-27   **(ArrayListDemo6.java)**

```
 1 import java.util.ArrayList; // Needed for ArrayList class
 2
 3 /**
 4    This program demonstrates how to store BankAccount
 5    objects in an ArrayList.
 6 */
 7
 8 public class ArrayListDemo6
 9 {
10    public static void main(String[] args)
11    {
12       // Create an ArrayList to hold BankAccount objects.
13       ArrayList<BankAccount> list = new ArrayList<BankAccount>();
14
15       // Add three BankAccount objects to the ArrayList.
16       list.add(new BankAccount(100.0));
17       list.add(new BankAccount(500.0));
18       list.add(new BankAccount(1500.0));
19
```

```
20          // Display each item.
21          for (int index = 0; index < list.size(); index++)
22          {
23             BankAccount account = list.get(index);
24             System.out.println("Account at index " + index +
25                          "\nBalance: " + account.getBalance());
26          }
27       }
28 }
```

Program Output

```
Account at index 0
Balance: 100.0
Account at index 1
Balance: 500.0
Account at index 2
Balance: 1500.0
```

Using the Diamond Operator for Type Inference (Java 7)

Beginning with Java 7, you can simplify the instantiation of an `ArrayList` by using the *diamond operator* (`<>`). For example, in this chapter you have seen several programs that create an `ArrayList` object with a statement such as this:

```
ArrayList<String> list = new ArrayList<String>();
```

Notice that the data type (in this case, `String`) appears between the angled brackets in two locations: first in the part that declares the reference variable, and then again in the part that calls the `ArrayList` constructor. Beginning with Java 7, you are no longer required to write the data type in the part of the statement that calls the `ArrayList` constructor. Instead, you can simply write a set of empty angled brackets, as shown here:

```
ArrayList<String> list = new ArrayList<>();
```

This set of empty angled brackets (`<>`) is called the diamond operator. It causes the compiler to infer the required data type from the reference variable declaration. Here is another example:

```
ArrayList<InventoryItem> list = new ArrayList<>();
```

This creates an `ArrayList` that can hold `InventoryItem` objects. Keep in mind that type inference was introduced in Java 7. If you are using an earlier version of the Java language, you will have to use the more lengthy form of the declaration statement to create an `ArrayList`.

 Checkpoint

MyProgrammingLab™ *www.myprogramminglab.com*

7.23   What `import` statement must you include in your code in order to use the `ArrayList` class?

7.24   Write a statement that creates an `ArrayList` object and assigns its address to a variable named `frogs`.

7.25 Write a statement that creates an `ArrayList` object and assigns its address to a variable named `lizards`. The `ArrayList` should be able to store `String` objects only.

7.26 How do you add items to an `ArrayList` object?

7.27 How do you remove an item from an `ArrayList` object?

7.28 How do you retrieve a specific item from an `ArrayList` object?

7.29 How do you insert an item at a specific location in an `ArrayList` object?

7.30 How do you determine an `ArrayList` object's size?

7.31 What is the difference between an `ArrayList` object's size and its capacity?

7.14 Common Errors to Avoid

The following list describes several errors that are commonly committed when learning this chapter's topics:

- **Using an invalid subscript.** Java does not allow you to use a subscript value that is outside the range of valid subscripts for an array.
- **Confusing the contents of an integer array element with the element's subscript.** An element's subscript and the value stored in the element are not the same thing. The subscript identifies an element, which holds a value.
- **Causing an off-by-one error.** When processing arrays, the subscripts start at zero and end at one less than the number of elements in the array. Off-by-one errors are commonly caused when a loop uses an initial subscript of one and/or uses a maximum subscript that is equal to the number of elements in the array.
- **Using the = operator to copy an array.** Assigning one array reference variable to another with the = operator merely copies the address in one variable to the other. To copy an array, you should copy the individual elements of one array to another.
- **Using the == operator to compare two arrays.** You cannot use the == operator to compare two array reference variables and determine whether the arrays are equal. When you use the == operator with reference variables, the operator compares the memory addresses that the variables contain, not the contents of the objects referenced by the variables.
- **Reversing the row and column subscripts when processing a two-dimensional array.** When thinking of a two-dimensional array as having rows and columns, the first subscript accesses a row and the second subscript accesses a column. If you reverse these subscripts, you will access the wrong element.

Review Questions and Exercises

Multiple Choice and True/False

1. In an array declaration, this indicates the number of elements that the array will have.
   a. subscript
   b. size declarator
   c. element sum
   d. reference variable

2. Each element of an array is accessed by a number known as a(n) _____.
   a. subscript
   b. size declarator
   c. address
   d. specifier

3. The first subscript in an array is always _____.
   a. 1
   b. 0
   c. −1
   d. 1 less than the number of elements

4. The last subscript in an array is always _____.
   a. 100
   b. 0
   c. −1
   d. 1 less than the number of elements

5. Array bounds checking happens _____.
   a. when the program is compiled
   b. when the program is saved
   c. when the program runs
   d. when the program is loaded into memory

6. This array field holds the number of elements that the array has.
   a. `size`
   b. `elements`
   c. `length`
   d. `width`

7. This search algorithm steps through an array, comparing each item with the search value.
   a. binary search
   b. sequential search
   c. selection search
   d. iterative search

8. This search algorithm repeatedly divides the portion of an array being searched in half.
   a. binary search
   b. sequential search
   c. selection search
   d. iterative search

9. This is the typical number of comparisons performed by the sequential search on an array of N elements (assuming the search values are consistently found).
   a. 2N
   b. N
   c. N^2
   d. N/2

10. When initializing a two-dimensional array, you enclose each row's initialization list in
    _____.
    a. braces
    b. parentheses
    c. brackets
    d. quotation marks

11. To insert an item at a specific location in an `ArrayList` object, you use this method.
    a. `store`
    b. `insert`
    c. `add`
    d. `get`

12. To delete an item from an `ArrayList` object, you use this method.
    a. `remove`
    b. `delete`
    c. `erase`
    d. `get`

13. To determine the number of items stored in an `ArrayList` object, you use this method.
    a. `size`
    b. `capacity`
    c. `items`
    d. `length`

14. **True or False:** Java does not allow a statement to use a subscript that is outside the range of valid subscripts for an array.

15. **True or False:** An array's sitze declarator can be a negative integer expression.

16. **True or False:** Both of the following declarations are legal and equivalent:
    ```
    int[] numbers;
    int numbers[];
    ```

17. **True or False:** The subscript of the last element in a single-dimensional array is one less than the total number of elements in the array.

18. **True or False:** The values in an initialization list are stored in the array in the order that they appear in the list.

19. **True or False:** The Java compiler does not display an error message when it processes a statement that uses an invalid subscript.

20. **True or False:** When an array is passed to a method, the method has access to the original array.

21. **True or False:** The first size declarator in the declaration of a two-dimensional array represents the number of columns. The second size declarator represents the number of rows.

22. **True or False:** A two-dimensional array has multiple `length` fields.

23. **True or False:** An `ArrayList` automatically expands in size to accommodate the items stored in it.

Find the Error

1. ```
   int[] collection = new int[-20];
   ```

2. ```
   int[] hours = 8, 12, 16;
   ```

3. ```
   int[] table = new int[10];
   for (int x = 1; x <= 10; x++)
   {
       table[x] = 99;
   }
   ```

4. ```
   String[] names = { "George", "Susan" };
   int totalLength = 0;
   for (int i = 0; i < names.length(); i++)
       totalLength += names[i].length;
   ```

5. ```
   String[] words = { "Hello", "Goodbye" };
   System.out.println(words.toUpperCase());
   ```

Algorithm Workbench

1. The variable `names` references an integer array with 20 elements. Write a `for` loop that prints each element of the array.

2. The variables `numberArray1` and `numberArray2` reference arrays that each have 100 elements. Write code that copies the values in `numberArray1` to `numberArray2`.

3. a. Write a statement that declares a `String` array initialized with the following strings: "Einstein", "Newton", "Copernicus", and "Kepler".
   b. Write a loop that displays the contents of each element in the array that you declared in Question 3(a).
   c. Write code that displays the total length of all the strings in the array that you declared in Question 3(a).

4. In a program you need to store the populations of 12 countries.
   a. Define two arrays that may be used in parallel to store the names of the countries and their populations.
   b. Write a loop that uses these arrays to print each country's name and its population.

5. In a program you need to store the identification numbers of ten employees (as `int` values) and their weekly gross pay (as `double` values).
   a. Define two arrays that may be used in parallel to store the 10 employee identification numbers and gross pay amounts.
   b. Write a loop that uses these arrays to print each of the employees' identification number and weekly gross pay.

6. Declare a two-dimensional `int` array named `grades`. It should have 30 rows and 10 columns.

7. Write code that calculates the average of all the elements in the `grades` array that you declared in Question 6.
   ```

8. Look at the following array declaration:

   ```
   int[][] numberArray = new int[9][11];
   ```

   a. Write a statement that assigns 145 to the first column of the first row of this array.
   b. Write a statement that assigns 18 to the last column of the last row of this array.

9. The `values` variable references a two-dimensional double array with 10 rows and 20 columns. Write code that sums all the elements in the array and stores the sum in the variable `total`.

10. An application uses a two-dimensional array declared as follows:

    ```
    int[][] days = new int[29][5];
    ```

    a. Write code that sums each row in the array and displays the results.
    b. Write code that sums each column in the array and displays the results.

11. Write code that creates an `ArrayList` that can hold `String` objects. Add the names of three cars to the `ArrayList`, and then display the contents of the `ArrayList`.

Short Answer

1. What is the difference between a size declarator and a subscript?

2. Look at the following array definition:

   ```
   int[] values = new int[10];
   ```

   a. How many elements does the array have?
   b. What is the subscript of the first element in the array?
   c. What is the subscript of the last element in the array?

3. Look at the following array definition:

   ```
   int[] values = { 4, 7, 6, 8, 2 };
   ```

   What does each of the following code segments display?

   ```
   System.out.println(values[4]);        a. _____
   
   x = values[2] + values[3];
   System.out.println(x);                b. _____
   
   x = ++values[1];
   System.out.println(x);                c. _____
   ```

4. How do you define an array without providing a size declarator?

5. Assuming that `array1` and `array2` are both array reference variables, why is it not possible to assign the contents of the array referenced by `array2` to the array referenced by `array1` with the following statement?

   ```
   array1 = array2;
   ```

6. How do you establish an array without providing a size declarator?

7. The following statement creates a `BankAccount` array:

   ```
   BankAccount[] acc = new BankAccount[10];
   ```

   Is it okay or not okay to execute the following statements?

   ```
   acc[0].setBalance(5000.0);
   acc[0].withdraw(100.0);
   ```

8. If a sequential search method is searching for a value that is stored in the last element of a 10,000-element array, how many elements will the search code have to read to locate the value?

9. Look at the following array definition:

```
double[][] sales = new double[8][10];
```

   a. How many rows does the array have?
   b. How many columns does the array have?
   c. How many elements does the array have?
   d. Write a statement that stores a number in the last column of the last row in the array.

Programming Challenges

MyProgrammingLab™ *Visit www.myprogramminglab.com to complete many of these Programming Challenges online and get instant feedback.*

1. Rainfall Class

Write a `RainFall` class that stores the total rainfall for each of 12 months into an array of `doubles`. The program should have methods that return the following:

- the total rainfall for the year
- the average monthly rainfall
- the month with the most rain
- the month with the least rain

Demonstrate the class in a complete program.

Input Validation: Do not accept negative numbers for monthly rainfall figures.

2. Payroll Class

Write a `Payroll` class that uses the following arrays as fields:

- **`employeeId`.** An array of seven integers to hold employee identification numbers. The array should be initialized with the following numbers:

  5658845 4520125 7895122 8777541
  8451277 1302850 7580489

- **`hours`.** An array of seven integers to hold the number of hours worked by each employee
- **`payRate`.** An array of seven `doubles` to hold each employee's hourly pay rate
- **`wages`.** An array of seven `doubles` to hold each employee's gross wages

The class should relate the data in each array through the subscripts. For example, the number in element 0 of the `hours` array should be the number of hours worked by the employee whose identification number is stored in element 0 of the `employeeId` array. That same employee's pay rate should be stored in element 0 of the `payRate` array.

In addition to the appropriate accessor and mutator methods, the class should have a method that accepts an employee's identification number as an argument and returns the gross pay for that employee.

Demonstrate the class in a complete program that displays each employee number and asks the user to enter that employee's hours and pay rate. It should then display each employee's identification number and gross wages.

Input Validation: Do not accept negative values for hours or numbers less than 6.00 for pay rate.

3. Charge Account Validation

Create a class with a method that accepts a charge account number as its argument. The method should determine whether the number is valid by comparing it to the following list of valid charge account numbers:

5658845	4520125	7895122	8777541	8451277	1302850
8080152	4562555	5552012	5050552	7825877	1250255
1005231	6545231	3852085	7576651	7881200	4581002

VideoNote

The Charge Account Validation Problem

These numbers should be stored in an array or an `ArrayList` object. Use a sequential search to locate the number passed as an argument. If the number is in the array, the method should return `true`, indicating the number is valid. If the number is not in the array, the method should return `false`, indicating the number is invalid.

Write a program that tests the class by asking the user to enter a charge account number. The program should display a message indicating whether the number is valid or invalid.

4. Charge Account Modification

Modify the charge account validation class that you wrote for Programming Challenge 3 so it reads the list of valid charge account numbers from a file. Use Notepad or another text editor to create the file.

5. Larger Than *n*

In a program, write a method that accepts two arguments: an array and a number *n*. Assume that the array contains integers. The method should display all of the numbers in the array that are greater than the number *n*.

6. Driver's License Exam

The local Driver's License Office has asked you to write a program that grades the written portion of the driver's license exam. The exam has 20 multiple choice questions. Here are the correct answers:

1. B	6. A	11. B	16. C
2. D	7. B	12. C	17. C
3. A	8. A	13. D	18. B
4. A	9. C	14. A	19. D
5. C	10. D	15. D	20. A

A student must correctly answer 15 of the 20 questions to pass the exam.

Write a class named `DriverExam` that holds the correct answers to the exam in an array field. The class should also have an array field that holds the student's answers. The class should have the following methods:

- `passed`. Returns true if the student passed the exam, or false if the student failed
- `totalCorrect`. Returns the total number of correctly answered questions

- `totalIncorrect`. Returns the total number of incorrectly answered questions
- `questionsMissed`. An `int` array containing the question numbers of the questions that the student missed

Demonstrate the class in a complete program that asks the user to enter a student's answers, and then displays the results returned from the `DriverExam` class's methods.

Input Validation: Only accept the letters A, B, C, or D as answers.

7. Quarterly Sales Statistics

Write a program that lets the user enter four quarterly sales figures for six divisions of a company. The figures should be stored in a two-dimensional array. Once the figures are entered, the program should display the following data for each quarter:

- A list of the sales figures by division
- Each division's increase or decrease from the previous quarter (this will not be displayed for the first quarter)
- The total sales for the quarter
- The company's increase or decrease from the previous quarter (this will not be displayed for the first quarter)
- The average sales for all divisions that quarter
- The division with the highest sales for that quarter

Input Validation: Do not accept negative numbers for sales figures.

8. Grade Book

A teacher has five students who have taken four tests. The teacher uses the following grading scale to assign a letter grade to a student, based on the average of his or her four test scores:

Test Score	Letter Grade
90–100	A
80–89	B
70–79	C
60–69	D
0–59	F

Write a class that uses a `String` array or an `ArrayList` object to hold the five students' names, an array of five characters to hold the five students' letter grades, and five arrays of four `doubles` each to hold each student's set of test scores. The class should have methods that return a specific student's name, the average test score, and a letter grade based on the average.

Demonstrate the class in a program that allows the user to enter each student's name and his or her four test scores. It should then display each student's average test score and letter grade.

Input Validation: Do not accept test scores less than zero or greater than 100.

9. Grade Book Modification

Modify the grade book application in Programming Challenge 8 so that it drops each student's lowest score when determining the test score averages and letter grades.

10. Lottery Application

Write a Lottery class that simulates a lottery. The class should have an array of five integers named lotteryNumbers. The constructor should use the Random class (from the Java API) to generate a random number in the range of 0 through 9 for each element in the array. The class should also have a method that accepts an array of five integers that represent a person's lottery picks. The method is to compare the corresponding elements in the two arrays and return the number of digits that match. For example, the following shows the lotteryNumbers array and the user's array with sample numbers stored in each. There are two matching digits (elements 2 and 4).

lotteryNumbers array:

User's array:

| 4 | 2 | 9 | 7 | 3 |

In addition, the class should have a method that returns a copy of the lotteryNumbers array.

Demonstrate the class in a program that asks the user to enter five numbers. The program should display the number of digits that match the randomly generated lottery numbers. If all of the digits match, display a message proclaiming the user a grand prize winner.

11. Array Operations

Write a program with an array that is initialized with test data. Use any primitive data type of your choice. The program should also have the following methods:

- getTotal. This method should accept a one-dimensional array as its argument and return the total of the values in the array.
- getAverage. This method should accept a one-dimensional array as its argument and return the average of the values in the array.
- getHighest. This method should accept a one-dimensional array as its argument and return the highest value in the array.
- getLowest. This method should accept a one-dimensional array as its argument and return the lowest value in the array.

Demonstrate each of the methods in the program.

12. Number Analysis Class

Write a class with a constructor that accepts a file name as its argument. Assume the file contains a series of numbers, each written on a separate line. The class should read the contents of the file into an array, and then displays the following data:

- The lowest number in the array
- The highest number in the array
- The total of the numbers in the array
- The average of the numbers in the array

This chapter's source code folder, available at www.pearsonhighered.com/gaddis, contains a text file named *Numbers.txt*. This file contains twelve random numbers. Write a program that tests the class by using this file.

13. Name Search

If you have downloaded this book's source code (the companion Web site is available at www.pearsonhighered.com/gaddis), you will find the following files in the *Chapter 07* folder:

- *GirlNames.txt* – This file contains a list of the 200 most popular names given to girls born in the United States for the years 2000 through 2009.
- *BoyNames.txt* – This file contains a list of the 200 most popular names given to boys born in the United States for the years 2000 through 2009.

Write a program that reads the contents of the two files into two separate arrays, or `ArrayLists`. The user should be able to enter a boy's name, a girl's name, or both, and the application will display messages indicating whether the names were among the most popular.

14. Population Data

If you have downloaded this book's source code (the companion Web site is available at www.pearsonhighered.com/gaddis), you will find a file named *USPopulation.txt* in the *Chapter 07* folder. The file contains the midyear population of the United States, in thousands, during the years 1950 through 1990. The first line in the file contains the population for 1950, the second line contains the population for 1951, and so forth.

Write a program that reads the file's contents into an array. The program should display the following data:

- The average annual change in population during the time period
- The year with the greatest increase in population during the time period
- The year with the smallest increase in population during the time period

15. World Series Champions

If you have downloaded this book's source code (the companion Web site is available at www.pearsonhighered.com/gaddis), you will find a file named *WorldSeriesWinners.txt*. This file contains a chronological list of the winning teams in the World Series from 1903 through 2009. (The first line in the file is the name of the team that won in 1903, and the last line is the name of the team that won in 2009. Note that the World Series was not played in 1904 or 1994, so those years are skipped in the file.)

Write a program that lets the user enter the name of a team, and then displays the number of times that team has won the World Series in the time period from 1903 through 2009.

TIP: Read the contents of the *WorldSeriesWinners.txt* file into an array, or an `ArrayList`. When the user enters the name of a team, the program should step through the array or `ArrayList`, counting the number of times the selected team appears.

16. 2D Array Operations

Write a program that creates a two-dimensional array initialized with test data. Use any primitive data type that you wish. The program should have the following methods:

- `getTotal`. This method should accept a two-dimensional array as its argument and return the total of all the values in the array.
- `getAverage`. This method should accept a two-dimensional array as its argument and return the average of all the values in the array.
- `getRowTotal`. This method should accept a two-dimensional array as its first argument and an integer as its second argument. The second argument should be the subscript of a row in the array. The method should return the total of the values in the specified row.
- `getColumnTotal`. This method should accept a two-dimensional array as its first argument and an integer as its second argument. The second argument should be the subscript of a column in the array. The method should return the total of the values in the specified column.
- `getHighestInRow`. This method should accept a two-dimensional array as its first argument and an integer as its second argument. The second argument should be the subscript of a row in the array. The method should return the highest value in the specified row of the array.
- `getLowestInRow`. This method should accept a two-dimensional array as its first argument and an integer as its second argument. The second argument should be the subscript of a row in the array. The method should return the lowest value in the specified row of the array.

Demonstrate each of the methods in this program.

17. Phone Book `ArrayList`

Write a class named `PhoneBookEntry` that has fields for a person's name and phone number. The class should have a constructor and appropriate accessor and mutator methods. Then write a program that creates at least five `PhoneBookEntry` objects and stores them in an `ArrayList`. Use a loop to display the contents of each object in the `ArrayList`.

18. Trivia Game

In this programming challenge, you will create a simple trivia game for two players. The program will work like this:

- Starting with player 1, each player gets a turn at answering 5 trivia questions. (There are 10 questions, 5 for each player.) When a question is displayed, four possible answers are also displayed. Only one of the answers is correct, and if the player selects the correct answer, he or she earns a point.
- After answers have been selected for all of the questions, the program displays the number of points earned by each player and declares the player with the highest number of points the winner.

You are to design a `Question` class to hold the data for a trivia question. The `Question` class should have `String` fields for the following data:

- A trivia question
- Possible answer 1
- Possible answer 2
- Possible answer 3
- Possible answer 4
- The number of the correct answer (1, 2, 3, or 4)

The `Question` class should have appropriate constructor(s), accessor, and mutator methods.

The program should create an array of 10 `Question` objects, one for each trivia question. (If you prefer, you can use an `ArrayList` instead of an array.) Make up your own trivia questions on the subject or subjects of your choice for the objects.

19. Lo Shu Magic Square

The Lo Shu Magic Square is a grid with 3 rows and 3 columns, shown in Figure 7-31. The Lo Shu Magic Square has the following properties:

- The grid contains the numbers 1 through 9 exactly.
- The sum of each row, each column, and each diagonal all add up to the same number. This is shown in Figure 7-32.

In a program you can simulate a magic square using a two-dimensional array. Write a method that accepts a two-dimensional array as an argument, and determines whether the array is a Lo Shu Magic Square. Test the function in a program.

Figure 7-31   Lo Shu Magic Square

4	9	2
3	5	7
8	1	6

Figure 7-32   Row, column, and diagonal sums in the Lo Shu Magic Square

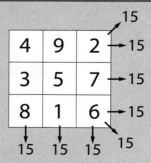

8

A Second Look at Classes and Objects

8.1 Static Class Members

CONCEPT: A static class member belongs to the class, not objects instantiated from the class.

A Quick Review of Instance Fields and Instance Methods

Recall from Chapter 6 that each instance of a class has its own set of fields, which are known as instance fields. You can create several instances of a class and store different values in each instance's fields. For example, the Rectangle class that we created in Chapter 6 has a length field and a width field. Let's say that box references an instance of the Rectangle class and we execute the following statement:

```
box.setLength(10);
```

This statement stores the value 10 in the length field that belongs to the instance that is referenced by box. You can think of instance fields as belonging to a specific instance of a class.

You will also recall that classes may have instance methods as well. When you call an instance method, it performs an operation on a specific instance of the class. For example, assuming that box references an instance of the Rectangle class, look at the following statement:

```
x = box.getLength();
```

This statement calls the getLength method, which returns the value of the length field that belongs to a specific instance of the Rectangle class: the one referenced by box. Both instance fields and instance methods are associated with a specific instance of a class, and they cannot be used until an instance of the class is created.

Static Members

It is possible to create a field or method that does not belong to any instance of a class. Such members are known as static fields and static methods. When a value is stored in a static field, it is not stored in an instance of the class. In fact, an instance of the class doesn't even have to exist in order for values to be stored in the class's static fields. Likewise, static methods do not operate on the fields that belong to any instance of the class. Instead, they can operate only on static fields. You can think of static fields and static methods as belonging to the class instead of an instance of the class. In this section, we will take a closer look at static members. First we will examine static fields.

Static Fields

When a field is declared with the key word static, there will be only one copy of the field in memory, regardless of the number of instances of the class that might exist. A single copy of a class's static field is shared by all instances of the class. For example, the Countable class shown in Code Listing 8-1 uses a static field to keep count of the number of instances of the class that are created.

Code Listing 8-1   **(Countable.java)**

```
 1  /**
 2      This class demonstrates a static field.
 3  */
 4
 5  public class Countable
 6  {
 7      private static int instanceCount = 0;
 8
 9      /**
10          The constructor increments the static
11          field instanceCount. This keeps track
12          of the number of instances of this
13          class that are created.
14      */
15
16      public Countable()
17      {
```

```
18    instanceCount++;
19   }
20
21   /**
22      The getInstanceCount method returns
23      the number of instances of this class
24      that have been created.
25      @return The value in the instanceCount field.
26   */
27
28   public int getInstanceCount()
29   {
30      return instanceCount;
31   }
32 }
```

First, notice in line 7 the declaration of the static field named `instanceCount` as follows:

```
private static int instanceCount = 0;
```

A static field is created by placing the key word `static` after the access specifier and before the field's data type. Notice that we have explicitly initialized the `instanceCount` field with the value 0. This initialization takes place only once, regardless of the number of instances of the class that are created.

> **NOTE:** Java automatically stores 0 in all uninitialized static member variables. The `instanceCount` field in this class is explicitly initialized so it is clear to anyone reading the code that the field starts with the value 0.

Next, look at the constructor in lines 16 through 19. The constructor uses the ++ operator to increment the `instanceCount` field. Each time an instance of the `Countable` class is created, the constructor will be called and the `instanceCount` field will be incremented. As a result, the `instanceCount` field will contain the number of instances of the `Countable` class that have been created. The `getInstanceCount` method, in lines 28 through 31, returns the value in `instanceCount`. The program in Code Listing 8-2 demonstrates this class.

Code Listing 8-2   (StaticDemo.java)

```
1  /**
2     This program demonstrates the Countable class.
3  */
4
5  public class StaticDemo
6  {
7     public static void main(String[] args)
8     {
9        int objectCount;
```

```
10
11          // Create three instances of the
12          // Countable class.
13          Countable object1 = new Countable();
14          Countable object2 = new Countable();
15          Countable object3 = new Countable();
16
17          // Get the number of instances from
18          // the class's static field.
19          objectCount = object1.getInstanceCount();
20          System.out.println(objectCount +
21                          " instances of the class " +
22                          "were created.");
23      }
24  }
```

Program Output

```
3 instances of the class were created.
```

The program creates three instances of the Countable class, referenced by the variables object1, object2, and object3. Although there are three instances of the class, there is only one copy of the static field. This is illustrated in Figure 8-1.

Figure 8-1 All instances of the class share the static field

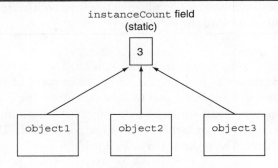

Instances of the Countable class

In line 19 the program calls the getInstanceCount method to retrieve the number of instances that have been created:

```
objectCount = object1.getInstanceCount();
```

Although the program calls the getInstanceCount method from object1, the same value would be returned from any of the objects.

Static Methods

When a class contains a static method, it isn't necessary for an instance of the class to be created in order to execute the method. The program in Code Listing 8-3 shows an example of a class with static methods.

Code Listing 8-3   (`Metric.java`)

```
 1 /**
 2    This class demonstrates static methods.
 3 */
 4
 5 public class Metric
 6 {
 7    /**
 8       The milesToKilometers method converts a
 9       distance in miles to kilometers.
10       @param m The distance in miles.
11       @return The distance in kilometers.
12    */
13
14    public static double milesToKilometers(double m)
15    {
16       return m * 1.609;
17    }
18
19    /**
20       The kilometersToMiles method converts
21       a distance in kilometers to miles.
22       @param k The distance in kilometers.
23       @return The distance in miles.
24    */
25
26    public static double kilometersToMiles(double k)
27    {
28       return k / 1.609;
29    }
30 }
```

A static method is created by placing the key word `static` after the access specifier in the method header. The `Metric` class has two static methods: `milesToKilometers` and `kilometersToMiles`. Because they are declared as `static`, they belong to the class and may be called without any instances of the class being in existence. You simply write the name of the class before the dot operator in the method call. Here is an example:

```
kilometers = Metric.milesToKilometers(10.0);
```

This statement calls the `milesToKilometers` method, passing the value `10.0` as an argument. Notice that the method is not called from an instance of the class, but is called directly from the `Metric` class. Code Listing 8-4 shows a program that uses the `Metric` class. Figure 8-2 shows an example of interaction with the program.

Code Listing 8-4 (MetricDemo.java)

```java
 1 import javax.swing.JOptionPane;
 2
 3 /**
 4    This program demonstrates the Metric class.
 5 */
 6
 7 public class MetricDemo
 8 {
 9    public static void main(String[] args)
10    {
11       String input; // To hold input
12       double miles; // A distance in miles
13       double kilos; // A distance in kilometers
14
15       // Get a distance in miles.
16       input = JOptionPane.showInputDialog("Enter " +
17                           "a distance in miles.");
18       miles = Double.parseDouble(input);
19
20       // Convert the distance to kilometers.
21       kilos = Metric.milesToKilometers(miles);
22       JOptionPane.showMessageDialog(null,
23         String.format("%,.2f miles equals %,.2f kilometers.",
24                      miles, kilos));
25
26       // Get a distance in kilometers.
27       input = JOptionPane.showInputDialog("Enter " +
28                        "a distance in kilometers: ");
29       kilos = Double.parseDouble(input);
30
31       // Convert the distance to kilometers.
32       miles = Metric.kilometersToMiles(kilos);
33       JOptionPane.showMessageDialog(null,
34         String.format("%,.2f kilometers equals %,.2f miles.",
35                      kilos, miles));
```

```
36
37        System.exit(0);
38    }
39 }
```

Figure 8-2   Interaction with the `MetricDemo.java` program

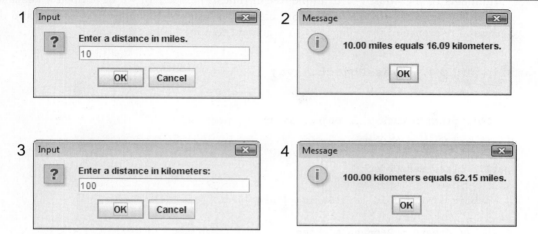

Static methods are convenient for many tasks because they can be called directly from the class, as needed. They are most often used to create utility classes that perform operations on data, but have no need to collect and store data. The `Metric` class is a good example. It is used as a container to hold methods that convert miles to kilometers and vice versa, but is not intended to store any data.

The only limitation that static methods have is that they cannot refer to non-static members of the class. This means that any method called from a static method must also be static. It also means that if the method uses any of the class's fields, they must be static as well.

 Checkpoint

MyProgrammingLab™ *www.myprogramminglab.com*

8.1   What is the difference between an instance field and a static field?

8.2   What action is possible with a static method that isn't possible with an instance method?

8.3   Describe the limitation of static methods.

8.2 Passing Objects as Arguments to Methods

CONCEPT: To pass an object as a method argument, you pass an object reference.

In Chapter 5, we discussed how primitive values, as well as references to String objects, can be passed as arguments to methods. You can also pass references to other types of objects as arguments to methods. For example, recall that in Chapter 6, we developed a Rectangle class. The program in Code Listing 8-5 creates an instance of the Rectangle class and then passes a reference to that object as an argument to a method.

Code Listing 8-5 (PassObject.java)

```java
1   /**
2       This program passes an object as an argument.
3   */
4
5   public class PassObject
6   {
7      public static void main(String[] args)
8      {
9         // Create a Rectangle object.
10        Rectangle box = new Rectangle(12.0, 5.0);
11
12        // Pass a reference to the object to
13        // the displayRectangle method.
14        displayRectangle(box);
15     }
16
17     /**
18         The displayRectangle method displays the
19         length and width of a rectangle.
20         @param r A reference to a Rectangle
21         object.
22     */
23
24     public static void displayRectangle(Rectangle r)
25     {
26        // Display the length and width.
27        System.out.println("Length : " + r.getLength() +
28                           " Width : " + r.getWidth());
29     }
30  }
```

Program Output

```
Length : 12.0 Width : 5.0
```

In this program's main method, the box variable is a Rectangle reference variable. In line 14 its value is passed as an argument to the displayRectangle method. The displayRectangle method has a parameter variable, r, which is also a Rectangle reference variable, that receives the argument.

Recall that a reference variable holds the memory address of an object. When the displayRectangle method is called, the address that is stored in box is passed into the r parameter variable. This is illustrated in Figure 8-3. This means that when the displayRectangle method is executing, box and r both reference the same object. This is illustrated in Figure 8-4.

Figure 8-3 Passing a reference as an argument

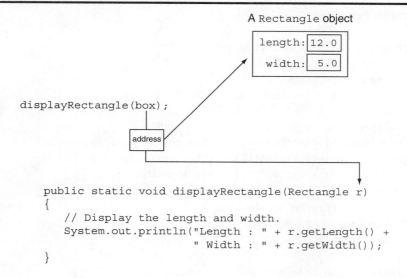

Figure 8-4 Both box and r reference the same object

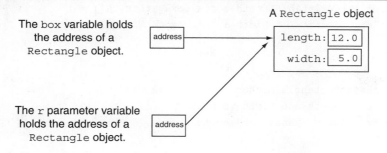

Recall from Chapter 5 that when a variable is passed as an argument to a method, it is said to be passed by value. This means that a copy of the variable's value is passed into the method's parameter. When the method changes the contents of the parameter variable, it does not affect the contents of the original variable that was passed as an argument. When a reference variable is passed as an argument to a method, however, the method has access to the object that the variable references. As you can see from Figure 8-4, the displayRectangle method has access to the same Rectangle object that the box variable references. When a method receives an object reference as an argument, it is possible for the method to modify the contents of the object referenced by the variable. This is demonstrated in Code Listing 8-6.

Code Listing 8-6 (PassObject2.java)

```java
 1 /**
 2    This program passes an object as an argument.
 3    The object is modified by the receiving method.
 4 */
 5
 6 public class PassObject2
 7 {
 8    public static void main(String[] args)
 9    {
10       // Create a Rectangle object.
11       Rectangle box = new Rectangle(12.0, 5.0);
12
13       // Display the object's contents.
14       System.out.println("Contents of the box object:");
15       System.out.println("Length : " + box.getLength() +
16                          " Width : " + box.getWidth());
17
18       // Pass a reference to the object to the
19       // changeRectangle method.
20       changeRectangle(box);
21
22       // Display the object's contents again.
23       System.out.println("\nNow the contents of the " +
24                          "box object are:");
25       System.out.println("Length : " + box.getLength() +
26                          " Width : " + box.getWidth());
27    }
28
29    /**
30       The changeRectangle method sets a Rectangle
31       object's length and width to 0.
32       @param r The Rectangle object to change.
33    */
34
35    public static void changeRectangle(Rectangle r)
36    {
37       r.setLength(0.0);
38       r.setWidth(0.0);
39    }
40 }
```

Program Output

Contents of the box object:
Length : 12.0 Width : 5.0

Now the contents of the box object are:
Length : 0.0 Width : 0.0

When writing a method that receives the value of a reference variable as an argument, you must take care not to accidentally modify the contents of the object that is referenced by the variable.

8.3 Returning Objects from Methods

CONCEPT: A method can return a reference to an object.

VideoNote
eturning Objects
from Methods

Just as methods can be written to return an int, double, float, or other primitive data type, they can also be written to return a reference to an object. For example, recall the BankAccount class that was discussed in Chapter 6. The program in Code Listing 8-7 uses a method, getAccount, which returns a reference to a BankAccount object. Figure 8-5 shows example interaction with the program.

Code Listing 8-7   (ReturnObject.java)

```
 1 import javax.swing.JOptionPane;
 2
 3 /**
 4    This program demonstrates how a method
 5    can return a reference to an object.
 6 */
 7
 8 public class ReturnObject
 9 {
10    public static void main(String[] args)
11    {
12       BankAccount account;
13
14       // Get a reference to a BankAccount object.
15       account = getAccount();
16
17       // Display the account's balance.
18       JOptionPane.showMessageDialog(null,
19             "The account has a balance of $" +
20             account.getBalance());
21
```

```
22          System.exit(0);
23      }
24
25      /**
26          The getAccount method creates a BankAccount
27          object with the balance specified by the
28          user.
29          @return A reference to the object.
30      */
31
32      public static BankAccount getAccount()
33      {
34          String input;         // To hold input
35          double balance;       // Account balance
36
37          // Get the balance from the user.
38          input = JOptionPane.showInputDialog("Enter " +
39                              "the account balance.");
40          balance = Double.parseDouble(input);
41
42          // Create a BankAccount object and return
43          // a reference to it.
44          return new BankAccount(balance);
45      }
46  }
```

Figure 8-5   Interaction with the `ReturnObject.java` program

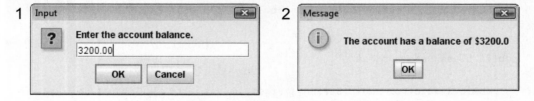

Notice that the `getAccount` method has a return data type of `BankAccount`. Figure 8-6 shows the method's return type, which is listed in the method header.

Figure 8-6   The `getAccount` method header

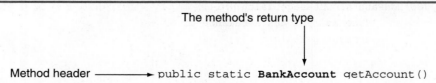

A return type of BankAccount means the method returns a reference to a BankAccount object when it terminates. The following statement, which appears in line 15, assigns the getAccount method's return value to account:

```
account = getAccount();
```

After this statement executes, the account variable will reference the BankAccount object that was returned from the getAccount method.

Now let's look at the getAccount method. In lines 38 and 39 the method uses a JOptionPane dialog box to get the account balance from the user. In line 40 the value entered by the user is converted to a double and assigned to balance, a local variable. The last statement in the method, in line 44, is the following return statement:

```
return new BankAccount(balance);
```

This statement uses the new key word to create a BankAccount object, passing balance as an argument to the constructor. The address of the object is then returned from the method, as illustrated in Figure 8-7. Back in line 15, where the method is called, the address is assigned to account.

Figure 8-7 The getAccount method returns a reference to a BankAccount object

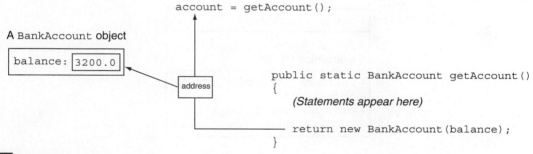

8.4 The toString Method

CONCEPT: Most classes can benefit from having a method named **toString**, which is implicitly called under certain circumstances. Typically, the method returns a string that represents the state of an object.

Quite often we need to display a message that indicates an object's state. An object's *state* is simply the data that is stored in the object's fields at any given moment. For example, recall that the BankAccount class has one field: balance. At any given moment, a BankAccount object's balance field will hold some value. The value of the balance field represents the object's state at that moment. The following might be an example of code that displays a BankAccount object's state:

```
BankAccount account = new BankAccount(1500.0);
System.out.println("The account balance is $" +
                account.getBalance());
```

The first statement creates a BankAccount object, passing the value 1500.0 to the constructor. Recall that the BankAccount constructor stores this value in the balance field. After this statement executes, the account variable will reference the BankAccount object. In the second statement, the System.out.println method displays a string showing the value of the object's balance field. The output of this statement will look like this:

```
The account balance is $1500.0
```

Let's take a closer look at the second statement, which displays the state of the object. The argument that is passed to System.out.println is a string, which is put together from two pieces. The concatenation operator (+) joins the pieces together. The first piece is the string literal "The account balance is $". To this, the value returned from the getBalance method is concatenated. The resulting string, which is displayed on the screen, represents the current state of the object.

Creating a string that represents the state of an object is such a common task that many programmers equip their classes with a method that returns such a string. In Java, it is standard practice to name this method toString. Let's look at an example of a class that has a toString method. Figure 8-8 shows the UML diagram for the Stock class, which holds data about a company's stock.

Figure 8-8 UML diagram for the Stock class

```
┌─────────────────────────────────────┐
│                Stock                  │
├─────────────────────────────────────┤
│ - symbol : String                     │
│ - sharePrice : double                 │
├─────────────────────────────────────┤
│ + Stock(sym : String, price : double) :│
│ + getSymbol() : String                │
│ + getSharePrice() : double            │
│ + toString() : String                 │
└─────────────────────────────────────┘
```

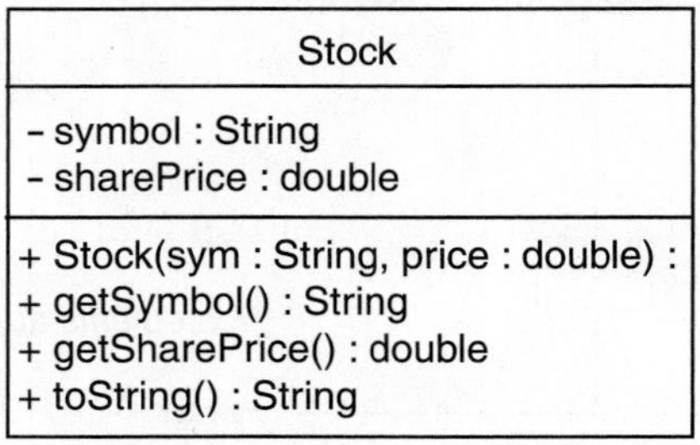

This class has two fields: symbol and sharePrice. The symbol field holds the trading symbol for the company's stock. This is a short series of characters that are used to identify the stock on the stock exchange. For example, the XYZ Company's stock might have the trading symbol XYZ. The sharePrice field holds the current price per share of the stock. Table 8-1 describes the class's methods.

Table 8-1 The Stock class methods

Method	Description
Constructor	This constructor accepts arguments that are assigned to the symbol and sharePrice fields.
getSymbol	This method returns the value in the symbol field.
getSharePrice	This method returns the value in the sharePrice field.
toString	This method returns a string representing the state of the object. The string will be appropriate for displaying on the screen.

Code Listing 8-8 shows the code for the Stock class. (This file is in the source code folder *Chapter 08\Stock Class Phase 1.*)

Code Listing 8-8   (Stock.java)

```java
 1 /**
 2    The Stock class holds data about a stock.
 3 */
 4
 5 public class Stock
 6 {
 7    private String symbol;        // Trading symbol of stock
 8    private double sharePrice;    // Current price per share
 9
10    /**
11       Constructor
12       @param sym The stock's trading symbol.
13       @param price The stock's share price.
14    */
15
16    public Stock(String sym, double price)
17    {
18       symbol = sym;
19       sharePrice = price;
20    }
21
22    /**
23       getSymbol method
24       @return The stock's trading symbol.
25    */
26
27    public String getSymbol()
28    {
29       return symbol;
30    }
31
32    /**
33       getSharePrice method
34       @return The stock's share price
35    */
36
37    public double getSharePrice()
38    {
39       return sharePrice;
40    }
41
42    /**
```

```
43          toString method
44          @return A string indicating the object's
45                  trading symbol and share price.
46     */
47
48     public String toString()
49     {
50        // Create a string describing the stock.
51        String str = "Trading symbol: " + symbol +
52                     "\nShare price: " + sharePrice;
53
54        // Return the string.
55        return str;
56     }
57 }
```

The `toString` method appears in lines 48 through 56. The method creates a string listing the stock's trading symbol and price per share. This string is then returned from the method. A call to the method can then be passed to `System.out.println`, as shown in the following code:

```
Stock xyzCompany = new Stock ("XYZ", 9.62);
System.out.println(xyzCompany.toString());
```

This code would produce the following output:

```
Trading symbol: XYZ
Share price: 9.62
```

In actuality, it is unnecessary to explicitly call the `toString` method in this example. If you write a `toString` method for a class, Java will automatically call the method when the object is passed as an argument to `print` or `println`. The following code would produce the same output as that previously shown:

```
Stock xyzCompany = new Stock ("XYZ", 9.62);
System.out.println(xyzCompany);
```

Java also implicitly calls an object's `toString` method any time you concatenate an object of the class with a string. For example, the following code would implicitly call the `xyzCompany` object's `toString` method:

```
Stock xyzCompany = new Stock ("XYZ", 9.62);
System.out.println("The stock data is:\n" + xyzCompany);
```

This code would produce the following output:

```
The stock data is:
Trading symbol: XYZ
Share price: 9.62
```

Code Listing 8-9 shows a complete program demonstrating the `Stock` class's `toString` method. (This file is in the source code folder *Chapter 08\Stock Class Phase 1.*)

Code Listing 8-9   (`StockDemo1.java`)

```
 1 /**
 2    This program demonstrates the Stock class's
 3    toString method.
 4 */
 5
 6 public class StockDemo1
 7 {
 8    public static void main(String[] args)
 9    {
10       // Create a Stock object for the XYZ Company.
11       // The trading symbol is XYZ and the current
12       // price per share is $9.62.
13       Stock xyzCompany = new Stock ("XYZ", 9.62);
14
15       // Display the object's values.
16       System.out.println(xyzCompany);
17    }
18 }
```

Program Output

```
Trading symbol: XYZ
Share price: 9.62
```

 NOTE: Every class automatically has a `toString` method that returns a string containing the object's class name, followed by the @ symbol, followed by an integer that is usually based on the object's memory address. This method is called when necessary if you have not provided your own `toString` method. You will learn more about this in Chapter 10.

8.5 Writing an equals Method

CONCEPT: You cannot determine whether two objects contain the same data by comparing them with the == operator. Instead, the class must have a method such as **equals** for comparing the contents of objects.

Recall from Chapter 3 that the `String` class has a method named `equals`, which determines whether two strings are equal. You can write an `equals` method for any of your own classes as well.

In fact, you must write an `equals` method (or one that works like it) for a class in order to determine whether two objects of the class contain the same values. This is because you cannot use the == operator to compare the contents of two objects. For example, the following code might appear to compare the contents of two Stock objects, but in reality does not:

```java
// Create two Stock objects with the same values.
Stock company1 = new Stock("XYZ", 9.62);
Stock company2 = new Stock("XYZ", 9.62);

// Use the == operator to compare the objects.
// (This is a mistake.)
if (company1 == company2)
   System.out.println("Both objects are the same.");
else
   System.out.println("The objects are different.");
```

When you use the == operator with reference variables, the operator compares the memory addresses that the variables contain, not the contents of the objects referenced by the variables. This is illustrated in Figure 8-9.

Figure 8-9 The if statement tests the contents of the reference variables, not the contents of the objects the variables reference

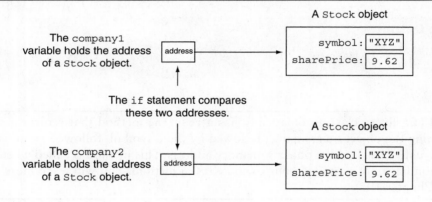

Because the two variables reference different objects in memory, they will contain different addresses. Therefore, the result of the boolean expression company1 == company2 is false and the code reports that the objects are not the same. Instead of using the == operator to compare the two Stock objects, we should write an equals method that compares the contents of the two objects.

In the source code folder *Chapter 08\Stock Class Phase 2,* you will find a revision of the Stock class. This version of the class has an equals method. The code for the method follows (no other part of the class has changed, so only the equals method is shown):

```java
public boolean equals(Stock object2)
{
   boolean status;

   // Determine whether this object's symbol and
   // sharePrice fields are equal to object2's
```

```
                 // symbol and sharePrice fields.
                 if (symbol.equals(object2.symbol) &&
                     sharePrice == object2.sharePrice)
                     status = true;    // Yes, the objects are equal.
                 else
                     status = false;   // No, the objects are not equal.

                 // Return the value in status.
                 return status;
          }
```

The equals method accepts a Stock object as its argument. The parameter variable object2 will reference the object that was passed as an argument. The if statement performs the following comparison: If the symbol field of the calling object is equal to the symbol field of object2, *and* the sharePrice field of the calling object is equal to the sharePrice field of object2, then the two objects contain the same values. In this case, the local variable status (a boolean) is set to true. Otherwise, status is set to false. Finally, the method returns the value of the status variable.

Notice that the method can access object2's symbol and sharePrice fields directly. Because object2 references a Stock object, and the equals method is a member of the Stock class, the method is allowed to access object2's private fields.

The program in Code Listing 8-10 demonstrates the equals method. (This file is also stored in the source code folder *Chapter 08\Stock Class Phase 2.*)

Code Listing 8-10   (**StockCompare.java**)

```
 1  /**
 2      This program uses the Stock class's equals
 3      method to compare two Stock objects.
 4  */
 5
 6  public class StockCompare
 7  {
 8      public static void main(String[] args)
 9      {
10          // Create two Stock objects with the same values.
11          Stock company1 = new Stock("XYZ", 9.62);
12          Stock company2 = new Stock("XYZ", 9.62);
13
14          // Use the equals method to compare the objects.
15          if (company1.equals(company2))
16              System.out.println("Both objects are the same.");
17          else
18              System.out.println("The objects are different.");
19      }
20  }
```

Program Output

Both objects are the same.

If you want to be able to compare the objects of a given class, you should always write an `equals` method for the class.

> **NOTE:** Every class automatically has an `equals` method, which works the same as the `==` operator. This method is called when necessary if you have not provided your own `equals` method. You will learn more about this in Chapter 10.

8.6 Methods That Copy Objects

CONCEPT: You can simplify the process of duplicating objects by equipping a class with a method that returns a copy of an object.

You cannot make a copy of an object with a simple assignment statement, as you would with a primitive variable. For example, look at the following code:

```
Stock company1 = new Stock("XYZ", 9.62);
Stock company2 = company1;
```

The first statement creates a `Stock` object and assigns its address to the `company1` variable. The second statement assigns `company1` to `company2`. This does not make a copy of the object referenced by `company1`. Rather, it makes a copy of the address that is stored in `company1` and stores that address in `company2`. After this statement executes, both the `company1` and `company2` variables will reference the same object. This is illustrated in Figure 8-10.

Figure 8-10 Both variables reference the same object

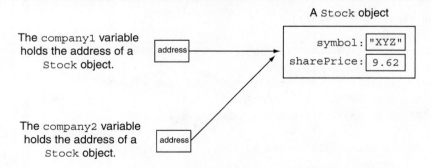

This type of assignment operation is called a *reference copy* because only the object's address is copied, not the actual object itself. To copy the object itself, you must create a new object and then set the new object's fields to the same values as the fields of the object that is being copied. This process can be simplified by equipping the class with a method that performs this operation. The method then returns a reference to the duplicate object.

In the source code folder *Chapter 08\Stock Class Phase 3*, you will find a revision of the `Stock` class. This version of the class has a method named `copy`, which returns a copy of a `Stock` object. The code for the method follows (no other part of the class has changed so only the copy method is shown):

```java
public Stock copy()
{
    // Create a new Stock object and initialize it
    // with the same data held by the calling object.
    Stock copyObject = new Stock(symbol, sharePrice);

    // Return a reference to the new object.
    return copyObject;
}
```

The `copy` method creates a new `Stock` object and passes the calling object's `symbol` and `sharePrice` fields as arguments to the constructor. This makes the new object a copy of the calling object. The program in Code Listing 8-11 demonstrates the `copy` method. (This file is also stored in the source code folder *Chapter 08\Stock Class Phase 3*.)

Code Listing 8-11   (`ObjectCopy.java`)

```java
 1 /**
 2    This program uses the Stock class's copy method
 3    to create a copy of a Stock object.
 4 */
 5
 6 public class ObjectCopy
 7 {
 8    public static void main(String[] args)
 9    {
10       // Create a Stock object.
11       Stock company1 = new Stock("XYZ", 9.62);
12
13       // Declare a Stock variable
14       Stock company2;
15
16       // Make company2 reference a copy of the object
17       // referenced by company1.
18       company2 = company1.copy();
19
20       // Display the contents of both objects.
21       System.out.println("Company 1:\n" + company1);
22       System.out.println();
23       System.out.println("Company 2:\n" + company2);
24
25       // Confirm that we actually have two objects.
26       if (company1 == company2)
```

```
27        {
28            System.out.println("The company1 and company2 " +
29                    "variables reference the same object.");
30        }
31        else
32        {
33            System.out.println("The company1 and company2 " +
34                    "variables reference different objects.");
35        }
36    }
37 }
```

Program Output

```
Company 1:
Trading symbol: XYZ
Share price: 9.62

Company 2:
Trading symbol: XYZ
Share price: 9.62
The company1 and company2 variables reference different objects.
```

Copy Constructors

Another way to create a copy of an object is to use a copy constructor. A *copy constructor* is simply a constructor that accepts an object of the same class as an argument. It makes the object that is being created a copy of the object that was passed as an argument.

In the source code folder *Chapter 08\Stock Class Phase 4,* you will find another revision of the Stock class. This version of the class has a copy constructor. The code for the copy constructor follows (no other part of the class has changed, so only the copy constructor is shown):

```
public Stock(Stock object2)
{
    symbol = object2.symbol;
    sharePrice = object2.sharePrice;
}
```

Notice that the constructor accepts a Stock object as an argument. The parameter variable object2 will reference the object that was passed as an argument. The constructor copies the values that are in object2's symbol and sharePrice fields to the symbol and sharePrice fields of the object that is being created.

The following code segment demonstrates the copy constructor. It creates a Stock object referenced by the variable company1. Then it creates another Stock object referenced by the variable company2. The object referenced by company2 is a copy of the object referenced by company1.

```
// Create a Stock object.
Stock company1 = new Stock("XYZ", 9.62);
// Create another Stock object that is a copy of the company1 object.
Stock company2 = new Stock(company1);
```

8.7 Aggregation

CONCEPT: Aggregation occurs when an instance of a class is a field in another class.

In real life, objects are frequently made of other objects. A house, for example, is made of door objects, window objects, wall objects, and much more. It is the combination of all these objects that makes a house object.

VideoNote

Aggregation

When designing software, it sometimes makes sense to create an object from other objects. For example, suppose you need an object to represent a course that you are taking in college. You decide to create a Course class, which will hold the following information:

- The course name
- The instructor's last name, first name, and office number
- The textbook's title, author, and publisher

In addition to the course name, the class will hold items related to the instructor and the textbook. You could put fields for each of these items in the Course class. However, a good design principle is to separate related items into their own classes. In this example, an Instructor class could be created to hold the instructor-related data and a TextBook class could be created to hold the textbook-related data. Instances of these classes could then be used as fields in the Course class.

Let's take a closer look at how this might be done. Figure 8-11 shows a UML diagram for the Instructor class. To keep things simple, the class has only the following methods:

- A constructor, which accepts arguments for the instructor's last name, first name, and office number
- A copy constructor
- A set method, which can be used to set all of the class's fields
- A toString method

Figure 8-11   UML diagram for the Instructor class

Instructor
– lastName : String – firstName : String – officeNumber : String

+ Instructor(lname : String, fname : String,
          office : String) :
+ Instructor(object2 : Instructor) :
+ set(lname : String, fname : String,
          office : String) : void
+ toString() : String

The code for the Instructor class is shown in Code Listing 8-12.

Code Listing 8-12 (Instructor.java)

```java
1 /**
2    This class stores data about an instructor.
3 */
4
5 public class Instructor
6 {
7    private String lastName;      // Last name
8    private String firstName;     // First name
9    private String officeNumber;  // Office number
10
11   /**
12      This constructor initializes the last name,
13      first name, and office number.
14      @param lname The instructor's last name.
15      @param fname The instructor's first name.
16      @param office The office number.
17   */
18
19   public Instructor(String lname, String fname,
20                     String office)
21   {
22      lastName = lname;
23      firstName = fname;
24      officeNumber = office;
25   }
26
27   /**
28      The copy constructor initializes the object
29      as a copy of another Instructor object.
30      @param object2 The object to copy.
31   */
32
33   public Instructor(Instructor object2)
34   {
35      lastName = object2.lastName;
36      firstName = object2.firstName;
37      officeNumber = object2.officeNumber;
38   }
39
40   /**
41      The set method sets a value for each field.
42      @param lname The instructor's last name.
43      @param fname The instructor's first name.
```

```
44            @param office The office number.
45        */
46
47        public void set(String lname, String fname,
48                        String office)
49        {
50            lastName = lname;
51            firstName = fname;
52            officeNumber = office;
53        }
54
55        /**
56            toString method
57            @return A string containing the instructor
58                    information.
59        */
60
61        public String toString()
62        {
63            // Create a string representing the object.
64            String str = "Last Name: " + lastName +
65                         "\nFirst Name: " + firstName +
66                         "\nOffice Number: " + officeNumber;
67
68            // Return the string.
69            return str;
70        }
71 }
```

Figure 8-12 shows a UML diagram for the TextBook class. As before, we want to keep the class simple. The only methods it has are a constructor, a copy constructor, a set method, and a toString method. The code for the TextBook class is shown in Code Listing 8-13.

Figure 8-12 UML diagram for the TextBook class

TextBook
- title : String - author : String - publisher : String

+ TextBook(textTitle : String, auth : String,
        pub : String) :
+ TextBook(object2 : TextBook) :
+ set(textTitle : String, auth : String,
    pub : String) : void
+ toString() : String

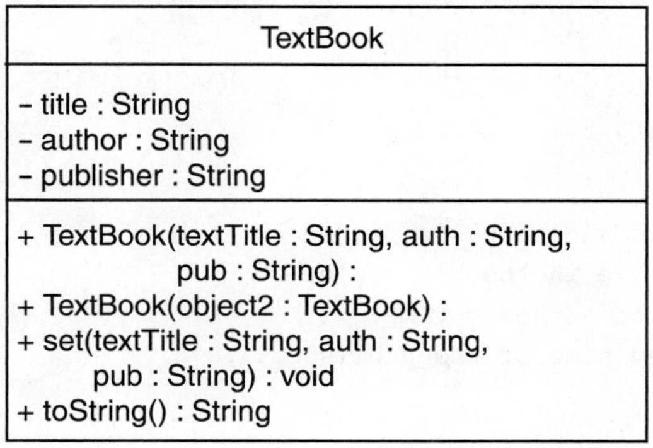

Code Listing 8-13 `(TextBook.java)`

```java
 1  /**
 2      This class stores data about a textbook.
 3  */
 4
 5  public class TextBook
 6  {
 7     private String title;        // Title of the book
 8     private String author;       // Author's last name
 9     private String publisher;    // Name of publisher
10
11     /**
12         This constructor initializes the title,
13         author, and publisher fields
14         @param textTitle The book's title.
15         @param auth The author's name.
16         @param pub The name of the publisher.
17     */
18
19     public TextBook(String textTitle, String auth,
20                     String pub)
21     {
22        title = textTitle;
23        author = auth;
24        publisher = pub;
25     }
26
27     /**
28         The copy constructor initializes the object
29         as a copy of another TextBook object.
30         @param object2 The object to copy.
31     */
32
33     public TextBook(TextBook object2)
34     {
35        title = object2.title;
36        author = object2.author;
37        publisher = object2.publisher;
38     }
39
40     /**
41         The set method sets a value for each field.
42         @param textTitle The book's title.
43         @param auth The author's name.
44         @param pub The name of the publisher.
45     */
```

```
46
47    public void set(String textTitle, String auth,
48                    String pub)
49    {
50       title = textTitle;
51       author = auth;
52       publisher = pub;
53    }
54
55    /**
56       toString method
57       @return A string containing the textbook
58              information.
59    */
60
61    public String toString()
62    {
63       // Create a string representing the object.
64       String str = "Title: " + title +
65                    "\nAuthor: " + author +
66                    "\nPublisher: " + publisher;
67
68       // Return the string.
69       return str;
70    }
71 }
```

Figure 8-13 shows a UML diagram for the Course class. Notice that the Course class has an Instructor object and a TextBook object as fields. Making an instance of one class a field in another class is called *object aggregation*. The word *aggregate* means "a whole which is made of constituent parts." In this example, the Course class is an aggregate class because it is made of constituent objects.

When an instance of one class is a member of another class, it is said that there is a "has a" relationship between the classes. For example, the relationships that exist among the Course, Instructor, and TextBook classes can be described as follows:

- The course *has an* instructor.
- The course *has a* textbook.

The "has a" relationship is sometimes called a *whole-part relationship* because one object is part of a greater whole. The code for the Course class is shown in Code Listing 8-14.

Figure 8-13 UML diagram for the Course class

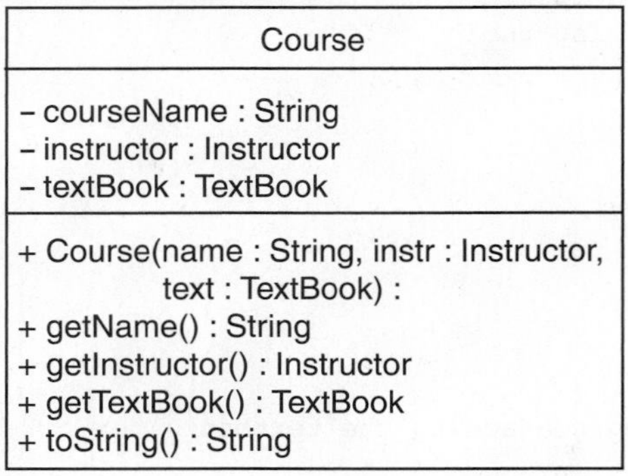

Course
– courseName : String – instructor : Instructor – textBook : TextBook
+ Course(name : String, instr : Instructor,   text : TextBook) : + getName() : String + getInstructor() : Instructor + getTextBook() : TextBook + toString() : String

Code Listing 8-14 (Course.java)

```java
1  /**
2     This class stores data about a course.
3  */
4
5  public class Course
6  {
7     private String courseName;      // Name of the course
8     private Instructor instructor;  // The instructor
9     private TextBook textBook;      // The textbook
10
11    /**
12       This constructor initializes the courseName,
13       instructor, and text fields.
14       @param name The name of the course.
15       @param instructor An Instructor object.
16       @param text A TextBook object.
17    */
18
19    public Course(String name, Instructor instr,
20                  TextBook text)
21    {
22       // Assign the courseName.
23       courseName = name;
24
25       // Create a new Instructor object, passing
26       // instr as an argument to the copy constructor.
27       instructor = new Instructor(instr);
28
29       // Create a new TextBook object, passing
30       // text as an argument to the copy constructor.
31       textBook = new TextBook(text);
32    }
```

```
33
34     /**
35        getName method
36        @return The name of the course.
37     */
38
39     public String getName()
40     {
41        return courseName;
42     }
43
44     /**
45        getInstructor method
46        @return A reference to a copy of this course's
47                Instructor object.
48     */
49
50     public Instructor getInstructor()
51     {
52        // Return a copy of the instructor object.
53        return new Instructor(instructor);
54     }
55
56     /**
57        getTextBook method
58        @return A reference to a copy of this course's
59                TextBook object.
60     */
61
62     public TextBook getTextBook()
63     {
64        // Return a copy of the textBook object.
65        return new TextBook(textBook);
66     }
67
68     /**
69        toString method
70        @return A string containing the course information.
71     */
72
73     public String toString()
74     {
75        // Create a string representing the object.
76        String str = "Course name: " + courseName +
77                     "\nInstructor Information:\n" +
78                     instructor +
79                     "\nTextbook Information:\n" +
80                     textBook;
81
```

```
82        // Return the string.
83        return str;
84    }
85 }
```

The program in Code Listing 8-15 demonstrates the Course class.

Code Listing 8-15   (CourseDemo.java)

```
1 /**
2     This program demonstrates the Course class.
3 */
4
5 public class CourseDemo
6 {
7    public static void main(String[] args)
8    {
9       // Create an Instructor object.
10      Instructor myInstructor =
11          new Instructor("Kramer", "Shawn", "RH3010");
12
13      // Create a TextBook object.
14      TextBook myTextBook =
15          new TextBook("Starting Out with Java",
16                      "Gaddis", "Pearson");
17
18      // Create a Course object.
19      Course myCourse =
20          new Course("Intro to Java", myInstructor,
21                      myTextBook);
22
23      // Display the course information.
24      System.out.println(myCourse);
25    }
26 }
```

Program Output

```
Course name: Intro to Java
Instructor Information:
Last Name: Kramer
First Name: Shawn
Office Number: RH3010
Textbook Information:
Title: Starting Out with Java
Author: Gaddis
Publisher: Pearson
```

Aggregation in UML Diagrams

You show aggregation in a UML diagram by connecting two classes with a line that has an open diamond at one end. The diamond is closest to the class that is the aggregate. Figure 8-14 is a UML diagram that shows the relationship among the `Course`, `Instructor`, and `TextBook` classes. The open diamond is closest to the `Course` class because it is the aggregate (the whole).

Figure 8-14   UML diagram showing aggregation

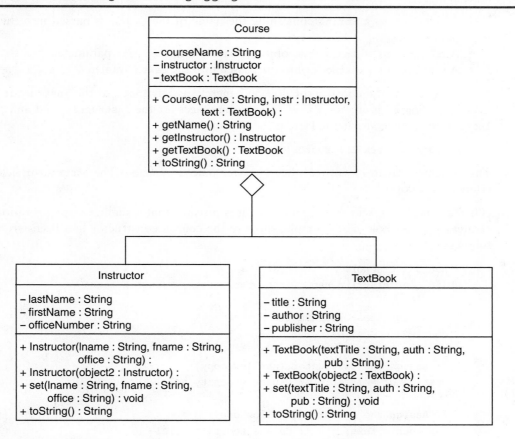

Security Issues with Aggregate Classes

When writing an aggregate class, you should be careful not to unintentionally create "security holes" that can allow code outside the class to modify private data inside the class. We will focus on the following two specific practices that can help prevent security holes in your classes:

- **Perform Deep Copies When Creating Field Objects**
  An aggregate object contains references to other objects. When you make a copy of the aggregate object, it is important that you also make copies of the objects it references. This is known as a *deep copy*. If you make a copy of an aggregate object, but only make a reference copy of the objects it references, then you have performed a *shallow copy*.

- **Return Copies of Field Objects, Not the Originals**
  When a method in the aggregate class returns a reference to a field object, return a reference to a copy of the field object.

Let's discuss each of these practices in more depth.

Perform Deep Copies When Creating Field Objects

Let's take a closer look at the `Course` class. First, notice the arguments that the constructor accepts in lines 19 and 20 as follows:

- A reference to a `String` containing the name of the course is passed into the `name` parameter.
- A reference to an `Instructor` object is passed into the `instr` parameter.
- A reference to a `TextBook` object is passed into the `text` parameter.

Next, notice that the constructor does not merely assign `instr` to the `instructor` field. Instead, in line 27 it creates a new `Instructor` object for the `instructor` field and passes `instr` to the copy constructor. Here is the statement:

```
instructor = new Instructor(instr);
```

This statement creates a copy of the object referenced by `instr`. The `instructor` field will reference the copy.

When a class has a field that is an object, it is possible that a shallow copy operation will create a security hole. For example, suppose the `Course` constructor had been written as follows:

```
// Bad constructor!
public Course(String name, Instructor instr, TextBook text)
{
   // Assign the courseName.
   courseName = name;

   // Assign the instructor (shallow copy)
   instructor = instr;  // Causes security hole!

   // Assign the textBook (shallow copy)
   textBook = text;     // Causes security hole!
}
```

In this example, the `instructor` and `textBook` fields are merely assigned the addresses of the objects passed into the constructor. This can cause problems because there may be variables outside the `Course` object that also contain references to these `Instructor` and `TextBook` objects. These outside variables would provide direct access to the `Course` object's private data.

At this point you might be wondering why a deep copy was not also done for the `courseName` field. In line 23 the `Course` constructor performs a shallow copy, simply assigning the address of the `String` object referenced by `name` to the `courseName` field. This is permissible because `String` objects are immutable. An *immutable* object does not provide a way to change its contents. Even if variables outside the Course class reference the same object that courseName references, the object cannot be changed.

Return Copies of Field Objects, Not the Originals

When a method in an aggregate class returns a reference to a field object, it should return a reference to a copy of the field object, not the field object itself. For example, look at the getInstructor method in the Course class. The code is shown here:

```
public Instructor getInstructor()
{
    // Return a copy of the instructor object.
    return new Instructor(instructor);
}
```

Notice that the return statement uses the new key word to create a new Instructor object, passing the instructor field to the copy constructor. The object that is created is a copy of the object referenced by instructor. The address of the copy is then returned. This is preferable to simply returning a reference to the field object itself. For example, suppose the method had been written this way:

```
// Bad method
public Instructor getInstructor()
{
    // Return a reference to the instructor object.
    return instructor;  // WRONG! Causes a security hole.
}
```

This method returns the value stored in the instructor field, which is the address of an Instructor object. Any variable that receives the address can then access the Instructor object. This means that code outside the Course object can change the values held by the Instructor object. This is a security hole because the Instructor object is a private field! Only code inside the Course class should be allowed to access it.

NOTE: It is permissible to return a reference to a String object, even if the String object is a private field. This is because String objects are immutable.

Avoid Using null References

By default, a reference variable that is an instance field is initialized to the value null. This indicates that the variable does not reference an object. Because a null reference variable does not reference an object, you cannot use it to perform an operation that would require the existence of an object. For example, a null reference variable cannot be used to call a method. If you attempt to perform an operation with a null reference variable, the program will terminate. For example, look at the FullName class shown in Code Listing 8-16.

Code Listing 8-16 (FullName.java)

```java
 1 /**
 2    This class stores a person's first, last, and middle
 3    names. The class is dangerous because it does not
 4    prevent operations on null reference fields.
 5 */
 6
 7 public class FullName
 8 {
 9    private String lastName;        // Last name
10    private String firstName;       // First name
11    private String middleName;      // Middle name
12
13    /**
14       The setLastName method sets the lastName field.
15       @param str The String to set lastName to.
16    */
17
18    public void setLastName(String str)
19    {
20       lastName = str;
21    }
22
23    /**
24       The setFirstName method sets the firstName field.
25       @param str The String to set firstName to.
26    */
27
28    public void setFirstName(String str)
29    {
30       firstName = str;
31    }
32
33    /**
34       The setMiddleName method sets the middleName field.
35       @param str The String to set middleName to.
36    */
37
38    public void setMiddleName(String str)
39    {
40       middleName = str;
41    }
42
43    /**
44       The getLength method returns the length of the
45       full name.
```

```
46          @return The length.
47       */
48
49    public int getLength()
50    {
51       return lastName.length() + firstName.length()
52              + middleName.length();
53    }
54
55    /**
56       The toString method returns the full name.
57       @return A reference to a String.
58    */
59
60    public String toString()
61    {
62       return firstName + " " + middleName + " "
63              + lastName;
64    }
65 }
```

First, notice that the class has three String reference variables as fields: lastName, firstName, and middleName. Second, notice that the class does not have a programmer-defined constructor. When an instance of this class is created, the lastName, firstName, and middleName fields will be initialized to null by the default constructor. Third, notice that the getLength method uses the lastName, firstName, and middleName variables to call the String class's length method in lines 51 and 52. Nothing is preventing the length method from being called while any or all of these reference variables are set to null. The program in Code Listing 8-17 demonstrates this.

Code Listing 8-17   (NameTester.java)

```
1  /**
2     This program creates a FullName object, and then
3     calls the object's getLength method before values
4     are established for its reference fields. As a
5     result, this program will crash.
6  */
7
8  public class NameTester
9  {
10    public static void main(String[] args)
11    {
12       int len;  // To hold the name length
13
14       // Create a FullName object.
```

```
15        FullName name = new FullName();
16
17        // Get the length of the full name.
18        len = name.getLength();
19    }
20 }
```

This program will crash when you run it because the getLength method is called before the name object's fields are made to reference String objects. One way to prevent the program from crashing is to use if statements in the getLength method to determine whether any of the fields are set to null. Here is an example:

```
public int getLength()
{
   int len = 0;

   if (lastName != null)
      len += lastName.length();

   if (firstName != null)
      len += firstName.length();

   if (middleName != null)
      len += middleName.length();

   return len;
}
```

Another way to handle this problem is to write a no-arg constructor that assigns values to the reference fields. Here is an example:

```
public FullName()
{
   lastName = "";
   firstName = "";
   middleName = "";
}
```

8.8 The this Reference Variable

CONCEPT: The this key word is the name of a reference variable that an object can use to refer to itself. It is available to all non-static methods.

The key word this is the name of a reference variable that an object can use to refer to itself. For example, recall the Stock class presented earlier in this chapter. The class has the following equals method that compares the calling Stock object to another Stock object that is passed as an argument:

```
public boolean equals(Stock object2)
{
   boolean status;

   // Determine whether this object's symbol and
   // sharePrice fields are equal to object2's
   // symbol and sharePrice fields.
   if (symbol.equals(object2.symbol) &&
       sharePrice == object2.sharePrice)
      status = true;   // Yes, the objects are equal.
   else
      status = false;  // No, the objects are not equal.

   // Return the value in status.
   return status;
}
```

When this method is executing, the this variable contains the address of the calling object. We could rewrite the if statement as follows, and it would perform the same operation (the changes appear in bold):

```
if (this.symbol.equals(object2.symbol) &&
    this.sharePrice == object2.sharePrice)
```

The this reference variable is available to all of a class's non-static methods.

Using this to Overcome Shadowing

One common use of the this key word is to overcome the shadowing of a field name by a parameter name. Recall from Chapter 6 that if a method's parameter has the same name as a field in the same class, then the parameter name shadows the field name. For example, look at the constructor in the Stock class:

```
public Stock(String sym, double price)
{
   symbol = sym;
   sharePrice = price;
}
```

This method uses the parameter sym to accept an argument that is assigned to the symbol field, and the parameter price to accept an argument that is assigned to the sharePrice field. Sometimes it is difficult (and even time-consuming) to think of a good parameter name that is different from a field name. To avoid this problem, many programmers give parameters the same names as the fields to which they correspond, and then use the this key word to refer to the field names. For example, the Stock class's constructor could be written as follows:

```
public Stock(String symbol, double sharePrice)
{
   this.symbol = symbol;
   this.sharePrice = sharePrice;
}
```

Although the parameter names `symbol` and `sharePrice` shadow the field names `symbol` and `sharePrice`, the `this` key word overcomes the shadowing. Because `this` is a reference to the calling object, the expression `this.symbol` refers to the calling object's `symbol` field, and the expression `this.sharePrice` refers to the calling object's `sharePrice` field.

Using `this` to Call an Overloaded Constructor from Another Constructor

You already know that a constructor is automatically called when an object is created. You also know that you cannot call a constructor explicitly, as you do other methods. However, there is one exception to this rule: You can use the `this` key word to call one constructor from another constructor in the same class.

To illustrate this, recall the `Stock` class that was presented earlier in this chapter. It has the following constructor:

```
public Stock(String sym, double price)
{
   symbol = sym;
   sharePrice = price;
}
```

This constructor accepts arguments that are assigned to the `symbol` and `sharePrice` fields. Let's suppose we also want a constructor that only accepts an argument for the `symbol` field, and assigns 0.0 to the `sharePrice` field. Here's one way to write the constructor:

```
public Stock(String sym)
{
   this(sym, 0.0);
}
```

This constructor simply uses the `this` variable to call the first constructor. It passes the value in `sym` as the first argument, and 0.0 as the second argument. The result is that the `symbol` field is assigned the value in `sym` and the `sharePrice` field is assigned 0.0.

Remember the following rules about using `this` to call a constructor:

- `this` can only be used to call a constructor from another constructor in the same class.
- It *must* be the first statement in the constructor that is making the call. If it is not the first statement, a compiler error will result.

 **Checkpoint**

MyProgrammingLab™ *www.myprogramminglab.com*

8.4   Look at the following code. (You might want to review the `Stock` class presented earlier in this chapter.)

```
Stock stock1 = new Stock("XYZ", 9.65);
Stock stock2 = new Stock("SUNW", 7.92);
```

While the `equals` method is executing as a result of the following statement, what object does `this` reference?

```
if (stock2.equals(stock1))
    System.out.println("The stocks are the same.");
```

8.9 Enumerated Types

> **CONCEPT:** An enumerated data type consists of a set of predefined values. You can use the data type to create variables that can hold only the values that belong to the enumerated data type.

You've already learned the concept of data types and how they are used with primitive variables. For example, a variable of the `int` data type can hold integer values within a certain range. You cannot assign floating-point values to an `int` variable because only `int` values may be assigned to `int` variables. A data type defines the values that are legal for any variable of that data type.

Sometimes it is helpful to create your own data type that has a specific set of legal values. For example, suppose you wanted to create a data type named `Day`, and the legal values in that data type were the names of the days of the week (Sunday, Monday, and so forth). When you create a variable of the `Day` data type, you can only store the names of the days of the week in that variable. Any other values would be illegal. In Java, such a type is known as an *enumerated data type*.

You use the `enum` key word to create your own data type and specify the values that belong to that type. Here is an example of an enumerated data type declaration:

```
enum Day { SUNDAY, MONDAY, TUESDAY, WEDNESDAY,
           THURSDAY, FRIDAY, SATURDAY }
```

An enumerated data type declaration begins with the key word enum, followed by the name of the type, followed by a list of identifiers inside braces. The example declaration creates an enumerated data type named `Day`. The identifiers `SUNDAY`, `MONDAY`, `TUESDAY`, `WEDNESDAY`, `THURSDAY`, `FRIDAY`, and `SATURDAY`, which are listed inside the braces, are known as *enum constants*. They represent the values that belong to the `Day` data type. Here is the general format of an enumerated type declaration:

```
enum TypeName { One or more enum constants }
```

Note that the enum constants are not enclosed in quotation marks; therefore, they are not strings. enum constants must be legal Java identifiers.

> **TIP:** When making up names for enum constants, it is not required that they be written in all uppercase letters. We could have written the `Day` type's enum constants as sunday, monday, and so forth. Because they represent constant values, however, the standard convention is to write them in all uppercase letters.

Once you have created an enumerated data type in your program, you can declare variables of that type. For example, the following statement declares workDay as a variable of the Day type:

```
Day workDay;
```

Because workDay is a Day variable, the only values that we can legally assign to it are the enum constants Day.SUNDAY, Day.MONDAY, Day.TUESDAY, Day.WEDNESDAY, Day.THURSDAY, Day.FRIDAY, and Day.SATURDAY. If we try to assign any value other than one of the Day type's enum constants, a compiler error will result. For example, the following statement assigns the value Day.WEDNESDAY to the workDay variable:

```
Day workDay = Day.WEDNESDAY;
```

Notice that we assigned Day.WEDNESDAY instead of just WEDNESDAY. The name Day.WEDNESDAY is the *fully qualified name* of the Day type's WEDNESDAY constant. Under most circumstances you must use the fully qualified name of an enum constant.

Enumerated Types Are Specialized Classes

When you write an enumerated type declaration, you are actually creating a special kind of class. In addition, the enum constants that you list inside the braces are actually objects of the class. In the previous example, Day is a class, and the enum constants Day.SUNDAY, Day.MONDAY, Day.TUESDAY, Day.WEDNESDAY, Day.THURSDAY, Day.FRIDAY, and Day.SATURDAY are all instances of the Day class. When we assigned Day.WEDNESDAY to the workDay variable, we were assigning the address of the Day.WEDNESDAY object to the variable. This is illustrated in Figure 8-15.

Figure 8-15 The workDay variable references the Day.WEDNESDAY object

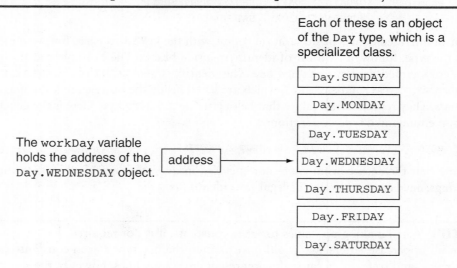

enum constants, which are actually objects, come automatically equipped with a few methods. One of them is the toString method. The toString method simply returns the name of the calling enum constant as a string. For example, assuming that the Day type has been declared as previously shown, both of the following code segments display the string WEDNESDAY (recall that the toString method is implicitly called when an object is passed to System.out.println):

```
// This code displays WEDNESDAY.
Day workDay = Day.WEDNESDAY;
System.out.println(workDay);

// This code also displays WEDNESDAY.
System.out.println(Day.WEDNESDAY);
```

enum constants also have a method named ordinal. The ordinal method returns an integer value representing the constant's ordinal value. The constant's *ordinal value* is its position in the enum declaration, with the first constant being at position 0. Figure 8-16 shows the ordinal value of each of the constants declared in the Day data type.

Figure 8-16 The Day enumerated data type and the ordinal positions of its enum constants

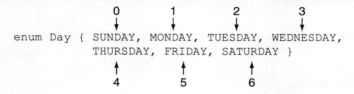

For example, assuming that the Day type has been declared as previously shown, look at the following code segment:

```
Day lastWorkDay = Day.FRIDAY;
System.out.println(lastWorkDay.ordinal());
System.out.println(Day.MONDAY.ordinal());
```

The ordinal value for Day.FRIDAY is 5 and the ordinal value for Day.MONDAY is 1, so this code will display:

```
5
1
```

The last enumerated data type methods that we will discuss here are equals and compareTo. The equals method accepts an object as its argument and returns true if that object is equal to the calling enum constant. For example, assuming that the Day type has been declared as previously shown, the following code segment will display "The two are the same":

```
Day myDay = Day.TUESDAY;
if (myDay.equals(Day.TUESDAY))
    System.out.println("The two are the same.");
```

The compareTo method is designed to compare enum constants of the same type. It accepts an object as its argument and returns the following:

- a negative integer value if the calling enum constant's ordinal value is less than the argument's ordinal value
- zero if the calling enum constant is the same as the argument
- a positive integer value if the calling enum constant's ordinal value is greater than the argument's ordinal value

For example, assuming that the Day type has been declared as previously shown, the following code segment will display "FRIDAY is greater than MONDAY":

```
Day myDay = Day.FRIDAY;
if (myDay.compareTo(Day.MONDAY) > 0)
    System.out.println(myDay + " is greater than "
                    + Day.MONDAY);
```

One place to declare an enumerated type is inside a class. If you declare an enumerated type inside a class, it cannot be inside a method. Code Listing 8-18 shows an example. It demonstrates the Day enumerated type.

Code Listing 8-18   (EnumDemo.java)

```java
 1 /**
 2    This program demonstrates an enumerated type.
 3 */
 4
 5 public class EnumDemo
 6 {
 7    // Declare the Day enumerated type.
 8    enum Day { SUNDAY, MONDAY, TUESDAY, WEDNESDAY,
 9             THURSDAY, FRIDAY, SATURDAY }
10
11    public static void main(String[] args)
12    {
13       // Declare a Day variable and assign it a value.
14       Day workDay = Day.WEDNESDAY;
15
16       // The following statement displays WEDNESDAY.
17       System.out.println(workDay);
18
19       // The following statement displays the ordinal
20       // value for Day.SUNDAY, which is 0.
21       System.out.println("The ordinal value for " +
22                     Day.SUNDAY + " is " +
23                     Day.SUNDAY.ordinal());
24
25       // The following statement displays the ordinal
26       // value for Day.SATURDAY, which is 6.
27       System.out.println("The ordinal value for " +
28                     Day.SATURDAY + " is " +
29                     Day.SATURDAY.ordinal());
```

```
30
31        // The following statement compares two enum constants.
32        if (Day.FRIDAY.compareTo(Day.MONDAY) > 0)
33           System.out.println(Day.FRIDAY + " is greater than " +
34                                Day.MONDAY);
35        else
36           System.out.println(Day.FRIDAY + " is NOT greater than " +
37                                Day.MONDAY);
38     }
39 }
```

Program Output

```
WEDNESDAY
The ordinal value for SUNDAY is 0
The ordinal value for SATURDAY is 6
FRIDAY is greater than MONDAY
```

You can also write an enumerated type declaration inside its own file. If you do, the file-name must match the name of the type. For example, if we stored the Day type in its own file, we would name the file *Day.java*. This makes sense because enumerated data types are specialized classes. For example, look at Code Listing 8-19. This file, *CarType.java*, contains the declaration of an enumerated data type named CarType. When it is compiled, a byte code file named *CarType.class* will be generated.

Code Listing 8-19   **(CarType.java)**

```
1 /**
2    CarType enumerated data type
3 */
4
5 enum CarType { PORSCHE, FERRARI, JAGUAR }
```

Also look at Code Listing 8-20. This file, *CarColor.java*, contains the declaration of an enumerated data type named CarColor. When it is compiled, a byte code file named *CarColor.class* will be generated.

Code Listing 8-20   **(CarColor.java)**

```
1 /**
2    CarColor enumerated data type
3 */
4
5 enum CarColor { RED, BLACK, BLUE, SILVER }
```

Code Listing 8-21 shows the SportsCar class, which uses these enumerated types. Code Listing 8-22 demonstrates the class.

Code Listing 8-21 (SportsCar.java)

```
1  /**
2     SportsCar class
3  */
4
5  public class SportsCar
6  {
7     private CarType make;     // The car's make
8     private CarColor color;   // The car's color
9     private double price;     // The car's price
10
11    /**
12       The constructor initializes the car's make,
13       color, and price.
14       @param aMake The car's make.
15       @param aColor The car's color.
16       @param aPrice The car's price.
17    */
18
19    public SportsCar(CarType aMake, CarColor aColor, double aPrice)
20    {
21       make = aMake;
22       color = aColor;
23       price = aPrice;
24    }
25
26    /**
27       getMake method
28       @return The car's make.
29    */
30
31    public CarType getMake()
32    {
33       return make;
34    }
35
36    /**
37       getColor method
38       @return The car's color.
```

```
39     */
40
41     public CarColor getColor()
42     {
43        return color;
44     }
45
46     /**
47        getPrice method
48        @return The car's price.
49     */
50
51     public double getPrice()
52     {
53        return price;
54     }
55
56     /**
57        toString method
58        @return A string indicating the car's make,
59               color, and price.
60     */
61
62     public String toString()
63     {
64        // Create a string representing the object.
65        String str = String.format("Make: %s\nColor: %s\nPrice: $%,.2f",
66                                   make, color, price);
67
68        // Return the string.
69        return str;
70     }
71 }
```

Code Listing 8-22   (SportsCarDemo.java)

```
1 /**
2    This program demonstrates the SportsCar class.
3 */
4
5 public class SportsCarDemo
6 {
```

```
 7      public static void main(String[] args)
 8      {
 9         // Create a SportsCar object.
10         SportsCar yourNewCar = new SportsCar(CarType.PORSCHE,
11                                         CarColor.RED, 100000);
12
13         // Display the object's values.
14         System.out.println(yourNewCar);
15      }
16   }
```

Program Output

```
Make: PORSCHE
Color: RED
Price: $100,000.00
```

Switching On an Enumerated Type

Java allows you to test an enum constant with a switch statement. For example, look at the program in Code Listing 8-23. It creates a SportsCar object, and then uses a switch statement to test the object's make field.

Code Listing 8-23   (SportsCarDemo2.java)

```
 1 /**
 2    This program shows that you can switch on an
 3    enumerated type.
 4 */
 5
 6 public class SportsCarDemo2
 7 {
 8    public static void main(String[] args)
 9    {
10       // Create a SportsCar object.
11       SportsCar yourNewCar = new SportsCar(CarType.PORSCHE,
12                                       CarColor.RED, 100000);
13
14       // Get the car make and switch on it.
15       switch (yourNewCar.getMake())
16       {
17          case PORSCHE :
18             System.out.println("Your car was made in Germany.");
19             break;
20          case FERRARI :
```

```
21          System.out.println("Your car was made in Italy.");
22          break;
23       case JAGUAR :
24          System.out.println("Your car was made in England.");
25          break;
26       default:
27          System.out.println("I'm not sure where that car "
28                               + "was made.");
29    }
30  }
31 }
```

Program Output

```
Your car was made in Germany.
```

In line 15 the switch statement tests the value returned from the yourNewCar.getMake()
method. This method returns a CarType enumerated constant. Based upon the value returned
from the method, the program then branches to the appropriate case statement. Notice in
the case statements that the enumerated constants are not fully qualified. In other words,
we had to write PORSCHE, FERRARI, and JAGUAR instead of CarType.PORSCHE, CarType.FERRARI,
and CarType.JAGUAR. If you give a fully qualified enum constant name as a case expression,
a compiler error will result.

 TIP: Notice that the switch statement in Code Listing 8-23 has a default section, even
though it has a case statement for every enum constant in the CarType type. This will
handle things in the event that more enum constants are added to the *CarType* file. This
type of planning is an example of "defensive programming."

 Checkpoint

MyProgrammingLab™ *www.myprogramminglab.com*

8.5   Look at the following statement, which declares an enumerated data type:

```
enum Flower { ROSE, DAISY, PETUNIA }
```

a)   What is the name of the data type?
b)   What is the ordinal value for the enum constant ROSE? For DAISY? For PETUNIA?
c)   What is the fully qualifed name of the enum constant ROSE? Of DAISY?
       Of PETUNIA?
d)   Write a statement that declares a variable of this enumerated data type.
       The variable should be named flora. Initialize the variable with the
       PETUNIA constant.

8.6   Assume that the following enumerated data type has been declared:

```
enum Creatures{ HOBBIT, ELF, DRAGON }
```

What will the following code display?

```
            System.out.println(Creatures.HOBBIT + " "
                            + Creatures.ELF + " "
                            + Creatures.DRAGON);
```

8.7   Assume that the following enumerated data type has been declared:

```
enum Letters { Z, Y, X }
```

What will the following code display?

```
if (Letters.Z.compareTo(Letters.X) > 0)
    System.out.println("Z is greater than X.");
else
    System.out.println("Z is not greater than X.");
```

8.10 Garbage Collection

CONCEPT: The Java Virtual Machine periodically runs a process known as the garbage collector, which removes unreferenced objects from memory.

When an object is no longer needed, it should be destroyed so the memory it uses can be freed for other purposes. Fortunately, you do not have to destroy objects after you are finished using them. The Java Virtual Machine periodically performs a process known as garbage collection, which automatically removes unreferenced objects from memory. For example, look at the following code:

```
// Declare two BankAccount reference variables.
BankAccount account1, account2;

// Create an object and reference it with account1.
account1 = new BankAccount(500.0);

// Reference the same object with account2.
account2 = account1;

// Store null in account1 so it no longer
// references the object.
account1 = null;

// The object is still referenced by account2, though.
// Store null in account2 so it no longer references
// the object.
account2 = null;

// Now the object is no longer referenced, so it
// can be removed by the garbage collector.
```

This code uses two reference variables, account1 and account2. A BankAccount object is created and referenced by account1. Then, account1 is assigned to account2, which causes account2 to reference the same object as account1. This is illustrated in Figure 8-17.

Figure 8-17   Both `account1` and `account2` reference the same object

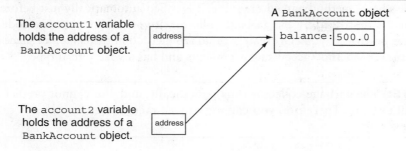

Next, the `null` value is assigned to `account1`. This removes the address of the object from the `account1` variable, causing it to no longer reference the object. Figure 8-18 illustrates this.

Figure 8-18   The object is only referenced by the `account2` variable

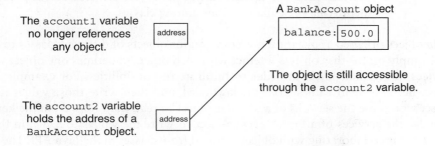

The object is still accessible, however, because it is referenced by the `account2` variable. The next statement assigns `null` to `account2`. This removes the object's address from `account2`, causing it to no longer reference the object. Figure 8-19 illustrates this. Because the object is no longer accessible, it will be removed from memory the next time the garbage collector process runs.

Figure 8-19   The object is no longer referenced

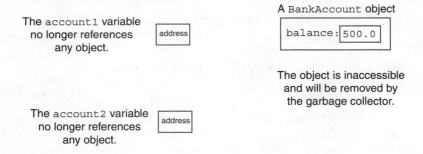

The `finalize` Method

If a class has a method named `finalize`, it is called automatically just before an instance of the class is destroyed by the garbage collector. If you wish to execute code just before an object is destroyed, you can create a `finalize` method in the class and place the code there. The `finalize` method accepts no arguments and has a `void` return type.

NOTE: The garbage collector runs periodically, and you cannot predict exactly when it will execute. Therefore, you cannot know exactly when an object's finalize method will execute.

8.11 Focus on Object-Oriented Design: Class Collaboration

CONCEPT: It is common for classes to interact, or collaborate, with each other to perform their operations. Part of the object-oriented design process is identifying the collaborations among classes.

In an object-oriented application it is common for objects of different classes to collaborate. This simply means that objects interact with each other. Sometimes one object will need the services of another object in order to fulfill its responsibilities. For example, let's say an object needs to read values from the keyboard, and then write those values to a file. The object would use the services of a `Scanner` object to read the values from the keyboard, and then use the services of a `PrintWriter` object to write the values to a file. In this example, the object is collaborating with objects created from classes in the Java API. The objects that you create from your own classes can also collaborate with each other.

If one object is to collaborate with another object, then it must know something about the other object's class methods and how to call them. For example, suppose we were to write a class named `StockPurchase`, which uses an object of the `Stock` class (presented earlier in this chapter) to simulate the purchase of a stock. The `StockPurchase` class is responsible for calculating the cost of the stock purchase. To do that, it must know how to call the `Stock` class's `getSharePrice` method to get the price per share of the stock. Code Listing 8-24 shows an example of the `StockPurchase` class. (This file is in the source code folder *Chapter 08\StockPurchase Class*.)

Code Listing 8-24   (`StockPurchase.java`)

```
1 /**
2    The StockPurchase class represents a stock purchase.
3 */
4
5 public class StockPurchase
6 {
7    private Stock stock;  // The stock that was purchased
```

```
 8      private int shares; // Number of shares owned
 9
10      /**
11         Constructor
12         @param stockObject The stock to purchase.
13         @param numShares The number of shares.
14      */
15
16      public StockPurchase(Stock stockObject, int numShares)
17      {
18         // Create a copy of the object referenced by
19         // stockObject.
20         stock = new Stock(stockObject);
21         shares = numShares;
22      }
23
24      /**
25         getStock method
26         @return A copy of the Stock object for the stock
27                 being purchased.
28      */
29
30      public Stock getStock()
31      {
32         // Return a copy of the object referenced by stock.
33         return new Stock(stock);
34      }
35
36      /**
37         getShares method
38         @return The number of shares being purchased.
39      */
40
41      public int getShares()
42      {
43         return shares;
44      }
45
46      /**
47         getCost method
48         @return The cost of the stock purchase.
49      */
50
51      public double getCost()
52      {
53         return shares * stock.getSharePrice();
54      }
55 }
```

The constructor for this class accepts a `Stock` object representing the stock that is being purchased, and an `int` representing the number of shares to purchase. In line 20 we see the first collaboration: The `StockPurchase` constructor makes a copy of the `Stock` object by using the `Stock` class's copy constructor. The copy constructor is used again in the `getStock` method, in line 33, to return a copy of the `Stock` object.

The next collaboration takes place in the `getCost` method. This method calculates and returns the cost of the stock purchase. In line 53 it calls the `Stock` class's `getSharePrice` method to determine the stock's price per share. The program in Code Listing 8-25 demonstrates this class. (This file is also stored in the source code folder *Chapter 08\ StockPurchase Class.*)

Code Listing 8-25   (`StockTrader.java`)

```java
1 import java.util.Scanner;
2
3 /**
4    This program allows you to purchase shares of XYZ
5    company's stock.
6 */
7
8 public class StockTrader
9 {
10    public static void main(String[] args)
11    {
12       int sharesToBuy;  // Number of shares to buy.
13
14       // Create a Stock object for the company stock.
15       // The trading symbol is XYZ and the stock is
16       // currently $9.62 per share.
17       Stock xyzCompany = new Stock("XYZ", 9.62);
18
19       // Create a Scanner object for keyboard input.
20       Scanner keyboard = new Scanner(System.in);
21
22       // Display the current share price.
23       System.out.printf("XYZ stock is currently $%,.2f.\n",
24                      xyzCompany.getSharePrice());
25
26       // Get the number of shares to purchase.
27       System.out.print("How many shares do you want to buy? ");
28       sharesToBuy = keyboard.nextInt();
29
30       // Create a StockPurchase object for the transaction.
31       StockPurchase buy =
32               new StockPurchase(xyzCompany, sharesToBuy);
```

```
33
34        // Display the cost of the transaction.
35        System.out.printf("Cost of the stock: $%,.2f",
36                        buy.getCost());
37   }
38 }
```

Program Output with Example Input Shown in Bold

```
XYZ stock is currently $9.62.
How many shares do you want to buy? 100 [Enter]
Cost of the stock: $962.00
```

Determining Class Collaborations with CRC Cards

During the object-oriented design process, you can determine many of the collaborations that will be necessary among classes by examining the responsibilities of the classes. In Chapter 6, Section 6.9, we discussed the process of finding the classes and their responsibilities. Recall from that section that a class's responsibilities are as follows:

- Things that the class is responsible for knowing
- Actions that the class is responsible for doing

Often you will determine that the class must collaborate with another class in order to fulfill one or more of its responsibilities. One popular method of discovering a class's responsibilities and collaborations is by creating CRC cards. CRC stands for class, responsibilities, and collaborations.

You can use simple index cards for this procedure. Once you have gone through the process of finding the classes (which is discussed in Chapter 6, Section 6.9), set aside one index card for each class. At the top of the index card, write the name of the class. Divide the rest of the card into two columns. In the left column, write each of the class's responsibilities. As you write each responsibility, think about whether the class needs to collaborate with another class to fulfill that responsibility. Ask yourself questions such as the following:

- Will an object of this class need to get data from another object in order to fulfill this responsibility?
- Will an object of this class need to request another object to perform an operation in order to fulfill this responsibility?

If collaboration is required, write the name of the collaborating class in the right column, next to the responsibility that requires it. If no collaboration is required for a responsibility, simply write "None" in the right column, or leave it blank. Figure 8-20 shows an example CRC card for the StockPurchase class.

Figure 8-20 CRC card

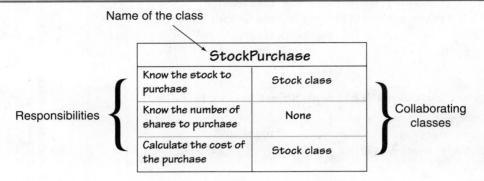

From the CRC card shown in the figure, we can see that the StockPurchase class has the following responsibilities and collaborations:

- **Responsibility:** To know the stock to purchase
  Collaboration: The Stock class
- **Responsibility:** To know the number of shares to purchase
  Collaboration: None
- **Responsibility:** To calculate the cost of the purchase
  Collaboration: The Stock class

When you have completed a CRC card for each class in the application, you will have a good idea of each class's responsibilities and how the classes must interact.

 8.12 Common Errors to Avoid

The following list describes several errors that are commonly committed when learning this chapter's topics:

- **Attempting to refer to an instance field or instance method in a static method.** Static methods can refer only to other class members that are static.
- **In a method that accepts an object as an argument, writing code that accidentally modifies the object.** When a reference variable is passed as an argument to a method, the method has access to the object that the variable references. When writing a method that receives a reference variable as an argument, you must take care not to accidentally modify the contents of the object that is referenced by the variable.
- **Allowing a null reference to be used.** Because a null reference variable does not reference an object, you cannot use it to perform an operation that would require the existence of an object. For example, a null reference variable cannot be used to call a method. If you attempt to perform an operation with a null reference variable, the program will terminate. This can happen when a class has a reference variable as a field, and it is not properly initialized with the address of an object.
- **Forgetting to use the fully qualified name of an enum constant.** Under most circumstances you must use the fully qualified name of an enum constant. One exception to this is when the enum constant is used as a case expression in a switch statement.

Review Questions and Exercises

Multiple Choice and True/False

1. This type of method cannot access any non-static member variables in its own class.
   a. instance
   b. void
   c. static
   d. non-static

2. When an object is passed as an argument to a method, this is actually passed.
   a. a copy of the object
   b. the name of the object
   c. a reference to the object
   d. none of these; you cannot pass an object

3. If you write this method for a class, Java will automatically call it any time you concatenate an object of the class with a string.
   a. `toString`
   b. `plusString`
   c. `stringConvert`
   d. `concatString`

4. Making an instance of one class a field in another class is called _____.
   a. nesting
   b. class fielding
   c. aggregation
   d. concatenation

5. This is the name of a reference variable that is always available to an instance method and refers to the object that is calling the method.
   a. `callingObject`
   b. `this`
   c. `me`
   d. `instance`

6. This enum method returns the position of an `enum` constant in the declaration.
   a. `position`
   b. `location`
   c. `ordinal`
   d. `toString`

7. Assuming the following declaration exists:

   ```
   enum Seasons { SPRING, WINTER, SUMMER, FALL }
   ```

   what is the fully qualified name of the `FALL` constant?
   a. `FALL`
   b. `enum.FALL`
   c. `FALL.Seasons`
   d. `Seasons.FALL`

8. You cannot use the fully qualified name of an `enum` constant for this.
   a. a `switch` expression
   b. a case expression
   c. an argument to a method
   d. all of these

9. The Java Virtual Machine periodically performs this process, which automatically removes unreferenced objects from memory.
   a. memory cleansing
   b. memory deallocation
   c. garbage collection
   d. object expungement

10. If a class has this method, it is called automatically just before an instance of the class is destroyed by the Java Virtual Machine.
    a. `finalize`
    b. `destroy`
    c. `remove`
    d. `housekeeper`

11. CRC stands for
    a. Class, Return value, Composition
    b. Class, Responsibilities, Collaborations
    c. Class, Responsibilities, Composition
    d. Compare, Return, Continue

12. **True or False:** A static member method may refer to non-static member variables of the same class, but only after an instance of the class has been defined.

13. **True or False:** All static member variables are initialized to –1 by default.

14. **True or False:** When an object is passed as an argument to a method, the method can access the argument.

15. **True or False:** A method cannot return a reference to an object.

16. **True or False:** You can declare an enumerated data type inside a method.

17. **True or False:** Enumerated data types are actually special types of classes.

18. **True or False:** `enum` constants have a `toString` method.

Find the Error

The following class definition has an error. What is it?

```
1. public class MyClass
   {
         private int x;
         private double y;

         public static void setValues(int a, double b)
         {
```

```
            x = a;
            y = b;
      }
}
```

2. Assume the following declaration exists :

    ```
    enum Coffee { MEDIUM, DARK, DECAF }
    ```

    Find the error(s) in the following switch statement:

    ```
    // This code has errors!
    Coffee myCup = DARK;
    switch (myCup)
    {
        case Coffee.MEDIUM :
            System.out.println("Mild flavor.");
            break;
        case Coffee.DARK :
            System.out.println("Strong flavor.");
            break;
        case Coffee.DECAF :
            System.out.println("Won't keep you awake.");
            break;
        default:
            System.out.println("Never heard of it.");
    }
    ```

Algorithm Workbench

1. Consider the following class declaration:

    ```
    public class Circle
    {
        private double radius;

        public Circle(double r)
        {
            radius = r;
        }

        public double getArea()
        {
            return Math.PI * radius * radius;
        }

        public double getRadius()
        {
            return radius;
        }
    }
    ```

    a. Write a `toString` method for this class. The method should return a string containing the radius and area of the circle.

    b. Write an `equals` method for this class. The method should accept a `Circle` object as an argument. It should return `true` if the argument object contains the same data as the calling object, or `false` otherwise.

    c. Write a `greaterThan` method for this class. The method should accept a `Circle` object as an argument. It should return `true` if the argument object has an area that is greater than the area of the calling object, or `false` otherwise.

2. Consider the following class declaration:

```java
public class Thing
{
    private int x;
    private int y;
    private static int z = 0;

    public Thing()
    {
        x = z;
        y = z;
    }
    static void putThing(int a)
    {
        z = a;
    }
}
```

Assume a program containing the class declaration defines three `Thing` objects with the following statements:

```java
Thing one = new Thing();
Thing two = new Thing();
Thing three = new Thing();
```

    a. How many separate instances of the x member exist?
    b. How many separate instances of the y member exist?
    c. How many separate instances of the z member exist?
    d. What value will be stored in the x and y members of each object?
    e. Write a statement that will call the `putThing` method.

3. A pet store sells dogs, cats, birds, and hamsters. Write a declaration for an enumerated data type that can represent the types of pets the store sells.

Short Answer

1. Describe one thing you cannot do with a static method.
2. Why are static methods useful in creating utility classes?
3. Describe the difference in the way variables and class objects are passed as arguments to a method.

4. Even if you do not write an `equals` method for a class, Java provides one. Describe the behavior of the `equals` method that Java automatically provides.

5. A "has a" relationship can exist between classes. What does this mean?

6. What happens if you attempt to call a method using a reference variable that is set to `null`?

7. Is it advisable or not advisable to write a method that returns a reference to an object that is a private field? What is the exception to this?

8. What is the `this` key word?

9. Look at the following declaration:

   ```
   enum Color { RED, ORANGE, GREEN, BLUE }
   ```

   a. What is the name of the data type declared by this statement?
   b. What are the `enum` constants for this type?
   c. Write a statement that defines a variable of this type and initializes it with a valid value.

10. Assuming the following enum declaration exists:

    ```
    enum Dog { POODLE, BOXER, TERRIER }
    ```

    what will the following statements display?

    a.
    ```
    System.out.println(Dog.POODLE + "\n" +
                       Dog.BOXER + "\n" +
                       Dog.TERRIER);
    ```

    b.
    ```
    System.out.println(Dog.POODLE.ordinal() + "\n" +
                       Dog.BOXER.ordinal() + "\n" +
                       Dog.TERRIER.ordinal());
    ```

    c.
    ```
    Dog myDog = Dog.BOXER;
    if (myDog.compareTo(Dog.TERRIER) > 0)
        System.out.println(myDog + " is greater than " +
                           Dog.TERRIER);
    else
        System.out.println(myDog + " is NOT greater than " +
                           Dog.TERRIER);
    ```

11. Under what circumstances does an object become a candidate for garbage collection?

Programming Challenges

MyProgrammingLab™   *Visit www.myprogramminglab.com to complete many of these Programming Challenges online and get instant feedback.*

1. Area Class

Write a class that has three overloaded static methods for calculating the areas of the following geometric shapes:

- circles
- rectangles
- cylinders

Here are the formulas for calculating the area of the shapes.

Area of a circle: $Area = \pi r^2$
                 where π is Math.PI and r is the circle's radius

Area of a rectangle: $Area = Width \times Length$

Area of a cylinder: $Area = \pi r^2 h$
                 where π is Math.PI, r is the radius of the cylinder's base, and
                                  h is the cylinder's height

Because the three methods are to be overloaded, they should each have the same name, but different parameter lists. Demonstrate the class in a complete program.

VideoNote

The BankAccount
Class Copy
Constructor
Problem

2. BankAccount **Class Copy Constructor**

Add a copy constructor to the BankAccount class. This constructor should accept a BankAccount object as an argument. It should assign to the balance field the value in the argument's balance field. As a result, the new object will be a copy of the argument object.

3. Carpet Calculator

The Westfield Carpet Company has asked you to write an application that calculates the price of carpeting for rectangular rooms. To calculate the price, you multiply the area of the floor (width times length) by the price per square foot of carpet. For example, the area of floor that is 12 feet long and 10 feet wide is 120 square feet. To cover that floor with carpet that costs $8 per square foot would cost $960. ($12 \times 10 \times 8 = 960$.)

First, you should create a class named RoomDimension that has two fields: one for the length of the room and one for the width. The RoomDimension class should have a method that returns the area of the room. (The area of the room is the room's length multiplied by the room's width.)

Next you should create a RoomCarpet class that has a RoomDimension object as a field. It should also have a field for the cost of the carpet per square foot. The RoomCarpet class should have a method that returns the total cost of the carpet.

Figure 8-21 is a UML diagram that shows possible class designs and the relationships among the classes. Once you have written these classes, use them in an application that asks the user to enter the dimensions of a room and the price per square foot of the desired carpeting. The application should display the total cost of the carpet.

4. LandTract **Class**

Make a LandTract class that has two fields: one for the tract's length and one for the width. The class should have a method that returns the tract's area, as well as an equals method and a toString method. Demonstrate the class in a program that asks the user to enter the dimensions for two tracts of land. The program should display the area of each tract of land and indicate whether the tracts are of equal size.

Figure 8-21   UML diagram for Programming Challenge 3

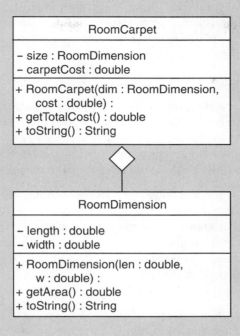

5. Month Class

Write a class named Month. The class should have an int field named monthNumber that holds the number of the month. For example, January would be 1, February would be 2, and so forth. In addition, provide the following methods:

- A no-arg constructor that sets the monthNumber field to 1.
- A constructor that accepts the number of the month as an argument. It should set the monthNumber field to the value passed as the argument. If a value less than 1 or greater than 12 is passed, the constructor should set monthNumber to 1.
- A constructor that accepts the name of the month, such as "January" or "February" as an argument. It should set the monthNumber field to the correct corresponding value.
- A setMonthNumber method that accepts an int argument, which is assigned to the monthNumber field. If a value less than 1 or greater than 12 is passed, the method should set monthNumber to 1.
- A getMonthNumber method that returns the value in the monthNumber field.
- A getMonthName method that returns the name of the month. For example, if the monthNumber field contains 1, then this method should return "January".
- A toString method that returns the same value as the getMonthName method.
- An equals method that accepts a Month object as an argument. If the argument object holds the same data as the calling object, this method should return true. Otherwise, it should return false.

- A greaterThan method that accepts a Month object as an argument. If the calling object's monthNumber field is greater than the argument's monthNumber field, this method should return true. Otherwise, it should return false.
- A lessThan method that accepts a Month object as an argument. If the calling object's monthNumber field is less than the argument's monthNumber field, this method should return true. Otherwise, it should return false.

6. CashRegister **Class**

Write a CashRegister class that can be used with the RetailItem class that you wrote in Chapter 6's Programming Challenge 4. The CashRegister class should simulate the sale of a retail item. It should have a constructor that accepts a RetailItem object as an argument. The constructor should also accept an integer that represents the quantity of items being purchased. In addition, the class should have the following methods:

- The getSubtotal method should return the subtotal of the sale, which is the quantity multiplied by the price. This method must get the price from the RetailItem object that was passed as an argument to the constructor.
- The getTax method should return the amount of sales tax on the purchase. The sales tax rate is 6 percent of a retail sale.
- The getTotal method should return the total of the sale, which is the subtotal plus the sales tax.

Demonstrate the class in a program that asks the user for the quantity of items being purchased, and then displays the sale's subtotal, amount of sales tax, and total.

7. Sales Receipt File

Modify the program you wrote in Programming Challenge 6 to create a file containing a sales receipt. The program should ask the user for the quantity of items being purchased, and then generate a file with contents similar to the following:

```
SALES RECEIPT
Unit Price: $10.00
Quantity: 5
Subtotal: $50.00
Sales Tax: $ 3.00
Total: $53.00
```

8. Parking Ticket Simulator

For this assignment you will design a set of classes that work together to simulate a police officer issuing a parking ticket. You should design the following classes:

- The ParkedCar **Class:** This class should simulate a parked car. The class's responsibilities are as follows:

  - To know the car's make, model, color, license number, and the number of minutes that the car has been parked.

- The ParkingMeter **Class:** This class should simulate a parking meter. The class's only responsibility is as follows:

  - To know the number of minutes of parking time that has been purchased.

- **The ParkingTicket Class:** This class should simulate a parking ticket. The class's responsibilities are as follows:

  - To report the make, model, color, and license number of the illegally parked car
  - To report the amount of the fine, which is $25 for the first hour or part of an hour that the car is illegally parked, plus $10 for every additional hour or part of an hour that the car is illegally parked
  - To report the name and badge number of the police officer issuing the ticket

- **The PoliceOfficer Class:** This class should simulate a police officer inspecting parked cars. The class's responsibilities are as follows:

  - To know the police officer's name and badge number
  - To examine a ParkedCar object and a ParkingMeter object, and determine whether the car's time has expired
  - To issue a parking ticket (generate a ParkingTicket object) if the car's time has expired

Write a program that demonstrates how these classes collaborate.

9. Geometry Calculator

Design a Geometry class with the following methods:

- A static method that accepts the radius of a circle and returns the area of the circle. Use the following formula:

  $Area = \pi r^2$

  Use Math.PI for π and the radius of the circle for r.

- A static method that accepts the length and width of a rectangle and returns the area of the rectangle. Use the following formula:

  $Area = Length \times Width$

- A static method that accepts the length of a triangle's base and the triangle's height. The method should return the area of the triangle. Use the following formula:

  $Area = Base \times Height \times 0.5$

The methods should display an error message if negative values are used for the circle's radius, the rectangle's length or width, or the triangle's base or height.

Next, write a program to test the class, which displays the following menu and responds to the user's selection:

```
Geometry Calculator
1. Calculate the Area of a Circle
2. Calculate the Area of a Rectangle
3. Calculate the Area of a Triangle
4. Quit

Enter your choice (1-4):
```

Display an error message if the user enters a number outside the range of 1 through 4 when selecting an item from the menu.

10. Car Instrument Simulator

For this assignment, you will design a set of classes that work together to simulate a car's fuel gauge and odometer. The classes you will design are the following:

- **The FuelGauge Class:** This class will simulate a fuel gauge. Its responsibilities are as follows:

  - To know the car's current amount of fuel, in gallons.
  - To report the car's current amount of fuel, in gallons.
  - To be able to increment the amount of fuel by 1 gallon. This simulates putting fuel in the car. (The car can hold a maximum of 15 gallons.)
  - To be able to decrement the amount of fuel by 1 gallon, if the amount of fuel is greater than 0 gallons. This simulates burning fuel as the car runs.

- **The Odometer Class:** This class will simulate the car's odometer. Its responsibilities are as follows:

  - To know the car's current mileage.
  - To report the car's current mileage.
  - To be able to increment the current mileage by 1 mile. The maximum mileage the odometer can store is 999,999 miles. When this amount is exceeded, the odometer resets the current mileage to 0.
  - To be able to work with a FuelGauge object. It should decrease the FuelGauge object's current amount of fuel by 1 gallon for every 24 miles traveled. (The car's fuel economy is 24 miles per gallon.)

Demonstrate the classes by creating instances of each. Simulate filling the car up with fuel, and then run a loop that increments the odometer until the car runs out of fuel. During each loop iteration, print the car's current mileage and amount of fuel.

11. First to One Game

This game is meant for two or more players. In the game, each player starts out with 50 points, as each player takes a turn rolling the dice; the amount generated by the dice is subtracted from the player's points. The first player with exactly one point remaining wins. If a player's remaining points minus the amount generated by the dice results in a value less than one, then the amount should be added to the player's points. (As an alternative, the game can be played with a set number turns. In this case, the player with the amount of points closest to one, when all rounds have been played, wins.)

Write a program that simulates the game being played by two players. Use the Die class that was presented in Chapter 6 to simulate the dice. Write a Player class to simulate the players.

12. Heads or Tails Game

This game is meant for two or more players. In this game, the players take turns flipping a coin. Before the coin is flipped, players should guess if the coin will land face up or face down. If a player guesses correctly, then that player is awarded a point. If a player guesses incorrectly, then that player will lose a point. The first player to score five points is the winner.

Write a program that simulates the game being played by two players. Use the Coin class that you wrote as an assignment in Chapter 6 (Programming Challenge 16) to simulate the coin. Write a Player class to simulate the players.

9 Text Processing and More about Wrapper Classes

9.1 Introduction to Wrapper Classes

CONCEPT: Java provides wrapper classes for the primitive data types. The wrapper class for a given primitive type contains not only a value of that type, but also methods that perform operations related to the type.

Recall from Chapter 2 that the primitive data types are called "primitive" because they are not created from classes. Instead of instantiating objects, you create variables from the primitive data types, and variables do not have attributes or methods. They are designed simply to hold a single value in memory.

Java also provides wrapper classes for all of the primitive data types. A *wrapper class* is a class that is "wrapped around" a primitive data type and allows you to create objects instead of variables. In addition, these wrapper classes provide methods that perform useful operations on primitive values. For example, you have already used the wrapper class "parse" methods to convert strings to primitive values.

Although these wrapper classes can be used to create objects instead of variables, few programmers use them that way. One reason is because the wrapper classes are immutable, which means that once you create an object, you cannot change the object's value. Another reason is because they are not as easy to use as variables for simple operations. For example, to get the value stored in an object you must call a method, whereas variables can be used directly in assignment statements, used in mathematical operations, passed as arguments to methods, and so forth.

Although it is not normally useful to create objects from the wrapper classes, they do provide static methods that are very useful. We examine several of Java's wrapper classes in this chapter. We begin by looking at the Character class, which is the wrapper class for the char data type.

9.2 Character Testing and Conversion with the Character Class

CONCEPT: The Character class is a wrapper class for the char data type. It provides numerous methods for testing and converting character data.

The Character class is part of the java.lang package, so no import statement is necessary to use this class. The class provides several static methods for testing the value of a char variable. Some of these methods are listed in Table 9-1. Each of the methods accepts a single char argument and returns a boolean value.

Table 9-1   Some static Character class methods for testing char values

Method	Description
boolean isDigit(char *ch*)	Returns true if the argument passed into *ch* is a digit from 0 through 9. Otherwise returns false.
boolean isLetter(char *ch*)	Returns true if the argument passed into *ch* is an alphabetic letter. Otherwise returns false.
boolean isLetterOrDigit(char *ch*)	Returns true if the character passed into *ch* contains a digit (0 through 9) or an alphabetic letter. Otherwise returns false.
boolean isLowerCase(char *ch*)	Returns true if the argument passed into *ch* is a lowercase letter. Otherwise returns false.
boolean isUpperCase(char *ch*)	Returns true if the argument passed into *ch* is an uppercase letter. Otherwise returns false.
boolean isSpaceChar(char *ch*)	Returns true if the argument passed into *ch* is a space character. Otherwise returns false.
boolean isWhiteSpace(char *ch*)	Returns true if the argument passed into *ch* is a whitespace character (a space, tab, or newline character). Otherwise returns false.

The program in Code Listing 9-1 demonstrates many of these methods. Figures 9-1 and 9-2 show example interactions with the program.

Code Listing 9-1   (CharacterTest.java)

```java
 1 import javax.swing.JOptionPane;
 2
 3 /**
 4    This program demonstrates some of the Character
 5    class's character testing methods.
 6 */
 7
 8 public class CharacterTest
 9 {
10    public static void main(String[] args)
11    {
12       String input;   // To hold the user's input
13       char ch;        // To hold a single character
14
15       // Get a character from the user and store
16       // it in the ch variable.
17       input = JOptionPane.showInputDialog("Enter " +
18                            "any single character.");
19       ch = input.charAt(0);
20
21       // Test the character.
22       if (Character.isLetter(ch))
23       {
24          JOptionPane.showMessageDialog(null,
25                      "That is a letter.");
26       }
27
28       if (Character.isDigit(ch))
29       {
30          JOptionPane.showMessageDialog(null,
31                      "That is a digit.");
32       }
33
34       if (Character.isLowerCase(ch))
35       {
36          JOptionPane.showMessageDialog(null,
37               "That is a lowercase letter.");
38       }
39
40       if (Character.isUpperCase(ch))
41       {
42          JOptionPane.showMessageDialog(null,
43               "That is an uppercase letter.");
44       }
45
```

```
46          if (Character.isSpaceChar(ch))
47          {
48              JOptionPane.showMessageDialog(null,
49                              "That is a space.");
50          }
51
52          if (Character.isWhitespace(ch))
53          {
54              JOptionPane.showMessageDialog(null,
55                "That is a whitespace character.");
56          }
57
58          System.exit(0);
59      }
60 }
```

Figure 9-1 Interaction with the `CharacterTest.java` program

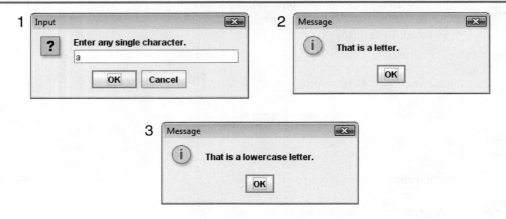

Code Listing 9-2 shows a more practical application of the character testing methods. It tests a string to determine whether it is a seven-character customer number in the proper format. Figures 9-3 and 9-4 show example interactions with the program.

Figure 9-2 Interaction with the `CharacterTest.java` program

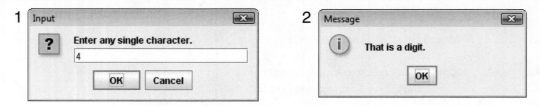

Code Listing 9-2   (`CustomerNumber.java`)

```java
 1  import javax.swing.JOptionPane;
 2
 3  /**
 4     This program tests a customer number to
 5     verify that it is in the proper format.
 6  */
 7
 8  public class CustomerNumber
 9  {
10     public static void main(String[] args)
11     {
12        String input;   // To hold the user's input
13
14        // Get a customer number.
15        input = JOptionPane.showInputDialog("Enter " +
16           "a customer number in the form LLLNNNN\n" +
17           "(LLL = letters and NNNN = numbers)");
18
19        // Validate the input.
20        if (isValid(input))
21        {
22           JOptionPane.showMessageDialog(null,
23                    "That's a valid customer number.");
24        }
25        else
26        {
27           JOptionPane.showMessageDialog(null,
28              "That is not the proper format of a " +
29              "customer number.\nHere is an " +
30              "example: ABC1234");
31        }
32
33        System.exit(0);
34     }
35
36     /**
37        The isValid method determines whether a
38        String is a valid customer number. If so, it
39        returns true.
40        @param custNumber The String to test.
41        @return true if valid, otherwise false.
42     */
43
44     private static boolean isValid(String custNumber)
45     {
```

```
46        boolean goodSoFar = true;     // Flag
47        int i = 0;                     // Control variable
48
49        // Test the length.
50        if (custNumber.length() != 7)
51           goodSoFar = false;
52
53        // Test the first three characters for letters.
54        while (goodSoFar && i < 3)
55        {
56           if (!Character.isLetter(custNumber.charAt(i)))
57              goodSoFar = false;
58           i++;
59        }
60
61        // Test the last four characters for digits.
62        while (goodSoFar && i < 7)
63        {
64           if (!Character.isDigit(custNumber.charAt(i)))
65              goodSoFar = false;
66           i++;
67        }
68
69        return goodSoFar;
70     }
71 }
```

Figure 9-3 Interaction with the `CustomerNumber.java` program

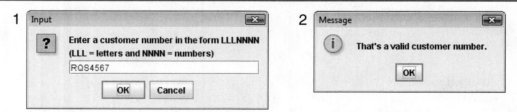

Figure 9-4 Interaction with the `CustomerNumber.java` program

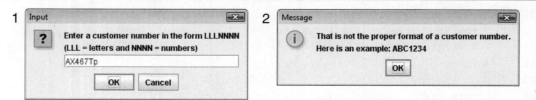

In this program, the customer number is expected to be seven characters long and consist of three alphabetic letters followed by four numeric digits. The isValid method accepts a String argument, which will be tested. The method uses the following local variables, which are declared in lines 46 and 47:

```
boolean goodSoFar = true;  // Flag
int i = 0;                 // Control variable
```

The goodSoFar variable is a flag variable that is initialized with true, but will be set to false immediately when the method determines the customer number is not in a valid format. The i variable is a loop control variable.

The first test is to determine whether the string is the correct length. In line 50 the method tests the length of the custNumber argument. If the argument is not seven characters long, it is not valid and the goodSoFar variable is set to false in line 51.

Next, the method uses the following loop, in lines 54 through 59, to validate the first three characters:

```
while (goodSoFar && i < 3)
{
    if (!Character.isLetter(custNumber.charAt(i)))
        goodSoFar = false;
    i++;
}
```

Recall from Chapter 2 that the String class's charAt method returns a character at a specific position in a string (position numbering starts at 0). This code uses the Character.isLetter method to test the characters at positions 0, 1, and 2 in the custNumber string. If any of these characters are not letters, the goodSoFar variable is set to false and the loop terminates. Next, the method uses the following loop, in lines 62 through 67, to validate the last four characters:

```
while (goodSoFar && i < 7)
{
    if (!Character.isDigit(custNumber.charAt(i)))
        goodSoFar = false;
    i++;
}
```

This code uses the Character.isDigit method to test the characters at positions 3, 4, 5, and 6 in the custNumber string. If any of these characters are not digits, the goodSoFar variable is set to false and the loop terminates. Last, the method returns the value of the goodSoFar method.

Character Case Conversion

The Character class also provides the static methods listed in Table 9-2 for converting the case of a character. Each method accepts a char argument and returns a char value.

Table 9-2 Some `Character` class methods for case conversion

Method	Description
`char toLowerCase(char ch)`	Returns the lowercase equivalent of the argument passed to `ch`.
`char toUpperCase(char ch)`	Returns the uppercase equivalent of the argument passed to `ch`.

If the `toLowerCase` method's argument is an uppercase character, the method returns the lowercase equivalent. For example, the following statement will display the character a on the screen:

```
System.out.println(Character.toLowerCase('A'));
```

If the argument is already lowercase, the `toLowerCase` method returns it unchanged. The following statement also causes the lowercase character a to be displayed:

```
System.out.println(Character.toLowerCase('a'));
```

If the `toUpperCase` method's argument is a lowercase character, the method returns the uppercase equivalent. For example, the following statement will display the character A on the screen:

```
System.out.println(Character.toUpperCase('a'));
```

If the argument is already uppercase, the `toUpperCase` method returns it unchanged.

Any non-letter argument passed to `toLowerCase` or `toUpperCase` is returned as it is. Each of the following statements displays the method argument without any change:

```
System.out.println(Character.toLowerCase('*'));
System.out.println(Character.toLowerCase('$'));
System.out.println(Character.toUpperCase('&'));
System.out.println(Character.toUpperCase('%'));
```

The program in Code Listing 9-3 demonstrates the `toUpperCase` method in a loop that asks the user to enter Y or N. The program repeats as long as the user enters Y or y in response to the question.

Code Listing 9-3 (`CircleArea.java`)

```
1 import java.util.Scanner;
2
3 /**
4    This program demonstrates the Character
5    class's toUpperCase method.
6 */
7
```

```
 8 public class CircleArea
 9 {
10    public static void main(String[] args)
11    {
12        double radius; // The circle's radius
13        double area;   // The circle's area
14        String input;  // To hold a line of input
15        char choice;   // To hold a single character
16
17        // Create a Scanner object to read keyboard input.
18        Scanner keyboard = new Scanner(System.in);
19
20        do
21        {
22            // Get the circle's radius.
23            System.out.print("Enter the circle's radius: ");
24            radius = keyboard.nextDouble();
25
26            // Consume the remaining newline character.
27            keyboard.nextLine();
28
29            // Calculate and display the area.
30            area = Math.PI * radius * radius;
31            System.out.printf("The area is %.2f.\n", area);
32
33            // Repeat this?
34            System.out.print("Do you want to do this " +
35                             "again? (Y or N) ");
36            input = keyboard.nextLine();
37            choice = input.charAt(0);
38
39        } while (Character.toUpperCase(choice) == 'Y');
40    }
41 }
```

Program Output with Example Input Shown in Bold

```
Enter the circle's radius: 10 [Enter]
The area is 314.16.
Do you want to do this again? (Y or N) y [Enter]
Enter the circle's radius: 15 [Enter]
The area is 706.86.
Do you want to do this again? (Y or N) n [Enter]
```

Checkpoint

MyProgrammingLab™ *www.myprogramminglab.com*

9.1   Write a statement that converts the contents of the char variable big to lowercase. The converted value should be assigned to the variable little.

9.2   Write an if statement that displays the word "digit" if the char variable ch contains a numeric digit. Otherwise, it should display "Not a digit."

9.3   What is the output of the following statement?

```
System.out.println(Character.toUpperCase(Character.toLowerCase('A')));
```

9.4   Write a loop that asks the user, "Do you want to repeat the program or quit? (R/Q)". The loop should repeat until the user has entered an R or Q (either uppercase or lowercase).

9.5   What will the following code display?

```
char var = '$';
System.out.println(Character.toUpperCase(var));
```

9.6   Write a loop that counts the number of uppercase characters that appear in the String object str.

9.3   More String Methods

CONCEPT: The String class provides several methods for searching and working with String objects.

Searching for Substrings

The String class provides several methods that search for a string inside of a string. The term *substring* commonly is used to refer to a string that is part of another string. Table 9-3 summarizes some of these methods. Each of the methods in Table 9-3 returns a boolean value indicating whether the string was found.

Let's take a closer look at each of these methods.

The startsWith and endsWith Methods

The startsWith method determines whether the calling object's string begins with a specified substring. For example, the following code determines whether the string "Four score and seven years ago" begins with "Four". The method returns true if the string begins with the specified substring, or false otherwise.

```
String str = "Four score and seven years ago";
if (str.startsWith("Four"))
    System.out.println("The string starts with Four.");
else
    System.out.println("The string does not start with Four.");
```

Table 9-3   String methods that search for a substring

Method	Description
boolean startsWith(String *str*)	This method returns true if the calling string begins with the string passed into *str*.
boolean endsWith(String *str*)	This method returns true if the calling string ends with the string passed into *str*.
boolean regionMatches(int *start*, String *str*, int *start2*, int *n*)	This method returns true if a specified region of the calling string matches a specified region of the string passed into *str*. The *start* parameter indicates the starting position of the region within the calling string. The *start2* parameter indicates the starting position of the region within *str*. The *n* parameter indicates the number of characters in both regions.
boolean regionMatches(Boolean *ignoreCase*, int *start*, String *str*, int *start2*, int *n*)	This overloaded version of the *regionMatches* method has an additional parameter, *ignoreCase*. If true is passed into this parameter, the method ignores the case of the calling string and *str* when comparing the regions. If false is passed into the *ignoreCase* parameter, the comparison is case-sensitive.

In the code, the method call str.startsWith("Four") returns true because the string does begin with "Four". The startsWith method performs a case-sensitive comparison, so the method call str.startsWith("four") would return false.

The endsWith method determines whether the calling string ends with a specified substring. For example, the following code determines whether the string "Four score and seven years ago" ends with "ago". The method returns true if the string does end with the specified substring or false otherwise.

```
String str = "Four score and seven years ago";
if (str.endsWith("ago"))
    System.out.println("The string ends with ago.");
else
    System.out.println("The string does not end with ago.");
```

In the code, the method call str.endsWith("ago") returns true because the string does end with "ago". The endsWith method also performs a case-sensitive comparison, so the method call str.endsWith("Ago") would return false.

The program in Code Listing 9-4 demonstrates a search algorithm that uses the startsWith method. The program searches an array of strings for an element that starts with a specified string.

Code Listing 9-4 (`PersonSearch.java`)

```java
 1 import java.util.Scanner;
 2
 3 /**
 4    This program uses the startsWith method to search using
 5    a partial string.
 6 */
 7
 8 public class PersonSearch
 9 {
10    public static void main(String[] args)
11    {
12       String lookUp;  // To hold a lookup string
13
14       // Create an array of names.
15       String[] people = { "Cutshaw, Will", "Davis, George",
16                           "Davis, Jenny", "Russert, Phil",
17                           "Russell, Cindy", "Setzer, Charles",
18                           "Smathers, Holly", "Smith, Chris",
19                           "Smith, Brad", "Williams, Jean" };
20
21       // Create a Scanner object for keyboard input.
22       Scanner keyboard = new Scanner(System.in);
23
24       // Get a partial name to search for.
25       System.out.print("Enter the first few characters of " +
26                        "the last name to look up: ");
27       lookUp = keyboard.nextLine();
28
29       // Display all of the names that begin with the
30       // string entered by the user.
31       System.out.println("Here are the names that match:");
32       for (String person : people)
33       {
34          if (person.startsWith(lookUp))
35             System.out.println(person);
36       }
37    }
38 }
```

Program Output with Example Input Shown in Bold

```
Enter the first few characters of the last name to look up: Davis [Enter]
```

```
Here are the names that match:
Davis, George
Davis, Jenny
```

Program Output with Example Input Shown in Bold

```
Enter the first few characters of the last name to look up: Russ [Enter]
Here are the names that match:
Russert, Phil
Russell, Cindy
```

The regionMatches Methods

The String class provides overloaded versions of the regionMatches method, which determines whether specified regions of two strings match. The following code demonstrates:

```
String str = "Four score and seven years ago";
String str2 = "Those seven years passed quickly";
if (str.regionMatches(15, str2, 6, 11))
    System.out.println("The regions match.");
else
    System.out.println("The regions do not match.");
```

This code will display "The regions match." The specified region of the str string begins at position 15, and the specified region of the str2 string begins at position 6. Both regions consist of 11 characters. The specified region in the str string is "seven years" and the specified region in the str2 string is also "seven years". Because the two regions match, the regionMatches method in this code returns true. This version of the regionMatches method performs a case-sensitive comparison. An overloaded version accepts an additional argument indicating whether to perform a case-insensitive comparison. The following code demonstrates:

```
String str = "Four score and seven years ago";
String str2 = "THOSE SEVEN YEARS PASSED QUICKLY";

if (str.regionMatches(true, 15, str2, 6, 11))
    System.out.println("The regions match.");
else
    System.out.println("The regions do not match.");
```

This code will also display "The regions match." The first argument passed to this version of the regionMatches method can be true or false, indicating whether a case-insensitive comparison should be performed. In this example, true is passed, so case will be ignored when the regions "seven years" and "SEVEN YEARS" are compared.

Each of these methods indicates by a boolean return value whether a substring appears within a string. The String class also provides methods that not only search for items within a string, but also report the location of those items. Table 9-4 describes overloaded versions of the indexOf and lastIndexOf methods.

Table 9-4 `String` methods for getting a character or substring's location

Method	Description
`int indexOf(char ch)`	Searches the calling `String` object for the character passed into `ch`. If the character is found, the position of its first occurrence is returned. Otherwise, −1 is returned.
`int indexOf(char ch, int start)`	Searches the calling `String` object for the character passed into `ch`, beginning at the position passed into `start` and going to the end of the string. If the character is found, the position of its first occurrence is returned. Otherwise, −1 is returned.
`int indexOf(String str)`	Searches the calling `String` object for the string passed into `str`. If the string is found, the beginning position of its first occurrence is returned. Otherwise, −1 is returned.
`int indexOf(String str, int start)`	Searches the calling `String` object for the string passed into `str`. The search begins at the position passed into `start` and goes to the end of the string. If the string is found, the beginning position of its first occurrence is returned. Otherwise, −1 is returned.
`int lastIndexOf(char ch)`	Searches the calling `String` object for the character passed into `ch`. If the character is found, the position of its last occurrence is returned. Otherwise, −1 is returned.
`int lastIndexOf(char ch, int start)`	Searches the calling `String` object for the character passed into `ch`, beginning at the position passed into `start`. The search is conducted backward through the string, to position 0. If the character is found, the position of its last occurrence is returned. Otherwise, −1 is returned.
`int lastIndexOf(String str)`	Searches the calling `String` object for the string passed into `str`. If the string is found, the beginning position of its last occurrence is returned. Otherwise, −1 is returned.
`int lastIndexOf(String str, int start)`	Searches the calling `String` object for the string passed into `str`, beginning at the position passed into `start`. The search is conducted backward through the string, to position 0. If the string is found, the beginning position of its last occurrence is returned. Otherwise, −1 is returned.

Finding Characters with the `indexOf` and `lastIndexOf` Methods

The `indexOf` and `lastIndexOf` methods can search for either a character or a substring within the calling string. If the item being searched for is found, its position is returned. Otherwise -1 is returned. Here is an example of code using two of the methods to search for a character:

```
String str = "Four score and seven years ago";
int first, last;

first = str.indexOf('r');
last = str.lastIndexOf('r');

System.out.println("The letter r first appears at " +
                   "position " + first);

System.out.println("The letter r last appears at " +
                   "position " + last);
```

This code produces the following output:

```
The letter r first appears at position 3
The letter r last appears at position 24
```

The following code shows another example. It uses a loop to show the positions of each letter 'r' in the string.

```
String str = "Four score and seven years ago";
int position;

System.out.println("The letter r appears at the " +
                   "following locations:");
position = str.indexOf('r');
while (position != -1)
{
    System.out.println(position);
    position = str.indexOf('r', position + 1);
}
```

This code will produce the following output:

```
The letter r appears at the following locations:
3
8
24
```

The following code is very similar, but it uses the `lastIndexOf` method and shows the positions in reverse order:

```
String str = "Four score and seven years ago";
int position;

System.out.println("The letter r appears at the " +
                   "following locations.");
```

```java
position = str.lastIndexOf('r');
while (position != -1)
{
   System.out.println(position);
   position = str.lastIndexOf('r', position - 1);
}
```

This code will produce the following output:

```
The letter r appears at the following locations.
24
8
3
```

Finding Substrings with the `indexOf` and `lastIndexOf` Methods

The `indexOf` and `lastIndexOf` methods can also search for substrings within a string. The following code shows an example. It displays the starting positions of each occurrence of the word "and" within a string.

```java
String str = "and a one and a two and a three";
int position;
System.out.println("The word and appears at the " +
                   "following locations.");
position = str.indexOf("and");
while (position != -1)
{
   System.out.println(position);
   position = str.indexOf("and", position + 1);
}
```

This code produces the following output:

```
The word and appears at the following locations.
0
10
20
```

The following code also displays the same results, but in reverse order:

```java
String str = "and a one and a two and a three";
int position;

System.out.println("The word and appears at the " +
                   "following locations.");
position = str.lastIndexOf("and");
while (position != -1)
{
   System.out.println(position);
   position = str.lastIndexOf("and", position - 1);
}
```

This code produces the following output:

```
The word and appears at the following locations.
20
10
0
```

Extracting Substrings

The `String` class provides several methods that allow you to retrieve a substring from a string. The methods we will examine are listed in Table 9-5.

Table 9-5   String methods for extracting substrings

Method	Description
`String substring(int start)`	This method returns a copy of the substring that begins at *start* and goes to the end of the calling object's string.
`String substring(int start,` `int end)`	This method returns a copy of a substring. The argument passed into *start* is the substring's starting position, and the argument passed into *end* is the substring's ending position. The character at the *start* position is included in the substring, but the character at the *end* position is not included.

`void getChars(int start,`
    `int end,`
    `char[] array,`
    `int arrayStart)`
	This method extracts a substring from the calling object and stores it in a `char` array. The argument passed into *start* is the substring's starting position, and the argument passed into *end* is the substring's ending position. The character at the *start* position is included in the substring, but the character at the *end* position is not included. (The last character in the substring ends at *end* − 1.) The characters in the substring are stored as elements in the array that is passed into the *array* parameter. The *arrayStart* parameter specifies the starting subscript within the array where the characters are to be stored.

`char[] toCharArray()`	This method returns all of the characters in the calling object as a `char` array.

The `substring` Methods

The `substring` method returns a copy of a substring from the calling object. There are two overloaded versions of this method. The first version accepts an `int` argument that is the starting position of the substring. The method returns a reference to a `String` object containing all of the characters from the starting position to the end of the string. The character at the starting position is part of the substring. Here is an example of the method's use:

```
String fullName = "Cynthia Susan Lee";
String lastName = fullName.substring(14);
System.out.println("The full name is " + fullName);
System.out.println("The last name is " + lastName);
```

This code will produce the following output:

```
The full name is Cynthia Susan Lee
The last name is Lee
```

Keep in mind that the substring method returns a new String object that holds a copy of the substring. When this code executes, the fullName and lastName variables will reference two different String objects, as shown in Figure 9-5.

Figure 9-5 The fullName and lastName variables reference separate objects

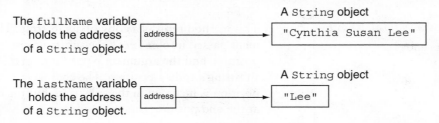

The second version of the method accepts two int arguments. The first specifies the substring's starting position and the second specifies the substring's ending position. The character at the starting position is included in the substring, but the character at the ending position is not. Here is an example of how the method is used:

```
String fullName = "Cynthia Susan Lee";
String middleName = fullName.substring(8, 13);
System.out.println("The full name is " + fullName);
System.out.println("The middle name is " + middleName);
```

The code will produce the following output:

```
The full name is Cynthia Susan Lee
The middle name is Susan
```

The getChars and toCharArray Methods

The getChars and toCharArray methods convert the calling String object to a char array. The getChars method can be used to convert a substring, while the toCharArray method converts the entire string. Here is an example of how the getChars method might be used:

```
String fullName = "Cynthia Susan Lee";
char[] nameArray = new char[5];
```

```
fullName.getChars(8, 13, nameArray, 0);
System.out.println("The full name is " + fullName);
System.out.println("The values in the array are:");
for (int i = 0; i < nameArray.length; i++)
    System.out.print(nameArray[i] + " ");
```

This code stores the individual characters of the substring "Susan" in the elements of the nameArray array, beginning at element 0. The code will produce the following output:

```
The full name is Cynthia Susan Lee
The values in the array are:
S u s a n
```

The toCharArray method returns a reference to a char array that contains all of the characters in the calling object. Here is an example:

```
String fullName = "Cynthia Susan Lee";
char[] nameArray;
nameArray = fullName.toCharArray();
System.out.println("The full name is " + fullName);
System.out.println("The values in the array are:");
for (int i = 0; i < nameArray.length; i++)
    System.out.print(nameArray[i] + " ");
```

This code will produce the following output:

```
The full name is Cynthia Susan Lee
The values in the array are:
C y n t h i a   S u s a n   L e e
```

These methods can be used when you want to use an array processing algorithm on the contents of a String object. The program in Code Listing 9-5 converts a String object to an array and then uses the array to determine the number of letters, digits, and whitespace characters in the string. Figure 9-6 shows an example of interaction with the program.

Code Listing 9-5   **(StringAnalyzer.java)**

```
 1 import javax.swing.JOptionPane;
 2
 3 /**
 4    This program displays the number of letters,
 5    digits, and whitespace characters in a string.
 6 */
 7
 8 public class StringAnalyzer
 9 {
10    public static void main(String [] args)
11    {
12       String input;       // To hold input
13       char[] array;       // Array for input
```

```
14          int letters = 0;      // Number of letters
15          int digits = 0;       // Number of digits
16          int whitespaces = 0;  // Number of whitespaces
17
18          // Get a string from the user.
19          input = JOptionPane.showInputDialog("Enter " +
20                                               "a string:");
21
22          // Convert the string to a char array.
23          array = input.toCharArray();
24
25          // Analyze the characters.
26          for (int i = 0; i < array.length; i++)
27          {
28             if (Character.isLetter(array[i]))
29                letters++;
30             else if (Character.isDigit(array[i]))
31                digits++;
32             else if (Character.isWhitespace(array[i]))
33                whitespaces++;
34          }
35
36          // Display the results.
37          JOptionPane.showMessageDialog(null,
38                          "That string contains " +
39                          letters + " letters, " +
40                          digits + " digits, and " +
41                          whitespaces +
42                          " whitespace characters.");
43
44          System.exit(0);
45       }
46 }
```

Figure 9-6 Interaction with the StringAnalyzer.java program

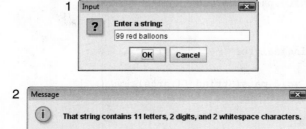

Methods That Return a Modified String

The String class methods listed in Table 9-6 return a modified copy of a String object.

Table 9-6 Methods that return a modified copy of a String object

Method	Description
String concat(String *str*)	This method returns a copy of the calling String object with the contents of *str* concatenated to it.
String replace(char *oldChar*, char *newChar*)	This method returns a copy of the calling String object, in which all occurrences of the character passed into *oldChar* have been replaced by the character passed into *newChar*.
String trim()	This method returns a copy of the calling String object, in which all leading and trailing whitespace characters have been deleted.

The concat method performs the same operation as the + operator when used with strings. For example, look at the following code, which uses the + operator:

```
String fullName;
String firstName = "Timothy ";
String lastName = "Haynes";
fullName = firstName + lastName;
```

Equivalent code can also be written with the concat method. Here is an example:

```
String fullName;
String firstName = "Timothy ";
String lastName = "Haynes";
fullName = firstName.concat(lastName);
```

The replace method returns a copy of a String object, where every occurrence of a specified character has been replaced with another character. For example, look at the following code:

```
String str1 = "Tom Talbert Tried Trains";
String str2;
str2 = str1.replace('T', 'D');
System.out.println(str1);
System.out.println(str2);
```

In this code, the replace method will return a copy of the str1 object with every occurrence of the letter 'T' replaced with the letter 'D'. The code will produce the following output:

```
Tom Talbert Tried Trains
Dom Dalbert Dried Drains
```

Remember that the `replace` method does not modify the contents of the calling `String` object, but returns a reference to a `String` that is a modified copy of it. After the previous code executes, the `str1` and `str2` variables will reference different `String` objects.

The `trim` method returns a copy of a `String` object with all leading and trailing whitespace characters deleted. A *leading* whitespace character is one that appears at the beginning, or left side, of a string. For example, the following string has three leading whitespace characters:

```
"   Hello"
```

A *trailing* whitespace character is one that appears at the end, or right side, of a string, after the non-space characters. For example, the following string has three trailing whitespace characters:

```
"Hello   "
```

Here is an example:

```
String greeting1 = "   Hello   ";
String greeting2;
greeting2 = greeting1.trim();
System.out.println("*" + greeting1 + "*");
System.out.println("*" + greeting2 + "*");
```

In this code, the first statement assigns the string "   Hello   " (with three leading spaces and three trailing spaces) to the `greeting1` variable. The `trim` method is called, which returns a copy of the string with the leading and trailing spaces removed. The code will produce the following output:

```
*   Hello   *
*Hello*
```

One common use of the `trim` method is to remove any leading or trailing spaces that the user might have entered while inputting data.

The Static `valueOf` Methods

The `String` class has several overloaded versions of a method named `valueOf`. This method accepts a value of any primitive data type as its argument and returns a string representation of the value. Table 9-7 describes these methods.

The following code demonstrates several of these methods:

```
boolean b = true;
char [] letters = { 'a', 'b', 'c', 'd', 'e' };
double d = 2.4981567;
int i = 7;

System.out.println(String.valueOf(b));
System.out.println(String.valueOf(letters));
System.out.println(String.valueOf(letters, 1, 3));
System.out.println(String.valueOf(d));
System.out.println(String.valueOf(i));
```

Table 9-7   Some of the String class's valueOf methods

Method	Description
String valueOf(boolean b)	If the boolean argument passed to b is true, the method returns the string "true". If the argument is false, the method returns the string "false".
String valueOf(char c)	This method returns a String containing the character passed into c.
String valueOf(char[] array)	This method returns a String that contains all of the elements in the char array passed into array.
String valueOf(char[] array, int subscript, int count)	This method returns a String that contains part of the elements in the char array passed into array. The argument passed into subscript is the starting subscript and the argument passed into count is the number of elements.
String valueOf(double number)	This method returns the String representation of the double argument passed into number.
String valueOf(float number)	This method returns the String representation of the float argument passed into number.
String valueOf(int number)	This method returns the String representation of the int argument passed into number.
String valueOf(long number)	This method returns the String representation of the long argument passed into number.

This code will produce the following output:

```
true
abcde
bcd
2.4981567
7
```

 Checkpoint

MyProgrammingLab™ *www.myprogramminglab.com*

9.7   Write a method that accepts a reference to a String object as an argument and returns true if the argument ends with the substring "ger". Otherwise, the method should return false.

9.8   Modify the method you wrote for Checkpoint 9.7 so it performs a case-insensitive test. The method should return true if the argument ends with "ger" in any possible combination of uppercase and lowercase letters.

9.9   Look at the following declaration:

```
String cafeName = "Broadway Cafe";
String str;
```

Which of the following methods would you use to make str reference the string "Broadway"?

```
startsWith
regionMatches
substring
indexOf
```

9.10 What is the difference between the indexOf and lastIndexOf methods?

9.11 What is the difference between the getChars and substring methods?

9.12 The + operator, when used with strings, performs the same operation as what String method?

9.13 What is the difference between the getChars and toCharArray methods?

9.14 Look at the following code:

```
String str1 = "To be, or not to be";
String str2 = str1.replace('o', 'u');
System.out.println(str1);
System.out.println(str2);
```

You hear a fellow student claim that the code will display the following:

```
Tu be ur nut tu be
Tu be ur nut tu be
```

Is your fellow student right or wrong? Why?

9.15 What will the following code display?

```
String str1 = "William ";
String str2 = " the ";
String str3 = " Conqueror";
System.out.println(str1.trim() + str2.trim() +
                        str3.trim());
```

9.16 Assume that a program has the following declarations:

```
double number = 9.47;
String str;
```

Write a statement that assigns a string representation of the number variable to str.

9.4 The StringBuilder Class

CONCEPT: The StringBuilder class is similar to the String class, except that you may change the contents of StringBuilder objects. The StringBuilder class also provides several useful methods that the String class does not have.

The StringBuilder class is similar to the String class. The main difference between the two is that you can change the contents of a StringBuilder object, but you cannot change the contents of a String object. Recall that String objects are immutable. This means that once you set the contents of a String object, you cannot change the string value that it holds. For example, look at the following code:

```
String name;
name = "George";
name = "Sally";
```

The first statement creates the name variable. The second creates a String object containing the string "George" and assigns its address to the name variable. Although we cannot change the contents of the String object, we can make the name variable reference a different String object. That's what the third statement does: It creates another String object containing the string "Sally", and assigns its address to name. This is illustrated by Figure 9-7.

Figure 9-7   The String object containing "George" is no longer referenced

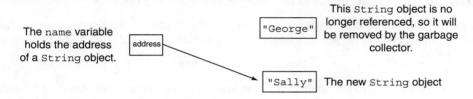

Unlike String objects, StringBuilder objects have methods that allow you to modify their contents without creating a new object in memory. You can change specific characters, insert characters, delete characters, and perform other operations. The StringBuilder object will grow or shrink in size, as needed, to accommodate the changes.

The fact that String objects are immutable is rarely a problem, but you might consider using StringBuilder objects if your program needs to make a lot of changes to one or more strings. This will improve the program's efficiency by reducing the number of String objects that must be created and then removed by the garbage collector. Now let's look at the StringBuilder class's constructors and methods.

The StringBuilder Constructors

Table 9-8 lists three of the StringBuilder constructors.

Table 9-8   StringBuilder constructors

Constructor	Description
StringBuilder()	This constructor accepts no arguments. It gives the object enough storage space to hold 16 characters, but no characters are stored in it.
StringBuilder(int *length*)	This constructor gives the object enough storage space to hold *length* characters, but no characters are stored in it.
StringBuilder(String *str*)	This constructor initializes the object with the string in str. The object's initial storage space will be the length of the string plus 16.

The first two constructors create empty `StringBuilder` objects of a specified size. The first constructor makes the `StringBuilder` object large enough to hold 16 characters, and the second constructor makes the object large enough to hold *length* characters. Remember, `StringBuilder` objects automatically resize themselves, so it is not a problem if you later want to store a larger string in the object. The third constructor accepts a `String` object as its argument and assigns the object's contents to the `StringBuilder` object. Here is an example of its use:

```
StringBuilder city = new StringBuilder("Charleston");
System.out.println(city);
```

This code creates a `StringBuilder` object and assigns its address to the `city` variable. The object is initialized with the string "Charleston". As demonstrated by this code, you can pass a `StringBuilder` object to the `println` and `print` methods.

One limitation of the `StringBuilder` class is that you cannot use the assignment operator to assign strings to `StringBuilder` objects. For example, the following code will not work:

```
StringBuilder city = "Charleston";  // ERROR!!! Will not work!
```

Instead of using the assignment operator, you must use the new key word and a constructor, or one of the `StringBuilder` methods, to store a string in a `StringBuilder` object.

Other `StringBuilder` Methods

The `StringBuilder` class provides many of the same methods as the `String` class. Table 9-9 lists several of the `StringBuilder` methods that work exactly like their `String` class counterparts.

Table 9-9   Methods that are common to the `String` and `StringBuilder` classes

```
char charAt(int position)
void getChars(int start, int end, char[] array, int arrayStart)
int indexOf(String str)
int indexOf(String str, int start)
int lastIndexOf(String str)
int lastIndexOf(String str, int start)
int length()
String substring(int start)
String substring(int start, int end)
```

In addition, the `StringBuilder` class provides several methods that the `String` class does not have. Let's look at a few of them.

The `append` Methods

The `StringBuilder` class has several overloaded versions of a method named `append`. These methods accept an argument, which may be of any primitive data type, a `char` array, or a `String` object. They append a string representation of their argument to the calling object's current contents. Because there are so many overloaded versions of `append`, we will examine the general form of a typical call to the method as follows:

```
object.append(item);
```

After the method is called, a string representation of *item* will be appended to *object*'s contents. The following code shows some of the `append` methods being used:

```
StringBuilder str = new StringBuilder();

// Append values to the object.
str.append("We sold ");          // Append a String object.
str.append(12);                  // Append an int.
str.append(" doughnuts for $");  // Append another String.
str.append(15.95);               // Append a double.

// Display the object's contents.
System.out.println(str);
```

This code will produce the following output:

```
We sold 12 doughnuts for $15.95
```

The `insert` Methods

The `StringBuilder` class also has several overloaded versions of a method named `insert`, which inserts a value into the calling object's string. These methods accept two arguments: an `int` that specifies the position in the calling object's string where the insertion should begin, and the value to be inserted. The value to be inserted may be of any primitive data type, a `char` array, or a `String` object. Because there are so many overloaded versions of `insert`, we will examine the general form of a typical call to the method as follows:

```
object.insert(start, item);
```

In the general form, *start* is the starting position of the insertion and *item* is the item to be inserted. The following code shows an example:

```
StringBuilder str = new StringBuilder("New City");
str.insert(4, "York ");
System.out.println(str);
```

The first statement creates a `StringBuilder` object initialized with the string `"New City"`. The second statement inserts the string `"York "` into the `StringBuilder` object, beginning at position 4. The characters that are currently in the object beginning at position 4 are moved to the right. In memory, the `StringBuilder` object is automatically expanded in size to accommodate the inserted characters. If these statements were in a complete program and we ran it, we would see `New York City` displayed on the screen.

The following code shows how a `char` array can be inserted into a `StringBuilder` object:

```
char cArray[] = { '2', '0', ' ' };
StringBuilder str = new StringBuilder("In July we sold cars.");
str.insert(16, cArray);
System.out.println(str);
```

The first statement declares a char array named cArray, containing the characters '2', '0', and ' '. The second statement creates a StringBuilder object initialized with the string "In July we sold cars." The third statement inserts the characters in cArray into the StringBuilder object, beginning at position 16. The characters that are currently in the object beginning at position 16 are moved to the right. If these statements were in a complete program and we ran it, we would see In July we sold 20 cars. displayed on the screen.

The replace Method

The StringBuilder class has a replace method that differs slightly from the String class's replace method. While the String class's replace method replaces the occurrences of one character with another character, the StringBuilder class's replace method replaces a specified substring with a string. Here is the general form of a call to the method:

```
object.replace(start, end, str);
```

In the general form, start is an int that specifies the starting position of a substring in the calling object, and end is an int that specifies the ending position of the substring. (The starting position is included in the substring, but the ending position is not.) The str parameter is a String object. After the method executes, the substring will be replaced with str. Here is an example:

```
StringBuilder str =
    new StringBuilder("We moved from Chicago to Atlanta.");
str.replace(14, 21, "New York");
System.out.println(str);
```

The replace method in this code replaces the word "Chicago" with "New York". The code will produce the following output:

```
We moved from New York to Atlanta.
```

The delete, deleteCharAt, and setCharAt Methods

The delete and deleteCharAt methods are used to delete a substring or a character from a StringBuilder object. The setCharAt method changes a specified character to another value. Table 9-10 describes these methods.

Table 9-10 The StringBuilder class's delete, deleteCharAt, and setCharAt methods

Method	Description
StringBuilder delete(int start, int end)	The start parameter is an int that specifies the starting position of a substring in the calling object, and the end parameter is an int that specifies the ending position of the substring. (The starting position is included in the substring, but the ending position is not.) The method will delete the substring.
StringBuilder deleteCharAt (int position)	The position parameter specifies the location of a character that will be deleted.
void setCharAt(int position, char ch)	This method changes the character at position to the value passed into ch.

The following code demonstrates all three of these methods:

```java
StringBuilder str =
    new StringBuilder("I ate 100 blueberries!");

// Display the StringBuilder object.
System.out.println(str);

// Delete the '0'.
str.deleteCharAt(8);

// Delete "blue".
str.delete(9, 13);

// Display the StringBuilder object.
System.out.println(str);

// Change the '1' to '5'
str.setCharAt(6, '5');

// Display the StringBuilder object.
System.out.println(str);
```

This code will produce the following output:

```
I ate 100 blueberries!
I ate 10 berries!
I ate 50 berries!
```

The toString Method

If you need to convert a StringBuilder object to a regular string, you can call the object's toString method. The following code shows an example of a StringBuilder object's contents being assigned to a String variable:

```java
StringBuilder strb = new StringBuilder("This is a test.");
String str = strb.toString();
```

In the Spotlight:

Formatting and Unformatting Telephone Numbers

Telephone numbers in the United States are commonly formatted to appear in the following manner:

(XXX)XXX-XXXX

In the format, x represents a digit. The three digits that appear inside the parentheses are the area code. The three digits following the area code are the prefix, and the four digits after the hyphen are the line number. Here is an example:

(919)555-1212

Although the parentheses and the hyphen make the number easier for people to read, those characters are unnecessary for processing by a computer. In a computer system, a telephone number is commonly stored as an unformatted series of digits, as shown here:

9195551212

A program that works with telephone numbers usually needs to unformat numbers that have been entered by the user. This means that the parentheses and the hyphen must be removed before the number is stored in a file or processed in some other way. In addition, such a program needs the ability to format the digits so that the number contains the parentheses and the hyphen when it appears on the screen or is printed on paper.

Code Listing 9-6 shows a class named `Telephone` that contains the following static methods:

- `isFormatted`—This method accepts a `String` argument and returns `true` if the argument is formatted as `(XXX)XXX-XXXX`. If the argument is not formatted this way, the method returns `false`.
- `unformat`—This method accepts a `String` argument. If the argument is formatted as `(XXX)XXX-XXXX`, the method returns an unformatted version of the argument with the parentheses and the hyphen removed. Otherwise, the method returns the original argument.
- `format`—This method's purpose is to format a sequence of digits as `(XXX)XXX-XXXX`. The sequence of digits is passed as a `String` argument. If the argument is 10 characters in length, then the method returns the argument with parentheses and a hyphen inserted. Otherwise, the method returns the original argument.

The program in Code Listing 9-7 demonstrates the `Telephone` class.

Code Listing 9-6   (`Telephone.java`)

```
 1 /**
 2     The Telephone class provides static methods
 3     for formatting and unformatting U.S. telephone
 4     numbers.
 5 */
 6
 7 public class Telephone
 8 {
 9    // These constant fields hold the valid lengths of
10    // strings that are formatted and unformatted.
11    public final static int FORMATTED_LENGTH = 13;
12    public final static int UNFORMATTED_LENGTH = 10;
13
14    /**
15       The isFormatted method determines whether a
16       string is properly formatted as a U.S. telephone
17       number in the following manner:
18       (XXX)XXX-XXXX
19       @param str The string to test.
```

```
20        @return true if the string is properly formatted,
21               or false otherwise.
22     */
23
24     public static boolean isFormatted(String str)
25     {
26        boolean valid;    // Flag to indicate valid format
27
28        // Determine whether str is properly formatted.
29        if (str.length() == FORMATTED_LENGTH &&
30            str.charAt(0) == '(' &&
31            str.charAt(4) == ')' &&
32            str.charAt(8) == '-')
33            valid = true;
34        else
35           valid = false;
36
37        // Return the value of the valid flag.
38        return valid;
39     }
40
41     /**
42        The unformat method accepts a string containing
43        a telephone number formatted as:
44        (XXX)XXX-XXXX.
45        If the argument is formatted in this way, the
46        method returns an unformatted string where the
47        parentheses and hyphen have been removed. Otherwise,
48        it returns the original argument.
49        @param str The string to unformat.
50        @return An unformatted string.
51     */
52
53     public static String unformat(String str)
54     {
55        // Create a StringBuilder initialized with str.
56        StringBuilder strb = new StringBuilder(str);
57
58        // If the argument is properly formatted, then
59        // unformat it.
60        if (isFormatted(str))
61        {
62           // First, delete the left paren at position 0.
63           strb.deleteCharAt(0);
64
65           // Next, delete the right paren. Because of the
66           // previous deletion it is now located at
67           // position 3.
```

```
68              strb.deleteCharAt(3);
69
70              // Next, delete the hyphen. Because of the
71              // previous deletions it is now located at
72              // position 6.
73              strb.deleteCharAt(6);
74          }
75
76          // Return the unformatted string.
77          return strb.toString();
78      }
79
80      /**
81         The format method formats a string as:
82         (XXX)XXX-XXXX.
83         If the length of the argument is UNFORMATTED_LENGTH
84         the method returns the formatted string. Otherwise,
85         it returns the original argument.
86         @param str The string to format.
87         @return A string formatted as a U.S. telephone number.
88      */
89
90      public static String format(String str)
91      {
92          // Create a StringBuilder initialized with str.
93          StringBuilder strb = new StringBuilder(str);
94
95          // If the argument is the correct length, then
96          // format it.
97          if (str.length() == UNFORMATTED_LENGTH)
98          {
99              // First, insert the left paren at position 0.
100             strb.insert(0, "(");
101
102             // Next, insert the right paren at position 4.
103             strb.insert(4, ")");
104
105             // Next, insert the hyphen at position 8.
106             strb.insert(8, "-");
107         }
108
109         // Return the formatted string.
110         return strb.toString();
111     }
112 }
```

Code Listing 9-7   (TelephoneTester.java)

```java
 1 import java.util.Scanner;
 2
 3 /**
 4    This program demonstrates the Telephone
 5    class's static methods.
 6 */
 7
 8 public class TelephoneTester
 9 {
10    public static void main(String[] args)
11    {
12       String phoneNumber;  // To hold a phone number
13
14       // Create a Scanner object for keyboard input.
15       Scanner keyboard = new Scanner(System.in);
16
17       // Get an unformatted telephone number.
18       System.out.print("Enter an unformatted telephone number: ");
19       phoneNumber = keyboard.nextLine();
20
21       // Format the telephone number.
22       System.out.println("Formatted: " +
23             Telephone.format(phoneNumber));
24
25       // Get a formatted telephone number.
26       System.out.println("Enter a telephone number formatted as");
27       System.out.print("(XXX)XXX-XXXX : ");
28       phoneNumber = keyboard.nextLine();
29
30       // Unformat the telephone number.
31       System.out.println("Unformatted: " +
32             Telephone.unformat(phoneNumber));
33    }
34 }
```

Program Output with Example Input Shown in Bold

Enter an unformatted telephone number: **9195551212 [Enter]**
Formatted: (919)555-1212
Enter a telephone number formatted as
(XXX)XXX-XXXX : **(828)555-1212 [Enter]**
Unformatted: 8285551212

NOTE: The Java API provides a class named StringBuffer, which is essentially the same as the StringBuilder class, with the same constructors and the same methods. The difference is that the methods in the StringBuffer class are *synchronized*. This means that the StringBuffer class is safe to use in a multithreaded application. Multithreaded programming is beyond the scope of this book, but in a nutshell, a *multithreaded application* is one that concurrently runs multiple threads of execution. In such an application, it is possible for more than one thread to access the same objects in memory at the same time. In multithreaded applications, it is important that the methods be synchronized, to prevent the possibility of data corruption.

Because synchronization requires extra steps to be performed, the StringBuffer class is slower than the StringBuilder class. In an application where the object will not be accessed by multiple threads, you should use the StringBuilder class to get the best performance. In an application where multiple threads will be accessing the object, you should use the StringBuffer class to ensure that its data does not become corrupted.

Checkpoint

MyProgrammingLab™ *www.myprogramminglab.com*

9.17 The String class is immutable. What does this mean?

9.18 In a program that makes lots of changes to strings, would it be more efficient to use String objects or StringBuilder objects? Why?

9.19 Look at the following statement:

```
String city = "Asheville";
```

Rewrite this statement so that city references a StringBuilder object instead of a String object.

9.20 You wish to add a string to the end of the existing contents of a StringBuilder object. What method do you use?

9.21 You wish to insert a string into the existing contents of a StringBuilder object. What method do you use?

9.22 You wish to delete a specific character from the existing contents of a StringBuilder object. What method do you use?

9.23 You wish to change a specific character in a StringBuilder object. What method do you use?

9.24 How does the StringBuilder class's replace method differ from the String class's replace method?

9.5 Tokenizing Strings

CONCEPT: Tokenizing a string is a process of breaking a string down into its components, which are called tokens. The `String` class's `split` method can be used to tokenize strings.

Sometimes a string will contain a series of words or other items of data separated by spaces or other characters. For example, look at the following string:

```
"peach raspberry strawberry vanilla"
```

This string contains the following four items of data: `peach`, `raspberry`, `strawberry`, and `vanilla`. In programming terms, items such as these are known as *tokens*. Notice that a space appears between the items. The character that separates tokens is known as a *delimiter*. Here is another example:

```
"17;92;81;12;46;5"
```

This string contains the following tokens: 17, 92, 81, 12, 46, and 5. Notice that a semicolon appears between each item. In this example the semicolon is used as a delimiter. Some programming problems require you to read a string that contains a list of items and then extract all of the tokens from the string for processing. For example, look at the following string that contains a date:

```
"3-22-2015"
```

The tokens in this string are 3, 22, and 2015, and the delimiter is the hyphen character. Perhaps a program needs to extract the month, day, and year from such a string. Another example is an operating system pathname, such as the following:

```
/home/rsullivan/data
```

The tokens in this string are `home`, `rsullivan`, and `data`, and the delimiter is the / character. Perhaps a program needs to extract all of the directory names from such a pathname.

The process of breaking a string into tokens is known as *tokenizing*. In this section, we will discuss the `String` class's `split` method, a tool that you can use to tokenize strings.

The `String` class has a method named `split`, which tokenizes a string and returns an array of `String` objects. Each element in the array is one of the tokens. As an example, look at Code Listing 9-8.

Code Listing 9-8

```
1 /**
2    This program demonstrates the String class's
3    split method.
4 */
5
6 public class SplitDemo1
```

```
7  {
8     public static void main(String[] args)
9     {
10        // Create a string to tokenize.
11        String str = "one two three four";
12
13        // Get the tokens, using a space delimiter.
14        String[] tokens = str.split(" ");
15
16        // Display the tokens.
17        for (String s : tokens)
18           System.out.println(s);
19     }
20 }
```

Program Output

```
one
two
three
four
```

In line 11, we assign the string "one two three four" to the str variable. Notice that the words are separated by spaces. Line 14 calls the str object's split method. The argument passed to the split method indicates the delimiter. In this example, a space is used as the delimiter. The method returns an array containing the strings "one", "two", "three", and "four". The array is assigned to the tokens variable. Then, the for loop in lines 17 and 18 displays the elements of the array.

The argument that you pass to the split method is a *regular expression*. A regular expression is a string that specifies a pattern of characters. Regular expressions can be powerful tools, and are commonly used to search for patterns that exist in strings, files, or other collections of text. A complete discussion of regular expressions is outside the scope of this book. However, we will discuss some basic uses of regular expressions for the purpose of tokenizing strings.

In the previous example, we passed a string containing a single space to the split method. This specified that the space character was the delimiter. The split method also allows you to use multi-character delimiters. This means you are not limited to a single character as a delimiter. Your delimiters can be entire words, if you wish. The following code, which is taken from the program *SplitDemo2.java* in this chapter's source code, demonstrates:

```
// Create a string to tokenize.
String str = "one and two and three and four";

// Get the tokens, using " and " as the delimiter.
String[] tokens = str.split(" and ");
```

```
// Display the tokens.
for (String s : tokens)
   System.out.println(s);
```

This code will produce the following output:

```
one
two
three
four
```

The previous code demonstrates multi-character delimiters (delimiters containing multiple characters). You can also specify a series of characters where each individual character is a delimiter. For example, look at the following email address:

```
joe@gaddisbooks.com
```

This string uses two delimiters: @ (the "at" character) and . (the period). To specify that both the @ character and the . character are delimiters, we must enclose them in brackets inside our regular expression. The regular expression will look like this:

```
"[@.]"
```

Because the @ and . characters are enclosed in brackets, they will each be considered as a delimiter. The following code, which is taken from the program *SplitDemo3.java* in this chapter's source code, demonstrates:

```
// Create a string to tokenize.
String str = "joe@gaddisbooks.com";

// Get the tokens, using @ and . as delimiters.
String[] tokens = str.split("[@.]");

// Display the tokens.
for (String s : tokens)
   System.out.println(s);
```

This code will produce the following output:

```
joe
gaddisbooks
com
```

Trimming a String before Tokenizing

When you are tokenizing a string that was entered by the user, and you are using characters other than whitespaces as delimiters, you will probably want to trim the string before tokenizing it. Otherwise, if the user enters leading whitespace characters, they will become part of the first token. Likewise, if the user enters trailing whitespace characters, they will become part of the last token. For example, look at the following code:

```
// Create a string with leading and trailing whitespaces.
String str = " one;two;three ";
```

```
// Tokenize the string using the semicolon as a delimiter.
String[] tokens = str.split(";");

// Display the tokens.
for (String s : tokens)
{
    System.out.println("*" + s + "*");
}
```

Notice that the string referenced by str contains a leading and a trailing space. This code will produce the following output:

```
* one*
*two*
*three *
```

Notice in the output that the first token contains the leading space and the last token contains the trailing space. To prevent leading and/or trailing whitespace characters from being included in the tokens, use the String class's trim method to remove them. Here is the same code, modified to use the trim method:

```
// Create a string with leading and trailing whitespaces.
String str = " one;two;three ";

// Trim leading and trailing whitespace.
str = str.trim();

// Tokenize the string using the semicolon as a delimiter.
String[] tokens = str.split(";");

// Display the tokens.
for (String s : tokens)
{
    System.out.println("*" + s + "*");
}
```

This code will produce the following output:

```
*one*
*two*
*three*
```

 Checkpoint

MyProgrammingLab™ *www.myprogramminglab.com*

9.25 The following string contains three tokens. What are they? What character is the delimiter?

```
"apples pears bananas"
```

9.26   Look at the following code:

```
String str = "one two three four";
String[] tokens = str.split(" ");
int x = tokens.length;
String first = tokens[0];
```

What value will be stored in x? What value will the `first` variable reference?

9.27   Look at the following string:

```
"/home/rjones/mydata.txt"
```

Write code using the `String` class's `split` method that can be used to extract the following tokens from the string: `home` , `rjones` , `mydata` , and `txt`.

9.28   Look at the following string:

```
"dog$cat@bird%squirrel"
```

Write code using the `String` class's `split` method that can be used to extract the following tokens from the string: `dog`, `cat`, `bird`, and `squirrel`.

9.6 Wrapper Classes for the Numeric Data Types

CONCEPT: The Java API provides wrapper classes for each of the numeric data types. These classes have methods that perform useful operations involving primitive numeric values.

Earlier in this chapter, we discussed the `Character` wrapper class and some of its static methods. The Java API also provides wrapper classes for all of the numeric primitive data types, as listed in Table 9-13.

You have already used many of these wrapper classes' "parse" methods, which convert strings to values of the primitive types. For example, the `Integer.parseInt` method converts a string to an `int`, and the `Double.parseDouble` method converts a string to a `double`. Now we will examine other methods and uses of the wrapper classes.

Table 9-13   Wrapper classes for the numeric primitive data types

Wrapper Class	Primitive Type It Applies To
Byte	byte
Double	double
Float	float
Integer	int
Long	long
Short	short

The Static `toString` Methods

Each of the numeric wrapper classes has a static `toString` method that converts a number to a string. The method accepts the number as its argument and returns a string representation of that number. The following code demonstrates:

```
int i = 12;
double d = 14.95;
String str1 = Integer.toString(i);
String str2 = Double.toString(d);
```

The `toBinaryString`, `toHexString`, and `toOctalString` Methods

The `toBinaryString`, `toHexString`, and `toOctalString` methods are static members of the `Integer` and `Long` wrapper classes. These methods accept an integer as an argument and return a string representation of that number converted to binary, hexadecimal, or octal. The following code demonstrates these methods:

```
int number = 14;
System.out.println(Integer.toBinaryString(number));
System.out.println(Integer.toHexString(number));
System.out.println(Integer.toOctalString(number));
```

This code will produce the following output:

```
1110
e
16
```

The `MIN_VALUE` and `MAX_VALUE` Constants

The numeric wrapper classes each have a set of static `final` variables named `MIN_VALUE` and `MAX_VALUE`. These variables hold the minimum and maximum values for a particular data type. For example, `Integer.MAX_VALUE` holds the maximum value that an `int` can hold. For example, the following code displays the minimum and maximum values for an `int`:

```
System.out.println("The minimum value for an " +
                   "int is " + Integer.MIN_VALUE);
System.out.println("The maximum value for an " +
                   "int is " + Integer.MAX_VALUE);
```

Autoboxing and Unboxing

It is possible to create objects from the wrapper classes. One way is to pass an initial value to the constructor, as shown here:

```
Integer number = new Integer(7);
```

This creates an `Integer` object initialized with the value 7, referenced by the variable `number`. Another way is to simply declare a wrapper class variable, and then assign a primitive value to it. For example, look at the following code:

```
Integer number;
number = 7;
```

The first statement in this code declares an `Integer` variable named `number`. It does not create an `Integer` object, just a variable. The second statement is a simple assignment statement. It assigns the primitive value 7 to the variable. You might suspect that this will cause an error. After all, `number` is a reference variable, not a primitive variable. However, because `number` is a wrapper class variable, Java performs an autoboxing operation. *Autoboxing* is Java's process of automatically "boxing up" a value inside an object. When this assignment statement executes, Java boxes up the value 7 inside an `Integer` object, and then assigns the address of that object to the `number` variable.

Unboxing is the opposite of boxing. It is the process of converting a wrapper class object to a primitive type. The following code demonstrates an unboxing operation:

```
Integer myInt = 5;          // Autoboxes the value 5
int primitiveNumber;
primitiveNumber = myInt;    // Unboxes the object
```

The first statement in this code declares `myInt` as an `Integer` reference variable. The primitive value 5 is autoboxed, and the address of the resulting object is assigned to the `myInt` variable. The second statement declares `primitiveNumber` as an `int` variable. Then, the third statement assigns the `myInt` object to `primitiveNumber`. When this statement executes, Java automatically unboxes the `myInt` wrapper class object and stores the resulting value, which is 5, in `primitiveNumber`.

Although you rarely need to create an instance of a wrapper class, Java's autoboxing and unboxing features make some operations more convenient. Occasionally, you will find yourself in a situation where you want to perform an operation using a primitive variable, but the operation can only be used with an object. For example, recall the `ArrayList` class that we discussed in Chapter 7. An `ArrayList` is an array-like object that can be used to store other objects. You cannot, however, store primitive values in an `ArrayList`. It is intended for objects only. If you try to compile the following statement, an error will occur:

```
ArrayList<int> list = new ArrayList<int>();   // ERROR!
```

However, you can store wrapper class objects in an `ArrayList`. If we need to store int values in an `ArrayList`, we have to specify that the `ArrayList` will hold `Integer` objects. Here is an example:

```
ArrayList<Integer> list = new ArrayList<Integer>(); // Okay.
```

This statement declares that `list` references an `ArrayList` that can hold `Integer` objects. One way to store an int value in the `ArrayList` is to instantiate an `Integer` object, initialize it with the desired int value, and then pass the `Integer` object to the `ArrayList`'s add method. Here is an example:

```
ArrayList<Integer> list = new ArrayList<Integer>();
Integer myInt = 5;
list.add(myInt);
```

However, Java's autoboxing and unboxing features make it unnecessary to create the Integer object. If you add an int value to the ArrayList, Java will autobox the value. The following code works without any problems:

```
ArrayList<Integer> list = new ArrayList<Integer>();
list.add(5);
```

When the value 5 is passed to the add method, Java boxes the value up in an Integer object. When necessary, Java also unboxes values that are retrieved from the ArrayList. The following code demonstrates this:

```
ArrayList<Integer> list = new ArrayList<Integer>();
list.add(5);
int primitiveNumber = list.get(0);
```

The last statement in this code retrieves the item at index 0. Because the item is being assigned to an int variable, Java unboxes it and stores the primitive value in the int variable.

Checkpoint

MyProgrammingLab™ *www.myprogramminglab.com*

9.29 Write a statement that converts the following integer to a string and stores it in the String object referenced by str:

```
int i = 99;
```

9.30 What wrapper class methods convert a number from decimal to another numbering system? What wrapper classes are these methods a member of?

9.31 What is the purpose of the MIN_VALUE and MAX_VALUE variables that are members of the numeric wrapper classes?

9.7 Focus on Problem Solving: The TestScoreReader Class

Professor Harrison keeps her students' test scores in a Microsoft Excel spreadsheet. Figure 9-8 shows a set of five test scores for five students. Each column holds a test score and each row represents the scores for one student.

Figure 9-8 Microsoft Excel spreadsheet

	A	B	C	D	E	F
1	87	79	91	82	94	
2	72	79	81	74	88	
3	94	92	81	89	96	
4	77	56	67	81	79	
5	79	82	85	81	90	
6						

In addition to manipulating the scores in Excel, Dr. Harrison wants to write a Java application that accesses them. Excel, like many commercial applications, has the ability to export data to a text file. When the data in a spreadsheet is exported, each row is written to a line, and the values in the cells are separated by commas. For example, when the data shown in Figure 9-8 is exported, it will be written to a text file in the following format:

```
87,79,91,82,94
72,79,81,74,88
94,92,81,89,96
77,56,67,81,79
79,82,85,81,90
```

This is called the *comma separated value* file format. When you save a spreadsheet in this format, Excel saves it to a file with the *.csv* extension. Dr. Harrison decides to export her spreadsheet to a *.csv* file, and then write a Java program that reads the file. The program will use the String class's split method to extract the test scores from each line, and a wrapper class to convert the tokens to numeric values. As an experiment, she writes the TestScoreReader class shown in Code Listing 9-9.

Code Listing 9-9   **(TestScoreReader.java)**

```java
 1 import java.io.*;
 2 import java.util.Scanner;
 3
 4 /**
 5    The TestScoreReader class reads test scores as
 6    tokens from a file and calculates the average
 7    of each line of scores.
 8 */
 9
10 public class TestScoreReader
11 {
12    private Scanner inputFile;
13    private String line;
14
15    /**
16       The constructor opens a file to read
17       the grades from.
18       @param filename The file to open.
19    */
20
21    public TestScoreReader(String filename)
22                           throws IOException
23    {
24       File file = new File(filename);
25       inputFile = new Scanner(file);
26    }
27
28    /**
29       The readNextLine method reads the next line
30       from the file.
31       @return true if the line was read, false
```

```
32      otherwise.
33   */
34
35   public boolean readNextLine() throws IOException
36   {
37      boolean lineRead; // Flag variable
38
39      // Determine whether there is more to read.
40      lineRead = inputFile.hasNext();
41
42      // If so, read the next line.
43      if (lineRead)
44         line = inputFile.nextLine();
45
46      return lineRead;
47   }
48
49   /**
50      The getAverage method calculates the average
51      of the last set of test scores read from the file.
52      @return The average.
53   */
54
55   public double getAverage()
56   {
57      int total = 0;    // Accumulator
58      double average;   // The average test score
59
60      // Tokenize the last line read from the file.
61      String[] tokens = line.split(",");
62
63      // Calculate the total of the test scores.
64      for (String str : tokens)
65      {
66         total += Integer.parseInt(str);
67      }
68
69      // Calculate the average of the scores.
70      // Use a cast to avoid integer division.
71      average = (double) total / tokens.length;
72
73      // Return the average.
74      return average;
75   }
76
77   /**
78      The close method closes the file.
79   */
```

```
80
81    public void close() throws IOException
82    {
83       inputFile.close();
84    }
85 }
```

The constructor accepts the name of a file as an argument and opens the file. The readNextLine method reads a line from the file and stores it in the line field. The method returns true if a line was successfully read from the file, or false if there are no more lines to read. The getAverage method tokenizes the last line read from the file, converts the tokens to int values, and calculates the average of the values. The average is returned. The program in Code Listing 9-10 uses the TestScoreReader class to open the file *Grades.csv* and get the averages of the test scores it contains.

Code Listing 9-10   (TestAverages.java)

```
1 import java.io.*;  // Needed for IOException
2
3 /**
4    This program uses the TestScoreReader class
5    to read test scores from a file and get
6    their averages.
7 */
8
9 public class TestAverages
10 {
11    public static void main(String[] args)
12                    throws IOException
13    {
14       double average;        // Test average
15       int studentNumber = 1;  // Control variable
16
17       // Create a TestScoreReader object.
18       TestScoreReader scoreReader =
19               new TestScoreReader("Grades.csv");
20
21       // Display the averages.
22       while (scoreReader.readNextLine())
23       {
24          // Get the average from the TestScoreReader.
25          average = scoreReader.getAverage();
26
27          // Display the student's average.
28          System.out.println("Average for student " +
29                          studentNumber + " is " +
30                          average);
```

```
31
32          // Increment the student number.
33          studentNumber++;
34       }
35
36       // Close the TestScoreReader.
37       scoreReader.close();
38       System.out.println("No more scores.");
39    }
40 }
```

Program Output

```
Average for student 1 is 86.6
Average for student 2 is 78.8
Average for student 3 is 90.4
Average for student 4 is 72.0
Average for student 5 is 83.4
No more scores.
```

Dr. Harrison's class works properly, and she decides that she can expand it to perform other, more complex, operations.

9.8 Common Errors to Avoid

The following list describes several errors that are commonly committed when learning this chapter's topics:

- **Using static wrapper class methods as if they were instance methods.** Many of the most useful wrapper class methods are static, and you should call them directly from the class.
- **Trying to use `String` comparison methods such as `startsWith` and `endsWith` for case-insensitive comparisons.** Most of the `String` comparison methods are case-sensitive. Only the `regionMatches` method performs a case-insensitive comparison.
- **Thinking of the first position of a string as 1.** Many of the `String` and `StringBuilder` methods accept a character position within a string as an argument. Remember, the position numbers in a string start at zero. If you think of the first position in a string as 1, you will cause an off-by-one error.
- **Thinking of the ending position of a substring as part of the substring.** Methods such as `getChars` accept the starting and ending position of a substring as arguments. The character at the *start* position is included in the substring, but the character at the *end* position is not included. (The last character in the substring ends at *end* − 1.)
- **Forgetting to trim a string before tokenizing it.** When tokenizing a string, and using characters other than whitespaces as delimiters, you will probably want to trim the string before tokenizing it. Otherwise, if the string contains leading and/or trailing whitespace characters, they will become part of the first and last tokens.

Review Questions and Exercises

Multiple Choice and True/False

1. The `isDigit`, `isLetter`, and `isLetterOrDigit` methods are members of this class.
   a. `String`
   b. `Char`
   c. `Character`
   d. `StringBuilder`

2. This method converts a character to uppercase.
   a. `makeUpperCase`
   b. `toUpperCase`
   c. `isUpperCase`
   d. `upperCase`

3. The `startsWith`, `endsWith`, and `regionMatches` methods are members of this class.
   a. `String`
   b. `Char`
   c. `Character`
   d. `Wrapper`

4. The `indexOf` and `lastIndexOf` methods are members of this class.
   a. `String`
   b. `Integer`
   c. `Character`
   d. `Wrapper`

5. The `substring`, `getChars`, and `toCharArray` methods are members of this class.
   a. `String`
   b. `Float`
   c. `Character`
   d. `Wrapper`

6. This `String` class method performs the same operation as the + operator when used on strings.
   a. `add`
   b. `join`
   c. `concat`
   d. `plus`

7. The `String` class has several overloaded versions of a method that accepts a value of any primitive data type as its argument and returns a string representation of the value. The name of the method is _____.
   a. `stringValue`
   b. `valueOf`
   c. `getString`
   d. `valToString`

8. If you do not pass an argument to the `StringBuilder` constructor, the object will have enough memory to store this many characters.
   a. 16
   b. 1
   c. 256
   d. Unlimited

9. This is one of the methods that are common to both the `String` and `StringBuilder` classes.
   a. `append`
   b. `insert`
   c. `delete`
   d. `length`

10. To change the value of a specific character in a `StringBuilder` object, use this method.
    a. `changeCharAt`
    b. `setCharAt`
    c. `setChar`
    d. `change`

11. To delete a specific character in a `StringBuilder` object, use this method.
    a. `deleteCharAt`
    b. `removeCharAt`
    c. `removeChar`
    d. `expunge`

12. The character that separates tokens in a string is known as a _____.
    a. separator
    b. tokenizer
    c. delimiter
    d. terminator

13. This `String` method breaks a string into tokens.
    a. `break`
    b. `tokenize`
    c. `getTokens`
    d. `split`

14. These static `final` variables are members of the numeric wrapper classes and hold the minimum and maximum values for a particular data type.
    a. `MIN_VALUE` and `MAX_VALUE`
    b. `MIN` and `MAX`
    c. `MINIMUM` and `MAXIMUM`
    d. `LOWEST` and `HIGHEST`

15. **True or False:** Character testing methods, such as `isLetter`, accept strings as arguments and test each character in the string.

16. **True or False:** If the `toUpperCase` method's argument is already uppercase, it is returned as is, with no changes.

17. **True or False:** If `toLowerCase` method's argument is already lowercase, it will be inadvertently converted to uppercase.

18. **True or False:** The startsWith and endsWith methods are case-sensitive.
19. **True or False:** There are two versions of the regionMatches method: one that is case-sensitive and one that can be case-insensitive.
20. **True or False:** The indexOf and lastIndexOf methods can find characters, but cannot find substrings.
21. **True or False:** The String class's replace method can replace individual characters, but cannot replace substrings.
22. **True or False:** The StringBuilder class's replace method can replace individual characters, but cannot replace substrings.
23. **True or False:** You can use the = operator to assign a string to a StringBuilder object.

Find the Error

Find the error in each of the following code segments:

1.
```
int number = 99;
String str;
// Convert number to a string.
str.valueOf(number);
```

2.
```
// Store a name in a StringBuilder object.
StringBuilder name = "Joe Schmoe";
```

3.
```
// Change the very first character of a
// StringBuilder object to 'Z'.
str.setCharAt(1, 'Z');
```

4.
```
// Tokenize a string that is delimited
// with semicolons. The string has 3 tokens.
String str = "one;two;three";
String tokens = str.split(";");
System.out.println(tokens);
```

Algorithm Workbench

1. The following if statement determines whether choice is equal to 'Y' or 'y':

   `if (choice == 'Y' || choice == 'y')`

   Rewrite this statement so it makes only one comparison and does not use the || operator. (*Hint: Use either the toUpperCase or toLowerCase method.*)
2. Write a loop that counts the number of space characters that appear in the String object str.
3. Write a loop that counts the number of digits that appear in the String object str.
4. Write a loop that counts the number of lowercase characters that appear in the String object str.
5. Write a method that accepts a reference to a String object as an argument and returns true if the argument ends with the substring ".com". Otherwise, the method should return false.
6. Modify the method you wrote for Algorithm Workbench 5 so it performs a case-insensitive test. The method should return true if the argument ends with ".com" in any possible combination of uppercase and lowercase letters.

7. Write a method that accepts a `StringBuilder` object as an argument and converts all occurrences of the lowercase letter 't' in the object to uppercase.

8. Look at the following string:

   `"cookies>milk>fudge:cake:ice cream"`

   Write code using the `String` class's `split` method that can be used to extract the following tokens from the string: `cookies`, `milk`, `fudge`, `cake`, and `ice cream`.

9. Assume that `d` is a `double` variable. Write an `if` statement that assigns `d` to the `int` variable `i` if the value in `d` is not larger than the maximum value for an `int`.

10. Write code that displays the contents of the `int` variable `i` in binary, hexadecimal, and octal.

Short Answer

1. Why should you use `StringBuilder` objects instead of `String` objects in a program that makes lots of changes to strings?

2. A program reads a string as input from the user for the purpose of tokenizing it. Why is it a good idea to trim the string before tokenizing it?

3. Each of the numeric wrapper classes has a static `toString` method. What do these methods do?

4. How can you determine the minimum and maximum values that may be stored in a variable of a given data type?

Programming Challenges

MyProgrammingLab™ *Visit www.myprogramminglab.com to complete many of these Programming Challenges online and get instant feedback.*

1. Backward String

Write a method that accepts a `String` object as an argument and displays its contents backward. For instance, if the string argument is "gravity" the method should display -"ytivarg". Demonstrate the method in a program that asks the user to input a string and then passes it to the method.

2. Word Counter

Write a method that accepts a `String` object as an argument and returns the number of words it contains. For instance, if the argument is "Four score and seven years ago" the method should return the number 6. Demonstrate the method in a program that asks the user to input a string and then passes it to the method. The number of words in the string should be displayed on the screen.

3. Sentence Capitalizer

VideoNote
The Sentence
Capitalizer
Problem

Write a method that accepts a `String` object as an argument and returns a copy of the string with the first character of each sentence capitalized. For instance, if the argument is "hello. my name is Joe. what is your name?" the method should return the string "Hello. My name is Joe. What is your name?" Demonstrate the method in a program that asks the user to input a string and then passes it to the method. The modified string should be displayed on the screen.

4. Vowels and Consonants

Write a class with a constructor that accepts a `String` object as its argument. The class should have a method that returns the number of vowels in the string, and another method that returns the number of consonants in the string. Demonstrate the class in a program that performs the following steps:

1. The user is asked to enter a string.
2. The program displays the following menu:
   a. Count the number of vowels in the string
   b. Count the number of consonants in the string
   c. Count both the vowels and consonants in the string
   d. Enter another string
   e. Exit the program
3. The program performs the operation selected by the user and repeats until the user selects e, to exit the program.

5. Password Verifier

Imagine you are developing a software package for Amazon.com that requires users to enter their own passwords. Your software requires that users' passwords meet the following criteria:

- The password should be at least six characters long.
- The password should contain at least one uppercase and at least one lowercase letter.
- The password should have at least one digit.

Write a class that verifies that a password meets the stated criteria. Demonstrate the class in a program that allows the user to enter a password and then displays a message indicating whether it is valid or not.

6. Telemarketing Phone Number List

Write a program that has two parallel arrays of `String` objects. One of the arrays should hold people's names and the other should hold their phone numbers. Here are example contents of both arrays:

name Array Example Contents	**phone** Array Example Contents
"Harrison, Rose"	"555-2234"
"James, Jean"	"555-9098"
"Smith, William"	"555-1785"
"Smith, Brad"	"555-9224"

The program should ask the user to enter a name or the first few characters of a name to search for in the array. The program should display all of the names that match the user's input and their corresponding phone numbers. For example, if the user enters "Smith", the program should display the following names and phone numbers from the list:

```
Smith, William: 555-1785
Smith, Brad: 555-9224
```

610 Chapter 9 Text Processing and More about Wrapper Classes

7. Check Writer

Write a program that displays a simulated paycheck. The program should ask the user to enter the date, the payee's name, and the amount of the check. It should then display a simulated check with the dollar amount spelled out, as shown here:

	Date: 11/24/2012
Pay to the Order of: John Phillips	$1920.85
One thousand nine hundred twenty and 85 cents	

8. Sum of Numbers in a String

Write a program that asks the user to enter a series of numbers separated by commas. Here is an example of valid input:

```
7,9,10,2,18,6
```

The program should calculate and display the sum of all the numbers.

9. Sum of Digits in a String

Write a program that asks the user to enter a series of single digit numbers with nothing separating them. The program should display the sum of all the single digit numbers in the string. For example, if the user enters 2514, the method should return 12, which is the sum of 2, 5, 1, and 4. The program should also display the highest and lowest digits in the string. (*Hint: Convert the string to an array.*)

10. Word Counter

Write a program that asks the user for the name of a file. The program should display the number of words that the file contains.

11. Sales Analysis

The file *SalesData.txt*, in this chapter's source code folder, contains the dollar amount of sales that a retail store made each day for a number of weeks. Each line in the file contains seven numbers, which are the sales numbers for one week. The numbers are separated by a comma. The following line is an example from the file:

```
2541.36,2965.88,1965.32,1845.23,7021.11,9652.74,1469.36
```

Write a program that opens the file and processes its contents. The program should display the following:

- The total sales for each week
- The average daily sales for each week
- The total sales for all of the weeks
- The average weekly sales
- The week number that had the highest amount of sales
- The week number that had the lowest amount of sales

12. Miscellaneous String Operations

Write a class with the following static methods:

- **WordCount.** This method should accept a reference to a `String` object as an argument and return the number of words contained in the object.
- **arrayToString.** This method accepts a `char` array as an argument and converts it to a `String` object. The method should return a reference to the `String` object.
- **mostFrequent.** This method accepts a reference to a `String` object as an argument and returns the character that occurs the most frequently in the object.
- **replaceSubstring.** This method accepts three references to `String` objects as arguments. Let's call them `string1`, `string2`, and `string3`. It searches `string1` for all occurrences of `string2`. When it finds an occurrence of `string2`, it replaces it with `string3`. For example, suppose the three arguments have the following values:

`string1:`	"the dog jumped over the fence"
`string2:`	"the"
`string3:`	"that"

With these three arguments, the method would return a reference to a `String` object with the value "that dog jumped over that fence".

Demonstrate each of these methods in a complete program.

13. Alphabetic Telephone Number Translator

Many companies use telephone numbers like 555-GET-FOOD so the number is easier for their customers to remember. On a standard telephone, the alphabetic letters are mapped to numbers in the following fashion:

A, B, and C = 2
D, E, and F = 3
G, H, and I = 4
J, K, and L = 5
M, N, and O = 6
P, Q, R, and S = 7
T, U, and V = 8
W, X, Y, and Z = 9

Write an application that asks the user to enter a 10-character telephone number in the format xxx-xxx-xxxx. The application should display the telephone number with any alphabetic characters that appeared in the original translated to their numeric equivalent. For example, if the user enters 555-GET-FOOD the application should display 555-438-3663.

14. Word Separator

Write a program that accepts as input a sentence in which all of the words are run together, but the first character of each word is uppercase. Convert the sentence to a string in which the words are separated by spaces and only the first word starts with an uppercase letter. For example, the string "StopAndSmellTheRoses." would be converted to "Stop and smell the roses."

15. Pig Latin

Write a program that reads a sentence as input and converts each word to "Pig Latin". In one version of Pig Latin, you convert a word by removing the first letter, placing that letter at the end of the word, and then appending "ay" to the word. Here is an example:

English: I SLEPT MOST OF THE NIGHT
Pig Latin: IAY LEPTSAY OSTMAY FOAY HETAY IGHTNAY

16. Morse Code Converter

Morse code is a code where each letter of the English alphabet, each digit, and various punctuation characters are represented by a series of dots and dashes. Table 9-14 shows part of the code. Write a program that asks the user to enter a string, and then converts that string to Morse code. Use hyphens for dashes and periods for dots.

Table 9-14   Morse code

Character	Code	Character	Code	Character	Code	Character	Code
space	*space*	6	-....	G	--.	Q	--.-
comma	--..--	7	--...	H	....	R	.-.
period	.-.-.-	8	---..	I	..	S	...
question mark	..--..	9	----.	J	.---	T	-
0	-----	A	.-	K	-.-	U	..-
1	.----	B	-...	L	.-..	V	...-
2	..---	C	-.-.	M	--	W	.--
3	...--	D	-..	N	-.	X	-..-
4	....-	E	.	O	---	Y	-.--
5	.....	F	..-.	P	.--.	Z	--..

10 Inheritance

TOPICS

10.1 What Is Inheritance?

CONCEPT: Inheritance allows a new class to extend an existing class. The new class inherits the members of the class it extends.

Generalization and Specialization

VideoNote
Inheritance

In the real world, you can find many objects that are specialized versions of other more general objects. For example, the term *insect* describes a very general type of creature with numerous characteristics. Because grasshoppers and bumblebees are insects, they have all the general characteristics of an insect. In addition, they have special characteristics of their own. For example, the grasshopper has its jumping ability, and the bumblebee has its stinger. Grasshoppers and bumblebees are specialized versions of an insect. This is illustrated in Figure 10-1.

Figure 10-1 Bumblebees and grasshoppers are specialized versions of an insect

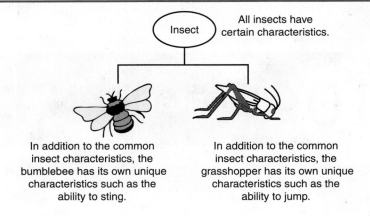

Inheritance and the "Is a" Relationship

When one object is a specialized version of another object, there is an "is a" relationship between them. For example, a grasshopper is an insect. Here are a few other examples of the "is a" relationship:

- A poodle is a dog.
- A car is a vehicle.
- A flower is a plant.
- A rectangle is a shape.
- A football player is an athlete.

When an "is a" relationship exists between objects, it means that the specialized object has all of the characteristics of the general object, plus additional characteristics that make it special. In object-oriented programming, inheritance is used to create an "is a" relationship among classes. This allows you to extend the capabilities of a class by creating another class that is a specialized version of it.

Inheritance involves a superclass and a subclass. The *superclass* is the general class and the *subclass* is the specialized class. You can think of the subclass as an extended version of the superclass. The subclass inherits fields and methods from the superclass without any of them having to be rewritten. Furthermore, new fields and methods may be added to the subclass, and that is what makes it a specialized version of the superclass.

> **NOTE:** At the risk of confusing you with too much terminology, it should be mentioned that superclasses are also called *base classes*, and subclasses are also called *derived classes*. Either set of terms is correct. For consistency, this text will use the terms *superclass* and *subclass*.

Let's look at an example of how inheritance can be used. Most teachers assign various graded activities for their students to complete. A graded activity can be given a numeric score such as 70, 85, 90, and so on, and a letter grade such as A, B, C, D, or F. Figure 10-2 shows a UML diagram for the GradedActivity class, which is designed to hold the numeric score of a graded activity. The setScore method sets a numeric score, and the getScore method returns the numeric score. The getGrade method returns the letter grade that corresponds to the numeric score. Notice that the class does not have a programmer-defined constructor, so Java will automatically generate a default constructor for it. This will be a point of discussion later. Code Listing 10-1 shows the code for the class.

Figure 10-2   UML diagram for the GradedActivity class

```
┌─────────────────────────────┐
│       GradedActivity         │
├─────────────────────────────┤
│ – score : double             │
├─────────────────────────────┤
│ + setScore(s : double) : void│
│ + getScore() : double        │
│ + getGrade() : char          │
└─────────────────────────────┘
```

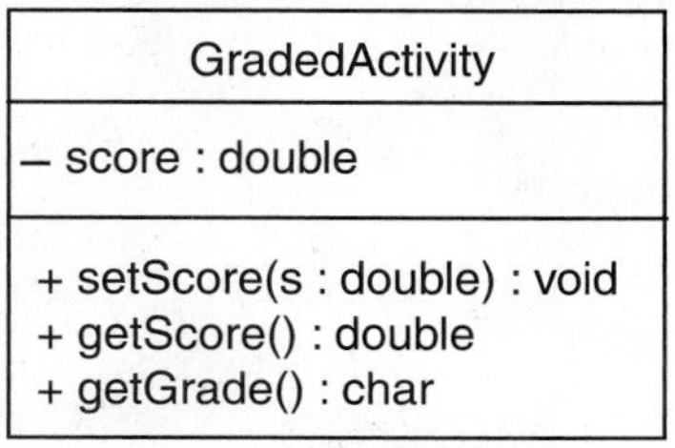

Code Listing 10-1   (GradedActivity.java)

```java
1   /**
2      A class that holds a grade for a graded activity.
3   */
4
5   public class GradedActivity
6   {
7      private double score;  // Numeric score
8
9      /**
10        The setScore method sets the score field.
11        @param s The value to store in score.
12     */
13
14     public void setScore(double s)
15     {
16        score = s;
17     }
18
19     /**
20        The getScore method returns the score.
21        @return The value stored in the score field.
22     */
23
```

```
24       public double getScore()
25       {
26          return score;
27       }
28
29       /**
30          The getGrade method returns a letter grade
31          determined from the score field.
32          @return The letter grade.
33       */
34
35       public char getGrade()
36       {
37          char letterGrade;
38
39          if (score >= 90)
40             letterGrade = 'A';
41          else if (score >= 80)
42             letterGrade = 'B';
43          else if (score >= 70)
44             letterGrade = 'C';
45          else if (score >= 60)
46             letterGrade = 'D';
47          else
48             letterGrade = 'F';
49
50          return letterGrade;
51       }
52 }
```

The program in Code Listing 10-2 demonstrates the class. Figures 10-3 and 10-4 show examples of interaction with the program.

Code Listing 10-2   (`GradeDemo.java`)

```
1 import javax.swing.JOptionPane;
2
3 /**
4    This program demonstrates the GradedActivity
5    class.
6 */
7
8 public class GradeDemo
9 {
10    public static void main(String[] args)
11    {
```

```
.12         String input;        // To hold input
13          double testScore;    // A test score
14
15          // Create a GradedActivity object.
16          GradedActivity grade = new GradedActivity();
17
18          // Get a test score.
19          input = JOptionPane.showInputDialog("Enter " +
20                           "a numeric test score.");
21          testScore = Double.parseDouble(input);
22
23          // Store the score in the grade object.
24          grade.setScore(testScore);
25
26          // Display the letter grade for the score.
27          JOptionPane.showMessageDialog(null,
28                       "The grade for that test is " +
29                       grade.getGrade());
30
31          System.exit(0);
32      }
33 }
```

Figure 10-3   Interaction with the `GradeDemo.java` program

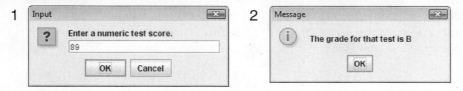

Figure 10-4   Interaction with the `GradeDemo.java` program

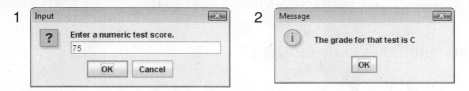

The `GradedActivity` class represents the general characteristics of a student's graded activity. Many different types of graded activities exist, however, such as quizzes, midterm exams, final exams, lab reports, essays, and so on. Because the numeric scores might be determined differently for each of these graded activities, we can create subclasses to handle each one. For example, we could create a `FinalExam` class that would be a subclass of the

GradedActivity class. Figure 10-5 shows the UML diagram for such a class, and Code Listing 10-3 shows its code. It has fields for the number of questions on the exam (numQuestions), the number of points each question is worth (pointsEach), and the number of questions missed by the student (numMissed).

Figure 10-5 UML diagram for the FinalExam class

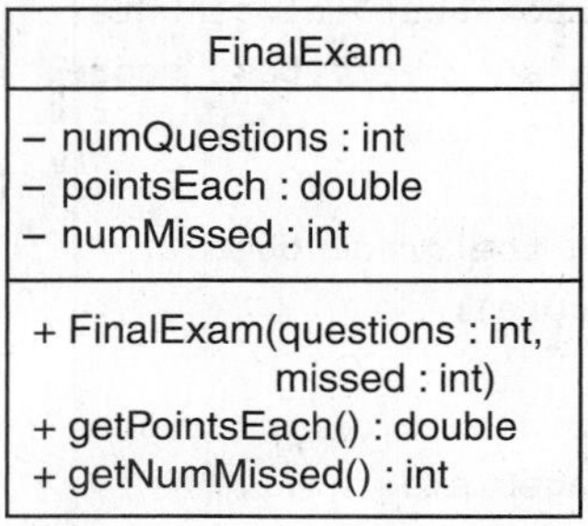

```
            FinalExam

   – numQuestions : int
   – pointsEach : double
   – numMissed : int

   + FinalExam(questions : int,
                    missed : int)
   + getPointsEach() : double
   + getNumMissed() : int
```

Code Listing 10-3   (FinalExam.java)

```java
 1 /**
 2     This class determines the grade for a final exam.
 3 */
 4
 5 public class FinalExam extends GradedActivity
 6 {
 7     private int numQuestions;      // Number of questions
 8     private double pointsEach;     // Points for each question
 9     private int numMissed;         // Questions missed
10
11     /**
12        The constructor sets the number of questions on the
13        exam and the number of questions missed.
14        @param questions The number of questions.
15        @param missed The number of questions missed.
16     */
17
18     public FinalExam(int questions, int missed)
19     {
20         double numericScore;       // To hold a numeric score
21
22         // Set the numQuestions and numMissed fields.
23         numQuestions = questions;
24         numMissed = missed;
25
26         // Calculate the points for each question and
```

```
27          // the numeric score for this exam.
28          pointsEach = 100.0 / questions;
29          numericScore = 100.0 - (missed * pointsEach);
30
31          // Call the inherited setScore method to
32          // set the numeric score.
33          setScore(numericScore);
34       }
35
36       /**
37          The getPointsEach method returns the number of
38          points each question is worth.
39          @return The value in the pointsEach field.
40       */
41
42       public double getPointsEach()
43       {
44          return pointsEach;
45       }
46
47       /**
48          The getNumMissed method returns the number of
49          questions missed.
50          @return The value in the numMissed field.
51       */
52
53       public int getNumMissed()
54       {
55          return numMissed;
56       }
57 }
```

Look at the header for the FinalExam class in line 5. The header uses the extends key word, which indicates that this class extends another class (a superclass). The name of the superclass is listed after the word extends. So, this line indicates that FinalExam is the name of the class being declared and GradedActivity is the name of the superclass it extends. This is illustrated in Figure 10-6.

Figure 10-6 FinalExam class header

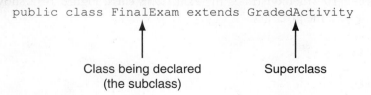

If we want to express the relationship between the two classes, we can say that a FinalExam is a GradedActivity.

Because the FinalExam class extends the GradedActivity class, it inherits all of the public members of the GradedActivity class. Here is a list of the members of the FinalExam class.

Fields:

int numQuestions;	Declared in FinalExam
double pointsEach;	Declared in FinalExam
int numMissed;	Declared in FinalExam

Methods:

Constructor	Declared in FinalExam
getPointsEach	Declared in FinalExam
getNumMissed	Declared in FinalExam
setScore	Inherited from GradedActivity
getScore	Inherited from GradedActivity
getGrade	Inherited from GradedActivity

Notice that the GradedActivity class's score field is not listed among the members of the FinalExam class. That is because the score field is private. Private members of the superclass cannot be accessed by the subclass, so technically speaking, they are not inherited. When an object of the subclass is created, the private members of the superclass exist in memory, but only methods in the superclass can access them. They are truly private to the superclass.

You will also notice that the superclass's constructor is not listed among the members of the FinalExam class. It makes sense that superclass constructors are not inherited because their purpose is to construct objects of the superclass. In the next section we discuss in more detail how superclass constructors operate.

To see how inheritance works in this example, let's take a closer look at the FinalExam constructor in lines 18 through 34. The constructor accepts two arguments: the number of test questions on the exam, and the number of questions missed by the student. In lines 23 and 24 these values are assigned to the numQuestions and numMissed fields. Then, in lines 28 and 29, the number of points for each question and the numeric test score are calculated. In line 33, the last statement in the constructor reads as follows:

```
setScore(numericScore);
```

This is a call to the setScore method. Although no setScore method appears in the FinalExam class, the method is inherited from the GradedActivity class. The program in Code Listing 10-4 demonstrates the FinalExam class. Figure 10-7 shows an example of interaction with the program.

Code Listing 10-4   (FinalExamDemo.java)

```java
1 import javax.swing.JOptionPane;
2
3 /**
4    This program demonstrates the FinalExam class,
5    which extends the GradedActivity class.
6 */
7
8 public class FinalExamDemo
9 {
10    public static void main(String[] args)
11    {
12       String input;        // To hold input
13       int questions;       // Number of questions
14       int missed;          // Number of questions missed
15
16       // Get the number of questions on the exam.
17       input = JOptionPane.showInputDialog("How many " +
18                   "questions are on the final exam?");
19       questions = Integer.parseInt(input);
20
21       // Get the number of questions the student missed.
22       input = JOptionPane.showInputDialog("How many " +
23                   "questions did the student miss?");
24       missed = Integer.parseInt(input);
25
26       // Create a FinalExam object.
27       FinalExam exam = new FinalExam(questions, missed);
28
29       // Display the test results.
30       JOptionPane.showMessageDialog(null,
31           "Each question counts " + exam.getPointsEach() +
32           " points.\nThe exam score is " +
33           exam.getScore() + "\nThe exam grade is " +
34           exam.getGrade());
35
36       System.exit(0);
37    }
38 }
```

Figure 10-7 Interaction with the `FinalExamDemo.java` program

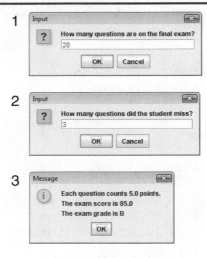

In line 27 the following statement creates an instance of the `FinalExam` class and assigns its address to the `exam` variable:

```
FinalExam exam = new FinalExam(questions, missed);
```

When a `FinalExam` object is created in memory, it not only has the members declared in the `FinalExam` class, but also the non-private members declared in the `GradedActivity` class. Notice in lines 30 through 34, shown here, that two public methods of the `GradedActivity` class, `getScore` and `getGrade`, are directly called from the exam object:

```
JOptionPane.showMessageDialog(null,
    "Each question counts " + exam.getPointsEach() +
    " points.\nThe exam score is " +
    exam.getScore() + "\nThe exam grade is " +
    exam.getGrade());
```

When a subclass extends a superclass, the public members of the superclass become public members of the subclass. In this program the `getScore` and `getGrade` methods can be called from the exam object because they are public members of the object's superclass.

As mentioned before, the private members of the superclass (in this case, the `score` field) cannot be accessed by the subclass. When the exam object is created in memory, a `score` field exists, but only the methods defined in the superclass, `GradedActivity`, can access it. It is truly private to the superclass. Because the `FinalExam` constructor cannot directly access the `score` field, it must call the superclass's `setScore` method (which is public) to store a value in it.

Inheritance in UML Diagrams

You show inheritance in a UML diagram by connecting two classes with a line that has an open arrowhead at one end. The arrowhead points to the superclass. Figure 10-8 is a UML diagram showing the relationship between the `GradedActivity` and `FinalExam` classes.

Figure 10-8   UML diagram showing inheritance

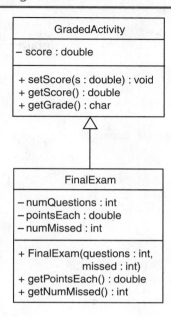

The Superclass's Constructor

You might be wondering how the constructors work together when one class inherits from another. In an inheritance relationship, the superclass constructor always executes before the subclass constructor. As was mentioned earlier, the GradedActivity class has only one constructor, which is the default constructor that Java automatically generated for it. When a FinalExam object is created, the GradedActivity class's default constructor is executed just before the FinalExam constructor is executed.

Code Listing 10-5 shows a class, SuperClass1, that has a no-arg constructor. The constructor simply displays the message "This is the superclass constructor." Code Listing 10-6 shows SubClass1, which extends SuperClass1. This class also has a no-arg constructor, which displays the message "This is the subclass constructor."

Code Listing 10-5   (SuperClass1.java)

```
1  public class SuperClass1
2  {
3     /**
4        Constructor
5     */
6
7     public SuperClass1()
8     {
```

```
 9          System.out.println("This is the " +
10                  "superclass constructor.");
11      }
12  }
```

Code Listing 10-6   (SubClass1.java)

```
 1  public class SubClass1 extends SuperClass1
 2  {
 3      /**
 4          Constructor
 5      */
 6
 7      public SubClass1()
 8      {
 9          System.out.println("This is the " +
10                  "subclass constructor.");
11      }
12  }
```

The program in Code Listing 10-7 creates a SubClass1 object. As you can see from the program output, the superclass constructor executes first, followed by the subclass constructor.

Code Listing 10-7   (ConstructorDemo1.java)

```
 1  /**
 2      This program demonstrates the order in which
 3      superclass and subclass constructors are called.
 4  */
 5
 6  public class ConstructorDemo1
 7  {
 8      public static void main(String[] args)
 9      {
10          SubClass1 obj = new SubClass1();
11      }
12  }
```

Program Output

```
This is the superclass constructor.
This is the subclass constructor.
```

If a superclass has either (a) a default constructor or (b) a no-arg constructor that was written into the class, then that constructor will be automatically called just before a subclass constructor executes. In a moment we will discuss other situations that can arise involving superclass constructors.

Inheritance Does Not Work in Reverse

In an inheritance relationship, the subclass inherits members from the superclass, not the other way around. This means it is not possible for a superclass to call a subclass's method. For example, if we create a GradedActivity object, it cannot call the getPointsEach or the getNumMissed methods because they are members of the FinalExam class.

Checkpoint

MyProgrammingLab™ *www.myprogramminglab.com*

10.1 Here is the first line of a class declaration. What is the name of the superclass? What is the name of the subclass?

```
public class Truck extends Vehicle
```

10.2 Look at the following class declarations and answer the questions that follow them:

```
public class Shape
{
    private double area;
    public void setArea(double a)
    {
        area = a;
    }
    public double getArea()
    {
        return area;
    }
}
public class Circle extends Shape
{
    private double radius;
    public void setRadius(double r)
    {
        radius = r;
        setArea(Math.PI * r * r);
    }
    public double getRadius()
    {
        return radius;
    }
}
```

a) Which class is the superclass? Which class is the subclass?
b) Draw a UML diagram showing the relationship between these two classes.
c) When a `Circle` object is created, what are its public members?
d) What members of the `Shape` class are not accessible to the `Circle` class's methods?
e) Assume a program has the following declarations:

```
Shape s = new Shape();
Circle c = new Circle();
```

Indicate whether the following statements are legal or illegal:

```
c.setRadius(10.0);
s.setRadius(10.0);
System.out.println(c.getArea());
System.out.println(s.getArea());
```

10.3 Class B extends class A. (Class A is the superclass and class B is the subclass.) Describe the order in which the class's constructors execute when a class B object is created.

10.2 Calling the Superclass Constructor

CONCEPT: The **super** key word refers to an object's superclass. You can use the super key word to call a superclass constructor.

In the previous section you saw examples illustrating how a superclass's default constructor or no-arg constructor is automatically called just before the subclass's constructor executes. But what if the superclass does not have a default constructor or a no-arg constructor? Or, what if the superclass has multiple overloaded constructors and you want to make sure a specific one is called? In either of these situations, you use the super key word to call a superclass constructor explicitly. The super key word refers to an object's superclass and can be used to access members of the superclass.

Code Listing 10-8 shows a class, `SuperClass2`, which has a no-arg constructor and a constructor that accepts an `int` argument. Code Listing 10-9 shows `SubClass2`, which extends `SuperClass2`. This class's constructor uses the super key word to call the superclass's constructor and pass an argument to it.

Code Listing 10-8   (SuperClass2.java)

```
1  public class SuperClass2
2  {
3     /**
4        Constructor #1
5     */
6
7     public SuperClass2()
8     {
```

```
 9          System.out.println("This is the superclass " +
10                             "no-arg constructor.");
11     }
12
13     /**
14        Constructor #2
15     */
16
17     public SuperClass2(int arg)
18     {
19         System.out.println("The following argument " +
20                            "was passed to the superclass " +
21                            "constructor: " + arg);
22     }
23  }
```

Code Listing 10-9   (SubClass2.java)

```
 1  public class SubClass2 extends SuperClass2
 2  {
 3     /**
 4        Constructor
 5     */
 6
 7     public SubClass2()
 8     {
 9        super(10);
10        System.out.println("This is the " +
11                           "subclass constructor.");
12     }
13  }
```

The statement in line 9 of the SubClass2 constructor calls the superclass constructor and passes the argument 10 to it. Here are three guidelines you should remember about calling a superclass constructor:

- The super statement that calls the superclass constructor may be written only in the subclass's constructor. You cannot call the superclass constructor from any other method.
- The super statement that calls the superclass constructor must be the first statement in the subclass's constructor. This is because the superclass's constructor must execute before the code in the subclass's constructor executes.
- If a subclass constructor does not explicitly call a superclass constructor, Java will automatically call the superclass's default constructor, or no-arg constructor, just

before the code in the subclass's constructor executes. This is equivalent to placing the following statement at the beginning of a subclass constructor:

```
super();
```

The program in Code Listing 10-10 demonstrates these classes.

Code Listing 10-10 (ConstructorDemo2.java)

```
1   /**
2      This program demonstrates how a superclass
3      constructor is called with the super key word.
4   */
5
6   public class ConstructorDemo2
7   {
8      public static void main(String[] args)
9      {
10         SubClass2 obj = new SubClass2();
11      }
12  }
```

Program Output

```
The following argument was passed to the superclass constructor: 10
This is the subclass constructor.
```

Let's look at a more meaningful example. Recall the Rectangle class from Chapter 6. Figure 10-9 shows a UML diagram for the class.

Figure 10-9 UML diagram for the Rectangle class

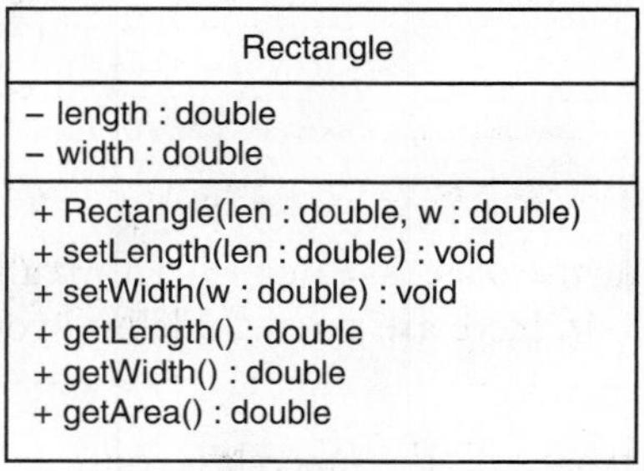

```
┌─────────────────────────────────────┐
│            Rectangle                 │
├─────────────────────────────────────┤
│ – length : double                    │
│ – width : double                     │
├─────────────────────────────────────┤
│ + Rectangle(len : double, w : double)│
│ + setLength(len : double) : void     │
│ + setWidth(w : double) : void        │
│ + getLength() : double               │
│ + getWidth() : double                │
│ + getArea() : double                 │
└─────────────────────────────────────┘
```

Here is part of the class's code:

```
public class Rectangle
{
    private double length;
    private double width;
    /**
```

```
     Constructor
     @param len The length of the rectangle.
     @param w The width of the rectangle.
  */

  public Rectangle(double len, double w)
  {
     length = len;
     width = w;
  }
  (Other methods follow . . .)
}
```

Next we will design a `Cube` class, which extends the `Rectangle` class. The `Cube` class is designed to hold data about cubes, which not only have a length, width, and area (the area of the base), but also a height, surface area, and volume. A UML diagram showing the inheritance relationship between the `Rectangle` and `Cube` classes is shown in Figure 10-10, and the code for the `Cube` class is shown in Code Listing 10-11.

Figure 10-10   UML diagram for the `Rectangle` and `Cube` classes

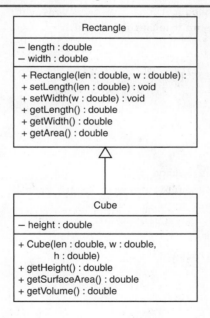

Code Listing 10-11   (`Cube.java`)

```
1  /**
2      This class holds data about a cube.
3  */
4
5  public class Cube extends Rectangle
6  {
```

```
 7       private double height;  // The cube's height
 8
 9       /**
10          The constructor sets the cube's length,
11          width, and height.
12          @param len The cube's length.
13          @param w The cube's width.
14          @param h The cube's height.
15       */
16
17       public Cube(double len, double w, double h)
18       {
19          // Call the superclass constructor.
20          super(len, w);
21
22          // Set the height.
23           height = h;
24       }
25
26       /**
27          The getHeight method returns the cube's height.
28          @return The value in the height field.
29       */
30
31       public double getHeight()
32       {
33          return height;
34       }
35
36       /**
37          The getSurfaceArea method calculates and
38          returns the cube's surface area.
39          @return The surface area of the cube.
40       */
41
42       public double getSurfaceArea()
43       {
44          return getArea() * 6;
45       }
46
47       /**
48          The getVolume method calculates and
49          returns the cube's volume.
50          @return The volume of the cube.
51       */
52
53       public double getVolume()
54       {
```

```
55           return getArea() * height;
56    }
57 }
```

The Cube constructor accepts arguments for the parameters len, w, and h. The values that are passed to len and w are subsequently passed as arguments to the Rectangle constructor in line 20:

```
super(len, w);
```

When the Rectangle constructor finishes, the remaining code in the Cube constructor is executed. The program in Code Listing 10-12 demonstrates the class.

Code Listing 10-12   (CubeDemo.java)

```
1 import java.util.Scanner;
2
3 /**
4    This program demonstrates passing arguments to a
5    superclass constructor.
6 */
7
8 public class CubeDemo
9 {
10    public static void main(String[] args)
11    {
12       double length;       // The cube's length
13       double width;        // The cube's width
14       double height;       // The cube's height
15
16       // Create a Scanner object for keyboard input.
17       Scanner keyboard = new Scanner(System.in);
18
19       // Get cube's length.
20       System.out.println("Enter the following " +
21                          "dimensions of a cube:");
22       System.out.print("Length: ");
23       length = keyboard.nextDouble();
24
25       // Get the cube's width.
26       System.out.print("Width: ");
27       width = keyboard.nextDouble();
28
29       // Get the cube's height.
30       System.out.print("Height: ");
31       height = keyboard.nextDouble();
32
```

```
33          // Create a cube object and pass the
34          // dimensions to the constructor.
35          Cube myCube =
36                  new Cube(length, width, height);
37
38          // Display the cube's properties.
39          System.out.println("Here are the cube's " +
40                              "properties.");
41          System.out.println("Length: " +
42                              myCube.getLength());
43          System.out.println("Width: " +
44                              myCube.getWidth());
45          System.out.println("Height: " +
46                              myCube.getHeight());
47          System.out.println("Base Area: " +
48                              myCube.getArea());
49          System.out.println("Surface Area: " +
50                              myCube.getSurfaceArea());
51          System.out.println("Volume: " +
52                              myCube.getVolume());
53      }
54 }
```

Program Output with Example Input Shown in Bold

```
Enter the following dimensions of a cube:
Length: 10 [Enter]
Width: 15 [Enter]
Height: 12 [Enter]
Here are the cube's properties.
Length: 10.0
Width: 15.0
Height: 12.0
Base Area: 150.0
Surface Area: 900.0
Volume: 1800.0
```

When the Superclass Has No Default or No-Arg Constructors

Recall from Chapter 6 that Java provides a default constructor for a class only when you provide no constructors for the class. This makes it possible to have a class with no default constructor. The Rectangle class we just looked at is an example. It has a constructor that accepts two arguments. Because we have provided this constructor, the Rectangle class does not have a default constructor. In addition, we have not written a no-arg constructor for the class.

If a superclass does not have a default constructor and does not have a no-arg constructor, then a class that inherits from it must call one of the constructors that the superclass does have. If it does not, an error will result when the subclass is compiled.

Summary of Constructor Issues in Inheritance

We have covered a number of important issues that you should remember about constructors in an inheritance relationship. The following list summarizes them:

- The superclass constructor always executes before the subclass constructor.
- You can write a super statement that calls a superclass constructor, but only in the subclass's constructor. You cannot call the superclass constructor from any other method.
- If a super statement that calls a superclass constructor appears in a subclass constructor, it must be the first statement.
- If a subclass constructor does not explicitly call a superclass constructor, Java will automatically call super() just before the code in the subclass's constructor executes.
- If a superclass does not have a default constructor and does not have a no-arg constructor, then a class that inherits from it must call one of the constructors that the superclass does have.

Checkpoint

MyProgrammingLab™ *www.myprogramminglab.com*

10.4   Look at the following classes:

```
public class Ground
{
    public Ground()
    {
        System.out.println("You are on the ground.");
    }
}
public class Sky extends Ground
{
    public Sky()
    {
        System.out.println("You are in the sky.");
    }
}
```

What will the following program display?

```
public class Checkpoint
{
    public static void main(String[] args)
    {
        Sky object = new Sky();
    }
}
```

10.5 Look at the following classes:

```java
public class Ground
{
    public Ground()
    {
        System.out.println("You are on the ground.");
    }
    public Ground(String groundColor)
    {
        System.out.println("The ground is " +
                            groundColor);
    }
}
public class Sky extends Ground
{
    public Sky()
    {
        System.out.println("You are in the sky.");
    }
    public Sky(String skyColor)
    {
        super("green");
        System.out.println("The sky is " + skyColor);
    }
}
```

What will the following program display?

```java
public class Checkpoint
{
    public static void main(String[] args)
    {
        Sky object = new Sky("blue");
    }
}
```

10.3 Overriding Superclass Methods

CONCEPT: A subclass may have a method with the same signature as a superclass method. In such a case, the subclass method overrides the superclass method.

Sometimes a subclass inherits a method from its superclass, but the method is inadequate for the subclass's purpose. Because the subclass is more specialized than the superclass, it is sometimes necessary for the subclass to replace inadequate superclass methods with more suitable ones. This is known as method *overriding*.

For example, recall the GradedActivity class that was presented earlier in this chapter. This class has a setScore method that sets a numeric score and a getGrade method that returns a letter grade based on that score. But, suppose a teacher wants to curve a numeric score before the letter grade is determined. For example, Dr. Harrison determines that in order to curve the grades in her class she must multiply each student's score by a certain percentage. This gives an adjusted score that is used to determine the letter grade. To satisfy this need we can design a new class, CurvedActivity, which extends the GradedActivity class and has its own specialized version of the setScore method. The setScore method in the subclass overrides the setScore method in the superclass. Figure 10-11 is a UML diagram showing the relationship between the GradedActivity class and the CurvedActivity class.

Figure 10-11 The GradedActivity and CurvedActivity classes

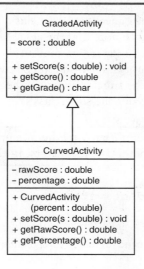

Table 10-1 summarizes the CurvedActivity class's fields, and Table 10-2 summarizes the class's methods.

Table 10-1 CurvedActivity class fields

Field	Description
rawScore	This field holds the student's unadjusted score.
percentage	This field holds the value that the unadjusted score must be multiplied by to get the curved score.

Table 10-2 CurvedActivity class methods

Method	Description
Constructor	The constructor accepts a double argument that is the curve percentage. This value is assigned to the percentage field and the rawScore field is assigned 0.0.
setScore	This method overrides the setScore method in the superclass. It accepts a double argument that is the student's unadjusted score. The method stores the argument in the rawScore field, and then passes the result of rawScore * percentage as an argument to the superclass's setScore method.
getRawScore	This method returns the value in the rawScore field.
getPercentage	This method returns the value in the percentage field.

Code Listing 10-13 shows the CurvedActivity class. The setScore method appears in lines 31 through 35. It is important to note that the setScore method in the CurvedActivity class has the same signature as the setScore method in the superclass, GradedActivity. In order for overriding to occur, the subclass method must have the same signature as the superclass method. When an object of the subclass invokes the setScore method, it invokes the subclass's version of the method, not the superclass's.

NOTE: Recall from Chapter 6 that a method's signature consists of the method's name and the data types of the method's parameters, in the order that they appear.

Code Listing 10-13 (CurvedActivity.java)

```java
1  /**
2      This class computes a curved grade. It extends
3      the GradedActivity class.
4  */
5
6  public class CurvedActivity extends GradedActivity
7  {
8      double rawScore;      // Unadjusted score
9      double percentage;    // Curve percentage
10
11     /**
12        The constructor sets the curve percentage.
13        @param percent The curve percentage.
14     */
15
16     public CurvedActivity(double percent)
17     {
18        percentage = percent;
19        rawScore = 0.0;
20     }
21
```

```
22      /**
23          The setScore method overrides the superclass setScore method.
24          This version accepts the unadjusted score as an argument. That
25          score is multiplied by the curve percentage and the result is
26          sent as an argument to the superclass's setScore method.
27          @param s The unadjusted score.
28      */
29
30      @Override
31      public void setScore(double s)
32      {
33          rawScore = s;
34          super.setScore(rawScore * percentage);
35      }
36
37      /**
38          The getRawScore method returns the raw score.
39          @return The value in the rawScore field.
40      */
41
42      public double getRawScore()
43      {
44          return rawScore;
45      }
46
47      /**
48          The getPercentage method returns the curve
49          percentage.
50          @return The value in the percentage field.
51      */
52
53      public double getPercentage()
54      {
55          return percentage;
56      }
57  }
```

Notice that in line 30, the @Override annotation appears just before the setScore method definition. This annotation tells the Java compiler that the setScore method is meant to override a method in the superclass.

The @Override annotation in line 30 is not required, but it is recommended that you use it. If the method fails to correctly override a method in the superclass, the compiler will display an error message. For example, suppose we had written the method header in line 31 like this:

```
public void setscore(double s)
```

If you look closely at the method name, you will see that all the letters are written in lowercase. This does not match the method's name in the superclass, which is setScore. Without the

@Override annotation, the code would still compile and execute, but we would not get the expected results because the method in the subclass would not override the method in the superclass. However, by using the @Override annotation in line 30, the compiler would generate an error letting us know that the subclass method does not override any method in the superclass.

Let's take a closer look at the setScore method in the CurvedActivity class. It accepts an argument, which is the student's unadjusted numeric score. This value is stored in the rawScore field. Then, in line 34, the following statement is executed:

```
super.setScore(rawScore * percentage);
```

As you already know, the super key word refers to the object's superclass. This statement calls the superclass's version of the setScore method with the result of the expression rawScore * percentage passed as an argument. This is necessary because the superclass's score field is private, and the subclass cannot access it directly. In order to store a value in the superclass's score field, the subclass must call the superclass's setScore method. A subclass may call an overridden superclass method by prefixing its name with the super key word and a dot (.). The program in Code Listing 10-14 demonstrates this class.

Code Listing 10-14   **(CurvedActivityDemo.java)**

```java
 1 import java.util.Scanner;
 2
 3 /**
 4    This program demonstrates the CurvedActivity class,
 5    which inherits from the GradedActivity class.
 6 */
 7
 8 public class CurvedActivityDemo
 9 {
10    public static void main(String[] args)
11    {
12       double score;              // Raw score
13       double curvePercent;       // Curve percentage
14
15       // Create a Scanner object to read keyboard input.
16       Scanner keyboard = new Scanner(System.in);
17
18       // Get the unadjusted exam score.
19       System.out.print("Enter the student's " +
20                        "raw numeric score: ");
21       score = keyboard.nextDouble();
22
23       // Get the curve percentage.
24       System.out.print("Enter the curve percentage: ");
25       curvePercent = keyboard.nextDouble();
26
27       // Create a CurvedActivity object.
28       CurvedActivity curvedExam =
29                new CurvedActivity(curvePercent);
```

```
30
31      // Set the exam score.
32      curvedExam.setScore(score);
33
34      // Display the raw score.
35      System.out.println("The raw score is " +
36                          curvedExam.getRawScore() +
37                          " points.");
38
39      // Display the curved score.
40      System.out.println("The curved score is " +
41                          curvedExam.getScore());
42
43      // Display the exam grade.
44      System.out.println("The exam grade is " +
45                          curvedExam.getGrade());
46   }
47 }
```

Program Output with Example Input Shown in Bold

```
Enter the student's raw numeric score: 87 [Enter]
Enter the curve percentage: 1.06 [Enter]
The raw score is 87.0 points.
The curved score is 92.22
The exam grade is A
```

This program uses the curvedExam variable to reference a CurvedActivity object. In line 32 the following statement is used to call the setScore method:

```
curvedExam.setScore(score);
```

Because curvedExam references a CurvedActivity object, this statement calls the CurvedActivity class's setScore method, not the superclass's version.

Even though a subclass may override a method in the superclass, superclass objects still call the superclass version of the method. For example, the following code creates an object of the GradedActivity class and calls the setScore method:

```
GradedActivity regularExam = new GradedActivity();
regularExam.setScore(85);
```

Because regularExam references a GradedActivity object, this code calls the GradedActivity class's version of the setScore method.

Overloading versus Overriding

There is a distinction between overloading a method and overriding a method. Recall from Chapter 6 that overloading is when a method has the same name as one or more other methods, but a different parameter list. Although overloaded methods have the same name, they have different signatures. When a method overrides another method, however, they both have the same signature.

Both overloading and overriding can take place in an inheritance relationship. You already know that overloaded methods can appear within the same class. In addition, a method in a subclass can overload a method in the superclass. If class A is the superclass and class B is the subclass, a method in class B may overload a method in class A, or another method in class B. Overriding, on the other hand, can only take place in an inheritance relationship. If class A is the superclass and class B is the subclass, a method in class B may override a method in class A. However, a method cannot override another method in the same class. The following list summarizes the distinction between overloading and overriding:

- If two methods have the same name but different signatures, they are overloaded. This is true where the methods are in the same class or where one method is in the superclass and the other method is in the subclass.
- If a method in a subclass has the same signature as a method in the superclass, the subclass method overrides the superclass method.

The distinction between overloading and overriding is important because it can affect the accessibility of superclass methods in a subclass. When a subclass overloads a superclass method, both methods may be called with a subclass object. However, when a subclass overrides a superclass method, only the subclass's version of the method can be called with a subclass object. For example, look at the SuperClass3 class in Code Listing 10-15. It has two overloaded methods named showValue. One of the methods accepts an int argument and the other accepts a String argument.

Code Listing 10-15 (SuperClass3.java)

```java
 1  public class SuperClass3
 2  {
 3     /**
 4        This method displays an int.
 5        @param arg An int.
 6     */
 7
 8     public void showValue(int arg)
 9     {
10        System.out.println("SUPERCLASS: " +
11                           "The int argument was " + arg);
12     }
13
14     /**
15        This method displays a String.
16        @param arg A String.
17     */
18
19     public void showValue(String arg)
20     {
21        System.out.println("SUPERCLASS: " +
22                           "The String argument was " + arg);
23     }
24  }
```

Now look at the `SubClass3` class in Code Listing 10-16. It inherits from the `SuperClass3` class.

Code Listing 10-16　　(SubClass3.java)

```
 1 public class SubClass3 extends SuperClass3
 2 {
 3    /**
 4       This method overrides one of the superclass methods.
 5       @param arg An int.
 6    */
 7
 8    @Override
 9    public void showValue(int arg)
10    {
11       System.out.println("SUBCLASS: " +
12            "The int argument was " + arg);
13    }
14
15    /**
16       This method overloads the superclass methods.
17       @param arg A double.
18    */
19
20    public void showValue(double arg)
21    {
22       System.out.println("SUBCLASS: " +
23            "The double argument was " + arg);
24    }
25 }
```

Notice that `SubClass3` also has two methods named `showValue`. The first one, in lines 9 through 13, accepts an `int` argument. This method overrides one of the superclass methods because they have the same signature. The second `showValue` method, in lines 20 through 24, accepts a `double` argument. This method overloads the other `showValue` methods because none of the others have the same signature. Although there is a total of four `showValue` methods in these classes, only three of them may be called from a `SubClass3` object. This is demonstrated in Code Listing 10-17.

Code Listing 10-17　　(ShowValueDemo.java)

```
 1 /**
 2    This program demonstrates the methods in the
 3    SuperClass3 and SubClass3 classes.
 4 */
 5
 6 public class ShowValueDemo
 7 {
```

```
 8      public static void main(String[] args)
 9      {
10         // Create a SubClass3 object.
11         SubClass3 myObject = new SubClass3();
12
13         myObject.showValue(10);          // Pass an int.
14         myObject.showValue(1.2);         // Pass a double.
15         myObject.showValue("Hello");     // Pass a String.
16      }
17   }
```

Program Output

```
SUBCLASS: The int argument was 10
SUBCLASS: The double argument was 1.2
SUPERCLASS: The String argument was Hello
```

When an int argument is passed to showValue, the subclass's method is called because it overrides the superclass method. In order to call the overridden superclass method, we would have to use the super key word in the subclass method. Here is an example:

```
public void showValue(int arg)
{
   super.showValue(arg);   // Call the superclass method.
   System.out.println("SUBCLASS: The int argument was " +
                      arg);
}
```

Preventing a Method from Being Overridden

When a method is declared with the final modifier, it cannot be overridden in a subclass. The following method header is an example that uses the final modifier:

```
public final void message()
```

If a subclass attempts to override a final method, the compiler generates an error. This technique can be used to make sure that a particular superclass method is used by subclasses and not a modified version of it.

 Checkpoint

MyProgrammingLab™ *www.myprogramminglab.com*

10.6   Under what circumstances would a subclass need to override a superclass method?

10.7   How can a subclass method call an overridden superclass method?

10.8   If a method in a subclass has the same signature as a method in the superclass, does the subclass method overload or override the superclass method?

10.9   If a method in a subclass has the same name as a method in the superclass, but uses a different parameter list, does the subclass method overload or override the superclass method?

10.10 How do you prevent a method from being overridden?

10.4 Protected Members

CONCEPT: Protected members of a class may be accessed by methods in a subclass, and by methods in the same package as the class.

Until now you have used two access specifications within a class: private and public. Java provides a third access specification, protected. A protected member of a class may be directly accessed by methods of the same class or methods of a subclass. In addition, protected members may be accessed by methods of any class that are in the same package as the protected member's class. A protected member is not quite private, because it may be accessed by some methods outside the class. Protected members are not quite public either because access to them is restricted to methods in the same class, subclasses, and classes in the same package as the member's class. A protected member's access is somewhere between private and public.

Let's look at a class with a protected member. Code Listing 10-18 shows the GradedActivity2 class, which is a modification of the GradedActivity class presented earlier. In this class, the score field has been made protected instead of private.

Code Listing 10-18   (GradedActivity2.java)

```java
1  /**
2      A class that holds a grade for a graded activity.
3  */
4
5  public class GradedActivity2
6  {
7      protected double score;  // Numeric score
8
9      /**
10         The setScore method sets the score field.
11         @param s The value to store in score.
12      */
13
14      public void setScore(double s)
15      {
16         score = s;
17      }
18
19      /**
20         The getScore method returns the score.
21         @return The value stored in the score field.
22      */
23
24      public double getScore()
25      {
26         return score;
```

```
27      }
28
29      /**
30         The getGrade method returns a letter grade
31         determined from the score field.
32         @return The letter grade.
33      */
34
35      public char getGrade()
36      {
37         char letterGrade;
38
39         if (score >= 90)
40            letterGrade = 'A';
41         else if (score >= 80)
42            letterGrade = 'B';
43         else if (score >= 70)
44            letterGrade = 'C';
45         else if (score >= 60)
46            letterGrade = 'D';
47         else
48            letterGrade = 'F';
49
50         return letterGrade;
51      }
52 }
```

Because in line 7 the score field is declared as protected, any class that inherits from this class has direct access to it. The FinalExam2 class, shown in Code Listing 10-19, is an example. This class is a modification of the FinalExam class, which was presented earlier. This class has a new method, adjustScore, which directly accesses the superclass's score field. If the contents of score have a fractional part of .5 or greater, the method rounds up score to the next whole number. The adjustScore method is called from the constructor.

Code Listing 10-19   (FinalExam2.java)

```
1 /**
2     This class determines the grade for a final exam.
3     The numeric score is rounded up to the next whole
4     number if its fractional part is .5 or greater.
5 */
6
7 public class FinalExam2 extends GradedActivity2
8 {
9     private int numQuestions;    // Number of questions
```

```
10      private double pointsEach;    // Points for each question
11      private int numMissed;        // Number of questions missed
12
13      /**
14         The constructor sets the number of questions on the
15         exam and the number of questions missed.
16         @param questions The number of questions.
17         @param missed The number of questions missed.
18      */
19
20      public FinalExam2(int questions, int missed)
21      {
22         double numericScore;         // To hold a numeric score
23
24         // Set the numQuestions and numMissed fields.
25         numQuestions = questions;
26         numMissed = missed;
27
28         // Calculate the points for each question and
29         // the numeric score for this exam.
30         pointsEach = 100.0 / questions;
31         numericScore = 100.0 - (missed * pointsEach);
32
33         // Call the inherited setScore method to
34         // set the numeric score.
35         setScore(numericScore);
36
37         // Adjust the score.
38         adjustScore();
39      }
40
41      /**
42         The getPointsEach method returns the number of
43         points each question is worth.
44         @return The value in the pointsEach field.
45      */
46
47      public double getPointsEach()
48      {
49         return pointsEach;
50      }
51
52      /**
53         The getNumMissed method returns the number of
54         questions missed.
55         @return The value in the numMissed field.
56      */
57
```

```
58    public int getNumMissed()
59    {
60       return numMissed;
61    }
62
63    /**
64       The adjustScore method adjusts a numeric score.
65       If score is within 0.5 points of the next whole
66       number, it rounds the score up.
67    */
68
69    private void adjustScore()
70    {
71       double fraction;
72
73       // Get the fractional part of the score.
74       fraction = score - (int) score;
75
76       // If the fractional part is .5 or greater,
77       // round the score up to the next whole number.
78       if (fraction >= 0.5)
79          score = score + (1.0 - fraction);
80    }
81 }
```

The program in Code Listing 10-20 demonstrates the class. Figure 10-12 shows an example of interaction with the program.

Code Listing 10-20   (ProtectedDemo.java)

```
1 import javax.swing.JOptionPane;
2
3 /**
4    This program demonstrates the FinalExam2 class,
5    which extends the GradedActivity2 class.
6 */
7
8 public class ProtectedDemo
9 {
10    public static void main(String[] args)
11    {
12       String input;       // To hold input
13       int questions;      // Number of questions
14       int missed;         // Number of questions missed
15
```

```
16          // Get the number of questions on the exam.
17          input = JOptionPane.showInputDialog("How many " +
18                          "questions are on the final exam?");
19          questions = Integer.parseInt(input);
20
21          // Get the number of questions the student missed.
22          input = JOptionPane.showInputDialog("How many " +
23                          "questions did the student miss?");
24          missed = Integer.parseInt(input);
25
26          // Create a FinalExam object.
27          FinalExam2 exam = new FinalExam2(questions, missed);
28
29          // Display the test results.
30          JOptionPane.showMessageDialog(null,
31              "Each question counts " + exam.getPointsEach() +
32              " points.\nThe exam score is " +
33              exam.getScore() + "\nThe exam grade is " +
34              exam.getGrade());
35
36          System.exit(0);
37      }
38 }
```

In the example running of the program in Figure 10-12, the student missed 5 out of 40 questions. The unadjusted numeric score would be 87.5, but the adjustScore method rounded up the score field to 88.

Figure 10-12   Interaction with the `ProtectedDemo.java` program

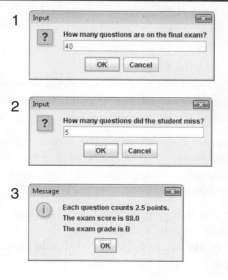

Protected class members may be denoted in a UML diagram with the # symbol. Figure 10-13 shows a UML diagram for the GradedActivity2 class, with the score field denoted as protected.

Figure 10-13   UML diagram for the GradedActivity2 class

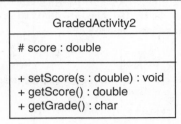

Although making a class member protected instead of private might make some tasks easier, you should avoid this practice when possible because any class that inherits from the class, or is in the same package, has unrestricted access to the protected member. It is always better to make all fields private and then provide public methods for accessing those fields.

Package Access

If you do not provide an access specifier for a class member, the class member is given package access by default. This means that any method in the same package may access the member. Here is an example:

```
public class Circle
{
    double radius;
    int centerX, centerY;

    (Method definitions follow . . .)
}
```

In this class, the radius, centerX, and centerY fields were not given an access specifier, so the compiler grants them package access. Any method in the same package as the Circle class may directly access these members.

There is a subtle difference between protected access and package access. Protected members may be accessed by methods in the same package or in a subclass. This is true even if the subclass is in a different package. Members with package access, however, cannot be accessed by subclasses that are in a different package.

It is more likely that you will give package access to class members by accident than by design, because it is easy to forget the access specifier. Although there are circumstances under which package access can be helpful, you should normally avoid it. Be careful always to specify an access specifier for class members.

Tables 10-3 and 10-4 summarize how each of the access specifiers affects a class member's accessibility within and outside of the class's package.

Table 10-3   Accessibility from within the class's package

Access Specifier	Accessible to a subclass inside the same package?	Accessible to all other classes in the same package?
default (no modifier)	Yes	Yes
public	Yes	Yes
protected	Yes	Yes
private	No	No

Table 10-4   Accessibility from outside the class's package

Access Specifier	Accessible to a subclass outside the same package?	Accessible to all other classes outside the same package?
default (no modifier)	No	No
public	Yes	Yes
protected	Yes	No
private	No	No

Checkpoint

MyProgrammingLab™ *www.myprogramminglab.com*

10.11   When a class member is declared as protected, what code may access it?

10.12   What is the difference between private members and protected members?

10.13   Why should you avoid making class members protected when possible?

10.14   What is the difference between private access and package access?

10.15   Why is it easy to give package access to a class member by accident?

10.5 Chains of Inheritance

CONCEPT: A superclass can also inherit from another class.

Sometimes it is desirable to establish a chain of inheritance in which one class inherits from a second class, which in turn inherits from a third class, as illustrated by Figure 10-14. In some cases, this chaining of classes goes on for many layers.

In Figure 10-14, ClassC inherits ClassB's members, including the ones that ClassB inherited from ClassA. Let's look at an example of such a chain of inheritance. Consider the PassFailActivity class, shown in Code Listing 10-21, which inherits from the GradedActivity class. The class is intended to determine a letter grade of 'P' for passing, or 'F' for failing.

Figure 10-14 A chain of inheritance

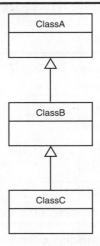

Code Listing 10-21 (`PassFailActivity.java`)

```java
1  /**
2      This class holds a numeric score and determines
3      whether the score is passing or failing.
4  */
5
6  public class PassFailActivity extends GradedActivity
7  {
8      private double minPassingScore; // Minimum passing score
9
10     /**
11         The constructor sets the minimum passing score.
12         @param mps The minimum passing score.
13     */
14
15     public PassFailActivity(double mps)
16     {
17         minPassingScore = mps;
18     }
19
20     /**
21         The getGrade method returns a letter grade
22         determined from the score field. This
23         method overrides the superclass method.
24         @return The letter grade.
25     */
26
27     @Override
28     public char getGrade()
29     {
```

```
30        char letterGrade;
31
32        if (super.getScore() >= minPassingScore)
33           letterGrade = 'P';
34        else
35           letterGrade = 'F';
36
37        return letterGrade;
38     }
39 }
```

The `PassFailActivity` constructor, in lines 15 through 18, accepts a `double` argument, which is the minimum passing grade for the activity. This value is stored in the `minPassingScore` field. The `getGrade` method, in lines 28 through 38, overrides the super-class method of the same name. This method returns a grade of `'P'` if the numeric score is greater-than or equal-to `minPassingScore`. Otherwise, the method returns a grade of `'F'`.

Suppose we wish to extend this class with another more specialized class. For example, the `PassFailExam` class, shown in Code Listing 10-22, determines a passing or failing grade for an exam. It has fields for the number of questions on the exam (`numQuestions`), the number of points each question is worth (`pointsEach`), and the number of questions missed by the student (`numMissed`).

Code Listing 10-22   (`PassFailExam.java`)

```
1 /**
2     This class determines a passing or failing grade for
3     an exam.
4 */
5
6 public class PassFailExam extends PassFailActivity
7 {
8     private int numQuestions;      // Number of questions
9     private double pointsEach;     // Points for each question
10    private int numMissed;         // Number of questions missed
11
12    /**
13       The constructor sets the number of questions, the
14       number of questions missed, and the minimum passing
15       score.
16       @param questions The number of questions.
17       @param missed The number of questions missed.
18       @param minPassing The minimum passing score.
19    */
20
21    public PassFailExam(int questions, int missed,
22                           double minPassing)
```

```
23    {
24        // Call the superclass constructor.
25        super(minPassing);
26
27        // Declare a local variable for the score.
28        double numericScore;
29
30        // Set the numQuestions and numMissed fields.
31        numQuestions = questions;
32        numMissed = missed;
33
34        // Calculate the points for each question and
35        // the numeric score for this exam.
36        pointsEach = 100.0 / questions;
37        numericScore = 100.0 - (missed * pointsEach);
38
39        // Call the superclass's setScore method to
40        // set the numeric score.
41        setScore(numericScore);
42    }
43
44    /**
45        The getPointsEach method returns the number of
46        points each question is worth.
47        @return The value in the pointsEach field.
48    */
49
50    public double getPointsEach()
51    {
52        return pointsEach;
53    }
54
55    /**
56        The getNumMissed method returns the number of
57        questions missed.
58        @return The value in the numMissed field.
59    */
60
61    public int getNumMissed()
62    {
63        return numMissed;
64    }
65 }
```

The PassFailExam class inherits the PassFailActivity class's members, including the ones that PassFailActivity inherited from GradedActivity. The program in Code Listing 10-23 demonstrates the class.

Code Listing 10-23   (`PassFailExamDemo.java`)

```java
 1  import java.util.Scanner;
 2
 3  /**
 4     This program demonstrates the PassFailExam class.
 5  */
 6
 7  public class PassFailExamDemo
 8  {
 9     public static void main(String[] args)
10     {
11        int questions;       // Number of questions
12        int missed;          // Number of questions missed
13        double minPassing;   // Minimum passing score
14
15        // Create a Scanner object for keyboard input.
16        Scanner keyboard = new Scanner(System.in);
17
18        // Get the number of questions on the exam.
19        System.out.print("How many questions are " +
20                          "on the exam? ");
21        questions = keyboard.nextInt();
22
23        // Get the number of questions missed.
24        System.out.print("How many questions did " +
25                          "the student miss? ");
26        missed = keyboard.nextInt();
27
28        // Get the minimum passing score.
29        System.out.print("What is the minimum " +
30                          "passing score? ");
31        minPassing = keyboard.nextDouble();
32
33        // Create a PassFailExam object.
34        PassFailExam exam =
35            new PassFailExam(questions, missed, minPassing);
36
37        // Display the points for each question.
38        System.out.println("Each question counts " +
39                          exam.getPointsEach() + " points.");
40
41        // Display the exam score.
42        System.out.println("The exam score is " +
43                          exam.getScore());
44
45        // Display the exam grade.
```

```
46          System.out.println("The exam grade is " +
47                          exam.getGrade());
48   }
49 }
```

Program Output with Example Input Shown in Bold

How many questions are on the exam? **100 [Enter]**
How many questions did the student miss? **25 [Enter]**
What is the minimum passing score? **60 [Enter]**
Each question counts 1.0 points.
The exam score is 75.0
The exam grade is P

Figure 10-15 is a UML diagram showing the inheritance relationship among the GradedActivity, PassFailActivity, and PassFailExam classes.

Figure 10-15 The GradedActivity, PassFailActivity, and PassFailExam classes

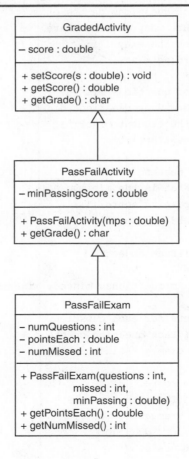

Class Hierarchies

Classes often are depicted graphically in a class hierarchy. Like a family tree, a class hierarchy shows the inheritance relationships between classes. Figure 10-16 shows a class hierarchy for the `GradedActivity`, `FinalExam`, `PassFailActivity`, and `PassFailExam` classes. The more general classes are toward the top of the tree and the more specialized classes are toward the bottom.

Figure 10-16 Class hierarchy

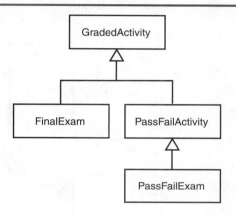

10.6 The Object Class

CONCEPT: The Java API has a class named `Object`, which all other classes directly or indirectly inherit from.

Every class in Java, including the ones in the API and the classes that you create, directly or indirectly inherits from a class named `Object`, which is part of the `java.lang` package. Here's how it happens: When a class does not use the `extends` key word to inherit from another class, Java automatically extends it from the `Object` class. For example, look at the following class declaration:

```
public class MyClass
{
    (Member Declarations ...)
}
```

This class does not explicitly extend any other class, so Java treats it as though it were written as follows:

```
public class MyClass extends Object
{
    (Member Declarations ...)
}
```

Ultimately, every class extends the `Object` class. Figure 10-17 shows how the `PassFailExam` class inherits from `Object`.

Figure 10-17 The line of inheritance from `Object` to `PassFailExam`

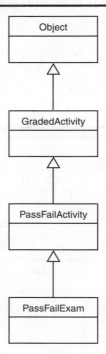

Because every class directly or indirectly extends the `Object` class, every class inherits the `Object` class's members. Two of the most useful are the `toString` and `equals` methods. In Chapter 8 you learned that every class has a `toString` and an `equals` method, and now you know why! It is because those methods are inherited from the `Object` class.

In the `Object` class, the `toString` method returns a reference to a `String` containing the object's class name, followed by the @ sign, followed by the object's hash code, which is a hexadecimal number. The `equals` method accepts a reference to an object as its argument. It returns `true` if the argument references the calling object. This is demonstrated in Code Listing 10-24.

Code Listing 10-24   (`ObjectMethods.java`)

```
 1  /**
 2      This program demonstrates the toString and equals
 3      methods that are inherited from the Object class.
 4  */
 5
 6  public class ObjectMethods
 7  {
 8     public static void main(String[] args)
 9     {
10        // Create two objects.
11        PassFailExam exam1 =
```

```
12                        new PassFailExam(0, 0, 0);
13          PassFailExam exam2 =
14                        new PassFailExam(0, 0, 0);
15
16          // Send the objects to println, which
17          // will call the toString method.
18          System.out.println(exam1);
19          System.out.println(exam2);
20
21          // Test the equals method.
22          if (exam1.equals(exam2))
23              System.out.println("They are the same.");
24          else
25              System.out.println("They are not the same.");
26      }
27 }
```

Program Output

```
PassFailExam@16f0472
PassFailExam@18d107f
They are not the same.
```

If you wish to change the behavior of either of these methods for a given class, you must override them in the class.

Checkpoint

MyProgrammingLab™ *www.myprogramminglab.com*

10.16 Look at the following class definition:

```
public class ClassD extends ClassB
{
    (Member Declarations . . .)
}
```

Because ClassD inherits from ClassB, is it true that ClassD does not inherit from the Object class? Why or why not?

10.17 When you create a class, it automatically has a toString method and an equals method. Why?

10.7 Polymorphism

CONCEPT: A superclass reference variable can reference objects of a subclass.

VideoNote
Polymorphism

Look at the following statement that declares a reference variable named exam:

```
GradedActivity exam;
```

This statement tells us that the exam variable's data type is GradedActivity. Therefore, we can use the exam variable to reference a GradedActivity object, as shown in the following statement:

```
exam = new GradedActivity();
```

The GradedActivity class is also used as the superclass for the FinalExam class. Because of the "is-a" relationship between a superclass and a subclass, an object of the FinalExam class is not just a FinalExam object. It is also a GradedActivity object. (A final exam is a graded activity.) Because of this relationship, we can use a GradedActivity variable to reference a FinalExam object. For example, look at the following statement:

```
GradedActivity exam = new FinalExam(50, 7);
```

This statement declares exam as a GradedActivity variable. It creates a FinalExam object and stores the object's address in the exam variable. This statement is perfectly legal and will not cause an error message because a FinalExam object is also a GradedActivity object.

This is an example of polymorphism. The term *polymorphism* means the ability to take many forms. In Java, a reference variable is polymorphic because it can reference objects of types different from its own, as long as those types are subclasses of its type. All of the following declarations are legal because the FinalExam, PassFailActivity, and PassFailExam classes inherit from GradedActivity:

```
GradedActivity exam1 = new FinalExam(50, 7);
GradedActivity exam2 = new PassFailActivity(70);
GradedActivity exam3 = new PassFailExam(100, 10, 70);
```

Although a GradedActivity variable can reference objects of any class that extends GradedActivity, there is a limit to what the variable can do with those objects. Recall that the GradedActivity class has three methods: setScore, getScore, and getGrade. So, a GradedActivity variable can be used to call only those three methods, regardless of the type of object the variable references. For example, look at the following code:

```
GradedActivity exam = new PassFailExam(100, 10, 70);
System.out.println(exam.getScore());        // This works.
System.out.println(exam.getGrade());        // This works.
System.out.println(exam.getPointsEach());   // ERROR! Won't work.
```

In this code, exam is declared as a GradedActivity variable and is assigned the address of a PassFailExam object. The GradedActivity class has only the setScore, getScore, and getGrade methods, so those are the only methods that the exam variable knows how to execute. The last statement in this code is a call to the getPointsEach method, which is defined in the PassFailExam class. Because the exam variable only knows about methods in the GradedActivity class, it cannot execute this method.

Polymorphism and Dynamic Binding

When a superclass variable references a subclass object, a potential problem exists. What if the subclass has overridden a method in the superclass, and the variable makes a call to that method? Does the variable call the superclass's version of the method, or the subclass's version? For example, look at the following code:

```java
GradedActivity exam = new PassFailActivity(60);
exam.setScore(70);
System.out.println(exam.getGrade());
```

Recall that the PassFailActivity class extends the GradedActivity class, and it overrides the getGrade method. When the last statement calls the getGrade method, does it call the GradedActivity class's version (which returns 'A', 'B', 'C', 'D', or 'F') or does it call the PassFailActivity class's version (which returns 'P' or 'F')?

Recall from Chapter 6 that the process of matching a method call with the correct method definition is known as binding. Java performs dynamic binding or late binding when a variable contains a polymorphic reference. This means that the Java Virtual Machine determines at runtime which method to call, depending on the type of object that the variable references. So, it is the object's type that determines which method is called, not the variable's type. In this case, the exam variable references a PassFailActivity object, so the PassFailActivity class's version of the getGrade method is called. The last statement in this code will display a grade of P.

The program in Code Listing 10-25 demonstrates polymorphic behavior. It declares an array of GradedActivity variables, and then assigns the addresses of objects of various types to the elements of the array.

Code Listing 10-25   (Polymorphic.java)

```java
1   /**
2       This program demonstrates polymorphic behavior.
3   */
4
5   public class Polymorphic
6   {
7      public static void main(String[] args)
8      {
9         // Create an array of GradedActivity references.
10        GradedActivity[] tests = new GradedActivity[3];
11
12        // The first test is a regular exam with a
13        // numeric score of 75.
14        tests[0] = new GradedActivity();
15        tests[0].setScore(95);
16
17        // The second test is a pass/fail test. The
18        // student missed 5 out of 20 questions, and
19        // the minimum passing grade is 60.
20        tests[1] = new PassFailExam(20, 5, 60);
21
```

```
22          // The third test is the final exam. There were
23          // 50 questions and the student missed 7.
24          tests[2] = new FinalExam(50, 7);
25
26          // Display the grades.
27          for (int i = 0; i < tests.length; i++)
28          {
29              System.out.println("Test " + (i + 1) + ": " +
30                                  "score " + tests[i].getScore() +
31                                  ", grade " + tests[i].getGrade());
32          }
33      }
34  }
```

Program Output

```
Test 1: score 95.0, grade A
Test 2: score 75.0, grade P
Test 3: score 86.0, grade B
```

You can also use parameters to accept arguments to methods polymorphically. For example, look at the following method:

```
public static void displayGrades(GradedActivity g)
{
    System.out.println("Score " + g.getScore() +
                       ", grade " + g.getGrade());
}
```

This method's parameter, g, is a GradedActivity variable. But, it can be used to accept arguments of any type that inherit from GradedActivity. For example, the following code passes objects of the FinalExam, PassFailActivity, and PassFailExam classes to the method:

```
GradedActivity exam1 = new FinalExam(50, 7);
GradedActivity exam2 = new PassFailActivity(70);
GradedActivity exam3 = new PassFailExam(100, 10, 70);
displayGrades(exam1);    // Pass a FinalExam object.
displayGrades(exam2);    // Pass a PassFailActivity object.
displayGrades(exam3);    // Pass a PassFailExam object.
```

The "Is-a" Relationship Does Not Work in Reverse

It is important to note that the "is-a" relationship does not work in reverse. Although the statement "a final exam is a graded activity" is true, the statement "a graded activity is a final exam" is not true. This is because not all graded activities are final exams. Likewise, not all GradedActivity objects are FinalExam objects. So, the following code will not work:

```
GradedActivity activity = new GradedActivity();
FinalExam exam = activity;    // ERROR!
```

You cannot assign the address of a `GradedActivity` object to a `FinalExam` variable. This makes sense because `FinalExam` objects have capabilities that go beyond those of a `GradedActivity` object. Interestingly, the Java compiler will let you make such an assignment if you use a type cast, as shown here:

```
GradedActivity activity = new GradedActivity();
FinalExam exam = (FinalExam) activity;  // Will compile but not run.
```

But, the program will crash when the assignment statement executes.

The `instanceof` Operator

There is an operator in Java named `instanceof` that you can use to determine whether an object is an instance of a particular class. Here is the general form of an expression that uses the `instanceof` operator:

```
refVar instanceof ClassName
```

In the general form, *refVar* is a reference variable and *ClassName* is the name of a class. This is the form of a `boolean` expression that will return `true` if the object referenced by *refVar* is an instance of *ClassName*. Otherwise, the expression returns `false`. For example, the `if` statement in the following code determines whether the reference variable `activity` references a `GradedActivity` object:

```
GradedActivity activity = new GradedActivity();
if (activity instanceof GradedActivity)
   System.out.println("Yes, activity is a GradedActivity.");
else
   System.out.println("No, activity is not a GradedActivity.");
```

This code will display `"Yes, activity is a GradedActivity."`

The `instanceof` operator understands the "is-a" relationship that exists when a class inherits from another class. For example, look at the following code:

```
FinalExam exam = new FinalExam(20, 2);
if (exam instanceof GradedActivity)
   System.out.println("Yes, exam is a GradedActivity.");
else
   System.out.println("No, exam is not a GradedActivity.");
```

Even though the object referenced by `exam` is a `FinalExam` object, this code will display `"Yes, exam is a GradedActivity."` The `instanceof` operator returns `true` because `FinalExam` is a subclass of `GradedActivity`.

 **Checkpoint**

MyProgrammingLab™ *www.myprogramminglab.com*

10.18 Recall the `Rectangle` and `Cube` classes discussed earlier, as shown in Figure 10-18.

Figure 10-18 Rectangle and Cube classes

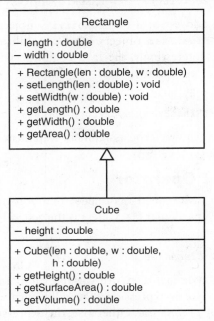

a) Is the following statement legal or illegal? If it is illegal, why?

```
Rectangle r = new Cube(10, 12, 5);
```

b) If you determined that the statement in part a is legal, are the following statements legal or illegal? (Indicate legal or illegal for each statement.)

```
System.out.println(r.getLength());
System.out.println(r.getWidth());
System.out.println(r.getHeight());
System.out.println(r.getSurfaceArea());
```

c) Is the following statement legal or illegal? If it is illegal, why?

```
Cube c = new Rectangle(10, 12);
```

10.8 Abstract Classes and Abstract Methods

CONCEPT: An abstract class is not instantiated, but other classes extend it. An abstract method has no body and must be overridden in a subclass.

An abstract method is a method that appears in a superclass, but expects to be overridden in a subclass. An abstract method has only a header and no body. Here is the general format of an abstract method header:

AccessSpecifier abstract *ReturnType MethodName(ParameterList)*;

Notice that the key word abstract appears in the header, and that the header ends with a semicolon. There is no body for the method. Here is an example of an abstract method header:

```
public abstract void setValue(int value);
```

When an abstract method appears in a class, the method must be overridden in a subclass. If a subclass fails to override the method, an error will result. Abstract methods are used to ensure that a subclass implements the method.

When a class contains an abstract method, you cannot create an instance of the class. Abstract methods are commonly used in abstract classes. An abstract class is not instantiated itself, but serves as a superclass for other classes. The abstract class represents the generic or abstract form of all the classes that inherit from it.

For example, consider a factory that manufactures airplanes. The factory does not make a generic airplane, but makes three specific types of airplanes: two different models of prop-driven planes and one commuter jet model. The computer software that catalogs the planes might use an abstract class named Airplane. That class has members representing the common characteristics of all airplanes. In addition, the software has classes for each of the three specific airplane models the factory manufactures. These classes all extend the Airplane class, and they have members representing the unique characteristics of each type of plane. The Airplane class is never instantiated, but is used as a superclass for the other classes.

A class becomes abstract when you place the abstract key word in the class definition. Here is the general format:

AccessSpecifier abstract class *ClassName*

An abstract class is not instantiated, but other classes extend it. An abstract method has no body and must be overridden in a subclass.

For example, look at the following abstract class Student shown in Code Listing 10-26. It holds data common to all students, but does not hold all the data needed for students of specific majors.

Code Listing 10-26   (Student.java)

```
 1  /**
 2      The Student class is an abstract class that holds
 3      general data about a student. Classes representing
 4      specific types of students should inherit from
 5      this class.
 6  */
 7
 8  public abstract class Student
 9  {
10      private String name;        // Student name
11      private String idNumber;    // Student ID
12      private int yearAdmitted;   // Year admitted
13
14      /**
15          The constructor sets the student's name,
16          ID number, and year admitted.
```

```
17          @param n The student's name.
18          @param id The student's ID number.
19          @param year The year the student was admitted.
20      */
21
22      public Student(String n, String id, int year)
23      {
24          name = n;
25          idNumber = id;
26          yearAdmitted = year;
27      }
28
29      /**
30          The toString method returns a String containing
31          the student's data.
32          @return A reference to a String.
33      */
34
35      public String toString()
36      {
37          String str;
38
39          str = "Name: " + name
40              + "\nID Number: " + idNumber
41              + "\nYear Admitted: " + yearAdmitted;
42          return str;
43      }
44
45      /**
46          The getRemainingHours method is abstract.
47          It must be overridden in a subclass.
48          @return The hours remaining for the student.
49      */
50
51      public abstract int getRemainingHours();
52 }
```

The Student class contains fields for storing a student's name, ID number, and year admitted. It also has a constructor, a toString method, and an abstract method named getRemainingHours.

This abstract method must be overridden in classes that inherit from the Student class. The idea behind this method is that it returns the number of hours remaining for a student to take in his or her major. It was made abstract because this class is intended to be the base for other classes that represent students of specific majors. For example, a CompSciStudent class might hold the data for a computer science student, and a BiologyStudent class might hold the data for a biology student. Computer science students must take courses in different disciplines than those taken by biology students. It stands to reason that the

CompSciStudent class will calculate the number of hours remaining to be taken differently than the BiologyStudent class. Let's look at an example of the CompSciStudent class, which is shown in Code Listing 10-27.

Code Listing 10-27 (CompSciStudent.java)

```java
 1 /**
 2    This class holds data for a computer science student.
 3 */
 4
 5 public class CompSciStudent extends Student
 6 {
 7    // Required hours
 8    private final int MATH_HOURS = 20;   // Math hours
 9    private final int CS_HOURS = 40;     // Comp sci hours
10    private final int GEN_ED_HOURS = 60; // Gen ed hours
11
12    // Hours taken
13    private int mathHours;  // Math hours taken
14    private int csHours;    // Comp sci hours taken
15    private int genEdHours; // General ed hours taken
16
17    /**
18       The Constructor sets the student's name,
19       ID number, and the year admitted.
20       @param n The student's name.
21       @param id The student's ID number.
22       @param year The year the student was admitted.
23    */
24
25    public CompSciStudent(String n, String id, int year)
26    {
27       super(n, id, year);
28    }
29
30    /**
31       The setMathHours method sets the number of
32       math hours taken.
33       @param math The math hours taken.
34    */
35
36    public void setMathHours(int math)
37    {
38       mathHours = math;
39    }
40
41    /**
```

```
42          The setCsHours method sets the number of
43          computer science hours taken.
44          @param cs The computer science hours taken.
45      */
46
47      public void setCsHours(int cs)
48      {
49          csHours = cs;
50      }
51
52      /**
53          The setGenEdHours method sets the number of
54          general ed hours taken.
55          @param genEd The general ed hours taken.
56      */
57
58      public void setGenEdHours(int genEd)
59      {
60          genEdHours = genEd;
61      }
62
63      /**
64          The getRemainingHours method returns the
65          the number of hours remaining to be taken.
66          @return The hours remaining for the student.
67      */
68
69      @Override
70      public int getRemainingHours()
71      {
72          int reqHours,          // Total required hours
73              remainingHours;    // Remaining hours
74
75          // Calculate the required hours.
76          reqHours = MATH_HOURS + CS_HOURS + GEN_ED_HOURS;
77
78          // Calculate the remaining hours.
79          remainingHours = reqHours - (mathHours + csHours
80                          + genEdHours);
81
82          return remainingHours;
83      }
84
85      /**
86          The toString method returns a string containing
87          the student's data.
88          @return A reference to a String.
89      */
```

```
90
91      @Override
92      public String toString()
93      {
94         String str;
95
96         str = super.toString() +
97            "\nMajor: Computer Science" +
98            "\nMath Hours Taken: " + mathHours +
99            "\nComputer Science Hours Taken: " + csHours +
100           "\nGeneral Ed Hours Taken: " + genEdHours;
101
102        return str;
103     }
104 }
```

The CompSciStudent class, which extends the Student class, declares the following final integer fields in lines 8 through 10: MATH_HOURS, CS_HOURS, and GEN_ED_HOURS. These fields hold the required number of math, computer science, and general education hours for a computer science student. It also declares the following fields in lines 13 through 15: mathHours, csHours, and genEdHours. These fields hold the number of math, computer science, and general education hours taken by the student. Mutator methods are provided to store values in these fields. In addition, the class overrides the toString method and the abstract getRemainingHours method. The program in Code Listing 10-28 demonstrates the class.

Code Listing 10-28   (CompSciStudentDemo.java)

```
1  /**
2      This program demonstrates the CompSciStudent class.
3  */
4
5  public class CompSciStudentDemo
6  {
7     public static void main(String[] args)
8     {
9        // Create a CompSciStudent object.
10       CompSciStudent csStudent =
11               new CompSciStudent("Jennifer Haynes",
12                                  "167W98337", 2015);
13
14       // Store values for math, CS, and gen ed hours.
15       csStudent.setMathHours(12);
16       csStudent.setCsHours(20);
17       csStudent.setGenEdHours(40);
18
19       // Display the student's data.
```

```
20          System.out.println(csStudent);
21
22          // Display the number of remaining hours.
23          System.out.println("Hours remaining: " +
24                          csStudent.getRemainingHours());
25      }
26  }
```

Program Output

```
Name: Jennifer Haynes
ID Number: 167W98337
Year Admitted: 2015
Major: Computer Science
Math Hours Taken: 12
Computer Science Hours Taken: 20
General Ed Hours Taken: 40
Hours remaining: 48
```

Remember the following points about abstract methods and classes:

- Abstract methods and abstract classes are defined with the abstract key word.
- Abstract methods have no body, and their header must end with a semicolon.
- An abstract method must be overridden in a subclass.
- When a class contains an abstract method, it cannot be instantiated. It must serve as a superclass.
- An abstract class cannot be instantiated. It must serve as a superclass.

Abstract Classes in UML

Abstract classes are drawn like regular classes in UML, except the name of the class and the names of abstract methods are shown in italics. For example, Figure 10-19 shows a UML diagram for the Student class.

Figure 10-19   UML diagram for the Student class

```
                Student
─────────────────────────────────
 − name : String
 − idNumber : String
 − yearAdmitted : int
─────────────────────────────────
 + Student(n : String, id : String,
                   year : int)
 + toString() : String
 + getRemainingHours() : int
```

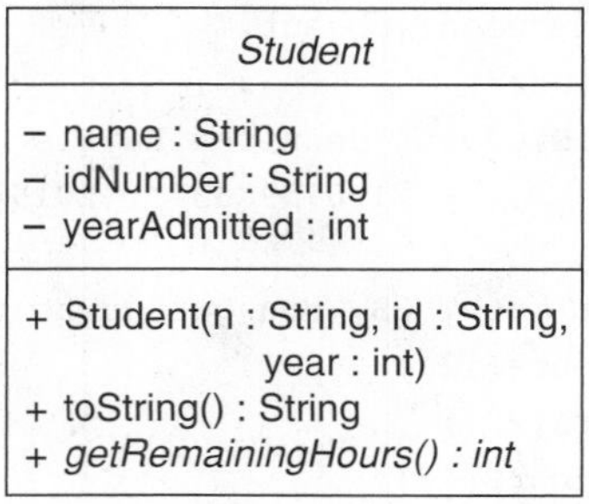

Checkpoint

MyProgrammingLab™ *www.myprogramminglab.com*

10.19 What is the purpose of an abstract method?

10.20 If a subclass extends a superclass with an abstract method, what must you do in the subclass?

10.21 What is the purpose of an abstract class?

10.22 If a class is defined as abstract, what can you not do with the class?

10.9 Interfaces

CONCEPT: An interface specifies behavior for a class.

In its simplest form, an interface is like a class that contains only abstract methods. An interface cannot be instantiated. Instead, it is *implemented* by other classes. When a class implements an interface, the class must override the methods that are specified by the interface.

An interface looks similar to a class, except the key word `interface` is used instead of the key word `class`, and the methods that are specified in an interface have no bodies, only headers that are terminated by semicolons. Here is the general format of an interface definition:

```
public interface InterfaceName
{
   (Method headers ...)
}
```

Code Listing 10-29 shows an example of an interface named `Displayable`. In line 3, the interface specifies a `void` method named `display()`.

Code Listing 10-29   (`Displayable.java`)

```
1  public interface Displayable
2  {
3     void display();
4  }
```

Notice that the `display` method header in line 3 does not have an access specifier. This is because all methods in an interface are implicitly `public`. You can optionally write `public` in the method header, but most programmers leave it out because all interface methods must be `public`.

Any class that implements the `Displayable` interface shown in Code Listing 10-29 *must* provide an implementation of the `display` method (with the exact signatures specified by the interface, and with the same return type). The `Person` class shown in Code Listing 10-30 is an example.

Code Listing 10-30   (`Person.java`)

```
 1 public class Person implements Displayable
 2 {
 3    private String name;
 4
 5    // Constructor
 6    public Person(String n)
 7    {
 8       name = n;
 9    }
10
11    // display method
12    public void display()
13    {
14       System.out.println("My name is " + name);
15    }
16 }
```

When you want a class to implement an interface, you use the `implements` key word in the class header. Notice in line 1 of Code Listing 10-30, the `Person` class header ends with the clause `implements Displayable`. Because the `Person` class implements the `Displayable` interface, it must provide an implementation of the interface's `display` method. This is done in lines 12 through 15 of the `Person` class. The program in Code Listing 10-31 demonstrates the `Person` class.

Code Listing 10-31   (`InterfaceDemo.java`)

```
 1 /**
 2    This program demonstrates a class that implements
 3    the Displayable interface.
 4 */
 5
 6 public class InterfaceDemo
 7 {
 8    public static void main(String[] args)
 9    {
10       // Create an instance of the Person class.
11       Person p = new Person("Antonio");
12
13       // Call the object's display method.
14       p.display();
15    }
16 }
```

Program Output

```
My name is Antonio
```

An Interface is a Contract

When a class implements an interface, it is agreeing to provide all of the methods that are specified by the interface. It is often said that an interface is like a "contract," and when a class implements an interface it must adhere to the contract.

For example, Code Listing 10-32 shows an interface named `Relatable`, which is intended to be used with the `GradedActivity` class presented earlier. This interface has three method headers: `equals`, `isGreater`, and `isLess`. Notice that each method accepts a `GradedActivity` object as its argument.

Code Listing 10-32   (`Relatable.java`)

```
 1  /**
 2      Relatable interface
 3  */
 4
 5  public interface Relatable
 6  {
 7     boolean equals(GradedActivity g);
 8     boolean isGreater(GradedActivity g);
 9     boolean isLess(GradedActivity g);
10  }
```

You might have guessed that the `Relatable` interface is named "Relatable" because it specifies methods that presumably, make relational comparisons with `GradedActivity` objects. The intent is to make any class that implements this interface "relatable" with `GradedActivity` objects by ensuring that it has an `equals`, an `isGreater`, and an `isLess` method that perform relational comparisons. But, the interface only specifies the headers for these methods, not what the methods should do. Although the programmer of a class that implements the `Relatable` interface can choose what those methods should do, he or she should provide methods that comply with this intent.

Code Listing 10-33 shows the code for the `FinalExam3` class, which implements the `Relatable` interface. The `equals`, `isGreater`, and `isLess` methods compare the calling object with the object passed as an argument. The program in Code Listing 10-34 demonstrates the class.

Code Listing 10-33   (`FinalExam3.java`)

```
 1  /**
 2      This class determines the grade for a final exam.
 3  */
 4
 5  public class FinalExam3 extends GradedActivity implements Relatable
 6  {
 7     private int numQuestions;   // Number of questions
 8     private double pointsEach;  // Points for each question
 9     private int numMissed;      // Questions missed
```

```
10
11     /**
12        The constructor sets the number of questions on the
13        exam and the number of questions missed.
14        @param questions The number of questions.
15        @param missed The number of questions missed.
16     */
17
18     public FinalExam3(int questions, int missed)
19     {
20        double numericScore;   // To hold a numeric score
21
22        // Set the numQuestions and numMissed fields.
23        numQuestions = questions;
24        numMissed = missed;
25
26        // Calculate the points for each question and
27        // the numeric score for this exam.
28        pointsEach = 100.0 / questions;
29        numericScore = 100.0 - (missed * pointsEach);
30
31        // Call the inherited setScore method to
32        // set the numeric score.
33        setScore(numericScore);
34     }
35
36     /**
37        The getPointsEach method returns the number of
38        points each question is worth.
39        @return The value in the pointsEach field.
40     */
41
42     public double getPointsEach()
43     {
44        return pointsEach;
45     }
46
47     /**
48        The getNumMissed method returns the number of
49        questions missed.
50        @return The value in the numMissed field.
51     */
52
53     public int getNumMissed()
54     {
55        return numMissed;
56     }
57
```

```
 58     /**
 59        The equals method compares the calling object
 60        to the argument object for equality.
 61        @return true if the calling
 62        object's score is equal to the argument's
 63        score.
 64     */
 65
 66     public boolean equals(GradedActivity g)
 67     {
 68        boolean status;
 69
 70        if (this.getScore() == g.getScore())
 71           status = true;
 72        else
 73           status = false;
 74
 75        return status;
 76     }
 77
 78     /**
 79        The isGreater method determines whether the calling
 80        object is greater than the argument object.
 81        @return true if the calling object's score is
 82        greater than the argument object's score.
 83     */
 84
 85     public boolean isGreater(GradedActivity g)
 86     {
 87        boolean status;
 88
 89        if (this.getScore() > g.getScore())
 90           status = true;
 91        else
 92           status = false;
 93
 94        return status;
 95     }
 96
 97     /**
 98        The isLess method determines whether the calling
 99        object is less than the argument object.
100        @return true if the calling object's score is
101        less than the argument object's score.
102     */
103
104     public boolean isLess(GradedActivity g)
105     {
```

```
106        boolean status;
107
108        if (this.getScore() < g.getScore())
109            status = true;
110        else
111            status = false;
112
113        return status;
114    }
115 }
```

Code Listing 10-34   (RelatableExams.java)

```
1  /**
2     This program demonstrates the FinalExam3 class which
3     implements the Relatable interface.
4  */
5
6  public class RelatableExams
7  {
8     public static void main(String[] args)
9     {
10        // Exam #1 had 100 questions and the student
11        // missed 20 questions.
12        FinalExam3 exam1 = new FinalExam3(100, 20);
13
14        // Exam #2 had 100 questions and the student
15        // missed 30 questions.
16        FinalExam3 exam2 = new FinalExam3(100, 30);
17
18        // Display the exam scores.
19        System.out.println("Exam 1: " + exam1.getScore());
20        System.out.println("Exam 2: " + exam2.getScore());
21
22        // Compare the exam scores.
23        if (exam1.equals(exam2))
24            System.out.println("The exam scores are equal.");
25
26        if (exam1.isGreater(exam2))
27            System.out.println("The Exam 1 score is the highest.");
28
29        if (exam1.isLess(exam2))
30            System.out.println("The Exam 1 score is the lowest.");
31    }
32 }
```

Program Output

```
Exam 1: 80.0
Exam 2: 70.0
The Exam 1 score is the highest.
```

Fields in Interfaces

An interface can contain field declarations, but all fields in an interface are treated as `final` and `static`. Because they automatically become `final`, you must provide an initialization value. For example, look at the following interface definition:

```
public interface Doable
{
    int FIELD1 = 1;
    int FIELD2 = 2;
    (Method headers . . .)
}
```

In this interface, FIELD1 and FIELD2 are `final static int` variables. Any class that implements this interface has access to these variables.

Implementing Multiple Interfaces

You might be wondering why we need both abstract classes and interfaces, since they are so similar to each other. The reason is that a class can extend only one superclass, but Java allows a class to implement multiple interfaces. When a class implements multiple interfaces, it must provide the methods specified by all of them.

To specify multiple interfaces in a class definition, simply list the names of the interfaces, separated by commas, after the `implements` key word. Here is the first line of an example of a class that implements multiple interfaces:

```
public class MyClass implements Interface1,
                                 Interface2,
                                 Interface3
```

This class implements three interfaces: Interface1, Interface2, and Interface3.

Interfaces in UML

In a UML diagram, an interface is drawn like a class, except the interface name and the method names are italicized, and the <<interface>> tag is shown above the interface name. The relationship between a class and an interface is known as a realization relationship (the class realizes the interfaces). You show a realization relationship in a UML diagram by connecting a class and an interface with a dashed line that has an open arrowhead at one end. The arrowhead points to the interface. This depicts the realization relationship. Figure 10-20 is a UML diagram showing the relationships among the GradedActivity class, the FinalExam3 class, and the Relatable interface.

Figure 10-20   Realization relationship in a UML diagram

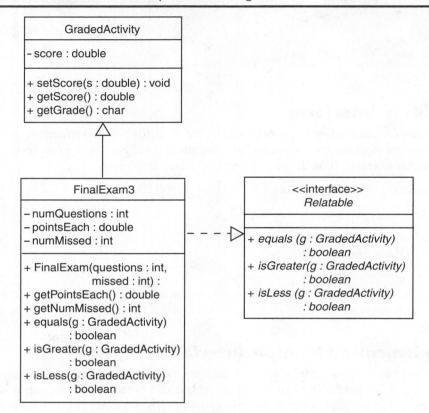

Default Methods

Beginning in Java 8, interfaces may have *default methods*. A default method is an interface method that has a body. Code Listing 10-35 shows another version of the Displayable interface, in which the display method is a default method.

Code Listing 10-35   (Displayable.java)

```
1 public interface Displayable
2 {
3    default void display()
4    {
5       System.out.println("This is the default display method.");
6    }
7 }
```

Notice in line 3 that the method header begins with the key word default. This is required for an interface method that has a body. When a class implements an interface with a default method, the class can override the default method, but it is not required to. For example, the Person class shown in Code Listing 10-36 implements the Displayable interface, but does not override the display method. The program in Code Listing 10-37 instantiates the Person class, and calls the display method. As you can see from the program output, the code in the interface's default method is executed.

Code Listing 10-36   (Person.java)

```
1  /**
2     This class implements the Displayable
3     interface, but does not override the
4     default display method.
5  */
6
7  public class Person implements Displayable
8  {
9     private String name;
10
11    // Constructor
12    public Person(String n)
13    {
14       name = n;
15    }
16 }
```

Code Listing 10-37   (InterfaceDemoDefaultMethod.java)

```
1  /**
2     This program demonstrates a class that implements
3     the Displayable interface (with a default method).
4  */
5
6  public class InterfaceDemoDefaultMethod
7  {
8     public static void main(String[] args)
9     {
10       // Create an instance of the Person class.
11       Person p = new Person("Antonio");
12
13       // Call the object's display method.
14       p.display();
15    }
16 }
```

Program Output

```
This is the default display method.
```

NOTE: One of the benefits of having default methods is that they allow you to add new methods to an existing interface without causing errors in the classes that already implement the interface. Prior to Java 8, when you added a new method header to an existing interface, all of the classes that already implement that interface had to be rewritten to override the new method. Now you can add default methods to an interface, and if an existing class (that implements the interface) does not need the new method, you do not have to rewrite the class.

Polymorphism and Interfaces

Just as you can create reference variables of a class type, Java allows you to create reference variables of an interface type. An interface reference variable can reference any object that implements that interface, regardless of its class type. This is another example of polymorphism. For example, look at the `RetailItem` interface in Code Listing 10-38.

Code Listing 10-38   (`RetailItem.java`)

```java
1  /**
2      RetailItem interface
3  */
4
5  public interface RetailItem
6  {
7     public double getRetailPrice();
8  }
```

This interface specifies only one method: `getRetailPrice`. Both the `CompactDisc` and `DvdMovie` classes, shown in Code Listings 10-39 and 10-40, implement this interface.

Code Listing 10-39   (`CompactDisc.java`)

```java
1  /**
2      Compact Disc class
3  */
4
5  public class CompactDisc implements RetailItem
6  {
7     private String title;        // The CD's title
8     private String artist;       // The CD's artist
9     private double retailPrice;  // The CD's retail price
10
11    /**
12       Constructor
13       @param cdTitle The CD title.
14       @param cdArtist The name of the artist.
15       @param cdPrice The CD's price.
16    */
```

```
17
18      public CompactDisc(String cdTitle, String cdArtist,
19                  double cdPrice)
20      {
21         title = cdTitle;
22         artist = cdArtist;
23         retailPrice = cdPrice;
24      }
25
26      /**
27         getTitle method
28         @return The CD's title.
29      */
30
31      public String getTitle()
32      {
33         return title;
34      }
35
36      /**
37         getArtist method
38         @return The name of the artist.
39      */
40
41      public String getArtist()
42      {
43         return artist;
44      }
45
46      /**
47         getRetailPrice method (Required by the RetailItem
48         interface)
49         @return The retail price of the CD.
50      */
51
52      public double getRetailPrice()
53      {
54         return retailPrice;
55      }
56   }
```

Code Listing 10-40 (DvdMovie.java)

```
1   /**
2      DvdMovie class
3   */
4
```

```
 5   public class DvdMovie implements RetailItem
 6   {
 7      private String title;         // The DVD's title
 8      private int runningTime;      // Running time in minutes
 9      private double retailPrice;   // The DVD's retail price
10
11      /**
12         Constructor
13         @param dvdTitle The DVD title.
14         @param runTime The running time in minutes.
15         @param dvdPrice The DVD's price.
16      */
17
18      public DvdMovie(String dvdTitle, int runTime,
19                                   double dvdPrice)
20      {
21         title = dvdTitle;
22         runningTime = runTime;
23         retailPrice = dvdPrice;
24      }
25
26      /**
27         getTitle method
28         @return The DVD's title.
29      */
30
31      public String getTitle()
32      {
33         return title;
34      }
35
36      /**
37         getRunningTime method
38         @return The running time in minutes.
39      */
40
41      public int getRunningTime()
42      {
43         return runningTime;
44      }
45
46      /**
47         getRetailPrice method (Required by the RetailItem
48         interface)
49         @return The retail price of the DVD.
50      */
51
52      public double getRetailPrice()
```

```
53    {
54        return retailPrice;
55    }
56 }
```

Because they implement the `RetailItem` interface, objects of these classes may be referenced by a `RetailItem` reference variable. The following code demonstrates:

```
RetailItem item1 = new CompactDisc("Songs From the Heart",
                                   "Billy Nelson",
                                   18.95);
RetailItem item2 = new DvdMovie("Planet X",
                                102,
                                22.95);
```

In this code, two `RetailItem` reference variables, `item1` and `item2`, are declared. The `item1` variable references a `CompactDisc` object and the `item2` variable references a `DvdMovie` object. This is possible because both the `CompactDisc` and `DvdMovie` classes implement the `RetailItem` interface. When a class implements an interface, an inheritance relationship known as interface inheritance is established. Because of this inheritance relationship, a `CompactDisc` object is a `RetailItem`, and likewise, a `DvdMovie` object is a `RetailItem`. Therefore, we can create `RetailItem` reference variables and have them reference `CompactDisc` and `DvdMovie` objects.

The program in Code Listing 10-41 demonstrates how an interface reference variable can be used as a method parameter.

Code Listing 10-41   (`PolymorphicInterfaceDemo.java`)

```java
 1 /**
 2    This program demonstrates that an interface type may
 3    be used to create a polymorphic reference.
 4 */
 5
 6 public class PolymorphicInterfaceDemo
 7 {
 8    public static void main(String[] args)
 9    {
10       // Create a CompactDisc object.
11       CompactDisc cd =
12             new CompactDisc("Greatest Hits",
13                             "Joe Looney Band",
14                             18.95);
15       // Create a DvdMovie object.
16       DvdMovie movie =
17             new DvdMovie("Wheels of Fury",
18                          137, 12.95);
19
20       // Display the CD's title.
```

```
21          System.out.println("Item #1: " +
22                              cd.getTitle());
23
24      // Display the CD's price.
25      showPrice(cd);
26
27      // Display the DVD's title.
28      System.out.println("Item #2: " +
29                          movie.getTitle());
30
31      // Display the DVD's price.
32      showPrice(movie);
33   }
34
35   /**
36      The showPrice method displays the price
37      of a RetailItem object.
38      @param item A reference to a RetailItem object.
39   */
40
41   private static void showPrice(RetailItem item)
42   {
43      System.out.printf("Price: $%,.2f\n", item.getRetailPrice());
44   }
45 }
```

Program Output

```
Item #1: Greatest Hits
Price: $18.95
Item #2: Wheels of Fury
Price: $12.95
```

There are some limitations to using interface reference variables. As previously mentioned, you cannot create an instance of an interface. In addition, when an interface variable references an object, you can use the interface variable to call only the methods that are specified in the interface. For example, look at the following code:

```
// Reference a CompactDisc object with a RetailItem variable.
RetailItem item = new CompactDisc("Greatest Hits",
                                  "Joe Looney Band",
                                  18.95);

// Call the getRetailPrice method . . .
System.out.println(item.getRetailPrice()); // OK, this works.
// Attempt to call the getTitle method . . .
System.out.println(item.getTitle()); // ERROR! Will not compile!
```

The last line of code will not compile because the `RetailItem` interface specifies only one method: `getRetailPrice`. So, we cannot use a `RetailItem` reference variable to call any other method.

TIP: It is possible to cast an interface reference variable to the type of the object it references, and then call methods that are members of that type. The syntax is somewhat awkward, however. The statement that causes the compiler error in the example code could be rewritten as:

```
System.out.println(((CompactDisc)item).getTitle());
```

Checkpoint

MyProgrammingLab™ *www.myprogramminglab.com*

10.23 What is the purpose of an interface?

10.24 How is an interface similar to an abstract class?

10.25 How is an interface different from an abstract class, or any class?

10.26 If an interface has fields, how are they treated?

10.27 Write the first line of a class named `Customer`, which implements an interface named `Relatable`.

10.28 Write the first line of a class named `Employee`, which implements interfaces named `Payable` and `Listable`.

10.10 Anonymous Inner Classes

CONCEPT: An inner class is a class that is defined inside another class. An anonymous inner class is an inner class that has no name. An anonymous inner class must implement an interface, or extend another class.

Sometimes you need a class that is simple, and to be instantiated only once in your code. When this is the case, you can use an *anonymous inner class*. An anonymous inner class is a class that has no name. It is called an inner class because it is defined inside another class. You use the `new` operator to simultaneously define an anonymous inner class and create an instance of it. Here is the general syntax for instantiating and defining an anonymous inner class:

```
new ClassOrInterfaceName() {

    (Fields and methods of the anonymous class...)

}
```

The `new` operator is followed by the name of an existing class or interface, followed by a set of parentheses. Next, you write the body of the class, enclosed in curly braces. The expression creates an object that is an instance of a class that either extends the specified superclass, or implements the specified interface. A reference to the object is returned. (Notice that you do *not* use the `extends` or `implements` key words in the expression.)

Before you look at an example, you must understand a few requirements and restrictions:

- An anonymous inner class must either implement an interface, or extend another class.
- If the anonymous inner class extends a superclass, the superclass's no-arg constructor is called when the object is created.
- An anonymous inner class must override all of the abstract methods specified by the interface it is implementing, or the superclass it is extending.
- Because an anonymous inner class's definition is written inside a method, it can access that method's local variables, but only if they are declared final, or if they are effectively final. (An effectively final variable is a variable whose value is never changed.) A compiler error will result if an anonymous inner class tries to use a variable that is not final, or not effectively final.

Let's look at an example of an anonymous inner class that implements an interface. Suppose we have the interface shown in Code Listing 10-42.

Code Listing 10-42   (IntCalculator.java)

```
1   interface IntCalculator
2   {
3       int calculate(int number);
4   }
```

The name of the interface is IntCalculator, and it specifies a method named calculate. The calculate method accepts an int argument, and returns an int value. Suppose we want to define a class that implements the IntCalculator interface, and overrides the calculate method so that it returns the square of the argument that is passed to it. The following code snippet shows how:

```
IntCalculator square = new IntCalculator() {
    public int calculate(int number)
    {
        return number * number;
    }};
```

The first line of the code snippet declares a variable named square, that is an IntCalculator reference variable (meaning that it can refer to any object that implements IntCalculator). On the right side of the = sign, the expression new IntCalculator() creates an instance of an anonymous class that implements the IntCalculator interface. The body of the anonymous class appears next, enclosed inside curly braces. In the class body, the calculate method is overridden. Because this is a complete statement, it ends with a semicolon. Figure 10-21 illustrates the different parts of the statement, and Code Listing 10-43 shows a complete program that uses it.

Figure 10-21 Creating an instance of an anonymous inner class

```
                              This creates an instance of
        Interface             an anonymous class that
   reference variable         implements IntCalculator.

   IntCalculator square = new IntCalculator() {
        public int calculate(int number)
        {                                          Method in the
            return number * number;                anonymous class
        }};

         Semicolon
```

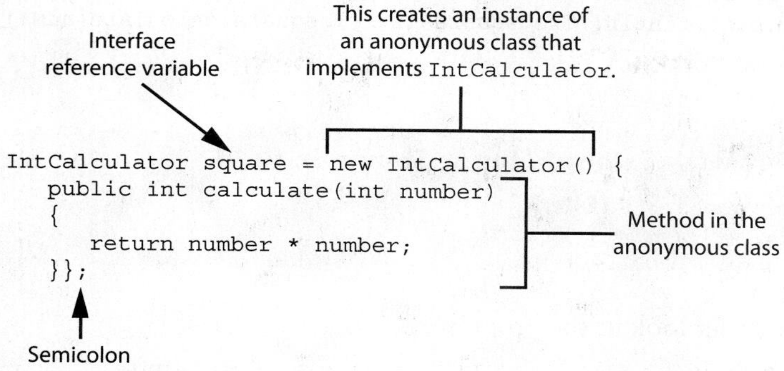

Code Listing 10-43   (**AnonymousClassDemo.java**)

```java
 1 import java.util.Scanner;
 2
 3 /**
 4  This program demonstrates an anonymous inner class.
 5 */
 6
 7 public class AnonymousClassDemo
 8 {
 9    public static void main(String[] args)
10    {
11       int num;
12
13       // Create a Scanner object for keyboard input.
14       Scanner keyboard = new Scanner(System.in);
15
16       // Create an object that implements IntCalculator.
17       IntCalculator square = new IntCalculator() {
18          public int calculate(int number)
19          {
20             return number * number;
21          }};
22
23       // Get a number from the user.
24       System.out.print("Enter an integer number: ");
25       num = keyboard.nextInt();
```

```
26
27        // Display the square of the number.
28        System.out.println("The square is " + square.calculate(num));
29    }
30 }
```

Program Output with Example Input Shown in Bold

Enter an integer number: **5 [Enter]**
The square is 25

Let's take a closer look at the program:

- Line 11 declares an int variable named num, which will be used to hold user input.
- Line 14 creates a Scanner object for keyboard input.
- Lines 17 through 21 instantiate an anonymous inner class that implements the IntCalculator interface. A variable named square is used to reference the object. In the class body, lines 18 through 21 override the calculate method to return the square of the method's argument.
- Line 24 prompts the user to enter an integer number, and line 25 reads the number from the keyboard. The number is assigned to the num variable.
- Line 28 calls the square object's calculate method, and displays the return value in a message.

10.11 Functional Interfaces and Lambda Expressions

CONCEPT: A functional interface is an interface that has one abstract method. You can use a special type of expression, known as a lambda expression, to create an object that implements a functional interface.

Java 8 introduces two new features that work together to simplify code, particularly in situations where you might use anonymous inner classes. These new features are functional interfaces and lambda expressions. A *functional interface* is simply an interface that has one abstract method. For example, let's take another look at the IntCalculator interface that we previously discussed in the section on anonymous classes. Because it has only one abstract method, it is considered a functional interface. For your convenience, Code Listing 10-44 shows the code for the interface.

Code Listing 10-44 (IntCalculator.java)

```
1  interface IntCalculator
2  {
3     int calculate(int number);
4  }
```

The name of the interface is `IntCalculator`, and it specifies one method named `calculate`. The `calculate` method accepts an `int` argument, and returns an `int` value.

Because `IntCalculator` is a functional interface, we do not have to go to the trouble of defining a class that implements the interface. We do not even have to use an anonymous inner class. Instead, we can use a *lambda expression* to create an object that implements the interface, and overrides its abstract method.

You can think of a lambda expression as an anonymous method, or a method with no name. Like regular methods, lambda expressions can accept arguments and return values. Here is the general format of a simple lambda expression that accepts one argument, and returns a value:

```
parameter -> expression
```

In this general format, the lambda expression begins with a parameter variable, followed by the *lambda operator* (`->`), followed by an expression that has a value. Here is an example:

```
x -> x * x
```

The `x` that appears on the left side of the `->` operator is the name of a parameter variable, and the expression `x * x` that appears on the right side of the `->` operator is the value that is returned.

This lambda expression works like a method that has a parameter variable named `x`, and it returns the value of `x * x`.

We can use this lambda expression to create an object that implements the `IntCalculator` interface. Here is an example:

```
IntCalculator square = x -> x * x;
```

On the left side of the `=` operator we declare an `IntCalculator` reference variable named `square`. On the right side of the `=` operator we have a lambda expression that creates an object with the following characteristics:

- Because we are assigning the object to an `IntCalculator` reference variable, the object automatically implements the `IntCalculator` interface.
- Because the `IntCalculator` interface has only one abstract method (named `calculate`), the lambda expression will be used to implement that one method.
- The parameter `x` that is used in the lambda expression represents the argument that is passed to the `calculate` method. We do not have to specify the data type of `x` because the compiler will determine it. Because the `calculate` method (in the`IntCalculator` interface) has an `int` parameter, the `x` parameter in the lambda expression will automatically become an `int`.
- The expression `x * x` is the value that is returned from the `calculate` method.

Code Listing 10-45 shows a complete program that uses the previously shown statement to create an object.

Code Listing 10-45 (`LambdDemo.java`)

```
1 import java.util.Scanner;
2
3 /**
```

```
4    This program demonstrates a simple
5    lambda expression.
6  */
7
8  public class LambdaDemo
9  {
10     public static void main(String[] args)
11     {
12        int num;
13
14        // Create a Scanner object for keyboard input.
15        Scanner keyboard = new Scanner(System.in);
16
17        // Create an object that implements IntCalculator.
18        IntCalculator square = x -> x * x;
19
20        // Get a number from the user.
21        System.out.print("Enter an integer number: ");
22        num = keyboard.nextInt();
23
24        // Display the square of the number.
25        System.out.println("The square is " + square.calculate(num));
26     }
27 }
```

Program Output with Example Input Shown in Bold

Enter an integer number: **5 [*Enter*]**
The square is 25

Let's take a closer look at the program:

- Line 12 declares an int variable named num, which will be used to hold user input.
- Line 15 creates a Scanner object for keyboard input.
- Line 18 uses a lambda expression to create an object that implements the IntCalculator interface. A variable named square is used to reference the object. The object's calculate method will return the square of the method's argument.
- Line 21 prompts the user to enter an integer number, and line 22 reads the number from the keyboard. The number is assigned to the num variable.
- Line 25 calls the square object's calculate method, and displays the return value in a message.

Lambda expressions provide a way to easily create and instantiate anonymous inner classes. If you compare Code Listing 10-45 with the program shown in Code Listing 10-43, you can see that the lambda expression is much more concise than the anonymous inner class declaration.

Lambda Expressions That Do Not Return a Value

If a functional interface's abstract method is void (does not return a value), any lambda expression that you use with the interface should also be void. Here is an example:

```
x -> System.out.println(x);
```

This lambda expression has a parameter, x. When the expression is invoked, it displays the value of x.

Lambda Expressions with Multiple Parameters

If a functional interface's abstract method has multiple parameters, any lambda expression that you use with the interface must also have multiple parameters. To use more than one parameter in a lambda expression, simply write a comma-separated list and enclose the list in parentheses. Here is an example:

```
(a, b) -> a + b;
```

This lambda expression has two parameters, a and b. The expression returns the value of a + b.

Lambda Expressions with No Parameters

If a functional interface's abstract method has no parameters, any lambda expression that you use with the interface must also have no parameters. Simply write a set of empty parentheses as the parameter list, as shown here:

```
() -> System.out.println();
```

When this lambda expression is invoked, it simply prints a blank line.

Explicitly Declaring a Parameter's Data Type

You do not have to specify the data type of a lambda expression's parameter because the compiler will determine it from the interface's abstract method header. However, you can explicitly declare the data type of a parameter, if you wish. Here is an example:

```
(int x) -> x * x;
```

Note that the parameter declaration (on the left side of the -> operator) must be enclosed in parentheses. Here is another example, involving two parameters:

```
(int a, int b) -> a + b;
```

Using Multiple Statements in the Body of a Lambda Expression

You can write multiple statements in the body of a lambda expression, but if you do, you must enclose the statements in a set of curly braces, and you must write a return statement if the expression returns a value. Here is an example:

```
(int x) -> {
    int a = x * 2;
    return a;
};
```

Accessing Variables Within a Lambda Expression

A lambda expression can access variables that are declared in the enclosing scope, as long as those variables are final, or effectively final. An *effectively* final variable is a variable whose value is never changed, but it isn't declared with the final key word.

In Code Listing 10-46, the main method uses a lambda expression that accesses a final variable named factor that is local to the main method.

Code Listing 10-46   (LambdDemo2.java)

```
 1 import java.util.Scanner;
 2
 3 /**
 4    This program demonstrates a lambda expression
 5    that uses a final local variable.
 6 */
 7
 8 public class LambdaDemo2
 9 {
10    public static void main(String[] args)
11    {
12       final int factor = 10;
13       int num;
14
15       // Create a Scanner object for keyboard input.
16       Scanner keyboard = new Scanner(System.in);
17
18       // Create an object that implements IntCalculator.
19       IntCalculator multiplier = x -> x * factor;
20
21       // Get a number from the user.
22       System.out.print("Enter an integer number: ");
23       num = keyboard.nextInt();
24
25       // Display the number multiplied by 10.
26       System.out.println("Multiplied by 10, that number is " +
27                           multiplier.calculate(num));
28    }
29 }
```

Program Output with Example Input Shown in Bold

Enter an integer number: **10 [*Enter*]**
Multiplied by 10, that number is 100

In Code Listing 10-46 we could remove the final key word from the variable declaration in line 12, and the program would still compile and execute correctly. This is because the factor variable is never modified, and therefore is effectively final.

10.12 Common Errors to Avoid

The following list describes several errors that are commonly committed when learning this chapter's topics:

- **Attempting to access a private superclass member directly from a subclass.** Private superclass members cannot be directly accessed by a method in a subclass. The subclass must call a public or protected superclass method in order to access the superclass's private members.
- **Forgetting to call a superclass constructor explicitly when the superclass does not have a default constructor or a programmer-defined no-arg constructor.** When a superclass does not have a default constructor or a programmer-defined no-arg constructor, the subclass's constructor must explicitly call one of the constructors that the superclass does have.
- **Allowing the superclass's no-arg constructor to be implicitly called when you intend to call another superclass constructor.** If a subclass's constructor does not explicitly call a superclass constructor, Java automatically calls the superclass's no-arg constructor.
- **Forgetting to precede a call to an overridden superclass method with super.** When a subclass method calls an overridden superclass method, it must precede the method call with the key word super and a dot (.). Failing to do so results in the subclass's version of the method being called.
- **Forgetting a class member's access specifier.** When you do not give a class member an access specifier, it is granted package access by default. This means that any method in the same package may access the member.
- **Writing a body for an abstract method.** An abstract method cannot have a body. It must be overridden in a subclass.
- **Forgetting to terminate an abstract method's header with a semicolon.** An abstract method header does not have a body, and it must be terminated with a semicolon.
- **Failing to override an abstract method.** An abstract method must be overridden in a subclass.
- **Overloading an abstract method instead of overriding it.** Overloading is not the same as overriding. When a superclass has an abstract method, the subclass must have a method with the same signature as the abstract method.
- **Trying to instantiate an abstract class.** You cannot create an instance of an abstract class.
- **Implementing an interface but forgetting to provide all of the methods specified by the interface.** When a class implements an interface, all of the methods specified by the interface must be provided in the class.
- **Writing a method specified by an interface but failing to use the exact signature and return type.** When a class implements an interface, the class must have methods with the same signature and return type as the methods specified in the interface.

Review Questions and Exercises

Multiple Choice and True/False

1. In an inheritance relationship, this is the general class.
   a. subclass
   b. superclass
   c. slave class
   d. child class

2. In an inheritance relationship, this is the specialized class.
   a. superclass
   b. master class
   c. subclass
   d. parent class

3. This key word indicates that a class inherits from another class.
   a. derived
   b. specialized
   c. based
   d. extends

4. A subclass does not have access to these superclass members.
   a. public
   b. private
   c. protected
   d. all of these

5. This key word refers to an object's superclass.
   a. super
   b. base
   c. superclass
   d. this

6. In a subclass constructor, a call to the superclass constructor must _____.
   a. appear as the very first statement
   b. appear as the very last statement
   c. appear between the constructor's header and the opening brace
   d. not appear

7. The following is an explicit call to the superclass's default constructor.
   a. default();
   b. class();
   c. super();
   d. base();

8. A method in a subclass that has the same signature as a method in the superclass is an example of _____.
   a. overloading
   b. overriding

    c. composition

    d. an error

9. A method in a subclass having the same name as a method in the superclass but a different signature is an example of _____.

    a. overloading

    b. overriding

    c. composition

    d. an error

10. These superclass members are accessible to subclasses and classes in the same package.

    a. private

    b. public

    c. protected

    d. all of these

11. All classes directly or indirectly inherit from this class.

    a. `Object`

    b. `Super`

    c. `Root`

    d. `Java`

12. With this type of binding, the Java Virtual Machine determines at runtime which method to call, depending on the type of the object that a variable references.

    a. static

    b. early

    c. flexible

    d. dynamic

13. This operator can be used to determine whether a reference variable references an object of a particular class.

    a. `isclass`

    b. `typeof`

    c. `instanceof`

    d. `isinstance`

14. When a class implements an interface, it must _____.

    a. overload all of the methods listed in the interface

    b. provide all of the nondefault methods that are listed in the interface, with the exact signatures and return types specified

    c. not have a constructor

    d. be an abstract class

15. Fields in an interface are _____.

    a. `final`

    b. `static`

    c. both `final` and `static`

    d. not allowed

16. Abstract methods must be _____.
    a. overridden
    b. overloaded
    c. deleted and replaced with real methods
    d. declared as private

17. Abstract classes cannot _____.
    a. be used as superclasses
    b. have abstract methods
    c. be instantiated
    d. have fields

18. You use the _____ operator to define an anonymous inner class.
    a. `class`
    b. `inner`
    c. `new`
    d. `anonymous`

19. An anonymous inner class must _____.
    a. be a superclass
    b. implement an interface
    c. extend a superclass
    d. either b or c.

20. A functional interface is an interface with _____.
    a. only one abstract method.
    b. no abstract methods.
    c. only private methods.
    d. no name.

21. You can use a lambda expression to instantiate an object that _____.
    a. that has no constructor.
    b. extends any superclass.
    c. implements a functional interface
    d. does not implement an interface.

22. **True or False:** Constructors are not inherited.

23. **True or False:** In a subclass, a call to the superclass constructor can only be written in the subclass constructor.

24. **True or False:** If a subclass constructor does not explicitly call a superclass constructor, Java will not call any of the superclass's constructors.

25. **True or False:** An object of a superclass can access members declared in a subclass.

26. **True or False:** The superclass constructor always executes before the subclass constructor.

27. **True or False:** When a method is declared with the `final` modifier, it must be overridden in a subclass.

28. **True or False:** A superclass has a member with package access. A class that is outside the superclass's package but inherits from the superclass can access the member.

29. **True or False:** A superclass reference variable can reference an object of a subclass that extends the superclass.

30. **True or False:** A subclass reference variable can reference an object of the superclass.
31. **True or False:** When a class contains an abstract method, the class cannot be instantiated.
32. **True or False:** A class may only implement one interface.
33. **True or False:** By default all members of an interface are public.

Find the Error

Find the error in each of the following code segments:

1.
```
// Superclass
public class Vehicle
{
    (Member declarations . . .)
}
// Subclass
public class Car expands Vehicle
{
    (Member declarations . . .)
}
```

2.
```
// Superclass
public class Vehicle
{
    private double cost;
    (Other methods . . .)
}
// Subclass
public class Car extends Vehicle
{
    public Car(double c)
    {
        cost = c;
    }
}
```

3.
```
// Superclass
public class Vehicle
{
    private double cost;
    public Vehicle(double c)
    {
        cost = c;
    }
    (Other methods . . .)
}
// Subclass
public class Car extends Vehicle
```

```
    {
        private int passengers;
        public Car(int p)
        {
            passengers = c;
        }
        (Other methods . . .)
    }
4.  // Superclass
    public class Vehicle
    {
        public abstract double getMilesPerGallon();
        (Other methods . . .)
    }
    // Subclass
    public class Car extends Vehicle
    {
        private int mpg;
        public int getMilesPerGallon();
        {
            return mpg;
        }
        (Other methods . . .)
    }
```

Algorithm Workbench

1. Write the first line of the definition for a Poodle class. The class should extend the Dog class.

2. Look at the following code, which is the first line of a class definition:

    `public class Tiger extends Felis`

    In what order will the class constructors execute?

3. Write the declaration for class B. The class's members should be as follows:

    - m, an integer. This variable should not be accessible to code outside the class or to any class that extends class B.
    - n, an integer. This variable should be accessible only to classes that extend class B or are in the same package as class B.
    - setM, getM, setN, and getN. These are the mutator and accessor methods for the member variables m and n. These methods should be accessible to code outside the class.
    - calc. This is a public abstract method.

    Next, write the declaration for class D, which extends class B. The class's members should be as follows:

    - q, a double. This variable should not be accessible to code outside the class.
    - r, a double. This variable should be accessible to any class that extends class D or is in the same package.

- `setQ`, `getQ`, `setR`, and `getR`. These are the mutator and accessor methods for the member variables `q` and `r`. These methods should be accessible to code outside the class.
- `calc`, a public method that overrides the superclass's abstract `calc` method. This method should return the value of `q` times `r`.

4. Write the statement that calls a superclass constructor and passes the arguments `x`, `y`, and `z`.

5. A superclass has the following method:

```
public void setValue(int v)
{
    value = v;
}
```

Write a statement that may appear in a subclass that calls this method, passing 10 as an argument.

6. A superclass has the following abstract method:

```
public abstract int getValue();
```

Write an example of a `getValue` method that can appear in a subclass.

7. Write the first line of the definition for a `Stereo` class. The class should extend the `SoundSystem` class, and it should implement the `CDplayable`, `TunerPlayable`, and `CassettePlayable` interfaces.

8. Write an interface named `Nameable` that specifies the following methods:

```
public void setName(String n)
public String getName()
```

9. Look at the following interface:

```
public interface Computable
{
    double compute(double x);
}
```

Write a statement that uses a lambda expression to create an object that implements the `Computable` interface. The object's name should be `half`. The `half` object's `compute` method should return the value of the x parameter divided by 2.

Short Answer

1. What is an "is-a" relationship?

2. A program uses two classes: `Animal` and `Dog`. Which class is the superclass and which is the subclass?

3. What is the superclass and what is the subclass in the following line?

```
public class Pet extends Dog
```

4. What is the difference between a protected class member and a private class member?

5. Can a subclass ever directly access the private members of its superclass?

6. Which constructor is called first, that of the subclass or the superclass?

7. What is the difference between overriding a superclass method and overloading a superclass method?

8. Reference variables can be polymorphic. What does this mean?

9. When does dynamic binding take place?

10. What is an abstract method?

11. What is an abstract class?

12. What are the differences between an abstract class and an interface?

13. When you instantiate an anonymous inner class, the class must do one of two things. What are they?

14. What is a functional interface?

15. What is a lambda expression?

Programming Challenges

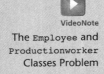

VideoNote
The Employee and
Productionworker
Classes Problem

Visit www.myprogramminglab.com to complete many of these Programming Challenges online and get instant feedback.

1. Employee and ProductionWorker Classes

Design a class named Employee. The class should keep the following information in fields:

- Employee name
- Employee number in the format XXX–L, where each X is a digit within the range 0–9 and the L is a letter within the range A–M.
- Hire date

Write one or more constructors and the appropriate accessor and mutator methods for the class.

Next, write a class named ProductionWorker that extends the Employee class. The ProductionWorker class should have fields to hold the following information:

- Shift (an integer)
- Hourly pay rate (a double)

The workday is divided into two shifts: day and night. The shift field will be an integer value representing the shift that the employee works. The day shift is shift 1 and the night shift is shift 2. Write one or more constructors and the appropriate accessor and mutator methods for the class. Demonstrate the classes by writing a program that uses a ProductionWorker object.

2. ShiftSupervisor Class

In a particular factory, a shift supervisor is a salaried employee who supervises a shift. In addition to a salary, the shift supervisor earns a yearly bonus when his or her shift meets production goals. Design a ShiftSupervisor class that extends the Employee class you created in Programming Challenge 1. The ShiftSupervisor class should have a field that holds the annual salary and a field that holds the annual production bonus that a shift supervisor has earned. Write one or more constructors and the appropriate accessor and mutator methods for the class. Demonstrate the class by writing a program that uses a ShiftSupervisor object.

3. TeamLeader Class

In a particular factory, a team leader is an hourly paid production worker that leads a small team. In addition to hourly pay, team leaders earn a fixed monthly bonus. Team leaders are required to attend a minimum number of hours of training per year. Design a TeamLeader class that extends the `ProductionWorker` class you designed in Programming Challenge 1. The `TeamLeader` class should have fields for the monthly bonus amount, the required number of training hours, and the number of training hours that the team leader has attended. Write one or more constructors and the appropriate accessor and mutator methods for the class. Demonstrate the class by writing a program that uses a `TeamLeader` object.

4. Essay Class

Design an `Essay` class that extends the `GradedActivity` class presented in this chapter. The `Essay` class should determine the grade a student receives for an essay. The student's essay score can be up to 100 and is determined in the following manner:

> Grammar: 30 points
> Spelling: 20 points
> Correct length: 20 points
> Content: 30 points

Demonstrate the class in a simple program.

5. Course Grades

In a course, a teacher gives the following tests and assignments:

- A **lab activity** that is observed by the teacher and assigned a numeric score.
- A **pass/fail exam** that has 10 questions. The minimum passing score is 70.
- An **essay** that is assigned a numeric score.
- A **final exam** that has 50 questions.

Write a class named `CourseGrades`. The class should have a `GradedActivity` array named `grades` as a field. The array should have four elements, one for each of the assignments previously described. The class should have the following methods:

`setLab:`	This method should accept a `GradedActivity` object as its argument. This object should already hold the student's score for the lab activity. Element 0 of the `grades` field should reference this object.
`setPassFailExam:`	This method should accept a `PassFailExam` object as its argument. This object should already hold the student's score for the pass/fail exam. Element 1 of the `grades` field should reference this object.
`setEssay:`	This method should accept an `Essay` object as its argument. (See Programming Challenge 4 for the `Essay` class. If you have not completed Programming Challenge 4, use a `GradedActivity` object instead.) This object should already hold the student's score for the essay. Element 2 of the `grades` field should reference this object.
`setFinalExam:`	This method should accept a `FinalExam` object as its argument. This object should already hold the student's score for the final exam. Element 3 of the `grades` field should reference this object.
`toString:`	This method should return a string that contains the numeric scores and grades for each element in the `grades` array.

Demonstrate the class in a program.

6. Analyzable **Interface**

Modify the CourseGrades class you created in Programming Challenge 5 so it implements the following interface:

```
public interface Analyzable
{
    double getAverage();
    GradedActivity getHighest();
    GradedActivity getLowest();
}
```

The getAverage method should return the average of the numeric scores stored in the grades array. The getHighest method should return a reference to the element of the grades array that has the highest numeric score. The getLowest method should return a reference to the element of the grades array that has the lowest numeric score. Demonstrate the new methods in a complete program.

7. Person **and** Customer **Classes**

Design a class named Person with fields for holding a person's name, address, and telephone number. Write one or more constructors and the appropriate mutator and accessor methods for the class's fields.

Next, design a class named Customer, which extends the Person class. The Customer class should have a field for a customer number and a boolean field indicating whether the customer wishes to be on a mailing list. Write one or more constructors and the appropriate mutator and accessor methods for the class's fields. Demonstrate an object of the Customer class in a simple program.

8. PreferredCustomer **Class**

A retail store has a preferred customer plan where customers can earn discounts on all their purchases. The amount of a customer's discount is determined by the amount of the customer's cumulative purchases in the store as follows:

- When a preferred customer spends $500, he or she gets a 5 percent discount on all future purchases.
- When a preferred customer spends $1,000, he or she gets a 6 percent discount on all future purchases.
- When a preferred customer spends $1,500, he or she gets a 7 percent discount on all future purchases.
- When a preferred customer spends $2,000 or more, he or she gets a 10 percent discount on all future purchases.

Design a class named PreferredCustomer, which extends the Customer class you created in Programming Challenge 7. The PreferredCustomer class should have fields for the amount of the customer's purchases and the customer's discount level. Write one or more constructors and the appropriate mutator and accessor methods for the class's fields. Demonstrate the class in a simple program.

9. BankAccount **and** SavingsAccount **Classes**

Design an abstract class named BankAccount to hold the following data for a bank account:

- Balance
- Number of deposits this month

- Number of withdrawals
- Annual interest rate
- Monthly service charges

The class should have the following methods:

Constructor:	The constructor should accept arguments for the balance and annual interest rate.
deposit:	A method that accepts an argument for the amount of the deposit. The method should add the argument to the account balance. It should also increment the variable holding the number of deposits.
withdraw:	A method that accepts an argument for the amount of the withdrawal. The method should subtract the argument from the balance. It should also increment the variable holding the number of withdrawals.
calcInterest:	A method that updates the balance by calculating the monthly interest earned by the account, and adding this interest to the balance. This is performed by the following formulas:

$$Monthly\ Interest\ Rate = (Annual\ Interest\ Rate\ /\ 12)$$
$$Monthly\ Interest = Balance\ *\ Monthly\ Interest\ Rate$$
$$Balance = Balance\ +\ Monthly\ Interest$$

monthlyProcess:	A method that subtracts the monthly service charges from the balance, calls the calcInterest method, and then sets the variables that hold the number of withdrawals, number of deposits, and monthly service charges to zero.

Next, design a SavingsAccount class that extends the BankAccount class. The SavingsAccount class should have a status field to represent an active or inactive account. If the balance of a savings account falls below $25, it becomes inactive. (The status field could be a boolean variable.) No more withdrawals may be made until the balance is raised above $25, at which time the account becomes active again. The savings account class should have the following methods:

withdraw:	A method that determines whether the account is inactive before a withdrawal is made. (No withdrawal will be allowed if the account is not active.) A withdrawal is then made by calling the superclass version of the method.
deposit:	A method that determines whether the account is inactive before a deposit is made. If the account is inactive and the deposit brings the balance above $25, the account becomes active again. A deposit is then made by calling the superclass version of the method.
monthlyProcess:	Before the superclass method is called, this method checks the number of withdrawals. If the number of withdrawals for the month is more than 4, a service charge of $1 for each withdrawal above 4 is added to the superclass field that holds the monthly service charges. (Don't forget to check the account balance after the service charge is taken. If the balance falls below $25, the account becomes inactive.)

10. `Ship`, `CruiseShip`, and `CargoShip` Classes

Design a `Ship` class that the following members:

- A field for the name of the ship (a string).
- A field for the year that the ship was built (a string).
- A constructor and appropriate accessors and mutators.
- A `toString` method that displays the ship's name and the year it was built.

Design a `CruiseShip` class that extends the `Ship` class. The `CruiseShip` class should have the following members:

- A field for the maximum number of passengers (an `int`).
- A constructor and appropriate accessors and mutators.
- A `toString` method that overrides the `toString` method in the base class. The `CruiseShip` class's `toString` method should display only the ship's name and the maximum number of passengers.

Design a `CargoShip` class that extends the `Ship` class. The `CargoShip` class should have the following members:

- A field for the cargo capacity in tonnage (an `int`).
- A constructor and appropriate accessors and mutators.
- A `toString` method that overrides the `toString` method in the base class. The `CargoShip` class's `toString` method should display only the ship's name and the ship's cargo capacity.

Demonstrate the classes in a program that has a `Ship` array. Assign various `Ship`, `CruiseShip`, and `CargoShip` objects to the array elements. The program should then step through the array, calling each object's `toString` method. (See Code Listing 10-25 as an example.)

11 Exceptions and Advanced File I/O

TOPICS

11.1 Handling Exceptions
11.2 Throwing Exceptions
11.3 Advanced Topics: Binary Files, Random Access Files, and Object Serialization
11.4 Common Errors to Avoid

11.1 Handling Exceptions

CONCEPT: An exception is an object that is generated as the result of an error or an unexpected event. To prevent exceptions from crashing your program, you must write code that detects and handles them.

VideoNote
Handling
Exceptions

There are many error conditions that can occur while a Java application is running that will cause it to halt execution. By now you have probably experienced this many times. For example, look at the program in Code Listing 11-1. This program attempts to read beyond the bounds of an array.

Code Listing 11-1 (BadArray.java)

```
1 /**
2    This program causes an error and crashes.
3 */
4
5 public class BadArray
6 {
7    public static void main(String[] args)
8    {
```

```
 9          // Create an array with 3 elements.
10          int[] numbers = { 1, 2, 3 };
11
12          // Attempt to read beyond the bounds
13          // of the array.
14          for (int i = 0; i <= 3; i++)
15              System.out.println(numbers[i]);
16      }
17 }
```

Program Output

```
1
2
3
Exception in thread "main" java.lang.ArrayIndexOutOfBoundsException
        at BadArray.main(BadArray.java:15)
```

The numbers array in this program has only three elements, with the subscripts 0 though 2. The program crashes when it tries to read the element at numbers[3], and displays an error message similar to that shown at the end of the program output. This message indicates that an exception occurred, and it gives some information about it. An *exception* is an object that is generated in memory as the result of an error or an unexpected event. When an exception is generated, it is said to have been "thrown." Unless an exception is detected by the application and dealt with, it causes the application to halt.

To detect that an exception has been thrown and prevent it from halting your application, Java allows you to create exception handlers. An *exception handler* is a section of code that gracefully responds to exceptions when they are thrown. The process of intercepting and responding to exceptions is called *exception handling*. If your code does not handle an exception when it is thrown, the *default exception handler* deals with it, as shown in Code Listing 11-1. The default exception handler prints an error message and crashes the program.

The error that caused the exception to be thrown in Code Listing 11-1 is easy to avoid. If the loop were written properly, it would not have tried to read outside the bounds of the array. Some errors, however, are caused by conditions that are outside the application and cannot be avoided. For example, suppose an application creates a file on the disk and the user deletes it. Later the application attempts to open the file to read from it, and because it does not exist, an error occurs. As a result, an exception is thrown.

Exception Classes

As previously mentioned, an exception is an object. Exception objects are created from classes in the Java API. The API has an extensive hierarchy of exception classes. A small part of the hierarchy is shown in Figure 11-1.

As you can see, all of the classes in the hierarchy inherit from the Throwable class. Just below the Throwable class are the classes Error and Exception. Classes that inherit from

`Error` are for exceptions that are thrown when a critical error occurs, such as an internal error in the Java Virtual Machine or running out of memory. Your applications should not try to handle these errors because they are the result of a serious condition.

All of the exceptions that you will handle are instances of classes that inherit from `Exception`. Figure 11-1 shows two of these classes: `IOException` and `RuntimeException`. These classes also serve as superclasses. `IOException` serves as a superclass for exceptions that are related to input and output operations. `RuntimeException` serves as a superclass for exceptions that result from programming errors, such as an out-of-bounds array subscript.

The chart in Figure 11-1 shows two of the classes that inherit from the `IOException` class: `EOFException` and `FileNotFoundException`. These are examples of classes that exception objects are created from. An `EOFException` object is thrown when an application attempts to read beyond the end of a file, and a `FileNotFoundException` object is thrown when an application tries to open a file that does not exist.

NOTE: The exception classes are in packages in the Java API. For example, `FileNotFoundException` is in the `java.io` package. When you handle an exception that is not in the `java.lang` package, you will need the appropriate `import` statement.

Figure 11-1   Part of the exception class hierarchy

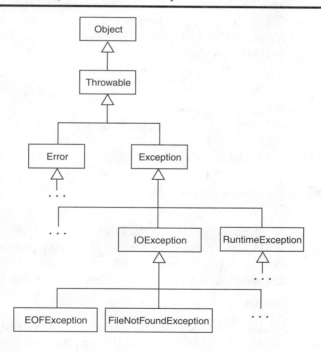

Handling an Exception

To handle an exception, you use a `try` statement. We will look at several variations of the `try` statement, beginning with the following general format:

```
try
{
    (try block statements . . .)
}
catch (ExceptionType parameterName)
{
    (catch block statements . . .)
}
```

First the key word `try` appears. Next, a block of code appears inside braces, which are required. This block of code is known as a *try block*. A *try block* is one or more statements that are executed and can potentially throw an exception. You can think of the code in the try block as being "protected" because the application will not halt if the try block throws an exception.

After the try block, a `catch` clause appears. A `catch` clause begins with the key word `catch`, followed by the code *(ExceptionType parameterName)*. This is a parameter variable declaration, where *ExceptionType* is the name of an exception class and *parameterName* is a variable name. If code in the try block throws an exception of the *ExceptionType* class, then the parameter variable will reference the exception object. In addition, the code that immediately follows the `catch` clause is executed. The code that immediately follows the catch clause is known as a `catch block`. Once again, the braces are required.

Let's look at an example of code that uses a `try` statement. The statement inside the following try block attempts to open the file *MyFile.txt*. If the file does not exist, the `Scanner` object throws an exception of the `FileNotFoundException` class. This code is designed to handle that exception if it is thrown.

```
try
{
    File file = new File("MyFile.txt");
    Scanner inputFile = new Scanner(file);
}
catch (FileNotFoundException e)
{
    System.out.println("File not found.");
}
```

Let's look closer. First, the code in the try block is executed. If this code throws an exception, the Java Virtual Machine searches for a `catch` clause that can deal with the exception. In order for a `catch` clause to be able to deal with an exception, its parameter must be of a type that is compatible with the exception's type. Here is this code's `catch` clause:

```
catch (FileNotFoundException e)
```

This `catch` clause declares a reference variable named e as its parameter. The e variable can reference an object of the `FileNotFoundException` class. So, this `catch` clause can deal with an exception of the `FileNotFoundException` class. If the code in the try block throws an exception of the `FileNotFoundException` class, the e variable will reference the exception object and the code in the catch block will execute. In this case, the message "File not found." will be printed. After the catch block is executed, the program will resume with the code that appears after the entire try/catch construct.

NOTE: The Java API documentation lists all of the exceptions that can be thrown from each method.

Code Listing 11-2 shows a program that asks the user to enter a file name, then attempts to open the file. If the file does not exist, an error message is printed. Figures 11-2 and 11-3 show examples of interaction with the program.

Code Listing 11-2   (OpenFile.java)

```java
 1 import java.io.*;     // For File class and FileNotFoundException
 2 import java.util.Scanner;          // For the Scanner class
 3 import javax.swing.JOptionPane;    // For the JOptionPane class
 4
 5 /**
 6    This program demonstrates how a FileNotFoundException
 7    exception can be handled.
 8 */
 9
10 public class OpenFile
11 {
12    public static void main(String[] args)
13    {
14       File file;               // For file input
15       Scanner inputFile;       // For file input
16       String fileName;         // To hold a file name
17
18       // Get a file name from the user.
19       fileName = JOptionPane.showInputDialog("Enter " +
20                       "the name of a file:");
21
22       // Attempt to open the file.
23       try
24       {
25          file = new File(fileName);
26          inputFile = new Scanner(file);
27          JOptionPane.showMessageDialog(null,
28                          "The file was found.");
29       }
30       catch (FileNotFoundException e)
31       {
32          JOptionPane.showMessageDialog(null,
33                          "File not found.");
34       }
35
36       JOptionPane.showMessageDialog(null, "Done.");
37       System.exit(0);
38    }
39 }
```

Figure 11-2 Interaction with the `OpenFile.java` program (assume that *BadFile.txt* does not exist)

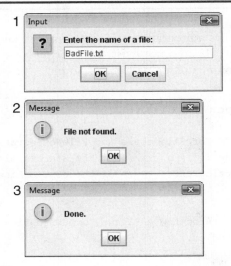

Figure 11-3 Interaction with the `OpenFile.java` program (assume that *GoodFile.txt* does exist)

Look at the example run of the program in Figure 11-2. The user entered *BadFile.txt* as the file name. In line 25, the first statement inside the try block, a `File` object is created and this name is passed to the `File` constructor. In line 26 a reference to the `File` object is passed to the `Scanner` constructor. Because *BadFile.txt* does not exist, an exception of the `FileNotFoundException` class is thrown by the `Scanner` class constructor. When the exception is thrown, the program immediately exits the try block, skipping the remaining statement in the block (lines 27 through 28). The program jumps to the `catch` clause in line 30, which has a `FileNotFoundException` parameter, and executes the catch block that follows it. Figure 11-4 illustrates this sequence of events.

Notice that after the catch block executes, the program resumes at the statement that immediately follows the try/catch construct. This statement, which is in line 36, displays the message "Done."

Figure 11-4 Sequence of events with an exception

```
                                try
                                {
    If this statement                  file = new File(fileName);
    throws an exception...              inputFile = new Scanner(file);
                                        JOptionPane.showMessageDialog(null,
    ... then this statement                           "The file was found.");
    is skipped.                 }
                                catch (FileNotFoundException e)
    If the exception is an object of    {
    the FileNotFoundException               JOptionPane.showMessageDialog(null,
    class, the program jumps to                          "File not found.");
    this catch clause.          }
```

Now look at the example run of the program in Figure 11-3. In this case, the user entered *GoodFile.txt*, which is the name of a file that exists. No exception was thrown in the try block, so the program skips the catch clause and its catch block and jumps directly to the statement in line 36, which follows the try/catch construct. This statement displays the message "Done." Figure 11-5 illustrates this sequence of events.

Figure 11-5 Sequence of events with no exception

```
                                try
                                {
                                    file = new File(fileName);
                                    inputFile = new Scanner(file);
                                    JOptionPane.showMessageDialog(null,
                                                      "The file was found.");
    If no exception is thrown in    }
    the try block, the program  catch (FileNotFoundException e)
    jumps to the statement that  {
    immediately follows the          JOptionPane.showMessageDialog(null,
    try/catch construct.                         "File not found.");
                                }
                                JOptionPane.showMessageDialog(null, "Done.");
```

Retrieving the Default Error Message

Each exception object has a method named getMessage that can be used to retrieve the default error message for the exception. This is the same message that is displayed when the exception is not handled and the application halts. The program in Code Listing 11-3 demonstrates the getMessage method. This is a modified version of the program in Code Listing 11-2. Figure 11-6 shows the program running. In the figure, the user entered the name of a file that does not exist.

Code Listing 11-3 (`ExceptionMessage.java`)

```java
 1 import java.io.*;              // For file I/O classes
 2 import java.util.Scanner;      // For the Scanner class
 3 import javax.swing.JOptionPane; // For the JOptionPane class
 4
 5 /**
 6    This program demonstrates how a FileNotFoundException
 7    exception can be handled.
 8 */
 9
10 public class ExceptionMessage
11 {
12    public static void main(String[] args)
13    {
14       File file;                // For file input
15       Scanner inputFile;        // For file input
16       String fileName;          // To hold a file name
17
18       // Get a file name from the user.
19       fileName = JOptionPane.showInputDialog("Enter " +
20                             "the name of a file:");
21
22       // Attempt to open the file.
23       try
24       {
25          file = new File(fileName);
26          inputFile = new Scanner(file);
27          JOptionPane.showMessageDialog(null,
28                      "The file was found.");
29       }
30       catch (FileNotFoundException e)
31       {
32          JOptionPane.showMessageDialog(null, e.getMessage());
33       }
34
35       JOptionPane.showMessageDialog(null, "Done.");
36       System.exit(0);
37    }
38 }
```

Code Listing 11-4 shows another example. This program forces the `parseInt` method of the `Integer` wrapper class to throw an exception.

Figure 11-6   Interaction with the `ExceptionMessage.java` program
(assume that *BadFile.txt* does not exist)

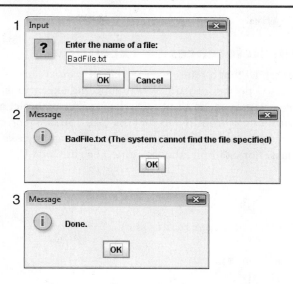

Code Listing 11-4	**(ParseIntError.java)**

```
 1 /**
 2    This program demonstrates how the Integer.parseInt
 3    method throws an exception.
 4 */
 5
 6 public class ParseIntError
 7 {
 8    public static void main(String[] args)
 9    {
10       String str = "abcde";
11       int number;
12
13       try
14       {
15          number = Integer.parseInt(str);
16       }
17       catch (NumberFormatException e)
18       {
19          System.out.println("Conversion error: " +
20                          e.getMessage());
21       }
22    }
23 }
```

Program Output

```
Conversion error: For input string: "abcde"
```

The numeric wrapper classes' "parse" methods all throw an exception of the `NumberFormatException` type if the string being converted does not contain a convertible numeric value.

Polymorphic References to Exceptions

Recall from Chapter 10 that a reference variable of a superclass type can reference subclass objects. This is called polymorphism. When handling exceptions, you can use a polymorphic reference as a parameter in the `catch` clause. For example, all of the exceptions that we have dealt with inherit from the `Exception` class. So, a `catch` clause that uses a parameter variable of the `Exception` type is capable of catching any exception that inherits from the `Exception` class. For example, the `try` statement in Code Listing 11-4 could be written as follows:

```
try
{
    number = Integer.parseInt(str);
}
catch (Exception e)
{
    System.out.println("Conversion error: " +
                    e.getMessage());
}
```

Although the `Integer` class's `parseInt` method throws a `NumberFormatException` object, this code still works because the `NumberFormatException` class inherits from the `Exception` class.

Using Multiple `catch` Clauses to Handle Multiple Exceptions

The programs we have studied so far test only for a single type of exception. In many cases, however, the code in the try block will be capable of throwing more than one type of exception. In such a case, you need to write a `catch` clause for each type of exception that could potentially be thrown.

For example, the program in Code Listing 11-5 reads the contents of a file named *SalesData.txt*. Each line in the file contains the sales amount for one month, and the file has several lines. Here are the contents of the file:

```
24987.62
26978.97
32589.45
31978.47
22781.76
29871.44
```

The program in Code Listing 11-5 reads each number from the file and adds it to an accumulator variable. The try block contains code that can throw different types of exceptions. For example, the Scanner class's constructor can throw a FileNotFoundException if the file is not found, and the Scanner class's nextDouble method can throw an InputMismatchException (which is in the java.util package) if it reads a non-numeric value from the file. To handle these exceptions, the try statement has two catch clauses. Figure 11-7 shows the dialog box displayed by the program when no errors occur. This dialog box is displayed by the statement in lines 51 through 56. Figure 11-8 shows the dialog box displayed by the statement in lines 62 through 64 when the file cannot be found.

Figure 11-7   Dialog box displayed by the SalesReport.java program when no error occurs

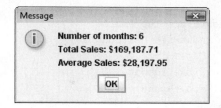

Figure 11-8   Dialog box displayed by the SalesReport.java program when the file cannot be found

Code Listing 11-5   (SalesReport.java)

```java
 1 import java.io.*;     // For File class and FileNotFoundException
 2 import java.util.*;   // For Scanner and InputMismatchException
 3 import javax.swing.JOptionPane; // For the JOptionPane class
 4
 5 /**
 6    This program demonstrates how multiple exceptions can
 7    be caught with one try statement.
 8 */
 9
10 public class SalesReport
11 {
12    public static void main(String[] args)
13    {
14       String filename = "SalesData.txt"; // File name
15       int months = 0;                    // Month counter
```

```
16        double oneMonth;              // One month's sales
17        double totalSales = 0.0;      // Total sales
18        double averageSales;          // Average sales
19
20        try
21        {
22           // Open the file.
23           File file = new File(filename);
24           Scanner inputFile = new Scanner(file);
25
26           // Process the contents of the file.
27           while (inputFile.hasNext())
28           {
29              // Get a month's sales amount.
30              oneMonth = inputFile.nextDouble();
31
32              // Accumulate the amount.
33              totalSales += oneMonth;
34
35              // Increment the month counter
36              months++;
37           }
38
39           // Close the file.
40           inputFile.close();
41
42           // Calculate the average.
43           averageSales = totalSales / months;
44
45           // Display the results.
46           JOptionPane.showMessageDialog(null,
47              String.format("Number of months: %d\n" +
48                       "Total Sales: $%,.2f\n" +
49                       "Average Sales: $%,.2f",
50                       months, totalSales, averageSales));
51        }
52        catch(FileNotFoundException e)
53        {
54           // Thrown by the Scanner constructor when
55           // the file is not found.
56           JOptionPane.showMessageDialog(null,
57              "The file " + filename + " does not exist.");
58        }
59        catch(InputMismatchException e)
60        {
61           // Thrown by the Scanner class's nextDouble
62           // method when a non-numeric value is found.
```

```
63            JOptionPane.showMessageDialog(null,
64                "Non-numeric data found in the file.");
65         }
66
67        System.exit(0);
68     }
69 }
```

When an exception is thrown by code in the try block, the JVM begins searching the try statement for a catch clause that can handle it. It searches the catch clauses from top to bottom and passes control of the program to the first catch clause with a parameter that is compatible with the exception.

Using Exception Handlers to Recover from Errors

The program in Code Listing 11-5 demonstrates how a try statement can have several catch clauses in order to handle different types of exceptions. However, the program does not use the exception handlers to recover from any of the errors. Regardless of whether the file is not found or a non-numeric item is encountered in the file, this program still halts. The program in Code Listing 11-6 is a better example of effective exception handling. It attempts to recover from as many of the exceptions as possible.

Code Listing 11-6   (`SalesReport2.java`)

```java
1  import java.io.*;      // For File class and FileNotFoundException
2  import java.util.*;   // For Scanner and InputMismatchException
3  import javax.swing.JOptionPane; // For the JOptionPane class
4
5  /**
6     This program demonstrates how exception handlers can
7     be used to recover from errors.
8  */
9
10 public class SalesReport2
11 {
12    public static void main(String[] args)
13    {
14       String filename = "SalesData.txt"; // File name
15       int months = 0;                    // Month counter
16       double oneMonth;                   // One month's sales
17       double totalSales = 0.0;           // Total sales
18       double averageSales;               // Average sales
19
20       // Attempt to open the file by calling the
21       // openfile method.
22       Scanner inputFile = openFile(filename);
```

```
23
24          // If the openFile method returned null, then
25          // the file was not found. Get a new file name.
26          while (inputFile == null)
27          {
28             filename = JOptionPane.showInputDialog(
29                          "ERROR: " + filename +
30                          " does not exist.\n" +
31                          "Enter another file name: ");
32             inputFile = openFile(filename);
33          }
34
35          // Process the contents of the file.
36          while (inputFile.hasNext())
37          {
38             try
39             {
40                // Get a month's sales amount.
41                oneMonth = inputFile.nextDouble();
42
43                // Accumulate the amount.
44                totalSales += oneMonth;
45
46                // Increment the month counter.
47                months++;
48             }
49             catch(InputMismatchException e)
50             {
51                // Display an error message.
52                JOptionPane.showMessageDialog(null,
53                   "Non-numeric data found in the file.\n" +
54                   "The invalid record will be skipped.");
55
56                // Skip past the invalid data.
57                inputFile.nextLine();
58             }
59          }
60
61          // Close the file.
62          inputFile.close();
63
64          // Calculate the average.
65          averageSales = totalSales / months;
66
67          // Display the results.
68          JOptionPane.showMessageDialog(null,
69             String.format("Number of months: %d\n" +
```

```
70                           "Total Sales: $%,.2f\n" +
71                           "Average Sales: $%,.2f",
72                           months, totalSales, averageSales));
73
74           System.exit(0);
75      }
76
77      /**
78          The opeFile method opens the specified file and
79          returns a reference to a Scanner object.
80          @param filename The name of the file to open.
81          @return A Scanner reference, if the file exists
82                  Otherwise, null is returned.
83      */
84
85      public static Scanner openFile(String filename)
86      {
87          Scanner scan;
88
89          // Attempt to open the file.
90          try
91          {
92              File file = new File(filename);
93              scan = new Scanner(file);
94          }
95          catch(FileNotFoundException e)
96          {
97              scan = null;
98          }
99
100         return scan;
101     }
102 }
```

Let's look at how this program recovers from a FileNotFoundException. The openFile method, in lines 85 through 101, accepts a file name as its argument. The method creates a File object (passing the file name to the constructor) and a Scanner object. If the Scanner class constructor throws a FileNotFoundException, the method returns null. Otherwise, it returns a reference to the Scanner object. In the main method, a loop is used in lines 26 through 33 to ask the user for a different file name in the event that the openFile method returns null.

Now let's look at how the program recovers from unexpectedly encountering a non-numeric item in the file. The statement in line 41, which calls the Scanner class's nextDouble method, is wrapped in a try statement that catches the InputMismatchException. If this exception is thrown by the nextDouble method, the catch block in lines 49 through 58 displays a message indicating that a non-numeric item was encountered and that the invalid record will be skipped. The invalid data is then read from the file with the `nextLine` method in line 57. Because the statement `months++` in line 47 is in the try block, it will not be executed when the exception occurs, so the number of months will still be correct. The loop continues processing with the next line in the file.

Let's look at some examples of how the program recovers from these errors. Suppose we rename *SalesData.txt* file as *SalesInfo.txt*. Figure 11-9 shows an example running of the program.

Figure 11-9 Interaction with the `SalesReport2.java` program

Now, suppose we change the name of the file back to *SalesData.txt* and edit its contents as follows:

```
24987.62
26978.97
abc
31978.47
22781.76
29871.44
```

Notice that the third item is no longer a number. Figure 11-10 shows an example running of the program.

Figure 11-10 Dialog boxes displayed by the `SalesReport2.java` program

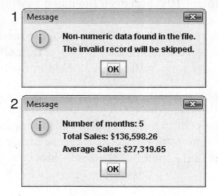

Handle Each Exception Only Once in a `try` Statement

Not including polymorphic references, a `try` statement may have only one `catch` clause for each specific type of exception. For example, the following `try` statement will cause the compiler to issue an error message because it handles a `NumberFormatException` object with two `catch` clauses:

```
try
{
    number = Integer.parseInt(str);
}
catch (NumberFormatException e)
{
    System.out.println("Bad number format.");
}
// ERROR!!! NumberFormatException has already been caught!
catch (NumberFormatException e)
{
    System.out.println(str + " is not a number.");
}
```

Sometimes you can cause this error by using polymorphic references. For example, look at Figure 11-11, which shows an inheritance hierarchy for the `NumberFormatException` class.

Figure 11-11   Inheritance hierarchy for the `NumberFormatException` class

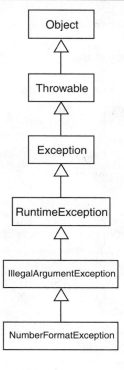

As you can see from the figure, the NumberFormatException class inherits from the IllegalArgumentException class. Now look at the following code:

```
try
{
    number = Integer.parseInt(str);
}
catch (IllegalArgumentException e)
{
    System.out.println("Bad number format.");
}
// This will also cause an error.
catch (NumberFormatException e)
{
    System.out.println(str + " is not a number.");
}
```

The compiler issues an error message regarding the second catch clause, reporting that NumberFormatException has already been caught. This is because the first catch clause, which catches IllegalArgumentException objects, will polymorphically catch NumberFormatException objects.

If you are handling multiple exceptions in the same try statement and some of the exceptions are related to each other through inheritance, then you should handle the more specialized exception classes before the more general exception classes. We can rewrite the previous code as follows, with no errors:

```
try
{
    number = Integer.parseInt(str);
}
catch (NumberFormatException e)
{
    System.out.println(str + " is not a number.");
}
catch (IllegalArgumentException e)
{
    System.out.println("Bad number format.");
}
```

The finally Clause

The try statement may have an optional finally clause, which must appear after all of the catch clauses. Here is the general format of a try statement with a finally clause:

```
try
{
    (try block statements . . .)
}
```

```
catch (ExceptionType ParameterName)
{
    (catch block statements . . .)
}
finally
{
    (finally block statements . . .)
}
```

The *finally block* is one or more statements that are always executed after the try block has executed and after any catch blocks have executed if an exception was thrown. The statements in the finally block execute whether an exception occurs or not. For example, the following code opens a file of doubles and reads its contents. The outer try statement opens the file and has a catch clause that catches the FileNotFoundException. The inner try statement reads values from the file and has a catch clause that catches the InputMismatchException. The finally block closes the file regardless of whether an InputMismatchException occurs.

```
try
{
    // Open the file.
    File file = new File(filename);
    Scanner inputFile = new Scanner(file);

    try
    {
        // Read and display the file's contents.
        while (inputFile.hasNext())
        {
            System.out.println(inputFile.nextDouble());
        }
    }
    catch (InputMismatchException e)
    {
        System.out.println("Invalid data found.");
    }
    finally
    {
        // Close the file.
        inputFile.close();
    }
}
catch (FileNotFoundException e)
{
    System.out.println("File not found.");
}
```

The Stack Trace

Quite often, a method will call another method, which will call yet another method. For example, method A calls method B, which calls method C. The *call stack* is an internal list of all the methods that are currently executing.

When an exception is thrown by a method that is executing under several layers of method calls, it is sometimes helpful to know which methods were responsible for the method being called. A *stack trace* is a list of all the methods in the call stack. It indicates the method that was executing when an exception occurred and all of the methods that were called in order to execute that method. For example, look at the program in Code Listing 11-7. It has three methods: main, myMethod, and produceError. The main method calls myMethod, which calls produceError. The produceError method causes an exception by passing an invalid position number to the String class's charAt method. The exception is not handled by the program, but is dealt with by the default exception handler.

Code Listing 11-7   (StackTrace.java)

```
 1 /**
 2    This program demonstrates the stack trace that is
 3    produced when an exception is thrown.
 4 */
 5
 6 public class StackTrace
 7 {
 8    public static void main(String[] args)
 9    {
10       System.out.println("Calling myMethod...");
11       myMethod();
12       System.out.println("Method main is done.");
13    }
14
15    /**
16       MyMethod
17    */
18
19    public static void myMethod()
20    {
21       System.out.println("Calling produceError...");
22       produceError();
23       System.out.println("myMethod is done.");
24    }
25
26    /**
27       produceError
28    */
29
```

```
30    public static void produceError()
31    {
32        String str = "abc";
33
34        // The following statement will cause an error.
35        System.out.println(str.charAt(3));
36        System.out.println("produceError is done.");
37    }
38 }
```

Program Output

```
Calling myMethod...
Calling produceError...
Exception in thread "main" java.lang.StringIndexOutOfBoundsException:
    String index out of range: 3
        at java.lang.String.charAt(Unknown Source)
        at StackTrace.produceError(StackTrace.java:35)
        at StackTrace.myMethod(StackTrace.java:22)
        at StackTrace.main(StackTrace.java:11)
```

When the exception occurs, the error message shows a stack trace listing the methods that were called in order to produce the exception. The first method that is listed in the stack trace, charAt, is the method that is responsible for the exception. The next method, produceError, is the method that called charAt. The next method, myMethod, is the method that called produceError. The last method, main, is the method that called myMethod. The stack trace shows the chain of methods that were called when the exception was thrown.

 NOTE: All exception objects have a printStackTrace method, inherited from the Throwable class, which can be used to print a stack trace.

Handling Multiple Exceptions with One catch Clause (Java 7)

In versions of Java prior to Java 7, each catch clause can handle only one type of exception. Beginning with Java 7, however, a catch clause can handle more than one type of exception. This can reduce a lot of duplicated code in a try statement that needs to catch multiple exceptions, but perform the same operation for each one. For example, suppose we have the following try statement in a program:

```
try
{
    (try block statements . . .)
}
catch(NumberFormatException ex)
{
    respondToError();
}
```

```
catch(IOException ex)
{
    respondToError();
}
```

This `try` statement has two `catch` clauses: one that handles a `NumberFormatException`, and another that handles an `IOException`. Notice that both catch blocks do the same thing: they call a method named `respondToError`. Because both catch blocks perform the same operation, the `catch` clauses can be combined into a single `catch` clause that handles both types of exception, as shown here:

```
try
{
    (try block statements . . .)
}
catch(NumberFormatException | IOException ex)
{
    respondToError();
}
```

Notice in the `catch` clause that the exception types are separated by a | symbol, which is the same symbol as that used for the logical OR operator. You can think of this as meaning that the clause will catch a `NumberFormatException` or an `IOException`. The following code shows a `catch` clause that handles three types of exceptions:

```
try
{
    (try block statements . . .)
}
catch(NumberFormatException | IOException | InputMismatchException ex)
{
    respondToError();
}
```

In this code, the `catch` clause will handle a `NumberFormatException` or an `IOException` or an `InputMismatchException`.

The ability to catch multiple types of exceptions with a single `catch` clause is known as *multi-catch*, and was introduced in Java 7. Code Listing 11-8 shows a complete program that uses multi-catch. The `catch` clause in line 34 can handle a `FileNotFoundException` or an `InputMismatchException`.

Code Listing 11-8   **(MultiCatch.java)**

```
1 import java.io.*;      // For File class and FileNotFoundException
2 import java.util.*;    // For Scanner and InputMismatchException
3
4 /**
5    This program demonstrates how multiple exceptions can
6    be caught with a single catch clause.
7 */
8
```

```
 9 public class MultiCatch
10 {
11    public static void main(String[] args)
12    {
13       int number;     // To hold a number from the file
14
15       try
16       {
17          // Open the file.
18          File file = new File("Numbers.txt");
19          Scanner inputFile = new Scanner(file);
20
21          // Process the contents of the file.
22          while (inputFile.hasNext())
23          {
24             // Get a number from the file.
25             number = inputFile.nextInt();
26
27             // Display the number.
28             System.out.println(number);
29          }
30
31          // Close the file.
32          inputFile.close();
33       }
34       catch(FileNotFoundException | InputMismatchException ex)
35       {
36          // Display an error message.
37          System.out.println("Error processing the file.");
38       }
39    }
40 }
```

 NOTE: If you are using a version of Java prior to Java 7, you cannot use multi-catch.

When an Exception Is Not Caught

When an exception is thrown, it cannot be ignored. It must be handled by the program, or by the default exception handler. When the code in a method throws an exception, the normal execution of that method stops and the JVM searches for a compatible exception handler inside the method. If there is no code inside the method to handle the exception, then control of the program is passed to the previous method in the call stack (that is, the method that called the offending method). If that method cannot handle the exception, then control is passed again, up the call stack, to the previous method. This continues until control reaches the main method. If the main method does not handle the exception, then the program is halted and the default exception handler handles the exception.

This was the case for the program in Code Listing 11-7. Because the produceError method did not handle the exception, control was passed back to myMethod. It didn't handle the exception either, so control was passed back to main. Because main didn't handle the exception, the program halted and the default exception handler displayed the error messages.

Checked and Unchecked Exceptions

In Java, there are two categories of exceptions: unchecked and checked. *Unchecked exceptions* are those that inherit from the Error class or the RuntimeException class. Recall that the exceptions that inherit from Error are thrown when a critical error occurs, such as running out of memory. You should not handle these exceptions because the conditions that cause them can rarely be dealt with in the program. Also recall that RuntimeException serves as a superclass for exceptions that result from programming errors, such as an out-of-bounds array subscript. It is best not to handle these exceptions either, because they can be avoided with properly written code. So, you should not handle unchecked exceptions.

All of the remaining exceptions (that is, those that do *not* inherit from Error or RuntimeException) are *checked exceptions*. These are the exceptions that you should handle in your program. If the code in a method can potentially throw a checked exception, then that method must meet one of the following requirements:

- It must handle the exception, or
- It must have a throws clause listed in the method header.

The throws clause informs the compiler of the exceptions that could get thrown from a method. For example, look at the following method:

```
// This method will not compile!
public void displayFile(String name)
{
   // Open the file.
   File file = new File(name);
   Scanner inputFile = new Scanner(file);

   // Read and display the file's contents.
   while (inputFile.hasNext())
   {
      System.out.println(inputFile.nextLine());
   }

   // Close the file.
   inputFile.close();
}
```

The code in this method is capable of throwing a FileNotFoundException, which is a checked exception. Because the method does not handle this exception, it must have a throws clause in its header or it will not compile.

The key word throws is written at the end of the method header, followed by a list of the types of exceptions that the method can throw. Here is the revised method header:

```
public void displayFile(String name) throws FileNotFoundException
```

The throws clause tells the compiler that this method can throw a FileNotFoundException. (If there is more than one type of exception, you separate them with commas.)

Now you know why you wrote a throws clause on methods that perform file operations in the previous chapters. We did not handle any of the checked exceptions that might occur, so we had to inform the compiler that our methods might pass them up the call stack.

 Checkpoint

MyProgrammingLab™ *www.myprogramminglab.com*

11.1   Briefly describe what an exception is.

11.2   What does it mean to "throw" an exception?

11.3   If an exception is thrown and the program does not handle it, what happens?

11.4   Other than the Object class, what is the superclass for all exceptions?

11.5   What is the difference between exceptions that inherit from the Error class and exceptions that inherit from the Exception class?

11.6   What is the difference between a try block and a catch block?

11.7   After the catch block has handled the exception, where does program execution resume?

11.8   How do you retrieve an error message from an exception?

11.9   If multiple exceptions can be thrown by code in a try block, how does the JVM know which catch clause it should pass the control of the program to?

11.10   When does the code in a finally block execute?

11.11   What is the call stack? What is a stack trace?

11.12   A program's main method calls method A, which calls method B. None of these methods performs any exception handling. The code in method B throws an exception. Describe what happens.

11.13   What are the differences between a checked and an unchecked exception?

11.14   When are you required to have a throws clause in a method header?

11.2 Throwing Exceptions

CONCEPT: You can write code that throws one of the standard Java exceptions, or an instance of a custom exception class that you have designed.

You can use the throw statement to throw an exception manually. The general format of the throw statement is as follows:

```
throw new ExceptionType(MessageString);
```

The throw statement causes an exception object to be created and thrown. In this general format, *ExceptionType* is an exception class name and *MessageString* is an optional String argument passed to the exception object's constructor. The *MessageString* argument contains a custom error message that can be retrieved from the exception object's getMessage method. If you do not pass a message to the constructor, the exception will have a null message. Here is an example of a throw statement:

```
throw new Exception("Out of fuel");
```

This statement creates an object of the Exception class and passes the string "Out of fuel" to the object's constructor. The object is then thrown, which causes the exception-handling process to begin.

> **NOTE:** Don't confuse the throw statement with the throws clause. The throw statement causes an exception to be thrown. The throws clause informs the compiler that a method throws one or more exceptions.

Recall the Die class from Chapter 6. The class simulates a gaming die, and its constructor accepts an argument specifying the number of sides for the die. Suppose we want to make sure that the number of sides is not less than a minimum value (after all, it wouldn't make sense to have a one-sided die, or a zero-sided die.)

One way to accomplish this is to have the constructor throw an exception when an invalid argument is passed. Code Listing 11-9 shows the modified code for the Die class:

Code Listing 11-9   (Die.java)

```java
 1 import java.util.Random;
 2
 3 /**
 4    The Die class simulates a six-sided die.
 5 */
 6
 7 public class Die
 8 {
 9    private final int MIN_SIDES = 4;
10    private int sides;   // Number of sides
11    private int value;   // The die's value
12
13    /**
14       The constructor performs an initial
15       roll of the die.
16       @param numSides The number of sides for this die.
17    */
18
19    public Die(int numSides)
20    {
21       // Validate the number of sides.
22       if (numSides < MIN_SIDES)
23       {
24          throw new IllegalArgumentException(
25             "The die must have at least " +
26             MIN_SIDES + " sides.");
27       }
```

```
28
29        // Store the number of sides and roll.
30        sides = numSides;
31        roll();
32      }
33
34      /**
35         The roll method simulates the rolling of
36         the die.
37      */
38
39      public void roll()
40      {
41         // Create a Random object.
42         Random rand = new Random();
43
44         // Get a random value for the die.
45         value = rand.nextInt(sides) + 1;
46      }
47
48      /**
49         getSides method
50         @return The number of sides for this die.
51      */
52
53      public int getSides()
54      {
55         return sides;
56      }
57
58      /**
59         getValue method
60         @return The value of the die.
61      */
62
63      public int getValue()
64      {
65         return value;
66      }
67 }
```

Line 9 declares a final field named MIN_SIDES, initialized with the value 4. This is the minimum value that the class will accept for the number of sides. In the constructor, in line 22 we test the value of the numSides parameter, to determine whether it is less than MIN_SIDES. If so, lines 24 through 26 throw an IllegalArgumentException. The message *The die must have at least 4 sides* is passed to the exception object's constructor. When we catch this exception, we can retrieve the message by calling the object's `getMessage` method. The `IllegalArgumentException` class was chosen for this error condition because it seems like the most appropriate exception to throw in response to an illegal argument being passed to the constructor. (Note that `IllegalArgumentException` inherits from `RuntimeException`, which inherits from `Exception`.)

 NOTE: Because the `IllegalArgumentException` class inherits from the `RuntimeException` class, it is unchecked. If we had chosen a checked exception class, we would have to put a throws clause in the constructor's header.

The program in Code Listing 11-10 demonstrates how the modified constructor works.

Code Listing 11-10   (DieExceptionDemo.java)

```
1  /**
2     This program demonstrates how the Die class throws
3     an exception when an invalid value is passed to the
4     constructor.
5  */
6
7  public class DiceExceptionDemo
8  {
9     public static void main(String[] args)
10    {
11       final int DIE_SIDES = 1;  // Number of sides
12
13       // Create an instance of the Die class.
14       Die die = new Die(DIE_SIDES);
15
16       System.out.println("Initial value of the die:");
17       System.out.println(die.getValue());
18    }
19 }
```

Program Output

```
Exception in thread "main" java.lang.IllegalArgumentException: The die must
have at least 4 sides.
        at Die.<init>(Die.java:24)
        at DiceExceptionDemo.main(DiceExceptionDemo.java:14)
```

Creating Your Own Exception Classes

To meet the needs of a specific class or application, you can create your own exception classes by extending the `Exception` class or one of its subclasses.

Let's look at an example that uses programmer-defined exceptions. Recall the `BankAccount` class from Chapter 6. This class holds the data for a bank account. A UML diagram for the class is shown in Figure 11-12.

There are a number of errors that could cause a `BankAccount` object to perform its duties incorrectly. Here are some specific examples:

- A negative starting balance is passed to the constructor.
- A negative number is passed to the `deposit` method.
- A negative number is passed to the `withdraw` method.
- The amount passed to the `withdraw` method exceeds the account's balance.

Figure 11-12   UML diagram for the `BankAccount` class

```
┌─────────────────────────────────────┐
│            BankAccount               │
├─────────────────────────────────────┤
│ – balance : double                   │
├─────────────────────────────────────┤
│ + BankAccount()                      │
│ + BankAccount(startBalance : double) │
│ + BankAccount(str : String)          │
│ + deposit(amount : double) : void    │
│ + deposit(str : String) : void       │
│ + withdraw(amount : double) : void   │
│ + withdraw(str : String) : void      │
│ + setBalance(b : double) : void      │
│ + setBalance(str : String) : void    │
│ + getBalance() : double              │
└─────────────────────────────────────┘
```

We can create our own exceptions that represent each of these error conditions. Then we can rewrite the class so it throws one of our custom exceptions when any of these errors occur. Let's start by creating an exception class for a negative starting balance. Code Listing 11-11 shows an exception class named `NegativeStartingBalance`.

Code Listing 11-11   **(NegativeStartingBalance.java)**

```java
 1  /**
 2      NegativeStartingBalance exceptions are thrown by the
 3      BankAccount class when a negative starting balance is
 4      passed to the constructor.
 5  */
 6
 7  public class NegativeStartingBalance
 8                      extends Exception
 9  {
10      /**
11          This constructor uses a generic
12          error message.
13      */
```

```
14
15      public NegativeStartingBalance()
16      {
17         super("Error: Negative starting balance");
18      }
19
20      /**
21         This constructor specifies the bad starting
22         balance in the error message.
23         @param The bad starting balance.
24      */
25
26      public NegativeStartingBalance(double amount)
27      {
28         super("Error: Negative starting balance: " +
29               amount);
30      }
31  }
```

Notice that this class extends the Exception class. It has two constructors. The no-arg constructor passes the string "Error: Negative starting balance" to the superclass constructor. This is the error message that is retrievable from an object's getMessage method. The second constructor accepts the starting balance as a double argument. This amount is used to pass a more detailed error message containing the starting balance amount to the superclass constructor.

The following code shows one of the BankAccount constructors rewritten to throw a NegativeStartingBalance exception when a negative value is passed as the starting balance.

```
public BankAccount(double startBalance)
                throws NegativeStartingBalance
{
    if (startBalance < 0)
        throw new NegativeStartingBalance(startBalance);

    balance = startBalance;
}
```

Note that NegativeStartingBalance extends the Exception class. This means that it is a checked exception class. Because of this, the constructor header must have a throws clause listing the exception type.

You will find the modified *BankAccount.java* file in this chapter's source code, available on the book's companion Web site at www.pearsonhighered.com/gaddis. The program in Code Listing 11-12 demonstrates the new constructor by forcing it to throw the NegativeStartingBalance exception.

Code Listing 11-12   **(AccountTest.java)**

```
1   /**
2       This program demonstrates how the BankAccount
3       class constructor throws custom exceptions.
4   */
5
6   public class AccountTest
7   {
8       public static void main(String [] args)
9       {
10          // Force a NegativeStartingBalance exception.
11          try
12          {
13              BankAccount account =
14                      new BankAccount(-100.0);
15          }
16          catch(NegativeStartingBalance e)
17          {
18              System.out.println(e.getMessage());
19          }
20      }
21  }
```

Program Output

```
Error: Negative starting balance: -100.0
```

Using the @exception Tag in Documentation Comments

When writing the documentation comments for a method, you can document the exceptions thrown by the method by using an @exception tag. When the javadoc utility sees an @exception tag inside a method's documentation comments, it knows that the name of an exception appears next, followed by a description of the events that cause the exception. The general format of an @exception tag comment is as follows:

@exception *ExceptionName Description*

ExceptionName is the name of an exception and *Description* is a description of the circumstances that cause the exception. Remember the following points about @exception tag comments:

- The @exception tag in a method's documentation comment must appear after the general description of the method.
- The description can span several lines. It ends at the end of the documentation comment (the */ symbol), or at the beginning of another tag.

When a method's documentation comments contain an @exception tag, the javadoc utility will create a Throws section in the method's documentation. This is where the descriptions of the exceptions thrown by the method will be listed. As an example, here are the documentation comments for the `BankAccount` class's constructor presented earlier:

```
/**
    This constructor sets the starting balance
    to the value passed as an argument.
    @param startBalance The starting balance.
    @exception NegativeStartingBalance When
               startBalance is negative.
*/
```

 Checkpoint

MyProgrammingLab™ *www.myprogramminglab.com*

11.15 What does the `throw` statement do?

11.16 What is the purpose of the argument that is passed to an exception object's constructor? What happens if you do not pass an argument to the constructor?

11.17 What is the difference between the `throw` statement and the `throws` clause?

11.18 If a method has a `throw` statement, does it always have to have a `throws` clause in its header? Why or why not?

11.19 If you are writing a custom exception class, how can you make sure it is checked? How can you make sure it is unchecked?

11.3 Advanced Topics: Binary Files, Random Access Files, and Object Serialization

CONCEPT: A file that contains raw binary data is known as a binary file. The content of a binary file is not formatted as text, and not meant to be opened in a text editor. A random access file is a file that allows a program to read data from any location within the file, or write data to any location within the file. Object serialization is the process of converting an object to a series of bytes and saving them to a file. Deserialization is the process of reconstructing a serialized object.

Binary Files

All the files you've been working with so far have been text files. This means that the data stored in the files has been formatted as text. Even a number, when stored in a text file with the `print` or `println` method, is converted to text. For example, consider the following program segment:

```
PrintWriter outputFile = new PrintWriter("Number.txt");
int x = 1297;
outputFile.print(x);
```

The last statement writes the contents of the variable x to the *Number.txt* file. When the number is written, however, it is stored as the characters '1', '2', '9', and '7'. This is illustrated in Figure 11-13.

Figure 11-13 The number 1297 expressed as characters

1297 expressed as characters

'1'	'2'	'9'	'7'

When a number such as 1297 is stored in the computer's memory, it isn't stored as text, however. It is formatted as a binary number. Figure 11-14 shows how the number 1297 is stored in memory, in an int variable, using binary. Recall that int variables occupy four bytes.

Figure 11-14 The number 1297 as a binary number, as it is stored in memory

1297 as a binary number

00000000	00000000	00000101	00010001

The binary representation of the number shown in Figure 11-14 is the way the raw data is stored in memory. In fact, this is sometimes called the *raw binary format*. Data can be stored in a file in its raw binary format. A file that contains binary data is often called a *binary file*.

Storing data in its binary format is more efficient than storing it as text because there are fewer conversions to take place. In addition, there are some types of data that should only be stored in their raw binary format. Images are an example. However, when data is stored in a binary file, you cannot open the file in a text editor such as Notepad. When a text editor opens a file, it assumes the file contains text.

Writing Data to a Binary File

To write data to a binary file you must create objects from the following classes:

FileOutputStream   This class, which is in the java.io package, allows you to open a file for writing binary data and establish a connection with it; however, it provides only basic functionality for writing bytes to the file.

DataOutputStream   This class which is in the java.io package, allows you to write data of any primitive type or String objects to a binary file. The DataOutputStream class by itself cannot directly access a file, however. It is used in conjunction with a FileOutputStream object that has a connection to a file.

You wrap a DataOutputStream object around a FileOutputStream object to write data to a binary file. The following code shows how a file named *MyInfo.dat* can be opened for binary output:

```
FileOutputStream fstream = new FileOutputStream("MyInfo.dat");
DataOutputStream outputFile = new DataOutputStream(fstream);
```

The first line creates an instance of the FileOutputStream class, which has the ability to open a file for binary output and establish a connection with it. You pass the name of the file that you wish open, as a string, to the constructor. The second line creates an instance of the DataOutputStream object that is connected to the FileOutputStream referenced by fstream. The result of this statement is that the outputFile variable will reference an object that is able to write binary data to the *MyInfo.dat* file.

 WARNING! If the file that you are opening with the FileOutputStream object already exists, it will be erased and an empty file by the same name will be created.

 NOTE: The FileOutputStream constructor throws an IOException if an error occurs when it attempts to open the file.

If there is no reason to reference the FileOutputStream object, then these statements can be combined into one, as follows:

```
DataOutputStream outputFile =
        new DataOutputStream(new FileOutputStream("MyInfo.dat"));
```

Once the DataOutputStream object has been created, you can use it to write binary data to the file. Table 11-1 lists some of the DataOutputStream methods. Note that each of the methods listed in the table throws an IOException if an error occurs.

Table 11-1 Some of the DataOutputStream methods

Method	Description
void close()	Closes the file.
void writeBoolean(boolean *b*)	Writes the boolean value passed to *b* to the file.
void writeByte(byte *b*)	Writes the byte value passed to *b* to the file.
void writeChar(int *c*)	This method accepts an int, which is assumed to be a character code. The character it represents is written to the file as a two-byte Unicode character.
void writeDouble(double *d*)	Writes the double value passed to *d* to the file.
void writeFloat(float *f*)	Writes the float value passed to *f* to the file.
void writeInt(int *i*)	Writes the int value passed to *i* to the file.
void writeLong(long *num*)	Writes the long value passed to *num* to the file.
void writeShort(short *s*)	Writes the short value passed to *s* to the file.
void writeUTF(String *str*)	Writes the String object passed to *str* to the file using the Unicode Text Format.

The program in Code Listing 11-13 shows a simple demonstration. An array of `int` values is written to the file *Numbers.dat*.

Code Listing 11-13   (WriteBinaryFile.java)

```java
 1  import java.io.*;
 2
 3  /**
 4     This program opens a binary file and writes the contents
 5     of an int array to the file.
 6  */
 7
 8  public class WriteBinaryFile
 9  {
10     public static void main(String[] args)
11                        throws IOException
12     {
13        // An array to write to the file
14        int[] numbers = { 2, 4, 6, 8, 10, 12, 14 };
15
16        // Create the binary output objects.
17        FileOutputStream fstream =
18                new FileOutputStream("Numbers.dat");
19        DataOutputStream outputFile =
20                new DataOutputStream(fstream);
21
22        System.out.println("Writing the numbers to the file...");
23
24        // Write the array elements to the file.
25        for (int i = 0; i < numbers.length; i++)
26           outputFile.writeInt(numbers[i]);
27
28        System.out.println("Done.");
29
30        // Close the file.
31        outputFile.close();
32     }
33  }
```

Program Output

```
Writing the numbers to the file...
Done.
```

Reading Data from a Binary File

To open a binary file for input, you use the following classes:

FileInputStream
:   This class, which is in the java.io package, allows you to open a file for reading binary data and establish a connection with it. It provides only the basic functionality for reading bytes from the file, however.

DataInputStream
:   This class, which is in the java.io package, allows you to read data of any primitive type, or String objects, from a binary file. The DataInputStream class by itself cannot directly access a file, however. It is used in conjunction with a FileInputStream object that has a connection to a file.

To open a binary file for input, you wrap a DataInputStream object around a FileInputStream object. The following code shows the file *MyInfo.dat* can be opened for binary input:

```
FileInputStream fstream = new FileInputStream("MyInfo.dat");
DataInputStream inputFile = new DataInputStream(fstream);
```

The following code, which combines these two statements into one, can also be used:

```
DataInputStream inputFile =
        new DataInputStream(new FileInputStream("MyInfo.dat"));
```

The FileInputStream constructor will throw a FileNotFoundException if the file named by the string argument cannot be found. Once the DataInputStream object has been created, you can use it to read binary data from the file. Table 11-2 lists some of the DataInputStream methods. Note that each of the methods listed in the table throws an EOFException if the end of the file has already been reached.

Table 11-2 Some of the DataInputStream methods

Method	Description
void close()	Closes the file.
boolean readBoolean()	Reads a boolean value from the file and returns it.
byte readByte()	Reads a byte value from the file and returns it.
char readChar()	Reads a char value from the file and returns it. The character is expected to be stored as a two-byte Unicode character, as written by the DataOutputStream class's writeChar method.
double readDouble()	Reads a double value from the file and returns it.
float readFloat()	Reads a float value from the file and returns it.
int readInt()	Reads an int value from the file and returns it.
long readLong()	Reads a long value from the file and returns it.
short readShort()	Reads a short value from the file and returns it.
String readUTF()	Reads a string from the file and returns it as a String object. The string must have been written with the DataOutputStream class's writeUTF method.

The program in Code Listing 11-14 opens the `Numbers.dat` file that was created by the program in Code Listing 11-13. The numbers are read from the file and displayed on the screen. Notice that the program must catch the `EOFException` in order to determine when the file's end has been reached.

Code Listing 11-14   (`ReadBinaryFile.java`)

```java
 1 import java.io.*;
 2
 3 /**
 4    This program opens a binary file, reads
 5    and displays the contents.
 6 */
 7
 8 public class ReadBinaryFile
 9 {
10    public static void main(String[] args)
11                throws IOException
12    {
13       int number;                   // A number read from the file
14       boolean endOfFile = false;    // EOF flag
15
16       // Create the binary file input objects.
17       FileInputStream fstream =
18                new FileInputStream("Numbers.dat");
19       DataInputStream inputFile =
20                new DataInputStream(fstream);
21
22       System.out.println("Reading numbers from the file:");
23
24       // Read the contents of the file.
25       while (!endOfFile)
26       {
27          try
28          {
29             number = inputFile.readInt();
30             System.out.print(number + " ");
31          }
32          catch (EOFException e)
33          {
34             endOfFile = true;
35          }
36       }
37
38       System.out.println("\nDone.");
39
40       // Close the file.
```

```
41          inputFile.close();
42    }
43 }
```

```
Reading numbers from the file:
2 4 6 8 10 12 14
Done.
```

Writing and Reading Strings

To write a string to a binary file you should use the `DataOutputStream` class's `writeUTF` method. This method writes its `String` argument in a format known as *UTF-8 encoding*. Here's how the encoding works: Just before writing the string, this method writes a two-byte integer indicating the number of bytes that the string occupies. Then it writes the string's characters in Unicode. (UTF stands for Unicode Text Format.)

When the `DataInputStream` class's `readUTF` method reads from the file, it expects the first two bytes to contain the number of bytes that the string occupies. Then it reads that many bytes and returns them as a `String`.

For example, assuming that `outputFile` references a `DataOutputStream` object, the following code uses the `writeUTF` method to write a string:

```
String name = "Chloe";
outputFile.writeUTF(name);
```

Assuming that `inputFile` references a `DataInputStream` object, the following statement uses the `readUTF` method to read a UTF-8 encoded string from the file:

```
String name = inputFile.readUTF();
```

Remember that the `readUTF` method will correctly read a string only when the string is written with the `writeUTF` method.

> This chapter's source code folder contains the example programs `WriteUTF.java` and `ReadUTF.java`, which demonstrate writing and reading strings using these methods.

Appending Data to an Existing Binary File

If you pass the name of an existing file to the `FileOutputStream` constructor, it will be erased and a new empty file with the same name will be created. Sometimes, however, you want to preserve an existing file and append new data to its current contents. The `FileOutputStream` constructor takes an optional second argument, which must be a `boolean` value. If the argument is `true`, the file will not be erased if it already exists and new data will be written to the end of the file. If the argument is `false`, the file will be erased if it already exists. For example, the following code opens the file *MyInfo.dat* for output. If the file exists, it will not be deleted, and any data written to the file will be appended to the existing data.

```
FileOutputStream fstream = new FileOutputStream("MyInfo.dat", true);
DataOutputStream outputFile = new DataOutputStream(fstream);
```

Random Access Files

All of the programs that you have created to access files so far have performed *sequential file access*. With sequential access, when a file is opened for input, its read position is at the very beginning of the file. This means that the first time data is read from the file, the data will be read from its beginning. As the reading continues, the file's read position advances sequentially through the file's contents.

The problem with sequential file access is that in order to read a specific byte from the file, all the bytes that precede it must be read first. For instance, if a program needs data stored at the hundredth byte of a file, it will have to read the first 99 bytes to reach it. If you've ever listened to a cassette tape player, you understand sequential access. To listen to a song at the end of the tape, you have to listen to all the songs that are before it, or fast-forward over them. There is no way to jump immediately to that particular song.

Although sequential file access is useful in many circumstances, it can slow down a program tremendously. If the file is very large, locating data buried deep inside it can take a long time. Alternatively, Java allows a program to perform *random file access*. In random file access, a program may immediately jump to any location in the file without first reading the preceding bytes. The difference between sequential and random file access is like the difference between a cassette tape and a compact disc. When listening to a CD, there is no need to listen to or fast-forward over unwanted songs. You simply jump to the track that you want to listen to. This is illustrated in Figure 11-15.

Figure 11-15   Sequential access versus random access

Items in a sequential access file are accessed one after the other.

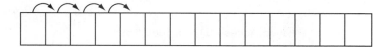

Items in a random access file are accessed in any order.

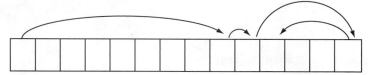

To create and work with random access files in Java, you use the `RandomAccessFile` class, which is in the `java.io` package. The general format of the class constructor is as follows:

```
RandomAccessFile(String filename, String mode)
```

The first argument is the name of the file. The second argument is a string indicating the mode in which you wish to use the file. The two modes are `"r"` for reading, and `"rw"` for reading and writing. When a file is opened with `"r"` as the mode, the program can only read from the file. When a file is opened with `"rw"` as the mode, the program can read from the file and write to it. Here are some examples of statements that open files using the `RandomAccessFile` class:

```
        // Open a file for random reading.
        RandomAccessFile randomFile =
                        new RandomAccessFile("MyData.dat", "r");
        // Open a file for random reading and writing.
        RandomAccessFile randomFile =
                        new RandomAccessFile("MyData.dat", "rw");
```

Here are some important points to remember about the two modes:

- If you open a file in "r" mode and the file does not exist, a FileNotFoundException will be thrown.
- If you open a file in "r" mode and try to write to it, an IOException will be thrown.
- If you open an existing file in "rw" mode, it will not be deleted. The file's existing contents will be preserved.
- If you open a file in "rw" mode and the file does not exist, it will be created.

Reading and Writing with the RandomAccessFile Class

A file that is opened or created with the RandomAccessFile class is treated as a binary file. In fact, the RandomAccessFile class has the same methods as the DataOutputStream class for writing data, and the same methods as the DataInputStream class for reading data. In fact, you can use the RandomAccessFile class to process a binary file sequentially. For example, the program in Code Listing 11-15 opens a file named *Letters.dat* and writes all of the letters of the alphabet to the file.

Code Listing 11-15   (WriteLetters.java)

```
 1 import java.io.*;
 2
 3 /**
 4    This program uses a RandomAccessFile object to
 5    create the file Letters.dat. The letters of the
 6    alphabet are written to the file.
 7 */
 8
 9 public class WriteLetters
10 {
11    public static void main(String[] args)
12                    throws IOException
13    {
14       // The letters array has all 26 letters.
15       char[] letters = {
16                        'a', 'b', 'c', 'd', 'e', 'f', 'g',
17                        'h', 'i', 'j', 'k', 'l', 'm', 'n',
18                        'o', 'p', 'q', 'r', 's', 't', 'u',
19                        'v', 'w', 'x', 'y', 'z' };
20
21       System.out.println("Opening the file.");
22
23       // Open a file for reading and writing.
```

```
24       RandomAccessFile randomFile =
25               new RandomAccessFile("Letters.dat", "rw");
26
27       System.out.println("Writing data to the file...");
28
29       // Sequentially write the letters array to the file.
30       for (int i = 0; i < letters.length; i++)
31           randomFile.writeChar(letters[i]);
32
33       // Close the file.
34       randomFile.close();
35
36       System.out.println("Done.");
37   }
38 }
```

Program Output

```
Opening the file.
Writing data to the file...
Done.
```

After this program executes, the letters of the alphabet will be stored in the *Letters.dat* file. Because the writeChar method was used, the letters will each be stored as two-byte characters. This is important to know later when we want to read the characters from the file.

The File Pointer

The RandomAccessFile class treats a file as a stream of bytes. The bytes are numbered, with the first byte being byte 0. The last byte's number is one less than the number of bytes in the file. These byte numbers are similar to an array's subscripts, and are used to identify locations in the file.

Internally, the RandomAccessFile class keeps a long integer value known as the file pointer. The *file pointer* holds the byte number of a location in the file. When a file is first opened, the file pointer is set to 0. This causes it to "point" to the first byte in the file. When an item is read from the file, it is read from the byte that the file pointer points to. Reading also causes the file pointer to advance to the byte just beyond the item that was read. For example, let's say the file pointer points to byte 0 and an int is read from the file with the readInt method. An int is four bytes in size, so four bytes will be read from the file, starting at byte 0. After the value is read, the file pointer will be advanced to byte number 4, which is the 5th byte in the file. If another item is immediately read, the reading will begin at byte number 4. If the file pointer refers to a byte number that is beyond the end of the file, an EOFException is thrown when a read operation is performed.

Writing also takes place at the location pointed to by the file pointer. If the file pointer points to the end of the file when a write operation is performed, then the data will be written to the end of the file. However, if the file pointer holds the number of a byte within the file, at a location where data is already stored, then a write operation will cause data to be written over the existing data at that location.

Not only does the `RandomAccessFile` class let you read and write data, but also it allows you to move the file pointer. This means that you can immediately read data from any byte location in the file. It also means that you can write data to any location in the file, over existing data. To move the file pointer, you use the `seek` method. Here is the method's general format:

```
void seek(long position)
```

The argument is the number of the byte that you want to move the file pointer to. For example, look at the following code:

```
RandomAccessFile file =
            new RandomAccessFile("MyInfo.dat", "r");
file.seek(99);
byte b = file.readByte();
```

This code opens the file *MyInfo.dat* for reading. The `seek` method is called to move the file pointer to byte number 99 (which is the 100th byte in the file). Then, the `readByte` method is called to read byte number 99 from the file. After that statement executes, the file pointer will be advanced by one byte, so it will point to byte 100. Suppose we continue processing the same file with the following code:

```
file.seek(49);
int i = file.readInt();
```

First, the `seek` method moves the file pointer to byte number 49 (which is the 50th byte in the file). Then, the `readInt` method is called. This reads an `int` from the file. An `int` is four bytes in size, so this statement reads four bytes, beginning at byte number 49. After the statement executes the file pointer will be advanced by four bytes, so it will point to byte 53.

Although a file might contain `chars`, `ints`, `doubles`, strings, and so forth, the `RandomAccessFile` class sees it only as a stream of bytes. The class is unaware of the data types of the data stored in the file, and it cannot determine where one item of data ends and another begins. When you write a program that reads data from a random access file, it is your responsibility to know how the data is structured.

For example, recall that the program in Code Listing 11-15 wrote the letters of the alphabet to the *Letters.dat* file. Let's say the first letter is character 0, the second letter is character 1, and so forth. Suppose we want to read character 5 (the sixth letter in the file). At first, we might be tempted to try the following code:

```
// Open the file for reading.
RandomAccessFile randomFile =
            new RandomAccessFile("Letters.dat", "r");
// Move the file pointer to byte 5, which is the 6th byte.
randomFile.seek(5);
// Read the character.
char ch = randomFile.readChar();
// What will this display?
System.out.println("The sixth letter is " + ch);
```

Although this code will compile and run, you might be surprised at the result. Recall that the `writeChar` method writes a character as two bytes. Because each character occupies two bytes in the file, the sixth character begins at byte 10, not byte 5. This is illustrated in

Figure 11-16. In fact, if we try to read a character starting at byte 5, we will read garbage because byte 5 is not at the beginning of a character.

Figure 11-16   Layout of the *Letters.dat* file

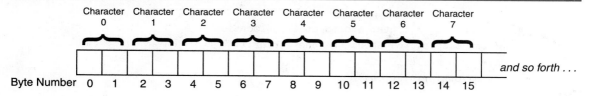

To determine the position of a character in the file, we must take each character's size into account. The following code will correctly read and display the sixth character. To determine the character's starting byte number, it multiplies the size of a character by the number of the character we want to locate.

```
final int CHAR_SIZE = 2;   // Each char uses two bytes
// Move the file pointer to character 5.
randomFile.seek(CHAR_SIZE * 5);
// Read the character.
char ch = randomFile.readChar();
// This will display the correct character.
System.out.println("The sixth character is " + ch);
```

The program in Code Listing 11-16 demonstrates further. It randomly reads characters 5, 10, and 3 from the file.

Code Listing 11-16   (`ReadRandomLetters.java`)

```java
 1 import java.io.*;
 2
 3 /**
 4    This program uses the RandomAccessFile class to open
 5    the file Letters.dat and randomly read letters from
 6    different locations.
 7 */
 8
 9 public class ReadRandomLetters
10 {
11    public static void main(String[] args) throws IOException
12    {
13       final int CHAR_SIZE = 2;    // 2 byte characters
14       long byteNum;               // The byte number
15       char ch;                    // A character from the file
16
17       // Open the file for reading.
18       RandomAccessFile randomFile =
19                 new RandomAccessFile("Letters.dat", "r");
```

```
20
21          // Move to the character 5. This is the 6th
22          // character from the beginning of the file.
23          byteNum = CHAR_SIZE * 5;
24          randomFile.seek(byteNum);
25
26          // Read the character stored at this location
27          // and display it. Should be the letter f.
28          ch = randomFile.readChar();
29          System.out.println(ch);
30
31          // Move to character 10 (the 11th character),
32          // read the character, and display it.
33          // Should be the letter k.
34          byteNum = CHAR_SIZE * 10;
35          randomFile.seek(byteNum);
36          ch = randomFile.readChar();
37          System.out.println(ch);
38
39          // Move to character 3 (the 4th character),
40          // read the character, and display it.
41          // Should be the letter d.
42          byteNum = CHAR_SIZE * 3;
43          randomFile.seek(byteNum);
44          ch = randomFile.readChar();
45          System.out.println(ch);
46
47          // Close the file.
48          randomFile.close();
49      }
50 }
```

Program Output

```
f
k
d
```

> See Appendix I—Working with Records and Random Access Files. The appendix is available on the book's companion Web site, at www.pearsonhighered.com.gaddis.

Object Serialization

In Appendix I, available on the book's companion Web site, at www.pearsonhighered.com.gaddis, you can see how an object's fields can be retrieved and saved to a file as fields in a record. If an object contains other types of objects as fields, however, the process of saving its contents can become complicated. Fortunately, Java allows you to *serialize* objects, which is a simpler way of saving objects to a file.

When an object is serialized, it is converted into a series of bytes that contain the object's data. If the object is set up properly, even the other objects that it might contain as fields are automatically serialized. The resulting set of bytes can be saved to a file for later retrieval.

In order for an object to be serialized, its class must implement the Serializable interface. The Serializable interface, which is in the java.io package, has no methods or fields. It is used only to let the Java compiler know that objects of the class might be serialized. In addition, if a class contains objects of other classes as fields, those classes must also implement the Serializable interface, in order to be serialized.

For example, in this chapter's source code folder there is a modified version of the BankAccount class named BankAccount2. The only modification to the class is that it implements the Serializable interface. Here are the modified lines of code from the file:

```
import java.io.Serializable;


public class BankAccount2 implements Serializable
```

This new code tells the compiler that we want to be able to serialize objects of the BankAccount2 class. To write a serialized object to a file, you use an ObjectOutputStream object. The ObjectOutputStream class is designed to perform the serialization process (converting an object to a series of bytes). To write the bytes to a file, you must also use an output stream object, such as FileOutputStream. Here is an example:

```
FileOutputStream outStream =
          new FileOutputStream("Objects.dat");
ObjectOutputStream objectOutputFile =
          new ObjectOutputStream(outStream);
```

To serialize an object and write it to the file, use the ObjectOutputStream class's writeObject method, as shown here:

```
BankAccount2 account = new BankAccount2(5000.0);
objectOutputFile.writeObject(account);
```

The writeObject method throws an IOException if an error occurs.

The process of reading a serialized object's bytes and constructing an object from them is known as *deserialization*. To deserialize an object you use an ObjectInputStream object, along with a FileInputStream object. Here is an example of how to set up the objects:

```
FileInputStream inStream =
          new FileInputStream("Objects.dat");
ObjectInputStream objectInputFile =
          new ObjectInputStream(inStream);
```

To read a serialized object from the file, use the ObjectInputStream class's readObject method. Here is an example:

```
BankAccount2 account;
account = (BankAccount2) objectInputFile.readObject();
```

The readObject method returns the deserialized object. Notice that you must cast the return value to the desired class type. (The readObject method throws a number of different exceptions if an error occurs. See the API documentation for more information.)

The following programs demonstrate how to serialize and deserialize objects. The program in Code Listing 11-17 serializes three BankAccount2 objects, and the program in Code Listing 11-18 deserializes them.

Code Listing 11-17   (SerializeObjects.java)

```java
 1 import java.io.*;
 2 import java.util.Scanner;
 3
 4 /**
 5    This program serializes the objects in an array of
 6    BankAccount2 objects.
 7 */
 8
 9 public class SerializeObjects
10 {
11    public static void main(String[] args)
12                      throws IOException
13    {
14       double balance;              // An account balance
15       final int NUM_ITEMS = 3;     // Number of accounts
16
17       // Create a Scanner object for keyboard input.
18       Scanner keyboard = new Scanner(System.in);
19
20       // Create a BankAccount2 array
21       BankAccount2[] accounts =
22                   new BankAccount2[NUM_ITEMS];
23
24       // Populate the array.
25       for (int i = 0; i < accounts.length; i++)
26       {
27          // Get an account balance.
28          System.out.print("Enter the balance for " +
29                       "account " + (i + 1) + ": ");
30          balance = keyboard.nextDouble();
31
32          // Create an object in the array.
33          accounts[i] = new BankAccount2(balance);
34       }
35
36       // Create the stream objects.
37       FileOutputStream outStream =
38                   new FileOutputStream("Objects.dat");
39       ObjectOutputStream objectOutputFile =
40                   new ObjectOutputStream(outStream);
41
42       // Write the serialized objects to the file.
```

```
43          for (int i = 0; i < accounts.length; i++)
44          {
45             objectOutputFile.writeObject(accounts[i]);
46          }
47
48          // Close the file.
49          objectOutputFile.close();
50
51          System.out.println("The serialized objects " +
52                  "were written to the Objects.dat file.");
53       }
54 }
```

Program Output with Example Input Shown in Bold

Enter the balance for account 1: **5000.0 [Enter]**
Enter the balance for account 2: **2500.0 [Enter]**
Enter the balance for account 3: **1800.0 [Enter]**
The serialized objects were written to the Objects.dat file.

Code Listing 11-18   (DeserializeObjects.java)

```
1 import java.io.*;
2
3 /**
4    This program deserializes the objects in the Objects.dat
5    file and stores them in an array.
6 */
7
8 public class DeserializeObjects
9 {
10    public static void main(String[] args)
11                      throws Exception
12    {
13       double balance;          // An account balance
14       final int NUM_ITEMS = 3;    // Number of accounts
15
16       // Create the stream objects.
17       FileInputStream inStream =
18              new FileInputStream("Objects.dat");
19       ObjectInputStream objectInputFile =
20              new ObjectInputStream(inStream);
21
22       // Create a BankAccount2 array
23       BankAccount2[] accounts =
24              new BankAccount2[NUM_ITEMS];
25
26       // Read the serialized objects from the file.
27       for (int i = 0; i < accounts.length; i++)
```

```
28        {
29            accounts[i] =
30               (BankAccount2) objectInputFile.readObject();
31        }
32
33        // Close the file.
34        objectInputFile.close();
35
36        // Display the objects.
37        for (int i = 0; i < accounts.length; i++)
38        {
39            System.out.println("Account " + (i + 1) +
40                       " $ " + accounts[i].getBalance());
41        }
42    }
43 }
```

Program Output

```
Account 1 $ 5000.0
Account 2 $ 2500.0
Account 3 $ 1800.0
```

Serializing Aggregate Objects

If a class implements the `Serializable` interface, then all of the fields in that class must be serializable. This isn't a problem for primitive variables because they are serializable just as they are. However, if the class has a reference variable as a field, then the object referenced by that variable should also be serializable. This means that the object's class should also implement the `Serializable` interface. If it doesn't, then the `transient` key word should be used in the reference variable's declaration. Here is an example:

```
private transient SomeClass refVar;
```

Because of the `transient` key word, the compiler will skip the object referenced by `refVar` during the serialization process. Fortunately, the `String` class, and most of the other classes found in the Java API, implement the `Serializable` interface.

 Checkpoint

MyProgrammingLab™ *www.myprogramminglab.com*

11.20 What is the difference between a text file and a binary file?

11.21 What classes do you use to write output to a binary file? What classes do you use to read from a binary file?

11.22 What is the difference between sequential and random access?

11.23 What class do you use to work with random access files?

11.24 What are the two modes that a random access file may be opened in? Explain the difference between them.

11.25 What must you do to a class in order to serialize objects of that class?

11.4 Common Errors to Avoid

- **Assuming that all statements inside a try block will execute.** When an exception is thrown, the try block is exited immediately. This means that statements appearing in the try block after the offending statement will not be executed.
- **Getting the `try`, `catch`, and `finally` clauses out of order.** In a `try` statement, the `try` clause must appear first, followed by all of the `catch` clauses, followed by the optional `finally` clause.
- **Writing two `catch` clauses that handle the same exception in the same `try` statement.** You cannot have more than one `catch` clause per exception type in the same `try` statement.
- **When catching multiple exceptions that are related to one another through inheritance, listing the more general exceptions first.** If you are handling multiple exceptions in the same `try` statement, and some of the exceptions are related to each other through inheritance, then you should handle the more specialized exception classes before the more general exception classes. Otherwise, an error will occur because the compiler thinks that you are handling the same exception more than once.
- **Forgetting to write a `throws` clause on a method that can throw a checked exception but does not handle the exception.** If a method is capable of throwing a checked exception but does not handle the exception, it must have a `throws` clause in its header that specifies the exception.
- **Calling a method but not handling an exception that it might throw.** You must either handle all of the checked exceptions that a method can throw, or list them in the calling method's `throws` clause.
- **In a custom exception class, forgetting to pass an error message to the superclass's constructor.** If you do not pass an error message to the superclass's constructor, the exception object will have a `null` error message.
- **Serializing an object with members that are not serializable.** If a class has fields that are objects of other classes, those classes must implement the `Serializable` interface in order to be serialized.

Review Questions and Exercises

Multiple Choice and True/False

1. When an exception is generated, it is said to have been _____.
   a. built
   b. thrown
   c. caught
   d. killed

2. This is a section of code that gracefully responds to exceptions.
   a. exception generator
   b. exception manipulator
   c. exception handler
   d. exception monitor

3. If your code does not handle an exception when it is thrown, it is dealt with by this.
   a. default exception handler
   b. the operating system
   c. system debugger
   d. default exception generator

4. All exception classes inherit from this class.
   a. `Error`
   b. `RuntimeException`
   c. `JavaException`
   d. `Throwable`

5. `FileNotFoundException` inherits from _____.
   a. `Error`
   b. `IOException`
   c. `JavaException`
   d. `FileException`

6. You can think of this code as being "protected" because the application will not halt if it throws an exception.
   a. try block
   b. catch block
   c. finally block
   d. protected block

7. This method can be used to retrieve the error message from an exception object.
   a. `errorMessage`
   b. `errorString`
   c. `getError`
   d. `getMessage`

8. The numeric wrapper classes' "parse" methods all throw an exception of this type.
   a. `ParseException`
   b. `NumberFormatException`
   c. `IOException`
   d. `BadNumberException`

9. This is one or more statements that are always executed after the try block has executed and after any catch blocks have executed if an exception was thrown.
   a. try block
   b. catch block
   c. finally block
   d. protected block

10. This is an internal list of all the methods that are currently executing.
    a. invocation list
    b. call stack
    c. call list
    d. list trace

11. This method may be called from any exception object, and it shows the chain of methods that were called when the exception was thrown.
    a. `printInvocationList`
    b. `printCallStack`
    c. `printStackTrace`
    d. `printCallList`

12. These are exceptions that inherit from the `Error` class or the `RuntimeException` class.
    a. unrecoverable exceptions
    b. unchecked exceptions
    c. recoverable exceptions
    d. checked exceptions

13. All exceptions that do *not* inherit from the `Error` class or the `RuntimeException` class are _____.
    a. unrecoverable exceptions
    b. unchecked exceptions
    c. recoverable exceptions
    d. checked exceptions

14. This informs the compiler of the exceptions that could get thrown from a method.
    a. `throws` clause
    b. parameter list
    c. `catch` clause
    d. method return type

15. You use this statement to throw an exception manually.
    a. `try`
    b. `generate`
    c. `throw`
    d. `System.exit(0)`

16. This is the process of converting an object to a series of bytes that represent the object's data.
    a. serialization
    b. deserialization
    c. dynamic conversion
    d. casting

17. **True or False:** You are not required to catch exceptions that inherit from the `RuntimeException` class.

18. **True or False:** When an exception is thrown by code inside a try block, all of the statements in the try block are always executed.

19. **True or False:** `IOException` serves as a superclass for exceptions that are related to programming errors, such as an out-of-bounds array subscript.

20. **True or False:** You cannot have more than one `catch` clause per `try` statement.

21. **True or False:** When an exception is thrown, the JVM searches the try statement's catch clauses from top to bottom and passes control of the program to the first catch clause with a parameter that is compatible with the exception.

22. **True or False:** Not including polymorphic references, a try statement may have only one catch clause for each specific type of exception.

23. **True or False:** When in the same try statement you are handling multiple exceptions and some of the exceptions are related to each other through inheritance, you should handle the more general exception classes before the more specialized exception classes.

24. **True or False:** The throws clause causes an exception to be thrown.

Find the Error

Find the error in each of the following code segments:

1.
```java
catch (FileNotFoundException e)
{
   System.out.println("File not found.");
}
try
{
   File file = new File("MyFile.txt");
   Scanner inputFile = new Scanner(file);
}
```

2.
```java
// Assume inputFile references a Scanner object.
try
{
   input = inputFile.nextInt();
}
finally
{
   inputFile.close();
}
catch (InputMismatchException e)
{
   System.out.println(e.getMessage());
}
```

3.
```java
try
{
   number=Integer.parseInt(str);
}
catch (Exception e)
{
   System.out.println(e.getMessage());
}
```

```
catch (IllegalArgumentException e)
{
   System.out.println("Bad number format.");
}
catch (NumberFormatException e)
{
   System.out.println(str + " is not a number.");
}
```

Algorithm Workbench

1. Look at the following program and tell what it will output when run:

```
public class ExceptionTest
{
   public static void main(String[] args)
   {

      int number;
      String str;

      try
      {
         str = "xyz";
         number = Integer.parseInt(str);
         System.out.println("A");
      }
      catch(NumberFormatException e)
      {
         System.out.println("B");
      }
      catch(IllegalArgumentException e)
      {
         System.out.println("C");
      }

      System.out.println("D");
   }
}
```

2. Look at the following program and tell what it will output when run:

```
public class ExceptionTest
{
   public static void main(String[] args)
   {
      int number;
      String str;
```

```
            try
            {
               str = "xyz";
               number = Integer.parseInt(str);
               System.out.println("A");
            }
            catch(NumberFormatException e)
            {
               System.out.println("B");
            }
            catch(IllegalArgumentException e)
            {
               System.out.println("C");
            }
            finally
            {
               System.out.println("D");
            }

            System.out.println("E");
         }
      }
```

3. Write a method that searches a numeric array for a specified value. The method should return the subscript of the element containing the value if it is found in the array. If the value is not found, the method should throw an exception of the `Exception` class with the error message "Element not found".

4. Write a statement that throws an `IllegalArgumentException` with the error message "Argument cannot be negative".

5. Write an exception class that can be thrown when a negative number is passed to a method.

6. Write a statement that throws an instance of the exception class that you created in Algorithm Workbench 5.

7. The method `getValueFromFile` is public and returns an `int`. It accepts no arguments. The method is capable of throwing an `IOException` and a `FileNotFoundException`. Write the header for this method.

8. Write a `try` statement that calls the `getValueFromFile` method described in Algorithm Workbench 7. Be sure to handle all the exceptions that the method can throw.

9. Write a statement that creates an object that can be used to write binary data to the file *Configuration.dat*.

10. Write a statement that opens the file *Customers.dat* as a random access file for both reading and writing.

11. Assume that the reference variable r refers to a serializable object. Write code that serializes the object to the file *ObjectData.dat*.

Short Answer

1. What is meant when it is said that an exception is thrown?
2. What does it mean to catch an exception?
3. What happens when an exception is thrown, but the try statement does not have a catch clause that is capable of catching it?
4. What is the purpose of a finally clause?
5. Where does execution resume after an exception has been thrown and caught?
6. When multiple exceptions are caught in the same try statement and some of them are related through inheritance, does the order in which they are listed matter?
7. What types of objects can be thrown?
8. When are you required to have a throws clause in a method header?
9. What is the difference between a checked exception and an unchecked exception?
10. What is the difference between the throw statement and the throws clause?
11. What is the difference between a text file and a binary file?
12. What is the difference between a sequential access file and a random access file?
13. What happens when you serialize an object? What happens when you deserialize an object?

Programming Challenges

MyProgrammingLab™ *Visit www.myprogramminglab.com to complete many of these Programming Challenges online and get instant feedback.*

1. TestScores Class

Write a class named TestScores. The class constructor should accept an array of test scores as its argument. The class should have a method that returns the average of the test scores. If any test score in the array is negative or greater than 100, the class should throw an IllegalArgumentException. Demonstrate the class in a program.

2. TestScores Class Custom Exception

Write an exception class named InvalidTestScore. Modify the TestScores class you wrote in Programming Challenge 1 so that it throws an InvalidTestScore exception if any of the test scores in the array are invalid.

3. RetailItem Exceptions

Programming Challenge 4 of Chapter 6 required you to write a RetailItem class that holds data pertaining to a retail item. Write an exception class that can be instantiated and thrown when a negative number is given for the price. Write another exception class that can be instantiated and thrown when a negative number is given for the units on hand. Demonstrate the exception classes in a program.

4. `Month` **Class Exceptions**

Programming Challenge 5 of Chapter 8 required you to write a `Month` class that holds information about the month. Write exception classes for the following error conditions:

- A number less than 1 or greater than 12 is given for the month number.
- An invalid string is given for the name of the month.

Modify the `Month` class so that it throws the appropriate exception when either of these errors occurs. Demonstrate the classes in a program.

5. `Payroll` **Class Exceptions**

Programming Challenge 5 of Chapter 6 required you to write a `Payroll` class that calculates an employee's payroll. Write exception classes for the following error conditions:

- An empty string is given for the employee's name.
- An invalid value is given for the employee's ID number. If you implemented this field as a string, then an empty string would be invalid. If you implemented this field as a numeric variable, then a negative number or zero would be invalid.
- An invalid number is given for the number of hours worked. This would be a negative number or a number greater than 84.
- An invalid number is given for the hourly pay rate. This would be a negative number or a number greater than 25.

Modify the `Payroll` class so that it throws the appropriate exception when any of these errors occurs. Demonstrate the exception classes in a program.

6. `FileArray` **Class**

Design a class that has a static method named `writeArray`. The method should take two arguments: the name of a file and a reference to an `int` array. The file should be opened as a binary file, the contents of the array should be written to the file, and then the file should be closed.

Write a second method in the class named `readArray`. The method should take two arguments: the name of a file and a reference to an `int` array. The file should be opened, data should be read from the file and stored in the array, and then the file should be closed. Demonstrate both methods in a program.

7. **File Encryption Filter**

File encryption is the science of writing the contents of a file in a secret code. Your encryption program should work like a filter, reading the contents of one file, modifying the data into a code, and then writing the coded contents out to a second file. The second file will be a version of the first file, but written in a secret code.

Although there are complex encryption techniques, you should come up with a simple one of your own. For example, you could read the first file one character at a time, and add 10 to the character code of each character before it is written to the second file.

8. **File Decryption Filter**

Write a program that decrypts the file produced by the program in Programming Challenge 7. The decryption program should read the contents of the coded file, restore the data to its original state, and write it to another file.

9. TestScores **Modification for Serialization**

Modify the TestScores class that you created for Programming Challenge 1 to be serializable. Write a program that creates an array of at least five TestScore objects and serializes them. Write another program that deserializes the objects from the file.

10. Exception Project

VideoNote
The Exception
Project
Problem

This assignment assumes you have completed Programming Challenge 1 of Chapter 10 (Employee and ProductionWorker Classes). Modify the Employee and ProductionWorker classes so they throw exceptions when the following errors occur:

- The Employee class should throw an exception named InvalidEmployeeNumber when it receives an invalid employee number.
- The ProductionWorker class should throw an exception named InvalidShift when it receives an invalid shift.
- The ProductionWorker class should throw an exception named InvalidPayRate when it receives a negative number for the hourly pay rate.

Write a test program that demonstrates how each of these exception conditions works.

12 A First Look at GUI Applications

TOPICS

12.1 Introduction

CONCEPT: In Java, you use the Java Foundation Classes (JFC) to create a graphical user interface for your application. Within the JFC you use the Abstract Windowing Toolkit (AWT) or Swing classes to create a graphical user interface.

In this chapter, we discuss the basics of creating a Java application with a *graphical user interface* or *GUI* (pronounced "gooey"). A GUI is a graphical window or a system of graphical windows that is presented by an application for interaction with the user. In addition to accepting input from the keyboard, GUIs typically accept input from a mouse as well.

A window in a GUI commonly consists of several *components* that present data to the user and/or allow interaction with the application. Some of the common GUI components are buttons, labels, text fields, check boxes, and radio buttons. Figure 12-1 shows an example of a window with a variety of components. Table 12-1 describes the components that appear in the window.

Figure 12-1 Various GUI components   (Oracle Corporate Counsel)

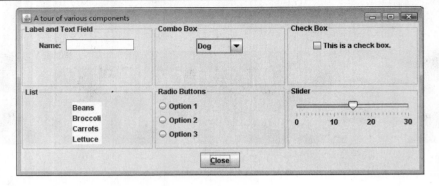

Table 12-1 Some GUI components

Component	Description
Label	An area that can display text.
Text field	An area in which the user may type a single line of input from the keyboard.
Combo box	A component that displays a drop-down list of items from which the user may select. A combo box also provides a text field in which the user may type input. It is called a combo box because it is the combination of a list and a text field.
Check box	A component that has a box that may be checked or unchecked.
List	A list from which the user may select an item.
Radio button	A component that can be either selected or deselected. Radio buttons usually appear in groups and allow the user to select one of several options.
Slider	A component that allows the user to select a value by moving a slider along a track.
Button	A button that can cause an action to occur when it is clicked.

The JFC, AWT, and Swing

Java programmers use the *Java Foundation Classes (JFC)* to create GUI applications. The JFC consists of several sets of classes, many of which are beyond the scope of this book. The two sets of JFC classes that we focus on are the AWT and Swing classes. First, we discuss the differences between them.

Java has been equipped, since its earliest version, with a set of classes for drawing graphics and creating GUIs. These classes are part of the *Abstract Windowing Toolkit (AWT)*. The AWT allows programmers to create applications and applets that interact with the user via windows and other GUI components.

Programmers are limited in what they can do with the AWT classes, however. This is because the AWT classes do not actually draw user interface components on the screen. Instead, the AWT classes communicate with another layer of software, known as the *peer classes*, which directs the underlying operating system to draw its own built-in components. Each version of Java that is developed for a particular operating system has its own set of peer classes. Although this means that Java programs have a look that is consistent with other applications on the same system, it also leads to some problems.

One problem is that not all operating systems offer the same set of GUI components. For example, one operating system might provide a sophisticated slider bar component that is not found on any other platform. Other operating systems might have their own unique components as well. In order for the AWT to retain its portability, it has to offer only those components that are common to all the operating systems that support Java.

Another problem is in the behavior of components across various operating systems. A component on one operating system might have slightly different behavior than the same component on a different operating system. In addition, the peer classes for some operating systems reportedly have bugs. As a result, programmers cannot be completely sure how their AWT programs will behave on different operating systems until they test each one.

A third problem is that programmers cannot easily customize the AWT components. Because these components rely on the appearance and behavior of the underlying operating system components, there is little that can be done by the programmer to change their properties.

To remedy these problems, Swing was introduced with the release of Java 2. *Swing* is a library of classes that do not replace the AWT, but provide an improved alternative for creating GUI applications and applets. Very few of the Swing classes rely on an underlying system of peer classes. Instead, Swing draws most of its own components on the screen. This means that Swing components can have a consistent look and predictable behavior on any operating system.

 NOTE: Swing applications can have the look of a specific operating system. The programmer may choose from a variety of "look and feel" themes.

Swing components can also be easily customized. The Swing library provides many sophisticated components that are not found in the AWT. In this chapter and in Chapter 13, we primarily use Swing to develop GUI applications. In Chapter 14, we use AWT to develop applets.

 NOTE: AWT components are commonly called heavyweight components because they are coupled with their underlying peer classes. Very few of the Swing components are coupled with peer classes, so they are referred to as lightweight components.

Event-Driven Programming

Programs that operate in a GUI environment must be *event-driven*. An *event* is an action that takes place within a program, such as the clicking of a button. Part of writing a GUI application is creating event listeners. An *event listener* is an object that automatically executes one of its methods when a specific event occurs. If you wish for an application to perform an operation when a particular event occurs, you must create an event listener object that responds when that event takes place.

The `javax.swing` and `java.awt` Packages

In this chapter, we use the Swing classes for all of the graphical components that we create in our GUIs. The Swing classes are part of the `javax.swing` package. (Take note of the letter x that appears after the word java.) The following `import` statement will be used in every applicaton:

```
import javax.swing.*;
```

We also use some of the AWT classes to determine when events, such as the clicking of a mouse, take place in our applications. The AWT classes are part of the `java.awt` package. (Note that there is no x after `java` in this package name.) Programs that use the AWT classes will have the following `import` statement:

```
import java.awt.*;
```

12.2 Creating Windows

> **CONCEPT:** You can use Swing classes to create windows containing various GUI components.

VideoNote

Creating a Simple GUI Application

The `JOptionPane` dialog boxes that you learned about in Chapter 2 allow you to easily display messages and gather input. If an application is to provide a full graphical user interface, however, much more is needed. Often, applications need one or more windows with various components that allow the user to enter and/or select data and interact with the application. For example, the window that is displayed in Figure 12-1 has several different components within it.

A window is a component, but because a window contains other components, it is more appropriately considered a container. A *container* is simply a component that holds other components. In GUI terminology, a container that can be displayed as a window is known as a *frame*. A frame appears as a basic window that has a border around it, a title bar, and a set of buttons for minimizing, maximizing, and closing the window. In a Swing application, you create a frame object from the `JFrame` class.

There are a number of steps involved in creating a window, so let's look at an example. The program in Code Listing 12-1 displays the window shown in Figure 12-2.

Code Listing 12-1   (`ShowWindow.java`)

```java
 1  import javax.swing.*;    // Needed for Swing classes
 2
 3  /**
 4     This program displays a simple window with a title. The
 5     application exits when the user clicks the close button.
 6  */
 7
 8  public class ShowWindow
 9  {
10     public static void main(String[] args)
11     {
12        final int WINDOW_WIDTH = 350;    // Window width in pixels
13        final int WINDOW_HEIGHT = 250;   // Window height in pixels
14
15        // Create a window.
16        JFrame window = new JFrame();
17
18        // Set the title.
19        window.setTitle("A Simple Window");
20
21        // Set the size of the window.
22        window.setSize(WINDOW_WIDTH, WINDOW_HEIGHT);
23
24        // Specify what happens when the close button is clicked.
25        window.setDefaultCloseOperation(JFrame.EXIT_ON_CLOSE);
26
27        // Display the window.
28        window.setVisible(true);
29     }
30  }
```

Figure 12-2   Window displayed by `ShowWindow.java`   (Oracle Corporate Counsel)

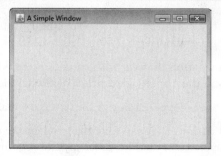

The window shown in Figure 12-2 was produced on a system running Microsoft Windows. Notice that the window has a border and a title bar with "A Simple Window" displayed in it. In addition, it has the standard Microsoft Windows buttons in the upper-right corner: a minimize button, a maximize button, and a close button. These standard features are sometimes referred to as *decorations*. If you run this program, you will see the window displayed on your screen. When you click on the close button, the window disappears and the program terminates.

Let's take a closer look at the code. First, notice that the following import statement is used in line 1:

```
import javax.swing.*;   // Needed for Swing classes
```

Any program that uses a Swing class, such as JFrame, must have this import statement. In lines 12 and 13 the two constants WINDOW_WIDTH and WINDOW_HEIGHT are declared as follows:

```
final int WINDOW_WIDTH = 350;   // Window width in pixels
final int WINDOW_HEIGHT = 250;  // Window height in pixels
```

We use these constants later in the program to set the size of the window. The window's size is measured in pixels. A *pixel* is one of the small dots that make up a screen display; the resolution of your monitor is measured in pixels. For example, if your monitor's resolution is 1024 by 768, that means the width of your screen is 1024 pixels, and the height of your screen is 768 pixels.

Next, we create an instance of the JFrame class with the following statement in line 16:

```
JFrame window = new JFrame();
```

This statement creates a JFrame object in memory and assigns its address to the window variable. This statement does not display the window on the screen, however. A JFrame is initially invisible.

In line 19 we call the JFrame object's setTitle method as follows:

```
window.setTitle("A Simple Window");
```

The string that is passed as an argument to setTitle will appear in the window's title bar when it is displayed. In line 22 we call the JFrame object's setSize method to set the window's size as follows:

```
window.setSize(WINDOW_WIDTH, WINDOW_HEIGHT);
```

The two arguments passed to setSize specify the window's width and height in pixels. In this program we pass the constants WINDOW_WIDTH and WINDOW_HEIGHT, which we declared earlier, to set the size of the window to 350 pixels by 250 pixels.

In line 25 we specify the action that we wish to take place when the user clicks on the close button, which appears in the upper-right corner of the window as follows:

```
window.setDefaultCloseOperation(JFrame.EXIT_ON_CLOSE);
```

There are a number of actions that can take place when the user clicks on the close button. The setDefaultCloseOperation method takes an int argument, which specifies the action. In this statement, we pass the constant JFrame.EXIT_ON_CLOSE, which causes the application to end with a `System.exit` method call. If we had passed `JFrame.HIDE_ON_CLOSE`, the window would be hidden from view, but the application would not end. The default action is `JFrame.HIDE_ON_CLOSE`.

Last, in line 28, we use the following code to display the window:

```
window.setVisible(true);
```

The `setVisible` method takes a `boolean` argument. If the argument is `true`, the window is made visible. If the argument is `false`, the window is hidden.

Using Inheritance to Extend the `JFrame` Class

The program in Code Listing 12-1 performs a very simple operation: It creates an instance of the `JFrame` class and displays it. Most of the time, your GUI applications will be much more involved than this. As you progress through this chapter, you will add numerous components and capabilities to the windows that you create.

Instead of simply creating an instance of the `JFrame` class, as shown in Code Listing 12-1, a more common technique is to use inheritance to create a new class that extends the `JFrame` class.

IF YOU'VE SKIPPED AHEAD TO THIS CHAPTER: This chapter is written so that you can skip ahead to it any time after Chapter 6. Reading about inheritance and interfaces in Chapter 10 would be helpful; but if you have not read that material yet, the following summarizes what you need to know for this chapter.

When a new class *extends* an existing class, it inherits many of the existing class's members just as if they were part of the new class. For example, you saw how the program in Code Listing 12-1 created a `JFrame` object and then called four of its methods: `setTitle`, `setSize`, `setDefaultCloseOperation`, and `setVisible`. These methods are all members of the `JFrame` class. If you create a new class that extends the `JFrame` class, the new class will automatically inherit these methods. Then these methods can be called from an instance of the new class just as if they were written into its declaration. You can add your own custom code to the new class, making it a specialized, or extended, version of the `JFrame` class. Programs can then create instances of your new specialized class instead of the more generic `JFrame` class.

Let's look at the `SimpleWindow` class in Code Listing 12-2. This is an example of a class that extends the `JFrame` class.

Code Listing 12-2   (`SimpleWindow.java`)

```
1  import javax.swing.*;    // Needed for Swing classes
2
3  /**
4     This class extends the JFrame class. Its constructor displays
5     a simple window with a title. The application exits when the
```

```
 6       user clicks the close button.
 7  */
 8
 9  public class SimpleWindow extends JFrame
10  {
11     /**
12        Constructor
13     */
14
15     public SimpleWindow()
16     {
17        final int WINDOW_WIDTH = 350;   // Window width in pixels
18        final int WINDOW_HEIGHT = 250;  // Window height in pixels
19
20        // Set this window's title.
21        setTitle("A Simple Window");
22
23        // Set the size of this window.
24        setSize(WINDOW_WIDTH, WINDOW_HEIGHT);
25
26        // Specify what happens when the close button is clicked.
27        setDefaultCloseOperation(JFrame.EXIT_ON_CLOSE);
28
29        // Display the window.
30        setVisible(true);
31     }
32  }
```

Notice the class header in line 9 as follows:

```
public class SimpleWindow extends JFrame
```

The words extends JFrame indicate that the SimpleWindow class extends the JFrame class. This means that the SimpleWindow class inherits members of the JFrame class, such as the setTitle, setSize, setDefaultCloseOperation, and setVisible methods, just as if they were written into the SimpleWindow class declaration. Now look at the constructor. In lines 17 and 18 we declare the WINDOW_WIDTH and WINDOW_HEIGHT constants, which will be used to establish the size of the window as follows:

```
final int WINDOW_WIDTH = 350;   // Window width in pixels
final int WINDOW_HEIGHT = 250;  // Window height in pixels
```

In line 21 we call the setTitle method to set the text for the window's title bar as follows:

```
setTitle("A Simple Window");
```

Notice that we are calling the method without an object reference and a dot preceding it. This is because the method was inherited from the JFrame class, and we can call it just as if it were written into the SimpleWindow class declaration.

The rest of the constructor calls the setSize, setDefaultCloseOperation, and setVisible methods. All that is necessary to display the window is to create an instance of the

SimpleWindow class, as shown in the program in Code Listing 12-3. When this program runs, the window that was previously shown in Figure 12-2 is displayed. Remember, the SimpleWindow class is an extended version of the JFrame class. When we create an instance of the SimpleWindow class, we are really creating an instance of the JFrame class, with some customized code added to its constructor.

Code Listing 12-3   (`SimpleWindowDemo.java`)

```
 1  /**
 2      This program creates an instance of the
 3      SimpleWindow class.
 4  */
 5
 6  public class SimpleWindowDemo
 7  {
 8      public static void main(String[] args)
 9      {
10          SimpleWindow myWindow = new SimpleWindow();
11      }
12  }
```

Equipping GUI Classes with a `main` Method

You know that a Java application always starts execution with a static method named main. The previous example consists of two separate files:

- SimpleWindow.java: This file contains the SimpleWindow class, which defines a GUI window.
- SimpleWindowDemo.java: This file contains a static main method that creates an object of the GUI window class, thus displaying it.

The purpose of the SimpleWindowDemo.java file is simply to create an instance of the SimpleWindow class. It is possible to eliminate the second file, SimpleWindowDemo.java, by writing the static main method directly into the SimpleWindow.java file. The EmbeddedMain class in Code Listing 12-4 shows an example.

Code Listing 12-4   (`EmbeddedMain.java`)

```
 1  import javax.swing.*; // Needed for Swing classes
 2
 3  /**
 4      This class defines a GUI window and has its own
 5      main method.
 6  */
 7
 8  public class EmbeddedMain extends JFrame
 9  {
10      final int WINDOW_WIDTH = 350;    // Window width in pixels
11      final int WINDOW_HEIGHT = 250;   // Window height in pixels
```

```
12
13    /**
14       Constructor
15    */
16
17    public EmbeddedMain()
18    {
19       // Set this window's title.
20       setTitle("A Simple Window");
21
22       // Set the size of this window.
23       setSize(WINDOW_WIDTH, WINDOW_HEIGHT);
24
25       // Specify what happens when the close button is clicked.
26       setDefaultCloseOperation(JFrame.EXIT_ON_CLOSE);
27
28       // Display the window.
29       setVisible(true);
30    }
31
32    /**
33       The main method creates an instance of the EmbeddedMain
34       class, which causes it to display its window.
35    */
36
37    public static void main(String[] args)
38    {
39       EmbeddedMain em = new EmbeddedMain();
40    }
41 }
```

The EmbeddedMain class contains its own static main method (in lines 37 through 40), which creates an instance of the class. Notice that the main method has exactly the same header as any other static main method that we have written. We can compile the *EmbeddedMain.java* file and then run the resulting *.class* file. When we do, we see the window shown in Figure 12-3.

Figure 12-3 Window displayed by the EmbeddedMain class (Oracle Corporate Counsel)

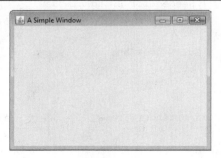

Notice that in line 39 the main method declares a variable named em to reference the instance of the class. Once the instance is created, however, the variable is not used again. Because we do not need the variable, we can instantiate the class *anonymously* as shown here:

```
public static void main(String[] args)
{
    new EmbeddedMain();
}
```

In this version of the method, an instance of the EmbeddedMain class is created in memory, but its address is not assigned to any reference variable.

Adding Components to a Window

Swing provides numerous GUI components that can be added to a window. Three fundamental components are the label, the text field, and the button. These are summarized in Table 12-2.

Table 12-2 Label, text field, and button controls

Component	Swing Class	Description
Label	JLabel	An area that can display text
Text field	JTextField	An area in which the user may type a single line of input from the keyboard
Button	JButton	A button that can cause an action to occur when it is clicked

In Swing, labels are created with the JLabel class, text fields are created with the JTextField class, and buttons are created with the JButton class. To demonstrate these components, we will build a simple GUI application: The Kilometer Converter. This application will present a window in which the user will be able to enter a distance in kilometers, and then click a button to see that distance converted to miles. The conversion formula is as follows:

Miles = Kilometers $\times$ 0.6214

When designing a GUI application, it is usually helpful to draw a sketch showing the window you are creating. Figure 12-4 shows a sketch of what the Kilometer Converter application's window will look like. As you can see from the sketch, the window will have a label, a text field, and a button. When the user clicks the button, the distance in miles will be displayed in a separate JOptionPane dialog box.

Figure 12-4 Sketch of the Kilometer Converter window (Oracle Corporate Counsel)

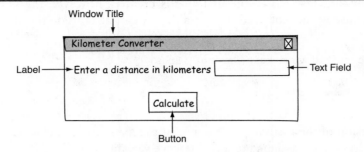

Content Panes and Panels

Before we start writing code, you should be familiar with content panes and panels. A *content pane* is a container that is part of every JFrame object. You cannot see the content pane and it does not have a border, but any component that is to be displayed in a JFrame must be added to its content pane.

A *panel* is also a container that can hold GUI components. Unlike JFrame objects, panels cannot be displayed by themselves; however, they are commonly used to hold and organize collections of related components. With Swing, you create panels with the JPanel class. In our Kilometer Converter application, we will create a panel to hold the label, text field, and button. Then we will add the panel to the JFrame object's content pane. This is illustrated in Figure 12-5.

Figure 12-5 A panel is added to the content pane (Oracle Corporate Counsel)

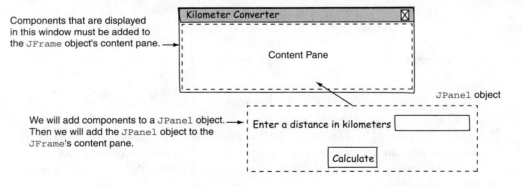

Code Listing 12-5 shows the initial code for the KiloConverter class. We will be adding to this code as we develop the application. This version of the class is stored in the source code folder *Chapter 12\KiloConverter Phase 1*.

Code Listing 12-5 (`KiloConverter.java`)

```
1 import javax.swing.*;
2
3 /**
4    The KiloConverter class displays a JFrame that
5    lets the user enter a distance in kilometers. When
```

```
 6       the Calculate button is clicked, a dialog box is
 7       displayed with the distance converted to miles.
 8 */
 9
10 public class KiloConverter extends JFrame
11 {
12     private JPanel panel;                  // To reference a panel
13     private JLabel messageLabel;           // To reference a label
14     private JTextField kiloTextField;      // To reference a text field
15     private JButton calcButton;            // To reference a button
16     private final int WINDOW_WIDTH = 310; // Window width
17     private final int WINDOW_HEIGHT = 100;// Window height
18
19     /**
20        Constructor
21     */
22
23     public KiloConverter()
24     {
25        // Set the window title.
26        setTitle("Kilometer Converter");
27
28        // Set the size of the window.
29        setSize(WINDOW_WIDTH, WINDOW_HEIGHT);
30
31        // Specify what happens when the close button is clicked.
32        setDefaultCloseOperation(JFrame.EXIT_ON_CLOSE);
33
34        // Build the panel and add it to the frame.
35        buildPanel();
36
37        // Add the panel to the frame's content pane.
38        add(panel);
39
40        // Display the window.
41        setVisible(true);
42     }
43
44     /**
45        The buildPanel method adds a label, a text field,
46        and a button to a panel.
47     */
48
49     private void buildPanel()
50     {
51        // Create a label to display instructions.
52        messageLabel = new JLabel("Enter a distance " +
53                                   "in kilometers");
```

```
54
55          // Create a text field 10 characters wide.
56          kiloTextField = new JTextField(10);
57
58          // Create a button with the caption "Calculate".
59          calcButton = new JButton("Calculate");
60
61          // Create a JPanel object and let the panel
62          // field reference it.
63          panel = new JPanel();
64
65          // Add the label, text field, and button
66          // components to the panel.
67          panel.add(messageLabel);
68          panel.add(kiloTextField);
69          panel.add(calcButton);
70       }
71
72       /**
73          main method
74       */
75
76       public static void main(String[] args)
77       {
78          new KiloConverter();
79       }
80  }
```

Let's take a closer look at this class. First, notice in line 10 that the KiloConverter class extends the JFrame class as follows:

```
public class KiloConverter extends JFrame
```

Next, in lines 12 through 17, notice in the following that the class declares a number of fields, and according to good class design principles, the fields are private:

```
private JPanel panel;                // To reference a panel
private JLabel messageLabel;         // To reference a label
private JTextField kiloTextField;    // To reference a text field
private JButton calcButton;          // To reference a button
private final int WINDOW_WIDTH = 310;  // Window width
private final int WINDOW_HEIGHT = 100; // Window height
```

The statement in line 12 declares a JPanel reference variable named panel, which we will use to reference the panel that will hold the other components. The messageLabel variable, declared in line 13, will reference a JLabel object that displays a message instructing the user to enter a distance in kilometers. The kiloTextField variable, declared in line 14, will reference a JTextField object that will hold a value typed by the user. The calcButton variable, declared in line 15, will reference a JButton object that will calculate and display the kilometers converted to miles when clicked. The WINDOW_WIDTH and WINDOW_HEIGHT fields, declared in lines 16 and 17, are constants that hold the width and height of the window.

Now let's look at the constructor. In line 26 the setTitle method, which was inherited from the JFrame class, is called to set the text for the window's title bar. Next, in line 29, the inherited setSize method is called to establish the size of the window. In line 32, the inherited setDefaultCloseOperation method is called to establish the action that should occur when the window's close button is clicked.

Line 35 calls the buildPanel method. The buildPanel method is defined in this class, in lines 49 through 70. The purpose of the buildPanel method is to create a label, a text field, and a button, and then add those components to a panel. Let's look at the method.

First, look at the method header in line 49 and notice that it is declared private. When a method is private, only other methods in the same class can call it. This method is not meant to be called by code outside the class, so it is declared private. In lines 52 and 53, the method uses the following statement to create a JLabel object and assign its address to the message field:

```
messageLabel = new JLabel("Enter a distance " +
                          "in kilometers");
```

The string that is passed to the JLabel constructor is the text that will be displayed in the label. The following statement appears in line 56. It creates a JTextField object, and assigns its address to the kiloTextField field:

```
kiloTextField = new JTextField(10);
```

The argument that is passed to the JTextField constructor is the width of the text field in columns. One column is enough space to hold the letter "m," which is the widest letter in the alphabet.

The following statement appears in line 59; it creates a JButton object, and assigns its address to the calcButton field:

```
calcButton = new JButton("Calculate");
```

The string that is passed as an argument to the JButton constructor is the text that will be displayed on the button.

Next, in line 63, the method uses the following statement to create a JPanel object and assign its address to the panel field, which is a private field in the class:

```
panel = new JPanel();
```

A JPanel object is used to hold other components. You add a component to a JPanel object with the add method. The following code, in lines 67 through 69, adds the objects referenced by the messageLabel, kiloTextField, and calcButton variables to the JPanel object:

```
panel.add(messageLabel);
panel.add(kiloTextField);
panel.add(calcButton);
```

At this point, the panel is fully constructed in memory. The `buildPanel` method ends, and control returns to the class constructor. Here's the next statement in the constructor, which appears in line 38:

```
add(panel);
```

This statement calls the `add` method, which was inherited from the `JFrame` class. The purpose of the `add` method is to add an object to the content pane. This statement adds the object referenced by `panel` to the content pane.

The constructor's last statement, in line 41, calls the inherited `setVisible` method to display the window on the screen as follows:

```
setVisible(true);
```

The class has a static `main` method, which appears in lines 76 through 79. Line 78 creates an instance of the `KiloConverter` class. When this program is executed, the window shown in Figure 12-6 is displayed on the screen.

Figure 12-6 Kilometer Converter window

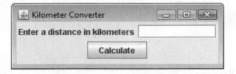

Figure 12-7 shows the window again, this time pointing out each of the components.

Although you can type input into the text field, the application does nothing when you click the Calculate button because we have not written an event handler that will execute when the button is clicked. That's the next step.

Figure 12-7 Components in the Kilometer Converter window   (Oracle Corporate Counsel)

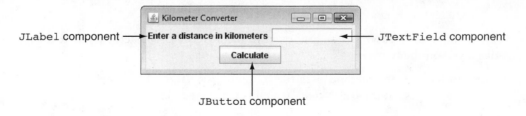

JLabel component

JTextField component

JButton component

NOTE: Recall that the size of the window in the `KiloConverter` class is set to 310 pixels wide by 100 pixels high. This is set with the `WINDOW_WIDTH` and `WINDOW_HEIGHT` constants. Figures 12-6 and 12-7 show the window as it appears on a system set at a video resolution of 1024 by 768 pixels. If your video resolution is lower, the window might not appear exactly as shown in the figures. If this is the case, you can increase the values of the `WINDOW_WIDTH` and `WINDOW_HEIGHT` constants and recompile the program. This is true for other applications in this chapter as well.

Handling Events with Action Listeners

VideoNote
Handling Events

An *event* is an action that takes place within a program, such as the clicking of a button. When an event takes place, the component that is responsible for the event creates an event object in memory. The *event object* contains information about the event. The component that generated the event object is known as the *event source*. For example, when the user clicks a button, the JButton component generates an event object. The JButton component that generated the event object is the event source.

But what happens to the event object once it is generated by a source component? It is possible that the source component is connected to one or more event listeners. An *event listener* is an object that responds to events. If the source component is connected to an event listener, then the event object is automatically passed, as an argument, to a specific method in the event listener. The method then performs any actions that it was programmed to perform in response to the event. This process is sometimes referred to as *event firing*.

When you are writing a GUI application, it is your responsibility to write the classes for the event listeners that your application needs. For example, if you write an application with a JButton component, an event will be generated each time the user clicks the button. Therefore, you should write an event listener class that can handle the event. In your application you would create an instance of the event listener class and connect it to the JButton component. Before looking at a specific example, we must discuss two important topics that arise when writing event listeners: private inner classes and interfaces.

Writing Event Listener Classes as Private Inner Classes

Java allows you to write a class definition inside of another class definition. A class that is defined inside of another class is known as an *inner class*. Figure 12-8 illustrates a class definition inside of another class definition.

Figure 12-8   A class with an inner class   (Oracle Corporate Counsel)

```
public class Outer
{
      Fields and methods of the Outer
      class appear here.

      private class Inner
      {
          Fields and methods of the Inner
          class appear here.
      }
}
```

When an inner class is private, as shown in the figure, it is accessible only to code in the class that contains it. For example, the Inner class shown in the figure would be accessible only to methods that belong to the Outer class. Code outside the Outer class would not be able to access the Inner class. A common technique for writing an event listener class is to write it as a private inner class, inside the class that creates the GUI. Although this is not the only way to write event listener classes, it is the approach we take in this book.

Event Listeners Must Implement an Interface

There is a special requirement that all event listener classes must meet: They must *implement an interface*.

We discussed interfaces in detail in Chapter 10, but in case you haven't read that material, you can think of an interface as something like a class, containing one or more method headers. Interfaces do not have actual methods, however, only their headers. When you write a class that implements an interface, you are agreeing that the class will have all of the methods that are specified in the interface.

Java provides numerous interfaces that you can use with event listener classes. There are several different types of events that can occur within a GUI application, and the specific interface that you use depends on the type of event you want to handle. JButton components generate *action events*, and an event listener class that can handle action events is also known as an *action listener* class. When you write an action listener class for a JButton component, it must implement an interface known as ActionListener. In case you are curious, this is what the code for the ActionListener interface looks like:

```
public interface ActionListener
{
    public void actionPerformed(ActionEvent e);
}
```

As you can see, the ActionListener interface contains the header for only one method: actionPerformed. Notice that the method has public access, is void, and has a parameter of the ActionEvent type. When you write a class that implements this interface, it *must* have a method named actionPerformed, with a header exactly like the one in the interface.

> **NOTE:** The *ActionListener* interface, as well as other event listener interfaces, is in the *java.awt.event* package. We will use the following *import* statement in order to use those interfaces:
>
> ```
> import java.awt.event.*;
> ```

You use the implements key word in a class header to indicate that it implements an interface. Here is an example of a class named MyButtonListener that implements the ActionListener interface:

```
private class MyButtonListener implements ActionListener
{
    public void actionPerformed(ActionEvent e)
    {
        Write code here to handle the event.
    }
}
```

Remember, when you write a class that implements an interface, you are "promising" that the class will have the methods specified in the interface. Notice that this class lives up to its promise. It has a method named actionPerformed, with a header that matches the actionPerformed header in the ActionListener interface exactly.

NOTE: In your action listener class, the only part of the `actionPerformed` method header that does not have to match that which is shown in the `ActionListener` interface exactly is the name of the parameter variable. Instead of using the name e, you can use any legal variable name that you wish.

Registering an Event Listener Object

Once you have written an event listener class, you can create an object of that class, and then connect the object with a GUI component. The process of connecting an event listener object to a GUI component is known as *registering* the event listener.

When a `JButton` component generates an event, it automatically executes the `actionPerformed` method of the event listener object that is registered with it, passing the event object as an argument. This is illustrated in Figure 12-9.

Figure 12-9   A `JButton` component firing an action event   (Oracle Corporate Counsel)

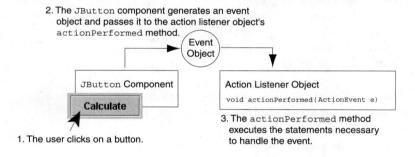

Writing an Event Listener for the `KiloConverter` Class

Now that we've gone over the basics of event listeners, let's continue to develop the `KiloConverter` class. Code Listing 12-6 shows the class with an action listener added to it. This version of the class is stored in the source code folder *Chapter 12\KiloConverter Phase 2*. The action listener is a private inner class named `CalcButtonListener`. The new code is shown in bold.

Code Listing 12-6   (`KiloConverter.java`)

```
1 import javax.swing.*;       // Needed for Swing classes
2 import java.awt.event.*; // Needed for ActionListener Interface
3
4 /**
5    The KiloConverter class displays a JFrame that
6    lets the user enter a distance in kilometers. When
7    the Calculate button is clicked, a dialog box is
8    displayed with the distance converted to miles.
```

```
 9   */
10
11   public class KiloConverter extends JFrame
12   {
13      private JPanel panel;              // To reference a panel
14      private JLabel messageLabel;       // To reference a label
15      private JTextField kiloTextField;  // To reference a text field
16      private JButton calcButton;        // To reference a button
17      private final int WINDOW_WIDTH = 310;   // Window width
18      private final int WINDOW_HEIGHT = 100;  // Window height
19
20      /**
21         Constructor
22      */
23
24      public KiloConverter()
25      {
26         // Set the window title.
27         setTitle("Kilometer Converter");
28
29         // Set the size of the window.
30         setSize(WINDOW_WIDTH, WINDOW_HEIGHT);
31
32         // Specify what happens when the close button is clicked.
33         setDefaultCloseOperation(JFrame.EXIT_ON_CLOSE);
34
35         // Build the panel and add it to the frame.
36         buildPanel();
37
38         // Add the panel to the frame's content pane.
39         add(panel);
40
41         // Display the window.
42         setVisible(true);
43      }
44
45      /**
46         The buildPanel method adds a label, a text field,
47         and a button to a panel.
48      */
49
50      private void buildPanel()
51      {
52         // Create a label to display instructions.
53         messageLabel = new JLabel("Enter a distance " +
54                                   "in kilometers");
55
56         // Create a text field 10 characters wide.
```

```
57        kiloTextField = new JTextField(10);
58
59        // Create a button with the caption "Calculate".
60        calcButton = new JButton("Calculate");
61
62        // Add an action listener to the button.
63        calcButton.addActionListener(new CalcButtonListener());
64
65        // Create a JPanel object and let the panel
66        // field reference it.
67        panel = new JPanel();
68
69        // Add the label, text field, and button
70        // components to the panel.
71        panel.add(messageLabel);
72        panel.add(kiloTextField);
73        panel.add(calcButton);
74     }
75
76     /**
77        CalcButtonListener is an action listener class for
78        the Calculate button.
79     */
80
81     private class CalcButtonListener implements ActionListener
82     {
83        /**
84           The actionPerformed method executes when the user
85           clicks on the Calculate button.
86           @param e The event object.
87        */
88
89        public void actionPerformed(ActionEvent e)
90        {
91           final double CONVERSION = 0.6214;
92           String input;  // To hold the user's input
93           double miles;  // The number of miles
94
95           // Get the text entered by the user into the
96           // text field.
97           input = kiloTextField.getText();
98
99           // Convert the input to miles.
100          miles = Double.parseDouble(input) * CONVERSION;
101
102          // Display the result.
103          JOptionPane.showMessageDialog(null, input +
104                  " kilometers is " + miles + " miles.");
```

```
105          }
106      }
107
108      /**
109         main method
110      */
111
112      public static void main(String[] args)
113      {
114          new KiloConverter();
115      }
116 }
```

First, notice that we've added the `import java.awt.event.*;` statement in line 2. This is necessary for our program to use the `ActionListener` interface. Next, look at the following code in line 81:

```
private class CalcButtonListener implements ActionListener
```

This is the header for an inner class that we will use to create event listener objects. The name of this class is `CalcButtonListener` and it implements the `ActionListener` interface. We could have named the class anything we wanted to, but because it will handle the `JButton` component's action events, it must implement the `ActionListener` interface. The class has one method, `actionPerformed`, which is required by the `ActionListener` interface. The header for the `actionPerformed` method appears in line 89 as follows:

```
public void actionPerformed(ActionEvent e)
```

This method will be executed when the user clicks the `JButton` component. It has one parameter, e, which is an `ActionEvent` object. This parameter receives the event object that is passed to the method when it is called. Although we do not actually use the e parameter in this method, we still have to list it inside the method header's parentheses because it is required by the `ActionListener` interface.

The `actionPerformed` method declares a constant for the conversion factor in line 91, and two local variables in lines 92 and 93: `input`, a reference to a `String` object; and `miles`, a `double`. The following statement appears in line 97:

```
input = kiloTextField.getText();
```

All `JTextField` objects have a `getText` method that returns the text contained in the text field. This will be any value entered into the text field by the user. The value is returned as a string. So, this statement retrieves any value entered by the user into the text field and assigns it to `input`.

The following statement appears in line 100:

```
miles = Double.parseDouble(input) * CONVERSION;
```

This statement converts the value in `input` to a `double`, and then multiplies it by the constant `CONVERSION`, which is set to 0.6214. This will convert the number of kilometers entered by the user to miles. The result is stored in the `miles` variable. The method's last statement, in lines 103 and 104, uses JOptionPane to display a dialog box showing the distance converted to miles as follows:

```
JOptionPane.showMessageDialog(null, input +
        " kilometers is " + miles + " miles.");
```

Writing an action listener class is only part of the process of handling a JButton component's action events. We must also create an object from the class and then register the object with the JButton component. When we register the action listener object with the JButton component, we are creating a connection between the two objects.

JButton components have a method named addActionListener, which is used for registering action event listeners. In line 63, which is in the buildPanel method, the following statement creates a CalcButtonListener object and registers that object with the calcButton object:

```
calcButton.addActionListener(new CalcButtonListener());
```

You pass the address of an action listener object as the argument to the addActionListener method. This statement uses the expression new CalcButtonListener() to create an instance of the CalcButtonListener class. The address of that instance is then passed to the addActionListener method. Now, when the user clicks the Calculate button, the CalcButtonListener object's actionPerformed method will be executed.

TIP: Instead of the one statement in line 63, we could have written the following two statements:

```
CalcButtonListener listener = new CalcButtonListener();
calcButton.addActionListener(listener);
```

The first statement shown here declares a CalcButtonListener variable named listener, creates a new CalcButtonListener object, and assigns the object's address to the listener variable. The second statement passes the address in listener to the addActionListener method. These two statements accomplish the same thing as the one statement in line 63, but they declare a variable, listener, that we will not use again in the program. A better way is to use the one statement that appears in line 63 as follows:

```
calcButton.addActionListener(new CalcButtonListener());
```

Recall that the new key word creates an object and returns the object's address. This statement uses the new key word to create a CalcButtonListener object, and passes the object's address directly to the addActionListener method. Because we do not need to refer to the object again in the program, we do not assign the object's address to a variable. It is known as an *anonymous object*.

When this program is executed, the first window shown in Figure 12-10 is displayed on the screen. If the user enters 2 in the text field and clicks the Calculate button, the second window shown in the figure (a dialog box) appears. To exit the application, the user clicks the OK button on the dialog box, and then clicks the close button in the upper-right corner of the main window.

Figure 12-10   Windows displayed by the `KiloConverter` class   (Oracle Corporate Counsel)

This window appears first. The user enters 2 in the text field and then clicks the Calculate button.

This dialog box appears next.

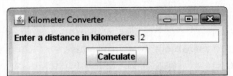

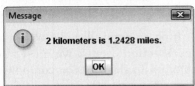

Background and Foreground Colors

Many of the Swing component classes have methods named `setBackground` and `setForeground`. You call these methods to change a component's color. The background color is the color of the component itself, and the foreground color is the color of text that might be displayed on the component.

The argument that you pass to the `setBackground` and `setForeground` methods is a color code. Table 12-3 lists several predefined constants that you can use for colors. To use these constants, you must have the `import java.awt.*;` statement in your code.

Table 12-3   Color constants   (Oracle Corporate Counsel)

Color.BLACK	Color.BLUE
Color.CYAN	Color.DARK_GRAY
Color.GRAY	Color.GREEN
Color.LIGHT_GRAY	Color.MAGENTA
Color.ORANGE	Color.PINK
Color.RED	Color.WHITE
Color.YELLOW	

For example, the following code creates a button with the text "OK" displayed on it. The `setBackground` and `setForeground` methods are called to make the button blue and the text yellow.

```
JButton okButton = new JButton("OK");
okButton.setBackground(Color.BLUE);
okButton.setForeground(Color.YELLOW);
```

The `ColorWindow` class in Code Listing 12-7 displays a window with a label and three buttons. When the user clicks a button, it changes the background color of the panel that contains the components and the foreground color of the label.

Code Listing 12-7   (`ColorWindow.java`)

```java
 1 import javax.swing.*;      // Needed for Swing classes
 2 import java.awt.*;         // Needed for Color class
 3 import java.awt.event.*;   // Needed for event listener interface
 4
 5 /**
 6    This class demonstrates how to set the background color of
 7    a panel and the foreground color of a label.
 8 */
 9
10 public class ColorWindow extends JFrame
11 {
12    private JLabel messageLabel;     // To display a message
13    private JButton redButton;       // Changes color to red
14    private JButton blueButton;      // Changes color to blue
15    private JButton yellowButton;    // Changes color to yellow
16    private JPanel panel;            // A panel to hold components
17    private final int WINDOW_WIDTH = 200;   // Window width
18    private final int WINDOW_HEIGHT = 125;  // Window height
19
20    /**
21       Constructor
22    */
23
24    public ColorWindow()
25    {
26       // Set the title bar text.
27       setTitle("Colors");
28
29       // Set the size of the window.
30       setSize(WINDOW_WIDTH, WINDOW_HEIGHT);
31
32       // Specify an action for the close button.
33       setDefaultCloseOperation(JFrame.EXIT_ON_CLOSE);
34
35       // Create a label.
36       messageLabel = new JLabel("Click a button to " +
37                                 "select a color.");
38
39       // Create the three buttons.
40       redButton = new JButton("Red");
41       blueButton = new JButton("Blue");
42       yellowButton = new JButton("Yellow");
43
44       // Register an event listener with all 3 buttons.
```

```
45        redButton.addActionListener(new RedButtonListener());
46        blueButton.addActionListener(new BlueButtonListener());
47        yellowButton.addActionListener(new YellowButtonListener());
48
49        // Create a panel and add the components to it.
50        panel = new JPanel();
51        panel.add(messageLabel);
52        panel.add(redButton);
53        panel.add(blueButton);
54        panel.add(yellowButton);
55
56        // Add the panel to the content pane.
57        add(panel);
58
59        // Display the window.
60        setVisible(true);
61     }
62
63     /**
64        Private inner class that handles the event when
65        the user clicks the Red button.
66     */
67
68     private class RedButtonListener implements ActionListener
69     {
70        public void actionPerformed(ActionEvent e)
71        {
72           // Set the panel's background to red.
73           panel.setBackground(Color.RED);
74
75           // Set the label's text to blue.
76           messageLabel.setForeground(Color.BLUE);
77        }
78     }
79
80     /**
81        Private inner class that handles the event when
82        the user clicks the Blue button.
83     */
84
85     private class BlueButtonListener implements ActionListener
86     {
87        public void actionPerformed(ActionEvent e)
88        {
89           // Set the panel's background to blue.
90           panel.setBackground(Color.BLUE);
```

```
91
92            // Set the label's text to yellow.
93            messageLabel.setForeground(Color.YELLOW);
94      }
95   }
96
97   /**
98      Private inner class that handles the event when
99      the user clicks the Yellow button.
100  */
101
102  private class YellowButtonListener implements ActionListener
103  {
104     public void actionPerformed(ActionEvent e)
105     {
106        // Set the panel's background to yellow.
107        panel.setBackground(Color.YELLOW);
108
109        // Set the label's text to black.
110        messageLabel.setForeground(Color.BLACK);
111     }
112  }
113
114  /**
115     main method
116  */
117
118  public static void main(String[] args)
119  {
120     new ColorWindow();
121  }
122 }
```

Notice that this class has three action listener classes, one for each button. The action listener classes are RedButtonListener, BlueButtonListener, and YellowButtonListener. The following statements, in lines 45 through 47, register instances of these classes with the appropriate button components:

```
redButton.addActionListener(new RedButtonListener());
blueButton.addActionListener(new BlueButtonListener());
yellowButton.addActionListener(new YellowButtonListener());
```

When you run the program, the window shown in Figure 12-11 appears.

Figure 12-11   The window produced by the `ColorWindow` class   (Oracle Corporate Counsel)

The window components first
appear in their default colors.

When the user clicks on the Red button, the
panel turns red and the label turns blue.

When the user clicks on the Blue button, the
panel turns blue and the label turns yellow.

When the user clicks on the Yellow button, the
panel turns yellow and the label turns black.

Changing the Background Color of a `JFrame` Object's Content Pane

Recall that a `JFrame` object has a content pane, which is a container for all the components that are added to the `JFrame`. When you add a component to a `JFrame` object, you are actually adding it to the object's content pane. In the example shown in this section, we added a label and some buttons to a panel, and then added the panel to the `JFrame` object's content pane. When we changed the background color, we changed the background color of the panel. In this example, the color of the content pane does not matter because it is completely filled up by the panel. The color of the panel covers up the color of the content pane.

In some cases, where you have not filled up the `JFrame` object's content pane with a panel, you might want to change the background color of the content pane. If you wish to change the background color of a `JFrame` object's content pane, you must call the content pane's `setBackground` method, not the `JFrame` object's `setBackground` method. For example, in a class that extends the `JFrame` class, the following statement can be used to change the content pane's background to blue:

```
getContentPane().setBackground(Color.BLUE);
```

In this statement, the `getContentPane` method is called to get a reference to the `JFrame` object's content pane. This reference is then used to call the content pane's `setBackground` method. As a result, the content pane's background color will change to blue.

The `ActionEvent` Object

The action listener's `actionPerformed` method has a parameter variable named e that is declared as follows:

```
ActionEvent e
```

`ActionEvent` is a class that is defined in the Java API. When an action event occurs, an object of the `ActionEvent` class is created, the action listener's `actionPerformed` method is called, and a reference to the `ActionEvent` object is passed into the e parameter variable. So, when the `actionPerformed` method executes, the e parameter references the event object that was generated in response to the event.

Earlier it was mentioned that the event object contains information about the event. If you wish, you can retrieve certain information about the event by calling one of the event object's methods. Two of the `ActionEvent` methods are listed in Table 12-4.

Table 12-4   ActionEvent methods

Method Name	Description
getActionCommand()	Returns the action command for this event as a `String`
getSource()	Returns a reference to the object that generated this event

The `getActionCommand` Method

The first method listed in Table 12-4, getActionCommand, returns the *action command* that is associated with the event. When a `JButton` component generates an event, the action command is the text that appears on the button. The getActionCommand returns this text as a `String`. You can use the getActionCommand method to determine which button was clicked when several buttons share the same action listener class.

To demonstrate, look at the `EventObjectWindow` class in Code Listing 12-8. It produces a window with three buttons. The buttons have the text "Button 1", "Button 2", and "Button 3". The action listener class displays the contents of the event object's action command when any of these buttons are clicked.

Code Listing 12-8   (EventObjectWindow.java)

```java
 1 import javax.swing.*;    // Needed for Swing classes
 2 import java.awt.event.*; // Needed for event listener interface
 3
 4 /**
 5    This class demonstrates how to retrieve the action command
 6    from an event object.
 7 */
 8
 9 public class EventObject extends JFrame
10 {
11    private JButton button1;    // Button 1
12    private JButton button2;    // Button 2
13    private JButton button3;    // Button 3
14    private JPanel panel;       // A panel to hold components
15    private final int WINDOW_WIDTH = 300; // Window width
16    private final int WINDOW_HEIGHT = 70; // Window height
```

```
17
18    /**
19         Constructor
20    */
21
22    public EventObject()
23    {
24       // Set the title bar text.
25       setTitle("Event Object Demonstration");
26
27       // Set the size of the window.
28       setSize(WINDOW_WIDTH, WINDOW_HEIGHT);
29
30       // Specify what happens when the close button is clicked.
31       setDefaultCloseOperation(JFrame.EXIT_ON_CLOSE);
32
33       // Create the three buttons.
34       button1 = new JButton("Button 1");
35       button2 = new JButton("Button 2");
36       button3 = new JButton("Button 3");
37
38       // Register an event listener with all 3 buttons.
39       button1.addActionListener(new ButtonListener());
40       button2.addActionListener(new ButtonListener());
41       button3.addActionListener(new ButtonListener());
42
43       // Create a panel and add the buttons to it.
44       panel = new JPanel();
45       panel.add(button1);
46       panel.add(button2);
47       panel.add(button3);
48
49       // Add the panel to the content pane.
50       add(panel);
51
52       // Display the window.
53       setVisible(true);
54    }
55
56    /**
57       Private inner class that handles the event when
58       the user clicks a button.
59    */
60
61    private class ButtonListener implements ActionListener
62    {
63       public void actionPerformed(ActionEvent e)
```

```
64          {
65              // Get the action command.
66              String actionCommand = e.getActionCommand();
67
68              // Determine which button was clicked and display
69              // a message.
70              if (actionCommand.equals("Button 1"))
71              {
72                  JOptionPane.showMessageDialog(null, "You clicked " +
73                                                  "the first button.");
74              }
75              else if (actionCommand.equals("Button 2"))
76              {
77                  JOptionPane.showMessageDialog(null, "You clicked " +
78                                                  "the second button.");
79              }
80              else if (actionCommand.equals("Button 3"))
81              {
82                  JOptionPane.showMessageDialog(null, "You clicked " +
83                                                  "the third button.");
84              }
85          }
86      }
87
88      /**
89         main method
90      */
91
92      public static void main(String[] args)
93      {
94          new EventObject();
95      }
96  }
```

Previously you saw the ColorWindow class, in Code Listing 12-7, which had three buttons and three different action listener classes. The EventObjectWindow class also has three buttons, but only one action listener class. In lines 39 through 41, we create and register three separate instances of the class with the three buttons as follows:

```
button1.addActionListener(new ButtonListener());
button2.addActionListener(new ButtonListener());
button3.addActionListener(new ButtonListener());
```

Figure 12-12 shows the output of the application when the user clicks Button 1, Button 2, and Button 3.

Figure 12-12 Output of `EventObjectWindow` class (Oracle Corporate Counsel)

This window appears first.

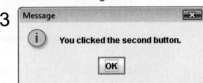

The user clicks Button 1 and this dialog box appears next. The user clicks the OK button to dismiss the dialog box.

The user clicks Button 2 and this dialog box appears next. The user clicks the OK button to dismiss the dialog box.

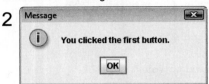

The user clicks Button 3 and this dialog box appears next. The user clicks the OK button to dismiss the dialog box.

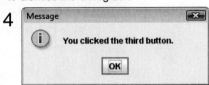

 TIP: The text that is displayed on a button is the default action command. You can change the action command by calling the `JButton` class's `setActionCommand` method. For example, assuming that `myButton` references a `JButton` component, the following statement would change the component's action command to "The button was clicked":

```
myButton.setActionCommand("The button was clicked");
```

 NOTE: Changing a `JButton` component's action command does not change the text that is displayed on the button. For a demonstration of how to change the action command, see the *ActionCommand.java* file in this chapter's source code folder.

The `getSource` Method

The second `ActionEvent` method listed in Table 12-4, `getSource`, returns a reference to the component that is the source of the event. As with the `getActionCommand` method, if you have several buttons and use objects of the same action listener class to respond to their events, you can use the `getSource` method to determine which button was clicked. For example, the `ButtonListener` class's `actionPerformed` method in Code Listing 12-8 could have been written as follows, to achieve the same result:

```
public void actionPerformed(ActionEvent e)
{
    // Determine which button was clicked and display
    // a message.
```

```
    if (e.getSource() == button1)
    {
        JOptionPane.showMessageDialog(null, "You clicked " +
                                       "the first button.");
    }
    else if (e.getSource() == button2)
    {
        JOptionPane.showMessageDialog(null, "You clicked " +
                                       "the second button.");
    }
    else if (e.getSource() == button3)
    {
        JOptionPane.showMessageDialog(null, "You clicked " +
                                       "the third button.");
    }
}
```

See the *EventObjectWindow2.java* file in this chapter's source code folder for a demonstration of this code.

Checkpoint

MyProgrammingLab™ *www.myprogramminglab.com*

12.1   What is a frame? How do you create a frame with Swing?

12.2   How do you set a frame's size?

12.3   How do you display a frame on the screen?

12.4   What is a content pane?

12.5   What is the difference between a frame and a panel?

12.6   What is an event listener?

12.7   If you are writing an event listener class for a JButton component, what interface must the class implement? What method must the class have? When is this method executed?

12.8   How do you register an event listener with a JButton component?

12.9   How do you change the background color of a component? How do you change the color of text displayed by a label or a button?

12.3 Layout Managers

CONCEPT: A layout manager is an object that governs the positions and sizes of components in a container. The layout manager automatically repositions and, in some cases, resizes the components when the container is resized.

An important part of designing a GUI application is determining the layout of the components that are displayed in the application's windows. The term *layout* refers to the positioning and sizing of components. In Java, you do not normally specify the exact location of a component within a window. Instead, you let a layout manager control the positions of components for you. A *layout manager* is an object that has its own rules about how components are to be positioned and sized, and it makes adjustments when necessary. For example, when the user resizes a window, the layout manager determines where the components should be moved to.

In order to use a layout manager with a group of components, you must place the components in a container, and then create a layout manager object. The layout manager object and the container work together. In this chapter we discuss the three layout managers described in Table 12-5. To use any of these classes, your code should have the following import statement: import java.awt.*;

Table 12-5 Layout managers

Layout Manager	Description
FlowLayout	Arranges components in rows; this is the default layout manager for JPanel objects
BorderLayout	Arranges components in five regions: north, south, east, west, and center; this is the default layout manager for a JFrame object's content pane
GridLayout	Arranges components in a grid with rows and columns

Adding a Layout Manager to a Container

You add a layout manager to a container, such as a content pane or a panel, by calling the setLayout method and passing a reference to a layout manager object as the argument. For example, the following code creates a JPanel object, then sets a BorderLayout object as its layout manager:

```
JPanel panel = new JPanel();
panel.setLayout(new BorderLayout());
```

Likewise, the following code might appear in the constructor of a class that extends the JFrame class. It sets a FlowLayout object as the layout manager for the content pane:

```
setLayout(new FlowLayout());
```

Once you establish a layout manager for a container, the layout manager governs the positions and sizes of the components that are added to the container.

The FlowLayout Manager

The FlowLayout manager arranges components in rows. This is the default layout manager for JPanel objects. Here are some rules that the FlowLayout manager follows:

- You can add multiple components to a container that uses a FlowLayout manager.
- When you add components to a container that uses a FlowLayout manager, the components appear horizontally, from left to right, in the order that they were added to the component.
- When there is no more room in a row but more components are added, the new components "flow" to the next row.

For example, the `FlowWindow` class shown in Code Listing 12-9 extends `JFrame`. This class creates a 200 pixel wide by 105 pixel high window. In the constructor, the `setLayout` method is called to give the content pane a `FlowLayout` manager. Then, three buttons are created and added to the content pane. The `main` method creates an instance of the `FlowWindow` class, which displays the window.

Code Listing 12-9   **(FlowWindow.java)**

```java
 1  import javax.swing.*; // Needed for Swing classes
 2  import java.awt.*;    // Needed for FlowLayout class
 3
 4  /**
 5     This class demonstrates how to use a FlowLayout manager
 6     with the content pane.
 7  */
 8
 9  public class FlowWindow extends JFrame
10  {
11     private final int WINDOW_WIDTH = 200;  // Window width
12     private final int WINDOW_HEIGHT = 105; // Window height
13
14     /**
15        Constructor
16     */
17
18     public FlowWindow()
19     {
20        // Set the title bar text.
21        setTitle("Flow Layout");
22
23        // Set the size of the window.
24        setSize(WINDOW_WIDTH, WINDOW_HEIGHT);
25
26        // Specify an action for the close button.
27        setDefaultCloseOperation(JFrame.EXIT_ON_CLOSE);
28
29        // Add a FlowLayout manager to the content pane.
30        setLayout(new FlowLayout());
31
32        // Create three buttons.
33        JButton button1 = new JButton("Button 1");
34        JButton button2 = new JButton("Button 2");
35        JButton button3 = new JButton("Button 3");
36
37        // Add the three buttons to the content pane.
38        add(button1);
39        add(button2);
40        add(button3);
```

```
41
42        // Display the window.
43        setVisible(true);
44    }
45
46    /**
47       The main method creates an instance of the FlowWindow
48       class, causing it to display its window.
49    */
50
51    public static void main(String[] args)
52    {
53        new FlowWindow();
54    }
55 }
```

Figure 12-13 shows the window that is displayed by this class. Notice that the buttons appear from left to right in the order they were added to the content pane. Because there is only enough room for the first two buttons in the first row, the third button is positioned in the second row. By default, the content of each row is centered and there is a five pixel gap between the components.

Figure 12-13   The window displayed by the `FlowWindow` class   (Oracle Corporate Counsel)

If the user resizes the window, the layout manager repositions the components according to its rules. Figure 12-14 shows the appearance of the window in three different sizes.

Figure 12-14   The arrangements of the buttons after resizing

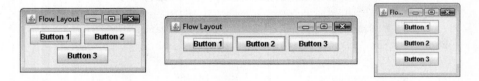

Adjusting the `FlowLayout` Alignment

The `FlowLayout` manager allows you to align components in the center of each row or along the left or right edge of each row. An overloaded constructor allows you to pass one of the following constants as an argument to set an alignment: `FlowLayout.CENTER`, `FlowLayout.LEFT`, or `FlowLayout.RIGHT`. Here is an example that sets left alignment:

```
setLayout(new FlowLayout(FlowLayout.LEFT));
```

Figure 12-15 shows examples of windows that use a FlowLayout manager with left, center, and right alignment.

Adjusting the FlowLayout Component Gaps

By default, the FlowLayout manager inserts a gap of five pixels between components, both horizontally and vertically. You can adjust this gap by passing values for the horizontal and vertical gaps as arguments to an overloaded FlowLayout constructor. The constructor has the following format:

```
FlowLayout(int alignment, int horizontalGap, int verticalGap)
```

You pass one of the alignment constants discussed in the previous section to the alignment parameter. The horizontalGap parameter is the number of pixels to separate components horizontally, and the verticalGap parameter is the number of pixels to separate components vertically. Here is an example of the constructor call:

```
setLayout(new FlowLayout(FlowLayout.LEFT, 10, 7));
```

This statement causes components to be left aligned with a horizontal gap of 10 pixels and a vertical gap of seven pixels.

Figure 12-15   Left, center, and right alignment   (Oracle Corporate Counsel)

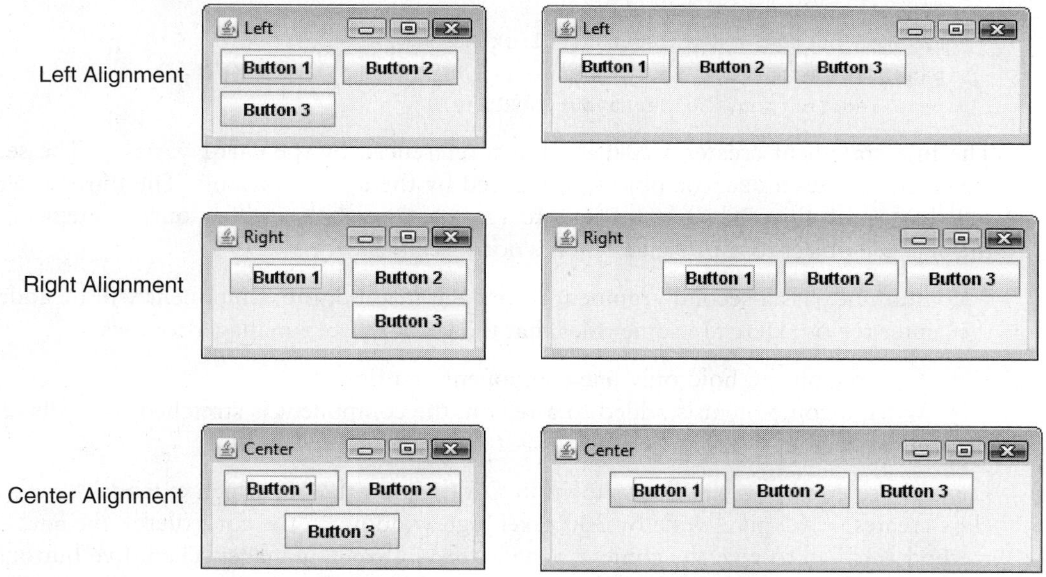

The BorderLayout Manager

The BorderLayout manager divides a container into five regions. The regions are known as north, south, east, west, and center. The arrangement of these regions is shown in Figure 12-16.

Figure 12-16 The regions of a `BorderLayout` manager (Oracle Corporate Counsel)

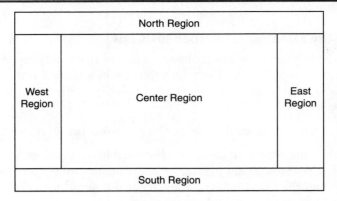

When a component is placed into a container that is managed by a `BorderLayout` manager, the component must be placed into one of these five regions. Only one component at a time may be placed into a region. When adding a component to the container, you specify the region by passing one of the following constants as a second argument to the container's add method: `BorderLayout.NORTH`, `BorderLayout.SOUTH`, `BorderLayout.EAST`, `BorderLayout.WEST`, or `BorderLayout.CENTER`.

For example, look at the following code:

```
JPanel panel = new JPanel();
JButton button = new JButton("Click Me");
panel.setLayout(new BorderLayout());
panel.add(button, BorderLayout.NORTH);
```

The first statement creates a `JPanel` object, referenced by the `panel` variable. The second statement creates a `JButton` object, referenced by the `button` variable. The third statement sets the `JPanel` object's layout manager to a `BorderLayout` object. The fourth statement adds the `JButton` object to the `JPanel` object's north region.

If you do not pass a second argument to the add method, the component will be added to the center region. Here are some rules that the `BorderLayout` manager follows:

- Each region can hold only one component at a time.
- When a component is added to a region, the component is stretched so it fills up the entire region.

Look at the `BorderWindow` class shown in Code Listing 12-10, which extends `JFrame`. This class creates a 400 pixel wide by 300 pixel high window. In the constructor, the `setLayout` method is called to give the content pane a `BorderLayout` manager. Then, five buttons are created and each is added to a different region.

Code Listing 12-10   (BorderWindow.java)

```
1 import javax.swing.*; // Needed for Swing classes
2 import java.awt.*;    // Needed for BorderLayout class
```

```
 3
 4   /**
 5       This class demonstrates the BorderLayout manager.
 6   */
 7
 8   public class BorderWindow extends JFrame
 9   {
10      private final int WINDOW_WIDTH = 400;    // Window width
11      private final int WINDOW_HEIGHT = 300;   // Window height
12
13      /**
14          Constructor
15      */
16
17      public BorderWindow()
18      {
19         // Set the title bar text.
20         setTitle("Border Layout");
21
22         // Set the size of the window.
23         setSize(WINDOW_WIDTH, WINDOW_HEIGHT);
24
25         // Specify an action for the close button.
26         setDefaultCloseOperation(JFrame.EXIT_ON_CLOSE);
27
28         // Add a BorderLayout manager to the content pane.
29         setLayout(new BorderLayout());
30
31         // Create five buttons.
32         JButton button1 = new JButton("North Button");
33         JButton button2 = new JButton("South Button");
34         JButton button3 = new JButton("East Button");
35         JButton button4 = new JButton("West Button");
36         JButton button5 = new JButton("Center Button");
37
38         // Add the five buttons to the content pane.
39         add(button1, BorderLayout.NORTH);
40         add(button2, BorderLayout.SOUTH);
41         add(button3, BorderLayout.EAST);
42         add(button4, BorderLayout.WEST);
43         add(button5, BorderLayout.CENTER);
44
45         // Display the window.
46         setVisible(true);
47      }
48
49      /**
```

```
50          The main method creates an instance of the BorderWindow
51          class, causing it to display its window.
52    */
53
54    public static void main(String[] args)
55    {
56       new BorderWindow();
57    }
58 }
```

NOTE: A JFrame object's content pane is automatically given a BorderLayout manager. We have explicitly added it in Code Listing 12-10 so it is clear that we are using a BorderLayout manager.

Figure 12-17 shows the window that is displayed. Normally the size of a button is just large enough to accommodate the text that is displayed on the button. Notice that the buttons displayed in this window did not retain their normal size. Instead, they were stretched to fill all of the space in their regions. If the user resizes the window, the sizes of the components will be changed as well. This is shown in Figure 12-18.

Figure 12-17 The window displayed by the BorderWindow class   (Oracle Corporate Counsel)

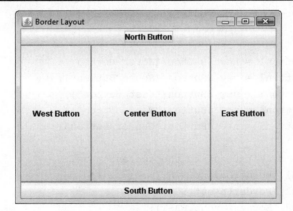

Here are the rules that govern how a BorderLayout manager resizes components:

- A component that is placed in the north or south regions may be resized horizontally so it fills up the entire region.
- A component that is placed in the east or west regions may be resized vertically so it fills up the entire region.

Figure 12-18 The window resized

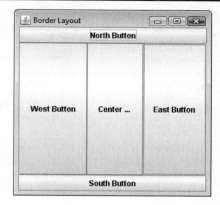

- A component that is placed in the center region may be resized both horizontally and vertically so it fills up the entire region.

> **TIP:** You do not have to place a component in every region of a border layout. To achieve the desired positioning, you might want to place components in only a few of the layout regions. In Chapter 13, you will see examples of applications that do this.

By default there is no gap between the regions. You can use an overloaded version of the `BorderLayout` constructor to specify horizontal and vertical gaps, however. Here is the constructor's format:

```
BorderLayout(int horizontalGap, int verticalGap)
```

The `horizontalGap` parameter is the number of pixels to separate the regions horizontally, and the `verticalGap` parameter is the number of pixels to separate the regions vertically. Here is an example of the constructor call:

```
setLayout(new BorderLayout(5, 10));
```

This statement causes the regions to appear with a horizontal gap of five pixels and a vertical gap of 10 pixels.

Nesting Panels Inside a Container's Regions

You might think that the `BorderLayout` manager is limiting because it allows only one component per region, and the components that are placed in its regions are automatically resized to fill up any extra space. These limitations are easy to overcome, however, by adding components to panels and then nesting the panels inside the regions.

For example, suppose we wish to modify the `BorderWindow` class in Code Listing 12-10 so the buttons retain their original size. We can accomplish this by placing each button in a separate `JPanel` object and then adding the `JPanel` objects to the content pane's five regions. This is illustrated in Figure 12-19. As a result, the `BorderLayout` manager resizes the `JPanel` objects to fill up the space in the regions, not the buttons contained within the `JPanel` objects.

Figure 12-19 Nesting `JPanel` objects inside each region (Oracle Corporate Counsel)

1. Five `JPanel` objects are created and a `JButton` object is added to each one.

2. The `JPanel` objects are then added to the content pane, one to each region.

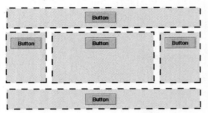

North Region		
West Region	Center Region	East Region
South Region		

The `BorderPanelWindow` class in Code Listing 12-11 demonstrates this technique. This class also introduces a new way of sizing windows. Notice that the constructor does not explicitly set the size of the window with the `setSize` method. Instead, it calls the `pack` method just before calling the `setVisible` method. The `pack` method, which is inherited from `JFrame`, automatically sizes the window to accommodate the components contained within it. Figure 12-20 shows the window that the class displays.

Code Listing 12-11 (`BorderPanelWindow.java`)

```
1  import java.awt.*;     // Needed for BorderLayout class
2  import javax.swing.*;  // Needed for Swing classes
3
4  /**
5     This class demonstrates how JPanels can be nested
6     inside each region of a content pane governed by
7     a BorderLayout manager.
8  */
9
10 public class BorderPanelWindow extends JFrame
11 {
12    /**
13       Constructor
14    */
15
16    public BorderPanelWindow()
17    {
18       // Set the title bar text.
19       setTitle("Border Layout");
20
21       // Specify an action for the close button.
22       setDefaultCloseOperation(JFrame.EXIT_ON_CLOSE);
23
24       // Add a BorderLayout manager to the content pane.
```

```
25        setLayout(new BorderLayout());
26
27        // Create five panels.
28        JPanel panel1 = new JPanel();
29        JPanel panel2 = new JPanel();
30        JPanel panel3 = new JPanel();
31        JPanel panel4 = new JPanel();
32        JPanel panel5 = new JPanel();
33
34        // Create five buttons.
35        JButton button1 = new JButton("North Button");
36        JButton button2 = new JButton("South Button");
37        JButton button3 = new JButton("East Button");
38        JButton button4 = new JButton("West Button");
39        JButton button5 = new JButton("Center Button");
40
41        // Add the buttons to the panels.
42        panel1.add(button1);
43        panel2.add(button2);
44        panel3.add(button3);
45        panel4.add(button4);
46        panel5.add(button5);
47
48        // Add the five panels to the content pane.
49        add(panel1, BorderLayout.NORTH);
50        add(panel2, BorderLayout.SOUTH);
51        add(panel3, BorderLayout.EAST);
52        add(panel4, BorderLayout.WEST);
53        add(panel5, BorderLayout.CENTER);
54
55        // Pack and display the window.
56        pack();
57        setVisible(true);
58     }
59
60     /**
61        The main method creates an instance of the
62        BorderPanelWindow class, causing it to display
63        its window.
64     */
65
66     public static void main(String[] args)
67     {
68        new BorderPanelWindow();
69     }
70 }
```

Figure 12-20 Window displayed by the `BorderPanelWindow` class   (Oracle Corporate Counsel)

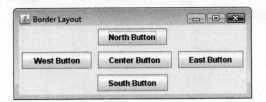

 NOTE: There are multiple layout managers at work in the `BorderPanelWindow` class. The content pane uses a `BorderLayout` manager, and each of the `JPanel` objects use a `FlowLayout` manager.

The `GridLayout` Manager

The `GridLayout` manager creates a grid with rows and columns, much like a spreadsheet. As a result, the container that is managed by a `GridLayout` object is divided into equally sized cells. Figure 12-21 illustrates a container with three rows and five columns. This means that the container is divided into 15 cells.

Figure 12-21 The `GridLayout` manager divides a container into cells

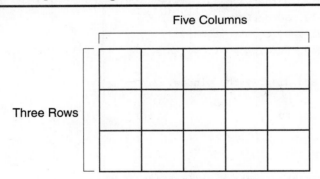

Here are some rules that the `GridLayout` manager follows:

- Each cell can hold only one component.
- All of the cells are the same size. This is the size of the largest component placed within the layout.
- A component that is placed in a cell is automatically resized to fill up any extra space.

You pass the number of rows and columns that a container should have as arguments to the GridLayout constructor. Here is the general format of the constructor:

```
GridLayout(int rows, int columns)
```

Here is an example of the constructor call:

```
setLayout(new GridLayout(2, 3));
```

This statement gives the container two rows and three columns, for a total of six cells. You can pass 0 as an argument for the rows or the columns, but not both. Passing 0 for both arguments will cause an error.

When adding components to a container that is governed by the GridLayout manager, you cannot specify a cell. Instead, the components are assigned to cells in the order they are added. The first component added to the container is assigned to the first cell, which is in the upper-left corner. As other components are added, they are assigned to the remaining cells in the first row, from left to right. When the first row is filled up, components are assigned to the cells in the second row, and so forth.

The GridWindow class shown in Code Listing 12-12 demonstrates. It creates a 400 pixel wide by 200 pixel high window, governed by a GridLayout manager. The content pane is divided into two rows and three columns, and a button is added to each cell. Figure 12-22 shows the window displayed by the class.

Code Listing 12-12   **(GridWindow.java)**

```java
1  import javax.swing.*; // Needed for Swing classes
2  import java.awt.*;    // Needed for GridLayout class
3
4  /**
5     This class demonstrates the GridLayout manager.
6  */
7
8  public class GridWindow extends JFrame
9  {
10    private final int WINDOW_WIDTH = 400;    // Window width
11    private final int WINDOW_HEIGHT = 200;   // Window height
12
13    /**
14       Constructor
15    */
16
17    public GridWindow()
18    {
19       // Set the title bar text.
20       setTitle("Grid Layout");
21
```

```
22        // Set the size of the window.
23        setSize(WINDOW_WIDTH, WINDOW_HEIGHT);
24
25        // Specify an action for the close button.
26        setDefaultCloseOperation(JFrame.EXIT_ON_CLOSE);
27
28        // Add a GridLayout manager to the content pane.
29        setLayout(new GridLayout(2, 3));
30
31        // Create six buttons.
32        JButton button1 = new JButton("Button 1");
33        JButton button2 = new JButton("Button 2");
34        JButton button3 = new JButton("Button 3");
35        JButton button4 = new JButton("Button 4");
36        JButton button5 = new JButton("Button 5");
37        JButton button6 = new JButton("Button 6");
38
39        // Add the six buttons to the content pane.
40        add(button1);   // Goes into row 1, column 1
41        add(button2);   // Goes into row 1, column 2
42        add(button3);   // Goes into row 1, column 3
43        add(button4);   // Goes into row 2, column 1
44        add(button5);   // Goes into row 2, column 2
45        add(button6);   // Goes into row 2, column 3
46
47        // Display the window.
48        setVisible(true);
49    }
50
51    /**
52       The main method creates an instance of the GridWindow
53       class, causing it to display its window.
54    */
55
56    public static void main(String[] args)
57    {
58        new GridWindow();
59    }
60 }
```

As previously mentioned, the GridLayout manager limits each cell to only one component and resizes components to fill up all of the space in a cell. To get around these limitations you can nest panels inside the cells and add other components to the panels. For example, the GridPanelWindow class shown in Code Listing 12-13 is a modification of the GridWindow class. It creates six panels and adds a button and a label to each panel. These panels are then added to the content pane's cells. Figure 12-23 shows the window displayed by this class.

Figure 12-22 Window displayed by the `GridWindow` class   (Oracle Corporate Counsel)

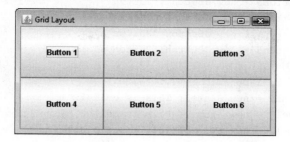

Code Listing 12-13   **(GridPanelWindow.java)**

```
 1 import javax.swing.*; // Needed for Swing classes
 2 import java.awt.*;    // Needed for GridLayout class
 3
 4 /**
 5    This class demonstrates how panels may be added to
 6    the cells created by a GridLayout manager.
 7 */
 8
 9 public class GridPanelWindow extends JFrame
10 {
11    private final int WINDOW_WIDTH = 400;   // Window width
12    private final int WINDOW_HEIGHT = 200;  // Window height
13
14    /**
15       Constructor
16    */
17
18    public GridPanelWindow()
19    {
20       // Set the title bar text.
21       setTitle("Grid Layout");
22
23       // Set the size of the window.
24       setSize(WINDOW_WIDTH, WINDOW_HEIGHT);
25
26       // Specify an action for the close button.
27       setDefaultCloseOperation(JFrame.EXIT_ON_CLOSE);
28
29       // Add a GridLayout manager to the content pane.
30       setLayout(new GridLayout(2, 3));
31
32       // Create six buttons.
33       JButton button1 = new JButton("Button 1");
```

```
34        JButton button2 = new JButton("Button 2");
35        JButton button3 = new JButton("Button 3");
36        JButton button4 = new JButton("Button 4");
37        JButton button5 = new JButton("Button 5");
38        JButton button6 = new JButton("Button 6");
39
40        // Create six labels.
41        JLabel label1 = new JLabel("This is cell 1.");
42        JLabel label2 = new JLabel("This is cell 2.");
43        JLabel label3 = new JLabel("This is cell 3.");
44        JLabel label4 = new JLabel("This is cell 4.");
45        JLabel label5 = new JLabel("This is cell 5.");
46        JLabel label6 = new JLabel("This is cell 6.");
47
48        // Create six panels.
49        JPanel panel1 = new JPanel();
50        JPanel panel2 = new JPanel();
51        JPanel panel3 = new JPanel();
52        JPanel panel4 = new JPanel();
53        JPanel panel5 = new JPanel();
54        JPanel panel6 = new JPanel();
55
56        // Add the labels to the panels.
57        panel1.add(label1);
58        panel2.add(label2);
59        panel3.add(label3);
60        panel4.add(label4);
61        panel5.add(label5);
62        panel6.add(label6);
63
64        // Add the buttons to the panels.
65        panel1.add(button1);
66        panel2.add(button2);
67        panel3.add(button3);
68        panel4.add(button4);
69        panel5.add(button5);
70        panel6.add(button6);
71
72        // Add the panels to the content pane.
73        add(panel1);  // Goes into row 1, column 1
74        add(panel2);  // Goes into row 1, column 2
75        add(panel3);  // Goes into row 1, column 3
76        add(panel4);  // Goes into row 2, column 1
77        add(panel5);  // Goes into row 2, column 2
78        add(panel6);  // Goes into row 2, column 3
79
80        // Display the window.
81        setVisible(true);
```

```
82    }
83
84    /**
85       The main method creates an instance of the
86       GridPanelWindow class, displaying its window.
87    */
88
89    public static void main(String[] args)
90    {
91       new GridPanelWindow();
92    }
93 }
```

Figure 12-23   Window displayed by the `GridPanelWindow` class

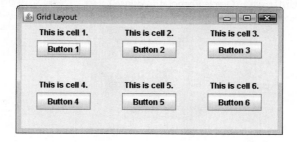

Because we have containers nested inside the content pane, there are multiple layout managers at work in the `GridPanelWindow` class. The content pane uses a `GridLayout` manager, and each of the `JPanel` objects uses a `FlowLayout` manager.

 **Checkpoint**

MyProgrammingLab™ *www.myprogramminglab.com*

12.10 How do you add a layout manager to a container?

12.11 Which layout manager divides a container into regions known as north, south, east, west, and center?

12.12 Which layout manager arranges components in a row, from left to right, in the order they were added to the container?

12.13 Which layout manager arranges components in rows and columns?

12.14 How many components can you have at one time in a `BorderLayout` region? In a `GridLayout` cell?

12.15 How do you prevent the `BorderLayout` manager from resizing a component that has been placed in its region?

12.16 How can you cause a content pane to be automatically sized to accommodate the components contained within it?

12.17 What is the default layout manager for a `JFrame` object's content pane? For a `JPanel` object?

12.4 Radio Buttons and Check Boxes

> **CONCEPT:** Radio buttons normally appear in groups of two or more and allow the user to select one of several possible options. Check boxes, which may appear alone or in groups, allow the user to make yes/no or on/off selections.

Radio Buttons

Radio buttons are useful when you want the user to select one choice from several possible options. Figure 12-24 shows a group of radio buttons.

Figure 12-24 Radio buttons   (Oracle Corporate Counsel)

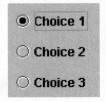

A radio button may be selected or deselected. Each radio button has a small circle that appears filled in when the radio button is selected and appears empty when the radio button is deselected. You use the JRadioButton class to create radio buttons. Here are the general formats of two JRadioButton constructors:

```
JRadioButton(String text)
JRadioButton(String text, boolean selected)
```

The first constructor shown creates a deselected radio button. The argument passed to the text parameter is the string that is displayed next to the radio button. For example, the following statement creates a radio button with the text "Choice 1" displayed next to it. The radio button initially appears deselected.

```
JRadioButton radio1 = new JRadioButton("Choice 1");
```

The second constructor takes an additional boolean argument, which is passed to the selected parameter. If true is passed as the selected argument, the radio button initially appears selected. If false is passed, the radio button initially appears deselected. For example, the following statement creates a radio button with the text "Choice 1" displayed next to it. The radio button initially appears selected.

```
JRadioButton radio1 = new JRadioButton("Choice 1", true);
```

Radio buttons are normally grouped together. When a set of radio buttons are grouped together, only one of the radio buttons in the group may be selected at any time. Clicking a radio button selects it and automatically deselects any other radio button in the same group. Because only one radio button in a group can be selected at any given time, the buttons are said to be *mutually exclusive*.

> **NOTE:** The name "radio button" refers to the old car radios that had push buttons for selecting stations. Only one of the buttons could be pushed in at a time. When you pushed a button in, it automatically popped out any other button that was pushed in.

Grouping with the ButtonGroup class

Once you have created the `JRadioButton` objects that you wish to appear in a group, you must create an instance of the `ButtonGroup` class, and then add the `JRadioButton` objects to it. The `ButtonGroup` object creates the mutually exclusive relationship among the radio buttons that it contains. The following code shows an example:

```
// Create three radio buttons.
JRadioButton radio1 = new JRadioButton("Choice 1", true);
JRadioButton radio2 = new JRadioButton("Choice 2");
JRadioButton radio3 = new JRadioButton("Choice 3");

// Create a ButtonGroup object.
ButtonGroup group = new ButtonGroup();

// Add the radio buttons to the ButtonGroup object.
group.add(radio1);
group.add(radio2);
group.add(radio3);
```

Although you add radio buttons to a `ButtonGroup` object, `ButtonGroup` objects are not containers like `JPanel` objects, or content frames. The function of a `ButtonGroup` object is to deselect all the other radio buttons when one of them is selected. If you wish to add the radio buttons to a panel or a content frame, you must add them individually, as shown here:

```
// Add the radio buttons to the JPanel referenced by panel.
panel.add(radio1);
panel.add(radio2);
panel.add(radio3);
```

Responding to Radio Button Events

Just like `JButton` objects, `JRadioButton` objects generate an action event when they are clicked. To respond to a radio button action event, you must write an action listener class and then register an instance of that class with the `JRadioButton` object. To demonstrate, we will look at the `MetricConverter` class, which is similar to the `KiloConverter` class shown earlier. The `MetricConverter` class presents a window in which the user can enter a distance in kilometers, and then click radio buttons to see that distance converted to miles, feet, or inches. The conversion formulas are as follows:

$Miles = Kilometers \times 0.6214$
$Feet = Kilometers \times 3281.0$
$Inches = Kilometers \times 39370.0$

Figure 12-25 shows a sketch of what the window will look like. As you can see from the sketch, the window will have a label, a text field, and three radio buttons. When the user clicks on one of the radio buttons, the distance will be converted to the selected units and displayed in a separate JOptionPane dialog box.

Figure 12-25 Metric Converter window (Oracle Corporate Counsel)

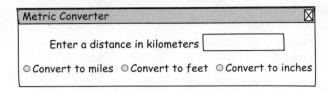

The MetricConverter class is shown in Code Listing 12-14. The class initially displays the window shown at the top of Figure 12-26. The figure also shows the dialog boxes that are displayed when the user clicks any of the radio buttons.

Code Listing 12-14 (MetricConverter.java)

```java
1 import javax.swing.*;
2 import java.awt.event.*;
3 import java.awt.*;
4
5 /**
6    The MetricConverter class lets the user enter a
7    distance in kilometers. Radio buttons can be selected to
8    convert the kilometers to miles, feet, or inches.
9 */
10
11 public class MetricConverter extends JFrame
12 {
13    private JPanel panel;                    // A holding panel
14    private JLabel messageLabel;             // A message to the user
15    private JTextField kiloTextField;        // To hold user input
16    private JRadioButton milesButton;        // To convert to miles
17    private JRadioButton feetButton;         // To convert to feet
18    private JRadioButton inchesButton;       // To convert to inches
19    private ButtonGroup radioButtonGroup;    // To group radio buttons
20    private final int WINDOW_WIDTH = 400;    // Window width
21    private final int WINDOW_HEIGHT = 100;   // Window height
22
23    /**
24       Constructor
25    */
26
27    public MetricConverter()
28    {
```

```
29          // Set the title.
30          setTitle("Metric Converter");
31
32          // Set the size of the window.
33          setSize(WINDOW_WIDTH, WINDOW_HEIGHT);
34
35          // Specify an action for the close button.
36          setDefaultCloseOperation(JFrame.EXIT_ON_CLOSE);
37
38          // Build the panel and add it to the frame.
39          buildPanel();
40
41          // Add the panel to the frame's content pane.
42          add(panel);
43
44          // Display the window.
45          setVisible(true);
46       }
47
48       /**
49          The buildPanel method adds a label, text field, and
50          and three buttons to a panel.
51       */
52
53       private void buildPanel()
54       {
55          // Create the label, text field, and radio buttons.
56          messageLabel = new JLabel("Enter a distance in kilometers");
57          kiloTextField = new JTextField(10);
58          milesButton = new JRadioButton("Convert to miles");
59          feetButton = new JRadioButton("Convert to feet");
60          inchesButton = new JRadioButton("Convert to inches");
61
62          // Group the radio buttons.
63          radioButtonGroup = new ButtonGroup();
64          radioButtonGroup.add(milesButton);
65          radioButtonGroup.add(feetButton);
66          radioButtonGroup.add(inchesButton);
67
68          // Add action listeners to the radio buttons.
69          milesButton.addActionListener(new RadioButtonListener());
70          feetButton.addActionListener(new RadioButtonListener());
71          inchesButton.addActionListener(new RadioButtonListener());
72
73          // Create a panel and add the components to it.
74          panel = new JPanel();
75          panel.add(messageLabel);
76          panel.add(kiloTextField);
```

```
77          panel.add(milesButton);
78          panel.add(feetButton);
79          panel.add(inchesButton);
80      }
81
82      /**
83         Private inner class that handles the event when
84         the user clicks one of the radio buttons.
85      */
86
87      private class RadioButtonListener implements ActionListener
88      {
89          public void actionPerformed(ActionEvent e)
90          {
91              String input;          // To hold the user's input
92              String convertTo = "";  // The units we're converting to
93              double result = 0.0;    // To hold the conversion
94
95              // Get the kilometers entered.
96              input = kiloTextField.getText();
97
98              // Determine which radio button was clicked.
99              if (e.getSource() == milesButton)
100             {
101                 // Convert to miles.
102                 convertTo = " miles.";
103                 result = Double.parseDouble(input) * 0.6214;
104             }
105             else if (e.getSource() == feetButton)
106             {
107                 // Convert to feet.
108                 convertTo = " feet.";
109                 result = Double.parseDouble(input) * 3281.0;
110             }
111             else if (e.getSource() == inchesButton)
112             {
113                 // Convert to inches.
114                 convertTo = " inches.";
115                 result = Double.parseDouble(input) * 39370.0;
116             }
117
118             // Display the conversion.
119             JOptionPane.showMessageDialog(null, input +
120                     " kilometers is " + result + convertTo);
121         }
122     }
```

```
123
124    /**
125        The main method creates an instance of the
126        MetricConverter class, displaying its window.
127    */
128
129    public static void main(String[] args)
130    {
131        new MetricConverter();
132    }
133 }
```

Figure 12-26   Window and dialog boxes displayed by the `MetricConverter` class

This window appears first. The user enters 2 into the text field.

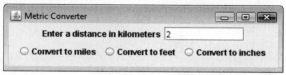

This dialog box appears when the user clicks the "Convert to miles" radio button.

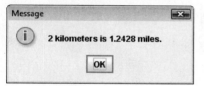

This dialog box appears when the user clicks the "Convert to feet" radio button.

This dialog box appears when the user clicks the "Convert to inches" radio button.

Determining in Code Whether a Radio Button Is Selected

In many applications you will merely want to know whether a radio button is selected. The `JRadioButton` class's `isSelected` method returns a boolean value indicating whether the radio button is selected. If the radio button is selected, the method returns `true`. Otherwise, it returns `false`. In the following code, the `radio` variable references a radio button. The `if` statement calls the `isSelected` method to determine whether the radio button is selected.

```
if (radio.isSelected())
{
   // Code here executes if the radio
   // button is selected.
}
```

Selecting a Radio Button in Code

It is also possible to select a radio button in code with the JRadioButton class's doClick method. When the method is called, the radio button is selected just as if the user had clicked on it. As a result, an action event is generated. In the following statement, the radio variable references a radio button. When this statement executes, the radio button will be selected.

```
radio.doClick();
```

Check Boxes

A *check box* appears as a small box with a label appearing next to it. The window shown in Figure 12-27 has three check boxes.

Figure 12-27   Check boxes   (Oracle Corporate Counsel)

Like radio buttons, check boxes may be selected or deselected at run time. When a check box is selected, a small check mark appears inside the box. Although check boxes are often displayed in groups, they are not usually grouped in a ButtonGroup like radio buttons. This is because check boxes are not normally used to make mutually exclusive selections. Instead, the user is allowed to select any or all of the check boxes that are displayed in a group.

You create a check box with the JCheckBox class. Here are the general formats of two JCheckBox constructors:

```
JCheckBox(String text)
JCheckBox(String text, boolean selected)
```

The first constructor shown creates a deselected check box. The argument passed to the text parameter is the string that is displayed next to the check box. For example, the following statement creates a check box with the text "Macaroni" displayed next to it. The check box initially appears deselected.

```
JCheckBox check1 = new JCheckBox("Macaroni");
```

The second constructor takes an additional `boolean` argument, which is passed to the `selected` parameter. If `true` is passed as the `selected` argument, the radio check box initially appears selected. If `false` is passed, the check box initially appears deselected. For example, the following statement creates a check box with the text "Macaroni" displayed next to it. The radio check box initially appears selected.

```
JCheckBox check1 = new JCheckBox("Macaroni", true);
```

Responding to Check Box Events

When a `JCheckBox` object is selected or deselected, it generates an *item event*. You handle item events in a manner similar to the way you handle the action events that are generated by `JButton` and `JRadioButton` objects. First, you write an *item listener* class, which must meet the following requirements:

- It must implement the `ItemListener` interface.
- It must have a method named `itemStateChanged` with the following header:

```
public void itemStateChanged(ItemEvent e)
```

> **NOTE:** When implementing the `ItemListener` interface, your code must have the following import statement: `import java.awt.event.*;`

Once you have written an item listener class, you create an object of that class, and then register the item listener object with the `JCheckBox` component. When a `JCheckBox` component generates an event, it automatically executes the `itemStateChanged` method of the item listener object that is registered to it, passing the event object as an argument.

Determining in Code Whether a Check Box Is Selected

As with `JRadioButton`, you use the `isSelected` method to determine whether a `JCheckBox` component is selected. The method returns a `boolean` value. If the check box is selected, the method returns `true`. Otherwise, it returns `false`. In the following code, the `checkBox` variable references a `JCheckBox` component. The `if` statement calls the `isSelected` method to determine whether the check box is selected.

```
if (checkBox.isSelected())
{
   // Code here executes if the check
   // box is selected.
}
```

The `ColorCheckBoxWindow` class, shown in Code Listing 12-15, demonstrates how check boxes are used. It displays the window shown in Figure 12-28. When the "Yellow background" check box is selected, the background color of the content pane, the label, and the check boxes turns yellow. When this check box is deselected, the background colors go back to light gray. When the "Red foreground" check box is selected, the color of the text displayed in the label and the check boxes turns red. When this check box is deselected, the foreground colors go back to black.

Code Listing 12-15   (`ColorCheckBoxWindow.java`)

```java
 1 import javax.swing.*;
 2 import java.awt.*;
 3 import java.awt.event.*;
 4
 5 /**
 6    The ColorCheckBoxWindow class demonstrates how check boxes
 7    can be used.
 8 */
 9
10 public class ColorCheckBoxWindow extends JFrame
11 {
12    private JLabel messageLabel;      // A message to the user
13    private JCheckBox yellowCheckBox; // To select yellow background
14    private JCheckBox redCheckBox;    // To select red foreground
15    private final int WINDOW_WIDTH = 300;    // Window width
16    private final int WINDOW_HEIGHT = 100;   // Window height
17
18    /**
19       Constructor
20    */
21
22    public ColorCheckBoxWindow()
23    {
24       // Set the text for the title bar.
25       setTitle("Color Check Boxes");
26
27       // Set the size of the window.
28       setSize(WINDOW_WIDTH, WINDOW_HEIGHT);
29
30       // Specify an action for the close button.
31       setDefaultCloseOperation(JFrame.EXIT_ON_CLOSE);
32
33       // Create a label.
34       messageLabel = new JLabel("Select the check " +
35                                  "boxes to change colors.");
36
37       // Create the check boxes.
38       yellowCheckBox = new JCheckBox("Yellow background");
39       redCheckBox = new JCheckBox("Red foreground");
40
41       // Add an item listener to the check boxes.
42       yellowCheckBox.addItemListener(new CheckBoxListener());
43       redCheckBox.addItemListener(new CheckBoxListener());
44
45       // Add a FlowLayout manager to the content pane.
46       setLayout(new FlowLayout());
```

```
47
48      // Add the label and check boxes to the content pane.
49      add(messageLabel);
50      add(yellowCheckBox);
51      add(redCheckBox);
52
53      // Display the window.
54      setVisible(true);
55   }
56
57   /**
58      Private inner class that handles the event when
59      the user clicks one of the check boxes.
60   */
61
62   private class CheckBoxListener implements ItemListener
63   {
64      public void itemStateChanged(ItemEvent e)
65      {
66         // Determine which check box was clicked.
67         if (e.getSource() == yellowCheckBox)
68         {
69            // Is the yellow check box selected? If so, we
70            // want to set the background color to yellow.
71            if (yellowCheckBox.isSelected())
72            {
73               // The yellow check box was selected. Set
74               // the background color for the content
75               // pane and the two check boxes to yellow.
76               getContentPane().setBackground(Color.YELLOW);
77               yellowCheckBox.setBackground(Color.YELLOW);
78               redCheckBox.setBackground(Color.YELLOW);
79            }
80            else
81            {
82               // The yellow check box was deselected. Set
83               // the background color for the content
84               // pane and the two check boxes to light gray.
85               getContentPane().setBackground(Color.LIGHT_GRAY);
86               yellowCheckBox.setBackground(Color.LIGHT_GRAY);
87               redCheckBox.setBackground(Color.LIGHT_GRAY);
88            }
89         }
90         else if (e.getSource() == redCheckBox)
91         {
92            // Is the red check box selected? If so, we want
93            // to set the foreground color to red.
94            if (redCheckBox.isSelected())
```

```
 95                 {
 96                     // The red check box was selected. Set the
 97                     // foreground color for the label and the
 98                     // two check boxes to red.
 99                     messageLabel.setForeground(Color.RED);
100                     yellowCheckBox.setForeground(Color.RED);
101                     redCheckBox.setForeground(Color.RED);
102                 }
103                 else
104                 {
105                     // The red check box was deselected. Set the
106                     // foreground color for the label and the
107                     // two check boxes to black.
108                     messageLabel.setForeground(Color.BLACK);
109                     yellowCheckBox.setForeground(Color.BLACK);
110                     redCheckBox.setForeground(Color.BLACK);
111                 }
112             }
113         }
114     }
115
116     /**
117         The main method creates an instance of the
118         ColorCheckBoxWindow class, displaying its window.
119     */
120
121     public static void main(String[] args)
122     {
123         new ColorCheckBoxWindow();
124     }
125 }
```

Figure 12-28 Window displayed by the `ColorCheckBoxWindow` class   (Oracle Corporate Counsel)

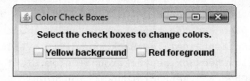

Selecting a Check Box in Code

As with radio buttons, it is possible to select check boxes in code with the `JCheckBox` class's `doClick` method. When the method is called, the radio check box is selected just as if the user had clicked on it. As a result, an item event is generated. In the following statement, the checkBox variable references a JCheckBox object. When this statement executes, the check box will be selected.

    checkBox.doClick();

 Checkpoint

MyProgrammingLab™ *www.myprogramminglab.com*

12.18 You want the user to be able to select only one item from a group of items. Which type of component would you use for the items, radio buttons or check boxes?

12.19 You want the user to be able to select any number of items from a group of items. Which type of component would you use for the items, radio buttons or check boxes?

12.20 What is the purpose of a ButtonGroup object?

12.21 Do you normally add radio buttons, check boxes, or both to a ButtonGroup object?

12.22 What type of event does a radio button generate when the user clicks on it?

12.23 What type of event does a check box generate when the user clicks on it?

12.24 How do you determine in code whether a radio button is selected?

12.25 How do you determine in code whether a check box is selected?

 12.5 Borders

CONCEPT: A component can appear with several different styles of borders around it. A **Border** object specifies the details of a border. You use the **BorderFactory** class to create **Border** objects.

Sometimes it is helpful to place a border around a component or a group of components on a panel. You can give windows a more organized look by grouping related components inside borders. For example, Figure 12-29 shows a group of check boxes that are enclosed in a border. In addition, notice that the border has a title.

Figure 12-29   A group of check boxes with a titled border

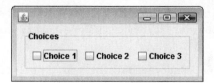

JPanel components have a method named setBorder, which is used to add a border to the panel. The setBorder method accepts a Border object as its argument. A Border object contains detailed information describing the appearance of a border.

Rather than creating Border objects yourself, you should use the BorderFactory class to create them for you. The BorderFactory class has methods that return various types of borders. Table 12-6 describes borders that can be created with the `BorderFactory` class. The table also lists the `BorderFactory` methods that can be called to create the borders. Note that there are several overloaded versions of each method.

NOTE: If you use the `BorderFactory` class in your code, you should have the following import statement: `import javax.swing.*;`

Table 12-6 Borders produced by the `BorderFactory` class

Border	`BorderFactory` Method	Description
Compound border	createCompoundBorder	A border that has two parts: an inside edge and an outside edge. The inside and outside edges can be any of the other borders.
Empty border	createEmptyBorder	A border that contains only empty space.
Etched border	createEtchedBorder	A border with a 3-D appearance that looks "etched" into the background.
Line border	createLineBorder	A border that appears as a line.
Lowered bevel border	createLoweredBevelBorder	A border that looks like beveled edges. It has a 3-D appearance that gives the illusion of being sunken into the surrounding background.
Matte border	createMatteBorder	A line border that can have edges of different thicknesses.
Raised bevel border	createRaisedBevelBorder	A border that looks like beveled edges. It has a 3-D appearance that gives the illusion of being raised above the surrounding background.
Titled border	createTitledBorder	An etched border with a title.

In this chapter, we will concentrate on empty borders, line borders, and titled borders.

Empty Borders

An empty border is simply empty space around the edges of a component. To create an empty border, call the `BorderFactory` class's `createEmtpyBorder` method. Here is the method's general format:

```
BorderFactory.createEmptyBorder(int top, int left,
                                int bottom, int right);
```

The arguments passed into `top`, `left`, `bottom`, and `right` specify in pixels the size of the border's top, left, bottom, and right edges. The method returns a reference to a `Border` object. The following is an example of a statement that uses the method. Assume that the `panel` variable references a `JPanel` object.

```
panel.setBorder(BorderFactory.createEmptyBorder(5, 5, 5, 5));
```

After this statement executes, the JPanel referenced by panel will have an empty border of five pixels around each edge.

> **NOTE:** In case you've skipped ahead to this chapter, the BorderFactory methods are static, which means that you call them without creating an instance of the BorderFactory class. (You simply write *BorderFactory.* before the method name to call the method.) This is similar to the way the Math class and wrapper class methods we have discussed are called. Static methods are covered in Chapter 8.

Line Borders

A line border is a line of a specified color and thickness that appears around the edges of a component. To create a line border, call the BorderFactory class's createLineBorder method. Here is the method's general format:

```
BorderFactory.createLineBorder(Color color, int thickness);
```

The arguments passed into color and thickness specify the color of the line and the size of the line in pixels. The method returns a reference to a Border object. The following is an example of a statement that uses the method. Assume that the panel variable references a JPanel object.

```
panel.setBorder(BorderFactory.createLineBorder(Color.RED, 1));
```

After this statement executes, the JPanel referenced by panel will have a red line border that is one pixel thick around its edges.

Titled Borders

A titled border is an etched border with a title displayed on it. To create a titled border, call the BorderFactory class's createTitledBorder method. Here is the method's general format:

```
BorderFactory.createTitledBorder(String title);
```

The argument passed into title is the text that is to be displayed as the border's title. The method returns a reference to a Border object. The following is an example of a statement that uses the method. Assume that the panel variable references a JPanel object.

```
panel.setBorder(BorderFactory.createTitledBorder("Choices"));
```

After this statement executes, the JPanel referenced by panel will have an etched border with the title "Choices" displayed on it.

Checkpoint

MyProgrammingLab™ *www.myprogramminglab.com*

12.26 What method do you use to set a border around a component?

12.27 What is the preferred way of creating a Border object?

12.6 Focus on Problem Solving: Extending Classes from JPanel

CONCEPT: By writing a class that is extended from the JPanel class, you can create a custom panel component that can hold other components and their related code.

In the applications that you have studied so far in this chapter, we have used the extends JFrame clause in the class header to extend the class from the JFrame class. Recall that the extended class is then a specialized version of the JFrame class, and we use its constructor to create the panels, buttons, and all of the other components needed. This approach works well for simple applications. But for applications that use many components, this approach can be cumbersome. Bundling all of the code and event listeners for a large number of components into a single class can lead to a large and complex class. A better approach is to encapsulate smaller groups of related components and their event listeners into their own classes.

A commonly used technique is to extend a class from the JPanel class. This allows you to create your own specialized panel component, which can contain other components and related code such as event listeners. A complex application that uses numerous components can be constructed from several specialized panel components. In this section we will examine such an application.

The Brandi's Bagel House Application

Brandi's Bagel House has a bagel and coffee delivery service for the businesses in her neighborhood. Customers may call in and order white and whole wheat bagels with a variety of toppings. In addition, customers may order three different types of coffee. (Delivery for coffee alone is not available, however.) Here is a complete price list:

Bagels: *White bagel $1.25, whole wheat bagel $1.50*
Toppings: *Cream cheese $0.50, butter $0.25, peach jelly $0.75, blueberry jam $0.75*
Coffee: *Regular coffee $1.25, decaf coffee $1.25, cappuccino $2.00*

Brandi, the owner, needs an "order calculator" application that her staff can use to calculate the price of an order as it is called in. The application should display the subtotal, the amount of a 6 percent sales tax, and the total of the order. Figure 12-30 shows a sketch of the application's window. The user selects the type of bagel, toppings, and coffee, then clicks the Calculate button. A dialog box appears displaying the subtotal, amount of sales tax, and total. The user can exit the application by clicking either the Exit button or the standard close button in the upper-right corner.

The layout shown in the sketch can be achieved using a BorderLayout manager with the window's content pane. The label that displays "Welcome to Brandi's Bagel House" is in the north region, the radio buttons for the bagel types are in the west region, the check boxes for the toppings are in the center region, the radio buttons for the coffee selection are in the east region, and the Calculate and Exit buttons are in the south region. To construct this window, we create the following specialized panel classes that are extended from JPanel:

Figure 12-30   Sketch of the Order Calculator window   (Oracle Corporate Counsel)

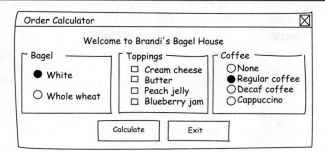

- **GreetingsPanel.** This panel contains the label that appears in the window's north region.
- **BagelPanel.** This panel contains the radio buttons for the types of bagels.
- **ToppingPanel.** This panel contains the check boxes for the types of bagels.
- **CoffeePanel.** This panel contains the radio buttons for the coffee selections.

(We will not create a specialized panel for the Calculate and Exit buttons. The reason is explained later.) After these classes have been created, we can create objects from them and add the objects to the correct regions of the window's content pane. Let's take a closer look at each of these classes.

The GreetingPanel Class

The GreetingPanel class holds the label displaying the text "Welcome to Brandi's Bagel House". Code Listing 12-16 shows the class, which extends JPanel.

Code Listing 12-16   **(GreetingPanel.java)**

```
1   import javax.swing.*;
2
3   /**
4      The GreetingPanel class displays a greeting in a panel.
5   */
6
7   public class GreetingPanel extends JPanel
8   {
9      private JLabel greeting; // To display a greeting
10
11     /**
12        Constructor
13     */
14
15     public GreetingPanel()
16     {
17        // Create the label.
```

```
18              greeting = new JLabel("Welcome to Brandi's Bagel House");
19
20              // Add the label to this panel.
21              add(greeting);
22          }
23      }
```

In line 21 the add method is called to add the JLabel component referenced by greeting. Notice that we are calling the method without an object reference and a dot preceding it. This is because the method was inherited from the JPanel class, and we can call it just as if it were written into the GreetingPanel class declaration.

When we create an instance of this class, we are creating a JPanel component that displays a label with the text "Welcome to Brandi's Bagel House". Figure 12-31 shows how the component will appear when it is placed in the window's north region.

Figure 12-31   Appearance of the GreetingPanel component

Welcome to Brandi's Bagel House

The BagelPanel Class

The BagelPanel class holds the radio buttons for the types of bagels. Notice that this panel uses a GridLayout manager with two rows and one column. Code Listing 12-17 shows the class, which is extended from JPanel.

Code Listing 12-17   (BagelPanel.java)

```java
1   import javax.swing.*;
2   import java.awt.*;
3
4   /**
5      The BagelPanel class allows the user to select either
6      a white or whole wheat bagel.
7   */
8
9   public class BagelPanel extends JPanel
10  {
11     // The following constants are used to indicate
12     // the cost of each type of bagel.
13     public final double WHITE_BAGEL = 1.25;
14     public final double WHEAT_BAGEL = 1.50;
15
16     private JRadioButton whiteBagel;  // To select white
17     private JRadioButton wheatBagel;  // To select wheat
```

```
18     private ButtonGroup bg;              // Radio button group
19
20     /**
21        Constructor
22     */
23
24     public BagelPanel()
25     {
26        // Create a GridLayout manager with
27        // two rows and one column.
28        setLayout(new GridLayout(2, 1));
29
30        // Create the radio buttons.
31        whiteBagel = new JRadioButton("White", true);
32        wheatBagel = new JRadioButton("Wheat");
33
34        // Group the radio buttons.
35        bg = new ButtonGroup();
36        bg.add(whiteBagel);
37        bg.add(wheatBagel);
38
39        // Add a border around the panel.
40        setBorder(BorderFactory.createTitledBorder("Bagel"));
41
42        // Add the radio buttons to the panel.
43        add(whiteBagel);
44        add(wheatBagel);
45     }
46
47     /**
48        getBagelCost method
49        @return The cost of the selected bagel.
50     */
51
52     public double getBagelCost()
53     {
54        double bagelCost = 0.0;
55
56        if (whiteBagel.isSelected())
57           bagelCost = WHITE_BAGEL;
58        else
59           bagelCost = WHEAT_BAGEL;
60
61        return bagelCost;
62     }
63 }
```

Notice that the `whiteBagel` radio button is automatically selected when it is created. This is the default choice. This class does not have an inner event listener class because we do not want to execute any code when the user selects a bagel. Instead, we want this class to be able to report the cost of the selected bagel. That is the purpose of the `getBagelCost` method, which returns the cost of the selected bagel as a `double`. (This method will be called by the Calculate button's event listener.) Figure 12-32 shows how the component appears when it is placed in the window's west region.

Figure 12-32   Appearance of the `BagelPanel` component   (Oracle Corporate Counsel)

The `ToppingPanel` Class

The `ToppingPanel` class holds the check boxes for the available toppings. Code Listing 12-18 shows the class, which is also extended from `JPanel`.

Code Listing 12-18   (`ToppingPanel.java`)

```
1   import javax.swing.*;
2   import java.awt.*;
3
4   /**
5      The ToppingPanel class allows the user to select
6      the toppings for the bagel.
7   */
8
9   public class ToppingPanel extends JPanel
10  {
11     // The following constants are used to indicate
12     // the cost of toppings.
13     public final double CREAM_CHEESE = 0.50;
14     public final double BUTTER = 0.25;
15     public final double PEACH_JELLY = 0.75;
16     public final double BLUEBERRY_JAM = 0.75;
17
18     private JCheckBox creamCheese;        // To select cream cheese
19     private JCheckBox butter;             // To select butter
20     private JCheckBox peachJelly;         // To select peach jelly
21     private JCheckBox blueberryJam;       // To select blueberry jam
22
```

```java
23      /**
24          Constructor
25      */
26
27      public ToppingPanel()
28      {
29         // Create a GridLayout manager with
30         // four rows and one column.
31         setLayout(new GridLayout(4, 1));
32
33         // Create the check boxes.
34         creamCheese = new JCheckBox("Cream cheese");
35         butter = new JCheckBox("Butter");
36         peachJelly = new JCheckBox("Peach jelly");
37         blueberryJam = new JCheckBox("Blueberry jam");
38
39         // Add a border around the panel.
40         setBorder(BorderFactory.createTitledBorder("Toppings"));
41
42         // Add the check boxes to the panel.
43         add(creamCheese);
44         add(butter);
45         add(peachJelly);
46         add(blueberryJam);
47      }
48
49      /**
50          getToppingCost method
51          @return The cost of the selected toppings.
52      */
53
54      public double getToppingCost()
55      {
56         double toppingCost = 0.0;
57
58         if (creamCheese.isSelected())
59            toppingCost += CREAM_CHEESE;
60         if (butter.isSelected())
61            toppingCost += BUTTER;
62         if (peachJelly.isSelected())
63            toppingCost += PEACH_JELLY;
64         if (blueberryJam.isSelected())
65            toppingCost += BLUEBERRY_JAM;
66
67         return toppingCost;
68      }
69   }
```

As with the BagelPanel class, this class does not have an inner event listener class because we do not want to execute any code when the user selects a topping. Instead, we want this class to be able to report the total cost of all the selected toppings. That is the purpose of the getToppingCost method, which returns the cost of all the selected toppings as a double. (This method will be called by the Calculate button's event listener.) Figure 12-33 shows how the component appears when it is placed in the window's center region.

Figure 12-33   Appearance of the ToppingPanel component   (Oracle Corporate Counsel)

The CoffeePanel Class

The CoffeePanel class holds the radio buttons for the available coffee selections. Code Listing 12-19 shows the class, which extends JPanel.

Code Listing 12-19   (CoffeePanel.java)

```
1   import javax.swing.*;
2   import java.awt.*;
3
4   /**
5      The CoffeePanel class allows the user to select coffee.
6   */
7
8   public class CoffeePanel extends JPanel
9   {
10     // The following constants are used to indicate
11     // the cost of coffee.
12     public final double NO_COFFEE = 0.0;
13     public final double REGULAR_COFFEE = 1.25;
14     public final double DECAF_COFFEE = 1.25;
15     public final double CAPPUCCINO = 2.00;
16
17     private JRadioButton noCoffee;        // To select no coffee
18     private JRadioButton regularCoffee;   // To select regular coffee
19     private JRadioButton decafCoffee;     // To select decaf
20     private JRadioButton cappuccino;      // To select cappuccino
21     private ButtonGroup bg;               // Radio button group
22
23     /**
24        Constructor
```

```
25      */
26
27      public CoffeePanel()
28      {
29          // Create a GridLayout manager with
30          // four rows and one column.
31          setLayout(new GridLayout(4, 1));
32
33          // Create the radio buttons.
34          noCoffee = new JRadioButton("None");
35          regularCoffee = new JRadioButton("Regular coffee", true);
36          decafCoffee = new JRadioButton("Decaf coffee");
37          cappuccino = new JRadioButton("Cappuccino");
38
39          // Group the radio buttons.
40          bg = new ButtonGroup();
41          bg.add(noCoffee);
42          bg.add(regularCoffee);
43          bg.add(decafCoffee);
44          bg.add(cappuccino);
45
46          // Add a border around the panel.
47          setBorder(BorderFactory.createTitledBorder("Coffee"));
48
49          // Add the radio buttons to the panel.
50          add(noCoffee);
51          add(regularCoffee);
52          add(decafCoffee);
53          add(cappuccino);
54      }
55
56      /**
57         getCoffeeCost method
58         @return The cost of the selected coffee.
59      */
60
61      public double getCoffeeCost()
62      {
63          double coffeeCost = 0.0;
64
65          if (noCoffee.isSelected())
66              coffeeCost = NO_COFFEE;
67          else if (regularCoffee.isSelected())
68              coffeeCost = REGULAR_COFFEE;
69          else if (decafCoffee.isSelected())
70              coffeeCost = DECAF_COFFEE;
71          else if (cappuccino.isSelected())
72              coffeeCost = CAPPUCCINO;
```

```
73
74        return coffeeCost;
75    }
76 }
```

As with the `BagelPanel` and `ToppingPanel` classes, this class does not have an inner event listener class because we do not want to execute any code when the user selects coffee. Instead, we want this class to be able to report the cost of the selected coffee. The `getCoffeeCost` method returns the cost of the selected coffee as a `double`. (This method will be called by the Calculate button's event listener.) Figure 12-34 shows how the component appears when it is placed in the window's east region.

Figure 12-34 Appearance of the `CoffeePanel` component

Putting It All Together

The last step in creating this application is to write a class that builds the application's window and adds the Calculate and Exit buttons. This class, which we name `OrderCalculatorGUI`, is extended from `JFrame` and uses a `BorderLayout` manager with its content pane. Figure 12-35 shows how instances of the `GreetingPanel`, `BagelPanel`, `ToppingPanel`, and `CoffeePanel` classes are placed in the content pane.

Figure 12-35 Placement of the custom panels

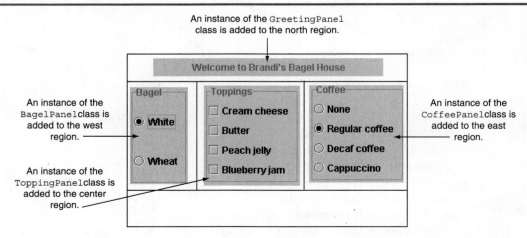

We have not created a custom panel class to hold the Calculate and Exit buttons. The reason is that the Calculate button's event listener must call the `getBagelCost`, `getToppingCost`, and `getCoffeeCost` methods. In order to call those methods, the event listener must have access to the `BagelPanel`, `ToppingPanel`, and `CoffeePanel` objects that are created in the `OrderCalculatorGUI` class. The approach taken in this example is to have the `OrderCalculatorGUI` class itself create the buttons. The code for the `OrderCalculatorGUI` class is shown in Code Listing 12-20.

Code Listing 12-20   **(OrderCalculatorGUI.java)**

```java
 1 import javax.swing.*;
 2 import java.awt.*;
 3 import java.awt.event.*;
 4
 5 /**
 6    The OrderCalculatorGUI class creates the GUI for the
 7    Brandi's Bagel House application.
 8 */
 9
10 public class OrderCalculatorGUI extends JFrame
11 {
12    private BagelPanel bagels;       // Bagel panel
13    private ToppingPanel toppings;   // Topping panel
14    private CoffeePanel coffee;      // Coffee panel
15    private GreetingPanel banner;    // To display a greeting
16    private JPanel buttonPanel;      // To hold the buttons
17    private JButton calcButton;      // To calculate the cost
18    private JButton exitButton;      // To exit the application
19    private final double TAX_RATE = 0.06; // Sales tax rate
20
21    /**
22       Constructor
23    */
24
25    public OrderCalculatorGUI()
26    {
27       // Display a title.
28       setTitle("Order Calculator");
29
30       // Specify an action for the close button.
31       setDefaultCloseOperation(JFrame.EXIT_ON_CLOSE);
32
33       // Create a BorderLayout manager.
34       setLayout(new BorderLayout());
```

```
35
36          // Create the custom panels.
37          banner = new GreetingPanel();
38          bagels = new BagelPanel();
39          toppings = new ToppingPanel();
40          coffee = new CoffeePanel();
41
42          // Create the button panel.
43          buildButtonPanel();
44
45          // Add the components to the content pane.
46          add(banner, BorderLayout.NORTH);
47          add(bagels, BorderLayout.WEST);
48          add(toppings, BorderLayout.CENTER);
49          add(coffee, BorderLayout.EAST);
50          add(buttonPanel, BorderLayout.SOUTH);
51
52          // Pack the contents of the window and display it.
53          pack();
54          setVisible(true);
55      }
56
57      /**
58          The buildButtonPanel method builds the button panel.
59      */
60
61      private void buildButtonPanel()
62      {
63          // Create a panel for the buttons.
64          buttonPanel = new JPanel();
65
66          // Create the buttons.
67          calcButton = new JButton("Calculate");
68          exitButton = new JButton("Exit");
69
70          // Register the action listeners.
71          calcButton.addActionListener(new CalcButtonListener());
72          exitButton.addActionListener(new ExitButtonListener());
73
74          // Add the buttons to the button panel.
75          buttonPanel.add(calcButton);
76          buttonPanel.add(exitButton);
77      }
78
79      /**
80          Private inner class that handles the event when
81          the user clicks the Calculate button.
```

```
82     */
83
84     private class CalcButtonListener implements ActionListener
85     {
86        public void actionPerformed(ActionEvent e)
87        {
88           // Variables to hold the subtotal, tax, and total
89           double subtotal, tax, total;
90
91           // Calculate the subtotal.
92           subtotal = bagels.getBagelCost() +
93                      toppings.getToppingCost() +
94                      coffee.getCoffeeCost();
95
96           // Calculate the sales tax.
97           tax = subtotal * TAX_RATE;
98
99           // Calculate the total.
100          total = subtotal + tax;
101
102          // Display the charges.
103          JOptionPane.showMessageDialog(null,
104             String.format("Subtotal: $%,.2f\n" +
105                           "Tax: $%,.2f\n" +
106                           "Total: $%,.2f",
107                           subtotal, tax, total));
108       }
109    }
110
111    /**
112       Private inner class that handles the event when
113       the user clicks the Exit button.
114    */
115
116    private class ExitButtonListener implements ActionListener
117    {
118       public void actionPerformed(ActionEvent e)
119       {
120          System.exit(0);
121       }
122    }
123
124    /**
125       main method
126    */
127
```

```
128    public static void main(String[] args)
129    {
130        new OrderCalculatorGUI();
131    }
132 }
```

When the application runs, the window shown in Figure 12-36 appears. Figure 12-37 shows the `JOptionPane` dialog box that is displayed when the user selects a wheat bagel with butter, cream cheese, and decaf coffee.

Figure 12-36 The Order Calculator window   (Oracle Corporate Counsel)

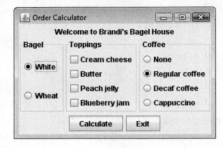

Figure 12-37 The subtotal, tax, and total displayed   (Oracle Corporate Counsel)

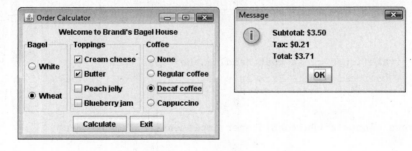

12.7 Splash Screens

CONCEPT: A splash screen is a graphic image that is displayed while an application loads into memory and starts up.

Most major applications display a splash screen, which is a graphic image that is displayed while the application is loading into memory. Splash screens usually show company logos and keep the user's attention while the application starts up. Splash screens are particularly important for large applications that take a long time to load, because they assure the user that the program is not malfunctioning.

Beginning with Java 6, you can display splash screens with your Java applications. First, you have to use a graphics program to create the image that you want to display. Java supports splash screens in the GIF, PNG, or JPEG formats. (If you are using Windows, you can create images with Microsoft Paint, which supports all of these formats.)

To display the splash screen you use the java command in the following way when you run the application:

```
java -splash:GraphicFileName ClassFileName
```

GraphicFileName is the name of the file that contains the graphic image, and *ClassFileName* is the name of the *.class* file that you are running. For example, in the same source code folder as the *Brandi's Bagel House* application, you will find a file named *BrandiLogo.jpg*. This image, which is shown in Figure 12-38, is a logo for the *Brandi's Bagel House* application. To display the splash screen when the application starts, you would use the following command:

```
java splash:BrandiLogo.jpg Bagel
```

When you run this command, the graphic file will immediately be displayed in the center of the screen. It will remain displayed until the application's window appears.

Figure 12-38 Splash screen for the *Brandi's Bagel House* application   (Oracle Corporate Counsel)

12.8 Using Console Output to Debug a GUI Application

CONCEPT: When debugging a GUI application, you can use `System.out.println` to send diagnostic messages to the console.

When an application is not performing correctly, programmers sometimes write statements that display *diagnostic messages* into the application. For example, if an application is not giving the correct result for a calculation, diagnostic messages can be displayed at various points in the program's execution showing the values of all the variables used in the calculation. If the trouble is caused by a variable that has not been properly initialized, or that has not been assigned the correct value, the diagnostic messages reveal this problem. This helps the programmer see what is going on "under the hood" while an application is running.

The `System.out.println` method can be a valuable tool for displaying diagnostic messages in a GUI application. Because the `System.out.println` method sends its output to the console, diagnostic messages can be displayed without interfering with the application's GUI windows.

Code Listing 12-21 shows an example. This is a modified version of the `KiloConverter` class, discussed earlier in this chapter. Inside the `actionPerformed` method, which is in the `CalcButtonListener` inner class, calls to the `System.out.println` method have been written. The new code, which appears in lines 99 through 104 and 113 through 115, is shown in bold. These new statements display the value that the application has retrieved from the text field, and is working within its calculation. (This file is stored in the source code folder *Chapter 12\KiloConverter Phase 3*.)

Code Listing 12-21   **(KiloConverter.java)**

```java
 1 import javax.swing.*;     // Needed for Swing classes
 2 import java.awt.event.*;  // Needed for ActionListener Interface
 3
 4 /**
 5    The KiloConverter class displays a JFrame that
 6    lets the user enter a distance in kilometers. When
 7    the Calculate button is clicked, a dialog box is
 8    displayed with the distance converted to miles.
 9 */
10
11 public class KiloConverter extends JFrame
12 {
13    private JPanel panel;           // To reference a panel
14    private JLabel messageLabel;    // To reference a label
15    private JTextField kiloTextField; // To reference a text field
16    private JButton calcButton;     // To reference a button
17    private final int WINDOW_WIDTH = 310;  // Window width
18    private final int WINDOW_HEIGHT = 100; // Window height
19
20    /**
21       Constructor
22    */
23
24    public KiloConverter()
25    {
26       // Set the window title.
27       setTitle("Kilometer Converter");
28
29       // Set the size of the window.
30       setSize(WINDOW_WIDTH, WINDOW_HEIGHT);
31
32       // Specify what happens when the close button is clicked.
33       setDefaultCloseOperation(JFrame.EXIT_ON_CLOSE);
```

```
34
35          // Build the panel and add it to the frame.
36          buildPanel();
37
38          // Add the panel to the frame's content pane.
39          add(panel);
40
41          // Display the window.
42          setVisible(true);
43       }
44
45    /**
46       The buildPanel method adds a label, a text field,
47       and a button to a panel.
48    */
49
50    private void buildPanel()
51    {
52       // Create a label to display instructions.
53       messageLabel = new JLabel("Enter a distance " +
54                                 "in kilometers");
55
56       // Create a text field 10 characters wide.
57       kiloTextField = new JTextField(10);
58
59       // Create a button with the caption "Calculate".
60       calcButton = new JButton("Calculate");
61
62       // Add an action listener to the button.
63       calcButton.addActionListener(new CalcButtonListener());
64
65       // Create a JPanel object and let the panel
66       // field reference it.
67       panel = new JPanel();
68
69       // Add the label, text field, and button
70       // components to the panel.
71       panel.add(messageLabel);
72       panel.add(kiloTextField);
73       panel.add(calcButton);
74    }
75
76    /**
77       CalcButtonListener is an action listener class for
78       the Calculate button.
79    */
80
81    private class CalcButtonListener implements ActionListener
```

```
 82   {
 83      /**
 84         The actionPerformed method executes when the user
 85         clicks on the Calculate button.
 86         @param e The event object.
 87      */
 88
 89      public void actionPerformed(ActionEvent e)
 90      {
 91         final double CONVERSION = 0.6214;
 92         String input;  // To hold the user's input
 93         double miles;  // The number of miles
 94
 95         // Get the text entered by the user into the
 96         // text field.
 97         input = kiloTextField.getText();
 98
 99         // For debugging, display the text entered, and
100         // its value converted to a double.
101         System.out.println("Reading " + input +
102                             " from the text field.");
103         System.out.println("Converted value: " +
104                             Double.parseDouble(input));
105
106         // Convert the input to miles.
107         miles = Double.parseDouble(input) * CONVERSION;
108
109         // Display the result.
110         JOptionPane.showMessageDialog(null, input +
111               " kilometers is " + miles + " miles.");
112
113         // For debugging, display a message indicating
114         // the application is ready for more input.
115         System.out.println("Ready for the next input.");
116      }
117   } // End of CalcButtonListener class
118
119   /**
120      The main method creates an instance of the
121      KiloConverter class, which displays
122      its window on the screen.
123   */
124
125   public static void main(String[] args)
126   {
127      new KiloConverter();
128   }
129 }
```

Let's take a closer look. In lines 101 and 102, a message is displayed to the console showing the value that was read from the text field. In lines 103 and 104, another message is displayed showing the value after it is converted to a double. Then, in line 115, a message is displayed indicating that the application is ready for its next input. Figure 12-39 shows an example session with the application on a computer running Microsoft Windows. Both the console window and the application windows are shown.

Figure 12-39 Messages displayed to the console during the application's execution

1. A command is typed in the console window to execute the application. The application's window appears.

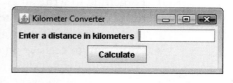

2. The user types a value into the text field and clicks the Calculate button. Debugging messages appear in the console window, and a message dialog appears showing the value converted to miles.

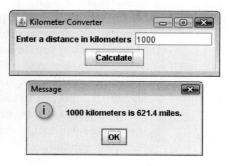

3. The user dismisses the dialog box and a message is displayed in the console window indicating that the application is ready for the next input.

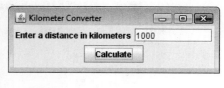

The messages that are displayed to the console are meant for only the programmer to see, while he or she is debugging the application. Once the programmer is satisfied that the application is running correctly, the calls to System.out.println can be taken out.

12.9   Common Errors to Avoid

- **Misspelling `javax.swing` in an `import` statement.** Don't forget the letter x that appears after java in this import statement.
- **Forgetting to specify the action taken when the user clicks on a `JFrame`'s close button.** By default, a window is hidden from view when the close button is clicked, but the application is not terminated. If you wish to exit the application when a `JFrame`'s close button is clicked, you must call the `setDefaultCloseOperation` method and pass `JFrame.EXIT_ON_CLOSE` as the argument.
- **Forgetting to write an event listener for each event you wish an application to respond to.** In order to respond to an event, you must write an event listener that implements the proper type of interface, registered to the component that generates the event.
- **Forgetting to register an event listener.** Even if you write an event listener, it will not execute unless it has been registered with the correct component.
- **When writing an event listener method that is required by an interface, not using the method header specified by the interface.** The header of an `actionPerformed` method must match that specified by the `ActionListener` interface. Also, the header of an `itemStateChanged` method must match that specified by the `ItemListener` method.
- **Placing components directly into the regions of a container governed by a `BorderLayout` manager when you do not want the components resized or you want to add more than one component per region.** If you do not want the components that you place in a `BorderLayout` region to be resized, place them in a `JPanel` component and then add the `JPanel` component to the region.
- **Placing components directly into the cells of a container governed by a `GridLayout` manager when you do not want the components resized or you want to add more than one component per cell.** If you do not want the components that you place in a `GridLayout` cell to be resized, place them in a `JPanel` component, and then add the `JPanel` component to the cell.
- **Forgetting to add `JRadioButton` components to a `ButtonGroup` object.** A mutually exclusive relationship is created between radio buttons only when they are added to a `ButtonGroup` object.

Review Questions and Exercises

Multiple Choice and True/False

1. With Swing, you use this class to create a frame.
   a. `Frame`
   b. `SwingFrame`
   c. `JFrame`
   d. `JavaFrame`

2. This is the part of a `JFrame` object that holds the components that have been added to the `JFrame` object.
   a. content pane
   b. viewing area
   c. component array
   d. object collection

3. This is a `JPanel` object's default layout manager.
   a. `BorderLayout`
   b. `GridLayout`
   c. `FlowLayout`
   d. None

4. This is the default layout manager for a `JFrame` object's content pane.
   a. `BorderLayout`
   b. `GridLayout`
   c. `FlowLayout`
   d. None

5. If a container is governed by a `BorderLayout` manager and you add a component to it, but you do not pass the second argument specifying the region, this is the region in which the component will be added.
   a. north
   b. south
   c. east
   d. center

6. Components in this/these regions of a `BorderLayout` manager are resized horizontally so they fill up the entire region.
   a. north and south
   b. east and west
   c. center only
   d. north, south, east, and west

7. Components in this/these regions of a `BorderLayout` manager are resized vertically so they fill up the entire region.
   a. north and south
   b. east and west
   c. center only
   d. north, south, east, and west

8. Components in this/these regions of a `BorderLayout` manager are resized both horizontally and vertically so they fill up the entire region.
   a. north and south
   b. east and west
   c. center only
   d. north, south, east, and west

9. This is the default alignment of a `FlowLayout` manager.
   a. left
   b. center
   c. right
   d. no alignment

10. Adding radio button components to this type of object creates a mutually exclusive relationship between them.
    a. `MutualExclude`
    b. `RadioGroup`
    c. `LogicalGroup`
    d. `ButtonGroup`

11. You use this class to create Border objects.
    a. BorderFactory
    b. BorderMaker
    c. BorderCreator
    d. BorderSource

12. **True or False:** A panel cannot be displayed by itself.

13. **True or False:** You can place multiple components inside a GridLayout cell.

14. **True or False:** You can place multiple components inside a BorderLayout region.

15. **True or False:** You can place multiple components inside a container governed by a FlowLayout manager.

16. **True or False:** You can place a panel inside a region governed by a BorderLayout manager.

17. **True or False:** A component placed in a GridLayout manager's cell will not be resized to fill up any extra space in the cell.

18. **True or False:** You normally add JCheckBox components to a ButtonGroup object.

19. **True or False:** A mutually exclusive relationship is automatically created among all JRadioButton components in the same container.

20. **True or False:** You can write a class that extends the JPanel class.

Find the Error

1. The following statement is in a class that uses Swing components:

```
import java.swing.*;
```

2. The following is an inner class that will be registered as an action listener for a JButton component:

```
private class ButtonListener implements ActionListener
{
    public void actionPerformed()
    {
        // Code appears here.
    }
}
```

3. The intention of the following statement is to give the panel object a GridLayout manager with 10 columns and 5 rows:

```
panel.setLayout(new GridLayout(10, 5));
```

4. The panel variable references a JPanel governed by a BorderLayout manager. The following statement attempts to add the button component to the north region of panel:

```
panel.add(button, NORTH);
```

5. The panel variable references a JPanel object. The intention of the following statement is to create a titled border around panel:

```
panel.setBorder(new BorderFactory("Choices"));
```

Algorithm Workbench

1. The variable myWindow references a JFrame object. Write a statement that sets the size of the object to 500 pixels wide and 250 pixels high.

2. The variable myWindow references a JFrame object. Write a statement that causes the application to end when the user clicks on the JFrame object's close button.

3. The variable myWindow references a JFrame object. Write a statement that displays the object's window on the screen.

4. The variable myButton references a JButton object. Write the code to set the object's background color to white and foreground color to red.

5. Assume that a class inherits from the JFrame class. Write code that can appear in the class constructor, which gives the content pane a FlowLayout manager. Components added to the content pane should be aligned with the left edge of each row.

6. Assume that a class inherits from the JFrame class. Write code that can appear in the class constructor, which gives the content pane a GridLayout manager with five rows and 10 columns.

7. Assume that the variable panel references a JPanel object that uses a BorderLayout manager. In addition, the variable button references a JButton object. Write code that adds the button object to the panel object's west region.

8. Write code that creates three radio buttons with the text "Option 1", "Option 2", and "Option 3". The radio button that displays the text "Option 1" should be initially selected. Make sure these components are grouped so that a mutually exclusive relationship exists among them.

9. Assume that panel references a JPanel object. Write code that creates a two pixel thick blue line border around it.

Short Answer

1. If you do not change the default close operation, what happens when the user clicks on the close button on a JFrame object?

2. Why is it sometimes necessary to place a component inside a panel and then place the panel inside a container governed by a BorderLayout manager?

3. In what type of situation would you present a group of items to the user with radio buttons? With check boxes?

4. How can you create a specialized panel component that can be used to hold other components and their related code?

Programming Challenges

MyProgrammingLab™ *Visit www.myprogramminglab.com to complete many of these Programming Challenges online and get instant feedback.*

1. Retail Price Calculator

Create a GUI application where the user enters the wholesale cost of an item and its markup percentage into text fields. (For example, if an item's wholesale cost is $5 and its markup percentage is 100 percent, then its retail price is $10.) The application should have a button that displays the item's retail price when clicked.

2. Monthly Sales Tax

VideoNote
The Monthly
Sales Tax
Problem

A retail company must file a monthly sales tax report listing the total sales for the month, and the amount of state and county sales tax collected. The state sales tax rate is 4 percent and the county sales tax rate is 2 percent. Create a GUI application that allows the user to enter the total sales for the month into a text field. From this figure, the application should calculate and display the following:

- The amount of county sales tax
- The amount of state sales tax
- The total sales tax (county plus state)

In the application's code, represent the county tax rate (0.02) and the state tax rate (0.04) as named constants.

3. Property Tax

A county collects property taxes on the assessment value of property, which is 60 percent of the property's actual value. If an acre of land is valued at $10,000, its assessment value is $6,000. The property tax is then $0.64 for each $100 of the assessment value. The tax for the acre assessed at $6,000 will be $38.40. Create a GUI application that displays the assessment value and property tax when a user enters the actual value of a property.

4. Travel Expenses

Create a GUI application that calculates and displays the total travel expenses of a business person on a trip. Here is the information that the user must provide:

- Number of days on the trip
- Amount of airfare, if any
- Amount of car rental fees, if any
- Number of miles driven, if a private vehicle was used
- Amount of parking fees, if any
- Amount of taxi charges, if any
- Conference or seminar registration fees, if any
- Lodging charges, per night

The company reimburses travel expenses according to the following policy:

- $37 per day for meals
- Parking fees, up to $10.00 per day
- Taxi charges up to $20.00 per day
- Lodging charges up to $95.00 per day
- If a private vehicle is used, $0.27 per mile driven

The application should calculate and display the following:

- Total expenses incurred by the business person
- The total allowable expenses for the trip
- The excess that must be paid by the business person, if any
- The amount saved by the business person if the expenses are under the total allowed

5. Theater Revenue

A movie theater only keeps a percentage of the revenue earned from ticket sales. The remainder goes to the movie company. Create a GUI application that allows the user to enter the following data into text fields:

- Price per adult ticket
- Number of adult tickets sold
- Price per child ticket
- Number of child tickets sold

The application should calculate and display the following data for one night's box office business at a theater:

- **Gross revenue for adult tickets sold.** This is the amount of money taken in for all adult tickets sold.
- **Net revenue for adult tickets sold.** This is the amount of money from adult ticket sales left over after the payment to the movie company has been deducted.
- **Gross revenue for child tickets sold.** This is the amount of money taken in for all child tickets sold.
- **Net revenue for child tickets sold.** This is the amount of money from child ticket sales left over after the payment to the movie company has been deducted.
- **Total gross revenue.** This is the sum of gross revenue for adult and child tickets sold.
- **Total net revenue.** This is the sum of net revenue for adult and child tickets sold.

Assume the theater keeps 20 percent of its box office receipts. Use a constant in your code to represent this percentage.

6. Joe's Automotive

Joe's Automotive performs the following routine maintenance services:

- Oil change—$26.00
- Lube job—$18.00
- Radiator flush—$30.00
- Transmission flush—$80.00
- Inspection—$15.00
- Muffler replacement—$100.00
- Tire rotation—$20.00

Joe also performs other nonroutine services and charges for parts and for labor ($20 per hour). Create a GUI application that displays the total for a customer's visit to Joe's.

7. Long Distance Calls

A long-distance provider charges the following rates for telephone calls:

Rate Category	Rate per Minute
Daytime (6:00 A.M. through 5:59 P.M.)	$0.07
Evening (6:00 P.M. through 11:59 P.M.)	$0.12
Off-Peak (12:00 A.M. through 5:59 A.M.)	$0.05

Create a GUI application that allows the user to select a rate category (from a set of radio buttons), and enter the number of minutes of the call into a text field. A dialog box should display the charge for the call.

8. Latin Translator

Look at the following list of Latin words and their meanings.

Latin	English
sinister	left
dexter	right
medium	center

Write a GUI application that translates the Latin words to English. The window should have three buttons, one for each Latin word. When the user clicks a button, the program displays the English translation in a label.

9. MPG Calculator

Write a GUI application that calculates a car's gas mileage. The application should let the user enter the number of gallons of gas the car holds, and the number of miles it can be driven on a full tank. When a *Calculate MPG* button is clicked, the application should display the number of miles that the car may be driven per gallon of gas. Use the following formula to calculate MPG:

$$MPG = \frac{Miles}{Gallons}$$

10. Celsius to Fahrenheit

Write a GUI application that converts Celsius temperatures to Fahrenheit temperatures. The user should be able to enter a Celsius temperature, click a button, and then see the equivalent Fahrenheit temperature. Use the following formula to make the conversion:

$$F = \frac{9}{5} C + 32$$

F is the Fahrenheit temperature and C is the Celsius temperature.

CHAPTER

13 Advanced GUI Applications

TOPICS

13.1 The Swing and AWT Class Hierarchy

Now that you have used some of the fundamental GUI components, let's look at how they fit into the class hierarchy. Figure 13-1 shows the parts of the Swing and AWT class hierarchy that contain the JFrame, JPanel, JLabel, JTextField, JButton, JRadioButton, and JCheckBox classes. Because of the inheritance relationships that exist, there are many other classes in the figure as well.

The classes that are in the unshaded top part of the figure are AWT classes and are in the java.awt package. The classes that are in the shaded bottom part of the figure are Swing classes and are in the javax.swing package. Notice that all of the components we have dealt with ultimately inherit from the Component class.

Figure 13-1 Part of the Swing and AWT class hierarchy   (Oracle Corporate Counsel)

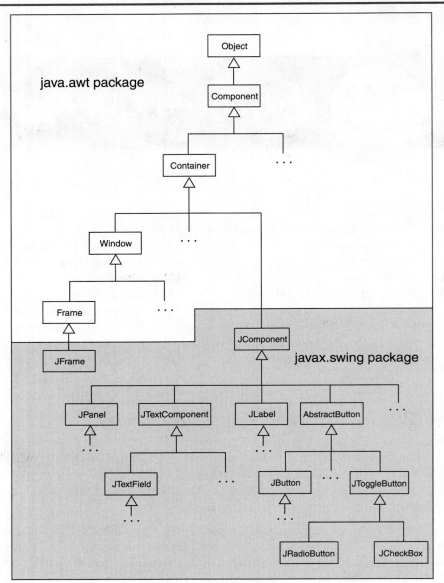

13.2 Read-Only Text Fields

CONCEPT: A read-only text field displays text that can be changed by code in the application, but cannot be edited by the user.

A read-only text field is not a new component, but a different way to use the JTextField component. The JTextField component has a method named setEditable, which has the following general format:

```
setEditable(boolean editable)
```

You pass a `boolean` argument to this method. By default a text field is editable, which means that the user can enter data into it. If you call the `setEditable` method and pass `false` as the argument, then the text field becomes read-only. This means it is not editable by the user. Figure 13-2 shows a window that has three read-only text fields.

Figure 13-2 A window with three read-only text fields   (Oracle Corporate Counsel)

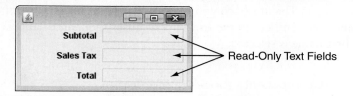

The following code could be used to create the read-only text fields shown in the figure:

```
// Create a read-only text field for the subtotal.
JTextField subtotalField = new JTextField(10);
subtotalField.setEditable(false);

// Create a read-only text field for the sales tax.
JTextField taxField = new JTextField(10);
taxField.setEditable(false);

// Create a read-only text field for the total.
JTextField totalField = new JTextField(10);
totalField.setEditable(false);
```

A read-only text field looks like a label with a border drawn around it. You can use the `setText` method to display data inside it. Here is an example:

```
subtotalField.setText("100.00");
taxField.setText("6.00");
totalField.setText("106.00");
```

This code causes the text fields to appear as shown in Figure 13-3.

Figure 13-3 Read-only text fields with data displayed   (Oracle Corporate Counsel)

13.3 Lists

> **CONCEPT:** A list component displays a list of items and allows the user to select an item from the list.

VideoNote

The JList Component

A list is a component that displays a list of items and also allows the user to select one or more items from the list. Java provides the JList component for creating lists. Figure 13-4 shows an example. The JList component in the figure shows a list of names. At runtime, the user may select an item in the list, which causes the item to appear highlighted. In the figure, the first name is selected.

Figure 13-4 A JList component (Oracle Corporate Counsel)

When you create an instance of the JList class, you pass an array of objects to the constructor. Here is the general format of the constructor call:

```
JList (Object[] array)
```

The JList component uses the array to create the list of items. In this text we always pass an array of String objects to the JList constructor. For example, the list component shown in Figure 13-4 could be created with the following code:

```
String[] names = { "Bill", "Geri", "Greg", "Jean",
                   "Kirk", "Phillip", "Susan" };
JList nameList = new JList(names);
```

Selection Modes

The JList component can operate in any of the following selection modes:

- Single Selection Mode. In this mode only one item can be selected at a time. When an item is selected, any other item that is currently selected is deselected.
- Single Interval Selection Mode. In this mode multiple items can be selected, but they must be in a single interval. An interval is a set of contiguous items.
- Multiple Interval Selection Mode. In this mode multiple items may be selected with no restrictions. This is the default selection mode.

Figure 13-5 shows an example of a list in each type of selection mode.

Figure 13-5 Selection modes (Oracle Corporate Counsel)

Single selection mode allows only one item to be selected at a time.

Single interval selection mode allows a single interval of contiguous items to be selected.

Multiple interval selection mode allows multiple items to be selected with no restrictions.

The default mode is multiple interval selection. To keep our applications simple, we will use single selection mode for now. You change a JList component's selection mode with the setSelectionMode method. The method accepts an int argument that determines the selection mode.

The ListSelectionModel class, which is in the javax.swing package, provides the following constants that you can use as arguments to the setSelectionMode method:

- ListSelectionModel.SINGLE_SELECTION
- ListSelectionModel.SINGLE_INTERVAL_SELECTION
- ListSelectionModel.MULTIPLE_INTERVAL_SELECTION

Assuming that nameList references a JList component, the following statement sets the component to single selection mode:

```
nameList.setSelectionMode(ListSelectionModel.SINGLE_SELECTION);
```

Responding to List Events

When an item in a JList object is selected it generates a list selection event. You handle list selection events with a list selection listener class, which must meet the following requirements:

- It must implement the ListSelectionListener interface.
- It must have a method named valueChanged. This method must take an argument of the ListSelectionEvent type.

NOTE: The ListSelectionListener interface is in the javax.swing.event package, so you must have an import statement for that package in your source code.

Once you have written a list selection listener class, you create an object of that class and then pass it as an argument to the JList component's addListSelectionListener method. When the JList component generates an event, it automatically executes the valueChanged method of the list selection listener object, passing the event object as an argument. You will see an example in a moment.

Retrieving the Selected Item

You may use either the `getSelectedValue` method or the `getSelectedIndex` method to determine which item in a list is currently selected. The `getSelectedValue` method returns a reference to the item that is currently selected. For example, assume that `nameList` references the `JList` component shown earlier in Figure 13-4. The following code retrieves a reference to the name that is currently selected and assigns it to the `selectedName` variable:

```
String selectedName;
selectedName = (String) nameList.getSelectedValue();
```

Note that the return value of the `getSelectedValue` method is an `Object` reference. In this code we had to cast the return value to the `String` type in order to store it in the `selectedName` variable. If no item in the list is selected, the method returns `null`.

The `getSelectedIndex` method returns the index of the selected item, or -1 if no item is selected. Internally, the items that are stored in a list are numbered. Each item's number is called its index. The first item (which is the item stored at the top of the list) has the index 0, the second item has the index 1, and so forth. You can use the index of the selected item to retrieve the item from an array. For example, assume that the following code was used to build the `nameList` component shown in Figure 13-4:

```
String[] names = { "Bill", "Geri", "Greg", "Jean",
                   "Kirk", "Phillip", "Susan" };
JList nameList = new JList(names);
```

Because the `names` array holds the values displayed in the `namesList` component, the following code could be used to determine the selected item:

```
int index;
String selectedName;
index = nameList.getSelectedIndex();
if (index != -1)
    selectedName = names[index];
```

The `ListWindow` class shown in Code Listing 13-1 demonstrates the concepts we have discussed so far. It uses a `JList` component with a list selection listener. When an item is selected from the list, it is displayed in a read-only text field. The `main` method creates an instance of the `ListWindow` class, which displays the window shown on the left in Figure 13-6. After the user selects October from the list, the window appears as that shown on the right in the figure.

Code Listing 13-1　**(ListWindow.java)**

```
1 import javax.swing.*;
2 import javax.swing.event.*;
3 import java.awt.*;
4
5 /**
6    This class demonstrates the List Component.
7 */
```

```
 8
 9  public class ListWindow extends JFrame
10  {
11      private JPanel monthPanel;              // To hold components
12      private JPanel selectedMonthPanel;      // To hold components
13      private JList monthList;                // The months
14      private JTextField selectedMonth;       // The selected month
15      private JLabel label;                   // A message
16
17      // The following array holds the values that will
18      // be displayed in the monthList list component.
19      private String[] months = { "January", "February",
20                          "March", "April", "May", "June", "July",
21                          "August", "September", "October", "November",
22                          "December" };
23
24      /**
25          Constructor
26      */
27
28      public ListWindow()
29      {
30          // Set the title.
31          setTitle("List Demo");
32
33          // Specify an action for the close button.
34          setDefaultCloseOperation(JFrame.EXIT_ON_CLOSE);
35
36          // Add a BorderLayout manager.
37          setLayout(new BorderLayout());
38
39          // Build the month and selectedMonth panels.
40          buildMonthPanel();
41          buildSelectedMonthPanel();
42
43          // Add the panels to the content pane.
44          add(monthPanel, BorderLayout.CENTER);
45          add(selectedMonthPanel, BorderLayout.SOUTH);
46
47          // Pack and display the window.
48          pack();
49          setVisible(true);
50      }
51
52      /**
53          The buildMonthPanel method adds a list containing
54          the names of the months to a panel.
55      */
```

```
56
57     private void buildMonthPanel()
58     {
59        // Create a panel to hold the list.
60        monthPanel = new JPanel();
61
62        // Create the list.
63        monthList = new JList(months);
64
65        // Set the selection mode to single selection.
66        monthList.setSelectionMode(
67                  ListSelectionModel.SINGLE_SELECTION);
68
69        // Register the list selection listener.
70        monthList.addListSelectionListener(
71                                  new ListListener());
72
73        // Add the list to the panel.
74        monthPanel.add(monthList);
75     }
76
77     /**
78        The buildSelectedMonthPanel method adds an
79        uneditable text field to a panel.
80     */
81
82     private void buildSelectedMonthPanel()
83     {
84        // Create a panel to hold the text field.
85        selectedMonthPanel = new JPanel();
86
87        // Create the label.
88        label = new JLabel("You selected: ");
89
90        // Create the text field.
91        selectedMonth = new JTextField(10);
92
93        // Make the text field uneditable.
94        selectedMonth.setEditable(false);
95
96        // Add the label and text field to the panel.
97        selectedMonthPanel.add(label);
98        selectedMonthPanel.add(selectedMonth);
99     }
100
101    /**
102       Private inner class that handles the event when
103       the user selects an item from the list.
```

```
104       */
105
106       private class ListListener
107                       implements ListSelectionListener
108       {
109          public void valueChanged(ListSelectionEvent e)
110          {
111             // Get the selected month.
112             String selection =
113                   (String) monthList.getSelectedValue();
114
115             // Put the selected month in the text field.
116             selectedMonth.setText(selection);
117          }
118       }
119
120       /**
121          The main method creates an instance of the
122          ListWindow class which causes it to display
123          its window.
124       */
125
126       public static void main(String[] args)
127       {
128             new ListWindow();
129       }
130    }
```

Figure 13-6 Window displayed by the `ListWindow` class   (Oracle Corporate Counsel)

Window as initially displayed.

Window after the user selects October.

Placing a Border around a List

As with other components, you can use the `setBorder` method, which was discussed in Chapter 12, to draw a border around a `JList`. For example the following statement can be used to draw a black 1-pixel thick line border around the `monthList` component:

```
monthList.setBorder(BorderFactory.createLineBorder(Color.BLACK, 1));
```

This code will cause the list to appear as shown in Figure 13-7.

Figure 13-7   List with a line border   (Oracle Corporate Counsel)

Adding a Scroll Bar to a List

By default, a list component is large enough to display all of the items it contains. Sometimes a list component contains too many items to be displayed at once, however. Most GUI applications display a scroll bar on list components that contain a large number of items. The user simply uses the scroll bar to scroll through the list of items.

List components do not automatically display a scroll bar. To display a scroll bar on a list component, you must follow the following general steps:

1. Set the number of visible rows for the list component.
2. Create a scroll pane object and add the list component to it.
3. Add the scroll pane object to any other containers, such as panels.

Let's take a closer look at how these steps can be used to apply a scroll bar to the list component created in the following code:

```
String[] names = { "Bill", "Geri", "Greg", "Jean",
                   "Kirk", "Phillip", "Susan" };
JList nameList = new JList(names);
```

First, we establish the size of the list component with the `JList` class's `setVisibleRowCount` method. The following statement sets the number of visible rows in the `nameList` component to three:

```
nameList.setVisibleRowCount(3);
```

This statement causes the nameList component to display only three items at a time.

Next, we create a scroll pane object and add the list component to it. A scroll pane object is a container that displays scroll bars on any component it contains. In Java we use the JScrollPane class to create a scroll pane object. We pass the object that we wish to add to the scroll pane as an argument to the JScrollPane constructor. The following statement demonstrates:

```
JScrollPane scrollPane = new JScrollPane(nameList);
```

This statement creates a JScrollPane object and adds the nameList component to it.

Next, we add the scroll pane object to any other containers that are necessary for our GUI. For example, the following code adds the scroll pane to a JPanel, which is then added to the JFrame object's content pane:

```
// Create a panel and add the scroll pane to it.
JPanel panel = new JPanel();
panel.add(scrollPane);

// Add the panel to this JFrame object's contentPane.
add(panel);
```

When the list component is displayed, it will appear as shown in Figure 13-8.

Although the list component displays only three items at a time, the user can scroll through all of the items it contains.

The ListWindowWithScroll class shown in Code Listing 13-2 is a modification of the ListWindow class. In this class, the monthList component shows only six items at a time, but displays a scroll bar. The code shown in bold is the new lines that are used to add the scroll bar to the list. The main method creates an instance of the class, which displays the window shown in Figure 13-9.

Figure 13-8   List component with a scroll bar   (Oracle Corporate Counsel)

Figure 13-9   List component with scroll bars   (Oracle Corporate Counsel)

Code Listing 13-2 (`ListWindowWithScroll.java`)

```java
 1 import javax.swing.*;
 2 import javax.swing.event.*;
 3 import java.awt.*;
 4
 5 /**
 6    This class demonstrates the List Component.
 7 */
 8
 9 public class ListWindowWithScroll extends JFrame
10 {
11    private JPanel monthPanel;           // To hold components
12    private JPanel selectedMonthPanel;   // To hold components
13    private JList monthList;             // The months
14    private JScrollPane scrollPane;      // A scroll pane
15    private JTextField selectedMonth;    // The selected month
16    private JLabel label;                // A message
17
18    // The following array holds the values that will
19    // be displayed in the monthList list component.
20    private String[] months = { "January", "February",
21             "March", "April", "May", "June", "July",
22             "August", "September", "October", "November",
23             "December" };
24
25    /**
26       Constructor
27    */
28
29    public ListWindowWithScroll()
30    {
31       // Set the title.
32       setTitle("List Demo");
33
34       // Specify an action for the close button.
35       setDefaultCloseOperation(JFrame.EXIT_ON_CLOSE);
36
37       // Add a BorderLayout manager.
38       setLayout(new BorderLayout());
39
40       // Build the month and selectedMonth panels.
41       buildMonthPanel();
42       buildSelectedMonthPanel();
43
44       // Add the panels to the content pane.
45       add(monthPanel, BorderLayout.CENTER);
```

```
46          add(selectedMonthPanel, BorderLayout.SOUTH);
47
48          // Pack and display the window.
49          pack();
50          setVisible(true);
51      }
52
53      /**
54          The buildMonthPanel method adds a list containing
55          the names of the months to a panel.
56      */
57
58      private void buildMonthPanel()
59      {
60          // Create a panel to hold the list.
61          monthPanel = new JPanel();
62
63          // Create the list.
64          monthList = new JList(months);
65
66          // Set the selection mode to single selection.
67          monthList.setSelectionMode(
68                  ListSelectionModel.SINGLE_SELECTION);
69
70          // Register the list selection listener.
71          monthList.addListSelectionListener(
72                                  new ListListener());
73
74          // Set the number of visible rows to 6.
75          monthList.setVisibleRowCount(6);
76
77          // Add the list to a scroll pane.
78          scrollPane = new JScrollPane(monthList);
79
80          // Add the scroll pane to the panel.
81          monthPanel.add(scrollPane);
82      }
83
84      /**
85          The buildSelectedMonthPanel method adds an
86          uneditable text field to a panel.
87      */
88
89      private void buildSelectedMonthPanel()
90      {
91          // Create a panel to hold the text field.
92          selectedMonthPanel = new JPanel();
```

```
 93
 94        // Create the label.
 95        label = new JLabel("You selected: ");
 96
 97        // Create the text field.
 98        selectedMonth = new JTextField(10);
 99
100        // Make the text field uneditable.
101        selectedMonth.setEditable(false);
102
103        // Add the label and text field to the panel.
104        selectedMonthPanel.add(label);
105        selectedMonthPanel.add(selectedMonth);
106    }
107
108    /**
109       Private inner class that handles the event when
110       the user selects an item from the list.
111    */
112
113    private class ListListener
114                      implements ListSelectionListener
115    {
116       public void valueChanged(ListSelectionEvent e)
117       {
118          // Get the selected month.
119          String selection =
120                 (String) monthList.getSelectedValue();
121
122          // Put the selected month in the text field.
123          selectedMonth.setText(selection);
124       }
125    }
126
127    /**
128       The main method creates an instance of the
129       ListWindowWithScroll class which causes it
130       to display its window.
131    */
132
133    public static void main(String[] args)
134    {
135       new ListWindowWithScroll();
136    }
137 }
```

NOTE: By default, when a JList component is added to a JScrollPane object, the scroll bar is only displayed when there are more items in the list than there are visible rows.

 NOTE: When a JList component is added to a JScrollPane object, a border will automatically appear around the list.

Adding Items to an Existing JList Component

The JList class's setListData method allows you to store items in an existing JList component. Here is the method's general format:

```
void setListData(Object[] data)
```

The argument passed into data is an array of objects that will become the items displayed in the JList component. Any items that are currently displayed in the component will be replaced by the new items.

In addition to replacing the existing items in a list, you can use this method to add items to an empty list. You can create an empty list by passing no argument to the JList constructor. Here is an example:

```
JList nameList = new JList();
```

This statement creates an empty JList component referenced by the nameList variable. You can then add items to the list, as shown here:

```
String[] names = { "Bill", "Geri", "Greg", "Jean",
                   "Kirk", "Phillip", "Susan" };
nameList.setListData(names);
```

Multiple Selection Lists

For simplicity, the previous examples used a JList component in single selection mode. Recall that the other two selection modes are single interval and multiple interval. Both of these modes allow the user to select multiple items. Let's take a closer look at each of these modes.

Single Interval Selection Mode

You put a JList component in single interval selection mode by passing the constant ListSelectionModel.SINGLE_INTERVAL_SELECTION to the component's setSelectionMode method. In single interval selection mode, single or multiple items can be selected. An interval is a set of contiguous items. (See Figure 13-5 to see an example of an interval.)

To select an interval of items, the user selects the first item in the interval by clicking on it, and then selects the last item in the interval by holding down the Shift key while clicking on it. All of the items that appear in the list from the first item through the last item are selected.

In single interval selection mode, the getSelectedValue method returns the first item in the selected interval. The getSelectedIndex method returns the index of the first item in the selected interval. To get the entire selected interval, use the getSelectedValues method. This method returns an array of objects. The array will hold the items in the selected interval. You can also use the getSelectedIndices method, which returns an array of int values. The values in the array will be the indices of all the selected items in the list.

Multiple Interval Selection Mode

You put a JList component in multiple interval selection mode by passing the constant ListSelectionModel.MULTIPLE_INTERVAL_SELECTION to the component's setSelectionMode method. In multiple interval selection mode, multiple items can be selected and the items do not have to be in the same interval. (See Figure 13-5 for an example.)

In multiple interval selection mode, the user can select single items or intervals. When the user holds down the Ctrl key while clicking on an item, it selects the item without deselecting any items that are currently selected. This allows the user to select multiple items that are not in an interval.

In multiple interval selection mode, the getSelectedValue method returns the first selected item. The getSelectedIndex method returns the index of the first selected item. The getSelectedValues method returns an array of objects containing the items that are selected. The getSelectedIndices method returns an int array containing the indices of all the selected items in the list.

The MultipleIntervalSelection class, shown in Code Listing 13-3, demonstrates a JList component used in multiple interval selection mode. The main method creates an instance of the class that displays the window shown on the left in Figure 13-10. When the user selects items from the top JList component and then clicks the Get Selections button, the selected items appear in the bottom JList component.

Code Listing 13-3   (MultipleIntervalSelection.java)

```
1 import javax.swing.*;
2 import java.awt.*;
3 import java.awt.event.*;
4
5 /**
6    This class demonstrates the List Component in
7    multiple interval selection mode.
8 */
9
10 public class MultipleIntervalSelection extends JFrame
11 {
12    private JPanel monthPanel;          // To hold components
13    private JPanel selectedMonthPanel;  // To hold components
14    private JPanel buttonPanel;         // To hold the button
15
```

```
16    private JList monthList;              // To hold months
17    private JList selectedMonthList;      // Selected months
18
19    private JScrollPane scrollPane1;      // Scroll pane - first list
20    private JScrollPane scrollPane2;      // Scroll pane - second list
21
22    private JButton button;               // A button
23
24    // The following array holds the values that
25    // will be displayed in the monthList list component.
26    private String[] months = { "January", "February",
27              "March", "April", "May", "June", "July",
28              "August", "September", "October", "November",
29              "December" };
30
31    /**
32       Constructor
33    */
34
35    public MultipleIntervalSelection()
36    {
37       // Set the title.
38       setTitle("List Demo");
39
40       // Specify an action for the close button.
41       setDefaultCloseOperation(JFrame.EXIT_ON_CLOSE);
42
43       // Add a BorderLayout manager.
44       setLayout(new BorderLayout());
45
46       // Build the panels.
47       buildMonthPanel();
48       buildSelectedMonthsPanel();
49       buildButtonPanel();
50
51       // Add the panels to the content pane.
52       add(monthPanel, BorderLayout.NORTH);
53       add(selectedMonthPanel,BorderLayout.CENTER);
54       add(buttonPanel, BorderLayout.SOUTH);
55
56       // Pack and display the window.
57       pack();
58       setVisible(true);
59    }
60
61    /**
62       The buildMonthPanel method adds a list containing the
63       names of the months to a panel.
```

```
64      */
65
66      private void buildMonthPanel()
67      {
68         // Create a panel to hold the list.
69         monthPanel = new JPanel();
70
71         // Create the list.
72         monthList = new JList(months);
73
74         // Set the selection mode to multiple
75         // interval selection.
76         monthList.setSelectionMode(
77           ListSelectionModel.MULTIPLE_INTERVAL_SELECTION);
78
79         // Set the number of visible rows to 6.
80         monthList.setVisibleRowCount(6);
81
82         // Add the list to a scroll pane.
83         scrollPane1 = new JScrollPane(monthList);
84
85         // Add the scroll pane to the panel.
86         monthPanel.add(scrollPane1);
87      }
88
89      /**
90         The buildSelectedMonthsPanel method adds a list
91         to a panel. This will hold the selected months.
92      */
93
94      private void buildSelectedMonthsPanel()
95      {
96         // Create a panel to hold the list.
97         selectedMonthPanel = new JPanel();
98
99         // Create the list.
100        selectedMonthList = new JList();
101
102        // Set the number of visible rows to 6.
103        selectedMonthList.setVisibleRowCount(6);
104
105        // Add the list to a scroll pane.
106        scrollPane2 =
107                new JScrollPane(selectedMonthList);
108
109        // Add the scroll pane to the panel.
110        selectedMonthPanel.add(scrollPane2);
```

```
111      }
112
113      /**
114         The buildButtonPanel method adds a
115         button to a panel.
116      */
117
118      private void buildButtonPanel()
119      {
120         // Create a panel to hold the list.
121         buttonPanel = new JPanel();
122
123         // Create the button.
124         button = new JButton("Get Selections");
125
126         // Add an action listener to the button.
127         button.addActionListener(new ButtonListener());
128
129         // Add the button to the panel.
130         buttonPanel.add(button);
131      }
132
133      /**
134         Private inner class that handles the event when
135         the user clicks the button.
136      */
137
138      private class ButtonListener implements ActionListener
139      {
140         public void actionPerformed(ActionEvent e)
141         {
142            // Get the selected values.
143            Object[] selections =
144                          monthList.getSelectedValues();
145
146            // Store the selected items in selectedMonthList.
147            selectedMonthList.setListData(selections);
148         }
149      }
150
151      /**
152         The main method creates an instance of the
153         MultipleIntervalSelection class which causes it
154         to display its window.
155      */
156
157      public static void main(String[] args)
```

```
158    {
159        new MultipleIntervalSelection();
160    }
161 }
```

Figure 13-10   The window displayed by the `MultipleIntervalSelection` class   (Oracle Corporate Counsel)

This is the window as it is intially displayed.

This is the window after the user has selected some items from the top list and clicked the Get Selections button.

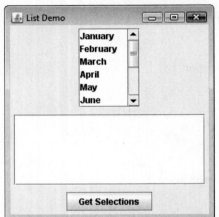
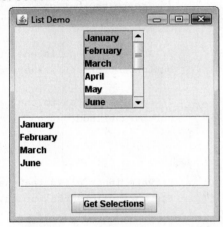

13.4 Combo Boxes

CONCEPT: A combo box allows the user to select an item from a drop-down list.

VideoNote

The JComboBox Component

A combo box presents a list of items that the user may select from. Unlike a list component, a combo box presents its items in a drop-down list. You use the `JComboBox` class, which is in the `javax.swing` package, to create a combo box. You pass an array of objects that are to be displayed as the items in the drop-down list to the constructor. Here is an example:

```
String[] names = { "Bill", "Geri", "Greg", "Jean",
                   "Kirk", "Phillip", "Susan" };
JComboBox nameBox = new JComboBox(names);
```

When displayed, the combo box created by this code will initially appear as the button shown on the left in Figure 13-11. The button displays the item that is currently selected. Notice that the first item in the list is automatically selected when the combo box is first displayed. When the user clicks the button, the drop-down list appears and the user may select another item.

Figure 13-11 A combo box

The combo box initially appears as a button that displays the selected item.

When the user clicks on the button, the list of items drops down. The user may select another item from the list.

As you can see, a combo box is a combination of two components. In the case of the combo box shown in Figure 13-11, it is the combination of a button and a list. This is where the name "combo box" comes from.

Responding to Combo Box Events

When an item in a `JComboBox` object is selected, it generates an action event. As with `JButton` components, you handle action events with an action event listener class, which must have an `actionPerformed` method. When the user selects an item in a combo box, the combo box executes its action event listener's `actionPerformed` method, passing an `ActionEvent` object as an argument.

Retrieving the Selected Item

There are two methods in the `JComboBox` class that you can use to determine which item in a combo box is currently selected: `getSelectedItem` and `getSelectedIndex`. The `getSelectedItem` method returns a reference to the item that is currently selected. For example, assume that `nameBox` references the `JComboBox` component shown earlier in Figure 13-11. The following code retrieves a reference to the name that is currently selected and assigns it to the `selectedName` variable:

```
String selectedName;
selectedName = (String) nameBox.getSelectedItem();
```

Note that the return value of the `getSelectedItem` method is an `Object` reference. In this code we had to cast the return value to the `String` type to store it in the `selectedName` variable.

The `getSelectedIndex` method returns the index of the selected item. As with `JList` components, the items that are stored in a combo box are numbered with indices that start at 0. You can use the index of the selected item to retrieve the item from an array. For example, assume that the following code was used to build the `nameBox` component shown in Figure 13-11:

```
String[] names = { "Bill", "Geri", "Greg", "Jean",
                   "Kirk", "Phillip", "Susan" };
JComboBox nameBox = new JComboBox(names);
```

Because the `names` array holds the values displayed in the `namesBox` component, the following code could be used to determine the selected item:

```
int index;
String selectedName;
index = nameList.getSelectedIndex();
selectedName = names[index];
```

The `ComboBoxWindow` class shown in Code Listing 13-4 demonstrates a combo box. It uses a `JComboBox` component with an action listener. When an item is selected from the combo box, it is displayed in a read-only text field. The `main` method creates an instance of the class, which initially displays the window shown at the top left of Figure 13-12. When the user clicks the combo box button, the drop-down list appears as shown in the top right of the figure. After the user selects Espresso from the list, the window appears as shown at the bottom of the figure.

Figure 13-12 The window displayed by the `ComboBoxWindow` class (Oracle Corporate Counsel)

This is the window that initially appears.

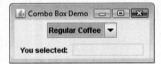

When the user clicks on the combo box button, the drop-down list appears.

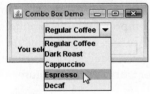

The item selected by the user appears in the read-only text field.

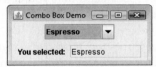

Code Listing 13-4 **(ComboBoxWindow.java)**

```
 1 import java.awt.*;
 2 import java.awt.event.*;
 3 import javax.swing.*;
 4
 5 /**
 6    This class demonstrates a combo box.
 7 */
 8
 9 public class ComboBoxWindow extends JFrame
10 {
```

```
11      private JPanel coffeePanel;            // To hold components
12      private JPanel selectedCoffeePanel;    // To hold components
13      private JComboBox coffeeBox;           // A list of coffees
14      private JLabel label;                  // Displays a message
15      private JTextField selectedCoffee;     // Selected coffee
16
17      // The following array holds the values that will
18      // be displayed in the coffeeBox combo box.
19      private String[] coffee = { "Regular Coffee",
20                                  "Dark Roast", "Cappuccino",
21                                  "Espresso", "Decaf"};
22
23      /**
24         Constructor
25      */
26
27      public ComboBoxWindow()
28      {
29         // Set the title.
30         setTitle("Combo Box Demo");
31
32         // Specify an action for the close button.
33         setDefaultCloseOperation(JFrame.EXIT_ON_CLOSE);
34
35         // Create a BorderLayout manager.
36         setLayout(new BorderLayout());
37
38         // Build the panels.
39         buildCoffeePanel();
40         buildSelectedCoffeePanel();
41
42         // Add the panels to the content pane.
43         add(coffeePanel, BorderLayout.CENTER);
44         add(selectedCoffeePanel, BorderLayout.SOUTH);
45
46         // Pack and display the window.
47         pack();
48         setVisible(true);
49      }
50
51      /**
52         The buildCoffeePanel method adds a combo box
53         with the types of coffee to a panel.
54      */
55
56      private void buildCoffeePanel()
57      {
58         // Create a panel to hold the combo box.
```

```
59          coffeePanel = new JPanel();
60
61          // Create the combo box.
62          coffeeBox = new JComboBox(coffee);
63
64          // Register an action listener.
65          coffeeBox.addActionListener(new ComboBoxListener());
66
67          // Add the combo box to the panel.
68          coffeePanel.add(coffeeBox);
69       }
70
71       /**
72          The buildSelectedCoffeePanel method adds a
73          read-only text field to a panel.
74       */
75
76       private void buildSelectedCoffeePanel()
77       {
78          // Create a panel to hold the components.
79          selectedCoffeePanel = new JPanel();
80
81          // Create the label.
82          label = new JLabel("You selected: ");
83
84          // Create the uneditable text field.
85          selectedCoffee = new JTextField(10);
86          selectedCoffee.setEditable(false);
87
88          // Add the label and text field to the panel.
89          selectedCoffeePanel.add(label);
90          selectedCoffeePanel.add(selectedCoffee);
91       }
92
93       /**
94          Private inner class that handles the event when
95          the user selects an item from the combo box.
96       */
97
98       private class ComboBoxListener
99                       implements ActionListener
100      {
101         public void actionPerformed(ActionEvent e)
102         {
103            // Get the selected coffee.
104            String selection =
105                    (String) coffeeBox.getSelectedItem();
106
```

```
107              // Display the selected coffee in the text field.
108              selectedCoffee.setText(selection);
109          }
110      }
111
112      /**
113          The main method creates an instance of the
114          ComboBoxWindow class, which causes it to display
115          its window.
116      */
117
118      public static void main(String[] args)
119      {
120          new ComboBoxWindow();
121      }
122  }
```

Editable Combo Boxes

There are two types of combo boxes: uneditable and editable. The default type of combo box is uneditable. An uneditable combo box combines a button with a list and allows the user to select items from its list only. This is the type of combo box used in the previous examples.

An editable combo box combines a text field and a list. In addition to selecting items from the list, the user may also type input into the text field. You make a combo box editable by calling the component's setEditable method, passing true as the argument. Here is an example:

```
String[] names = { "Bill", "Geri", "Greg", "Jean",
                   "Kirk", "Phillip", "Susan" };
JComboBox nameBox = new JComboBox(names);
nameBox.setEditable(true);
```

When displayed, the combo box created by this code initially appears as shown on the left of Figure 13-13. An editable combo box appears as a text field with a small button displaying an arrow joining it. The text field displays the item that is currently selected. When the user clicks the button, the drop-down list appears, as shown in the center of the figure. The user may select an item from the list. Alternatively, the user may type a value into the text field, as shown on the right of the figure. The user is not restricted to the values that appear in the list, and may type any input into the text field.

You can use the getSelectedItem method to retrieve a reference to the item that is currently selected. This method returns the item that appears in the combo box's text field, so it may or may not be an item that appears in the combo box's list.

The getSelectedIndex method returns the index of the selected item. However, if the user has entered a value in the text field that does not appear in the list, this method will return -1.

Figure 13-13 An editable combo box (Oracle Corporate Counsel)

The editable combo box initially appears as a text field that displays the selected item. A small button with an arrow appears next to the text field.

When the user clicks on the button, the list of items drops down. The user may select another item from the list.

Alternatively, the user may type input into the text field. The user may type a value that does not appear in the list.

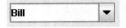

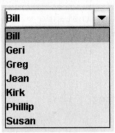

 Checkpoint

MyProgrammingLab™ *www.myprogramminglab.com*

13.1 How do you make a text field read-only? In code, how do you store text in a text field?

13.2 What is the index of the first item stored in a JList or a JComboBox component? If one of these components holds 12 items, what is the index of the 12th item?

13.3 How do you retrieve the selected item from a JList component? How do you get the index of the selected item?

13.4 How do you cause a scroll bar to be displayed with a JList component?

13.5 How do you retrieve the selected item from a JComboBox component? How do you get the index of the selected item?

13.6 What is the difference between an uneditable and an editable combo box? Which of these is a combo box by default?

13.5 Displaying Images in Labels and Buttons

CONCEPT: Images may be displayed in labels and buttons. You use the **ImageIcon** class to get an image from a file.

In addition to displaying text in a label, you can also display an image. For example, Figure 13-14 shows a window with two labels. The top label displays a smiley face image and no text. The bottom label displays a smiley face image and text.

Figure 13-14 Labels displaying an image icon (Oracle Corporate Counsel)

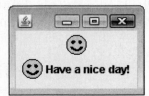

To display an image, first you create an instance of the `ImageIcon` class, which can read the contents of an image file. The `ImageIcon` class is part of the `javax.swing` package. The constructor accepts a `String` argument that is the name of an image file. The supported file types are JPEG, GIF, and PNG. The name can also contain path information. Here is an example:

```
ImageIcon image = new ImageIcon("Smiley.gif");
```

This statement creates an `ImageIcon` object that reads the contents of the file *Smiley.gif*. Because no path was given, it is assumed that the file is in the current directory or folder. Here is an example that uses a path:

```
ImageIcon image = new ImageIcon("C:\\Chapter 13\\Images\\Smiley.gif");
```

Next, you can display the image in a label by passing the `ImageIcon` object as an argument to the `JLabel` constructor. Here is the general format of the constructor:

```
JLabel(Icon image)
```

The argument passed to the image parameter can be an `ImageIcon` object or any object that implements the `Icon` interface. Here is an example:

```
ImageIcon image = new ImageIcon("Smiley.gif");
JLabel label = new JLabel(image);
```

This creates a label with an image, but no text. You can also create a label with both an image and text. An easy way to do this is to create the label with text, as usual, and then use the `JLabel` class's `setIcon` method to add an image to the label. The `setIcon` method accepts an `ImageIcon` object as its argument. Here is an example:

```
JLabel label = new JLabel("Have a nice day!");
label.setIcon(image);
```

The text will be displayed to the right of the image. The `JLabel` class also has the following constructor:

```
JLabel(String text, Icon image, int horizontalAlignment)
```

The first argument is the text to be displayed, the second argument is the image to be displayed, and the third argument is an `int` that specifies the horizontal alignment of the label contents. You should use the constants `SwingConstants.LEFT`, `SwingConstants.CENTER`, or `SwingConstants.RIGHT` to specify the horizontal alignment. Here is an example:

```
ImageIcon image = new ImageIcon("Smiley.gif");
JLabel label = new JLabel("Have a nice day!",
                          image,
                          SwingConstants.RIGHT);
```

You can also display images in buttons, as shown in Figure 13-15.

Figure 13-15 Buttons displaying an image icon (Oracle Corporate Counsel)

The process of creating a button with an image is similar to that of creating a label with an image. You use an `ImageIcon` object to read the image file, then pass the `ImageIcon` object as an argument to the `JButton` constructor. To create a button with an image and no text, pass only the `ImageIcon` object to the constructor. Here is an example:

```
// Create a button with an image, but no text.
ImageIcon image = new ImageIcon("Smiley.gif");
JButton button = new JButton(image);
```

To create a button with an image and text, pass a `String` and an `ImageIcon` object to the constructor. Here is an example:

```
// Create a button with an image and text.
ImageIcon image = new ImageIcon("Smiley.gif");
JButton button = new JButton("Have a nice day!", image);
```

To add an image to an existing button, pass an `ImageIcon` object to the button's `setIcon` method. Here is an example:

```
// Create a button with an image and text.
JButton button = new JButton("Have a nice day!");
ImageIcon image = new ImageIcon("Smiley.gif");
button.setIcon(image);
```

You are not limited to small graphical icons when placing images in labels or buttons. For example, the `MyCatImage` class in Code Listing 13-5 displays a digital photograph in a label when the user clicks a button. The `main` method creates an instance of the class, which displays the window shown at the left in Figure 13-16. When the user clicks the Get Image button, the window displays the image shown at the right in the figure.

Code Listing 13-5 (`MyCatImage.java`)

```
1 import java.awt.*;
2 import java.awt.event.*;
3 import javax.swing.*;
4
5 /**
6    This class demonstrates how to use an ImageIcon
7    and a JLabel to display an image.
8 */
9
```

```
10  public class MyCatImage extends JFrame
11  {
12     private JPanel imagePanel;        // To hold the label
13     private JPanel buttonPanel;       // To hold a button
14     private JLabel imageLabel;        // To show an image
15     private JButton button;           // To get an image
16
17
18     /**
19        Constructor
20     */
21
22     public MyCatImage()
23     {
24        // Set the title.
25        setTitle("My Cat");
26
27        // Specify an action for the close button.
28        setDefaultCloseOperation(JFrame.EXIT_ON_CLOSE);
29
30        // Create a BorderLayout manager.
31        setLayout(new BorderLayout());
32
33        // Build the panels.
34        buildImagePanel();
35        buildButtonPanel();
36
37        // Add the panels to the content pane.
38        add(imagePanel, BorderLayout.CENTER);
39        add(buttonPanel, BorderLayout.SOUTH);
40
41        // Pack and display the window.
42        pack();
43        setVisible(true);
44     }
45
46     /**
47        The buildImagePanel method adds a label to a panel.
48     */
49
50     private void buildImagePanel()
51     {
52        // Create a panel.
53        imagePanel = new JPanel();
54
55        // Create a label.
56        imageLabel = new JLabel("Click the button to " +
57                                "see an image of my cat.");
```

```
58
59          // Add the label to the panel.
60          imagePanel.add(imageLabel);
61      }
62
63      /**
64         The buildButtonPanel method adds a button
65         to a panel.
66      */
67
68      private void buildButtonPanel()
69      {
70          ImageIcon smileyImage;
71
72          // Create a panel.
73          buttonPanel = new JPanel();
74
75          // Get the smiley face image.
76          smileyImage = new ImageIcon("Smiley.gif");
77
78          // Create a button.
79          button = new JButton("Get Image");
80          button.setIcon(smileyImage);
81
82          // Register an action listener with the button.
83          button.addActionListener(new ButtonListener());
84
85          // Add the button to the panel.
86          buttonPanel.add(button);
87      }
88
89      /**
90         Private inner class that handles the event when
91         the user clicks the button.
92      */
93
94      private class ButtonListener implements ActionListener
95      {
96          public void actionPerformed(ActionEvent e)
97          {
98              // Read the image file into an ImageIcon object.
99              ImageIcon catImage = new ImageIcon("Cat.jpg");
100
101             // Display the image in the label.
102             imageLabel.setIcon(catImage);
103
104             // Remove the text from the label.
105             imageLabel.setText(null);
```

```
106    )
107            // Pack the frame again to accommodate the
108            // new size of the label.
109            pack();
110        }
111    }
112
113    /**
114       The main method creates an instance of the
115       MyCatImage class, which causes it to display
116       its window.
117    */
118    public static void main(String[] args)
119    {
120        new MyCatImage();
121    }
122 }
```

Figure 13-16   Window displayed by the `MyCatImage` class

This window initially appears.

When the user clicks the Get Image button, this image appears.

Let's take a closer look at the `MyCatImage` class. After some initial setup, the constructor calls the `buildImagePanel` method in line 34. Inside the `buildImagePanel` method, line 53 creates a `JPanel` component, referenced by the `imagePanel` variable, and then lines 56 and 57 create a `JLabel` component, referenced by the `imageLabel` variable. This is the label that will display the image when the user clicks the button. The last statement in the method, in line 60, adds the `imageLabel` component to the `imagePanel` panel.

Back in the constructor, line 35 calls the `buildButtonPanel` method, which creates the Get Image button and adds it to a panel. An instance of the `ButtonListener` inner class is also registered as the button's action listener. Let's look at the `ButtonListener` class's `actionPerformed` method. This method is executed when the user clicks the Get Image button. First, in line 99, an `ImageIcon` object is created from the file *Cat.jpg*. This file is in the same directory as the class. Next, in line 102, the image is stored in the `imageLabel` component. In line 105 the text that is currently displayed in the label is removed by passing `null` to the `imageLabel` component's `setText` method. The last statement, in line 109, calls the `JFrame` class's `pack` method. When the image was loaded into the `JLabel` component, the component resized itself to accommodate its new contents. The `JFrame` that encloses the window does not automatically resize itself, so we must call the `pack` method. This forces the `JFrame` to resize itself.

 Checkpoint

MyProgrammingLab™ *www.myprogramminglab.com*

13.7   How do you store an image in a `JLabel` component? How do you store both an image and text in a `JLabel` component?

13.8   How do you store an image in a `JButton` component? How do you store both an image and text in a `JButton` component?

13.9   What method do you use to store an image in an existing `JLabel` or `JButton` component?

 13.6   Mnemonics and Tool Tips

CONCEPT: A mnemonic is a key that you press while holding down the Alt key to interact with a component. A tool tip is text that is displayed in a small box when the user holds the mouse cursor over a component.

Mnemonics

A mnemonic is a key on the keyboard that you press in combination with the Alt key to access a component such as a button quickly. These are sometimes referred to as shortcut keys, or hot keys. When you assign a mnemonic to a button, the user can click the button by holding down the Alt key and pressing the mnemonic key. Although users can interact with components with either the mouse or their mnemonic keys, those who are quick with the keyboard usually prefer to use mnemonic keys instead of the mouse.

You assign a mnemonic to a component through the component's `setMnemonic` method, which is inherited from the `AbstractButton` class. The method's general format is as follows:

```
void setMnemonic(int key)
```

The argument that you pass to the method is an integer code that represents the key you wish to assign as a mnemonic. The `KeyEvent` class, which is in the `java.awt.event` package, has predefined constants that you can use. These constants take the form `KeyEvent.VK_x`, where x is a key on the keyboard. For example, to assign the A key as a mnemonic, you would use `KeyEvent.VK_A`. (The letters VK in the constants stand for "virtual key".) Here is an example of code that creates a button with the text "Exit" and assigns the X key as the mnemonic:

```
JButton exitButton = new JButton("Exit");
exitButton.setMnemonic(KeyEvent.VK_X);
```

The user may click this button by pressing +X on the keyboard. (This means holding down the Alt key and pressing X.)

If the letter chosen as the mnemonic is in the component's text, the first occurrence of that letter will appear underlined when the component is displayed. For example, the button created with the previous code has the text "Exit". Because X was chosen as the mnemonic, the letter x will appear underlined, as shown in Figure 13-17.

Figure 13-17   Button with mnemonic X   (Oracle Corporate Counsel)

If the mnemonic is a letter that does not appear in the component's text, then no letter will appear underlined.

> **NOTE:** The KeyEvent class also has constants for symbols. For example, the constant for the ! symbol is VK_EXCLAMATION_MARK, and the constant for the & symbol is VK_AMPERSAND. See the Java API documentation for the KeyEvent class for a list of all the constants.

You can also assign mnemonics to radio buttons and check boxes, as shown in the following code:

```
//Create three radio buttons and assign mnemonics.
JRadioButton rb1 = new JRadioButton("Breakfast");
rb1.setMnemonic(KeyEvent.VK_B);
JRadioButton rb2 = new JRadioButton("Lunch");
rb2.setMnemonic(KeyEvent.VK_L);
JRadioButton rb3 = new JRadioButton("Dinner");
rb3.setMnemonic(KeyEvent.VK_D);

// Create three check boxes and assign mnemonics.
JCheckBox cb1 = new JCheckBox("Monday");
cb1.setMnemonic(KeyEvent.VK_M);
JCheckBox cb2 = new JCheckBox("Wednesday");
cb2.setMnemonic(KeyEvent.VK_W);
JCheckBox cb3 = new JCheckBox("Friday");
cb3.setMnemonic(KeyEvent.VK_F);
```

This code will create the components shown in Figure 13-18.

Figure 13-18 Radio buttons and check boxes with mnemonics assigned (Oracle Corporate Counsel)

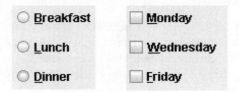

Tool Tips

A tool tip is text that is displayed in a small box when the user holds the mouse cursor over a component. The box usually gives a short description of what the component does. Most GUI applications use tool tips as a way of providing immediate and concise help to the user. For example, Figure 13-19 shows a button with its tool tip displayed.

Figure 13-19 Button with tool tip displayed (Oracle Corporate Counsel)

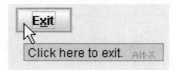

You assign a tool tip to a component with the setToolTipText method, which is inherited from the JComponent class. Here is the method's general format:

```
void setToolTipText(String text)
```

The String that is passed as an argument is the text that will be displayed in the component's tool tip. For example, the following code creates the Exit button shown in Figure 13-19 and its associated tool tip:

```
JButton exitButton = new JButton("Exit");
exitButton.setToolTipText("Click here to exit.");
```

 Checkpoint

 *www.myprogramminglab.com*

13.10 What is a mnemonic? How do you assign a mnemonic to a component?

13.11 What is a tool tip? How do you assign a tool tip to a component?

13.7 File Choosers and Color Choosers

CONCEPT: Java provides components that equip your applications with standard dialog boxes for opening files, saving files, and selecting colors.

File Choosers

A file chooser is a specialized dialog box that allows the user to browse for a file and select it. Figure 13-20 shows an example of a file chooser dialog box.

Figure 13-20   A file chooser dialog box for opening a file   (Oracle Corporate Counsel)

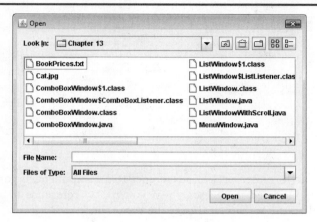

You create an instance of the JFileChooser class, which is part of the javax.swing package, to display a file chooser dialog box. The class has several constructors. We will focus on two of them, which have the following general formats:

```
JFileChooser()
JFileChooser(String path)
```

The first constructor shown takes no arguments. This constructor uses the default directory as the starting point for all of its dialog boxes. If you are using Windows, this will probably be the "My Documents" folder under your account. If you are using UNIX, this will be your login directory. The second constructor takes a String argument containing a valid path. This path will be the starting point for the object's dialog boxes.

A JFileChooser object can display two types of predefined dialog boxes: an open file dialog box and a save file dialog box. Figure 13-20 shows an example of an open file dialog box. It lets the user browse for an existing file to open. A save file dialog box, as shown in Figure 13-21, is employed when the user needs to browse to a location to save a file. Both of these dialog boxes appear the same, except the open file dialog box displays "Open" in its title bar, and the save file dialog box displays "Save." Also, the open file dialog box has an Open button, and the save file dialog box has a Save button. There is no difference in the way they operate.

Displaying a File Chooser Dialog Box

To display an open file dialog box, use the showOpenDialog method. The method's general format is as follows:

```
int showOpenDialog(Component parent)
```

Figure 13-21   A save file dialog box   (Oracle Corporate Counsel)

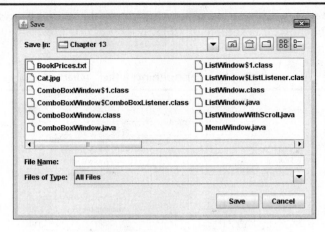

The argument can be either `null` or a reference to a component. If you pass `null`, the dialog box is normally centered in the screen. If you pass a reference to a component, such as `JFrame`, the dialog box is displayed over the component.

To display a save file dialog box, use the `showSaveDialog` method. The method's general format is as follows:

```
int showSaveDialog(Component parent)
```

Once again, the argument can be either `null` or a reference to a component. Both the `showOpenDialog` and `showSaveDialog` methods return an integer that indicates the action taken by the user to close the dialog box. You can compare the return value to one of the following constants:

- **`JFileChooser.CANCEL_OPTION`**. This return value indicates that the user clicked the Cancel button.
- **`JFileChooser.APPROVE_OPTION`**. This return value indicates that the user clicked the Open or Save button.
- **`JFileChooser.ERROR_OPTION`**. This return value indicates that an error occurred, or the user clicked the standard close button on the window to dismiss it.

If the user selected a file, you can use the `getSelectedFile` method to determine the file that was selected. The `getSelectedFile` method returns a `File` object, which contains data about the selected file. The `File` class is part of the `java.io` package. You can use the `File` object's `getPath` method to get the path and file name as a `String`. Here is an example:

```
JFileChooser fileChooser = new JFileChooser();
int status = fileChooser.showOpenDialog(null);
if (status == JFileChooser.APPROVE_OPTION)
{
    File selectedFile = fileChooser.getSelectedFile();
    String filename = selectedFile.getPath();
    JOptionPane.showMessageDialog(null, "You selected " + filename);
}
```

Color Choosers

A color chooser is a specialized dialog box that allows the user to select a color from a predefined palette of colors. Figure 13-22 shows an example of a color chooser. By clicking the HSB tab you can select a color by specifying its hue, saturation, and brightness. By clicking the RGB tab you can select a color by specifying its red, green, and blue components.

Figure 13-22 A color chooser dialog box   (Oracle Corporate Counsel)

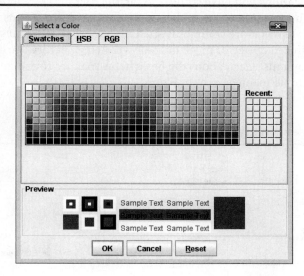

You use the `JColorChooser` class, which is part of the `javax.swing` package, to display a color chooser dialog box. You do not create an instance of the class, however. It has a static method named `showDialog`, with the following general format:

```
Color showDialog(Component parent, String title, Color initial)
```

The first argument can be either `null` or a reference to a component. If you pass `null`, the dialog box is normally centered in the screen. If you pass a reference to a component, such as `JFrame`, the dialog box is displayed over the component. The second argument is text that is displayed in the dialog box's title bar. The third argument indicates the color that appears initially selected in the dialog box. This method returns the color selected by the user. The following code is an example. This code allows the user to select a color, and then that color is assigned as a panel's background color.

```
JPanel panel = new JPanel();
Color selectedColor;
selectedColor = JColorChooser.showDialog(null,
             "Select a Background Color", Color.BLUE);
panel.setBackground(selectedColor);
```

13.8 Menus

CONCEPT: Java provides classes for creating systems of drop-down menus. Menus can contain menu items, checked menu items, radio button menu items, and other menus.

In the GUI applications you have studied so far, the user initiates actions by clicking components such as buttons. When an application has several operations for the user to choose from, a menu system is more commonly used than buttons. A menu system is a collection of commands organized in one or more drop-down menus. Before learning how to construct a menu system, you must learn about the basic items that are found in a typical menu system. Look at the example menu system in Figure 13-23.

Figure 13-23   Example menu system   (Oracle Corporate Counsel)

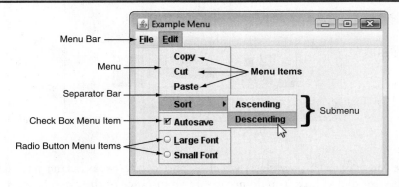

The menu system in the figure consists of the following items:

- **Menu Bar.** At the top of the window, just below the title bar, is a menu bar. The menu bar lists the names of one or more menus. The menu bar in Figure 13-23 shows the names of two menus: File and Edit.
- **Menu.** A menu is a drop-down list of menu items. The user may activate a menu by clicking on its name on the menu bar. In the figure, the Edit menu has been activated.
- **Menu Item.** A menu item can be selected by the user. When a menu item is selected, some type of action is usually performed.
- **Check box menu item.** A check box menu item appears with a small box beside it. The item may be selected or deselected. When it is selected, a check mark appears in the box. When it is deselected, the box appears empty. Check box menu items are normally used to turn an option on or off. The user toggles the state of a check box menu item each time he or she selects it.
- **Radio button menu item.** A radio button menu item may be selected or deselected. A small circle appears beside it that is filled in when the item is selected and empty when the item is deselected. Like a check box menu item, a radio button menu item can be used to turn an option on or off. When a set of radio button menu items are grouped

with a `ButtonGroup` object, only one of them can be selected at a time. When the user selects a radio button menu item, the one that was previously selected is deselected.

- **Submenu.** A menu within a menu is called a submenu. Some of the commands on a menu are actually the names of submenus. You can tell when a command is the name of a submenu because a small right arrow appears to its right. Activating the name of a submenu causes the submenu to appear. For example, in Figure 13-23, clicking on the Sort command causes a submenu to appear.
- **Separator bar.** A separator bar is a horizontal bar that is used to separate groups of items on a menu. Separator bars are only used as a visual aid and cannot be selected by the user.

A menu system is constructed with the following classes:

- **`JMenuItem`.** Use this class to create a regular menu item. A `JMenuItem` component generates an action event when the user selects it.
- **`JCheckBoxMenuItem`.** Use this class to create a check box menu item. The class's `isSelected` method returns `true` if the item is selected, or `false` otherwise. A `JCheckBoxMenuItem` component generates an action event when the user selects it.
- **`JRadioButtonMenuItem`.** Use this class to create a radio button menu item. `JRadioButtonMenuItem` components can be grouped in a `ButtonGroup` object so that only one of them can be selected at a time. The class's `isSelected` method returns `true` if the item is selected, or `false` otherwise. A `JRadioButtonMenuItem` component generates an action event when the user selects it.
- **`JMenu`.** Use this class to create a menu. A `JMenu` component can contain `JMenuItem`, `JCheckBoxMenuItem`, and `JRadioButton` components, as well as other `JMenu` components. A submenu is a `JMenu` component that is inside another `JMenu` component.
- **`JMenuBar`.** Use this class to create a menu bar. A `JMenuBar` object can contain `JMenu` components.

All of these classes are in the `javax.swing` package. A menu system is a `JMenuBar` component that contains one or more `JMenu` components. Each `JMenu` component can contain `JMenuItem`, `JRadioButtonMenuItem`, and `JCheckBoxMenuItem` components, as well as other `JMenu` components. The classes contain all of the code necessary to operate the menu system.

To see an example of an application that uses a menu system, we look at the `MenuWindow` class shown in Code Listing 13-6. The class displays the window shown in Figure 13-24.

Figure 13-24   Window displayed by the `MenuWindow` class

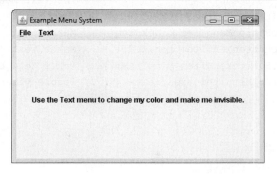

The class demonstrates how a label appears in different colors. Notice that the window has a menu bar with two menus: File and Text. Figure 13-25 shows a sketch of the menu system. When the user opens the Text menu, he or she can select a color using the radio button menu items and the label will change to the selected color. The Text menu also contains a Visible item, which is a check box menu item. When this item is selected (checked), the label is visible. When this item is deselected (unchecked), the label is invisible.

Figure 13-25 Sketch of the MenuWindow class's menu system   (Oracle Corporate Counsel)

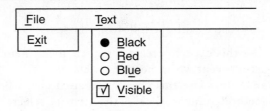

Code Listing 13-6   (MenuWindow.java)

```java
 1 import javax.swing.*;
 2 import java.awt.*;
 3 import java.awt.event.*;
 4
 5 /**
 6    The MenuWindow class demonstrates a menu system.
 7 */
 8
 9 public class MenuWindow extends JFrame
10 {
11    private JLabel messageLabel;           // Displays a message
12    private final int LABEL_WIDTH = 400;   // Label's width
13    private final int LABEL_HEIGHT = 200;  // Label's height
14
15    // The following will reference menu components.
16    private JMenuBar menuBar;              // The menu bar
17    private JMenu fileMenu;                // The File menu
18    private JMenu textMenu;                // The Text menu
19    private JMenuItem exitItem;            // To exit
20    private JRadioButtonMenuItem blackItem; // Makes text black
21    private JRadioButtonMenuItem redItem;  // Makes text red
22    private JRadioButtonMenuItem blueItem; // Makes text blue
23    private JCheckBoxMenuItem visibleItem; // Toggle visibility
24
25    /**
26       Constructor
27    */
28
```

```
29    public MenuWindow()
30    {
31       // Set the title.
32       setTitle("Example Menu System");
33
34       // Specify an action for the close button.
35       setDefaultCloseOperation(JFrame.EXIT_ON_CLOSE);
36
37       // Create the messageLabel label.
38       messageLabel = new JLabel("Use the Text menu to " +
39                   "change my color and make me invisible.",
40                   SwingConstants.CENTER);
41
42       // Set the label's preferred size.
43       messageLabel.setPreferredSize(
44                   new Dimension(LABEL_WIDTH, LABEL_HEIGHT));
45
46       // Set the label's foreground color.
47       messageLabel.setForeground(Color.BLACK);
48
49       // Add the label to the content pane.
50       add(messageLabel);
51
52       // Build the menu bar.
53       buildMenuBar();
54
55       // Pack and display the window.
56       pack();
57       setVisible(true);
58    }
59
60    /**
61       The buildMenuBar method builds the menu bar.
62    */
63
64    private void buildMenuBar()
65    {
66       // Create the menu bar.
67       menuBar = new JMenuBar();
68
69       // Create the file and text menus.
70       buildFileMenu();
71       buildTextMenu();
72
73       // Add the file and text menus to the menu bar.
74       menuBar.add(fileMenu);
75       menuBar.add(textMenu);
76
```

```
77          // Set the window's menu bar.
78          setJMenuBar(menuBar);
79       }
80
81       /**
82          The buildFileMenu method builds the File menu
83          and returns a reference to its JMenu object.
84       */
85
86       private void buildFileMenu()
87       {
88          // Create an Exit menu item.
89          exitItem = new JMenuItem("Exit");
90          exitItem.setMnemonic(KeyEvent.VK_X);
91          exitItem.addActionListener(new ExitListener());
92
93          // Create a JMenu object for the File menu.
94          fileMenu = new JMenu("File");
95          fileMenu.setMnemonic(KeyEvent.VK_F);
96
97          // Add the Exit menu item to the File menu.
98          fileMenu.add(exitItem);
99       }
100
101      /**
102         The buildTextMenu method builds the Text menu
103         and returns a reference to its JMenu object.
104      */
105
106      private void buildTextMenu()
107      {
108         // Create the radio button menu items to change
109         // the color of the text. Add an action listener
110         // to each one.
111         blackItem = new JRadioButtonMenuItem("Black", true);
112         blackItem.setMnemonic(KeyEvent.VK_B);
113         blackItem.addActionListener(new ColorListener());
114
115         redItem = new JRadioButtonMenuItem("Red");
116         redItem.setMnemonic(KeyEvent.VK_R);
117         redItem.addActionListener(new ColorListener());
118
119         blueItem = new JRadioButtonMenuItem("Blue");
120         blueItem.setMnemonic(KeyEvent.VK_U);
121         blueItem.addActionListener(new ColorListener());
122
123         // Create a button group for the radio button items.
124         ButtonGroup group = new ButtonGroup();
```

```
125        group.add(blackItem);
126        group.add(redItem);
127        group.add(blueItem);
128
129        // Create a check box menu item to make the text
130        // visible or invisible.
131        visibleItem = new JCheckBoxMenuItem("Visible", true);
132        visibleItem.setMnemonic(KeyEvent.VK_V);
133        visibleItem.addActionListener(new VisibleListener());
134
135        // Create a JMenu object for the Text menu.
136        textMenu = new JMenu("Text");
137        textMenu.setMnemonic(KeyEvent.VK_T);
138
139        // Add the menu items to the Text menu.
140        textMenu.add(blackItem);
141        textMenu.add(redItem);
142        textMenu.add(blueItem);
143        textMenu.addSeparator();     // Add a separator bar.
144        textMenu.add(visibleItem);
145    }
146
147    /**
148       Private inner class that handles the event that
149       is generated when the user selects Exit from
150       the File menu.
151    */
152
153    private class ExitListener implements ActionListener
154    {
155       public void actionPerformed(ActionEvent e)
156       {
157          System.exit(0);
158       }
159    }
160
161    /**
162       Private inner class that handles the event that
163       is generated when the user selects a color from
164       the Text menu.
165    */
166
167    private class ColorListener implements ActionListener
168    {
169       public void actionPerformed(ActionEvent e)
170       {
171          if (blackItem.isSelected())
172             messageLabel.setForeground(Color.BLACK);
```

```
173              else if (redItem.isSelected())
174                  messageLabel.setForeground(Color.RED);
175              else if (blueItem.isSelected())
176                  messageLabel.setForeground(Color.BLUE);
177          }
178      }
179
180      /**
181         Private inner class that handles the event that
182         is generated when the user selects Visible from
183         the Text menu.
184      */
185
186      private class VisibleListener implements ActionListener
187      {
188          public void actionPerformed(ActionEvent e)
189          {
190              if (visibleItem.isSelected())
191                  messageLabel.setVisible(true);
192              else
193                  messageLabel.setVisible(false);
194          }
195      }
196
197      /**
198         The main method creates an instance of the
199         MenuWindow class, which causes it to display
200         its window.
201      */
202
203      public static void main(String[] args)
204      {
205          MenuWindow mw = new MenuWindow();
206      }
207 }
```

Let's take a closer look at the MenuWindow class. Before we examine how the menu system is constructed, we should explain the code in lines 38 through 44. Lines 38 through 40 create the messageLabel component and align its text in the label's center. Then, in lines 43 and 44, the setPreferredSize method is called. The setPreferredSize method is inherited from the JComponent class, and it establishes a component's preferred size. It is called the *preferred size* because the layout manager adjusts the component's size when necessary. Normally, a label's preferred size is determined automatically, depending on its contents. We want to make this label larger, however, so the window will be larger when it is packed around the label.

The setPreferredSize method accepts a Dimension object as its argument. A Dimension object specifies a component's width and height. The first argument to the Dimension class constructor is the component's width, and the second argument is the component's height. In this class, the LABEL_WIDTH and LABEL_HEIGHT constants are defined with the values 400 and 200 respectively. So, this statement sets the label's preferred size to 400 pixels wide by 200 pixels high. (The Dimension class is part of the java.awt package.) Notice from Figure 13-24 that this code does not affect the size of the text that is displayed in the label, only the size of the label component.

To create the menu system, the constructor calls the buildMenuBar method in line 53. Inside this method, the statement in line 67 creates a JMenuBar component and assigns its address to the menuBar variable. The JMenuBar component acts as a container for JMenu components. The menu bar in this application has two menus: File and Text.

Next, the statement in line 70 calls the buildFileMenu method. The buildFileMenu method creates the File menu, which has only one item: Exit. The statement in line 89 creates a JMenuItem component for the Exit item, which is referenced by the exitItem variable. The String that is passed to the JMenuItem constructor is the text that will appear on a menu for this menu item. The statement in line 90 assigns the x key as a mnemonic to the exitItem component. Then, line 91 creates an action listener for the component (an instance of ExitListener, a private inner class), which causes the application to end.

Next, line 94 creates a JMenu object for the File menu. Notice that the name of the menu is passed as an argument to the JMenu constructor. Line 95 assigns the F key to the File menu as a mnemonic. The last statement in the buildFileMenu method, in line 98, adds exitItem to the fileMenu component.

Back in the buildMenuBar method, the statement in line 71 calls the buildTextMenu method. The buildTextMenu method builds the Text menu, which has three radio button menu items (Black, Red, and Blue), a separator bar, and a check box menu item (Visible). The code in lines 111 through 121 creates the radio button menu items, assigns mnemonic keys to them, and adds an action listener to each.

The JRadioButtonItem constructor accepts a String argument, which is the menu item's text. By default, a radio button menu item is not initially selected. The constructor can also accept an optional second argument, which is a boolean value indicating whether the item should be initially selected. Notice that in line 111, true is passed as the second argument to the JRadioButtonItem constructor. This causes the Black menu item to be initially selected.

Next, in lines 124 through 127, a button group is created and the radio button menu items are added to it. As with JRadioButton components, JRadioButtonMenuItem components may be grouped in a ButtonGroup object. As a result, only one of the grouped menu items may be selected at a time. When one is selected, any other menu item in the group is deselected.

Next, the Visible item, a check box menu item, is created in line 131. Notice that true is passed as the second argument to the constructor. This causes the item to be initially selected. A mnemonic key is assigned in line 132, and an action listener is added to the component in line 133.

Line 136 creates a JMenu component for the Text menu, and line 137 assigns a mnemonic key to it. Lines 140 through 142 add the blackItem, redItem, and blueItem radio button menu items to the Text menu. In line 143, the addSeparator method is called to add a separator bar to the menu. Because the addSeparator method is called just after the blueItem component is added and just before the visibleItem component is added, it will appear between the Blue and Visible items on the menu. Line 144 adds the Visible item to the Text menu.

Back in the buildMenuBar method, in lines 74 and 75, the File menu and Text menu are added to the menu bar. In line 78, the setJMenuBar method is called, passing menuBar as an argument. The setJMenuBar method is a JFrame method that places a menu bar in a frame. You pass a JMenuBar component as the argument. When the JFrame is displayed, the menu bar will appear at its top.

Figure 13-26 shows how the class's window appears with the File menu and the Text menu opened. Selecting a color from the Text menu causes an instance of the ColorListener class to execute its actionPerformed method, which changes the color of the text. Selecting the Visible item causes an instance of the VisibleListener class to execute its actionPerformed method, which toggles the label's visibility.

Figure 13-26 The window with the File menu and Text menu opened   (Oracle Corporate Counsel)

The window with the File menu opened.

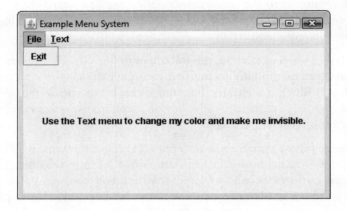

The window with the Text menu opened.

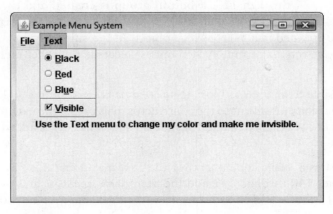

Checkpoint

MyProgrammingLab™ *www.myprogramminglab.com*

13.12 Briefly describe each of the following menu system items:
   a) Menu bar
   b) Menu item
   c) Check box menu item
   d) Radio button menu item
   e) Submenu
   f) Separator bar

13.13 What class do you use to create a regular menu item? What do you pass to the class constructor?

13.14 What class do you use to create a radio button menu item? What do you pass to the class constructor? How do you cause it to be initially selected?

13.15 How do you create a relationship between radio button menu items so that only one may be selected at a time?

13.16 What class do you use to create a check box menu item? What do you pass to the class constructor? How do you cause it to be initially selected?

13.17 What class do you use to create a menu? What do you pass to the class constructor?

13.18 What class do you use to create a menu bar?

13.19 How do you place a menu bar in a JFrame?

13.20 What type of event do menu items generate when selected by the user?

13.21 How do you change the size of a component such as a JLabel after it has been created?

13.22 What arguments do you pass to the Dimension class constructor?

13.9 More about Text Components: Text Areas and Fonts

CONCEPT: A text area is a multi-line text field that can accept several lines of text input. Components that inherit from the **JComponent** class have a **setFont** method that allows you to change the font and style of the component's text.

Text Areas

In Chapter 12, you were introduced to the JTextField class, which is used to create text fields. A text field is a component that allows the user to enter a single line of text. A text area is like a text field that can accept multiple lines of input. You use the JTextArea class to create a text area. Here is the general format of two of the class's constructors:

```
JTextArea(int rows, int columns)
JTextArea(String text, int rows, int columns)
```

In both constructors, rows is the number of rows or lines of text that the text area is to display, and columns is the number of columns or characters that are to be displayed per line. In the second constructor, text is a string that the text area will initially display. For example, the following statement creates a text area with 20 rows and 40 columns:

```
JTextArea textInput = new JTextArea(20, 40);
```

The following statement creates a text area with 20 rows and 40 columns that will initially display the text stored in the String object info:

```
JTextArea textInput = new JTextArea(info, 20, 40);
```

As with the JTextField class, the JTextArea class provides the getText and setText methods for getting and setting the text contained in the component. For example, the following statement gets the text stored in the textInput text area and stores it in the String object userText:

```
String userText = textInput.getText();
```

The following statement stores the text that is in the String object info in the textInput text area:

```
textInput.setText(info);
```

JTextArea components do not automatically display scroll bars. To display scroll bars on a JTextArea component, you must add it to the scroll pane. As you already know, you create a scroll pane with the JScrollPane class. Here is an example of code that creates a text area and adds it to a scroll pane:

```
JTextArea textInput = new JTextArea(20, 40);
JScrollPane scrollPane = new JScrollPane(textInput);
```

The JScrollPane object displays both vertical and horizontal scroll bars on a text area. By default, the scroll bars are not displayed until they are needed; however, you can alter this behavior with two of the JScrollPane class's methods. The setHorizontalScrollBarPolicy method takes an int argument that specifies when a horizontal scroll bar should appear in the scroll pane. You can pass one of the following constants as an argument:

- **JScrollPane.HORIZONTAL_SCROLLBAR_AS_NEEDED.** This is the default setting. A horizontal scroll bar is displayed only when there is not enough horizontal space to display the text contained in the text area.
- **JScrollPane.HORIZONTAL_SCROLLBAR_NEVER.** This setting prevents a horizontal scroll bar from being displayed in the text area.
- **JScrollPane.HORIZONTAL_SCROLLBAR_ALWAYS.** With this setting, a horizontal scroll bar is always displayed, even when it is not needed.

The setVerticalScrollBarPolicy method also takes an int argument, which specifies when a vertical scroll bar should appear in the scroll pane. You can pass one of the following constants as an argument:

- **JScrollPane.VERTICAL_SCROLLBAR_AS_NEEDED.** This is the default setting. A vertical scroll bar is displayed only when there is not enough vertical space to display the text contained in the text area.

- **JScrollPane.VERTICAL_SCROLLBAR_NEVER.** This setting prevents a vertical scroll bar from being displayed in the text area.
- **JScrollPane.VERTICAL_SCROLLBAR_ALWAYS.** With this setting, a vertical scroll bar is always displayed, even when it is not needed.

For example, the following code specifies that a vertical scroll bar should always appear on a scroll pane's component, but a horizontal scroll bar should not appear:

```
scrollPane.setHorizontalScrollBarPolicy(
           JScrollPane.HORIZONTAL_SCROLLBAR_NEVER);
scrollPane.setVerticalScrollBarPolicy(
           JScrollPane.VERTICAL_SCROLLBAR_ALWAYS);
```

Figure 13-27 shows a text area without scroll bars, a text area with a vertical scroll bar, and a text area with both a horizontal and a vertical scroll bar.

Figure 13-27   Text areas with and without scroll bars   (Oracle Corporate Counsel)

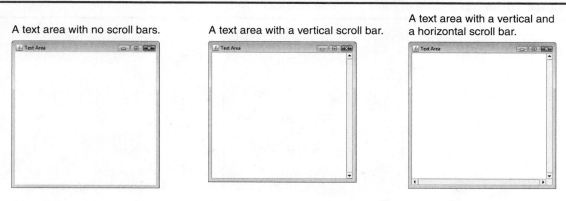

By default, JTextArea components do not perform line wrapping. This means that when text is entered into the component and the end of a line is reached, the text does not wrap around to the next line. If you want line wrapping, you use the JTextArea class's setLineWrap method to turn it on. The method accepts a boolean argument. If you pass true, line wrapping is turned on. If you pass false, line wrapping is turned off. Here is an example of a statement that turns a text area's line wrapping on:

```
textInput.setLineWrap(true);
```

There are two different styles of line wrapping: word wrapping and character wrapping. When word wrapping is performed, the line breaks always occur between words, never in the middle of a word. When character wrapping is performed, lines are broken between characters. This means that lines can be broken in the middle of a word. You specify the style of line wrapping that you prefer with the JTextArea class's setWrapStyleWord method. This method accepts a boolean argument. If you pass true, the text area will perform word wrapping. If you pass false, the text area will perform character wrapping. The default style is character wrapping.

Fonts

The appearance of a component's text is determined by the text's font, style, and size. The font is the name of the typeface—the style can be plain, bold, and/or italic—and the size is the size of the text in points. To change the appearance of a component's text you use the component's `setFont` method, which is inherited from the `JComponent` class. The general format of the method is as follows:

```
void setFont(Font appearance)
```

You pass a `Font` object as an argument to this method. The `Font` class constructor has the following general format:

```
Font(String fontName, int style, int size);
```

The first argument is the name of a font. Although the fonts that are available vary from system to system, Java guarantees that you will have Dialog, DialogInput, Monospaced, SansSerif, and Serif. Figure 13-28 shows an example of each of these.

Figure 13-28   Examples of fonts   (Oracle Corporate Counsel)

The second argument to the `Font` constructor is an `int` that represents the style of the text. The `Font` class provides the following constants that you can use: `Font.PLAIN`, `Font.BOLD`, and `Font.ITALIC`. The third argument is the size of the text in points. (There are 72 points per inch, so a 72-point font has a height of one inch. Ten- and twelve-point fonts are normally used for most applications.) Here is an example of a statement that changes the text of a label to a 24-point bold serif font:

```
label.setFont(new Font("Serif", Font.BOLD, 24));
```

You can combine styles by mathematically adding them. For example, the following statement changes a label's text to a 24-point bold and italic serif font:

```
label.setFont(new Font("Serif", Font.BOLD + Font.ITALIC, 24));
```

Figure 13-29 shows an example of the serif font in plain, bold, italic, and bold plus italic styles. The following code was used to create the labels:

```
JLabel label1 = new JLabel("Serif Plain", SwingConstants.CENTER);
label1.setFont(new Font("Serif", Font.PLAIN, 24));

JLabel label2 = new JLabel("Serif Bold", SwingConstants.CENTER);
label2.setFont(new Font("Serif", Font.BOLD, 24));
```

```
JLabel label3 = new JLabel("Serif Italic", SwingConstants.CENTER);
label3.setFont(new Font("Serif", Font.ITALIC, 24));

JLabel label4 = new JLabel("Serif Bold + Italic",
                    SwingConstants.CENTER);
label4.setFont(new Font("Serif", Font.BOLD + Font.ITALIC, 24));
```

Figure 13-29 Examples of serif plain, bold, italic, and bold plus italic   (Oracle Corporate Counsel)

 **Checkpoint**

MyProgrammingLab™ *www.myprogramminglab.com*

13.23 What arguments do you pass to the JTextArea constructor?

13.24 How do you retrieve the text that is stored in a JTextArea component?

13.25 Does the JTextArea component automatically display scroll bars? If not, how do you accomplish this?

13.26 What is line wrapping? What are the two styles of line wrapping? How do you turn a JTextArea component's line wrapping on? How do you select a line wrapping style?

13.27 What type of argument does a component's setFont method accept?

13.28 What are the arguments that you pass to the Font class constructor?

> See the Simple Text Editor Application case study on this book's companion Web site (www.pearsonhighered.com/gaddis) for an in-depth example that uses menus and other topics from this chapter.

 13.10 Sliders

CONCEPT: A slider is a component that allows the user to adjust a number graphically within a range of values.

Sliders, which are created from the JSlider class, display an image of a "slider knob" that can be dragged along a track. Sliders can be horizontally or vertically oriented, as shown in Figure 13-30.

A slider is designed to represent a range of numeric values. At one end of the slider is the range's minimum value and at the other end is the range's maximum value. Both of the sliders shown in Figure 13-30 represent a range of 0 through 50. Sliders hold a numeric value in a field, and as the user moves the knob along the track, the numeric value is adjusted accordingly. Notice that the sliders in Figure 13-30 have accompanying tick marks. At every tenth value, a major tick mark is displayed along with a label indicating the value at that tick mark. Between the major tick marks are minor tick marks, which in this example are displayed at every second value. The appearance of tick marks, their spacing, and the appearance of labels can be controlled through methods in the JSlider class. The JSlider constructor has the following general format:

```
JSlider(int orientation, int minValue,
        int maxValue, int initialValue)
```

Figure 13-30 A horizontal and a vertical slider (Oracle Corporate Counsel)

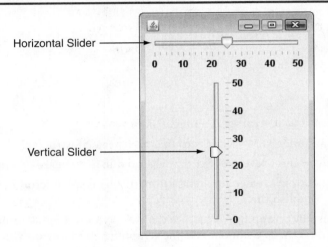

The first argument is an int specifying the slider's orientation. You should use one of the constants JSlider.HORIZONTAL or JSlider.VERTICAL. The second argument is the minimum value of the slider's range and the third argument is the maximum value of the slider's range. The fourth argument is the initial value of the slider, which determines the initial position of the slider's knob. For example, the following code could be used to create the sliders shown in Figure 13-30:

```
JSlider slider1 = new JSlider(JSlider.HORIZONTAL, 0, 50, 25);
JSlider slider2 = new JSlider(JSlider.VERTICAL, 0, 50, 25);
```

You set the major and minor tick mark spacing with the methods setMajorTickSpacing and setMinorTickSpacing. Each of these methods accepts an int argument that specifies the intervals of the tick marks. For example, the following code sets the slider1 object's major tick mark spacing at 10, and its minor tick mark spacing at 2:

```
slider1.setMajorTickSpacing(10);
slider1.setMinorTickSpacing(2);
```

If the slider1 component's range is 0 through 50, then these statements would cause major tick marks to be displayed at values 0, 10, 20, 30, 40, and 50. Minor tick marks would be displayed at values 2, 4, 6, and 8, then at values 12, 14, 16, and 18, and so forth.

By default, tick marks are not displayed, and setting their spacing does not cause them to be displayed. You display tick marks by calling the setPaintTicks method, which accepts a boolean argument. If you pass true, then tick marks are displayed. If you pass false, they are not displayed. Here is an example:

```
slider1.setPaintTicks(true);
```

By default, labels are not displayed either. You display numeric labels on the slider component by calling the setPaintLabels method, which accepts a boolean argument. If you pass true, then numeric labels are displayed at the major tick marks. If you pass false, labels are not displayed. Here is an example:

```
slider1.setPaintLabels(true);
```

When the knob's position is moved, the slider component generates a change event. To handle the change event, you must write a change listener class. When you write a change listener class, it must meet the following requirements:

- It must implement the ChangeListener interface. This interface is in the javax.swing.event package.
- It must have a method named stateChanged. This method must take an argument of the ChangeEvent type.

To retrieve the current value stored in a JSlider, use the getValue method. This method returns the slider's value as an int. Here is an example:

```
currentValue = slider1.getValue();
```

The TempConverter class shown in Code Listing 13-7 demonstrates the JSlider component. This class displays the window shown in Figure 13-31. Two temperatures are initially shown: 32.0 degrees Fahrenheit and 0.0 degrees Celsius. A slider, which has the range of 0 through 100, allows you to adjust the Celsius temperature and immediately see the Fahrenheit conversion. The main method creates an instance of the class and displays the window.

Figure 13-31 Window displayed by the TempConverterWindow class

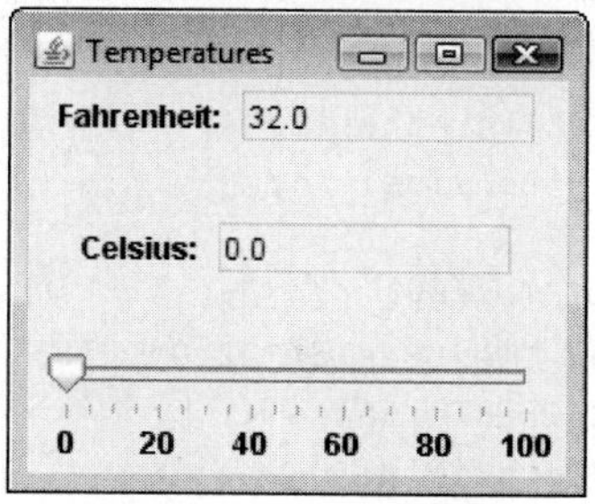

Code Listing 13-7 (TempConverter.java)

```java
 1  import javax.swing.*;
 2  import javax.swing.event.*;
 3  import java.awt.*;
 4
 5  /**
 6     This class displays a window with a slider component.
 7     The user can convert the Celsius temperatures from
 8     0 through 100 to Fahrenheit by moving the slider.
 9  */
10
11  public class TempConverter extends JFrame
12  {
13      private JLabel label1, label2;       // Message labels
14      private JTextField fahrenheitTemp;   // Fahrenheit temp
15      private JTextField celsiusTemp;      // Celsius temp
16      private JPanel fpanel;               // Fahrenheit panel
17      private JPanel cpanel;               // Celsius panel
18      private JPanel sliderPanel;          // Slider panel
19      private JSlider slider;              // Temperature adjuster
20
21      /**
22         Constructor
23      */
24
25      public TempConverter()
26      {
27          // Set the title.
28          setTitle("Temperatures");
29
30          // Specify an action for the close button.
31          setDefaultCloseOperation(JFrame.EXIT_ON_CLOSE);
32
33          // Create the message labels.
34          label1 = new JLabel("Fahrenheit: ");
35          label2 = new JLabel("Celsius: ");
36
37          // Create the read-only text fields.
38          fahrenheitTemp = new JTextField("32.0", 10);
39          fahrenheitTemp.setEditable(false);
40          celsiusTemp = new JTextField("0.0", 10);
41          celsiusTemp.setEditable(false);
42
43          // Create the slider.
44          slider = new JSlider(JSlider.HORIZONTAL, 0, 100, 0);
45          slider.setMajorTickSpacing(20); // Major tick every 20
```

```
46        slider.setMinorTickSpacing(5);   // Minor tick every 5
47        slider.setPaintTicks(true);      // Display tick marks
48        slider.setPaintLabels(true);     // Display numbers
49        slider.addChangeListener(new SliderListener());
50
51        // Create panels and place the components in them.
52        fpanel = new JPanel();
53        fpanel.add(label1);
54        fpanel.add(fahrenheitTemp);
55        cpanel = new JPanel();
56        cpanel.add(label2);
57        cpanel.add(celsiusTemp);
58        sliderPanel = new JPanel();
59        sliderPanel.add(slider);
60
61        // Create a GridLayout manager.
62        setLayout(new GridLayout(3, 1));
63
64        // Add the panels to the content pane.
65        add(fpanel);
66        add(cpanel);
67        add(sliderPanel);
68
69        // Pack and display the frame.
70        pack();
71        setVisible(true);
72    }
73
74    /**
75       Private inner class to handle the change events
76       that are generated when the slider is moved.
77    */
78
79    private class SliderListener implements ChangeListener
80    {
81        public void stateChanged(ChangeEvent e)
82        {
83            double fahrenheit, celsius;
84
85            // Get the slider value.
86            celsius = slider.getValue();
87
88            // Convert the value to Fahrenheit.
89            fahrenheit = (9.0 / 5.0) * celsius + 32.0;
90
91            // Store the celsius temp in its display field.
92            celsiusTemp.setText(Double.toString(celsius));
```

```
93
94           // Store the Fahrenheit temp in its display field.
95           fahrenheitTemp.setText(String.format("%.1f", fahrenheit));
96      }
97   }
98
99   /*
100      The main method creates an instance of the
101      class, which displays a window with a slider.
102   */
103
104   public static void main(String[] args)
105   {
106      new TempConverter();
107   }
108 }
```

Checkpoint

MyProgrammingLab™ *www.myprogramminglab.com*

13.29 What type of event does a `JSlider` generate when its slider knob is moved?

13.30 What `JSlider` methods do you use to perform each of these operations?
- a) Establish the spacing of major tick marks.
- b) Establish the spacing of minor tick marks.
- c) Cause tick marks to be displayed.
- d) Cause labels to be displayed.

13.11 Look and Feel

CONCEPT: A GUI application's appearance is determined by its look and feel. Java allows you to select an application's look and feel.

Most operating systems' GUIs have their own unique appearance and style conventions. For example, if a Windows user switches to a Macintosh, UNIX, or Linux system, the first thing he or she is likely to notice is the difference in the way the GUIs on each system appear. The appearance of a particular system's GUI is known as its look and feel.

Java allows you to select the look and feel of a GUI application. The default look and feel for Java is called *Ocean*. This is the look and feel that you have seen in all of the GUI applications that we have written in this book. Some of the other look and feel choices are Metal, Motif, and Windows. Metal was the default look and feel for previous versions of Java. Motif is similar to a UNIX look and feel. Windows is the look and feel of the Windows operating system. Figure 13-32 shows how the `TempConverterWindow` class window, presented earlier in this chapter, appears in each of these looks and feels.

NOTE: Ocean is actually a special theme of the Metal look and feel.

 NOTE: Currently the Windows look and feel is available only on computers running the Microsoft Windows operating system.

Figure 13-32 Metal, Motif, and Windows looks and feels (Oracle Corporate Counsel)

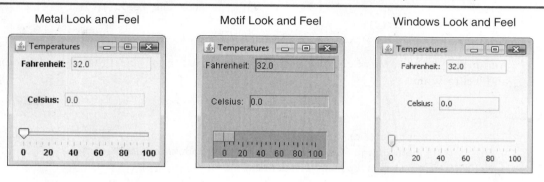

To change an application's look and feel, you call the `UIManager` class's static `setLookAndFeel` method. Java has a class for each look and feel, and this method takes the fully qualified class name for the desired look and feel as its argument. The class name must be passed as a string. Table 13-1 lists the fully qualified class names for the Metal, Motif, and Windows looks and feels.

Table 13-1 Look and feel class names

Class Name	Look and Feel
`"javax.swing.plaf.metal.MetalLookAndFeel"`	Metal
`"com.sun.java.swing.plaf.motif.MotifLookAndFeel"`	Motif
`"com.sun.java.swing.plaf.windows.WindowsLookAndFeel"`	Windows

When you call the `UIManager.setLookAndFeel` method, any components that have already been created need to be updated. You do this by calling the `SwingUtilities.updateComponentTreeUI` method, passing a reference to the component that you want to update as an argument.

The `UIManager.setLookAndFeel` method throws a number of exceptions. Specifically, it throws `ClassNotFoundException`, `InstantiationException`, `IllegalAccessException`, and `UnsupportedLookAndFeelException`. Unless you want to trap each of these types of exceptions, you can simply trap exceptions of type `Exception`. Here is an example of code that can be run from a `JFrame` object that changes its look and feel to Motif:

```
try
{
    UIManager.setLookAndFeel(
        "com.sun.java.swing.plaf.motif.MotifLookAndFeel");
    SwingUtilities.updateComponentTreeUI(this);
}
catch (Exception e)
{
    JOptionPane.showMessageDialog(null, "Error setting " +
                                  "the look and feel.");
    System.exit(0);
}
```

And here is an example of code that can be run from a `JFrame` object that changes its look and feel to Windows:

```
try
{
    UIManager.setLookAndFeel(
        "com.sun.java.swing.plaf.windows.WindowsLookAndFeel");
    SwingUtilities.updateComponentTreeUI(this);
}
catch (Exception e)
{
    JOptionPane.showMessageDialog(null, "Error setting " +
                                  "the look and feel.");
    System.exit(0);
}
```

13.12 Common Errors to Avoid

- **Only retrieving the first selected item from a list component in which multiple items have been selected.** If multiple items have been selected in a list component, the `getSelectedValue` method returns only the first selected item. Likewise, the `getSelectedIndex` method returns only the index of the first selected item. You should use the `getSelectedValues` or `getSelectedIndices` methods instead.
- **Using 1 as the beginning index for a list or combo box.** The indices for a list or combo box start at 0, not 1.
- **Forgetting to add a list or text area to a scroll pane.** The `JList` and `JTextArea` components do not automatically display scroll bars. You must add these components to a scroll pane object in order for them to display scroll bars.
- **Using the add method instead of the constructor to add a component to a scroll pane.** To add a component to a scroll pane, you must pass a reference to the component as an argument to the `JScrollPane` constructor.
- **Adding a component to a scroll pane and then adding the component (not the scroll pane) to another container, such as a panel.** If you add a component to a scroll pane and then intend to add that same component to a panel or other container, you must add the scroll pane instead of the component. Otherwise, the scroll bars will not appear on the component.

- Forgetting to call the `setEditable` method to give a combo box a text field. By default, a combo box is the combination of a button and a list. To make it a combination of a text field and a list, you must call the `setEditable` method and pass `true` as an argument.
- Trying to open an image file of an unsupported type. Currently, an `ImageIcon` object can open image files that are stored in JPEG, GIF, or PNG formats.
- Loading an image into an existing `JLabel` component and clipping part of the image. If you have not explicitly set the preferred size of a `JLabel` component, it resizes itself automatically when you load an image into it. The `JFrame` that encloses the `JLabel` does not automatically resize, however. You must call the `JFrame` object's `pack` method or `setPreferredSize` method to resize it.
- Assigning the same mnemonic to more than one component. If you assign the same mnemonic to more than one component in a window, it works only for the first component that you assigned it to.
- Forgetting to add menu items to a `JMenu` component, and `JMenu` components to a `JMenuBar` component. After you create a menu item, you must add it to a `JMenu` component in order for it to be displayed on the menu. Likewise, `JMenu` components must be added to a `JMenuBar` component in order to be displayed on the menu bar.
- Not calling the `JFrame` object's `setJMenuBar` method to place the menu bar. To display a menu bar, you must call the `setJMenuBar` method and pass it as an argument.
- Not grouping `JRadioButtonMenuItems` in a `ButtonGroup` object. Just like regular radio button components, you must group radio button menu items in a button group in order to create a mutually exclusive relationship among them.

Review Questions and Exercises

Multiple Choice and True/False

1. You can use this method to make a text field read-only.
   a. setReadOnly
   b. setChangeable
   c. setUneditable
   d. setEditable

2. A `JList` component generates this type of event when the user selects an item.
   a. action event
   b. item event
   c. list selection event
   d. list change event

3. To display a scroll bar with a `JList` component, you must _____.
   a. do nothing; the `JList` automatically appears with scroll bars if necessary
   b. add the `JList` component to a `JScrollPane` component
   c. call the `setScrollBar` method
   d. none of the above; you cannot display a scroll bar with a `JList` component

4. This is the `JList` component's default selection mode.
   a. single selection
   b. single interval selection
   c. multiple selection
   d. multiple interval selection

5. A list selection listener must have this method.
   a. `valueChanged`
   b. `selectionChanged`
   c. `actionPerformed`
   d. `itemSelected`

6. The `ListSelectionListener` interface is in this package.
   a. `java.awt`
   b. `java.awt.event`
   c. `javax.swing.event`
   d. `javax.event`

7. This `JList` method returns -1 if no item in the list is selected.
   a. `getSelectedValue`
   b. `getSelectedItem`
   c. `getSelectedIndex`
   d. `getSelection`

8. A `JComboBox` component generates this type of event when the user selects an item.
   a. action event
   b. item event
   c. list selection event
   d. list change event

9. You can pass an instance of this class to the `JLabel` constructor if you want to display an image in the label.
   a. `ImageFile`
   b. `ImageIcon`
   c. `JLabelImage`
   d. `JImageFile`

10. This method can be used to store an image in a `JLabel` or a `JButton` component.
    a. `setImage`
    b. `storeImage`
    c. `getIcon`
    d. `setIcon`

11. This is text that appears in a small box when the user holds the mouse cursor over a component.
    a. mnemonic
    b. instant message
    c. tool tip
    d. pop-up mnemonic

12. This is a key that activates a component just as if the user clicked it with the mouse.
    a. mnemonic
    b. key activator
    c. tool tip
    d. click simulator

13. To display an open file or save file dialog box, you use this class.
    a. JFileChooser
    b. JOpenSaveDialog
    c. JFileDialog
    d. JFileOptionPane

14. To display a dialog box that allows the user to select a color, you use this class.
    a. JColor
    b. JColorDialog
    c. JColorChooser
    d. JColorOptionPane

15. You use this class to create a menu bar.
    a. MenuBar
    b. JMenuBar
    c. JMenu
    d. JBar

16. You use this class to create a radio button menu item.
    a. JMenuItem
    b. JRadioButton
    c. JRadioButtonItem
    d. JRadioButtonMenuItem

17. You use this method to place a menu bar on a JFrame.
    a. setJMenuBar
    b. setMenuBar
    c. placeMenuBar
    d. setJMenu

18. The setPreferredSize method accepts this as its argument(s).
    a. a Size object
    b. two int values
    c. a Dimension object
    d. one int value

19. Components of this class are multi-line text fields.
    a. JMultiLineTextField
    b. JTextArea
    c. JTextField
    d. JEditField

20. This method is inherited from JComponent and changes the appearance of a component's text.
    a. setAppearance
    b. setTextAppearance
    c. setFont
    d. setText

21. This method sets the intervals at which major tick marks are displayed on a JSlider component.
    a. setMajorTickSpacing
    b. setMajorTickIntervals
    c. setTickSpacing
    d. setIntervals

22. **True or False:** You can use code to change the contents of a read-only text field.

23. **True or False:** A JList component automatically appears with a line border drawn around it.

24. **True or False:** In single interval selection mode, the user may select multiple items from a JList component.

25. **True or False:** With an editable combo box the user may only enter a value that appears in the component's list.

26. **True or False:** You can store either text or an image in a JLabel object, but not both.

27. **True or False:** You can store large images as well as small ones in a JLabel component.

28. **True or False:** Mnemonics are useful for users who are good with the keyboard.

29. **True or False:** A JMenuBar object acts as a container for JMenu components.

30. **True or False:** A JMenu object cannot contain other JMenu objects.

31. **True or False:** A JTextArea component does not automatically display scroll bars.

32. **True or False:** By default, a JTextArea component does not perform line wrapping.

33. **True or False:** A JSlider component generates an action event when the slider knob is moved.

34. **True or False:** By default, a JSlider component displays labels and tick marks.

35. **True or False:** When labels are displayed on a JSlider component, they are displayed on the major tick marks.

Find the Error

1. ```
   // Create a read-only text field.
   JTextField textField = new JTextField(10);
   textField.setEditable(true);
   ```

2. ```
   // Create a black 1-pixel border around list, a JList component.
   list.setBorder(Color.BLACK, 1);
   ```

3. ```
   // Create a JList and add it to a scroll pane.
   // Assume that array already exists.
   JList list = new JList(array);
   JScrollPane scrollPane = new JScrollPane();
   scrollPane.add(list);
   ```
   ```

4. `// Assume that nameBox is a combo box and is properly set up`
   `// with a list of names to choose from.`
   `// Get value of the selected item.`
   `String selectedName = nameBox.getSelectedIndex();`

5. `JLabel label = new JLabel("Have a nice day!");`
   `label.setImage(image);`

6. `// Add a menu to the menu bar.`
   `JMenuBar menuBar = new JMenuBar(menuItem);`

7. `// Create a text area with 20 columns and 5 rows.`
   `JTextArea textArea = new JTextArea (20, 5);`

Algorithm Workbench

1. Give an example of code that creates a read-only text field.

2. Write code that creates a list with the following items: Monday, Tuesday, Wednesday, Thursday, Friday, Saturday, and Sunday.

3. Write code that adds a scroll bar to the list you created in your answer to Algorithm Workbench 2.

4. Assume that the variable myList references a JList component, and selection is a String variable. Write code that assigns the selected item in the myList component to the selection variable.

5. Assume that the variable myComboBox references an uneditable combo box, and selectionIndex is an int variable. Write code that assigns the index of the selected item in the myComboBox component to the selectionIndex variable.

6. Write code that stores the image in the file *dog.jpg* in a label.

7. Assume that label references an existing JLabel object. Write code that stores the image in the file *picture.gif* in the label.

8. Write code that creates a button with the text "Open File." Assign the O key as a mnemonic and assign "This button opens a file" as the component's tool tip.

9. Write code that displays a file open dialog box. If the user selects a file, the code should store the file's path and name in a String variable.

10. Write code that creates a text area displaying 10 rows and 15 columns. The text area should be capable of displaying scroll bars, when necessary. It should also perform word style line wrapping.

11. Write the code that creates a menu bar with one menu named File. The File menu should have the F key assigned as a mnemonic. The File menu should have three menu items: Open, Print, and Exit. Assign mnemonic keys of your choice to each of these items. Register an instance of the OpenListener class as an action listener for the Open menu item, an instance of the PrintListener class as an action listener for the Print menu item, and an instance of the ExitListener class as an action listener for the Exit menu item. Assume these classes have already been created.

12. Write code that creates a JSlider component. The component should be horizontally oriented and its range should be 0 through 1000. Labels and tick marks should be displayed. Major tick marks should appear at every 100th number, and minor tick marks should appear at every 25th number. The initial value of the slider should be set at 500.

Short Answer

1. What selection mode should you select if you want the user to select a single item only in a list?

2. You want to provide 20 items in a list for the user to select from. Which component would take up less space, a `JList` or a `JComboBox`?

3. What is the difference between an uneditable combo box and an editable combo box? Which one is a combo box by default?

4. Describe how you can store both an image and text in a `JLabel` component.

5. What is a mnemonic? How does the user use it?

6. What happens when the mnemonic that you assign to a component is a letter that appears in the component's text?

7. What is a tool tip? What is its purpose?

8. What do you do to a group of radio button menu items so that only one of them can be selected at a time?

9. When a checked menu item shows a check mark next to it, what happens when the user clicks on it?

10. What fonts does Java guarantee you have?

11. Why would a `JSlider` component be ideal when you want the user to enter a number, but you want to make sure that the number is within a range?

12. What are the standard GUI looks and feels that are available in Java?

Programming Challenges

MyProgrammingLab™ *Visit www.myprogramminglab.com to complete many of these Programming Challenges online and get instant feedback.*

1. Scrollable Tax Calculator

Create an application that allows you to enter the amount of a purchase and then displays the amount of sales tax on that purchase. Use a slider to adjust the tax rate between 0 percent and 10 percent.

VideoNote
The Image
Viewer Problem

2. Image Viewer

Write an application that allows the user to view image files. The application should use either a button or a menu item that displays a file chooser. When the user selects an image file, it should be loaded and displayed.

3. Dorm and Meal Plan Calculator

A university has the following dormitories:

Allen Hall: $1,500 per semester
Pike Hall: $1,600 per semester
Farthing Hall: $1,200 per semester
University Suites: $1,800 per semester

The university also offers the following meal plans:

> 7 meals per week: $560 per semester
> 14 meals per week: $1,095 per semester
> Unlimited meals: $1,500 per semester

Create an application with two combo boxes. One should hold the names of the dormitories, and the other should hold the meal plans. The user should select a dormitory and a meal plan, and the application should show the total charges for the semester.

4. Skateboard Designer

The Skate Shop sells the skateboard products listed in Table 13-2.

Table 13-2   Skateboard products

Decks	Truck Assemblies	Wheels
The Master Thrasher $60	7.75 inch axle $35	51 mm $20
The Dictator $45	8 inch axle $40	55 mm $22
The Street King $50	8.5 inch axle $45	58 mm $24
		61 mm $28

In addition, the Skate Shop sells the following miscellaneous products and services:

> Grip tape: $10
> Bearings: $30
> Riser pads: $2
> Nuts & bolts kit: $3

Create an application that allows the user to select one deck, one truck assembly, and one wheel set from either list components or combo boxes. The application should also have a list component that allows the user to select multiple miscellaneous products. The application should display the subtotal, the amount of sales tax (at 6 percent), and the total of the order.

5. Shopping Cart System

Create an application that works like a shopping cart system for a bookstore. In this chapter's source code folder (available on the book's companion Web site at www.pearsonhighered.com/gaddis), you will find a file named *BookPrices.txt*. This file contains the names and prices of various books, formatted in the following fashion:

> I Did It Your Way, 11.95
> The History of Scotland, 14.50
> Learn Calculus in One Day, 29.95
> Feel the Stress, 18.50

Each line in the file contains the name of a book, followed by a comma, followed by the book's retail price. When your application begins execution, it should read the contents of the file and store the book titles in a list component. The user should be able to select a title from the list and add it to a shopping cart, which is simply another list component. The application should have buttons or menu items that allow the user to remove items from the shopping cart, clear the shopping cart of all selections, and check out. When the user checks out, the application should calculate and display the subtotal of all the books in the shopping cart, the sales tax (which is 6 percent of the subtotal), and the total.

6. Cell Phone Packages

Cell Solutions, a cell phone provider, sells the following packages:

> 300 minutes per month: $45.00 per month
> 800 minutes per month: $65.00 per month
> 1500 minutes per month: $99.00 per month

The provider sells the following phones (a 6 percent sales tax applies to the sale of a phone):

> Model 100: $29.95
> Model 110: $49.95
> Model 200: $99.95

Customers may also select the following options:

> Voice mail: $5.00 per month
> Text messaging: $10.00 per month

Write an application that displays a menu system. The menu system should allow the user to select one package, one phone, and any of the options desired. As the user selects items from the menu, the application should show the prices of the items selected.

7. Shade Designer

A custom window shade designer charges a base fee of $50 per shade. In addition, charges are added for certain styles, sizes, and colors as follows:

Styles:

> Regular shades: Add $0
> Folding shades: Add $10
> Roman shades: Add $15

Sizes:

> 25 inches wide: Add $0
> 27 inches wide: Add $2
> 32 inches wide: Add $4
> 40 inches wide: Add $6

Colors:

> Natural: Add $5
> Blue: Add $0
> Teal: Add $0
> Red: Add $0
> Green: Add $0

Create an application that allows the user to select the style, size, color, and number of shades from lists or combo boxes. The total charges should be displayed.

8. Conference Registration System

Create an application that calculates the registration fees for a conference. The general conference registration fee is $895 per person, and student registration is $495 per person. There is also an optional opening night dinner with a keynote speech for $30 per person. In addition, the optional preconference workshops listed in Table 13-3 are available.

Table 13-3   Optional preconference workshops

Workshop	Fee
Introduction to E-commerce	$295
The Future of the Web	$295
Advanced Java Programming	$395
Network Security	$395

The application should allow the user to select the registration type, the optional opening night dinner and keynote speech, and as many preconference workshops as desired. The total cost should be displayed.

9. Dice Simulator

Write a GUI application that simulates a pair of dice, similar to that shown in Figure 13-33. Each time the button is clicked, the application should roll the dice, using random numbers to determine the value of each die. (This chapter's source code folder contains images that you can use to display the dice.)

Figure 13-33   Dice simulator

10. Card Dealer

This chapter's source code folder contains images for a complete deck of poker cards. Write a GUI application, similar to the one shown in Figure 13-34, that randomly selects a card from the deck and displays it each time the user clicks the button. When a card has been selected, it is removed from the deck and cannot be selected again. Display a message when no more cards are left in the deck.

Figure 13-34 Card dealer

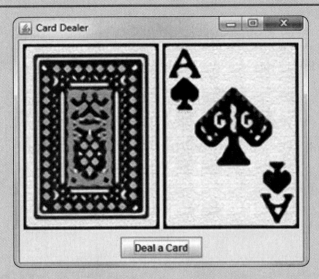

11. Tic Tac Toe Simulator

Create a GUI application that simulates a game of tic tac toe. Figure 13-35 shows an example of the application's window. The window shown in the figure uses nine large `JLabel` components to display the Xs and Os.

One approach in designing this application is to use a two-dimensional `int` array to simulate the game board in memory. When the user clicks the *New Game* button, the application should step through the array, storing a random number in the range of 0 through 1 in each element. The number 0 represents the letter O, and the number 1 represents the letter X. The `JLabel` components should then be updated to display the game board. The application should display a message indicating whether player X won, player Y won, or the game was a tie.

Figure 13-35 The Tic Tac Toe application   (Oracle Corporate Counsel)

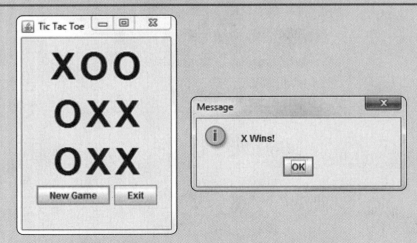

(14) Applets and More

14.1 Introduction to Applets

CONCEPT: An applet is a Java program that is associated with a Web page and is executed in a Web browser as part of that Web page.

Recall from Chapter 1 that there are two types of programs you can create with Java: applications and applets. An *application* is a stand-alone program that runs on your computer. So far in this book, we have concentrated exclusively on writing applications.

Applets are Java programs that are usually part of a Web site. If a user opens the Web site with a Java-enabled browser, the applet is executed inside the browser window. It appears to the user that the applet is part of the Web site. This is how it works: Applets are stored on a Web server along with the site's Web pages. When a user accesses a Web page on a server with his or her browser, any applets associated with the Web page are transmitted over the Internet from the server to the user's system. This is illustrated in Figure 14-1. Once the applets are transmitted, the user's system executes them.

Applets are important because they can be used to extend the capabilities of a Web page. Web pages are normally written in Hypertext Markup Language (HTML). HTML is limited, however, because it merely describes the content and layout of a Web page, and creates links to other files and Web pages. HTML does not have sophisticated abilities such as performing math calculations and interacting with the user. A programmer can write a Java applet to perform these types of operations and associate it with a Web page. When someone visits the Web page, the applet is downloaded to the visitor's browser and executed.

Figure 14-1 Applets are transmitted along with Web pages

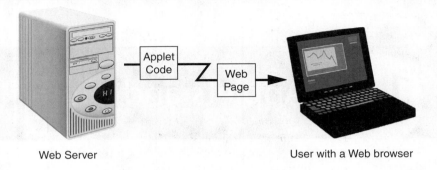

Web Server   User with a Web browser

Figure 14-2 shows an example of a Web page that has an applet. In the figure, the Web page is being viewed with Internet Explorer. This Web page briefly explains the Fahrenheit and Celsius temperature scales. The area with the text boxes and the button at the bottom of the page is generated by an applet. To see a Fahrenheit temperature converted to Celsius, the user can enter the Fahrenheit temperature into the top text box and click the Convert button. The Celsius temperature will be displayed in the read-only text box.

> An applet does not have to be on a Web server to be executed. The Web page shown in Figure 14-2 is in the source code folder *Chapter 14\TempConverter*. Open the *TempConverter.html* file in your Web browser to try it. Later in this chapter, we will take a closer look at this Web page and its applet.

Figure 14-2 A Web page with an applet   (Microsoft Corporation)

This part of the Web page is generated by an applet.

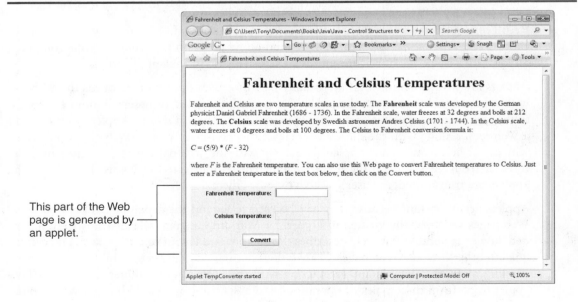

Most Web browsers have a special version of the JVM for running applets. For security purposes, this version of the JVM greatly restricts what an applet can do. Here is a summary of the restrictions placed on applets:

- Applets cannot delete files, read the contents of files, or create files on the user's system.
- Applets cannot run any other program on the user's system.
- Applets cannot execute operating system procedures on the user's system.
- Applets cannot retrieve information about the user's system, or the user's identity.
- Applets cannot make network connections with any system except the server from which the applet was transmitted.
- If an applet displays a window, it will automatically have a message such as "Warning: Applet Window" displayed in it. This lets the user know that the window was not displayed by an application on his or her system.

These restrictions might seem severe, but they are necessary to prevent malicious code from attacking or spying on unsuspecting users. If an applet attempts to violate one of these restrictions, an exception is thrown.

Checkpoint

MyProgrammingLab™ *www.myprogramminglab.com*

14.1   How is an applet that is associated with a Web page executed on a user's system?

14.2   Why do applets run in a restricted environment?

14.2 A Brief Introduction to HTML

CONCEPT: When creating a Web page, you use Hypertext Markup Language (HTML) to create a file that can be read and processed by a Web browser.

Hypertext Markup Language (HTML) is the language that Web pages are written in. Although it is beyond the scope of this book to teach you everything about HTML, this section will give you enough of the fundamentals so that you can write simple Web pages. You will need to know a little about HTML in order to run Java applets. If you are already familiar with HTML, this section is optional.

Before we continue, let's look at the meanings of the terms *hypertext* and *markup language*.

Hypertext

Web pages can contain regular text and hypertext, which are both displayed in the browser window. In addition, *hypertext* can contain a link to another Web page, or perhaps another location in the same Web page. When the user clicks on the hypertext, it loads the Web page or the location that the hypertext is linked to.

Markup Language

Although HTML is called a language, it is not a programming language like Java. Instead, HTML is a *markup language*. It allows you to "mark up" a text file by inserting special instructions. These instructions tell the browser how to format the text and create any hypertext links.

To make a Web page, you create a text file that contains HTML instructions, which are known as *tags*, as well as the text that should be displayed on the Web page. The resulting file is known as an *HTML document*, and it is usually saved with the *.html* file name extension. When a Web browser reads the HTML document, the tags instruct it how to format the text, where to place images, what to do when the user clicks on a link, and more.

Most HTML tags come in pairs. The first is known as the opening tag and the second is known as the closing tag. The general format of a simple tag is as follows:

```
<tag_name>
Text
</tag_name>
```

In this general format, `tag_name` is the name of the tag. The opening tag is `<tag_name>` and the closing tag is `</tag_name>`. Both the opening and closing tags are enclosed in angle brackets (< >). Notice that in the closing tag, the tag name is preceded by a forward slash (/). The `Text` that appears between the opening and closing tags is text that is formatted or modified by the tags.

Document Structure Tags

Some of the HTML tags are used to establish the structure of an HTML document. The first of the structure tags that you should learn is the `<html></html>` tag. This tag marks the beginning and ending of an HTML document. Everything that appears between these tags, including other tags, is the content of the Web page. When you are writing an HTML document, place an `<html>` tag at the very beginning, and an `</html>` tag at the very end.

The next tag is `<head></head>`. Everything that appears between `<head>` and `</head>` is considered part of the document head. The *document head* is a section of the HTML file that contains information about the document. For example, key words that search engines use to identify a document are often placed in the document's head. The only thing that we will use the document head for is to display a title in the Web browser's title bar. You do this with the `<title></title>` tag. Any text that you place between `<title>` and `</title>` becomes the title of the page and is displayed in the browser's title bar. Code Listing 14-1 shows the contents of an HTML document with the title "My First Web Page".

Notice that the `<title></title>` tag is inside of the `<head></head>` tag. The only output displayed by this Web page is the title. Figure 14-3 shows how this Web page appears when opened in a browser.

Code Listing 14-1   (`BasicWebPage1.html`)

```html
<html>
<head>
    <title>My First Web Page</title>
</head>
</html>
```

Figure 14-3   Web page with a title only   (Microsoft Corporation)

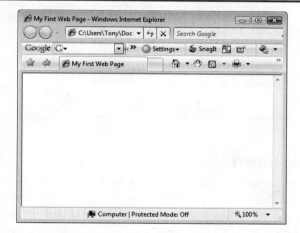

After the document head comes the document body, which is enclosed in the `<body></body>` tag. The *document body* contains all of the tags and text that produce output in the browser window. Code Listing 14-2 shows an HTML document with text placed in its body. Figure 14-4 shows the document when opened in a browser.

Code Listing 14-2   (`BasicWebPage2.html`)

```html
<html>
<head>
    <title>Java Applications and Applets</title>
</head>
<body>
    There are two types of programs you can create with Java: applications
    and applets. An application is a stand-alone program that runs on your
    computer. Applets are Java programs that are usually part of a Web site.
    They are stored on a Web server along with the site's Web pages. When a
    remote user accesses a Web page with his or her browser, any applets
```

```
    associated with the Web page are transmitted over the Internet from the
    server to the remote user's system.
</body>
</html>
```

Figure 14-4   Web page produced by *BasicWebPage2.html*   (Microsoft Corporation)

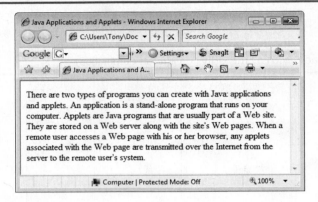

Text Formatting Tags

The text displayed in the Web page in Figure 14-4 is unformatted, which means it appears as plain text. There are many HTML tags that you can use to change the appearance of text. For example, there are six different header tags that you can use to format text as a heading of some type. The <h1></h1> tag creates a level one header. A level one header appears in boldface, and is much larger than regular text. The <h2></h2> tag creates a level two header. A level two header also appears in boldface, but is smaller than a level one header. This pattern continues with the <h3></h3>, <h4></h4>, <h5></h5>, and <h6></h6> tags. The higher a header tag's level number is, the smaller the text that it formats appears. For example, look at the following HTML:

```
<h1>This is an h1 Header</h1>
<h2>This is an h2 Header</h2>
<h3>This is an h3 Header</h3>
<h4>This is an h4 Header</h4>
<h5>This is an h5 Header</h5>
<h6>This is an h6 Header</h6>
This is regular unformatted text.
```

When this appears in the body of an HTML document, it produces the Web page shown in Figure 14-5.

You can use the tag to center a line of text in the browser window. To demonstrate, we will add the following line to the document that was previously shown in Code Listing 14-2:

```
<center><h1>Java</h1></center>
```

Figure 14-5   Header levels   (Microsoft Corporation)

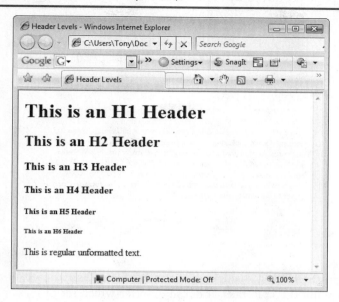

This will cause the word "Java" to appear centered and as a level one header. The modified document is shown in Code Listing 14-3, and the Web page it produces is shown in Figure 14-6.

Code Listing 14-3   **(BasicWebPage3.html)**

```
<html>
<head>
    <title>Java Applications and Applets</title>
</head>
<body>
    <center>
        <h1>Java</h1>
    </center>
    There are two types of programs you can create with Java: applications
    and applets. An application is a stand-alone program that runs
    on your computer. Applets are Java programs that are usually
    part of a Web site. They are stored on a Web server along with
    the site's Web pages. When a remote user accesses a Web page
    with his or her browser, any applets associated with the Web
    page are transmitted over the Internet from the server to the
    remote user's system.
</body>
</html>
```

Figure 14-6   Web page produced by *BasicWebPage3.html*   (Microsoft Corporation)

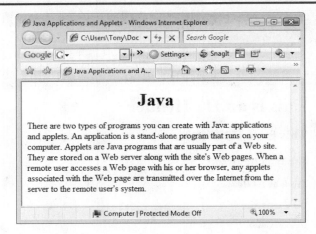

Notice that in the HTML document, the word "Java" is enclosed in two sets of tags: the `<center>` tags and the `<h1>` tags. It doesn't matter which set of tags is used first. If we had written the line as follows, we would have gotten the same result:

```
<h1><center>Java</center></h1>
```

You can display text in boldface by using the `<b></b>` tag, and in italics by using the `<i></i>` tag. For example, the following will cause the text "Hello World" to be displayed in boldface:

```
<b>Hello World</b>
```

The following will cause "Hello World" to be displayed in italics:

```
<i>Hello World</i>
```

The following will display "Hello World" in boldface and italics:

```
<b><i>Hello World</i></b>
```

Creating Breaks in Text

We will look at three HTML tags that are used to create breaks in a document's text. These three tags are unique from the ones we previously studied because they do not occur in pairs. When you use one of these tags, you only insert an opening tag.

The `<br />` tag causes a line break to appear at the point in the text where it is inserted. It is often necessary to insert `<br />` tags in an HTML document because the browser usually ignores the newline characters that are created when you press the Enter key. For example, if the following line appears in the body of an HTML document, it will cause the output shown in Figure 14-7.

```
First line<br />Second line<br />Third line
```

Figure 14-7   Line breaks in an HTML document   (Microsoft Corporation)

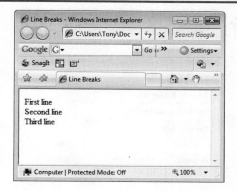

The `<p />` tag causes a paragraph break to appear at the point in the text where it is inserted. A paragraph break typically inserts more space into the text than a line break. For example, if the following line appears in the body of an HTML document, it will cause the output shown in Figure 14-8.

```
First paragraph<p />Second paragraph<p />Third paragraph
```

Figure 14-8   Paragraph breaks in an HTML document   (Microsoft Corporation)

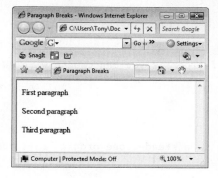

The `<hr />` tag causes a horizontal rule to appear at the point in the text where it is inserted. A horizontal rule is a thin, horizontal line that is drawn across the Web page. For example, if the following text appears in the body of an HTML document, it will cause the output shown in Figure 14-9.

```
This is the first line of text.
<hr />
This is the second line of text.
<hr />
This is the third line of text.
```

Figure 14-9 Horizontal rules in a Web page   (Microsoft Corporation)

The HTML document shown in Code Listing 14-4 demonstrates each of the tags we have discussed. The Web page it produces is shown in Figure 14-10.

Code Listing 14-4   **(BasicWebPage4.html)**

```html
<html>
<head>
    <title>Java Applications and Applets</title>
</head>
<body>
    <center>
        <h1>Java</h1>
    </center>
    There are two types of programs you can create with Java: applications
    and applets.
    <p />
    <b>Applications</b>
    <br />
    An <i>application</i> is a stand-alone program that runs on
    your computer.
    <p />
    <b>Applets</b>
    <br />
    <i>Applets</i> are Java programs that are usually part of a
    Web site. They are stored on a Web server along with the site's
    Web pages. When a remote user accesses a Web page with his or
    her browser, any applets associated with the Web page are
    transmitted over the Internet from the server to the remote
    user's system.
    <hr />
</body>
</html>
```

Figure 14-10   Web page produced by *BasicWebPage4.html*   (Microsoft Corporation)

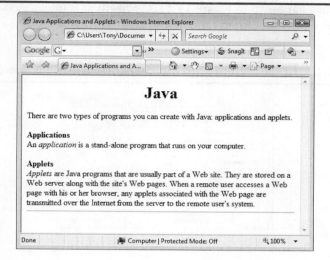

Inserting Links

As previously mentioned, a link is some element in a Web page that can be clicked on by the user. When the user clicks the link, another Web page is displayed, or some sort of action is initiated. We now look at how to insert a simple link that causes another Web page to be displayed. The tag that is used to insert a link has the following general format:

```
<a href="Address">Text</a>
```

The *Text* that appears between the opening and closing tags is the text that will be displayed in the Web page. When the user clicks on this text, the Web page that is located at *Address* will be displayed in the browser. This address is often referred to as a *uniform resource locator* (*URL*). Notice that the address is enclosed in quotation marks. Here is an example:

```
<a href="http://www.pearsonhighered.com/gaddis/">Click here to go to
the textbook's web site.</a>
```

The HTML document shown in Code Listing 14-5 uses this link, and Figure 14-11 shows how the page appears in the browser.

Code Listing 14-5   (**LinkDemo.html**)

```html
<html>
<head>
    <title>Link Demonstration</title>
</head>
<body>
    This demonstrates a link.
    <br />
    <a href="http://www.aw.com/gaddis">Click here to go to
    the textbook's web site.</a>
</body>
</html>
```

The text that is displayed by a link is usually highlighted in some way to let the user know that it is not ordinary text. In Figure 14-11, the link text is underlined. When the user clicks on this text, the browser displays the Web page at www.aw.com/gaddis

Figure 14-11 Web page produced by *LinkDemo.html* (Microsoft Corporation)

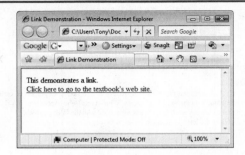

 Checkpoint

MyProgrammingLab™ *www.myprogramminglab.com*

14.3 What tag marks the beginning and end of an HTML document?

14.4 What tag marks the beginning and end of an HTML document's head section?

14.5 What statement would you use in an HTML document to display the text "My Web Page" in the browser's title bar? What section of the HTML document would this statement be written in?

14.6 What tag marks the beginning and end of an HTML document's body section?

14.7 What statement would you write in an HTML document to display the text "Student Roster" as a level one header?

14.8 What statement would you write in an HTML document to display the text "My Resume" in bold and centered on the page?

14.9 What statement would you write in an HTML document to display the text "Hello World" in bold and italic?

14.10 What tag causes a line break? What tag causes a paragraph break? What tag displays a horizontal rule?

14.11 Suppose you wanted to display the text "Click Here" as a link to the Web site http://java.sun.com. What statement would you write to create the text?

14.3 Creating Applets with Swing

CONCEPT: You extend a class from `JApplet` to create an applet, just as you extend a class from `JFrame` to create a GUI application.

By now you know almost everything necessary to create an applet. That is because applets are very similar to GUI applications. You can think of an applet as a GUI application that runs under the control of a Web browser. Instead of displaying its own window, an applet appears in the browser's window. The differences between GUI application code and applet code are summarized here:

VideoNote
Creating
an Applet

- A GUI application class inherits from JFrame. An applet class inherits from JApplet. The JApplet class is part of the javax.swing package.
- A GUI application class has a constructor that creates other components and sets up the GUI. An applet class does not normally have a constructor. Instead, it has a method named init that performs the same operations as a constructor. The init method accepts no arguments and has a void return type.
- The following methods, which are commonly called in a GUI application's constructor, are not called in an applet:

```
setTitle
setSize
setDefaultCloseOperation
pack
setVisible
```

The methods listed here are used in a GUI application to affect the application's window in some way. They are not usually applicable to an applet because the applet does not have a window of its own.

- There is no static main method needed to create an instance of the applet class. The browser creates an instance of the class automatically.

Let's look at a simple applet. Code Listing 14-6 shows an applet that displays a label.

Code Listing 14-6   (SimpleApplet.java)

```
 1 import javax.swing.*;
 2 import java.awt.*;
 3
 4 /**
 5    This is a simple applet.
 6 */
 7
 8 public class SimpleApplet extends JApplet
 9 {
10    /**
11       The init method sets up the applet, much
12       like a constructor.
13    */
14
15    public void init()
16    {
17       // Create a label.
18       JLabel label =
19          new JLabel("This is my very first applet.");
20
```

```
21        // Set the layout manager.
22        setLayout(new FlowLayout());
23
24        // Add the label to the content pane.
25        add(label);
26    }
27 }
```

This code is very much like a regular GUI application. Although this class extends `JApplet` instead of `JFrame`, you still add components to the content pane and use layout managers in the same way.

Running an Applet

The process of running an applet is different from that of running an application. To run an applet, you create an HTML document with an `applet` tag, which has the following general format:

```
<applet code="Filename.class" width=Wide height=High></applet>
```

In the general format, *Filename.class* is the name of the applet's *.class* file. This is the file that contains the compiled byte code. Note that you do not specify the *.java* file, which contains the Java source code. You can optionally specify a path along with the file name. If you specify only the file name, it is assumed that the file is in the same directory as the HTML document. *Wide* is the width of the applet in pixels, and *High* is the height of the applet in pixels. When a browser processes an `applet` tag, it loads specified byte code and executes it in an area that is the size specified by the *Wide* and *High* values.

The HTML document shown in Code Listing 14-7 uses an `applet` tag to load the applet shown in Code Listing 14-6. This document specifies that the applet should be displayed in an area that is 200 pixels wide by 50 pixels high. Figure 14-12 shows this document when it is displayed in a Web browser.

Code Listing 14-7   (`SimpleApplet.html`)

```html
<html>
<head>
    <title>A Simple Applet</title>
</head>
<body>
    <applet code="SimpleApplet.class" width="200" height="50">
    </applet>
</body>
</html>
```

Figure 14-12 The Web page produced by *SimpleApplet.html* (Microsoft Corporation)

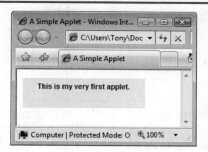

 NOTE: When you load a Web page that uses an applet into your browser, you will most likely get a security warning. For example, Figure 14-13 shows the warning you get from Internet Explorer. To run the applet, click the warning message and then select Allow Blocked Content . . . from the pop-up menu that appears.

Figure 14-13 Security warning in Internet Explorer (Microsoft Corporation)

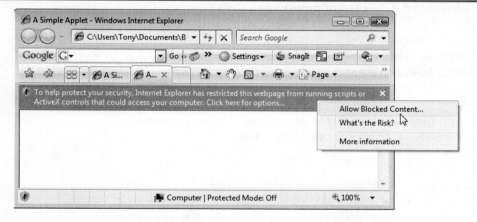

Running an Applet with `appletviewer`

The Sun JDK comes with an applet viewer program that loads and executes an applet without the need for a Web browser. This program can be run from a command prompt with the `appletviewer` command. When you run the program, you specify the name of an HTML document as a command line argument. For example, the following command passes `SimpleApplet.html` as the command line argument:

```
appletviewer SimpleApplet.html
```

This command executes any applet that is referenced by an `applet` tag in the file *SimpleApplet.html*. The window shown in Figure 14-14 will be displayed.

Figure 14-14 Applet executed by `appletviewer`

 NOTE: The applet viewer does not display any output generated by text or tags in the HTML document. It only executes applets. If the applet viewer opens an HTML document with more than one `applet` tag, it will execute each applet in a separate window.

Handling Events in an Applet

In an applet, events are handled with event listeners exactly as they are in GUI applications. To demonstrate, we will examine the `TempConverter` class, which is shown in Code Listing 14-8. This class is the applet displayed in the Web page we examined at the beginning of this chapter. It has a text field where the user can enter a Fahrenheit temperature and a Convert button that converts the temperature to Celsius and displays it in a read-only text field. The temperature conversion is performed in an action listener class that handles the button's action events.

Code Listing 14-8   (`TempConverter.java`)

```java
 1 import javax.swing.*;
 2 import java.awt.*;
 3 import java.awt.event.*;
 4
 5 /**
 6    The TempConverter class is an applet that converts
 7    Fahrenheit temperatures to Celsius.
 8 */
 9
10 public class TempConverter extends JApplet
11 {
12    private JPanel fPanel;        // To hold a text field
13    private JPanel cPanel;        // To hold a text field
14    private JPanel buttonPanel;   // To hold a button
15    private JTextField fahrenheit; // Fahrenheit temperature
16    private JTextField celsius;    // Celsius temperature
17
18    /**
19       init method
20    */
21
22    public void init()
23    {
24       // Build the panels.
25       buildFpanel();
```

```
26        buildCpanel();
27        buildButtonPanel();
28
29        // Create a layout manager.
30        setLayout(new GridLayout(3, 1));
31
32        // Add the panels to the content pane.
33        add(fPanel);
34        add(cPanel);
35        add(buttonPanel);
36    }
37
38    /**
39        The buildFpanel method creates a panel with a text
40        field in which the user can enter a Fahrenheit
41        temperature.
42    */
43
44    private void buildFpanel()
45    {
46        // Create the panel.
47        fPanel = new JPanel();
48
49        // Create a label to display a message.
50        JLabel message1 =
51                new JLabel("Fahrenheit Temperature:");
52
53        // Create a text field for the Fahrenheit temp.
54        fahrenheit = new JTextField(10);
55
56        // Create a layout manager for the panel.
57        fPanel.setLayout(new FlowLayout(FlowLayout.RIGHT));
58
59        // Add the label and text field to the panel.
60        fPanel.add(message1);
61        fPanel.add(fahrenheit);
62    }
63
64    /**
65        The buildCpanel method creates a panel that
66        displays the Celsius temperature in a
67        read-only text field.
68    */
69
70    private void buildCpanel()
71    {
72        // Create the panel.
73        cPanel = new JPanel();
```

```
 74
 75        // Create a label to display a message.
 76        JLabel message2 =
 77               new JLabel("Celsius Temperature:");
 78
 79        // Create a text field for the celsius temp.
 80        celsius = new JTextField(10);
 81
 82        // Make the text field read-only.
 83        celsius.setEditable(false);
 84
 85        // Create a layout manager for the panel.
 86        cPanel.setLayout(new FlowLayout(FlowLayout.RIGHT));
 87
 88        // Add the label and text field to the panel.
 89        cPanel.add(message2);
 90        cPanel.add(celsius);
 91    }
 92
 93    /**
 94       The buildButtonPanel method creates a panel with
 95       a button that converts the Fahrenheit temperature
 96       to Celsius.
 97    */
 98
 99    private void buildButtonPanel()
100    {
101        // Create the panel.
102        buttonPanel = new JPanel();
103
104        // Create a button with the text "Convert".
105        JButton convButton = new JButton("Convert");
106
107        // Add an action listener to the button.
108        convButton.addActionListener(new ButtonListener());
109
110        // Add the button to the panel.
111        buttonPanel.add(convButton);
112    }
113
114    /**
115       Private inner class that handles the action event
116       that is generated when the user clicks the convert
117       button.
118    */
119
120    private class ButtonListener implements ActionListener
```

```
121    {
122        public void actionPerformed(ActionEvent e)
123        {
124            double ftemp, ctemp;  // To hold the temperatures
125
126            // Get the Fahrenheit temperature and convert it
127            // to a double.
128            ftemp = Double.parseDouble(fahrenheit.getText());
129
130            // Calculate the Celsius temperature.
131            ctemp = (5.0 / 9.0) * (ftemp - 32);
132
133            // Display the Celsius temperature.
134            celsius.setText(String.format("%.1f",  ctemp));
135        }
136    }
137 }
```

Code Listing 14-9 shows the contents of TempConverter.html, an HTML document that uses this applet. Figure 14-15 shows the Web page produced by this document. In the figure, the user has entered a Fahrenheit temperature and converted it to Celsius.

Code Listing 14-9   (TempConverter.html)

```html
<html>
<head>
    <title>Fahrenheit and Celsius Temperatures</title>
</head>
<body>
    <center>
        <h1>Fahrenheit and Celsius Temperatures</h1>
    </center>
    Fahrenheit and Celsius are two temperature scales in use today.
    The <b>Fahrenheit</b> scale was developed by the German physicist
    Daniel Gabriel Fahrenheit (1686 - 1736). In the Fahrenheit scale,
    water freezes at 32 degrees and boils at 212 degrees. The
    <b>Celsius</b> scale was developed by Swedish astronomer Andres Celsius
    (1701 - 1744). In the Celsius scale, water freezes at 0 degrees and
    boils at 100 degrees. The Celsius to Fahrenheit conversion formula
    is:
    <p />
    <i>C</i> = (5/9) * (<i>F</i> - 32)
    <p />
    where <i>F</i> is the Fahrenheit temperature. You can also use
    this Web page to convert Fahrenheit temperatures to Celsius.
    Just enter a Fahrenheit temperature in the text box below, then
```

```
        click on the Convert button.
        <p />
        <applet code="TempConverter.class" width="300" height="150">
        </applet>
        <hr />
    </body>
</html>
```

Figure 14-15 Web page produced by *TempConverter.html* (Microsoft Corporation)

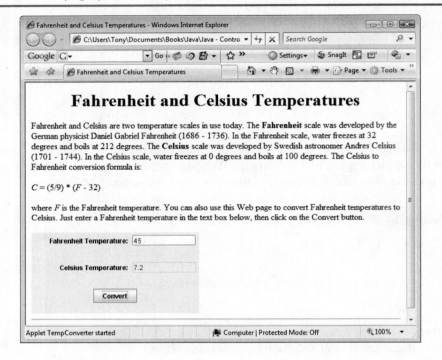

Checkpoint

MyProgrammingLab™ *www.myprogramminglab.com*

14.12 Instead of JFrame, an applet class is extended from what class?

14.13 Instead of a constructor, an applet class uses what method?

14.14 Why is there no need for a static main method to create an instance of an applet class?

14.15 Suppose the file *MyApplet.java* contains the Java source code for an applet. What tag would you write in an HTML document to run the applet in an area that is 400 pixels wide by 200 pixels high?

14.4 Using AWT for Portability

CONCEPT: Applets that use Swing components may be incompatible with some browsers. If you want to make sure that an applet is compatible with all Java-enabled browsers, use AWT components instead of Swing.

Java provides two libraries of classes that GUI components may be created from. Recall from Chapter 12 that these libraries are AWT and Swing. AWT is the original library that has been part of Java since its earliest version. Swing is an improved library that was introduced with Java 2. All of the GUI applications in Chapters 12 and 13, as well as the applets we have studied so far in this chapter, use Swing classes for their components.

Some browsers, do not directly support the Swing classes in applets. These browsers require a *plug-in*, which is software that extends or enhances another program, in order to run applets that use Swing components. Fortunately, this plug-in is automatically installed on a computer when the Sun JDK is installed. If you have installed the JDK, you should be able to write applets that use Swing and run them with no problems.

If you are writing an applet for other people to run on their computers, however, there is no guarantee that they will have the required plug-in. If this is the case, you should use the AWT classes instead of the Swing classes for the components in your applet. Fortunately, the AWT component classes are very similar to the Swing classes, so learning to use them is simple if you already know how to use Swing.

There is a corresponding AWT class for each of the Swing classes that you have learned so far. The names of the AWT classes are the same as those of the Swing classes, except the AWT class names do not start with the letter J. For example, the AWT class to create a frame is named Frame, and the AWT class to create a panel is named Panel. Table 14-1 lists several of the AWT classes. All of these classes are in the java.awt package.

Table 14-1   Several AWT classes

AWT Class	Description	Corresponding Swing Class
Applet	Used as a superclass for all applets. Unlike JApplet objects, Applet objects do not have a content pane.	JApplet
Frame	Creates a frame container that may be displayed as a window. Unlike JFrame objects, Frame objects do not have a content pane.	JFrame
Panel	Creates a panel container.	JPanel
Button	Creates a button that may be clicked.	JButton
Label	Creates a label that displays text.	JLabel
TextField	Creates a single line text field, which the user may type into.	JTextField
Checkbox	Creates a check box that may be selected or deselected.	JCheckBox

The Swing classes were intentionally designed with constructors and methods that are similar to those of their AWT counterparts. In addition, events are handled in the same way for each set of classes. This makes it easy for you to use either set of classes without learning a completely different syntax for each. For example, Code Listing 14-10 shows a version of the TempConverter applet that has been rewritten to use AWT components instead of Swing components.

Code Listing 14-10   (AWTTempConverter.java)

```java
 1 import java.applet.Applet;
 2 import java.awt.*;
 3 import java.awt.event.*;
 4
 5 /**
 6    The AWTTempConverter class is an applet that converts
 7    Fahrenheit temperatures to Celsius.
 8 */
 9
10 public class AWTTempConverter extends Applet
11 {
12    private Panel fPanel;          // To hold a text field
13    private Panel cPanel;          // To hold a text field
14    private Panel buttonPanel;     // To hold a button
15    private TextField fahrenheit;  // Fahrenheit temperature
16    private TextField celsius;     // Celsius temperature
17
18    /**
19       init method
20    */
21
22    public void init()
23    {
24       // Build the panels.
25       buildFpanel();
26       buildCpanel();
27       buildButtonPanel();
28
29       // Create a layout manager.
30       setLayout(new GridLayout(3, 1));
31
32       // Add the panels to the applet.
33       add(fPanel);
34       add(cPanel);
35       add(buttonPanel);
36    }
```

```
37
38     /**
39        The buildFpanel method creates a panel with a text
40        field in which the user can enter a Fahrenheit
41        temperature.
42     */
43
44     private void buildFpanel()
45     {
46        // Create the panel.
47        fPanel = new Panel();
48
49        // Create a label to display a message.
50        Label message1 = new Label("Fahrenheit Temperature:");
51
52        // Create a text field for the Fahrenheit temp.
53        fahrenheit = new TextField(10);
54
55        // Create a layout manager for the panel.
56        fPanel.setLayout(new FlowLayout(FlowLayout.RIGHT));
57
58        // Add the label and text field to the panel.
59        fPanel.add(message1);
60        fPanel.add(fahrenheit);
61     }
62
63     /**
64        The buildCpanel method creates a panel that
65        displays the Celsius temperature in a
66        read-only text field.
67     */
68
69     private void buildCpanel()
70     {
71        // Create the panel.
72        cPanel = new Panel();
73
74        // Create a label to display a message.
75        Label message2 = new Label("Celsius Temperature:");
76
77        // Create a text field for the Celsius temp.
78        celsius = new TextField(10);
79
80        // Make the text field read-only.
81        celsius.setEditable(false);
82
```

```
 83            // Create a layout manager for the panel.
 84            cPanel.setLayout(new FlowLayout(FlowLayout.RIGHT));
 85
 86            // Add the label and text field to the panel.
 87            cPanel.add(message2);
 88            cPanel.add(celsius);
 89         }
 90
 91         /**
 92            The buildButtonPanel method creates a panel with
 93            a button that converts the Fahrenheit temperature
 94            to Celsius.
 95         */
 96
 97
 98         private void buildButtonPanel()
 99         {
100            // Create the panel.
101            buttonPanel = new Panel();
102
103            // Create a button with the text "Convert".
104            Button convButton = new Button("Convert");
105
106            // Add an action listener to the button.
107            convButton.addActionListener(new ButtonListener());
108
109            // Add the button to the panel.
110            buttonPanel.add(convButton);
111         }
112
113         /**
114            Private inner class that handles the action event
115            that is generated when the user clicks the convert
116            button.
117         */
118
119         private class ButtonListener implements ActionListener
120         {
121            public void actionPerformed(ActionEvent e)
122            {
123               double ftemp, ctemp;  // To hold the temperatures
124
125               // Get the Fahrenheit temperature and convert it
126               // to a double.
127               ftemp = Double.parseDouble(fahrenheit.getText());
128
```

```
129              // Calculate the Celsius temperature.
130              ctemp = (5.0 / 9.0) * (ftemp - 32);
131
132              // Display the Celsius temperature.
133              celsius.setText(String.format("%.1f",  ctemp));
134         }
135    }
136 }
```

The only modifications that were made were as follows:

- The JApplet, JPanel, JLabel, JTextField, and JButton classes were replaced with the Applet, Panel, Label, TextField, and Button classes.
- The import javax.swing.*; statement was removed.

To run the applet in a browser, the APPLET tag in the *TempConverter.html* file must be modified to read as follows:

```
<applet code="AWTTempConverter.class" width=300 height=150>
</applet>
```

Once this change is made, the *TempConverter.html* file produces the Web page shown in Figure 14-16.

Figure 14-16 Web page running the AWTTempConverter applet   (Microsoft Corporation)

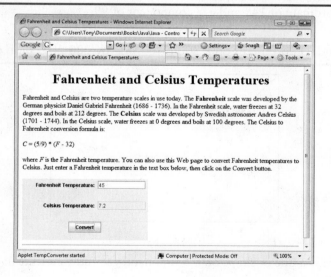

Checkpoint

MyProgrammingLab™ *www.myprogramminglab.com*

14.16 To create an applet using AWT, what class do you inherit your applet class from?

14.17 In Swing, if an object's class extends JFrame or JApplet, you add components to its content pane. How do you add components to an object if its class extends Frame or Applet?

14.5 Drawing Shapes

CONCEPT: Components have an associated `Graphics` object that may be used to draw lines and shapes.

In addition to displaying standard components such as buttons and labels, Java allows you to draw lines and graphical shapes such as rectangles, ovals, and arcs. These lines and shapes are drawn directly on components. This allows a frame or a panel to become a canvas for your drawings. Before we examine how to draw graphics on a component, however, we must discuss the *XY* coordinate system. You use the *XY* coordinate system to specify the location of your graphics.

The *XY* Coordinate System

The location of each pixel in a component is identified with an *X* coordinate and a *Y* coordinate. The coordinates are usually written in the form (*X*, *Y*). The *X* coordinate identifies a pixel's horizontal location, and the *Y* coordinate identifies its vertical location. The coordinates of the pixel in the upper-left corner of a component are usually (0, 0). The *X* coordinates increase from left to right, and the *Y* coordinates increase from top to bottom. For example, Figure 14-17 illustrates a component such as a frame or a panel that is 300 pixels wide by 200 pixels high. The *X* and *Y* coordinates of the pixels in each corner, as well as the pixel in the center of the component are shown. The pixel in the center of the component has an X coordinate of 149 and a Y component of 99.

Figure 14-17 *X* and *Y* coordinates on a 300 pixel wide by 200 pixel high component

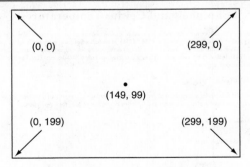

When you draw a line or shape on a component, you must indicate its position using *X* and *Y* coordinates.

Graphics Objects

Each component has an internal object that inherits from the `Graphics` class, which is part of the `java.awt` package. This object has numerous methods for drawing graphical shapes on the surface of the component. Table 14-2 lists some of these methods.

Table 14-2 Some of the Graphics class methods

Method	Description
`void setColor(Color c)`	Sets the drawing color for this object to that specified by the argument.
`Color getColor()`	Returns the current drawing color for this object.
`void drawLine(int x1, int y1,` `           int x2, int y2)`	Draws a line on the component starting at the coordinate $(x1, y1)$ and ending at the coordinate $(x2, y2)$. The line will be drawn in the current drawing color.
`void drawRect(int x, int y,` `     int width, int height)`	Draws the outline of a rectangle on the component. The upper-left corner of the rectangle will be at the coordinate (x, y). The `width` parameter specifies the rectangle's width in pixels, and `height` specifies the rectangle's height in pixels. The rectangle will be drawn in the current drawing color.
`void fillRect(int x, int y,` `     int width, int height)`	Draws a filled rectangle. The parameters are the same as those used by the `drawRect` method. The rectangle will be filled with the current drawing color.
`void drawOval(int x, int y,` `     int width, int height)`	Draws the outline of an oval on the component. The shape and size of the oval is determined by an invisible rectangle that encloses it. The upper-left corner of the rectangle will be at the coordinate (x, y). The `width` parameter specifies the rectangle's width in pixels, and `height` specifies the rectangle's height in pixels. The oval will be drawn in the current drawing color.
`void fillOval(int x, int y,` `     int width, int height)`	Draws a filled oval. The parameters are the same as those used by the `drawOval` method. The oval will be filled in the current drawing color.

`void drawArc(int x, int y,`
`     int width, int height,`
`     int startAngle,`
`     int arcAngle)`
	This method draws an arc, which is considered to be part of an oval. The shape and size of the oval are determined by an invisible rectangle that encloses it. The upper-left corner of the rectangle will be at the coordinate (x, y). The `width` parameter specifies the rectangle's width in pixels, and `height` specifies the rectangle's height in pixels. The arc begins at the angle `startAngle`, and ends at the angle `arcAngle`. The arc will be drawn in the current drawing color.

`void fillArc(int x, int y,`
`     int width, int height,`
`     int startAngle,`
`     int arcAngle)`
	This method draws a filled arc. The parameters are the same as those used by the `drawArc` method. The arc will be filled with the current drawing color.

(table continues next page)

Table 14-2   Some of the `Graphics` class methods (continued)

Method	Description

`void drawPolygon(int[] xPoints,`
`    int[] yPoints,`
`    int numPoints)`
	This method draws the outline of a closed polygon on the component. The *xPoints* array contains the X-coordinates for each vertex, and the *yPoints* array contains the Y coordinates for each vertex. The argument passed into *numPoints* is the number of vertices in the polygon.

`void fillPolygon(int[] xPoints,`
`    int[] yPoints,`
`    int numPoints)`
	This method draws a filled polygon. The parameters are the same as those used by the `drawPolygon` method. The polygon will be filled with the current drawing color.

`void drawstring(String str,` `    int x, int y)`	Draws the string passed into *str* using the current font. The bottom left of the string is drawn at the coordinates passed into *x* and *y*.
`void setFont(Font f)`	Sets the current font, which is used by the `drawString` method.

In order to call any of these methods, you must get a reference to a component's `Graphics` object. One way to do this is to override the `paint` method. You can override the `paint` method in any class that extends as follows:

- `JApplet`
- `JFrame`
- Any AWT class, including `Applet` and `Frame`

The `paint` method is responsible for displaying, or "painting," a component on the screen. This method is automatically called when the component is first displayed and is called again any time the component needs to be redisplayed. For example, when the component is completely or partially obscured by another window, and the obscuring window is moved, then the component's `paint` method is called to redisplay it. The header for the `paint` method is:

```
public void paint(Graphics g)
```

Notice that the method's argument is a `Graphics` object. When this method is called for a particular component, the `Graphics` object that belongs to that component is automatically passed as an argument. By overriding the `paint` method, you can use the `Graphics` object argument to draw your own graphics on the component. For example, look at the applet class in Code Listing 14-11.

This class inherits from `JApplet`, and it overrides the `paint` method. The `Graphics` object that is passed into the `paint` method's g parameter is the object that is responsible for drawing the entire applet window. Notice that in line 29 the method first calls the superclass version of the `paint` method, passing the object g as an argument. When overriding the `paint` method, you should always call the superclass's `paint` method before doing anything else. This ensures that the component will be displayed properly on the screen.

Code Listing 14-11　　(LineDemo.java)

```java
 1 import javax.swing.*;
 2 import java.awt.*;
 3
 4 /**
 5    This class is an applet that demonstrates how lines
 6    can be drawn.
 7 */
 8
 9 public class LineDemo extends JApplet
10 {
11    /**
12       init method
13    */
14
15    public void init()
16    {
17       // Set the background color to white.
18       getContentPane().setBackground(Color.white);
19    }
20
21    /**
22       paint method
23       @param g The applet's Graphics object.
24    */
25
26    public void paint(Graphics g)
27    {
28       // Call the superclass paint method.
29       super.paint(g);
30
31       // Draw a red line from (20, 20) to (280, 280).
32       g.setColor(Color.red);
33       g.drawLine(20, 20, 280, 280);
34
35       // Draw a blue line from (280, 20) to (20, 280).
36       g.setColor(Color.blue);
37       g.drawLine(280, 20, 20, 280);
38    }
39 }
```

In line 32 the method sets the drawing color to red. In line 33 a line is drawn from the coordinates (20, 20) to (280, 280). This is a diagonal line drawn from the top-left area of the applet window to the bottom-right area. Next, in line 36, the drawing color is set to blue. In line 37 a line is drawn from (280, 20) to (20, 280). This is also a diagonal line. It is drawn from the top-right area of the applet window to the bottom-left area.

We can use the *LineDemo.html* file, which is in the same folder as the applet class, to execute the applet. The following line in the file runs the applet in an area that is 300 pixels wide by 300 pixels high:

```
<applet code="LineDemo.class" width=300 height=300>
</applet>
```

Figure 14-18 shows the applet running in the applet viewer.

Figure 14-18   `LineDemo` applet

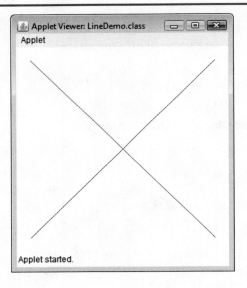

Notice that the `paint` method is not explicitly called by the applet. It is automatically called when the applet first executes. As previously mentioned, it is also called any time the applet window needs to be redisplayed.

Code Listing 14-12 shows the `RectangleDemo` class, an applet that draws two rectangles: one as a black outline and one filled with red. Each rectangle is 120 pixels wide and 120 pixels high. The file *RectangleDemo.html*, which is in the same folder as the applet class, executes the applet with the following tag:

```
<applet code="RectangleDemo.class" width=300 height=300>
</applet>
```

Figure 14-19 shows the applet running in the applet viewer.

Code Listing 14-12   (`RectangleDemo.java`)

```
 1 import javax.swing.*;
 2 import java.awt.*;
 3
 4 /**
 5    This class is an applet that demonstrates how
 6    rectangles can be drawn.
 7 */
 8
 9 public class RectangleDemo extends JApplet
10 {
11    /**
12       init method
13    */
14
15    public void init()
16    {
17       // Set the background color to white.
18       getContentPane().setBackground(Color.white);
19    }
20
21    /**
22       paint method
23       @param g The applet's Graphics object.
24    */
25
26    public void paint(Graphics g)
27    {
28       // Call the superclass paint method.
29       super.paint(g);
30
31       // Draw a black unfilled rectangle.
32       g.setColor(Color.black);
33       g.drawRect(20, 20, 120, 120);
34
35       // Draw a red filled rectangle.
36       g.setColor(Color.red);
37       g.fillRect(160, 160, 120, 120);
38    }
39 }
```

Figure 14-19 RectangleDemo applet

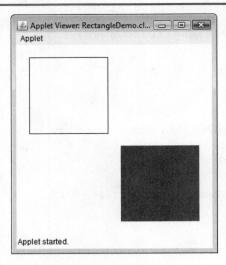

Code Listing 14-13 shows the OvalDemo class, an applet that draws two ovals. An oval is enclosed in an invisible rectangle that establishes the boundaries of the oval. The width and height of the enclosing rectangle defines the shape and size of the oval. This is illustrated in Figure 14-20.

When you call the drawOval or fillOval method, you pass the X and Y coordinates of the enclosing rectangle's upper-left corner, and the width and height of the enclosing rectangle as arguments.

Code Listing 14-13   (OvalDemo.java)

```
 1 import javax.swing.*;
 2 import java.awt.*;
 3
 4 /**
 5    This class is an applet that demonstrates how
 6    ovals can be drawn.
 7 */
 8
 9 public class OvalDemo extends JApplet
10 {
11    /**
12       init method
13    */
14
15    public void init()
16    {
```

```
17          // Set the background color to white.
18          getContentPane().setBackground(Color.white);
19       }
20
21       /**
22          paint method
23          @param g The applet's Graphics object.
24       */
25
26       public void paint(Graphics g)
27       {
28          // Call the superclass paint method.
29          super.paint(g);
30
31          // Draw a black unfilled oval.
32          g.setColor(Color.black);
33          g.drawOval(20, 20, 120, 75);
34
35          // Draw a green filled oval.
36          g.setColor(Color.green);
37          g.fillOval(80, 160, 180, 75);
38       }
39 }
```

Figure 14-20   An oval and its enclosing rectangle

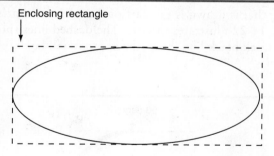

Enclosing rectangle

The file *OvalDemo.html*, which is in the same folder as the applet class, executes the applet with the following tag:

```
<applet code="OvalDemo.class" width=300 height=255>
</applet>
```

Figure 14-21 shows the applet running in the applet viewer.

Figure 14-21 `OvalDemo` applet

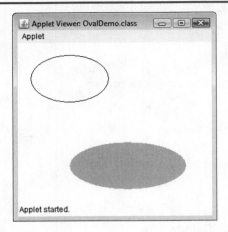

 TIP: To draw a circle, simply draw an oval with an enclosing rectangle that is square. In other words, the enclosing rectangle's width and height should be the same.

The `drawArc` method draws an arc, which is part of an oval. You pass the same arguments to `drawArc` as you do to `drawOval`, plus two additional arguments: the arc's starting angle and ending angle. The angles are measured in degrees, with 0 degrees being at the 3 o'clock position. For example, look at the following statement:

```
g.drawArc(20, 20, 100, 100, 0, 90);
```

This statement creates an enclosing rectangle with its upper-left corner at (20, 20) and with a width and height of 100 pixels each. The oval constructed from this enclosing rectangle is a circle. The arc that is drawn is the part of the oval that starts at 0 degrees and ends at 90 degrees. Figure 14-22 illustrates this arc. The dashed lines show the enclosing rectangle and the oval. The thick black line shows the arc that will be drawn.

Figure 14-22 An arc

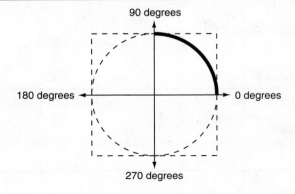

Code Listing 14-14 shows the `ArcDemo` class, which is an applet that draws four arcs: two unfilled and two filled. The filled arcs are drawn with the `fillArc` method.

> The file *ArcDemo.html*, which is in the same folder as the applet class, executes the applet with the following tag:
>
> ```
> <applet code="ArcDemo.class" width=300 height=220>
> </applet>
> ```

Figure 14-23 shows the applet running in the applet viewer.

Code Listing 14-14   (`ArcDemo.java`)

```java
 1 import javax.swing.*;
 2 import java.awt.*;
 3
 4 /**
 5    This class is an applet that demonstrates how
 6    arcs can be drawn.
 7 */
 8
 9 public class ArcDemo extends JApplet
10 {
11    /**
12       init method
13    */
14
15    public void init()
16    {
17       // Set the background color to white.
18       getContentPane().setBackground(Color.white);
19    }
20
21    /**
22       paint method
23       @param g The applet's Graphics object.
24    */
25
26    public void paint(Graphics g)
27    {
28       // Call the superclass paint method.
29       super.paint(g);
30
31       // Draw a black unfilled arc from 0 degrees
32       // to 90 degrees.
33       g.setColor(Color.black);
34       g.drawArc(0, 20, 120, 120, 0, 90);
35
36       // Draw a red filled arc from 0 degrees
37       // to 90 degrees.
```

```
38        g.setColor(Color.red);
39        g.fillArc(140, 20, 120, 120, 0, 90);
40
41        // Draw a green unfilled arc from 0 degrees
42        // to 45 degrees.
43        g.setColor(Color.green);
44        g.drawArc(0, 120, 120, 120, 0, 45);
45
46        // Draw a blue filled arc from 0 degrees
47        // to 45 degrees.
48        g.setColor(Color.blue);
49        g.fillArc(140, 120, 120, 120, 0, 45);
50    }
51 }
```

Figure 14-23 ArcDemo applet

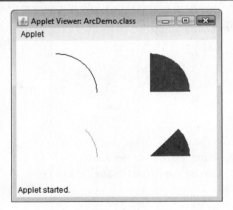

The drawPolygon method draws an outline of a closed polygon and the fillPolygon method draws a closed polygon filled with the current drawing color. A polygon is constructed of multiple line segments that are connected. The point where two line segments are connected is called a *vertex*. These methods accept two int arrays as arguments. The first array contains the X coordinates of each vertex, and the second array contains the Y coordinates of each vertex. The third argument is an int that specifies the number of vertices, or connecting points.

For example, suppose we use the following arrays as arguments for the X and Y coordinates of a polygon:

```
int[] xCoords = {60, 100, 140, 140, 100, 60, 20, 20 };
int[] yCoords = {20, 20, 60, 100, 140, 140, 100, 60 };
```

The first point specified by these arrays is (60, 20), the second point is (100, 20), and so forth. There are a total of eight points specified by these arrays, and if we connect each of these points we get the octagon shown in Figure 14-24.

Figure 14-24   Points of each vertex in an octagon

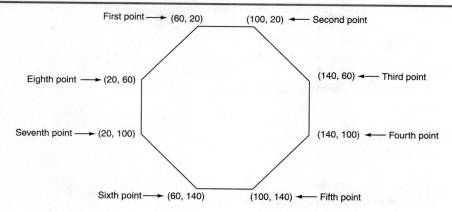

If the last point specified in the arrays is different from the first point, as in this example, then the two points are automatically connected to close the polygon. The PolygonDemo class in Code Listing 14-15 draws a filled polygon using these arrays as arguments.

Code Listing 14-15   (PolygonDemo.java)

```
 1 import javax.swing.*;
 2 import java.awt.*;
 3
 4 /**
 5    This class is an applet that demonstrates how a
 6    polygon can be drawn.
 7 */
 8
 9 public class PolygonDemo extends JApplet
10 {
11    /**
12       init method
13    */
14
15    public void init()
16    {
17       // Set the background color to white.
18       getContentPane().setBackground(Color.white);
19    }
20
21    /**
22       paint method
23       @param g The applet's Graphics object.
24    */
25
26    public void paint(Graphics g)
```

```
27  {
28      int[] xCoords = {60, 100, 140, 140,
29                        100, 60, 20, 20 };
30      int[] yCoords = {20, 20, 60, 100,
31                        140, 140, 100, 60 };
32
33      // Call the superclass paint method.
34      super.paint(g);
35
36      // Set the drawing color.
37      g.setColor(Color.red);
38
39      // Draw the polygon.
40      g.fillPolygon(xCoords, yCoords, 8);
41  }
42 }
```

The file *PolygonDemo.html*, which is in the same folder as the applet class, executes the applet with the following tag:

```
<applet code="PolygonDemo.class" width=160 height=160>
</applet>
```

Figure 14-25 shows the applet running in the applet viewer.

Figure 14-25 PolygonDemo applet

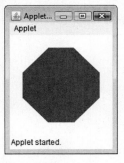

The drawString method draws a string as a graphic. The string is specified by its first argument, a String object. The X and Y coordinates of the lower-left point of the string are specified by the second and third arguments. For example, assuming that g references a Graphics object, the following statement draws the string "Hello World", starting at the coordinates 100, 50:

```
g.drawstring("Hello World", 100, 50);
```

You can set the font for the string with the setFont method. This method accepts a Font object as its argument. Here is an example:

```
g.setFont(new Font("Serif", Font.ITALIC, 20));
```

The Font class was covered in Chapter 13. Recall that the Font constructor's arguments are the name of a font, the font's style, and the font's size in points. You can combine font styles with the + operator, as follows:

```
g.setFont(new Font("Serif", Font.BOLD + Font.ITALIC, 24));
```

The GraphicStringDemo class in Code Listing 14-16 demonstrates the drawString method. It draws the same octagon that the PolygonDemo class drew, and then draws the string "STOP" over it to create a stop sign. The string is drawn in a bold 35-point sanserif font.

Code Listing 14-16   (`GraphicStringDemo.java`)

```java
 1 import javax.swing.*;
 2 import java.awt.*;
 3
 4 /**
 5    This class is an applet that demonstrates how a
 6    string can be drawn.
 7 */
 8
 9 public class GraphicStringDemo extends JApplet
10 {
11    /**
12       init method
13    */
14
15    public void init()
16    {
17       // Set the background color to white.
18       getContentPane().setBackground(Color.white);
19    }
20
21    /**
22       paint method
23       @param g The applet's Graphics object.
24    */
25
26    public void paint(Graphics g)
27    {
28       int[] xCoords = {60, 100, 140, 140,
29                           100, 60, 20, 20 };
30       int[] yCoords = {20, 20, 60, 100,
31                           140, 140, 100, 60 };
32
```

```
33        // Call the superclass paint method.
34        super.paint(g);
35
36        // Set the drawing color.
37        g.setColor(Color.red);
38
39        // Draw the polygon.
40        g.fillPolygon(xCoords, yCoords, 8);
41
42        // Set the drawing color to white.
43        g.setColor(Color.white);
44
45        // Set the font and draw "STOP".
46        g.setFont(new Font("SansSerif", Font.BOLD, 35));
47        g.drawString("STOP", 35, 95);
48     }
49 }
```

The file *GraphicStringDemo.html*, which is in the same folder as the applet class, executes the applet with the following tag:

```
<applet code="GraphicStringDemo.class" width=160 height=160>
</applet>
```

Figure 14-26 shows the applet running in the applet viewer.

Figure 14-26 GraphicStringDemo applet

The repaint Method

As previously mentioned, you do not call a component's paint method. It is automatically called when the component must be redisplayed. Sometimes, however, you might want to force the application or applet to call the paint method. You do this by calling the repaint method, which has the following header:

```
public void repaint()
```

The `repaint` method clears the surface of the component and then calls the `paint` method. You will see an applet that uses this method in a moment.

Drawing on Panels

Each of the preceding examples uses the entire `JApplet` window as a canvas for drawing. Sometimes, however, you might want to confine your drawing space to a smaller region within the window, such as a panel. To draw on a panel, you simply get a reference to the panel's `Graphics` object and then use that object's methods to draw. The resulting graphics are drawn only on the panel.

Getting a reference to a `JPanel` component's `Graphics` object is similar to the technique you saw in the previous examples. Instead of overriding the `JPanel` object's `paint` method, however, you should override its `paintComponent` method. This is true not only for `JPanel` objects, but also for all Swing components except `JApplet` and `JFrame`. The `paintComponent` method serves for `JPanel` and most other Swing objects the same purpose as the `paint` method: It is automatically called when the component needs to be redisplayed. When it is called, the component's `Graphics` object is passed as an argument. Here is the method's header:

```
public void paintComponent(Graphics g)
```

When you override this method, first you should call the superclass's `paintComponent` method to ensure that the component is properly displayed. Here is an example call to the superclass's version of the method:

```
super.paintComponent(g);
```

After this you can call any of the `Graphics` object's methods to draw on the component. As an example, we look at the `GraphicsWindow` class in Code Listing 14-17. When this applet is run (via the *GraphicsWindow.html* file, which is in the same folder as the applet class), the window shown in Figure 14-27 is displayed. A set of check boxes is displayed in a `JPanel` component on the right side of the window. The white area that occupies the majority of the window is a `DrawingPanel` object. The `DrawingPanel` class inherits from `JPanel`, and its code is shown in Code Listing-14-18. When one of the check boxes is selected, a shape appears in the `DrawingPanel` object. Figure 14-28 shows how the applet window appears when all of the check boxes are selected.

Figure 14-27   `GraphicsWindow` applet

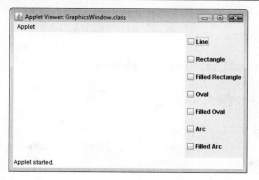

Figure 14-28   `GraphicsWindow` applet with all graphics selected

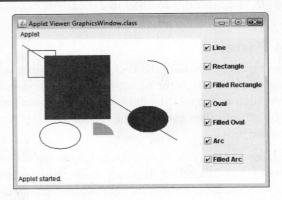

Code Listing 14-17   **(GraphicsWindow.java)**

```
 1 import javax.swing.*;
 2 import java.awt.*;
 3 import java.awt.event.*;
 4
 5 /**
 6    This class displays a drawing panel and a set of
 7    check boxes that allow the user to select shapes.
 8    The selected shapes are drawn on the drawing panel.
 9 */
10
11 public class GraphicsWindow extends JApplet
12 {
13    // Declare an array of check box components
14    private JCheckBox[] checkBoxes;
15
16    // The following titles array contains the
17    // titles of the check boxes.
18    private String[] titles = { "Line", "Rectangle",
19                                "Filled Rectangle",
20                                "Oval", "Filled Oval",
21                                "Arc", "Filled Arc" };
22
23    // The following will reference a panel to contain
24    // the check boxes.
25    private JPanel checkBoxPanel;
26
27    // The following will reference an instance of the
28    // DrawingPanel class. This will be a panel to draw on.
29    private DrawingPanel drawingPanel;
```

```
30
31      /**
32         init method
33      */
34
35      public void init()
36      {
37         // Build the check box panel.
38         buildCheckBoxPanel();
39
40         // Create the drawing panel.
41         drawingPanel = new DrawingPanel(checkBoxes);
42
43         // Add the check box panel to the east region
44         // and the drawing panel to the center region.
45         add(checkBoxPanel, BorderLayout.EAST);
46         add(drawingPanel, BorderLayout.CENTER);
47      }
48
49      /**
50         The buildCheckBoxPanel method creates the array of
51         check box components and adds them to a panel.
52      */
53
54      private void buildCheckBoxPanel()
55      {
56         // Create the panel.
57         checkBoxPanel = new JPanel();
58         checkBoxPanel.setLayout(new GridLayout(7, 1));
59
60         // Create the check box array.
61         checkBoxes = new JCheckBox[7];
62
63         // Create the check boxes and add them to the panel.
64         for (int i = 0; i < checkBoxes.length; i++)
65         {
66            checkBoxes[i] = new JCheckBox(titles[i]);
67            checkBoxes[i].addItemListener(
68                                new CheckBoxListener());
69            checkBoxPanel.add(checkBoxes[i]);
70         }
71      }
72
73      /**
74         A private inner class to respond to changes in the
75         state of the check boxes.
76      */
77
```

```
78     private class CheckBoxListener implements ItemListener
79     {
80        public void itemStateChanged(ItemEvent e)
81        {
82           drawingPanel.repaint();
83        }
84     }
85  }
```

Code Listing 14-18   (`DrawingPanel.java`)

```
1  import javax.swing.*;
2  import java.awt.*;
3
4  /**
5     This class creates a panel that example shapes are
6     drawn on.
7  */
8
9  public class DrawingPanel extends JPanel
10 {
11    // Declare a check box array.
12    private JCheckBox[] checkBoxArray;
13
14    /**
15       Constructor
16    */
17
18    public DrawingPanel(JCheckBox[] cbArray)
19    {
20       // Reference the check box array.
21       checkBoxArray = cbArray;
22
23       // Set the background color to white.
24       setBackground(Color.white);
25
26       // Set the preferred size of the panel.
27       setPreferredSize(new Dimension(300, 200));
28    }
29
30    /**
31       paintComponent method
32       @param g The panel's Graphics object.
33    */
34
35    public void paintComponent(Graphics g)
```

```
36    {
37        // Call the superclass paintComponent method.
38        super.paintComponent(g);
39
40        // Draw the selected shapes.
41        if (checkBoxArray[0].isSelected())
42        {
43            g.setColor(Color.black);
44            g.drawLine(10, 10, 290, 190);
45        }
46        if (checkBoxArray[1].isSelected())
47        {
48            g.setColor(Color.black);
49            g.drawRect(20, 20, 50, 50);
50        }
51        if (checkBoxArray[2].isSelected())
52        {
53            g.setColor(Color.red);
54            g.fillRect(50, 30, 120, 120);
55        }
56        if (checkBoxArray[3].isSelected())
57        {
58            g.setColor(Color.black);
59            g.drawOval(40, 155, 75, 50);
60        }
61        if (checkBoxArray[4].isSelected())
62        {
63            g.setColor(Color.blue);
64            g.fillOval(200, 125, 75, 50);
65        }
66        if (checkBoxArray[5].isSelected())
67        {
68            g.setColor(Color.black);
69            g.drawArc(200, 40, 75, 50, 0, 90);
70        }
71        if (checkBoxArray[6].isSelected())
72        {
73            g.setColor(Color.green);
74            g.fillArc(100, 155, 75, 50, 0, 90);
75        }
76    }
77 }
```

Let's take a closer look at the applet's code. First, notice in lines 14 through 21 of the GraphicsWindow class (in Code Listing 14-17) that two of the class's fields are array reference variables. The checkBoxes variable references an array of JCheckBox components, and the titles variable references an array of strings. The strings in the titles array are the titles that the check boxes will display.

The first statement in the init method, line 38, is a call to the buildCheckBoxPanel method, which creates a panel for the check boxes, creates the array of check boxes, adds an item listener to each element of the array, and adds each element to the panel.

After the buildCheckBoxPanel method executes, the init method creates a DrawingPanel object with the statement in line 41. Notice that the checkBoxes variable is passed to the DrawingPanel constructor. The drawingPanel object needs a reference to the array so its paintComponent method can determine which check boxes are selected and draw the corresponding shape.

The only times that the paintComponent method is automatically called is when the component is initially displayed and when the component needs to be redisplayed. In order to display a shape immediately when the user selects a check box, we need the check box item listener to force the paintComponent method to be called. This is accomplished by the statement in line 82, in the CheckBoxListener class's itemStateChanged method. This statement calls the drawingPanel object's repaint method, which causes the drawingPanel object's surface to be cleared, and then causes the object's paintComponent method to execute. Because it is in the item listener, it is executed each time the user clicks on a check box.

Checkpoint

MyProgrammingLab™ *www.myprogramminglab.com*

14.18 In an AWT component, or a class that extends JApplet or JFrame, if you want to get a reference to the Graphics object, do you override the paint or paintComponent method?

14.19 In a JPanel object, do you override the paint or paintComponent method to get a reference to the Graphics object?

14.20 When are the paint and paintComponent method called?

14.21 In the paint or paintComponent method, what should be done before anything else?

14.22 How do you force the paint or paintComponent method to be called?

14.23 When using a Graphics object to draw an oval, what invisible shape is the oval enclosed in?

14.24 What values are contained in the two arrays that are passed to a Graphics object's drawPolygon method?

14.25 What Graphics class methods do you use to perform the following tasks?
   a) Draw a line.
   b) Draw a filled rectangle.
   c) Draw a filled oval.
   d) Draw a filled arc.
   e) Set the drawing color.
   f) Draw a rectangle.
   g) Draw an oval.
   h) Draw an arc.
   i) Draw a string.
   j) Set the font.

14.6 Handling Mouse Events

CONCEPT: Java allows you to create listener classes that handle events generated by the mouse.

Handling Mouse Events

The mouse generates two types of events: mouse events and mouse motion events. To handle mouse events you create a *mouse listener* class and/or a *mouse motion listener* class. A mouse listener class can respond to any of the follow events:

- The mouse button is pressed.
- The mouse button is released.
- The mouse button is clicked (pressed, then released without moving the mouse).
- The mouse cursor enters a component's screen space.
- The mouse cursor exits a component's screen space.

A mouse listener class must implement the MouseListener interface, which is in the java.awt.event package. The class must also have the methods listed in Table 14-3.

Table 14-3 Methods required by the MouseListener interface

Method	Description
public void mousePressed(MouseEvent e)	If the mouse cursor is over the component and the mouse button is pressed, this method is called.
public void mouseClicked(MouseEvent e)	A mouse click is defined as pressing the mouse button and releasing it without moving the mouse. If the mouse cursor is over the component and the mouse is clicked on, this method is called.
public void mouseReleased(MouseEvent e)	This method is called when the mouse button is released after it has been pressed. The mousePressed method is always called before this method.
public void mouseEntered(MouseEvent e)	This method is called when the mouse cursor enters the screen area belonging to the component.
public void mouseExited(MouseEvent e)	This method is called when the mouse cursor leaves the screen area belonging to the component.

Notice that each of the methods listed in Table 14-3 accepts a MouseEvent object as its argument. The MouseEvent object contains data about the mouse event. We will use two of the `MouseEvent` object's methods: `getX` and `getY`. These methods return the *X* and *Y* coordinates of the mouse cursor when the event occurs.

Once you create a mouse listener class, you can register it with a component using the `addMouseListener` method, which is inherited from the `Component` class. The appropriate methods in the mouse listener class are automatically called when their corresponding mouse events occur.

A mouse motion listener class can respond to the following events:

- The mouse is dragged (the button is pressed and the mouse is moved while the button is held down).
- The mouse is moved.

A mouse motion listener class must implement the `MouseMotionListener` interface, which is in the `java.awt.event` package. The class must also have the methods listed in Table 14-4. Notice that each of these methods also accepts a `MouseEvent` object as an argument.

Table 14-4 Methods required by the `MouseMotionListener` interface

Method	Description
`public void mouseDragged(MouseEvent e)`	The mouse is dragged when its button is pressed and the mouse is moved while the button is held down. This method is called when a dragging operation begins over the component. The `mousePressed` method is always called just before this method.
`public void mouseMoved(MouseEvent e)`	This method is called when the mouse cursor is over the component and it is moved.

Once you create a mouse motion listener class, you can register it with a component using the `addMouseMotionListener` method, which is inherited from the `Component` class. The appropriate methods in the mouse motion listener class are automatically called when their corresponding mouse events occur.

The `MouseEvents` class, shown in Code Listing 14-19, is an applet that demonstrates both a mouse listener and a mouse motion listener. The file *MouseEvents.html*, which is in the same folder as the applet class, can be used to start the applet. Figure 14-29 shows the applet running. The window displays a group of read-only text fields that represent the different mouse and mouse motion events. When an event occurs, the corresponding text field turns yellow. The last two text fields constantly display the mouse cursor's *X* and *Y* coordinates. Run this applet and experiment by clicking the mouse inside the window, dragging the mouse, moving the mouse cursor in and out of the window, and moving the mouse cursor over the text fields.

Code Listing 14-19   (MouseEvents.java)

```java
 1 import javax.swing.*;
 2 import java.awt.event.*;
 3 import java.awt.*;
 4
 5 /**
 6    This applet shows the mouse events as they occur.
 7 */
 8
 9 public class MouseEvents extends JApplet
10 {
11    private JTextField[] mouseStates;
12    private String[] text = {
13                  "Pressed", "Clicked", "Released",
14                  "Entered", "Exited", "Dragged",
15                  "X:", "Y:" };
16
17    /**
18       init method
19    */
20
21    public void init()
22    {
23       // Create a layout manager.
24       setLayout(new FlowLayout());
25
26       // Create the array of text fields.
27       mouseStates = new JTextField[8];
28       for (int i = 0; i < mouseStates.length; i++)
29       {
30          mouseStates[i] = new JTextField(text[i], 10);
31          mouseStates[i].setEditable(false);
32          add(mouseStates[i]);
33       }
34
35       // Add a mouse listener to this applet.
36       addMouseListener(new MyMouseListener());
37
38       // Add a mouse motion listener to this applet.
39       addMouseMotionListener(new MyMouseMotionListener());
40    }
41
42    /**
43       The clearTextFields method sets all of the text
44       backgrounds to light gray.
45    */
```

```
46
47     public void clearTextFields()
48     {
49        for (int i = 0; i < 6; i++)
50           mouseStates[i].setBackground(Color.lightGray);
51     }
52
53     /**
54        Private inner class that handles mouse events.
55        When an event occurs, the text field for that
56        event is given a yellow background.
57     */
58
59     private class MyMouseListener
60                            implements MouseListener
61     {
62        public void mousePressed(MouseEvent e)
63        {
64           clearTextFields();
65           mouseStates[0].setBackground(Color.yellow);
66        }
67
68        public void mouseClicked(MouseEvent e)
69        {
70           clearTextFields();
71           mouseStates[1].setBackground(Color.yellow);
72        }
73
74        public void mouseReleased(MouseEvent e)
75        {
76           clearTextFields();
77           mouseStates[2].setBackground(Color.yellow);
78        }
79
80        public void mouseEntered(MouseEvent e)
81        {
82           clearTextFields();
83           mouseStates[3].setBackground(Color.yellow);
84        }
85
86        public void mouseExited(MouseEvent e)
87        {
88           clearTextFields();
89           mouseStates[4].setBackground(Color.yellow);
90        }
91     }
92
```

```
93      /**
94          Private inner class to handle mouse motion events.
95      */
96
97      private class MyMouseMotionListener
98                        implements MouseMotionListener
99      {
100         public void mouseDragged(MouseEvent e)
101         {
102            clearTextFields();
103            mouseStates[5].setBackground(Color.yellow);
104         }
105
106         public void mouseMoved(MouseEvent e)
107         {
108            mouseStates[6].setText("X: " + e.getX());
109            mouseStates[7].setText("Y: " + e.getY());
110         }
111      }
112 }
```

Figure 14-29 MouseEvents applet

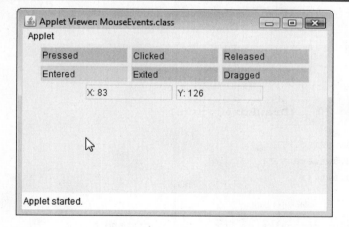

Using Adapter Classes

Many times when you handle mouse events, you will not be interested in handling every event that the mouse generates. This is the case with the DrawBoxes applet, which handles only mouse pressed and mouse dragged events.

This applet lets you draw rectangles by pressing the mouse button and dragging the mouse inside the applet window. When you initially press the mouse button, the position of the mouse cursor becomes the upper-left corner of a rectangle. As you drag the mouse, the lower-right corner of the rectangle follows the mouse cursor. When you release the mouse cursor, the rectangle stops following the mouse. Figure 14-30 shows an example of the applet's window. You can run the applet with the *DrawBoxes.html* file, which is in the same folder as the applet class. Code Listing 14-20 shows the code for the DrawBoxes class.

 NOTE: To draw the rectangle, you must drag the mouse cursor to the right and below the position where you initially pressed the mouse button.

Figure 14-30   DrawBoxes applet

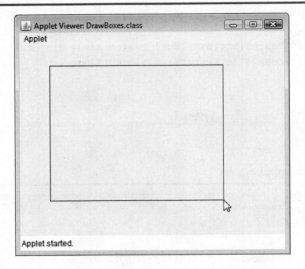

Code Listing 14-20   (**DrawBoxes.java**)

```
 1 import javax.swing.*;
 2 import java.awt.event.*;
 3 import java.awt.*;
 4
 5 /**
 6    This applet demonstrates how mouse events and mouse
 7    motion events can be handled. It lets the user draw
 8    boxes by dragging the mouse.
 9 */
10
11 public class DrawBoxes extends JApplet
12 {
13    private int currentX = 0;     // Mouse cursor's X position
14    private int currentY = 0;     // Mouse cursor's Y position
15    private int width = 0;        // The rectangle's width
```

```
16      private int height = 0;         // The rectangle's height
17
18      /**
19         init method
20      */
21
22      public void init()
23      {
24         // Add a mouse listener and a mouse motion listener.
25         addMouseListener(new MyMouseListener());
26         addMouseMotionListener(new MyMouseMotionListener());
27      }
28
29      /**
30         paint method
31         @param g The applet's Graphics object.
32      */
33
34      public void paint(Graphics g)
35      {
36         // Call the superclass's paint method.
37         super.paint(g);
38
39         // Draw a rectangle.
40         g.drawRect(currentX, currentY, width, height);
41      }
42
43      /**
44         Mouse listener class
45      */
46
47      private class MyMouseListener
48                         implements MouseListener
49      {
50         public void mousePressed(MouseEvent e)
51         {
52            // Get the mouse cursor coordinates.
53            currentX = e.getX();
54            currentY = e.getY();
55         }
56
57         //
58         // The following methods are unused, but still
59         // required by the MouseListener interface.
60         //
61
62         public void mouseClicked(MouseEvent e)
63         {
```

```
64          }
65
66          public void mouseReleased(MouseEvent e)
67          {
68          }
69
70          public void mouseEntered(MouseEvent e)
71          {
72          }
73
74          public void mouseExited(MouseEvent e)
75          {
76          }
77       }
78
79       /**
80          Mouse Motion listener class
81       */
82
83       private class MyMouseMotionListener
84                      implements MouseMotionListener
85       {
86          public void mouseDragged(MouseEvent e)
87          {
88             // Calculate the size of the rectangle.
89             width = e.getX() - currentX;
90             height = e.getY() - currentY;
91
92             // Repaint the window.
93             repaint();
94          }
95
96          /**
97             The mouseMoved method is unused, but still
98             required by the MouseMotionListener interface.
99          */
100
101         public void mouseMoved(MouseEvent e)
102         {
103         }
104      }
105 }
```

Notice in the mouse listener and mouse motion listener classes that several of the methods are empty. Even though the applet handles only two mouse events, the MyMouseListener and MyMouseMotionListener classes must have all of the methods required by the interfaces they implement. If any of these methods are omitted, a compiler error results.

The Java API provides an alternative technique for creating these listener classes, which eliminates the need to define empty methods for the events you are not interested in. Instead of implementing the MouseListener or MouseMotionListener interfaces, you can extend your classes from the MouseAdapter or MouseMotionAdapter classes. These classes implement the MouseListener and MouseMotionListener interfaces and provide empty definitions for all of the required methods. When you extend a class from one of these adapter classes, it inherits the empty methods. In your extended class, you can override the methods you want and forget about the others. Both the MouseAdapter and MouseMotionAdapter classes are in the java.awt.event package.

The DrawBoxes2 class shown in Code Listing 14-21 is a modification of the DrawBoxes class previously shown. In this version, the MyMouseListener class extends MouseAdapter and the MyMouseMotionListener class extends MouseMotionAdapter. This applet operates exactly the same as the DrawBoxes applet. The only difference is that this class does not have the empty methods in the listener classes.

NOTE: Java provides an adapter class for all of the interfaces in the API that have more than one method.

Code Listing 14-21   (**DrawBoxes2.java**)

```
 1 import javax.swing.*;
 2 import java.awt.event.*;
 3 import java.awt.*;
 4
 5 /**
 6    This applet demonstrates how the mouse adapter
 7    classes can be used.
 8 */
 9
10 public class DrawBoxes2 extends JApplet
11 {
12    private int currentX = 0;    // Mouse cursor's X position
13    private int currentY = 0;    // Mouse cursor's Y position
14    private int width = 0;       // The rectangle's width
15    private int height = 0;      // The rectangle's height
16
17    /**
18       init method
19    */
20
21    public void init()
22    {
23       // Add a mouse listener and a mouse motion listener.
24       addMouseListener(new MyMouseListener());
25       addMouseMotionListener(new MyMouseMotionListener());
26    }
```

```
27
28    /**
29       paint method
30       @param g The applet's Graphics object.
31    */
32
33    public void paint(Graphics g)
34    {
35       // Call the superclass's paint method.
36       super.paint(g);
37
38       // Draw a rectangle.
39       g.drawRect(currentX, currentY, width, height);
40    }
41
42    /**
43       Mouse listener class
44    */
45
46    private class MyMouseListener extends MouseAdapter
47    {
48       public void mousePressed(MouseEvent e)
49       {
50          // Get the coordinates of the mouse cursor.
51          currentX = e.getX();
52          currentY = e.getY();
53       }
54    }
55
56    /**
57       Mouse Motion listener class
58    */
59
60    private class MyMouseMotionListener
61                        extends MouseMotionAdapter
62    {
63       public void mouseDragged(MouseEvent e)
64       {
65          // Calculate the size of the rectangle.
66          width = e.getX() - currentX;
67          height = e.getY() - currentY;
68
69          // Repaint the window.
70          repaint();
71       }
72    }
73 }
```

Checkpoint

14.26 What is the difference between a mouse press event and a mouse click event?

14.27 What interface would a listener class implement to handle a mouse click event? A mouse press event? A mouse dragged event? A mouse release event? A mouse move event?

14.28 What type of object do mouse listener and mouse motion listener methods accept? What methods do these types of objects provide for determining a mouse cursor's location?

14.29 If a class implements the MouseListener interface but does not need to use all of the methods specified by the interface, can the definitions for those methods be left out? If not, how are these methods dealt with?

14.30 What is an adapter class, and how does it make some programming tasks easier?

14.7 Timer **Objects**

CONCEPT: A Timer object regularly generates action events at programmer-specified time intervals.

Timer objects automatically generate action events at regular time intervals. This is useful when you want a program to perform an operation at certain times or after an amount of time has passed.

Timer objects are created from the Timer class, which is in the javax.swing package. Here is the general format of the Timer class's constructor:

```
Timer(int delay, ActionListener listener)
```

The argument passed into the *delay* parameter is the amount of time between action events, measured in milliseconds. A millisecond is a thousandth of a second, so a *delay* value of 1000 causes an action event to be generated every second. The argument passed into the *listener* parameter is a reference to an action listener that is to be registered with the Timer object. If you want to add an action listener at a later time, you can pass null as this argument, then use the Timer object's addActionListener method to register an action listener. Table 14-5 lists the Timer class's methods.

An application can use a Timer object to execute code automatically at regular time intervals. For example, a Timer object can be used to perform simple animation by moving a graphic image across the screen by a certain amount at regular time intervals. This is demonstrated in the BouncingBall class, shown in Code Listing 14-22. This class is an applet that displays a bouncing ball, as shown in Figure 14-31.

Table 14-5   Timer class methods

Method	Description
void addActionListener (ActionListener *listener*)	Registers the object referenced by *listener* as an action listener.
int getDelay()	Returns the current time delay in milliseconds.
Boolean isRunning()	Returns true if the Timer object is running. Otherwise, it returns false.
void setDelay(int delay)	Sets the time delay. The argument is the amount of the delay in milliseconds.
void start()	Starts the Timer object, which causes it to generate action events.
void stop()	Stops the Timer object, which causes it to stop generating action events.

Figure 14-31   BouncingBall applet

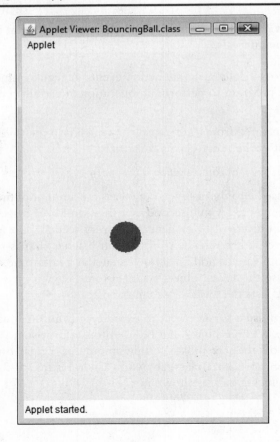

Code Listing 14-22   (`BouncingBall.java`)

```java
 1 import javax.swing.*;
 2 import java.awt.event.*;
 3 import java.awt.*;
 4
 5 /**
 6    This applet uses a Timer object to animate
 7    a bouncing ball.
 8 */
 9
10 public class BouncingBall extends JApplet
11 {
12    private final int X = 109;            // Ball's X coordinate
13    private final int WIDTH = 40;         // Ball's width
14    private final int HEIGHT = 40;        // Ball's height
15    private final int TIME_DELAY = 30;    // Time delay
16    private final int MOVE = 20;          // Pixels to move ball
17    private final int MINIMUM_Y = 50;     // Max height of ball
18    private final int MAXIMUM_Y = 400;    // Min height of ball
19    private int y = 400;                  // Ball's Y coordinate
20    private boolean goingUp = true;       // Direction indicator
21    private Timer timer;                  // Timer object
22
23
24    /**
25       init method
26    */
27
28    public void init()
29    {
30       timer = new Timer(TIME_DELAY, new TimerListener());
31       timer.start();
32    }
33
34    /**
35       paint method
36       @param g The applet's Graphics object.
37    */
38
39    public void paint(Graphics g)
40    {
41       // Call the superclass paint method.
42       super.paint(g);
43
44       // Set the drawing color to red.
45       g.setColor(Color.red);
46
```

```
47            // Draw the ball.
48            g.fillOval(X, y, WIDTH, HEIGHT);
49        }
50
51        /**
52            Private inner class that handles the Timer object's
53            action events.
54        */
55
56        private class TimerListener implements ActionListener
57        {
58            public void actionPerformed(ActionEvent e)
59            {
60                // Update the ball's Y coordinate.
61                if (goingUp)
62                {
63                    if (y > MINIMUM_Y)
64                        y -= MOVE;
65                    else
66                        goingUp = false;
67                }
68                else
69                {
70                    if (y < MAXIMUM_Y)
71                        y += MOVE;
72                    else
73                        goingUp = true;
74                }
75
76                // Force a call to the paint method.
77                repaint();
78            }
79        }
80 }
```

The BouncingBall class's init method creates a Timer object with the following statement in line 30:

```
timer = new Timer(TIME_DELAY, new TimerListener());
```

This initializes the object with a time delay of 30 milliseconds (the value of TIME_DELAY) and registers an instance of the TimerListener class as an action listener. This means that once the object is started, every 30 milliseconds it generates an action event, causing the action listener's actionPerformed method to execute. The next statement in the init method, in line 31, starts the Timer object as follows:

```
timer.start();
```

This causes the `Timer` object to commence generating action events. The `TimerListener` class's `actionPerformed` method calculates the new position of the bouncing ball and repaints the screen.

 Checkpoint

MyProgrammingLab™ *www.myprogramminglab.com*

14.31 What type of events do `Timer` objects generate?

14.32 How are the time intervals between a `Timer` object's action events measured?

14.33 How do you cause a `Timer` object to begin generating action events?

14.34 How to you cause a `Timer` object to cease generating action events?

14.8 Playing Audio

CONCEPT: Sounds that have been stored in an audio file may be played from a Java program.

Java applets can play audio that is stored in a variety of popular sound file formats. The file formats directly supported are as follows:

- *.aif* or *.aiff* (Macintosh Audio File)
- *.au* (Sun Audio File)
- *.mid* or *.rmi* (MIDI File)
- *.wav* (Windows Wave File)

To play audio files, your computer must be equipped with a sound card and speakers. One way to play an audio file is to use the `play` method, which the `JApplet` class inherits from the `Applet` class. The version of the method that we will use is as follows:

```
void play(URL baseLocation, String fileName)
```

The argument passed to *baseLocation* is a URL object that specifies the location of the file. The argument passed to *fileName* is the name of the file. The sound that is recorded in the file is played one time.

When calling the `play` method, it is common to use either the `getDocumentBase` or `getCodeBase` method (both of which the `JApplet` class inherits from the `Applet` class) to get a URL object for the first argument. The `getDocumentBase` method returns a URL object containing the location of the HTML file that invoked the applet. Here is an example of a call to the `play` method, using a call to `getDocumentBase` for the first argument:

```
play(getDocumentBase(), "mysound.wav");
```

This statement will load and play the *mysound.wav* sound file, stored at the same location as the HTML file that invoked the applet.

The `getCodeBase` method returns a URL object containing the location of the applet's *.class* file. Here is an example of its use:

```
play(getCodeBase(), "mysound.wav");
```

This statement will load and play the *mysound.wav* sound file, stored at the same location as the applet's *.class* file. The *AudioDemo1* folder contains an example applet that plays a sound file using the play method.

NOTE: If the sound file specified by the arguments to the play method cannot be found, no sound will be played.

Using an AudioClip **Object**

The Applet class's play method loads a sound file, plays it one time, and then releases it for garbage collection. If you need to load a sound file to be played multiple times, you should use an *AudioClip object*.

An AudioClip object is an object that implements the AudioClip interface. The AudioClip interface is in the java.applet package, and it specifies the following three methods: play, loop, and stop. The play method plays a sound one time. The loop method repeatedly plays a sound, and the stop method causes a sound to stop playing.

The Applet class's getAudioClip method can be used to create an AudioClip object for a given sound file as follows:

```
AudioClip getAudioClip(URL baseLocation, String fileName)
```

The argument passed to *baseLocation* is a URL object that specifies the location of a sound file, and the argument passed to *fileName* is the name of the file. The method returns an AudioClip object that can be used to play the sound file.

As before, we can use the getDocumentBase or getCodeBase method to get a URL object for the first argument. Here is an example of a statement that uses the getAudioClip method:

```
AudioClip clip = getAudioClip(getDocumentBase(), "mysound.wav");
```

This statement declares clip as an AudioClip reference variable. The object returned by the getAudioClip method will load the *mysound.wav* file, stored at the same location as the HTML file that invoked the applet. The address of the object will be assigned to clip. The following statement can then be used to play the sound file:

```
clip.play();
```

The sound file can be played repeatedly with the following statement:

```
clip.loop();
```

Any time the sound file is being played, the following statement can be used to stop it:

```
clip.stop();
```

The AudioDemo2 class shown in Code Listing 14-23 is an applet that uses an AudioClip object to play a sound file. The file *AudioDemo2.html* can be used to start the applet. Figure 14-32 shows the applet running. The Play button calls the AudioClip object's play method, causing the sound file to play once. The Loop button calls the loop method, causing the sound file to be played repeatedly. The Stop button stops the sound file from playing. The sound file that is played is a famous NASA transmission from the Moon. NASA provides a wealth of public domain audio, video, and image files. You can find such items by going to www.nasa.gov, and then search the site using search terms such as "audio clips", "video clips", etc.

Code Listing 14-23   (AudioDemo2.java)

```
1  import java.awt.*;
2  import java.applet.*;
3  import java.awt.event.*;
4  import javax.swing.*;
5
6  /**
7     This applet uses the AudioClip class to play a
8     sound. Sound source: NASA
9  */
10
11 public class AudioDemo2 extends JApplet
12 {
13    private JLabel credit;          // Displays NASA credit
14    private JButton playButton;     // Plays the sound clip
15    private JButton loopButton;     // Loops the clip
16    private JButton stopButton;     // Stops the clip
17    private AudioClip sound;         // Holds the sound clip
18
19    /**
20       init method
21    */
22
23    public void init()
24    {
25       // Create a layout manager.
26       setLayout(new FlowLayout());
27
28       // Make the credit label and add it.
29       credit = new JLabel("Audio source: NASA");
30       add(credit);
31
32       // Make the buttons and add them.
33       makeButtons();
34
35       // Get an AudioClip object for the sound file.
36       sound = getAudioClip(getDocumentBase(), "step.wav");
37    }
38
```

```
39    /**
40       The makeButtons method creates the Play, Loop, and
41       Stop buttons, and adds them to the content pane.
42    */
43
44    private void makeButtons()
45    {
46       // Create the Play, Loop, and Stop buttons.
47       playButton = new JButton("Play");
48       loopButton = new JButton("Loop");
49       stopButton = new JButton("Stop");
50
51       // Register an action listener with each button.
52       playButton.addActionListener(new ButtonListener());
53       loopButton.addActionListener(new ButtonListener());
54       stopButton.addActionListener(new ButtonListener());
55
56       // Add the buttons to the content pane.
57       add(playButton);
58       add(loopButton);
59       add(stopButton);
60    }
61
62    /**
63       Private inner class that handles the action event
64       that is generated when the user clicks one of the
65       buttons.
66    */
67
68    private class ButtonListener implements ActionListener
69    {
70       public void actionPerformed(ActionEvent e)
71       {
72          // Determine which button was clicked and
73          // perform the selected action.
74          if (e.getSource() == playButton)
75             sound.play();
76          else if (e.getSource() == loopButton)
77             sound.loop();
78          else if (e.getSource() == stopButton)
79             sound.stop();
80       }
81    }
82 }
```

Figure 14-32 AudioDemo2 applet

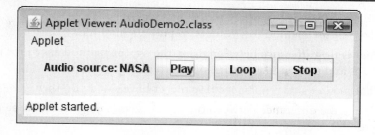

Playing Audio in an Application

The previous examples show how to play an audio file in an applet. You can play audio in an application as well. The process of getting a reference to an AudioClip object is different, however, in a class that does not extend JApplet. In the *Chapter 14\AudioDemo3* source code folder you will find a Swing application named *AudioFrame.java* that demonstrates how to do it. The following code segment is from the application.

```
43        // Create a file object for the step.wav file.
44        File file = new File("step.wav");
45
46        // Get a URI object for the audio file.
47        URI uri = file.toURI();
48
49        // Get a URL for the audio file.
50        URL url = uri.toURL();
51
52        // Get an AudioClip object for the sound
53        // file using the Applet class's static
54        // newAudioClip method.
55        sound = Applet.newAudioClip(url);
```

In line 44, we create a File object representing the audio file. Then, in line 47 we call the File class's toURI method to create a URI object representing the audio file. The URI class is in the java.net package. (URI stands for Uniform Resource Identifier.)

Then, in line 50, we call the URI class's toURL method to create a URL object representing the audio file. Note that if this method cannot construct a URL it throws a checked exception—MalformedURLException. The MalformedURLException class is in the java.net package.

Last, in line 55, we call the Applet class's static newAudioClip method, passing the URL object as an argument. The method returns a reference to an AudioClip object which can be used as previously demonstrated to play the audio file.

Checkpoint

MyProgrammingLab™ *www.myprogramminglab.com*

14.35 What `Applet` method can you use to play a sound file?

14.36 What is the difference between using the `Applet` method asked for in Checkpoint 14.35, and using an `AudioClip` object to play a sound file?

14.37 What methods does an `AudioClip` object have? What do they do?

14.38 What is the difference between the `Applet` class's `getDocumentBase` and `getCodeBase` methods?

14.9 Common Errors to Avoid

- **Forgetting a closing tag in an HTML document.** Most HTML tags have an opening tag and a closing tag. The page will not appear properly if you forget a closing tag.
- **Confusing the `<head></head>` tag with `<h1></h1>` or another header tag.** The `<head></head>` tag marks a document's head section, whereas the `<h1></h1>` tag marks a header, which is large bold text.
- **Using X and/or Y coordinates that are outside of the component when drawing a shape.** If you use coordinates that are outside the component to draw a shape, the shape will not appear.
- **Not calling the superclass's `paint` or `paintComponent` method.** When you override the `paint` or `paintComponent` method, the overriding method should call the superclass's version of the method before doing anything else.
- **Overriding the `paint` method with a component extended from `JComponent`.** You should override the `paint` method only with AWT components, `JFrame` components, or `JApplet` components.
- **Not calling the `repaint` method to redisplay a window.** When you update the data used to draw shapes on a component, you must call the `repaint` method to force a call to the `paint` or `paintComponent` method.
- **Not providing empty definitions for the unneeded methods in a mouse listener or mouse motion listener class.** When writing mouse listeners or mouse motion listeners, you must provide definitions for all the methods specified by the listener interfaces. To avoid this you can write a listener as a class that inherits from an adapter class.
- **Forgetting to start a `Timer` object.** A `Timer` object does not begin generating action events until it is started with a call to its `start` method.

Review Questions and Exercises

Multiple Choice and True/False

1. This section of an HTML document contains all of the tags and text that produce output in the browser window.
   a. head
   b. content
   c. body
   d. output

2. You place the `<title></title>` tag in this section of an HTML document.
   a. head
   b. content
   c. body
   d. output

3. Everything that appears between these tags in an HTML document is the content of the Web page.
   a. `<content></content>`
   b. `<html></html>`
   c. `<head></head>`
   d. `<page></page>`

4. To create a level one header you use this tag.
   a. `<level1></level1>`
   b. `<header1></header1>`
   c. `<h1></h1>`
   d. `<head></head>`

5. When using Swing to write an applet, you extend the applet's class from this class.
   a. `Applet`
   b. `JApplet`
   c. `JFrame`
   d. `JAppletFrame`

6. When using AWT to write an applet, you extend the applet's class from this class.
   a. `Applet`
   b. `JApplet`
   c. `JFrame`
   d. `JAppletFrame`

7. This applet method is invoked instead of a constructor.
   a. `startUp`
   b. `beginApplet`
   c. `invoke`
   d. `init`

8. The Sun JDK comes with this program, which loads and executes an applet without the need for a Web browser.
   a. `applettest`
   b. `appletload`
   c. `appletviewer`
   d. `viewapplet`

9. A class that inherits from `Applet` or `Frame` does not have one of these.
   a. an `add` method
   b. an `init` method
   c. a content pane
   d. a layout manager

10. What location on a component usually has the coordinates (0, 0)?
    a. upper-right corner
    b. upper-left corner
    c. center
    d. lower-right corner

11. In a class that extends `JApplet` or `JFrame` you override this method to get a reference to the `Graphics` object.
    a. `paint`
    b. `paintComponent`
    c. `getGraphics`
    d. `graphics`

12. In a class that extends `JPanel` you override this method to get a reference to the `Graphics` object.
    a. `paint`
    b. `paintComponent`
    c. `getGraphics`
    d. `graphics`

13. The `drawLine` method is a member of this class.
    a. `JApplet`
    b. `Applet`
    c. `JFrame`
    d. `Graphics`

14. To force the `paint` method to be called to update a component's display, you _____.
    a. call the `paint` method
    b. call the `repaint` method
    c. call the `paintAgain` method
    d. do nothing; you cannot force the `paint` method to be called

15. A class that implements this interface can handle mouse dragged events.
    a. `MouseListener`
    b. `ActionListener`
    c. `MouseMotionListener`
    d. `MouseDragListener`

16. A class that implements this interface can handle mouse click events.
    a. `MouseListener`
    b. `ActionListener`
    c. `MouseMotionListener`
    d. `MouseDragListener`

17. This `MouseEvent` method returns the X coordinate of the mouse cursor at the moment the mouse event is generated.
    a. `getXCoord`
    b. `getMouseX`
    c. `getPosition`
    d. `getX`

18. If a class implements a standard API interface that specifies more than one method but does not need many of the methods, this should be used instead of the interface.
    a. your own detailed versions of the needed methods
    b. an adapter class
    c. a different interface
    d. there is no other choice

19. A `Timer` object's time delay between events is specified in this unit of time.
    a. seconds
    b. microseconds
    c. milliseconds
    d. minutes

20. A `Timer` object generates this type of event.
    a. action events
    b. timer events
    c. item events
    d. interval events

21. The following `Applet` class method returns a URL object with the location of the HTML file that invoked the applet.
    a. `getHTMLlocation`
    b. `getDocumentBase`
    c. `getAppletBase`
    d. `getCodeBase`

22. The following `Applet` class method returns a URL object with the location of the applet's *.class* file.
    a. `getHTMLlocation`
    b. `getDocumentBase`
    c. `getAppletBase`
    d. `getCodeBase`

23. **True or False:** Applets cannot create files on the user's system.

24. **True or False:** Applets can read files on the user's system.

25. **True or False:** Applets cannot make network connections with any system except the server from which the applet was transmitted.

26. **True or False:** Applets can retrieve information about the user's system or the user's identity.

27. **True or False:** The `<h6>` tag produces larger text than the `<h1>` tag.

28. **True or False:** You use a static `main` method to create an instance of an applet class.

29. **True or False:** In a class that extends `JApplet`, you add components to the content pane.

30. **True or False:** In an applet, events are handled differently than in a GUI application.

31. **True or False:** An object of the `Frame` class does not have a content pane.

32. **True or False:** In an overriding `paint` method, you should never call the superclass's version of the `paint` method.

33. **True or False:** Once a `Timer` object has been started, it cannot be stopped without shutting down the program.

34. **True or False:** The `Applet` class's play method loads and plays an audio file once and then releases the memory it occupies for garbage collection.

35. **True or False:** The `loop` and `stop` methods, for use with audio files, are part of the `Applet` class.

Find the Error

Find the errors in the following code:

1.
```
<applet code="MyApplet.java" width=100 height=50>
</applet>
```

2.
```
public void paint(Graphics g)
{
    drawLine(0, 0, 100, 100);
}
```

3.
```
// Force a call to the paint method.
paint();
```

4.
```
public class MyPanel extends JPanel
{
    public MyPanel()
    {
        // Constructor code...
    }

    public void paint(Graphics g)
    {
        //paint method code...
    {
}
```

5.
```
private class MyMouseListener implements MouseListener
{
    public void mouseClicked(MouseEvent e)
    {
        mouseClicks += 1;
    }
}
```

6.
```
private class MyMouseListener implements MouseAdapter
{
    public void mouseClicked(MouseEvent e)
    {
        mouseClicks += 1;
    }
}
```

Algorithm Workbench

1. Write the text and HTML tags necessary to display "My Home Page" as a level one header, centered in the browser window.

2. You have written an applet and saved the source code in a file named `MyApplet.java`. Write the HTML tag needed to execute the applet in an area that is 300 pixels wide by 200 pixels high. Assume that the compiled applet code is stored in the same directory as the HTML document.

3. Look at the following GUI application class and indicate by line number the changes that should be made to convert this to an applet using Swing:

```
1 public class SimpleWindow extends JFrame
2 {
3    public SimpleWindow()
4    {
5       // Set the title.
6       setTitle("A Simple Window");
7
8       // Specify what happens when the close button is clicked.
9       setDefaultCloseOperation(JFrame.EXIT_ON_CLOSE);
10
11       // Add a label.
12       JLabel label = new JLabel("This is a simple window.");
13       add(label);
14
15       // Pack and display the window.
16       pack();
17       setVisible(true);
18    }
19 }
```

4. Assume that `g` references a `Graphics` object. Write code that performs the following:
   a. Draws an outline of a rectangle that is 100 pixels wide by 200 pixels high, with its upper-left corner at (50, 75).
   b. Draws a filled rectangle that is 300 pixels wide by 100 pixels high, with its upper-left corner at (10, 90).
   c. Draws a blue outline of an oval with an enclosing rectangle that is 100 pixels wide by 50 pixels high, with its upper-left corner at (10, 25).
   d. Draws a red line from (0, 5) to (150, 175).
   e. Draws the string "Greetings Earthling". The lower-left point of the string should be at (80, 99). Use a bold, 20-point serif font.
   f. Draws a polygon with vertices at the following points: (10, 10), (10, 25), (50, 25), and (50, 10). What shape does this code result in?

5. Rewrite the following mouse motion listener so it uses an adapter class:

```
private class MyMouseMotionListener implements MouseMotionListener
{
    public void mouseDragged(MouseEvent e)
    {
    }
```

```
            public void mouseMoved(MouseEvent e)
            {
                mouseMovements += 1;
            }
        }
```

6. Assume that a class has an inner class named `MyTimerListener` that can be used to handle the events generated by a `Timer` object. Write code that creates a `Timer` object with a time delay of one half second. Register an instance of `MyTimerListener` with the class.

Short Answer

1. When a user accesses a Web page on a remote server with his or her browser, and that Web page has an applet associated with it, is the applet executed by the server or by the user's system?

2. List at least three security restrictions imposed on applets.

3. Why are applets sometimes necessary in Web page development?

4. Why isn't it necessary to call the `setVisible` method to display an applet?

5. Why would you ever need to use the older AWT library instead of Swing to develop an applet?

6. A panel is 600 pixels wide by 400 pixels high. What are the X and Y coordinates of the pixel in the upper-left corner? The upper-right corner? The lower-left corner? The lower-right corner? The center of the panel?

7. When is a component's `paint` or `paintComponent` method called?

8. What is an adapter class? How does it make some programming tasks more convenient? Under what circumstances does the Java API provide an adapter class?

9. Under what circumstances would you want to use an `AudioClip` object to play a sound file, rather than the `Applet` class's play method?

Programming Challenges

MyProgrammingLab™   *Visit www.myprogramminglab.com to complete many of these Programming Challenges online and get instant feedback.*

1. `FollowMe` Applet

Write an applet that initially displays the word "Hello" in the center of a window. The word should follow the mouse cursor when it is moved inside the window.

VideoNote
The House
Applet
Problem

2. `House` Applet

Write an applet that draws the house shown on the left in Figure 14-33. When the user clicks on the door or windows, they should close. The figure on the right shows the house with its door and windows closed.

Figure 14-33   House drawing

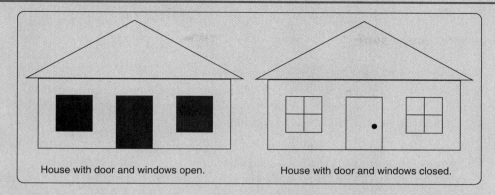

House with door and windows open.   House with door and windows closed.

3. `WatchMe` **Applet**

Write an applet that displays a drawing of two eyes in the center of its window. When the mouse cursor is not inside the window, the eyes should look ahead. When the mouse cursor is inside the window, the eyes should follow the cursor. This is illustrated in Figure 14-34.

4. Thermometer Applet

Write an applet that displays a thermometer. The user should be able to control the temperature with a slider component. When the user moves the slider, the thermometer should show the corresponding temperature.

5. Polygon Drawer

Write an applet that lets the user click on six points. After the sixth point is clicked, the applet should draw a polygon with a vertex at each point the user clicked.

Figure 14-34   Eyes following the mouse cursor

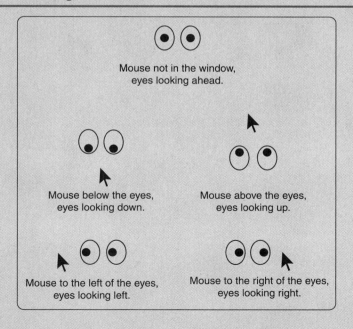

Mouse not in the window,
eyes looking ahead.

Mouse below the eyes,
eyes looking down.

Mouse above the eyes,
eyes looking up.

Mouse to the left of the eyes,
eyes looking left.

Mouse to the right of the eyes,
eyes looking right.

6. `GridFiller` **Applet**

Write an applet that displays a 4 × 4 grid. When the user clicks on a square in the grid, the applet should draw a filled circle in it. If the square already has a circle, clicking on it should cause the circle to disappear.

7. `DrinkMachine` **Applet**

Write an applet that simulates a soft drink vending machine. The simulated machine dispenses the following soft drinks: cola, lemon-lime soda, grape soda, root beer, and bottled water. These drinks cost $0.75 each to purchase.

When the applet starts, the drink machine should have a supply of 20 of each of the drinks. The applet should have a text field where the user can enter the amount of money he or she is giving the machine. The user can then click on a button to select a drink to dispense. The applet should also display the amount of change it is giving back to the user. The applet should keep track of its inventory of drinks and inform the user whether he or she has selected a drink that is out of stock. Be sure to handle operator errors such as selecting a drink with no money entered and selecting a drink with an inadequate amount of money entered.

8. `Stopwatch` **Applet**

Write an applet that simulates a stopwatch. It should have a Start button and a Stop button. When the Start button is clicked the applet should count the seconds that pass. When the Stop button is clicked, the applet should stop counting seconds.

9. **Slideshow Application**

Write an application that displays a slideshow of images, one after the other, with a time delay between each image. The user should be able to select up to 10 images for the slide show and specify the time delay in seconds.

15.1 Introduction

CONCEPT: In Java, you can use the JavaFX library to create GUI and graphical
applications. JavaFX is the next generation GUI toolkit for Java developers.

In this chapter, we discuss the basics of creating a Java application with a *graphical user interface*
or *GUI* (pronounced "gooey") using JavaFX. *JavaFX* is a standard Java library for developing
rich applications that employ graphics. It is fully integrated into Java, beginning with Java 7.
You can use it to create GUI applications, as well as applications that display 2D and 3D graphics. You can use JavaFX to create standalone graphics applications that run on your local computer, applications that run from a remote server, or applications that are embedded in a Web
page. This chapter introduces you to JavaFX as a tool for creating standalone GUI applications.

Compared with Swing (which is covered in Chapters 11 and 12), JavaFX is a relatively new
part of the Java library. Although JavaFX does not replace Swing, it is the next generation
of GUI toolkit for Java.

NOTE: It is not required that you read Chapters 11 and 12 before reading this chapter. This book is designed so you can choose either approach: Swing or JavaFX. If you
have already read Chapter 11, you can skip the rest of this section, and jump directly
to Section 15.2.

A GUI is a graphical window or a system of graphical windows presented by an application
for interaction with the user. In addition to accepting input from the keyboard, GUIs typically
accept input from a mouse, or a touch screen.

A window in a GUI commonly consists of several *components* that present data to the user and/or allow interaction with the application. Some of the common GUI components are Buttons, Labels, TextFields, CheckBoxes, and RadioButtons. Figure 15-1 shows an example of a window with a variety of components. Table 15-1 describes the components that appear in the window.

Figure 15-1 Various GUI components

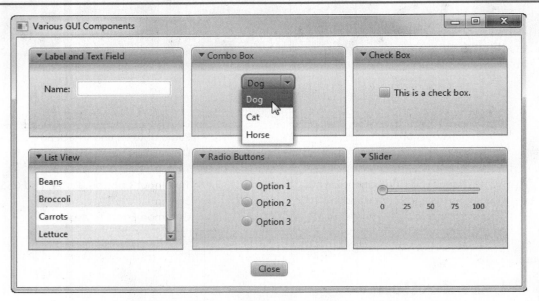

Table 15-1 Some GUI components

Component	Description
AnchorPane	A container for other components. The components that are contained inside an AnchorPane can be "anchored" at a certain distance from one or more of the AnchorPane's edges.
Button	A button that can cause an action to occur when it is clicked.
CheckBox	A component that has a box that may be checked or unchecked.
ComboBox	A component that displays a drop-down list of items from which the user may select. A ComboBox also provides a TextField in which the user may type input. It is called a ComboBox because it can behave as the combination of a list and a TextField.
Label	An area that can display text.
List	A list from which the user may select an item.
RadioButton	A component that can be either selected or deselected. RadioButtons usually appear in groups and allow the user to select one of several options.
Slider	A component that allows the user to select a value by moving a slider along a track.
TextField	An area in which the user may type a single line of input from the keyboard.
TitledPane	A container for other components. A TitledPane has a title bar at its top, in which a title can be displayed. A TitledPane may also be closed or opened.

Event-Driven Programming

Programs that operate in a GUI environment must be *event-driven*. An *event* is an action that takes place within a program, such as the clicking of a button. Part of writing a GUI application is creating event listeners. An *event listener* is a method that automatically executes when a specific event occurs. If you wish for an application to perform an operation when a particular event occurs, you must create an event listener that responds when that event takes place.

Checkpoint

15.1   What is a GUI?

15.2   What is JavaFX?

15.3   What is a component?

15.4   What is an event? What is an event listener?

15.2 Stages and Scenes

CONCEPT: The user interface for a JavaFX application can be likened to a stage on which actors act out a scene.

A JavaFX GUI application is based on the metaphor of a scene being played out on a stage in a theatre. In a desktop application, the stage is the top-level window while the various user interface components are the actors on the stage.

A JavaFX application is based on a class called `Application`. This class has two important methods:

```
static void launch(String ... args)
abstract void start(Stage stage)
```

The simplest way to write an application is to extend the `Application` class and call `launch` from the `main` method of your `Application` subclass:

```
public class SimpleJavaFXApp extends Application
{
    public static void main(String []args)
    {
        launch(args);
    }
    @Override
    public void start(Stage stage)
    {

    }
}
```

Because the `launch` method is inherited from `Application`, you do not have to write it. The `launch` method performs some initialization and set-up work, creates an "empty" `Stage` object, and calls the start method. To make your program useful, you must override the start method. Code Listing 15-1 is an example of a simple JavaFX application. Its start() method does not do much: it just sets the title of the stage and makes the stage visible.

Code Listing 15-1   (`SimpleJavaFXApp.java`)

```
1 import javafx.application.Application;
2 import javafx.stage.Stage;
3
4 /**
5     Simple JavaFX program displaying an empty stage.
6 */
7 public class SimpleJavaFXApp extends Application
8 {
9     public static void main(String []args)
10    {
11        launch(args);
12    }
13    @Override
14    public void start(Stage stage)
15    {
16        stage.setTitle("Simple JavaFX Application");
17        stage.show();
18    }
19 }
```

Upon execution, the program may display an empty window as shown in Figure 15-2.

Figure 15-2   A `JavaFX Application` showing an empty stage.   (Mark Schrier. Copyright Oracle, Inc.)

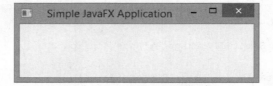

 NOTE: Displaying a stage on which no scene has been set may lead to unpredictable results; for example, the screen background beneath the application window may show through.

If you are using version 8 or later of the Netbeans IDE as your development environment, you can select JavaFX application as the type of project. JavaFX applications generated by Netbeans in that manner omit the main method and begin execution at the start() method. From now on, our example programs will also omit the main method to save space.

Checkpoint

15.5   In a desktop program, what user interface component does the JavaFX stage represent?

15.6   What is the purpose of the `launch()` method of the `Application` class?

15.7   Name two methods found in the `Stage` class.

15.8   Name two methods found in the `Application` class.

 15.3   Scene Graphs and Nodes

CONCEPT: A GUI consists of a scene graph, which is itself comprised of scene graph nodes.

The GUI application of Code Listing 15-1 shows a stage with no content. To have content, you must create a *scene*, add content to the scene, and set the scene on the stage. No object can be displayed by the application unless it is part of a scene that is attached to the stage.

An object that can be displayed as part of a scene is called a *node*. A node corresponds to a visual element of the application's user interface. A node can contain other nodes in the same way that a visual part of the user interface can be comprised of smaller visual parts nested inside it. If a node *P* contains another node *C*, then *P* is said to be the *parent* of *C* and *C* is said to be a *child* of *P*.

A scene is always formed from a single node called the *root* of the scene. The root node will usually have children, and some of those children may have children of their own. With the exception of the root, every node that is part of a scene will have a unique parent. Together, all nodes that are part of a scene form a hierarchical tree-like structure called a *scene graph*. Naturally, a node that is part of a scene graph is called a *scene graph node*. A scene graph node that has children is called a *branch node*, and a node with no children is called a *leaf node*. Figure 15-3 shows an example.

Figure 15-3   Nodes in a scene graph

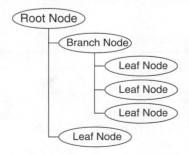

The JavaFX package contains a variety of classes that can be used to represent the visual elements that make up a scene. Among the most important are the classes `Node`, `Parent`, `Region`, `Pane`, `Control`, and `Labeled`. Figure 15-4 depicts the inheritance relationships among these classes.

Figure 15-4   Subclasses of the Node class

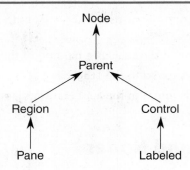

Node is the base class (super class) of all objects that can be used to display content in a JavaFX scene. The Parent class represents those nodes that can contain other nodes. Objects that are instances of Parent correspond to visual elements that have smaller visual elements nested within them, and when part of a scene graph, they correspond to the branch nodes shown in Figure 15-3. In particular, the root node of a scene must be an instance of the Parent class.

Objects of the Region class can be decorated with borders and have their appearance styled using styling rules written in a language known as *Cascading Style Sheets*, or CSS for short. CSS was originally designed to be used by web browsers to format web pages.

Objects of the Pane class have the ability to organize their children in a collection that allows programmers to add or remove nodes. In addition, different subclasses of Pane are able to automatically arrange their children according to specific layout rules.

The Control class represents nodes that have the ability to interact with users. Some controls are associated with a piece of descriptive text called a *label* that tells the user how to use the control: such controls descend from the Labeled class. Commonly used subclasses of Labeled include Label, Button, CheckBox, and RadioButton. A portion of the inheritance hierarchy rooted at Labeled is shown in Figure 15-5.

Figure 15-5   Subclasses of the Labeled class

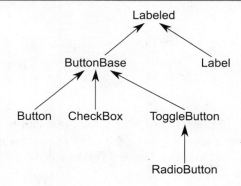

Creating a Scene

A scene is created by calling one of the Scene class constructors

```
Scene(Parent root, double width, double height)
Scene(Parent root)
```

and passing a node to be used as the root node of the scene. The width and height parameters specify the size of the scene. If the size parameters are omitted, the scene defaults to its *preferred size*, which is a size that is just large enough to hold its contents. The following statements create a scene that uses a Label control for its root node:

```
Label label = new Label("Hello World");
Scene scene = new Scene(label);
```

Code Listing 15-2 is a program that displays a label with the text "Hello World" in a scene on a JavaFX stage.

Code Listing 15-2   **(JavaFXHelloWorld.java)**

```
 1 import javafx.application.Application;
 2 import javafx.scene.Scene;
 3 import javafx.scene.control.Label;
 4 import javafx.stage.Stage;
 5
 6 /**
 7     Java FX Hello World using a Label.
 8 */
 9
10 public class JavaFXHelloWorld extends Application
11 {
12     @Override
13     public void start(Stage stage)
14     {
15         // Create label.
16         Label label = new Label("Hello World!");
17
18         // Set the label as the root of the scene graph.
20         Scene scene = new Scene(label, 300, 80);
21         stage.setScene(scene);
22
23         // Set the stage title and show the stage.
24         stage.setTitle("Hello World!");
25         stage.show();
26     }
27 }
```

When the program of Code Listing 15-2 runs, it displays the graphic shown in Figure 15-6.

Figure 15-6 Stage displayed by JavaFXHelloWorld.java (Mark Schrier. Copyright Oracle, Inc.)

The text shown in the label in Figure 15-6 is centered vertically and left-justified. This type of alignment is called *center-left*. If you look in the Labeled class, the super class of Label, you will find a method

```
void setAlignment(Pos value)
```

which can be used to align the text within a Labeled object. It takes a parameter of type Pos. This is an enumeration type in the javafx.geometry package with values:

```
TOP_LEFT        TOP_CENTER        TOP_RIGHT
CENTER_LEFT     CENTER            CENTER_RIGHT
BOTTOM_LEFT     BOTTOM_CENTER     BOTTOM_RIGHT
```

These values can be used to align the text in nine different ways within the label. For example, adding the statement

```
label.setAlignment(Pos.CENTER);
```

to Code Listing 15-2 immediately after the creation of the label will center the text in the label shown in Figure 15-7.

Figure 15-7 A label with its text centered (Mark Schrier. Copyright Oracle, Inc.)

 **Checkpoint**

15.9 Name two examples of direct or indirect subclasses of the Labeled class.

15.10 Look up the online documentation for the Labeled class and identify a method that can be used to change the text of a label.

15.11 Point out two important uses of the Pane class.

15.4 Panes and Component Layout

CONCEPT: Panes expose their collection of children to the programmer and have the ability to layout their children.

Although every subclass of `Parent` has a collection of children, not all of them expose that collection to the programmer. In `Parent` and `Region`, the collection is protected and the programmer cannot access it to add or remove children. The `Pane` class exposes its collection of children through the method:

```
ObservableList<Node> getChildren()
```

The `ObservableList<Node>` class has two methods that can be used to add nodes:

```
boolean add(Node child)
boolean addAll(Node ... children)
```

The `Pane` class has several subclasses, each with its own way of arranging its children. These include `VBox`, `HBox`, `GridPane`, `BorderPane`, and `TilePane`.

`VBox` and `HBox`

A `VBox` pane arranges its children in a vertical column. A `VBox` pane can be created using one of the class's two constructors:

```
VBox(double spacing)
VBox()
```

The spacing parameter specifies the length of a vertical gap inserted between two children when the pane contains more than one child. The default spacing is zero.

Like `Labeled`, the `VBox` class has a method

```
void setAlignment(Pos value)
```

that tells the pane how to align its children. When not specified, the alignment defaults to top-left.

The program in Code Listing 15-3 builds the user interface shown on the left in Figure 15-8. It adds a label and a button to a `VBox` pane that uses the default alignment and spacing. To add the two controls to the pane, the program calls `getChildren()` to obtain the pane's collection of children and then invokes the `addAll()` method on that collection:

```
pane.getChildren().addAll(label, button);
```

Once this is done, the program sets the pane as the root node of the scene and sets the scene onto the stage.

Code Listing 15-3 (`VBoxLayout.java`)

```java
 1 import javafx.application.Application;
 2 import javafx.scene.Scene;
 3 import javafx.scene.control.Button;
 4 import javafx.scene.control.Label;
 5 import javafx.scene.layout.VBox;
 6 import javafx.stage.Stage;
 7
 8 /**
 9    This program demonstrates use of the VBox pane.
10 */
11
12 public class VBoxLayout extends Application
13 {
14     @Override
15     public void start(Stage stage)
16     {
17         // Create label, button and pane.
18         Label label = new Label("This is a label");
19         Button button = new Button("Button");
20
21         // Create a VBox with default spacing and alignment.
22         VBox pane = new VBox();
23
24         // Add the label and button to the children of the pane.
25         pane.getChildren().addAll(label, button);
26
27         // Set pane as root of scene and set the scene on the stage.
28         Scene scene = new Scene(pane, 220, 80);
29         stage.setTitle("VBox Layout");
30         stage.setScene(scene);
31         stage.show();
32     }
33 }
```

When run, the user interface of this program will appear as shown in the graphic on the left in Figure 15-8.

Figure 15-8 Two layouts using the VBox pane   (Mark Schrier. Copyright Oracle, Inc.)

You can insert some spacing between children and align all the children to the center of the VBox pane by passing a spacing value to the constructor and setting the alignment of the pane to center like this:

```
// Create a VBox with a spacing of 10 and centered alignment.
VBox pane = new VBox(10);
pane.setAlignment(Pos.CENTER);

// Add the label and button to the children of the pane.
pane.getChildren().addAll(label, button);
```

The resulting layout will be as shown in the right side of Figure 15-8.

The following properties of the VBox class determine how it lays out its children:

- A VBox pane expands to fill the space made available to it by its container, which in this case is the stage.
- The children of a VBox pane gather together in a huddle, separated only by the inter-child spacing, in the area of the pane determined by the alignment setting.

The HBox class is similar to VBox, except that it lays out its children in a horizontal row. For example, we can modify Code Listing 15-3 to use HBox with a spacing of 10 and an alignment of Pos.CENTER like this:

```
// Create label, button and pane.
Label label = new Label("This is a label");
Button button = new Button("Button");

// Create HBox with center alignment and add children.
HBox pane = new HBox(10);
pane.setAlignment(Pos.CENTER);
pane.getChildren().addAll(label, button);
```

You can see the effect of this in the graphic on the left in Figure 15-9.

Figure 15-9 Two layouts using the HBox pane   (Mark Schrier. Copyright Oracle, Inc.)

 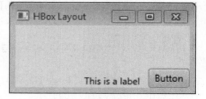

Alternatively, if we were to change the alignment on the HBox pane to bottom-right, the user interface would look as shown in the graphic on the right in Figure 15-9.

Margin and Padding

The typical node has a border (which may not be visible) and content. (In the case of a button, the text that appears on the button is its content.) To achieve a layout that looks attractive, we often want to set some extra space *around* and *inside* the border of node. JavaFX nodes have margin and padding properties that can be used for this purpose. The *margin* of a node is the space around its border that separates it from nearby nodes. The *padding* of a node is the space just inside the border that surrounds its content. These concepts are illustrated in Figure 15-10.

Figure 15-10   Margin and padding of a node

Margins and paddings are specified using instances of the `Insets` class. This class has a constructor that takes parameters for the width of the top, right, bottom, and left sides of a margin or padding:

```
Insets(double top, double right, double bottom, double left)
```

A second constructor takes a single parameter and creates insets of uniform size all around:

```
Insets(double width)
```

Every pane inherits from the `Region` class an instance method

```
void setPadding(Insets value)
```

that can be used to set its padding. For example, adding the line

```
pane.setPadding(new Insets(5));
```

right after the statement that creates the pane in the program of Code Listing 15-3 will put a space of 5 pixels between the pane and its contents. Interestingly, there is no instance method for setting the margin of a node. Instead, most subclasses of `Pane` have a static method

```
static void setMargin(Node child, Insets value)
```

that is used to set margins for child nodes. Code Listing 15-4 modifies Code Listing 15-3 by adding code to set margins for the label and button. The effect is to transform the user interface from the graphic on the left side of Figure 15-8 to what is seen in Figure 15-11.

Code Listing 15-4   **(MarginExample.java)**

```
 1 import javafx.application.Application;
 2 import javafx.geometry.Insets;
 3 import javafx.scene.Scene;
 4 import javafx.scene.control.Button;
 5 import javafx.scene.control.Label;
 6 import javafx.scene.layout.VBox;
 7 import javafx.stage.Stage;
 8
 9 /**
10    This program illustrates how to set margins
```

```
11      on children of a VBox.
12  */
13  public class MarginExample extends Application
14  {
15      @Override
16      public void start(Stage stage)
17      {
18          // Create label and button.
19          Label label = new Label("This is a label");
20          Button button = new Button("Button");
21
22          // Set margins for a VBox pane on the label and button.
23          Insets insets = new Insets(10);
24          VBox.setMargin(label, insets);
25          VBox.setMargin(button, insets);
26
27          // Create a VBox with default spacing and alignment
28          VBox pane = new VBox();
29
30          // Add the label and button to the children of the pane.
31          pane.getChildren().addAll(label, button);
32
33          // Set pane as root of scene and set the scene on the stage.
34          Scene scene = new Scene(pane, 240, 80);
35          stage.setTitle("Margin Example");
36          stage.setScene(scene);
37          stage.show();
38      }
39  }
```

The program sets a uniform margin of 10 pixels around both the label and the button to separate them from each other and from the borders of the enclosing pane. Notice that the VBox pane used in the program has the default spacing of 0.

Figure 15-11   The result of setting margins in a VBox pane   (Mark Schrier. Copyright Oracle, Inc.)

Nested Layouts

Different types of panes can be nested to achieve very elaborate layouts. As a simple example, consider the layout shown in Figure 15-12.

Figure 15-12 A layout using nested panes (Mark Schrier. Copyright Oracle, Inc.)

You can build this layout as follows. Begin by creating a vertical box that center-aligns its children. Next, create the label and add it as the first child of the vertical box. Finally, create the two buttons, add them to a center-aligned horizontal box, and add the horizontal box as the second child of the vertical box.

 Checkpoint

15.12 What is the difference between HBox and VBox?

15.13 Write code that creates a HBox pane and adds two labels to it.

15.14 What is the difference between *margin* and *padding*?

 15.5 Events and Event Handling

CONCEPT: Programs respond to events by calling event-handling methods.

An *event* is something that occurs during execution of a program that requires a response. For example, a user expects a program to respond when he or she clicks on a button, so clicking on a button is an event. Other events occur when a user types into a text field, drags on a scrollbar thumb, or selects a menu item. A program responds to an event by calling a method of an object designated as the *event handler* for that type of event. Event handlers are also called *event listeners*.

In JavaFX, events are described by subclasses of the Event class in the javafx.event package. Each event type is associated with an *event listener interface* that lists methods that can be called to respond to events of that type. An event handler object is created by instantiating a class that implements the listener interface.

For example, the button click event is described by a subclass of Event called ActionEvent. The ActionEvent class is associated with the interface,

```
interface EventHandler<ActionEvent>
{
    void handle(ActionEvent event);
}
```

which has a single method handle(). To handle click events on a button *B*, you create a class that implements this interface, instantiate the class to get a handler *H*, and set *H* as the handler for ActionEvent on *B*. Thereafter, the program will automatically call the handle method of *H* whenever the button *B* is clicked.

Let us illustrate this process with the program whose user interface is shown on the left in Figure 15-13. When the button is clicked, the program will pop up the message box shown on the right side of the same figure.

Figure 15-13 A simple event-handling program   (Mark Schrier. Copyright Oracle, Inc.)

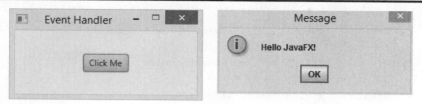

The program consists of two classes: the usual subclass of `Application`, and another class that implements the event handler interface. Here is the code for the event handler class:

```java
class SimpleEventHandler implements EventHandler<ActionEvent>
{
    @Override
    public void handle(ActionEvent event)
    {
        JOptionPane.showMessageDialog(null, "Hello JavaFX!");
    }
}
```

Assuming we already have a button named `button` created, we can create an event handler and set it on the button like this:

```java
Button button = new Button("Click Me");
button.setOnAction(new SimpleEventHandler());
```

The `setOnAction()` method is inherited from the `ButtonBase` class.

To complete the program, we add a button to a `VBox` pane, attach an event handler to the button, and set the `VBox` pane to be the stage scene. The details appear in Code Listing 15-5.

Code Listing 15-5   (`EventHandlerExample.java`)

```java
1 import javafx.application.Application;
2 import javafx.event.ActionEvent;
3 import javafx.event.EventHandler;
4 import javafx.geometry.Pos;
5 import javafx.scene.Scene;
6 import javafx.scene.control.Button;
7 import javafx.scene.layout.VBox;
8 import javafx.stage.Stage;
9 import javax.swing.JOptionPane;
10 /**
```

```
11    This program illustrates event handling.
12  */
13  public class EventHandlerExample extends Application
14  {
15      @Override
16      public void start(Stage stage)
17      {
18          // Create a button and set a handler on the button.
19          Button button = new Button("Click Me");
20          button.setOnAction(new SimpleEventHandler());
21
22          // Create VBox with center alignment.
23          VBox vBox = new VBox();
24          vBox.setAlignment(Pos.CENTER);
25
26          // Add button to VBox and set the VBox as scene.
27          vBox.getChildren().add(button);
28          stage.setScene(new Scene(vBox, 250, 90));
29          stage.setTitle("Event Handler");
30          stage.show();
31      }
32  }
33
34  // Handler class.
35  class SimpleEventHandler implements EventHandler<ActionEvent>
36  {
37      @Override
38      public void handle(ActionEvent event)
39      {
40          JOptionPane.showMessageDialog(null, "Hello JavaFX!");
41      }
42  }
```

Passing Information to Event Handlers

The event handler in the previous program does not need to access any information in another part of the program. For a more realistic example, consider the program of Figure 15-14, which has a button and a label. The label displays a number that is incremented every time the button is clicked.

Figure 15-14   A program that counts button clicks   (Mark Schrier. Copyright Oracle, Inc.)

Each time the button is clicked, an event handler set on the button accesses the label, retrieves the number from the label, increments it, and writes it back onto the label. Here is an outline for a class that implements such an event handler:

```
class ClickHandler implements EventHandler<ActionEvent>
{
    // Reference to label that will be updated
    private Label rLabel;

    @Override
    public void handle(ActionEvent event)
    {
        int count = Integer.parseInt(rLabel.getText());
        count ++;
        rLabel.setText(String.valueOf(count));
    }
}
```

An event handler from this class will have a label rLabel that references the label that has the number that needs updating. Every time the button is clicked, the handle() method is called and rLabel is updated.

But how does the private reference rLabel get to point to the label that needs updating? This is where the constructor parameter comes in. When the constructor is called to create the object, it is passed a reference to the label to be updated. The constructor uses this parameter value to set the rLabel field.

```
private Label rLabel;
public ClickHandler(Label cParamLabel)
{
    rLabel = cParamLabel;
}
```

The complete class that implements the handler interface now looks like this:

```
class ClickHandler implements EventHandler<ActionEvent>
{
    // Reference to label that will be updated
    private Label rLabel;
    public ClickHandler(Label cParamLabel)
    {
        rLabel = cParamLabel;
    }

    @Override
    public void handle(ActionEvent event)
    {
        int count = Integer.parseInt(rLabel.getText());
        count ++;
        rLabel.setText(String.valueOf(count));
    }
}
```

Assuming that the label to be updated is called `label`, we can pass it to the event handler via its constructor parameter like this:

```
new ClickHandler(label);
```

Putting all this together, and adding code to the `start()` method to create the label and button and set the event handler on the button, we get the program shown in Code Listing 15-6.

Code Listing 15-6 (`ClickCounter.java`)

```java
 1 import javafx.application.Application;
 2 import javafx.event.ActionEvent;
 3 import javafx.event.EventHandler;
 4 import javafx.geometry.Pos;
 5 import javafx.scene.Scene;
 6 import javafx.scene.control.Button;
 7 import javafx.scene.control.Label;
 8 import javafx.scene.layout.VBox;
 9 import javafx.stage.Stage;
10
11 /**
12    This program illustrates the passing of information
13    to an event handler class constructor.
14 */
15
16 public class ClickCounter extends Application
17 {
18     @Override
19     public void start(Stage stage)
20     {
21         // Create label, button, and attach event handler to the button.
22         Label label = new Label("0");
23         Button button = new Button("Click");
24         button.setOnAction(new ClickHandler(label));
25
26         // Add the label and button to a pane.
27         VBox pane = new VBox(10);
28         pane.setAlignment(Pos.CENTER);
29         pane.getChildren().addAll(label, button);
30
31         // Set up the stage.
32         stage.setScene(new Scene(pane, 200, 80));
33         stage.setTitle("Click Count");
34         stage.show();
35     }
36 }
37
38 // Handler class
```

```
39 class ClickHandler implements EventHandler<ActionEvent>
40 {
41     // Reference to label that will be updated
42     private Label rLabel;
43     public ClickHandler(Label cParamLabel)
44     {
45         rLabel = cParamLabel;
46     }
47     @Override
48     public void handle(ActionEvent event)
49     {
50         int count = Integer.parseInt(rLabel.getText());
51         count ++;
52         rLabel.setText(String.valueOf(count));
53     }
54 }
```

The technique used here to share information with an event handler, although illustrated here for only one variable, can be used to provide an event handler with access to any number of variables.

Using Inner Classes for Event Handling

The technique used above to share information with event handlers through constructor parameters is very powerful. If the variables to be shared are effectively final, we can dispense with the constructor parameters and use inner classes. Doing this requires us to define the event handler class as an inner class *after* all variables to be shared have been defined. The program in Code Listing 15-7, which works identically the same as the last program, illustrates this technique.

Code Listing 15-7   (`ClickCounter2.java`)

```
 1 import javafx.application.Application;
 2 import javafx.event.ActionEvent;
 3 import javafx.event.EventHandler;
 4 import javafx.geometry.Pos;
 5 import javafx.scene.Scene;
 6 import javafx.scene.control.Button;
 7 import javafx.scene.control.Label;
 8 import javafx.scene.layout.VBox;
 9 import javafx.stage.Stage;
10
11 /**
12    This program illustrates the use of inner classes
13    for event handling.
14 */
15 public class ClickCounter2 extends Application
```

```
16 {
17      @Override
18      public void start(Stage stage)
19      {
20          // Create label, button, and attach event handler to the button.
21          Label label = new Label("0");
22          Button button = new Button("Click");
23
24          // Define an inner class to use as event handler.
25          class ClickHandler implements EventHandler<ActionEvent>
26          {
27              public void handle(ActionEvent event)
28              {
29                  int count = Integer.parseInt(label.getText());
30                  count++;
31                  label.setText(String.valueOf(count));
32              }
33          }
34          // Create a handler object based on the inner class
35          // and set on the button.
36          button.setOnAction(new ClickHandler());
37
38          // Add the label and button to a pane.
39          VBox pane = new VBox(10);
40          pane.setAlignment(Pos.CENTER);
41          pane.getChildren().addAll(label, button);
42
43          // Set up the stage.
44          stage.setScene(new Scene(pane, 200, 80));
45          stage.setTitle("Click Count");
46          stage.show();
47      }
48 }
```

The `ClickHandler` class, shown in Lines 25-33, is much simpler due to the elimination of its class field and constructor. Notice also that the definition of `ClickHandler` class comes after the definition of all local variables that it accesses.

Using Anonymous Local Inner Classes for Event Handling

As you learned in Chapter 10, we can omit the definition of a class that is instantiated only once and use an anonymous inner class instead. In particular, we can replace Lines 24-36 with a single (albeit unwieldy) statement, resulting in a `start` method that looks like this:

```
public void start(Stage stage)
{
    // Create label, button, and attach event handler to the button.
    Label label = new Label("0");
```

```
        Button button = new Button("Click");
        // Use an object of anonymous class that implements EventHandler
        // to handle the ActionEvent on the button.
        button.setOnAction(new EventHandler<ActionEvent>()
        {
            public void handle(ActionEvent event)
            {
                int count = Integer.parseInt(label.getText());
                count++;
                label.setText(String.valueOf(count));
            }
        });

        // Add the label and button to a pane.
        VBox pane = new VBox(10);
        pane.setAlignment(Pos.CENTER);
        pane.getChildren().addAll(label, button);

        // Set up the stage.
        stage.setScene(new Scene(pane, 200, 80));
        stage.setTitle("Click Count");
        stage.show();
    }
```

Using Lambda Expressions for Event Handling

As you also learned in Chapter 10, the use of anonymous classes that implement functional interfaces can be replaced with lambda expressions. Code Listing 15-8 uses a lambda expression as an event handler for ActionEvent, but is otherwise equivalent to the programs of Code Listings 15-6 and 15-7.

Code Listing 15-8   (LambdaExpClickCounter.java)

```
 1 import javafx.application.Application;
 2 import javafx.geometry.Pos;
 3 import javafx.scene.Scene;
 4 import javafx.scene.control.Button;
 5 import javafx.scene.control.Label;
 6 import javafx.scene.layout.VBox;
 7 import javafx.stage.Stage;
 8
 9 /**
10    This program illustrates the use of Lambda
11    Expressions for event handling.
12 */
13 public class LambdaExpClickCounter extends Application
```

```
14 {
15     @Override
16     public void start(Stage stage)
17     {
18         // Create label, button, and attach event handler to the button.
19         Label label = new Label("0");
20         Button button = new Button("Click");
21
22         // Use a lambda expression for the event handler.
23         button.setOnAction(
24             event ->
25             {
26                 int count = Integer.parseInt(label.getText());
27                 count++;
28                 label.setText(String.valueOf(count));
29             });
30
31         // Add the label and button to a pane.
32         VBox pane = new VBox(10);
33         pane.setAlignment(Pos.CENTER);
34         pane.getChildren().addAll(label, button);
35
36         // Set up the stage.
37         stage.setScene(new Scene(pane, 200, 80));
38         stage.setTitle("Click Count");
39         stage.show();
40     }
41 }
```

Although lambda expressions and inner classes as event handlers are convenient to use, they do have some limitations. As already mentioned, they cannot be used to access program variables that are not effectively final. Also, programs that use them become difficult to read when the inner class or lambda expression contains a lot of code.

 Checkpoint

15.15 What is the name of the method in the EventHandler<ActionEvent> interface?

15.16 What is the parameter type of the method in the EventHandler<ActionEvent> interface?

15.17 What are the different ways of sharing information with an event handler?

15.6 Determining the Target of an Event

CONCEPT: The component that calls an event handler is called the event target. The parameter to an event-handling method contains information that identifies the event target.

Recall that the interface for handling action events looks like this:

```
interface EventHandler<ActionEvent>
{
    void handle(ActionEvent event);
}
```

Until now, we have not used the `ActionEvent` parameter that is passed to the `handle` method. The `ActionEvent` class has a method

```
EventTarget getTarget()
```

that returns a reference to the node that caused the `handle` method to be called. In the case of a button click, the event target will be the button that was clicked. This method can be used to identify the calling button when a single event handler has been set on more than one button.

To illustrate, consider a program that displays a stage with two buttons when it begins execution, as shown in Figure 15-15.

Figure 15-15 Event target example at start of execution   (Mark Schrier. Copyright Oracle, Inc.)

The program will have a single event handler set on both buttons. When it is called, the handler determines which button was clicked and sets the text of that button as the title of the stage, as shown in Figure 15-16.

Figure 15-16 Event target example after some user interaction   (Mark Schrier. Copyright Oracle, Inc.)

The two buttons trigger similar functions, so it makes sense to avoid duplication of code and use a single event handler to handle both of them. The program uses a lambda expression to create the handler, and then assigns it to an `EventHander<ActionEvent>` reference named `handler` so it can be used more than once:

```
EventHandler<ActionEvent> handler =
        event ->
        {
            Button clickedButton = (Button) event.getTarget();
            String newTitle = clickedButton.getText();
            stage.setTitle(newTitle);
        };
```

The body of the lambda expression invokes getTarget on the event parameter and casts the returned value to Button to allow the text of the button to be retrieved. The returned text is then used to set the stage title.

The reference to the handler can be re-used as many times as needed to set the same handler on different buttons:

```
button1.setOnAction(handler);
button2.setOnAction(handler);
```

Code Listing 15-9 has the complete program.

Code Listing 15-9   (EventTargetExample.java)

```java
 1 import javafx.application.Application;
 2 import javafx.event.*;
 3 import javafx.geometry.*;
 4 import javafx.scene.Scene;
 5 import javafx.scene.control.Button;
 6 import javafx.scene.layout.HBox;
 7 import javafx.stage.Stage;
 8
 9 /**
10    This program illustrates how to determine the
11    event target.
12 */
13
14 public class EventTargetExample extends Application
15 {
16     @Override
17     public void start(Stage stage)
18     {
19         // Create the two buttons.
20         Button button1 = new Button("One");
21         Button button2 = new Button("Two");
22
23         // Create the event handler using a lambda expression.
24         EventHandler<ActionEvent> handler =
25                 event ->
26                 {
27                     // Use getTarget to determine the clicked button.
28                     Button clickedButton = (Button) event.getTarget();
29                     // Get the text of the clicked button.
30                     String newTitle = clickedButton.getText();
31                     // set the new stage title.
32                     stage.setTitle(newTitle);
33                 };
34
35         // Add the same event handler to BOTH buttons
```

```
36          button1.setOnAction(handler);
37          button2.setOnAction(handler);
38
39          // Create a pane and add the two buttons to it.
40          HBox pane = new HBox(10);
41          pane.setAlignment(Pos.CENTER);
42          pane.setPadding(new Insets(5, 50, 5, 50));
43          pane.getChildren().addAll(button1, button2);
44
45          // Set the  scene to the stage and show.
46          stage.setScene(new Scene(pane));
47          stage.show();
48      }
49 }
```

The program uses a center-aligned horizontal box to hold its two buttons. Notice in Line 42 that the two buttons are set off from the border of the pane by margins of 5 pixels at the top and bottom, and 50 pixels on the left and right. The left and right margins force the pane to be 100 pixels wider than is required to hold the two buttons with the spacing between them. Finally, notice in Line 46 that the values for the width and height of the scene are not specified. This leaves the scene free to assume its preferred size, which is the size that is just large enough to hold its contents.

 Checkpoint

15.18 Why might you want to use a single handler to handle action events on more than one button?

15.19 If you put one event handler on two different buttons, how can you tell which button called the handler?

15.20 What is the preferred size of a scene?

15.7 Radio Buttons and Check Boxes

CONCEPT: Radio buttons normally appear in groups of two or more and are used to select one of several possible options. Check boxes, which may appear alone or in groups, are used to make yes/no or on/off selections.

Radio buttons are useful when you want the user to select one choice from several possible options. The following figure shows a group of radio buttons. A radio button may be selected or deselected. Each radio button has a small circle that appears filled-in when the radio button is selected and appears empty when the radio button is deselected.

Figure 15-17 Radio buttons (Mark Schrier. Copyright Oracle, Inc.)

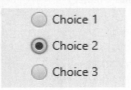

Figure 15-5, earlier in this chapter, depicts the inheritance pedigree of the `RadioButton` and `CheckBox` classes. Both of these classes have methods

```
void setSelected(boolean value)
boolean isSelected()
```

that can be used to select or deselect the radio button or check box; or to query it to see if it is currently selected. In addition, the `RadioButton` class has a

```
void setToggleGroup(ToggleGroup value)
```

method that can be used to set a *toggle group* for a radio button. The job of a toggle group is to make sure that among all radio buttons with the same toggle group, at most one can be selected at any given time. To create a radio button, use one of the constructors

```
RadioButton(String text)
RadioButton()
```

to create a radio button with a given label, or if you prefer, one with no label.

To illustrate the use of radio buttons, we will build the application shown in Figure 15-18. Its user interface consists of a group of three radio buttons, a button with the text *Show Selection*, and a label.

Figure 15-18 Radio button example program (Mark Schrier. Copyright Oracle, Inc.)

A person using this program will first use the radio buttons to select one of a set of transportation options. When the person clicks on the *Show Selection* button, the program responds by displaying the text of the selected radio button in the label at the bottom.

To write this program, we begin by creating and configuring a vertical box to hold the radio buttons:

```
VBox radiosBox = new VBox(10);
radiosBox.setPadding(new Insets(10, 10, 10, 10));
```

We want to provide a visual cue that the radio buttons form a functional group, so we will use CSS to style the pane containing them with a gray border:

```
radiosBox.setStyle("-fx-border-color: gray;");
```

The setStyle method, inherited from the Node class, can be used to apply certain CSS styling rules to a JavaFX node. We will use it from time to time to set borders and change background colors of controls.

Because radio buttons (and check boxes) often come in groups, it is convenient to use arrays when working with them. We begin by defining an array of strings of labels:

```
String [] optionLabels =
                {"Walk", "Drive", "Take Public Transportation"};
```

Following this, we create a radio button for each label, storing each radio button in an array as it is created, and setting all of them to the same toggle group property:

```
ToggleGroup radiosGroup = new ToggleGroup();
RadioButton [] radioButtons = new RadioButton[optionLabels.length];
for (int k = 0; k < radioButtons.length; k++)
{
    radioButtons[k] = new RadioButton(optionLabels[k]);
    radioButtons[k].setToggleGroup(radiosGroup);
}
```

Now that we have all the radio buttons we need in an array, we add them to the previously created vertical box:

```
radiosBox.getChildren().addAll(radioButtons);
```

Next, we create a top-level vertical box to serve as the root node of the scene graph. This box will hold the box with the radio buttons, the *Show Selection* button, and the label:

```
Button showSelectionButton = new Button("Show Selection");
Label selectionLabel = new Label();
topLevelBox.getChildren()
        .addAll(radiosBox, showSelectionButton, selectionLabel);
```

Finally, we use a lambda expression to set an event handler on the button. The handler searches through the array of radio buttons, picks the one that is currently selected, and sets its text as the text of the label:

```
// Create the handler for the showSelectionButton
EventHandler<ActionEvent> handler = event ->
{
    for (RadioButton rb : radioButtons)
    {
        if (rb.isSelected())
        {
            selectionLabel.setText(rb.getText());
            return;
        }
    }
};
showSelectionButton.setOnAction(handler);
```

The complete program can be found in Code Listing 15-10.

Code Listing 15-10 (`RadioButtonDemo.java`)

```
1 import javafx.application.Application;
2 import javafx.event.*;
3 import javafx.geometry.*;
4 import javafx.scene.Scene;
5 import javafx.scene.control.*;
6 import javafx.scene.layout.VBox;
7 import javafx.stage.Stage;
8
9 /**
10    This program illustrates how to use radio buttons.
11 */
12
13 public class RadioButtonDemo extends Application
14 {
15     @Override
16     public void start(Stage stage) throws Exception
17     {
18         // Vertical Box to hold the radio buttons.
19         VBox radiosBox = new VBox(10);
20         radiosBox.setPadding(new Insets(10, 10, 10, 10));
21         // Set a gray border around the radio button box.
22         radiosBox.setStyle("-fx-border-color: gray;");
23
24         // Labels to use for the radio buttons.
25         String [] optionLabels =
26             {"Walk", "Drive", "Take Public Transportation"};
27
28         // Create the radioButtons and
29         // set their toggleGroup property.
30         ToggleGroup radiosGroup = new ToggleGroup();
31         RadioButton [] radioButtons =
32                 new RadioButton[optionLabels.length];
33         for (int k = 0; k < radioButtons.length; k++)
34         {
35             radioButtons[k] = new RadioButton(optionLabels[k]);
36             radioButtons[k].setToggleGroup(radiosGroup);
37         }
38         // Add the radio Buttons to the box.
39         radiosBox.getChildren().addAll(radioButtons);
40         // Pre-select the first choice.
41         radioButtons[0].setSelected(true);
42
43         // Construct the top-level vertical box.
```

```
44          VBox topLevelBox = new VBox(10);
45          topLevelBox.setAlignment(Pos.CENTER);
46          topLevelBox.setPadding(new Insets(10, 50, 10, 50));
47
48          // Create the button and selectionlabel
49          // and add to the top-level box.
50          Button showSelectionButton = new Button("Show Selection");
51          Label selectionLabel = new Label();
52          topLevelBox.getChildren().
53              addAll(radiosBox,showSelectionButton, selectionLabel);
54
55          // Set the handler for the show selection button.
56          EventHandler<ActionEvent> handler = event ->
57          {
58              for (RadioButton rb : radioButtons)
59              {
60                  if (rb.isSelected())
61                  {
62                      selectionLabel.setText(rb.getText());
63                      return;
64                  }
65              }
66          };
67          showSelectionButton.setOnAction(handler);
68
69          // Set the scene and the stage
70          Scene scene = new Scene(topLevelBox);
71          stage.setScene(scene);
72          stage.setTitle("RadioButton Demo");
73          stage.show();
74      }
75 }
```

Programming with Check Boxes

Like radio buttons, check boxes may be selected or deselected at run time. Check boxes are displayed as small square boxes; a checkmark appears within the box when the check box is selected. Although check boxes are often used in groups, they are not used with a toggle group like radio buttons are. This is because check boxes are not normally used to make mutually exclusive selections. Instead, a user can select any number of the check boxes displayed in a group.

Using check boxes in your program is similar to how you use radio buttons. The main differences are that you use the CheckBox class instead of RadioButton, and you do not need to use a ToggleGroup object.

Figure 15-19 Check boxes (Mark Schrier. Copyright Oracle, Inc.)

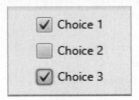

Responding to Radio Button and Check Box events

In many cases, radio buttons and check boxes are used with a separate "commit" button like the *Show Selection* button in Figure 15-18. The user tries different combinations of selections before eventually committing. In such cases, the program does not need to respond to selection and deselections until the user clicks on the commit button. That is how the program in Code Listing 15-9 works.

Even so, there are times when your program will want to respond as soon as there is a change in the selection state of a radio button or check box. A simple way to do this is note that all subclasses of `ButtonBase`, radio buttons, and check boxes included, generate action events when they are clicked. By setting an `ActionEvent` handler on a check box or radio button, you can receive notification whenever the component is clicked. You can then examine the component to see if it is selected or deselected and take appropriate action.

 Checkpoint

15.21 How are radio buttons different from check boxes?

15.22 Why do you need to use a toggle group with radio buttons?

15.23 Write statements that create an `HBox` pane and add a red border to it.

 15.8 **Displaying Images**

CONCEPT: The `Image` class is used to load graphical images into memory, and the `ImageView` class is used to display the images.

JavaFX has an `Image` class that supports the in-memory representation of images. The class has two constructors

```
Image(InputStream stream)
Image(String location)
```

that can load an image into memory by reading it from an input stream, or by fetching it from a local or an online location. The location may be a URL of an image on the Internet, or the path name of a file that contains the image. For example, you can create images in your program like this:

```
Image image1 = new Image("tiger.jpg");
Image image2 = new Image("c:\\Temp\\Images\\tiger.jpg");
```

The first statement does not specify a full path name, so the file is searched for in the current directory or folder. If you are running the program from within an IDE (Integrated Development Environment), the file will be searched for in the folder that contains the source code.

The Image class is not a subclass of Node, so Image objects cannot be displayed as part of a scene graph. To display an image, you must embed the image inside an object of the ImageView class. This class has three constructors:

```
ImageView(Image image)
ImageView(String location)
ImageView()
```

You use the first constructor if you want to embed a previously created image. The second constructor will create and embed an Image object from a file or an online location, and the last constructor creates an empty ImageView object. The class also has a

```
void setImage(Image image)
```

method that can be used to set the image to be displayed in an ImageView object.

Code Listing 15-11 is a simple program that uses an ImageView component to display an image. Its user interface is shown in Figure 15-20.

Figure 15-20   Displaying an image

Code Listing 15-11   (**ImageExample**)

```
 1 import javafx.application.Application;
 2 import javafx.geometry.Pos;
 3 import javafx.scene.Scene;
 4 import javafx.scene.image.ImageView;
 5 import javafx.scene.layout.VBox;
 6 import javafx.stage.Stage;
 7
 8 /**
 9    This program demonstrates the ImageView class.
10 */
11
```

```
12 public class ImageExample extends Application
13 {
14     @Override
15     public void start(Stage stage)
16     {
17         // Create a pane.
18         VBox vBox = new VBox();
19         vBox.setAlignment(Pos.CENTER);
20
21         // Add image view to the pane.
22         vBox.getChildren().add(new ImageView("tiger.jpg"));
23
24         // Set the stage and show.
25         Scene scene = new Scene(vBox);
26         stage.setTitle("Image Demo");
27         stage.setScene(scene);
28         stage.show();
29     }
30 }
```

Checkpoint

15.24 What is the difference between the `Image` and `ImageView` classes?

15.25 If you create an `ImageView` using the default no-arg constructor, how can you get it to display an image?

15.9 Timeline Animation

CONCEPT: A Timeline animation is a process for keying changes in a collection of object properties to the passage of time.

There are times when we want a program to

(a) change the values of certain variables, and/or
(b) call a previously designated method

at the expiration of some interval of time. An example of (a) is the need to change the position of an object with time to make the object appear to be moving across the screen. An example of (b) is a stock market monitoring application that needs to check for updates every 30 seconds. Both of these tasks can be achieved using the JavaFX `Timeline` animation class. In this section, we consider the use of the `TimeLine` animation class to trigger calls to a method at specified points in time.

In its simplest form, a *timeline animation* can be viewed as a process for the controlled updating of a collection of object property values along a progression of time. The timeline updates the properties in such a way that they achieve specified target values at specified points in time.

Timeline animation uses the concept of key frames. A *key frame* is used to specify, for each object property P that is being updated by the timeline, a *target value* for P at a *certain point in time*. These target values are referred to as *key values* of the key frame. Thus a key frame is defined as a point in time together with a collection of key values. A key value is also called an *end value*. A timeline animation is defined by a sequence of key frames.

An example will help clarify these concepts. Suppose that an object has width and height properties whose values are 80 and 100 pixels respectively, and you want an animation to shrink both the width and height to zero in 20 seconds. A simple timeline animation would consist of a single key frame at the 20-second mark and two key values. The key value for the height property would specify a target value of 0 at the 20-second mark. Likewise, the key value for the width property would also specify a target value of 0 at the 20-second mark.

When the animation is run, the timeline uses a process of interpolation to determine that the width and height properties have to decrease at rates of 4 and 5 pixels per second in order to hit their target values of 0 in 20 seconds. Using this information, the timeline can compute target values for both properties at each point in time between 0 and 20 seconds. In this way, the time-line animation can compute a display *frame* with target values for each property at all points in time that are intermediate between its key frames. To run smoothly, an animation must have at least 30 evenly-spaced frames in each one-second interval in the duration of the animation.

To create an animation, you must first determine the *duration* of the animation – this is how long the animation will run. Next, you specify key frames for key points along the duration. The animation will then interpolate between the supplied key frames and compute enough frames so that there is a frame to display every 1/30th of a second.

Although our illustration is a timeline with only one key frame, timeline animations are not limited to a single key frame. You can exert greater control over the animation by providing more key frames. For example, in our example, we could have a key frame with end values of 40 for the width and 50 for the height at the 15 second mark on the timeline; and another key frame with end values of 0 for both properties at the 20 second mark. The result would be an animation that shrinks the object to half its size over the first 15 seconds of the animation, and then rapidly shrinks the size to 0 over the next 5 seconds.

In addition to the set of key values and a point in time, a key frame can optionally be associated with an action event handler to be called when the animation reaches that key frame. Thus a key frame provides a way for a method to be called at a specific point in time.

To specify a point in time for a key frame, you use an object of the `Duration` class. You can use the constructor for this class to specify a duration in milliseconds:

```
Duration(double millis)
```

The `Duration` class also has a couple of static methods

```
static Duration minutes(double min)
static Duration millis(double ms)
```

that you can use to specify a duration in minutes or milliseconds.

The `KeyFrame` class is used to represent key frames. The most general constructor for this class requires you to specify a duration for the key frame, an event handler to be executed when the key frame is reached, and a list of key values:

```
KeyFrame(Duration time,
    EventHandler<ActionEvent> handler, KeyValue ... values)
```

The third parameter, the list of key values, can be omitted if you are only interested in executing the handler at that point in time.

As we have mentioned, a timeline is just a list of key frames. To create a timeline, use the constructor:

```
Timeline(KeyFrame ... keyFrames)
```

The `Timeline` class is a subclass of the `Animation` class, from which it inherits the following methods:

```
void playFromStart()
void play()
void pause()
void stop()
void setCycleCount(int count)
```

These methods can be used to play an animation from the start; to play an animation from its current position; to pause an animation that is already playing; to stop an animation and reset its position to the beginning; and to set the number of times the animation should be repeated.

The call

```
setCycleCount(Animation.INDEFINITE);
```

will cause the animation to be repeated indefinitely until the `stop()` method is called.

As an example, let us write a program that displays a counter that goes from 0 to 15, incrementing at one second intervals, and then stops. The key design points for the program are as follows:

1. The program uses a label whose initial text is the string "0" to represent the counter.
2. The program uses a timeline with a single key frame. The key frame has a duration of one second (1000 milliseconds) and an event handler. The event handler method reads the number from the label, increments it, and updates the label.
3. The timeline has a cycle count of 15.

The program can be seen in Code Listing 15-12.

Code Listing 15-12   (`AnimationCounter1.java`)

```java
1 import javafx.animation.KeyFrame;
2 import javafx.animation.Timeline;
3 import javafx.application.Application;
4 import javafx.event.ActionEvent;
5 import javafx.event.EventHandler;
6 import javafx.geometry.Pos;
7 import javafx.scene.Scene;
8 import javafx.scene.control.Label;
9 import javafx.stage.Stage;
```

```
10  import javafx.util.Duration;
11
12  /**
13      This program illustrates simple animation.
14  */
15
16  public class AnimationCounter1 extends Application
17  {
18      @Override
19      public void start(Stage stage) throws Exception
20      {
21          // Create the label and align its contents
22          Label label = new Label("0");
23          label.setAlignment(Pos.CENTER);
24
25          // This is the keyframe handler.
26          EventHandler<ActionEvent> handler = event->
27          {
28              int count = Integer.parseInt(label.getText());
29              count ++;
30              label.setText(String.valueOf(count));
31          };
32          // Build the keyframe.
33          Duration sec = new Duration(1000);
34          KeyFrame keyFrame = new KeyFrame(sec, handler);
35
36          // Build the time line animation.
37          Timeline timeline = new Timeline(keyFrame);
38          timeline.setCycleCount(15);
39
40          // Set the stage and show, and play the animation
41          stage.setScene(new Scene(label, 250, 30));
42          stage.setTitle("Animation Counter");
43          stage.show();
44          timeline.playFromStart();
45      }
46  }
```

 Checkpoint

15.26 What are the values that are needed to define a KeyFrame object?

15.27 What is the class whose objects are used to define a point in time during an animation?

15.28 Write a JavaFX expression that defines a point in time 3.5 seconds from the start of an animation.

15.10 Text Input Controls, Panes, and CSS Styling

CONCEPT: JavaFX has a wide variety of controls for user input and a wide variety of panes for layout management. Panes and controls can be styled using CSS.

JavaFX has a wide variety of controls that can be used for user input. These include text fields, text areas, scrollbars, combo-boxes, tabbed panes, and menus. All of these controls descend from the `Control` class. There is also a wide variety of panes, each with its own layout discipline, that can be used in your application. JavaFX also supports the use of CSS to style both controls and panes. In this section, we will look at text input controls, study a number of useful layout panes, and learn how CSS can be used to change the background colors of user interface components.

Text Input Controls

Many applications require the user to enter text input. JavaFX has a `TextField` control that can be used to enter a single line of input and a `TextArea` control that allows multiple lines of input. Both are subclasses of `TextInputControl`, which is itself a subclass of `Control`.

`TextInputControl` is an abstract class, so it cannot be instantiated. It does, however, define several methods, including:

```
void setText(String text)
String getText()
void setEditable(boolean value)
boolean isEditable()
void clear()
```

The above methods are inherited by both `TextField` and `TextArea`. You can set the text in a text input control using `setText()`, and you can retrieve the text in such a control by calling `getText()`. A text input control is said to be *editable* if it allows the user to change its text; you can make the text input control editable or un-editable by passing a boolean flag to the `setEditable()` method.

Among the constructors and methods defined by `TextField` are

```
TextField()
TextField(String text)

void setPrefColumnCount(int value)
void setOnAction(EventHandler<ActionEvent> handler)
```

The two constructors allow you to create a text field with empty initial text content, or with initial text content of your choice. You can also set the *preferred column count* of the text field: This value is the approximate number of text characters the text field will be able to hold. The `setOnAction()` method allows you to set an `ActionEvent` handler on the text field. Such a handler, when set, will be called every time a user types the ENTER key inside the text field.

To illustrate the use of text fields, we will write a program that computes the square of a number entered by the user. Its user interface is shown in Figure 15-21.

Figure 15-21 The TextField demo program   (Mark Schrier. Copyright Oracle, Inc.)

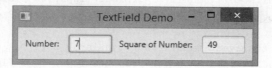

The program uses two labels and two text fields. The text field on the left is for user input. The text field on the right is not editable and is used to display the output. The program itself is shown in Code Listing 15-13.

Code Listing 15-13   (`TextFieldDemo.java`)

```
1  import javafx.application.Application;
2  import javafx.event.ActionEvent;
3  import javafx.event.EventHandler;
4  import javafx.geometry.Insets;
5  import javafx.geometry.Pos;
6  import javafx.scene.Scene;
7  import javafx.scene.control.Label;
8  import javafx.scene.control.TextField;
9  import javafx.scene.layout.HBox;
10 import javafx.stage.Stage;
11
12 /**
13    This program demonstrates the use of Text fields.
14 */
15
16 public class TextFieldDemo extends Application
17 {
18    @Override
19    public void start(Stage stage)
20    {
21       // Create labels for the user interface.
22       Label inputLabel = new Label("Number: ");
23       Label outputLabel = new Label("Square of Number: ");
24
25       // Create the text fields for the user interface.
26       TextField inputTextField = new TextField();
27       TextField outputTextField = new TextField();
28       inputTextField.setPrefColumnCount(4);
29       outputTextField.setPrefColumnCount(4);
30       outputTextField.setEditable(false);
31
32       // Create HBox and add the labels and textfields.
33       HBox hBox = new HBox(10);
34       hBox.setAlignment(Pos.CENTER);
```

```
35              hBox.setPadding(new Insets(10));
36              hBox.getChildren().addAll(inputLabel, inputTextField,
37                                        outputLabel, outputTextField);
38
39              // Create the event handler for the input text field.
40              // The handler read a number from the input text field,
41              // squares it, and writes it to the output text field.
42              EventHandler<ActionEvent> handler = event ->
43              {
44                  // Get Number from input text field.
45                  String inputText = inputTextField.getText().trim();
46                  int number = Integer.parseInt(inputText);
47
48                  // Write the square to the output text field.
49                  int square = number*number;
50                  outputTextField.setText(String.valueOf(square));
51              };
52              // Set the handler on the input text field
53              inputTextField.setOnAction(handler);
54
55              // Set the stage and show.
56              stage.setScene(new Scene(hBox));
57              stage.setTitle("TextField Demo");
58              stage.show();
59          }
60  }
```

The program begins by creating the user interface in Lines 21-37. Lines 42-51 are the creation of the event handler. The event handler is attached to the input text field in line 53, so it can be called whenever the user types the ENTER key into the input text field.

NOTE: It is not often necessary to put an event handler on a text field. Normally, the contents of the text field are read by an event handler attached to a button, or to some other control in the program.

Using CSS to Style Nodes

Earlier in this chapter, you learned that CSS (*Cascading Style Sheets*) is a language that is used to specify style rules for nodes in HTML documents. *Style rules* are used to modify aspects of nodes that affect appearance. Examples of such aspects are background and foreground colors, the color and width of a border, the size of margin and padding, and so on. JavaFX supports a variant of CSS for styling scene graph nodes.

A certain amount of CSS is useful to the JavaFX programmer because certain tasks, such as changing the background color or border of a node, are much more easily accomplished with CSS than by writing Java code. Changing the border of a node was covered in section 15.7.

Changing the background color of a node is similar. The following statement will change the background color of the HBox used in TextFieldDemo program to white:

```
hBox.setStyle("-fx-background-color: white");
```

Additional information on CSS and its use in JavaFX can be found online.

Preferred Width and Height of Components

The *preferred width* (or *height*) of a components is the least width (or height) that is just large enough to contain both its content and its padding. These concepts are important in understanding how different types of panes lay out their children.

TilePane

TilePane is a subclass of Pane that lays out its children in a grid of uniformly sized "tiles." In imagining what a TilePane would look like, you will not be far off if you think of a tiled bathroom wall. All the "tiles" are the same size, and each tile holds a single component.

Each TilePane has an *orientation*. If the orientation is *horizontal* (this is the default), children are added to the pane by rows, starting a new row when the current row reaches the pane's *preferred column size*. The preferred column size of a horizontal *TilePane* defaults to 5.

A TilePane with *vertical orientation* is similar. Children are added by columns, and a new column is started when the number of children added to a column reaches the pane's *preferred row size*. The default preferred row size is also 5.

A TilePane has a *vertical gap* and a *horizontal gap*. The vertical gap is the space that separates the rows, while the horizontal gap separates the columns. Both gaps default to 0 when they are not specified.

With these explanations, we can understand how to use the TilePane constructors:

```
TilePane(Orientation orientation, double hgap, double vgap)
TilePane(Orientation orientation)
TilePane(double hgap, double vgap)
TilePane()
```

To specify the orientation, use one of the following two values:

```
Orientation.HORIZONTAL
Orientation.VERTICAL.
```

Any value not specified as a constructor parameter assumes its default value. Thus the default constructor builds a horizontal TilePane with a preferred column size of 5, and with values of 0 for both the horizontal and vertical gaps.

Because all tiles must be the same size, the width of each tile is the preferred size of the widest child, and the height of each tile is the preferred height of the tallest child.

To illustrate this, we will create an array of buttons to use as children. The buttons are purposely built to have different preferred sizes.

```
String [] labels =
        {"zero", "one", " two ", "three", "four",
         " six ", "seven", "eight", "nine"
        };

Button [] buttons = new Button[labels.length];
for (int k = 0; k < buttons.length; k++)
{
    buttons[k] = new Button(labels[k]);
}
```

This code creates an array of buttons named `buttons`, with the individual buttons within the array having labels of different lengths. If the code

```
TilePane tilePane = new TilePane();
tilePane.getChildren().addAll(buttons);

stage.setScene(new Scene(tilePane));
stage.setTitle("TilePane 1");
stage.show();
```

were to be inserted into a program and executed, it would create a `TilePane` with all default settings, as shown in Figure 15-22.

Figure 15-22   Default `TilePane` settings   (Mark Schrier. Copyright Oracle, Inc.)

Notice that the pane has horizontal orientation, and it has the default number of 5 columns. Notice also that each child is center-aligned inside the tile that contains it. The fact that all tiles have the same height makes it easy to see that the vertical gap is 0.

A `TilePane` is not forced to adhere to its preferred column or row size: If the application stage is resized, a pane with a horizontal orientation will reconfigure itself so that as many children as possible fit on a single row. Figure 15-23 shows the effect of resizing the stage to make it wider:

Figure 15-23   The effect of increasing the width of the stage   (Mark Schrier. Copyright Oracle, Inc.)

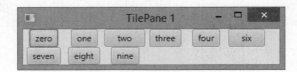

BorderPane

A BorderPane divides its regions into five areas as shown in Figure 15-24.

Figure 15-24 The five areas of a BorderPane   (Mark Schrier. Copyright Oracle, Inc.)

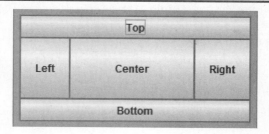

Each of the five regions is able to store at most one component. The *Top* and *Bottom* areas take up the entire width of the pane, and assume the preferred height of the component stored in them.

If no component is stored in the *Top* or *Bottom* area, its height will be 0 and it will not be visible. The *Left* and *Right* areas occupy the space from the bottom edge of the *Top* area to the top edge of the *Bottom* area, and assume the preferred width of the component stored in them. If a *Left* or *Right* area contains no component, its width becomes 0 and it is not visible.

When you add a child to a BorderPane, you must specify one of the 5 regions for the child to go into. You do this using one of the following methods:

```
void setTop(Node child)
void setBottom(Node child)
void setLeft(Node child)
void setRight(Node child)
void setCenter(Node child)
```

There are also methods for retrieving the child in a particular region:

```
Node getTop()
Node getBottom()
Node getLeft()
Node getRight()
Node getCenter()
```

Children of a BorderPane retain their preferred sizes. With the exception of the center child, each child is aligned top-left in the area assigned to it. To change the default alignment, use the static BorderPane method:

```
static setAlignment(Node child, Pos value)
```

As an illustration, consider this code that adds a button to each of the 5 areas of a BorderPane using the default alignments.

```
// Create the border pane.
BorderPane pane = new BorderPane();
```

```
// Add the children.
pane.setCenter(new Button("Center"));
pane.setTop(new Button("Top"));
pane.setBottom(new Button("Bottom"));
pane.setLeft(new Button("Left"));
pane.setRight(new Button("Right"));

// Set the stage and show
stage.setScene(new Scene(pane));
stage.setTitle("BorderPane Demo");
stage.show();
```

Executing this code yields an interface that looks like Figure 15-25.

Figure 15-25 `BorderPane` with default alignments   (Mark Schrier. Copyright Oracle, Inc.)

Notice that the center button is center-aligned in its area, while all the other buttons are aligned top-left in the areas assigned to them. Now, we can change the alignment of the four nodes that are not in the center like this:

```
BorderPane.setAlignment(pane.getRight(), Pos.CENTER);
BorderPane.setAlignment(pane.getTop(), Pos.CENTER);
BorderPane.setAlignment(pane.getBottom(), Pos.CENTER);
BorderPane.setAlignment(pane.getLeft(), Pos.CENTER);
```

These statements can be executed at any time after the nodes have been added to the pane. The result of this change is shown in Figure 15-26.

Figure 15-26 `BorderPane` with center alignment   (Mark Schrier. Copyright Oracle, Inc.)

The real power of `BorderPane` lies in its ability to nest other panes. Consider the program of Figure 15-21. We can redo its interface by putting each text field, together with its label, in a horizontal box. We can then put the horizontal box with the input text field in the *Top*

region of a `BorderPane`, and the horizontal box with the output text field in the *Bottom* region. The result will be as shown in Figure 15-27.

Figure 15-27   The square program using a `BorderPane`   (Mark Schrier. Copyright Oracle, Inc.)

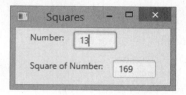

GridPane

`GridPane` is a two-dimensional grid that allows you to specify the row and column at which a child should be placed. Moreover, the columns of a `GridPane` do not all to have the same width: each column assumes for its width the preferred width of its widest child. Similarly, each row will take for its height the preferred height of the tallest child in that row. Like `TilePane`, a `GridPane` has vertical gaps to separate its rows and horizontal gaps to separate its columns. Both types of gaps default to 0 if not specified.

One way to add a node to a `GridPane` is to use the method:

```
void add(Node child, int column, int row)
```

Nodes can be added in any order: for example, you might have a `GridPane` to which you only add two children: one in column 10 and row 8, and another in column 4 and row 0. Rows in which no nodes have been placed will have a height of 0 and will not be visible; and likewise, columns with no nodes will not be visible either.

Code Listing 15-14 is a very simple program that uses a `GridPane`.

Code Listing 15-14   (GridPaneExample.java)

```java
1  import javafx.application.Application;
2  import javafx.scene.Scene;
3  import javafx.scene.control.Button;
4  import javafx.scene.layout.GridPane;
5  import javafx.stage.Stage;
6
7  /**
8     GridPane Example
9  */
10 public class GridPaneExample extends Application
11 {
12    @Override
13    public void start(Stage stage)
14    {
15       // Create a GridPane.
16       GridPane gridPane = new GridPane();
```

```
17
18          // Add three buttons.
19          gridPane.add(new Button(" long (1, 0) button  "), 1, 0);
20          gridPane.add(new Button("(0, 1)"), 0, 1);
21          gridPane.add(new Button("(3, 1)"), 3, 1);
22
23          // Make the grid lines visible.
24          gridPane.setGridLinesVisible(true);
25
26          // Set the stage and show.
27          stage.setScene(new Scene(gridPane));
28          stage.setTitle("GridPane Example 1");
29          stage.show();
30      }
31 }
```

The program first places a child in column 1, then in column 0, and then in column 3. No child is placed in column 2. The user interface is shown in Figure 15-28

Figure 15-28   `GridPane` example   (Mark Schrier. Copyright Oracle, Inc.)

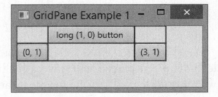

Notice that column 2, which has no nodes in it, is not visible. If the `GridPane` is bigger than its contents, the contents are (by default) aligned top-left. `GridPane` provides a method to change the default alignment of its contents. You can learn more about `GridPane` in the online JavaFX documentation at the Oracle website.

Additional Panes

There other types of panes, such as `FlowPane` and `AnchorPane` that you might find useful. You can learn about them by consulting the online JavaFX documentation.

 Checkpoint

15.29 Name two ways CSS can be used in a JavaFX application.

15.30 Define the concept of *preferred width* and *preferred height* of a node.

15.31 Name the method that is used to set the number of characters a text field can hold.

15.32 Name the five regions of a `BorderPane` container.

15.11 Common Errors to Avoid

- **Importing a non-JavaFX class with the same name.** Many of the classes used in JavaFX have the same names as classes in other packages. You will get an error if you import the wrong class. JavaFX package names start with the `javafx` prefix.
- **Trying to access a variable that is not effectively final from an inner class.** Lambda expressions are created from anonymous inner classes, so an attempt to access a variable that is not effectively final from a lambda expression will also result in an error.
- **Forgetting to use a toggle group with radio buttons.** If you have a set of radio buttons and you want the user to be able to select only one at a time, you must assign all the radio buttons to the same toggle group.

Review Questions and Exercises

Multiple Choice and True/False

1. A tree-like data structure that contains the components of a JavaFX GUI is called a
   a. directory tree
   b. node tree
   c. node graph
   d. scene graph

2. A node in a scene graph that contains other nodes is called a
   a. root node
   b. branch node
   c. leaf node
   d. terminal node

3. A node in a scene graph that has no children is called a
   a. root node
   b. branch node
   c. leaf node
   d. terminal node

4. An object that can be used to ensure that at most one of a group of radio buttons can be selected is called a(n)
   a. singular object
   b. toggle group
   c. toggle button
   d. exclusion enforcer

5. A language used to style web pages, which can also be used to style JavaFX components is called
   a. Component Styling System
   b. Cascading Style Sheets
   c. Common Styling Statements
   d. CDC

6. Spacing around the border of a component is called
   a. padding
   b. border spacing
   c. margin
   d. insets

7. Spacing inside the border of a component that surrounds its content is called
   a. padding
   b. border spacing
   c. margin
   d. insets

8. The class that is the super class of containers that are able to arrange their children is called
   a. `Pane`
   b. `Parent`
   c. `Region`
   d. `AnchorPane`

9. The class to use when you want to represent an image in JavaFX is
   a. `ImageView`
   b. `Image`
   c. `PictureBox`
   d. none of the above

10. The class to use when you want to display an image in JavaFX is
    a. `ImageView`
    b. `Image`
    c. `PictureBox`
    d. none of the above

11. The `Image` class is able to load images from
    a. online sources
    b. a file stored on your computer
    c. all of the above
    d. none of the above

12. If you use a lambda expression as an event handler, you can only access
    a. integer variables
    b. static variables
    c. variables that are local
    d. variables that are effectively final

13. A point in time, a set of key values, and an event handler are often used to define
    a. an animation
    b. a timeline
    c. a subclass of `KeyValue` that implements the time interface using an event handler
    d. a key frame

14. A JavaFX timeline is
    a. a sequence of key frames
    b. an interface that operates in time
    c. an object that keeps track of time in milliseconds
    d. a set of key values

15. A container that lays out its children in a horizontal row can be defined using the class
     a. `VBox`
     b. `HBox`
     c. `HorizontalBox`
     d. none of the above

16. Event handlers of type `EventHandler<ActionEvent>` can be used with objects of the class
     a. `Pane`
     b. `RadioButton`
     c. `Node`
     d. none of the above

17. In a JavaFX application, the values needed to construct a scene are
     a. a stage
     b. an instance of the `Node` class, with optional width and height values to define the dimensions of the scene
     c. an instance of the `Parent` class, with optional width and height values to define the dimensions of the scene
     d. a `VBox` object

18. In a JavaFX application,
     a. the developer must write code to create the stage
     b. the stage object is created while the program is being compiled
     c. the stage is created by the system without the developer writing code to create it
     d. none of the above

19. In a JavaFX application,
     a. you are allowed to make one pane the child of another pane
     b. you can use any object of the `Node` class to contain other nodes
     c. you can add an `Image` object to a `VBox` pane
     d. none of the above

20. Something that occurs while your program is executing that requires a response from your program is called
     a. an exception
     b. an event
     c. an event listener
     d. an event handler

Short Answer

1. What is a scene graph?
2. What characterizes a branch node in a scene graph?
3. What characterizes a leaf node in a scene graph?
4. What is an event?
5. What is an event handler?
6. Why do you need to use a toggle group with radio buttons?
7. Give a short description of timeline animation.
8. What is the main difference between radio buttons and check boxes?
9. Why do you get an error when you try to add an `Image` to a pane such as a `VBox`?
10. What is the difference between margin and padding?

Programming Challenges

1. Nested Layouts 1

Write a program that creates the layout of Figure 15-12.

VideoNote
Nested
Layouts 2

2. Nested Layouts 2

Write a program that creates the layout of Figure 15-27 by nesting horizontal boxes inside of a BorderPane.

3. Two Dimensional Square of Consecutive Numbers 1

Write a program that takes a positive integer n and displays the first n^2 positive integers in *row* order in an $n \times n$ square. Write the program in such a way that it works for different values of n by changing only one line in your code. For example, when $n = 5$, the program displays as in Figure 15-29. *Hint:* Use un-editable TextField objects in a GridPane.

Figure 15-29 Square of consecutive numbers (Mark Schrier. Copyright Oracle, Inc.)

4. Two Dimensional Square of Consecutive Numbers 2

Write a program that takes a positive integer n and displays the first n^2 positive integers in *column* order in an $n \times n$ square. Write the program in such a way that it works for different values of n by changing only one line in your code.

5. Checkerboard

Write a program that takes a positive integer n and displays an $n \times n$ checkerboard. For example, when $n = 5$, the program displays as in Figure 15-30. Make sure that adjacent squares differ in color regardless of whether n is odd or even. Write the program in such a way that it works for different values of n by changing only one line in your code. *Hint:* Use un-editable TextField objects in a GridPane, and use CSS to set background colors.

Figure 15-30 Checkerboard (Mark Schrier. Copyright Oracle, Inc.)

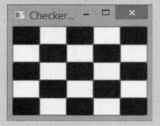

6. Color Changing Buttons

Write a program that displays two buttons in a horizontal box. The first button should be labeled *White* while the second is labeled *Yellow* (Or use any two different colors of your choice).

Clicking the *White* button changes the background color of the horizontal box to white, while clicking on the *Yellow* button changes the color of the horizontal box to yellow.

7. Color Changing Radio buttons

Write a program that displays two radio buttons in a horizontal box. The first radio button should be labeled *White* while the second is labeled *Yellow* (Or use any two different colors of your choice). Selecting the *White* radio button changes the background color of the horizontal box to white, while selecting the *Yellow* radio button changes the pane's color to yellow.

8. Game Clock

Imagine a person who is being timed to solve a Sudoku game puzzle. A game clock *starts* at 0, and begins to count up in seconds while the person plays the game. The player is allowed to *pause* the clock so he or she can go get a cup of coffee. Upon return, the game clock *resumes* counting from where it was when it was paused. If the player gets hopelessly confused, he or she is allowed to *reset* the clock to 0 in order to restart the game. The player can *stop* the clock as soon as the puzzle is solved. At any time, the player can give up and *quit* the game.

Write a game clock application with an un-editable text field that shows the number of seconds on the clock; a button labeled *Start/Resume* that can be used to start or resume a game; a *Reset* button that resets the seconds counter to 0; a *Pause/Stop* button that stops the clock but keeps the seconds counter where it is; and a *Quit* button that exits the program.

9. Digital Picture Frame

Obtain a collection of n small images in PNG or JPG format, where n is an integer between 3 and 10. Index the images with numbers 1,... n. Write a program that displays the images in order of increasing index, holding each image on the screen for two seconds before moving on to the next. When it gets to the highest index, the program cycles and begins again at 1. Write your program in such a way that it will work for different values of n by changing a single line in your code.

16 Recursion

TOPICS

16.1 Introduction to Recursion

CONCEPT: A recursive method is a method that calls itself.

You have seen instances of methods calling other methods. Method A can call method B, which can then call method C. It's also possible for a method to call itself. A method that calls itself is a recursive method. Look at the message method in Code Listing 16-1.

Code Listing 16-1 (EndlessRecursion.java)

```java
1  /**
2      This class has a recursive method.
3  */
4
5  public class EndlessRecursion
6  {
7     public static void message()
8     {
9        System.out.println("This is a recursive method.");
10       message();
11    }
12 }
```

This method displays the string "This is a recursive method." and then calls itself. Each time it calls itself, the cycle is repeated. Can you see a problem with the method? There's no way to stop the recursive calls. This method is like an infinite loop because there is no code to stop it from repeating.

Like a loop, a recursive method must have some way to control the number of times it repeats. The class in Code Listing 16-2 has a modified version of the message method. It passes an integer argument, which holds the number of times the method should call itself.

Code Listing 16-2 (Recursive.java)

```
1 /**
2    This class has a recursive method, message,
3    which displays a message n times.
4 */
5
6 public class Recursive
7 {
8    public static void message(int n)
9    {
10       if (n > 0)
11       {
12          System.out.println("This is a recursive method.");
13          message(n - 1);
14       }
15    }
16 }
```

This method contains an if statement that controls the repetition. As long as the n parameter is greater than zero, the method displays the message and calls itself again. Each time it calls itself, it passes n - 1 as the argument. For example, look at the program in Code Listing 16-3.

Code Listing 16-3 (RecursionDemo.java)

```
1 /**
2    This class demonstrates the Recursive.message method.
3 */
4
5 public class RecursionDemo
6 {
7    public static void main(String[] args)
8    {
9       Recursive.message(5);
10    }
```

```
11 }
12
```

Program Output

```
This is a recursive method.
This is a recursive method.
This is a recursive method.
This is a recursive method.
This is a recursive method.
```

The `main` method in this class calls the `Recursive.message` method with the argument 5, which causes the method to call itself five times. The first time the method is called, the `if` statement displays the message and then calls itself with 4 as the argument. Figure 16-1 illustrates this.

The diagram in Figure 16-1 illustrates two separate calls of the `message` method. Each time the method is called, a new instance of the n parameter is created in memory. The first time the method is called, the n parameter is set to 5. When the method calls itself, a new instance of n is created, and the value 4 is passed into it. This cycle repeats until finally, zero is passed to the method. This is illustrated in Figure 16-2.

Figure 16-1 First two calls of the method

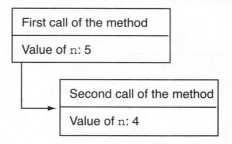

As you can see from Figure 16-2, the method is called a total of six times. The first time it is called from the `main` method of the `RecursionDemo` class, and the other five times it calls itself. The number of times that a method calls itself is known as the *depth of recursion*. In this example, the depth of recursion is five. When the method reaches its sixth call, the n parameter is set to 0. At that point, the `if` statement's conditional expression is `false`, so the method returns. Control of the program returns from the sixth instance of the method to the point in the fifth instance directly after the recursive method call. This is illustrated in Figure 16-3.

Because there are no more statements to be executed after the method call, the fifth instance of the method returns control of the program back to the fourth instance. This repeats until all instances of the method return.

Figure 16-2 Total of six calls to the `message` method

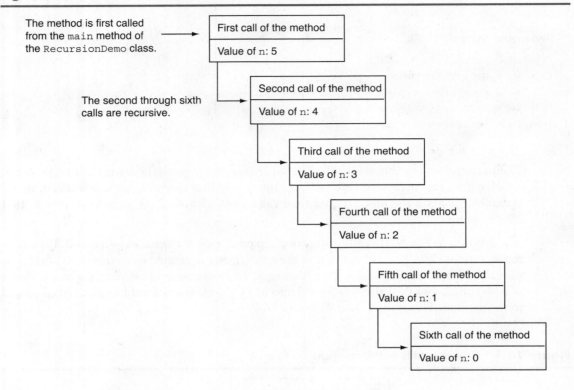

Figure 16-3 Control returns to the point after the recursive method call

```
            public static void message(int n)
            {
                if (n > 0)
                {
                    System.out.println("This is a recursive method.");
Recursive method call ──────►  message(n - 1);
                }                        ◄──────── Control returns here from the recursive call.
            }                                      There are no more statements to execute
                                                   in this method, so the method returns.
```

16.2 Solving Problems with Recursion

CONCEPT: A problem can be solved with recursion if it can be broken down into
successive smaller problems that are identical to the overall problem.

The Recursive and RecursionDemo classes shown in the previous section demonstrate the
mechanics of a recursive method. Recursion can be a powerful tool for solving repetitive
problems and is an important topic in upper-level computer science courses. What might
not be clear to you yet is how to use recursion to solve a problem. First, it should be noted
that recursion is never absolutely required to solve a problem. Any problem that can be

solved recursively can also be solved iteratively, with a loop. In fact, recursive algorithms are usually less efficient than iterative algorithms. This is because a method call requires several actions to be performed by the JVM. These actions include allocating memory for parameters and local variables, and storing the address of the program location where control returns after the method terminates. These actions, which are sometimes referred to as overhead, take place with each method call. Such overhead is not necessary with a loop.

Some repetitive problems, however, are more easily solved with recursion than with iteration. Where an iterative algorithm might result in faster execution time, the programmer might be able to design a recursive algorithm faster.

In general, a recursive method works like this:

VideoNote
Reducing a
Problem with
Recursion

- If the problem can be solved now, without recursion, then the method solves it and returns.
- If the problem cannot be solved now, then the method reduces it to a smaller but similar problem and calls itself to solve the smaller problem.

In order to apply this approach, first we identify at least one case in which the problem can be solved without recursion. This is known as the *base case*. Second, we determine a way to solve the problem in all other circumstances using recursion. This is called the *recursive case*. In the recursive case, we must always reduce the problem to a smaller version of the original problem. By reducing the problem with each recursive call, the base case will eventually be reached and the recursion will stop.

Let's take an example from mathematics to examine an application of recursion. In mathematics, the notation $n!$ represents the factorial of the number n. The factorial of a nonnegative number can be defined by the following rules:

If $n = 0$ then $n! = 1$
If $n > 0$ then $n! = 1 \times 2 \times 3 \times \ldots \times n$

Let's replace the notation $n!$ with factorial(n), which looks a bit more like computer code, and rewrite these rules as follows:

If $n = 0$ then   factorial(n) = 1
If $n > 0$ then   factorial(n) = $1 \times 2 \times 3 \times \ldots \times n$

These rules state that when n is 0, its factorial is 1. When n is greater than 0, its factorial is the product of all the positive integers from 1 up to n. For instance, factorial(6) is calculated as $1 \times 2 \times 3 \times 4 \times 5 \times 6$.

When designing a recursive algorithm to calculate the factorial of any number, first we identify the base case, which is the part of the calculation that we can solve without recursion. That is the case where n is equal to 0 as follows:

If $n = 0$ then   factorial(n) = 1

This tells how to solve the problem when n is equal to 0, but what do we do when n is greater than 0? That is the recursive case, or the part of the problem that we use recursion to solve. This is how we express it:

If $n > 0$ then   factorial(n) = $n \times$ factorial($n - 1$)

This states that if *n* is greater than 0, the factorial of *n* is *n* times the factorial of $n - 1$. Notice how the recursive call works on a reduced version of the problem, $n - 1$. So, our recursive rule for calculating the factorial of a number might look like this:

If $n = 0$ then $\qquad\qquad\qquad\qquad$ factorial(n) = 1

If $n > 0$ then $\qquad\qquad\qquad\qquad$ factorial(n) = $n \times$ factorial $(n - 1)$

The following code shows how this might be implemented in a Java method:

```java
private static int factorial(int n)
{
    if (n == 0)
        return 1;    // Base case
    else
        return n * factorial(n - 1);
}
```

The program in Code Listing 16-4 demonstrates the method. Figure 16-4 shows example interaction with the program.

Code Listing 16-4　　(FactorialDemo.java)

```java
 1 import javax.swing.JOptionPane;
 2
 3 /**
 4    This program demonstrates the recursive
 5    factorial method.
 6 */
 7
 8 public class FactorialDemo
 9 {
10    public static void main(String[] args)
11    {
12       String input;  // To hold user input
13       int number;    // To hold a number
14
15       // Get a number from the user.
16       input = JOptionPane.showInputDialog("Enter a " +
17                                 "nonnegative integer:");
18       number = Integer.parseInt(input);
19
20       // Display the factorial of the number.
21       JOptionPane.showMessageDialog(null,
22                 number + "! is " + factorial(number));
23
24       System.exit(0);
25    }
26
```

```
27    /**
28        The factorial method uses recursion to calculate
29        the factorial of its argument, which is assumed
30        to be a nonnegative number.
31        @param n The number to use in the calculation.
32        @return The factorial of n.
33    */
34
35    private static int factorial(int n)
36    {
37       if (n == 0)
38          return 1;   // Base case
39       else
40          return n * factorial(n - 1);
41    }
42 }
```

Figure 16-4   Interaction with the `FactorialDemo.java` program

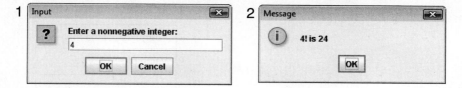

In the example run of the program, the factorial method is called with the argument 4 passed into n. Because n is not equal to 0, the `if` statement's `else` clause executes the following statement:

```
return n * factorial(n - 1);
```

Although this is a `return` statement, it does not immediately return. Before the return value can be determined, the value of `factorial(n - 1)` must be determined. The `factorial` method is called recursively until the fifth call, in which the n parameter will be set to zero. The diagram in Figure 16-5 illustrates the value of n and the return value during each call of the method.

This diagram illustrates why a recursive algorithm must reduce the problem with each recursive call. Eventually the recursion has to stop in order for a solution to be reached. If each recursive call works on a smaller version of the problem, then the recursive calls work toward the base case. The base case does not require recursion, so it stops the chain of recursive calls.

Usually, a problem is reduced by making the value of one or more parameters smaller with each recursive call. In our `factorial` method, the value of the parameter n gets closer to 0 with each recursive call. When the parameter reaches 0, the method returns a value without making another recursive call.

Figure 16-5 Recursive calls to the factorial method   (Oracle Corporate Counsel)

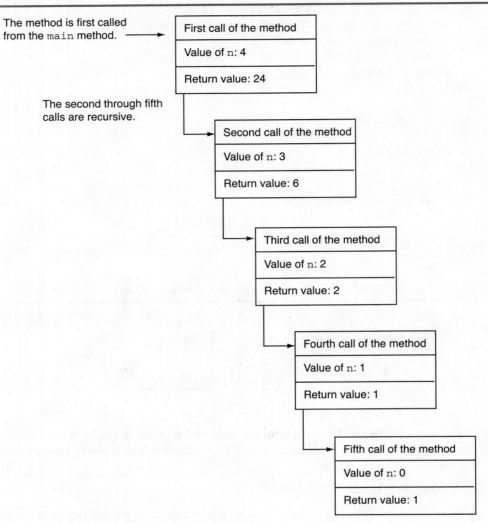

Direct and Indirect Recursion

The examples we have discussed so far show recursive methods that directly call themselves. This is known as direct recursion. There is also the possibility of creating indirect recursion in a program. This occurs when method A calls method B, which in turn calls method A. There can even be several methods involved in the recursion. For example, method A could call method B, which could call method C, which calls method A.

 Checkpoint

MyProgrammingLab™ *www.myprogramminglab.com*

16.1   It is said that a recursive algorithm has more overhead than an iterative algorithm. What does this mean?

16.2   What is a base case?

16.3 What is a recursive case?

16.4 What causes a recursive algorithm to stop calling itself?

16.5 What is direct recursion? What is indirect recursion?

16.3 Examples of Recursive Methods

Summing a Range of Array Elements with Recursion

In this example we look at a method, rangeSum, that uses recursion to sum a range of array elements. The method takes the following arguments: an int array that contains the range of elements to be summed, an int specifying the starting element of the range, and an int specifying the ending element of the range. Here is an example of how the method might be used:

```
int[] numbers = {1, 2, 3, 4, 5, 6, 7, 8, 9};
int sum;
sum = rangeSum(numbers, 3, 7);
```

This code specifies that rangeSum should return the sum of elements 3 through 7 in the numbers array. The return value, which in this case would be 30, is stored in sum. Here is the definition of the rangeSum method:

```
public static int rangeSum(int[] array, int start, int end)
{
   if (start > end)
      return 0;
   else
      return array[start] + rangeSum(array, start + 1, end);
}
```

This method's base case is when the start parameter is greater than the end parameter. If this is true, the method returns the value 0. Otherwise, the method executes the following statement:

```
return array[start] + rangeSum(array, start + 1, end);
```

This statement returns the sum of array[start] plus the return value of a recursive call. Notice that in the recursive call, the starting element in the range is start + 1. In essence, this statement says "return the value of the first element in the range plus the sum of the rest of the elements in the range." The program in Code Listing 16-5 demonstrates the method.

Code Listing 16-5   **(RangeSum.java)**

```
1 /**
2    This program demonstrates the recursive rangeSum method.
3 */
4
```

```
 5 public class RangeSum
 6 {
 7
 8    public static void main(String[] args)
 9    {
10       int[] numbers = { 1, 2, 3, 4, 5, 6, 7, 8, 9 };
11
12       System.out.print("The sum of elements 2 through " +
13                        "5 is "+ rangeSum(numbers, 2, 5));
14    }
15
16    /**
17       The rangeSum method calculates the sum of a specified
18       range of elements in array.
19       @param start Specifies the starting element.
20       @param end Specifies the ending element.
21       @return The sum of the range.
22    */
23
24    public static int rangeSum(int[] array, int start, int end)
25    {
26       if (start > end)
27          return 0;
28       else
29          return array[start] +
30                       rangeSum(array, start + 1, end);
31    }
32 }
```

Program Output

The sum of elements 2 through 5 is 18

Drawing Concentric Circles

In this example we look at the Circles applet, which uses recursion to draw concentric circles. Concentric circles are circles of different sizes, one inside another, all with a common center point. Figure 16-6 shows the applet's output. The applet code is shown in Code Listing 16-6.

Code Listing 16-6   (Circles.java)

```
1 import javax.swing.*;
2 import java.awt.*;
3
4 /**
5    This applet uses a recursive method to
6    draw concentric circles.
```

```
 7  */
 8
 9  public class Circles extends JApplet
10  {
11     /**
12        init method
13     */
14
15     public void init()
16     {
17        getContentPane().setBackground(Color.white);
18     }
19
20     /**
21        paint method
22        @param g The applet's Graphics object.
23     */
24
25     public void paint(Graphics g)
26     {
27        // Draw 10 concentric circles. The outermost
28        // circle's enclosing rectangle should be at
29        // (5, 5), and it should be 300 pixels wide
30        // by 300 pixels high.
31        drawCircles(g, 10, 5, 300);
32     }
33
34     /**
35        The drawCircles method draws concentric circles.
36        @param g A Graphics object.
37        @param n The number of circles to draw.
38        @param topXY The top left coordinates of the
39               outermost circle's enclosing rectangle.
40        @size The width and height of the outermost
41               circle's enclosing rectangle.
42     */
43
44     private void drawCircles(Graphics g, int n,
45                          int topXY, int size)
46     {
47        if (n > 0)
48        {
49           g.drawOval(topXY, topXY, size, size);
50           drawCircles(g, n - 1, topXY + 15, size - 30);
51        }
52     }
53  }
```

Figure 16-6   `Circles applet`

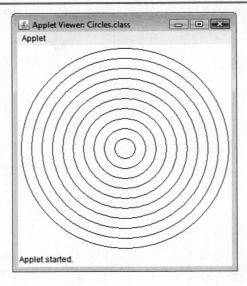

The `drawCircles` method, which is called from the applet's `paint` method, uses recursion to draw the concentric circles. The `n` parameter holds the number of circles to draw. When this parameter is set to 0, the method has reached its base case. Otherwise, it calls the `g` object's `drawOval` method to draw a circle. The `topXY` parameter holds the value to use as the X and Y coordinate of the enclosing rectangle's upper-left corner. The `size` parameter holds the value to use as the enclosing rectangle's width and height. After the circle is drawn, the `drawCircles` method is recursively called with parameter values adjusted for the next circle.

The Fibonacci Series

Some mathematical problems are designed to be solved recursively. One well-known example is the calculation of Fibonacci numbers. The Fibonacci numbers, named after the Italian mathematician Leonardo Fibonacci (born circa 1170), are the following sequence:

0, 1, 1, 2, 3, 5, 8, 13, 21, 34, 55, 89, 144, 233, . . .

Notice that after the second number, each number in the series is the sum of the two previous numbers. The Fibonacci series can be defined as follows:

If $n = 0$ then $Fib(n) = 0$
If $n = 1$ then $Fib(n) = 1$
If $n >= 2$ then $Fib(n) = Fib(n - 1) + Fib(n - 2)$

A recursive Java method to calculate the nth number in the Fibonacci series is shown here:

```java
public static int fib(int n)
{
    if (n == 0)
        return 0;
```

```
        else if (n == 1)
            return 1;
        else
            return fib(n - 1) + fib(n - 2);
    }
```

Notice that this method actually has two base cases: when n is equal to 0 and when n is equal to 1. In either case, the method returns a value without making a recursive call. The program in Code Listing 16-7 demonstrates this method by displaying the first 10 numbers in the Fibonacci series.

Code Listing 16-7   (`FibNumbers.java`)

```
 1 /**
 2    This program demonstrates the recursive fib method.
 3 */
 4
 5 public class FibNumbers
 6 {
 7    public static void main(String[] args)
 8    {
 9       System.out.println("The first 10 numbers in " +
10                          "the Fibonacci series are:");
11
12       for (int i = 0; i < 10; i++)
13          System.out.print(fib(i) + " ");
14
15       System.out.println();
16    }
17
18    /**
19       The fib method calculates the nth
20       number in the Fibonacci series.
21       @param n The nth number to calculate.
22       @return The nth number.
23    */
24
25    public static int fib(int n)
26    {
27       if (n == 0)
28          return 0;
29       else if (n == 1)
30          return 1;
31       else
32          return fib(n - 1) + fib(n - 2);
33    }
34 }
```

Program Output

```
The first 10 numbers in the Fibonacci series are:
0 1 1 2 3 5 8 13 21 34
```

Finding the Greatest Common Divisor

Our next example of recursion is the calculation of the greatest common divisor, or GCD, of two numbers. The GCD of two positive integers, x and y, is as follows:

if y divides x evenly, then $gcd(x, y) = y$
Otherwise, $gcd(x, y) = gcd(y$, remainder of $x/y)$

This definition states that the GCD of x and y is y if x/y has no remainder. This is the base case. Otherwise, the answer is the GCD of y and the remainder of x/y. The program in Code Listing 16-8 shows a recursive method for calculating the GCD.

Code Listing 16-8   (GCDdemo.java)

```java
 1 import java.util.Scanner;
 2
 3 /**
 4    This program demonstrates the recursive gcd method.
 5 */
 6
 7 public class GCDdemo
 8 {
 9    public static void main(String[] args)
10    {
11       int num1, num2; // Two numbers for GCD calculation
12
13       // Create a Scanner object for keyboard input.
14       Scanner keyboard = new Scanner(System.in);
15
16       // Get the first number from the user.
17       System.out.print("Enter an integer: ");
18       num1 = keyboard.nextInt();
19
20       // Get the second number from the user.
21       System.out.print("Enter another integer: ");
22       num2 = keyboard.nextInt();
23
24       // Display the GCD.
25       System.out.println("The greatest common divisor " +
26                          "of these two numbers is " +
27                          gcd(num1, num2));
28    }
29
30    /**
```

```
31          The gcd method calculates the greatest common
32          divisor of the arguments passed into x and y.
33          @param x A number.
34          @param y Another number.
35          @returns The greatest common divisor of x and y.
36      */
37
38      public static int gcd(int x, int y)
39      {
40          if (x % y == 0)
41              return y;
42          else
43              return gcd(y, x % y);
44      }
45 }
```

Program Output with Example Input Shown in Bold

```
Enter an integer: 49 [Enter]
Enter another integer: 28 [Enter]
The greatest common divisor of these two numbers is 7
```

16.4 A Recursive Binary Search Method

CONCEPT: The recursive binary search algorithm is more elegant and easier to understand than its iterative version.

In Chapter 7 you learned about the binary search algorithm and saw an iterative example written in Java. The binary search algorithm can also be implemented recursively. For example, the procedure can be expressed as:

If array[middle] *equals the search value, then the value is found.*
Else if array[middle] *is less than the search value, perform*
    a binary search on the upper half of the array.
Else if array[middle] *is greater than the search value, perform*
    a binary search on the lower half of the array.

When you compare the recursive algorithm to its iterative counterpart, it becomes evident that the recursive version is much more elegant and easier to understand. The recursive binary search algorithm is also a good example of repeatedly breaking a problem down into smaller pieces until it is solved. Here is the code for the method:

```
public static int binarySearch(int[] array, int first,
                               int last, int value)
{
    int middle;     // Mid point of search
    // Test for the base case where the
    // value is not found.
```

```
       if (first > last)
          return -1;
       // Calculate the middle position.
       middle = (first + last) / 2;
       // Search for the value.
       if (array[middle] == value)
          return middle;
       else if (array[middle] < value)
          return binarySearch(array, middle + 1,
                               last, value);
       else
          return binarySearch(array, first,
                               middle - 1, value);
    }
```

The first parameter, array, is the array to be searched. The next parameter, first, holds the subscript of the first element in the search range (the portion of the array to be searched). The next parameter, last, holds the subscript of the last element in the search range. The last parameter, value, holds the value to be searched for. Like the iterative version, this method returns the subscript of the value if it is found, or –1 if the value is not found. Code Listing 16-9 demonstrates the method.

Code Listing 16-9   (`RecursiveBinarySearch.java`)

```java
 1  import java.util.Scanner;
 2
 3  /**
 4      This program demonstrates the recursive
 5      binary search method.
 6  */
 7
 8  public class RecursiveBinarySearch
 9  {
10     public static void main(String [] args)
11     {
12        int searchValue;    // The value to search for
13        int result;         // The search result
14        String input;       // A line of input
15        char again;         // To hold a single character
16
17        // The values in the following array are sorted
18        // in ascending order.
19        int numbers[] = {101, 142, 147, 189, 199, 207, 222,
20                         234, 289, 296, 310, 319, 388, 394,
21                         417, 429, 447, 521, 536, 600};
22
23        // Create a Scanner object for keyboard input.
24        Scanner keyboard = new Scanner(System.in);
```

```
25
26        do
27        {
28           // Get a value to search for.
29           System.out.print("Enter a value to " +
30                            "search for: ");
31           searchValue = keyboard.nextInt();
32
33           // Search for the value
34           result = binarySearch(numbers, 0,
35                                 (numbers.length - 1),
36                                 searchValue);
37
38           // Display the results.
39           if (result == -1)
40           {
41              System.out.println(searchValue +
42                                 " was not found.");
43           }
44           else
45           {
46              System.out.println(searchValue +
47                                 " was found at " +
48                                 "element " + result);
49           }
50
51           // Does the user want to search again?
52           System.out.print("Do you want to search again? " +
53                            "(Y or N): ");
54           // Consume the remaining newline.
55           keyboard.nextLine();
56           // Read a line of input.
57           input = keyboard.nextLine();
58
59        } while (input.charAt(0) == 'y' ||
60                 input.charAt(0) == 'Y');
61     }
62
63     /**
64        The binarySearch method performs a binary search
65        on an integer array.
66        @param array The array to search.
67        @param first The first element in the search range.
68        @param last The last element in the search range.
69        @param value The value to search for.
70        @return The subscript of the value if found,
71               otherwise -1.
72     */
```

```
73
74    public static int binarySearch(int[] array, int first,
75                                    int last, int value)
76    {
77       int middle;      // Mid point of search
78
79       // Test for the base case where the
80       // value is not found.
81       if (first > last)
82          return -1;
83
84       // Calculate the middle position.
85       middle = (first + last) / 2;
86
87       // Search for the value.
88       if (array[middle] == value)
89          return middle;
90       else if (array[middle] < value)
91          return binarySearch(array, middle + 1,
92                              last, value);
93       else
94          return binarySearch(array, first,
95                              middle - 1, value);
96    }
97 }
```

Program Output with Example Input Shown in Bold

Enter a value to search for: **289 [Enter]**
289 was found at element 8
Do you want to search again? (Y or N): **y [Enter]**
Enter a value to search for: **388 [Enter]**
388 was found at element 12
Do you want to search again? (Y or N): **y [Enter]**
Enter a value to search for: **101 [Enter]**
101 was found at element 0
Do you want to search again? (Y or N): **y [Enter]**
Enter a value to search for: **999 [Enter]**
999 was not found.
Do you want to search again? (Y or N): **n [Enter]**

16.5 The Towers of Hanoi

CONCEPT: The repetitive steps involved in solving the Towers of Hanoi game can be easily implemented in a recursive algorithm.

The Towers of Hanoi is a mathematical game that is often used in computer science textbooks to illustrate the power of recursion. The game uses three pegs and a set of discs with holes through their centers. The discs are stacked on one of the pegs as shown in Figure 16-7.

Figure 16-7   The pegs and discs in the Towers of Hanoi game

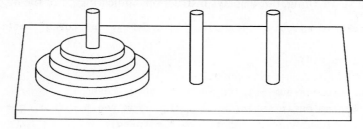

Notice that the discs are stacked on the leftmost peg, in order of size with the largest disc at the bottom. The game is based on a legend where a group of monks in a temple in Hanoi have a similar set of pegs with 64 discs. The job of the monks is to move the discs from the first peg to the third peg. The middle peg can be used as a temporary holder. Furthermore, the monks must follow these rules while moving the discs:

- Only one disk may be moved at a time.
- A disk cannot be placed on top of a smaller disc.
- All discs must be stored on a peg except while being moved.

According to the legend, when the monks have moved all of the discs from the first peg to the last peg, the world will come to an end.

To play the game, you must move all of the discs from the first peg to the third peg, following the same rules as the monks. Let's look at some example solutions to this game, for different numbers of discs. If you have only one disc, the solution to the game is simple: move the disc from peg 1 to peg 3. If you have two discs, the solution requires three moves:

- Move disc 1 to peg 2.
- Move disc 2 to peg 3.
- Move disc 1 to peg 3.

Notice that this approach uses peg 2 as a temporary location. The complexity of the moves continues to increase as the number of discs increases. To move three discs requires the seven moves shown in Figure 16-8.

The following statement describes the overall solution to the problem:

Move n discs from peg 1 to peg 3 using peg 2 as a temporary peg.

The following algorithm can be used as the basis of a recursive method that simulates the solution to the game. Notice that in this algorithm we use the variables A, B, and C to hold peg numbers.

To move n discs from peg A to peg C, using peg B as a temporary peg:
If n > 0 then

Move n − 1 discs from peg A to peg B, using peg C as a temporary peg.
Move the remaining disc from peg A to peg C.
Move n − 1 discs from peg B to peg C, using peg A as a temporary peg.
End if

The base case for the algorithm is reached when there are no more discs to move. The following code is for a method that implements this algorithm. Note that the method does not actually move anything, but displays instructions indicating all of the disc moves to make.

```java
private void moveDiscs(int num, int fromPeg, int toPeg, int tempPeg)
{
    if (num > 0)
    {
        moveDiscs(num - 1, fromPeg, tempPeg, toPeg);
        System.out.println("Move a disc from peg " + fromPeg +
                           " to peg " + toPeg);
        moveDiscs(num - 1, tempPeg, toPeg, fromPeg);
    }
}
```

Figure 16-8 Steps for moving three pegs

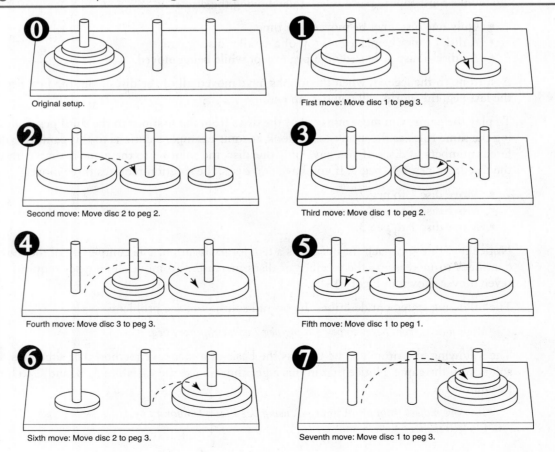

❶ Original setup.

❷ First move: Move disc 1 to peg 3.

❸ Second move: Move disc 2 to peg 2.

❹ Third move: Move disc 1 to peg 2.

❺ Fourth move: Move disc 3 to peg 3.

❻ Fifth move: Move disc 1 to peg 1.

❼ Sixth move: Move disc 2 to peg 3.

❽ Seventh move: Move disc 1 to peg 3.

This method accepts arguments into the following four parameters:

num   The number of discs to move.

fromPeg   The peg to move the discs from.

toPeg   The peg to move the discs to.

tempPeg   The peg to use as a temporary peg.

If num is greater than 0, then there are discs to move. The first recursive call is as follows:

```
moveDiscs(num - 1, fromPeg, tempPeg, toPeg);
```

This statement is an instruction to move all but one disc from fromPeg to tempPeg, using toPeg as a temporary peg. The next statement is as follows:

```
System.out.println("Move a disc from peg " + fromPeg +
                   " to peg " + toPeg);
```

This simply displays a message indicating that a disc should be moved from fromPeg to toPeg. Next, another recursive call is executed as follows:

```
moveDiscs(num - 1, tempPeg, toPeg, fromPeg);
```

This statement is an instruction to move all but one disc from tempPeg to toPeg, using fromPeg as a temporary peg. Code Listing 16-10 shows the Hanoi class, which uses this method.

Code Listing 16-10   (Hanoi.java)

```
 1 /**
 2    This class displays a solution to the Towers of
 3    Hanoi game.
 4 */
 5
 6 public class Hanoi
 7 {
 8    private int numDiscs;   // Number of discs
 9
10    /**
11       Constructor.
12       @param n The number of discs to use.
13    */
14
15    public Hanoi(int n)
16    {
17       // Assign the number of discs.
18       numDiscs = n;
19
20       // Move the number of discs from peg 1 to peg 3
21       // using peg 2 as a temporary storage location.
22       moveDiscs(numDiscs, 1, 3, 2);
23    }
```

```
24
25    /**
26        The moveDiscs method displays a disc move.
27        @param num The number of discs to move.
28        @param fromPeg The peg to move from.
29        @param toPeg The peg to move to.
30        @param tempPeg The temporary peg.
31    */
32
33    private void moveDiscs(int num, int fromPeg,
34                            int toPeg, int tempPeg)
35    {
36        if (num > 0)
37        {
38            moveDiscs(num - 1, fromPeg, tempPeg, toPeg);
39            System.out.println("Move a disc from peg " +
40                            fromPeg + " to peg " + toPeg);
41            moveDiscs(num - 1, tempPeg, toPeg, fromPeg);
42        }
43    }
44 }
```

The class constructor accepts an argument, which is the number of discs to use in the game. It assigns this value to the numDiscs field, and then calls the moveDiscs method in line 22. In a nutshell, this statement is an instruction to move all the discs from peg 1 to peg 3, using peg 2 as a temporary peg. The program in Code Listing 16-11 demonstrates the class. It displays the instructions for moving three discs.

Code Listing 16-11   (HanoiDemo.java)

```
1 /**
2    This class demonstrates the Hanoi class, which
3    displays the steps necessary to solve the Towers
4    of Hanoi game.
5 */
6
7 public class HanoiDemo
8 {
9    static public void main(String[] args)
10   {
11       Hanoi towersOfHanoi = new Hanoi(3);
12   }
13 }
```

Program Output

```
Move a disc from peg 1 to peg 3
Move a disc from peg 1 to peg 2
Move a disc from peg 3 to peg 2
Move a disc from peg 1 to peg 3
Move a disc from peg 2 to peg 1
Move a disc from peg 2 to peg 3
Move a disc from peg 1 to peg 3
```

16.6 Common Errors to Avoid

- **Not coding a base case.** When the base case is reached, a recursive method stops calling itself. Without a base case, the method will continue to call itself infinitely.
- **Not reducing the problem with each recursive call.** Unless the problem is reduced (which usually means that the value of one or more critical parameters is reduced) with each recursive call, the method will not reach the base case. If the base case is not reached, the method will call itself infinitely.
- **Writing the recursive call in such a way that the base case is never reached.** You might have a base case and a recursive case that reduces the problem, but if the calculations are not performed in such a way that the base case is ultimately reached, the method will call itself infinitely.

Review Questions and Exercises

Multiple Choice and True/False

1. A method is called once from a program's `main` method, and then it calls itself four times. The depth of recursion is _____.
    a. one
    b. four
    c. five
    d. nine

2. This is the part of a problem that can be solved without recursion.
    a. base case
    b. solvable case
    c. known case
    d. iterative case

3. This is the part of a problem that is solved with recursion.
    a. base case
    b. iterative case
    c. unknown case
    d. recursion case

4. This is when a method explicitly calls itself.
   a. explicit recursion
   b. modal recursion
   c. direct recursion
   d. indirect recursion

5. This is when method A calls method B, which calls method A.
   a. implicit recursion
   b. modal recursion
   c. direct recursion
   d. indirect recursion

6. This refers to the actions taken internally by the JVM when a method is called.
   a. overhead
   b. set up
   c. clean up
   d. synchronization

7. **True or False:** An iterative algorithm will usually run faster than an equivalent recursive algorithm.

8. **True or False:** Some problems can be solved through recursion only.

9. **True or False:** It is not necessary to have a base case in all recursive algorithms.

10. **True or False:** In the base case, a recursive method calls itself with a smaller version of the original problem.

Find the Error

1. Find the error in the following program:

```java
public class FindTheError
{
    public static void main(String[] args)
    {
        myMethod(0);
    }
    public static void myMethod(int num)
    {
        System.out.print(num + " ");
        myMethod(num + 1);
    }
}
```

Algorithm Workbench

1. Write a method that accepts a `String` as an argument. The method should use recursion to display each individual character in the `String`.

2. Modify the method you wrote in Algorithm Workbench 1 so it displays the `String` backwards.

3. What will the following program display?

```java
public class Checkpoint
{
    public static void main(String[] args)
    {
        int num = 0;
        showMe(num);
    }
    public static void showMe(int arg)
    {
        if (arg < 10)
            showMe(arg + 1);
        else
            System.out.println(arg);
    }
}
```

4. What will the following program display?

```java
public class Checkpoint
{
    public static void main(String[] args)
    {
        int num = 0;
        showMe(num);
    }
    public static void showMe(int arg)
    {
        System.out.println(arg);
        if (arg < 10)
            showMe(arg + 1);
    }
}
```

5. What will the following program display?

```java
public class ReviewQuestion5
{
    public static void main(String[] args)
    {
        int x = 10;
        System.out.println(myMethod(x));
    }
    public static int myMethod(int num)
    {
        if (num <= 0)
            return 0;
        else
```

```
                        return myMethod(num - 1) + num;
            }
    }
```

6. Convert the following iterative method to one that uses recursion:

```
public static void sign(int n)
{
    while (n > 0)
    {
        System.out.println("No Parking");
        n--;
    }
}
```

7. Write an iterative version (using a loop instead of recursion) of the `factorial` method shown in this chapter.

Short Answer

1. What is the difference between an iterative algorithm and a recursive algorithm?

2. What is a recursive algorithm's base case? What is the recursive case?

3. What is the base case of each of the recursive methods listed in Algorithm Workbench 3, 4, and 5?

4. What type of recursive method do you think would be more difficult to debug: one that uses direct recursion or one that uses indirect recursion? Why?

5. Which repetition approach is less efficient: a loop or a recursive method? Why?

6. When recursion is used to solve a problem, why must the recursive method call itself to solve a smaller version of the original problem?

7. How is a problem usually reduced with a recursive method?

Programming Challenges

MyProgrammingLab™   *Visit www.myprogramminglab.com to complete many of these Programming Challenges online and get instant feedback.*

1. Recursive Multiplication

Write a recursive function that accepts two arguments into the parameters x and y. The function should return the value of x times y. Remember, multiplication can be performed as repeated addition as follows:

$$7 * 4 = 4 + 4 + 4 + 4 + 4 + 4 + 4$$

2. isMember Method

Write a recursive `boolean` method named `isMember`. The method should search an array for a specified value, and return `true` if the value is found in the array, or `false` if the value is not found in the array. Demonstrate the method in a program.

3. String Reverser

Write a recursive method that accepts a string as its argument and prints the string in reverse order. Demonstrate the method in a program.

4. `maxElement` Method

Write a method named `maxElement`, which returns the largest value in an array that is passed as an argument. The method should use recursion to find the largest element. Demonstrate the method in a program.

5. Palindrome Detector

A palindrome is any word, phrase, or sentence that reads the same forward and backward. Here are some well-known palindromes:

> Able was I, ere I saw Elba
> A man, a plan, a canal, Panama
> Desserts, I stressed
> Kayak

Write a `boolean` method that uses recursion to determine whether a `String` argument is a palindrome. The method should return `true` if the argument reads the same forward and backward. Demonstrate the method in a program.

6. Character Counter

Write a method that uses recursion to count the number of times a specific character occurs in an array of characters. Demonstrate the method in a program.

VideoNote

The Recursive
Power Problem

7. Recursive Power Method

Write a method that uses recursion to raise a number to a power. The method should accept two arguments: the number to be raised and the exponent. Assume that the exponent is a nonnegative integer. Demonstrate the method in a program.

8. Sum of Numbers

Write a method that accepts an integer argument and returns the sum of all the integers from 1 up to the number passed as an argument. For example, if 50 is passed as an argument, the method will return the sum of 1, 2, 3, 4, . . . 50. Use recursion to calculate the sum. Demonstrate the method in a program.

9. Ackermann's Function

Ackermann's function is a recursive mathematical algorithm that can be used to test how well a computer performs recursion. Write a method `ackermann(m, n)`, which solves Ackermann's function. Use the following logic in your method:

> If $m = 0$ then return $n + 1$
> If $n = 0$ then return `ackermann(m − 1, 1)`
> Otherwise, return `ackermann(m − 1, ackermann(m, n − 1))`

Test your method in a program that displays the return values of the following method calls:

```
ackermann(0, 0)      ackermann(0, 1)      ackermann(1, 1)      ackermann(1, 2)
ackermann(1, 3)      ackermann(2, 2)      ackermann(3, 2)
```

10. Recursive Population Class

In Programming Challenge 9 of Chapter 4 you wrote a population class that predicts the size of a population of organisms after a number of days. Modify the class so it uses a recursive method instead of a loop to calculate the number of organisms.

17 Sorting, Searching, and Algorithm Analysis

17.1 Introduction to Sorting Algorithms

CONCEPT: Sorting algorithms are used to arrange data into some order.

Often, the data in an array must be sorted in some order. Customer lists, for instance, are commonly sorted in alphabetical order. Student grades might be sorted from highest to lowest. Product codes could be sorted so all the products of the same color are stored together. To sort the data in an array, the programmer must use an appropriate *sorting algorithm*. A sorting algorithm is a technique for scanning through an array and rearranging its contents in some specific order.

The data in an array can be sorted in either ascending or descending order. If an array is sorted in *ascending order*, it means the values in the array are stored from lowest to highest. If the values are sorted in *descending order*, they are stored from highest to lowest. This section will introduce four sorting algorithms that can be used to sort the data in an array: the *bubble sort*, the *selection sort*, the *insertion sort*, and the *Quicksort*.

The Bubble Sort

VideoNote
The Bubble Sort
Algorithm

The bubble sort is an easy way to arrange data in ascending or descending order. In this section we will see how the bubble sort can be used to sort an array in ascending order. This particular algorithm is called the *bubble sort* because it makes several passes through the elements of the array and the larger values "bubble" toward the end of the array with each pass.

Suppose we have the array shown in Figure 17-1. Let's see how the bubble sort can be used in arranging the array's elements in ascending order.

Figure 17-1 An array

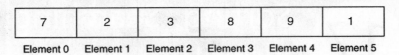

The bubble sort starts by comparing the first two elements in the array. If element 0 is greater than element 1, they are exchanged. After the exchange, the array would appear as shown in Figure 17-2.

Figure 17-2 Elements 0 and 1 are exchanged

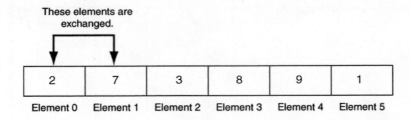

This step is repeated with elements 1 and 2. If element 1 is greater than element 2, they are exchanged. The array would then appear as shown in Figure 17-3.

Figure 17-3 Elements 1 and 2 are exchanged

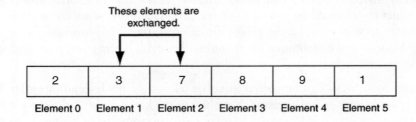

Next, elements 2 and 3 are compared. In this array, these elements are already in the proper order (element 2 is less than element 3), so no exchange takes place. As the cycle continues, elements 3 and 4 are compared. Once again, no exchange is necessary because they are already in the proper order.

When elements 4 and 5 are compared, however, an exchange must take place because element 4 is greater than element 5. The array now appears as shown in Figure 17-4.

Figure 17-4   Elements 4 and 5 are exchanged

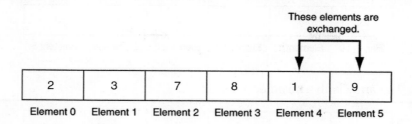

At this point, the entire array has been scanned, and the largest value, 9, is in the correct position. There are other elements, however, that are not yet in their final positions. So, we make another pass through the array, comparing each element with its neighbor. In the next pass we can stop comparing after we reach the next-to-last element because the last element is already at the correct position.

The second pass starts by comparing elements 0 and 1. Because those two are in the proper order, no exchange takes place. Elements 1 and 2 are compared next, but once again, no exchange takes place. This continues until elements 3 and 4 are compared. Because element 3 is greater than element 4, they are exchanged. Element 4 is the last element that we will compare during this pass, so this pass stops. The array now appears as shown in Figure 17-5.

Figure 17-5   Elements 3 and 4 are exchanged

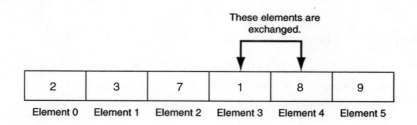

At the end of the second pass, the last two elements in the array are in their correct positions. The third pass starts now, comparing each element with its neighbor. The third pass will not involve the last two elements, however, because they are already in their correct positions. When the third pass is finished, the last three elements will also have been correctly placed, as shown in Figure 17-6.

Each time the algorithm makes a pass through the array, the portion of the array that is scanned is decreased in size by one element, and the largest value in the scanned portion of the array is moved to its final position. When all of the passes have been made, the array will appear as shown in Figure 17-7.

Figure 17-6   The array after the third pass

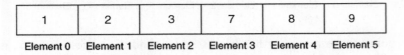

2	3	1	7	8	9
Element 0	Element 1	Element 2	Element 3	Element 4	Element 5

Figure 17-7   The array with all elements sorted

1	2	3	7	8	9
Element 0	Element 1	Element 2	Element 3	Element 4	Element 5

The following pseudocode shows the logic of the bubble sort.

For lastPosition = last subscript in the array, decremented down to 0
    For index = 0 up through lastPosition – 1
        If array[index] > array[index + 1]
            Swap array[index] with array[index + 1]
        End If
    End For
End For

Code Listing 17-1 shows the `IntBubbleSorter` class, which has a public static method, `bubbleSort`. You pass an `int` array to the method and it uses the bubble sort algorithm to sort the array's contents in ascending order.

Code Listing 17-1   (`IntBubbleSorter.java`)

```
1 /**
2    The IntBubbleSorter class provides a public static
3    method for performing a bubble sort on an int array.
4 */
5
6 public class IntBubbleSorter
7 {
8
9    /**
10       The bubbleSort method uses the bubble sort algorithm
11       to sort an int array.
12       @param array The array to sort.
13    */
14
15    public static void bubbleSort(int[] array)
16    {
17       int lastPos;   // Position of the last element to compare
18       int index;     // Index of an element to compare
```

```
19          int temp;       // Used to swap to elements
20
21      // The outer loop positions lastPos at the last element
22      // to compare during each pass through the array. Initially
23      // lastPos is the index of the last element in the array.
24      // During each iteration, it is decreased by one.
25      for (lastPos = array.length - 1; lastPos >= 0; lastPos--)
26      {
27          // The inner loop steps through the array, comparing
28          // each element with its neighbor. All of the elements
29          // from index 0 through lastPos are involved in the
30          // comparison. If two elements are out of order, they
31          // are swapped.
32          for (index = 0; index <= lastPos - 1; index++)
33          {
34              // Compare an element with its neighbor.
35              if (array[index] > array[index + 1])
36              {
37                  // Swap the two elements.
38                  temp = array[index];
39                  array[index] = array[index + 1];
40                  array[index + 1] = temp;
41              }
42          }
43      }
44   }
45 }
```

Lines 17, 18, and 19 declare three variables: lastPos, index, and temp. Here are the purposes of the variables:

- The lastPos variable will hold the index of the last element that is to be compared to its neighbor during a pass through the array.
- The index variable is used as an index into the array during each pass.
- The temp variable is used to hold the value of an element temporarily during a swap.

The method uses two for loops, one nested inside another. The outer loop begins in line 25 as follows:

```
for (lastPos = array.length - 1; lastPos >= 0; lastPos--)
```

This loop will iterate once for each element in the array. It causes the lastPos variable to take on all of the array's subscripts, from the highest subscript down to 0. After each iteration, lastPos is decremented by one.

The second loop, which is nested inside the first loop, begins in line 32 as follows:

```
for (index = 0; index <= lastPos - 1; index++)
```

This loop iterates once for each element in the portion of the array that is still unsorted. It starts index at 0 and increments it up through lastPos - 1. During each iteration, the comparison in line 35 is performed:

```
if (array[index] > array[index + 1])
```

This if statement compares the element at array[index] with its neighbor array[index + 1]. If the element's neighbor is less, then the two are swapped by the code in lines 38 through 40.

The program in Code Listing 17-2 tests the method.

Code Listing 17-2   (BubbleSortTest.java)

```
 1  /**
 2      This program tests the bubbleSort method in the
 3      IntBubbleSorter class.
 4  */
 5
 6  public class BubbleSortTest
 7  {
 8      public static void main(String[] args)
 9      {
10          // Create an int array with test values.
11          int[] values = { 5, 1, 3, 6, 4, 2 };
12
13          // Display the array's contents.
14          System.out.println("Original order: ");
15          for (int element : values)
16              System.out.print(element + " ");
17
18          // Sort the array.
19          IntBubbleSorter.bubbleSort(values);
20
21          // Display the array's contents.
22          System.out.println("\nSorted order: ");
23          for (int element : values)
24              System.out.print(element + " ");
25
26          System.out.println();
27      }
28  }
```

Program Output

```
Original order:
5 1 3 6 4 2
Sorted order:
1 2 3 4 5 6
```

Using the Bubble Sort to Sort Objects

The previous example demonstrated how the bubble sort algorithm can be used to sort an array of `int` values. But, suppose we have an array of objects that we wish to sort. How could we modify the `bubbleSort` method shown previously so it can work with objects?

To sort an array of objects, we must have a consistent way to compare the objects. In the `IntBubbleSorter` class, line 35 of the `bubbleSort` method compares two elements of the array and determines whether one is greater than the other. Because that method is comparing primitive `int` values, it simply compares the two elements with the greater than (>) operator. This approach will not work with object references, however. Reference variables hold only the addresses of objects, and you cannot use operators like greater than (>) or less than (<) to compare them. (Even if you could use these operators with object references, it would not make sense to do so. When you compare two objects, you usually want to compare the data contained within those objects.)

The Java API has an interface named `Comparable`, which helps in a situation like this. The `Comparable` interface, which is in the `java.lang` package, specifies a method named `compareTo`, which is used to compare the calling object with another object that is passed as an argument. The method returns an `int` value that specifies whether the calling object is greater than (>), less than (<), or equal to (=) the object that was passed as an argument.

Many of the classes in the Java API implement this interface, including `String` and the wrapper classes. You might recall from our discussion of the `String` class in Chapter 3 how the `compareTo` method works:

- If the calling object is less than the object passed as an argument, the method returns a negative number.
- If the calling object is equal to the object passed as an argument, the method returns 0.
- If the calling object is greater than the object passed as an argument, the method returns a positive number.

If we want to write a `bubbleSort` method that can accept an array of objects, a good solution is to require that the objects in the array implement the `Comparable` interface. That way we can use the `compareTo` method to compare the elements. Code Listing 17-3 shows the `ObjectBubbleSorter` class, which has a `bubbleSort` method that sorts an array of `Comparable` objects.

Code Listing 17-3   (`ObjectBubbleSorter.java`)

```
1  /**
2      The ObjectBubbleSorter class provides a public static
3      method for performing a bubble sort on an array of
4      objects implementing the Comparable interface.
5  */
6
7  public class ObjectBubbleSorter
8  {
```

```
 9
10      /**
11          The bubbleSort method uses the bubble sort algorithm
12          to sort an array of objects implementing Comparable
13          @param array The array to sort.
14      */
15
16      public static void bubbleSort(Comparable[] array)
17      {
18          int lastPos;     // Marks the last position to compare
19          int index;       // Index of an element to compare
20          Comparable temp; // Used to swap to elements
21
22          // The outer loop positions lastPos at the last element
23          // to compare during each pass through the array. Initially
24          // lastPos is the index of the last element in the array.
25          // During each iteration, it is decreased by one.
26          for (lastPos = array.length - 1; lastPos >= 0; lastPos--)
27          {
28              // The inner loop steps through the array, comparing
29              // each element with its neighbor. All of the elements
30              // from index 0 through lastPos are involved in the
31              // comparison. If two elements are out of order, they
32              // are swapped.
33              for (index = 0; index <= lastPos - 1; index++)
34              {
35                  // Compare an element with its neighbor.
36                  if (array[index].compareTo(array[index + 1]) > 0)
37                  {
38                      // Swap the two elements.
39                      temp = array[index];
40                      array[index] = array[index + 1];
41                      array[index + 1] = temp;
42                  }
43              }
44          }
45      }
46 }
```

NOTE: If you compile the class shown in Code Listing 17-3 you will likely see a warning such as:

```
ObjectBubbleSorter.java uses unchecked or unsafe operations.
Note: Recompile with -Xlint:unchecked for details.
```

For now, ignore this warning. In Chapter 18, when we discuss generic types, you will learn how to eliminate these warnings.

Notice in line 16 that the `bubbleSort` method's parameter is declared as `Comparable[]` array. When we call this method, the argument that we pass must be an array of objects that implement `Comparable`. The comparison that is made in line 36 reads as follows:

```
if (array[index].compareTo(array[index + 1]) > 0)
```

This statement uses the `array[index]` object's `compareTo` method to determine whether it is greater than the object at `array[index + 1]`. If it is, the two elements are swapped. (Also notice that the `temp` variable's data type has been changed. It is now a `Comparable` reference variable.)

Because the `String` class implements the `Comparable` interface, an easy way to test the method is to pass an array of `String` objects to it, as shown in Code Listing 17-4.

Code Listing 17-4   **(ObjectBubbleSortTest.java)**

```
1  /**
2      This program tests the bubbleSort method in the
3      ObjectBubbleSorter class.
4  */
5
6  public class ObjectBubbleSortTest
7  {
8      public static void main(String[] args)
9      {
10         // Create a String array with test values.
11         // Note that String implements Comparable.
12         String[] values = { "David", "Abe", "Katherine",
13                             "Beth", "Jeff", "Daisy" };
14
15         // Display the array's contents.
16         System.out.println("Original order:");
17         for (String element : values)
18            System.out.print(element + " ");
19
20         // Sort the array.
21         ObjectBubbleSorter.bubbleSort(values);
22
23         // Display the array's contents.
24         System.out.println("\nSorted order:");
25         for (String element : values)
26            System.out.print(element + " ");
27
28         System.out.println();
29      }
30 }
```

Program Output

```
Original order:
David Abe Katherine Beth Jeff Daisy
Sorted order:
Abe Beth Daisy David Jeff Katherine
```

When you are designing a class of your own, and you want to be able to sort objects of that class using the `bubbleSort` method shown in the `ObjectBubbleSorter` class (Code Listing 17-3), your class must implement the `Comparable` interface, and provide a `compareTo` method. In Chapter 18, Generics, we will take a closer look at the `Comparable` interface and how to implement it.

The Selection Sort

The *selection sort* works like this: The smallest value in the array is located and moved to position 0. Then, the next smallest value is located and moved to position 1. This process continues until all of the elements have been placed in their proper order. Let's see how the selection sort works when arranging the elements of the array in Figure 17-8.

Figure 17-8 Values in an array

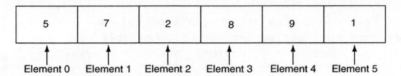

The selection sort scans the array, starting at position 0, and locates the element with the smallest value. Then, this smallest element is swapped with the element at position 0. In this example, the 1 stored at position 5 is swapped with the 5 stored at position 0. After the exchange, the array appears as shown in Figure 17-9.

Figure 17-9 Values in the array after the first swap

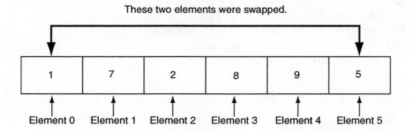

Then, the algorithm repeats the process, but because the element at position 0 is already the smallest value in the array, it can be left out of the procedure. This time, the algorithm begins the scan at position 1. In this example, the element at 2 is exchanged with the element at position 1. Then, the array appears as shown in Figure 17-10.

Figure 17-10   Values in the array after the second swap

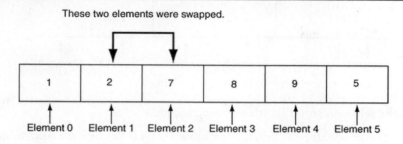

Once again the process is repeated, but this time the scan begins at position 2. The algorithm will find that position 5 contains the next smallest value. This element is swapped with the element at position 2, causing the array to appear as shown in Figure 17-11.

Figure 17-11   Values in the array after the third swap

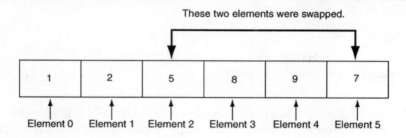

Next, the scanning begins at position 3. Its value is swapped with that at position 5, causing the array to appear as shown in Figure 17-12.

Figure 17-12   Values in the array after the fourth swap

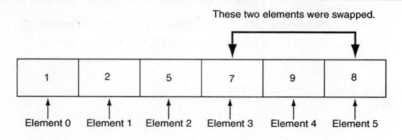

At this point, there are only two elements left in the unsorted portion of the array. The algorithm finds that the value at 5 is smaller than that at position 4, so the two are swapped. This puts the array in its final arrangement, as shown in Figure 17-13.

Figure 17-13 Values in the array after the fifth swap

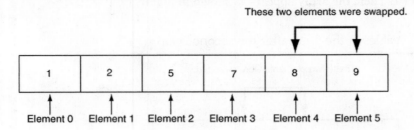

Here is the selection sort algorithm in pseudocode:

For startScan *equals each subscript in array from 0 through the next-to-last subscript*
 Set index *variable to* startScan.
 Set minIndex *variable to* startScan.
 Set minValue *variable to* array[startScan].
 For index *is each subscript in array from* (startScan + 1) *through the last subscript*
  If array[index] *is less than* minValue
   Set minValue *to* array[index].
   Set minIndex *to* index.
  End If.
  Increment index.
 End For.
 Set array[minIndex] *to* array[startScan].
 Set array[startScan] *to* minValue.
End For.

Code Listing 17-5 shows the IntSelectionSorter class, which has a public static method, selectionSort. You pass an int array to the method and it uses the selection sort algorithm to sort the array's contents in ascending order. The program in Code Listing 17-6 tests the method.

Code Listing 17-5 **(IntSelectionSorter.java)**

```
 1 /**
 2    The IntSelectionSorter class provides a public static
 3    method for performing a selection sort on an int array.
 4 */
 5
 6 public class IntSelectionSorter
 7 {
 8
 9    /**
10       The selectionSort method performs a selection sort on an
11       int array. The array is sorted in ascending order.
```

```
12         @param array The array to sort.
13      */
14
15      public static void selectionSort(int[] array)
16      {
17         int startScan;  // Starting position of the scan
18         int index;      // To hold a subscript value
19         int minIndex;   // Element with smallest value in the scan
20         int minValue;   // The smallest value found in the scan
21
22         // The outer loop iterates once for each element in the
23         // array. The startScan variable marks the position where
24         // the scan should begin.
25         for (startScan = 0; startScan < (array.length-1); startScan++)
26         {
27            // Assume the first element in the scannable area
28            // is the smallest value.
29            minIndex = startScan;
30            minValue = array[startScan];
31
32            // Scan the array, starting at the 2nd element in
33            // the scannable area. We are looking for the smallest
34            // value in the scannable area.
35            for(index = startScan + 1; index < array.length; index++)
36            {
37               if (array[index] < minValue)
38               {
39                  minValue = array[index];
40                  minIndex = index;
41               }
42            }
43
44            // Swap the element with the smallest value
45            // with the first element in the scannable area.
46            array[minIndex] = array[startScan];
47            array[startScan] = minValue;
48         }
49      }
50  }
```

Code Listing 17-6   (`SelectionSortTest.java`)

```
1  /**
2      This program tests the selectionSort method in the
3      IntSelectionSorter class.
4  */
```

```
5
6  public class SelectionSortTest
7  {
8     public static void main(String[] args)
9     {
10        // Create an int array with test values.
11        int[] values = { 5, 1, 3, 6, 4, 2 };
12
13        // Display the array's contents.
14        System.out.println("Original order:");
15        for (int element : values)
16           System.out.print(element + " ");
17
18        // Sort the array.
19        IntSelectionSorter.selectionSort(values);
20
21        // Display the array's contents.
22        System.out.println("\nSorted order:");
23        for (int element : values)
24           System.out.print(element + " ");
25
26        System.out.println();
27     }
28  }
```

Program Output

```
Original order:
5 1 3 6 4 2
Sorted order:
1 2 3 4 5 6
```

Using the Selection Sort to Sort Objects

Previously, we demonstrated how the bubbleSort method could be written to accept an array of Comparable objects, and then use the compareTo method in the bubble sort algorithm to compare the objects. We can take the same approach with the selection sort, as shown in Code Listing 17-7. This class has a public static selectionSort method that accepts an array of Comparable objects.

Code Listing 17-7   (ObjectSelectionSorter.java)

```
1  /**
2     The ObjectSelectionSorter class provides a public static
3     method for performing a selection sort on an array of
4     objects that implement the Comparable interface.
5  */
```

```
 6
 7 public class ObjectSelectionSorter
 8 {
 9
10    /**
11       The selectionSort method performs a selection sort on an
12       array of objects that implement the Comparable interface.
13       @param array The array to sort.
14    */
15
16    public static void selectionSort(Comparable[] array)
17    {
18       int startScan;        // Starting position of the scan
19       int index;            // To hold a subscript value
20       int minIndex;         // Element with smallest value in the scan
21       Comparable minValue;  // The smallest value found in the scan
22
23       // The outer loop iterates once for each element in the
24       // array. The startScan variable marks the position where
25       // the scan should begin.
26       for (startScan = 0; startScan < (array.length-1); startScan++)
27       {
28          // Assume the first element in the scannable area
29          // is the smallest value.
30          minIndex = startScan;
31          minValue = array[startScan];
32
33          // Scan the array, starting at the 2nd element in
34          // the scannable area. We are looking for the smallest
35          // value in the scannable area.
36          for(index = startScan + 1; index < array.length; index++)
37          {
38             if (array[index].compareTo(minValue) < 0)
39             {
40                minValue = array[index];
41                minIndex = index;
42             }
43          }
44
45          // Swap the element with the smallest value
46          // with the first element in the scannable area.
47          array[minIndex] = array[startScan];
48          array[startScan] = minValue;
49       }
50    }
51 }
```

The program in Code Listing 17-8 tests the selectionSort method with an array of String objects.

Code Listing 17-8   (ObjectSelectionSortTest.java)

```
 1 /**
 2    This program tests the selectionSort method in the
 3    ObjectSelectionSorter class.
 4 */
 5
 6 public class ObjectSelectionSortTest
 7 {
 8    public static void main(String[] args)
 9    {
10       // Create a String array with test values.
11       // Note that String implements Comparable.
12       String[] values = { "David", "Abe", "Katherine",
13                           "Beth", "Jeff", "Daisy" };
14
15       // Display the array's contents.
16       System.out.println("Original order:");
17       for (String element : values)
18          System.out.print(element + " ");
19
20       // Sort the array.
21       ObjectSelectionSorter.selectionSort(values);
22
23       // Display the array's contents.
24       System.out.println("\nSorted order:");
25       for (String element : values)
26          System.out.print(element + " ");
27
28       System.out.println();
29    }
30 }
```

Program Output

```
Original order:
David Abe Katherine Beth Jeff Daisy
Sorted order:
Abe Beth Daisy David Jeff Katherine
```

The Insertion Sort

In the insertion sort, we begin by looking at the first two elements of the array. We compare these elements and, if necessary, we swap them so they are in the proper order. This becomes a sorted portion of the array.

Then, our objective is to incorporate the third element of the array into the part of the array already sorted. We do this by inserting it into proper position, relative to the first two elements. If we need to shift either of the first two elements to accommodate the third element, we do so. Once we have inserted the third element into the correct position (relative to the first two elements), the initial portion of the array consisting of the first three elements will be sorted.

This process continues with the fourth and subsequent elements, until all of the elements have been inserted into their proper positions. Let's look at an example. Suppose we start with the `int` array shown in Figure 17-14. As shown in the figure, the values in the first and second elements are out of order, so they will be swapped.

Figure 17-14   An unsorted array

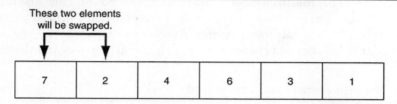

After the swap takes place, the first and second elements will be in sorted order. The next step is to move the value of the third element so it is in the correct position, relative to the first two elements. As shown in Figure 17-15, the value in the third element must be positioned between the values in the first and second elements.

Figure 17-15   The third element must be moved

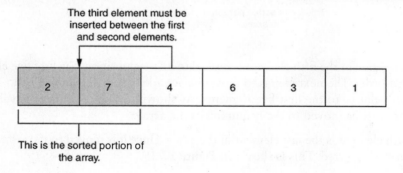

After the value in the third element is moved to its new position, the first three elements will be in sorted order. The next step is to move the value of the fourth element so it is in the correct position, relative to the first three elements. As shown in Figure 17-16, the value in the fourth element must be positioned between the values in the second and third elements.

Figure 17-16   The fourth element must be moved

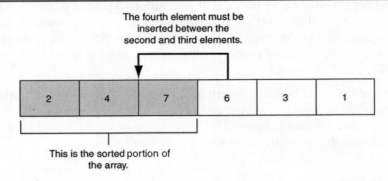

After the value in the fourth element is moved to its new position, the first four elements will be in sorted order. The next step is to move the value of the fifth element so it is in the correct position, relative to the first four elements. As shown in Figure 17-17, the value in the fifth element must be positioned between the values in the first and second elements.

Figure 17-17   The fifth element must be moved

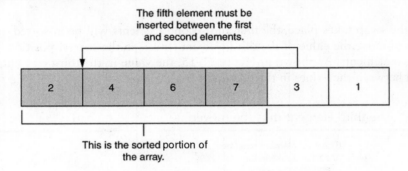

After the value in the fifth element is moved to its new position, the first five elements will be in sorted order. The next step is to move the value of the sixth element so it is in the correct position, relative to the first five elements. As shown in Figure 17-18, the value in the sixth element must be moved to the beginning of the array.

The sixth element is the last element in the array. Once it is moved to its correct position, the entire array is sorted. This is shown in Figure 17-19.

Figure 17-18 The sixth element must be moved

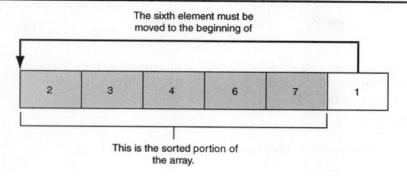

The sixth element must be moved to the beginning of

| 2 | 3 | 4 | 6 | 7 | 1 |

This is the sorted portion of the array.

Figure 17-19 All of the elements are in the correct position

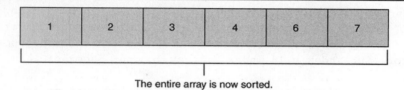

| 1 | 2 | 3 | 4 | 6 | 7 |

The entire array is now sorted.

Here is the insertion sort algorithm in pseudocode:

For index *equals each subscript in* array *from 1 through the last subscript*
  Save the value in index *in* scan
  Save the value in array[index] *in* unsortedValue
  While scan *is greater than 0 and* array[scan - 1] *is greater than* unsortedValue
    Move array[scan - 1] *to* array[scan]
    Subtract 1 from scan
  End While
  Store the value in unsortedValue *in* array[scan]
End For

Code Listing 17-9 shows the IntInsertionSorter class, which has a public static method, insertionSort. You pass an int array to the method and it uses the insertion sort algorithm to sort the array's contents in ascending order. The program in Code Listing 17-10 tests the method.

Code Listing 17-9   (IntInsertionSorter.java)

```
1  /**
2     The IntInsertionSorter class provides a public static
3     method for performing an insertion sort on an int array.
4  */
```

```
 5
 6 public class IntInsertionSorter
 7 {
 8
 9    /**
10       The insertionSort method performs an insertion sort on
11       an int array. The array is sorted in ascending order.
12       @param array The array to sort.
13    */
14
15    public static void insertionSort(int[] array)
16    {
17       int unsortedValue;   // The first unsorted value
18       int scan;            // Used to scan the array
19
20       // The outer loop steps the index variable through each
21       // subscript in the array, starting at 1. The portion of the
22       // array consisting of element 0 by itself is already sorted.
23       for (int index = 1; index < array.length; index++)
24       {
25          // The first element outside the sorted portion is
26          // array[index]. Store the value of this element
27          // in unsortedValue.
28          unsortedValue = array[index];
29
30          // Start scan at the subscript of the first element
31          // in the still unsorted part.
32          scan = index;
33
34          // Move the first element in the still unsorted part
35          // into its proper position within the sorted part.
36          while (scan > 0 && array[scan - 1] > unsortedValue)
37          {
38             array[scan] = array[scan-1];
39             scan--;
40          }
41
42          // Insert the unsorted value in its proper position
43          // within the sorted part.
44          array[scan] = unsortedValue;
45       }
46    }
47 }
```

Code Listing 17-10   (`InsertionSortTest.java`)

```
 1 /**
 2     This program tests the insertionSort method in the
 3     IntInsertionSorter class.
 4 */
 5
 6 public class InsertionSortTest
 7 {
 8    public static void main(String[] args)
 9    {
10       // Create an int array with test values.
11       int[] values = { 5, 1, 3, 6, 4, 2 };
12
13       // Display the array's contents.
14       System.out.println("Original order:");
15       for (int element : values)
16          System.out.print(element + " ");
17
18       // Sort the array.
19       IntInsertionSorter.insertionSort(values);
20
21       // Display the array's contents.
22       System.out.println("\nSorted order:");
23       for (int element : values)
24          System.out.print(element + " ");
25
26       System.out.println();
27    }
28 }
```

Program Output

```
Original order:
5 1 3 6 4 2
Sorted order:
1 2 3 4 5 6
```

Using the Insertion Sort to Sort Objects

We have demonstrated how the `bubbleSort` and `selectionSort` methods can be written to accept an array of `Comparable` objects, and then use the `compareTo` method to compare the objects. A similar approach can be taken with the `insertionSort` method. This will be left as a programming exercise for you at the end of the chapter.

The Quicksort Algorithm

The Quicksort algorithm is a popular sorting routine developed in 1960 by C. A. R. Hoare. It sorts an array by dividing it into two sublists. Between the sublists is a selected value known as the *pivot*, as shown in Figure 17-20.

Figure 17-20 Sublists and pivot

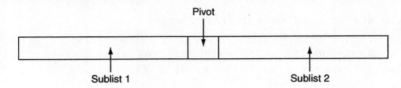

Notice in the figure that sublist 1 is positioned to the left of (before) the pivot, and sublist 2 is positioned to the right of (after) the pivot. Once a pivot value has been selected, the algorithm reorders the other values in the array until all the elements in the left sublist are less than the pivot, and all the elements in the right sublist are greater than or equal to the pivot. This does not mean that the elements in the sublists are sorted in order, just that the smaller values in the array are in the left sublist and the larger values are in the right sublist.

Once this is done, the algorithm recursively repeats the procedure on sublist 1, and then on sublist 2. During this process, the sublists are themselves divided into sublists with a pivot. All the elements less than the pivot are moved to the left sublist, and all the elements greater than the pivot are moved to the right sublist. The recursion stops when there is at most one element in a sublist. When all of the recursive calls have completed, the array is completely sorted.

To demonstrate the Quicksort algorithm we have provided a class, `IntQuickSorter.java`. This class has the following public static method:

```
14      public static void quickSort(int array[])
15      {
16          doQuickSort(array, 0, array.length - 1);
17      }
```

This method accepts an `int` array as its argument. Then it calls a private static method, `doQuickSort`. The reason we have this extra method call is that the Quicksort algorithm requires the starting subscript and the ending subscript of the area of the array that is to be sorted. When you first invoke the Quicksort algorithm, you provide the starting and ending subscripts of the entire array. As a convenience to anyone using the `IntQuickSorter` class, we have provided the `quickSort` method, which simply accepts an array. Then it calls the `doQuickSort` method, providing the starting and ending subscripts as arguments.

The pseudocode for the doQuickSort method is shown here:

doQuickSort:
  If Starting Index < Ending Index
    Partition the List around a Pivot.
    doQuickSort Sublist 1.
    doQuickSort Sublist 2.
  End If.
End doQuickSort

Here is the Java code for the doQuickSort method:

```
27      private static void doQuickSort(int array[], int start, int end)
28      {
29          int pivotPoint;
30
31          if (start < end)
32          {
33              // Get the pivot point.
34              pivotPoint = partition(array, start, end);
35
36              // Sort the first sublist.
37              doQuickSort(array, start, pivotPoint - 1);
38
39              // Sort the second sublist.
40              doQuickSort(array, pivotPoint + 1, end);
41          }
42      }
```

The first argument is the array holding the list that is to be sorted. The second and third arguments are the starting and ending subscripts of the list.

The subscript of the pivot element is returned by the partition method in line 34. The partition method not only determines which element will be the pivot, but also rearranges the other values in the list. The method selects the element in the middle of the array as the pivot, and then scans the remainder of the array searching for values less than the pivot.

The code for the partition method is shown here:

```
56      private static int partition(int array[], int start, int end)
57      {
58          int pivotValue;      // To hold the pivot value
59          int endOfLeftList;   // Last element in the left sublist.
60          int mid;             // To hold the mid-point subscript
61
62          // Find the subscript of the middle element.
63          // This will be our pivot value.
64          mid = (start + end) / 2;
65
```

```
66          // Swap the middle element with the first element.
67          // This moves the pivot value to the start of
68          // the list.
69          swap(array, start, mid);
70
71          // Save the pivot value for comparisons.
72          pivotValue = array[start];
73
74          // For now, the end of the left sublist is
75          // the first element.
76          endOfLeftList = start;
77
78          // Scan the entire list and move any values that
79          // are less than the pivot value to the left
80          // sublist.
81          for (int scan = start + 1; scan <= end; scan++)
82          {
83              if (array[scan] < pivotValue)
84              {
85                  endOfLeftList++;
86                  swap(array, endOfLeftList, scan);
87              }
88          }
89
90          // Move the pivot value to end of the
91          // left sublist.
92          swap(array, start, endOfLeftList);
93
94          // Return the subscript of the pivot value.
95          return endOfLeftList;
96      }
```

The partition method does not initially sort the values into their final order. Its job is only to move the values that are less than the pivot to the pivot's left, and move the values that are greater than the pivot to the pivot's right. As long as that condition is met, they may appear in any order. The ultimate sorting order of the entire array is achieved cumulatively, through the recursive calls to the doQuickSort method.

There are many different ways of partitioning the array. As previously stated, the technique shown in this partition method selects the middle value as the pivot. That value is then moved to the beginning of the array (by swapping it with the value stored there). This simplifies the next step, which is to scan the array.

A for loop scans the remainder of the array, and when an element is found whose value is less than the pivot, that value is moved to a location left of the pivot point. A third method, swap, is used to swap the values found in any two elements of the array. The method is shown here:

```
106    private static void swap(int[] array, int a, int b)
107    {
108        int temp;
109
110        temp = array[a];
111        array[a] = array[b];
112        array[b] = temp;
113    }
```

The program shown in Code Listing 17-11 uses these methods to test the Quicksort algorithm.

Code Listing 17-11 (QuickSortTest.java)

```
 1  /**
 2      This program tests the quickSort method in the
 3      IntQuickSorter class.
 4  */
 5
 6  public class QuickSortTest
 7  {
 8      public static void main(String[] args)
 9      {
10          // Create an int array with test values.
11          int[] values = { 5, 1, 3, 6, 4, 2 };
12
13          // Display the array's contents.
14          System.out.println("Original order:");
15          for (int element : values)
16              System.out.print(element + " ");
17
18          // Sort the array.
19          IntQuickSorter.quickSort(values);
20
21          // Display the array's contents.
22          System.out.println("\nSorted order:");
23          for (int element : values)
24              System.out.print(element + " ");
25
26          System.out.println();
27      }
28  }
```

Program Output

```
Original order:
5 1 3 6 4 2
Sorted order:
1 2 3 4 5 6
```

Using Quicksort to Sort Objects

As with the other sorting algorithms shown in this chapter, the Quicksort methods we have demonstrated can be modified to accept an array of `Comparable` objects, and then we can use the `compareTo` method to make comparisons. Modifying these Quicksort methods to accept an array of `Comparable` objects will be left as a programming exercise for you at the end of the chapter.

 Checkpoint

17.1   Which of the sorting algorithms that we discussed makes several passes through an array and causes the larger values to move gradually toward the end of the array with each pass?

17.2   One of the sorting algorithms that we discussed works like this: It begins by putting the initial portion of the array consisting of the first two elements in sorted order. Then the third element is moved to its correct position, relative to the first two elements. At that point the first three elements are in sorted order. This process continues with the fourth and subsequent elements until the entire array is sorted. Which algorithm is this?

17.3   One of the sorting algorithms that we discussed works like this: The smallest value in the array is located and moved to element 0. Then the next smallest value is located and moved to element 1. This process continues until all of the elements have been placed in their proper order. Which algorithm is this?

17.4   One of the algorithms we discussed divides an array into two sublists, with a pivot value between them. It arranges the sublists so that all the values less than the pivot are stored in the left sublist and all the values greater than the pivot are stored in the right sublist. The algorithm recursively sorts the sublists in this same way. When all of the recursive calls have completed, the array is completely sorted. Which algorithm is this?

 Introduction to Search Algorithms

> **CONCEPT:** A search algorithm is a method of locating a specific item in a larger collection of data. This section discusses two algorithms for searching the contents of an array.

It's very common for programs not only to store and process data stored in arrays, but also to search arrays for specific items. This section will show you two methods of searching an array: the sequential search and the binary search. Each has its advantages and disadvantages.

The Sequential Search Algorithm

The *sequential search algorithm* uses a loop to step sequentially through an array, starting with the first element. It compares each element with the value being searched for and stops when the value is found or the end of the array is encountered. If the value being searched for is not in the array, the algorithm unsuccessfully searches to the end of the array.

Here is the pseudocode for a method that performs the sequential search:

Set found *to false.*
Set position *to –1.*
Set index *to 0.*
While found *is false and* index < *number of elements*
   If list[index] *is equal to search value*
     found = *true.*
     position = index.
   End If
   Add 1 to index.
End While.
Return position.

This pseudocode method returns the subscript of the element holding the value. If the value is not found, however, it returns –1. The reason –1 is returned when the value is not found is that –1 is not a valid array subscript, and it cannot be mistaken as a position within the array.

The IntSequentialSearcher class in Code Listing 17-12 has a public static method that performs a sequential search on an int array. The program in Code Listing 17-13 tests the method.

Code Listing 17-12   (IntSequentialSearcher.java)

```
 1  /**
 2      The IntSequentialSearcher class provides a public static
 3      method for performing a sequential search on an int array.
 4  */
 5
 6  public class IntSequentialSearcher
 7  {
 8      /**
 9          The search method searches an array for a value.
10          @param array The array to search.
11          @param value The value to search for.
12          @return The subscript of the value if found in the
13                  array, otherwise -1.
14      */
15
16      public static int search(int[] array, int value)
17      {
18          int index;      // Loop control variable
19          int position;   // Position the value is found at
20          boolean found;  // Flag indicating search results
21
22          // Element 0 is the starting point of the search.
23          index = 0;
```

```
24
25        // Store the default values position and found.
26        position = -1;
27        found = false;
28
29        // Search the array.
30        while (!found && index < array.length)
31        {
32           if (array[index] == value)
33           {
34              found = true;
35              position = index;
36           }
37           index++;
38        }
39
40        // Return the found element's position,
41        // or -1 if not found.
42        return position;
43     }
44 }
```

Code Listing 17-13   (`SequentialSearchTest.java`)

```
 1 /**
 2     This program sequentially searches an
 3     int array for a specified value.
 4 */
 5
 6 public class SequentialSearchTest
 7 {
 8     public static void main(String[] args)
 9     {
10        int[] tests = { 87, 75, 98, 100, 82 };
11        int results;
12
13        // Search the array for the value 100.
14        results = IntSequentialSearcher.search(tests, 100);
15
16        // Determine whether 100 was found and
17        // display an appropriate message.
18        if (results == -1)
19        {
20           System.out.println("You did not " +
21                              "earn 100 on any test.");
22        }
```

```
23          else
24          {
25              System.out.println("You earned 100 " +
26                                  "on test " + (results + 1));
27          }
28      }
29  }
```

Program Output

You earned 100 on test 4

Average Case Analysis of the Sequential Search

The advantage of the sequential search is its simplicity. It is very easy to understand and implement. Sequential search is very flexible, and can be used on any array. But this flexibility comes at a cost: If the array being searched contains 20,000 elements, the algorithm may have to look at all 20,000 elements. This might happen, for example, when the value being searched for is not in the array, or when it is found in the very last array entry.

In an average case, an item is just as likely to be found near the beginning of the array as near the end. Typically, for an array of n items, the sequential search will locate an item in $n/2$ attempts. If an array has 50,000 elements, the sequential search will make a comparison with 25,000 of them in a typical case. This is assuming, of course, that the search item has equal probability of being found at any position in the array. ($n/2$ is the average number of comparisons. The maximum number of comparisons is always n.)

The Binary Search

The *binary search* is a clever algorithm that is much more efficient than the sequential search. Its only requirement is that the values in the array must be sorted in some order. Let us suppose the input array is sorted in ascending order. Instead of testing the array's first element, this algorithm starts with the element in the middle. If that element happens to contain the desired value, then the search is over. Otherwise, the value in the middle element is either greater than or less than the value being searched for. If it is greater, then the desired value (if it is in the list) will be found somewhere in the first half of the array. If it is less, then the desired value (again, if it is in the list) will be found somewhere in the last half of the array. In either case, half of the array's elements have been eliminated from further searching.

If the desired value isn't found in the middle element, the procedure is repeated for the half of the array that potentially contains the value. For instance, if the last half of the array is to be searched, the algorithm tests *its* middle element. If the desired value isn't found there, the search is narrowed to the quarter of the array that resides before or after that element. This process continues until the value being searched for is either found, or there are no more elements to test. Here is the pseudocode for a method that performs a binary search on an array:

Set first *to 0.*
Set last *to the last subscript in the array.*
Set found *to false.*
Set position *to –1.*
While found *is not true and* first *is less than or equal to* last
    Set middle *to the subscript half-way between* array[first] *and* array[last].
    If array[middle] *equals the desired value*
        Set found *to* true.
        Set position *to* middle.
    Else If array[middle] *is greater than the desired value*
        Set last *to* middle – 1.
    Else
        Set first *to* middle + 1.
    End If.
End While.
Return position.

This algorithm uses three variables to mark positions within the array: first, last, and middle. The first and last variables mark the boundaries of the portion of the array currently being searched. They are initialized with the subscripts of the array's first and last elements. The subscript of the element halfway between first and last is calculated and stored in the middle variable. If the element in the middle of the array does not contain the search value, the first or last variables are adjusted so that only the top or bottom half of the array is searched during the next iteration. This cuts the portion of the array being searched in half each time the loop fails to locate the search value.

The IntBinarySearcher class shown in Code Listing 17-14 has a public static method that performs a binary search on an integer array. The first parameter, array, is searched for an occurrence of the number stored in value. If the number is found, its array subscript is returned. Otherwise, –1 is returned indicating the value did not appear in the array. The program in Code Listing 17-15 tests the method.

Code Listing 17-14   **(IntBinarySearcher.java)**

```
1  /**
2     The IntBinarySearcher class provides a public static
3     method for performing a binary search on an int array.
4  */
5
6  public class IntBinarySearcher
7  {
8     /**
9        The search method performs a binary search on an int
10       array. The array is searched for the number passed to
11       value. If the number is found, its array subscript is
```

```
12          returned. Otherwise, -1 is returned indicating the
13          value was not found in the array.
14          @param array The array to search.
15          @param value The value to search for.
16       */
17
18       public static int search(int[] array, int value)
19       {
20          int first;       // First array element
21          int last;        // Last array element
22          int middle;      // Mid point of search
23          int position;    // Position of search value
24          boolean found;   // Flag
25
26          // Set the initial values.
27          first = 0;
28          last = array.length - 1;
29          position = -1;
30          found = false;
31
32          // Search for the value.
33          while (!found && first <= last)
34          {
35             // Calculate midpoint
36             middle = (first + last) / 2;
37
38             // If value is found at mid point...
39             if (array[middle] == value)
40             {
41                found = true;
42                position = middle;
43             }
44             // else if value is in lower half...
45             else if (array[middle] > value)
46                last = middle - 1;
47             // else if value is in upper half....
48             else
49                first = middle + 1;
50          }
51
52          // Return the position of the item, or -1
53          // if it was not found.
54          return position;
55       }
56 }
```

Code Listing 17-15 (BinarySearchTest.java)

```java
 1 import java.util.Scanner;
 2
 3 /**
 4    This program demonstrates the search method in
 5    the IntBinarySearcher class.
 6 */
 7
 8 public class BinarySearchTest
 9 {
10    public static void main(String[] args)
11    {
12       int result, searchValue;
13       String input;
14
15       // An array of numbers to search.
16       int numbers[] = { 536, 289, 296, 429, 319, 142, 394,
17                         101, 388, 147, 417, 199, 207, 222,
18                         189, 310, 447, 521, 234, 600};
19
20       // Create a Scanner object for keyboard input.
21       Scanner keyboard = new Scanner(System.in);
22
23       // First we must sort the array in ascending order.
24       IntQuickSorter.quickSort(numbers);
25
26       do
27       {
28          // Get a value to search for.
29          System.out.print("Enter a value to search for: ");
30          searchValue = keyboard.nextInt();
31
32          // Search for the value
33          result = IntBinarySearcher.search(numbers, searchValue);
34
35          // Display the results.
36          if (result == -1)
37             System.out.println(searchValue + " was not found.");
38          else
39          {
40             System.out.println(searchValue + " was found at " +
41                                "element " + result);
42          }
43
```

```
44                // Consume the remaining newline...
45                keyboard.nextLine();
46
47                // Does the user want to search again?
48                System.out.print("Do you want to search again? (Y or N): ");
49                input = keyboard.nextLine();
50       } while (input.charAt(0) == 'y' || input.charAt(0) == 'Y');
51    }
52 }
```

Program Output with Example Input Shown in Bold

```
Enter a value to search for: 289 [Enter]
289 was found at element 8
Do you want to search again? (Y or N): y [Enter]
Enter a value to search for: 101 [Enter]
101 was found at element 0
Do you want to search again? (Y or N): y [Enter]
Enter a value to search for: 999 [Enter]
999 was not found.
Do you want to search again? (Y or N): n [Enter]
```

Efficiency of the Binary Search

For sorted arrays, the binary search is much more efficient than the sequential search. Every time it makes a comparison and fails to find the desired item, it eliminates half of the remaining portion of the array that must be searched. For example, consider an array with 1,000 elements.

If the binary search fails to find an item on the first attempt, the number of elements that remains to be searched is 500. If the item is not found on the second attempt, the number of elements that remains to be searched is 250. This process continues until the binary search has either located the desired item or determined that it is not in the array. With 1,000 elements this takes no more than 10 comparisons. (Compare this to the sequential search, which would make an average of 500 comparisons!)

Powers of 2 are used to calculate the maximum number of comparisons the binary search will make on an array of any size. Simply find the smallest power of 2 that is greater than or equal to the number of elements in the array. For example, a maximum of 16 comparisons will be made on an array of 50,000 elements ($2^{16} = 65,536$), and a maximum of 20 comparisons will be made on an array of 1,000,000 elements ($2^{20} = 1,048,576$).

A Recursive Binary Search

The binary search algorithm that we previously examined used an iterative approach, meaning that it used a loop to step through the array. The binary search algorithm can also be implemented recursively. For example, the procedure can be expressed as follows:

If array[middle] *equals the search value, then the value is found.*
Else if array[middle] *is less than the search value, perform a binary*
  search on the upper half of the array.
Else if array[middle] *is greater than the search value, perform*
  a binary search on the lower half of the array.
End If

When you compare the recursive algorithm to its iterative counterpart, it becomes evident that the recursive version is much more elegant and easier to understand. The recursive binary search algorithm is also a good example of repeatedly breaking a problem down into smaller pieces until it is solved. Code Listing 17-16 shows the RecursiveBinarySearcher class. This class provides a public static method named search, which calls the recursive binarySearch method to find a value in an int array. The program in Code Listing 17-17 tests the method.

Code Listing 17-16   (`RecursiveBinarySearcher.java`)

```
1  /**
2     The RecursiveBinarySearcher class provides a public static
3     method for performing a recursive binary search on an int array.
4  */
5
6  public class RecursiveBinarySearcher
7  {
8     /**
9        The search method calls the doBinarySearch method
10       to search for a value in an array.
11       @param array The array to search.
12       @param value The value to search for.
13    */
14
15    public static int search(int[] array, int value)
16    {
17       return binarySearch(array, 0, array.length - 1, value);
18    }
19
20    /**
21       The binarySearch method performs a recursive binary
22       search on an integer array.
23       @param array The array to search.
24       @param first The first element in the search range.
25       @param last The last element in the search range.
26       @param value The value to search for.
27       @return The subscript of the value if found,
28              otherwise -1.
29    */
30
```

```
31      private static int binarySearch(int[] array, int first,
32                                      int last, int value)
33      {
34         int middle;      // Mid point of search
35
36         // Test for the base case where the
37         // value is not found.
38         if (first > last)
39            return -1;
40
41         // Calculate the middle position.
42         middle = (first + last) / 2;
43
44         // Search for the value.
45         if (array[middle] == value)
46            return middle;
47         else if (array[middle] < value)
48            return binarySearch(array, middle + 1,
49                                last, value);
50         else
51            return binarySearch(array, first,
52                                middle - 1, value);
53      }
54
55   }
```

Code Listing 17-17   **(RecursiveBinarySearchTest.java)**

```
1  import java.util.Scanner;
2
3  /**
4     This program tests the search method in the
5     RecursiveBinarySearcher class.
6  */
7
8  public class RecursiveBinarySearchTest
9  {
10    public static void main(String [] args)
11    {
12       int result, searchValue;
13       String input;
14
15       // An array of numbers to search.
16       int numbers[] = { 536, 289, 296, 429, 319, 142, 394,
17                         101, 388, 147, 417, 199, 207, 222,
18                         189, 310, 447, 521, 234, 600};
```

```
19
20        // Create a Scanner object to read keyboard input.
21        Scanner keyboard = new Scanner(System.in);
22
23        // First we must sort the array in ascending order.
24        IntQuickSorter.quickSort(numbers);
25
26        do
27        {
28           // Get a value to search for.
29           System.out.print("Enter a value to search for: ");
30           searchValue = keyboard.nextInt();
31
32           // Search for the value
33           result =
34              RecursiveBinarySearcher.search(numbers, searchValue);
35
36           // Display the results.
37           if (result == -1)
38              System.out.println(searchValue + " was not found.");
39           else
40           {
41              System.out.println(searchValue + " was found at " +
42                                 "element " + result);
43           }
44
45           // Consume the remaining newline.
46           keyboard.nextLine();
47
48           // Does the user want to search again?
49           System.out.print("Do you want to search again? (Y or N): ");
50           input = keyboard.nextLine();
51        } while (input.charAt(0) == 'y' || input.charAt(0) == 'Y');
52     }
53 }
```

Program Output with Example Input Shown in Bold

```
Enter a value to search for: 289 [Enter]
289 was found at element 8
Do you want to search again? (Y or N): y [Enter]
Enter a value to search for: 101 [Enter]
101 was found at element 0
Do you want to search again? (Y or N): y [Enter]
Enter a value to search for: 999 [Enter]
999 was not found.
Do you want to search again? (Y or N): n [Enter]
```

 **Checkpoint**

17.5 Describe the difference between the sequential search and the binary search.

17.6 On average, with an array of 20,000 elements, how many comparisons will the sequential search perform? (Assume the items being searched have equal probability of being found at any of the positions in the array.)

17.7 With an array of 20,000 elements, what is the maximum number of comparisons the binary search will perform?

17.8 If a sequential search is performed on an array, and it is known that some items are searched for more frequently than others, how can the contents of the array be reordered to improve the average performance of the search?

 17.3 ## Analysis of Algorithms

CONCEPT: We can estimate the efficiency of an algorithm by counting the number of steps that the algorithm requires to solve a problem.

An algorithm is a mechanical step-by-step procedure for solving a problem and is the basic strategy used in designing a program. There is often more than one algorithm that can be used to solve a given problem. For example, we saw in the previous section that the problem of searching a sorted array can be solved by two different methods: *sequential search* and *binary search*.

How can we decide which of two algorithms for solving a problem is better? To answer this question, we need to establish criteria for judging the "goodness" or efficiency of an algorithm. The two criteria that are most often used are space and time. The *space* criterion refers to the amount of memory the algorithm requires to solve the problem, while the *time* criterion refers to the length of execution time. In this chapter, we will use the time criterion to evaluate the efficiency of algorithms.

One possibility for comparing two algorithms is to code them and then time the execution of the resulting Java programs. This experimental approach can yield useful information, but it has the following shortcomings:

- It measures the efficiency of programs rather than algorithms.
- The results obtained depend on the programming language used to code the algorithms, and on the quality of the compiler used to generate machine code. The programs may run faster or slower if they are coded in a different language, or compiled by a different compiler.
- The results obtained depend on how the operating system executes programs, and on the nature of the hardware on which the programs are executing. The execution times may be different if we run the programs on a different computer and a different operating system.
- The results obtained apply only to those inputs that were part of the execution runs and may not be representative of the performance of the algorithms on a different set of inputs.

A better approach is to count the number of basic steps an algorithm requires to process an input of a given size. To make sense of this approach, we need more precise definitions of the concepts of a computational problem, problem input, input size, and basic step.

Computational Problems and Basic Steps

A *computational problem* is a problem to be solved using an algorithm. Such a problem is a collection of *instances*, with each instance being specified by input data given in some prescribed format. For example, if the problem P is to sort an array of integers, then an instance of P is just a specific integer array. The *size* of an instance refers to the amount of memory needed to hold the input data. The input size is usually given as a number that allows us to infer the total number of bits occupied by the input data. If the number of bits occupied by an entry of the array is fixed, say at 64 bits, then the length of the array is a good measure of input size. In contrast, the length of the array is not a good measure of input size if there is no a priori bound on the size of array elements.

A step executed by an algorithm is a *basic step* (also called a *basic operation*) if the algorithm can execute the step in time bounded by a constant regardless of the size of the input. In sorting an array of integers, the step

Swap the elements in positions k and k+1

is basic because the time required to swap two array elements remains constant even if the length of the array increases. In contrast, a step such as

Find the largest element of the array

is not basic because the time required to complete the step depends on the length of the array. Intuitively, a basic step is one that can conceivably be built into the hardware of some physical computers.

The definition of a basic step does not specify the size of the constant that bounds the time required to execute the step. Ignoring the exact value of these constants reflects the reality that the same operation may be executed with different speeds on different hardware, and that an operation that can be executed with one hardware instruction on one computer may require several hardware instructions on another computer. A consequence of this definition is that we can count any constant number of basic steps as one basic step. In particular, an algorithm that executes $500n$ basic steps can accurately be described as executing n basic steps.

It is important to realize that ordinary arithmetic and logic operations such as addition and comparison are not basic unless a constant bound is put on the size of the numbers being added or compared. The size of the bound does not matter as long as the bound is constant: it may be 32, 64, 128, 1024 bits, or even larger, and these operations will still be basic. In the following discussion, we assume that numbers that occur in our algorithms as inputs, outputs, or are computed as intermediate results are all bounded in size. This allows us to consider operations on them as basic.

It only makes sense to describe an algorithm after we have described the problem the algorithm is supposed to solve. A computational problem is described by giving, for each positive integer n, the format of a typical input of size n followed by a description of output to be produced by an algorithm that solves the problem. For example, the problem of summing an integer array can be described as follows:

INPUT: An integer array $a[\ ]$ of size n
SIZE OF INPUT: The number n of array entries
OUTPUT: An integer *sum* representing the sum total of the array entries

In this context, an algorithm for solving the problem can be given as follows:

ALGORITHM:
```
1:   sum = 0
2:   k = 0    //array index
3:   While k < n do
4:       sum = sum + a[k]
5:       k = k + 1
6:   End While
```

Complexity of Algorithms

We can determine the number of basic steps executed by this algorithm on an input of size n by reasoning as follows. The algorithm consists of two statements (Statements 1 and 2) and a loop (Statements 3–6). The two statements before the loop can be counted as one basic operation. Clearly, the amount of time the algorithm takes to execute a *single* iteration of the loop does not depend on n, and so is constant. (This can also be seen by noting that each statement inside the loop is a basic operation.) This allows us to count each loop iteration as a single basic operation. Because the algorithm executes the loop n times, it executes $n + 1$ basic operations altogether. For large problem sizes, the number of basic operations performed is approximately n. Because of the hidden constant factors, we say that the algorithm requires time proportional to n to process an input of size n.

Notice that in our analysis of the array-summing algorithm, we could have gotten the same result by counting the number of loop iterations performed by the algorithm. Moreover, notice that the crucial operation in summing an array is the addition of array elements (Statement 4), and that there are as many additions of array elements as there are loop iterations. Thus, we could have gotten the same result by just counting additions of array elements. It turns out that for most algorithms, it suffices to identify and count only one or two basic operations that are in some way crucial to the problem being solved. For example, in many array searching and sorting algorithms, it suffices to count the number of comparisons between array elements.

The array-summing algorithm just considered is particularly simple to analyze because it performs the same amount of work for all inputs of a given size. Consider the problem of searching an array of integers for a given integer X, solved here by the familiar sequential search algorithm:

INPUT: An integer array $a[\ ]$ of size n, and an integer X
SIZE OF INPUT: The number n of array entries
OUTPUT: An integer k in the range $0 \le k \le n - 1$ such that $a[k] = X$, or $k = n$

ALGORITHM:
```
k = 0
While k < n and a[k] != X do
  k = k + 1;
End While
```

This algorithm starts at one end and searches sequentially through the array. The algorithm stops as soon as it encounters X, but will search the entire array if X is not in the array. The algorithm may stop after making only one comparison (X is found in the first entry examined), or it may stop after making n comparisons (X is found in the last place examined, or is not in the array). In fact, the algorithm may perform m comparisons for any value of m between 1 and n. In cases where the algorithm may perform different amounts of work for different inputs of the same size, it is common to measure the efficiency of the algorithm by the work done on an input of size n that requires the most work. This is called measuring the algorithm by its *worst-case complexity function*.

Worst Case Complexity of Algorithms

The worst-case complexity function $f(n)$ of an algorithm is the number of steps it performs on an input of size n that requires the most work. It gives an indication of the longest time an algorithm will ever take to solve an instance of size n, and is a good measure of efficiency to use when we are looking for a performance guarantee.

Let us determine the worst-case complexity of binary search. This algorithm is used to locate an item X in an array sorted in ascending order. The worst case occurs when X is not found in the array. We will show that in this case, the algorithm performs $L + 1$ steps, where L is the number of loop iterations.

As shown earlier in this chapter, this algorithm consists of some initialization of some variables followed by a loop. The initialization requires constant time, and can therefore be considered to be one basic operation. Likewise, each iteration of the loop is a basic step (increasing the number of entries in the array does not increase the amount of time required by a single iteration of the loop). This shows that the number of steps required by binary search is $L + 1$. Now L is approximately equal to the integer part of log n, the logarithm of n to the base 2. To see this, notice that the size of the array to be searched is initially n, and each iteration reduces the size of the remaining portion of the array by one half. Because each loop iteration performs at most two comparisons, binary search performs a total of 2 log n comparisons. By ignoring the constant factor, we can summarize our findings as follows:

In the worst case, binary search requires time proportional to log n.

For our last example of determining the complexity of an algorithm, consider the following outline of a variant of the selection sort algorithm, also studied earlier in this chapter:

INPUT: An array $a[\ ]$ of n integers
SIZE OF INPUT: The number n of array entries
OUTPUT: The array $a[\ ]$ rearranged so that $a[0] \leq a[1] \leq \cdots \leq a[n-1]$

ALGORITHM:
```
1:   For (k = n-1; k ≥1; k--)
2:       // a[0..k] is what remains to be sorted
3:       determine position p of largest entry in a[0..k]
4:          swap a[p] with a[k]
5:   End For
```

Let us determine the number of comparisons (involving array entries) executed by this algorithm in sorting an array of n entries. All such comparisons occur in step 3, which is clearly not a basic step (it requires time proportional to k, which can be as large as n). Let us express step 3 using operations that are clearly basic:

INPUT: array $a[0..k]$ of $k + 1$ entries
SIZE OF INPUT: number $k + 1$ of array entries

```
6:  p = 0     //position of largest
7:  For (m = 1; m ≤ k; m++)
8:     If a[m] > a[p] Then
9:        p = m
10:    End if
11: End For
```

It is clear that this algorithm requires k comparisons between array entries.

Now returning to the main sorting algorithm, we observe that there will be $n - 1$ iterations of the loop that starts at line 1 and ends at line 5, with one such iteration for each value of k in the range $n - 1$ to 1. Moreover, on the k-th such iteration, the step on line 3 will perform k comparisons:

$k = n - 1$: step 3 performs $n - 1$ comparisons
$k = n - 2$: step 3 performs $n - 2$ comparisons

.
.
.

$k = 1$: step 3 performs 1 comparison

Now we see that the total number of comparisons performed by this simple sorting algorithm is given by the expression

$$1 + 2 + 3 + \cdots + n - 1 = (n - 1)n/2$$

For large n, this expression is very close to $n^2 / 2$. We have proved the following:

In the worst case, selection sort requires time proportional to n^2.

Average Case Complexity

The worst-case complexity will not give a good indication of how an algorithm will perform in practical situations in which inputs that yield worst case performance are rare. An alternative method, the *average case complexity function*, can be used if the relative frequencies with which the different inputs are likely to occur in practice are known. The average case complexity function uses such frequencies to form a weighted average of the number of steps performed on each input. Although it yields a good measure of the expected performance of an algorithm, it is difficult to use in practice because reliable estimates of input frequencies are usually not available.

Asymptotic Complexity and the Big O Notation

We can compare two algorithms F and G for solving a problem by comparing their complexity functions. More specifically, if $f(n)$ and $g(n)$ are the complexity functions for the two algorithms, we can compare the algorithms against each other by looking at what happens to the ratio $f(n)/g(n)$ when n gets large. This is easiest to understand if this ratio tends to some limit. Let us consider some specific examples. Throughout, we assume that $f(n) \geq 1$ and $g(n) \geq 1$ for all $(n) \geq 1$.

- $f(n) = 3n^2 + 5n$ and $g(n) = n^2$. In this case

$$\frac{f(n)}{g(n)} = \frac{3n^2 + 5n}{n^2} = 3 + \frac{5}{n} \to 3 \text{ as } n \to \infty$$

That is, the value of $f(n)/g(n)$ gets closer and closer to 3 as n gets large. What this means is that for very large input sizes F performs three times as many basic operations as G. Because the two algorithms differ in performance by a constant factor, we consider them to be equivalent in efficiency.

- $f(n) = 3n^2 + 5n$ and $g(n) = n$. In this case

$$\frac{f(n)}{g(n)} = \frac{3n^2 + 5n}{n} = 3n + 5 \to \infty \text{ as } n \to \infty$$

Here, the ratio $f(n)/g(n)$ gets larger and larger as n gets large. This means F does a lot more work than G on large input sizes. This makes G the better algorithm for large inputs.

- $f(n) = 3n^2 + 5n$ and $g(n) = n^3$. In this case

$$\frac{f(n)}{g(n)} = \frac{3n^2 + 5n}{n^3} = \frac{3}{n} + \frac{5}{n^2} \to 0 \text{ as } n \to \infty$$

This means that for large inputs the algorithm G is doing a lot more work than F, making F the more efficient algorithm.

In general, we can compare two complexity functions $f(n)$ and $g(n)$ by looking at what happens to $f(n)/g(n)$ as n gets large. Although thinking in terms of a limit of this ratio is helpful in comparing the two algorithms, we cannot assume that such a limit will always exist. It turns out that a limit does not have to exist for us to gain useful information from this ratio: we can usefully compare the two complexity functions if we can find a positive constant K such that

$$\frac{f(n)}{g(n)} \leq K \text{ for all } n \geq 1. \tag{17.1}$$

If this can be done, it means that the algorithm F is no worse than G for large problems, or in other words, F is at least as good as G. In this case, we say that $f(n)$ is in $O(g(n))$, pronounced "f is in Big O of g." The condition that defines $f(n)$ is in $O(g(n))$ is often written in the equivalent form shown in Equation (17.2).

$$f(n) \leq Kg(n) \text{ whenever } n \geq 1. \tag{17.2}$$

Showing that $f(n)$ is in $O(g(n))$ is usually straightforward: you look at the ratio $f(n)/g(n)$ and try to find a positive constant K that satisfies Equation (17.1) for all $n \geq 1$. For example, to show that $3n^2 + 5n$ is in $O(n^2)$, look at the ratio

$$\frac{3n^2 + 5n}{n} = 3 + \frac{5}{n}$$

and notice that $5/n$ will be at most 5 for all $n \geq 1$. You can then use $K = 8$ in Equation (17.1).

To show that $f(n)$ is *not* in $O(g(n))$, you have to show that there is no way to find a positive K that will satisfy Equation (17.1) for all $n \geq 1$. For example, the function $3n^2 + 5n$ is not in $O(n)$ because there is no constant K that satisfies

$$\frac{3n^2 + 5n}{n} = 3n + 5 \leq K \text{ for all } n \geq 1.$$

Although defined for functions, the "Big O" notation and terminology is also used to characterize algorithms and computational problems. Thus, we say that an algorithm F is in $O(g(n))$ for some function $g(n)$ if the complexity function $f(n)$ of F is in Big O of $g(n)$. Accordingly, sequential search of an array is in $O(n)$ whereas binary search is in $O(\log n)$.

Similarly, a computational problem is said to be in $O(g(n))$ if there exists an algorithm for the problem whose worst case complexity function is in $O(g(n))$. Thus, the problem of sorting an array is in $O(n^2)$, whereas the problem of searching a sorted array is in $O(\log n)$.

If $g(n)$ is a function, $O(g(n))$ can be regarded as a family of functions that grow no faster than $g(n)$. These families are called complexity classes, and a few of them are important enough to merit specific names. We list them here in order of their rate of growth:

1. $O(1)$: A function $f(n)$ is in this class if there is a constant $K > 0$ such that $f(n) \leq K$ for all $n \geq 1$. An algorithm whose worst case complexity function is in this class is said to run in *constant time*.

2. $O(\log n)$: Algorithms in this class run in *logarithmic time*. Because $\log n$ grows much slower than n, a huge increase in the size of the problem results in a small increase in the running time of the algorithm. This complexity is characteristic of search problems that eliminate half of the search space with each operation. The *binary search* algorithm is in this class.

3. $O(n)$: Algorithms in this class run in *linear time*. Any increase in the size of the problem results in a proportionate increase in the running time of the algorithm. This complexity is characteristic of algorithms like *sequential search* that make a single pass, or a constant number of passes, over their input.

4. $O(n\log n)$: This class is called "*n log n*" *time*. An increase in the size of the problem results in a slightly greater increase in the running time of the algorithm. The average case complexity of *Quicksort* lies in this class. Two well-known sorting algorithms, *Mergesort* and *Heapsort*, have worst case complexity functions that also lie in this class. We will discuss the *Heapsort* algorithm in Chapter 22.

5. $O(n^2)$: This class is called *quadratic time*. This performance is characteristic of algorithms that make multiple passes over the input data using two nested loops. An increase in the size of the problem causes a much greater increase in the running time of the algorithm. The worst case complexity functions of *bubble sort*, *selection sort*, *insertion sort*, and *Quicksort* all lie in this class.

6. The union of all classes $O(n^1)$, $O(n^2)$, $O(n^3)$, . . . , forms a class called *polynomial time*.

In the Spotlight:
The Importance of Choosing an Efficient Algorithm

The algorithm selected for a particular task can have a significant impact on the running time of a program. As an example, let us consider the task of computing terms of the Fibonacci sequence. You first encountered this sequence in Chapter 16, and as you may recall, its terms can be computed by this method:

```java
public static long fib(long n)
{
    if (n <= 1)
        return 1;
    else
        return fib(n-2) + fib(n-1);
}
```

This implementation has the advantages of being short and easy to understand, and for that reason, it is often used to illustrate recursion. It is, however, very inefficient. We can get an idea of how inefficient it is by embedding it in a program that determines the time required to execute calls to the method. The following program allows a user to specify six consecutive values to be passed as arguments to the method and prints the time needed by the computer to execute each call.

Code Listing 17-18   **(RecursiveFibonacciTimer.java)**

```java
1 import java.util.Scanner;
2
3 /**
4    This program times calls to the recursive Fibonacci method
5    for 6 consecutive calls and displays the results.
6 */
7
8 public class RecursiveFibonacciTimer
9 {
10    public static void main(String[] args)
11    {
12        // Get the starting argument
13        System.out.print("Enter a positive integer: ");
14        Scanner sc = new Scanner(System.in);
15        int number = sc.nextInt();
16
17        // Variables used to determine time for a function call
18        long currentTime = System.currentTimeMillis();
19        long previousTime;
20        long elapsedTime = 0;
21
22        for (int k = 0; k <= 5; k++)
23        {
24            // Record time before calling the method
```

```
25              previousTime = currentTime;
26              System.out.print("The Fibonacci term at position ");
27              System.out.print((number + k) + " is " );
28
29              // Compute and print fib term for the next argument
30              System.out.println(fib(number + k));
31
32              // Record time after calling the method
33              currentTime = System.currentTimeMillis();
34
35              // Compute and print elapsed time in seconds
36              elapsedTime = (currentTime - previousTime) / 1000;
37              System.out.println("Computed in " + elapsedTime + " seconds.");
38          }
39      }
40
41      /**
42          Computes a term of the Fibonacci sequence
43          @param n
44          @return nth term of the sequence
45      */
46      public static long fib(long n)
47      {
48          if (n <= 1)
49              return 1;
50          else
51              return fib(n-2) + fib(n-1);
52      }
53 }
```

Program Output with Example Input Shown in Bold

Enter a positive integer: **45 [Enter]**
The Fibonacci term at position 45 is 1836311903
Computed in 17 seconds.
The Fibonacci term at position 46 is 2971215073
Computed in 27 seconds.
The Fibonacci term at position 47 is 4807526976
Computed in 43 seconds.
The Fibonacci term at position 48 is 7778742049
Computed in 67 seconds.
The Fibonacci term at position 49 is 12586269025
Computed in 110 seconds.
The Fibonacci term at position 50 is 20365011074
Computed in 179 seconds.

In line 18, the program uses the System.currentTimeMillis() method to get the current time in milliseconds since midnight January 1, 1970. The value obtained is stored in the currentTime variable. At the beginning of each loop iteration, the current time is assigned to the previousTime variable in line 25. Then, after the call to the fib method, the current time is obtained again in line 33 and assigned to the currentTime variable. The time difference, in milliseconds, is calculated in line 36 by subtracting previousTime from currentTime. This difference is divided by 1000 to yield the time elapsed during the method call in seconds.

You can tell that the time required to compute a term of the sequence increases significantly for each successive term. For example, the computation of the term at position 45 requires a quarter of a minute, and five terms later, the 50th term requires nearly three minutes. And it gets worse from there. Clearly, this algorithm, although simple to write, is so inefficient as to be unusable for problems of moderately large sizes.

Checkpoint

17.9   What is a basic operation?

17.10   What is the worst case complexity function of an algorithm?

17.11   One algorithm needs $100n$ basic operations to process an input of size n, and another algorithm needs $25n$ basic operations to process the same input. Which of the two algorithms is more efficient?

17.12   What does it mean to say that $f(n)$ is not in $O(g(n))$?

17.13   What does it mean to say that $f(n)$ is in $O(g(n))$?

17.14   Show that $100n^3 + 50n^2 + 75$ is in $O(20n^3)$ by finding a positive K that satisfies Equation (17.1) in this section.

17.15   Let $a[\ ]$ and $b[\ ]$ be two integer arrays of size n. Following the examples of this section, give a formal description of the problem of determining if every element of $a[\ ]$ is also an element of $b[\ ]$. The output of the algorithm should be one of the words "true" or "false."

17.16   Give an algorithm for solving the problem you defined in Checkpoint 17.15, and determine its worst case complexity.

17.17   Show that every function in $O(20)$ also is in $O(1)$.

17.18   Assuming $g(n) \geq 1$ for all $n \geq 1$, show that every function in $O(g(n) + 100)$ is also in $O(g(n))$.

17.4   Common Errors to Avoid

- **Using an inefficient sort or search algorithm on a large array.** Simple algorithms like the bubble sort and the sequential search are inefficient because they access array elements so many times. More efficient algorithms like Quicksort and the binary search are preferable, especially on large arrays.
- **Forgetting to sort the data in an array before using the binary search algorithm.** The binary search algorithm requires that its data already be sorted.
- **Using timing to determine the efficiency of an algorithm.** The results obtained from timing an application depend on many variables, including the programming language used and on the quality of the compiler used to generate machine code. A better approach is to count the number of basic steps an algorithm requires to process an input of a given size.

Review Questions and Exercises

Multiple Choice and True/False

1. This search algorithm steps sequentially through an array, comparing each item with the search value.
   a. sequential search
   b. binary search
   c. natural order search
   d. selection search

2. This search algorithm repeatedly divides the portion of an array being searched in half.
   a. sequential search
   b. binary search
   c. natural order search
   d. selection search

3. This search algorithm will search half the array on average.
   a. sequential search
   b. binary search
   c. natural order search
   d. selection search

4. This search algorithm requires that the array's contents be sorted.
   a. sequential search
   b. binary search
   c. natural order search
   d. selection search

5. If an array is sorted in this order, the values are stored from lowest to highest.
   a. asymptotic
   b. logarithmic
   c. ascending
   d. descending

6. If an array is sorted in this order, the values are stored from highest to lowest.
   a. asymptotic
   b. logarithmic
   c. ascending
   d. descending

7. This sorting algorithm makes several passes through an array and causes the larger values to gradually move toward the end of the array with each pass.
   a. bubble sort
   b. selection sort
   c. insertion sort
   d. Quicksort

8. This sorting algorithm recursively divides an array into sublists.

   a. bubble sort
   b. selection sort
   c. insertion sort
   d. Quicksort

9. In this sorting algorithm, the smallest value in the array is located and moved to position 0. Then the next smallest value is located and moved to position 1. This process continues until all of the elements have been placed in their proper order.

   a. bubble sort
   b. selection sort
   c. insertion sort
   d. Quicksort

10. This sorting algorithm begins by sorting the initial portion of the array consisting of two elements. Then, the third element is moved to its correct position, relative to the first two elements. At that point, the first three elements are in sorted order. This process continues with the fourth and subsequent elements until the entire array is sorted.

    a. bubble sort
    b. selection sort
    c. insertion sort
    d. Quicksort

11. **True or False:** If data is sorted in ascending order, it means it is ordered from lowest value to highest value.

12. **True or False:** If data is sorted in descending order, it means it is ordered from lowest value to highest value.

13. **True or False:** The *average* number of comparisons performed by the sequential search on an array of n elements is $n/2$.

14. **True or False:** The *maximum* number of comparisons performed by the sequential search on an array of n elements is $n/2$.

Find the Error

1. Assume this code is using the `IntBinarySearcher` class presented in this chapter:

```
int[] numbers = { 8, 0, 9, 4, 3, 7, 2 };
// Search for 7.
int location = IntBinarySearcher.search(numbers, 7);
// Display the result.
if (location != -1)
   System.out.println("7 was found in the array.");
else
   System.out.println("7 was NOT found in the array.");
```

Algorithm Workbench

1. Complete the following table calculating the average and maximum number of comparisons the sequential search will perform, and the maximum number of comparisons the binary search will perform.

	Array Size: 50 elements	Array Size: 500 elements	Array Size: 10,000 elements	Array Size: 100,000 elements	Array Size: 10,000,000 elements
Sequential Search (Average Comparisons)					
Sequential Search (Maximum Comparisons)					
Binary Search (Maximum Comparisons)					

Short Answer

1. If a sequential search method is searching for a value that is stored in the last element of a 10,000-element array, how many elements will the search code have to examine to locate the value?

2. In an average case involving an array of n elements, how many array elements does a sequential search algorithm have to access to locate a specific value?

3. A binary search method is searching for a value that is stored in the middle element of an array. How many array elements have to be examined before finding the value?

4. What is the maximum number of comparisons that a binary search method will make when searching for a value in a 1,000-element array?

5. Why is the bubble sort inefficient for large arrays?

6. Under what conditions might the insertion sort be more efficient than the bubble sort?

7. List the steps that the selection sort algorithm would make in sorting the following values: 4, 1, 3, 2.

8. List the steps that the insertion sort algorithm would make in sorting the following values: 4, 1, 3, 2.

Programming Challenges

1. Sorting Objects with the Insertion Sort Algorithm

The insertionSort method in the IntInsertionSorter class presented in this chapter sorts an array of int values. Create an ObjectInsertionSorter class that can sort Comparable objects. Demonstrate the class in a program that sorts an array of String objects.

2. Sorting Objects with the Quicksort Algorithm

The IntQuickSorter class presented in this chapter sorts an array of int values. Create an ObjectQuickSorter class that can sort Comparable objects. Demonstrate the class in a program that sorts an array of String objects.

VideoNote
Searching for
Objects with the
Binary Search
Algorithm

3. Searching for Objects with the Binary Search Algorithm

The IntBinarySearcher class presented in this chapter searches an int array for a specific value. Create an ObjectBinarySearcher class that can search an array of Comparable objects. Demonstrate the class in a program that searches for a String in an array of String objects.

4. Charge Account Validation

Create a class with a method that accepts a charge account number as its argument. The method should determine whether the number is valid by comparing it to the following list of valid charge account numbers:

5658845	4520125	7895122	8777541	8451277	1302850
8080152	4562555	5552012	5050552	7825877	1250255
1005231	6545231	3852085	7576651	7881200	4581002

These numbers should be stored in an array. Use a sequential search to locate the number passed as an argument. If the number is in the array, the method should return true, indicating the number is valid. If the number is not in the array, the method should return false, indicating the number is invalid.

Write a program that tests the class by asking the user to enter a charge account number. The program should display a message indicating whether the number is valid or invalid.

5. Charge Account Validation Modification

Modify the program you wrote for Programming Challenge 4 (Charge Account Validation) so it performs a binary search to locate valid account numbers. Use your choice of sorting algorithm to sort the array before the binary search is performed.

6. Name Search

Download the Chapter 17 source code from www.pearsonhighered.com/gaddis, and, you will find a text file by the name of *names.txt*. This file contains a list of the 65 most popular female first names in the United States according to the 1990 census. Write a program that reads these names into a String array. Use the Quicksort algorithm to sort the names in ascending order. Then allow the user to search for a name in the array. Use the binary search algorithm to perform the search.

7. Search Benchmarks

Write an application that has an array of at least 20 integers. It should call a method that uses the sequential search algorithm to locate one of the values. The method should keep a count of the number of comparisons it makes until it finds the value. Then the program should call another method that uses the binary search algorithm to locate the same value. It should also keep count of the number of comparisons it makes. Display these values on the screen.

8. Sorting Benchmarks

Modify the methods presented in this chapter that perform the bubble sort, selection sort, insertion sort, and Quicksort algorithms on an `int` array, such that each method keeps a count of the number of swaps it makes.

Then, write an application that uses four identical arrays of at least 20 integers. It should call each method on a different array, and display the number of exchanges made by each algorithm.

9. Efficient Computation of Fibonacci Numbers

Modify the application in Code Listing 17-18 by replacing the recursive method for computing Fibonacci terms with an iterative version and try to make it as efficient as possible. Modify the application so it outputs the elapsed time in both seconds and milliseconds. Finally, run the application and generate output showing the time required to compute the terms of the sequence in positions 45, 46, 47, 48, 49, and 50. Comment on the results.

18 Generics

TOPICS

18.1 Introduction to Generics

CONCEPT: A generic class or method is one that permits you to specify the allowable types of objects that the class or method may work with. If you attempt to use the class or method with an object that is not of an allowable type, an error occurs at compile time.

In Chapter 8, you were introduced to the `ArrayList` class, which is in the `java.util` package. Once you create an `ArrayList` object, you can use it as a container to hold other objects. An `ArrayList` object automatically expands in size to accommodate the number of objects that are stored in it, which is an advantage over traditional arrays. The `ArrayList` class can be used in such a way that a mixture of objects, of any type, can be simultaneously stored in it. For example, look at Code Listing 18-1. This program stores a `String` object, a `Double` object, and a `Rectangle` object in the same `ArrayList`.

Code Listing 18-1 (`UnsafeArrayList.java`)

```
1   import java.util.ArrayList;
2
3   /**
4      This program demonstrates that an ArrayList can accept
5      a mixture of object types as its elements.
6   */
```

```
 7
 8    public class UnsafeArrayList
 9    {
10       public static void main(String[] args)
11       {
12          // Create an ArrayList object.
13          ArrayList list = new ArrayList();
14
15          // Store a variety of objects in the list.
16          list.add("Java is fun!");         // Add a String
17          list.add(new Double(2.5));         // Add a Double
18          list.add(new Rectangle(10, 12));   // Add a Rectangle
19
20          // Retrieve a reference to each object in the list.
21          // Note that the reference returned from the get
22          // method must be cast to the correct type.
23          String s = (String)list.get(0);
24          Double d = (Double)list.get(1);
25          Rectangle r = (Rectangle)list.get(2);
26       }
27    }
```

In lines 16, 17, and 18 the `ArrayList` class's `add` method is called to add a `String`, a `Double`, and a `Rectangle` to the `ArrayList`. In lines 23, 24, and 25 the `get` method is called to get a reference to each object stored in the `ArrayList`. The statement in line 23 gets a reference to element 0 (the `String`), line 24 gets a reference to element 1 (the `Double`), and line 25 gets a reference to element 2 (the `Rectangle`).

The `get` method returns an `Object` reference, so it is necessary to cast the method's return value to the desired type. Line 23 casts the method's return type to a `String` reference, line 24 casts it to a `Double` reference, and line 25 casts it to a `Rectangle` reference. If we do not cast the `get` method's return value, an error will occur at compile time. This is because the compiler does not know the exact type of the object being returned; only that it is an `Object`.

Even though the cast operator prevents an error from occurring at compile time, it does not prevent an error at runtime. We can still have problems if we inadvertently cast the `get` method's return value to the wrong type. For example, look at the following code:

```
12       // Create an ArrayList object.
13       ArrayList list = new ArrayList();
14
15       // Store a variety of objects in the list.
16       list.add("Java is fun!");         // Store a String at element 0
17       list.add(new Double(2.5));         // Store a Double at element 1
18       list.add(new Rectangle(10, 12));   // Store a Rectangle at element 2
19
20       // Retrieve a reference to each object in the list.
21       Double d = (Double)list.get(0);    // Error! Element 0 is a String
```

```
22    String s = (String)list.get(1);
23    Rectangle r = (Rectangle)list.get(2);
```

This code starts out just like the `main` method in Code Listing 18-1. An `ArrayList` is created, and then a `String`, a `Double`, and a `Rectangle` are stored in it. An error occurs in line 21, however. This statement gets a reference to the object at element 0. The problem is that it casts the return value of the `get` method to a `Double`, when the object that is actually returned is a `String`. The error that results from this statement does not happen at compile time, however. It happens at runtime. When the code runs, a `ClassCastException` will be thrown.

Starting with Java 5, the Java language provides a feature known as generic classes and methods, commonly referred to as generics. *Generics* allow the compiler to perform type-checking and report type incompatibilities. Rather than waiting for your finished application to throw an exception, it is far better to discover at compile time the places in your code where types have been mismatched.

A generic class or method is one that permits you to specify the allowable types of objects that the class or method may work with. If you attempt to use the class or method with an object that is not of an allowable type, an error occurs at compile time. Recall from Chapter 8 that the `ArrayList` class can also be used as a generic class. It allows you to specify the type of object that you want to store in an `ArrayList`, and the Java compiler will make sure that only objects of the specified type are stored in it. For example, we can create an `ArrayList` that will hold only `String` objects with a statement such as the following:

```
ArrayList<String> myList = new ArrayList<String>();
```

This statement creates an `ArrayList` object referenced by the variable `myList`. Because we have written the notation `<String>` immediately after the word `ArrayList`, we will only be allowed to store `String` objects in the `ArrayList`. If we try to store any other type of object in the `ArrayList`, an error will occur at compile time.

 TIP: The notation `ArrayList<String>` is pronounced "`ArrayList of String`."

Similarly, if we wish to create an `ArrayList` object that can hold only `Student` objects, we would use a statement such as the following:

```
ArrayList<Student> myStudents = new ArrayList<Student>();
```

If we write a statement that stores an object of any type other than `Student` in `myStudents`, the compiler will generate an error. In these two examples, we can provide the notation `<String>` or `<Student>` because the `ArrayList` class can be used as a generic class.

Because the compiler knows the type of every element, we do not have to use a cast operator when retrieving an element from a generic `ArrayList`. For example, the following code creates an `ArrayList` that can hold only `String` objects, stores a string in it, and then retrieves the string. Notice that the last statement does not use a cast operator.

```
ArrayList<String> myList = new ArrayList<String>();
myList.add("Java is fun!");
String str = myList.get(0);
```

Using the Diamond Operator for Type Inference

Java allows you to use the diamond operator (<>) to simplify the instantiation of a generic class. Previously, you saw the following statement that creates an `ArrayList` object:

```
ArrayList<String> list = new ArrayList<String>();
```

Notice that the data type `String` is written between the angled brackets in two locations: first in the part that declares the reference variable (on the left side of the = operator), and then again in the part that calls the `ArrayList` constructor (on the right side of the = operator). You can use the diamond operator to simplify this statement, as follows:

```
ArrayList<String> list = new ArrayList<>();
```

By using the diamond operator, you are not required to write the data type in the part of the statement that calls the `ArrayList` constructor. The diamond operator causes the compiler to infer the required data type from the reference variable declaration. Here is another example:

```
ArrayList<Student> list = new ArrayList<>();
```

Assuming that we have a class named `Student`, this statement creates an `ArrayList` that can hold `Student` objects.

Checkpoint

18.1 Why is it risky to store objects of different types in an `ArrayList`?

18.2 When `ArrayList` is used as a non-generic class, why must you use the cast operator with the `get` method?

18.3 Suppose we use the following statement to instantiate the `ArrayList` class. What type of objects will we be allowed to store in the `ArrayList`?

```
ArrayList<Rectangle> myList = new ArrayList<>();
```

18.4 Assume we have used the statement shown in Checkpoint 18.3 to instantiate the `ArrayList` class. If we attempt to store an object that is not of the allowable type in the `ArrayList`, will we see an error message at compile time or at runtime?

18.2 Writing a Generic Class

CONCEPT: In Java you can write your own generic classes that accept data type arguments.

Not only does Java provide several generic classes for you to use, such as `ArrayList`, but it also allows you to write your own generic classes. Code Listing 18-2 shows the `Point` class, which is a simple example of a generic class. (This version of the class is stored in the source code folder *Chapter 18\Point Class Version 1*.) An instance of the class holds two values: an X coordinate and a Y coordinate.

Code Listing 18-2   (Point.java)

```
1  /**
2     The Point class holds X and Y coordinates. The data type
3     of the coordinates is generic.
4  */
5
6  public class Point<T>
7  {
8     private T xCoordinate;   // The X coordinate
9     private T yCoordinate;   // The Y coordinate
10
11    /**
12       Constructor
13       @param x The X coordinate.
14       @param y The Y coordinate.
15    */
16
17    public Point(T x, T y)
18    {
19       xCoordinate = x;
20       yCoordinate = y;
21    }
22
23    /**
24       The setX method sets the X coordinate.
25       @param x The value for the X coordinate.
26    */
27
28    public void setX(T x)
29    {
30       xCoordinate = x;
31    }
32
33    /**
34       The setY method sets the Y coordinate.
35       @param y The value for the Y coordinate.
36    */
37
38    public void setY(T y)
39    {
40       yCoordinate = y;
41    }
42
43    /**
44       The getX method returns the X coordinate.
45       @return The value of the X coordinate.
46    */
```

```
47
48    public T getX()
49    {
50       return xCoordinate;
51    }
52
53    /**
54       The getY method returns the Y coordinate.
55       @return The value of the Y coordinate.
56    */
57
58    public T getY()
59    {
60       return yCoordinate;
61    }
62 }
```

Let's take a closer look at the class header in line 6:

```
public class Point<T>
```

After the name of the class, T appears inside angled brackets. In this class declaration, T is a type parameter. A *type parameter* is an identifier that represents an actual type. When you instantiate the class, you use an actual type as an argument for the type parameter. You do this by writing the type name inside angled brackets, immediately following the name of the class. For example, consider the following code:

```
Integer intX = new Integer(10);
Integer intY = new Integer(20);
Point<Integer> myPoint = new Point<>(intX, intY);
```

Recall that Integer is a wrapper class. In this statement we are passing Integer as a type argument to the T parameter. This is illustrated in Figure 18-1.

Figure 18-1   Passing a type argument to a type parameter

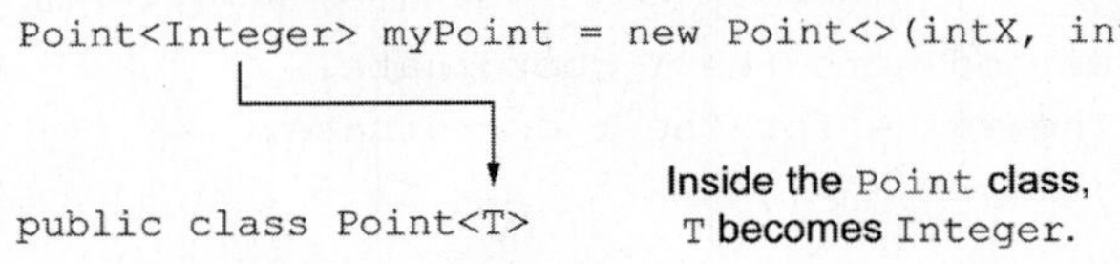

For this instance of the Point class, the type parameter T will become Integer. There are several places in the Point class where T is used, as shown in Figure 18-2. In each place, T will become the type that was passed to it as an argument.

Figure 18-2 The type parameter T in the Point class

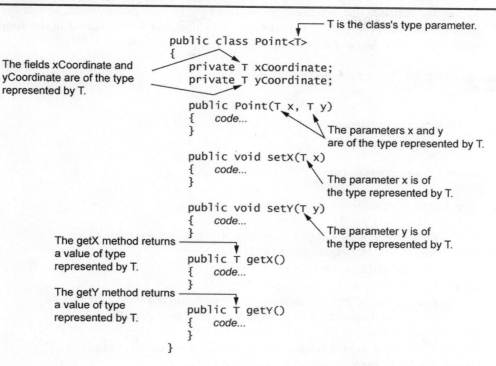

For example, look at the following declarations of the xCoordinate and yCoordinate fields in lines 8 and 9:

```
private T xCoordinate;      // The X coordinate
private T yCoordinate;      // The Y coordinate
```

If we pass Integer as a type argument to T, these declarations will become as follows:

```
private Integer xCoordinate;  // The X coordinate
private Integer yCoordinate;  // The Y coordinate
```

The T type parameter is also used in the following method headers:

```
public Point(T x, T y)
public void setX(T x)
public void setY(T y)
public T getX()
public T getY()
```

If we pass Integer as a type parameter to T, these method headers will become as follows:

```
public Point(Integer x, Integer y)
public void setX(Integer x)
public void setY(Integer y)
public Integer getX()
public Integer getY()
```

The program in Code Listing 18-3 tests the Point class by creating two instances of it. In the first instance, the Double type is passed to the type parameter T, and in the second instance the Integer type is passed to T. (This program is also stored in the source code folder *Chapter 18\Point Class Version 1*.)

Code Listing 18-3 (TestPoint.java)

```java
 1 /**
 2     This program demonstrates the Point class.
 3 */
 4
 5 public class TestPoint
 6 {
 7    public static void main(String[] args)
 8    {
 9       // Create two Double objects to use as coordinates.
10       Double dblX = new Double(1.5);
11       Double dblY = new Double(2.5);
12
13       // Create a Point object that can hold Doubles.
14       Point<Double> dPoint = new Point<>(dblX, dblY);
15
16       // Create two Integer objects to use as coordinates.
17       Integer intX = new Integer(10);
18       Integer intY = new Integer(20);
19
20       // Create a Point object that can hold Integers.
21       Point<Integer> iPoint = new Point<>(intX, intY);
22
23       // Display the Double values stored in dPoint.
24       System.out.println("Here are the values in dPoint.");
25       System.out.println("X Coordinate: " + dPoint.getX());
26       System.out.println("Y Coordinate: " + dPoint.getY());
27       System.out.println();
28
29       // Display the Integer values stored in iPoint.
30       System.out.println("Here are the values in iPoint.");
31       System.out.println("X Coordinate: " + iPoint.getX());
32       System.out.println("Y Coordinate: " + iPoint.getY());
33    }
34 }
```

Program Output

```
Here are the values in dPoint.
X Coordinate: 1.5
Y Coordinate: 2.5
Here are the values in iPoint.
X Coordinate: 10
Y Coordinate: 20
```

When the following statement is executed in line 14, the `Double` type is passed as an argument to the type parameter `T`:

```
Point<Double> dPoint = new Point<>(dblX, dblY);
```

For this particular instance of the `Point` class, the `T` type parameter is replaced with `Double`. The method header for this particular object's constructor becomes the following:

```
public Point(Double x, Double y)
```

Notice that in line 14 references to two `Double` objects, `dblX` and `dblY`, are passed as arguments to the constructor. If we had passed anything other than `Double` references, the compiler would have generated an error.

Another instance of the class is created with the following statement in line 21:

```
Point<Integer> iPoint = new Point<>(intX, intY);
```

For this particular instance of the `Point` class, the `T` type parameter is replaced with `Integer`. The method header for this particular object's constructor becomes the following:

```
public Point(Integer x, Integer y)
```

In this statement we have passed two `Integer` references, `intX` and `intY`, as arguments to the constructor. If we had passed anything other than `Integer` references, an error would have occurred at compile time.

Only Reference Types Can Be Passed to Type Parameters

When you create an instance of a generic class, you can only pass a reference type to the class's type parameter. This is the reason that in Code Listing 18-3 we passed the `Double` and `Integer` types to the `Point` class instead of the primitive `double` and `int` types. The only way to use a generic type to hold a primitive value is to wrap the primitive value up in a wrapper class, as we demonstrated in Code Listing 18-3.

Autoboxing and Unboxing

Although we can only pass reference types to a generic class's type parameter, we can use Java's autoboxing and unboxing feature to simplify our code if we need to store primitive values in a generic type. We briefly introduced autoboxing and unboxing in Chapter 10. Recall that *autoboxing* is Java's process of automatically "boxing up" a primitive value inside an object of an appropriate wrapper class. For example, the statement in line 14 of Code Listing 18-3 could have been written as follows:

```
Point<Double> dPoint = new Point<>(1.5, 2.5);
```

Because the `Point` constructor accepts two `Double` arguments, the literal values 1.5 and 2.5 are autoboxed into two objects of the `Double` class. References to those objects are then passed as arguments to the constructor.

Unboxing is the opposite of boxing. It is the process of automatically converting a wrapper class object to a primitive type, when needed. For example, look at the following code:

```
// Use autoboxing to pass doubles to the constructor.
Point<Double> dPoint = new Point<>(1.5, 2.5);
```

```
// Use unboxing to retrieve the X and Y coordinates
// and assign them to double variables.
double x = dPoint.getX();
double y = dPoint.getY();
```

In the last two statements, the getX and getY methods are called, which will return references to Double objects. Because the methods' return values are being assigned to double variables, however, Java will unbox the Double objects and store their values in the double variables. After this code executes the variables x and y will hold the values 1.5 and 2.5.

Instantiating a Generic Class without Specifying a Type Argument

Although it is not recommended, it is possible to create an instance of a generic class without providing a type argument. When you do this, you are using the class as a *raw type*. For example, look at the program in Code Listing 18-4. (This program is stored in the source code folder *Chapter 18\Point Class Version 1.*)

Code Listing 18-4   (TestPoint2.java)

```
 1  /**
 2      This demonstrates the Point class without a type argument.
 3  */
 4
 5  public class TestPoint2
 6  {
 7      public static void main(String[] args)
 8      {
 9          // Create an Integer and a Double
10          // to use as coordinates.
11          Integer x = new Integer(1);
12          Double y = new Double(7.5);
13
14          // Create a Point object with an
15          // Integer x coordinate and a Double
16          // y coordinate.
17          Point myPoint = new Point(x, y);
18
19          // Display the object's X and Y
20          // coordinate values
21          System.out.println("X Coordinate: " +
22                              myPoint.getX());
23          System.out.println("Y Coordinate: " +
24                              myPoint.getY());
25      }
26  }
```

Program Output

```
X Coordinate: 1
Y Coordinate: 7.5
```

An instance of the `Point` class is created with the following statement in line 17:

```
Point myPoint = new Point(x, y);
```

Notice that there is no type argument provided in angled brackets. When a type argument is not provided for an instance of a generic class, Java will provide `Object` as the type argument by default. This means that for the `myPoint` object, the declarations for the `xCoordinate` and `yCoordinate` fields will become the following:

```
private Object xCoordinate;   // The X coordinate
private Object yCoordinate;   // The Y coordinate
```

Likewise, each occurrence of `T` in the class methods will become `Object`.

> **NOTE:** If you compile the `TestPoint2.java` program shown in Code Listing 18-4 you will see a warning such as the following:
>
> ```
> TestPoint2.java uses unchecked or unsafe operations.
> Note: Recompile with -Xlint:unchecked for details.
> ```
>
> The Java compiler issues this warning when we compile code that instantiates a generic class without specifying a type argument.

It is not recommended that you instantiate a generic class without providing a type argument, because you give up the benefits of type-safety that you would have otherwise. For example, in line 17 of Code Listing 18-4, an `Integer` object is passed to the `Point` class constructor as the X coordinate, and a `Double` object is passed as the Y coordinate. This is legal because the constructor's parameter variables are of the `Object` type, and we can polymorphically pass references of any type to them.

It also means that the class's `xCoordinate` and `yCoordinate` fields can reference objects of any type. This opens up the door for runtime errors if we attempt to perform an unsupported operation on one of the class's fields.

Another reason that we should avoid instantiating a generic class without providing a type argument is that we have to use a cast operator to assign an `Object` reference to a variable of any other type. The following code illustrates this:

```
// Create an Integer and a Double.
Integer x = new Integer(1);
Double y = new Double(7.5);

// Create a Point object with no type argument.
Point myPoint = new Point(x, y);

// Retrieve the X and Y coordinates.
Integer xx = (Integer) myPoint.getX();
Double yy = (Double) myPoint.getY();
```

The last two statements shown here use the `myPoint` object to call the `getX` and `getY` methods. Because these methods return an `Object` reference, we must cast the reference to the proper type in order to assign it to a variable. This is not necessary when we instantiate the `Point` class with a type argument.

Commonly Used Type Parameter Names

The generic Point class that we examined defines a type parameter named T. There's nothing magic about the name T. When you are defining a generic type parameter, you can use any legal identifier you wish. By convention, however, type parameters are usually single letters written in uppercase. This helps distinguish the name of a type parameter from the name of a class. Also, there are some names that are commonly used, depending on the purpose of the type parameter. Table 18-1 lists the commonly used parameter names and briefly describes their meaning.

Table 18-1 Common Type Parameter Names

Name	Usual Meaning
T	T is commonly used for a general type.
S	S is commonly used for a general type when T has already been used.
E	E is commonly used to represent the type of an element, such as an element in an ArrayList or other collection.
K	K is commonly used to represent the type of a key in a class that keeps key/value pairs.
V	V is commonly used to represent the type of a value in a class that keeps key/value pairs.

As we progress through this chapter you will see several of these type parameter names being used.

 Checkpoint

18.5   What is a type parameter?

18.6   When you create an instance of a generic class, can you pass reference types, primitive types, or either to the class's type parameter?

18.7   Is it possible to create an instance of a generic class without providing a type argument? If so, is this recommended?

18.8   Is it required that type parameters be single letters written in uppercase?

 18.3

Passing Objects of a Generic Class to a Method

CONCEPT: When you create instances of a generic class, you must be able to pass those instances as arguments to methods. Method parameter variables can be declared to be of a generic type.

Suppose you want to write a method that accepts an instance of a generic class as an argument. For example, the following printPoint method accepts an instance of Point<Integer> as an argument and displays the X and Y coordinate values in that object.

```
public static void printPoint(Point<Integer> point)
{
    System.out.println("X Coordinate: " + point.getX());
    System.out.println("Y Coordinate: " + point.getY());
}
```

In this method, the parameter point is a reference to a Point<Integer> object. We can call the method and pass a reference to any Point<Integer> object, as shown here:

```
Point<Integer> iPoint = new Point<>(7, 12);
printPoint(iPoint);
```

A problem arises, however, if we want to pass an instance of Point<Double> to the method. The method's parameter is a reference to Point<Integer>, so only Point<Integer> objects can be passed to it.

If the printPoint method is intended to be a general purpose method that can display the X and Y coordinates of any Point object, this limitation will be too restrictive. It seems reasonable that any numeric wrapper class could be used as a valid type argument when creating an instance of the Point class. For example, we should expect that instances of Point<Integer>, Point<Double>, Point<Long>, Point<Float>, and Point<Short> are all valid. In that case, we would want the printPoint method to be able to accept instances of any of these types as an argument.

At this point you know something about inheritance and polymorphism, and you might be thinking along these lines: "I just checked the Java API documentation and found that all of the numeric wrapper classes extend the Number class, which is in the java.lang package. Why not use Number as the type argument in the method's parameter? That way we can use polymorphism to accept any Point object whose type argument extends the Number class."

In other words, why not write the printPoint method like this?

```
// Will this do what we want?
public static void printPoint(Point<Number> point)
{
    System.out.println("X Coordinate: " + point.getX());
    System.out.println("Y Coordinate: " + point.getY());
}
```

Unfortunately, this will not give us the results we want. The Java compiler will allow us to pass *only* Point<Number> objects to this method. If we try to pass a Point<Integer> or Point<Double> object, we will get an error at compile time. One way to solve our problem is to use the ? type wildcard with the parameter, as shown here:

```
public static void printPoint(Point<?> point)
{
    System.out.println("X Coordinate: " + point.getX());
    System.out.println("Y Coordinate: " + point.getY());
}
```

Notice that the parameter's type is Point<?>. The ? character that appears inside the angled brackets is a *type wildcard*, and it indicates that any type argument can be used in its place.

Now we can pass any `Point` object as an argument to the method, regardless of its type argument. The following statements will compile and execute without errors:

```
Point<Integer> iPoint = new Point<>(1, 2);
Point<Double> dPoint = new Point<>(1.5, 2.5);
printPoint(iPoint);
printPoint(dPoint);
```

Constraining a Type Parameter

Recall that the header for our original version of the `printPoint` method header looked like the following:

```
public static void printPoint(Point<Integer> point)
```

Because the parameter's type, `Point<Integer>`, was too restrictive, we changed the method header to the following:

```
public static void printPoint(Point<?> point)
```

The method now allows us to pass any `Point` object as an argument. However, this leads to a different problem: The parameter's new type, `Point<?>`, might not be restrictive enough. Suppose we only want to accept `Point` objects whose type argument is a numeric wrapper class. In other words, we only want to accept `Point` objects whose type argument is a subclass of `Number`. This can be accomplished by modifying the method once more, as shown here:

```
public static void printPoint(Point<? extends Number> point)
{
    System.out.println("X Coordinate: " + point.getX());
    System.out.println("Y Coordinate: " + point.getY());
}
```

In this version of the method, the parameter's type is `Point<? extends Number>`. This means that the `Point` object's type argument may be `Number`, or any type that extends `Number`. The following statements will compile and execute without errors:

```
Point<Integer> iPoint = new Point<>(1, 2);
Point<Double> dPoint = new Point<>(1.5, 2.5);
printPoint(iPoint);
printPoint(dPoint);
```

However, the following code will not compile because the `String` class is not a subclass of `Number`:

```
Point<String> sPoint = new Point<>("1", "2");
printPoint(sPoint);    // Error!
```

Code Listing 18-5 shows the `TestPoint3.java` program, which demonstrates this version of the `printPoint` method. (This program is stored in the source code folder *Chapter 18\ Point Class Version 1.*)

Code Listing 18-5   `(TestPoint3.java)`

```java
 1   /**
 2       This program demonstrates the printPoint method.
 3   */
 4
 5   public class TestPoint3
 6   {
 7       public static void main(String[] args)
 8       {
 9           // Create various Point objects.
10           Point<Integer> iPoint = new Point<>(1, 2);
11           Point<Double> dPoint = new Point<>(1.5, 2.5);
12           Point<Long> lPoint = new Point<>(10L, 20L);
13           Point<Float> fPoint = new Point<>(7.9f, 9.9f);
14
15           // Display each object's coordinates.
16           System.out.println("iPoint:");
17           printPoint(iPoint);
18
19           System.out.println("\ndPoint:");
20           printPoint(dPoint);
21
22           System.out.println("\nlPoint:");
23           printPoint(lPoint);
24
25           System.out.println("\nfPoint:");
26           printPoint(fPoint);
27       }
28
29       /**
30           The printPoint method prints a Point object's
31           X and Y coordinates.
32           @param point A Point object.
33       */
34
35       public static void printPoint(Point<? extends Number> point)
36       {
37           System.out.println("X Coordinate: " + point.getX());
38           System.out.println("Y Coordinate: " + point.getY());
39       }
40   }
```

Program Output

```
iPoint:
Coordinate: 1
Coordinate: 2
```

```
dPoint:
Coordinate: 1.5
Coordinate: 2.5

lPoint:
Coordinate: 10
Coordinate: 20

fPoint:
Coordinate: 7.9
Coordinate: 9.9
```

NOTE: In line 12 the values being passed as arguments to the `Point` class constructor are `10L` and `20L`. The "L" suffix tells the compiler to treat these literal values as long integers. Without the "L" suffix, these literals would be treated as `int` values, and an error would occur. Similarly, in line 13 the values `7.9f` and `9.9f` are being passed as arguments to the constructor. The "f" suffix tells the compiler to treat these literals as `float` values. Without the "f" suffix, these literals would be treated as `double` values and an error would occur.

Defining a Type Parameter in a Method Header

In the previous example you saw how the notation `<? extends Number>` means "any type that is `Number` or a subclass of `Number`." As an alternative to using the wildcard in this notation, you can actually define a type parameter in a method header. For example, the `printPoint` method could have been written as follows:

```
public static <T extends Number> void printPoint(Point<T> point)
{
    System.out.println("X Coordinate: " + point.getX());
    System.out.println("Y Coordinate: " + point.getY());
}
```

Notice that between the words `static` and `void`, the notation `<T extends Number>` appears. This defines a type parameter named `T`, and specifies that `T` can accept any type that is `Number` or a subclass of `Number`. Then notice that the type of the method's parameter is `Point<T>`. This means that the method can accept any `Point` object whose type argument is `Number` or a subclass of `Number`. This is illustrated in Figure 18-3.

Using this alternative syntax can simplify methods that accept multiple arguments of generic types. For example, look at the following method header:

```
public static void doSomething(Point<? extends Number> arg1,
                               Point<? extends Number> arg2,
                               Point<? extends Number> arg3)
```

Figure 18-3   Type parameter defined in a method header

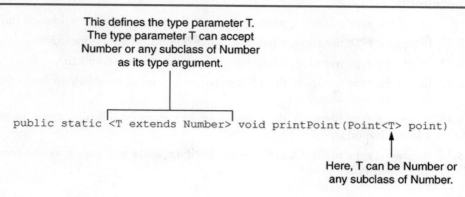

This method accepts three arguments, each of which is a `Point<? extends Number>` object. We had to write `Point<? extends Number>` as the type for each parameter variable. We can simplify the notation by defining a type parameter, as shown here:

```
public static <T extends Number> void doSomething(Point<T> arg1,
                                                  Point<T> arg2,
                                                  Point<T> arg3)
```

The `extends` Key Word Constrains a Type to an Upper Bound

When you use the `extends` key word with a generic type parameter, as we have shown in this section, it is said that you are constraining the type parameter to an *upper bound*. For example, in the notation `<T extends Number>` we are constraining `T` to the upper bound `Number`. This means that `T` can be any type that is below `Number` in the class hierarchy (or `Number` itself), but it cannot be a type that is above `Number` in the class hierarchy.

The `super` Key Word Constrains a Type to a Lower Bound

In addition to the `extends` key word, you can use the `super` key word to restrict a type parameter. Here is an example of how it might be used in a method header:

```
public static void doSomething(Point<? super Integer> arg)
```

In this method, the `arg` parameter's type is `Point<? super Integer>`. This means that the `Point` object's type argument may be `Integer`, or any superclass of `Integer`. Because the type can be any class that appears above `Integer` in the class hierarchy, it is said that we are constraining the type to a *lower bound*. The `Integer` class has only two superclasses: `Number` and `Object`. So, this method will only accept as arguments objects that are `Point<Integer>`, `Point<Number>`, or `Point<Object>`.

NOTE: You can use either `extends` to constrain a type to an upper bound, or `super` to constrain a type to a lower bound, but not both.

Checkpoint

18.9 In generic type notation, what does the ? character (the type wildcard) indicate?

18.10 In generic type notation, what does <? extends Number> mean?

18.11 In generic type notation, what does <? super Integer> mean?

18.12 In generic type notation, does the extends key word establish an upper boundary or a lower boundary?

18.13 In generic type notation, does the super key word establish an upper boundary or a lower boundary?

18.14 In generic type notation, can you use both extends and super to constrain a type to a set of boundaries?

 18.4 Writing Generic Methods

CONCEPT: In addition to classes, methods can also be generic.

Previously, you saw how a method can accept an object of a generic class as an argument. Methods themselves can also be generic. This means that they can have their own type parameters, and can use those type parameters to represent the types of arguments, the types of local variables, and their return type. Code Listing 18-6 shows a class with a generic method.

Code Listing 18-6   **(GenericMethodDemo.java)**

```
1   /**
2       This program demonstrates a simple generic method.
3   */
4
5   public class GenericMethodDemo
6   {
7       public static void main(String[] args)
8       {
9           String[] names = { "Alfonso", "Beatrice", "Celine" };
10          displayArray(names);
11      }
12
13      /**
14          The displayArray method displays each element
15          in an array.
16          @param array The array to display.
17      */
18
19      public static <E> void displayArray(E[] array)
20      {
21          for (E element : array)
```

```
22            System.out.println(element);
23        }
24    }
```

Program Output

```
Alfonso
Beatrice
Celine
```

Line 19 shows the header for the displayArray method. Notice that the method defines a type parameter named E. The method has a parameter variable, array, which is a reference to an array of E objects. The E type parameter is also used in line 21, in the enhanced for loop. Notice in line 10 that the displayArray method is called like a regular method. Even though it is a generic method, no type argument is passed to it. When you call a generic method, the compiler determines which type to use from the context in which you are using the method. For example, in line 10 we are passing names as an argument to the method. Because names is a String array, the compiler uses the String type for E in the method.

You can constrain a type parameter in a generic method. For example, suppose the displayArray method had been written as follows:

```
public static <E extends Number> void displayArray(E[] array)
{
    for (E element : array)
        System.out.println(element);
}
```

In this version of the method, we have constrained the type parameter E to any type that is Number or a subclass of Number. When calling this version of the method, we can only pass an array of Number objects, or of objects of a subclass of Number.

 Checkpoint

18.15 When an instance of a generic class is created, a type argument is explicitly passed to the class's type parameter. When a generic method is called, how is a type argument provided for the method's type parameter?

18.5 Constraining a Type Parameter in a Generic Class

CONCEPT: You can constrain the type parameter in a generic class so that only certain type arguments can be used to create an instance of the class.

Previously you saw how we used generic notation in the printPoint method header so the method can accept an instance of the generic Point class as an argument. You also saw how we used generic notation to constrain the method so that it will only accept Point objects whose type argument is Number or a subclass of Number.

Suppose we wish to constrain the Point class itself so that only certain type arguments can be used to create an instance of the class. For example, suppose we want to allow instances of the Point class to be created using only the numeric wrapper classes as type arguments. That would prevent a programmer from using classes such as String as the type argument when instantiating the Point class. We can impose such a restriction by using the extends key word to constrain the class's type parameter.

Code Listing 18-7 shows a modified version of the Point class, which uses the extends key word in its generic type notation. (This version of the class is stored in the source code folder *Chapter 18\Point Class Version 2.*)

Code Listing 18-7   (Point.java)

```
1   /**
2       The Point class holds X and Y coordinates. The data type
3       of the coordinates is generic, but restricted to
4       Number or a subclass of Number.
5   */
6
7   public class Point<T extends Number>
8   {
9       private T xCoordinate;   // The X coordinate
10      private T yCoordinate;   // The Y coordinate
11
12      /**
13          Constructor
14          @param x The X coordinate.
15          @param y The Y coordinate.
16      */
17
18      public Point(T x, T y)
19      {
20          xCoordinate = x;
21          yCoordinate = y;
22      }
23
24      /**
25          The setX method sets the X coordinate.
26          @param x The value for the X coordinate.
27      */
28
29      public void setX(T x)
30      {
31          xCoordinate = x;
32      }
33
34      /**
35          The setY method sets the Y coordinate.
```

```
36          @param y The value for the Y coordinate.
37       */
38
39       public void setY(T y)
40       {
41          yCoordinate = y;
42       }
43
44       /**
45          The getX method returns the X coordinate.
46          @return The value of the X coordinate.
47       */
48
49       public T getX()
50       {
51          return xCoordinate;
52       }
53
54       /**
55          The getY method returns the Y coordinate.
56          @return The value of the Y coordinate.
57       */
58
59       public T getY()
60       {
61          return yCoordinate;
62       }
63    }
```

The only difference between this Point class and the one we studied earlier is the following type parameter notation in line 7:

```
public class Point<T extends Number>
```

The notation <T extends Number> defines a type parameter T, which is constrained with Number as its upper bound. In other words, only Number or a subclass of Number may be passed as a type argument to this parameter. The following statements will compile without error because each of the type arguments being used is a subclass of Number:

```
Point<Integer> iPoint = new Point<>(1, 2);
Point<Double> dPoint = new Point<>(1.5, 2.5);
Point<Long> lPoint = new Point<>(10L, 20L);
Point<Float> fPoint = new Point<>(7.9f, 9.9f);
```

These statements, however, will cause an error at compile time because the type arguments String and Character are not subclasses of Number:

```
// These statements will cause an error.
Point<String> iPoint = new Point<>("1", "2");
Point<Character> dPoint = new Point<>('1', '2');
```

You can also use the `super` key word in a generic class, to constrain a type parameter to a lower bound. For example, suppose we had constrained the `Point` class's type parameter as follows:

```
public class Point<T super Double>
```

This specifies that the type argument must be `Double`, or any superclass of `Double`. Otherwise, an error will occur at compile time.

Checkpoint

18.16 Why would you want to constrain the type parameter in a generic class?

18.17 Can you constrain a generic class's type parameter with an upper bound? With a lower bound?

18.6 Inheritance and Generic Classes

CONCEPT: A generic class can be a superclass, and it can extend other classes.

VideoNote
Inheritance and
Generic classes

Inheritance can be used with generic classes. For example, Code Listing 18-8 shows the `Point3D` class, which extends the `Point` class. This class inherits the `Point` class's `xCoordinate` and `yCoordinate` fields, and has its own field for a Z coordinate, named `zCoordinate`. (This version of the class is stored in the source code folder *Chapter 18\Point Class Version 2.*)

Code Listing 18-8   (`Point3D.java`)

```
 1   /**
 2       The Point3D class holds a Z coordinate. The data type
 3       of the coordinate is generic.
 4   */
 5
 6   public class Point3D<T extends Number> extends Point<T>
 7   {
 8       private T zCoordinate;  // The z coordinate
 9
10       /**
11          Constructor
12          @param x The X coordinate.
13          @param y The Y coordinate.
14          @param z The Z coordinate.
15       */
16
17       public Point3D(T x, T y, T z)
18       {
```

```
19            // Call the Point class constructor.
20            super(x, y);
21
22            // Assign the Z coordinate.
23            zCoordinate = z;
24        }
25
26        /**
27            The setZ method sets the Z coordinate.
28            @param z The value for the Z coordinate.
29        */
30
31        public void setZ(T z)
32        {
33            zCoordinate = z;
34        }
35
36        /**
37            The getZ method returns the Z coordinate.
38            @return The value of the Z coordinate.
39        */
40
41        public T getZ()
42        {
43            return zCoordinate;
44        }
45    }
```

Take a closer look at the class header in line 6:

```
public class Point3D<T extends Number> extends Point<T>
```

The first part of this statement reads as follows:

```
public class Point3D<T extends Number>
```

This indicates that the class we are defining is `Point3D`, and the type parameter is `T`. The notation `<T extends Number>` is used to define the type parameter, so any type argument passed to `T` must be `Number` or a subclass of `Number`. The next part of the statement is as follows:

```
extends Point<T>
```

This indicates that the class we are defining (`Point3D`) extends the `Point` class, with `T` passed as a type argument to the `Point` class. Figure 18-4 illustrates the parts of this code.

The program in Code Listing 18-9 demonstrates the class. (This program is stored in the source code folder *Chapter 18\Point Class Version 2*.)

Figure 18-4 Generic subclass header

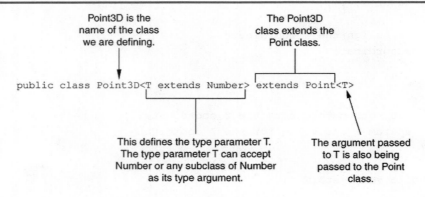

Code Listing 18-9 (TestPoint3D.java)

```
 1   /**
 2       This program demonstrates the Point3D class.
 3   */
 4
 5   public class TestPoint3D
 6   {
 7      public static void main(String[] args)
 8      {
 9         // Create a Point3D object that can hold Integers.
10         Point3D<Integer> point = new Point3D<>(10, 20, 30);
11
12         // Display the coordinates stored in point.
13         System.out.println("Here are the values in point.");
14         System.out.println("X Coordinate: " + point.getX());
15         System.out.println("Y Coordinate: " + point.getY());
16         System.out.println("Z Coordinate: " + point.getZ());
17      }
18   }
```

Program Output
```
Here are the values in point.
X Coordinate: 10
Y Coordinate: 20
Z Coordinate: 30
```

The "is-a" relationship is in effect between the Point3D class and the Point class. A Point3D object *is a* Point object. So, we can assign a Point3D object to a Point reference variable, or pass a Point3D object to a method that accepts Point objects. The program in Code Listing 18-10 demonstrates this. (This program is also stored in the source code folder *Chapter 18\Point Class Version 2.*)

Code Listing 18-10   (`PassPoint3D.java`)

```
 1   /**
 2       This program passes a Point3D object to a method
 3       with a Point parameter variable.
 4   */
 5
 6   public class PassPoint3D
 7   {
 8       public static void main(String[] args)
 9       {
10           // Create a Point3D object that can hold Integers.
11           Point3D<Integer> point = new Point3D<>(10, 20, 30);
12
13           // Display the X and Ycoordinates stored in point.
14           System.out.println("Here are the X and Y coordinates.");
15           printPoint(point);
16       }
17
18       /**
19           The printPoint method prints a Point object's
20           X and Y coordinates.
21           @param point A Point object.
22       */
23
24       public static void printPoint(Point<?> point)
25       {
26           System.out.println("X Coordinate: " + point.getX());
27           System.out.println("Y Coordinate: " + point.getY());
28       }
29   }
```

Program Output

```
Here are the X and Y coordinates.
X Coordinate: 10
Y Coordinate: 20
```

The `Point3D` class is an example of a generic class that extends another generic class. Both generic and non-generic classes may be used together in an inheritance hierarchy, in any of the following ways:

- A generic class may extend another generic class
- A generic class may extend a non-generic class
- A non-generic class may extend a generic class

Checkpoint

18.18 Can a generic class be a superclass? Can it be a subclass?

18.19 A generic class extends another generic class. Can you assign a reference to an instance of the subclass to a superclass variable?

18.20 Can you mix generic and non-generic classes in a class hierarchy?

18.7 Defining Multiple Type Parameters

CONCEPT: A generic class or method can have multiple type parameters, allowing it to accept multiple types as arguments.

It is possible to define multiple type parameters in a generic class or method. Different type arguments can then be passed to each type parameter. Here is an example of a class that defines two type parameters:

```java
public class MyClass<T, S>
{
    class code here...
}
```

In this example the type parameters are T and S. Inside the angled brackets the type parameters are listed, separated by commas. You can also apply constraints to the type parameters. Here is an example:

```java
public class MyClass<T extends Number, S extends Date>
{
    class code here...
}
```

In this example the type parameters are T and S. Any type that is passed to T must be Number or a subclass of Number. Any type that is passed to S must be Date or a subclass of Date.

Code Listing 18-11 shows the Pair class, which uses two type parameters. The Pair class is designed to hold a pair of items. Each of the items can be of a different type.

Code Listing 18-11 (Pair.java)

```java
1  /**
2     The Pair class demonstrates a generic class
3     with two type parameters.
4  */
5
6  public class Pair<T, S>
7  {
```

```
 8        private T first;          // The first item
 9        private S second;         // The second item
10
11        /**
12           Constructor
13           @param firstArg  Assigned to the first item.
14           @param secondArg Assigned to the second item.
15        */
16
17        public Pair(T firstArg, S secondArg)
18        {
19           first = firstArg;
20           second = secondArg;
21        }
22
23        /**
24           getFirst method
25           @return The first item in the pair.
26        */
27
28        public T getFirst()
29        {
30           return first;
31        }
32
33        /**
34           getSecond method
35           @return The second item in the pair.
36        */
37
38        public S getSecond()
39        {
40           return second;
41        }
42     }
```

Take a closer look at the class header in line 6:

```
public class Pair<T, S>
```

The notation `<T, S>` defines two type parameters, `T` and `S`. Notice that the first field is of the `T` type and the second field is of the `S` type. When we instantiate the class we must pass a type argument for each of these parameters. Code Listing 18-12 demonstrates the class.

Code Listing 18-12   (`PairTest.java`)

```
 1   /**
 2       This program demonstrates the Pair class which
 3       has two type parameters.
 4   */
 5
 6   public class PairTest
 7   {
 8      public static void main(String[] args)
 9      {
10         // Create an Integer to hold an ID number.
11         Integer idNumber = new Integer(475);
12
13         // Create a String to hold a name.
14         String name = "Smith, Sally";
15
16         // Create a Pair object to hold the ID
17         // number and the name.
18         Pair<Integer, String> myPair =
19                 new Pair<>(idNumber, name);
20
21         // Display the pair of items.
22         System.out.println("ID Number: " +
23                               myPair.getFirst());
24         System.out.println("Name: " +
25                               myPair.getSecond());
26      }
27   }
```

Program Output

```
ID Number: 475
Name: Smith, Sally
```

Line 11 creates an `Integer` object initialized with the value 475, referenced by the variable `idNumber`. Line 14 creates a `String` object referenced by the name variable. Lines 18 and 19 create a `Pair` object using the generic notation `<Integer, String>`. This passes `Integer` to the `T` parameter and `String` to the `S` parameter. This means that the `first` field will be an `Integer` and the `second` field will be a `String`.

The statement in lines 18 and 19 also pass `idNumber` and `name` to the `Pair` constructor, storing those items in the `myPair` object.

18.8 Generics and Interfaces

CONCEPT: Interfaces, as well as classes, may be generic.

So far, all of the generic types that we have examined have been classes. Interfaces can be generic too. For example, the Java API has an interface named `Comparable`, which is defined as follows:

```
public interface Comparable<T>
{
    int compareTo(T o);
}
```

This interface specifies a method named `compareTo`, which is used to compare the calling object with another object that is passed as an argument into the o parameter. Notice that the interface defines a type parameter, `T`. In the `compareTo` method header, `T` is the type of the o parameter.

Many of the classes in the Java API implement this interface, including `String` and the wrapper classes. You might recall from our discussion of the `String` class in Chapter 3 how the `compareTo` method works:

- If the calling object is less than the object passed to o, the method returns a negative number.
- If the calling object is equal to the object passed to o, the method returns 0.
- If the calling object is greater than the object passed to o, the method returns a positive number.

Suppose we are writing a class named `Tree`, and we want the `Tree` class to implement the `Comparable` interface. We would write the class in the following manner:

```
public class Tree implements Comparable<Tree>
{
    public int compareTo(Tree o)
    {
        Method code here...
    }

    Other class code here...
}
```

In the class header we are passing `Tree` as the type argument to the `Comparable` interface. So, the header for the `compareTo` method in the `Tree` class must be written as follows:

```
int compareTo(Tree o)
```

Any `Tree` object that calls the `compareTo` method will have to pass another `Tree` object as an argument to the method.

Constraining a Type Parameter to a Type That Implements an Interface

It is common for a method to have a parameter variable that is an interface reference rather than a class reference. For example, suppose we wish to write a generic method named `greatest`, which will compare two objects and determine which one is the "greater" of the two. Of course, the notion of "greater" depends entirely on the objects that are being compared. If we are comparing two `LuxuryCar` objects, the one that is the most expensive might be considered the greater one. However, if we are comparing two `RaceCar` objects, the one that has the highest top speed might be considered the greater one. Any objects that are passed as arguments to our method will have to support a standard method of comparison so we can determine which is the greater.

The `Comparable` interface helps in a situation like this. For example, let's assume that the `LuxuryCar` class implements the `Comparable` interface. The class header would be written as follows:

```
public class LuxuryCar implements Comparable<LuxuryCar>
{
    Class code here...
}
```

If we have two `LuxuryCar` objects, `mercedes` and `jaguar`, we can compare the two objects with an expression such as:

```
mercedes.compareTo(jaguar)
```

This expression will return a negative number, 0, or a positive number, indicating that the `mercedes` object is less than, equal to, or greater than the `jaguar` object.

The way we should write our `greatest` method is to make sure that only objects that implement the `Comparable` interface are passed to it as arguments. That way, we can safely use one of the objects to call the `compareTo` method, and determine which object is the greatest. With generics, we could write the method as follows:

```
public static < T extends Comparable<T> > T greatest(T arg1, T arg2)
{
    if (arg1.compareTo(arg2) > 0)
        return arg1;
    else
        return arg2;
}
```

This method defines a type parameter `T` with the following notation:

```
< T extends Comparable<T> >
```

In generic notation, the key word `extends` also means "implements." This specifies that the type passed to `T` must implement the `Comparable` interface. The method has two parameter variables, `arg1` and `arg2`. Because these parameter variables are of type `T`, any objects passed to them must implement the `Comparable` interface. Notice that the method's return type is also `T`, meaning that the method will return a reference to an object of type `T`.

Code Listing 18-13 shows a program that uses a generic method to search an array for a value. Both the array and the search value must be of a type that implements the `Comparable` interface. This is because the method uses the `compareTo` method to determine whether an element contains the search value.

Code Listing 18-13   `(GenericSearchArray.java)`

```java
 1  /**
 2      This program uses a generic method to sequentially
 3      search an array for a value.
 4  */
 5
 6  public class GenericSearchArray
 7  {
 8      public static void main(String[] args)
 9      {
10          int position;  // To hold a string's position in the array
11
12          // Array of strings to search
13          String[] names = { "Jack", "Kelly", "Beth",
14                             "Chris", "Kenny", "Britainy" };
15
16          // Search the array for Chris.
17          position = sequentialSearch(names, "Chris");
18
19          // Determine whether Chris was found.
20          if (position == -1)
21              System.out.println("Chris is not in the array. ");
22          else
23              System.out.println("Chris is at position " + position);
24      }
25
26      /**
27          The sequentialSearch method searches an array for
28          a value.
29          @param array The array to search.
30          @param value The value to search for.
31          @return The subscript of the value if found in the
32                  array, otherwise -1.
33      */
34
35      public static < E extends Comparable<E> >
36              int sequentialSearch(E[] array, E value)
37      {
38          int index;       // Loop control variable
39          int position;    // Position the value is found at
40          boolean found;   // Flag indicating search results
```

```
41
42         // Position 0 is the starting point of the search.
43         index = 0;
44
45         // Store the default values for position and found.
46         position = -1;
47         found = false;
48
49         // Search the array.
50         while (!found && index < array.length)
51         {
52             if (array[index].compareTo(value) == 0)
53             {
54                 found = true;
55                 position = index;
56             }
57             index++;
58         }
59         return position;
60     }
61 }
```

Program Output

Chris is at position 3

Take a closer look at the sequentialSearch method header, which appears in lines 35 and 36:

```
public static < E extends Comparable<E> >
             int sequentialSearch(E[] array, E value)
```

This method header defines a type parameter, E, which is constrained to types that implement the Comparable interface. The method's first parameter variable, array, is an array of type E. The second parameter variable, value, is a reference to an object of type E. If value is found in the array, the method returns the subscript of the element containing it. If value is not found in the array, the method returns –1.

 Checkpoint

18.21 Can interfaces be defined as generic?

18.22 Assume that you must define the type parameter T in a generic method. How would you constrain the type parameter T so it only accepts type arguments that implement the Comparable interface?

In the Spotlight:
Generic Subsets

Consider the task of generating a random subset of a set of some type. You might need to do this if you are writing a game of chance or if you are simulating certain types of real-world phenomena.

Let us suppose the set whose random subset we are to generate is in the form of a generic list,

```
List<T> argList
```

where `T` is a type parameter. There are different strategies we can use to pick a random subset: Here is one approach.

If the set has size N, it will have 2^N subsets. Each subset will correspond to a bit string of length N; and in turn, each bit string will correspond to a binary number in the range $0..2^N-1$. For example, if the set is $S = \{A, B, C\}$, then $N = 3$ and each of the eight subsets of S corresponds to a bit string of length 3. This three-way correspondence between subsets, bit strings, and numbers is illustrated in the following table.

Subset	{A, B, C}	{A, B}	{A, C}	{A}	{B, C}	{B}	{C}	{ }
Bit string	111	110	101	100	011	010	001	000
Number	7	6	5	4	3	2	1	0

Briefly, each element of the original set is assigned a position. A bit string has a 1 in that position whenever the corresponding subset includes the element at that position. For a set of size N, we can use the `nextInt()` method of the `java.util.Random` class to select a random integer k in the range $0..2^N-1$. We can next convert k to the binary string that represents it and then map this binary string to its corresponding subset. For example, if the random number selected is 5, then the bit string is 101, and the selected random subset is $\{A, C\}$. In this way, we can select random subsets of a set of size N by selecting random integers in the range $0..2^N-1$.

There are two static methods of the `Integer` class that will prove useful. The first is as follows:

```
int rotateLeft(int i, int N)
```

Calling this method with a value of 1 for the first parameter i and a value of N less than 32 will return 2^N, the number of subsets in a set of size N. This is shown in Line 41 of the following code listing. To convert an integer to the corresponding bit string, we use the method

```
String toBinaryString(int i);
```

as shown in line 47. Contrary to what you might expect, the length of the string returned, `subsetStr`, may not be the same as the size of the `argList`, the input set. This is because leading zeroes are omitted. For example, the bit string corresponding to $\{B, C\}$ will be 11 rather than 011. To compensate, the code that maps 1 bits to list elements must shift the index into `argList` by the number of zero bits omitted. This code appears in lines 50–55.

The following code listing demonstrates a generic class with a generic method for constructing a random subset. The `main` method exercises the method by calling the method three times, passing it the same list of strings on each call. As the output of the program shows, each call to the method is likely to return a different subset.

Code Listing 18-14   `(GenericRandomSubset.java)`

```java
1 import java.util.*;
2
3 /**
4   This program shows how to generate a random subset of a set S
5   when S is given as a generic list.
6 */
7
8 public class GenericRandomSubset <T>
9 {
10    public static void main(String[] args)
11    {
12       // Create a random subsets object specialized for strings
13       Subsets<String> strSubsets = new Subsets<>();
14
15       String [] people = {"Moe", "Curly", "Larry", "Bobby", "Stinky"};
16
17       // Transform the array into a list
18       List<String> peopleList = Arrays.asList(people);
19       System.out.println(strSubsets.getRandomSubset(peopleList));
20       System.out.println(strSubsets.getRandomSubset(peopleList));
21       System.out.println(strSubsets.getRandomSubset(peopleList));
22    }
23 }
24
25 class Subsets<T>
26 {
27    Random rand = new Random();
28
29    /**
30       This method computes a random subset of an input set.
31       @param argList: represents the input set
32       @return a list representing a random subset of a set
33    */
34
35    List<T> getRandomSubset(List<T> argList)
36    {
37       List<T> resultList = new ArrayList<T>();
38       int argListSize = argList.size();
39
40       // Compute the size of the power set of the input set.
41       int powerSetSize = Integer.rotateLeft(1,argListSize);
42
43       // Select a random integer in the range 0 to powerSetSize-1.
44       int randomInt = rand.nextInt(powerSetSize);
45
46       // Convert the random integer to a subset
47       String subsetStr = Integer.toBinaryString(randomInt);
```

```
48
49        // Interpret each bit in the string as an element
50        int length = subsetStr.length();
51        for (int k = 0; k < length; k++)
52        {
53            if (subsetStr.charAt(k) == '1')
54                resultList.add(argList.get(k + argList.size()-length));
55        }
56        return resultList;
57    }
58 }
```

Program Output

```
[Moe, Curly, Larry, Bobby]
[Moe, Curly, Bobby]
[Bobby, Stinky]
```

18.9 Erasure

CONCEPT: When the Java compiler processes a generic class or method, it erases the generic notation and substitutes an actual type for each type parameter.

When the Java compiler encounters generic code, it uses a process known as *erasure* to compile the code. The process is called erasure because the compiler erases the generic notation and substitutes an actual type for each type parameter. Here's how erasure works: When the compiler encounters a generic class, interface, or method with an unbound type parameter, such as <T> or <E>, it replaces all occurrences of the type parameter with Object. For example, the following class:

```java
public class Point<T>
{
    private T xCoordinate;
    private T yCoordinate;

    public Point(T x, T y)
    { code... }

    public void setX(T x)
    { code... }

    public void setY(T y)
    { code... }

    public T getX()
    { code... }
```

```
    public T getY()
    { code... }
}
```

would be converted by the process of erasure to this code:

```
public class Point
{
    private Object xCoordinate;
    private Object yCoordinate;

    public Point(Object x, Object y)
    { code... }

    public void setX(Object x)
    { code... }

    public void setY(Object y)
    { code... }

    public Object getX()
    { code... }

    public Object getY()
    { code... }
}
```

And, the following generic method:

```
    public static <E> void displayArray(E[] array)
    {
        for (E element : array)
            System.out.println(element);
    }
```

would be converted to:

```
    public static void displayArray(Object[] array)
    {
        for (Object element : array)
            System.out.println(element);
    }
```

When the compiler encounters a class, interface, or method with a bound type parameter, such as `<T extends Number>` or `<E extends Comparable>`, it replaces all occurrences of the type parameter with the bound that is applied to the parameter. For example, the following class:

```
    public class Point<T extends Number>
    {
        private T xCoordinate;
        private T yCoordinate;
```

```
            public Point(T x, T y)
            { code... }

            public void setX(T x)
            { code... }

            public void setY(T y)
            { code... }

            public T getX()
            { code... }

            public T getY()
            { code... }
        }
```

would be converted by the process of erasure to this code:

```
    public class Point
    {
        private Number xCoordinate;
        private Number yCoordinate;

        public Point(Number x, Number y)
        { code... }

        public void setX(Number x)
        { code... }

        public void setY(Number y)
        { code... }

        public Number getX()
        { code... }

        public Number getY()
        { code... }
    }
```

And, the following generic method:

```
    public static <E extends Comparable<E>>
        int sequentialSearch(E[] array, E value)
    {
        method code here...
    }
```

would be converted to:

```
    public static
            int sequentialSearch(Comparable[] array, Comparable value)
    {
        method code here...
    }
```

As you can see, generic notation exists only in the source code that is written by the programmer. Once the compiler confirms that a generic type is being used safely, it converts it into a raw type, which is simply a non-generic type. At the bytecode level, only raw types exist.

When working with generic types, the compiler also inserts cast operators, where necessary, in the code that uses the generic type. For example, suppose we use the following code to create an instance of the `Point` class:

```
Integer x = new Integer(1);
Integer y = new Integer(2);
Point<Integer> myPoint = new Point<>(x, y);
```

Then, later in the same program we write the following statement:

```
Integer tempX = myPoint.getX();
```

Because the translated `getX` method returns an `Object` reference, the compiler will modify this statement to read the following:

```
Integer tempX = (Integer)myPoint.getX();
```

Generics were introduced in Java 5. Older versions of Java did not support generics, so programmers could only write raw classes. The process of erasure ensures that newer code utilizing generics can coexist with older code that was written before Java 5.

 Checkpoint

18.23 During the process of erasure, when the compiler encounters a generic class, interface, or method with an unbound type parameter, such as `<T>` or `<E>`, what does it replace the type parameter with?

18.24 During the process of erasure, when the compiler encounters a class, interface, or method with a bound type parameter, such as `<T extends Number>` or `<E extends Comparable>`, what does it replace the type parameter with?

18.25 Do generic types still exist at the bytecode level?

 # 18.10 Restrictions on the Use of Generic Types

CONCEPT: Type parameters cannot be used in every way that a real type can be used.

Because of the erasure process, there are restrictions on how and when generic types and type parameters can be used. In this section we will examine some of those restrictions.

You cannot create an instance of a type parameter.

Let's say that a generic class has a type parameter named `T`. In the class you cannot create an instance of `T`. For example, the following code will not compile:

```
1   public class MyClass<T>
2   {
3      public MyClass()
4      {
5         // The following statement causes an ERROR.
6         T myObject = new T();
7      }
8   }
```

In this code the statement in line 6 causes an error at compile time. The expression `new T()` implies that `T` is the name of a constructor, but it is not.

You cannot create an array of generic class objects.

The Java compiler will not allow you to create an array of objects that are instances of a generic type. For example, the following statement will not compile:

```
ArrayList<String>[] a = new ArrayList<>[100];
```

At runtime, arrays in Java carry internal information about the data type of their elements. Because of erasure, an array of generic class instances would not have the necessary runtime type information, so the compiler will not allow such arrays to be created.

A generic class's type parameter cannot be the type of a static field, and cannot be referred to in a static method.

You cannot use a type parameter as the type of a static field. For example, the following code will not compile:

```
1   public class MyClass<T>
2   {
3      // The following statement will cause an ERROR.
3      private static T value;
4   }
```

Regardless of the number of instances of `MyClass`, there is only one instance of the static variable `value`, and therefore `value` can have only one type. The compiler also prohibits a static method from referring to a class's type parameter. The following code is illegal:

```
1   public class MyClass<T>
2   {
3      public static void doSomething()
4      {
5         // The following statement causes an ERROR.
6         T myValue;
7      }
8   }
```

You cannot make an exception class generic.

Let's imagine what would have to take place in order for a Java application to use generic exception classes. First, you would have to be able to use generic type notation in a catch clause. Then, when a generic exception was thrown, the system would have to check the type argument used to create the exception class to see if it matches the type specified in the catch clause. This is not possible because at runtime, generic type information has already been erased by the compiler. Because the compiler cannot know at compile time where an exception will come from, or what type argument will be used to create it, you are not allowed to create a generic exception class. Specifically, you are not allowed to create a generic subclass of Throwable. You are also not allowed to use generic type notation in a catch clause.

18.11 Common Errors to Avoid

- **Forgetting to pass a type argument when instantiating a generic class.** When you instantiate a generic class without passing a type argument, you are using the class as a raw type. When you do this, you give up the benefits of type-safety that you normally have with a generic class.
- **Using a primitive type as a type argument.** Generic classes and methods can accept only reference types as type arguments.
- **Misusing inheritance when passing an instance of a generic class as an argument to a method.** If a method's parameter variable is declared as the Point<Number> type, you cannot pass an instance of Point<Integer> to the parameter. Even though Integer is a subclass of Number, Point<Integer> is not a subclass of Point<Number>. When a parameter variable is declared as Point<Number>, the only arguments that can be passed to it are instances of Point<Number>.
- **Being too type-restrictive when using a generic class to declare a parameter variable.** Suppose in a method you declare a parameter variable as Point<Integer> myPoint. The only arguments that can be passed to this parameter are those of the Point<Integer> type. If you try to pass a Point<Double> object, an error will occur. By declaring the parameter as Point<?> myPoint, you will be able to pass any Point object to the method. By declaring the parameter variable as Point<? extends Number> myPoint, you will be able to pass any Point object with a type argument that is Number or a subclass of Number.
- **Trying to use the implements key word to constrain a type parameter to types that implement an interface.** You do not use the implements key word in generic type notation. To constrain a type parameter to types that implement a particular interface, you use the extends key word. In generic notation, the extends key word means "extends" or "implements."
- **Forgetting to define a type parameter in a generic method.** If a generic method has its own type parameter, you must write a definition for the type parameter in the method header.
- **Defining a type parameter in the wrong place in a generic method.** Type parameter definitions in a generic method must appear just before the method's return type.

Review Questions and Exercises

Multiple Choice and True/False

1. When you create an instance of a generic class, what types can you pass as arguments to the class's type parameter?

    a. primitive types only
    b. reference types only
    c. interface types only
    d. primitive, reference, and interface types

2. In a generic method, a type parameter is defined _____.

    a. inside the parentheses, along with the method's parameter variables
    b. after the method's return type, and before the method's name
    c. before the method's return type
    d. inside the body of the method, but before any local variables are declared

3. Look at the following method header:

    ```
    void displayPoint(Point<Number> myPoint)
    ```

    Which of the following objects would we be allowed to pass as an argument to the `displayPoint` method? (Select all that apply.)

    a. `Point<Number> p;`
    b. `Point<Integer> p;`
    c. `Point <Double> p;`
    d. `Point <String> p;`

4. Look at the following method header:

    ```
    void displayPoint(Point<?> myPoint)
    ```

    Which of the following objects would we be allowed to pass as an argument to the `displayPoint` method? (Select all that apply.)

    a. `Point<Number> p;`
    b. `Point<Integer> p;`
    c. `Point <Double> p;`
    d. `Point <String> p;`

5. Look at the following method header:

    ```
    void displayPoint(Point<? extends Number> myPoint)
    ```

    Which of the following objects would we be allowed to pass as an argument to the `displayPoint` method? (Select all that apply.)

    a. `Point<Number> p;`
    b. `Point<Integer> p;`
    c. `Point <Double> p;`
    d. `Point <String> p;`

6. Look at the following method header:

```
void displayPoint(Point<? super Double> myPoint)
```

Which of the following objects would we be allowed to pass as an argument to the displayPoint method? (Select all that apply.)

   a. `Point<Number> p;`
   b. `Point<Integer> p;`
   c. `Point <Double> p;`
   d. `Point <String> p;`

7. In the generic type notation `<T extends Number>` to what type of bound is `T` constrained?

   a. an upper bound
   b. a lower bound
   c. both an upper bound and lower bound
   d. `T` is not constrained to a bound

8. In the generic type notation `<T super Integer>` to what type of bound is `T` constrained?

   a. an upper bound
   b. a lower bound
   c. both an upper bound and lower bound
   d. `T` is not constrained to a bound

9. Which of the following generic type notations uses a wildcard?

   a. `Point<W>`
   b. `Point<T extends Number>`
   c. `Point<T super Integer>`
   d. `Point<?>`

10. The process used by the Java compiler to remove generic notation and substitute an actual type for type parameters is known as _____.

    a. erasure
    b. removal
    c. substitution
    d. masking

11. **True or False:** It is better to discover an error at runtime than at compile time.

12. **True or False:** It is possible to instantiate a generic class without specifying a type argument.

13. **True or False:** Type parameters must be single character identifiers, written in uppercase.

14. **True or False:** You can constrain a type parameter to both an upper bound and lower bound.

15. **True or False:** A generic class can extend a non-generic class.

16. **True or False:** You cannot create an array of generic class objects.

17. **True or False:** A generic class's type parameter can be the type of a static field.

18. **True or False:** An exception class cannot be generic.

Find the Error

1. ```
   ArrayList myList = new ArrayList<String>();
   ```

2. Assume the following is a method header in a class:
   ```
   public < T implements Comparable<T> > T greatest(T arg1, T arg2)
   ```

3. ```
   public class MyClass<T>
   {
       public static void displayValue(T value)
       {
           System.out.println(value);
       }
   }
   ```

4. ```
   public class Point<T extends Number super Integer>
   {
       Class code . . .
   }
   ```

Algorithm Workbench

1. Assume there is a class named `Customer`. Write a statement that creates an `ArrayList` that can hold only `Customer` objects.

2. Assume `names` references an object of the `ArrayList<String>` class. Write a statement that adds the string `"William Jefferson"` to the `names` object.

3. Write the header for a generic class named `MyType`. The class should have one type parameter. The type parameter's upper bound should be the `String` class.

4. Write the header for a generic class named `MyType`. The class should have one type parameter. The type parameter's lower bound should be the `Integer` class.

5. Modify the following `max` method so its arguments can be of any type that implements the `Comparable` interface. The method's return type should be the same as the type of its parameter variables.
   ```
   public static int max(int a, int b)
   {
       if (a > b)
           return a;
       else
           return b;
   }
   ```

6. Write the header for a generic class named `MyType`. The class should have two type parameters.
   ```

7. Write the header for a generic class named `MyType`. The class should have two type parameters. The first type parameter's upper bound should be the `Number` class. The second type parameter's upper bound should be the `String` class.

Short Answer

1. When a generic class is used in a program, when does type checking take place?

2. Look at the following method header:

   `public < T extends Comparable<T> > T least(T arg1, T arg2)`

   What constraint is placed on the type parameter `T`?

3. What is erasure?

4. Do generic types exist at the bytecode level?

5. When the compiler encounters a generic class, interface, or method with an unbound type parameter, such as `<T>` or `<E>`, it replaces all occurrences of the type parameter with what type?

6. When the compiler encounters a class, interface, or method with a bound type parameter, such as `<T extends Number>` or `<E extends Comparable>`, it replaces all occurrences of the type parameter with what type?

Programming Challenges

1. `MyList` Class

Write a generic class named `MyList`, with a type parameter `T`. The type parameter `T` should be constrained to an upper bound: the `Number` class. The class should have as a field an `ArrayList` of `T`. Write a public method named `add`, which accepts a parameter of type `T`. When an argument is passed to the method, it is added to the `ArrayList`. Write two other methods, `largest` and `smallest`, which return the largest and smallest values in the `ArrayList`.

2. `MyList` Modification

Modify the `MyList` class that you wrote for Programming Challenge 1 so the type parameter `T` should accept any type that implements the `Comparable` interface. Test the class in a program that creates one instance of `MyList` to store `Integers`, and another instance to store `Strings`.

3. `PointList` Class

Write a class named `PointList` that keeps a list of `Point` objects in an `ArrayList`. The `PointList` class should accept any object that is an instance of the `Point` class, or a subclass of `Point`. Demonstrate the class in an application.

4. Generic Insertion Sort

In Programming Challenge 1 of Chapter 16 you wrote an `ObjectInsertionSorter` class that can sort `Comparable` objects. Modify the sorting method so it is a generic method. The method should use generic notation to accept an array of any objects that implement the `Comparable` interface. Demonstrate the class in an application.

5. Generic Binary Search

In Programming Challenge 3 of Chapter 16 you wrote an `ObjectBinarySearcher` class. Modify the search method so it is a generic method. The method should use generic notation to accept an array of any objects that implement the `Comparable` interface. Demonstrate the class in an application.

VideoNote
Highest and
Lowest
Elements

6. Highest and Lowest Elements

Write a generic class with a type parameter constrained to any type that implements `Comparable`. The constructor should accept an array of such objects. The class should have methods that return the highest and lowest values in the array. Demonstrate the class in an application.

7. Number Analyzer

Write a generic class with a type parameter constrained to the `Number` class or any subclass of `Number`. The constructor should accept an array of such objects. The class should have methods that return the highest and lowest values in the array, the total of the elements, and the average value of all the elements. Demonstrate the class in an application.

8. Generic Random Permutation

Write a generic class with a generic method that returns a random permutation of a list passed to it as a parameter. Demonstrate the working of the method in an application that displays random permutations of lists of strings and of lists of numbers.

19 Collections and the Stream API

18

19 → 18 throughout

19.1 Introduction to the Java Collections Framework

CONCEPT: The Java API provides numerous interfaces and classes that allow you to create collections, which are objects that act as containers for groups of other objects.

It is common for an application to create a group of similar objects and work with that group of objects throughout the application's execution. Suppose, a teacher uses an application to manage student grades. That application might create several Student objects, with each object holding information about a particular student. Another example would be a payroll application that creates a group of Employee objects, with each object holding information about a specific employee.

Working with groups of objects is so common in programming that the Java API provides a set of interfaces and classes specifically for this purpose. These interfaces and classes, which are in the java.util package, are known as the *Java Collections Framework (JCF)*. You can use these interfaces and classes to create *collections*, which are objects that act as *containers* of other objects. You can use a collection to store a group of objects. Each object that is stored in a collection is referred to as an *element*. Collections allow you to add, retrieve, and delete objects.

Lists, Sets, and Maps

There are three general types of collections: *lists*, *sets*, and *maps*. Each of these is described here:

- List—A *list* is an *ordered collection* that orders its elements by position. The *position* of an element *x* within the list, also called its *index*, is the number of elements that precede x within the list. A list permits duplicate elements: two objects that are equal can be added to the list. The list distinguishes equal objects by their index.

- Set—A *set* in an *unordered collection* of objects that does not permit duplicates. Unlike a list, a set has no concept of position for its elements. Implementations of sets are usually optimized for searching so you can quickly find a specific stored value.
- Map—A *map* is a collection that stores every object x according to a property of x called its *key*. This means that each element in a map is a *key-value pair*. The *key* is a property of the object and the *value* is the object itself. A map allows a value to be quickly retrieved based on its key.

Java Functional Interfaces

The `java.util.function` package defines a number of functional interfaces that are referred to by methods defined in JCF interfaces and classes. In practice, the functional interfaces are used to declare the types of lambda expressions to be passed as a parameter to a collection class method. Knowing the naming system used to name these functional interfaces will help you to better understand the JCF methods that refer to them. The naming system uses the words *supplier*, *consumer*, *predicate*, *operator*, and *function* as root words, and employs a set of prefixes that includes *binary*, *bi*, *unary*, and the names of primitive types to modify the meaning of the root words.

A *function* takes at least one parameter and returns a value. The generic interface `Function<T, R>` takes a parameter of type `T` and returns a value of type `R`. A *bi-function* takes two parameters and returns a value: the generic interface `BiFunction<T, U, R>` takes two parameters of type `T` and `U`, in that order, and returns a value of type `R`.

It is useful to have a short hand notation for functional types. We will use the notation $T \to R$ for the type `Function<T, R>` and $(T, U) \to R$ for the type `BiFunction<T, U, R>`. Similar shorthand notation will be used for other functional types.

There are also functional interfaces that involve the primitive types `int`, `long`, and `double`. For example, the interface `IntFunction<R>` is the type $int \to R$, the interface `LongFunction<R>` is the type $long \to R$, and `IntToLongFunction` is the type $int \to long$.

An *operator* is a function whose parameters and return value have the same type. A *binary operator* is an operator that takes two parameters, and a *unary operator* is an operator that takes a single parameter. Thus `BinaryOperator<T>` has type $(T, T) \to T$, the interface `UnaryOperator<T>` has type $T \to T$, and `LongUnaryOperator` has type $long \to long$.

A *consumer* takes at least one parameter and returns no result. The interface `Consumer<T>` has type $T \to void$, while the interface `BiConsumer<T, U>` has type $(T, U) \to void$.

A *supplier* is the opposite of a consumer: it takes no parameters and returns a value. The interface `Supplier<T>` has type $( ) \to T$ and `IntSupplier` has type $( ) \to int$.

A *predicate* is a function that returns a boolean value. Thus `Predicate<T>` has type $T \to boolean$, while `BiPredicate<T, U>` has type $(T, U) \to boolean$.

JCF Interfaces

The Java Collection Framework defines interfaces and classes to facilitate the creation and use of collections. The classes and interfaces are generic so they can be used with different element types. Four of these interfaces are shown in Figure 19-1.

Figure 19-1 The main JCF interfaces

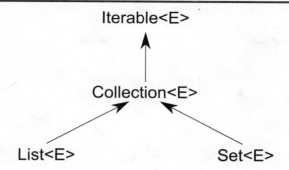

Iterating a Collection

Figure 19-1 shows that lists and sets are special types of collections, and that every collection is iterable. *Iteration* is the successive retrieval of elements from a collection until all elements have been examined. A collection that provides methods for iteration is said to be *iterable*. The JCF Iterable<E> interface defines methods for iterating a collection that stores elements of type E. The Collection interface extends Iterable and adds many methods for working with collections. The List interface is implemented by all collections that order their elements by position. It defines methods for adding, removing, and retrieving elements by index. Finally, the Set interface serves as the interface for all unordered collections. The Set interface does not add any methods to those that it inherits from Collection.

There is also a Map<K,V> interface that defines methods for a map that stores key-value pairs with K as the type of key and V as the type of value. This interface does not extend Collection, and will be covered later.

The Iterable Interface and the forEach method

The Iterable<E> interface provides two methods that can be used to iterate through a collection. The first of these is the method:

```
void forEach(Consumer<? super E> action)
```

The action parameter must be an object that implements the Consumer<? Super E> interface. In practice, this will usually be a lambda expression that takes a single parameter and returns no value. Moreover, the type of the parameter must be a superclass of E, the collection's element type.

We can illustrate the use of forEach() using ArrayList, a class that you learned about in Chapter 7. The program in Code Listing 19-1 creates a list with four names, and then uses forEach() to invoke the consumer function defined by the lambda expression

```
x ->
{
    System.out.printf("%s %d\n", x, x.length());
}
```

on each element of the list. The effect is to print the name and length of each element in the list.

Code Listing 19-1   (ForEachDemo.java)

```java
 1 import java.util.ArrayList;
 2
 3 /**
 4    This program demonstrates Iterable forEach().
 5 */
 6
 7 public class ForEachDemo
 8 {
 9    public static void main(String [] args)
10    {
11       // Array of names.
12       String [] names = {"Anna", "Bob", "Carlos", "Debby"};
13
14       // Create list and add names.
15       ArrayList<String> nameList = new ArrayList<>();
16       for (String name : names)
17       {
18          nameList.add(name);
19       }
20
21       // Use forEach with lambda expression to print.
22       nameList.forEach(
23             x ->
24             {
25                System.out.printf("%s %d\n", x, x.length());
26             });
27    }
28 }
```

Program Output

```
Anna 4
Bob 3
Carlos 6
Debby 5
```

Iterators

Another method in the Iterable<E> is as follows:

```
Iterator<E> iterator()
```

Calling this method on a collection returns an iterator for that collection. An *iterator* for a collection *C* is an object that provides controlled iteration through the elements of *C*. Unlike the forEach() method, which applies an action to *all* elements of a collection, an iterator provides finer control, letting you call for the next element only when you need it, and allowing you to stop the iteration at any stage of the process. An iterator is defined by the `Iterator<E>` interface, whose methods are defined in Table 19-1.

Table 19-1 Methods of the `Iterator<E>` interface

`boolean hasNext()`	Returns `true` if there are elements that have not yet been returned by the iterator, and `false` otherwise.
`E next()`	Returns the next element from the collection, or throws `NoSuchElementException` if no more elements remain.
`void remove()`	Removes from the underlying collection the element that was returned by the last call to `next()`. You can only call this method once after each call to `next()`.
`void forEachRemaining(Consumer<? super E> action)`	Calls the specified action method for each element that has not yet been returned by the iterator.

You get an iterator by calling the `iterator()` method on a collection. This method will take a snapshot of the elements in the collection at the time of the call and return an iterator that is ready to provide access to those elements. You typically use the iterator in a loop, calling `hasNext()` to see if there are more elements yet to be examined, and calling `next()` to fetch the next available element. The `remove()` method is optional, so it is not supported by all iterators. If supported, it will remove the element returned by the last call to `next()` from the underlying collection. The `forEachRemaining()` method applies an action to every element that has not yet been returned by the iterator.

The program in Code Listing 19-2 is a variation of the one in Code Listing 19-1. It prints names and lengths until `"Bob"` has been printed, then it prints the name without the length for each remaining list element.

To make the code more readable, the program defines the lambda expression in a separate statement:

```
Consumer<String> action = x ->
           {
                System.out.printf("%s\n", x);
           };
```

Notice that the functional interface must be specialized to the element type of the collection, which is `String`. The iterator is created like this:

```
Iterator<String> iter = nameList.iterator();
```

The call `iter.hasNext()` checks to if there are still elements to be returned by the iterator, and the call to `iter.next()` returns the next available element.

Code Listing 19-2   (`IteratorDemo.java`)

```
1 import java.util.ArrayList;
2 import java.util.Iterator;
3 import java.util.function.Consumer;
```

```
4
5  /**
6     This program demonstrates Iterators.
7  */
8
9  public class IteratorDemo
10 {
11     public static void main(String [] args)
12     {
13         // Array of names.
14         String [] names = {"Anna", "Bob", "Carlos", "Debby"};
15
16         // Create list and add names.
17         ArrayList<String> nameList = new ArrayList<>();
18         for (String name : names)
19         {
20             nameList.add(name);
21         }
22
23         // Define an action for the "remaining" elements.
24         Consumer<String> action = x ->
25                 {
26                     System.out.printf("%s\n", x);
27                 };
28
29         // Get the iterator to the list.
30         Iterator<String> iter = nameList.iterator();
31
32         // Process list elements with the iterator.
33         while (iter.hasNext())
34         {
35             String name = iter.next();
36             System.out.printf("%s %d\n", name, name.length());
37             if (name.equals("Bob"))
38             {
39                 // Act differently for names after "Bob".
40                 iter.forEachRemaining(action);
41             }
42         }
43     }
44 }
```

Program Output

```
Anna 4
Bob 3
Carlos
Debby
```

You can think of an iterator as having a list of all elements in the collection and a cursor that is initially positioned just before the first element of that list. Every call to next() returns the element at the cursor position and moves the cursor past the element returned. The hasNext() method returns false when the cursor gets past the last element in the list.

> **NOTE:** The next() method throws NoSuchElementException if it is called when there are no elements left to return.

The Enhanced For Loop

In Chapter 7, you learned that the enhanced for loop can be used with arrays and ArrayList collections. In fact, the enhanced for loop will work with any object of any class that implements the Iterable interface. In particular, it can be used with any collection.

The Collection Interface

The Collection<E> interface defines methods for working with collections. Some of these methods, with brief explanations of their use, are shown in Table 19-2.

Table 19-2 Methods of the Collection<E> interface

boolean add(E e)	Adds the object referenced by e to this collection. Some collections restrict the objects that can be added as elements. This method returns true if the object was added to the collection. It returns false if the collection did not allow the object to be added. This would be the case if the collection is a set and the add() is attempting to add a duplicate.
boolean addAll(Collection<? extends E> c)	The parameter c is another Collection object. This method adds all of the elements of c to this collection. The method returns true if the elements of c were added to this collection. It returns false otherwise.
void clear()	Removes all of the elements in this collection.
boolean contains(Object o)	Returns true if this collection contains the specified object, or false otherwise.
boolean containsAll(Collection<?> c)	Returns true if this collection contains all of the elements in the collection c, and returns false otherwise.
boolean equals(Object o)	Returns true if this collection is equal to the object o, and false otherwise.
boolean isEmpty()	Returns true if this collection contains no elements, and false otherwise.
boolean remove(Object o)	Removes a single instance of the object o from this collection if found, and returns true. If o is not found, the method returns false.

(table continues next page)

Table 19-2 Methods of the `Collection<E>` interface (continued)

`boolean removeAll(Collection<?> c)`	Removes every element in the collection c from this collection. Returns `true` if at least one element was removed from this collection, and `false` otherwise.
`boolean removeIf(Predicate<? super E> filter)`	Removes all of the elements of this collection that satisfy the given predicate. Returns `true` if at least one element was removed from this collection, and `false` otherwise.
`boolean retainAll(Collection<?> c)`	The parameter c is another collection. This collection will retain all of its elements that are also elements of the collection c. All other elements in this collection are removed. Returns `true` if at least one element was removed.
`int size()`	Returns the number of elements in this collection.
`Stream<E> stream()`	Returns a sequential stream with this collection as its source. Streams are discussed later in this chapter.
`Object[] toArray()`	This method converts the collection into an array of `Object` and returns the array.
`<T> T[] toArray(T[] a)`	The parameter to this method is an array of some reference type T. The elements of this collection are stored as objects of type T in the array a and the array a is returned. If this collection contains more elements than the array a, then a new array is created to hold the elements of this collection and the new array is returned. If this collection holds fewer elements than the array a, then the elements of this collection are stored in a and the element of a that immediately follows the last collection element is set to `null`.

The `removeIf` method uses a predicate as a filter. This method filters out all elements that satisfy the collection, leaving in the collection only those elements on which the predicate returns a value of false. Code Listing 19-3 uses this method to remove from a list of names all names whose length is at most 4. First, we define a lambda expression to be used as the filter:

```
Predicate<String> filter = x -> x.length() <= 4;
```

The lambda expression returns the value of the boolean expression `x.length() <= 4`. The filter function will return `true` when the length of the string x is at most 4, and `false` when the length of x is greater than 4.

Code Listing 19-3 (`FilterDemo.java`)

```
1 import java.util.ArrayList;
2 import java.util.function.Predicate;
3
4 /**
```

```
 5     This program demonstrates the Collection removeIf.
 6  */
 7
 8  public class FilterDemo
 9  {
10      public static void main(String [] args)
11      {
12          // Array of names.
13          String [] names = {"Anna", "Bob", "Carlos", "Debby"};
14
15          // Create list and add names.
16          ArrayList<String> nameList = new ArrayList<>();
17          for (String name : names)
18          {
19              nameList.add(name);
20          }
21          // Use forEach with lambda expression to print.
22          Predicate<String> filter = x -> x.length() <= 4;
23
24          // Remove strings with length at most 4 from nameList
25          nameList.removeIf(filter);
26
27          // Print the array list to show remaining strings.
28          System.out.println(nameList);
29      }
30  }
```

Program Output

```
[Carlos, Debby]
```

Checkpoint

19.1 The interfaces and classes in the Java Collections Framework are part of what package?

19.2 What are the three general types of collections?

19.3 Describe the differences between a list and a set.

19.4 A map's elements are comprised of how many parts? What are they?

19.5 The `List` and `Set` interfaces extend what other interface?

19.6 Name two methods in the `Iterable` interface.

19.7 What is an iterator?

19.2 Lists

—**CONCEPT:** There are two different ways to implement the `List` interface. The `ArrayList` class uses an implementation based on contiguous memory allocation, while the `LinkedList` implementation is based on linked allocation.

A list is a collection that stores its elements as a sequence. Each element in a sequence is assigned a nonnegative integer called its index. The first element in the sequence is assigned an index of 0, the next an index of 1, and so on.

The `List` Interface

The `List` interface specifies the operations that a list must support. It extends the `Collection` interface, so it inherits all of the methods specified by `Collection`. It also adds additional methods, shown in Table 19-3, specifically for working with lists. In a nutshell, the `List` interface specifies methods for the following:

- Adding an element at a specific index
- Retrieving an element from a specific index
- Changing the value of an element at a specific index
- Removing an element that is at a specific index
- Searching for an element in the list and returning its index
- Retrieving a segment of the list as a sublist

Table 19-3 Methods of the `List<E>` interface

`void add(int index, E element)`	
	Adds `element` to this list at the position specified by `index`.
`boolean addAll(int index, Collection<? extends E> c)`	
	The parameter `c` is a `Collection` object. This method adds all of the elements of `c` to this list, starting at the position specified by `index`. Any elements that are currently stored in this list, beginning at the position specified by `index`, are shifted into positions of higher index. The method returns `true` if the elements of `c` were added to this list. It returns `false` otherwise.
`E get(int index)`	Returns a reference to the element at the position specified by `index`.
`int indexOf(Object o)`	Returns the position of the first occurrence of the object o in the list. If o does not exist in the list, the method returns –1.
`int lastIndexOf(Object o)`	Returns the position of the last occurrence of the object o in the list. If o does not exist in the list, the method returns –1.
`E remove(int index)`	This method removes the element at the position specified by `index`, and returns a reference to the element that was removed.
`E set(int index, E element)`	This method stores the object referenced by `element` at the position specified by `index`. The object currently stored at the specified position is replaced.
`void sort(Comparator<? super E> c)`	
	Sorts this list according to the order induced by the specified comparator.
`List<E> subList(int fromIndex, int toIndex)`	
	This method returns a `List` object containing the elements of this `List`, starting with the element at `fromIndex` and ending with the element at `toIndex`.

Notice that many of the methods in Table 19-3 take an integer parameter for an index. The value of the index must be within the proper bounds, or the method will throw an `IndexOutBoundsException`. Elements already in the list have nonnegative indices that are less than the length of the list, so `get()`, `remove()`, and `set()` will throw this exception if the index passed to them is negative or greater or equal to the length of the list. The `add()` and `addAll()` methods throw the exception if the index is less than 0, or greater than the length of the list.

The `ArrayList` and `LinkedList` Classes

The purpose of an interface is to allow different classes to provide different implementations for the methods defined in the interface. JCF provides two implementations of the `List` interface. One of these is the `ArrayList` class, which you encountered in Chapter 7. An array list internally uses a backing array to keep track of references to its elements. The `ArrayList` class overcomes the fixed-size limitation of arrays by automatically allocating a bigger array whenever its backing array is about to overflow, and copying all its elements to the bigger array. The `ArrayList` implementation is said to use *contiguous memory allocation* because all the elements in the backing array occupy successive locations in memory.

Another implementation of the `List` interface is the `LinkedList` class. This class uses *linked allocation*: it keeps track of a reference to the first element in the list, and each element contains a reference to its successor. These successor references are called *links*. Thus, the element at index 0 contains a link to the element at index 1, which contains a link to the element at index 2, and so on. The last element in the list has no successor, so its successor reference is `null`. A list that uses linked allocation is called a *linked list*. Linked lists are studied further in Chapter 20.

Because of the nature of linked allocation, it takes longer to access an element near the end of the list than one near the beginning. This is because to get to an element at position k, you must start at zero and follow the successor links through all elements of lower index. In contrast, `ArrayList` can jump directly to the desired element by using k to index the backing array. Because of this, `ArrayList` is said to provide *random access* to its elements.

The `ArrayList` implementation performs best when most of the elements added to the list are added at the end (the position with the highest index), and most of the elements being removed are removed from the end. This is because inserting an element in the middle of the backing array requires space to be created for the new element by moving all elements with index equal or greater to the insertion point up by one. Similarly, deleting an element in the middle leaves a gap in the backing array, and requires all elements after the deletion point to move down by one to close the gap.

The `LinkedList` implementation performs best when many elements need to be added or removed at a position in the middle of the list. Such an operation can be carried out by reassigning a few successor links, unlike contiguous allocation where lots of elements may need to be shifted.

Creating and Initializing Lists

To create a list using the `ArrayList<E>` implementation, you need to use one of the following constructors:

```
ArrayList()
ArrayList(int initialCapacity)
ArrayList(Collection<? extends E> c)
```

The first constructor creates an empty list with the default initial capacity of 10, while the second constructor creates a list with the specified initial capacity. The *capacity* of an array list is the maximum number of elements it can hold before its backing array overflows. The capacity should not be confused with the *size* of the list, which is the number of elements currently stored in the list. The last constructor creates a list containing the same elements as the specified collection, in the order returned by that collection's iterator.

To create a list using the `LinkedList<E>` implementation, you need to use one of its two constructors:

```
LinkedList()
LinkedList(Collection<? extends E> c)
```

These constructors allow you to create an empty list, or a list whose elements come from a specified collection.

If you need to initialize a list to a long list of values, you can save yourself some typing by first initializing an array and then copying the array elements to a list using a loop:

```
// Initialize array of names.
String [] namesArray = {"Anna", "Bob", "Carlos", "Debby"};

// Create empty list.
LinkedList<String> list1 = new LinkedList<>();

// Populate the list using a loop.
for (String s : namesArray)
{
    list1.add(s);
}
System.out.println(list1);
```

Here we have created a linked list, added some elements to it, and printed the list. All implementations of collections in Java provide a `toString()` method, so collections can be printed without resorting to a loop to print the individual elements of the collection.

We can simplify this code further by using the constructor that takes an existing collection to initialize a list. The `Arrays` class has a method

```
static <T> List<T> asList(T ... a)
```

that takes an array of a reference type `T` and returns a fixed-size list backed by that array. So you can create a list from an array like this:

```
List<String> aList = Arrays.asList(namesArray);
```

You cannot add elements or remove elements from a fixed-size list, but you can use it as a parameter to a `LinkedList` or `ArrayList` constructor. Thus, you can initialize a list with names from an array, and a new name to the list, and print the list like this:

```
String [] namesArray = {"Anna", "Bob", "Carlos", "Debby"};
List<String> fixedList = Arrays.asList(namesArray);
LinkedList list2 = new LinkedList<>(fixedList);
list2.add("Ephraim");
System.out.println(list2);
```

This code will print the line:

```
[Anna, Bob, Carlos, Debby, Ephraim]
```

Because the `asList` method takes a var-args parameter, you can shorten the code to create and initialize the list further:

```
LinkedList list2 =
    new LinkedList<>(Arrays.asList("Anna", "Bob", "Carlos", "Debby"));
```

List Iterators

For lists, the iterator inherited from `Collection` returns list elements in order of increasing index, and its `next()` method always moves "forward" through the list. The `List<E>` interface defines a method:

```
ListIterator<E> listIterator()
```

When called on a list, this method returns a special *list iterator* that is able to move both forward and backwards through a list. In addition to a `next()` method, a list iterator has a `previous()` method that returns an element while moving backwards. A list iterator has a cursor position that always lies between the element that would be returned by a call to `previous()` and the element that would be returned a call to `next()`. Initially, the cursor is just before the element with index 0. When `next()` is called, the cursor returns the element at 0 and moves forward past the returned element to the position between elements 0 and 1. At this point, a call to `previous()` will return the element 0 and move the cursor back to the beginning, but a call to `next()` will return element 1 and move the cursor forward to the position between elements 1 and 2. If the cursor is already past the last element, a call to `next()` will throw `NoSuchElementException`. Likewise, a call to `previous()` will throw the same exception if the cursor position is before the element 0.

The `remove()` method in a list iterator removes from the list the element that was returned by the last call to `next()` or `previous()`. The `remove()` method can only be called once after a call to either of those two methods. A list iterator also has an `add()` method that adds a new element to the list at the current cursor position. The new element goes just after the element that would be returned by a call to `previous()`, and just before the element that would be returned by a call to `next()`.

The methods of a list iterator are defined in the `ListIterator` interface. This interface extends `Iterator` and adds the methods shown in Table 19-4.

Table 19-4   Methods of the `ListIterator<E>` interface

`void add(E e)`	Adds the specified element into the list at the current cursor position.
`E previous()`	Returns the element just before the cursor position and moves the cursor position backwards.
`boolean hasPrevious()`	Returns `true` if there is an element before the current cursor position, `false` otherwise.
`int nextIndex()`	Returns the index of the element that would be returned by a subsequent call to `next()`.
`int previousIndex()`	Returns the index of the element that would be returned by a subsequent call to `previous()`.
`void set(E e)`	Replaces the last element returned by `next()` or `previous()`.

The program in Code Listing 19-4 demonstrates how to use a list iterator to traverse a list and add a new element.

Code Listing 19-4   (`ListIteratorDemo.java`)

```java
 1 import java.util.*;
 2
 3 /**
 4    Demonstrates the list iterator
 5 */
 6
 7 public class ListIteratorDemo
 8 {
 9     public static void main(String [] args)
10     {
11         // Create an array list to hold strings.
12         String []names = {"Chris", "David", "Katherine", "Kenny"};
13         List<String> nameList = new ArrayList<>(Arrays.asList(names));
14
15         // Display the names in the list.
16         System.out.println("Here are the original names.");
17         System.out.println(nameList);
18
19         // Get a list iterator.
20         ListIterator<String> it = nameList.listIterator();
21
22         // Add "Darlene" to the list right after "Chris".
23         while (it.hasNext())
24         {
25             String str = it.next();
```

```
26                    // If the last name retrieved was "Chris"
27                    // then insert "Darlene".
28                    if (str.equalsIgnoreCase("Chris"))
29                    {
30                        it.add("Darlene");
31                        // We are done
32                        break;
33                    }
34              }
35          //Display the names in the list again.
36          System.out.println("\nHere are the new names now.");
37          System.out.println(nameList);
38      }
39 }
```

Program Output

```
Here are the original names.
[Chris, David, Katherine, Kenny]

Here are the new names now.
[Chris, Darlene, David, Katherine, Kenny]
```

The program in Code Listing 19-5 demonstrates using the set() method to replace an element, and the remove() method to remove an element. In this program, the first name in the list is replaced with "Alfonso" and the last name is removed.

Code Listing 19-5   **(ListIteratorDemo2.java)**

```
1 import java.util.*;
2
3 /**
4    This program demonstrates setting and removing list
5    elements with a ListIterator.
6 */
7
8 public class ListIteratorDemo2
9 {
10     public static void main(String[] args)
11     {
12         // Create an ArrayList to hold String objects.
13         List<String> nameList = new ArrayList<>();
14
15         // Add some names to the ArrayList.
16         nameList.add("Chris");
17         nameList.add("David");
18         nameList.add("Katherine");
19         nameList.add("Kenny");
20
```

```
21          // Display the names in the list
22          System.out.println("Here are the original names.");
23          System.out.println(nameList);
24
25          // Get a list iterator.
26          ListIterator<String> it = nameList.listIterator();
27
28          // Replace the first element with "Alfonso".
29          if (it.hasNext())
30          {
31              // Get the first element.
32              it.next();
33
34              // Replace it.
35              it.set("Alfonso");
36          }
37          // Move the iterator to the end of the list.
38          while (it.hasNext())
39          {
40              it.next();
41          }
42
43          // Remove the last element that was retrieved.
44          it.remove();
45
46          // Display the names in the list again. The list
47          // should read Alfonso, David, and Katherine.
48          System.out.println("\nHere are the names now.");
49          System.out.println(nameList);
50      }
51 }
```

Program Output

```
Here are the original names.
[Chris, David, Katherine, Kenny]

Here are the names now.
[Alfonso, David, Katherine]
```

Methods of the LinkedList Class

Linked allocation makes it easy to move *forward* in a list; you can easily pass from one element to the next by following the successor link. The Java implementation of a linked list is actually a doubly linked list. In addition to each element having a link to its successor, every element has a link to its *predecessor*. The predecessor links make it easy to move *backward* in the list. Also, in addition to keeping a reference to the first element in the list, the Java implementation keeps a reference to the last element of the list. This makes it as easy to locate the last element as it is to locate the first.

To understand why a linked list should maintain predecessor as well as successor links, imagine an application that prints the element of a linked list of length 5 in reverse order. Suppose that the application accesses the elements by index, using the `get()` method of the `List` interface.

```
String [] namesArray = {"Anna", "Bob", "Carlos", "Debby", "Ephraim"};
LinkedList list2 = new LinkedList<>(Arrays.asList(namesArray));

for (int k = list2.size()-1; k >= 0; k--)
{
    System.out.printf("%s ", list2.get(k));
}
```

With each call to `get(k)`, the list would start at index 0 and traverse k links to get to the node at index k. Altogether, this code would require the traversal of $4 + 3 + 2 + 1 = 10$ links. For a long list, the code would need to traverse a lot of links.

To facilitate the backward and forward traversals of a linked list, and to guarantee quick access to the first and last elements, the `LinkedList` class adds several methods not found in `List`.

Table 19-5 Methods of the `LinkedList<E>` class

`void addFirst(E e)`	Inserts the specified element at the beginning of this list.
`void addLast(E e)`	Appends the specified element to the end of this list.
`E getFirst()`	Returns the first element in this list.
`E getLast()`	Returns the last element in this list.
`E removeFirst()`	Removes and returns the first element in this list.
`E removeLast()`	Removes and returns the last element in this list.
`Iterator<E> descendingIterator()`	Returns an iterator that traverses the list in reverse order.

 NOTE: The methods of Table 19-5 for getting and removing the first and last elements will throw `NoSuchElementException` if called on an empty list.

Using an Interface Variable to Reference a `Collection` Object

Take a closer look at the statement in line 13 of Code Listing 19-5:

```
List<String> nameList = new ArrayList<>();
```

Notice that `nameList` is a `List` variable, not an `ArrayList` variable. Because the `ArrayList` class implements the `List` interface, we can use a `List` variable to reference an `ArrayList` object. This is a common practice. By always using interface variables to reference collection objects, our code will be easier to maintain if it becomes necessary to use a different concrete class to create the object.

Either one of the `ArrayList` and `LinkedList` class can be used to create a list. Internally, however, there are differences in the way that these classes handle list operations. Suppose we write a program that at first uses an `ArrayList` to store a large number of `String` objects. We use the following statement to instantiate the `ArrayList`:

```
List<String> myList = new ArrayList<>();
```

Also, assume that in the program we pass the `ArrayList` object as an argument to numerous methods. Each of the methods uses a `List` variable as a parameter, such as the following:

```
public void displayList(List<String> somelist)
{
    method code here...
}
```

Once we put the program into use, we determine that the `ArrayList` is performing slowly because a large number of objects are constantly being inserted in the middle. After doing a little research, we determine that the `LinkedList` class performs faster under these circumstances, and we decide to use it instead of the `ArrayList` class. Because the `LinkedList` class also implements the `List` interface, and we have only used `List` variables to reference the `ArrayList`, making the change is simple. In the statement that instantiates the list object, we only have to change `ArrayList` to `LinkedList`, as shown here:

```
List<String> myList = new LinkedList<>();
```

Changes in other parts of the program are not necessary because we only used `List` variables to reference the list object.

Checkpoint

19.8 What kind of memory allocation is used by the `ArrayList` class?

19.9 What kind of memory allocation is used by the `LinkedList` class?

19.10 Why is it a common practice to use an interface variable to reference a collection object?

19.11 `ListIterator` is a subinterface of what other JCF interface?

19.12 When it comes to moving through the elements of a collection, describe a difference between an `Iterator` and a `ListIterator`.

19.13 When you need a list iterator, how do you get one?

19.14 When stepping through the elements of a list with a list iterator's `next` method, how do you determine whether there are more elements in the list to visit?

19.15 Which method should you call to determine `previous()` can be called without throwing an exception?

19.16 What element does the `remove` method (in the `Iterator` interface) remove?

19.17 What element does the `set` method (in the `ListIterator` interface) change?

19.18 What is the difference between the *size* and *capacity* of an `ArrayList`?

19.19 Which concrete list class stores its elements in a *linked list*?

19.20 Which concrete list class would be a good choice to use when your application will be storing a large amount of data in a list, and a lot of insertions and/or deletions in the middle of the list are likely to take place?

19.3 Sets

> **CONCEPT:** A set is a collection that lets you quickly find a value in a large amount of data. A set stores elements in an unordered sequence, and does not allow duplicates.

Sometimes when data is stored in a list, you know the exact location of specific items. For example, suppose we have a list that holds the total sales for each month of the year. The list has twelve elements, with the indices 0 through 11. We know that January's sales amount is stored at index 0, February's sales amount is stored at index 1, and so forth. If we want to retrieve the sales amount for December, we know that we have to retrieve the element at index 11. In the list, the sales for month n is stored at index $n - 1$.

Sometimes, we need to retrieve a particular element from a collection, but we do not know the location of that element. For example, suppose we have a collection of Customer objects, and we need to search for a particular object by the customer's name. Customer objects are added to and removed from the collection on a daily basis, and we have no way of knowing where a particular object is stored. If the objects are stored in a list, finding a particular customer means sequentially searching the list until we find the element we are looking for. This could be a time-consuming process if there are a large number of objects in the list.

Perhaps a set is the best type of collection to use in this situation—if fast retrieval is important. Sets are useful when you have a large collection of data, and you must retrieve an element from the collection by searching for its value. The elements in a set are stored in a data structure that is optimized for this type of retrieval.

It is helpful to compare sets to lists. A list will allow you to append an element at the end, add an element at the beginning, or insert an element at a specific position within the list. In contrast, a set element is not associated with a position within the set. Sets are also different from lists in another way: they do not allow duplicate elements. Each element in a set must be unique.

The Set Interface

The Set interface extends the Collection interface, so it inherits all of the methods specified by Collection. (See Table 19-2 for a description of the methods specified by the Collection interface.) The Set interface does not add any additional methods of its own, but it does place restrictions on many of the methods inherited from Collection. These restrictions enforce the requirement that a set cannot contain duplicate elements.

The HashSet Class

The first concrete set class that we will study is the HashSet class, which implements the Set interface. The HashSet class uses hash codes to store its elements in a way that makes searching faster. To understand how a HashSet works, first you must understand the concept of a hash code.

A *hash code* is an integer value that is characteristic of an object. You use a *hashing algorithm* to calculate a hash code for an object. There are many different hashing algorithms, ranging from the simple to the complex. Although we will not conduct an in-depth study of hashing algorithms, later in this section we will look at some simple techniques for calculating hash codes.

Hashing algorithms typically use the data that is stored in an object to calculate the object's hash code. For example, if we were to calculate the hash code for a string, we would somehow use the characters making up the string in the calculation. Perhaps we would use each character's Unicode value in a mathematical formula that would give us an integer value.

Ideally, our hashing algorithm would produce different hash codes for different strings. For example, the hash code for "Fred" would be different from the hash code for "Wilma".

In addition to producing different hash codes for different objects, an ideal hashing algorithm should produce the same hash code for objects that are equal in value. For example, suppose we have the following two String objects, str1 and str2:

```
String str1 = new String("Fred");
String str2 = new String("Fred");
```

Although str1 and str2 are different objects, they contain equal data and a hashing algorithm should produce the same hash code for both.

In Java, every object has a hashCode method that is inherited from the Object class. This method returns a hash code for the object. The hashCode method that is inherited from the Object class, however, is rarely adequate because it returns a value that is based on the object's memory address. The value that is returned from the Object class's hashCode method is unique for every object, even objects that contain the same data. For this reason, the Object class's hashCode method must usually be overridden so that it returns the same hash code for equivalent objects.

Hash codes are at the heart of how the HashSet class works. When an object is added to a HashSet, the HashSet calls the object's hashCode method to get its hash code. Then it checks to see if an object with the same hash code has already been stored in the set. (Remember, a set does not allow duplicates.) If it finds that an object with the same hash code is already in the set, it performs one more test: it calls the object's equals method to see if it reports that the two objects are equal. If they are, the HashSet does not store the object in the set.

You might be wondering why a HashSet does not simply refuse to store an object as soon as it finds another object with the same hash code already in the set. Earlier, we said that an ideal hashing algorithm would produce different hash codes for different values. That is true, but hashing algorithms are not usually ideal. Occasionally, a hashing algorithm will produce the same hash code for two objects that are not equal. This is called a *collision*.

Because collisions can occur, the HashSet performs two tests, one using the hashCode method and the other using the equals method, to determine whether an object's value is already in the set.

Because collisions sometimes occur with hashing algorithms, it is possible that when a new object is added to a HashSet it will have the same hash code as an object already in the set, but it will not be equal to that object (the two objects will contain different data). In this case, the HashSet must allow the new object to be added to the set.

One popular way of thinking about hash codes is that they identify "buckets" in the HashSet. Each individual hash code has its own bucket, and all objects in the set that have that hash code are stored in that hash code's bucket. So, some buckets will have only one object stored in them, while other buckets will contain multiple objects. In pseudocode, the following is the procedure followed by the HashSet class to add a new object:

Call the new object's hashCode *method to get the object's hash code.*
If that hash code's bucket is empty, Then
    Store the object in the bucket for that hash code.
Else
    Use the object's equals *method to compare it to each object in the bucket.*
    If it is not equal to any other object in the bucket, Then
        Store the object in the bucket.
    Else
        Do not store the new object.
    End If
End If

TIP: Because the hashCode and equals methods are used together like this, any time you override the Object class's equals method you should also override the hashCode method.

The HashSet class has four constructors, which are summarized in Table 19-6. Note that when a HashSet is constructed, it has an initial capacity and a load factor. The *initial capacity* is the number of "buckets" that the HashSet initially has. The *load factor* is the percentage of the buckets that have to be occupied before the capacity is increased. For example, with a load factor of 0.75, the capacity will be increased when 75 percent of the buckets have a value stored in them.

Table 19-6 HashSet constructors

HashSet()	This constructor creates an empty HashSet object with an initial capacity of 16 and a load factor of 0.75.
HashSet(Collection<? extends E> c)	This constructor creates a HashSet object and stores the elements of the collection c in it. The initial capacity will be at least enough to hold the elements of c, and the load factor will be 0.75. Throws a NullPointerException if c is a null reference.
HashSet(int initialCapacity, float loadFactor)	This constructor creates an empty HashSet object with the specified initial capacity and load factor.
HashSet(int initialCapacity)	This constructor creates an empty HashSet object with the specified initial capacity and a load factor of 0.75.

Now, let's look at a simple example of how we can store String objects in a HashSet. The program in Code Listing 19-6 creates a HashSet and adds a group of String objects to it. Then it attempts to add a duplicate String object to the set.

Code Listing 19-6   (HashSetDemo1.java)

```
1 import java.util.*;
2
3 /**
```

```
 4    This program demonstrates how to add elements to a HashSet.
 5    It also shows that duplicate elements are not allowed.
 6 */
 7 public class HashSetDemo1
 8 {
 9     public static void main(String[] args)
10     {
11         // Create a HashSet to hold String objects.
12         Set<String> fruitSet = new HashSet<>();
13
14         // Add some strings to the set.
15         fruitSet.add("Apple");
16         fruitSet.add("Banana");
17         fruitSet.add("Pear");
18         fruitSet.add("Strawberry");
19
20         // Display the elements in the set.
21         System.out.println("Here are the elements.");
22         System.out.println(fruitSet);
23
24         // Try to add a duplicate element.
25         System.out.println("\nTrying to add Banana to"
26                 + "the set again . . .");
27         if (!fruitSet.add("Banana"))
28         {
29             System.out.println("Banana was not added again.");
30         }
31
32         // Display the elements in the set.
33         System.out.println("\nHere are the elements once more.");
34         System.out.println(fruitSet);
35     }
36 }
```

Program Output

```
Here are the elements.
[Apple, Pear, Strawberry, Banana]

Trying to add Banana to the set again...
Banana was not added again.

Here are the elements once more.
[Apple, Pear, Strawberry, Banana]
```

Take a closer look at lines 27–30:

```
if (!fruitSet.add("Banana"))
{
    System.out.println("Banana was not added again.");
}
```

The HashSet class's add method does not throw an exception if it is called with a duplicate item. It simply does not add the item. The method does return a boolean value, however, indicating whether the item was added. The statement shown here calls the add method, passing "Banana" as an argument. Because "Banana" is already in the set, the method returns false indicating that it was not added again.

The program in Code Listing 19-7 shows another demonstration. It uses the second constructor shown in Table 19-6 to create a HashSet from a previously created collection of names, and then gets an iterator to step through the set and print its elements. The program also calls the HashSet class's contains method to determine whether an object has been stored in the set.

Code Listing 19-7

```
 1 import java.util.*;
 2
 3 /**
 4    This program creates a HashSet with names in it,
 5    gets an iterator for the set, and searches the
 6    set for names.
 7 */
 8
 9 public class HashSetDemo2
10 {
11     public static void main(String[] args)
12     {
13         // Create a HashSet to hold names.
14         List<String> nameList =
15                 Arrays.asList("Chris", "David", "Katherine", "Kenny");
16         Set<String> nameSet = new HashSet<>(nameList);
17
18         // Get an iterator for the set.
19         Iterator<String> it = nameSet.iterator();
20
21         // Display the elements in the set.
22         System.out.println("Here are the names in the set.");
23         while (it.hasNext())
24         {
25             System.out.println(it.next());
26         }
27         System.out.println();
28
```

```
29              // Search for "Katherine". We should find this
30              // name in the set.
31              if (nameSet.contains("Katherine"))
32              {
33                  System.out.println("Katherine is in the set.");
34              } else
35              {
36                  System.out.println("Katherine is NOT in the set.");
37              }
38
39              // Search for "Bethany". We should not find
40              // this name in the set.
41              if (nameSet.contains("Bethany"))
42              {
43                  System.out.println("Bethany is in the set.");
44              } else
45              {
46                  System.out.println("Bethany is NOT in the set.");
47              }
48      }
49  }
```

Program Output

```
Here are the names in the set.
Chris
Katherine
David
Kenny

Katherine is in the set.
Bethany is NOT in the set.
```

Implementing Your Own `hashCode` Method

When you design a class, you will need to override the `hashCode` and `equals` methods if you want to store objects of the class in a `HashSet`. Here are three guidelines that you should follow when writing your own `hashCode` and `equals` methods:

1. If you call an object's `hashCode` method more than once during the execution of an application, the method should consistently return the same value. The only exception is when something in the object has changed, which would affect the way the `equals` method makes comparisons.
2. If the `equals` method reports that two objects are equal, then both objects' `hashCode` methods should return the same value.
3. If the `equals` method reports that two objects are *not* equal, it is permissible for both objects to have the same hash code. You should be aware, however, that having too many unequal objects with the same hash code will degrade the performance of an algorithm that uses the hash codes for searching.

The String class uses the following formula to calculate a hash code for a string:

$$hashCode = S_0 * 31^{(n-1)} + S_1 * 31^{(n-2)} + \ldots + S_{n-1}$$

In the formula, n is the number of characters in the string, S_0 is the Unicode value of the character at position 0, S_1 is the Unicode value of the character at position 1, and S_{n-1} is the Unicode value of the character at position $n-1$.

The algorithm used by the String class is moderately complex. Other classes use a simpler approach. For example, the Character class simply uses the character's Unicode value as its hash code. The Integer class uses the actual integer value of the object as its hash code.

Code Listing 19-8 shows a Car class that we will use to hold a VIN (vehicle identification number) and description of a car. These fields are stored as the String objects vin and description. In this class, we have overridden the hashCode method to simply return the hash code of vin. This should be adequate because each car has its own unique VIN. We have also overridden the equals method to return true if both objects have the same VIN.

Code Listing 19-8   **(Car.java)**

```
 1 /**
 2    The Car class stores a VIN (Vehicle Identification Number)
 3    and a description for a car.
 4 */
 5 public class Car
 6 {
 7     private String vin; // Vehicle Identification Number
 8     private String description; // Car description
 9
10     /**
11        Constructor
12
13        @param v The VIN for the car.
14        @param desc The description of the car.
15     */
16     public Car(String v, String desc)
17     {
18         vin = v;
19         description = desc;
20     }
21
22     /**
23        getVin method
24
25        @return The car's VIN.
26     */
27     public String getVin()
28     {
29         return vin;
```

```
30        }
31
32        /**
33          getDescription method
34
35          @return The car's description.
36        */
37        public String getDescription()
38        {
39            return description;
40        }
41
42        /**
43          toString method
44
45          @return A string containing the VIN and description.
46        */
47        public String toString()
48        {
49            return "VIN:" + vin
50                    + "\tDescription:"
51                    + description;
52        }
53
54        /**
55          hashCode method
56
57          @return A hash code for this car.
58        */
59        public int hashCode()
60        {
61            return vin.hashCode();
62        }
63
64        /**
65          equals method
66
67          @param obj Another object to compare this object to.
68          @return true if the two objects are equal, false otherwise.
69        */
70        public boolean equals(Object obj)
71        {
72            // Make sure the other object is a Car.
73            if (obj == null || !(obj instanceof Car) )
74                return false;
75            else
76            {
77                // Both are cars: Get a reference to other
```

```
78               // object as a car and check if their VIN
79               // numbers are the same.
80               Car tempCar = (Car) obj;
81               return vin.equalsIgnoreCase(tempCar.vin);
82        }
83    }
84 }
```

The program in Code Listing 19-9 tests the class by adding several Car objects to a HashSet. Then the HashSet is searched for two Car objects: one that is in the set, and one that is not.

Code Listing 19-9   (CarHashSet.java)

```
1 import java.util.*;
2
3 /**
4    This program stores Car objects in a HashSet and then
5    searches for various objects.
6 */
7 public class CarHashSet
8 {
9     public static void main(String[] args)
10    {
11        // Create a HashSet to store Car objects.
12        Set<Car> carSet = new HashSet<>();
13
14        // Add some Car objects to the HashSet.
15        carSet.add(new Car("227H54", "1997 Volkswagen"));
16        carSet.add(new Car("448A69", "1965 Mustang"));
17        carSet.add(new Car("453B55", "2007 Porsche"));
18        carSet.add(new Car("177R60", "1980 BMW"));
19
20        // Display the elements in the HashSet.
21        System.out.println("Here are the cars in the set:");
22        for (Car c : carSet)
23        {
24            System.out.println(c);
25        }
26        System.out.println();
27
28        // Search for a specific car. This one is in the set.
29        Car mustang = new Car("448A69", "1965 Mustang");
30        System.out.println("Searching for" + mustang);
31        if (carSet.contains(mustang))
32        {
33            System.out.println("The Mustang is in the set.");
34        } else
```

```
35              {
36                  System.out.println("The Mustang is NOT in the set.");
37              }
38
39              // Search for another car. This one is not in the set.
40              Car plymouth = new Car("911C87", "2000 Plymouth");
41              System.out.println("Searching for" + plymouth);
42              if (carSet.contains(plymouth))
43              {
44                  System.out.println("The Plymouth is in the set.");
45              } else
46              {
47                  System.out.println("The Plymouth is NOT in the set.");
48              }
49          }
50  }
```

Program Output

```
Here are the cars in the set:
VIN: 177R60 Description: 1980 BMW
VIN: 227H54 Description: 1997 Volkswagen
VIN: 448A69 Description: 1965 Mustang
VIN: 453B55 Description: 2007 Porsche

Searching for VIN: 448A69  Description: 1965 Mustang
The Mustang is in the set.
Searching for VIN: 911C87  Description: 2000 Plymouth
The Plymouth is NOT in the set.
```

The `LinkedHashSet` Class

You might have noticed that in the program output of Code Listings 19-6, 19-7, and 19-9, the order in which the `HashSet` elements are displayed does not match the order in which they were added to the set. Sets have no concept of internal position of their elements, and they do not keep track of the order of insertion. When you iterate through a `HashSet`, you should not expect the iterator to return elements in the order of their insertion.

If you need to access set elements in the order that they were inserted, you can use the `LinkedHashSet` class instead of `HashSet`. The `LinkedHashSet` class, which extends `HashSet`, keeps an internal linked list that references the elements of the set in the order that they were inserted. This gives you the ability of iterating through the set in that order.

The `LinkedHashSet` class's constructors and methods are identical to those of the `HashSet` method. The program in Code Listing 19-10 creates two sets: a `HashSet` and a `LinkedHashSet`. The same `String` objects are stored in each set.

Code Listing 19-10   (`LinkedHashSetDemo.java`)

```java
 1 import java.util.*;
 2
 3 /**
 4   This program demonstrates how a LinkedHashSet
 5   preserves the order in which elements are added.
 6 */
 7 public class LinkedHashSetDemo
 8 {
 9     public static void main(String[] args)
10     {
11         // List of fruits to put in hash sets.
12         List<String> fruitList =
13                 Arrays.asList("Apple", "Strawberry", "Pear", "Banana");
14
15         // Create the HashSet.
16         Set<String> set1 = new HashSet<>(fruitList);
17
18         // Now create the LinkedHashSet.
19         Set<String> set2 = new LinkedHashSet<>(fruitList);
20
21         // Display the elements in the HashSet.
22         System.out.println("Here are the elements in"
23                 + "the HashSet:");
24         System.out.println(set1);
25
26         // Now display the elements in the LinkedHashSet.
27         System.out.println("\nAnd here are the elements"
28                 + "in the LinkedHashSet:");
29          System.out.println(set2);
30     }
31 }
```

Program Output

```
Here are the elements in the HashSet:
[Apple, Pear, Strawberry, Banana]

And here are the elements in the LinkedHashSet:
[Apple, Strawberry, Pear, Banana]
```

The `SortedSet` Interface and the `TreeSet` Class

The `Set` interface has a subinterface called `SortedSet` whose methods are shown in Table 19-7.

Table 19-7 `SortedSet<E>` methods

`Comparator <? super E> comparator()`	This method returns a reference to the comparator used with this `SortedSet`. We discuss comparators later in this section.
`E first()`	Returns the first element in this set. This will be the element with the lowest value.
`SortedSet<E> headSet(E toElement)`	Returns a `SortedSet` that serves as a "view" into this `SortedSet`. The elements in the set that are returned are all less in value than the element specified by `toElement`. The elements in the set that are returned are merely references to elements in this set, so any changes made to the elements in the returned set are reflected in this set.
`E last()`	Returns the last element in this set. This will be the element with the highest value.
`SortedSet<E> subSet(E fromElement, E toElement)`	Returns a `SortedSet` that serves as a "view" into this `SortedSet`. The elements in the set that are returned are greater than or equal to the element specified by `fromElement`, and less than the element specified by `toElement`. The elements in the set that are returned are merely references to elements in this set, so any changes made to the elements in the returned set are reflected in this set.
`SortedSet<E> tailSet(E fromElement)`	Returns a `SortedSet` that serves as a "view" into this `SortedSet`. The elements in the set that are returned are all greater in value than the element specified by `fromElement`. The elements in the set that are returned are merely references to elements in this set, so any changes made to the elements in the returned set are reflected in this set.

A `SortedSet` is a set in which the elements are sorted according to their natural order. A class of objects has a *natural order* if it is possible to determine for any two objects of the class whether one object is equal to, or "less than," or "greater than" the other. In this context, *less than* and *greater than* refers to which element should precede the other on the natural ordering of that class. For example, the natural order of numbers is to order them in increasing order. For strings, the natural order is alphabetic order.

A class imposes a natural order on its objects by implementing the `Comparable` interface. We looked at this interface in Chapter 18 when we were studying generics. Recall that the `Comparable` interface specifies a method named `compareTo`, which is used to compare the calling object with another object that is passed as an argument to the method. This is how the `compareTo` method works:

- If the calling object is less than the object passed as an argument, the method returns a negative number.
- If the calling object is equal to the object passed as an argument, the method returns 0.
- If the calling object is greater than the object passed as an argument, the method returns a positive number.

There is a JCF class called `TreeSet` that implements the `SortedSet` interface. If you create a `TreeSet` using that class's no-arg constructor, the tree set will sort objects added to it by their natural order. The program in Code Listing 19-11 demonstrates this by creating a `TreeSet` and using it to sort strings. This works because the `String` class implements the `Comparable` interface.

Code Listing 19-11   (`TreeSetDemo1.java`)

```java
 1 import java.util.*;
 2
 3 /**
 4    This program demonstrates how a TreeSet sorts
 5    its elements in ascending order.
 6 */
 7 public class TreeSetDemo1
 8 {
 9     public static void main(String[] args)
10     {
11         // Create a TreeSet and store some values in it.
12         SortedSet<String> mySet = new TreeSet<>();
13         mySet.add("Pear");
14         mySet.add("Apple");
15         mySet.add("Strawberry");
16         mySet.add("Banana");
17
18         // Display the elements in the TreeSet.
19         System.out.println("Here are the TreeSet elements"
20                 + "in ascending order:");
21         System.out.println(mySet);
22
23         // Add a new element to the TreeSet.
24         System.out.println("\nAdding Blueberry to the set.");
25         mySet.add("Blueberry");
26
27         // Display the elements again.
28         System.out.println("\nHere are the TreeSet elements"
29                 + "again:");
30         System.out.println(mySet);
31     }
32 }
```

Program Output

```
Here are the TreeSet elements in ascending order:
[Apple, Banana, Pear, Strawberry]

Adding Blueberry to the set.

Here are the TreeSet elements again:
[Apple, Banana, Blueberry, Pear, Strawberry]
```

Using a Comparator to Compare Objects

If the objects that you wish to store in a `TreeSet` do not implement the `Comparable` interface, you can still store them in the `TreeSet` by creating a comparator. A *comparator* is an object that can compare two other objects and determine whether one is greater than, less than, or equal to the other. A comparator implements the `Comparator` interface, which is in the `java.util` package. The `Comparator` interface has two abstract methods:

```
public interface Comparator<T>
{
    public int compare(T obj1, T obj2);
    public boolean equals(Object obj);
}
```

 NOTE: Beginning with Java 8, the `Comparator` interface contains other methods besides `compare` and `equals`.

Table 19-8 describes the two abstract methods specified by the `Comparator` interface.

Table 19-8   Abstract methods of the `Comparator<T>` interface

`public int compare(T obj1, T obj2)`	This method compares `obj1` with `obj2` and returns 0 if the two objects are equal, a negative value if `obj1` is less than `obj2`, and a positive value if `obj1` is greater than `obj2`.
`public boolean equals(Object obj)`	This method determines whether this comparator is equal to the object `obj`. If the two are equal, it returns `true`.

Code Listing 19-12 shows an example of a `Comparator` class that can compare `Car` objects. The compare method accepts references to two `Car` objects. It gets each car's VIN, which is a `String`, and then uses the `String` class's `compareToIgnoreCase` method to compare the two VINs.

Code Listing 19-12   **(CarComparator.java)**

```
1  import java.util.Comparator;
2
3  public class CarComparator
4         implements Comparator<Car>
5  {
6      public int compare(Car car1, Car car2)
7      {
8          // Get the two cars' VINs.
9          String vin1 = car1.getVin();
10         String vin2 = car2.getVin();
```

```
11
12          // Compare the VINs and return the
13          // result of the comparison.
14          return vin1.compareToIgnoreCase(vin2);
15      }
16 }
```

> **NOTE:** We did not provide an `equals` method in the `CarComparator` class, even though it is specified in the `Comparator` interface. The `Object` class provides an `equals` method, so we will not get an error when we compile this class. If we wanted to be able to compare objects of this class with other comparators, we would have provided an `equals` method.

The program in Code Listing 19-13 demonstrates how to create a `TreeSet` that uses a `CarComparator` to compare its elements. If you pass a comparator object as an argument to the `TreeSet` constructor, the `TreeSet` will use the comparator to perform comparisons.

Code Listing 19-13   **(TreeSetDemo2.java)**

```
1 import java.util.*;
2
3 /**
4    This program demonstrates how a TreeSet can use
5    a Comparator to sort its elements.
6 */
7 public class TreeSetDemo2
8 {
9      public static void main(String[] args)
10     {
11         // Create a TreeSet and pass an instance of
12         // CarComparator to it.
13         SortedSet<Car> carSet
14                 = new TreeSet<>(new CarComparator());
15
16         // Add some Car objects to the TreeSet.
17         carSet.add(new Car("227H54", "1997 Volkswagen"));
18         carSet.add(new Car("453B55", "2007 Porsche"));
19         carSet.add(new Car("177R60", "1980 BMW"));
20         carSet.add(new Car("448A69", "1965 Mustang"));
21
22         // Display the elements in the TreeSet.
23         System.out.println("Here are the cars sorted in"
24                 + "order of their VINs:");
25         for (Car car : carSet)
26         {
27             System.out.println(car);
```

```
28          }
29     }
30 }
```

Program Output

```
Here are the cars sorted in order of their VINs:
VIN: 177R60 Description: 1980 BMW
VIN: 227H54 Description: 1997 Volkswagen
VIN: 448A69 Description: 1965 Mustang
VIN: 453B55 Description: 2007 Porsche
```

Table 19-9 summarizes some of the most frequently used `TreeSet` constructors.

Table 19-9 `TreeSet<E>` constructors

`TreeSet()`	This constructor creates an empty `TreeSet` object. Any objects added to the `TreeSet` must implement the `Comparable` interface.
`TreeSet(Collection<? extends E> c)`	This constructor creates a `TreeSet` object and stores the elements of the collection c in it. The elements of c must implement the `Comparable` interface.
`TreeSet(Comparator<? extends E> c)`	This constructor creates a `TreeSet` object and uses c, a comparator, to compare its elements.

 Checkpoint

19.21 What is a hash code?

19.22 What method do you call to get an object's hash code?

19.23 In hashing, what is a collision?

19.24 What does the `HashSet` class's `add` method do when you try to add a duplicate item?

19.25 Any time you override the `Object` class's `equals` method, what other method should you also override?

19.26 Which concrete set class should you use if you need to access its elements in the order that they were inserted?

19.27 Which concrete set class should you use if you need to retrieve its elements in their natural order?

19.28 What is a comparator? What interface must it implement?

 **19.4 Maps**

CONCEPT: Each element in a map has two parts: a key and a value. Each key is associated with a specific value, and can be used to locate that value.

Each element in a *map* has two parts: a key and a value. Each key is associated with a specific value, and can be used to locate that value. For example, suppose we wish to store employee names in a map, and we want to search for specific employees by their ID numbers. Each time we store an employee's name in the map as a value, we also store that employee's ID number as a key. The map creates an association between the value and the key, and allows us to retrieve the name by searching for the ID number. The elements in a map are referred to as *mappings*.

There are a number of similarities between sets and maps. In fact, you can think of a map as storing a set of keys, with each key in the map's *key set* being associated with a value. Just as the JCF has a `Set` interface, there is a `Map` interface. Just as the `HashSet` and `LinkedHashSet` classes implement the `Set` interface; there are `HashMap` and `LinkedHashMap` classes that implement the `Map` interface. Just as `Set` has a `SortedSet` subinterface; `Map` has a `SortedMap` subinterface. Finally, there is a `TreeMap` class that implements the `SortedMap` interface, mirroring the way that `TreeSet` implements the `SortedSet` interface.

The map interface is generic, and is parameterized by two type variables K and V. These respectively stand for the classes representing the key and value objects. Table 19-10 lists some of the more commonly used methods specified by the `Map<K,V>` interface.

Table 19-10   Methods specified by the `Map<K,V>` interface

`void clear()`	Clears the map of all its elements. (This is an optional method. If the map does not support it, it throws an `UnsupportedOperationException`.)
`boolean containsKey(Object key)`	Returns `true` if this map contains a value that is associated with the specified key.
`boolean containsValue(Object value)`	Returns `true` if this map contains one or more keys mapped to the specified value.
`Set< Map.Entry<K,V> > entrySet()`	Returns a set that serves as a "view" into this map, containing all of the map's mappings. The elements in the set that is returned all implement the `Map.Entry` interface. (`Entry` is defined as an inner interface in the `Map` interface.) The elements in the set that is returned are merely references to elements in this set, so any changes made to the elements in the returned set are reflected in this map.
`void forEach(BiConsumer<? super K,? super V> action)`	Calls the action method on each key and value pair in this map.
`V get(Object key)`	Returns the value that is associated with the specified key. If the key does not map to a value, the method returns null.
`boolean isEmpty()`	Returns `true` if this map contains no mappings.
`Set<K> keySet()`	Returns a set that contains all of the keys in this map. The set that is returned serves as a "view" into this map. The elements in the set are merely references to the keys in this map, so any changes made to the elements in the returned set are reflected in this map.

(table continues next page)

Table 19-10 Methods specified by the `Map<K,V>` interface (continued)

`V put(K key, V value)`	This method puts a mapping in the map. The specified key is mapped to the specified value. If an existing mapping for this key exists, it is replaced by this mapping. The method returns the previous value that was associated with this key, or `null` if there was no value associated with this key previously.
`V remove(Object key)`	If a mapping for the specified key exists, it is removed. A reference to the value that the key was previously mapped to is returned.
`int size()`	Returns the number of mappings in this map.
`Collection<V> values()`	Returns a collection that contains all of the values in this map. The collection that is returned serves as a "view" into this map. The elements in the collection are merely references to the values in this map, so any changes made to the elements in the returned collection are reflected in this map.

The `HashMap` Class

VideoNote
The HashMap
Class

The `HashMap` class is a concrete class that implements the `Map` interface. Like a `HashSet`, a `HashMap` uses hash codes to store and retrieve data. Specifically, the `HashMap` class stores keys by their hash codes. Table 19-11 summarizes the `HashMap` constructors. Some of these constructors will look familiar because they are similar to the `HashSet` constructors. Because the `HashMap` class uses hash codes to store keys, it provides constructors that allow you to specify initial capacity and load factor. (See the previous section on the `HashSet` class for a discussion of initial capacity and load factor.)

Table 19-11 `HashMap<K, V>` constructors

`HashMap()`	This constructor creates an empty `HashMap` object with an initial capacity of 16 and a load factor of 0.75.
`HashMap(Map<? Extends K, ? extends V> m)`	This constructor creates a `HashMap` object and stores the mappings of the map m in it. The initial capacity will be at least enough to hold the elements of m, and the load factor will be 0.75. Throws a `NullPointerException` if m is a null reference.
`HashMap(int initialCapacity, float loadFactor)`	This constructor creates an empty `HashMap` object with the specified initial capacity and load factor.
`HashMap(int initialCapacity)`	This constructor creates an empty `HashMap` object with the specified initial capacity and a load factor of 0.75.

The program in Code Listing 19-14 demonstrates a simple `HashMap` for storing `Car` objects. This application uses VINs (vehicle identification numbers) as keys, and `Car` objects as values. As a result, the `HashMap` will allow us to search for a specific `Car` object by specifying its VIN.

Code Listing 19-14 (`CarHashMap1.java`)

```java
1 import java.util.*;
2
3 /**
4    This program stores mappings in a HashMap and then
5    searches for various objects.
6 */
7
8 public class CarHashMap1
9 {
10    public static void main(String[] args)
11    {
12       // Create a HashMap to store Car objects.
13       Map<String, Car> carMap = new HashMap<>();
14
15       // Create some Car objects.
16       Car vw = new Car("227H54", "1997 Volkswagen");
17       Car mustang = new Car("448A69", "1965 Mustang");
18       Car porsche = new Car("453B55", "2007 Porsche");
19       Car bmw = new Car("177R60", "1980 BMW");
20
21       // Put some mappings into the HashMap. In each
22       // mapping, the car's VIN is the key and the
23       // Car object containing that VIN is the value.
24       carMap.put(vw.getVin(), vw);
25       carMap.put(mustang.getVin(), mustang);
26       carMap.put(porsche.getVin(), porsche);
27       carMap.put(bmw.getVin(), bmw);
28
29       // Search for the Mustang by its VIN.
30       System.out.println("\nSearching for the car with" +
31                          "VIN" + mustang.getVin());
32       Car foundCar = carMap.get(mustang.getVin());
33
34       // If the car was found, display it.
35       if (foundCar != null)
36          System.out.println(foundCar);
37       else
38          System.out.println("The Mustang is NOT in the set.");
39
40       // Search for another VIN. This one is not in the set.
41       System.out.println("\nSearching for the car with" +
42                          "VIN 911C87");
43       foundCar = carMap.get("911C87");
44
45       // If the car was found display it.
```

```
46          if (foundCar != null)
47              System.out.println(foundCar);
48          else
49              System.out.println("That car is NOT in the set.");
50      }
51  }
```

Program Output

```
Searching for the car with VIN 448A69
VIN: 448A69 Description: 1965 Mustang

Searching for the car with VIN 911C87
That car is NOT in the set.
```

The statement in line 13 creates the `HashMap`:

```
Map<String, Car> carMap = new HashMap<>();
```

Note that the `Map<K, V>` interface has been specialized to `Map<String, Car>` because `String` is the data type of the keys and `Car` is the data type of the values.

The statements in lines 16 through 19 create four `Car` objects: one for a VW, one for a Mustang, one for a Porsche, and one for a BMW. Then, the statements in lines 24 through 27 use the `put` method to create several mappings in the `HashMap`. For example, look at the statement in line 24:

```
carMap.put(vw.getVin(), vw);
```

The `put` method puts a mapping into the `HashMap`. The first argument is the key, and the second argument is the value to associate with the key. In this program, we are creating mappings between VINs and `Car` objects. In each mapping, the key is a VIN and the value is the `Car` object that goes with that VIN. In this statement, we are creating a mapping that associates the VW's VIN with the VW's `Car` object. The statements in lines 24 through 27 create similar mappings for the other `Car` objects.

Line 32 shows how we can search for a specific `Car` object:

```
Car foundCar = carMap.get(mustang.getVin());
```

This statement creates a `Car` reference variable, `foundCar`, and assigns to it the value returned from the `carMap.get` method. The `get` method accepts a key as its argument and it returns the value that the key is mapped to. In this statement, we are passing the Mustang's VIN as the argument. We are basically saying to the `HashMap` "Give me the `Car` object that is associated with this VIN." If the key is found in the `HashMap`, the method returns a reference to the value that is associated with that key. Because the Mustang's VIN is indeed found as a key in the `HashMap`, this statement returns a reference to the mustang object and assigns to `foundCar`.

In line 43 we aren't so lucky. Here we pass to the `get` method a VIN that does not exist in the `HashMap`:

```
foundCar = carMap.get("911C87");
```

As a result, the method will return `null`.

Unlike the Set<E> and List<E> interfaces, Map<K, V> does not extend the Collection<E> interface. And unlike the other collections, maps do not provide iterators. One way to iterate over the contents of a map is to convert its mappings to some other type of collection. For example, you can use the keyset() method to get a set that contains all of the keys in a map, and you can use the values() method to get a collection that contains all of the map's values. Then you can iterate over the resulting set or collection. Code Listing 19-15 shows an example.

Code Listing 19-15 (CarHashMap2.java)

```
1 import java.util.*;
2
3 /**
4    This program retrieves a set of keys and a
5    collection of values from a HashMap.
6 */
7
8 public class CarHashMap2
9 {
10     public static void main(String[] args)
11     {
12         // Create a HashMap to store Car objects.
13         Map<String, Car> carMap =  new HashMap<>();
14
15         // Create some Car objects.
16         Car vw = new Car("227H54", "1997 Volkswagen");
17         Car mustang = new Car("448A69", "1965 Mustang");
18         Car porsche = new Car("453B55", "2007 Porsche");
19         Car bmw = new Car("177R60", "1980 BMW");
20
21         // Put some mappings into the HashMap. In each
22         // mapping, the car's VIN is the key and the
23         // Car object containing that VIN is the value.
24         carMap.put(vw.getVin(), vw);
25         carMap.put(mustang.getVin(), mustang);
26         carMap.put(porsche.getVin(), porsche);
27         carMap.put(bmw.getVin(), bmw);
28
29         // Get a set containing the keys in this map.
30         Set<String> keys = carMap.keySet();
31
32         // Iterate through the keys, printing each one.
33         System.out.println("Here are the keys:");
34         for (String k : keys)
35             System.out.println(k);
36
37         // Get a collection containing the values.
```

```
38          Collection<Car> values = carMap.values();
39
40          // Iterate through the values, printing each one.
41          System.out.println("\nHere are the values:");
42          for (Car c : values)
43              System.out.println(c);
44      }
45 }
```

Program Output

```
Here are the keys:
177R60
227H54
448A69
453B55

Here are the values:
VIN: 177R60    Description: 1980 BMW
VIN: 227H54    Description: 1997 Volkswagen
VIN: 448A69    Description: 1965 Mustang
VIN: 453B55    Description: 2007 Porsche
```

 NOTE: The set and the collection that are returned from the keyset and values methods serve as "views" into the map. The elements in the set and collection are merely references to the entries in the map, so any changes made to the elements in the set or collection are reflected in the map, and vice versa.

In Code Listing 19-15, the keys and values of the map are retrieved separately. You can also retrieve a single set that contains all the key-value pairs stored in the map. This is done by the map's entrySet method.

The entrySet method returns a set of Map.Entry objects. Entry is an inner interface in the Map interface. Two of the methods specified by Map.Entry are getKey and getValue. The getKey method returns the key and getValue returns the value. The program in Code Listing 19-16 demonstrates the entrySet method and how to access the keys and values of the Set elements it returns.

Code Listing 19-16   (CarHashMap3.java)

```
1 import java.util.*;
2
3 /**
4    This program retrieves the mappings from a HashMap
5    as a Set of Map.Entry objects.
6 */
7
```

```
 8 public class CarHashMap3
 9 {
10    public static void main(String[] args)
11    {
12       // Create a HashMap to store Car objects.
13       Map<String, Car> carMap = new HashMap<>();
14
15       // Create some Car objects.
16       Car vw = new Car("227H54", "1997 Volkswagen");
17       Car mustang = new Car("448A69", "1965 Mustang");
18       Car porsche = new Car("453B55", "2007 Porsche");
19       Car bmw = new Car("177R60", "1980 BMW");
20
21       // Put some mappings into the HashMap. In each
22       // mapping, the car's VIN is the key and the
23       // Car object containing that VIN is the value.
24       carMap.put(vw.getVin(), vw);
25       carMap.put(mustang.getVin(), mustang);
26       carMap.put(porsche.getVin(), porsche);
27       carMap.put(bmw.getVin(), bmw);
28
29       // Get a set containing the mappings in this map.
30       Set<Map.Entry<String, Car>> cars = carMap.entrySet();
31
32       // Iterate through the mappings, printing each one.
33       System.out.println("Here are the mappings:");
34       for (Map.Entry<String, Car> entry : cars)
35       {
36          System.out.println("Key =" + entry.getKey());
37          System.out.println("Value =" + entry.getValue());
38          System.out.println();
39       }
40    }
41 }
```

Program Output

```
Here are the mappings:
Key = 177R60
Value = VIN: 177R60    Description: 1980 BMW


Key = 227H54
Value = VIN: 227H54    Description: 1997 Volkswagen


Key = 448A69
Value = VIN: 448A69    Description: 1965 Mustang


Key = 453B55
Value = VIN: 453B55    Description: 2007 Porsche
```

> **NOTE:** The set that is returned from the entrySet()method also serves as a "view" into the map. The elements in the set are merely references to the entries in the map, so any changes made to the elements in the set are reflected in the map, and vice versa.

Java 8 adds to the Map<K, V> interface a default method

```
void forEach(BiConsumer<? super K,? super V> action)
```

that can be used to invoke an action on each key-value pair stored in a map. The action must implement the BiConsumer<? super K,? super V> interface. This means that the action function must have a type that is appropriately related to the type $(K, V) \rightarrow$ void; its parameters are a key and a value, and its return type is void. As usual, we can use a lambda expression for the action. If we adopt this technique, Lines 29-39 of Code Listing 19-16 can be replaced with:

```
System.out.println("Here are the mappings:");
carMap.forEach( (key, value) ->
            {
                System.out.println("Key = " + key);
                System.out.println("Value = " + value);
                System.out.println();
            });
```

The LinkedHashMap Class

Hashmap objects, like sets, have no concept of order for their elements. You will notice, for example, that the order in which the mappings are displayed in Code Listing 19-16 does not match the order in which they were put into the HashMap.

The LinkedHashMap class, which extends HashMap, allows you to access its mappings in one of two orders:

- Insertion order, which is the order in which the mappings were inserted into the map
- Access order, which is the order in which the mappings were last accessed

A LinkedHashMap keeps an internal linked list that references mappings. If you are using the map in insertion order mode, the linked list references the mappings in the order that they were inserted. If you are using the map in access order mode, the linked list references the mappings in the order that they were accessed with either put or get.

In access order mode, the mappings that have been accessed the most are placed at the end of the linked list, and the mappings that have been accessed the least are placed at the beginning. This mode is useful in applications that need to know which data items are being accessed the most or the least.

You indicate which sorting order you prefer with the appropriate LinkedHashMap constructor. Table 19-12 summarizes them.

Table 19-12 `LinkedHashMap` constructors

`LinkedHashMap()`	This constructor creates an empty `LinkedHashMap` using insertion-order mode, an initial capacity of 16, and a load factor of 0.75.
`LinkedHashMap(int initialCapacity)`	This constructor creates an empty `LinkedHashMap` using insertion-order mode, an initial capacity of the specified amount, and a load factor of 0.75.
`LinkedHashMap(int initialCapacity, float loadFactor)`	This constructor creates an empty `LinkedHashMap` using insertion-order mode and the specified values for initial capacity and a load factor.
`LinkedHashMap(int initialCapacity, float loadFactor, boolean accessOrder)`	This constructor creates an empty `LinkedHashMap` using the specified values for initial capacity and a load factor. If `accessOrder` is true, the map will use access-order mode. If `accessOrder` is false, the map will use insertion-order mode.
`LinkedHashMap(Map<? extends K, ? extends V> m)`	This constructor creates a `LinkedHashMap` and stores the mappings of the map m in it. The initial capacity will be at least enough to hold the elements of m, and the load factor will be 0.75. It throws a `NullPointerException` if m is a null reference.

The program in Code Listing 19-17 is a modification of Code Listing 19-16. In this version, a `LinkedHashMap` is used in insertion-ordering mode, and the `forEach()` method is used to display the mappings. In the program output, the mappings are displayed in the order that they were inserted into the map.

Code Listing 19-17 (`CarHashMap4.java`)

```
 1 import java.util.*;
 2
 3 /**
 4    This program retrieves the mappings from a HashMap
 5    as a Set of Map.Entry objects.
 6 */
 7
 8 public class CarHashMap4
 9 {
10    public static void main(String[] args)
11    {
12       // Create a HashMap to store Car objects.
13       Map<String, Car> carMap = new LinkedHashMap<>();
14
```

```
15        // Create some Car objects.
16        Car vw = new Car("227H54", "1997 Volkswagen");
17        Car mustang = new Car("448A69", "1965 Mustang");
18        Car porsche = new Car("453B55", "2007 Porsche");
19        Car bmw = new Car("177R60", "1980 BMW");
20
21        // Put some mappings into the HashMap. In each
22        // mapping, the car's VIN is the key and the
23        // Car object containing that VIN is the value.
24        carMap.put(vw.getVin(), vw);
25        carMap.put(mustang.getVin(), mustang);
26        carMap.put(porsche.getVin(), porsche);
27        carMap.put(bmw.getVin(), bmw);
28
29        // Iterate through the mappings, printing each one.
30        System.out.println("Here are the mappings:");
31        carMap.forEach( (key, value) ->
32                        {
33                            System.out.println("Key =" + key);
34                            System.out.println("Value =" + value);
35                            System.out.println();
36                        });
37    }
38 }
```

Program Output

```
Here are the mappings:
Key = 227H54
Value = VIN: 227H54  Description: 1997 Volkswagen

Key = 448A69
Value = VIN: 448A69  Description: 1965 Mustang

Key = 453B55
Value = VIN: 453B55  Description: 2007 Porsche

Key = 177R60
Value = VIN: 177R60  Description: 1980 BMW
```

The SortedMap Interface and the TreeMap Class

SortedMap<K, V> is a subinterface of Map<K, V> that allows maps to store mappings by key order. The TreeMap class implements SortedMap. Table 19-13 lists some of its constructors.

Table 19-13 TreeMap<K, V> constructors

TreeMap()	This constructor creates a tree map that orders keys by their natural order. The key type K must implement the Comparable interface.
TreeMap(Comparator<? super K> c)	This constructor creates a tree map that uses the comparator c to order the keys.

Using TreeMap is no different from using the other types of maps. For example, we can replace Line 13 of Code Listing 19-17 with:

```
SortedMap<String, Car> carMap = new TreeMap<>();
```

The program will create a tree map that will order its entries in alphabetical order of the VIN number. If we run the resulting program, the output will be as shown below.

Program Output for TreeMap version of Code Listing 19-17

```
Here are the mappings:
Key = 177R60
Value = VIN: 177R60  Description: 1980 BMW

Key = 227H54
Value = VIN: 227H54  Description: 1997 Volkswagen

Key = 448A69
Value = VIN: 448A69  Description: 1965 Mustang

Key = 453B55
Value = VIN: 453B55  Description: 2007 Porsche
```

 Checkpoint

19.29 Each element in a map is comprised of what two parts?

19.30 What part of a mapping does the HashMap store by its hash code?

19.31 The LinkedHashMap class allows you to retrieve mappings in what two orders?

19.32 How are the keys in a SortedMap sorted?

19.5 The Collections Class

CONCEPT: The Collections class provides numerous static methods for performing algorithms and utility operations on collections.

The JCF has a class named Collections which provides numerous static methods that perform useful operations on collections. Note that the name of this class, Collections, is plural, and should not be confused with the Collection interface.

Many of the methods in the `Collections` class perform operations on lists. There are methods for copying, sorting, searching, randomly shuffling, filling with a value, and many other procedures. Table 19-14 describes several of the `Collections` methods.

Table 19-14 Some of the static methods in the `Collections` class

`static <T> int binarySearch(List<? extends Comparable<? super T>> list, T key)`	
	Performs a binary search for the element specified by `key` in the list specified by `list`.
	Note that the elements in the list must implement the `Comparable` interface and be sorted according to their natural order. If the element is found, the method returns its index. Otherwise it returns a negative number.
`static <T> int binarySearch(List<? extends T> list, T key, Comparator<? super T> c)`	
	Performs a binary search for the element specified by `key` in the list specified by `list`.
	This version of the method uses the comparator `c` to make comparisons. If the element is found, the method returns its index. Otherwise, it returns a negative number. The list must be sorted in comparator order before it is passed to this method.
`static boolean disjoint (Collection<?> c1, Collection<?> c2)`	
	Returns `true` if the collections `c1` and `c2` have no elements in common.
`static <T extends Object & Comparable<? super T>> T max(Collection<? extends T> coll)`	
	Returns the maximum element in the collection `coll`. This method requires that all elements of `coll` implement the `Comparable` interface. There is a similar method `min` that returns the minimum.
`static <T> T max(Collection<? extends T>coll, Comparator<? super T> comp)`	
	Returns the maximum element in the collection `coll`. This method uses the comparator `comp` to compare the elements. There is a similar method `min` that returns the minimum.
`static void shuffle(List<?> list)`	
	This method rearranges the elements of list in a random order.
`public static <T extends Comparable<? super T>> void sort(List<T> list)`	
	Sorts the elements in `list` by their natural order. This method requires that the elements of list implement the `Comparable` interface.
`public static <T> void sort(List<T> list,Comparator<? super T> c)`	
	Sorts the elements in `list` according to the order imposed by the comparator `c`.

In the Spotlight:
Using Anonymous Subclasses to Initialize Collections

Normally, you create anonymous classes from interfaces or abstract superclasses because you want to override their methods. You can also create an anonymous class from a concrete class and override some of its methods. In particular, you can do this with sets, lists, and maps. For example, here is the syntax for creating an anonymous subclass of `HashMap`:

```
Map<String, Integer> myMap = new HashMap<String, Integer>()
{
    // optional initialization block
    {
        // initialization code
    }
    // optional method overrides
};
```

As the example syntax shows, you can have a block of code to initialize the instance that is being created from the anonymous class. If you are instantiating a set, list, or map, you can use the initialization block to add elements. Here is an example that initializes a map and prints its contents.

```
Map<String, Integer> myMap = new HashMap<String, Integer>()
{
    {
        put("Mary", 4);
        put("Sam", 3);
    }
};
// Print the map
System.out.println(myMap);
```

19.6 The Stream API

CONCEPT: A stream is an object that permits a pipeline of operations to be performed on a sequence of elements drawn from a source.

A *stream* is an object that permits a pipeline of operations to be performed on a sequence of elements drawn from a source. The *source* of elements may be an array, a collection, or a function that is able to generate an element each time it is called. By a *pipeline* of operations, we mean a sequence of operations where the output of one operation becomes the input to the next operation in the sequence.

The operations in a stream pipeline may be of two kinds. An *intermediate* operation acts on the stream and turns it into another stream with the same source: this resulting stream may then be acted on by the next operation in the pipeline. A *terminal* operation, also called a *reduction*, acts on the stream and yields a non-stream result. A stream pipeline always begins with a source of elements, followed by zero or more intermediate operations, and ends with a single terminal operation.

The Stream Package

The java.util.stream package defines a number of interfaces and classes. Among them is Stream<T>, a generic interface that defines the methods supported by streams whose elements are objects of type T. Unlike the collection API, which only supports reference types and requires primitive types to be boxed, the stream API has direct support for streams of primitive types through the IntStream, DoubleStream, and LongStream interfaces. There is also a Collectors class that has static methods for implementing useful reduction operations that accumulate stream elements into different type of collections or summary values.

Creating a Stream

There are many ways to create a stream. The Stream interfaces, the Arrays class, the Collection interface, and the Random class, all have methods that can be used to create streams.

1. The Arrays class has several static stream() methods that take an array parameter and return a stream whose source is the array:

   ```
   static Stream<T> stream(T[] array)
   static DoubleStream  stream(double[] array)
   static IntStream stream(int[] array)
   static LongStream stream(long[] array)
   ```

   The first of these methods is used to obtain a stream from an array whose elements are reference types. The other three stream() methods return streams of primitive types.

2. The Collection<E> interface defines an instance method

   ```
   Stream<E> stream()
   ```

   that returns a stream whose source is the collection.

3. All stream interfaces have a static of( ) method with a var-args parameter that lets you create a stream from a specified list of values:

   ```
   static Stream<T> of(T ... values)
   static IntStream of(int ... values)
   static DoubleStream of(double ... values)
   static LongStream of(long ... values)
   ```

4. All Stream interfaces have a static generate() method that creates a potentially infinite stream of elements by repeatedly calling on a *supplier* function:

   ```
   static Stream<T> generate(Supplier<T> s)
   static IntStream generate(IntSupplier s)
   ```

```
static DoubleStream generate(DoubleSupplier s)
static LongStream generate(LongSupplier s)
```

5. Each of the `IntStream` and `LongStream` interfaces has two static methods that create a stream from a sequence of consecutive integers beginning at m and ending at n:

```
static IntStream range(int m, int n)            // n excluded
static IntStream rangeClosed(int m, int n)       // n included
static LongStream range(long m, long n)          // n excluded
static LongStream rangeClosed(long m, long n)    // n included
```

The `rangeClosed()`methods include the upper bound n, while the `range()`methods exclude it.

6. Objects of the `java.util.Random` class have methods that can return `IntStream`, `DoubleStream`, and `LongStream` streams of random numbers. As an example, we list the following methods of `Random` that return an `IntStream` object:

```
IntStream ints()
IntStream ints(int m, int n)
IntStream ints(long count)
IntStream ints(long count, int m, int n)
```

The `ints()` method returns a stream that can generate infinitely many random integers. The `ints(m,n)` method returns a stream that can generate infinitely many integers bounded below by m and above by n. The versions of `ints()` that take a count parameter are similar, except that they generate a finite stream of count elements.

In addition to these methods for creating a stream, the stream interfaces define many intermediate operations that transform an existing stream into another stream. We will look at those later.

Terminal Operations

A *terminal* operation, also called a *reduction*, operates on a stream and produces a non-stream result. The result produced by a reduction is often an aggregate of some type, or a summary of some characteristics of the stream elements. Some terminal operations may perform actions on stream elements (such as printing or updating other program variables) without returning a value.

One of the simplest reduction operators is `long count()`, which returns the number of elements in a stream. The following code creates a stream of string elements stooges and invokes the reduction operator `long()` on it.

```
Stream<String> stooges = Stream.of("Larry", "Curly", "Moe");
System.out.println(stooges.count());
```

Table 19-15 lists some of the simpler stream reduction operators.

Table 19-15   Stream reduction operators

`long count()`	Returns the number of elements in this stream.
`void forEach(Consumer<? super T> action)`	Calls the specified action for each element of this stream.
`Optional<T> max(Comparator<? super T> c)`	Returns the maximum of all elements in this stream according to the comparator c.
`Optional<T> min(Comparator<? super T> c)`	Returns the minimum of all elements in this stream according to the comparator c.
`boolean noneMatch(Predicate<? super T> p)`	Returns true if no elements of this stream satisfy the predicate p, false otherwise.
`boolean allMatch(Predicate<? super T> p)`	Returns true if all elements of this stream satisfy the predicate p, false otherwise.
`boolean anyMatch(Predicate<? super T> p)`	Returns true if at least one element of this stream satisfies the predicate p, false otherwise.
`<A> A[] toArray(IntFunction<A[]> generator)`	Returns an array containing the elements of this stream. The array is created using a function that takes an int parameter x and returns an array of x elements of type A.

Consider the reduction operator:

```
Optional<T> max(Comparator<? super T> c)
```

This operator requires a comparator for elements of type T as parameter and returns a value of type `Optional<T>`. This type represents a value of type T that may not exist. The maximum of all elements in a stream does not exist if the stream has *no* elements. The class `Optional<T>` has a method

```
boolean isPresent()
```

that returns true if the optional value is actually present. The class also has a method

```
T get()
```

that returns the value if it is indeed present. If `get()` is called when the value is not present, it will throw `NoSuchElementException`.

Now, suppose we want to find and print the string in the `stooges` stream that comes first in alphabetic order. We can use the statements:

```
stooges = Stream.of("Larry", "Curly", "Moe");
Optional<String> min = stooges.min( (x, y) -> x.compareTo(y) );
System.out.printf("First stooge by alphabetic order: %s\n", min.get());
```

Here we have used the lambda expression

```
(String x, String y) -> s.compareTo(y)
```

to create an object that implements the `Comparator` interface for string types. It turns out that Java 8 allows a shorter way to write such a lambda expression: you can just write `String::compareTo`. The call to the `min` reduction can therefore be written like this:

```
Optional<String> min1 = stooges.min(String::compareTo);
```

In the code above, we do not bother to call `min.isPresent()` before we call `min.get()` because we know our `stooges` stream is not empty. You should call `isPresent()` before calling `get()` whenever there is a possibility that the stream is empty.

The reduction operator

```
<A> A[] toArray(IntFunction<A[]> generator)
```

collects stream elements into an array that is created by an array *generator*. This is a function that takes an integer x and returns an array of length x, whose elements have type A. In our case, the type A is `String`, so we want the lambda expression:

```
x -> new String [x]
```

Again, Java 8 provides a convenient notation for such a function: simply write `String[]::new`. In general, for any type A, the expression `A[]::new` represents a function that takes an integer parameter x and returns an array of type A that has x elements.

Code Listing 19-18 illustrates how to use some of the reduction operators in Table 19-15.

Code Listing 19-18 **(StreamReductionsDemo.java)**

```
 1 import java.util.Arrays;
 2 import java.util.Optional;
 3 import java.util.stream.Stream;
 4 /**
 5  This program illustrates the use of a
 6  number of stream reduction operators.
 7 */
 8
 9 public class StreamReductionsDemo
10 {
11     public static void main(String[] args)
12     {
13         // Create the source.
14         String[] stoogesArray0 =
15         {
16             "Larry", "Curly", "Moe"
17         };
18         System.out.printf("The Stream source is the array: %s \n",
19                 Arrays.toString(stoogesArray0));
20         // Variable for the stream.
```

```
21          Stream<String> stooges;
22
23          // Get a stream and reduce with count.
24          stooges = Stream.of(stoogesArray0);
25          System.out.printf("The count is %d\n", stooges.count());
26
27          // Get a stream and reduce with forEach.
28          stooges = Stream.of(stoogesArray0);
29          stooges.forEach(x ->
30          {
31              System.out.printf("%s has length %d\n", x, x.length());
32          });
33
34          System.out.println("The stream reduced to an array (2 ways):");
35
36          // Get a stream and reduce with toArray().
37          stooges = Stream.of(stoogesArray0);
38          String[] stoogesArray1 = stooges.toArray(x -> new String[x]);
39          System.out.println(Arrays.toString(stoogesArray1));
40
41          // Get a stream and reduce with toArray().
42          stooges = Stream.of(stoogesArray0);
43          String[] stoogesArray2 = stooges.toArray(String[]::new);
44          System.out.println(Arrays.toString(stoogesArray2));
45
46          // Get a stream and reduce with min.
47          stooges = Stream.of(stoogesArray0);
48          Optional<String> min = stooges.min((x, y) -> x.compareTo(y));
49          System.out.printf("First stooge by alphabetic order: %s\n",
50                                                          min.get());
51          // Get a stream and reduce with min.
52          stooges = Stream.of(stoogesArray0);
53          Optional<String> min1 = stooges.min(String::compareTo);
54          System.out.printf("First stooge by alphabetic order: %s\n",
55                                                          min1.get());
56          // Get a stream and reduce with max.
57          stooges = Stream.of(stoogesArray0);
58          Optional<String> max = stooges.max(String::compareTo);
59          System.out.printf("Last stooge by alphabetic order: %s\n",
60                                                          max.get());
61      }
62 }
```

Program Output

```
The Stream source is the array: [Larry, Curly, Moe]
The count is 3
Larry has length 5
```

```
Curly has length 5
Moe has length 3
The stream reduced to an array (2 ways):
[Larry, Curly, Moe]
[Larry, Curly, Moe]
First stooge by alphabetic order: Curly
First stooge by alphabetic order: Curly
Last stooge by alphabetic order: Moe
```

In Code Listing 19-18, we have to recreate the stream from the source every time we execute a reduction operation on it:

```
stooges = Stream.of(stoogesArray0);
```

This is because a stream object can be reduced only one time. Once it is reduced, the stream is drained of all its elements and becomes unuseable.

The `IntStream`, `DoubleStream`, and `LongStream` have additional reduction operators. Because of the close similarity, we will list only the operators for `DoubleStream`. Analogous operators exist for the other two streams.

```
OptionalDouble average()
OptionalDouble max()
OptionalDouble min()
Double sum()
double[] toArray()
```

These operators respectively reduce a stream of numbers of type `double` to their average, maximum, minimum, and sum. The `max()` and `min()` are similar to the corresponding operators of the same name in `Stream<T>`, but do not require a comparator because the natural order of numbers is used. The last operator collects stream elements into an array of type `double`.

Intermediate Operations on Streams

An intermediate operation acts on an existing stream and produces a new stream. Table 19-16 lists some of the intermediate operations defined in the `Stream<T>` interface.

Table 19-16   `Stream<T>` intermediate operators

`Stream<T> distinct()`	Removes duplicates and returns the resulting stream.
`Stream<T> filter(Predicate<? super T> predicate)`	Returns a stream consisting of only those elements that satisfy the given predicate.
`Stream<T> limit(long n)`	Returns a stream consisting of at most the first n elements of this stream.
`<R> Stream<R> map(Function<? super T,? extends R> mappingFunction)`	Returns a stream whose elements are the result of calling the mapping function on elements of this stream.

(table continues next page)

Table 19-16 `Stream<T>` intermediate operators (continued)

`Stream<T> peek(Consumer<? super T> action)`	
	Returns a stream consisting of the same elements as this stream. The given action method will be called on each element of the resulting stream as the element is being drawn from the stream.
`Stream<T> skip(long n)`	Returns this stream after discarding the first n elements.
`Stream<T> sorted()`	Returns a stream with the same elements as this stream, but sorted according to their natural order.
`Stream<T> sorted(Comparator <? super T> comparator)`	
	Returns a stream with the same elements as this stream, but sorted according to the given comparator.

Code Listing 19-19 illustrates some of these intermediate operators. The program creates a stream that is able to produce infinitely many random integers less than 10. A filter operation is then plugged onto that stream to filter for even numbers, followed by a `limit(15)` operation that will ask for only 15 of those numbers. The last operation in the pipeline reduces the resulting stream to an array, which is then printed.

Code Listing 19-19   (`StreamIntermediateOpsDemo.java`)

```
1 import java.util.Arrays;
2 import java.util.Random;
3 import java.util.stream.IntStream;
4
5 /**
6   This program illustrates intermediate Stream operations.
7 */
8
9 public class StreamIntermediateOpsDemo
10 {
11     public static void main(String [] args)
12     {
13         // Random number generator.
14         Random randy = new Random();
15
16         // Potentially infinite stream of random
17         // numbers all of which are less than 10.
18         IntStream infRandom = randy.ints(0, 10);
19
20         // Filter out all the odd numbers, keep only even numbers.
21         IntStream intEvenRandom = infRandom.filter(x -> x % 2 == 0);
22
23         // Keep only the first 15 of the infinite
24         // stream of random even numbers.
25         IntStream first15 = intEvenRandom.limit(15);
26
```

```
27          // Reduce to an array and print.
28          int [] evenRandomArr = first15.toArray();
29          System.out.println("The result of stream operations is: ");
30          System.out.println(Arrays.toString(evenRandomArr));
31      }
32  }
```

Program Output

```
The result of stream operations is:
[0, 2, 6, 2, 2, 6, 8, 4, 8, 8, 6, 4, 6, 6, 4]
```

Intermediate Stream Operations are Lazy

You may well be wondering how the stream

```
randy.ints(0,10)
```

can represent an infinite stream of numbers as claimed. The reason is that all intermediate stream operations are *lazy*: the intermediate operations will produce an element only when the element is being demanded by a reduction operation. To see how this works, let us remove all the "temporary" variables that are keeping track of the streams at intermediate stages. We end up with the pipeline expression:

```
evenRandomArr = randy.ints(0, 10)
                    .filter(x -> x% 2 == 0)
                    .limit(15)
                    .toArray();
```

When this is executed, the `toArray()` reduction demands all elements in the aggregate stream.

The `limit(15)` operation will then demand 15 elements from the filter operation, which will keep demanding elements from `int(0,10)` until it has passed 15 even numbers to `limits(15)`. At that point, `limits(15)` is satisfied and stops asking for elements from filter, which stops asking for elements from `ints(0,10)`.

You can think of a stream as a conduit through which objects flow, beginning at a source and ending at some terminal operation. The `peek()` operation executes an action on each element as it passes by. Consider Code Listing 19-20, and the output that follows the code listing. We have modified the stream pipeline shown above by placing a `peek()` on elements as they leave the `ints(0,10)` stream, and another `peek()` as the elements leave the `filter()`. To cut down on the volume of the output, we limit the size of the final stream to 5 elements.

Code Listing 19-20   (`PeekDemo.java`)

```
1  import java.util.Arrays;
2  import java.util.Random;
3  import java.util.stream.IntStream;
4
5  /**
```

```
 6    This program illustrates the working of the
 7    peek intermediate operation.
 8 */
 9
10 public class PeekOpDemo
11 {
12     public static void main(String [] args)
13     {
14         // Random number generator.
15         Random randy = new Random();
16
17         // Potentially infinite stream of random
18         // numbers all of which are less than 10.
19         IntStream infRandom = randy.ints(0, 10);
20
21         int [] evenRandomArr =
22                 randy.ints(0, 10)
23                     .peek(x -> {System.out.printf("ints: %d\n", x);})
24                     .filter(x -> x% 2 == 0)
25                     .peek(x-> {System.out.printf("filter: %d\n", x);})
26                     .limit(5)
27                     .toArray();
28         System.out.println("The result of stream operations is: ");
29         System.out.println(Arrays.toString(evenRandomArr));
30     }
31 }
```

Program Output

```
ints: 9
ints: 0
filter: 0
ints: 9
ints: 1
ints: 5
ints: 6
filter: 6
ints: 3
ints: 9
ints: 4
filter: 4
ints: 4
filter: 4
ints: 6
filter: 6
The result of stream operations is:
[0, 6, 4, 4, 6]
```

Notice that ints() produces 11 elements altogether, 6 odd and 5 even. All odd elements make it out of the int() stream, but get filtered out by filter().

The Stream map Operation

The map operation

```
<R> Stream<R> map(Function<? super T,? extends R> mappingFunction)
```

applies a function of type $T \rightarrow R$ to transform a stream of elements of type T into a stream of type R. Actually the input type of the function needs only be a superclass of T, and the return type only needs to be a subclass of R.

A simple example of this is the following. If you have a stream of consecutive integers

```
[1,  2,  3,  4,  5,  6]
```

you can apply the mapping function x -> 2*x-1 to every element of the stream and get the stream of consecutive odd numbers

```
[1,  3,  5,  7,  9,  11]
```

The code for this is:

```
int n = sc.nextInt();
IntStream odds = IntStream.rangeClosed(1, n).map(x -> 2*x -1);
System.out.println(Arrays.toString(odds.toArray()));
```

Now, suppose you want to turn a stream of strings into a string of integers by mapping each string to its length. The map operation $T \rightarrow R$ requires that R be a reference type. If you use map, the compiler will automatically box the integer length of each string, creating a stream of type Stream<Integer> instead of one of type IntStream.

```
Stream<String> names = Stream.of("Abby", "Bob", "Christopher",
                                 "David", "Elizabeth");
Stream<Integer> lengths = names.map(x -> x.length());
```

This means that executing the lines of code above will result in lengths being a stream of Integer rather than int elements. If you want to map a Stream<T> object to a stream whose elements are primitive types, you need to use the following mapToXXX() methods of the Stream<T> interface.

```
DoubleStream mapToDouble(ToDoubleFunction<? super T> mapper)
IntStream mapToInt(ToIntFunction<? super T> mapper)
LongStream mapToLong(ToLongFunction<? super T> mapper)
```

These methods take as input a function that takes a parameter of type T and returns a double, an int, or long value. The proper way to map a stream of strings to an IntStream is like this:

```
Stream<String> names = Stream.of("Abby", "Bob", "Christopher",
                                 "David", "Elizabeth");
IntStream lengths = names.mapToInt(x -> x.length());
System.out.println(Arrays.toString(lengths.toArray()));
```

The Stream reduce Methods

Many reduction operations can be viewed as a process of "accumulating" stream elements into a single value of the same type. The simplest example of this is when the elements of a stream of integers are processed to yield another integer that is the sum of the stream elements. Another example is the processing of a stream of integers to yield a product.

To perform an accumulation reduction on a stream of type T, you need an *accumulation operator* p of type $(T, T) \rightarrow T$ that will be used to combine two values of type T into a single value. You also need a value i of type T to represent the result of performing the accumulation reduction on an empty stream. This value is called the *identity* value for p and must satisfy the relation $p(i, x) = x$ for all values x of type T. The accumulation process uses an internal variable a to represent the value of stream elements already accumulated. Initially, no elements have been accumulated and a is set to i. The process proceeds by setting $a = p(a, x)$ for each stream element x. The final value of a is returned at the end of the process.

As an example, suppose we want to reduce a stream of integers to the sum of its elements. The accumulation operator p is a function that returns the sum of two integers. For example, p might be the lambda expression (x,y)-> x+y. The identity value for addition is the integer zero. Initially, the internal variable a would be 0. At each stage of the reduction, the current stream element would be added to a by setting $a = a + x$.

All three interfaces for streams of primitive types define reduce() methods that implement accumulation reductions of this nature:

```
int reduce(int identity, IntBinaryOperator op)
long reduce(long identity, LongBinaryOperator op)
double reduce(double identity, DoubleBinaryOperator op)
```

When you are accumulating an integer stream to find the sum, you use (x,y)-> x+y for the binary operator and take 0 for the identity. However, if you are accumulating by multiplying, the appropriate binary operator is (x,y)-> x*y and the identity value is 1. The following code uses reductions to find the sum of the first 4 positive odd integers, and also the product of the first 4 positive integers.

```
int n = 4;
// Create streams of integers.
IntStream odds = IntStream.rangeClosed(1, n).map(x-> 2*x -1);
IntStream ints = IntStream.rangeClosed(1, n);

// Reduce the streams.
int oddsSum = odds.reduce(0, (x,y)->x+y );
int intsProduct = ints.reduce(1, (x, y)-> x*y);

// Print the results.
System.out.printf("The sum is %d and the product is %d\n",
                                    oddsSum, intsProduct);
```

When executed, this code will print 14 for the sum and 24 for the product.

The Stream<T> interface has a similar reduce() method:

```
T reduce(T identity, BinaryOperator<T> accumulator)
```

This method works similarly to the ones we have already discussed.

The `reduce()` methods require the binary accumulator operator *p* to be associative. A binary operator *p* is *associative* if for any sequence of values *a, b, c,* the two values *p(a, p(b, c))* and *p(p(a, b), c)* are equal. The requirement allows for the parallelization of the reduction operation. The implementation may split the stream into segments, reduce these segments in parallel, and later combine the result. The associativity of the accumulator operator ensures that final result will not be affected by the order in which the results are combined.

There are times when you want to reduce the elements of a stream of type *T* to a single value of a different type *U*. To meet this need, the `Stream<T>` interface defines a method:

```
<U> U reduce(U identity, BiFunction<U,? super T,U> accumulator,
                                    BinaryOperator<U> combiner)
```

This method requires an *accumulator* bi-function *f* of type *(U, T)* → *U* to "add" a current value of type *T* to the accumulated value of type *U*. It also requires a value *i* of type *U* to act as the initial accumulation value to get the process started. At each stream element *x*, the reduction replaces the current accumulation value *a* with *f(a, x)* by setting *a = f(a, x)*. The reduction may split the stream into segments and reduce the segments in parallel, with each segment producing an accumulated value of type *U*. These values are combined two at a time by using a binary *combiner* operator *c*, which must be associative. Moreover, the accumulation value *i* must be an *identity* value for the operator *c*.

As an example, suppose that we want to reduce a stream of `String` elements by collecting them into a set. We will see shortly that there is a stream `Collectors` method that will do that, but let us push ahead for the sake of illustration. Here the type *T* is `String`, while the type *U* is `Set`. At each stage, the accumulated value will be a set, and the accumulator bi-function will be a function that takes a set and a string, adds the string to the set, and returns the resulting set:

```
(Set s, String x) -> { s.add(x); return s; }
```

The combiner operator will take two sets, add all the elements of the first set to the second set, and return the second set:

```
(Set s, Set t) -> { t.addAll(s); return t; }
```

Finally, the identity value that gets the set-building process started is an empty set:

```
new HashSet<String>();
```

Code Listing 19-21 shows the complete program.

Code Listing 19-21   (ReduceToSetDemo.java)

```
1 import java.util.HashSet;
2 import java.util.Set;
3 import java.util.function.BiFunction;
4 import java.util.function.BinaryOperator;
5 import java.util.stream.Stream;
6
```

```
 7  /**
 8     This program demonstrates how to use the Stream
 9     reduce method.
10  */
11
12  public class ReducetoSetDemo
13  {
14      public static void main(String [] args)
15      {
16          Stream<String> stooges = Stream.of("Larry", "Curly", "Moe");
17
18          // The accumulator for the reduction.
19          BiFunction<Set<String>, String, Set<String>> accumulator =
20                  (s, x) -> { s.add(x); return s;};
21
22          // The combiner for the reduction
23          BinaryOperator<Set<String>> combiner =
24                  (s, t) -> { t.addAll(s); return t;};
25
26          // Reduce the stream to a set.
27          Set<String> stoogeSet = stooges.reduce(new HashSet<String>(),
28                                          accumulator, combiner);
29          // Print the set
30          System.out.printf("The set of stooges is %s\n", stoogeSet);
31      }
32  }
```

Program Output

```
The set of stooges is [Moe, Larry, Curly]
```

Notice, we can easily convert a stream into a set using the forFach() reduction method that we learned about earlier. The advantage of the reduce() methods lies in the potential for parallelization. When working with large quantities of data, parallelization may result in significant savings in time.

Stream Collectors

Collectors are a slightly different approach to reductions. *Collectors* are typically used to accumulate stream elements into a collection, although they can perform other types of reductions.

The Stream<T> interface has a method

```
    <R,A> R collect(Collector<? super T,A,R> collector)
```

that uses a collector object to reduce a stream of elements of type *T* into a single value of type *R*. The collector accumulates stream elements into a value of type *A*, and then transforms the type *A* value into a final result of type *R* when all stream elements have been processed.

The `Stream` package has a `Collectors` class that provides static methods that return different types of collectors. Among them are the two methods:

```
static <T> Collector<T,?,List<T>>  toList()
static <T> Collector<T,?,Set<T>>  toSet()
```

The `toList()` method returns a collector that will reduce a stream of elements of type *T* by collecting them into a list of type `List<T>`. Here the final type *R* is `List<T>`, and the intermediate type *A* is an unspecified implementation detail. This is because the user of the collector does not need to know the internal type used for the intermediate accumulated values. The `toSet()` method is similar.

Let us illustrate the use of the `toSet()` collector. The following code collects the elements of a stream of strings into a set and prints the set:

```
Stream<String> stooges = Stream.of("Larry", "Curly", "Moe");
Set<String> stoogesSet = stooges.collect(Collectors.toSet());
System.out.printf("The set of stooges is %s\n", stoogesSet);
```

As you can see, the `collect` method takes a lot less code than the program of Code Listing 19-21.

Another interesting method is `toMap()`:

```
static <T,K,U> Collector<T,?,Map<K,U>>
    toMap(
            Function<? super T,? extends K> keyMapper,
            Function<? super T,? extends U> valueMapper
          )
```

This method returns a collector that can reduce a stream to a map. The method takes as parameters two functions: a key mapper that determines the key for a stream element, and a value mapper that determines the value associated with the key. It is these key-value pairs that are stored in the map.

To illustrate, suppose we have a stream of strings, and we want to create a map that stores the strings as values, with each string being keyed by its length. For example, a stream of the strings

```
"Larry", "Moe", "Al"
```

would result in a map that stores the following key-value pairs:

```
(5, Larry)
(3, Moe)
(2, Al)
```

In the syntax of the definition of `toMap()`, the stream element type *T* is `String`, the key type *K* is `Integer`, and the value type *U* is `String`. Our key-mapping function is the lambda expression,

```
(String x)-> x.length()
```

while the value-mapping function is the lambda expression

```
(String x) -> x
```

A program that reduces a stream of strings to such a map is shown in Code Listing 19-22.

Code Listing 19-22 (`ReduceToMapDemo1.java`)

```java
 1 import java.util.Map;
 2 import java.util.function.Function;
 3 import java.util.stream.Collectors;
 4 import java.util.stream.Stream;
 5
 6 /**
 7   This program demonstrates the Collectors.toMap method.
 8 */
 9
10 public class ReduceToMapDemo1
11 {
12     public static void main(String [] args)
13     {
14         // This is the stream to reduce.
15         Stream<String> names = Stream.of("Larry", "Moe", "Al");
16
17         // key of a string is its length.
18         Function<String, Integer> keyMapper = x -> x.length();
19
20         // The value of a string is the string itself.
21         Function<String, String> valueMapper = x -> x;
22
23         // Reduce the stream to a ma
24         Map<Integer, String> namesMap =
25             names.collect(Collectors.toMap(keyMapper, valueMapper));
26
27         // Print the map.
28         System.out.printf("The map of stooges is %s\n", namesMap);
29     }
30 }
```

Program Output

```
The map of stooges is {2=Al, 3=Moe, 5=Larry}
```

In the input to the program of Code Listing 19-22, there is at most one string with a given length. This is because the lengths of the strings are keys of a map, and maps require keys to be unique. A more realistic reduction would allow any number of strings of a given length and groups the strings according to their length. Such a reduction would reduce a stream of strings to a map whose values are lists of strings, and the key of a value is the common length of all strings in the list. For example, the stream of strings

```
"Larry", "Curly", "Moe", "Al"
```

would be reduced to the map

```
(5, [Larry, Curly])
(3, [Moe])
(2, [Al])
```

The `Streams<T>` interface has such a method:

```
static <T,K,U> Collector<T,?,Map<K,U>>
    toMap(
            Function<? super T,? extends K> keyMapper,
            Function<? super T,? extends U> valueMapper,
            BinaryOperator<U> mergeFunction
        )
```

This method is just like the last one, except it has a *merge function* parameter that is a binary operator on the type U. The merge function m has type $(U, U) \rightarrow U$, meaning that m takes two parameters of type U and returns a single result of the same type. If two values u_1 and u_2 have the same key k, the `toMap()` method will call the merge function on the two values and use the result $m(u_1, u_2)$ as the "merged" value for k.

Let's look at how this plays out if we want to reduce a stream of strings into a map that groups strings by their lengths. First, note that the type U of the final result is no longer `String`, but `List<String>`. The key mapper is the same as before, but the value mapper now assigns to each string x a list whose only member is x:

```
Function<String, List<String>> valueMapper = x->
    {
        List<String> listOfOne = new ArrayList<>();
        listOfOne.add(x);
        return listOfOne;
    };
```

The merge function takes two lists that would have the same key and returns a single list that is the concatenation of the two lists:

```
BinaryOperator<List<String>> mergeFunction = (list1, list2) ->
    {
        list1.addAll(list2);
        return list1;
    };
```

Code Listing 19-23 shows a complete program that implements the reduction.

Code Listing 19-23   (ReduceToDemo2.java)

```
1 import java.util.ArrayList;
2 import java.util.List;
3 import java.util.Map;
4 import java.util.function.BinaryOperator;
5 import java.util.function.Function;
6 import java.util.stream.Collectors;
```

```
 7 import java.util.stream.Stream;
 8
 9 /**
10
11   This program demonstrates the Collectors.toMap method.
12 */
13
14 public class ReduceToMapDemo2
15 {
16     public static void main(String [] args)
17     {
18         // This is the stream to reduce to a map.
19         Stream<String> names = Stream.of("Larry", "Curly", "Moe", "Al");
20
21         // The key for a string is the length of the string.
22         Function<String, Integer> keyMapper  = x -> x.length();
23
24         // The value for a string is a list of all strings in
25         // the stream with the same length. Every string is initially
26         // mapped to list containing just that string.
27         Function<String, List<String>> valueMapper =  x->
28         {
29             List<String> listOfOne = new ArrayList<>();
30             listOfOne.add(x);
31             return listOfOne;
32         };
33
34         // When two values have the same key, the merge function
35         // is used to merge the two values and the merged result
36         // becomes the value of the key.
37         BinaryOperator<List<String>> mergeFunction = (list1, list2) ->
38         {
39             list1.addAll(list2);
40             return list1;
41         };
42
43         //Reduce the stream and get a map.
44         Map<Integer, List<String>> namesMap =
45         names.collect(Collectors.toMap(
46                                          keyMapper, valueMapper,
47                                          mergeFunction));
48
49         // Print the map.
50         System.out.printf("The map of names is %s\n", namesMap);
51     }
52 }
```

Program Output

```
The map of names is {2=[Al], 3=[Moe], 5=[Larry, Curly]}
```

The `Stream<T>` interface has a second `collect` method that takes as parameters the ingredients needed to build a collector. The method internally builds the collector and uses it to reduce the stream. You can use this method in the event that none of the collectors in the `Collectors` class suit your needs.

```
<R> R collect(
        Supplier<R> supplier,
        BiConsumer<R,? super T> accumulator,
        BiConsumer<R,R> combiner
    )
```

Briefly, the supplier is a method that is called to provide an initial value of the final type *R*; the role of the supplier is similar to the role of the identity in the reduce methods. The accumulator and combiners play roles similar to those of the accumulator and combiner in the reduce methods. You can learn more about this and other methods by studying the streams API documentation.

Checkpoint

19.33 How do you define a stream of elements?

19.34 How does a stream intermediate operation differ from a terminal operation?

19.35 Name at least two different classes or interfaces that have methods for creating streams.

19.36 What is a stream pipeline?

19.37 What is the difference between a terminal operation and a reduction?

19.38 What is a collector?

19.39 How many reduction operations can be in a stream pipeline?

19.7 Common Errors to Avoid

- **Not calling an iterator's `hasNext` method before calling `next`.** To prevent an exception from being thrown, you should always call an iterator's `hasNext` method before calling its `next` method. This ensures that the `next` method will actually return a reference.
- **Not calling an iterator's `next` method before calling `remove`.** An iterator's `remove` method removes the last element that was returned by the `next` method. The `next` method must be called before the `remove` method can be called.
- **Not calling a `ListIterator`'s `hasPrevious` method before calling `previous`.** To prevent an exception from being thrown, you should always call a `ListIterator`'s `hasPrevious` method before calling its `previous` method.
- **Not calling a `ListIterator`'s `hasNext` or `hasPrevious` method immediately before calling `set`.** To prevent an exception from being thrown, you should always call a `ListIterator`'s `hasNext` or `hasPrevious` method before calling its `set` method.
- **Modifying a collection via one of its methods after an iterator has been created for the collection.** After an iterator has been created for a collection, you cannot modify the collection using one of the collection's methods and then continue to use the iterator. Doing so will cause an exception to be thrown. If you wish to modify a collection

while it is being iterated over, you should use the iterator to perform the modifications. For example, the Iterator interface specifies a remove method, and the ListIterator interface specifies add and set methods.

- **Designing a class so objects of the class can be stored in a HashSet, but not overriding both the equals and hashCode methods.** When an object is stored in a HashSet, both the hashCode and the equals methods are used to find a location for the object in the HashSet. If you are designing a class so objects of the class can be stored in a HashSet, you should override both the hashCode and the equals methods.
- **Storing objects that cannot be compared in a TreeSet.** In a TreeSet, objects are compared using the compareTo method. An error will occur if you attempt to store in a TreeSet an object of a class that does not implement the compareTo method.
- **Attempting to store duplicate keys in a map.** The keys in a map must be unique.
- **Trying to reuse a stream after it has been reduced.** A stream becomes drained of its elements when it is reduced. Trying to use it after that will result in an error.

Review Questions and Exercises

Multiple Choice and True/False

1. This type of collection stores elements in an ordered sequence, and allows duplicates.
   a. list
   b. set
   c. map
   d. hash set

2. Each element in one of these is comprised of two parts: a key and a value.
   a. list
   b. set
   c. map
   d. hash set

3. This type of collection is optimized for searching, stores elements in an unordered sequence, and does not allow duplicates.
   a. list
   b. set
   c. map
   d. hash set

   bad question b, d and possibly c can be regarded as correct answers! but map is technically not a collection

4. This interface specifies the basic operations of a list.
   a. ListCollection
   b. List
   c. Set
   d. ArrayList

5. A terminal operation in a stream pipeline is also called
   a. the stream end
   b. a reduction
   c. the sink
   d. an iterator

6. This is an object that can be used to retrieve the elements in a collection, one after the other.
   a. iterator
   b. manipulator
   c. comparator
   d. concrete collection class

7. `ListIterator` is a subinterface of
   a. `Iterator`
   b. `Collection`
   c. `Comparator`
   d. `List`

8. This `ListIterator` method replaces an existing element with a new element.
   a. replace
   b. update
   c. set
   d. add

9. A stream collector is an object that
   a. implements the `Collection` interface
   b. implements the `Map` interface
   c. is used to reduce a stream
   d. uses lambda expressions

10. This list class stores its elements by connecting each element to its successor.
    a. `ArrayList`
    b. `LinkedList`
    c. `HashList`
    d. `ConnectedList`

11. This is an object that can compare two other objects and determine whether one is greater than, less than, or equal to the other.
    a. `Comparator`
    b. `Comparer`
    c. `Sorter`
    d. `Sequencer`

12. This class provides numerous static methods that perform useful operations on collections.
    a. `Collection`
    b. `CollectionUtilities`
    c. `Collections`
    d. `Util`

13. This JCF interface is not a subinterface of `Collection`.
    a. `List`
    b. `Set`
    d. `Map`
    c. `SortedSet`

14. This class is a good choice to use when your application is storing data in a list and is doing lots of insertions and deletions in the middle of the list.
    a. `ArrayList`
    b. `Vector`
    c. `LargeList`
    d. `LinkedList`

15. True or False: Duplicates can be stored in a list.

16. True or False: Duplicates can be stored in a set.

17. True or False: `Collection` is a subinterface of `List`.

18. True or False: A `ListIterator` can move backward through a list.

19. True or False: A `ListIterator` can be used to modify the contents of a list.

20. True or False: When the Java compiler processes an enhanced `for` loop, it actually converts it to a traditional loop that uses an iterator.

21. True or False: You can randomly access the elements in a linked list.

22. True or False: When you iterate through a `HashSet`, the objects will be retrieved in the same order that they were added to the `HashSet`.

Find the Error

1. `List<String> nameList = new LinkedHashSet<>();`

2. `List<String> nameList = new ArrayList<>();`
   `ListIterator it = new ListIterator(nameList);`

3. `Set<String> nameSet = new HashSet<>();`
   `nameSet.add("Chris");`
   `nameSet.add("Kenny");`
   `ListIterator it = nameSet.listIterator();`

4. `List<String> nameList = new ArrayList<>();`
   `ListIterator it = new ListIterator(nameList);`
   `it.set("Herbert");`

Algorithm Workbench

1. Write a statement that declares a `List` reference variable, instantiates an `ArrayList` object that can hold `String` objects, and assigns the address of the `ArrayList` object to the reference variable.

2. Assume that `myList` references a `List` object. Write a statement that gets a list iterator from the `myList` object.

3. Assume that `it` references a newly created iterator for a list of `String` objects. Write code that uses the iterator to display each of the `String` objects in the list.

4. In pseudocode, outline the procedure followed by a `HashSet` object to add a new object.

Short Answer

1. What do you call an object that provides the elements that make up a stream?

2. What is the essential difference between a stream intermediate operation and a stream terminal operation?

3. What is the benefit of using an interface variable to reference a collection object?

4. What is an iterator?

5. How do you get an iterator for a list?

6. Which element does the `ListIterator` method set replace in a list?

7. How does the Java compiler process an enhanced `for` loop?

8. Which is more efficient—inserting an element in the middle of an `ArrayList`, or inserting a node into the middle of a `LinkedList`?

9. Why do we need `IntStream` when we have `Stream<Integer>`?

10. What is the purpose of the `map()` method in the `Stream<T>` interface?

11. Look at the following code:

```
String str1 = new String("Barney");
String str2 = new String("Barney");
```

Will the methods `str1.hashCode()` and `str2.hashCode()` return the same value?

12. In hashing, what is a collision?

13. How does a map work?

14. What are the three guidelines that you should follow when overriding the `hashCode` and `equals` methods in a class?

Programming Challenges

1. Word Set

Write an application that reads a line of input from the keyboard, and then displays each unique word that was entered, sorted in ascending order. You can do this by tokenizing the line of input and adding each token to an appropriate `Set` object.

2. Instructor Set

Chapter 8 presented an `Instructor` class that holds information about an instructor. (See Section 8.7—Aggregation) Modify the `Instructor` class by overriding the `hashCode` and `equals` methods. Then write a class that stores several `Instructor` objects in a `HashSet`. The class should be able to display all the instructors in the set, and allow the user to search for an instructor. Demonstrate the class in an application.

3. `EmployeeMap` Class

Create an `Employee` class that stores an employee's ID number and name. Then create an `EmployeeMap` class that allows you to add `Employee` objects and look them up by their ID numbers. The `EmployeeMap` class should use a `Map` object to map ID numbers to `Employee` objects. Create an application to demonstrate the classes.

4. Stock Map

Chapter 8 presented a `Stock` class that holds information about a stock. (See Section 8.4—The `toString` Method) Write a class that keeps `Stock` objects in a `Map`. The class should be able to retrieve a particular `Stock` object from the `Map` by searching on its stock symbol. Demonstrate the class in an application.

5. Prime Number List

A prime number is an integer (other than 1) that is only evenly divisible by itself and 1. For example, the number 5 is prime because it can only be evenly divided by 1 and 5. The number 6, however, is not prime because it can be divided evenly by 1, 2, 3, and 6. Write an application that calculates and stores the first 100 prime numbers (starting at 2) in a list. Use an iterator to display the numbers.

6. Dealing Cards

Write a class named `Card`, which can be used to represent a card from a deck of cards. The class should be able to store a card's suit and face value. A card's suit can be one of the following: Hearts, Diamonds, Spades, or Clubs. A card's face value can be Ace, Jack, Queen, King, or a value in the range of two through ten.

Next write a `Deck` class. This class constructor should create a list of 52 `Card` objects, each representing a valid card in a deck of cards. The class should have a `shuffle` method that randomly shuffles the `Card` objects in the list. It should also have a `deal` method that "deals" a card from the deck. It does this by removing the `Card` object at the beginning of the list and returning a reference to that object.

Next, write `CardPlayer` class. This class should keep a list of `Card` objects that have been dealt to it. This represents a hand of cards. A method named `getCard` should accept a reference to a `Card` object, which is added to the list. A method named `showCards` displays the `Card` objects in the list.

Demonstrate these classes in an application that creates a `Deck` object, shuffles the cards it contains, and deals five cards from the `Deck` to a `CardPlayer` object. The `CardPlayer` should then display its cards.

7. `Action` and `AbstractAction`

replace

Java defines a subinterface of the `ActionListener` interface called `Action`. Among the methods that `Action` adds to `ActionListener` are

```
Object getValue(String key);
void putValue(String key, Object value);
```

These two methods assume the existence of a maplike structure that uses strings to access objects. Java provides an abstract class called `AbstractAction` that implements the methods in `Action`, leaving only the

```
void actionPerformed(ActionEvent e)
```

method to be implemented by the programmer. Research the `AbstractAction` class online and then write a subclass of `AbstractAction` called `ColorAction` that maps names of colors to `Color` objects. Write a GUI program with a `JTextfield` in a panel and add the panel to a `JFrame`. `JTextfields` fire `Action` events when a user types a string and presses the Enter key. Add an object of `ColorAction` as an `ActionListener` to the `JTextfield` to handle such `Action` events. Whenever the user enters the name of a color in the `JTextfield`, the `ColorAction` object should map the string in the `JTextfield` to a color and then use that color to set the background of the panel.

8. `groupingBy` Collector

Consult the online Stream API documentation and read about the `groupingBy()` method of the `Collectors` class, and use that method to get a simpler and shorter solution to the problem of classifying strings that was solved in the program of Code Listing 19-23.

20 Linked Lists

TOPICS

20.1 Introduction to Linked Lists

CONCEPT: A linked list is an implementation of a list in which elements are stored in nodes, and each node contains a link to its successor.

As you learned in Chapter 19, a list is a collection that stores its elements in a position-based sequence. Each element in a list is associated with an index that corresponds to its position within the list. The first element has index 0, the second element has index 1, and so forth.

This position-based order gives rise to the notion of a predecessor and a successor for each element: if X is a list element with index k, then its *successor* is the element with index $k + 1$ and its *predecessor* is the element with index $k - 1$. The first element in the list has no predecessor and the last element in the list has no successor.

There are two ways to allocate storage for the elements of a list: contiguous allocation, and linked allocation. Array-based lists use *contiguous allocation*, which allocates storage for successive list elements in consecutive memory locations. A drawback of contiguous allocation is the necessity to move large numbers of elements when inserting elements into, or deleting elements from, the middle of the list.

Linked allocation does not need consecutive memory locations to store list elements. Instead, it stores with each element, a pointer to the memory location of its successor. A *linked list* is a list that uses linked allocation. In Java, a linked list is implemented as a sequence of *nodes*, where each node stores a list element and a reference to the next node in the list. For example, to implement a linked list of `String` elements, we can use a class such as the following:

```
class Node
{
    String value;          // Value of a list element
    Node next;             // Link to next node in the list

    Node(String val, Node n)
    {
        value = val;
        next = n;
    }
    Node(String val)
    {
        value = val;
        next = null;
    }
}
```

A linked list is represented by a reference to its first node. The first element of the list is called the *head* of the list, so this reference is often called the *head reference*. An empty linked list is indicated by setting its head reference to `null`.

Our examples in this chapter will involve linked lists of strings. Working with linked lists of other types of elements, and even with generic linked lists, is similar.

Creating Lists and Adding Nodes

Once we have a suitable node class, we can create linked lists by creating nodes and setting their successor links to reflect the order that the list imposes on its elements. A sequence of statements that builds a linked list is shown in Figure 20-1. In the figure, a `Node` object is shown as a rectangular box with a compartment for the element and a second compartment for the successor reference `next`.

The first statement in Figure 20-1

```
Node myList = new Node("Bob");
```

creates a linked list with the single element `"Bob"`. At this point, `myList` refers to a `Node` object that contains a field `myList.next`, which can itself be made to point to another node:

```
myList.next = new Node("Carol");
```

This creates a linked list whose two elements form the sequence `"Bob Carol"`. The newly added node contains its own `next` field, which can be accessed by using the expression `myList.next.next` and made to point to yet another node:

```
myList.next.next = new Node("Debby");
```

We are not limited to the end of a list when adding nodes. The statement

```
Node p = new Node("Allan", myList);
```

adds a new node `"Allan"` to the beginning of the list of elements already accumulated. This statement uses the two-parameter constructor, which allows the successor of a node to be specified. The result of executing this sequence of four statements is the list of four elements shown at the bottom of Figure 20-1. The figure shows the `next` field of a `Node` object as an arrow pointing to a successor node. A backward diagonal drawn through the `next` field indicates a `null` value, and signifies that the node has no successor.

Figure 20-1 Adding nodes to a linked list

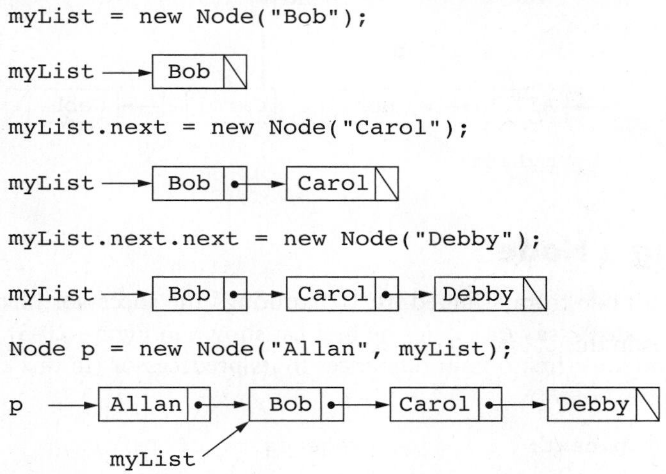

In addition to adding nodes at the beginning and end of a list, we can insert nodes into the middle. Given the final scenario shown in Figure 20-1, we can add the string `"Brad"` immediately after `"Bob"` by writing

```
Node b = p.next;        // b points to "Bob"
Node c = b.next;        // c points to "Carol"
b.next = new Node("Brad", c);
```

Execution of these statements gives us the sequence of scenarios shown in Figure 20-2.

In the example just shown, we used two auxiliary references, `b` and `c`, to insert a node in the middle of a list. In general, adding a new node at any place other than the beginning requires a reference to the node that will be the predecessor (in this case, `b`) and to a node that will be the successor of the new node (in this case, `c`). The auxiliary variables are not always needed, however. For example, instead of using the three statements shown in Figure 20-2, we can add `"Brad"` to the list by writing

```
myList.next = new Node("Brad", myList.next);
```

Figure 20-2 Inserting a node in the middle of a linked list

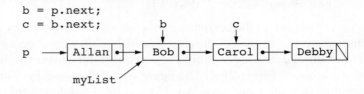

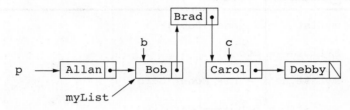

Removing a Node

You remove a node from a linked list by "routing" the successor link around it. Basically, to remove a node X (say Carol in the first list shown in Figure 20-3) from the middle of a linked list, you must first obtain references to its predecessor (In this case, Bob) and successor (In this case, Debby).

```
Node b = p.next;         // Predecessor of Carol
Node d = b.next.next;    // Successor of Carol
```

Then you remove the targeted node X by manipulating references to bypass X and make the successor of X the successor of its predecessor:

```
b.next = d;
```

This sequence of events is illustrated in Figure 20-3.

Figure 20-3 Removing a node from the middle of a linked list

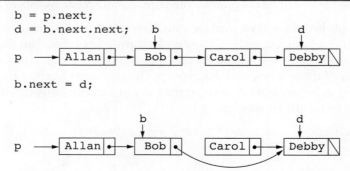

As you may already have guessed, the removal of a node does not require an explicit reference to the successor of the targeted node. The following code fragment also removes `Carol` from the list, and is shorter:

```
b = p.next;
b.next = b.next.next;
```

The procedure we have just outlined for removing a node from the middle of a list will not work when the node being targeted for removal is the first in the list. This is because the first node has no predecessor. You remove a node at the beginning of a list by moving the head reference one node forward. For instance, to remove `"Allan"` from the list at the beginning of Figure 20-3, simply write:

```
p = p.next;
```

As we have seen, both addition and removal require a reference to the node just before the point of the addition or removal. You can obtain such a reference by setting a reference to the head of the list and then walking the reference forward, one node at a time, to get it to the desired place. The process of walking a reference along the nodes of a list is called traversing the list.

Traversing Linked Lists

A *traversal* of a collection is a systematic method of doing some processing at each element of the collection. To traverse a linked list, set a reference, say `ref`, to the first node in the list, process the value at that node (by accessing `ref.value`) and then move on to the next node by setting `ref` to the successor of the current node:

```
ref = ref.next;
```

In this way, the reference `ref` moves from each node to the next until it becomes `null` at the end of the list. The following code fragment traverses a linked list `myList` and prints all of its elements:

```
Node ref = myList;
while (ref != null)
{
    System.out.println(ref.value);
    ref = ref.next;
}
```

Code Listing 20-1 builds a simple linked list and then traverses it to print its contents. The centerpiece of the program is the `LinkedList0` class. This class contains a private declaration of `Node`, which it uses to represent the linked list. `LinkedList0` uses a private field `first` to point to the first node of the linked list.

Code Listing 20-1 (LinkedList0.java)

```java
1   public class LinkedList0
2   {
3      /**
4          The Node class represents a list node.
5      */
6
7      private class Node
8      {
9         String value;
10        Node next;
11
12        /**
13           Constructor.
14           @param val The element to store in this node.
15           @param n The reference to the next node.
16        */
17
18        Node(String val, Node n)
19        {
20           value = val;
21           next = n;
22        }
23
24        /**
25           Constructor.
26           @param val The element to store in this node.
27        */
28
29        Node(String val)
30        {
31           value = val;
32           next = null;
33        }
34     }
35
36     //Reference to the first node in the list
37     private Node first = null;
38
39     /**
40        Constructor.
41        Builds a linked list.
42     */
43
44     public LinkedList0()
45     {
46        // Incrementally build the list
```

```
47            // Chuck Debby Elaine Fred
48            first = new Node("Debby");
49            first.next = new Node("Elaine");
50            first.next.next = new Node ("Fred");
51            first = new Node ("Chuck", first);
52
53            String [ ] names = {"Bob", "Allan"};
54
55            // Use a loop to add all names in the array to the
56            // front of the linked list to build the list
57            // Allan Bob Chuck Debby Elaine Fred
58            for (String s : names)
59                first = new Node(s, first);
60        }
61
62        /**
63            The print method traverses the list
64            and prints all of its elements.
65        */
66
67        public void print()
68        {
69            Node ref = first;
70            while (ref!= null)
71            {
72                System.out.print(ref.value + " ");
73                ref = ref.next;
74            }
75        }
76
77        /**
78            The main method creates the linked list
79            and invokes its print method.
80        */
81
82        public static void main(String [] args)
83        {
84            LinkedList0 ll = new LinkedList0();
85            String str = "The contents of the list are:";
86            System.out.println(str);
87            ll.print();
88        }
89    }
```

Program Output

```
The contents of the list are:
Allan Bob Chuck Debby Elaine Fred
```

Checkpoint

20.1 Give a sequence of statements that creates a linked list of strings
"red green blue" by creating a node with "green", then a node with "blue",
then a node with "red", in that order.

20.2 Consider the following statements:

```
Node colorList = new Node("Yellow", new Node("Purple"));
colorList = new Node("Brown", colorList);
System.out.print(colorList.value);
System.out.print(colorList.next.value);
System.out.print(colorList.next.next.value);
```

What is the output?

20.2 Operations on Linked Lists

CONCEPT: The most basic operations on linked lists are traversing the list, moving
to a position determined by an index, adding an element, removing an
element, and searching for an element.

Let us write a linked list class that implements a subset of the methods of the `java.util.List`
interface. Our class will implement the following methods:

- `boolean isEmpty()`: check if the list is empty.
- `int size()`: return the number of elements in the list.
- `void add(String e)`: add an element e to the end of the list.
- `void add(int index, String e)`: add the specified element e to the list at the
  position given by index.
- `String remove(int index)`: remove and return the element at the position given
  by index.
- `boolean remove(String e)`: remove the specified element e and return true if the
  item was successfully removed.

The `LinkedList1` class uses the same `Node` class as `LinkedList0`. The class also uses
two references

```
Node first;
Node last;
```

to keep track of the first and last nodes in the list. The reference `first` serves as the head of
the list, and `last` is used to enable elements to be added quickly to the end of the list. Both
references will be set to `null` when the list is empty.

The `isEmpty` Method

We can check to see if the list is empty by evaluating the expression `first == null`. The
`isEmpty` method simply returns the value of that expression:

```
boolean isEmpty()
{
    return first == null;
}
```

The `size` Method

The number of elements in a linked list can be determined by initializing a counter to 0 and then incrementing the counter at each step of a traversal of the linked list.

The `add` Methods

The `add(String e)` method adds a new element e to the end of the linked list. If the list is empty, the new node containing e becomes both the first and last node:

```
first = new Node(e);
last = first;
```

If the list is nonempty, the new node is made the successor of the last node, and then the reference `last` is set to point to the new node:

```
last.next = new Node(e);
last = last.next;
```

The `add(int index, String e)` method is a little more involved. We consider several cases:

- *The index is invalid.* If the index is negative, or greater than the size of the list, the method throws an exception.
- *The index is zero.* The new node becomes the first node of the list. If the list was previously empty, then `last` must be set to `first`.
- *The index is greater than zero.* The method must find the right place to add the new node. It does this by skipping index−1 nodes to get to the node that is to be the predecessor of the new node as follows:

```
Node pred = first;
for (int k = 1; k <= index − 1; k++)
{
    pred = pred.next;
}
```

Once the predecessor is found, the new node is created and spliced in as follows:

```
pred.next = new Node(e, pred.next);
```

At this point, the method checks to see if the new node is now the last node. If so, `last` must be updated to point to the new node as follows:

```
if (pred.next.next == null)
    last = pred.next;
```

The remove Methods

The remove methods follow logic similar to the corresponding add methods. Let us consider the remove(int index) method. Again, we consider a number of different cases:

- *The index is invalid.* If the index is negative, or greater or equal to the size of the list, the method throws an exception.
- *The index is zero.* Here the element to be removed is the first on the list. The method moves first down to remove the first node. If the list is now empty, then last must be set to null.
- *The index is greater than zero.* In this case the method sets a reference pred to the predecessor of the node being targeted for removal. The target node is then removed. If the removed node was at the end of the list, then last must be reset to point to its predecessor:

```
pred.next == pred.next.next;
if (pred.next == null)
    last = pred;
```

The toString Method

This method returns a string representation of the contents of the list, and is useful for displaying the list in a GUI component. The method appends the string value of each list element to a StringBuilder object and returns the string value representation of that object.

The LinkedList1 class and all of its methods can be seen in Code Listing 20-2.

Code Listing 20-2 (LinkedList1.java)

```
1   /**
2       The LinkedList1 class implements a Linked list.
3   */
4
5   class LinkedList1
6   {
7       /**
8           The Node class stores a list element
9           and a reference to the next node.
10      */
11
12      private class Node
13      {
14          String value;
15          Node next;
16
17          /**
18              Constructor.
```

```
19                @param val The element to store in the node.
20                @param n The reference to the successor node.
21           */
22
23           Node(String val, Node n)
24           {
25              value = val;
26              next = n;
27           }
28
29           /**
30              Constructor.
31              @param val The element to store in the node.
32           */
33
34           Node(String val)
35           {
36              // Call the other (sister) constructor.
37              this(val, null);
38           }
39       }
40
41       private Node first;    // list head
42       private Node last;     // last element in list
43
44       /**
45          Constructor.
46       */
47
48       public LinkedList1()
49       {
50          first = null;
51          last = null;
52       }
53
54       /**
55          The isEmpty method checks to see
56          if the list is empty.
57          @return true if list is empty,
58          false otherwise.
59       */
60
61       public boolean isEmpty()
62       {
63          return first == null;
64       }
65
66       /**
```

```
67          The size method returns the length of the list.
68          @return The number of elements in the list.
69       */
70
71       public int size()
72       {
73          int count = 0;
74          Node p = first;
75          while (p != null)
76          {
77             // There is an element at p
78             count ++;
79             p = p.next;
80          }
81          return count;
82       }
83
84       /**
85          The add method adds an element to
86          the end of the list.
87          @param e The value to add to the
88          end of the list.
89       */
90
91       public void add(String e)
92       {
93          if (isEmpty())
94          {
95             first = new Node(e);
96             last = first;
97          }
98          else
99          {
100            // Add to end of existing list
101            last.next = new Node(e);
102            last = last.next;
103         }
104      }
105
106      /**
107         The add method adds an element at a position.
108         @param e The element to add to the list.
109         @param index The position at which to add
110         the element.
111         @exception IndexOutOfBoundsException When
112         index is out of bounds.
113      */
114
```

```
115     public void add(int index, String e)
116     {
117         if (index < 0  || index > size())
118         {
119             String message = String.valueOf(index);
120             throw new IndexOutOfBoundsException(message);
121         }
122
123         // Index is at least 0
124         if (index == 0)
125         {
126             // New element goes at beginning
127             first = new Node(e, first);
128             if (last == null)
129                 last = first;
130             return;
131         }
132
133         // Set a reference pred to point to the node that
134         // will be the predecessor of the new node
135         Node pred = first;
136         for (int k = 1; k <= index - 1; k++)
137         {
138             pred = pred.next;
139         }
140
141         // Splice in a node containing the new element
142         pred.next = new Node(e, pred.next);
143
144         // Is there a new last element ?
145         if (pred.next.next == null)
146             last = pred.next;
147     }
148
149     /**
150         The toString method computes the string
151         representation of the list.
152         @return The string form of the list.
153     */
154
155     public String toString()
156     {
157         StringBuilder strBuilder = new StringBuilder();
158
159         // Use p to walk down the linked list
160         Node p = first;
161         while (p != null)
162         {
```

```
163            strBuilder.append(p.value + "\n");
164            p = p.next;
165         }
166         return strBuilder.toString();
167      }
168
169      /**
170         The remove method removes the element at an index.
171         @param index The index of the element to remove.
172         @return The element removed.
173         @exception IndexOutOfBoundsException When index is
174                    out of bounds.
175      */
176
177      public String remove(int index)
178      {
179         if (index < 0 || index >= size())
180         {
181            String message = String.valueOf(index);
182            throw new IndexOutOfBoundsException(message);
183         }
184
185         String element;   // The element to return
186         if (index == 0)
187         {
188            // Removal of first item in the list
189            element = first.value;
190            first = first.next;
191            if (first == null)
192               last = null;
193         }
194         else
195         {
196            // To remove an element other than the first,
197            // find the predecessor of the element to
198            // be removed.
199            Node pred = first;
200
201            // Move pred forward index - 1 times
202            for (int k = 1; k <= index -1; k++)
203               pred = pred.next;
204
205            // Store the value to return
206            element = pred.next.value;
207
208            // Route link around the node to be removed
209            pred.next = pred.next.next;
210
```

```
211            // Check if pred is now last
212            if (pred.next == null)
213               last = pred;
214         }
215         return element;
216      }
217
218      /**
219         The remove method removes an element.
220         @param element The element to remove.
221         @return true if the remove succeeded,
222         false otherwise.
223      */
224
225      public boolean remove(String element)
226      {
227         if (isEmpty())
228            return false;
229
230         if (element.equals(first.value))
231         {
232            // Removal of first item in the list
233            first = first.next;
234            if (first == null)
235               last = null;
236            return true;
237         }
238
239         // Find the predecessor of the element to remove
240         Node pred = first;
241         while (pred.next != null &&
242                !pred.next.value.equals(element))
243         {
244            pred = pred.next;
245         }
246
247         // pred.next == null OR pred.next.value is element
248         if (pred.next == null)
249            return false;
250
251         // pred.next.value  is element
252         pred.next = pred.next.next;
253
254         // Check if pred is now last
255         if (pred.next == null)
256            last = pred;
257
258         return true;
```

```
259        }
260
261        public static void main(String [] args)
262        {
263            LinkedList1 ll = new LinkedList1();
264            ll.add("Amy");
265            ll.add("Bob");
266            ll.add(0, "Al");
267            ll.add(2, "Beth");
268            ll.add(4, "Carol");
269            System.out.println("The members of the list are:");
270            System.out.print(ll);
271        }
272    }
```

Program Output

```
The members of the list are:
Al
Amy
Beth
Bob
Carol
```

Graphical Interfaces for the Linked List Program

Now we describe graphical user interfaces that can be used to test the LinkedList1 class
and other classes like it. The user interfaces are shown in Figure 20-4. The screenshot shows
a scenario in which the user has given commands to add the strings Amy, Bob, Carol, and
David to the list, followed by a command to remove the string at index 1 (Bob). The window
on the left shows the Swing version of the user interface, while the one on the right shows
the JavaFX version.

Figure 20-4   Graphical Interfaces for testing linked list classes   (Mark Schrier. Copyright Oracle, Inc.)

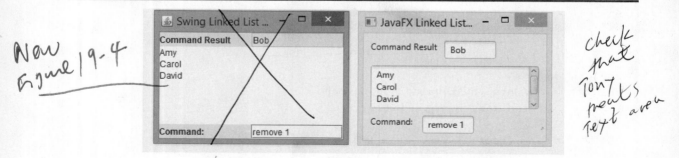

The interfaces have a command entry text field at the bottom of the window, a text area in
the center of the window, and an un-editable text field at the top. The text field at the top is
used to display values returned by some of the list class methods.

Code Listing 20-3 builds the Swing version of the interface while Code Listing 20-4 builds the JavaFX version. Both programs attach an event handler to the command text field at the bottom of the window, causing the handler to be called when the user types a command into the text field and presses the ⌜Enter⌝ key. The event handler method retrieves the typed command, analyzes it to determine its meaning, and calls the appropriate LinkedList1 class method.

The program recognizes simple commands that are closely patterned after the methods they are intended to test. The list of recognized commands:

- isempty: This command calls the isEmpty() method and displays the returned value in the result text field at the top of the frame.
- size: This command calls size() and displays the returned value in the result text field.
- add s: This command calls the add(String e) method and passes it s in place of e. For example, the user might type add Amy.
- add i s: This command calls the add(int index, string e) method and passes it the argument i for index and s for e. As an example, the user might type add 2 Brad to add "Brad" as the third element in the list.
- remove s: This command calls the remove(String e) method and passes s for e.
- remove i: This command calls the remove(int index) method and passes i for index.

The listener method works by separating the text retrieved from the command entry text field into a command followed by its arguments. For example, the command text

```
add 2 Brad
```

is separated into three tokens: the command add, the integer index 2, and the element Brad. The method creates a Scanner object that will read from the command string and then uses the usual Scanner methods to read strings and numbers from the command. This is done as follows:

```
String cmdText = cmdTextField.getText();
// Create a Scanner to read from the string
Scanner sc = new Scanner(cmdText);
```

Full details of the implementation can be found in Code Listings 20-3 and 20-4. The Swing version, shown next, uses an inner class for the event listener. This allows the action listener method to access the linked list object, the text area used for the list view, the text field used for command entry, and the text field used to show the results.

Code Listing 20-3   (SwingLinkedList1Demo.java)

```java
1  import java.awt.*;
2  import java.awt.event.*;
3  import javax.swing.*;
4  import java.util.*;
5
6  /**
7     This Swing class is used to demonstrate
8     the operations in the LinkedList1 class.
9  */
10
```

```
11  public class SwingLinkedList1Demo extends JFrame
12  {
13      private LinkedList1 ll;
14      private JTextArea  listView;
15      private JTextField cmdTextField;
16      private JTextField resultTextField;
17
18      public SwingLinkedList1Demo()
19      {
20          ll = new LinkedList1();
21          listView = new JTextArea();
22          cmdTextField = new JTextField();
23          resultTextField = new JTextField();
24
25          // Create a panel and label for result field
26          JPanel resultPanel = new JPanel(new GridLayout(1,2));
27          resultPanel.add(new JLabel("Command Result"));
28          resultPanel.add(resultTextField);
29          resultTextField.setEditable(false);
30          add(resultPanel, BorderLayout.NORTH);
31
32          // Put the textArea in the center of the frame
33          add(listView);
34          listView.setEditable(false);
35          listView.setBackground(Color.WHITE);
36
37          // Create a panel and label for the command text field
38          JPanel cmdPanel = new JPanel(new GridLayout(1,2));
39          cmdPanel.add(new JLabel("Command:"));
40          cmdPanel.add(cmdTextField);
41          add(cmdPanel, BorderLayout.SOUTH);
42          cmdTextField.addActionListener(new CmdTextListener());
43
44          // Set up the frame
45          setTitle("Swing Linked List Demo");
46          setDefaultCloseOperation(JFrame.EXIT_ON_CLOSE);
47          pack();
48          setVisible(true);
49      }
50
51      /**
52         Private class that responds to the command that
53         the user types into the command entry text field.
54      */
55
56      private class CmdTextListener implements ActionListener
57      {
58          public void actionPerformed(ActionEvent evt)
```

delete

```
59          {
60              // Get the command from the command textfield.
61              String cmdText = cmdTextField.getText();
62
63              // Use a scanner to read the method in the command
64              // and do a switch on it.
65              Scanner sc = new Scanner(cmdText);
66              String cmd = sc.next();
67              switch(cmd)
68              {
69                  case "add":
70                      if (sc.hasNextInt())
71                      {
72                          // add index element
73                          int index = sc.nextInt();
74                          String element = sc.next();
75                          ll.add(index, element);
76                      }
77                      else
78                      {
79                          // add element
80                          String element = sc.next();
81                          ll.add(element);
82                      }
83                      listView.setText(ll.toString());
84                      pack();
85                      return;
86                  case "remove":
87                      if (sc.hasNextInt())
88                      {
89                          // remove index
90                          int index = sc.nextInt();
91                          String res = ll.remove(index);
92                          resultTextField.setText(res);
93                      }
94                      else
95                      {
96                          // remove element
97                          String element = sc.next();
98                          boolean res = ll.remove(element);
99                          String resText = String.valueOf(res);
100                         resultTextField.setText(resText);
101                     }
102                     listView.setText(ll.toString());
103                     pack();
104                     return;
105                 case "isempty" :
106                     String resText = String.valueOf(ll.isEmpty());
```

```
107                    resultTextField.setText(resText);
108                    return;
109                case "size":
110                    String resText1 = String.valueOf(ll.size());
111                    resultTextField.setText(resText1);
112                    return;
113            }
114        }
115    }
116
117    /**
118        The main method creates an instance of the
119        SwingLinkedList1Demo class which causes it to
120        display its window.
121    */
122
123    public static void main(String [ ] args)
124    {
125        new SwingLinkedList1Demo();
126    }
127 }
```

The program

The ~~JavaFX version shown in Code Listing 20-4~~ uses a separate, non-nested class for the event handler. The class uses constructor parameters to pass the linked list object, the text area to be used for the list view, and the text filed used to display results. The text field used for command entry is accessed through the getTarget() method of the event parameter of the event handler method. — ↑ ⌐ line 89

20-7 19.3

Code Listing 20-4 (~~JavaFXLinkedListDemo.java~~)

```
 1 import java.util.Scanner;
 2 import javafx.application.Application;
 3 import javafx.event.*;
 4 import javafx.geometry.Insets;
 5 import javafx.scene.Scene;
 6 import javafx.scene.control.*;
 7 import javafx.scene.layout.*;
 8 import javafx.stage.Stage;
 9
10 /**
11  This JavaFX class is used to demonstrate
12  the operations in the LinkedList1 class.
13 */
14
15 public class ~~JavaFX~~LinkedListDemo extends Application
16 {
17     @Override
18     public void start(Stage stage) throws Exception
```

replace with new version

```
19        {
20              // Reference to linked list.
21              LinkedList1 ll = new LinkedList1();
22
23              // listView shows current list elements.
24              TextArea  listView = new TextArea();
25              listView.setEditable(false);
26
27              // Input for user command.
28              TextField cmdTextField = new TextField();
29              cmdTextField.setPrefColumnCount(5);
30
31              // Displays result of list method that was
32              // invoked by the user command.
33              TextField resultTextField = new TextField();
34              resultTextField.setPrefColumnCount(5);
35              resultTextField.setEditable(false);
36
37              // Attach event handler to cmdTextField
38              EventHandler<ActionEvent> handler =
39                      new CommandHandler(ll, listView, resultTextField);
40              cmdTextField.setOnAction(handler);
41
42              // HBox to contain command result label and text field.
43              HBox hBox1 = new HBox(10);
44              Label resultLabel = new Label("Command Result");
45              hBox1.getChildren().addAll(resultLabel, resultTextField);
46
47              // HBox to contain label and text field for command input.
48              HBox hBox2 = new HBox(10);
49              Label cmdLabel = new Label("Command: ");
50              hBox2.getChildren().addAll(cmdLabel, cmdTextField);
51
52              // VBox to contain the user interface components
53              VBox vBox = new VBox(10);
54              vBox.setPadding(new Insets(10));
55              vBox.getChildren().addAll(hBox1, listView, hBox2);
56
57              // Set up the scene and show the stage.
58              stage.setScene(new Scene(vBox));
59              stage.setTitle("JavaFX Linked List Demo");
60              stage.show();
61        }
62
63        public static void main(String [] args)
64        {
65              launch();
66        }
67 }
```

```
68
69
70  // Event Handler class for the command text field.
71  class CommandHandler implements EventHandler<ActionEvent>
72  {
73      // private fields to hold information passed to the constructor.
74      private LinkedList1 ll;
75      private TextField resultTextField;
76      private TextArea listView;
77
78      CommandHandler(LinkedList1 lList, TextArea lView, TextField rTfield)
79      {
80          ll = lList;
81          resultTextField = rTfield;
82          listView = lView;
83      }
84
85      @Override
86      public void handle(ActionEvent event)
87      {
88          // Get the command from the command textfield.
89          TextField cmdTextField = (TextField)event.getTarget();
90          String cmdText =  cmdTextField.getText();
91
92          // Use a scanner to read the name of the linked list
93          // method and do a switch on it.
94          Scanner sc = new Scanner(cmdText);
95          String cmd = sc.next();
96          switch(cmd)
97          {
98              case "add" :
99                  if (sc.hasNextInt())
100                 {
101                     // add index element
102                     int index = sc.nextInt();
103                     String element = sc.next();
104                     ll.add(index, element);
105                 }
106                 else
107                 {
108                     // add element
109                     String element = sc.next();
110                     ll.add(element);
111                 }
112                 listView.setText(ll.toString());
113                 return;
114             case "remove" :
115                 if (sc.hasNextInt())
116                 {
```

```
117                    // remove index
118                    int index = sc.nextInt();
119                    String res = ll.remove(index);
120                    resultTextField.setText(res);
121                 }
122             else
123             {
124                    // remove element
125                    String element = sc.next();
126                    boolean res = ll.remove(element);
127                    String resText = String.valueOf(res);
128                    resultTextField.setText(resText);
129             }
130             listView.setText(ll.toString());
131             return;
132         case "isempty":
133             String resText = String.valueOf(ll.isEmpty());
134             resultTextField.setText(resText);
135             return;
136         case "size":
137             String resText1 = String.valueOf(ll.size());
138             resultTextField.setText(resText1);
139             return;
140         }
141     }
142 }
```

20.3 Doubly Linked and Circularly Linked Lists

CONCEPT: A singly linked list makes it easy to move from any node to its successor. A doubly linked list makes it easy to move from any node to its successor or predecessor. A circularly linked list makes it easy to move from one end of the list to the other.

The singly linked lists we have been studying allow us to move from any node to its successor in one step. If we want to move from a node to its predecessor, though, we must start at the head of the list and then move all the way down to the predecessor of the current node. That gets costly if the current node is near the end of a long list. Moving to the predecessor can be done in one step if we add a predecessor reference to each node. Linked lists with successor and predecessor references are said to be *doubly linked*. Nodes in a doubly linked list look like this:

```
class Node
{
    String value; // Element
    Node next;    // Reference to successor
    Node prev;    // Reference to predecessor
```

```
            Node(String val, Node n, Node p)
            {
               value = val;
               next = n;
               prev = p;
            }

            Node(String val)
            {
               // Call the other constructor
               this(val, null, null);
            }
         }
```

A node with next and prev references is shown in Figure 20-5.

Figure 20-5 A node for a doubly linked list

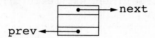

Working with doubly linked lists is not much different from working with singly linked lists. You use a null reference to represent an empty list and a reference to the head of the list to represent a nonempty list. You set next to null if the node has no successor, and set prev to null if the node has no predecessor. An example of a doubly linked list with the names Alan, Bob, and Carol is shown in Figure 20-6. The list uses a head pointer named first and a pointer to the last element named last.

Figure 20-6 A doubly linked list

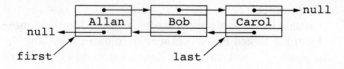

Adding a Node to a Doubly Linked List

VideoNote
Adding a
Node to a
Doubly Linked
List

Adding a node to a doubly linked list is similar to adding a node to a singly linked one. Say we want to add an element e to a doubly linked list. If the list is empty, the new node will have neither successor nor predecessor, so we can write the following:

```
first = new Node(e, null, null);
last = first;
```

Alternatively, we can use the one-arg constructor as follows:

```
first = new Node(e);
last = first;
```

There are two cases to consider when the list is nonempty: when the new node is to be added *before* the first element, and when the new node is to be added *after*. To add the new node before the first element, we can write

```
first = new Node(e, first, null);
first.next.prev = first;
```

Now let us consider the latter case. One way to proceed is first to obtain a reference to the node that will become the predecessor of the new node. Let us say such a reference, pred, has already been obtained. Now take another reference, succ, and set it to the node following pred:

```
Node succ = pred.next;
```

The new node to be added will go between pred and succ. Create this new node using a reference named middle:

```
Node middle = new Node(e, succ, pred);
```

Executing this sequence results in the scenario shown in Figure 20-7, with Alex playing the role of the element e. The goal is to insert Alex right after Allan.

Figure 20-7 The first step in inserting a node into a doubly linked list

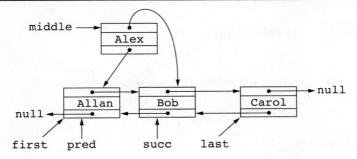

Once the situation in Figure 20-7 is achieved, it only remains to set pred.next to middle and succ.prev to middle. But we must be careful: while we know that pred is not null, we cannot say the same about succ. Moreover, if succ is null, it means that the new node was added at the end of the list, and last must be set to point to it. The correct code to finish the job follows:

```
pred.next = middle;
if (succ == null)
    last = middle
else
    succ.prev = middle;
```

Removing a Node from a Doubly Linked List

Removing a node from a doubly linked list is not difficult, although it needs to be done with some care. First, obtain a reference to the node you want to remove. Given such a reference, say target, obtain references to the nodes on either side:

```
Node pred = target.prev;
Node succ = target.next;
```

Now you want to make succ the successor of pred, and pred the predecessor of succ:

```
pred.next = succ;
succ.prev = pred;
```

Unfortunately, this code does not work if the targeted node is either the first or the last in the list. For example, if the targeted node is the last in the list, then succ will be null and trying to set succ.prev to pred will cause an exception to be thrown. The correct code follows:

```
if (pred == null)
    first = succ;
else
    pred.next = succ;

if (succ == null)
    last = pred;
else
    succ.prev = pred;
```

Note that this code works correctly even when the node being removed is the only one in the list. An implementation of a doubly linked list class is given in Code Listing 20-5.

Code Listing 20-5   (DLinkedList.java)

```
1   /**
2       The DLinkedList class implements a doubly
3       Linked list.
4   */
5
6   class DLinkedList
7   {
8       /**
9           The Node class stores a list element
10          and a reference to the next node.
11      */
12      private class Node
13      {
14          String value;       // Value of a list element
15          Node next;          // Next node in the list
16          Node prev;          // Previous element in the list
17
18          /**
19              Constructor.
20              @param val The element to be stored in the node.
21              @param n The reference to the successor node.
22              @param p The reference to the predecessor node.
23          */
```

```
24
25          Node(String val, Node n, Node p)
26          {
27              value = val;
28              next = n;
29              prev = p;
30          }
31
32          /**
33              Constructor.
34              @param val The element to be stored in the node.
35          */
36
37          Node(String val)
38          {
39              // Just call the other (sister) constructor
40              this(val, null, null);
41          }
42      }
43
44      private Node first;            // Head of the list
45      private Node last;            // Last element on the list
46
47      /**
48          Constructor.
49      */
50
51      public DLinkedList()
52      {
53          first = null;
54          last = null;
55      }
56
57      /**
58          The isEmpty method checks to see if the list
59          is empty.
60          @return true if list is empty, false otherwise.
61      */
62
63      public boolean isEmpty()
64      {
65          return first == null;
66      }
67
68      /**
69          The size method returns the length of the list.
70          @return The number of elements in the list.
71      */
```

```
 72
 73     public int size()
 74     {
 75        int count = 0;
 76        Node p = first;
 77        while (p != null)
 78        {
 79           // There is an element at p
 80           count ++;
 81           p = p.next;
 82        }
 83        return count;
 84     }
 85
 86     /**
 87        The add method adds to the end of the list.
 88        @param e The value to add.
 89     */
 90
 91     public void add(String e)
 92     {
 93        if (isEmpty())
 94        {
 95           last = new Node(e);
 96           first = last;
 97        }
 98        else
 99        {
100           // Add to end of existing list
101           last.next = new Node(e, null, last);
102           last = last.next;
103        }
104     }
105
106     /**
107        This add method adds an element at an index.
108        @param e The element to add to the list.
109        @param index The index at which to add.
110        @exception IndexOutOfBoundsException
111        When the index is out of bounds.
112     */
113
114     public void add(int index, String e)
115     {
116        if (index < 0  || index > size())
117        {
118           String message = String.valueOf(index);
119           throw new IndexOutOfBoundsException(message);
```

```
120            }
121
122         // Index is at least 0
123         if (index == 0)
124         {
125            // New element goes at beginning
126            Node p = first;              // Old first
127            first = new Node(e, p, null);
128            if (p != null)
129               p.prev = first;
130            if (last == null)
131               last = first;
132            return;
133         }
134
135         // pred will point to the predecessor
136         // of the new node.
137         Node pred = first;
138         for (int k = 1; k <= index - 1; k++)
139         {
140            pred = pred.next;
141         }
142
143         // Splice in a node with the new element
144         // We want to go from  pred-- succ to
145         // pred--middle--succ
146         Node succ = pred.next;
147         Node middle = new Node(e, succ, pred);
148         pred.next = middle;
149         if (succ == null)
150            last = middle;
151         else
152            succ.prev = middle;
153      }
154
155      /**
156         The toString method computes the string
157         representation of the list.
158         @return The string representation of the
159         linked list.
160      */
161
162      public String toString()
163      {
164         StringBuilder strBuilder = new StringBuilder();
165
166         // Use p to walk down the linked list
167         Node p = first;
```

```
168        while (p != null)
169        {
170            strBuilder.append(p.value + "\n");
171            p = p.next;
172        }
173        return strBuilder.toString();
174    }
175
176    /**
177        The remove method removes the element
178        at a given position.
179        @param index The position of the element
180        to remove.
181        @return The element removed.
182        @exception IndexOutOfBoundsException When
183        index is out of bounds.
184    */
185
186    public String remove(int index)
187    {
188        if (index < 0 || index >= size())
189        {
190            String message = String.valueOf(index);
191            throw new IndexOutOfBoundsException(message);
192        }
193
194        // Locate the node targeted for removal
195        Node target = first;
196        for (int k = 1; k <= index; k++)
197            target = target.next;
198
199        String element = target.value;   // Element to return
200        Node pred = target.prev;          // Node before the target
201        Node succ = target.next;          // Node after the target
202
203        // Route forward and back pointers around
204        // the node to be removed
205        if (pred == null)
206            first = succ;
207        else
208            pred.next = succ;
209
210        if (succ == null)
211            last = pred;
212        else
213            succ.prev = pred;
214
215        return element;
```

```
216        }
217
218        /**
219            The remove method removes an element from the list.
220            @param element The element to remove.
221            @return true if the element was removed, false otherwise.
222        */
223
224        public boolean remove(String element)
225        {
226            if (isEmpty())
227                return false;
228
229            // Locate the node targeted for removal
230            Node target = first;
231            while (target != null
232                    && !element.equals(target.value))
233                target = target.next;
234
235            if (target == null)
236                return false;
237
238            Node pred = target.prev;          // Node before the target
239            Node succ = target.next;          // Node after the target
240
241            // Route forward and back pointers around
242            // the node to be removed
243            if (pred == null)
244                first = succ;
245            else
246                pred.next = succ;
247
248            if (succ == null)
249                last = pred;
250            else
251                succ.prev = pred;
252
253            return true;
254        }
255
256        public static void main(String [] args)
257        {
258            DLinkedList ll = new DLinkedList();
259            ll.add("Amy");
260            ll.add("Bob");
261            ll.add(0, "Al");
262            ll.add(2, "Beth");
263            ll.add(4, "Carol");
```

```
264                 System.out.println("The elements of the list are:");
265                 System.out.println(ll);
266          }
267    }
```

Program Output

```
The elements of the list are:
Al
Amy
Beth
Bob
Carol
```

This class can be used through a graphical user interfaces similar to the those used with the LinkedList1 class. The code that implements these user interfaces is in the files *Swing-DLinkedListDemo.java and JavaFXDLinkedListDemo.java*, and can be found in the book's source code, available at www.pearsonhighered.com/gaddis.

Circularly Linked Lists

A singly linked list is *circularly linked* if the successor of the last node is the first. A doubly linked list is *circularly linked* if the successor of the last node is the first, and the predecessor of the first node is the last. Working with circularly linked lists is similar to working with non–circularly linked lists: the main differences are when you are adding to an empty list and when you are removing the last node from a list.

Checkpoint

20.3 Consider adding an element e to a nonempty doubly linked list with head pointer first and a pointer last pointing to the last node. The new node is to be added before some node that is already in the list. Let succ be a reference to the node in the list that will be the successor of the new node. Write code that can be used to add e to the list.

20.4 Consider adding an element e to a nonempty doubly linked list with head pointer first and a pointer last pointing to the last node. Write code that can be used to add e to the end of the list.

20.4 Recursion on Linked Lists

CONCEPT: A linked list is an inherently recursive data structure, and many operations on linked lists have natural recursive implementations.

The *tail* of a nonempty linked list *L* is the linked list that remains when the head of *L* is removed. The fact that the tail of a linked list is itself a linked list means that linked lists have a recursive structure. Many operations on linked lists can be given recursive formulations that process the element at the head of the list and then recursively operate on the tail. The base case for such recursive formulations is usually the case in which the list to be operated on is empty. This fact is very useful in formulating recursive methods that work on linked lists, so we restate it for emphasis:

A linked list is either empty (base case), or consists of a head and a tail. The head is the first element of the list, and the tail is the linked list consisting of all the other elements.

Consider a linked list class `RLinkedList` whose outline is shown here:

```
class RLinkedList
{
    private Node
    {

    }
    private Node first = null;
}
```

This class differs from the `LinkedList1` class of Section 20.2 in that it omits the reference that points to the last node in the list. We want to write recursive implementations of the `size`, `add`, and `remove` methods.

A Recursive Implementation of `size`

The recursive strategy to compute the size of a list mirrors the recursive nature of the linked list: If the list is empty, its size is 0; otherwise, the size of the list is the size of the tail plus 1. Note that the tail of a list `list` is `list.next`. A recursive implementation of `size` follows:

```
private int size(Node list)
{
    if (list == null)
        return 0;                      // Base case
    else
        return size(list.next) + 1;    // Add 1 to size of tail
}
```

The public `size` method simply calls the private recursive version of `size`, passing it the reference to the head of the list as follows:

```
public int size( )
{
    return size(first);
}
```

Other recursive methods of this class will similarly be private, and will be called by a corresponding public method.

A Recursive Implementation of the add(String e, Node list) Method

The RLinkedList class will have a recursive private method

```
Node add(String e, Node list)
```

that will be called by its public counterpart, void add(String e). The recursive method will take a list list and an element e as parameters, and will return the list that results from adding e to the end of list. As in the case of size, the recursive strategy is based on the recursive nature of a linked list. If the list is empty, then the method returns a list of one item containing e as its only element. If the list is nonempty, then the element e is added to the end of the tail of the list as follows:

```
private Node add(String e, Node list)
{
    if (list == null)
    {
        // Base case
        return new Node(e);
    }
    else
    {
        // Add e to the end of the tail and use
        // the result to replace the tail
        list.next = add(e, list.next);
        return list;
    }
}
```

Notice the sequence of events in the nonbase case. First, the recursive call is used to return the result of adding e to the end of the tail:

```
add(e, list.next);
```

Second, this modified tail is used to replace the current tail in list:

```
list.next = add(e, list.next);
```

Third and finally, the method returns the original list with the tail thus replaced:

```
return list;
```

A Recursive Implementation of add(int index, String e, Node list)

This method inserts an element e at a given index within a list and returns the resulting list. First the method checks that index is within the proper range and throws an exception if it is not. Suppose therefore that the index is nonnegative, and that the size of the list is greater than or equal to the index. Consider two cases:

- *The index is zero.* The method needs to put e at the beginning of the list (which may or may not be empty) and return the result. This is accomplished by

    ```
    return new Node(e, list);
    ```

- *The index is greater than zero.* Because the size of the list is greater than or equal to the index, the list cannot be empty, and therefore must have a head and a tail. The method needs to replace the tail with the result of adding e at position index-1 in the tail and return the modified list:

    ```
    list.next = add(index-1, e, list.next);
    return list;
    ```

In this method, the recursion is on the index parameter rather than on the list, and the base case is when the index is zero. The complete method is as follows:

```
private Node add(int index, String e, Node list)
{
    if (index < 0  || index > size())
    {
        String message = String.valueOf(index);
        throw new IndexOutOfBoundsException(message);
    }

    if (index == 0)
        return new Node(e, list);

    list.next = add(index-1, e, list.next);
    return list;
}
```

A Recursive Implementation of the remove Methods

Each of the two recursive remove methods returns a pair of results: the node removed from the list, and the list that remains after said node has been removed. These two results can be embodied in a single object of type RemovalResult:

```
private class RemovalResult
{
    Node node;   // The node removed from the list
    Node list;   // The list remaining after the removal

    RemovalResult(Node remNode, Node remList)
    {
        node = remNode;
        list = remList;
    }
}
```

First, consider the method

```
RemovalResult remove(int index, Node list)
```

This method is supposed to return the node at the given index, and the remaining list, packaged together in a single `RemovalResult` object. Assume that `index` is nonnegative and is less or equal to one less than the size of list. Again, consider the following cases:

- *The index is zero.* Then the size of the list must be greater or equal to 1, so the list is nonempty. The method needs to remove the first node from `list`, package the node and remaining list (which will be `list.next`), and return the resulting `RemovalResult` object.

  ```
  if (index == 0)
  {
      // Remove the first node on list
      RemovalResult remRes;
      remRes = new RemovalResult(list, list.next);
      list.next = null;
      return remRes;
  }
  ```

- *The index is nonzero.* In this case, the method needs to recursively remove the node at `index-1` from the tail:

  ```
  RemovalResult remRes;
  remRes = remove(index-1, list.next);
  ```

  The method then replaces the tail with the results of the recursive call:

  ```
  list.next = remRes.list;
  ```

  Before returning to its caller, the method must modify the `RemovalResult` object returned from the recursive call by setting its remaining list field to `list` (as modified by the replacement of its tail):

  ```
  remRes.list = list;
  return remRes;
  ```

The second removal method is similar and can be found in Code Listing 20-6.

Code Listing 20-6 (RLinkedList.java)

```
1   /**
2       Linked List class with recursive methods.
3   */
4
5   class RLinkedList
6   {
7       /**
8           The Node class will store a list element
9           and a reference to the next node.
10      */
11
12      private class Node
13      {
14          String value;
```

```
15          Node next;
16
17          /**
18             Constructor.
19             @param val The element to store in the node.
20             @param n The reference to the successor node.
21          */
22
23          Node(String val, Node n)
24          {
25             value = val;
26             next = n;
27          }
28
29          /**
30             Constructor.
31             @param val The element to be stored in the node.
32          */
33
34          Node(String val)
35          {
36             // Just call the other (sister) constructor
37             this(val, null);
38          }
39       }
40
41       private Node first;  // List head
42
43       /**
44          Constructor.
45       */
46
47       public RLinkedList()
48       {
49          first = null;
50       }
51
52       /**
53          The isEmpty method checks to see if the list is empty.
54          @return true if list is empty, false otherwise.
55       */
56
57       public boolean isEmpty()
58       {
59          return first == null;
60       }
61
62       /**
```

```
63          The size method returns the length of the list.
64          @return The number of elements in the list.
65       */
66
67      public int size()
68      {
69          return size(first);
70      }
71
72      /**
73          This size method recursively computes the
74          length of a linked list passed to it.
75          @param The linked list.
76          @return The number of items in the linked list.
77       */
78
79      private int size(Node list)
80      {
81          if (list == null)
82             return 0;
83          else
84             return size(list.next) + 1;
85      }
86
87      /**
88          The add method adds an element to the end of the list.
89          @param e The value to add to the end of the list.
90       */
91
92      public void add(String e)
93      {
94          // Replace first with result of adding e to first
95          first = add(e, first);
96      }
97
98      /**
99          This recursive private add method adds
100         an element e to the end of a list.
101         @param e The element to add to the list.
102         @param list The list to add e to.
103         @return The list resulting from adding e to its end.
104      */
105
106     private Node add(String e, Node list)
107     {
108         if (list == null)
109         {
110             // Base case
```

```
111            return new Node(e);
112        }
113        else
114        {
115            // Add e to the end of the tail and use
116            // the result to replace the tail
117            list.next = add(e, list.next);
118            return list;
119        }
120    }
121
122    /**
123        The add method adds an element e at place index
124        in this linked list.
125        @param index The place in the list to add an element.
126        @param e The element to add this the linked list.
127        @exception IndexOutOfBoundsException When index is
128                    out of bounds.
129    */
130
131    public void add(int index, String e)
132    {
133        // Replace first with the result of adding
134        // e at index in first
135        first = add(index, e, first);
136    }
137
138    /**
139        This add method adds an element at an index in a list.
140        @param e The element to add to the list.
141        @param index The index at which to add the element.
142        @param list The list to add e to.
143        @return The list resulting from adding e.
144        @exception IndexOutOfBoundsException When index is
145                    out of bounds.
146    */
147
148    private Node add(int index, String e, Node list)
149    {
150        if (index < 0  || index > size())
151        {
152            String message = String.valueOf(index);
153            throw new IndexOutOfBoundsException(message);
154        }
155        if (index == 0)
156            return new Node(e, list);
157
158        // 0 < index and index <= size so list is not empty
```

```
159            // Replace the tail with result of adding e at index - 1
160            // in the tail
161            list.next = add(index-1, e, list.next);
162            return list;
163        }
164
165        /**
166            The toString method computes the string
167            representation of the list.
168            @return The string representation of the linked list.
169        */
170
171        public String toString()
172        {
173            StringBuilder strBuilder = new StringBuilder();
174
175            // Use p to walk down the linked list
176            Node p = first;
177            while (p != null)
178            {
179                strBuilder.append(p.value + "\n");
180                p = p.next;
181            }
182            return strBuilder.toString();
183        }
184
185        /**
186            The RemovalResult class describes the results of
187            removing a node from a linked list.
188        */
189
190        private class RemovalResult
191        {
192            Node node;    // The node removed from the list
193            Node list;    // The list remaining after the removal
194            RemovalResult(Node remNode, Node remList)
195            {
196                node = remNode;
197                list = remList;
198            }
199        }
200
201        /**
202            The remove method removes the element at an index.
203            @param index The index of the element to remove.
204            @return The element removed.
205            @exception IndexOutOfBoundsException When index is
206                        out of bounds.
```

```
207        */
208
209        public String remove(int index)
210        {
211           // Pass the job on to the recursive version
212           RemovalResult  remRes = remove(index, first);
213           String element = remRes.node.value;  // Element to return
214           first = remRes.list;                 // Remaining list
215           return element;
216        }
217
218        /**
219           The private remove method recursively removes
220           the node at the given index from a list.
221           @param index The position of the node to remove.
222           @param list The list from which to remove a node.
223           @return The result of removing the node from the list.
224           @exception IndexOutOfBoundsException When index is
225                        out of bounds.
226        */
227        private RemovalResult remove(int index, Node list)
228        {
229           if (index < 0 || index >= size())
230           {
231              String message = String.valueOf(index);
232              throw new IndexOutOfBoundsException(message);
233           }
234
235           if (index == 0)
236           {
237              // Remove the first node on list
238              RemovalResult remRes;
239              remRes = new RemovalResult(list, list.next);
240              list.next = null;
241              return remRes;
242           }
243
244           // Recursively remove the element at index-1 in the tail
245           RemovalResult remRes;
246           remRes = remove(index-1, list.next);
247
248           // Replace the tail with the results and return
249           // after modifying the list part of RemovalResult
250           list.next = remRes.list;
251           remRes.list = list;
252           return remRes;
253        }
254
```

```
255     /**
256        The remove method removes a given
257        element from linked list.
258     */
259
260     public boolean remove(String e)
261     {
262        RemovalResult remRes;
263        remRes = remove(e, first);
264
265        // Replace the list by the results of the removal
266        first = remRes.list;
267        if (remRes.node != null)
268           return true;
269        else
270           return false;
271     }
272
273     /**
274        The remove method recursively removes a
275        node containing a given element from
276        a specified list.
277        @param element The element to remove.
278        @param list The list to remove from.
279        @return the list containing
280     */
281
282     private RemovalResult remove(String e, Node list)
283     {
284        if (list == null)
285           return new RemovalResult(null, null);
286
287        // Is the first node on list the target of the removal?
288        if (list.value.equals(e))
289        {
290           RemovalResult remRes;
291           remRes = new RemovalResult(list, list.next);
292           list.next = null;
293           return remRes;
294        }
295
296        // Node to be removed is after the first node on list
297        // Recursively remove it from the tail
298        RemovalResult remRes;
299        remRes = remove(e, list.next);
300
301        list.next = remRes.list;
302        remRes.list = list;
```

```
303            return remRes;
304        }
305
306        public static void main(String [] args)
307        {
308            RLinkedList ll = new RLinkedList();
309            ll.add("Amy");
310            ll.add("Bob");
311            ll.add(0, "Al");
312            ll.add(2, "Beth");
313            ll.add(4, "Carol");
314            System.out.println("The members of the list are:");
315            System.out.print(ll);
316        }
317    }
```

The book's source code, available at www.pearsonhighered.com/gaddis, contains files ~~SwingRLinkedListDemo.java~~ and *JavaFXRLinkedListDemo.java* that implement graphical user interfaces for this class.

In the Spotlight:
Directed Graphs

A linked list defines a one-way relation among a set of nodes in such a way that from any of the nodes you can move to at most one other node. If you can move from a node *A* to another node *B*, we say that *A* is *adjacent to B*, or that *B* is a *neighbor* of *A*. Using this terminology, we can see that a linked list is a collection of nodes in which every node may have at most one neighbor, and in which there is a path from a distinguished *head node* to every other node, as shown in Figure 20-8.

Figure 20-8   The adjacency relation for nodes of a linked list

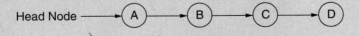

A directed graph is a data structure that is similar to a linked list, but with a much more general type of adjacency relation among its nodes. Specifically, a *directed graph* is a collection of nodes with an adjacency relation in which any node may have any number of neighbors. Directed graphs are often referred to as *digraphs,* and links between their nodes are called *edges.* An example of a directed graph is depicted in Figure 20-9.

Figure 20-9   An example of a digraph

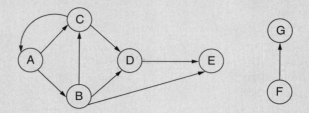

A digraph does not have to have a head node from which you can reach every other node, nor does it have to be "connected." Digraphs are very useful in modeling different types of systems. For example, a digraph can be used to model a computer network. In such a model, the nodes represent computers and the edges represent communication links.

The ideas we learned in this and preceding chapters can be used to create computer representations of digraphs. One such representation associates with each node *X* the list of its neighbors: that is, the list of nodes that can be reached from *X* by traversing a single edge. Such a list is called an *adjacency list* for *X*. For example, the digraph of Figure 20-9 can be represented as shown in Table 20-1.

Table 20-1   Representing a digraph by adjacency lists

Node	Neighbors
A	B, C
B	C, D, E
C	A, D
D	E
E	
F	G
G	

The adjacency list representation can be realized by using a map that associates nodes with their adjacency lists. Code Listing 20-7 initializes an adjacency list for the digraph of Figure 20-9 and then prints it out. The program uses a `Map` of `String` to `List<String>`, which is defined in lines 12 and 13. In lines 22 through 27, the program acquires an entry set for the `Map` object and then uses the enhanced for loop to print out the adjacency list information. Entry sets for maps were discussed in Section 18.4.

Code Listing 20-7   (`AdjacencyList.java`)

```
1 import java.util.*;
2 /**
3    This program demonstrates how to initialize an adjacency list
```

```
 4    structure whose nodes are strings. It uses a map of strings (nodes)
 5    to Lists of strings (nodes)
 6 */
 7
 8 public class AdjacencyList
 9 {
10     public static void main(String[] args)
11     {
12         Map<String, List<String>>
13                         adjList = new HashMap<String, List<String>>();
14         adjList.put("A", Arrays.asList("B", "C"));
15         adjList.put("B", Arrays.asList("C", "D", "E"));
16         adjList.put("C", Arrays.asList("A", "D"));
17         adjList.put("D", Arrays.asList("E"));
18         adjList.put("E", new ArrayList<String>());
19         adjList.put("F", Arrays.asList("G"));
20         adjList.put("G", new ArrayList<String>());
21
22         Set< Map.Entry<String, List<String>>>
23                         entries = adjList.entrySet();
24         for (Map.Entry<String, List<String>> e : entries)
25         {
26             System.out.println(e.getKey() + ": " + e.getValue()) ;
27         }
28     }
29 }
```

Program Output

```
D: [E]
E: []
F: [G]
G: []
A: [B, C]
B: [C, D, E]
C: [A, D]
```

In practice, we do not build adjacency lists of strings, as shown here. Instead, we establish a mapping between the set of names of the nodes and a set of nonnegative integers $0..N-1$, where N is the number of nodes. In our example, if we number the nodes A through G in order, the adjacency list structure might be as shown in Table 20-2.

Table 20-2   An adjacency list using integers to represent digraph nodes

Node	Neighbors
0	1, 2
1	2, 3, 4
2	0, 3
3	4
4	
5	6
6	

The reason for the change is that, in practice, algorithms that work with adjacency lists often need to compare different nodes of the digraph for equality. It is more efficient to compare integers than it is to compare strings.

Data describing adjacency lists is usually stored in text files. Programs that work with digraphs read the data from such files and construct an in-memory representation of the adjacency list. The data stored in the file should follow a format that makes it easy for programs to *parse* the data. *Parsing* is the process of recognizing meaningful structure from syntax. In this case, we need to parse the file data to recognize which parts of the data represent nodes and which parts represent the adjacency lists for the nodes. Table 20-3 uses the example digraph of Figure 20-9 to illustrate a format that is relatively easy to parse.

Table 20-3   Storing digraph information in a file to simplify parsing

7			
A	0		
B	1		
C	2		
D	3		
E	4		
F	5		
G	6		
0	2	1	2
1	3	2	3	4
2	2	0	3
3	1	4	
4	0		
5	1	6	
6	0		

The file starts with the number *N* of nodes in the graph, in this case 7. This number is followed by *N* lines, with each line showing the name of a node and the number that will be used to represent the node in the adjacency list. Following this is another set of *N* lines, with each line specifying the neighbors reachable from a single node. Each line has the form

(node)   (number of reachable neighbors)   (list of reachable neighbors)

For example, the line for node 1 is

    1   3   2 3 4

This line shows that the node with number 1 has 3 reachable neighbors and that these neighbors form the list 2 3 4.

20.5 Common Errors to Avoid

- **Forgetting to check that a reference to a node is not null.** Before you attempt to access the value stored in a node, or the `next` or `prev` references, make sure the reference is not null.
- **Forgetting to check for special cases.** Algorithms that operate on linked lists usually have to handle one or more special cases. Among the special cases to watch for are the following: an empty list when adding an element, a list of one element when removing an element, and the first or last node in the list when adding or removing a node.
- **Incorrect handling of base cases in recursive linked list algorithms.** Most recursive linked list algorithms do the recursion on the list parameter. In that case, the base case is usually when the list is empty. Algorithms that manipulate a list based on an index sometimes do the recursion on the index parameter: in that case the base case is when the index is zero.
- **Using the head of the list to traverse the list.** Do not use the head reference to walk down the list when you are traversing it, as it will destroy the structure of the list. Use an auxiliary reference initialized to the head.

Review Questions and Exercises

Multiple Choice and True/False

1. A list is a collection that _____.
   a. associates keys with elements
   b. assigns an index to each of its elements
   c. is implemented by the `JList` class
   d. none of the above

2. In Java, the first (head) element of a list _____.
   a. has a predecessor but no successor
   b. has both a predecessor and a successor
   c. has index 0
   d. has index 1

3. To add an element e just after a node referenced by `ref`, you should use the statement _____.

   a. `add(ref);`
   b. `ref.next = new Node(e);`
   c. `ref.next = new Node(e, ref.next);`
   d. `ref = new Node(e, ref.next);`

4. In general, adding an element e in *one step* to a singly linked list just before a node referenced by `ref` _____.

   a. cannot be done
   b. can be done if you use a loop
   c. can only be done when `ref` is the last node in the list
   d. can be done if you check for exceptions

5. To remove a node that is not the head of a singly linked list conveniently, you need to have a reference to _____.

   a. the node that precedes it
   b. the node that comes after it
   c. the node itself
   d. none of the above

6. To easily move from any node to its successor, and from any node to its predecessor, and from the first to the last node and from the last to the first node, you need _____.

   a. a singly linked list
   b. a singly and circularly linked list
   c. a doubly linked list
   d. a doubly and circularly linked list

7. A systematic method that starts at the beginning of the list and processes every node is called _____.

   a. a walk down the list
   b. a list processing function
   c. a travesty of list processing
   d. a traversal

8. A method for removing the element at an index k in a list throws an exception unless _____.

   a. k is negative
   b. k is nonnegative and less than the size of the list
   c. k is nonnegative and less than or equal to the size of the list
   d. k is positive and less than or equal to the size of the list

9. A method for adding an element at an index k in a list throws an exception unless _____.

   a. k is negative
   b. k is nonnegative and less than the size of the list
   c. k is nonnegative and less than or equal to the size of the list
   d. k is positive and less than or equal to the size of the list

10. A method that determines if a list is empty in a consistently written linked list class that uses a reference `first` to point to the first element, and a reference `last` to point to the last element, can return the value _____.

    a. `first == null`
    b. `last == null;`
    c. `first == null || last == null`
    d. all of the above

11. **True or False:** A linked list is a recursive data structure.

12. **True or False:** A linked list is a looping data structure.

13. **True or False:** The head of a linked list is also a linked list.

14. **True or False:** The tail of a linked list is also a linked list.

15. **True or False:** The index of an element to be added to a list can be the same as the size of the list.

16. **True or False:** The index of an element to be removed from a list can be the same as the size of the list.

17. **True or False:** The statement

```
myList = new Node("Zoe", myList);
```

    adds `"Zoe"` to the end of the linked list `myList;`

18. **True or False:** There is a natural way to write a recursive method to check whether a linked list is empty.

19. **True or False:** The last item in a doubly linked list can sometimes have a successor.

20. **True or False:** The first item in a doubly linked list can sometimes have a successor.

Find the Error

Find the error in each of the following code segments.

1.
```
// Print the second element on
// a list myList of 3 elements
Node ref = myList;
ref ++ ;
System.out.print(ref.value);
```

2.
```
// Print all elements in a list myList
Node ref = myList;
while (ref.next != null)
{
    System.out.print(ref.value + " ");
    ref = ref.next;
}
```

3.
```
// Add a node to the beginning of
// a doubly linked list myList
myList = new Node("Abraham", myList, null);
```

4. // Remove the first node of a nonempty
   // doubly linked list myList
   myList = myList.next;

5. // The reference last points to the last
   // node in a nonempty doubly linked list.
   // Remove the last node from the list
   last = last.prev;

Algorithm Workbench

1. Write a recursive method `void print(Node ref)` that prints the values of all elements in the linked list whose first node is `ref`.

2. Write a nonrecursive method `reverse()` that reverses the order of the elements in a list. Assume that this method is to be added to the `LinkedList1` class in this chapter.

3. Write a method `reverse()` as in Algorithm Workbench 2, except implement the method to call a private recursive method `Node reverse(Node list)`. Implement this recursive method as well.

4. Add a method `String removeMin()` to the `LinkedList1` class in this chapter. The method removes and returns the minimum string (according to the usual dictionary order on strings) from the list. If the list is empty, the method returns `null`.

Short Answer

1. Explain why recursive linked list methods should not be made public.

2. Explain how to modify the linked list classes in this chapter so that the size of the list can be computed more efficiently. Describe specifically the changes that have to be made to the fields and methods of the class.

3. What is the index of an element in a list?

4. Explain how contiguous allocation works to store elements of a list.

5. Explain how linked allocation works to store elements of a list.

6. Consult the online Java documentation and determine the differences between the `StringBuffer` and `StringBuilder` classes.

Programming Challenges

1. Generic Linked Lists

Modify the doubly linked list class presented in this chapter so it works with generic types. Add the following methods drawn from the `java.util.List` interface:

- `void clear()`: remove all elements from the list.
- `E get(int index)`: return the element at position `index` in the list.
- `E set(int index, E element)`: replace the element at the specified position with the specified element and return the previous element.

Test your generic linked list class by processing a list of numbers of type `double`.

2. Linked List Sorting and Reversing

Modify the `LinkedList1` class presented in this chapter by adding `sort()` and `reverse()` methods. The `reverse` method reverses the order of the elements in the list, and the `sort` method rearranges the elements in the list so they are sorted in alphabetical order. Do not use recursion to implement either of these operations. Extend the graphical interface in the `LinkedList1Demo` class to support sort and reverse commands, and use it to test the new methods.

3. Recursive Linked List Operations

Modify the `LinkedList1` class presented in this chapter by adding `sort()` and `reverse()` methods. The `reverse` method reverses the order of the elements in the list, and the `sort` method rearranges the elements in the list so they are sorted in alphabetical order. The class should use recursion to implement the sort and reverse operations. Extend the graphical interface in the `LinkedList1Demo` class to support sort and reverse commands, and use it to test the new methods.

4. Top Ten Gamers

Implement a class that maintains a list of the top ten performers in a video game. An entry on the list consists of a name and score, and the list is kept sorted in descending order of scores. Here is an example of such a list when it has only four elements.

Spike	120
Whiz	105
G-Man	99
JediMaster	95

Use a class based on linked lists. The class should have a constructor that sets up an empty list, and a `void insert(String name, int score)` method that adds a name and a score pair to the list. The `insert` method puts the entry in the proper position so that the list stays sorted by score. The list should have a maximum size of 10. After the list has 10 elements, an attempt to add a name with a score that is less than or equal to the minimum score on the list is ignored, and adding a score that is greater than the minimum score causes an entry with the minimum score to be dropped from the list.

Test the score with a graphical user interface similar to `LinkedList1Demo.java`. The graphical interface should support a single command of the form

> *insert name score*

An example of such a command is "insert Whiz 105."

5. Wedding Lottery

A beautiful princess is to select a husband from n suitors. The suitors are assigned numbers $0, \ldots, n-1$ and seated at a round table, and a random sequence of $n-1$ numbers $x_0, x_1, \ldots, x_{n-2}$, all of them in the range $0, \ldots, n-1$ is selected. The princess starts at suitor 0, and moving in a clockwise direction, she counts off x_0 positions and eliminates the suitor at that position. From there, she counts off another x_1 positions and eliminates the suitor at that position. She continues doing this until one lucky guy is left: she marries him and they live happily ever after.

Assume that the princess' position is always between two suitors. As an example, assume the suitors are A, B, C, and D, with A being numbered 0 and D being numbered 3. Let the random sequence be 0, 2, 1. Then the suitors will be eliminated in the order A, D, and C, and the lucky suitor will be B.

Write a class that uses linked lists to help the princess make her decision. The constructor for the class will be passed the number n of suitors (say 4), followed by a list of n suitors' names (say A, B, C, D), followed by a list of n – 1 numbers used to "rotate" among the suitors (0, 2, 1). The current position starts at the beginning of the list. The class should have a method rotate(int x) that counts off x steps in the clockwise direction beginning at the current position. The class should have a method

```
List<String> getEliminated()
```

that returns a list, in order of elimination, of the names of the suitors already eliminated. The class should also have a method

```
List <String> getHopeful()
```

that returns a list of suitors not yet eliminated.

Write a driver program that obtains the input n, a list of n suitors' names, and a list of n – 1 integers to be used as "rotate steps." Using the class you have written, the program prints the names of the rejected suitors (in the order of rejection), and then prints the name of the lucky guy.

6. Wedding Lottery II

Write an appropriate graphical user interface for the Wedding Lottery problem. The interface should allow the princess to specify the list of suitors using commands of the form *add name*. Once the princess has entered all the names, she presses a button labeled "Choose" to move from the input phase to the selection phase. In the selection phase, the user interface displays a list of suitors already rejected and another list of suitors still under consideration. The interface will have a text field in which the princess can enter a number for the next rotate step. As long as there is more than one suitor left, the program eliminates a suitor each time the princess types a number into the rotate step text field.

7. Adjacency List Input

Create a file containing the adjacency list data given at the end of this chapter, and then modify the program in Code Listing 20-6 so that it reads the file and uses the data found in the file to build the adjacency list structure. Use an array of strings to keep track of the association between node names and node numbers that is given at the beginning of the file, and then use an array or an ArrayList of lists of numbers for the adjacency list structure. Print the adjacency list twice: once using numbers to name the nodes (as in Table 20-3) and again using the string names of the nodes, as in Table 20-3.

21 Stacks and Queues

21.1 Stacks and Their Applications

CONCEPT: A stack is a collection of items that allows addition and removal of items in a last-in-first-out manner.

In Chapter 18 you learned about linked lists, array lists, vectors, and other types of collection classes that are part of the Java Collection Framework. The List classes you learned about in that chapter are very general, and allow elements to be added and removed at any position in the list. There are many applications that use lists of objects in more restricted ways. For example, an application may need to maintain a list of objects that requires additions and removals only at the ends, or even at only one end of the list. In a list that requires additions and removals to take place at only one end, the only item available for removal is the item that was last added. Such a list is called a *stack*, and the end of the list at which additions and removals take place is called the *top of the stack*.

Examples and Applications of Stacks

There are many examples of stacks in real life. For example, when a number of cars are parked single file in a narrow driveway, the last car parked must be the first one to leave. Another example is a stack of plates in a cafeteria. Workers add plates to the top of the stack, and each patron removes a plate from the top of the stack.

There are many problems, both in computer science and out of it, that can be solved with the use of stacks. For example, all programming languages allow programmers to define methods and call them from different places within the program. The computer must keep track of the *return address* for each method call, that is, the place in the program from which the method was called. The computer then uses this return address when the method executes a return statement. Whenever a method is called, the computer adds its return address to a stack. Later, when the method executes a return, the computer removes an address from the stack and uses it as the target address for the return statement. The stack is the right data structure to use because the last method called is the first to return.

Stack Operations

A stack can be viewed as an abstract data type that supports three main operations, traditionally called push, peek, and pop. The *push* operation takes a single item and adds it to the top of the stack. The *peek* operation returns the item currently at the top of the stack, but does not remove it. The *pop* operation removes (and returns) the item currently stored at the top of the stack.

The Java Collection Framework provides a `Stack` class that supports generic types. The class is in the `java.util` package. Table 21-1 lists most of its methods.

Table 21-1   Stack class methods

`Stack<E>()`	Constructor.
`E push(E item)`	Adds `item` to the top of the stack and returns the item added.
`E pop()`	Removes and returns the item at the top of the stack. If the stack is empty, pop throws `EmptyStackException`.
`E peek()`	Returns the item that is currently at the top of the stack, but does not remove it from the stack. If the stack is empty, `peek` throws `EmptyStackException`.
`boolean empty()`	Returns `true` if this stack is empty and `false` otherwise.

Code Listing 21-1 is a simple demonstration of the use of the `Stack` class. The program creates a stack and pushes `String` objects onto it. Then it keeps popping the stack and printing the values popped until the stack is empty. Notice that the last-in-first-out nature of the stack causes the strings to be popped in the reverse of the order in which they were pushed.

Code Listing 21-1   (StackDemo1.java)

```
1   import java.util.*;
2
3   /**
4      This program demonstrates the java.util.Stack class.
5   */
6
7   public class StackDemo1
8   {
```

```
 9      public static void main(String [] args)
10      {
11          // Create a stack of strings and add some names
12          Stack<String> stack = new Stack<>();
13          String [ ] names = {"Al", "Bob", "Carol"};
14          System.out.println("Pushing onto the stack the names:");
15          System.out.println("Al Bob Carol");
16          for (String s : names)
17              stack.push(s);
18
19          // Now pop and print everything on the stack
20          String message = "Popping and printing all stack values:";
21          System.out.println(message);
22          while (!stack.empty())
23              System.out.print(stack.pop() + " ");
24      }
25  }
```

Program Output

```
Pushing onto the stack the names:
Al Bob Carol
Popping and printing all stack values:
Carol Bob Al
```

Stacks of Primitive Types

The Stack class provided by the Java Collections Framework does not directly accept values of primitive type. To use it with a primitive type such as int or double, you must use the corresponding wrapper class. For example, to have a stack of int, you must create a stack of Integer:

```
Stack<Integer> intStack = new Stack<>();
```

Then you can pass values of the appropriate primitive type to the push method, and the value will automatically be boxed as explained in Chapter 17. Likewise, popping a value from the stack and assigning to a variable of the appropriate primitive type will cause it to be unboxed. The use of stacks of primitive types is illustrated in the program of Code Listing 21-2. The program pushes some numbers onto a stack, then pops and prints them.

Code Listing 21-2   (StackDemo2.java)

```
1  import java.util.*;
2
3  /**
4     This program demonstrates the use
5     of stacks with primitive types.
6  */
7
```

```
 8   public class StackDemo2
 9   {
10      public static void main(String [] args)
11      {
12         Stack<Integer> intStack = new Stack<>();
13
14         // Push some numbers onto the stack
15         for (int k = 1; k < 10; k++)
16            intStack.push(k*k);
17
18         // Pop and print all numbers
19         while (!intStack.empty())
20         {
21            int x = intStack.pop();
22            System.out.print( x + "   ");
23         }
24      }
25   }
```

Program Output

```
81   64   49   36   25   16   9   4   1
```

21.2 Array Implementation of Stacks

CONCEPT: A stack can be implemented by using an array to hold the stack items and an integer to keep track of the top of the stack.

A stack is just a list that enforces last-in-first-out access. In this section and the next, we look at how arrays and linked lists can be used to implement stacks.

The idea is simple. You create an array large enough to hold the largest number of items you will need to have in the stack at any given time, say, four (the capacity of a stack in a real application would likely be much larger), and you use an integer index, top, to point to the next slot in the array that is available to receive an item. Thus, for a stack of integers, you would have:

```
int [ ] s = new int [4];      // Array holds stack elements
int top = 0;                  // Pointer to top of stack
```

The variable top, when used in this manner, is traditionally called the *stack top pointer*, or simply, the *stack pointer*.

The Stack Push Operation

To push a new item x, first we check to see if there is room in the stack. If so, we place it in the slot pointed to by top and then increment top to point to the next slot. If the stack has no room, we throw an exception as follows:

```
if (top == s.length)
    throw new StackOverFlowException();
else
{
    // Add the new item to the stack and update top
    s[top] = x;
    top ++;
}
```

StackOverFlowException is not a Java exception: it is one that we have to define. Figure 21-1 illustrates a sequence of events that starts with an empty stack and adds two items.

Figure 21-1 Pushing items onto a stack

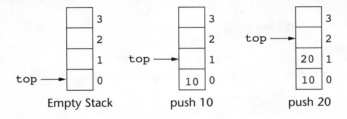

The Stack empty Method

The boolean expression top == 0 is true when the stack is empty and false when it is not, so the empty method simply returns the value of that expression:

```
return top == 0;
```

The Stack peek and pop Methods

The two stack methods peek and pop are similar: both check to see if the stack is empty before attempting to access the item at the top of the stack, and throw EmptyStackException if the stack is empty. The peek method returns the item at the top of the stack as follows:

```
return s[top-1];
```

The pop method needs to return the same value as peek, but in addition, it needs to decrement the stack pointer to indicate that the stack slot currently holding the item at the top of the stack is becoming available. This is accomplished as follows:

```
top --;
return s[top];
```

The code we have outlined here will correctly implement a stack of integers. The stack class makes use of a separate file, *StackExceptions.java*, containing definitions of the following subclasses of the `RuntimeException` class. These two exception classes will be thrown by our stack methods.

```
class StackOverFlowException extends RuntimeException
{
}
class EmptyStackException extends RuntimeException
{
}
```

The code for the stack class is given next, as Code Listing 21-3.

Code Listing 21-3   **(ArrayStack.java)**

```
1   /**
2       Array Implementation of a stack.
3   */
4
5   public class ArrayStack
6   {
7       private int [] s; // Holds stack elements
8       private int top;  // Stack top pointer
9
10      /**
11          Constructor.
12          @param capacity The capacity of the stack.
13      */
14
15      public ArrayStack (int capacity)
16      {
17          s = new int[capacity];
18          top = 0;
19      }
20
21      /**
22          The empty method checks for an empty stack.
23          @return true if stack is empty.
24      */
25
26      public boolean empty()
27      {
28          return top == 0;
29      }
30
31      /**
32          The push method pushes a value onto the stack.
```

```
33              @param x The value to push onto the stack.
34              @exception StackOverflowException When the
35              stack is full.
36          */
37
38          public void push(int x)
39          {
40              if (top == s.length)
41                  throw new StackOverFlowException();
42              else
43              {
44                  s[top] = x;
45                  top ++;
46              }
47          }
48
49          /**
50              The pop method pops a value off the stack.
51              @return The value popped.
52              @exception EmptyStackException When the
53              stack is empty.
54          */
55
56          public int pop()
57          {
58              if (empty())
59                  throw new EmptyStackException();
60              else
61              {
62                  top--;
63                  return s[top];
64              }
65          }
66
67          /**
68              The peek method returns the value at the
69              top of the stack.
70              @return value at top of the stack.
71              @exception EmptyStackException When the
72              stack is empty.
73          */
74
75          int peek()
76          {
77              if (empty())
78                  throw new EmptyStackException();
79              else
80              {
```

```
81              return s[top-1];
82         }
83    }
84  }
```

The `ArrayStackDemo` class, shown in Code Listing 21-4, demonstrates the use of this stack. It has a main method that creates a stack with capacity 5, stores some integers on it, and then pops and prints them.

Code Listing 21-4   (`ArrayStackDemo.java`)

```
1   /**
2       This class demonstrates the
3       use of the ArrayStack class.
4   */
5
6   public class ArrayStackDemo
7   {
8       public static void main(String [] arg)
9       {
10          String str;   // Use for output
11          ArrayStack   st = new ArrayStack(5);
12          str = "Pushing 10 20 onto the stack.";
13          System.out.println(str);
14          st.push(10);
15          st.push(20);
16          str = "Value at top of the stack is ";
17          System.out.println(str + st.peek());
18          str = "Popping and printing all values:";
19          System.out.println(str);
20          while (!st.empty())
21              System.out.print(st.pop() + " ");
22      }
23  }
```

Program Output

```
Pushing 10 20 onto the stack.
Value at top of the stack is 20
Popping and printing all values:
20 10
```

Stacks of Objects

The stack in Code Listing 21-3 is a stack of integers. Writing a stack that works with other types is similar. For example, to write a stack that works with `String` objects, we would modify the `ArrayStack` class by changing all occurrences of `int` that refer to the type of the items being stored in the stack to `String`. In particular, the parameter and return types of `peek`, `pop`, and `push` would change as follows:

`int peek()`	*becomes*	`String peek()`
`int pop()`	*becomes*	`String pop()`
`void push(int x)`	*becomes*	`void push(String x)`

The type of array that holds the stack items also needs to change as follows:

`int [ ] s;`	*becomes*	`String [ ] s;`
`s = new int[capacity]`	*becomes*	`s = new String[capacity];`

One other change must be made to the `pop` method when the stack is being used to store object types: the array entry referring to the stack item being removed must be set to `null` to facilitate garbage collection of the item being removed from the stack as follows:

```
s[top-1] = null;
```

For example, the `pop` method modified to work with string objects would look like this:

```java
public String pop()
{
   if (empty())
      throw new EmptyStackException();
   else
   {
      String retVal = s[top-1];
      s[top-1] = null; // Facilitate garbage collection
      top--;
      return retVal;
   }
}
```

Later in this chapter we will look at how we can use generic types to write a single stack class that works with values of all types.

A disadvantage of using an array implementation is the need to fix the size of the array at the time the stack is created. This causes a problem if the application using the stack needs to store more items than the size of the stack will allow. Basing the implementation of an array on a linked list avoids this problem.

21.3 Linked Implementation of Stacks

CONCEPT: A stack can be implemented by using a singly linked list to hold the stack items, and having the head of the list serve as the top of the stack.

A stack can be implemented by using any type of list object, including the `LinkedList` class in the `java.util` package, to hold the stack items. The `LinkedList` class, however, supports many operations that are not needed when all we need is a stack: for example, most applications of stacks do not need iterators, or the ability to add and remove items from the middle of the list. We can avoid this additional overhead by basing a stack on a simple linked list that we code ourselves.

The linked list will be based on the following `Node` class, declared private inside a `LinkedStack` class:

```
private class Node
{
    String value;
    Node next;
    Node(String val, Node n)
    {
        value = val;
        next = n;
    }
}
```

Inside the `LinkedStack` class, we will have a reference to a linked list of items. A reference `top` will point to the node at the front of the list: this node will be the one removed by the next call to `pop`. For example, starting with an empty stack and pushing the strings `"Alice"` and `"Bob"` in succession will result in the scenario shown in Figure 21-2.

Figure 21-2 A linked stack after pushing two items

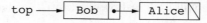

A further operation of pushing `"Carol"` on the stack would give the result shown in Figure 21-3:

Figure 21-3 The linked stack of Figure 21-2 after push of the string `"Carol"`

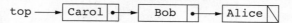

At this point, executing a pop operation would remove `"Carol"` from the stack and return us to the scenario shown in Figure 21-2.

Implementation of Stack Methods

The LinkedStack class will have a field top that points to the item at the top of the stack and simultaneously serves as the head of the linked list. The stack will be empty whenever the expression

```
top == null
```

is true, so the empty method simply returns the value of that expression:

```
public boolean empty()
{
    return top == null;
}
```

The push operation adds a new item s to the front of the list:

```
top = new Node(s, top);
```

The peek method returns the value field of the node at the front of the list:

```
return top.value;
```

The pop method saves the value in the node at the top, removes the top node from the list by moving the head pointer past it, and returns the saved value:

```
String retValue = top.value;
top = top.next;
return retValue;
```

Both peek and pop throw an exception if they are called on an empty stack. Finally, the LinkedStack class is equipped with a toString method that uses a StringBuilder object to create a string representation of the class. Having this method allows the contents of the entire stack st to be displayed by passing it to the System.out.print method:

```
System.out.println(st);
```

The LinkedStack class can be seen in Code Listing 21-5.

Code Listing 21-5   (**LinkedStack.java**)

```
1   /**
2       This program demonstrates how to write and
3       use a stack class based on linked lists.
4   */
5
6   class LinkedStack
7   {
8       /**
9           The Node class is used to implement the
10          linked list.
11      */
12
```

```
13      private class Node
14      {
15         String value;
16         Node next;
17         Node(String val, Node n)
18         {
19            value = val;
20            next = n;
21         }
22      }
23
24      private Node top = null;  // Top of the stack
25
26      /**
27         The empty method checks for an empty stack.
28         @return true if stack is empty, false otherwise.
29      */
30
31      public boolean empty()
32      {
33         return top == null;
34      }
35
36      /**
37         The push method adds a new item to the stack.
38         @param s The item to be pushed onto the stack.
39      */
40
41      public void push(String s)
42      {
43         top = new Node(s, top);
44      }
45
46      /**
47         The Pop method removes the value at the
48         top of the stack.
49         @return The value at the top of the stack.
50         @exception EmptyStackException When the
51         stack is empty.
52      */
53
54      public String pop()
55      {
56         if (empty())
57            throw new EmptyStackException();
58         else
59         {
60            String retValue = top.value;
```

```
61              top = top.next;
62              return retValue;
63          }
64      }
65
66      /**
67          The peek method returns the top value
68          on the stack.
69          @return The value at the top of the stack.
70          @exception EmptyStackException When the
71          stack is empty.
72      */
73
74      public String peek()
75      {
76          if (empty())
77              throw new EmptyStackException();
78          else
79              return top.value;
80      }
81
82      /**
83          The toString method computes a string
84          representation of the contents of the stack.
85          @return The string representation of the
86          stack contents.
87      */
88
89      public String toString()
90      {
91          StringBuilder sBuilder = new StringBuilder();
92          Node p = top;
93          while (p != null)
94          {
95              sBuilder.append(p.value);
96              p = p.next;
97              if (p != null)
98                  sBuilder.append("\n");
99          }
100         return sBuilder.toString();
101     }
102 }
```

Code Listing 21-6 gives the LinkedStackDemo class, which demonstrates the use of the LinkedStack class.

Code Listing 21-6 (`LinkedStackDemo.java`)

```
1   /**
2       This class demonstrates the use of the
3       LinkedStack class.
4   */
5
6   public class LinkedStackDemo
7   {
8       public static void main(String [ ] args)
9       {
10          LinkedStack st = new LinkedStack();
11          System.out.println("Pushing: Amy Bob Chuck");
12          System.out.println("Contents of Stack:");
13          st.push("Amy");
14          st.push("Bob");
15          st.push("Chuck");
16          System.out.println(st);
17          String name = st.pop();
18          System.out.println("Popped: " + name);
19          System.out.println("Contents of Stack:");
20          System.out.println(st);
21      }
22  }
```

Program Output

```
Pushing: Amy Bob Chuck
Contents of Stack:
Chuck
Bob
Amy
Popped: Chuck
Contents of Stack:
Bob
Amy
```

 Checkpoint

21.1 What is the common name for an operation that adds an element to a stack?

21.2 What is the common name for an operation that removes an element from a stack?

21.3 What should a stack method for removing an item do when the stack is empty?

21.4 In what order are elements added and removed from a stack?

21.5 Cite an example from everyday life where a collection of items behaves like a stack.

21.4 Queues and Their Applications

CONCEPT: A queue is a collection of items that is accessed in a first-in-first-out fashion.

You saw in the last section that a stack is a collection of items that is accessed in a last-in-first-out fashion. A queue is like a stack, except its items are added and removed in a first-in-first-out fashion. Queues, like stacks, have many applications in the real world. For example, at a grocery store checkout line, the first customer in the line is the first to be served.

Queues find many applications in computer science. Consider, for example, a network of computers that must share one printer. The printer server associates a queue with the printer, and print jobs that arrive from the various computers are added to this queue. Print jobs are removed from this queue and are serviced in a first-come-first-served fashion.

A queue can be viewed as a list where one end is designated as the *front* of the queue, and the other end is designated as the *rear*. We add items at the rear of the queue and remove items from the front. A queue is required to support the following operations:

- *enqueue(x)*: add a new item *x* to the rear of the queue
- *dequeue( )*: remove and return the item at the front of the queue
- *empty( )*: check if the queue is empty
- *peek( )*: return, but do not remove, the item at the front of the queue

21.5 Array Implementation of Queues

CONCEPT: Fixed size arrays can be used to implement queues.

VideoNote

Array
Implementation
of Queues

To implement a queue using an array, we need an array q, and two integer indices `front` and `rear`. Assuming we want to implement a queue that will hold strings, we declare these variables as follows:

```
String [ ] q;
int front, rear;
```

It is useful to establish a condition that specifies how the variables `front` and `rear` are being used, and require that all queue methods that manipulate `front` and `rear` preserve this condition. This condition, which we will refer to as the *queue invariant*, is as follows:

- `front` is the index of the slot in q that holds the next item that will be dequeued. This slot will normally be *filled*.
- `rear` is the index of the slot in q that will hold the next item that will be enqueued. This slot will normally be *empty*.

Initially, the queue is empty, and both `front` and `rear` are initialized to 0 as required by the queue invariant (the first element stored will be placed at 0, and the first element removed will come from 0). The queue invariant is illustrated in Figure 21-4.

Now suppose we want to add an item s to the queue. The queue invariant says that we should store s in the slot q[rear] and then increment rear so it points to the next empty slot as follows:

```
q[rear] = s;
rear ++;
```

Thus, after adding one item, rear will be 1, and after adding a second, rear will be 2. At this point front will still be 0. This is illustrated in the first two rows of Figure 21-4.

Figure 21-4 Use of an array-based queue

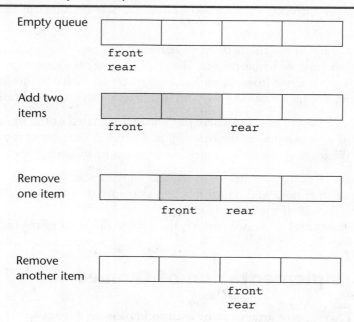

Now consider the operation of removing an item. The item to be removed is q[front]. We save the value at that position so it can be returned to the caller, set the queue entry to null, and increment front so that it points to the next item that will be dequeued.

```
String value = q[front];
q[front] = null;
front ++;
```

This is illustrated in the third and fourth rows of Figure 21-4. Notice that as long as we have not reached the end of the array, rear will increase as items are added, and front will increase as items are removed, and rear and front will be equal precisely when the queue is empty.

Now suppose we start with the queue shown in the last row of Figure 21-4 and add two more items. At that point front will still be 2, and rear will be 0 because that is the next available empty slot in the array. That situation is shown in the top row of Figure 21-5. We see that to make the best use of available space in the array, the indices `front` and `rear` need to wrap around to 0 whenever they get to the end of the array. Accordingly, the correct code for adding an item to the queue is

```
q[rear]= s;
rear ++;
if (rear == q.length) rear = 0;
```

and the correct code for removing an item is

```
String value = q[front];
q[front] = null;
front ++;
if (front == q.length) front = 0;
```

When array indices wrap around to the beginning of the array in this fashion, we say that we are using the array as a *circular buffer*.

Figure 21-5   Use of an array as a circular buffer

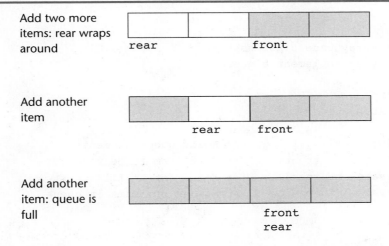

Notice in Figure 21-5 that `front` is also equal to `rear` when the array is completely full. This makes it impossible to distinguish a queue that is full from one that is empty just by looking at `front` and `rear`. One way to work around this is to have the queue keep a count of the number of items it contains: an enqueue operation increments this counter, and a dequeue operation decrements it. Then we can tell that the queue is empty when this count is 0, and that the queue is full when the count is equal to the length of the array.

A complete implementation of a queue is given in Code Listing 21-7. It uses a variable named `size` to keep track of the number of items in the queue, and has a method named `capacity` that returns the length of the array used inside the queue. Notice that the `enqueue` and `dequeue` methods check for an empty or full queue, and throw appropriately named exceptions when they cannot accomplish their designated task. The exceptions thrown are in a separate file named *QueueExceptions.java*:

```
class QueueOverFlowException extends RuntimeException
{
}

class EmptyQueueException extends RuntimeException
{
}
```

The `ArrayQueue` class in Code Listing 21-7 overrides the `toString` method to return a readable string representation of the contents of the queue. The string returned from this method encodes the current value of the `front` and `rear` indices, together with the value and position of each item in the queue. You can see the format of the string returned by the `toString` method, and how it encodes the state of the queue, in the Program Output following Code Listing 21-8.

Code Listing 21-7   (`ArrayQueue.java`)

```
1   import java.util.*;
2
3   /**
4      The ArrayQueue class uses an
5      array to implement a queue.
6   */
7
8   class ArrayQueue
9   {
10     private String [ ] q;   // Holds queue elements
11     private int front;      // Next item to be removed
12     private int rear;       // Next slot to fill
13     private int size;       // Number of items in queue
14
15     /**
16        Constructor.
17        @param capacity   The capacity of the queue.
18     */
19
20     ArrayQueue(int capacity)
21     {
22        q = new String[capacity];
23        front = 0;
24        rear = 0;
25        size = 0;
26     }
27
28     /**
29        The capacity method returns the length of
30        the array used to implement the queue.
31        @return The capacity of the queue.
```

```
32        */
33
34        public int capacity()
35        {
36            return q.length;
37        }
38
39        /**
40            The enqueue method adds an element to the queue.
41            @param s The element to be added to the queue.
42            @exception QueueOverFlowException When there
43            is no more room in the queue.
44        */
45
46        public void enqueue(String s)
47        {
48            if (size == q.length)
49                throw new QueueOverFlowException();
50            else
51            {
52                // Add to rear
53                size ++;
54                q[rear] = s;
55                rear ++;
56                if (rear == q.length) rear = 0;
57            }
58        }
59
60        /**
61            The peek method returns the item
62            at the front of the queue.
63            @return element at front of queue.
64            @exception EmptyQueueException When
65            the queue is empty.
66        */
67
68        public String peek()
69        {
70            if (empty())
71                throw new EmptyQueueException();
72            else
73                return q[front];
74        }
75
76        /**
77            The dequeue method removes and returns
78            the element at the front of the queue.
79            @return The element at the front of the queue.
```

```
80          @exception EmptyQueueException When
81          the queue is empty.
82       */
83
84       public String dequeue()
85       {
86          if (empty())
87             throw new EmptyQueueException();
88          else
89           {
90             size--;
91             // Remove from front
92             String value = q[front];
93
94             // Facilitate garbage collection
95             q[front] = null;
96
97             // Update front
98             front++;
99             if (front == q.length) front = 0;
100
101            return value;
102          }
103      }
104
105      /**
106         The empty method checks to see if
107         this queue is empty.
108         @return true if the queue is empty and
109         false otherwise.
110      */
111
112      public boolean empty()
113      {
114         return size == 0;
115      }
116
117      /**
118         The toString method returns a
119         readable representation of the
120         contents of the queue.
121         @return  The string representation
122         of the contents of the queue.
123      */
124
125      public String toString()
126      {
127         StringBuilder sBuilder = new StringBuilder();
```

```
128          sBuilder.append("front = " + front + "; ");
129          sBuilder.append("rear = " + rear + "\n");
130          for (int k = 0; k < q.length; k++)
131          {
132             if (q[k] != null)
133                sBuilder.append(k + " " + q[k]);
134             else
135                sBuilder.append(k + " ?");
136             if (k != q.length - 1)
137                sBuilder.append("\n");
138          }
139          return sBuilder.toString();
140       }
141    }
```

The program shown in Code Listing 21-8 demonstrates the use of the ArrayQueue class.

Code Listing 21-8   (ArrayQueueDemo.java)

```
1    /**
2        The ArrayQueueDemo demonstrates the use
3        of the ArrayQueue class.
4    */
5
6    public class ArrayQueueDemo
7    {
8       public static void main(String [] args)
9       {
10         String str;  // Holds various string values
11
12         ArrayQueue queue = new ArrayQueue(4);
13         str = "Queue has capacity ";
14         System.out.println(str + queue.capacity());
15
16         // Add 4 names
17         String [ ] names
18            = {"Alfonso", "Bob", "Carol", "Deborah"};
19         System.out.println("Adding names: ");
20         for (String s : names)
21         {
22            System.out.print(s + " ");
23            queue.enqueue(s);
24         }
25         System.out.println("\nState of queue is: ");
26         System.out.println(queue);
27
```

```
28              // Remove 2 names
29              System.out.println("Removing 2 names.");
30              queue.dequeue(); queue.dequeue();
31              System.out.println("State of queue is: ");
32              System.out.println(queue);
33
34              // Add a name
35              System.out.println("Adding the name Elaine:");
36              queue.enqueue("Elaine");
37              System.out.println("State of queue is: ");
38              System.out.println(queue);
39          }
40      }
```

Program Output

```
Queue has capacity 4
Adding names:
Alfonso Bob Carol Deborah
State of queue is:
front = 0; rear = 0
0 Alfonso
1 Bob
2 Carol
3 Deborah
Removing 2 names.
State of queue is:
front = 2; rear = 0
0 ?
1 ?
2 Carol
3 Deborah
Adding the name Elaine:
State of queue is:
front = 2; rear = 1
0 Elaine
1 ?
2 Carol
3 Deborah
```

GUI Front End for the Queue Demo Program

Now we describe a graphical user interface to the queue implemented in Code Listing 21-7. A screenshot of the user interface after the user starts with a queue of size four, adds three names, and then removes a name, is shown in Figure 21-6.

Figure 21-6 Screenshot of GUI front end for the queue program   (Mark Schrier. Copyright Oracle, Inc.)

Make this a JavaFx screen Shot

The user interface consists of a window with a pane at the top that has an array of text fields. At the bottom of the window, there is a text field used by the user to enter commands. The program recognizes the following commands:

- enqueue x: add x to the queue
- add x: add x to the queue (same as enqueue x)
- dequeue: remove an item from the queue
- remove: remove an item from the queue (same as dequeue)

Swing Version of the GUI Front End

The program attaches an action listener to the command entry text field. This action listener is called whenever the user types a command. The listener retrieves the text of the command, parses it by using a Scanner object, identifies the command and its argument, and calls the appropriate queue method. Then the listener calls the refresh method, passing it a string that represents the current state of the queue. The refresh method examines its argument to determine the position and value of each queue element, and then updates the queue view text fields at the top of the frame. Code Listing 21-9 gives the rest of the details.

Code Listing 21-9   (GUIQueueDemo.java)

```
1   import java.awt.event.*;
2   import java.awt.*;
3   import javax.swing.*;
4   import java.util.*;
5
6   /**
7      This program is a graphical user interface
8      to the ArrQueue class.
9   */
10
11  public class GUIQueueDemo extends JFrame
12  {
13      private JTextField [ ] qViewTextField;
14      private ArrayQueue queue;
15
16      private JTextField commandEntryTextField;
17
```

```
18      /**
19         Constructor.
20      */
21
22      GUIQueueDemo()
23      {
24         setTitle("Array Based Queue Demo");
25
26         // Create queue
27         queue = new ArrayQueue(4);
28         int qSize = queue.capacity();
29
30         // Create view for queue and put
31         // it at top of frame.
32         qViewTextField = new JTextField[qSize];
33         LayoutManager layout = new GridLayout(1, qSize);
34         JPanel qViewPanel = new JPanel(layout);
35         for (int k = 0; k < qViewTextField.length; k++)
36         {
37            qViewTextField[k] = new JTextField();
38            JTextField t = qViewTextField[k];
39            qViewPanel.add(t);
40            t.setEditable(false);
41            t.setBackground(Color.WHITE);
42         }
43         add(qViewPanel, BorderLayout.NORTH);
44
45         // Create commandEntryTextField and put it
46         // in a panel at the bottom of the frame.
47         commandEntryTextField = new JTextField(15);
48         ActionListener lis = new CmdTextListener();
49         commandEntryTextField.addActionListener(lis);
50         JPanel commandEntryPanel = new JPanel();
51         commandEntryPanel.add(new JLabel("Command: "));
52         commandEntryPanel.add(commandEntryTextField);
53         add(commandEntryPanel, BorderLayout.SOUTH);
54
55         // Finish setting up frame
56         pack();
57         setDefaultCloseOperation(JFrame.EXIT_ON_CLOSE);
58         setVisible(true);
59      }
60
61      /**
62         This private inner class responds to the
63         commands typed into command entry text field.
```

```java
64     */
65    private class CmdTextListener
66       implements ActionListener
67    {
68       public void actionPerformed(ActionEvent evt)
69       {
70          String cmdText = commandEntryTextField.getText();
71          Scanner sc = new Scanner(cmdText);
72          if (!sc.hasNext()) return;
73          String cmd = sc.next();
74          if (cmd.equals("add") || cmd.equals("enqueue"))
75          {
76             String item = sc.next();
77             queue.enqueue(item);
78             refresh(queue.toString());
79             return;
80          }
81          if (cmd.equals("remove") || cmd.equals("dequeue"))
82          {
83             queue.dequeue();
84             refresh(queue.toString());
85             return;
86          }
87       }
88    }
89
90    /**
91       The refresh  method stores the current
92       queue entries in the corresponding text
93       fields of the queue view.
94       @param The string encoding the current
95       contents of the queue.
96    */
97
98    private void refresh(String qStr)
99    {
100       Scanner sc = new Scanner(qStr);
101       sc.nextLine();    // Skip first, rear info
102       while (sc.hasNext())
103       {
104          int k = sc.nextInt();
105          String qEntry = sc.next();
106          qViewTextField[k].setText(qEntry);
107       }
108    }
109
```

```
110     /**
111         The main method creates the frame so the user
112         can start interacting with the program.
113     */
114
115     public static void main(String [] arg)
116     {
117         new GUIQueueDemo();
118     }
119 }
```

JavaFX Version of the GUI Front End

This program is similar to its Swing counterpart. The program sets an event handler on the command entry text field that is called whenever the user types a command. The handler retrieves the text of the command, parses it by using a Scanner object, identifies the command and its argument, and calls the appropriate queue method. The handler then calls the refresh method, passing it a string that represents the current state of the queue. The refresh method examines its argument to determine the position and value of each queue element, and then updates the queue view text fields at the top of the frame. Code Listing 21-10 gives the rest of the details.

Code Listing 21-10 (JavaFXQueueDemo.java)

```
 1 import java.util.Scanner;
 2 import javafx.application.Application;
 3 import javafx.event.*;
 4 import javafx.geometry.*;
 5 import javafx.scene.Scene;
 6 import javafx.scene.control.*;
 7 import javafx.scene.layout.*;
 8 import javafx.stage.Stage;
 9
10 /**
11    This program demonstrates the graphical display of a queue.
12 */
13
14 public class JavaFXQueueDemo extends Application
15 {
16     @Override
17     public void start(Stage stage) throws Exception
18     {
19         // Create a queue.
20         ArrayQueue queue = new ArrayQueue(4);
21         int qSize = queue.capacity();
```

```
22
23          // Create the GUI to display the queue.
24          TextField[] qViewTextField = new TextField[4];
25          TextField commandEntryTextField = new TextField();
26
27          // Put the queue view text fields in a horizontal box.
28          HBox topHBox = new HBox(10);
29
30          for (int k = 0; k < qViewTextField.length; k++)
31          {
32              TextField tF = new TextField();
33              tF.setPrefColumnCount(5);
34              tF.setEditable(false);
35              topHBox.getChildren().add(tF);
36              qViewTextField[k] = tF;
37          }
38
39          // Put the label and commandEntryTextField in
40          // a horizontal box.
41          HBox hBox = new HBox(10);
42          hBox.setAlignment(Pos.CENTER);
43          hBox.getChildren().addAll(new Label("Command"),
44                                    commandEntryTextField);
45
46          // Use an outer VBox to hold all the GUI components
47          VBox outerPane = new VBox(10);
48          outerPane.setPadding(new Insets(10));
49          outerPane.getChildren().addAll(topHBox, hBox);
50
51          // Set the event handler on the text field
52          EventHandler<ActionEvent> handler
53                  = new CmdTextHandler(queue, qViewTextField);
54          commandEntryTextField.setOnAction(handler);
55
56          stage.setScene(new Scene(outerPane));
57          stage.setTitle("JavaFX Queue Demo");
58          stage.show();
59      }
60 }
61
62 /**
63    The handler for the command entry text field uses
64    constructor parameters to store reference to
65    the queue and the queue view text fields.
66 */
67 class CmdTextHandler implements EventHandler<ActionEvent>
```

```
68  {
69      private ArrayQueue queue;
70      private TextField[] qViewTextField;
71
72      public CmdTextHandler(ArrayQueue queue1, TextField[] qViewTfs)
73      {
74          queue = queue1;
75          qViewTextField = qViewTfs;
76      }
77
78      public void handle(ActionEvent evt)
79      {
80          TextField cmdTextField = (TextField) evt.getTarget();
81          String cmdText = cmdTextField.getText();
82          Scanner sc = new Scanner(cmdText);
83          if (!sc.hasNext())
84          {
85              return;
86          }
87          String cmd = sc.next();
88          if (cmd.equals("add") || cmd.equals("enqueue"))
89          {
90              String item = sc.next();
91              queue.enqueue(item);
92              refresh(queue.toString());
93              return;
94          }
95          if (cmd.equals("remove") || cmd.equals("dequeue"))
96          {
97              queue.dequeue();
98              refresh(queue.toString());
99              return;
100         }
101     }
102
103     /**
104         The refresh method stores the current queue
105         entries in the corresponding text fields of
106         the queue view.
107
108         @param The string encoding the current contents of the queue.
109     */
110     private void refresh(String qStr)
111     {
112         Scanner sc = new Scanner(qStr);
113         sc.nextLine();    // Skip first, rear info
114         while (sc.hasNext())
```

```
115              {
116                    int k = sc.nextInt();
117                    String qEntry = sc.next();
118                    qViewTextField[k].setText(qEntry);
119              }
120         }
121 }
```

21.6   Linked List Implementation of Queues

CONCEPT: Singly linked lists can be used to implement queues.

A simple linked list can be used to implement a queue. A reference *front* is used as the head of the linked list, and marks the end of the list from which items will be removed. A second reference, *rear*, is used to mark the end at which additions will take place. Figure 21-7 shows a queue with three elements.

Figure 21-7   A linked list representing a queue with three elements

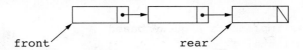

front   rear

Notice that *front* and *rear* will be pointing to the same node whenever there is only one node in the list, and will both be set to `null` whenever the list is empty.

Queue Initialization and Enqueuing of Items

Using the same `Node` class as in the `LinkedStack` program, we can define a class `LinkedQueue` that has two fields, `front` and `rear`, to keep track of the list of queue items:

```
Node front = null;
Node rear = null;
```

To add an item s to an empty queue, we create a node containing s and set both `rear` and `front` to point to it as follows:

```
rear = new Node(s, null);
front = rear;
```

To add an item s to a nonempty queue, we create a node containing s, set `rear.next` to point to that node, and then move `rear` so that it points to the newly added node as follows:

```
rear.next = new Node(s, null);
rear = rear.next;
```

Dequeuing Items

To remove and return a value from the queue, first we store the value to be returned. Then we move front down past the node being removed and return the stored value as follows:

```
String value = front.value;
front = front.next;
return value;
```

This code, however, will leave rear pointing to an item that has been removed if the item being removed is the last one in the list. In this case, rear must be set to null. The correct code for removing is therefore

```
String value = front.value;
front = front.next;
if (front == null)
    rear = null;
return value;
```

The code that implements the LinkedQueue class, with appropriate driver code is given in Code Listing 21-11.10

Code Listing 21-11   (LinkedQueue.java)

```
1   /**
2       This class implements a queue based
3       on linked lists.
4   */
5
6   public class LinkedQueue
7   {
8       private class Node
9       {
10          String value;
11          Node next;
12          Node(String val, Node n)
13          {
14              value = val;
15              next = n;
16          }
17      }
18
19      private Node front = null;
20      private Node rear = null;
21
22      /**
23          The method enqueue adds a value
24          to the queue.
```

```
25          @param s The value to be added
26          to the queue.
27       */
28
29       public void enqueue(String s)
30       {
31          if (rear != null)
32          {
33             rear.next = new Node(s, null);
34             rear = rear.next;
35          }
36          else
37          {
38             rear = new Node(s, null);
39             front = rear;
40          }
41       }
42
43       /**
44          The empty method checks to see if
45          the queue is empty.
46          @return true if and only if queue
47          is empty.
48       */
49
50       public boolean empty()
51       {
52          return front == null;
53       }
54
55       /**
56          The method peek returns value at the
57          front of the queue.
58          @return item at front of queue.
59          @exception EmptyQueueException When the
60          queue is empty.
61       */
62
63       public String peek()
64       {
65          if (empty())
66             throw new EmptyQueueException();
67          else
68             return front.value;
69       }
70
```

```
71     /**
72         The dequeue method removes and returns
73         the item at the front of the queue.
74         @return item at front of queue.
75         @exception EmptyQueueException When
76         the queue is empty.
77     */
78
79     public String dequeue()
80     {
81         if (empty())
82             throw new EmptyQueueException();
83         else
84         {
85             String value = front.value;
86             front = front.next;
87             if (front == null) rear = null;
88             return value;
89         }
90     }
91
92     /**
93         The toString method concatenates all strings
94         in the queue to give a string representation
95         of the contents of the queue.
96         @return string representation of this queue.
97     */
98
99     public String toString()
100    {
101        StringBuilder sBuilder = new StringBuilder();
102
103        // Walk down the list and append all values
104        Node p = front;
105        while (p != null)
106        {
107            sBuilder.append(p.value + " ");
108            p = p.next;
109        }
110        return sBuilder.toString();
111    }
112 }
```

Code Listing 21-12 demonstrates the use of the LinkedQueue class.

11

Code Listing 21-12   **(LinkedQueueDemo.java)**

```
1    /**
2       The LinkedQueueDemo class demonstrates
3       the use of the LinkedQueue class.
4    */
5
6    public class LinkedQueueDemo
7    {
8       public static void main(String [] args)
9       {
10         LinkedQueue queue = new LinkedQueue();
11
12         // Add 4 names
13         String [ ] names =
14             {"Alfonso", "Bob", "Carol", "Deborah"};
15         System.out.println("Adding names: ");
16         for (String s : names)
17         {
18             System.out.print(s + " ");
19             queue.enqueue(s);
20         }
21
22         System.out.println("\nState of queue is: ");
23         System.out.println(queue);
24
25         // Remove 2 names
26         System.out.println("Removing 2 names.");
27         queue.dequeue(); queue.dequeue();
28         System.out.println("State of queue is: ");
29         System.out.println(queue);
30
31         // Add another name
32         System.out.println("Adding the name Elaine:");
33         queue.enqueue("Elaine");
34         System.out.println("State of queue is: ");
35         System.out.println(queue);
36      }
37   }
```

Program Output

```
Adding names:
Alfonso Bob Carol Deborah
State of queue is:
Alfonso Bob Carol Deborah
Removing 2 names.
```

```
State of queue is:
Carol Deborah
Adding the name Elaine:
State of queue is:
Carol Deborah Elaine
```

Checkpoint

21.6 What is the common name for an operation that adds an element to a queue?

21.7 In what order are elements added and removed from a queue?

21.8 Cite an example of a queue from everyday life.

21.9 In an array implementation of a queue, why is it necessary to treat the array as a circular buffer?

21.7 Generic Implementation of Stacks and Queues

CONCEPT: Classes that implement collections should be written to use generic types.

A generic collection class, whether a stack or a queue, has a great advantage: it can be used to hold items of any type. Implementing a generic collection is not much different from implementing a type-specific one: you simply parameterize the name of the class with a type parameter, say T, and then use T wherever you would need to use the type of the items being stored in the collection. For example, a skeleton for an array implementation of a generic stack class looks like this:

```
class GenStack<T>
{
    private T [] s;      // Holds stack elements
    private int top;     // Stack top pointer
    public GenStack (int capacity)
    {

    }
    public boolean empty() { return top == 0; }
    public T push(T x)
    {

    }
    public T pop()
    {

    }
}
```

There is a complication, however, because Java does not allow arrays of generic type to be instantiated. For example, the following statement to instantiate an array to hold the stack items will not compile:

```
T[ ] s = new T[capacity];
```

As explained in Chapter 19, there is a workaround: first instantiate an array of Object, and then cast it to the desired generic type as follows:

```
T[ ] s = (T[ ]) new Object[capacity];
```

This compiles, albeit with a compiler warning. Code Listing 21-13 shows a complete implementation of an array-based generic stack. The code uses the exception classes declared in the StackExceptions.java encountered earlier.

Code Listing 21-13   (GenStack.java)

```java
1   /**
2      This class implements a generic array
3      based stack.
4   */
5
6   public class GenStack<T>
7   {
8      private T [] s;    // Body of stack
9      private int top;   // Stack top pointer
10
11     /**
12        Constructor.
13        @param capacity The capacity of the stack.
14     */
15
16     public GenStack (int capacity)
17     {
18        s = (T[ ]) new Object [capacity];
19        top = 0;
20     }
21     /**
22        The empty method checks to see if
23        the stack is empty.
24        @return true if and only if the
25        stack is empty.
26     */
27
28     public boolean empty() { return top == 0; }
29
30     /**
31        The push  method adds x to the stack.
```

```
32          @param x the value to be pushed onto
33          the stack.
34          @return the value that was pushed
35          onto the stack.
36          @exception StackOverFlowException When
37          the stack is full.
38       */
39
40       public T push(T x)
41       {
42          if (top == s.length)
43             throw new StackOverFlowException();
44          else
45          {
46             s[top] = x;
47             top ++;
48             return x;
49          }
50       }
51
52       /**
53          The pop method removes and returns the
54          item at the top of the stack.
55          @return item at the top of the stack.
56          @exception EmptyStackException When the
57          stack is empty.
58       */
59
60       public T pop()
61       {
62          if (empty())
63             throw new EmptyStackException();
64          else
65          {
66             T retVal = s[top-1];
67             s[top-1] = null;
68             top--;
69             return retVal;
70          }
71       }
72    }
```

The program in Code Listing 21-14 shows how to use the GenericStack class.

13

Code Listing 21-14   (`GenericStackDemo.java`)

```
 1  /**
 2     This class demonstrates the use of
 3     the generic stack class GenStack
 4  */
 5
 6  public class GenericStackDemo
 7  {
 8     public static void main(String [] arg)
 9     {
10        GenStack <String> st = new GenStack<String>(5);
11        st.push("George");
12        st.push("Washington");
13        System.out.println(st.pop());
14        System.out.println(st.pop());
15     }
16  }
```

Program Output

```
Washington
George
```

21.8 Queues and Breadth-First Search

You do not need to implement your own queue if you need to use one in your program. The Java Collection Framework provides many different classes that implement the Queue interface. One such class is the familiar `LinkedList` class that we encountered in Chapter 20. The Queue interface declares the methods shown in Table 21-2.

Table 21-2 Some methods in the Queue interface

`boolean add(E, e)`	Adds an element to the rear of the queue (*enqueue*)
`E peek()`	Returns, but does not remove, the element at the front of the queue
`E remove()`	Removes and returns the element at the front of the queue (*dequeue*)
`boolean isEmpty()`	Checks to see if the queue is empty

In the Spotlight:
Directory Searching Using Breadth-First Search

Queues are very useful in solving problems that involve *breadth-first search,* a type of search through the nodes of a digraph. (Digraphs were introduced in the Spotlight section of Chapter 20.) Breadth-first search starts searching at one node and then continues the search through other nodes in order of increasing distance from the start node. Here we show how breadth-first search can be used to search a directory and all contained subdirectories for a specified file or subdirectory. It is not necessary to understand what a digraph is to follow this presentation.

Files and directories in a computer system are stored in a hierarchical fashion, in which a directory may contain files and other directories. When a directory D is contained in another directory E, we say that D is a child directory of E. This creates a situation in which directories can have children, children of children, and, in general, *descendants.* The problem here is to search through some initial directory and all its descendants to find a specified file F and print the path to F if it is found.

Breadth-first search is based on using a queue to store directories that are descendants of the initial directory. A descendant directory is placed on the queue if it has been encountered, but has not yet been searched. Initially, the queue contains only one directory: the initial directory. We proceed in stages. At each stage, we remove the directory X at the front of the queue and search it. If we find the desired file, we stop the search. Otherwise, we add all the child directories of X to the (rear of the) queue.

Suppose that the initial directory is X. In the beginning, the queue contains only X, and X will be removed from the queue and searched. If the process does not stop there, then all the children of X will be added to the queue. The children of X are the first-generation descendants. At the second stage, one of the first-generation descendants, say Y, will be removed and searched. If the desired file is not found, then all the children of Y (which are second-generation descendants of X) will be added to the rear of the queue for later processing. Because nodes will be removed from the queue and searched in the order in which they are added, all directories will be searched in increasing order of their generation. You can see from this that breadth-first search searches nodes in order of increasing distance from the start node.

We need several methods from the `java.util.File` class, as shown in Table 21-3.

Table 21-3 Some methods of the `File` class

`String [] list()`	Returns an array of strings representing names of the files or directories stored in this directory. Returns `null` if the `File` object is not a directory or if there is an IO error in trying to determine the directory listing.
`File [] listFiles()`	Returns an array of `File` objects representing the files or subdirectories stored in this directory. Returns `null` if the `File` object is not a directory or if there is an IO error in trying to determine the directory listing.
`boolean isDirectory()`	Returns `true` if this `File` object is a directory and not a regular file.
`String getAbsolutePath()`	Returns the full pathname of the file or directory.

The program in Code Listing 21-14 follows closely the preceding description of breadth-first search. For brevity, the test data is hard coded into the main method, and the program searches for a file named "Menu.tex" starting in the directory "C:/Users/gcm". As shown by the program output, this file is found in a descendant subdirectory named "Backup\ CSC531".

Code Listing 21-14   (DirSearch.java)

```java
1 /**
2     This program shows how to use breadth-first search
3     based on a queue to do a directory search.
4 */
5 import java.io.File;
6 import java.util.*;
7
8 public class DirSearch
9 {
10     public static void main(String[] args)
11     {
12         File initDir = new File("C:/Users/gcm");
13         String filePath = search(initDir, "Menus.tex");
14         if (filePath == null)
15             System.out.println("Not found");
16         else
17             System.out.println(filePath);
18     }
19
20     /**
21         This method searches a given directory and all its
22         subdirectories looking for specified file or subdirectory.
23         @param initDir : the initial directory to search.
24         @param searchFileName : the name of the file or subdirectory
25                                 to search for.
26         @return the full path name of the searched for file or directory.
27     */
28     static String search(File initDir, String searchFileName)
29     {
30         Queue<File> directoriesToSearch = new LinkedList<File>();
31         directoriesToSearch.add(initDir);
32
33         while (!directoriesToSearch.isEmpty())
34         {
35             // Get next directory to search
36             File currDir = directoriesToSearch.remove();
37             // Get contents of current directory
38             String[] dirContents = currDir.list();
39             // Directory contents will be null if there is
```

```
40              // a problem listing the directory contents
41              if (dirContents == null) continue;
42              // Do the directory contents contain the desired file?
43              if (Arrays.asList(dirContents).contains(searchFileName))
44              {
45                  return currDir.getAbsolutePath();
46              }
47              // Desired file not in current directory
48              // Add all the children of this directory to the queue
49              // of directories to be searched
50              File [] childDirectories = currDir.listFiles();
51              for (File f : childDirectories)
52              {
53                  if (f.isDirectory())
54                      directoriesToSearch.add(f);
55              }
56          }
57          // No more directories left to search, so not found
58          return null;
59      }
60  }
```

Program Output

```
C:\Users\gcm\Backup\CSC531
```

21.9 Common Errors to Avoid

- **Forgetting to check for an empty stack or queue.** You should always check to see if a stack is empty before calling peek or pop, and you should always check to see if a queue is empty before attempting to access or dequeue an element from the queue. If you forget to do this, the exception thrown will terminate your program.
- **Handling an empty stack or queue by catching the exception thrown.** Exception handling should be reserved for conditions your program cannot anticipate and prevent. Use the methods for checking if a collection is empty instead.
- **Not maintaining the stack or queue invariant.** If you are writing a stack or queue, establish a convention (invariant) for how you use the fields of your stack or queue class, and make sure all methods preserve the invariant.

Review Questions and Exercises

Multiple Choice and True/False

1. A collection that is accessed in *first-in-first-out* fashion is called _____.
   a. a stack
   b. a queue
   c. a linked list
   d. an array-based collection

2. A collection that is accessed in *last-in-first-out* fashion is called _____.
   a. a stack
   b. a queue
   c. a linked list
   d. none of the above

3. The order in which cars go through a toll booth is best described as _____.
   a. a stack
   b. a queue
   c. a linked list
   d. none of the above

4. The concept of seniority, which some employers use to hire and fire workers is _____.
   a. a stack
   b. a queue
   c. a linked list
   d. none of the above

5. The stack method that returns an element from the stack without removing it is _____.
   a. pop
   b. push
   c. peek
   d. spy

6. If the stack method push is called on an empty stack, _____.
   a. it throws an EmptyStackException
   b. it adds its argument to the stack
   c. it calls the stack method empty
   d. none of the above

7. **True or False:** You can use the JCF stack to directly create a stack of int.

8. **True or False:** If pop is called on an empty stack, it will not return until the user puts something on the stack.

9. **True or False:** When using an array to implement a stack, the push method will wrap around to the beginning of the stack when it reaches the end.

10. **True or False:** In a linked implementation of a queue, the references front and rear can only be equal if the queue is empty.

Find the Error

Find the error in each of the following code segments:

1.
```
// An array implementation of a stack
int pop()
{
    if (top == 0)
        throw new EmptyStackException( );
    else
    {
        return s[top-1];
        top --;
    }
}
```

2.
```
// A linked implementation of a queue
void enqueue(int x)
{
    if (empty())
    {
        rear = new Node(x);
        front = rear;
    }
    else
    {
        rear = new Node(x);
        rear = rear.next;
    }
}
```

3.
```
//A linked implementation of a stack
int pop()
{
    if(empty())
        throw new EmptyStackException();
    return top.value;
}
```

4.
```
// A linked implementation of a queue
int dequeue()
{
    if(empty())
        throw new EmptyQueueException();
    int value = front.value;
    front ++;
    return value;
}
```

error

```
5. // An array implementation of a queue
   int dequeue()
   {
       if (empty())
           throw new EmptyQueueException();
           int val = q[rear];
           rear ++;
           return val;
   }
```

Algorithm Workbench

1. A palindrome is a word that reads the same backward as forward. For example, the words *madam*, *radar*, *dad*, and *kayak* are all palindromes. Write a method that takes a parameter s of type String and uses a stack to see if s is a palindrome.

2. Write a class that uses an array to implement a stack of integers. The stack should have the following fields:

   ```
   int [ ]s;            // Holds stack elements
   int top = -1;        // Points to last item pushed
   ```

   The field top will point to an item that is actually stored on the stack, instead of pointing to the next available slot. The stack will set top to –1 when it is empty. Write the constructor for this class, and all the usual stack methods.

3. Suppose that you have two stacks but no queues. You have an application that needs to use a queue. Explain how to use the two stacks to simulate a single queue.

Short Answer

1. What is the name for a last-in-first-out collection?

2. What is the name for a first-in-first-out collection?

3. What is the name for a first-in-last-out collection?

4. What does the pop method do when it is called on an empty stack?

5. Why does the array entry containing an item that is being popped have to be set to null?

6. What problem would you encounter if you tried to use the head of a linked list for the rear of a queue, and use the other end of the list for the front?

Programming Challenges

1. Double-Ended Queue

A *deque* (pronounced "deck") is a list-based collection that allows additions and removals to take place at both ends. A deque supports the operations *addFront(x)*, *removeFront( )*, *addRear(x)*, *removeRear( )*, *size( )*, and *empty( )*. Write a class that implements a deque that stores strings using a doubly linked list that you code yourself. Demonstrate your class with a graphical user interface that allows users to manipulate the deque by typing appropriate commands in a `JTextField` component, and see the current state of the deque displayed in a `JTextArea` component. Consult the documentation for the `JTextArea` class for methods you can use to display each item in the deque on its own line.

2. Array-Based Deque

VideoNote
Array-Based
Deque

Implement a deque as described in Programming Challenge 1, except base your implementation on an array. The constructor for the class should accept an integer parameter for the capacity of the deque and create an array of that size. Use a graphical user interface based on an array of text fields similar to what is shown in Figure 21-6. Test your deque class by constructing a deque with capacity 10.

3. Prefix Expressions

An expression is in *prefix form* when operators are written before their operands. Here are some examples of prefix expressions and the values they evaluate to:

Expression	Value
12	12
+ 2 51	53
* 5 7	35
* + 16 4 + 3 1	80

An expression (such as 12) that begins with an integer is a prefix expression that evaluates to itself. Otherwise, an expression is a prefix expression if it begins with an operator and is followed by two prefix expressions. In this latter case, the value of the expression is recursively computed from the values of its constituent prefix sub-expressions.

Write a program that allows the user to enter prefix expressions in a text field. The program reads the expression, evaluates it, and displays the value in a suitable GUI component. Assume that the user enters expressions that use only positive integers and the two operators + and *. Your program should use a stack to store values of sub-expressions as they are computed, and another stack to store operators that have not yet been applied.

4. Properly Nested Delimiters

A Java program can have the following type of delimiters: {, }, (,), [, and]. In a correct Java program, these delimiters must be properly nested. Think of each left delimiter {, (, and [as opening a scope, and think of each right delimiter },), and] as closing a scope opened by a corresponding left delimiter. A string of characters containing these delimiters *has proper nesting of delimiters* if each scope that is opened is eventually closed, and the scopes are opened and closed in a last-opened-first-closed fashion.

Write a program that reads a file containing Java source code and checks it for proper nesting of delimiters. Your program should read the source code from the file and print it to the screen. If the file is properly nested, all of it is printed to the screen and a message is printed that the file is properly nested. If the file is not properly nested, then copying of the file to the screen stops as soon as improper nesting is detected, and your program prints a message that the file has errors. To simplify your task, you may assume these delimiters do not appear inside of comments and string literals, and that they do not appear in the program as character literals.

5. Tracing Genealogies

A file has genealogy data for a collection of N people. The first line of the file contains the integer N followed by N additional lines of data. Each of these additional lines specifies a list of children for a single person. The line starts with the name of the person, followed by the number of that person's children, followed by the names of the children. Here is an example of a file specifying genealogy information for ten people.

```
10
Al       3    Beth Carol Dino
Beth     1    Pablo
Carol    3    Ben Alex Mary
Dino     0
Pablo    1    Angela Miguel
Ben      0
Alex     0
Mary     0
Angela   0
Miguel   0
```

For example, Al has three children named Beth, Carol, and Dino; Beth has one child named Pablo; and Dino has no children. You may assume that all names are unique.

Write a program which reads a file of genealogy information and then allows the user to enter pairs of names X and Y. The program then determines whether Y is a descendant of X, and if so, prints a list of names beginning with X and ending with Y, such that each person in the chain is a child of person preceding them on the list. Otherwise, the program states that Y is not a descendant of X.

22 Binary Trees, AVL Trees, and Priority Queues

22.1 Binary Trees and Their Applications

CONCEPT: A binary tree is like a list in which every node can have up to two successors.

A *binary tree* is a collection of nodes in which each node is associated with up to two successor nodes, respectively called the *left* and *right child*. Not every node in a binary tree will have two children: the left child may be missing, or the right child may be missing, or both nodes may be missing. A node in a binary tree that has no children is called a *leaf*.

A node that has children is said to be the *parent* of its children. For a nonempty collection of nodes to qualify as a binary tree, every node must have at most one parent, and there must be exactly one node with no parent. The one node that has no parent is called the *root* of the binary tree. An empty collection of nodes is regarded as constituting an empty binary tree.

A binary tree is similar in some ways to a linked list: the root of the binary tree corresponds to the head of the list, a child of a node in a binary tree corresponds to the successor of a node in a list, and the parent of a node in a binary tree corresponds to the *predecessor* of a node in a list. And of course, the analogue of the empty list is the empty binary tree.

Figure 22-1 shows an example of a binary tree. The node labeled *A* is the root, and each arrow points from a parent to a child.

Figure 22-1 A binary tree

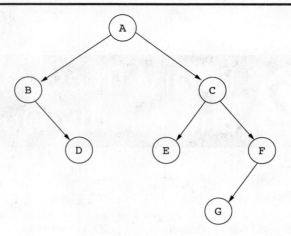

Binary Tree Concepts

Let X be a node in a binary tree T. A node Y is a *descendant* of X if Y is on a path from X to a leaf of T. Thus, the descendants of X are X itself, all the children of X, all the children of the children of X, and so on. In Figure 22-1, the descendants of C are C, E, F, and G. Any node X together with all its descendants forms a binary tree with root X: such a binary tree is called a *subtree* of T. In particular, the set of all descendants of the left child of the root of T forms a binary tree called the *left subtree* of T. Likewise, the set of all descendants of the right child of the root of T comprises the *right subtree* of T. Figure 22-2 illustrates the left and right subtrees of the binary tree of Figure 22-1.

Figure 22-2 Left and right subtrees

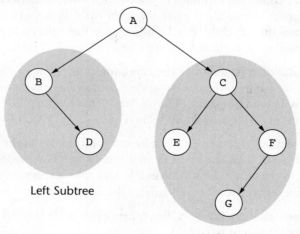

Although it is an abuse of language, we will sometimes speak of a subtree rooted at a child of a node X as being a subtree of X. According to this, {B, D} is the left subtree of A, and {F, G} is the right subtree of C.

An *ancestor* of X is any node on the path from X to the root of T. The ancestors of F in the binary tree of Figure 22-1 are F, C, and A.

Applications of Binary Trees

Binary trees and their generalizations have many applications. They can be used to organize information in ways that allow efficient search and retrieval. Other forms of trees closely related to binary trees are used in database management systems to represent data, and in programming language compilers and interpreters to represent expressions. Figure 22-3 shows the use of binary trees to represent arithmetic expressions.

Figure 22-3   Binary tree representation of expressions

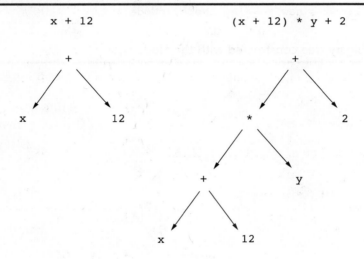

Representing Nodes of Binary Trees

A node in a binary tree is an object that contains a field for storing a value and two other fields for storing references to the left and right children. Here is a class that can be used to create nodes for a binary tree that stores integer data:

```
class Node
{
    int value;             // Value to be stored
    Node left, right;      // Left and right children
    Node(int val)
    {
        value = val;
        left = null;
        right = null;
    }
}
```

```
        Node(int val, Node left1, Node right1)
        {
            value = val;
            left = left1;
            right = right1;
        }
    }
```

Notice the two constructors in the `Node` class. The constructor with one parameter is convenient when we need to create leaf nodes.

A binary tree is represented by a reference to its root node. Assuming we have integer values A, B, C, and D, we can build the binary tree shown in Figure 22-4 by executing the following sequence of statements:

```
Node dNode = new Node(D);
Node cNode = new Node(C, dNode, null);
Node bNode = new Node(B);
Node aNode = new Node(A, bNode, cNode);
```

Figure 22-4 A binary tree constructed with the Node class

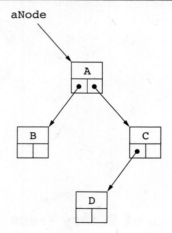

Traversing a Binary Tree

A *binary tree traversal* is a systematic method of doing some processing at every node of a binary tree. A common reason for traversing a binary tree is to print the values stored in it. There are three standard techniques for traversing binary trees. Each of these is most easily implemented as a recursive method called on the root node of the binary tree. They are as follows:

- *Preorder traversal*: process the data at the root node, traverse the left subtree, and then traverse the right subtree
- *Inorder traversal*: traverse the left subtree, process the data at the root node, and then traverse the right subtree
- *Postorder traversal*: traverse the left subtree, traverse the right subtree, and then process the data at the root node

Processing the data at a node is often called *visiting* the node.

A traversal method takes as parameter a reference `btree` to the root of a subtree. The method returns immediately if `btree` is `null`, otherwise, it visits the root and recursively traverses the two subtrees in the order prescribed by the traversal technique being used. Here is an implementation of inorder traversal that prints out all values stored in binary tree:

```java
void inorder(Node btree)
{
    // If the tree is empty do nothing
    if (btree != null)
    {
        // Traverse the left subtree
        inorder(btree.left);
        // Visit the node
        System.out.print(btree.value + " ");
        // Traverse the right subtree
        inorder(btree.right);
    }
}
```

Code Listing 22-1 shows a `Node` class that can be used as a basis for building a binary tree that stores integer values.

Code Listing 22-1   (`Node.java`)

```java
1  /**
2     Node class.
3  */
4  public class Node
5  {
6      int value;
7      Node left, right;
8
9      // Constructor for leaf nodes.
10     Node(int val)
11     {
12         value = val;
13         left = null;
14         right = null;
15     }
16
17     // Constructor for non-leaf nodes.
18     Node(int val, Node leftChild, Node rightChild)
19     {
20         value = val;
21         left = leftChild;
```

```
22              right = rightChild;
23          }
24  }
```

Code Listing 22-2 shows a class called `NodeUtilities`. This class can be used as a repository for various methods for working with node-based structures.

Code Listing 22-2 (`NodeUtilities.java`)

```java
1  /**
2     This class has various utility methods for working with nodes.
3  */
4  public class NodeUtilities
5  {
6      /**
7         Inorder traversal of a binary tree rooted at a node.
8         @param btree : The root of the binary tree.
9      */
10     static public void inorder(Node btree)
11     {
12         if (btree != null)
13         {
14             inorder(btree.left);
15             System.out.print(btree.value + " ");
16             inorder(btree.right);
17         }
18     }
19 }
```

Code Listing 22-3 uses these two classes. The program creates a collection of nodes, links them together to form a binary tree, and then traverses the binary tree in inorder.

Code Listing 22-3 (`BinaryTreeNodes.java`)

```java
1  /**
2     This program demonstrates construction and traversal of binary trees.
3  */
4
5  public class BinaryTreeNodes
6  {
7      // Creates a binary tree from nodes and traverses it in
8      // in inorder.
9      public static void main(String[] args)
```

```
10        {
11            Node root = null;  // Will be root of the binary tree.
12
13            Node aNode = new Node(10);
14            aNode.left = new Node(20);
15            Node dNode = new Node(40);
16            Node cNode = new Node(30, dNode, new Node(50));
17            aNode.right = cNode;
18            root = aNode;
19
20            System.out.print("Inorder traversal is: ");
21            NodeUtilities.inorder(root);
22            System.out.println();
23        }
24 }
```

Program Output

```
Inorder traversal is: 20 10 40 30 50
```

 Checkpoint

22.1   Consider the binary tree *T* shown in Figure 22-1.

   a)   List the ancestors of each node of *T*.
   b)   List the descendants of each node of *T*.
   c)   List all the leaves of *T*.
   d)   List all the nonleaf nodes of *T*.
   e)   Show the nodes of *T* as output by a preorder traversal.
   f)   Show the nodes of *T* as output by a postorder traversal.
   g)   Show the nodes of *T* as output by an inorder traversal.

22.2   Show the output from a postorder traversal of the two trees in Figure 22-3.

22.3   Show the output from a preorder traversal of the two trees in Figure 22-3.

22.4   Using the Node class defined in this section, draw the binary tree constructed by the following statements:

```
Node left = new Node(10, new Node(20), new Node(50));
Node right = new Node(60, new Node(180), null);
Node tree = new Node(160, left, right);
```

   and list the nodes of the resulting binary tree in preorder.

Graphical Display of Binary Trees

You can graphically display a binary tree with the same recursive logic that is used to traverse the tree. The main idea is to recursively partition a view into three sections as shown in Figure 22-5.

Figure 22-5 Partitioning a view to display a binary tree

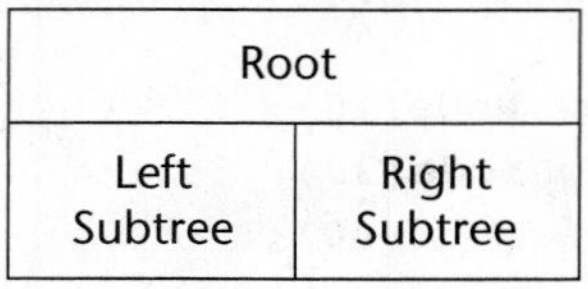

Root	
Left Subtree	Right Subtree

The partitioning is done by nesting views within views. An empty binary tree is displayed using a blank view. If the tree to be displayed is not empty, the display view is partitioned as in Figure 22-5, the root is displayed at the top, and the left and right subtrees are recursively displayed in subviews nested side by side in the lower part of the containing view.

Graphical Display of Binary Trees Using Swing

Code Listing 22-4 shows a `SwingNodeUtilities` class that has a recursive method for displaying a graphical view of a binary tree rooted at a node. If the tree is empty, its graphical representation is a blank `JPanel`. A leaf node is displayed as a `JPanel` containing a single un-editable text field that displays the value in the leaf node. A non-leaf node with a value v is displayed using a panel with a `BorderLayout`: the value v is displayed in the NORTH region, while the WEST and EAST regions recursively display the left and right subtrees.

Code Listing 22-4   (`SwingNodeUtilities.java`)

```
1  /**
2     This class is a utility for the graphical display
3     of a binary tree using Swing.
4  */
5  import java.awt.BorderLayout;
6  import java.awt.Color;
7  import javax.swing.JPanel;
8  import javax.swing.JTextField;
9
10 class SwingNodeUtilities
11 {
12     // Returns a component that displays a binary tree
13     public static JPanel getView(Node root)
14     {
15         // Empty tree is displayed as a blank JPanel.
16         if (root == null) { return new JPanel(); }
17
18         // Leaf node displayed as a panel containing a single text field.
19         if (root.left == null && root.right == null)
20         {
21             JTextField tF = new JTextField(String.valueOf(root.value));
22             tF.setEditable(false);
23             tF.setBackground(Color.WHITE);
24             JPanel leafPanel = new JPanel();
```

```
25              leafPanel.add(tF);
26              return leafPanel;
27          }
28
29          // Non-leaf node displayed in BorderLayout JPanel whose
30          // NORTH region displays the node's value, and whose WEST
31          // and EAST regions display the left and right subtree at
32          // node.
33          JPanel panel = new JPanel(new BorderLayout());
34
35          // Display the value in the node in NORTH.
36          String value = String.valueOf(root.value);
37          JTextField tF = new JTextField(String.valueOf(root.value));
38          tF.setEditable(false);
39          tF.setBackground(Color.WHITE);
40          JPanel valuePanel = new JPanel();
41          valuePanel.add(tF);
42          panel.add(valuePanel, BorderLayout.NORTH);
43
44          // Display the left and right subtrees in WEST and EAST.
45          panel.add(getView(root.left), BorderLayout.WEST);
46          panel.add(getView(root.right), BorderLayout.EAST);
47
48          return panel;
49      }
50  }
```

Code Listing 22-5 shows a program that uses this utility method to display a binary tree in a JFrame. The result of running the program can be seen in Figure 22-6.

Code Listing 22-5   (`SwingBtreeDisplayDemo.java`)

```
1  import javax.swing.JFrame;
2  /**
3     This class demonstrates the Swing Display of
4     a binary tree.
5  */
6
7  public class SwingBtreeDisplayDemo
8  {
9      public static void main(String [] args)
10     {
11         // Create the tree.
12         Node root;
13         Node aNode = new Node(10);
14         aNode.left = new Node(20);
```

```
15            Node dNode = new Node(40);
16            Node cNode = new Node(30, dNode, new Node(50));
17            aNode.right = cNode;
18            root = aNode;
19
20            // Display the tree in a JFrame.
21            JFrame frame = new JFrame("Swing Display of Binary Tree");
22            frame.add(SwingNodeUtilities.getView(root));
23            frame.pack();
24            frame.setDefaultCloseOperation(JFrame.EXIT_ON_CLOSE);
25            frame.setVisible(true);
26        }
27 }
```

Figure 22-6 Swing display of a binary tree (Mark Schrier. Copyright Oracle, Inc.)

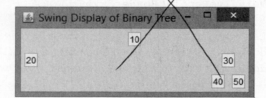

deleted

Graphical Display of Binary Trees Using JavaFX

Code Listing 22-6 shows a ~~JavaFXNodeUtilities~~ class that has a recursive method for displaying a graphical view of a binary tree rooted at a node. If the tree is empty, its graphical representation is a blank HBox pane. A leaf node is displayed as a HBox containing a single un-editable text field that displays the value in the leaf node. A non-leaf node with a value v is displayed using a BorderPane: the value v is displayed in the TOP region, while the LEFT and RIGHT regions recursively display the left and right subtrees.

A pane containing a subtree with more than one node is given a border

Code Listing 22-6 (JavaFXNodeUtilities.java)

```
1 import javafx.geometry.Insets;
2 import javafx.geometry.Pos;
3 import javafx.scene.control.TextField;
4 import javafx.scene.layout.BorderPane;
5 import javafx.scene.layout.HBox;
6 import javafx.scene.layout.Pane;
7
8 /**
9    This class has a utility method for displaying a
10    binary tree using JavaFX.
11 */
12
```

replace with new version

Insert 1344

```java
13 public class JavaFXNodeUtilities
14 {
15     public static Pane getView(Node root)
16     {
17         // Empty tree is displayed as an empty HBox
18         if (root == null) { return new HBox(); }
19
20         // Leaf node displayed as a single un-editabel text field
21         // in a HBox.
22         if (root.left == null && root.right == null)
23         {
24             TextField tF = new TextField(String.valueOf(root.value));
25             tF.setPrefColumnCount(2);
26             tF.setEditable(false);
27             HBox hBox = new HBox();
28             hBox.setAlignment(Pos.CENTER);
29             hBox.getChildren().add(tF);
30             hBox.setPadding(new Insets(5));
31             return hBox;
32         }
33         // Non-leaf node uses a BorderPane
34         // that puts the value in the TOP region, and left and right
35         // subtrees in the LEFT and RIGHT regions.
36         BorderPane pane = new BorderPane();
37
38         // Value of a non-leaf node is displayed in a text field
39         // in a HBox in the TOP region of the BorderPane.
40         String value = String.valueOf(root.value);
41         TextField tF2 = new TextField(value);
42         tF2.setPrefColumnCount(2);
43         tF2.setEditable(false);
44         HBox valueHBox = new HBox();
45         valueHBox.setAlignment(Pos.CENTER);
46         valueHBox.getChildren().add(tF2);
47         valueHBox.setPadding(new Insets(5));
48         pane.setTop(valueHBox);
49
50         // Left and right subtrees are recursively displayed
51         // in the LEFT and RIGHT region of the BorderPane.
52         pane.setLeft(getView(root.left));
53         pane.setRight(getView(root.right));
54
55         return pane;
56     }
57 }
```

Code Listing 22-7 shows a program that uses this utility method to display a binary tree in a scene on a JavaFX stage. The result of running the program can be seen in Figure 22-7.

Code Listing 22-7 (`JavaFXBtreeDisplayDemo.java`)

```java
1  import javafx.application.Application;
2  import javafx.scene.Scene;
3  import javafx.stage.Stage;
4
5  /**
6     This program demonstrates the JavaFX display of a
7     binary tree.
8  */
9
10 public class JavaFXBtreeDisplayDemo extends Application
11 {
12     @Override
13     public void start(Stage stage) throws Exception
14     {
15         // Create the tree.
16         Node root;
17         Node aNode = new Node(10);
18         aNode.left = new Node(20);
19         Node dNode = new Node(40);
20         Node cNode = new Node(30, dNode, new Node(50));
21         aNode.right = cNode;
22         root = aNode;
23
24         // Display the binary tree in a scene on the stage.
25         Scene scene = new Scene(JavaFXNodeUtilities.getView(root));
26         stage.setScene(scene);
27         stage.setTitle("JavaFX Display of Binary Tree");
28         stage.show();
29     }
30 }
```

Figure 22-7 JavaFX display of a binary tree   (Mark Schrier. Copyright Oracle, Inc.)

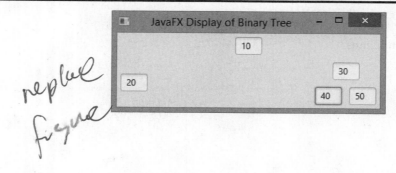

Class Implementation of Binary Trees

As we have seen, a binary tree is implemented as a reference to a root node that is an object of a suitable `Node` class such as shown in Code Listing 22-1. A simple class implementation might use a private nested `Node` class like this:

```
class BinaryTree
{
    private Node {  /* Node fields and methods */ }
    private Node root;
}
```

The class used to represent nodes is usually an implementation detail that should not concern users of the class, so the above approach makes sense. The class could then proceed to add public methods to work with binary tree objects.

Even so, it will be convenient for us to take a different approach. We will not nest the `Node` class, and we will declare the `root` field as *protected* instead of *private*:

```
class Node
{
    /* Node fields and methods */
}

class BinaryTree
{
    protected Node root;
}
```

Making `root` protected will make it accessible to subclasses, allowing us to use inheritance to write different types of binary trees. Not nesting Node will allow us to have different binary tree classes that refer to the same `Node` class, thus avoiding unnecessary repetition of code.

22.2 Binary Search Trees

CONCEPT: Binary search trees organize information to facilitate efficient search.

In Chapter 17, you saw how binary search can be used to search quickly for a given item in a sorted array. Binary search trees are special types of binary trees that can be used to implement a form of binary search that does not require arrays. Look at the binary tree in Figure 22-8.

Figure 22-8   A binary search tree

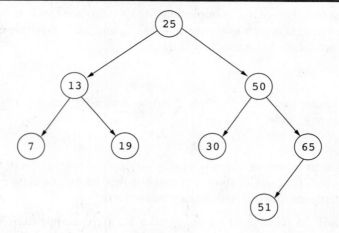

Notice that the values stored in the left subtree (7, 13, and 19) are all less than the value stored at the root (25), and that the values stored in the right subtree (30, 50, 51, and 65) are all greater than the value stored in the root. In fact, the tree has the following property: at every node N, all values stored in the left subtree of N are less than the value stored at N, and all values stored in the right subtree of N are greater than the value stored at N. A binary tree with this property is called a *binary search tree*.

Binary search trees have the potential to facilitate rapid searches. Suppose we want to determine if X is in the tree. Starting at the root, we make our way down some path of the binary tree, comparing X to each node that we come to. At each node N, we continue the search in the left subtree if X is less than N, or in the right subtree if X is greater. We stop when we find X at some node, or when we come to a leaf that is not X. Assuming that the tree is reasonably balanced, we see that we will discard approximately half of the remaining tree every time we make a comparison. Thus, searching a binary tree with *n* nodes will require approximately log *n* comparisons. Naturally, binary search can only be used with items that support a comparison operation with the property that for any two distinct elements *x* and *y*, either *x* "is less than" *y* or *x* "is greater than" *y*. Sets that support such a comparison operation are said to be *totally* or *linearly* ordered.

The following method searches a binary search tree for an element *x*. It returns true if the tree contains *x* and false otherwise.

```
private boolean contains(int x, Node bstree)
{
    if (bstree == null)
        return false;
    if (x == bstree.value)
        return true;
    if (x < bstree.value)
    {
        // Recursively look in left subtree
        return contains(x, bstree.left);
    }
```

```
    else
    {
        // Recursively look in right subtree
        return contains(x, bstree.right);
    }
}
```

Adding a Value to a Binary Search Tree

Like most operations on binary trees, adding a value to a binary search tree has a natural recursive implementation. The method

```
Node add(int x, Node bstree)
```

adds x to the binary search tree rooted at `bstree` and returns a reference to the root of the resulting binary search tree. First, the method checks to see if `bstree` is empty: if so, it creates and returns a new node containing x. If `bstree` is not empty, the method compares x to the element stored in the root: if x is less, it adds x to the left subtree and makes the resulting tree the new left subtree. If x is greater, it adds x to the right subtree and makes the resulting tree the new right subtree. Then it returns a reference to the root:

```
private Node add(int x, Node bstree)
{
    if (bstree == null)
        return new Node(x);
        // bstree is not null.
    if (x < bstree.value)
    {
        // Add x to the left subtree and replace the
        // current left subtree with the result
        bstree.left = add(x, bstree.left);
    }
    else
    {
        // Add x to the right subtree
        bstree.right = add(x, bstree.right);
    }
    return bstree;
}
```

Removing a Value from a Binary Search Tree

VideoNote
Removing a
Value from
a Binary
Search Tree

To remove a value from a binary search tree, you must locate the node N that contains the value and remove it from the tree. There are three cases to consider:

- The node N has no children. Remove N by setting the reference to it in its parent node to null.
- The node N has one child. Remove N and promote the child of N to take the place of its parent in the tree, as shown in Figure 22.9.

- The node N has two children. Remove N and replace it with the largest node in its left subtree, as shown in Figure 22-10. Notice that the largest node in the left subtree of N cannot have a right child, so removing it reduces it to the simpler case of removing a node with at most one child.

Figure 22-9   Before and after removal of a node with one child

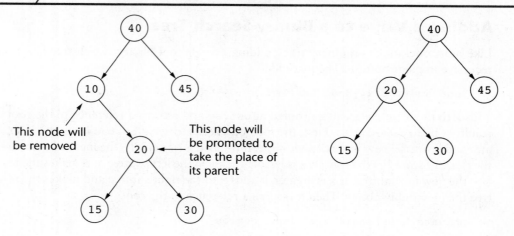

Figure 22-10   Removing a node with two children

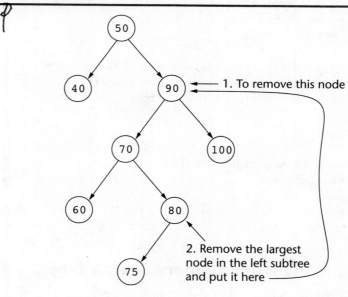

The tree that results from removing the node with 90 in the tree of Figure 22-10 is shown in Figure 22-11.

Figure 22-11 The tree of Figure 22-10 after removing 90

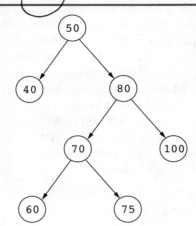

Let us now consider the task of coding the removal of a value x from a binary search tree T. This operation yields two objects: a node N that contains x, and the tree that remains after N has been removed from T. The following class will be used to represent the result of such an operation:

```
private class RemovalResult
{
    Node node;      // Removed node
    Node tree;      // Remaining tree
    RemovalResult(Node node, Node tree)
    {
        this.node = node;
        this.tree = tree;
    }
}
```

This class will be private to the class that represents the binary search tree. The method that performs the actual removal,

```
RemovalResult remove(Node bTree, int x)
```

will take a reference `bTree` to the root of a binary search tree and an integer value `x`. The remove method returns `null` if `x` is not found in `bTree`.

The algorithm for removing x considers three cases:

1. The relation `x < bTree.value` holds. In this case x is recursively removed from the left subtree:

```
RemovalResult result = remove(bTree.left, x);
if (result == null)
    return null;
bTree.left = result.tree;
result.tree = bTree;
return result;
```

If the recursive call returns null, then x is not in the left subtree and therefore cannot be in the tree, so the original call also returns null. Otherwise, the remaining tree from the recursive call becomes the left subtree of the remaining tree from the original call, and the result object is accordingly modified and returned.

2. The relation x > bTree.value holds. In this case x is recursively removed from the right subtree. This case is a mirror image of the preceding.

3. The relation x == bTree.value holds, so that the root node bTree contains the value to be removed. In this case, bTree becomes the removed node and the remaining tree is assembled from the left and right subtrees of bTree. The assembly of the remaining tree differs according to whether bTree has zero, one, or two children, and proceeds as previously explained and shown in Figures 22-8, 22-9, and 22-10. The programming details are as follows:

Consider first the case where bTree has zero children. The removed node is just bTree, and the remaining tree is empty:

```
if (bTree.right == null && bTree.left == null)
    return new RemovalResult(bTree, null);
```

Next, consider the case of bTree having one child. In this case bTree is the removed node, and the nonempty subtree of bTree becomes the remaining tree:

```
Node node = bTree;      // Removed node
Node tree;              // Remaining tree

// Remaining tree is the one nonempty subtree
if (bTree.left != null)
    tree = bTree.left;
else
    tree = bTree.right;
node.left = null;
node.right = null;
return new RemovalResult(node, tree);
```

Finally, consider the case of bTree having two children. Again, bTree becomes the removed node. The removal of bTree leaves two subtrees, and we have to find a way to combine these two subtrees into one binary search tree. This can be done by removing the largest node from the left subtree and using it to replace the removed root. The removal of the largest node from a binary search tree is accomplished by the following recursive method:

```
RemovalResult removeLargest(Node bTree)
```

To see the logic behind the algorithm used by this method, observe that the largest node in a nonempty binary search tree is the root if the root has no right subtree; otherwise, it is the largest node in the right subtree.

```
RemovalResult removeLargest(Node bTree)
{
    if (bTree == null)
        return null;
    if (bTree.right == null)
    {
```

```
        // Root is the largest node
        Node tree = bTree.left;          // Remaining tree
        bTree.left = null;
        return new RemovalResult(bTree, tree);
    }
    else
    {
        // Remove the largest node from the right subtree
        RemovalResult remResult = removeLargest(bTree.right);
        bTree.right = remResult.tree;
        remResult.tree = bTree;
        return remResult;
    }
}
```

Implementation of Binary Search Trees

We are now ready to implement a binary tree search class. We begin with a base binary tree class, shown in Code Listing 22-8, that contains a single method for checking whether the tree is empty.

Code Listing 22-8   (BinaryTree.java)

```java
1  /**
2      Base binary tree class
3  */
4  public class BinaryTree
5  {
6      protected Node root;
7
8      // Check if the binary tree is empty.
9      public boolean isEmpty()
10     {
11         return root == null;
12     }
13 }
```

A binary search tree is a special type of binary tree, so it makes sense to make the BinarySearchTree class a subclass of BinaryTree. Code Listing 22-9 shows the implementation of that class, together with all the methods that we have already discussed.

Code Listing 22-9   (BinarySearchTree.java)

```java
1  /**
2      This class implements a binary search tree.
3  */
```

```
 4
 5   public class BinarySearchTree extends BinaryTree
 6   {
 7       /**
 8           This class represents the result of removing
 9           a node from a binary tree.
10       */
11       private class RemovalResult
12       {
13           Node node;      // Removed node
14           Node tree;      // Remaining tree
15
16           RemovalResult(Node node, Node tree)
17           {
18               this.node = node;
19               this.tree = tree;
20           }
21       }
22
23       /**
24           The public add method adds a value to the tree by
25           calling a private add method and passing it the
26           root of the tree.
27           @param x The value to add to the tree.
28           @return true.
29       */
30       public boolean add(int x)
31       {
32           root = add(x, root);
33           return true;
34       }
35
36       /**
37           The contains method checks to see if a value is
38           in the binary tree.
39           @param x The value to check for.
40           @return true if x is in the tree, false otherwise.
41       */
42       public boolean contains(int x)
43       {
44           // Call the private recursive method.
45           return contains(x, root);
46       }
47
48       /**
49           The add method adds a value to the search tree.
50           @x the value to add.
51           @param bstree The root of the binary search tree.
```

```
52          @return The root of the resulting binary search tree.
53      */
54      private Node add(int x, Node bstree)
55      {
56          if (bstree == null)
57          {
58              return new Node(x);
59          }
60          // bstree is not null.
61          if (x < bstree.value)
62          {
63              // Add x to the left subtree and replace
64              // the current left subtree with the result.
65              bstree.left = add(x, bstree.left);
66          } else
67          {
68              // Add x to the right subtree.
69              bstree.right = add(x, bstree.right);
70          }
71          return bstree;
72      }
73
74      /**
75         The method contains checks whether an item is in
76         a binary search tree.
77         @param x The item to check for.
78         @param bstree The binary tree to look in.
79         @return true if found, false otherwise.
80      */
81      private boolean contains(int x, Node bstree)
82      {
83          if (bstree == null)
84          {
85              return false;
86          }
87          if (x == bstree.value)
88          {
89              return true;
90          }
91          if (x < bstree.value)
92          {
93              // Recursively look in left subtree.
94              return contains(x, bstree.left);
95          } else
96          {
97              // Recursively look in right subtree.
98              return contains(x, bstree.right);
99          }
```

```
100          }
101
102          /**
103             The remove method removes a value from the
104             binary search tree.
105             @param x The value to remove.
106             @returns true if x was removed, false if x not found.
107          */
108          public boolean remove(int x)
109          {
110              RemovalResult result = remove(root, x);
111              if (result == null)
112              {
113                  return false;
114              } else
115              {
116                  root = result.tree;
117                  return true;
118              }
119          }
120
121          /**
122             This remove method removes a value a from a
123             binary search tree and returns the removed node
124             and the remaining tree wrapped in a RemovalResult object.
125
126             @param bTree The binary search tree.
127             @param x The value to be removed.
128             @return null if x is not found in bTree.
129          */
130          private RemovalResult remove(Node bTree, int x)
131          {
132              if (bTree == null)
133              {
134                  return null;
135              }
136              if (x < bTree.value)
137              {
138                  // Remove x from the left subtree.
139                  RemovalResult result = remove(bTree.left, x);
140                  if (result == null)
141                  {
142                      return null;
143                  }
144                  bTree.left = result.tree;
145                  result.tree = bTree;
146                  return result;
147              }
148              if (x > bTree.value)
```

```
149              {
150                  // Remove x from the right subtree.
151                  RemovalResult result = remove(bTree.right, x);
152                  if (result == null)
153                  {
154                      return null;
155                  }
156                  bTree.right = result.tree;
157                  result.tree = bTree;
158                  return result;
159              }
160              // x is in this root node.
161              // Is it a leaf?
162              if (bTree.right == null && bTree.left == null)
163              {
164                  return new RemovalResult(bTree, null);
165              }
166
167              // Does the node have two children?
168              if (bTree.right != null && bTree.left != null)
169              {
170                  // Remove largest node in left subtree and
171                  // make it the root of the remaining tree.
172                  RemovalResult remResult = removeLargest(bTree.left);
173                  Node newRoot = remResult.node;
174                  newRoot.left = remResult.tree;
175                  newRoot.right = bTree.right;
176
177                  // Prepare the result to be returned.
178                  bTree.left = null;
179                  bTree.right = null;
180                  return new RemovalResult(bTree, newRoot);
181              }
182              // The node has one child
183              Node node = bTree;
184              Node tree;
185              if (bTree.left != null)
186              {
187                  tree = bTree.left;
188              } else
189              {
190                  tree = bTree.right;
191              }
192              node.left = null;
193              node.right = null;
194              return new RemovalResult(node, tree);
195      }
196
```

```
197      /**
198         The removeLargest method removes the largest node
199         from a binary search tree.
200         @param bTree: The binary search tree.
201         @return The result of removing the largest node.
202      */
203      private RemovalResult removeLargest(Node bTree)
204      {
205          if (bTree == null)
206          {
207              return null;
208          }
209          if (bTree.right == null)
210          {
211              // Root is the largest node
212              Node tree = bTree.left;
213              bTree.left = null;
214              return new RemovalResult(bTree, tree);
215          } else
216          {
217              // Remove the largest node from the right subtree.
218              RemovalResult remResult
219                      = removeLargest(bTree.right);
220              bTree.right = remResult.tree;
221              remResult.tree = bTree;
222              return remResult;
223          }
224      }
225  }
```

Graphical Display of Binary Search Trees

The graphical display of binary trees can be achieved by using the getView() method of the ~~SwingNodeUtililties and JavaFX~~NodeUtilities classes of Code Listings 22-4 and 22-6. The getView() method requires access to the root node of the binary tree to be displayed. Because the root field of BinaryTree is protected, the getView() method must be called from a subclass of BinaryTree.

What we need is a DisplayableBtree class, a subclass of BinaryTree that is able to wrap a pre-existing binary tree and produce a graphical view of the wrapped binary tree. The definition of this class starts out like this:

```
public class DisplayableBtree extends BinaryTree
{
    private BinaryTree tree;
    public DisplayableBtree(BinaryTree t)
    {
        tree = t;
    }
}
```

Notice that this class has only one constructor, so you cannot create an instance of `DisplayableBtree` unless you already have an existing binary tree that you want to display:

```
BinarySearchTree  tree1 = new BinarySearchTree();
tree1.add(50);
DisplayableBtree dTree = new DisplayableBTree(tree1);
```

Notice also that `DisplayableBtree` has two fields: a protected field root that it inherits from `Binarytree`, and a private field tree that references another binary tree. So, `DisplayableBtree` is a binary tree that contains, or wraps, another binary tree. Moreover, the inherited root field will always be `null`, because unlike `BinarySearchTree`, our BinaryTree class has no add method that can be used to add elements. To make the inherited `isEmpty()` method useful, we override it so that it checks the emptiness of the wrapped binary tree:

```
public class DisplayableBtree extends BinaryTree
{
    private BinaryTree tree;
    public DisplayableBtree(BinaryTree t)
    {
        tree = t;
    }


    @Override
    public boolean isEmpty()
    {
        return tree.isEmpty();
    }
}
```

Finally, we complete the class by adding a two `getView()` methods: ~~one to return a Swing view and the other a JavaFX view~~ to return a graphical view of the binary tree. The completed class is shown in Code Listing 22-10.

Insert 1359

Code Listing 22-10   (`DisplayableBtree.java`)

replace with new version

```
 1  import javafx.scene.layout.Pane;
 2  import javax.swing.JPanel;
 3
 4  public class DisplayableBtree extends BinaryTree
 5  {
 6      private BinaryTree tree;
 7      public DisplayableBtree(BinaryTree t)
 8      {
 9          tree = t;
10      }
11
12      @Override
13      public boolean isEmpty()
14      {
15          return tree.isEmpty();
16      }
```

```
17
18      /**
19          Return a view of the binary tree suitable for
20          display in Swing.
21      */
22      public JPanel getSwingView()
23      {
24          return  SwingNodeUtilities.getView(tree.root);
25      }
26
27      /**
28          Return a view of the binary tree suitable for
29          display in JavaFX.
30      */
31      public Pane getJavaFXView()
32      {
33          return  JavaFXNodeUtilities.getView(tree.root);
34      }
35  }
```

A Program for Testing the Binary Search Tree Class

The program for testing the class of Code Listing 22-10 will have a graphical user interface that allows users to type commands to add, remove, and search for items in the binary search tree. The user interface consists of a main window with a command entry text field at the bottom and an un-editable text field at the top used to display the results from executing user commands. The center of the window is used to display in a hierarchical tree form, the elements that are currently in the search tree. Figure 22-12 shows the interface after the user has executed commands to add 50, 100, 75, 80, 12, 105, and 77 in succession.

Figure 22-12 A binary tree after adding some values   (Mark Schrier. Copyright Oracle, Inc.)

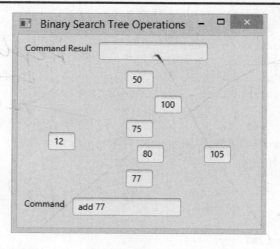

Removing the node with 100 causes the program to replace it with 80, resulting in the display shown in Figure 22-13.

Figure 22-13   The binary tree of Figure 22-12 after removing 100   (Mark Schrier. Copyright Oracle, Inc.)

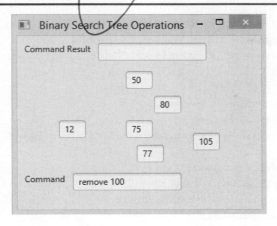

The program allows the following commands:

- add x: Adds the number x to the binary search tree, for example: add 12.
- remove x: Removes x from the tree, for example: remove 12.
- contains x: Checks if x is in the tree, for example: contains 12. The program will display true in the command result label at the top of the frame if x is found in the tree, and false otherwise.
- isempty: Checks if there are any values in the tree, for example: isempty. The program will display true in the command result text field if the tree is empty, and false otherwise.

Swing and JavaFX programs for testing the BinarySearchTree class follow. Both create a binary search tree on which the add, remove, and other operations will be performed, and then wrap the search tree with a DisplayableBtree:

```
BinarySearchTree binTree = new BinarySearchTree();
DisplayableBtree displayBinTree = new DisplayableBtree(binTree);
```

The programs then build the user interface and attach an event handler on the command entry text field at the bottom of the window. Every time the user enters a command, the handler method reads the command from the text field and executes the command on the binary search tree binTree. The old view of the tree is then removed from the user interface and replaced with the new view. The details are in Code Listings 22-11 and 22-12.

Code Listing 22-11   (SwingBSearchTreeDemo.java)

```
1 import javax.swing.*;
2 import java.awt.*;
3 import java.awt.event.*;
4 import java.util.*;
5
6 /**
7    This class is a Swing interface to testing the
8    binary search tree class.
9 */
```

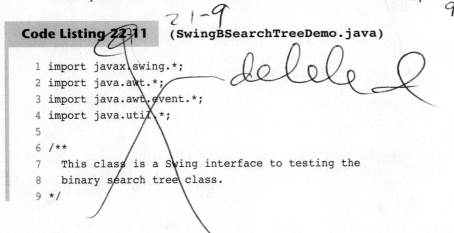

```
10 public class SwingBSearchTreeDemo extends JFrame
11 {
12     // The binary tree to be manipulated.
13     private BinarySearchTree
14             binTree = new BinarySearchTree();
15
16     // This binary tree wraps the real binary
17     // tree so it can be displayed.
18     private DisplayableBtree
19             displayBinTree = new DisplayableBtree(binTree);
20
21     // User interface components
22     private JLabel cmdResultLabel;
23     private JTextField cmdResultTextField;
24     private JLabel cmdLabel;
25     private JTextField cmdTextField;
26
27     // Constructor builds the user interface and sets the
28     // event listener.
29     public SwingBSearchTreeDemo()
30     {
31         setTitle("Binary Search Tree Operations");
32
33         //cmd text and cmd Result label in North.
34         JPanel resultPanel = new JPanel(new GridLayout(1, 2));
35         cmdResultLabel = new JLabel("Command Result: ");
36         cmdResultTextField = new JTextField();
37         resultPanel.add(cmdResultLabel);
38         resultPanel.add(cmdResultTextField);
39         cmdResultTextField.setEditable(false);
40         add(resultPanel, BorderLayout.NORTH);
41
42         // Leave center for binary tree view
43         // cmd label and cmd text field go in South.
44         cmdLabel = new JLabel("Command: ");
45         cmdTextField = new JTextField();
46         JPanel cmdPanel = new JPanel(new GridLayout(1, 2));
47         cmdPanel.add(cmdLabel);
48         cmdPanel.add(cmdTextField);
49         ActionListener cmdLis = new CmdTextListener();
50         cmdTextField.addActionListener(cmdLis);
51         add(cmdPanel, BorderLayout.SOUTH);
52
53         // Set up the frame.
54         pack();
55         setDefaultCloseOperation(JFrame.EXIT_ON_CLOSE);
56         setVisible(true);
57     }
58
```

```
59      // View of the binary tree to be displayed in the frame.
60      JPanel view = null;
61
62      /**
63       This private inner class responds to commands typed
64       into the command entry text field. It executes the
65       commands on the real binary tree and then displays
66       the view from the displayable binary tree.
67      */
68      private class CmdTextListener implements ActionListener
69      {
70          @Override
71          public void actionPerformed(ActionEvent evt)
72          {
73              String cmdStr = cmdTextField.getText();
74              Scanner sc = new Scanner(cmdStr);
75              String cmd = sc.next();
76              switch (cmd)
77              {
78                  case "add":
79                  {
80                      // Add the new value to the tree.
81                      int value = sc.nextInt();
82                      binTree.add(value);
83
84                      // Remove the old view and replace it with a
85                      // new view.
86                      if (view != null) { remove(view); }
87                      view = displayBinTree.getSwingView();
88                      add(view);
89                      // Tell the frame to resize itself.
90                      pack();
91                      validate();
92                      cmdResultTextField.setText(" ");
93                  }
94                  return;
95                  case "isempty":
96                  {
97                      String resultText
98                          = "Tree empty? " + binTree.isEmpty();
99                      cmdResultTextField.setText(resultText);
100                 }
101                 return;
102                 case "contains":
103                 {
104                     int value = sc.nextInt();
105                     String resultText = "Contains " + value + "?: "
106                         + binTree.contains(value);
```

```java
107                           cmdResultTextField.setText(resultText);
108                       }
109                       return;
110                   case "remove":
111                   {
112                       // Similar to case for "add".
113                       int value = sc.nextInt();
114                       binTree.remove(value);
115
116                       if (view != null) {remove(view); }
117                       view =  displayBinTree.getSwingView();
118                       add(view);
119
120                       pack();
121                       validate();
122                       cmdResultTextField.setText(" ");
123                   }
124                   return;
125               }
126           }
127       }
128
129       /**
130          The main method creates an instance of the
131          SwingBSearchTreeDemo class  which causes it
132          to display its window.
133       */
134       public static void main(String[] args)
135       {
136           new SwingBSearchTreeDemo();
137       }
138 }
```

Code Listing 22-12 (JavaFXBSearchTreeDemo.java)

GUI

replace

Insert

1364

```java
1 import java.util.Scanner;
2 import javafx.application.Application;
3 import javafx.event.ActionEvent;
4 import javafx.event.EventHandler;
5 import javafx.geometry.Insets;
6 import javafx.geometry.Pos;
7 import javafx.scene.Scene;
8 import javafx.scene.control.Label;
9 import javafx.scene.control.TextField;
10 import javafx.scene.layout.HBox;
```

```
11  import javafx.scene.layout.VBox;
12  import javafx.stage.Stage;
13
14  /**
15     This class is a JavaFX interface for testing the
16     the binary search tree class.
17  */
18
19  public class JavaFXBSearchTreeDemo extends Application
20  {
21      @Override
22      public void start(Stage stage) throws Exception
23      {
24          // Set up the binary tree to manipulate
25          BinarySearchTree binTree = new BinarySearchTree();
26
27          // This binary tree wraps the real binary tree
28          // so it can be displayed.
29          DisplayableBtree
30              displayBinTree = new DisplayableBtree(binTree);
31
32          // Displays the result of the user command.
33          TextField cmdResultTextField = new TextField();
34          cmdResultTextField.setEditable(false);
35
36          // Used by the user to enter a command.
37          TextField cmdTextField = new TextField();
38
39          // HBox1 holds cmdResultTextField and its label.
40          HBox hBox1 = new HBox(10);
41          Label cmdResultLabel = new Label("Command Result");
42          hBox1.getChildren().addAll(cmdResultLabel, cmdResultTextField);
43
44          // Place holder for the binary tree view.
45          HBox bTreeView = new HBox();
46          bTreeView.setAlignment(Pos.CENTER);
47
48          // HBox2 holds the cmdTextField and its label
49          HBox hBox2 = new HBox(10);
50          Label cmdLabel = new Label("Command");
51          hBox2.getChildren().addAll(cmdLabel, cmdTextField);
52
53          // Put the three HBox objects in a VBox
54          VBox outerPane = new VBox(10);
55          outerPane.setPadding(new Insets(10));
56          outerPane.getChildren().addAll(hBox1, bTreeView, hBox2);
57
```

```
58          // Command hander needs to access to the bTreeView
59          // so it can set the binary tree view, and to the
60          // cmdResultTextField so it can set the command result.
61          // Also needs access to the binary tree and its displayable
62          // twin.
63          EventHandler<ActionEvent>
64              handler = new CmdHandler(bTreeView, cmdResultTextField,
65                                          binTree, displayBinTree);
66          cmdTextField.setOnAction(handler);
67
68          // Set up the stage
69          stage.setTitle("Binary Search Tree Operations");
70          stage.setScene(new Scene(outerPane));
71          stage.show();
72      }
73
74      public static void main(String [] args)
75      {
76          launch(args) ;
77      }
78
79  }
80
81  // Event Handler class
82  class CmdHandler implements EventHandler<ActionEvent>
83  {
84      // These class variables reference
85      // data in the calling environment.
86      private HBox view;
87      private TextField cmdResultTextField;
88      private BinarySearchTree binTree;
89      private DisplayableBtree displayBinTree;
90
91      // Constructor stores references to data in
92      // the calling enviroment.
93      public CmdHandler(HBox tView, TextField cmdResTf,
94                      BinarySearchTree tree,
95                      DisplayableBtree dTree)
96      {
97          view = tView;
98          cmdResultTextField = cmdResTf;
99          binTree = tree;
100         displayBinTree = dTree;
101     }
102
103     public void handle(ActionEvent evt)
104     {
105         // Get the command from the event target.
```

```
106             TextField cmdTf = (TextField)evt.getTarget();
107             String cmdStr =  cmdTf.getText();
108
109             // Use a scanner to read the command and its parts.
110             Scanner sc = new Scanner(cmdStr);
111             String cmd = sc.next();
112             switch (cmd)
113             {
114                 case "add":
115                 {
116                     // Perform the operation on the tree.
117                     int value = sc.nextInt();
118                     binTree.add(value);
119
120                     // Replace the old view of the tree.
121                     view.getChildren().clear();
122                     view.getChildren().add(displayBinTree.getJavaFXView());
123                     cmdResultTextField.setText(" ");
124                 }
125                 return;
126                 case "isempty":
127                 {
128                     String resultText
129                             = "Tree empty? " + binTree.isEmpty();
130                     cmdResultTextField.setText(resultText);
131                 }
132                 return;
133                 case "contains":
134                 {
135                     int value = sc.nextInt();
136                     String resultText = "Contains " + value + "?: "
137                             + binTree.contains(value);
138                     cmdResultTextField.setText(resultText);
139                 }
140                 return;
141                 case "remove":
142                 {
143                     int value = sc.nextInt();
144                     binTree.remove(value);
145
146                     // Replace the old view of the tree.
147                     view.getChildren().clear();
148                     view.getChildren().add(displayBinTree.getJavaFXView());
149                     cmdResultTextField.setText(" ");
150                 }
151                 return;
152             }
153         }
154 }
```

22.3 AVL Trees

CONCEPT: Operations on binary search trees are more efficient when the tree is balanced. An AVL tree is a binary search tree that satisfies a balance condition at each one of its nodes.

Because most operations on binary search trees trace out a path from the root to some node, the amount of work they do is proportional to the length of the path. Therefore it is desirable to have binary search trees that are "shallow" rather than "deep." A binary tree can be kept shallow by imposing conditions on the height of its subtrees. The *height* of a binary tree is the length of the longest path from the root to a leaf. (The length of a path is the number of edges, or links, in the path: it is one less than the number of nodes in the path.) A binary tree with one node has height 0, and by convention, the empty binary tree has height –1.

An *AVL tree* is a binary search tree in which the heights of the left and right subtree of every node differ by at most 1. Figure 22-14 shows two examples of AVL trees.

Figure 22-14 Examples of AVL trees

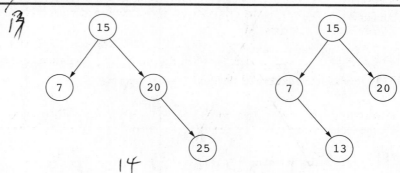

The tree of Figure 22-15 fails to be an AVL tree because the right subtree of the root has height 2 whereas the left subtree has height 0.

Figure 22-15 An example of a non-AVL tree

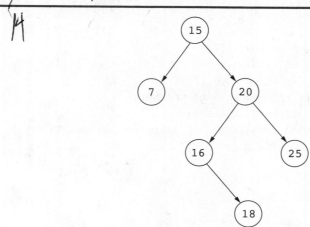

Adding New Elements to AVL Trees

AVL trees support the same operations as regular binary search trees: addition of new elements, removal, and search. To add a new element to an AVL tree, we simply add the new element using the same algorithm used to add elements to a regular binary search tree. It is possible, however, that the addition may upset the AVL balance condition, so we must check for this and rebalance the tree as necessary. We only need to check the balance condition at nodes that lie on the path between the newly inserted node and the root.

There are four types of imbalance that can result from adding a new node to an existing AVL tree:

- An *LL imbalance* occurs at a node N with a left child K when N and K are both left-heavy: that is, the height of the left subtree of N is greater than the height of the right subtree of N; and the height of the left subtree of K is greater than the height of the right subtree of K. An LL imbalance is fixed by performing a *single right rotation* at N: this is illustrated in Figure 22-16.
- An *RR imbalance* occurs at a node N with a right child M when N and M are both right-heavy. This situation is the mirror image of an LL imbalance: it is fixed by performing a *single left rotation* at N.
- An *LR imbalance* occurs at a node N with a left child K when N is left-heavy and K is right-heavy. An LR imbalance is fixed by performing a *double LR rotation* at N. This is illustrated in Figure 22-17.
- An *RL imbalance* occurs at a node N with a right child M when N is right-heavy and M is left-heavy. This situation is a mirror image of an LR imbalance, and can be fixed by performing a *double RL rotation* at M.

Figure 22-16   A single right rotation is performed at a node with an LL imbalance

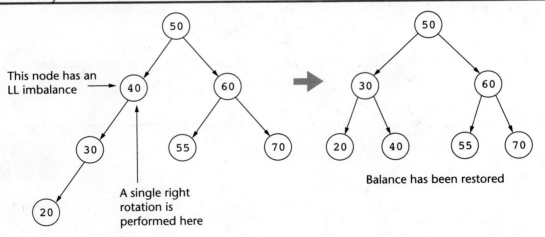

This node has an
LL imbalance

A single right
rotation is
performed here

Balance has been restored

Figure 22-17 A double LR rotation is performed at a node with an LR imbalance

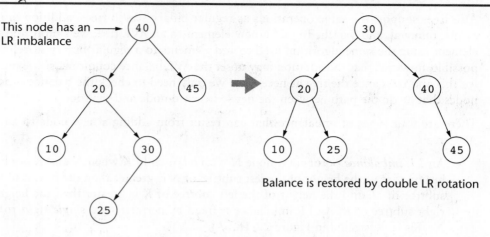

Balance is restored by double LR rotation

Consider now a general strategy for removing an LL imbalance that occurs after a new node has been added to an AVL tree. Let N be the node with the LL imbalance, let K be the left child of N, and let J be the left child of K. As shown in Figure 22-18, let p, q, r, and s be respectively the left subtree of J, the right subtree of J, the right subtree of K, and the right subtree of N. Letting h be the height of s, we deduce that the height of the left subtree of N must be $h + 2$. We can further deduce that the height of r must be h, and that one of p and q must have height h while the other has height $h - 1$. Let us assume that p has height h and q has height $h - 1$.

Figure 22-18 A node with an LL imbalance

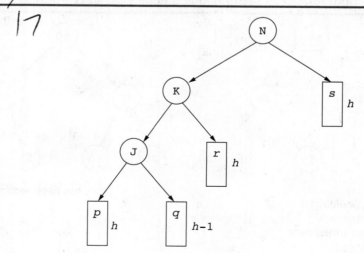

In general, this situation occurs when a new node has been added to the subtree p, and the imbalance is discovered at N as we are tracing our way back to the root. At this point, we fix the imbalance by performing a single right rotation at N, that is, we rearrange the parent child relationships among the nodes and subtrees shown to yield the tree shown in Figure 22-19.

Figure 22-19 Effect of a single right rotation

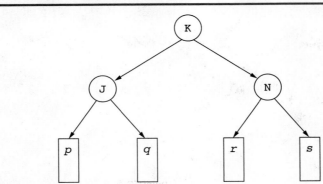

Notice that the rearranged tree is still a binary search tree, and moreover, it now obeys the AVL balance condition at every node. An RR imbalance can similarly be fixed using a single left rotation.

Consider now how to remove an LR imbalance at a node N. Any such node N will have a left child J, which will in turn have a right child K. Let p, q, r, and s represent the left and right subtrees of these nodes as shown in Figure 22-20. Assuming that s has height h, we deduce that the subtree rooted at J must have height $h + 2$. We can further deduce that the height of p is h. Because the subtree rooted at K has height $h + 1$, at least one of the subtrees of K, say q, will have height h. The other subtree, r, must have height $h - 1$ (r cannot have a height less than $h - 1$ because then the imbalance would be found at K rather than at N.)

Figure 22-20 A node with an LR imbalance

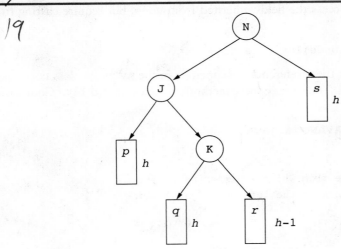

The LR imbalance shown in Figure 22-20 is removed by executing a double LR rotation, which rearranges the tree into the form shown in Figure 22-21.

Figure 22-21   Effect of a double LR rotation on the tree of Figure 22-20

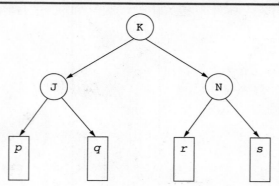

The reconfigured tree is now an AVL tree. An RL imbalance can similarly be removed by performing a double RL rotation.

Implementation of AVL Trees

An AVL node is a binary tree node with a height field. Our implementation of an AVL tree is based on the AVLNode class, which is a subclass of Node. The AVLNode class inherits the

```
int value;
Node left;
Node right;
```

fields from its superclass and adds an integer field to keep track of the height of the node in the AVL tree. The Node references `left` and `right` work fine when being assigned to, or when being used to access the fields inherited from `Node`, but require casting to access the height field:

```
int h =  ((AVLNode)left).height;
```

To simplify the use of these references, we include in the AVLNode class convenience methods that apply the cast. You can see these methods in Lines 12 and 13 of Code Listing 22-13.

Code Listing 22-13   (`AVLNode.java`)

```
1  /**
2     AVLNode extends Node from which it inherits
3     the value field, and also the left and right links.
4  */
5
6  class AVLNode extends Node
7  {
8      int height;
9
10     // These methods cast the inhertied NODE links
11     // AVLNode links.
```

```
12      AVLNode getLeft(){ return (AVLNode) left; }
13      AVLNode getRight(){ return (AVLNode) right; }
14
15      public AVLNode(int value)
16      {
17          // Call the other (sister) constructor.
18          this(value, null, null);
19      }
20
21      public AVLNode(int val, AVLNode left1, AVLNode right1)
22      {
23          // Pass the parameters to the superclass constructor.
24          super(val, left1, right1);
25          height = 0;
26      }
27
28      /**
29        The resetHeight methods recomputes height if the
30        left or right subtrees have changed.
31      */
32      void resetHeight()
33      {
34          int leftHeight = -1;
35          int rightHeight = -1;
36          if (left != null)
37          {
38              leftHeight = getLeft().height;
39          }
40          if (right != null)
41          {
42              rightHeight = getRight().height;
43          }
44          height = 1 + Math.max(leftHeight, rightHeight);
45      }
46  }
```

The implementation of AVL trees is similar to that of binary search trees, except that the add and remove methods must be modified to ensure that the tree stays balanced. Code Listing 22-14 shows an AVL class AVLTree with the add method implemented. The class extends the BinaryTree class of Code Listing 22-8, from which it inherits the root field. Although declared as being of type Node, the root field will point to AVLNode objects. Accordingly, the AVLTree class has a getRoot() method that retrieves root and automatically applies a cast to AVLNode. The getRoot() method appears in Lines 8-11 of Code Listing 22-14.

The add(bTree,x) method is a straightforward implementation of the strategy already discussed. If bTree is empty, add creates and returns a new AVL tree with a single node. Otherwise, the method recursively adds the new value to one of the subtrees, recomputes the height of the subtrees, and checks the balance condition at `bTree`. If the `bTree` is out of balance, add calls the balance method on it.

The balance method determines the type of imbalance existing at the node passed to it and calls one of four methods to perform the appropriate rotation. The methods that perform the rotations are named `llBalance`, `lrBalance`, `rlBalance`, and `rrBalance` after the type of imbalance they correct.

Code Listing 22-14 (`AVLTree.java`)

```java
1  /**
2     This class implements AVLTrees.
3  */
4  public class AVLTree extends BinaryTree
5  {
6      // Convenience method casts the inherited root
7      // from Node to AVLNode.
8      private AVLNode getRoot()
9      {
10         return (AVLNode) root;
11     }
12
13     /**
14        The getHeight method computes the height of an AVL tree.
15        @param tree An AVL tree.
16        @return The height of the AVL tree.
17     */
18     static int getHeight(AVLNode tree)
19     {
20         if (tree == null)
21             return -1;
22         else
23             return tree.height;
24     }
25
26     /**
27        The add method adds a value to this AVL tree.
28        @param x The value to add.
29        @return true.
30     */
31     public boolean add(int x)
32     {
33         root = add((AVLNode) root, x);
34         return true;
35     }
36
37     /**
38        The add method adds a value to an AVL tree.
```

```
39         @return The root of the augmented AVL tree.
40      */
41      private AVLNode add(AVLNode bTree, int x)
42      {
43          if (bTree == null)
44          {
45              return new AVLNode(x);
46          }
47          if (x < bTree.value)
48          {
49              bTree.left = add(bTree.getLeft(), x);
50          } else
51          {
52              bTree.right = add(bTree.getRight(), x);
53          }
54
55          // Compute heights of the left and right subtrees
56          // and rebalance the tree if needed.
57          int leftHeight = getHeight(bTree.getLeft());
58          int rightHeight = getHeight(bTree.getRight());
59          if (Math.abs(leftHeight - rightHeight) == 2)
60          {
61              return balance(bTree);
62          } else
63          {
64              bTree.resetHeight();
65              return bTree;
66          }
67      }
68
69      /**
70          The balance method rebalances an AVL tree.
71          @param bTree The AVL tree needing to be balanced.
72          @return The balanced AVL tree.
73      */
74      private AVLNode balance(AVLNode bTree)
75      {
76          int rHeight = getHeight(bTree.getRight());
77          int lHeight = getHeight(bTree.getLeft());
78
79          if (rHeight > lHeight)
80          {
81              AVLNode rightChild = bTree.getRight();
82              int rrHeight = getHeight(rightChild.getRight());
83              int rlHeight = getHeight(rightChild.getLeft());
84              if (rrHeight > rlHeight)
85              {
86                  return rrBalance(bTree);
```

```
 87                 } else
 88                 {
 89                     return rlBalance(bTree);
 90                 }
 91             } else
 92             {
 93                 AVLNode leftChild = bTree.getLeft();
 94                 int llHeight = getHeight(leftChild.getLeft());
 95                 int lrHeight = getHeight(leftChild.getRight());
 96                 if (llHeight > lrHeight)
 97                 {
 98                     return llBalance(bTree);
 99                 } else
100                 {
101                     return lrBalance(bTree);
102                 }
103             }
104     }
105
106     /**
107        The rrBlance method corrects an RR imbalance.
108        @param bTree The AVL tree wih an RR imbalance.
109        @return The balanced AVL tree.
110     */
111     private AVLNode rrBalance(AVLNode bTree)
112     {
113         AVLNode rightChild = bTree.getRight();
114         AVLNode rightLeftChild = rightChild.getLeft();
115         rightChild.left = bTree;
116         bTree.right = rightLeftChild;
117         bTree.resetHeight();
118         rightChild.resetHeight();
119         return rightChild;
120     }
121
122     /**
123        The rlBalance method corrects an RL imbalance.
124        @parame bTree The AVL tree with an RL imbalance.
125        @return The balanced AVL tree.
126     */
127     private AVLNode rlBalance(AVLNode bTree)
128     {
129         AVLNode root = bTree;
130         AVLNode rNode = root.getRight();
131         AVLNode rlNode = rNode.getLeft();
132         AVLNode rlrTree = rlNode.getRight();
133         AVLNode rllTree = rlNode.getLeft();
134
```

```
135           // Build the restructured tree.
136           rNode.left = rlrTree;
137           root.right = rllTree;
138           rlNode.left = root;
139           rlNode.right = rNode;
140
141           // Adjust heights
142           rNode.resetHeight();
143           root.resetHeight();
144           rlNode.resetHeight();
145
146           return rlNode;
147       }
148
149       /**
150          The llBalance method corrects an LL imbalance.
151          @param bTree The AVL tree with an LL imbalance.
152          @return The balanced AVL tree.
153       */
154       private AVLNode llBalance(AVLNode bTree)
155       {
156           AVLNode leftChild = bTree.getLeft();
157           AVLNode lrTree = leftChild.getRight();
158           leftChild.right = bTree;
159           bTree.left = lrTree;
160           bTree.resetHeight();
161           leftChild.resetHeight();
162           return leftChild;
163       }
164
165       /**
166          The lrBalance method corrects an LR imbalance.
167          @param bTree The AVL tree with an LR imbalance.
168          @return The balanced AVL tree.
169       */
170       private AVLNode lrBalance(AVLNode bTree)
171       {
172           AVLNode root = bTree;
173           AVLNode lNode = root.getLeft();
174           AVLNode lrNode = lNode.getRight();
175           AVLNode lrlTree = lrNode.getLeft();
176           AVLNode lrrTree = lrNode.getRight();
177
178           // Build the restructured tree.
179           lNode.right = lrlTree;
180           root.left = lrrTree;
181           lrNode.left = lNode;
182           lrNode.right = root;
```

```
183
184        // Adjust heights.
185        lNode.resetHeight();
186        root.resetHeight();
187        lrNode.resetHeight();
188
189        return lrNode;
190    }
191 }
192
```

Code Listing 22-15 implements the Swing version of the graphical interface to the AVLTree class. The program is a simple modification of the one in Code Listing 22-11.

Code Listing 22-15 (`AVLTreeDemo.java`)

```java
1  import java.util.*;
2  import java.awt.*;
3  import java.awt.event.*;
4  import javax.swing.*;
5
6  /**
7     The AVLFrame class builds the user interface and
8     supports user interaction.
9  */
10
11 public class AVLTreeDemo extends JFrame
12 implements ActionListener
13 {
14     // AVL Tree and a Displayable wrapper.
15     private AVLTree avlTree = new AVLTree();
16     private DisplayableBtree
17         displayAvlTree = new DisplayableBtree(avlTree);
18
19     // User interface components.
20     private JLabel cmdResultLabel;
21     private JTextField cmdResultTextField;
22     private JLabel cmdLabel;
23     private JTextField cmdTextField;
24
25     public AVLTreeDemo()
26     {
27         setTitle("AVL Trees");
28
29         // cmd text and cmd Result label in North Region.
30         JPanel resultPanel = new JPanel(new GridLayout(1,2));
```

[handwritten: replace this with a JavaFX version]

[handwritten: Insert 1378]

```
31        cmdResultLabel = new JLabel("Command Result: ");
32        cmdResultTextField = new JTextField();
33        resultPanel.add(cmdResultLabel);
34        resultPanel.add(cmdResultTextField);
35        cmdResultTextField.setEditable(false);
36        add(resultPanel, BorderLayout.NORTH);
37
38        // Leave center for binary tree view.
39
40        // cmd label and cmd text field in South Region.
41        cmdLabel = new JLabel("Command: ");
42        cmdTextField = new JTextField();
43        JPanel cmdPanel = new JPanel(new GridLayout(1,2));
44        cmdPanel.add(cmdLabel);
45        cmdPanel.add(cmdTextField);
46        cmdTextField.addActionListener(this);
47        add(cmdPanel, BorderLayout.SOUTH);
48
49        // Set up the frame.
50        pack();
51        setDefaultCloseOperation(JFrame.EXIT_ON_CLOSE);
52        setVisible(true);
53    }
54
55    JPanel view = null;
56
57    /**
58       This method interprets user commands entered in the
59       command entry text field.
60       @return evt The action event from the
61       command entry text field.
62    */
63
64    public void actionPerformed(ActionEvent evt)
65    {
66        String cmdStr = cmdTextField.getText();
67        Scanner sc = new Scanner(cmdStr);
68        String cmd = sc.next();
69        if (cmd.equals("add"))
70        {
71            int value = sc.nextInt();
72            avlTree.add(value);
73            if (view != null)
74                remove(view);
75            view = displayAvlTree.getSwingView();
76            add(view);
77            pack();
78            validate();
```

```
79              cmdResultTextField.setText(" ");
80          }
81      }
82
83      /**
84          The main method creates an instance of the
85          AVLTreeDemo class which causes it to display
86          its window.
87      */
88
89      public static void main(String [] args)
90      {
91          AVLTreeDemo atd = new AVLTreeDemo();
92      }
93 }
```

A screenshot of this user interface after the user has issued commands to add the first six multiples of 10 to an initially empty AVL tree is shown in Figure 22-22. A JavaFX version would be a simple modification of Code Listing 22-12 and is not shown.

Figure 22-22   Sample interaction with AVL program   (Mark Schrier. Copyright Oracle, Inc.)

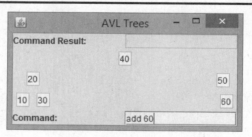

22.4 Priority Queues

CONCEPT: A priority queue is a collection that stores elements according to some order. Priority queues support addition and removal of elements, and a removal always returns the least element in the collection.

An *order* on a set of values is a way of establishing, for any two elements *x* and *y*, whether *x* is "less than" *y* or *y* is "less than" *x*. Many sets have a *natural order*: for example, the set of integers is ordered by the usual "less than" relation <, that is, in the natural order for the integers, *x* is "less than" *y* if and only if $x < y$. Likewise, in the natural order for strings, a string *s* is "less than" string *t* if *s* comes before *t* in alphabetical order. In an ordered set, an element that is "less than" every other element is called the *least* element, or the *minimum*.

All orders referred to in this chapter will be assumed to be *total* (or *linear*), meaning that for any two elements x and y, exactly one of the following conditions must hold:

1. x is "less than" y
2. x is equal to y
3. y is "less than" y

As an example of an order that is not natural, we can stipulate, for any two numbers x and y, that x is "less than" y if x > y. In this case, for a set such as {1, 2, 3, 4}, the defined order turns the set into the sequence {4, 3, 2, 1}, and makes 4 the "least" element of the set.

The natural order of primitive types in Java is specified by the built-in comparison operator <. A class type such as `Integer` or `String` specifies its natural order by implementing the `Comparable` interface.

A *priority queue* is a collection that stores elements and provides access to those elements according to some order. A remove operation executed on a priority queue always returns a minimum element. The queue element that will be returned by the next call to remove is said to be at the *head of the queue*.

The main operations supported by a priority queue when regarded as an abstract data structure are as follows:

- *add(x)*: Adds x to the priority queue.
- *removeMin( )*: Removes and returns the element at the head of the queue; this will be an element that is less than, or equal to, any other element in the queue.

The Java Collection Framework provides an implementation of a priority queue in a class called `PriorityQueue`. It provides more methods than the two we have listed, and some of the method names are different. Most of its methods are listed in Table 22-1.

Table 22-1 `PriorityQueue` **class methods**

`PriorityQueue<E>()`	Creates a queue that stores items of class type E and orders them according to their natural ordering (using the Comparable interface as implemented by E).
`PriorityQueue<E>(int capacity, Comparator<? Super E> comp)`	Creates a queue that stores items of class E and orders them by the specified comparator.
`boolean add(E item)`	Adds `item` to the priority queue and returns `true`.
`E poll()`	Removes and returns a minimum element from the priority queue. This method returns `null` if the queue is empty.
`E peek()`	Returns the item that is currently at the head of the queue, but does not remove it from the queue. If the queue is empty, `peek` returns `null`.
`int size()`	Returns the number of items currently stored in this priority queue.

Applications of Priority Queues

Priority queues are useful whenever items have to be processed according to some priority. For example, a personal information manager application might keep a list of tasks to be completed in a priority queue ordered by deadline, with the minimum task being the one with the closest deadline. Priority queues are also used by computer operating systems to schedule tasks for execution, and in computer networks to schedule data packets for transmission.

If you store a set of items in a priority queue and then retrieve them, they will come out in sorted order. This is the basis of a very efficient sorting algorithm named *Heapsort*. Code Listing 22-16 illustrates the use of a priority queue to sort an array.

Code Listing 22-16   **(Heapsort.java)**

```java
1    import java.util.*;
2
3    /**
4       This program demonstrates the Heapsort algorithm.
5    */
6
7    public class Heapsort
8    {
9       public static void main(String [] args)
10      {
11         // Create and display an array of random integers
12         Random randy = new Random();
13         int [ ] arr = new int[10];
14         System.out.println("Here is the array to be sorted:");
15         for (int k = 0; k < arr.length; k++)
16         {
17            arr[k] = randy.nextInt(100);
18            System.out.print(arr[k] + "   ");
19         }
20
21         // Create a priority queue of integers
22         // and use it to sort the array
23         PriorityQueue<Integer> pQueue =
24            new PriorityQueue<Integer>();
25         for (int x : arr) pQueue.add(x);
26         for (int k = 0; k < arr.length; k++)
27            arr[k] = pQueue.poll();
28
29         // Print the array
30         System.out.println("\nHere is the sorted array:");
31         for (int x : arr) System.out.print(x + "   ");
32      }
33   }
```

Program Output

```
Here is the array to be sorted:
13   81   78   93   94   60   2   32   88   58
Here is the sorted array:
2   13   32   58   60   78   81   88   93   94
```

Using Comparators with Priority Queues

The no-argument constructor of the `PriorityQueue` class used in Code Listing 22-16 orders items according to their natural ordering. This is the order specified by the < operator if the type of items is primitive, or specified by the `Comparable` interface for class types that implement it. If we need to use a different order, we must use the second constructor shown in Table 22-1. That constructor takes two parameters: an integer specifying the capacity of the queue to be created, and a `Comparator` object. `Comparator` is a generic interface defined as follows:

```
interface Comparator<T>
{
    int compare (T x, T y);
    boolean equals(Object o);
}
```

A class implementing this interface provides a definition of `compare` that returns a negative integer if *x* should be regarded as less than *y*, a positive integer if *x* should be regarded as greater than *y*, and 0 if *x* is equal to *y*. The `equals` method of the `Comparator` interface exists to allow two `Comparator` objects to be checked for equality, and does not have to be implemented if the default implementation inherited from `Object` is adequate.

As an example, let us look at a version of Heapsort that sorts integers in alphabetical order of their string representation. This is done by creating a `PriorityQueue` object that uses a `Comparator` object defined from the following class:

```
class AlphaOrder implements Comparator<Integer>
{
    public int compare(Integer x, Integer y)
    {
        return x.toString().compareTo(y.toString());
    }
}
```

The `AlphaOrder` class is defined inside `Alphaheapsort` as a static inner class. `AlphaOrder` is made static because it will be instantiated by the `main` method, which is itself static. In Java, static methods cannot instantiate non-static inner classes.

The following code fragment creates a priority queue that uses `AlphaOrder` as a comparator, and the program in Code Listing 22-17 demonstrates its use:

```
AlphaOrder comp = new AlphaOrder();
PriorityQueue<Integer>
        pQueue = new PriorityQueue<Integer>(arr.length, comp);
```

Code Listing 22-14 (Alphaheapsort.java)

```
1    import java.util.*;
2
3    /**
4       This program shows the use of a PriorityQueue with
5       a custom Comparator object.
6    */
7
8    public class Alphaheapsort
9    {
10      /**
11         Specialized Comparator.
12      */
13
14      static class AlphaOrder implements Comparator<Integer>
15      {
16         public int compare(Integer x, Integer y)
17         {
18            return x.toString().compareTo(y.toString());
19         }
20      }
21
22      public static void main(String [] args)
23      {
24         // Create and display an array of random integers
25         Random randy = new Random();
26         int [ ] arr = new int[10];
27         String str = "Here is the original list of numbers:";
28         System.out.println(str);
29         for (int k = 0; k < arr.length; k++)
30         {
31            arr[k] = randy.nextInt(10000);
32            System.out.print(arr[k] + "   ");
33         }
34
35         // Create a priority queue of integers
36         // and use it to sort the array
37         AlphaOrder c = new AlphaOrder();
38         PriorityQueue<Integer>
39            pQueue = new PriorityQueue<Integer>(arr.length, c);
40         for (int x : arr)
41            pQueue.add(x);
42         for (int k = 0; k < arr.length; k++)
43            arr[k] = pQueue.poll();
44
45         // Print the array
46         System.out.println("\nHere are the numbers sorted " +
```

```
47                          "in alphabetical order:");
48          for (int x : arr)
49              System.out.print(x + "   ");
50      }
51  }
```

Program Output

```
Here is the original list of numbers:
1065   8433   743   4962   9954   31   1815   4135   489   3094
Here are the numbers sorted alphabetical in order:
1065   1815   3094   31   4135   489   4962   743   8433   9954
```

Analysis of Heapsort

We can analyze the efficiency of Heapsort by counting the number of comparisons of array elements that it causes the priority queue to perform. It turns out that a properly implemented priority queue holding n elements requires at most log n comparisons to add or remove an item. Given an array of n elements, we can add all of them to a priority queue using $n$log n comparisons, and then remove all of them using another $n$log n comparisons, for a total of $2n$log n comparisons. In the language of Chapter 17, Heapsort is a O($n$log n) algorithm. In practice, an $n$log n algorithm is a lot faster than a O(n^2) algorithm such as Selectionsort or Bubblesort. It can be shown that no algorithm that sorts by comparing items can sort an array of n items in less than $n$log n comparisons. This means that, within a constant factor, the performance of Heapsort is the best possible.

Implementation of Priority Queues

Our goal in implementing a priority queue is to find a data structure that allows each of the two main priority queue operations, *add* and *removeMin*, to be performed with no more than log n comparisons when the priority queue has n items. Two possibilities immediately come to mind:

1. We can use an unsorted linked list to hold the n items. This will allow us to add a new element to the list quickly, but will force us to perform $n - 1$ comparisons to find and remove the minimum element.
2. We can use a linked list sorted in increasing order to hold the n items. This allows us to quickly find and remove the minimum, but will force us, in the worst case, to perform n comparisons while looking for the right place to insert the new item.

Neither of these achieves the desired O(log n) complexity for both operations, so we must look for another approach.

Binary Trees with the Heap Order Property

A third possibility is to use a binary tree to hold the elements of the queue. Consider a binary tree T that satisfies the following condition, which we will dub *the heap order property*:

At every node N of T, the value stored in N is greater than the value stored in the parent of N.

Intuitively, a binary tree with this property is a tree in which every path from the root to a leaf is sorted in increasing order. Figure 22-23 shows an example of such a tree.

Figure 22-23 A binary tree with the heap order property

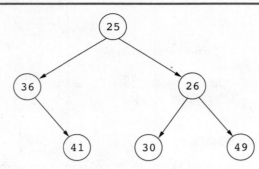

We need to impose a condition on such a tree that will keep it shallow; that is, we want the length of the longest path through the tree to be approximately log *n* rather than *n*. This will ensure that an addition operation that has to traverse a path from the root to a leaf can be performed in log *n* time. We need to introduce some terminology before we can proceed.

Let *T* be a binary tree. The *level* of a node *N* in *T* is the length of a path from the root to *N*. For example, the level of the root is 0, and the level of a child of a root is 1. The *depth* of *T* is the maximum level of a node in *T*; that is, it is the length of the longest path from the root to a leaf. A binary tree with depth *d* has *d* + 1 levels, because it has a level for each value of *l* in the range $0 \le l \le d$. We are looking for a family of trees whose depth is at most log *n* when the tree has *n* nodes.

Complete Binary Trees and Heaps

A binary tree with depth *d* is *complete* if it satisfies two conditions:

- *T* has 2^l nodes for all levels $0 \le l \le d - 1$; that is, each level other than the last has the maximum number of nodes possible
- All leaf nodes at level *d* are as far to the left as possible

Basically, a complete binary tree is one that you get when you build a binary tree by starting with the root and adding nodes level by level, following these rules:

R1. No node gets a child until each node at the previous level has two children.
R2. No node gets a child unless its left sibling already has two children.
R3. No node gets a right child unless it already has a left child.

The first rule ensures that there are no "holes" in the first *d* levels of the tree. The next two rules ensure that there are no "holes" as you move from left to right through the last level.

The tree of Figure 22-23 is not complete because the node that contains 36 has a right child but no left child. Figure 22-24 shows an example of a complete binary tree.

Figure 22-24 A complete binary tree that is also a heap

23

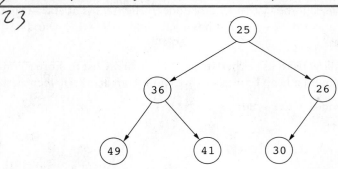

A complete binary tree that stores values from an ordered set is called a *heap* if it satisfies the heap order property.

The Depth of Complete Binary Trees

A complete binary tree T with n nodes is shallow in the sense that it cannot have depth much greater than $\log n$. If we disregard the last level, what remains of T is perfectly balanced in the sense that at each node, there are just as many nodes in the left subtree as in the right subtree. This means that if we start at the root and descend along any path, we retain less than half of the remaining nodes each time we pass to a new (numerically higher) level. This shows that the length of any path can be at most $\log n + 1$. We state this as follows:

A complete binary tree with n nodes has depth $d \leq \log n + 1$.

Storing a Complete Binary Tree in an Array

The fact that a complete binary tree has no "holes" has an interesting consequence. If you build the binary tree using rules R1 to R3 and store each node in an array A as it is added to the tree, you get the pattern shown in Figure 22-25.

24

Figure 22-25 Storing a complete binary tree in an array

24

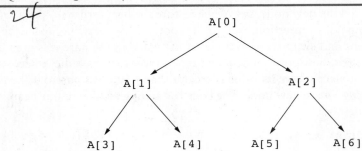

This pattern has the following characteristics:

- The root of the tree is $A[0]$
- The parent of a node $A[k]$ that is not the root is $A[(k-1)/2]$

- The left child and right children of a node A[k] are A[$2k + 1$] and A[$2k + 2$], respectively
- The rightmost leaf in the last level (last node in the tree) is at A[$n - 1$]
- A node A[k] is a leaf if $2k + 1 \geq n$, it has a left child if $2k + 1 < n$, and has a right child if $2k + 2 < n$

These observations allow us to use either an array or an array list to store a complete binary tree. In particular, to build a heap of integers, we can use an array list such as the following:

```
ArrayList<Integer> arrayHeap;
```

Adding an Item to a Heap

An addition of a new item to a heap must maintain the structure of a complete binary tree as well as the heap order property. We can preserve the structure of the tree by adding the new node according to rules R1, R2, and R3. This means that the new node will be added as a leaf at the last level of the tree, and will be as far to the left as possible within that level. For example, adding 12 to the tree of Figure 22-24 yields the tree of Figure 22-26.

Figure 22-26 Adding a new value may violate the heap order property

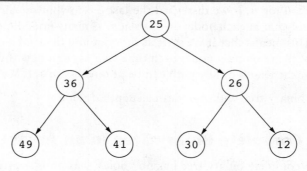

In terms of our array list representation, this means that the new value is added to the end of the array list as follows:

```
arrayHeap.add(x);
```

Once we have added the new node, say X, we restore the heap order property by traversing the path from the point of insertion back to the root. As we go, we compare the value of X to that of its parent and swap the two nodes if the value in the parent is greater. Then we climb up the tree to the new position of X and repeat. We stop when the X becomes the root, or when it gets to a place where its value is greater than that of its parent. When we do this, we say we are *sifting up* the new node. The code for adding a value to our heap is embodied in the following method:

```
boolean add(int x)
{
    // Add x at the end of the array list
    arrayHeap.add(x);
    // Sift up
```

```java
        siftUp();
        return true;
    }
```

The sifting up procedure is performed by the following method:

```java
    private void siftUp()
    {
        int p = arrayHeap.size()-1;  // Position to sift up
        while (p != 0)
        {
            int parent = (p-1) / 2;    // Index of parent
            if (valueAt(p) >= valueAt(parent))
            {
                // We are done
                return;
            }
            else
            {
                // Do a swap
                Integer temp = arrayHeap.get(parent);
                arrayHeap.set(parent, arrayHeap.get(p));
                arrayHeap.set(p, temp);
                // Move up
                p = parent;
            }
        }
    }
```

Removing the Minimum Element

To remove an element from a heap, we delete the root node and replace it with the node in the last place of the queue, that is, the rightmost leaf at the deepest level of the tree. If we do this to the heap of Figure 22-24, we get the complete binary tree shown in Figure 22-27.

Figure 22-27 The heap of Figure 22-24 after replacing the root with the deepest rightmost leaf

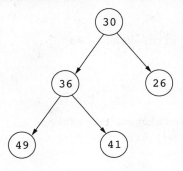

In general, the tree will violate the heap order property when the root is replaced in this manner, and we must perform a *sift down* operation to remake the heap. Say that X is the value that is currently stored in the root and needs to be sifted down. We start at the root and make our way down some branch of the tree. If we get to a place where X is smaller than its children, or is a leaf, we stop the procedure. Otherwise, we swap X with its smallest child, and then follow X down to the next level. In this way, we sift X down the tree until we get it to where it belongs. At that point, the heap order property is restored and we have remade the tree into a heap.

In terms of our array implementation, we must first save the value at position 0, and then remove the value at the end of the array list and store it at position 0. The `removeMin` method is as follows:

```java
public int removeMin()
{
  if (isEmpty())
    throw new RuntimeException("Priority Queue is empty.");
  else
  {
    int val = arrayHeap.get(0);

    // Replace root by last leaf
    arrayHeap.set(0, arrayHeap.get(arrayHeap.size()-1));

    // Remove the last leaf
    arrayHeap.remove(arrayHeap.size()-1);
    siftDown();
    return val;
  }
}
```

You can see the `siftDown` method, together with the methods for `add` and `removeMin`, in Code Listing 22-18.

Code Listing 22-18 **(Arrayheap.java)**

```java
1   import java.util.*;
2
3   /**
4      This class is an array-based heap
5   */
6
7   public class ArrayHeap
8   {
9      private ArrayList<Integer> arrayHeap
10                 = new ArrayList<>();
11
```

```
12      /**
13          The siftUp method sifts up the element
14          at arrayHeap[size()-1].
15      */
16      private void siftUp()
17      {
18          int p = arrayHeap.size()-1;  // Position to sift up
19          while (p != 0)
20          {
21              int parent = (p-1) / 2;
22              if (valueAt(p) >= valueAt(parent))
23              {
24                  // We are done
25                  break;
26              }
27              else
28              {
29                  // Do a swap
30                  Integer temp = arrayHeap.get(parent);
31                  arrayHeap.set(parent, arrayHeap.get(p));
32                  arrayHeap.set(p, temp);
33
34                  // Move up
35                  p = parent;
36              }
37          }
38      }
39
40      /**
41          The siftDown method sifts down the
42          element at arrayHeap[0].
43      */
44
45      private void siftDown()
46      {
47          int p = 0; // Position to sift down
48          int size = arrayHeap.size();
49          while (2*p + 1 < size)
50          {
51              int leftChildPos = 2*p + 1;
52              int rightChildPos = leftChildPos + 1;
53              int minChildPos = leftChildPos;
54
55              // Is there a right child?
56              if (rightChildPos < size)
57              {
58                  // Which child is smaller
59                  if (valueAt(rightChildPos) < valueAt(leftChildPos))
```

```
60                    {
61                        minChildPos = rightChildPos;
62                    }
63                }
64                // If less than children we are done,
65                // otherwise swap node with smaller child
66                if (valueAt(p) <= valueAt(minChildPos))
67                    break;
68                else
69                {
70                    // Do the swap
71                    Integer temp = arrayHeap.get(p);
72                    arrayHeap.set(p, arrayHeap.get(minChildPos));
73                    arrayHeap.set(minChildPos, temp);
74                }
75                // Go down to the child position
76                p = minChildPos;
77            }
78        }
79
80        /**
81            The add method adds a value to the heap.
82            @param x The value to add.
83            @return true.
84        */
85
86        boolean add(int x)
87        {
88            // Add x at the end of the array list
89            arrayHeap.add(x);
90
91            // Sift up
92            siftUp();
93            return true;
94        }
95
96        /**
97            The removeMin method removes an item from the heap.
98            @return The minimum element in the heap.
99            @exception RuntimeException When priority
100           queue is empty.
101       */
102
103       public int removeMin()
104       {
105           if (isEmpty())
106           {
107               String message = "Priority Queue is empty.";
```

```
108              throw new RuntimeException(message);
109          }
110          else
111          {
112              int val = arrayHeap.get(0);
113
114              // Replace root by last leaf
115              int lastPos = arrayHeap.size()-1;
116              arrayHeap.set(0, arrayHeap.get(lastPos));
117
118              // Remove the last leaf
119              arrayHeap.remove(arrayHeap.size()-1);
120              siftDown();
121              return val;
122          }
123      }
124
125      /**
126          The isEmpty method checks if the heap is empty.
127          @return true if the heap is empty
128          and false otherwise.
129      */
130
131      public boolean isEmpty()
132      {
133          return arrayHeap.size() == 0;
134      }
135
136      /**
137          The valueAt method is a convenience method,
138          it makes the code more readable.
139          @return value stored at given position in the heap.
140      */
141
142      private int valueAt(int pos)
143      {
144          return arrayHeap.get(pos);
145      }
146 }
```

The `ArrayHeapsort` program, given in Code Listing 22-19 demonstrates the use of the `ArrayHeap` class to sort an array. No output is shown for this program because it is similar to that of other programs in this chapter.

Code Listing 22-19   (ArrayHeapsort.java)

```java
1   import java.util.*;
2
3   /**
4      This program demonstrates the use of the
5      ArrayHeap class.
6   */
7
8   public class ArrayHeapsort
9   {
10     public static void main(String [] args)
11     {
12        // Create and display an array of random integers
13        Random randy = new Random();
14        int [ ] arr = new int[10];
15        System.out.println("Here is the array to be sorted:");
16        for (int k = 0; k < arr.length; k++)
17        {
18           arr[k] = randy.nextInt(100);
19           System.out.print(arr[k] + "   ");
20        }
21
22        // Create a heap of integers
23        // and use it to sort the array
24        ArrayHeap heap = new ArrayHeap();
25        for (int x : arr) heap.add(x);
26        for (int k = 0; k < arr.length; k++)
27           arr[k] = heap.removeMin();
28
29        // Print the array
30        System.out.println("\nHere is the sorted array:");
31        for (int x : arr)
32           System.out.print(x + "   ");
33     }
34  }
```

In the Spotlight:

Rooted Trees and the JTree Component

A rooted tree is a generalization of a binary tree in which nodes may have more than two children. A familiar example of a rooted tree is the hierarchical file and directory system used on almost all computers. Figure 22-28 shows a simple example of a rooted tree that might be a part of a genealogy tree.

Figure 22-28 A rooted tree

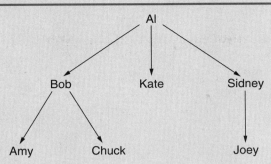

Many programs need to display rooted trees as part of their user interface. The Java Swing libraries provide a `JTree` component that can be used to fill this need. Actually, the `JTree` component provides only the *view* part of the rooted tree component. The view is the part that actually appears as part of the graphical interface. The data that makes up the tree must be stored separately from the view, in what is called the *data model* or, simply, the *model*. The `javax.swing.tree` package contains the `TreeModel` interface, which describes the methods for tree model objects. There is also a `TreeNode` interface describing the node objects that make up the tree. A subinterface of `TreeNode`, called `MutableTreeNode`, describes tree nodes that can be modified after they have been created. The libraries also provide classes with default implementations of the `TreeModel` and `MutableTreeNode` interfaces. These classes, `Default-TreeModel` and `DefaultMutableTreeNode`, make it easy to create the models for rooted trees.

To create a node, use the `DefaultMutableTreeNode` constructor

```
DefaultMutableTreeNode(Object userObject)
```

and pass to it an object that will serve as the data to be stored in the node. This creates a node that has no children. You can add a child node to a node by calling the method

```
void add(MutableTreeNode newChild)
```

For example, to create the portion of the tree of Figure 22-28 that shows `Sidney` as the parent of `Joey`, you can proceed as follows:

```
// Create the joey node
DefaultMutableTreeNode joey = new DefaultMutableTreeNode("Joey");
// Create the Sydney node and add its child joey
DefaultMutableTreeNode sydney = new DefaultMutableTreeNode("Sydney");
sydney.add(joey);
```

In this way, you can create a system of interconnected nodes, beginning with the leaves and culminating with the root of the tree, in this case, the node `al` containing the data for the patriarch, `Al`.

Once you have the root node, you can create the tree model by passing the root node to the `DefaultTreeModel` constructor. Then, you can create the `JTree` component by passing the tree model to the `JTree` constructor:

```
// Create a default tree model to hold the tree data rooted at al
DefaultTreeModel myTreeModel = new DefaultTreeModel(al);
// Create the JTree using the the tree model
JTree myTree = new JTree(myTreeModel);
```

Code listing 22-20 illustrates the complete process involved in creating and displaying a JTree component.

Code Listing 22-20 (JTreeExample.java)

```java
1  import javax.swing.*;
2  import javax.swing.tree.*;
3  /**
4     This program shows how to build a JTree component.
5  */
6  public class JTreeExample
7  {
8     public static void main(String[] args)
9     {
10        //Create all the leaf nodes
11        DefaultMutableTreeNode kate = new DefaultMutableTreeNode("Kate");
12        DefaultMutableTreeNode amy = new DefaultMutableTreeNode("Amy");
13        DefaultMutableTreeNode chuck = new DefaultMutableTreeNode("Chuck");
14        DefaultMutableTreeNode joey = new DefaultMutableTreeNode("Joey");
15
16        //Create the Bob node and add its children amy and chuck
17        DefaultMutableTreeNode bob = new DefaultMutableTreeNode("Bob");
18        bob.add(amy);
19        bob.add(chuck);
20
21        // Create the Sydney node and add its child joey
22        DefaultMutableTreeNode sydney =
23                new DefaultMutableTreeNode("Sydney");
24        sydney.add(joey);
25
26        // Create the root node al and add children bob, kate and sidney
27        DefaultMutableTreeNode al = new DefaultMutableTreeNode("Al");
28        al.add(bob);
29        al.add(kate);
30        al.add(sydney);
31
32        // Create a default tree model to hold the tree rooted at al
33        DefaultTreeModel myTreeModel = new DefaultTreeModel(al);
34        // Create the JTree using the the tree model
35        JTree myTree = new JTree(myTreeModel);
36
37        //Display the tree in a JFrame
38        JFrame myFrame  = new JFrame("Tree Exhibition Program");
39        myFrame.add(myTree);
40        myFrame.setDefaultCloseOperation(JFrame.EXIT_ON_CLOSE);
41        myFrame.pack();
42        myFrame.setVisible(true);
43     }
44 }
```

The user interface displayed when this program is run is shown in Figure 22-29.

Figure 22-29 Screen shot of the `JTree` example program   (Mark Schrier. Copyright Oracle, Inc.)

We have shown how to build and display a `JTree` component. As you might expect, you can do a lot more with `JTree` objects. You can add listeners that will respond to various user actions and events as nodes in the tree are selected or unselected. You can find more information on using `JTree` components online.

22.5 Common Errors to Avoid

- **Forgetting to check for an empty tree.** Make sure a reference to a node is not `null` before you try to access the value or children of the node.
- **Forgetting to replace a subtree with a modified subtree.** If you have to alter a tree, you will often have to recursively alter one or both subtrees. Make sure that you replace the current subtree with the altered version.
- **Trying to use a loop when recursion is the best way to go.** Most problems on binary trees have simple and elegant recursive solutions. Very often you don't need to use both iteration and recursion on the same problem.

Review Questions and Exercises

Multiple Choice and True/False

1. A binary tree is a collection of items in which each item _____.
   a. has no successor
   b. has one successor
   c. has exactly two successors
   d. has at most two successors

2. The three standard techniques for traversing a binary tree are _____.
   a. preorder, inorder, and postorder
   b. prefix, infix, and postfix

   c. left-to-right, top-down, and parent-to-child

   d. none of the above

3. The set of all descendants of a node in a binary tree form _____.

   a. a path from the node to the end of the tree

   b. a path from the node to the root

   c. a subtree rooted at that node

   d. a set that is best traversed using inorder traversal

4. A binary search tree is structured in such a way that _____.

   a. for each node, the left subtree holds values that are less than the node, and the right subtree holds values that are greater

   b. for each node, the left child holds a value that is less than the node, and the right child holds a value that is greater

   c. the value stored at each node is less than values stored in the children

   d. the heights of the subtrees at any node differ by at most 1

5. An AVL tree is _____.

   a. a kind of priority queue

   b. a kind of heap

   c. a kind of binary search tree

   d. none of the above

6. When a node with two children is removed from a binary search tree, it can be replaced with _____.

   a. the rightmost leaf at the deepest level of the tree

   b. the smallest node in its right subtree

   c. the smallest node in its left subtree

   d. the smallest ancestor of the node

7. In a binary tree that is a heap, _____.

   a. every non root node must have a value greater than that of its parent

   b. every left child must be less than its parent, and every right child must be greater

   c. the height of the left and right subtrees of each node must differ by at most one

   d. leaf nodes must be greater or equal to every other node

8. In a complete binary tree, _____.

   a. every level l other than the last must have 2^l nodes

   b. the depth d of the tree satisfies $d \leq \log n + 1$, where n is the number of nodes in the tree

   c. every node that has a right child also has a left child

   d. all of the above

9. The Heapsort method _____.

   a. is based on a complete binary search tree structure with the heap order property

   b. makes $O(n \log n)$ comparisons when sorting an array of n entries

   c. is a very good sorting method, but there are other general sorting methods that are much faster

   d. all of the above

10. To add a new value to a heap, you should _____.
    a. add it as a leaf and then sift up
    b. sift the root down to make room for the new node
    c. replace the root with the deepest and rightmost leaf, and then sift down
    d. none of the above

11. **True or False:** A node in a binary tree can have two parents.

12. **True or False:** A node in a binary tree can have no parents.

13. **True or False:** The depth of a binary tree is always the same as the height of its root.

14. **True or False:** The level of a node is the height of the tree minus the height of the node.

15. **True or False:** Removing an item from a priority queue gives you the minimum element.

16. **True or False:** The height of an empty binary tree is not defined.

17. **True or False:** A heap is a complete binary tree that has the heap order property.

18. **True or False:** An ancestor of a node can never be in a subtree of the node.

19. **True or False:** A descendant of a node must belong to at least one subtree of the node.

20. **True or False:** The subtrees of a node in an AVL tree can be equal in height.

21. **True or False:** The subtrees of a node in a complete binary tree must be equal in height.

Find the Error

Find the error in each of the following code segments.

1.
```
// return number of nodes in a binary tree
int NodeCount(Node tree)
{
    int count = 0;
    if (tree != null)
    {
        count ++;
        NodeCount(tree.left);
        NodeCount(tree.right);
    }
    return count;
}
```

2.
```
// Add a value to a binary search tree
// Return root of resulting search tree
Node add(Node tree, int value)
{
    if (tree == null)
```

```
        return new Node(x);
    if (value < tree.value)
        return add(tree.left, value);
    else
        return add(tree.right, value);
}
```

3. ```
   // Add 1 to the value in each node of the tree
   void incrementAll(Node tree)
   {
       incrementAll(tree.left);
       incrementAll(tree.right);
       tree.Value ++;
   }
   ```

Short Answer

1. Why is it good for binary search trees to be balanced?

2. A binary search tree has a right subtree but no left subtree. What node contains the least element in the tree?

3. What is the height of a binary tree?

4. Explain the concept of *order* as used with priority queues.

5. What is a priority queue?

6. Explain why the depth of a complete binary tree with n nodes is at most log n + 1.

7. How does an AVL tree differ from an ordinary binary search tree?

Algorithm Workbench

1. Write a method
   ```
   void preorder(Node bTree)
   ```
   that uses a preorder traversal to print all values stored in a binary tree.

2. Write a method
   ```
   void postorder(Node bTree)
   ```
   that uses a postorder traversal to print all values stored in a binary tree.

3. Write a method
   ```
   int treeSize(Node bTree)
   ```
   that computes and returns the number of nodes in a binary tree.

4. Write a method
   ```
   int leafCount(Node btree)
   ```
   that computes and returns the number of leaves in a binary tree.

5. Assume that data is stored in a binary tree, but that unlike the case of a binary search tree, no attempt is made to maintain any sort of order in the data stored. Give
   ```

an algorithm for a method `contains` that searches a binary tree for a particular value x and returns `true` or `false` according to whether x is found in the tree.

6. Define a `Comparator` class `DecOrder` that orders integers in decreasing order, and give the code that shows how to create a `PriorityQueue` object that uses such a `Comparator` object.

7. Define an order on strings where a string s is less than t if the length of s is less than the length of t. If s and t have the same length, then s is less than t if s comes before t in alphabetic order. Write a `Comparator` class that corresponds to this order.

Programming Challenges

1. AVL Trees

Add a `remove` method to the AVL tree class of this chapter. Use a graphical user interface that allows a user to work interactively with the AVL tree, adding and removing items as desired.

2. Family Tree

Write a program, with a graphical user interface, that allows users to create genealogy trees and work with them. Each person in this genealogy tree will be restricted to having at most two children. The nodes of the tree will store string values, which are interpreted as names of people. The program should support the following commands:

- `root name`: Adds `name` as the root of the tree. This must be the first command entered: it creates a tree with a single node, whose value field holds `name`. The created node becomes the root of the genealogy tree. The command is ignored if it is entered after the tree has been created.
- `left parent child`: Adds a new node `child` as the left child of the node with name `parent`. The command is ignored if there is no node with name `parent` in the tree, or if there is such a node, but it already has a left child.
- `right parent child`: Adds a new node `child` as the right child of the node with name `parent`. The command is ignored if there is no node with name `parent` in the tree, or if there is such a node, but it already has a right child.
- `descendants person`: Displays a list of all descendants of the node with name `person`. The command is ignored if there is no node in the tree with that name.
- `ancestors person`: Displays a list of all ancestors of the node with the name `person`. The command is ignored if there is no node in the tree with that name.

3. Balanced Search Tree

Write a program that can convert a sorted array into a balanced binary search tree. For this project, a balanced binary tree is one where the size of the left and right subtrees at each node differs by at most one. Your program should have a graphical user interface. The program allows the user to enter a number n, generates an array of n random integers, sorts the array, and then converts the sorted array into a balanced binary search tree. The program should display a graphical representation of the binary search tree.

4. Prefix Calculator

VideoNote
Prefix
Calculator

An arithmetic expression is in *prefix form* when operators are written before their operands. Here are some examples of prefix expressions and the values they evaluate to:

Expression	Value
12	12
+ 2 51	53
* 5 7	35
* + 16 4 + 3 1	80

An expression (such as 12) that begins with an integer is a prefix expression that evaluates to itself. Otherwise, an expression is a prefix expression if it begins with an operator and is followed by two prefix expressions. In this latter case, the value of the expression is recursively computed from the values of its constituent prefix sub-expressions.

Write a program that allows the user to enter prefix expressions in a text field. The program reads the expression, evaluates it, and displays the value in a suitable GUI component. Assume that the user enters expressions that use only positive integers and the two operators + and *. Your program should internally convert the prefix expression into a binary tree before evaluating it.

5. Levels in an AVL Tree

Extend the AVL tree class presented in this chapter by adding a method that takes a value, locates it in the AVL tree, and displays its level. Do this by extending the list of commands supported by the program to include commands of the form *level value*. For example, if the user types in

```
level 12
```

the program displays the level of a node containing 12. The program should display −1 if the user types a value not in the tree. If there is more than one instance of the value in the tree, the program displays the level of any one of them.

6. Binary Tree Input and Display

You are given a file that contains data describing a binary tree whose nodes are strings. The file begins with an integer N, the number of nodes in the tree, on a line by itself. This first line is followed by N additional lines where each line specifies child information for a node in the tree. The line for a node X starts with X itself followed by a list of the children of X. Names of nodes are separated by whitespace. For example, the data set

```
5
Al  Bob  Carol
Bob  Debby  Elaine
Carol
Debby
Elaine
```

represents a binary tree in which Al has two children named Bob and Carol; Bob has two children named Debby and Elaine; and Carol, Debby, and Elaine have no children. Write a program that reads in data from such a file and displays it in a JTree component.

7. Breadth-First Traversal of Binary trees

Write a program that reads a file that describes a binary tree using the format of Programming Challenge 6. The program then lists all the nodes in the tree by their distance from the root: first the root, then all the children of the root, then all nodes that are children of a child of the root, and so on. For the example tree in Programming Challenge 6, the program might output the nodes in any of the following orders:

```
Al Bob Carol Debby Elaine
Al Carol Bob Elaine Debby
Al Bob Carol Debby Elaine
```

Such ordering are called breadth-first orders. Note that these three are not the only possible breadth-first orders.

Index

A

abstract classes and methods,
662–669
Abstract Windowing Toolkit
(AWT)
See also specific classes
applets created with, 937–941
classes, list of, 937
class hierarchy, 849–850
defined, 761, 762–763
portability, 937–941
access
package, 648–649
sequential file, 741
specification in UML
diagrams, 341
accessing variables, within lambda
expressions, 690
accessor method, 340
access specifiers
private, 328
protected, 643–649
public, 28, 328
accumulators, 217, 219, 429
action command, 789, 792
`ActionEvent` class, 1004
`getActionCommand()`, 789–792
`getSource()`, 789, 792–793
`ActionEvent` object, 788–789
action events, 778
`ActionListener` interface,
777–784
action listeners, handling events
with, 764, 777–784
`actionPerformed()`, 777–778
actual parameters, 281
adapter classes, 967–972
`addActionListener()`, 783,
786–790, 791, 974
adding/inserting items in
`ArrayList`, 475, 479–480

addition operator, 55
`addListSelectionListener()`, 853
address, 4
adjacency list, 1280–1282
aggregation
description of, 517–527
security issues, 525–527
in UML diagrams, 525
algorithm analysis, 1105–1114
algorithms, 6, 1112–1114
array, 428–435
binary search, 468–470
binary search, recursive, 1055–
1058
selection sort, 465–468
sequential search, 449–451
ALU (arithmetic and logic unit), 3
analysis of algorithms, 1105–1114
asymptotic complexity,
1110–1111
average case complexity, 1109
basic steps, 1106
Big O notation, 1110–1112
complexity of algorithms,
1107–1108
computational problems,
1106–1107
constant time, 1111
instances, 1106
linear time, 1111
logarithmic time, 1111
n log n time, 1111
polynomial time, 1112
quadratic time, 1111
space criterion, 1105
time criterion, 1105
worst case complexity,
1108–1109
`AnchorPane` class, 1034
`AnchorPane` component, JavaFX
GUI, 992, 994

AND (`&&`), 137, 138–140
animation, timeline, 1022–1025
duration, 1023
key frame, 1022–1023
key value, 1023
anonymous inner classes,
683–686
event handling, 1010–1011
anonymous subclasses, 1213
anonymous object, 771, 783
API (application programmer
interface), 33
standard packages, 383
appearance, 904–906
`append()`, 584–585
appending data to files, 236–237,
740
`Applet` class, 937
See also `AudioClip` interface
applets
audio, playing, 977–980
AWT, creating with, 937–941
defined, 8–9, 917–918
differences between GUI and,
929
events, handling in, 932–936
restrictions on, 919
running, 930–932
running with `appletviewer`,
931–932
security, 919, 931
Swing, creating with, 928–936
`appletviewer`, 931–932
`Application` class, 993–994
application programmer interface.
See API
applications
defined, 917
Java, 8–9
playing audio in, 981
software, 5